GALE ENCYCLOPEDIA OF

MULTICULTURAL AMERICA

THIRD EDITION

EDITED BY THOMAS RIGGS

GALE ENCYCLOPEDIA OF
MULTICULTURAL AMERICA

VOLUME **2**

DANISH AMERICANS–JORDANIAN AMERICANS

EDITED BY THOMAS RIGGS

GALE
CENGAGE Learning·

Detroit • New York • San Francisco • New Haven, Conn • Waterville, Maine • London

© 2014 Gale, Cengage Learning
WCN: 01-100-101

Gale Encyclopedia of Multicultural America

Thomas Riggs, Editor

Project Editor: Marie Toft

Editorial: Jeff Hunter, Carol Schwartz

Technical Assistance: Luann Brennan, Grant Eldridge, Jeffrey Muhr, Rebecca Parks

Rights Acquisition and Management: Sheila Spencer

Composition: Evi Abou-El-Seoud

Manufacturing: Wendy Blurton

Imaging: John Watkins

Product Design: Kristine Julien

Index: Shana Milkie

For product information and technology assistance, contact us at
Gale Customer Support, 1-800-877-4253.
For permission to use material from this text or product,
submit all requests online at **www.cengage.com/permissions.**
Further permissions questions can be emailed to
permissionrequest@cengage.com.

Cover photographs and art reproduced with the following permission:
For Asian business man, © aslysun/Shutterstock.com; for Indian businessman, © Kenneth Man/Shutterstock.com; for young Sephardic Jewish man, © Howard Sandler/Shutterstock.com; for African American female, © Flashon Studio/Shutterstock.com; for Rastafarian male, © Alan Bailey/Shutterstock.com; for Muslim woman (side view), © szefei/Shutterstock.com; for young woman in white t-shirt and jeans, © Vlasov Volodymyr/Shutterstock.com; for Hispanic woman in white blouse, © Warren Goldswaini/Shutterstock.com; for puzzle vector illustration, © VikaSuh/Shutterstock.com.

While every effort has been made to ensure the reliability of the information presented in this publication, Gale, a part of Cengage Learning, does not guarantee the accuracy of the data contained herein. Gale accepts no payment for listing; and inclusion in the publication of any organization, agency, institution, publication, service, or individual does not imply endorsement of the editors or publisher. Errors brought to the attention of the publisher and verified to the satisfaction of the publisher will be corrected in future editions.

Library of Congress Cataloging-in-Publication Data

Gale Encyclopedia of Multicultural America / Thomas Riggs, editor. — 3rd edition.
    pages cm
  Includes bibliographical references and index.
    ISBN 978-0-7876-7550-9 (set : hardcover) — ISBN 978-0-7876-7551-6 (vol. 1 : hardcover) — ISBN 978-0-7876-7552-3 (vol. 2 : hardcover) — ISBN 978-0-7876-7553-0 (vol. 3 : hardcover) — ISBN 978-1-4144-3279-3 (vol. 4 : hardcover)
  1. Cultural pluralism—United States—Encyclopedias. 2. Ethnology—United States—Encyclopedias. 3. Minorities—United States—Encyclopedias. 4. United States—Ethnic relations—Encyclopedias. 5. United States—Race relations—Encyclopedias. I. Riggs, Thomas.
  E184.A1G14 2014
  305.800973—dc23
                                                                    2013049273

Gale
27500 Drake Rd.
Farmington Hills, MI, 48331-3535

ISBN-13: 978-0-7876-7550-9 (set)
ISBN-13: 978-0-7876-7551-6 (vol. 1)
ISBN-13: 978-0-7876-7552-3 (vol. 2)
ISBN-13: 978-0-7876-7553-0 (vol. 3)
ISBN-13: 978-1-4144-3279-3 (vol. 4)

This title is also available as an e-book.
ISBN-13: 978-1-4144-3806-1
Contact your Gale, a part of Cengage Learning sales representative for ordering information.

Printed in the United States of America
1 2 3 4 5 6 7 18 17 16 15 14

TABLE OF CONTENTS

Contents of All Volumes **vii**

Editor's Note **xi**

Advisory Board **xiii**

List of Academic Reviewers **xv**

List of Contributors **xix**

Introduction **xxiii**

D

Danish Americans **1**
Dominican Americans **15**
Druze Americans **27**
Dutch Americans **35**

E

Ecuadorian Americans **47**
Egyptian Americans **61**
English Americans **73**
Eritrean Americans **87**
Estonian Americans **97**
Ethiopian Americans **107**

F

Filipino Americans **119**
Finnish Americans **137**
French Americans **153**
French-Canadian Americans **167**

G

Garifuna Americans **185**
Georgian Americans **197**
German Americans **207**

Ghanaian Americans **225**
Greek Americans **237**
Grenadian Americans **255**
Guamanian Americans **263**
Guatemalan Americans **275**
Guyanese Americans **293**

H

Haitian Americans **305**
Hawaiians **317**
Hmong Americans **331**
Honduran Americans **345**
Hopis **357**
Hungarian Americans **373**

I

Icelandic Americans **387**
Indonesian Americans **401**
Indos **413**
Inupiat **421**
Iranian Americans **433**
Iraqi Americans **445**
Irish Americans **459**
Iroquois Confederacy **477**
Israeli Americans **493**
Italian Americans **505**

J

Jamaican Americans **523**
Japanese Americans **537**
Jewish Americans **557**
Jordanian Americans **579**

Annotated Bibliography **591**

CONTENTS OF ALL VOLUMES

VOLUME 1

A

Acadians 1
Afghan Americans 17
African Americans 31
Albanian Americans 61
Aleuts 75
Algerian Americans 87
Amish 97
Apache 113
Arab Americans 125
Argentinean Americans 141
Armenian Americans 151
Asian Indian Americans 165
Australian Americans 179
Austrian Americans 189
Azerbaijani Americans 203

B

Bahamian Americans 211
Bangladeshi Americans 221
Barbadian Americans 237
Basque Americans 251
Belarusan Americans 265
Belgian Americans 275
Belizean Americans 289
Blackfoot 301
Bolivian Americans 319
Bosnian Americans 331

Brazilian Americans 343
Bulgarian Americans 357
Burmese Americans 373

C

Cambodian Americans 381
Canadian Americans 395
Cape Verdean Americans 407
Carpatho-Rusyn Americans 419
Catawba Indian Nation 433
Chaldean Americans 441
Cherokees 453
Cheyenne 465
Chilean Americans 479
Chinese Americans 491
Choctaws 507
Colombian Americans 519
Congolese Americans 531
Costa Rican Americans 543
Creeks 553
Creoles 567
Croatian Americans 577
Cuban Americans 591
Cypriot Americans 607
Czech Americans 619

VOLUME 2

D

Danish Americans 1
Dominican Americans 15

Druze Americans 27

Dutch Americans 35

E

Ecuadorian Americans 47

Egyptian Americans 61

English Americans 73

Eritrean Americans 87

Estonian Americans 97

Ethiopian Americans 107

F

Filipino Americans 119

Finnish Americans 137

French Americans 153

French-Canadian Americans 167

G

Garifuna Americans 185

Georgian Americans 197

German Americans 207

Ghanaian Americans 225

Greek Americans 237

Grenadian Americans 255

Guamanian Americans 263

Guatemalan Americans 275

Guyanese Americans 293

H

Haitian Americans 305

Hawaiians 317

Hmong Americans 331

Honduran Americans 345

Hopis 357

Hungarian Americans 373

I

Icelandic Americans 387

Indonesian Americans 401

Indos 413

Inupiat 421

Iranian Americans 433

Iraqi Americans 445

Irish Americans 459

Iroquois Confederacy 477

Israeli Americans 493

Italian Americans 505

J

Jamaican Americans 523

Japanese Americans 537

Jewish Americans 557

Jordanian Americans 579

VOLUME 3

K

Kenyan Americans 1

Klamaths 11

Korean Americans 23

Kurdish Americans 41

L

Laotian Americans 53

Latvian Americans 65

Lebanese Americans 79

Liberian Americans 91

Libyan Americans 101

Lithuanian Americans 111

Luxembourger Americans 129

M

Macedonian Americans 141

Malaysian Americans 155

Maltese Americans 163

Mennonites 171

Menominee 183

Mexican Americans 195

Mongolian Americans 219

Mormons 231

Moroccan Americans 245

N

Navajos 259

Nepalese Americans 277

New Zealander Americans 289

Nez Percé 301

Nicaraguan Americans 315

Nigerian Americans 329

Norwegian Americans 343

O

Ojibwe 359

Oneidas 375

Osages 389

P

Pacific Islander Americans 401

Paiutes 411

Pakistani Americans 425

Palestinian Americans 437

Panamanian Americans 449

Paraguayan Americans 459

Peruvian Americans 467

Polish Americans 477

Portuguese Americans 493

Pueblos 509

Puerto Rican Americans 525

VOLUME 4

R

Romani Americans 1

Romanian Americans 14

Russian Americans 31

S

Salvadoran Americans 47

Samoan Americans 59

Saudi Arabian Americans 75

Scotch-Irish Americans 87

Scottish Americans 101

Seminoles 113

Senegalese Americans 121

Serbian Americans 133

Sicilian Americans 151

Sierra Leonean Americans 165

Sikh Americans 179

Sioux 193

Slovak Americans 209

Slovenian Americans 223

Somali Americans 241

South African Americans 255

Spanish Americans 271

Sri Lankan Americans 283

Sudanese Americans 295

Swedish Americans 305

Swiss Americans 319

Syrian Americans 331

T

Taiwanese Americans 343

Thai Americans 357

Tibetan Americans 369

Tlingit 387

Tongan Americans 403

Trinidadian and Tobagonian Americans 411

Tunisian Americans 427

Turkish Americans 437

U

Ugandan Americans 449

Ukrainian Americans 459

Uruguayan Americans 475

V

Venezuelan Americans 485

Vietnamese Americans 499

Virgin Islander Americans 513

Welsh Americans **523**

Yemeni Americans **533**
Yupik **545**

Zuni **555**

EDITOR'S NOTE

The third edition of the *Gale Encyclopedia of Multicultural America*—a major revision to the previous editions published in 1995 and 2000—includes 175 entries, each focusing on an immigrant or indigenous group in the United States. Some entries provide historical and cultural overviews of commonly recognized groups, such as Mexican Americans and Japanese Americans, while others discuss much smaller groups—for example, Cape Verdean Americans, Jordanian Americans, and the Ojibwe. The third edition has 23 new entries; the 152 entries from the second edition were thoroughly revised and reorganized, creating up-to-date coverage and a more consistent approach throughout the book. The writing or revision of each entry was reviewed by a scholar with extensive research background in the group.

The structure and content of the *Gale Encyclopedia of Multicultural America* was planned with the help of the project's advisory board. Joe Feagin—professor of sociology at Texas A&M University and a member of the advisory board—revised and updated the encyclopedia's introduction, originally written by Rudolph Vecoli. The introduction provides a broad historical overview of race and ethnicity in the United States, explaining how cultural and legal influences, especially racism, helped shape the experience of indigenous and immigrant groups.

ORGANIZATION

The 175 entries are arranged alphabetically across three volumes. The length of the entries varies from about 4,000 to 20,000 words. All entries share a common structure, providing consistent coverage of the groups and a simple way of comparing basic elements of one entry with another. Birth and death dates are provided for people mentioned in the entries except when dates could not be found or verified. The encyclopedia has more than 400 color images.

Each entry has 14 sections:

Overview: Basic information about the group's origins, homeland, immigration to or migration within the United States, and population and principal areas of settlement.

History of the People: Significant historical events of the group in its original region or country.

Settlement in the United States: For immigrant groups, waves of immigration and notable settlement patterns; for indigenous groups, original area of settlement, as well as migration within North America after the group's contact with Europeans.

Language: Native languages and their influence on the present-day group. Some entries have a section on greetings and popular expressions.

Religion: Religions and religious practices of the group, both in the original country or region and in the United States.

Culture and Assimilation: Traditional beliefs and customs, as well as the status of these traditions in the present-day group; topics include cuisine, dress, dances and songs, holidays, and health care issues and practices. Some entries have a sidebar on proverbs.

Family and Community Life: Topics include family structure and traditions; gender roles; education; dating practices, marriage, and divorce; and relations with other Americans.

Employment and Economic Conditions: Types of jobs commonly done by early immigrants or by indigenous people as they came into contact with European settlers, as well as notable employment trends among later generations of the group.

Politics and Government: Topics include the group's involvement in American politics and government (including voting patterns, significant events, and legislation) and contemporary interest in the parent country.

Notable Individuals: Examples of accomplished members of the group in various fields, with brief summaries.

Media: List of television and radio stations, as well as newspapers and periodicals, that are directed toward the group or provide significant coverage of it.

Organizations and Associations: List of organizations and associations related to the group.

Museums and Research Centers: List of museums and research centers related to the group.

Sources for Additional Study: A bibliography of books and articles about the group, including recent sources.

ACKNOWLEDGMENTS

Many people contributed time, effort, and ideas to the third edition of the *Gale Encyclopedia of Multicultural America*. Marie Toft, senior content project editor at Cengage Gale, served as in-house manager for the project. The quality of the book owes much to her ideas and feedback, as well as to her oversight of the book's production.

We would like to express our appreciation to the advisors, who, in addition to creating the list of new entry topics, helped evaluate the second edition and proposed ideas for producing an improved third edition. We would also like to thank the contributors for their carefully prepared essays and for their efforts to summarize the cultural life of ethnic groups without stereotyping. We are grateful to the many scholars who reviewed entries for accuracy and coverage.

The long process of reorganizing and revising the second-edition entries, as well as preparing the new ones, was overseen by Joseph Campana, project editor, who also helped identify and correspond with the advisors. Anne Healey, senior editor, managed the editing process and was helped by Mary Beth Curran, David Hayes, and Lee Esbenshade, all associate editors. Hannah Soukup, assistant editor, identified and corresponded with the academic reviewers. Other important assistance came from Mariko Fujinaka, managing editor, and Jake Schmitt and Theodore McDermott, assistant editors. The line editors were Robert Anderson, Cheryl Collins, Tony Craine, Gerilee Hunt, Amy Mortensen, Jill Oldham, Kathy Peacock, Donna Polydoros, Natalie Ruppert, and Will Wagner.

Thomas Riggs

# Advisory Board

CHAIR

David R. M. Beck
Professor, Department of Native American Studies, University of Montana, Missoula.

ADVISORS

Joe Feagin
Ella C. McFadden Professor, Department of Sociology, Texas A&M University.

Patricia Fernandez-Kelly
Professor, Department of Sociology, Office of Population Research, Princeton University.

David Gerber
University at Buffalo Distinguished Professor Emeritus, Department of History, University at Buffalo, The State University of New York.

Rebecca Stuhr
Coordinator for Humanities Collections, Librarian for Classical Studies and History, University of Pennsylvania Libraries, Member, Ethnic & Multicultural Information Exchange Round Table, American Library Association.

Vladimir F. Wertsman
Retired Chair, Publishing and Multicultural Materials Committee, Ethnic and Multicultural Information Exchange Round Table, American Library Association.

LIST OF ACADEMIC REVIEWERS

HOLLY ACKERMAN

Ph. D. Librarian for Latin American, Iberian, & Latino Studies, Duke University, Durham, North Carolina

DEIRDRE ALMEIDA

Director of the American Indian Studies Program, Eastern Washington University, Cheney

BARBARA WATSON ANDAYA

Professor of Asian Studies, University of Hawai'i, Manoa

BARBARA A. ANDERSON

Ronald Freedman Collegiate Professor of Sociology and Population Studies, University of Michigan, Ann Arbor

JOSEPH ARBENA

Professor Emeritus of History, Clemson University, South Carolina

LAURIE ARNOLD

Director of Native American Studies, Gonzaga University, Spokane, Washington

CHRISTOPHER P. ATWOOD

Associate Professor of Central Eurasian Studies, Indiana University, Bloomington

ANNY BAKALIAN

Associate Director of the Graduate Center, City University of New York

CARINA BANDHAUER

Professor of Sociology, Western Connecticut State University, Danbury, Connecticut

CARL L. BANKSTON III

Professor of Sociology, Tulane University, New Orleans, Louisiana

LAURA BARBAS-RHODEN

Associate Professor of Foreign Languages, Wofford College, Spartanburg, South Carolina

DAVID BECK

Department Chair of the Native American Studies Department and Professor of Native American Studies, University of Montana, Missoula

JOHN BIETER

Associate Professor of History, Boise State University, Idaho

ADRIAN VILIAMI BELL

Visiting Assistant Professor of Anthropology, University of Utah, Salt Lake City

BRIAN BELTON

Ph.D., as well as Senior Lecturer, YMCA George Williams College, London, United Kingdom

SAMIR BITAR

Lecturer of Arabic Language and Cultures, Department of Anthropology, and Assistant Director of Outreach-Central and Southwest Asian Studies Center, University of Montana, Missoula

LASZLO BORHI

Senior Research Fellow, Institute of History Hungarian Academy of Sciences, Budapest, Hungary

GREGORY CAMPBELL

Professor of Anthropology, University of Montana, Missoula

MAURICE CARNEY

Independent scholar, Friends of the Congo, Washington D.C

JUAN MANUEL CASAL

Professor and Chair, Department of History, Universidad de Montevideo, Uruguay

ELIZABETH CHACKO

Associate Professor of Geography and International Affairs and Chair of the Department of Geography, George Washington University, Washington, D.C.

ALLAN CHRISTELOW

Professor of History, Idaho State University, Pocatello

STEPHEN CRISWELL

Associate Professor of English and Native American Studies, University of South Carolina, Lancaster

JAMSHEED CHOKSY

Professor of Iranian and Islamic Studies, Indiana University, Bloomington

RICHMOND CLOW

Professor of Native American Studies, University of Montana, Missoula

STEPHANIE COX

Visiting Assistant Professor of French, Carleton College, Northfield, Minnesota

SHAHYAR DANESHGAR

Senior Lecturer of Central Eurasian Studies, Indiana University, Bloomington

JEAN DENNISON

Assistant Professor of Anthropology, University of North Carolina, Chapel Hill

JOSE R. DEUSTUA

Associate Professor of History, Eastern Illinois University, Charleston, Illinois

MUNROE EAGLES

Program Director of Canadian Studies and Professor of Political Science, State University of New York, Buffalo

SARAH ENGLAND

Associate Professor of Anthropology and Director of Social and Behavioral Sciences, Soka University of America, Alisa Viejo, California

PHYLLIS FAST

Professor of Anthropology, University of Alaska, Anchorage

SUJATHA FERNANDES

Associate Professor of Sociology, Queens College and the Graduate Center of the City University of New York

ANN FIENUP-RIORDAN

Independent scholar, Calista Elders Council, Bethel, Alaska

SEAN FOLEY

Associate Professor of History, Middle Tennessee State University, Murfreesboro

JAMES GIGANTINO

Assistant Professor of History, University of Arkansas, Fayetteville

EDWARD GOBETZ

Professor Emeritus of Sociology, Kent State University, Ohio

STEVEN J. GOLD

Professor of Sociology and Associate Chair in the Department of Sociology, Michigan State University, East Lansing

ANGELA A. GONZALES

Associate Professor of Development Sociology and American Indian Studies, Cornell University, Ithaca, New York

JONATHAN GOSNELL

Associate Professor of French Studies, Smith College, Northampton, Massachusetts

ISHTAR GOVIA

Lecturer of Psychology, University of the West Indies, Mona, Jamaica

YVONNE HADDAD

Professor of the History of Islam and Christian-Muslim Relations, Georgetown University, Washington, D.C.

JEFFREY HADLER

Associate Professor of South and Southeast Asian Studies, University of California, Berkeley

MARILYN HALTER

Professor of History, Institute on Culture, Religion, and World Affairs, Boston University, Brookline, Massachusetts

ANNE PEREZ HATTORI

Professor of History and Chamorro Studies, University of Guam, Mangilao

MICHAEL HITTMAN

Professor of Anthropology, Long Island University, Brooklyn, New York

INEZ HOLLANDER

Lecturer of Dutch Studies, University of California, Berkeley

JON D. HOLTZMAN

Associate Professor of Anthropology, Western Michigan University, Kalamazoo

KATHLEEN HOOD

Publications Director and Events Coordinator, The UCLA Herb Alpert School of Music, Department of Ethnomusicology, University of California, Los Angeles

MAREN HOPKINS

Director of Research, Anthropological Research, LLC, Tucson, Arizona

GUITA HOURANI

Director of the Lebanese Emigration Research Center, Notre Dame University, Kesrwan, Lebanon

SALLY HOWELL

Assistant Professor of History, University of Michigan, Dearborn

TARA INNISS

Lecturer in History, University of the West Indies, Cave Hill Campus, Barbados

ALPHINE JEFFERSON

Professor of History, Randolph-Macon College, Ashland, Virginia

PETER KIVISTO

Richard A. Swanson Professor of Social Thought, Augustana College, Rock Island, Illinois

MICHAEL KOPANIC, JR.

Adjunct Full Professor of History, University of Maryland University College, Adelphi, and Adjunct Associate Professor of History, St. Francis University, Loretto, Pennsylvania

DONALD B. KRAYBILL

Distinguished College Professor and Senior Fellow, Young Center for Anabaptist and

Pietist Studies, Elizabethtown College, Pennsylvania

GARY KUNKELMAN

Senior Lecturer, Professional Writing, Penn State Berks, Wyomissing, Pennsylvania

AL KUSLIKIS

Senior Program Associate for Strategic Initiatives, American Indian Higher Education Consortium, Alexandria, Virginia

WILLIAM LAATSCH

Emeritus Professor of Urban and Regional Studies, University of Wisconsin, Green Bay

BRUCE LA BRACK

Professor Emeritus of Anthropology, University of the Pacific, Stockton, California

SARAH LAMB

Professor of Anthropology, Brandeis University, Waltham, Massachusetts

LAURIE RHONDA LAMBERT

Doctoral candidate in English and American Literature, New York University

JOHN LIE

C. K. Cho Professor, University of California, Berkeley

HUPING LING

Changjiang Scholar Chair Professor and Professor of History, Truman State University, Kirksville, Missouri

JOSEPH LUBIG

Associate Dean for Education, Leadership and Public Service, Northern Michigan University, Marquette

ALEXANDER LUSHNYCKY

President of the Shevchenko Scientific Society Study Center, Elkins Park, Pennsylvania

NEDA MAGHBOULEH

Assistant Professor, Department of Sociology, University of Toronto, Ontario

WILLIAM MEADOWS

Professor of Anthropology, Missouri State University, Springfield

MARIANNE MILLIGAN

Visiting Assistant Professor of Linguistics, Macalester College, Saint Paul, Minnesota

NAEEM MOHAIEMEN
Doctoral student in Anthropology at Columbia University, New York

ALEXANDER MURZAKU
Professor and Chair of World Cultures and Languages, College of Saint Elizabeth, Morristown, New Jersey

GEORGE MUSAMBIRA
Associate Professor of Communication, University of Central Florida, Orlando

GHIRMAI NEGASH
Professor of English & African Literature, Ohio University, Athens

JENNY NELSON
Associate Professor of Media Studies, Ohio University, Athens

RAFAEL NÚÑEZ-CEDEÑO
Coeditor of Probus: International Journal of Latin and Romance Linguistics and Professor Emeritus of Hispanic Studies, University of Illinois, Chicago

GREG O'BRIEN
Associate Professor of History, University of North Carolina, Greensboro

GRANT OLSON
Coordinator of Foreign Language Multimedia Learning Center, Northern Illinois University, DeKalb

THOMAS OWUSU
Professor and Chair of Geography, William Paterson University, Wayne, New Jersey

JODY PAVILACK
Associate Professor of History, University of Montana, Missoula

BARBARA POSADAS
College of Liberal Arts and Sciences Distinguished Professor of History, Northern Illinois University, DeKalb

JASON PRIBILSKY
Associate Professor of Anthropology, Whitman College, Walla Walla, Washington

LAVERN J. RIPPLEY
Professor of German, St. Olaf College, Northfield, Minnesota

MIKA ROINILA
Ph.D., as well as International Baccalaureate Program Coordinator and Fulbright

Specialist, John Adams High School, South Bend, Indiana

WILL ROSCOE
Ph.D., Independent scholar, San Francisco, California

LEONID RUDNYTZKY
Professor and Director of Central and Eastern European Studies Program, La Salle University, Philadelphia

NICHOLAS RUDNYTZKY
Independent scholar and Board member of the St. Sophia Religious Association of Ukrainian Catholics, Elkins Park, Pennsylvania

YONA SABAR
Professor of Hebrew, University of California, Los Angeles

LOUKIA K. SARROUB
Associate Professor of Education, University of Nebraska, Lincoln

RICHARD SATTLER
Adjunct Assistant Professor, University of Montana, Missoula

RICHARD SCAGLION
UCIS Research Professor, University of Pittsburgh, Pennsylvania

HELGA SCHRECKENBERGER
Chair of the Department of German and Russian and Professor of German, University of Vermont, Burlington

BRENDAN SHANAHAN
Doctoral student in North American history, University of California, Berkeley

KEMAL SILAY
Professor of Central Eurasian Studies and Director of the Turkish Studies Program, Indiana University, Bloomington

JEANNE SIMONELLI
Professor of Cultural and Applied Anthropology, Wake Forest University, Winston-Salem, North Carolina

GUNTIS ŠMIDCHENS
Kazickas Family Endowed Professor in Baltic Studies, Associate Professor of Baltic Studies, and Head of Baltic Studies Program, University of Washington, Seattle

MATTHEW SMITH
Senior Lecturer in History, University of the West Indies, Mona, Jamaica

MARY S. SPRUNGER
Professor of History, Eastern Mennonite University, Harrisonburg, Virginia

THOMAS THORNTON
Director for the MSc in Environmental Change and Management, University of Oxford, United Kingdom

ELAISA VAHNIE
Executive Director at the Burmese American Community Institute, Indianapolis, Indiana

DOUGLAS VELTRE
Professor Emeritus of Anthropology, University of Alaska, Anchorage

MILTON VICKERMAN
Associate Professor of Sociology, University of Virginia, Charlottesville

KRINKA VIDAKOVIC-PETROV
Principal Research Fellow, Institute for Literature and Arts, Belgrade, Serbia

BETH VIRTANEN
President, Finnish North American Literature Association

MARTIN VOTRUBA
Director of the Slovak Studies Program, University of Pittsburgh, Pennsylvania

MARY WATERS
M. E. Zukerman Professor of Sociology, Harvard University, Cambridge, Massachusetts

MARVIN WEINBAUM
Professor Emeritus of Political Science, University of Illinois, Urbana-Champaign

BRENT WEISMAN
Professor of Anthropology, University of South Florida, Tampa

THOMAS L. WHIGHAM
Professor of History, University of Georgia, Athens

BRADLEY WOODWORTH
Assistant Professor of History, University of New Haven, West Haven, Connecticut

KRISTIN ELIZABETH YARRIS
Assistant Professor of International Studies and Women's & Gender Studies, University of Oregon, Eugene

XIAOJIAN ZHAO
Professor of Asian American Studies, University of California, Santa Barbara

LIST OF CONTRIBUTORS

NABEEL ABRAHAM

Abraham holds a PhD in anthropology and is a university professor.

JUNE GRANATIR ALEXANDER

Alexander holds a PhD and has been a university professor.

DONALD ALTSCHILLER

Altschiller holds a PhD in library science and works as a university librarian.

DIANE ANDREASSI

Andreassi is a journalist and freelance writer

GREG BACH

Bach holds an MA in classics and is a freelance writer.

CARL L. BANKSTON III

Bankston holds a PhD in sociology and is a university professor.

CRAIG BEEBE

Beebe holds an MA in geography and works in nonprofit communications.

DIANE E. BENSON ("LXEIS")

Benson holds an MFA in creative writing and is a playwright, actor, and director.

BARBARA C. BIGELOW

Bigelow is an author of young adult books and a freelance writer and editor.

D. L. BIRCHFIELD

Birchfield was a university professor and novelist.

BENJAMIN BLOCH

Bloch holds an MFA in creative writing and an MFA in painting.

ELIZABETH BOEHEIM

Boeheim holds an MA in English literature and has been a university instructor.

CAROL BRENNAN

Brennan is a freelance writer with a background in history.

HERBERT J. BRINKS

Brinks was an author and editor and served as a curator at a university library.

K. MARIANNE WARGELIN BROWN

Wargelin Brown holds a PhD in history and is an independent scholar.

SEAN T. BUFFINGTON

Buffington holds an MA and is the president of The University of the Arts.

PHYLLIS J. BURSON

Burson holds a PhD in psychology and works as an independent consultant.

HELEN BUSH CAVER

Caver held a PhD and worked as a university librarian.

CIDA S. CHASE

Chase holds a PhD and is a university professor.

CLARK COLAHAN

Colahan holds a PhD and is a university professor.

ROBERT J. CONLEY

Conley holds an MA in English, is an award-winning novelist, and has served as a university professor.

JANE STEWART COOK

Cook is a freelance writer.

CHRISTINA COOKE

Cooke holds an MFA in creative nonfiction and works as a university instructor and freelance writer.

AMY COOPER

Cooper holds a PhD in anthropology and is a university professor.

PAUL ALAN COX

Cox holds a PhD in biology and is the director of the Institute of Ethnomedicine.

GIANO CROMLEY

Cromley holds an MFA in creative writing and is a university instructor.

KEN CUTHBERTSON

Cuthbertson is a writer, editor, and freelance broadcaster.

ROSETTA SHARP DEAN

Dean is a former school counselor and president of the Sharp-Dean School of Continuing Studies, Inc.

CHAD DUNDAS

Dundas holds an MFA in creative writing and has been a university instructor and freelance writer.

STANLEY E. EASTON

Easton holds a PhD and is a university professor.

TIM EIGO

Eigo holds a law degree and is writer and editor.

LUCIEN ELLINGTON

Ellington holds an EdD and is a university professor.

JESSIE L. EMBRY

Embry holds a PhD in history and is a research professor.

ALLAN ENGLEKIRK

Englekirk holds a PhD in Spanish and is a university professor.

RICHARD ESBENSHADE

Esbenshade holds a PhD in history and has been a university professor and freelance writer.

MARIANNE P. FEDUNKIW

Fedunkiw holds a PhD in strategic communications and is a university instructor and consultant.

DENNIS FEHR

Fehr holds a PhD in art education and is a university professor.

DAISY GARD

Gard is a freelance writer with a background in English literature.

CLINT GARNER

Garner holds an MFA in creative writing and is a freelance writer.

CHRISTOPHER GILES

Giles holds an MA in classics and an MA in history and is a college instructor and administrator.

MARY GILLIS

Gillis holds an MA has worked as a freelance writer and is a painter and sculptor.

EDWARD GOBETZ

Gobetz holds a PhD in sociology and is a retired university professor and former executive director of the Slovenian Research Center of America.

MARK A. GRANQUIST

Granquist holds a PhD and is a university professor.

DEREK GREEN

Green is a freelance writer and editor.

PAULA HAJAR

Hajar holds an EdD and has worked as a university professor and high school teacher.

LORETTA HALL

Hall is a freelance writer and the author of five works of nonfiction.

FRANCESCA HAMPTON

Hampton is a freelance writer and university instructor.

RICHARD C. HANES

Hanes holds a PhD and has served as the Division Chief of Cultural, Paleontological Resources, and Tribal Consultation for the Bureau of Land Management.

SHELDON HANFT

Hanft holds a PhD in history and is a university professor.

RODNEY HARRIS

Harris is a PhD candidate in history.

JOSH HARTEIS

Harteis holds an MA in English literature and is a freelance writer.

KARL HEIL

Heil is a freelance writer.

EVAN HEIMLICH

Heimlich is a freelance writer and university instructor.

ANGELA WASHBURN HEISEY

Heisey is a freelance writer.

MARY A. HESS

Hess is a freelance writer.

LAURIE COLLIER HILLSTROM

Hillstrom is a freelance writer and editor. She has published more than twenty works of history and biography.

MARIA HONG

Hong is a freelance writer and poet and was a Bunting Fellow at Harvard University in 2010-2011.

RON HORTON

Horton holds an MFA in creative writing and has been a high school English instructor and freelance writer.

EDWARD IFKOVIĆ

Ifković is a professor of creative writing and the author of four novels.

ALPHINE W. JEFFERSON

Jefferson holds a PhD in history and is a university professor.

CHARLIE JONES

Jones is a high school librarian.

J. SYDNEY JONES

Jones has worked as a freelance writer and correspondent and has published twelve works of fiction and nonfiction.

JANE JURGENS

Jurgens has been a university instructor.

JIM KAMP

Kamp is a freelance writer and editor.

OSCAR KAWAGLEY

Kawagley held a PhD in social and educational studies and was a university professor.

CLARE KINBERG

Kinberg holds a masters in library and information science and has been a literary journal editor.

KRISTIN KING-RIES

King-Ries holds an MFA in creative writing and has been a university instructor.

VITAUT KIPEL

Kipel held a PhD in mineralogy and an MLS and worked in the Slavic and Baltic Division of the New York Public Library.

JUDSON KNIGHT

Knight holds BIS in international studies, works as a freelance writer, and is co-owner of The Knight Agency, a literary sales and marketing firm.

PAUL S. KOBEL

Kobel is a freelance writer.

DONALD B. KRAYBILL

Kraybill holds a PhD in sociology and is a university professor.

LISA KROGER

Kroger holds a PhD in English literature and has been a university instructor.

KEN KURSON

Kurson is the editor-in-chief of the New York Observer.

ODD S. LOVOLL

Lovoll holds a PhD in U.S. history and is a university professor.

LORNA MABUNDA

Mabunda is a freelance writer.

PAUL ROBERT MAGOCSI

Magocsi holds a PhD in history and is the chair of Ukrainian Studies at the University of Toronto.

MARGUERITE MARÍN

Marín holds a PhD in sociology and is a university professor.

WILLIAM MAXWELL

Maxwell is a freelance writer who has worked as an editor at A Gathering of the Tribes magazine.

THEODORE MCDERMOTT

McDermott holds an MFA in creative writing and has been a university instructor and freelance writer.

JAQUELINE A. MCLEOD

McLeod holds a JD and PhD and is a university professor.

H. BRETT MELENDY

Melendy held a PhD in history and served as university professor and administrator.

MONA MIKHAIL

Mikhail holds a PhD in comparative literature and is a writer, translator, and university professor.

OLIVIA MILLER

Miller is a freelance writer, consultant, and university instructor.

CHRISTINE MOLINARI

Molinari is a freelance writer and editor and an independent researcher.

AARON MOULTON

Moulton holds an MA in Latin American studies. He is a PhD candidate in history and a university instructor.

LLOYD E. MULRAINE

Mulraine holds a DA in English and is a university professor.

JEREMY MUMFORD

Mumford holds a PhD in history and has worked as a university professor.

N. SAMUEL MURRELL

Murrell holds a PhD in biblical and theological studies and is a university professor.

AMY NASH

Nash is a published poet and has worked as a freelance writer and communications manager for Meyer, Scherer, & Rockcastle, Ltd., an architecture firm.

JOHN MARK NIELSEN

Nielsen is the executive director at the Danish Immigrant Museum.

ERNEST E. NORDEN

Norden holds a PhD and is a retired university professor.

SONYA SCHRYER NORRIS

Norris has worked as a freelance writer and website developer.

LOLLY OCKERSTROM

Ockerstrom holds a PhD in English and is a university professor.

KATRINA OKO-ODOI

Oko-Odoi is a PhD candidate in Spanish language literature and a university instructor.

JOHN PACKEL

Packel has worked as a freelance writer and is an associate director at American Express.

TINAZ PAVRI

Pavri holds a PhD in political science and is a university professor.

RICHARD E. PERRIN

Perrin was a university reference librarian.

PETER L. PETERSEN

Petersen holds a PhD in history and is a university professor.

MATTHEW T. PIFER

Pifer holds a PhD in composition and is a university professor.

GEORGE POZETTA

Pozetta held a PhD in history and was a university professor.

NORMAN PRADY

Prady is a freelance writer.

ELIZABETH RHOLETTER PURDY

Purdy is an independent scholar and has published numerous articles on political science and women's issues.

BRENDAN A. RAPPLE

Rapple holds an MBA and PhD and is a university librarian.

MEGAN RATNER

Ratner is a film critic and an associate editor at Bright Lights Film Journal.

WYLENE RHOLETTER

Rholetter holds a PhD in English literature and is a university professor.

LAVERN J. RIPPLEY

Rippley holds a PhD in German studies and is a university professor.

JULIO RODRIGUEZ

Rodriguez is a freelance writer.

PAM ROHLAND

Rohland is a freelance writer.

LORIENE ROY

Roy holds a PhD and MLS and is a university professor.

LAURA C. RUDOLPH

Rudolph is a freelance writer.

ANTHONY RUZICKA

Ruzicka is pursuing an MFA in poetry and has worked as a university instructor.

KWASI SARKODIE-MENSAH

Sarkodie-Mensah holds a PhD, is an author of research guides, and works as a university librarian.

LEO SCHELBERT

Schelbert holds a PhD in history and is a retired university professor.

JACOB SCHMITT

Schmitt holds an MA in English literature and has been a freelance writer.

MARY C. SENGSTOCK

Sengstock holds a PhD in sociology and is a university professor.

ELIZABETH SHOSTAK

Shostak is a freelance writer and editor.

STEFAN SMAGULA

Smagula has written for The Austin Chronicle and Zymurgy magazine and has designed software for Google, Bloomberg L.P., and The Economist. He works as software product designer in Austin, Texas.

HANNAH SOUKUP

Soukup holds an MFA in creative writing.

JANE E. SPEAR

Spear holds an MD and is a freelance writer and copyeditor.

TOVA STABIN

Stabin holds a Masters of Library and Information Science and works as a writer, editor, researcher, and diversity trainer.

BOSILJKA STEVANOVIĆ

Stevanović holds an MS in Library Science and is an independent translator.

SARAH STOECKL

Stoeckl holds a PhD in English literature and is a university instructor and freelance writer.

ANDRIS STRAUMANIS

Straumanis is a freelance writer and editor, as well as a university instructor.

PAMELA STURNER

Sturner is the executive director of the Leopold Leadership Program.

LIZ SWAIN

Swain has worked as a freelance writer and crime reporter and is a staff writer for the San Diego Reader.

MARK SWARTZ

Swartz holds an MA in art history, has served as writer for numerous nonprofits (including the American Hospital Association), and has published two novels.

THOMAS SZENDREY

Szendrey is a freelance writer.

HAROLD TAKOOSHIAN

Takooshian holds a PhD in psychology and is a university professor.

BAATAR TSEND

Tsend is an independent scholar and writer.

FELIX UME UNAEZE

Unaeze is a university librarian.

STEVEN BÉLA VÁRDY

Várdy holds a PhD in history and is a university professor.

GRACE WAITMAN

Waitman is pursuing a PhD in educational psychology. She holds an MA in English literature and has been a university instructor.

DREW WALKER

Walker is a freelance writer.

LING-CHI WANG

Wang holds a PhD and is a social activist and retired university professor.

KEN R. WELLS

Wells is a freelance writer and editor and has published works of young adult science fiction and nonfiction.

VLADIMIR F. WERTSMAN

Wertsman is a member of the American Library Association and the retired chair of the Publishing and Multicultural Materials Committee.

MARY T. WILLIAMS

Williams has worked as a university professor.

ELAINE WINTERS

Winters is a freelance writer, editor, and program facilitator. She has provided professional training for a number of Fortune 500 companies, including Apple, Nokia, and Nortel.

EVELINE YANG

Yang holds an MA in international and public affairs and is a PhD candidate in the Department of Central Eurasian Studies at Indiana University.

ELEANOR YU

Yu is the Supervising Producer at Monumental Mysteries at Optomen Productions.

INTRODUCTION

The term multiculturalism is used to describe a society characterized by a diversity of cultures. Religion, language, customs, traditions, and values are some components of culture, and culture also includes the perspectives through which people perceive and interpret society. A shared culture and common historical experience form the basis for a sense of peoplehood.

Over the course of U.S. history two divergent paths have led to this sense of peoplehood. All groups except indigenous Americans (Native Americans), have entered North America as voluntary or involuntary immigrants. Some of these immigrant groups and their descendants have been oppressed by the dominant group—white Americans that have been for centuries primarily of northern European descent   and were defined as inferior racial groups. A *racial group* is a societal group that people inside or outside that group distinguish as racially inferior or superior, usually on the basis of arbitrarily selected physical characteristics (for example, skin color). Historically whites have rationalized the subordination of other racial groups, viewing them as biologically and culturally inferior, uncivilized, foreign, and less than virtuous. To the present day Asian, African, Native, and Mexican Americans have been regularly "racialized" by the dominant white group. Even some non-British European immigrant groups (for example, Italian Americans) were for a short period of time defined as inferior racial groups, but within a generation or two they were defined as white.

Another term often used for certain distinctive social groups is *ethnic group*. While some social scientists have used it broadly to include racial groups, the more accurate use of the term is a group that is distinguished or set apart, by others or its own members, primarily on the basis of national-origin characteristics and cultural characteristics that are subjectively selected. "Ethnic" is an English word derived from the Greek word *ethnos* (for "nation") and was originally used for European immigrants entering in the early twentieth century. Examples are Polish Americans and Italian Americans, groups with a distinctive national origin and cultural heritage. Both racial groups and ethnic groups are socially constructed under particular historical circumstances and typically have a distinctive sense of peoplehood and cultural history. However, the lengthy historical and contemporary experiences of racial discrimination and subordination differentiate certain groups, such as African Americans and Native Americans, from the experiences and societal status of the ethnic groups of European origin that are now part of the white umbrella racial group.

"Multicultural America," the subject of this encyclopedia, is the product of the interaction of many different indigenous and immigrant peoples over the course of four centuries in what is now the United States. Cultural diversity was characteristic of the continent prior to the coming of European colonists and the Africans they enslaved. The indigenous inhabitants of North America numbered at least 7 million, and perhaps as many as 18 million, in the sixteenth century and were divided into hundreds of indigenous societies with distinctive cultures. Although the numbers of "Indians," as they were named by European colonizers, declined precipitously over the centuries as a result of European genocidal killings and diseases, their population has rebounded over the last century. As members of particular indigenous groups (such as Navajo, Ojibwa, and Choctaw) and as Native Americans, they are very much a part of today's cultural pluralism.

Most North Americans, in contrast, are the descendants of immigrants from other continents. Since the sixteenth century, from the early Spanish settlement at St. Augustine, Florida, the process of repopulating the continent has gone on apace. Several hundred thousand Europeans and Africans were recruited or enslaved and transported across the Atlantic Ocean during the colonial period to what eventually became the United States. The first census of 1790 revealed the racial and national origin diversity that marked the U.S. population. Almost a fifth of Americans were of African ancestry. (The census did not include Native Americans.) A surname analysis of the white population revealed that about 14 percent were Scottish and Scotch-Irish Americans and about 9 percent were German Americans—with smaller percentages of French, Irish, Dutch, Swedish, and Welsh Americans. English Americans comprised about 60 percent of the white population. At the time of its birth in 1776, the United States was already a complex racial and ethnic mosaic, with a wide variety of communities differentiated by the extent of racial oppression and by their national ancestry, culture, language, and religion.

The present United States includes not only the original 13 colonies but lands that were subsequently purchased or conquered by an often imperialistic U.S. government. Through this territorial expansion, other peoples and their lands were brought within the boundaries of the country. These included, in addition to many Native American societies, French, Hawaiian, Inuit, Mexican, and Puerto Rican groups, among others. Since 1790 great population growth, other than by natural increase, has come primarily through three eras of large-scale immigration. Arriving in the first major era of immigration (1841–1890) were almost 15 million newcomers: more than 4 million Germans, 3 million each of Irish and British (English, Scottish, and Welsh), and 1 million Scandinavians. A second major era of immigration (1891–1920) brought an additional 18 million immigrants: almost 4 million from Italy, 3.6 million from Austria-Hungary, and 3 million from Russia. In addition, more than 2 million Canadians immigrated prior to 1920. The following decades, from 1920 to 1945, marked a hiatus in immigration because of restrictive and discriminatory immigration policies, economic depression, and World War II. A modest postwar influx of European refugees was followed by a new era of major immigration resulting from the U.S. government abandoning in 1965 its openly discriminatory immigration policy favoring northern European immigrants. Totaling more than 40 million immigrants from 1965 to 2013—and still in progress—this third major era of immigration has encompassed about 20 million newcomers from Mexico and other parts of Central and South America and the Caribbean, as well as roughly 10 million newcomers from Asia. The rest have come from Canada, Europe, the Middle East, and Africa. While almost all the immigrants in the first two eras originated in Europe, a substantial majority since 1965 have come from Latin America, the Caribbean, Asia, Africa, and the Middle East.

Immigration has introduced a great diversity of racial-ethnic groups and cultures into the United States. The 2000 U.S. Census, the latest national census to report on ancestry, provides an interesting portrait of the complex origins of the people of the United States. Responses to the question "What is your ancestry or ethnic origin?" were tabulated for many groups. The largest ancestry groups reported were, in order of magnitude, German, Irish, African American, and English, all with more than 24 million individuals. Other groups reporting more than 4 million were Mexican, Italian, Polish, French, Native American, Scottish, Dutch, Norwegian, Scotch-Irish, and Swedish, with many other groups reporting more than 1 million each. There is also an array of smaller groups: Hmong, Maltese, Honduran, and Nigerian, among scores of others. Only 7 percent identified themselves simply as "American"—and less than one percent only as "white."

Immigration has contributed to the transformation of the religious character of the United States. The dominant Anglo-Protestantism (itself divided among numerous denominations and sects) of early English colonists was over time reinforced by the arrival of millions of Lutherans, Methodists, and Presbyterians and diluted by the heavy influx of Roman Catholics—first by the Irish and Germans, then by eastern Europeans and Italians, and more recently by Latin Americans. These immigrants have made Roman Catholicism the largest U.S. denomination. Meanwhile, Slavic Christian and Jewish immigrants from central and eastern Europe established Orthodox Christianity and Judaism as major religious bodies. As a consequence of Middle Eastern immigration—and the conversion of many African Americans to Islam—there are currently several million Muslims in the United States. Smaller numbers of Buddhists, Hindus, and followers of other religions have also arrived. In many U.S. cities houses of worship now include mosques and temples, as well as churches and synagogues. Religious pluralism is an important source of U.S. multiculturalism.

The immigration and naturalization policies pursued by a country's central government are revealing about the dominant group's public conception of the country. By determining who to admit to residence and citizenship, the dominant group defines the future racial and ethnic composition of the population. Each of the three great eras of immigration inspired much soul-searching and intense debate, especially in the dominant European American group, over the consequences of immigration for the U.S. future. If the capacity of this society to absorb tens of millions of immigrants over the course of more than 17 decades is impressive, it is also true that U.S. history has been punctuated by major episodes of vicious and violent nativism and xenophobia. With the exception of the British, it is difficult to find an immigrant group that has not been subject to significant racial or ethnic prejudice and discrimination. From early violent conflicts with Native Americans to the enslavement of Africans, Americans of northern European ancestry sought to establish "whiteness" as an essential marker of racial difference and superiority. They crafted a racial framing of society in order to legitimate and rationalize their subordination of numerous racial and ethnic groups. For example, the Naturalization Act (1790), one of the first passed in the new U.S. Congress, specified that citizenship in the United States was available only to an immigrant who was "a free white person." By this dramatic provision not only were African Americans ineligible for naturalization but also future immigrants who were deemed not to be "white." From that time to the present, the greater the likeness of immigrants to the northern European Protestants, the more readily they were welcomed by the dominant group.

There were, however, opposing, liberty-and-justice views held by racially and ethnically oppressed groups, as well as a version of this outlook supported by a minority of the dominant European American group. For example, in the nineteenth century, citing democratic ideals and universal brotherhood, many African Americans and some white Americans advocated the abolition of slavery and the human rights of those freed from slavery.

Since at least the 1880s debates over immigration policy have periodically brought contrasting views of the United States into collision. The ideal of the United States as a shelter and asylum for the oppressed of the world has exerted a powerful influence for a liberal reception of diverse newcomers. Early support for this liberal framing of immigration came from the descendants of early immigrants who were racially or ethnically different from the then dominant British American group. Poet Emma Lazarus's sonnet, which began "Give me your tired, your poor, your huddled masses yearning to breathe free, the wretched refuse of your teeming shore," struck a responsive chord among many Americans and was placed on the Statue of Liberty, a gift to the United States by the people of France. Emma Lazarus (1849-87) herself was the daughter of early Sephardic (Portuguese) Jewish immigrants to the colonies.

Over the centuries many U.S. businesses have depended upon the immigrant workers of Europe, Latin America, and Asia to develop the country's factories, mines, and railroads. Periodically, nonetheless, many white Americans have framed this immigration in negative terms—as posing a threat to societal stability, to their jobs, or U.S. cultural and biological integrity. Historically the strength of organized anti-immigrant movements has waxed and waned with the volume of immigration, as well as with fluctuations in the condition of the U.S. economy. Although the immigrant targets of nativistic attacks have changed over time, a constant theme in the framing of them by the dominant group has been the "danger" posed by "foreigners" to the core U.S. values and institutions.

For example, coming in large numbers from the 1830s to the 1850s, Irish Catholics were viewed as the dependent minions of the Catholic pope and thus as enemies of the Protestant character of the United States. A Protestant crusade against these immigrants culminated in the formation of the "Know-Nothing" Party in the 1850s, whose political battle cry was "America for the Americans!" This anti-Catholicism continued to be a powerful strain of nativism well into the middle of the twentieth century, including during the election and presidency of John F. Kennedy, an Irish Catholic American, in the early 1960s.

Despite frequent episodes of xenophobia, during its first decades of existence, the U.S. government generally welcomed newcomers with minimal regulation. In the 1880s, however, two important laws passed by a Congress controlled by (northern) European American politicians initiated a significant tightening of restrictions on some immigration. The first law established certain health and "moral" standards by excluding criminals, prostitutes, lunatics, idiots, and paupers. The second, the openly racist Chinese Exclusion Act, was the culmination of an anti-Chinese movement among European Americans centered on the West Coast. It denied admission to new Chinese laborers and barred Chinese workers already here from acquiring citizenship. Following the law's enactment, agitation for exclusion of Asian immigrants continued as the new Japanese and other Asian immigrant workers arrived. This European American nativism soon resulted in the blatantly racist provisions of the 1924 Immigration Law, which denied entry to "aliens ineligible for citizenship" (that is, those who were not "white"). It was not until 1950s and 1960s that a combination of international politics and civil rights movements, with their democratic ideals, resulted in the elimination of the more overtly racial restrictions from U.S. immigration and naturalization policies.

In the mid- to late-nineteenth century "scientific racism," which reiterated the superiority of whites of northern European origin, was embraced by many scientists and political leaders as justification for immigration restrictions and growing U.S. imperialism on the continent and overseas. By the late-nineteenth century the second immigration era was quite evident, as large numbers of immigrants from southern and eastern Europe entered the country. Nativists of northern European ancestry campaigned for a literacy test and other measures to restrict the entry of what they termed "inferior" European nationalities (sometimes termed "inferior races"). World War I created a xenophobic climate that prepared the way for the immigration acts of 1921 and 1924. Inspired by nativistic ideas, these laws established a national quota system designed to greatly reduce the number of southern and eastern Europeans entering the United States and to bar Asians. The statutes intentionally sought to maintain the northern European racial-ethnic identity of the country by protecting it from "contamination" from abroad.

Until 1965 the U.S. government pursued a very restrictive immigration policy that kept the country from becoming more diverse racially, ethnically, and religiously. The 1965 Immigration Act finally did away with the discriminatory national origins quotas and opened the country to immigration from throughout the world, establishing preferences for family members of citizens, skilled workers, entrepreneurs, and refugees. One consequence was the third wave of immigration. Since then, the annual volume of authorized immigration has increased steadily to about 1 million arrivals each year, and the majority of these new residents have come from Asia and Latin America.

The cumulative impact of the immigration of tens of millions of non-European immigrants since 1965 has aroused intense concerns, mostly in the dominant white group, regarding the demographic, cultural, and racial future of the United States. The skin color, as well as the languages and cultures, of most of the newcomers and their descendants have again been viewed negatively by many whites. Nativistic white advocates of tighter immigration restriction have warned that if current rates of immigration continue, white Americans will likely be a minority of the U.S. population by 2050.

One particular cause of white anxiety is the number of undocumented immigrants from Mexico (down to about 140,000 per year by 2013). Contrary to popular belief, the majority of undocumented immigrants do not cross the border from Mexico but enter the country with student or tourist visas and stay. Indeed, many are Europeans and Asians. The 1986 Immigration Reform and Control Act (IRCA) sought to solve the problem by extending amnesty for undocumented immigrants under certain conditions, imposing penalties on employers who hired them, and making provision for temporary agricultural migrant workers. Although more than 3 million people qualified for consideration for amnesty, employer sanctions failed for lack of enforcement, and for a time the number of undocumented immigrants did not decrease. Congress subsequently enacted the Immigration Act of 1990, which established a cap on immigrants per year, maintained preferences based on family reunification, and expanded the number of skilled workers admitted. The Illegal Immigration Reform and Immigrant Responsibility Act (IIRIRA), passed in 1996, established yet more regulations restricting legal and undocumented immigration and increased border control agents.

In 2006 Congress passed yet more restrictive legislation, the Secure Fence Act. It mandated the building of a billion-dollar border fence and other expensive surveillance technology and increased border enforcement personnel. Over recent decades the extensive border surveillance procedures have played a role in many of the estimated 5,100 lives lost as undocumented men, women, and children have tried to cross an ever more difficult U.S.-Mexico border—with its intensively policed and often extremely hot and waterless conditions--to improve their dire economic situations. Latin American immigration has continued to be a hotly debated U.S. political issue. Responding to the nativist mood of the country, politicians have advocated yet more restrictive measures to reduce immigration, as well as limiting access to government programs by legal and undocumented immigrants.

Forebodings about an "unprecedented immigrant invasion," however, have been greatly exaggerated. In the early 1900s the rate of immigration (the number of immigrants measured against the total population) was higher than in recent decades. While the number of foreign-born individuals in the United States reached nearly 40 million in 2010, an all-time high, they accounted for only 12.9 percent of the population, compared with 14.7 percent in 1910, giving the United States a smaller percentage of foreign-born individuals than some other contemporary nations. Moreover, in the early twenty-first century, Mexican immigration to the United States has been decreasing significantly, to the point that in 2005-10 there was a net zero migration to United States—that is, as many Mexicans were leaving the United States as were coming in. A persuasive argument has also been made that immigrants contribute much more than they take from the U.S. economy and pay more in taxes than they receive in social services. As in the past, new immigrants are often made the scapegoats for the country's broader economic and political problems.

Difficult questions face analysts of U.S. history. How have these millions of immigrants with such differing backgrounds and cultures been incorporated into the society? What changes have they wrought in the character of United States? The problematical concept of "assimilation" has traditionally been used to try to understand the process through which immigrants have adapted to U.S. society. Assimilation theorists view cultural assimilation (acculturation) as the one-way process whereby newcomers assume U.S. cultural attributes, such as the English language and political values, and social-group assimilation as the process of immigrant incorporation into important social networks (work, residence, and families) of the dominant group. In many cases such adaptation has not come easily. Many immigrants of color have culturally adapted to a significant degree but have experienced only limited incorporation into many mainstream networks and institutions because of persisting white racial bias and discrimination.

Indeed, since they have always wielded great social and political power, white Americans as a group have been able to decide who to include and exclude in the country. "Race" (especially skin color) has been the major barrier to full acceptance into historically white-controlled institutions. Asian and Latino Americans, as well as African Americans and Native Americans, have long been excluded from full integration into major white-dominated institutions. Race, language, religion, and national origin have been impediments to access. Social class has also strongly affected interactions among U.S. racial and ethnic groups. Historically, U.S. society has been highly strati-fied, with a close congruence between social class and racial or ethnic group. Thus, a high degree of employment and residential segregation has been central to maintaining the United States as a racially segregated society, with white Americans very disproportionately in the powerful upper and upper-middle classes.

The status of women within American society, as well as within particular racial and ethnic groups, has affected the ability of female immigrants to adapt to their new country. Historically, to a greater or lesser extent depending on their group, women have been restricted to traditional gender roles or have had limited freedom to pursue opportunities in the larger society. The density and location of immigrant settlements have also influenced the incorporation of immigrants into the dominant culture and institutions. Concentrated urban settlements and isolated rural settle-ments, by limiting contacts between immigrants and native-born Americans, tend to inhibit the processes of assimilation.

Historically one important variable is the determination of immigrants themselves whether or not to shed important aspects of their cultures. Through chain migrations, relatives and friends have often regrouped in cities, towns, and the countryside for mutual assistance and to maintain their customary ways in a sometimes hostile and difficult U.S. society. Establishing churches, news-papers, and other institutions, they have built communities and have developed an enlarged sense of peoplehood. Thus, national origin and home cultures have been important in many immigrants' attempts to cope with life in the United States. Theirs is often a selective adaptation, in which they have taken from the dominant U.S. culture what they needed and have kept significant aspects of their home culture that they value. The children and grandchildren of immigrants usually retain less of their ancestral cultures (languages are first to go) and have assumed more attributes of the dominant culture. Still, many have retained, to a greater or lesser degree, a sense of identity with a particular nationality or racial group. These patterns of societal adaptation vary greatly for differ-ent groups, historically and in the present. Immigrant groups of color and their descendants have been racialized by the dominant white group and have thus had quite different experiences from immigrants who are part of distinctive national origin groups within a white America. Racialized immigrant groups often use their home culture and its values and perspectives for resources in fight-ing against the racism and discrimination they face in their everyday lives.

For centuries the core culture of the colonies and early United States was essentially British American in most important aspects, and the immigrants (almost all European until the 1850s) and their offspring had to adapt to that dominant culture. Over time a few aspects of that core culture—such as music, food, and literature—have experienced some significant changes. These aspects of the core culture are today products of syncretism—the melding of different, sometimes discordant elements of the cultures of European and non-European immigrants and their descend-ants. Multiculturalism today is not a museum of immigrant cultures but rather a complex of the living, multitudinous cultures of the contemporary United States interacting with each other. Nonetheless, most of the central social, political, and economic realities of the U.S. core culture are still very much European American (especially British American) in their institutional structures, normative operation, and folkways. These include the major economic, legal, political, and educa-tional institutions.

The country's ideological heritage includes the ideals of freedom and equality from the American Revolution. Such ideals have often been just abstract principles, especially for the dominant white group, that have been handed down from the eighteenth century to the present. However, subordi-nated racial and ethnic groups, taking these ideals very seriously, have employed them as weapons to combat economic exploitation and racial and ethnic discrimination. If the United States has been the "promised land" for many immigrants, that promise has been realized, if only in part, after prolonged and collective societal struggles. Through civil rights and labor movements, they have contributed greatly to keeping alive and enlarging the ideals of freedom, equality, and justice. If the

United States has transformed the numerous immigrant and indigenous groups in significant ways, these groups have on occasion significantly transformed the United States.

How has the dominant white American group historically conceived of this polyglot, kaleidoscopic society? Over the centuries two major models of a society comprised of various racial and ethnic groups have competed with each other. The dominant white model long envisioned a society based on racial "caste"— a society constitutionally and legally divided into those who were free and those who were not. Such a societal order existed for about 85 percent of this country's history (until the late 1960s). While the Civil War destroyed slavery, the Jim Crow system of segregation maintained extreme white oppression of black Americans for another hundred years. This model of intensive racial-ethnic oppression was not limited to black-white relationships. The industrial economy created a caste-like structure in much of the North. For a century prior to the progressive "New Deal" era of the 1930s, U.S. power, wealth, and status in the North were concentrated in the hands of a British-American elite, while U.S. workers there, made up largely of European immigrants and their children, were the low-paid serfs of factories, railroads, and farms. In subsequent decades this pattern has shifted as immigrants of color and their children have often filled many of these jobs on farms and in factories in the North and the South. By the 1960s official Jim Crow segregation ended in Southern and border states, and African Americans continued their movement out of the South to the North, which had begun in earnest in the 1930s and 1940s.

Over the centuries, since at least the 1700s, immigrants to this country have been expected by the dominant group to adapt and conform to the British-American ("Anglo-Saxon") core culture. Convinced of their cultural and biological superiority, Americans of British and other northern European descent have pressured Native Americans, African Americans, Latinos, and Asian Americans to modify or abandon their distinctive linguistic and cultural patterns and conform in a more or less one-way adaptive pattern to the dominant culture and folkways. However, even as they have demanded this conformity, European Americans have erected racial barriers that have severely limited egalitarian social intercourse and integration with those they have framed as racially inferior. Indeed, a prime objective of the U.S. public school system has been the one-way "assimilation" of "alien" children to the dominant cultural values and behaviors. The intensity of this pressure can be seen in the successful attacks, mostly white-led, on various programs of bilingual education, especially those involving the Spanish language of many Latin American immigrants and their descendants.

Nonetheless, over the course of U.S. history, and especially since the early 1900s, this intense one-way adaptation model has been countered by variations on a melting pot perspective. The "melting pot" symbolizes the process in which diverse immigrant groups are assimilated into a new "American blend." There have been many variants of this ideology of the melting pot, including the prevailing one in which the European American is still the cook stirring and determining the immigrant ingredients. In all versions the United States is viewed as becoming a distinctive amalgam of varied cultures and peoples emerging from the racial-ethnic crucible. Expressing confidence in the capacity of the country to incorporate diverse newcomers, the melting pot ideology has also provided the rationale for a more liberal approach to immigrants and immigration policy. Even so, this liberal melting pot ideology has periodically come under increasing attacks from anti-immigrant and other nativist groups, even after the progressive changes in U.S. immigration laws in the 1960s.

A third model of immigrant adaptation emerged during World War I in opposition to intensive pressures on immigrants for one-way "Americanization," a model often termed "cultural pluralism." In this model, while sharing a common U.S. citizenship and loyalty, racial and ethnic groups should be able to maintain and foster their particular languages and distinctive cultures. The metaphors employed for the cultural pluralism model have included a symphony orchestra, a flower garden, and a mosaic. All suggest a reconciliation of group diversity with an encompassing harmony and coherence of racial and ethnic groups. During the 1930s, when cultural democracy was more in vogue, pluralist ideas were more popular. Again during the social movements of the

1960s and the 1970s, cultural pluralism attracted a considerable following. By the early twenty-first century, heightened fears, especially among white Americans, that U.S. society is fragmenting and moving away from the dominance of the English language and Euro-American culture have caused many people to reject any type of significant cultural pluralism.

Questions about racial and ethnic matters loom large as the United States moves ever more deeply into the twenty-first century. Its future as a racially and ethnically plural society and socially just society is vigorously debated. Is the United States more diverse today than in the past? Can discriminatory racial and ethnic barriers be finally removed? Can this multiracial society really be made more just and democratic? The old model of one-way conformity to the white-controlled core culture has lost its ideological and symbolic value for a great many Americans who believe we need to implement a more egalitarian societal model. These Americans see the United States as a respectfully multicultural and truly democratic people in the context of a multicultural world.

Suggested Reading On issues of systemic racism and the creation of U.S. racial groups, see Joe R. Feagin, *Systemic Racism: A Theory of Oppression* (2006) and *The White Racial Frame* (2nd edition, 2013). On conventional assimilation theory, see Milton Gordon's *Assimilation in American Life: The Role of Race, Religion, and National Origins* (1964). On recent assimilation theory and applicable data, see Richard Alba, *Blurring the Color Line: The New Chance for a More Integrated America* (2009). For discussion of racial and ethnic group definitions, see Joe R. Feagin and Clairece B. Feagin, *Racial and Ethnic Relations (2011). Harvard Encyclopedia of American Ethnic Groups* (1980), edited by Stephan Thernstrom, is a standard reference work with articles on racial-ethnic themes and specific groups. Roger Daniels's *Coming to America: A History of Immigration and Ethnicity in American Life* (1991) is a comprehensive history. For a comparative history of racial-ethnic groups, see Ronald Takaki's *A Different Mirror: A History of Multicultural America* (1993). A classic work on nativism is John Higham's *Strangers in the Land: Patterns of American Nativism: 1860-1925* (1963). On the British American elite's history, see E. Digby Baltzell's *The Protestant Establishment: Aristocracy and Caste in America* (1964). On contemporary ancestry groups, see Angela Brittingham and G. Patricia de la Cruz, *Ancestry: 2000* (2004).

Rudolph Vecoli
Updated and revised by Joe Feagin

DANISH AMERICANS

John Mark Nielsen and Peter L. Petersen

OVERVIEW

Danish Americans are immigrants or descendants of people from Denmark, the southernmost of the Nordic nations, which also include Finland, Iceland, Norway, and Sweden. Its land mass includes Jutland, a peninsula extending north from Germany, and more than 480 islands. With the exception of its 42-mile southern border with Germany, Denmark is surrounded by water. Sweden lies to the east across the Oresund, a narrow body of water that links the North and Baltic seas; Norway lies to the north; and the North Sea is to the west. Denmark has nearly 4,500 miles of coastline, and no part of the nation is more than 45 miles from the sea. Denmark also possesses Greenland, the world's largest island, and the Faeroe Islands, both of which are semiautonomous. Denmark's total land area is 6,630 square miles (43,094 square kilometers), roughly half the size of the state of Indiana.

According to the *CIA World Factbook*, the Danish population in 2012 was an estimated 5.5 million. One-fourth of the population lives in the capital city of Copenhagen and surrounding suburbs. The majority of Danes are of Nordic stock, and 90 percent are members of the Danish State Church, which is Lutheran. Like many other northern European countries, Denmark has seen an influx of immigration to meet employment needs. By 2011, 10 percent of the population consisted of immigrants or the children of immigrants, with the majority coming from Turkey, Germany, and Iraq. Denmark is one of the twenty wealthiest nations in the world. In addition to agricultural products, Danish industry is noted for pharmaceuticals, high-tech manufacturing, and global shipping. Although Danes pay high taxes, averaging about 50 percent of their income, the people benefit from a welfare system that provides education, health care, and care for the elderly.

The first wave of Danish immigration to the United States occurred in the 1850s after the Book of Mormon was translated into Danish. These immigrants were Mormon converts who settled in Utah. Major Danish immigration to the United States began in the late 1860s after the American Civil War and lasted until the mid-1920s. Because many were farmers or skilled craftspeople, most Danes arriving during this period settled on farms in the Midwest or found jobs in cities such as Chicago, Minneapolis, and Omaha. By 1900 the majority of Danish immigrants lived in a "Danish Belt" stretching from Chicago and Racine, Wisconsin, to Grand Island, Nebraska. Other Danes, however, settled in the New York City area and on the West Coast. Following the Great Depression and World War II, Danes who were highly skilled in engineering and the technical trades immigrated to the United States. Since the 1970s the average number of Danes coming to the United States has dropped to 1,000 per decade, and the population of Danish Americans has steadily declined, from 1,635,000 in 1990, to 1,431,250 in 2000, and 1,375,500 in 2010, suggesting that a number of Danish Americans have chosen to return to their home country in recent years or that some Danish Americans no longer identify with their heritage on census questionnaires. However, between 1990 and the early 2000s many Danes working for Danish and multinational corporations lived and worked in the United States with no intention of becoming U.S. citizens.

According to 2011 American Community Survey estimates, the number of Americans claiming Danish ancestry is about 1.3 million (a number roughly equivalent to the entire population of Dallas, Texas). Although many Danish Americans live in midwestern states (Illinois, Wisconsin, Minnesota, Iowa, and Nebraska), the immigrant population remains widely scattered. Danes are notable for having assimilated rather quickly in comparison to other immigrant groups in the United States. This is because they were educated, Anglo-Saxon in background, Protestant, and—with the exception of a few communities—did not settle in concentrated areas. Today there are small but active Danish American organizations and clubs in New York City, Atlanta, Houston, Los Angeles, San Francisco, Seattle, Minneapolis, and Chicago. Museums and archives that document the history of Danish Americans are located in Elk Horn, Iowa, and Blair, Nebraska, which were popular destinations for Danish immigrants during the earlier and major wave of Danish immigration to this country.

HISTORY OF THE PEOPLE

Early History It was not until the Viking Era of the ninth and tenth centuries that Danes, along with Swedes and Norwegians—collectively known as Norsemen or Vikings—had a significant impact upon world history. Sailing in their magnificent ships, Vikings traveled west to North America, south to the Mediterranean, and east to the Caspian Sea. They plundered, conquered, traded, and colonized. For a brief period in the eleventh century, a Danish king ruled England and Norway.

While Vikings roamed far and wide, those Danes who stayed at home cleared fields, built villages, and gradually created a nation. After a king with the colorful name of Harald Bluetooth (circa 935–985) was baptized circa 965, Christianity began to spread across Denmark. Many Vikings encountered the religion on their voyages and were receptive to it. The current queen of Denmark, Margrethe II (1940–), traces her sovereignty back to Harald's father, Gorm the Old (d. 950), thus making Denmark one of the oldest monarchies in the world. Slowly, the forces of Crown and Church helped make Denmark a major power in northern Europe. Under the leadership of Margrethe I (1353–1412), Denmark, Norway, and Sweden were joined in 1397 in the Kalmar Union. The growth of nationalism ultimately led Sweden to abandon the union in 1523, but Norway and Denmark remained allied until 1814. Like much of Europe in the early sixteenth century, Denmark struggled with the religious and political issues set in motion by the Protestant Reformation, with Catholics and Protestants battling for control. In 1536 a two-year civil war ended when the Lutheran King Christian III defeated the Catholic forces and established Lutheranism as the official religion of Denmark.

Growing rivalry with Sweden and various rulers along the north German coast created new problems for Denmark, but the greatest international disaster to befall the country came during the Napoleonic Wars (1804–1814), when an ill-fated alliance with France left the nation bankrupt; Norway was lost to Sweden. New threats to Danish territory soon followed from the south. After decades of intrigue and diplomatic maneuvering, Denmark and Prussia went to war in 1864 over the status of the Danish-ruled Duchies of Schleswig and Holstein. The Prussians quickly gained the upper hand, and Denmark was forced to surrender both Duchies, which meant a loss of about 40 percent of its territory and more than 30 percent of its population. This defeat reduced Denmark to the smallest size in its history and dashed any remaining dreams of international power.

The nineteenth century was also a time of great domestic change for Denmark. A liberal constitution, which took effect on June 5, 1849, brought an end to centuries of absolute monarchy. Danes could now form political parties, elect representatives to a parliament, and were guaranteed freedom of religion, assembly, and speech. The country also underwent an economic revolution. Danish farmers found it difficult to compete with the low-priced grains offered in European markets by American and Russian exports, and they increasingly turned to dairy and pork production. The growth of industry attracted many job-hungry Danes to developing urban centers. But agricultural change and the rise of industrialism were not enough to stop rising discontent; eventually one out of every ten Danes felt compelled to emigrate, with most traveling to the United States.

Modern Era Throughout the first half of the twentieth century, Denmark pursued a policy of neutrality in international affairs. Although this policy enabled the country to remain a non-belligerent in World War I (1914–1918), it did not prevent a German occupation during much of World War II (1939–1945). It was during this occupation that the Danish people won the admiration of much of the world by rescuing 7,200 of some 7,800 Danish Jews from Nazi forces in 1943. After World War II, Denmark moved away from neutrality, and in 1949 it joined with the United States, Canada, and nine other European nations to form the North Atlantic Treaty Organization (NATO), a pact aimed at containing the expansion of the Soviet Union. In 1973 Denmark became the first and only Scandinavian country to join the European Economic Community (EEC).

The twentieth century also witnessed great economic and social change. Danish agriculture became more specialized and moved toward increased exports while industrial development transformed most urban areas. Denmark gradually became a prosperous nation, and with the development of a welfare system that provides education, health care, and social security from cradle to grave, its citizens now enjoy one of the highest living standards in the world. Since 1972 Queen Margrethe II has presided over this small, peaceful, and civilized land, the character of which is best symbolized by its most famous author, Hans Christian Andersen (1805–1875), a writer of fairy tales with profound psychological depths, and by one of its modern exports—the small, colorful plastic bricks called Lego.

In the early years of the twenty-first century, Denmark continued to work closely with other Western nations even as it continued to enjoy economic success and address evolving social issues at home. Following the September 11, 2001, terrorist attacks that took place on U.S. soil, Denmark passed the most restrictive immigration laws of any country, making it very difficult for immigrants to become citizens. This trend was reinforced in 2005 when protests and riots broke out in the Middle East following the publication of twelve Danish cartoons depicting the Prophet Muhammad. These measures came in response to a growing immigrant population—non-Danes and their children now make up about 10 percent of the Danish population, according to a 2011 report by Statistics Denmark. In August 2009, Anders Fogh Rasmussen, who served as Danish prime minister from 2001 to 2009, became the twelfth Secretary General of NATO.

SETTLEMENT IN THE UNITED STATES

Although it is clear that Vikings reached the coast of Newfoundland early in the eleventh century, it is impossible to determine whether there were any Danes among these early voyagers. In 1619—twelve years after the English first settled at Jamestown—Danish explorer Jens Munk (1579–1628) reached North America; he had been sent by Danish King Christian IV (1577–1648) to find a trade route to the Orient via the Northwest Passage. With two ships and sixty-five men, Munk reached Hudson Bay before winter halted his exploration. Members of the expedition celebrated a traditional Danish Christmas, the first Lutheran Christmas service in North America, near the mouth of the Churchill River. Another Danish explorer, Vitus Jonassen Bering (1681–1741), discovered in 1728 that a narrow body of water separated the North American and Asian continents. Today this strait is named the Bering Sea in his honor. Bering was also the first European to find Alaska in 1741.

Other Danes sought warmer climes. In 1666 the Danish West Indies Company took possession of the island of St. Thomas in the Caribbean. Eventually, Danes took control of nearby St. John (1717) and St. Croix (1733). Danish planters imported slaves from Africa; raised cotton, tobacco, and sugar on the islands; and engaged in a lively commerce with England's North American colonies and, later, the United States. In 1792 Denmark became the first country to abolish the slave trade in overseas possessions. Denmark sold the islands—today called the Virgin Islands—to the United States in 1917 for $25 million.

Individual Danish immigrants reached North America early in the seventeenth century. By the 1640s approximately 50 percent of the 1,000 people living in the Dutch colony of New Netherlands (later New York) were Danes. It has long been believed that Jonas Bronck—for whom the borough of the Bronx was named—was a Dane, but recent research suggests that he may have been a Swede. After 1750 several Danish families who were members of a religious denomination called the Moravian Brethren immigrated to Pennsylvania, where they settled among German Moravians in the Bethlehem area.

From colonial times through 1850, most Danish immigrants to North America were single men, and they quickly blended into the general population. Rarely, with few exceptions, does the name of a Danish immigrant appear in the historical annals of this period. Hans Christian Febiger or Fibiger (1749–1796), often called "Old Denmark," was one of George Washington's most trusted officers during the American Revolution. Charles Zanco (1808–1836) gained a degree of immortality by dying at the Alamo in March 1836 during the struggle for Texan independence. A Danish flag stands today in one corner of the Alamo Chapel as a reminder of Zanco's sacrifice. Peter Lassen (1800–1859), a blacksmith from Copenhagen, led a group of adventurers from Missouri to California in 1839, establishing a trail soon to be followed by "forty-niners." Lassen is considered one of the most important of California's early settlers. Today a volcano in northern California, a California county, and a national park bear his name.

Between 1820 and 1850, only about sixty Danes entered the United States each year. But soon this trickle became a steady stream. From 1820 to 1990, more than 375,000 Danes came to the United States, the vast majority arriving between 1860 and 1930. The peak year was 1882, when 11,618 Danes entered the country. Converts to the Church of Jesus Christ of Latter-day Saints (Mormons) represent the first significant wave of Danish immigrants to the United States. Mormon missionaries from Utah arrived in Denmark in 1850, only months after the Constitution of 1849 granted the Danish people religious freedom. Between 1849 and 1904, when Mormons stopped recruiting immigrants, some 17,000 Danish converts and their children made the hazardous journey to the Mormon Zion in Utah, making Danes second only to the British in number of foreigners recruited by the church to the state. Many of these Danes settled in the small farming communities of Sanpete and Sevier counties, south of Salt Lake City; today these counties rank second and third, respectively, among all the counties in the United States in terms of percentage of Danish ancestry in their population.

Another source of sizable Danish emigration was the Schleswig area of Jutland. As noted earlier, Denmark had been forced to surrender Schleswig to Prussia in 1864. Some 150,000 residents of North Schleswig were thoroughly Danish, and many bitterly resented their area's new status. After Wilhelm I, king of Prussia, became emperor of Germany in 1871, the policy of Prussia in Schleswig was essentially that of Germany. This meant the abolition of the Danish language in the schools and the conscription of young Danish men for the German military. Between 1864 and 1920, when North Schleswig was returned to Denmark as a result of a plebiscite following Germany's defeat in World War I, some 50,000 North Sleswigers immigrated to the United States. Ironically, most of these Danes appear in census statistics as immigrants from Germany rather than Denmark.

Most Danes who immigrated to the United States after 1865 were motivated more by economic than religious or political motives. Like much of nineteenth-century Europe, Denmark experienced a steep rise in population. Better nutrition and medical care had produced a sharp decline in infant mortality, and Denmark's population rose from approximately 900,000 in 1800 to more than 2,500,000 by 1910. Denmark's economy was unable to absorb much of this increase, and the result was the rise of restless and dissatisfied elements within the population. For these

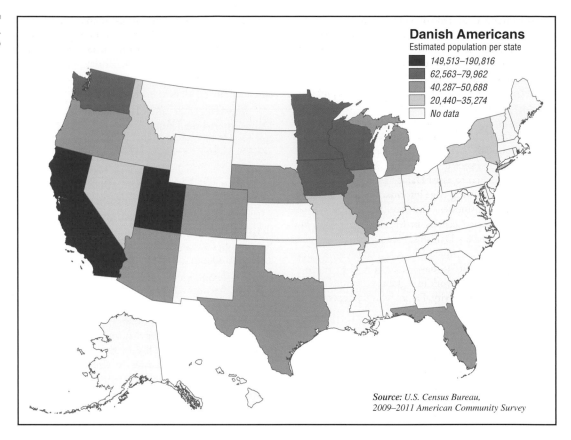

Danish Americans
Estimated population per state
- 149,513–190,816
- 62,563–79,962
- 40,287–50,688
- 20,440–35,274
- No data

*Source: U.S. Census Bureau,
2009–2011 American Community Survey*

people, migration to a nearby city or to the United States appeared to offer the only chance for a better life. Many used the Homestead Act or other generous land policies to become farmers in the United States. The work of emigration agents, often employed by steamship companies and American railroads with land to sell, and a steady stream of letters (some containing prepaid tickets) from earlier immigrants to relatives who had remained in Denmark, stimulated the exodus. During the 1870s almost half of all Danish immigrants to the United States traveled in family groups, but by the 1890s family immigration made up only 25 percent of the total. Perhaps more than 10 percent of these later immigrants, largely single and male, would eventually return to Denmark.

By 1900 a Danish belt of settlement had spread from Wisconsin across northern Illinois and southern Minnesota and into Iowa, Nebraska, and South Dakota. The largest concentration of these settlers was in western Iowa; according to the 2000 U.S. Census the adjacent counties of Audubon and Shelby rank first and fourth, respectively, in the United States in percentage of population with Danish ancestry. Communities with Danish names—Viborg and Thisted, South Dakota; Dannebrog and Nysted, Nebraska; and Ringsted, Iowa—attest to the role of Danes in settling the Midwest.

As the midwestern and eastern Great Plains began to fill with settlers, a variety of immigrant leaders and

organizations sought to establish Danish agricultural colonies elsewhere by arranging for land companies to restrict sales in specific tracts to Danes. The Dansk Folkesamfund (Danish Folk Society) sponsored several of these colonies, including settlements at Tyler, Minnesota, in 1886; Danevang, Texas, 1894; Askov, Minnesota, 1905; Dagmar, Montana, 1906; and Solvang, California, 1911. Similar colonies were established in Mississippi, North Dakota, Oregon, Washington, and Alberta, Canada. Most of these colonies were quite small and eventually blended into the surrounding community. An exception is Solvang, 45 miles north of Santa Barbara, which has become a major tourist attraction and bills itself as "A Quaint Danish Village."

Not all Danish emigrants sought land; a significant minority settled in American cities. Chicago led the way in 1900 with more than 11,000 Danish-born residents; New York counted 5,621. Omaha, Nebraska, and its neighboring city of Council Bluffs, Iowa, also had sizable Danish populations. Smaller concentrations of Danes could be found in Racine, Wisconsin (the city with the highest percentage of Danes among its population), the Twin Cities of Minneapolis and St. Paul, and San Francisco. By 1930 political and economic reform in Denmark, along with the closing of the American farming frontier, had brought this wave of immigration to an end.

The latest wave of immigrants came during the 1950s and the 1960s, when some 25,000 Danes, mostly highly educated young professionals, moved to the United States. They settled in major cities, particularly New York, Chicago, Los Angeles, and San Francisco. With the growth of a global economy, many Danes now legally work and live in the United States for Danish, American, and international corporations without ever planning to become U.S. citizens. There are also very active Danish American chambers of commerce, especially in New York, Chicago, Atlanta, and Houston. In 2006 the Danish government opened up an innovation center in Silicon Valley (Palo Alto, California) to assist Danish companies in taking advantage of cutting-edge information technologies to grow global businesses. The Danish government subsequently opened centers in Munich, Shanghai, and Hong Kong. Many Danish students study or complete internships in the United States, as Danish universities encourage students to have international experiences to prepare them to work in a global economy. Due to global corporate activity, Danes who do become U.S. citizens typically live in major cities.

LANGUAGE

Danish is a North Germanic language closely related to Norwegian and Swedish, and is also related to the West Germanic languages, including German and English. Contemporary Danish has adopted many English and American words such as *weekend*, *handicap*, *film*, and *hamburger*. Danish, however, has also had an influence on English. When Danish Vikings settled in England in the ninth century and established the Danelaw, many of their words became a part of the English language. Examples include: *by*, *fellow*, *hit*, *law*, *sister*, *take*, *thrive*, and *want*. The English town of Rugby is Danish for "rye town," and the word *bylaw* means "town law." Modern Danish has three vowels not found in English: æ (pronounced like the drawn-out "ei" in the English word *eight*); "ø" (pronounced like the "oi" in coil or the "oo" in cool), and å, formerly spelled *aa* (pronounced like the "o" in the English word *or*).

There is a popular saying among Danes that "Danish is not a language at all; it's a throat disease." Unlike the other Scandinavian languages, Danish makes use of the guttural "r" and the glottal stop, a sound produced by a momentary closure of the back of the throat followed by a quick release. The language is not as melodic as Norwegian or Swedish. Danes or Danish Americans challenge people who do not speak the language to say the name of a popular dessert, a fruit pudding made from raspberries or currants called *rødgrød med fløde* ("roidth groidth meth floodthe")—literally, red gruel with cream. The guttural "r" and the "ø" sound, made deep in the back of the throat, make this phrase virtually impossible to say for someone who does not speak Danish.

Because the Danish language is similar to English in syntax and the use of regular and irregular verbs, Danish immigrants did not have as much difficulty learning English as many other immigrants did. Almost all Danish immigrants were literate when they arrived, which also contributed to rapid linguistic assimilation. Today most Danish Americans do not read, speak, or write Danish, whereas most Danes speak English fluently. There are, however, Danish-language "Saturday" schools for children in Washington, D.C., Houston, and other cities; Danish-language classes at such universities as the University of Washington, the University of Wisconsin, and the University of Texas; and Danish-language summer camps in Oregon and Minnesota where students can learn Danish.

Greetings and Popular Expressions Although Danes in the United States quickly acquired English, many phrases and expressions remain popular and are understood within the Danish American community. Common greetings and other expressions (with pronunciation) include: *goddag* ("go'-day")—good day; *godmorgen* ("go'-mo'-ren")—good morning; *godaften* ("go'-af-ten")—good evening; *farvel* ("fa'-vel")—goodbye; *på gensyn* ("po gen-soon")—see you later; *værsgo* ("vairs-go")—please, or would you be so kind?; *til lykke* ("til looka")—congratulations; *tak* ("tuck")—thanks; *mange tak* ("monga tuck")—many thanks; *velkommen* ("vel-komin")—welcome; *glædelig jul* ("gla-le yool")—Merry Christmas; *godt nytår* ("got newt'-or")—Happy New Year. When toasting each other, the Danes, like other Scandinavians, use the word *skål* ("skoal"), which literally means "bowl." One popular tradition suggests that the expression was used when Vikings celebrated victory by drinking from the skulls of their enemy. A more civilized Danish word for which there is no exact English equivalent is *hyggelig* ("hoo'-ga-le"). *Hyggelig* describes a warm, cozy environment in which friends eat, drink, and converse.

> He who can do a little of everything gets along best. He must not shirk hard work, and he must not shirk being treated like a dog. He must be willing to be anyone's servant, just like any other newcomer here.
>
> Peter Sørensen in a letter dated April 14, 1885.

RELIGION

With the exception of the Mormons in Utah and small numbers of Methodists, Baptists, and Seventh-day Adventists, most Danish immigrants were Lutheran and at least nominal members of the *Folkekirke*, the Danish National Church. After the adoption of the liberal constitution of 1849, the Church of Denmark was no longer a state church; however, it has always been state-supported. For many years there was no established Danish Lutheran organization in the United States, and those immigrants who were religiously inclined frequently worshiped with Norwegian or Swedish Lutherans. In 1872, however, two clergymen from Denmark met with some laymen in Neenah, Wisconsin, and organized what became the Danish Evangelical Lutheran Church. The church faced many difficulties, including slow growth. By one estimate, only about one out of every ten Danish immigrants joined a Danish Lutheran church.

Along with a slow rate of growth, another problem in establishing a strong Danish Lutheran congregation in the United States involved the development within the Danish National Church of a factionalism, which immigrants carried to the United States. On one side were the followers of the aforementioned Grundtvig, the Danish educator and church leader, who emphasized the Apostle's Creed and the sacraments. These people were called Grundtvigians. Their opponents were identified as members of the Inner Mission. They stressed biblical authority, repentance, and the development of a personal faith. Eventually the theological disputes within the Danish Church in the United States grew so serious that in 1892 the Church was forced to close its seminary at West Denmark, Wisconsin. Two years later many of the Inner Mission members left the church and formed their own organization. In 1896 this faction joined with another Inner Mission group that had started a small Danish Lutheran church headquartered at Blair, Nebraska, in 1884. This new body called itself the United Danish Evangelical Lutheran Church. The divisions among Danish Lutherans in the United States weakened the church's role as a rallying point, thus contributing to the immigrant's rapid assimilation.

The Danish Church (*Grundtvigian*) was more inclined than the United Danish Church to stress its immigrant heritage. It opened Grand View Seminary in Des Moines, Iowa. The seminary also offered nontheological courses, and in 1938 it became an accredited junior college. The seminary function of the college ceased in 1959 and its name was ultimately changed to Grand View University. The Danish Church and its 24,000 members joined with three non-Danish Lutheran bodies in 1962 to form the Lutheran Church in America.

The United Church (Inner Mission) operated Trinity Seminary (founded in 1884) and Dana College on the same campus at Blair, Nebraska. In 1956 Trinity moved to Dubuque, Iowa, where four years later it merged with Wartburg Seminary. The 60,000-member United Church joined with German and Norwegian churches to form the American Lutheran Church in 1960.

In 1988, when the Lutheran Church in America and the American Lutheran Church merged to create the Evangelical Lutheran Church in America, the century-long organizational division among Danish Lutherans in the United States came to an end.

CULTURE AND ASSIMILATION

Historians agree that the Danes were among the most easily acculturated and assimilated of all American ethnic groups. A variety of studies indicate that in comparison to other immigrants Danes were more likely to speak English, become naturalized citizens, and marry outside their nationality. Several factors explain the relative ease of Danish assimilation. In comparison to people from many other countries, the number of Danish immigrants to the United States was quite small. Danes were generally literate and understood the democratic process, were Protestant in their religion, and easily blended with the northern and western European majority. Because Danes offered little challenge to the more established Americans, they seldom encountered resistance.

Traditions and Customs Danes have a variety of traditions and customs that have been adapted or preserved in Danish American society. Everyday life customs include men and women shaking hands with everyone when entering or leaving a group. Danes and Danish Americans take great pleasure in setting a proper table and following proper dining etiquette. This often means using fine Danish porcelain from one of the two famous Danish porcelain makers, Royal Copenhagen or Bing and Grøndahl. Being a guest requires that one bring flowers for the hostess. When a guest meets the host or hostess shortly after being entertained, the proper greeting is *Tak for sidst* ("tuck for seest")—Thanks for the last time.

Cuisine Danes love to eat and often do so six times a day. This includes morning and afternoon coffee and cookies and *natmad* ("nat-madth"), a snack eaten before going to bed. Many Danish Americans continue this routine. A Danish breakfast consists of an array of breads, cheeses, jellies, and plenty of butter. This is often topped off with pastry that in no way resembles what has come to be known in the United States as a "Danish." This pastry is baked fresh, with flaky, golden brown crust, and rich fillings.

Lunch often includes open-faced sandwiches or *smørrebrød* ("smoorbroidth"). These are artfully created to be both a feast for eye and palate. Combinations include: sliced, smoked beef, fried onions and a mayonnaise topping; carrots and peas mixed with mayonnaise topped with mushrooms; parboiled egg slices topped with anchovies or smoked eel; and a children's favorite, liver paste and slices of pickled red beets, which is eaten like peanut butter and jelly sandwiches in the United States. Beer, *sodavand* ("soda-van")—soda—and coffee are popular beverages.

The most important and time-consuming meal of the day is *middag* ("mid-da'")—midday, though it is eaten in the evening. Danes linger for at least an hour over this meal. *Middag* might include stuffed pork, fish (often plaice or cod), or *frikadeller* ("fre-ka-della'")—Danish meatballs of pork, beef, flour, and egg. Inevitably, the meal would also include *brunede kartofler* ("bru'-na-the car-tof-ler")—potatoes browned in butter and sugar; *rødkål* ("roidth-coal")—red cabbage; marinated fresh cucumbers; beer or a glass of red wine; and a dessert of cookies and fruit pudding, *rød grød med fløde*.

Other popular Danish dishes served in Danish American communities are: *rullepølse* ("rol'-la-poolsa")—spiced, pressed veal; *medisterpølse* ("ma-dis'-ta-poolsa")—pork sausage; *sød suppe* ("sooth soopa")—sweet soup made with fruit; *æbleskiver* ("able skeever")—Danish pancake balls; and *kringler* ("cringla")—almond-filled pastry.

Danes and Danish Americans welcome any excuse for gathering together and eating. Formal dinners are held at Christmas, confirmations, wedding anniversaries, and "round" birthdays—birthdays that can be divided by ten. Formal dinners normally last at least four to five hours and include toasts, lighthearted speeches, singing, and much conversation.

Traditional Dress Danish peasant costumes were colorful, yet practical. A woman's costume consisted of headdress, scarf, outer bodice, knitted jacket, apron, shift, and leather shoes with clasps of silver or pewter. The scarf was often embroidered in bright colors of red and yellow on one side and with more somber, mourning colors on the other so that it could be reversed depending on the occasion. The cut and design of headdress, scarf, and apron reflected regional identities. Men wore hats or caps, a kirtle or knee-length coat, shirt, waistcoat, trousers, woolen stockings, and shoes or high boots. By the 1840s these folk costumes of rural Denmark had become a thing of the past. On special occasions in the Danish American community, some will dress in "traditional" costumes, but these often reflect a nostalgic recreation of the past rather than a true authenticity.

Dances and Songs Danish folk dancing mirrors other northern European countries with both spirited and courtly dances. On the Faeroe Islands, a stately line dance dates back to the time of the Vikings. Singing is a part of many Danish and Danish American gatherings. Popular are songs from the period of Danish Romanticism (1814–1850), which celebrate former national greatness or the gently rolling Danish countryside. The two Danish national anthems capture these important themes: "*Kong Christian stod ved højen mast*" ("King Christian Stood by Lofty Mast") by Johannes Ewald (1743–1781) and "*Der er et yndigt land*" ("There Is a Lovely Land") by Adam Oehlenschlager (1779–1850).

Holidays Entertaining and tradition merge in the many customs surrounding Christmas. Because of the dark Scandinavian winter nights, Christmas, with its message of hope, light, and love, is especially welcomed and celebrated in Denmark. Danish Christmas customs are also celebrated by Danish Americans. December begins with baking. No home is without

DANISH KRINGLE

Ingredients
Dough:

1 package yeast

¼ cup warm water

1½ tablespoon sugar

½ cup scalded milk, cooled

2 egg yolks, beaten slightly

½ cup lard or cold butter

2 cups flour

½ teaspoon salt

Nut filling:

1 cup nuts (pecan or walnut)

½ cup brown sugar

½ cup butter

2 egg whites

Preparation

Dissolve yeast in warm water, add sugar. Add cooled milk and eggs and mix. Cut in lard or butter. Add flour and salt. Knead dough for 3 minutes. Place the dough in a bowl, cover, and let rise until doubled in size.

Mix filling ingredients together with hands into a nut paste.

When dough has risen, divide in half and roll out into two long rectangular shapes approximately 6 inches wide by 27 or so inches long.

Beat egg whites until foamy. With knife, spread foam down center of dough only. (not out to edges). Add half the nut mixture down the center of dough. Fold edges of dough over the filling mixture, then fold up ends so filling will not seep out.

Carefully lift Kringle and place on a cookie sheet in a U shape. Bake at 375°F for 20–30 minutes. Glaze while still warm.

at least seven different kinds of Christmas cookies. These treats are shared with guests, and it is customary to take decorated plates of cookies to friends and relatives. This custom is the origin of the well-known porcelain Danish Christmas plates that can be found in many homes. Often associated with the Royal Copenhagen porcelain company, which has been manufacturing Christmas plates since 1895, these festive plates are manufactured with unique winter and Christmas-related scenes and have become collectors' items around the world.

The celebration of Christmas culminates on Christmas Eve, a holiday traditionally shared with close family. Usually the family attends church in the

Danish Americans gather to celebrate the 4th of July and Constitution Day (July 5) at the same time. AP PHOTO / HENNING BAGGER / SCANPIX NORDFOTO

year. While Danish Americans may have special decorations depicting the *nisse*, they have largely adopted the American tradition of eagerly awaiting the arrival of Santa Claus.

In addition to Christmas, many Danish Americans celebrate Grundlovsdag, or Constitution Day, on June 5, marking the date in 1849 when the modern Danish state was born. Rebildfest is an unusual celebration held on the fourth of July in Denmark and attended by many Danish Americans. It was begun by Danish Americans in 1912 and is billed as the largest celebration of American independence held outside the United States.

Death and Burial Rituals In Denmark funerals are typically held in churches, which are often surrounded by graveyards. The order of service for funerals is similar to that of Protestant denominations in the United States. The deceased is either placed in a coffin or cremated and buried in the church graveyard. Gravesites are tended for twenty years. After that time, if the family does not pay for annual upkeep, gravestones are removed, and reburial occurs in the plot. This practice differs from what is customary in the United States.

FAMILY AND COMMUNITY LIFE

Danish family life has changed dramatically over the twentieth century. Prior to World War II, Danish families, both nuclear and extended, were very traditional in structure. Although women in Denmark have been afforded respect and certain property rights since the Viking era, Danish society was patriarchal. Danish immigrants to the United States brought this patriarchal family structure with them. Changes in Danish American family structure have been influenced by the evolution of the American family structure and not by what has occurred in Denmark, particularly since World War II.

Since the 1960s, family life has evolved in Denmark. This is due in part to the sexual revolution that took place during the 1950s and 1960s. Indeed, sexuality is viewed very differently in Denmark than it is in the United States, even among Danish Americans. The period of adolescence is recognized as a time of sexual awakening, and today Danish parents seem to accept that their teenage children will engage in sexual activity. Birth control methods are readily available to all, including teenagers. Danish American families are typically more conservative, particularly regarding sexuality, but also politically as well.

Gender Roles Family life has also evolved in Denmark due to greater gender equity. Danish women received the right to vote in local elections in 1908 and in all elections in 1915. Beginning in 1924, women have played an important role in government, and after Danish elections in September 2011, Helle Thorning-Schmidt became the country's first female prime minister. Since 1980, Danish law has assured

late afternoon and then returns to a feast of roast goose and all the trimmings. A special dessert is prepared: "*risengrød*" ("reesingroidth"), a rice pudding in which one whole almond is placed. The person who discovers the almond will have good luck throughout the coming year. After dinner, the family gathers around the Christmas tree, which is typically decorated on the day before Christmas Eve. It is lit with candles and decorated with paper cuttings of angels, woven straw ornaments, heart-shaped baskets, and strings of Danish flags. In Danish American homes, the tree is often decorated earlier and lit with electric lights. The family joins hands and dances around the tree, singing favorite carols. Gifts are exchanged, and the family enjoys coffee and cookies. The celebration does not end until a bowl of porridge is taken to the *nisse* ("nisa")—the mythical little people of Denmark who inhabit the lofts and attics of homes. This ritual assures happiness and good fortune in the coming equality of pay and working conditions for men and women. This has resulted in almost 80 percent of Danish women participating in the workforce, the highest participation rate in Europe. For Danish families, this has meant that men are increasingly playing a greater role in the home.

Education Education has played an important role in the Danish American community. Folk high schools were a significant early influence. Inspired by the writings of Bishop Nicolai Frederik Severin Grundtvig (1783–1872)—a Danish poet, pastor, and educator—these schools offered an education that sought to instill a love of learning in its students, though they offered no diplomas and no tests or grades were given. Folk schools were established in Elk Horn, Iowa (1878–1899); Ashland, Michigan (1882–1888); West Denmark, Wisconsin (1884); Nysted, Nebraska (1887–1934); Tyler, Minnesota (1888–1935); Kenmare, North Dakota (1902–1916); and Solvang, California (1910–1931). Because the educational philosophy differed significantly from many American institutions, folk high schools eventually ceased to exist. Grundtvig's philosophy lives on in adult education programs and in the work of the Highlander Research and Education Center in Tennessee, which played an important role in the Civil Rights Movement of the 1950s and 1960s. Elderhostel, a popular program offering senior citizens one-week educational experiences on college and university campuses, has roots in the folk high school experience and the writings of Grundtvig. Two liberal arts colleges founded by Danish Americans were Dana College and Grand View College. Founded in 1884 in Blair, Nebraska, Dana College was forced to close in 2010 due to financial difficulties. Grand View, in Des Moines, Iowa, was originally a seminary and two-year college before it became a four-year college in 1975. The school changed its name to Grand View University in 2008 because it had become a master's degree-granting institution.

Courtship and Weddings Individuals are free to choose whom they wish to marry. Prior to World War II, marriage typically occurred in the State Lutheran Church. Although church attendance has declined, particularly in urban areas, church weddings remain popular. However, today many couples will live together and even become parents prior to getting married. It is not unusual to see wedding portraits that also include children at the time of their baptism, with both ceremonies being held at the same time. Gays and lesbians have the right to register their partnerships with the government and enjoy rights equal to those of married couples. As in the United States, the divorce rate in Denmark is high, with about 40 percent of Danish marriages ending in divorce. Because Danish Americans have assimilated so easily, their wedding practices reflect those of American society. These practices differ little from traditions in Denmark, such as a short church ceremony and a reception featuring food, drinks, speeches, and dancing.

EMPLOYMENT AND ECONOMIC CONDITIONS

The majority of the Danes who immigrated to the United States looked to agriculture for a livelihood. Many who were farm laborers in Denmark soon became landowners in the United States. Danish immigrants contributed to American agriculture, particularly dairying, in a variety of ways. Danes had experience with farmers' cooperatives and helped spread that concept in the United States. The first centrifugal cream separator in the United States was brought to Iowa by a Dane in 1882. Danes worked as butter makers, served as government inspectors, and taught dairy courses at agricultural colleges.

The majority of the Danes who immigrated to the United States looked to agriculture for a livelihood. Many who were farm laborers in Denmark soon became landowners in the United States. Danish immigrants contributed to American agriculture, particularly dairying, in a variety of ways. Danes had experience with farmers' cooperatives and helped spread that concept in the United States.

Among Danish immigrants, young, single women often took jobs as domestic servants, but few remained single very long, as they were in demand as spouses. Men who sought nonfarm work found it in construction, manufacturing, and various business enterprises. With the exception of small concentrations in a Danish-owned terracotta factory in Perth Amboy, New Jersey, and in several farm equipment manufacturing companies in Racine, Wisconsin, urban Danes were rarely identified with a specific occupation.

Following the Great Depression and World War II, many Danish immigrants were highly skilled in engineering and the technical trades. Today there are Danes who legally live and work in the United States for short periods of time, following already-established careers working for Danish or multinational corporations. These Danes tend to be highly educated and highly skilled, and often return to Denmark or to other global postings after a few years rather than settling permanently in the United States.

POLITICS AND GOVERNMENT

Given their small numbers and widespread distribution across the United States, Danes have seldom been able to form any kind of voting bloc beyond local elections in a few rural areas. Nevertheless, politicians of Danish descent have served as governors of Iowa, Minnesota, Nebraska, and California. Several others have served in the U.S. Congress. In every election these Danish American politicians have had to depend upon non-Danish voters for a majority of their

The sculpting of the Mount Rushmore National Memorial was overseen by Gutzon Borglum, the son of Mormon Danish immigrants. After his death, Gutzon's son Lincoln continued the work. FUSE / GETTY IMAGES

support. Danes have not displayed any collective allegiance to a particular political party.

Two events in the twentieth century involving Denmark have attracted significant political interest among Danish Americans. The first of these was the status of Schleswig after World War I. Danish Americans organized to lobby the administration of President Woodrow Wilson to ensure that a provision granting Schleswigers the right to vote on their status be included in any peace treaty with Germany. Accordingly, in February 1920, residents of North Schleswig voted to return to Denmark after fifty-six years of foreign rule. Danish Americans expressed considerable concern about the German occupation of Denmark during World War II. After the war many Americans sent relief parcels to their Danish relatives.

Relations between Denmark and the United States have been unusually cordial. In 1791 Denmark became the eighth nation to recognize the independence of the United States, and it has maintained uninterrupted diplomatic relations since 1801, longer than any other country. In 1916, by a margin of nearly two to one, Danes voted to approve sale of the Danish West Indies (the U.S. Virgin Islands) to the United States. During World War II the United States and Denmark signed a treaty authorizing the United States to build two air bases in Greenland. After the war the United States provided Denmark with $271 million in Marshall Plan aid. In 1949 both nations joined the North Atlantic Treaty Organization (NATO) and thereafter jointly operated several military installations in Greenland.

NOTABLE INDIVIDUALS

Academia Peter Sørensen "P. S." Vig (1854–1929), church leader and teacher, wrote six books on the Danish immigrant experience and contributed to and edited the two-volume *Danske i Amerika* (*Danes in America*), published circa 1908. Marcus Lee Hansen (1892–1938) is acclaimed as a scholar who—early on—understood the importance of the immigrant experience in American life; his book *The Atlantic Migration* was awarded the Pulitzer Prize for History in 1941. The preeminent historian Henry Steele Commager (1902–1998) wrote of the influence his maternal grandfather, the Danish-born Adam Dan (1848–1931), had on him as a child; Dan was one of the founders of the Danish Lutheran Church in America and an important writer in the immigrant community.

Alvin Harvey Hansen (1887–1975), a Harvard economist influenced by the economic theories of John Maynard Keynes, played a role in the formation of the Social Security System in 1935 and in the Full Employment Act of 1946 that established the Council of Economic Advisors. Economist Alvin Johnson (1874–1971), a child of Danish parents, was cofounder of the New School in New York City. Johnson became director of the school in 1922, creating a division known as "the University in Exile" and bringing over European scholars who suffered Nazi persecution in their home countries in the 1930s and 1940s.

Activism Frequently described as the "mother of the consumer movement," Esther Peterson (1906–1997) was a daughter and granddaughter of Danish Mormons who immigrated to Utah. She spent much of her life fighting for better working conditions, rights for women and minorities, and corporate transparency that would provide more information on consumer products and allow for more informed decision making by consumers. In 1981 she received the Presidential Medal of Freedom, the nation's highest civilian honor for public service. Twelve years later she was among thirty-six women inducted into the National Women's Hall of Fame at Seneca Falls, New York. At the ceremony she was characterized as "one of the nation's most effective and beloved catalysts for change."

Art One of the most important monuments in the United States is Mount Rushmore National Memorial in South Dakota. The heads of presidents George Washington, Thomas Jefferson, Abraham Lincoln, and Theodore Roosevelt were sculpted by Gutzon Borglum (1867–1941), the son of Danish immigrants. Christian Gullager (1759–1826), the earliest of Danish American artists, painted George Washington's portrait in 1789. A Danish Mormon, Carl Christian Anton Christensen (1831–1912), created a panorama of works depicting important events in the history of the Mormon trek to Utah. Benedicte Wrensted (1859–1949), born in Hjørring, Denmark, photographed many Native Americans at her studio in Pocatello, Idaho.

More recently, two artists, Olaf Seltzer (1877–1957) and Olaf Wieghorst (1899–1988), have been recognized for their depictions of the Old West. Marshall Fredericks (1908–1998) was a contemporary, award-winning sculptor of Danish descent who has exhibited in the United States and Europe.

Broadcasting Individuals of Danish descent have made important contributions to American media. The A. C. Nielsen Company, founded in 1923 by Arthur C. Nielsen Sr., pioneered media market listener surveys for radio and television. The Nielsen Ratings have become an integral part of programming decisions both by the networks and cable companies. Bill Rasmussen and Scott Rasmussen (1956–), a father-and-son team with roots in Chicago's Danish American community, founded the Entertainment and Sports Programming Network (ESPN) in 1979.

Commerce and Industry Peter L. Jensen (1886?–1961) and an American partner invented the loudspeaker system and founded the Magnavox Company; later, Jensen established the Jensen Radio Manufacturing Company, which makes Jensen Speakers. A Danish-born blacksmith who settled in Nebraska, William Petersen (1882–1962) invented and registered the name Vise-Grip. In 2008 the manufacture of this widely used tool was moved from De Witt, Nebraska, to Shenzhen, China. William S. Knudsen (1879–1947), who was born in Copenhagen, became president of General Motors in 1937 and was chosen by President Franklin D. Roosevelt to lead the development of defense production programs during World War II.

Government Several Danish Americans have served multiple terms in the U.S. Congress. For example, Ben Jensen (1892–1970) represented Iowa's Seventh District from 1938 to 1964, while voters in Minnesota's Second District sent Ancher Nelsen (1904–1992) to Congress for eight terms between 1958 and 1974. Lloyd Bentsen (1921–2006), the grandson of a Danish immigrant to South Dakota, was elected to the House of Representatives for Texas in 1948; the twenty-seven-year-old was the youngest member of Congress at that time. In 1970 Bentsen won election to the Senate, and in 1988 he was the vice presidential candidate on the Democratic ticket headed by Michael Dukakis. President Bill Clinton appointed Bentsen as secretary of the Treasury in 1992.

Another high-profile member of the Clinton Cabinet, Attorney General Janet Reno (1938–), is also of Danish descent; her father, Henry Reno, was an immigrant who changed his surname from Rasmussen to Reno after his arrival in the United States. Prior to her appointment, Reno served as the state's attorney in Dade County, Florida. Although she never reached full Cabinet rank, Esther (Eggertsen) Peterson (1906–1997) held a variety of important governmental posts. An outspoken consumer advocate, Peterson was named by President John F. Kennedy as assistant secretary of labor and director of the Women's Bureau in the U.S. Department of Labor; in 1977 President Jimmy Carter appointed her as special assistant to the president for consumer affairs.

Journalism Jacob A. Riis (1849–1914), the most important Danish American journalist, fought for the rights of the poor; his work *How the Other Half Lives* (1890) described the impoverished conditions of laborers in New York City. Riis had a powerful ally in the person of President Theodore Roosevelt. Two important newspaper men in the Danish American community were Christian Rasmussen (1852–1926) and Sophus Neble (1862–1931). Rasmussen, a Republican, founded or purchased a number of papers in Minnesota, Wisconsin, and Illinois, and his printing company, headquartered in Minneapolis, published magazines and books as well. Neble's newspaper, *Den Danske Pioneer* (*The Danish Pioneer*), published in Omaha, championed the Democratic Party and had the largest circulation of any Danish American newspaper, reaching an estimated readership of 100,000.

Literature A number of writers have described the Danish immigrant experience. Most, however, have written in Danish. Kristian Østergaard (1855–1931) wrote both poetry and fiction; his five novels combine fantastic tales of Indians, horse thieves, and bank robbers with accounts of Danish immigrants struggling to create Danish communities on the prairies. The poet Anton Kvist (1878–1965) found audiences through the Danish American press; many of his poems were set to music and sung within Danish immigrant circles. Enok Mortensen (1902–1984) published several collections of stories, novels, and an important history, *The Danish Lutheran Church in America* (1967); his novel *Den lange plovfure* (*The Long Plow Furrow*), published in Denmark in 1984, is the last novel written by an immigrant who participated in the major wave of Danish immigration.

The most important Danish American novelist writing in English was Sophus Keith Winther (1893–1983); three of his novels, *Take All to Nebraska* (1936), *Mortgage Your Heart* (1937), and *This Passion Never Dies* (1937), portray the struggles of the Grimsen family, which arrives in Nebraska in the 1890s. The novels illustrate the darker side of the rural experience as fluctuating grain prices drive the family into bankruptcy. Julie Jensen McDonald's novel *Amalie's Story* (1970) recounts the story of an immigrant woman whose poor parents are forced to give her up for adoption. Later she finds success as an immigrant in the Danish American community in Iowa.

Music Lauritz Melchior (1890–1973), the great heroic tenor, won worldwide acclaim on European and American stages for his roles in the operas of Richard Wagner. Born in Copenhagen, Melchior began his career with the Metropolitan Opera in 1926; shortly before World War II, he immigrated to the United States with his German-born wife and settled in California, where he starred in a number of films; he continued to perform with the Metropolitan Opera until his retirement in 1950. Libby Larsen (1950–), an award-winning composer and the granddaughter of Danish immigrants, was named composer in residence with the Minnesota Orchestra in 1983.

Performance The most famous Danish American entertainer was Victor Borge (1909–2000). Fleeing Copenhagen after the Nazi occupation of Denmark in 1940, Borge came to New York; in 1941 a successful guest appearance on Bing Crosby's *Kraft Music Hall* radio program launched his career. Known as "The Clown Prince of the Piano," Borge entertained audiences with a unique blend of music and humor.

Science and Medicine Max Henius (1859–1935), a chemist, specialized in fermentation processes; proud of his Danish heritage, he was the prime mover in founding the Danes Worldwide Archives in Ålborg, Denmark, and establishing the Rebild Celebration of the Fourth of July in Denmark. Niels Ebbesen Hansen (1866–1950), a horticulturist, did pioneering work in the development of drought-resistant strains of alfalfa.

Sports Although there have been a number of Danish Americans of later generations who have played in professional sports, the most famous recent Danish American immigrant to play professionally is Morten Andersen (1960–), a kicker for five National Football League teams, primarily the New Orleans Saints and the Atlanta Falcons, between 1982 and his retirement in 2007. With a total of 2,544 points, as of 2012 he remained the NFL's all-time leading scorer. Born in Denmark, Andersen came to the United States at the age of seventeen as a high school exchange student; before immigrating, he had never kicked a football.

Stage and Screen Jean Hersholt (1886–1956) appeared in more than 200 films between 1914 and 1955; he is best remembered for his creation in the 1930s of the popular radio character "Dr. Christian." Another well-known actor of Danish descent is Buddy Ebsen (1908–2003), who starred in three long-running television series: *Davy Crockett*, *The Beverly Hillbillies*, and *Barnaby Jones*. Leslie Nielsen (1926–1997), a descendant of Danish immigrants to Canada (born in Canada, he later became a U.S. citizen), gained wide popularity in the comedic *Naked Gun* films.

MEDIA

Bien

Founded in 1882 in San Francisco, *Bien* was known in its early days as "the West Coast's Scandinavian newspaper."

Jytte Madsen, Publisher and Editor in Chief
19360 Rinaldi Street
Porter Ranch, California 91326
Phone: (818) 366-4100
Fax: (818) 368-6068
Email: Biendk@aol.com
URL: www.biendk.com

Church and Life

This periodical is published ten times a year by the Danish Interest Conference of the Evangelical Lutheran Church in America at Askov, Minnesota.

Joy Ibsen, Editor
123 NW 7th Street
Grand Rapids, Michigan 55744-2639
Phone: (218) 326-6776
Email: churchandlife@danamerica.com
URL: www.churchandlife.org

Den Danske Pioneer

Founded in Omaha in 1872, this publication has maintained the largest circulation of any Danish American newspaper throughout its history. In 1958 it was purchased by Chicago investors, the publication was moved to Illinois.

Linda Steffensen, Editor in Chief
1582 Glen Lake Road
Hoffman Estates, Illinois 60169-4023
Phone: (847) 882-2552
Fax: (847) 882-7082
Email: dpioneer@aol.com
URL: www.dendanskepioneer.com

ORGANIZATIONS AND ASSOCIATIONS

Danish American Heritage Society (DAHS)

Founded in 1977 to explore and record the history of Danish immigrants to North America.

Egon Bodtker
925 NE 15th Street
Salem, Oregon 97301
Phone: (503) 588-1331
Email: egonb@teleport.com
URL: www.danishamericanheritagesociety.org

Danish American Society

Since 1959, when the Danish American Society (DAS) was incorporated as a nonprofit, nonpolitical membership organization, it has pursued the goal of promoting friendship and understanding between the peoples of Denmark and the United States.

Lisa Resling Halpern, President
One Dag Hammerskjolds Plaza
885 Second Avenue
18th Floor
New York, New York 10017
Phone: (856) 912-3105
Email: info@das-ny.org
URL: www.das-ny.org

Danish Brotherhood in America (DBIA) (Woodmen of the World/Assured Life Association

A fraternal organization founded in 1882. It merged with the Woodmen of the World fraternal benefit society in 1992 and offers private insurance to members and their families.

Jerry Christensen
6030 Greenwood Plaza Boulevard
Suite 100
Greenwood Village, Colorado 80111
Phone: (800) 777-9777
Email: fraternal@denverwoodmen.com
URL: www.denverwoodmen.com

Rebild National Park Society

A Danish American friendship society founded in 1912 that encourages interaction between Danish Americans and the community at large.

Linda Steffensen, Corporate Secretary
1582 Glen Lake Road
Hoffman Estates, Illinois 60169
Phone: (847) 882-2552
Email: usrebildoffice@gmail.com
URL: www.rebildfesten.dk

Society for the Advancement of Scandinavian Studies (SASS)

An association of scholars and others interested in the cultures of the Nordic countries: Denmark, Finland, Iceland, Norway, and Sweden.

Mark Sandberg, President
SASS
Brigham Young University
3168 JFSB
Provo, Utah 84602-6702

Phone: (801) 422-5598
Email: sandberg@berkeley.edu
URL: www.scandinavianstudy.org

Supreme Lodge of the Danish Sisterhood of America (DSA)

Organized in 1883 in Negaunee, Michigan. Early lodges were organized to provide social and financial aid to fellow Danish countrymen in this new land.

Lizette Burtis
1462 Trombetta Street
Santa Rosa, California 95407
Email: lburtis@sbcglobal.net
URL: www.danishsisterhood.org

MUSEUMS AND RESEARCH CENTERS

Danish American Archive and Library (DAAL)

Houses a collection of unpublished written materials, photographs, and audio recordings that highlight the experiences of early Danish immigrants.

Jill Hennick, Director
1738 Washington
Blair, Nebraska 68008
Phone: (402) 426-7910
Email: info@danishamericanarchive.com
URL: www.danishamericanarchive.com

Danish Immigrant Archives, Grand View University

Contains personal accounts, photographs, and books and newspapers that trace the history of Danish immigrants and their contributions in America.

Sherri Muller
1351 Grandview Avenue
Des Moines, Iowa 50310
Phone: (515) 263-6199
Email: smuller@grandview.edu
URL: www.grandview.edu/aspx/audience/content.aspx?pageid=420

The Danish Immigrant Museum

Opened in 1994, the Danish Immigrant Museum houses records of Danish immigrant arrivals and documents the story of nineteenth-century Danish immigration to the United States.

John Mark Nielsen, Director
2212 Washington Street
Elk Horn, Iowa 51531
Phone: (712) 764-7001
Fax: (712) 764-7002
Email: director@danishmuseum.org
URL: www.danishmuseum.org

Family History and Genealogy Center of the Danish Immigrant Museum

This extension of the Danish Immigrant Museum provides resources for Danish Americans to trace their lineage.

Michele McNabb, FHGC Manager
4210 Main Street

PO Box 249
Elk Horn, Iowa 51531-0249
Phone: (712) 764-7008
Fax: (712) 764-7010
Email: librarian@danishmuseum.org
URL: www.danishmuseum.org

SOURCES FOR ADDITIONAL STUDY

Hale, Frederick Hale. *Danes in North America*. Seattle: University of Washington Press, 1984.

Hvidt, Kristian. *Flight to America*.New York: Academic Press, 1975.

Kjølhede, Peder, P. S. Vig, and I. M. Hansen. *Danes Go West*. Skørping, Denmark: Rebild National Park Society, Inc., 1976.

————. *Danes in America: Danish Lutheranism from 1860–1909*. Blair, NE: Lur Publications, 2001.

Larsen, Birgit Flemming, and Henning Bender, eds. *Danish Emigration to the U.S.A.* Ålborg, Denmark: Danes Worldwide Archives, 1992.

MacHaffie, Ingeborg, and Margaret Nielsen. *Of Danish Ways*. Minneapolis: Dillon Press, Inc., 1976.

Mussari, Mark. *The Danish Americans*. New York: Chelsea House Publishers, 1988.

Nielsen, George. *The Danish Americans*. Boston: G. K. Hall & Co., 1981.

Petersen, Peter L. *The Danes in America*. Minneapolis: Lerner Publication Company, 1987.

Petersen, Peter S. *Peter S. Petersen's Memoirs*. Blair, NE: Lur Publications, 2003.

Stilling, Niels Peter, and Anne Lisbeth Olsen. *A New Life*. Ålborg, Denmark: Danes Worldwide Archives, 1994.

DOMINICAN AMERICANS

Sean T. Buffington

OVERVIEW

Dominican Americans are immigrants or descendants of immigrants from the Dominican Republic, a nation that occupies the eastern portion of the Caribbean island of Hispaniola. The Dominican Republic takes up approximately two-thirds of the island, while the nation of Haiti occupies the western portion. Hispaniola is part of the Greater Antilles, one of two island groups in the Caribbean Sea. The Greater Antilles also include Cuba and Jamaica, located to the west of Hispaniola, and Puerto Rico, Hispaniola's eastern neighbor. The four highest peaks in the Caribbean are located in the Dominican Republic's Cordillera Central, or Central Mountain Range. The Dominican Republic is the second largest Caribbean nation. At 18,704 square miles (48,442 square kilometers), the country is roughly the size of New Hampshire and Vermont combined.

According to a 2010 census conducted by the country's Office of National Statistics, the Dominican Republic has a population of approximately 9.4 million. A 2010 report on international religious freedom conducted by the United Nations High Commissioner of Refugees (UNHCR) indicated that, although the Dominican Republic has traditionally been a predominantly Roman Catholic nation, with 68.9 percent of the population still declaring that as their religion, other religious denominations have seen a significant increase in followers. Evangelical Protestant groups account for close to 18 percent of the population, while the country maintains small but growing Jewish, Muslim, Hindu, and Buddhist communities. An indeterminable portion of the population practices a syncretic version of Catholicism and Afro-Caribbean beliefs. Due to the country's colonial history, 74 percent of the Dominican Republic's population is multiracial, with many inhabitants possessing both European and African ancestry. The U.S. State Department ranks the Dominican Republic's as the second largest economy in the Central America and Caribbean region; it relies primarily on tourism and agriculture.

Following the assassination of dictator Rafael Trujillo in 1961, Dominicans immigrated to the United States in unprecedented numbers, settling predominantly in New York, New Jersey, Massachusetts,

Pennsylvania, Rhode Island, and Florida. Many of the first wave of male immigrants worked in unskilled or semiskilled labor in the manufacturing industry. Female immigrants worked primarily in the service industry or in garment shops. As they became more established, Dominican Americans branched out into the service industry and a variety of small businesses, including grocery stores, travel agencies, and beauty shops. During the 1990s the majority of Dominicans who immigrated to the United States were in pursuit of employment and educational opportunities. This trend continued throughout the last decade of the twentieth century and into the twenty-first century as Dominicans continued to immigrate to the United States with hopes of securing higher wages and stable employment.

According to the U.S. Census Bureau, approximately 1.4 million people claiming Dominican ancestry were living in the United States as of 2010. These Dominican American communities are predominantly urban. For example, most Dominican Americans in New York and New Jersey live in either New York City (the Washington Heights neighborhood of Manhattan is one prominent location) or the New Jersey suburbs of New York City. Similarly, Dominican Americans in Massachusetts tend to live in Boston, while those in Florida reside mostly in Miami. Since the early 2000s, sizeable communities have emerged throughout the United States, including in Washington, D.C.; Baltimore, Maryland; New Orleans; Philadelphia and Allentown, Pennsylvania; and Portland, Oregon.

HISTORY OF THE PEOPLE

Early History The nation now called the Dominican Republic was colonized by the Spanish in the late fifteenth and early sixteenth centuries. The island of Hispaniola's previous inhabitants, known as the Taínos, were decimated primarily by diseases carried by the Spanish, but also through war, enslavement, and intermarriage. To replenish the population and provide workers for the plantations, the Spanish brought African slaves to the island in the early sixteenth century. In the late seventeenth century, France occupied and colonized the western third of the island, a region then called Saint-Domingue, which would later become the nation of Haiti.

Like the other Spanish Caribbean colonies at that time, the region of Hispaniola under Spanish rule was sparsely populated, mainly by those of Spanish descent (including Spanish "creoles," a term for people of Spanish descent born in the Americas) and relatively small numbers of African and African-descended slaves. Isolated from a distant Spanish monarch, underpopulated, and with little investment from the outside, the region languished, particularly in comparison to its French and British West Indian neighbors, Barbados and Saint-Domingue. In the seventeenth and eighteenth centuries, respectively, those regions became centers of sugar production based on slavery and generated great wealth for the British and French planters who owned the land. It was not until the nineteenth century that the region of Hispaniola now known as the Dominican Republic developed into a central presence in the Western Hemisphere.

In 1822 the newly founded nation of Haiti, which had won its independence from France at the turn of the century and become the first black sovereign nation in the Americas, invaded and occupied the Spanish portion of Hispaniola. For the remainder of the century, the Spanish portion of Hispaniola—including its capital city, Santo Domingo—passed into and out of sovereignty, winning independence from Haiti in 1844 and then voluntarily resubmitting to Spanish colonial rule in 1861. After regaining independence in 1865, the Dominican government discussed the possibilities of annexation with U.S. officials.

At the same time that the government was discussing new political directions, the Dominican economy began to experience new growth after centuries of slow progress. Cuban immigrants, along with others from North America and Europe, brought new capital into the country. They invested heavily in the sugar industry, which soon became the most important productive industry in the nation.

Modern Era The Dominican Republic's claims to sovereignty did not go unchallenged in the twentieth century. The United States invaded and occupied the Caribbean island twice, first in 1916 (in an occupation that lasted until 1924), and again in 1965. The second invasion played a significant role in launching the most recent migration of Dominicans to the United States. The assassination of military ruler Rafael Trujillo in 1961 marked the start of a period of political uncertainty in the Dominican Republic that ended when U.S. paratroops intervened by order of President Lyndon B. Johnson. The U.S. intervention brought to a close a civil war between supporters of democratically elected President Juan Bosch and his right-wing opponents in the Dominican military and oversaw the election of former Trujillo aide Joaquin Balaguer to the presidency.

That civil war and subsequent intervention by the United States on the side of the conservative military led to an outflux of Bosch supporters and other like-minded political activists from the Dominican

Republic in the 1960s. Most of those emigrants relocated to the United States and became the first of many Dominicans to arrive in the country over the next several decades.

In 1965 the United States sent additional forces to the Dominican Republic to prevent what President Johnson perceived to be a communist threat in the region and to monitor the transition of power from Bosch to Joaquin Balaguer. Between 1966 and 1978, President Balaguer and the Reformist Party established a repressive regime, which was challenged by Dominican Revolutionary Party (PRD) candidate Antonio Guzmán. Balaguer resisted Guzmán's election and attempted to retain his political power until external pressure from the United States forced him to yield his presidency to Guzmán. Guzmán remained in power until 1982, and PRD candidate Salvador Jorge Blanco won the presidential election that same year. With the Dominican Republic facing considerable debt and a struggling economy, Blanco enrolled the country in an austerity program with the International Monetary Fund (IMF). Despite Blanco's efforts, the Dominican Republic faced growing economic instability that increased the cost of food and led to massive riots in 1984.

Balaguer returned to power in 1986 and attempted to revitalize the economy through a variety of public works efforts. However, the country continued to face severe economic depression, and by 1989 the government was unable to supply people with basic services, leading to violent protests and a nationwide strike in the summer of 1989. The violence increased leading up to the 1990 elections. Although Balaguer secured his reelection, the elections were tainted by suspicions of fraud. In response to the increasing economic and political turmoil, Balaguer sought an agreement with the IMF, which helped to bring a period of stability to the country's economy. Balaguer won reelection in 1994, but observers of the election as well as the opposition questioned the legitimacy of the electoral process. The United States pressured Balaguer to hold new elections in 1996. Balaguer agreed to withhold his name from the ballot, but his vice president failed to garner sufficient popular support, forcing Balaguer to lend his support to PLD candidate Leonel Fernández. The so-called Patriotic Front between Balaguer and Fernández insured the latter's victory against the PRD candidate, José Francisco Peña Gómez.

Under Fernández's leadership, the Dominican Republic was a more active participant in regional affairs and organizations, including the Organization of American States (OAS) and the Summit of the Americas. Fernández's efforts helped to bring relative political stability to the country and sparked an extended period of considerable economic growth. The PRD regained control when Hipólito Mejía was elected in 2000. Mejía broadened the Dominican Republic's international involvement by signing the

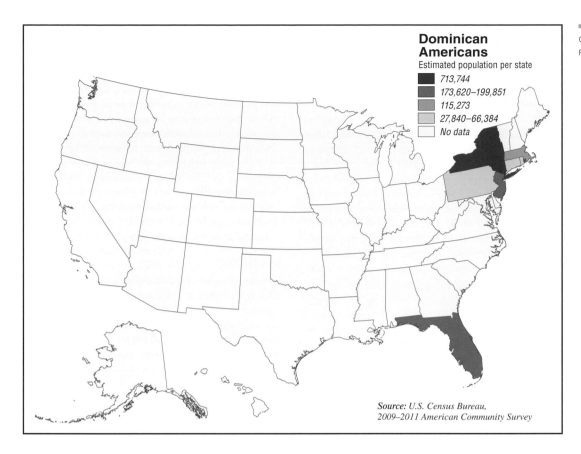

Dominican Americans
Estimated population per state

- 713,744
- 173,620–199,851
- 115,273
- 27,840–66,384
- No data

*Source: U.S. Census Bureau,
2009–2011 American Community Survey*

Central America Free Trade Agreement (CAFTA-DR) between the United States, Costa Rica, El Salvador, Guatemala, Honduras, and Nicaragua, as well as by committing troops for Operation Iraqi Freedom. Mejía presided over a tumultuous era of domestic and economic problems during which the country was plagued by bank fraud and power shortages. Fernández defeated Mejía and regained the presidency in 2004, broadening the Dominican Republic's international relationships and working closely with the United Nations, the OAS, and the United States to strengthen the country's security, law enforcement, and immigration policies. Fernández served as president until 2012, when he was succeeded by Danilo Medina.

SETTLEMENT IN THE UNITED STATES

Although Dominicans established small immigrant communities in the United States in the early twentieth century, greater numbers began arriving in the 1950s. Close to 10,000 Dominicans, mostly political exiles, fled their home country over the course of the 1950s. The numbers increased dramatically following the assassination of Trujillo in 1961. Immigration numbers averaged close to 9,330 Dominicans per year between 1961 and 1965. As the political situation in the Dominican Republic stabilized, Dominicans continued to emigrate because of limited employment opportunities and poor economic conditions in their country. Studies

have shown that Dominicans who emigrated in the 1960s were better educated than those who continued to live on the island and were more likely to have been employed when they left the Dominican Republic. Up to the end of the 1960s, these urban and usually professional migrants left the Caribbean to find better opportunities elsewhere.

At the end of the 1960s, the United States instituted a series of measures to curb the rising tide of Caribbean immigrants. The numbers for Dominican immigrants, however, continued to rise over the next few decades. Of the 169,147 Dominican-born persons residing in the United States at the time of the 1980 U.S. Census, only 6.1 percent had come to the United States before 1960. More than one-third had emigrated during the 1960s, the Dominican Republic's decade of political instability, and 56 percent had arrived in the 1970s. During the 1980s, Dominican immigration soared once again. In those ten years, more than 250,000 Dominicans were legally admitted to the United States. The number of new immigrants in that ten-year period was 50 percent greater than the entire Dominican-born population of the United States at the start of the decade. The 1990 U.S. Census reported that of the 506,000 persons of Dominican descent living in the United States, the vast majority were Dominican-born. Thus, the Dominican American community at that time was comprised primarily of recent immigrants.

According to the 2010 U.S. Census, most Dominican immigrants, or 86.3 percent, have settled in the northeast. Although the greatest number reside in New York and New Jersey (nearly 873,000), there are significantly sized Dominican communities in Massachusetts (103,292) and Florida (172,451).

No reliable figures exist on the number of undocumented Dominican immigrants in the United States. However, many who have studied Dominican immigration believe the number to be quite high. One scholar writing in 1986 suggested that there were some 300,000 undocumented Dominicans in the United States at that time. Although that number seems high given the statistics collected by the U.S. Census Bureau in 1990, it does suggest the significance of undocumented immigrants in the Dominican American community.

Many Dominican migrants return to the Dominican Republic to visit or to resettle permanently. Again, no recent or reliable statistics show exactly how many Dominicans have returned to the Caribbean or for how long. Some indicators, however, suggest that the return movement is significant. For example, the tourism secretariat in the Dominican Republic reported in 1985 that 20 percent of visitors to the island from abroad were Dominicans who had previously emigrated. Moreover, certain businesses and institutions—including schools, apartment buildings, and discos—have been opened in the Caribbean nation to cater specifically to returning emigrants.

Dominicans who settle in the United States maintain a strong interest in their country of origin. Many emigrants and *retornados*, or returned migrants, have invested heavily in the Dominican Republic, establishing real estate brokerages and grocery stores, among other businesses, on the island. Even those who do not start businesses contribute vitally to the economic life of the Dominican Republic. Remittances, monies sent back to family members still resident on the island, bring more foreign currency into the Dominican economy than any industry except tourism.

According to the results of the 2010 U.S. Census, the largest Dominican populations live in New York (674,787), New Jersey (197,922), Florida (172,451), Massachusetts (103,292), and Pennsylvania (62,348). Additionally, Dominican communities have emerged in the Midwest, with the 2010 Census reporting over 25,000, out of which 5,600 were reported for Chicago alone with the rest distributed through Milwaukee, Wisconsin; Grand Rapids, Michigan; St. Paul, Minnesota; and Indianapolis, Indiana. Similar to much of the country, Dominicans and other Hispanic immigrants are altering many regional demographics, such as in Alaska, where military bases and seasonal fishing have attracted immigrant communities, including Dominicans. Of the more than 39,000 people in Alaska who identified as Hispanic, close to 2,000 claimed Dominican ancestry.

LANGUAGE

Dominican migrants are primarily Spanish speakers. The 2010 U.S. Census showed that close to 92 percent of Dominican American homes listed Spanish as their primary language, although approximately 55 percent of those homes reported that they speak English well or very well. Given the propensity of immigrants to speak their native tongue, second-generation Dominicans typically live in bilingual environments. As with many immigrant populations, however, the dominance of U.S. culture has led many Dominicans to accept English as a first language. Similarly, due to interactions with their fellow students, employees, and neighbors, approximately 70 percent of third generation children speak mainly English.

RELIGION

Similar to Dominicans in their native country, more than 90 percent of Dominican Americans identify themselves as Roman Catholic. Some Dominicans also participate in an Afro-Catholic religion known as Santería, but in the United States this religion is primarily associated with Cuban and Puerto Rican immigrant communities and there are no reliable statistics showing how many Dominican Americans practice it. Santería combines certain aspects of Catholic belief with aspects of West African, chiefly Yoruba, belief and practice. Participating in Santería rites does not preclude belonging to a Catholic church and practicing that religion. The UNHCR's 2010 study found that while a majority of Dominican Americans identify themselves as religious and nearly half reported that they attend religious services three or more times per month, approximately one-third stated that they do not attend a religious service.

CULTURE AND ASSIMILATION

The Dominican Republic has an ongoing and often contentious relationship with the United States, its culture, and its citizens. Because of U.S. cultural and political hegemony in the Caribbean basin and extended periods of U.S. occupation, Dominicans are familiar with the United States and its culture. American movies and television programs are shown regularly in the Dominican Republic, baseball is the most popular sport in the country, and U.S. values are admired and emulated by many Dominicans. Thus, Dominicans who immigrate to the United States often have more than a passing familiarity with the country. However, those migrants who return home to the Dominican Republic are often disparaged for the degree to which they have adopted U.S. cultural forms.

The available evidence suggests that Dominican migrants do not have a simple and wholly positive relationship with Americans and U.S. culture. Most Dominican Americans work in nonunionized workplaces for wages that most "established" Americans would refuse. Many Dominican Americans have also encountered racial prejudice in the United States. The mixed Afro-Hispanic heritage of many Dominicans has led them to be categorized by white Americans as black, making them susceptible to the same racial prejudice that African Americans have experienced for centuries. Despite their compatriots' accusations of assimilation into U.S. culture, Dominican Americans tend to be viewed by other Americans as especially committed to their country, culture, and language of origin and particularly resistant to assimilation.

Dominican Americans are one of the newer national-cultural communities in the United States and are thus still in the process of creating a unique place for themselves in their adopted country. The relationships Dominican Americans have with the United States, the Dominican Republic, and those respective cultures are still evolving, and the character of the space the community carves out for itself still remains to be seen.

The evidence so far does suggest, however, that Dominicans in the United States have neither abandoned their country and culture of origin nor wholly embraced the culture of their adopted land. The accusations from nonmigrant Dominicans that migrants are too "American" clearly indicate that migrants have adopted certain highly visible characteristics of U.S. culture. Dominicans residing in the Caribbean who criticize Dominican migrants point to several aspects of Dominican American culture as "foreign" or "un-Dominican." According to Luis E. Guarnizo, "Migrants' style of living, their tastes, and their manners, especially those of youngsters and the most prosperous … are judged as tasteless and revolting especially by the upper classes." This may suggest that the children of migrants are abandoning traditional children's roles and adopting distinctly "American" models of proper behavior and attitudes for children. At least one young Dominican migrant has noted that young people in the United States behave differently than Dominican youngsters, that they are "too 'liberal'—so preoccupied with boyfriends, clothes, and the latest fads". Studies have also shown that the occupational profile of a migrant is different from that of an islander. Additionally, Dominican American women are more likely to find steady employment than their male counterparts, which positions the mother or daughter as the primary wage earner in the household. Nevertheless, certain behaviors among Dominican Americans—such as their regular return to the Caribbean and their tendency to settle in mostly Dominican communities in the United States—suggest that they retain a strong connection to their homeland, its customs, and its people.

Like many other immigrant groups, Dominican migrants have been regarded by many Americans as coming from the poorest, least educated segment of their country of origin. They have also been accused of placing a substantial burden on federal and state social

DOMINICAN PROVERBS

A buen hambre no hay pan duro.

When you are really hungry, no bread is too hard to eat.

Creerse que el maco es peje por estar en el agua.

To believe that a frog is a fish because it lives in the water (meaning that appearances can be deceiving).

Después de la excusa, nadie queda mal.

After the excuses were given, everybody got along fine.

El que anda con perro a ladrar aprende.

He who hangs out with a dog will learn how to bark.

El que quiere moños bonitos tiene que aguantar halones.

If you want nice hair, you have to pull it tight (meaning that if you want something, you need to work hard for it).

Entrar a comer ojos.

Between a rock and a hard place.

Es mejor andar solo que mal acompañado.

Better to go alone than to keep bad company.

Lo agarraron asando batatas.

He got caught with his pants down.

Lo que va, viene.

What goes around, comes around.

Si la vaca la venden por libras, por qué comprar la vaca entera?

If you can buy the cow by the pound, why buy the entire cow?

services. Research conducted in the 1980s showed both of these ideas to be false at the time. That research indicated that the proportion of highly educated Dominicans was greater among the migrant community than among island Dominicans. In the group of Dominicans who entered the United States between 1986 and 1991, there were 15,000 professionals. As a group, Dominican migrants were also shown to have more schooling than island Dominicans. Likewise, 99 percent of undocumented Hispanic immigrants and 85.9 percent of documented Hispanic immigrants surveyed in 1981 reported that they had never received welfare payments in the United States. A majority of both groups also reported that they had never received unemployment compensation or food stamps.

By the late 1990s, however, these statistics had changed, with poverty among Dominican Americans on the rise. As a whole, the American family was changing, reflected in the growth of single-parent households headed by women, up 8.6 percent in New York City between 1989 and 1997. Consequently, more families were relying on public assistance, including Dominican Americans. In 1997 a survey conducted by City College of New York (CCNY) and Columbia University showed that 50 percent of Dominican American households in New York City had a woman at their head, while the poverty rate among those households was 45.7 percent. This trend toward poverty was not sudden. In 1990 the only immigrants in New York City receiving more public assistance than Dominicans were those from the former Soviet Union.

As with many immigrant groups, second-generation Dominican Americans experience greater financial and professional success than the first generation of immigrants. According to multiple studies, second generation Dominican Americans are fluent in English and have made great strides in assimilating to the larger culture. While such assimilation assists second generation Dominican Americans in achieving financial success, those populations still face marked racism and social stigmas that inhibit their upward movement.

Cuisine Dominican dishes are similar to those in other Latin American countries. Many traditional dishes, such as *arepa*, *sancocho*, and *chapea*, rely on rice, beans, and meat or seafood. Due to the Dominican Republic's colonial heritage, some dishes also have African influences, including *mangu* (boiled, mashed plantains) and a variety of stews. Little specific information about the Dominican American diet is available. However, many Dominican Americans operate small independent grocery stores, or bodegas, in Dominican neighborhoods. These grocery stores, in addition to selling toiletries and American food products, sell Caribbean and Latin American products and ingredients commonly used in Dominican cooking. The presence of these stores indicates that Dominicans in the United States continue to prepare traditional Dominican dishes with some frequency.

Holidays Although it is not an official Dominican American holiday, the annual Dominican Day Parade in New York City is one of the best places to witness the growth of the Dominican American population. An annual event held every August since 1981, the parade has grown from a small festival confined to one avenue in the Washington Heights neighborhood to a much larger affair. The parade now includes merengue music, food delicacies like plantains, and rituals like the *gaga* ceremony (a rite for the sugar cane harvest). In 2012 the parade attracted more than 500,000 people.

Many Dominican Americans observe traditional Roman Catholic holidays, such as Easter and Christmas. It is difficult to ascertain what percentage of the Dominican American population continues to observe Dominican holidays, such as Restoration Day

At the Antillana Meat Warehouse, a Dominican supermarket in the Washington Heights Inwood neighborhood of Manhattan, the butcher stands with a whole, suckling pig. FRANCES ROBERTS / ALAMY

(August 16), which commemorates the restoration of Dominican sovereignty following the 1863–1865 war with Spain, and Dominican Independence Day (February 27). On both days, however, Dominican communities throughout the United States, including in New York, Boston, Chicago, Milwaukee, Indianapolis, and Providence, hold events to mark the day. Celebrations include the raising of the Dominican flag and galas that focus on Dominican cuisine, music, and dance.

Health Issues No reliable sources address in a systematic and complete way the topic of the state of Dominican Americans' health. Reports by the American Medical Association (AMA) that focus on the health of Hispanic people in the United States do not generally distinguish Dominican Americans from the group. Some targeted studies, however, have used Dominican Americans as a control group. In a 2006 National Institute of Health (NIH) study titled "Immigration and HIV/AIDS in the New York Metropolitan Area," researchers found that Dominican Americans, like other Caribbean groups, were more likely to have HIV/AIDs than their white counterparts. Another study, titled "Access Barriers to Health Care for Latino Children," found that Latino parents encountered a variety of barriers—including language problems, poverty, lack of health insurance, and transportation difficulties—that could lead to poor medical care, including misdiagnosis and incorrect medication.

FAMILY AND COMMUNITY LIFE

The Dominican family in the United States is a different institution than the family unit in the Dominican Republic. Although kin relationships continue to be important to Dominican migrants in the United States, their families become smaller and more nuclear the longer they remain in the country. In contrast, Dominican families in the Caribbean are more likely to be large and nonnuclear. In contrast, Dominican migrants tend to marry after some period of residence in the United States and that, after marrying, they tend to live in smaller, less nuclear families. Other studies have shown that Dominican women in the United States tend to have fewer children than women in the Dominican Republic.

Gender roles within the Dominican American family also seem to transform through emigration. The Dominican family tends to be patriarchal. Male heads of household exercise control over household budgets and have final authority over family members. Women in Dominican households are responsible for domestic tasks and maintenance. Among Dominican migrants, however, these roles seem to be changing. Dominican women in the United States have demanded greater control over budgets and have wrested some authority from their husbands. Their new role as co-breadwinners has empowered

Dominican American women to challenge male authority in the household more effectively.

These changes in the structure and organization of the Dominican family in the United States suggest that the process of courting and the institution of marriage have changed. While there are no authoritative or specific treatments of these topics, it seems reasonable to conclude from the noted studies concerning gender relations within marriages that gender relations among dating couples in the Dominican American community may be changing as well.

By the late 1990s, researchers had identified a trend toward single-parent households headed by women among Dominican Americans in New York City. A 2004 survey found that nearly 40 percent of Dominican American households were helmed by a woman. Almost the same percentage of households lived in poverty. Some experts blame the immigration process for the long-term separation of families. Others point to economic pressures in the United States and the lack of formal marriages among many Dominican Americans, claiming that men who fail to fulfill their role as providers tend to abandon their families, often leaving them destitute. Many of the abandoned women are left with no job skills, do not speak English, and are forced to use public assistance to help support themselves and their children. Seeing that their children get an education in the United States is often seen as these women's only hope.

Education seems to occupy a place of importance in the Dominican migrant worldview. Dominican migrants as a group are better educated than Dominicans who remain in their home country, and Dominicans in the United States have fought some of their most significant political battles over education. In the Washington Heights neighborhood of Manhattan in New York City, Dominican Americans organized to gain a voice on the local school board. The board at that time was dominated by non-Dominicans, even though Dominicans represented a majority of school-aged children in the district. Dominican residents of the neighborhood campaigned for and succeeded in putting representatives of their community on the board. This political mobilization around education marked one of the New York City Dominican American community's early forays into city politics, and at least one Dominican city leader began his political career on the Washington Heights board of education.

Prior to 2000 the U.S. Census Bureau classified Dominican Americans as "Central/South Americans." These groups are not comparable—their forebears came from radically different cultures, and they inhabit very different socioeconomic "worlds" in the United States. Since 2000, however, statistics on the level of education of native-born Dominican Americans have been easier to find, because the Census Bureau has provided additional space for respondents

Dominican women perform at the Hispanic Parade. DAVID GROSSMAN / ALAMY

to indicate their exact country of origin (for example, "Dominican" or "Salvadoran"). The 1990 U.S. Census found that 62 percent of Americans of Central or South American origin had graduated from high school and that 13 percent had graduated from college. The 2010 census showed that, of the respondents who identified themselves as Dominican immigrants, 21 percent were college graduates.

Besides education, baseball is another important institution in the Dominican American community. It is far more than a sport or recreational activity to Dominicans in both the Caribbean and the United States. Scholars who study baseball in the Dominican Republic have noted that becoming a professional baseball player is the dream of many Dominicans. Baseball represents a way out of poverty for the largely poor population of the Caribbean nation. As the national pastime, baseball also represents a way for Dominicans to demonstrate the pride they have in their nation. Between 1990 and 2010, Major League Baseball (MLB) experienced an influx of Dominicans and Dominican Americans into its ranks. The promise of high salaries and potential celebrity status has led many Dominican American and Dominican children to pursue baseball as a means to alleviate their financial hardships. Due to the Dominican Republic's large talent pool and the country's passion for the sport, almost every MLB

team maintains a scouting academy on the island. As the academies attempt to foster talent on the island, scouts comb the inner cities of the United States hoping to find the next star. According to multiple sources, these international academies have taken a significant toll on youth baseball in the United States, with participation dropping by 25 percent. However, Dominicans and other Latin Americans continue to play baseball in the United States in organized leagues and in pick-up games. Once signed to a major-league team, Dominicans are often sent to small towns in states across the United States, including Iowa, Montana, and Kansas. The increase of Dominican and Latino players in these towns has not only created small Latino communities in unlikely places, but has also transformed the makeup of the game, as entire teams might now consist of players born in Latin American and the Caribbean.

EMPLOYMENT AND ECONOMIC CONDITIONS

While significant numbers of those who emigrate from the Dominican Republic to the United States were professionals in their home country, most are employed in low-wage, low-prestige jobs once they are in the United States. The 1980 U.S. Census showed that, among foreign-born Dominicans, only 6.9 percent occupied "upper white-collar" positions, while 33.5 percent occupied "lower blue-collar" positions. Rates among the U.S. population as a whole were quite different, with 22.7 percent in upper white-collar positions and 18.3 percent in lower blue-collar positions. Similarly, 22.1 percent of foreign-born Dominican families were living in poverty, compared with 9.6 percent of the total U.S. population. In New York City in 1997, those numbers were considerably higher, with approximately 45.7 percent of Dominicans living in poverty, compared to a city-wide rate of 23.8 percent. Between 2000 and 2008, however, researchers noted that employment rates stabilized for Dominican Americans. Following a steep decline in male employment between 1998 and 2000, a steady increase in employment occurred, with nearly two-thirds of the Dominican population maintaining a position in the workforce in 2008.

A study conducted around the same time provides more detailed information about Dominican migrants. That study showed that the proportion of professionals among migrants decreased markedly as migrants moved from the Dominican Republic to the United States. At the same time, the proportion of laborers increased dramatically. The study also showed that among those employed as laborers, the majority worked in manufacturing, with a sizable number of men also working in restaurants and hotels. These laborers worked primarily for smaller firms, with 40 percent earning less than $150 a week and 45 percent working in nonunionized workplaces. In other words, Dominican Americans earned less and were less protected at their workplaces than the general U.S. population. The reasons for the economic position of Dominican Americans are easy to guess—the language barrier, discrimination, the illegal status of many in the community, and the lower level of education of the Dominican American community as a whole relative to the average level of education of the U.S. population.

The garment industry employs the greatest number of Dominican women in the New York City area. Many of these Dominican garment workers are employed in what is called the "informal sector" of the garment industry, in small firms that are not regulated or unionized. Women who work for these firms are paid low wages and enjoy little job security or protection while on the job. Many other Dominican American women clean houses and do other odd jobs outside the organized labor market.

Despite the fact that most in the Dominican American community work in low-paid, low-status jobs, a significant number own businesses that draw many customers from the immigrant and ethnic communities. In 1992 the New York City grocery store chain C-Town Group said that half of its stores were owned and operated by Dominican Americans. Other similar associations in New York report high levels of Dominican ownership as well. The Dominican involvement in the groceries trade goes even further, with many Dominicans owning and operating bodegas in their neighborhoods that are not affiliated with any grocery association.

POLITICS AND GOVERNMENT

The Dominican American community has taken up several important political issues in the United States and in the Dominican Republic. The most important of these issues have been education, the status of undocumented migrants in the United States, citizenship status, and police violence against Dominicans. In the 1970s a union of several Dominican associations called *Concilio de Organizaciones Dominicanas* (Council of Dominican Organizations) began to push for greater rights for undocumented Dominicans in the United States. In the same decade, a group called *Asociación Nacional de Dominicanos Ausentes* (National Association of Absent Dominicans) lobbied the Dominican government for the right of migrants in the United States to vote in Dominican elections. More recently, Dominican migrants have pushed the Dominican Republic to permit Dominicans in the United States to retain their Dominican citizenship so that they will be considered citizens when they return home to visit or to live, as many do.

The Union of Young Dominicans, has sought to address issues faced by Dominican immigrants. The Dominican Women's Development Center promotes self-sufficiency and helps Dominican American women organize around critical issues in their community. Dominican Americans have also made impressive strides in politics on the national and local levels. The 1990s saw the election of New York City's first Dominican American city councilman, Guillermo Linares. In 2009 President Barack Obama appointed Thomas E. Perez, a Dominican American, to Assistant Attorney General for the Civil Rights Division of the United States Department of Justice. In 2011 Angel Taveras, also a Dominican American, became the first Hispanic mayor of Providence, Rhode Island.

NOTABLE INDIVIDUALS

Academia Elsa Gomez (1938–) served as president of Kean College of New Jersey between 1989 and 1994. Born in 1938 in New York City, Gomez catapulted into the national spotlight when Jewish students at Kean College expressed outrage over a Nation of Islam speaker who made remarks that many regarded as anti-Semitic. Anthony Stevens-Acevedo is one of the founders of the City College of New York (CUNY) Dominican Studies Institute and as of 2012 served as assistant director of the institute along with fellow founding member and director Ramona Hernández.

Fashion Oscar de la Renta, born in 1932 in the Dominican Republic, is a world-renowned fashion designer and creator of a line of high-end women's clothing.

Fashion designer and Dominican American, Oscar de la Renta ©, with models on the runway after his fall 2013 show. FAIRCHILD PHOTO SERVICE

born in the Dominican Republic and immigrated to New Jersey as a child. By focusing on how immigrants adjust to their new lives in the United States, Díaz's work illuminates the joys and disappointments that many Dominicans experience when they pursue the American dream. In addition to his literary work, Díaz is a prominent advocate for young Latinos in the United States.

Politics Guillermo Linares, born in 1950 in the Dominican Republic, was the first Dominican American city councilman in New York City, serving from 1992 to 2001. Linares has since enjoyed a distinguished career as a politician. In 2004 he was appointed New York City Commissioner of Immigrant Affairs, and in 2010 Linares was elected State Assemblyman for the 72nd District of Manhattan.

In 2005 Grace Diaz, born in 1957, was elected to the Rhode Island House of Representatives, making her the first Dominican American woman to be elected to state office.

In 1996 Adriano Espaillat, born in 1954, became the first Dominican American to be elected to the New York State Assembly. In 2011 Espaillat was elected to the New York State Senate.

Sports Mary Joe Fernández, born in 1971 in the Dominican Republic, is a former professional tennis player. Fernández played in her first Grand Slam tennis tournament at the age of fourteen and went on to win two Grand Slam women's doubles titles. She also won Olympic gold medals in 1992 and 1996.

Juan Marichal, born in 1937 in the Dominican Republic, is a baseball Hall of Famer and a former pitcher for the San Francisco Giants, the Boston Red Sox, and the Los Angeles Dodgers. Marichal served as a scout for the Oakland Athletics for twelve years.

Since the 1990s numerous Dominicans have found success in Major League Baseball (MLB), including perennial all-stars José Bautista (1980–), Adrián Beltré (1979–), Robinson Canó (1982–), Pedro Martínez (1971–), David Ortiz (1975–), Albert Pujols (1980–), Hanley Ramírez (1983–), Alex Rodriguez (1975–), and Sammy Sosa (1968–). Dominicans have also made headway in other sports, such as Francisco García (1981–) and Al Horford (1986–) in the National Basketball Association (NBA).

Stage and Screen Agustin Rodriguez, born in 1967 in New York City, is frequently seen on network television and in movies. He has had small roles in the movies *Final Analysis* and *Falling Down* and has guest-starred on the television series *Street Justice* and *Sirens*. He was also a regular on the TV series *Moon Over Miami*.

Michelle Rodríguez, born in 1978 in San Antonio, Texas, played a high-profile role in the television series *Lost* and starred in the movies *The Fast and the Furious*, *S.W.A.T.*, and *Resident Evil*. Dania Ramirez, born in 1979 in the Dominican Republic, is known for her

Journalism and Literature Born in 1950 in the United States and raised in part in the Dominican Republic, Julia Alvarez is a prominent and critically acclaimed writer and poet. Alvarez is the author of several novels, including the much-lauded *How the Garcia Girls Lost Their Accents*. Much of her work explores the experience of growing up in two cultures. Tony Marcano (1960–) has served as a reporter for several nationally known newspapers during his career as a journalist. Marcano was born in 1960 in New York City and is former editor of the "City Times" section of the *Los Angeles Times*. In 2008 Junot Díaz (1968–) became the first Dominican American to win the Pulitzer Prize for Fiction for his novel *The Brief Wondrous Life of Oscar Wao*. Díaz was appearances in the TV series *The Sopranos, Entourage,* and *Heroes* and for starring in the movies *X-Men: The Last Stand* and *Quarantine.* Zoe Saldaña, born in 1978 in Passaic, New Jersey, of Dominican and Puerto Rican parents, has been featured in significant roles as Anamaría in *Pirates of the Caribbean: The Curse of the Black Pearl,* as the alien Neytiri in *Avatar,* and as Uhura in the 2009 film *Star Trek.*

In 2003 Susie Castillo, born in 1979 in Methuen, Massachusetts, was named Miss USA, while that same year Dominican Amelia Vega (1984–) was crowned Miss Universe.

MEDIA

Online newspapers published for Dominican Americans include the following:

Listín Diario

Oldest newspaper published in the Dominican Republic. Founded in 1889 by Arturo Pellerano Alfau and Julian Atiles, the newspaper is published daily.

URL: www.listin.com.do

El Viajero Digital

Online publication that maintains daily updated content.

URL: www.elviajero.com.do

ORGANIZATIONS AND ASSOCIATIONS

Dominican-American National Foundation (DANF)

Established in 1989, the DANF assists Dominican Americans with immigration assistance, educational and employment training, and access to a variety of social services.

2885 NW 36 Street
Miami, Florida 33142
URL: www.danf-usa.org

Dominican American National Roundtable (DANR)

Founded in 1999, the DANR provides a national forum for analysis, planning, and action to advance the educational, economic, legal, social, cultural, and political interests of Dominican Americans.

1050 17th Street, N.W., Suite 600
Washington, D.C. 20036
URL: www.darn.org

Dominican Women's Development Center (DWDC)

Founded in 1988, the DWDC seeks to empower Dominican American women by supporting them in education, employment, and health issues.

519 West 189th Street, Ground Floor
New York, New York 10040
URL: www.dwdc.org

MUSEUMS AND RESEARCH CENTERS

The Dominican Studies Institute of the City University of New York (CUNY DSI)

Founded in 1992, CUNY DSI provides a multidisciplinary approach to research and scholarship devoted to people of Dominican descent.

The City College of New York
North Academic Center (NAC) 4/107160
Convent Avenue at 138th Street
New York, New York 10031
Phone: Institute Main Office: (212) 650-7496
Archives and Library: (212) 650-7170
Email: dsi@ccny.cuny.edu
URL: www.ccny.cuny.edu/dsi

SOURCES FOR ADDITIONAL STUDY

Aparicio, Ana. *Dominican-Americans and the Politics of Empowerment.* Gainesville: UP of Florida, 2009.

Del Castillo, José, and Martin F. Murphy. "Migration, National Identity and Cultural Policy in the Dominican Republic." *Journal of Ethnic Studies* 15, no. 3 (1987): 49–69.

Garcia, John A. "Caribbean Migration to the Mainland: A Review of Adaptive Experiences," *Annals of the American Academy of Political and Social Science,* vol. 487 (1986): 114–125.

Gonzalez, David. "New Country Is Like Prison to Asenhat, 18," *New York Times,* April 20 (1993): A1.

Grasmuck, Sherri. "Immigration, Ethnic Stratification, and Native Working Class Discipline: Comparisons of Documented and Undocumented Dominicans," *International Migration Review,* vol. 18, no. 3, (1984): 692–713.

Guarnizo, Luis E. "Los Dominicanyorks: The Making of a Binational Society," *Annals of the American Academy of Political and Social Science,* vol. 533 (1994): 70–86.

Hernández, Ramona. *The Mobility of Workers under Advanced Capitalism: Dominican Migration to the United States.* New York: Columbia University Press, 2002.

Itzigsohn, José. *Encountering American Faultlines: Race, Class, and Dominican Experience in Providence.* New York: Russell Sage Foundation, 2009.

Kasinitz, Philip, John H. Mollenkopf, Mary Waters, and Jennifer Holdaway. *Inheriting the City: The Children of Immigrants Come of Age.* New York: Russell Sage Foundation, 2008.

Klein, Alan M. *Sugarball: The American Game, the Dominican Dream.* New Haven: Yale University Press, 1991.

Ojito, Mirta. "Dominicans, Scrambling for Hope." *New York Times,* December 16, 1997.

Stepan, Alfred, ed. *Americas: New Interpretive Essays.* Oxford: Oxford University Press, 1992.

Sutton, Constance R., and Elsa M. Chaney, eds. *Caribbean Life in New York City: Sociocultural Dimensions.* New York: Center for Migration Studies of New York, 1992.

Torres-Saillant, Silvio, and Ramona Hernández. *The Dominican Americans.* Westport, CT: Greenwood Press, 1998.

DRUZE AMERICANS

Pam Rohland

OVERVIEW

Druze Americans are members of a small religious community called the Druze, or, as they prefer to be called, al-Muwaḥḥidūn (Arabic for Unitarians or monotheists) or Banī Maʻrūf (the Sons of Beneficence). They are a religious sect that branched out from Shia Islam, whose origins can be traced to Cairo, Egypt, in the early eleventh century. A tightly knit, secretive group, the Druze have not accepted converts since 1043 CE. The Druze do not have their own homeland. In an attempt to avoid religious persecution, a majority of them migrated to the isolated mountains of Lebanon, Syria, and Israel, and by 1174 there was no trace of the group in Cairo. Due to political unrest in the Middle East, some Druze families and communities have been separated by these countries' borders, making it hard for families to visit or communicate with one another on a regular basis.

According to the U.S. Department of State's *International Religious Freedom Report* for 2012, there are approximately one million Druze living in the Middle East. The largest number, roughly 700,000, live in Syria; 250,000 live in Lebanon; 100,000 live in Israel; and smaller numbers live in Jordan (14,000, according to Minority Rights Group International) and the Israeli-occupied Golan Heights (20,000, according to the Israeli Central Bureau of Statistics). The Druze are a mixed race. They are largely of Arab descent but also have Iranian, Kurdish, and European heritage. Economically, the Druze in the Middle East have tended to be poor and have limited opportunity for advancement, but as a people they are not without ambition, and some have attained financial success, mostly as entrepreneurs overseeing small businesses. The Druze have fared best in Lebanon, where significant numbers have risen to the middle class and higher.

The overwhelming majority of Druze in the United States have immigrated from Lebanon. The first immigrants were men who came in the late 1800s and early 1900s hoping to make money and return to Lebanon. They found work as manual laborers and peddlers. Most ended up staying and made arrangements to have their families join them. The second period of immigration lasted from 1947 until the late 1980s, when many Druze sought to escape the political tension that was pervasive in the Middle East. The third wave of immigration occurred from 1990 to the early 2000s with a number of younger immigrants entering the United States to attend universities and seek employment. There are currently significant Druze communities in California, Florida, Michigan, New York, Texas, Virginia, and Washington.

In 2000 the American Druze Society estimated the number of Druze in the United States to be between 15,000 and 20,000. (As a basis for comparison, this number is roughly the capacity of Madison Square Garden in New York City.) Although the Druze American population has most likely grown since then, it is difficult to track the number of Druze immigrants in the United States, as they have not been counted in any formal census since the 1930s.

HISTORY OF THE PEOPLE

Early History In 1017 the ruler of the Fatimid dynasty, al-Ḥākim bi-Amr Allāh, announced that he was the earthly incarnation of God. He began attracting followers, and the Druze sect was born in Cairo, Egypt. The last years of al-Ḥākim's life were marked by unusual, irrational actions, which led outsiders to stereotype the Druze as madmen. The Druze themselves found al-Ḥākim's actions to be further evidence of his divinity. Druze historians believe that al-Ḥākim's reputation for instability was exaggerated, but they do describe him variously as capricious, whimsical, enigmatic, and prone to violence. Al-Ḥākim disappeared in 1021. The widely accepted theory is that he was murdered by conspirators with the help of his sister. Others believe he simply vanished while despairing that his goals would ever be reached.

After Al-Ḥākim disappeared, his apostle Ḥamzah ibn ʻAlī ibn Aḥmad formed al-Ḥākim's various dogmas and pronouncements into a creed. Despite the emergence of a more measured, rational leader, fear was rife among the Druze, and for six years following their founder's disappearance, they hid. They slowly re-entered public life, but most began migrating to remote mountainous regions in Lebanon, Syria, and what became Israel, where they hoped they could practice their faith without persecution. Because of their fear of outsiders, no new members have been admitted to the sect since 1043.

Despite trying to avoid conflict with large religious groups, Druze living among other Islamic sects in the Middle East faced retribution for their heterodox beliefs. Tribal skirmishes have been sporadic but ongoing for nearly a thousand years. Over the years, Druze who did not want to contend with the hostility publicly adopted the doctrine of the mainstream Muslims, while privately practicing their own religion.

During the mid-1800s, Protestant American missionaries traveled to Syria to convert the Druze, but they failed. During the same era, the Druze in Lebanon worked their way into a position of power, some becoming feudal lords. However, an insurrection by the Christians turned many of the Druze into serfs. The Druze in Syria fared somewhat better, remaining autonomous, mainly because of their self-imposed isolation. This detachment also led to poverty, as Syrian Druze attempted to make a living from farming. They were considered more militant than their Lebanese counterparts and were involved in various tribal wars with other sects.

Modern Era The Druze developed a fierce loyalty to each other because of their isolation. It also made them an easier target for French, British, and, later, Israeli occupying forces that wanted to undermine Arab nationalism after World War I. After the fall of the Ottoman Empire in 1918, the Druze lived under French and British Christian rulers. The Druze in Syria officially had their own Druze governor, but a French officer, Captain Carbillet, was temporarily appointed governor in 1923. Discontent with Carbillet's oppressive governance and taxation was one of many factors that led the Druze to rebellion.

In 1925 the Syrian Druze, led by well-known Druze leader Sulṭān al-Aṭrash, rose up against the French in what is called the Great Syrian Revolt of 1925–1927, or the Druze Revolt. This insurrection failed, and French authority was restored. Tensions continued to simmer until 1936, when France recognized both Lebanon and Syria as independent states and sovereign members of the League of Nations. The French remained a presence in both countries until the end of World War II.

The Druze had no geographical base from which to lobby for an autonomous regional authority. They were also too small in number to take any kind of powerful role in national affairs, which were dominated by two large sects, the Maronite Christians and Sunni Muslims. They had one privilege granted by the French that they had not enjoyed under the Ottomans: the right to officially administer their own civil affairs according to the laws and customs of their community. Despite this, a long and complicated number of coups and upheavals continued in Syria and Lebanon.

Later, the growing Druze population in Israel was permitted to exercise separate jurisdiction in matters of marriage and divorce, though they had to participate in the same compulsory military service required of all residents. During the period of civil and political unrest in the 1960s and 1970s, some Druze protested Israel's annexation of the Golan Heights, and a minority of Druze were involved in violent acts. It was at this point that the rest of the world began hearing about the Druze from media reports, and modern misconceptions of the Druze as radical and violent emerged. While unrest in this area has greatly subsided, most Syrian Druze living in Israeli-occupied Golan Heights admit their allegiance to the Syrian government although young Druze men are forced by Israeli law to serve in the Israeli military. In the wake of the September 11, 2001, terrorist attacks in the United States, many Druze Americans have been persecuted for their skin color and appearance.

SETTLEMENT IN THE UNITED STATES

The first wave of Druze immigrants arrived in the United States in the early 1900s. They were scattered acros the country, with a significant group in the Seattle, Washington area who in 1908 established a fraternal organization called El-Bakaurat Ed-Dirziyat, to build a sense of community in their new home. Shortly after it was founded, new branches were created in Cleveland, Ohio; Detroit, Michigan; and Danbury, Connecticut; Princeton, West Virginia; and Kingsport, Tennessee. There were also small Druze communities in Seminole, Oklahoma; and Dallas, Texas. In each of these places, the Druze remained a secretive, tight-knit community, often adopting other religions, particularly the Protestant sect of Christianity, in order to maintain a low religious profile to avoid persecution for their beliefs.

When subsequent waves of Druze immigrated to the United States in the latter half of the twentieth century, the new arrivals tended to settle in areas where they already had some connection to their fellow Druze who had come before them. Many Druze Americans still send money to relatives in their homeland and visit as often as they can. Some arrange marriages with women from their home village. Their cultural ties, more than their religious bonds, are what bind the Druze together in their adopted countries. There are significant Druze communities in California, Florida, Michigan, New York, Texas, Virginia, and Washington, and the ADS helps keep these localized Druze communities unified through magazines, newsletters, websites, and conventions.

LANGUAGE

The Druze speak a dialect of Arabic. In everyday speech, the Druze are easily recognizable by the use of the *qaf*, a strong guttural "k" sound that is found

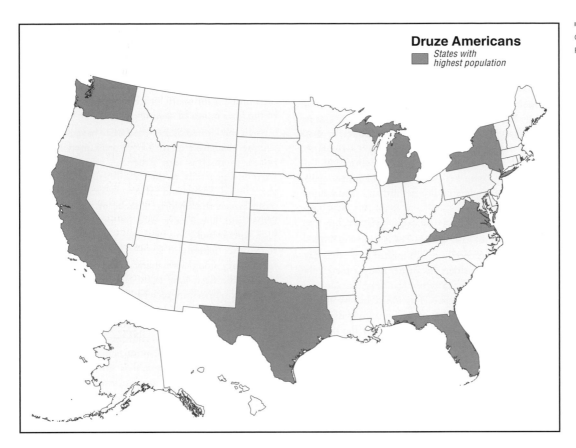

Druze Americans
■ States with
highest population

in Arabic and transliterated as *q* in English. Outside the Middle East, the Druze may consciously drop the qaf and other distinct speech characteristics to avoid identification or to appear more sophisticated. Druze living in the United States are generally fluent in English.

RELIGION

The origins of the Druze faith can be traced to the early eleventh century in Cairo, Egypt, where it began as an offshoot of Ismā'īlī Shiism. The faith subsequently spread to many regions in the Middle East and North Africa, although the adherents eventually became concentrated in the areas of what are now the nations of Lebanon, Syria, Jordan, and Israel. The basis of the religion is the belief that at various times God has been divinely incarnated as a living person. His last, and final, incarnation was al-Ḥākim bi-Amr Allāh, who announced himself as the earthly incarnation of God in 1017. His followers helped shaped a creed that is still followed.

The Druze religion is an outgrowth of Islam, although mainstream Muslims disavow it as a heterodox sect. The religion also incorporates elements of Judaism and Christianity. When the religion was established, its founders were influenced by Greek philosophy and Asiatic thought. Their progressive ideas—including the abolition of slavery and the separation of church and state—were considered unorthodox and placed the Druze at risk of persecution.

The tenets of the Druze religion are secret and mysterious, even to many Druze themselves, since the faith allows only a limited number of elite men and sometimes women, called *uqqāl* ("the enlightened"), to study and learn all of its aspects. The *uqqāl* oversee the religious life of their particular community, acting almost as intermediaries with God. Other Druze, known as the *juhhāl* ("the unenlightened"), are given a simplified outline of their faith in the form of a strict code of moral and ethical behavior.

The seven duties that all Druze are required to observe are recognition of al-Ḥākim and strict adherence to monotheism; negation of all non-Druze tenets; rejection of Satan and unbelief; acceptance of God's acts; submission to God for good or ill; truthfulness; and mutual solidarity and help between fellow Druze. While they are respectful of other religions, the Druze believe that a severe judgment awaits all non-Druze.

Religious meetings are held on Thursday nights in inconspicuous buildings without embellishments or furniture, except a small lectern to lay books on during meditation. Men and women may sit together, but with a divider between them. During the first part of the service, community affairs are discussed, and everyone may attend. However, the *juhhāl* must leave when prayer, study, and meditation begin. The secrecy surrounding the Druze faith is meant to protect its followers from persecution.

In order to protect their religion and not divulge its teachings, the Druze worship as Muslims when among Muslims, and as Christians when among Christians. They allow no outside converts to their religion: one must be born into the Druze faith. What is known is that the Druze are Muwaḥḥidūn, or Unitarians, who believe in one God whose qualities cannot be understood or defined and who renders justice impartially.

Reincarnation is a key belief of the faith. The Druze believe that the number of days of one's life is fixed, not to be exceeded or diminished by a single day. Since a Druze considers his or her body a mere robe for the soul, he or she does not fear death because it is only a tearing of the robe. The Druze believe that as soon as a person dies, his or her soul immediately is reborn into another human body (never the body of an animal). In addition, Druze believe that they will always be reborn as another Druze, further strengthening the solidarity of their community. Reincarnation continues until one's soul achieves purification and merges with the Holy One. Hell is the failure to achieve this state.

The Druze believe in the coexistence of all religious, national, and ethnic groups living under one flag. The sect's beliefs include loyalty to the country in which they reside, although all maintain close ties with their homeland.

CULTURE AND ASSIMILATION

Since leaving Egypt and settling elsewhere in the Middle East, the Druze have established a reputation of being a cooperative, hardworking people. They have tended to live among themselves and at a remove from the rest of the population at large, but they have also attempted to blend in and be unobtrusive. They have dressed in a manner similar to the people around them, performed well at their jobs in their host communities, and patronized all of the local establishments. To some degree, the Druze have even made efforts to blend in religiously. Because their faith is a mix of elements of Islam and Christianity, they have tended outwardly to emphasize the aspects of their religion that are most consistent with the religion of the host culture. Druze people living in Christian nations have been known to tell people, when asked, that they are Christians. The same has been true of some Druze living in Muslim countries. Over the course of their long history they are known to be loyal to the governments of the countries where they live, and they have a history of helping those governments

fight invading armies and occupying colonial powers. At the same time, throughout the centuries, Druze have also established a history of being a secretive, isolated society. It is difficult for outsiders to learn a tremendous amount about the Druze faith. It is, in fact, difficult for many Druze to find out about some of the finer points of their religion.

In the United States, the Druze have faced some unique challenges as they have attempted to incorporate themselves into American society. This has been due, generally, to the tense relationship between the United States and many nations in the Arab world since the terrorist attacks of September 11, 2001, and, specifically, to a long-standing trend in U.S. foreign policy to be more sympathetic to Israel than other nations in the Arab world. Since 9/11, the Druze, along with many other expatriates from the Middle East, have been stigmatized as potential threats to American society. U.S. support of Israel tends to divide Druze loyalty; they feel compelled to act as good citizens and support the government, but they also feel allegiance to countries such as Lebanon, Syria, and Jordan that have clashed with Israel. Such abiding tensions have made it difficult for Druze Americans to maintain their centuries-old habit of both blending in and living relatively unbothered at a remove from society.

Cuisine The Druze have traditionally been farmers who maintain olive groves and cherry and apple orchards on terraced hillsides in the Middle East. They also grow wheat. Most families grow their own vegetables and fruit, bake their own bread, and have a largely vegetarian diet, eating meat, primarily lamb, on special occasions.

A typical meal consists of dishes common throughout the Middle East, including pita bread (although the Druze version, *sagg pita*, is larger and thinner than elsewhere), hummus (chickpea and sesame-paste spread), tabbouleh (a salad made with bulgur, parsley, cucumber, tomatoes, mint, and olive oil), yogurt, and *baklava* (a pastry with syrup and chopped nuts), and seasonal fruit. Strong Turkish coffee, while not drunk as part of a meal, is often served to visiting guests along with nuts, fruits, and cookies or other sweets.

Animals are butchered following *halal* methods (that is, according to Muslim law). The basic cooking ingredients are olive oil, clarified butter, and, sometimes, animal fat. The Druze favor lamb but also eat chicken and beef. While Druze Americans often cook these traditional dishes at home, many choose to eat a Western diet, as there are no strict dietary rules that must be followed as per their religious beliefs. They frown upon eating pork, but many Westernized Druze do not object to eating it.

Traditional Costumes In most of the Middle East, many Druze women still wear the traditional long black or blue dress with a white head covering called a *keffiyeh*, although increasingly, younger women wear Western attire. Traditional dress for uninitiated men consists of *shirwāl* (traditional baggy pants, tight around the ankles) and *ḥaṭṭah* (white headscarf). Men who are religious initiates wear a tall white cylindrical head covering known as a *laffa*. Most Druze men grow mustaches, but some American Druze immigrants choose to not follow this tradition. Druze men and women living in the United States typically wear Western dress, although traditional costumes are often worn for religious ceremonies, weddings, funerals, and other important cultural occasions.

Names The Druze are often given a name that could be Christian or Islamic. In the past, boys were given Islamic names such as Maḥmūd, ʿAlī, or Muḥammad; today a Druze boy is more likely to be called Samīr, Samīḥ, Amīn, or Fawzī, names of no particular religious significance. The same is true for Druze girls. Islamic names such as ʿĀʾishah and Fāṭimah have all but disappeared in favor of neutral or even Christian names. Few family names are predictably Druze, aside from Arslan, Junbalat (or Jumblat), and al-Atrash. Because the Druze believe in honoring their country, Druze immigrants in the United States have taken to using names from their respective homelands of Lebanon, Jordan, Israel, and Syria as well as more Western names of their new American home.

Housing In keeping with their belief in austerity, the Druze traditionally furnished their homes sparsely, with low wooden tables and thin cushions lining the walls. Druze Americans live in more modern dwellings, including apartments, condominiums, and houses, although their home decor is often not elaborate.

FAMILY AND COMMUNITY LIFE

The life of the average Druze revolves closely around his or her family and his or her relationship with others in the Druze community. Apart from Thursday night religious meetings, the Druze enjoy spending time together through visits to each other's homes. Hospitality is an important feature of the culture, and Druze will offer coffee and food to guests in their homes, be they Christian, Muslim, or Druze. An old Druze adage states that people should always cook as if they are expecting company, because a guest could arrive at any moment. The Druze are known for their generosity and are guided by a sense of chivalry and honor. This concept compels the Druze to look after each other, including widows, orphans, and the destitute. If the extended family cannot take care of a member, the larger community will find a means of support.

Among the Druze the birth of a baby, especially a son, is cause for celebration, with a typical gathering including family members and friends and gift giving.

CONTESTANT NO. 2

The PBS television show *Wide Angle* aired an episode titled "Contestant No. 2" on August 8, 2009, that followed Duah Fares, a teenage Druze girl competing in the 2007 Miss Israel pageant. While her parents supported her quest to win the pageant, they were also concerned for her honor, as the competition required her to wear a swimsuit in public, a practice that is not permitted for Druze women. Fares received death threats from members of the Druze community and ultimately withdrew from the pageant. The incident provides a vivid example of how the role of women in traditional Druze culture is tested in this modern age.

Sons have traditionally been considered an asset, socially and economically. If a Druze couple has only daughters, they often keep having children until sons are born. This leads to large families. In the past, the average Druze family would have five or six children. More recent generations of Druze see the logic of having fewer children and providing for them, so the size of modern Druze families is shrinking. Male circumcision is practiced among the Druze and is celebrated with a gathering of family of friends.

Gender Roles Druze women have always had the right to own and dispose of property freely. However, although Druze women traditionally enjoy a privileged status of near-equality with men, there is no compromise in the matter of female chastity. Druze women are expected to marry within their faith and maintain their virginity until marriage. A young woman is expected to be faithful to her husband throughout her whole life. A woman's honor is the single most important factor in Druze family life, and its defilement is cause for great humiliation. If a woman's dishonor becomes public knowledge, it is the responsibility of her father or brother to take what is considered appropriate action in their culture. It is not unknown, even today, for a Druze woman living in the Middle East to be murdered by her nearest male relative for shaming the family. While this practice has not followed by Druze immigrants in the United States, female honor is still held in the highest esteem, and a woman whose honor is tarnished will be banished from her family and excommunicated from the community.

In Israel, Druze judges have forced the government to waive the requirement for a Druze woman's photograph to appear on official documents, such as identity cards. The Druze also object to male doctors treating or autopsying women. Many conservative Druze consider these acts—in addition to things such as going to a cinema—as a shaming of a woman's honor. It is becoming more common, however, for women to leave the house with other women in pursuit of innocent pleasures such as shopping or going to lectures.

Education Historically, the Druze have been literate and well-educated. At the end of the twentieth century, literacy was almost universal for Druze under the age of twenty-five. Druze living in the United States attend American schools and universities and hold jobs in a variety of fields, including academia, law, medicine, entertainment, and education.

Courtship and Weddings Marriage is expected of all Druze women at a relatively early age, usually between seventeen and twenty-one years old, although a few marry at as early as fifteen and in recent years many marry later than twenty-one. The marriage, which often is arranged by the families, is usually preceded by an engagement that can last one or two years, or sometimes less. Marriage partners are chosen from eligible young people within the same community. This fact holds true of female Druze immigrants in the United States, and marriages are often arranged from their respective homelands or through American Druze Society conventions that are held yearly for this purpose, among others.

Weddings and funerals provide another opportunity to bond and usually involve the whole community. Traditional Druze village weddings in the Middle East featured many varieties of song and dance that served to increase communal solidarity. Among the Syrian Druze, war songs were (and sometimes still are) often sung by men at weddings. A traditional Druze war song cited in William Seabrook's *Adventures in Arabia* (1927) proclaims, "We are the Children of Maruf! / Among our rocks is sanctuary. / When our spears grow rusty, we make them bright / with the blood of our enemies." Because the Druze often had to defend themselves against persecution, the war songs are a means to remind the community that the men can still protect them. Marriage celebrations can be quite extensive, depending on the means of the families involved. Guests expect large quantities of food and drink. The dishes served are copious and extravagant; at modern urban weddings, wine and other spirits may be served, unless there are too many disapproving attendees. Although frowned upon, the uninitiated (*juhhāl*) Druze may drink alcohol on occasion (men more frequently than women). The religious initiates (*uqqāl*), however, are expected to abstain from drinking alcohol and smoking.

In the past, wedding festivities also provided one of the few social occasions in which young Druze men and women were allowed to mix socially and eye each other as potential marriage partners. In recent years, however, young people may meet each other while studying at a university. In the Internet age, a couple may also meet on the Internet (for instance, on a Druze dating site such as druzedate.com). Both the bride and the groom are expected to be virgins at the time of marriage, although men find opportunities to engage in premarital sex. The subject of sexual relations is taboo in a traditional Druze household. Nothing of a physical or sexual nature is ever brought up in conversation, especially with elders. The telling of even a slightly off-color anecdote is considered a breach of manners.

Marriage Marriage outside of the Druze faith is forbidden in theory. "If you marry out, you convert out," said Haeyl Azaam, a thirty-year-old Israeli Druze who was quoted in the *Jewish Bulletin of Northern California*. "You're excommunicated. There's just no place for you in the community anymore." Although the injunction against outmarriage, or exogamy, is very strong, it occasionally happens, especially in the Druze diaspora communities outside the Middle East. According to Fuad I. Khuri in his book *Being a Druze* (2004), Druze outmarriage in the United States is estimated to be "a little below 5 percent among Druze immigrants in the United States." However, it is more likely that a woman will be excommunicated for outmarriage than a man.

To keep the faith strong, a Druze will marry a spouse from another country rather than wed a local non-Druze. In an event arranged by the International Committee of the Red Cross in 1993, seven Druze brides in elaborate white gowns crossed the Israeli-Syrian border to marry bridegrooms in the Israeli-occupied Golan Heights. From both sides of the cease-fire lines, hundreds of Druze danced and cheered as the couples married in the United Nations zone. The couples had met each other through videotapes.

The Druze may marry within their family, including first cousins. Polygamy is forbidden among the Druze.

Divorce Divorce is not easy for Druze. Although a Druze woman can initiate divorce proceedings, it is rarely done. The most frequent grounds for divorce by men are the failure of a wife to bear children, especially sons; disobedience; immodest behavior; and some chronic mental or physical illness that makes intercourse impossible. The wife may ask for divorce based on impotence, non-support, and desertion or lengthy absence. If a woman is divorced through her own failings, the husband is permitted to reclaim the dowry and the marriage expenses, although these are often not factors in American Druze weddings. In most cases, the Druze follow the custom of compensating the divorced wife for her "exertions." This benefit is especially important for the older woman who has few prospects of remarriage and cannot return to her father's house or expect other support in her old age.

Funerals Funerals are major events in the Druze community, even more so than marriage. Funeral arrangements are made immediately after death, and ceremonies are held that day, or the next day at the latest. The body is washed and dressed in the finest clothes. At the funeral, women lament loudly and at length, and acquaintances tell stories of the departed's virtues. Bodies are interred above ground, marked by monuments ranging from the very simple to the highly elaborate. While Druze Americans maintain some of these rituals, the Druze are very secretive about their religious practices and often blend into their surrounding communities, observing the ceremonies and traditions of their neighbors in order to avoid persecution.

EMPLOYMENT AND ECONOMIC CONDITIONS

Although the Druze are still a largely rural people with a long tradition of farming, younger Druze are seeking more professional occupations as they arrive in the United States and other countries, where many study and establish businesses. Today, the Druze work in banking, trade, small business, and transportation services. Druze students at U.S. universities are likely to major in business administration, economics, or engineering. In Saudi Arabia and the Gulf states, Druze men are prominent members of the local business community, particularly in American and European firms. They have a reputation for being especially hardworking and trustworthy. Education is highly esteemed in the Druze community, and a number of Druze have joined the ranks of academia and can be found on the faculties of high schools and universities, particularly in the Middle East.

POLITICS AND GOVERNMENT

Since 1977 Walid Jumblatt of the Progressive Socialist Party has been the predominant political leader of the Lebanese Druze, although his political leanings often vary from those of high-ranking Druze clerics, the religious leaders of the Druze faith.

The Druze believe in the coexistence of all religious, national, and ethnic groups living under one flag. The sect's beliefs include loyalty to the country in which they reside, although all maintain close ties with their homeland. In Syria and Israel, where military service is mandatory, Druze citizens serve in the armed forces; the Israeli Army's "Herev" battalion is made of mostly of Druze soldiers. Lebanese Druze also serve in the Lebanese military, although it is no longer mandatory in that country. However, Druze are reluctant to battle other Druze, and some defected from the Lebanese and Syrian armies when those countries were at war. Having been subjected to onslaughts from other sects, Druze also form their own militias to defend their territory when necessary. When called upon, Druze living in the United States have served in the U.S. armed forces.

NOTABLE INDIVIDUALS

Art Walter Hamady (1940–) is a descendant of Druze American immigrants in Flint, Michigan, who became a famous fiber artist, papermaker, and book designer.

Druze American Casey Kasem (1932–) became an American household mainstay after several decades presiding over America's Top-40 music scene. HULTON ARCHIVE / GETTY IMAGES

His handmade books have been shown in museums and libraries including the Library of Congress and the Whitney Museum of American Art. In 2004 he was named one of the top fifty designers in the United States by *ID: The International Design Magazine*.

Broadcasting Kemal Amin "Casey" Kasem (1932–) is an internationally renowned radio personality born to Lebanese Druse parents in Detroit, Michigan. He is famous for the *American Top 40* radio program, which aired off and on from 1970 to 2004. He is also famous as the voice of Shaggy in the popular American cartoon *Scooby-Doo*.

Film Ziad H. Hamzeh (1959–) is a Druze American filmmaker and writer who has received multiple accolades for his work, including best producer and best director awards at the Abu Dhabi and Alexandria film festivals, respectively.

Literature Rabih Alameddine (1959–), writer and artist, was born to Druze parents in Jordan before moving to California to attend UCLA. He received a Guggenheim Fellowship in 2002 and is the author of several novels, including *The Hakawati* (2008) and short stories.

Politics Selwa S. "Lucky" Roosevelt (1929–), the elder daughter of Druze immigrants from Lebanon, was appointed the State Department's chief of protocol by President Ronald Reagan in 1982, a position she held until 1989. She has also worked as a freelance writer, contributing editor, chairperson of the Blair House Restoration Fund, and member of the Executive Committee of the Washington Opera. In 1990 she published *Keeper of the Gate*, a memoir about her work in the Reagan administration.

Druze American writer Rabih Alameddine (1959–) is depicted in 2009 while in Paris, France, to promote his book, *The Hakawati*. Alameddine was born in Jordan to Lebanese Druze parents. ULF ANDERSEN / GETTY IMAGES ENTERTAINMENT / GETTY IMAGES

MEDIA

There is no established Druze media in the United States, but Druze around the world stay connected through the Internet. Most Druze get news of what is going on in their native country and within their community in the United States through websites maintained by the American Druze Society, the American Druze Foundation, the American Druze Youth, and, increasingly, through Facebook. *Our Heritage* is a publication of the American Druze Society, and *Actadruze* is a quarterly publication of the Druze Research and Publications Institute. It includes articles of special interest to the Druze community and general information about Druze around the world.

ORGANIZATIONS AND ASSOCIATIONS

American Druze Society

This society addresses issues related to Druze immigrants to the United States and has more than twenty chapters across the United States. The society holds annual regional and national conventions to keep members of the Druze faith

in contact with one another. It also publishes the magazine *Our Heritage*.

P.O. Box 960220
Miami, Florida 33296-0220
Email: Director@AmericanDruzeSociety.org
URL: www.druze.com

American Druze Society–Michigan Chapter

One of the regional chapters of the American Druze Society. It sponsors activities and events for Druze in the Michigan area.

4945 South Beech Daly Street
Dearborn Heights, Michigan 48125
URL: www.druze.org

MUSEUMS AND RESEARCH CENTERS

Druze Heritage Foundation

Established in 1999 in London, England, the Druze Heritage Foundation (DHF) aims to study and preserve Druze culture, history, and lore, as well as to provide information about the Druze.

Ms. Lina Yehia
48 Park Street
United Kingdom, W1K 2JH
Phone: +44 20 491 2974
Fax: +44 20 7493 0747
Email: info@druzeheritage.org
URL: www.druzeheritage.org

SOURCES FOR ADDITIONAL STUDY

Abu Izzeddin, Nejla M. *The Druzes: A New Study of Their History, Faith and Society*. New York, Leiden: E. J. Brill, 1984.

Azzam, Intisar. *Change for Continuity: The Druze in America*. Beirut: M. A. J. D., 1997.

———. *Gender and Religion: Druze Women*. London: Druze Heritage Foundation, 2007.

Betts, Robert Brenton. *The Druze*. New Haven, CT: Yale University Press, 1988.

Firro, Kais. *A History of the Druzes*. Leiden, Netherlands: E. J. Brill, 1999.

Khuri, Fuad I. *Being a Druze*. London: Druze Heritage Foundation, 2004.

Sālibī, Kamāl. *The Druze: Realities & Perceptions*. London: Druze Heritage Foundation, 2006.

Seabrook, William B. *Adventures in Arabia among the Bedouins, Druses, Whirling Dervishes, & Yezidee Devil Worshipers*. New York: Harcourt, Brace and Company, 1927.

Westheimer, Ruth K., and Gil Sedan. *The Olive and the Tree: The Secret Strength of the Druze*. New York: Lantern Books, 2007.

DUTCH AMERICANS

Herbert J. Brinks

OVERVIEW

Dutch Americans are immigrants or descendants of people from the Netherlands, a country in northwestern Europe. The Netherlands is bounded to the east by Germany, to the south by Belgium, and to the north and west by the North Sea. A coastal region incorporating two major harbors (Rotterdam and Amsterdam), the Netherlands has an economy that is heavily dependent upon shipping. The Netherlands has about 16,000 square miles of landmass, making it roughly the size New Jersey and Maryland combined.

According to census data compiled by Statistics Netherlands, the Netherlands had a population of about 16.7 million people as of January 2012. As of 2009, the largest religious group was Roman Catholic, which made up 27 percent of the population. Significantly smaller numbers of people belonged to the Protestant Church of the Netherlands or were Dutch Reformed Protestant, Calvinist, and other religions. Fully 44 percent of Dutch citizens were not affiliated with any religious denomination. The Netherlands typically ranks as one of the top five or six most prosperous nations in Europe and is a founding member of the European Union.

Dutch immigrants began to arrive in the United States during the early 1600s after the Dutch West India Company gained colonization rights in the Hudson River area and founded New Netherland (New York). Following World War II, when a war-ravaged economy and a severe housing shortage gripped the Netherlands, a new wave of 80,000 Dutch immigrants came to the United States. Since then, Dutch Americans have largely assimilated into mainstream American culture. From the 1960s to the present day, approximately 3,000 people per year move from the Netherlands to the United States.

The U.S. Census Bureau estimates that in 2011 there were more than 4.4 million Dutch Americans living in the United States, a number roughly equal to the population of South Carolina. Dutch Americans are widely dispersed throughout the United States. As a result of traditional Dutch immigration patterns, however, some states remain strongholds for Dutch Americans, most notably New York, New Jersey, Illinois, Wisconsin, Michigan, Iowa, Washington, and California.

HISTORY OF THE PEOPLE

Early History During the New Stone Age (circa 8000–3500 BCE), the Netherlands' landmass roughly equaled the nation's current 16,000 square miles, but by 55 BCE, when Rome's legions gained hegemony in the area, rising sea levels and erosion from winds, tides, and rivers reduced the coastal areas by at least 30 percent. Since then, the Dutch have employed various strategies to regain the land lost to the sea. Simple earthen hills linked by dikes long preceded the complex drainage systems that today drain the enclosed lowlands with electrically powered pumps.

While historians believe that nomadic peoples hunted and fished in the Netherlands as early as 16,000 BCE, the area was not settled until about 4000 BCE. Around 60 BCE, Roman armies under Julius Caesar conquered the Saxon, Celtic, and Frisian groups occupying the Netherlands. The Romans built roads and made improvements to existing dikes in the lowlands. In the fifth century CE, as Rome weakened, the Germanic Franks conquered the area and later introduced the Dutch to Christianity.

From the 700s to the 1100s, the Dutch were subjected to violent raids by Viking sailors from Scandinavia. During this unstable period, power passed to local nobles, whose arms and castles offered protection in return for rent, labor, and taxes. This system gradually declined when, beginning in the 1300s, much of the Netherlands was taken by the dukes of Burgundy, a powerful French feudal dynasty. In the early 1500s, Charles V, Duke of Burgundy, inherited the thrones of both Spain and the Holy Roman Empire. While he was well liked by the Dutch, his successors were not. In 1568 the Dutch prince William the Silent (1533–1584) led a rebellion against the Spanish Habsburgs (Phillip II, 1527–1621), initiating the Eighty Years' War (1568–1648). Although William was assassinated in 1584, his efforts eventually resulted in Dutch independence. For this reason, he is often regarded as the Father of the Netherlands.

Resistance to the Spanish united the lowlanders, who previously had local (rather than national) loyalties. In 1579, the Union of Utrecht unified the seven northern lowland provinces. (Their 1580 agreement, essentially a defensive alliance, served as a national constitution until 1795.) In 1581 those provinces declared the Netherlands an independent country. Meanwhile, Dutch exploration and trade had flourished, and by the 1620s, the Dutch shipping fleet was the world's largest. This golden age lasted until the 1700s, after which the Netherlands underwent a gradual decline as the balance of colonial power shifted to England. The beginning of this change can be traced to the 1664 sale of New Netherland (New York) to England.

Modern Era The Netherlands was occupied by the French during the Napoleonic Era (1795–1813). Afterward, in 1814, descendants of the House of Orange established a monarchy, which was reformed successively in 1848, 1896, and 1919 to create a broadly based democracy. Today the Netherlands has a constitutional monarchy with a bicameral, multiparty system administered by a premier and a coalition cabinet of ministers. Queen Beatrix (1938–), the titular head of state, performs largely ceremonial duties.

Viable habitation of the western provinces (South Holland, Zeeland, and North Holland) required flood control along the Rhine River delta and along the North Sea's shifting shoreline, and windmills—preserved currently as historic monuments—were used to pump water as part of flood control efforts for some five centuries (1400–1900). The massive Delta Works, stretching across the islands of South Holland and Zeeland, were constructed to protect the Netherlands from storms and high water following disastrous floods in 1953. Because the most productive farm land and the most populous commercial and industrial districts are as much as twenty feet below sea level, hydrological science has become a hallmark of Dutch achievement.

The Netherlands has struggled in the twenty-first century to accommodate and acculturate its own immigrant population. In 2002 anti-immigration politician Pim Fortuyn, who sought to bar immigration of Muslims to the Netherlands, was assassinated. Two years later a Dutch Moroccan immigrant assassinated filmmaker Theo Van Gogh (a descendant of Vincent's Van Gogh's brother, Theo) because of a film he made that is skeptical of the way Islam treats women. Since these developments, anti-immigration parties in the Netherlands typically receive a significant portion of the popular vote. However, in the 2012 elections, Geert Wilders' anti-immigration party lost a significant number of seats in parliament.

Despite recent divisiveness among member countries of the European Union, the Netherlands has remained a strong supporter of the union. It is closely allied with Germany in demanding member countries' strict adherence to the union's budgetary regulations. The Netherlands has retained its triple-A bond credit rating, indicating its relative economic soundness and stability.

SETTLEMENT IN THE UNITED STATES

After the Dutch West India Company gained colonization rights in the Hudson River area in 1621, New Netherland (later renamed New York) was founded.

The Dutch West India Company was chartered specifically to trade in the New World, where the Dutch had acquired colonies in Brazil, the Caribbean, and the east coast of North America. Pursuing its commercial interest in New Netherland, the company established Fort Orange (Albany), Breuckelen (Brooklyn), and Vlissingen (Flushing). In Delaware it established Swanendael (Lewes). In 1624 thirty Dutch families, sponsored by the company, settled on the island now known as Manhattan. These early settlers focused their economic activities on the flourishing fur trade. At the same time, the Dutch West India Company also founded the Dutch Reformed Church (the Reformed Church in America), which exercised a significant influence in the Dutch American community.

In New Amsterdam (New York City), Governor Peter Stuyvesant (1592–1672) attempted to eliminate all worship except for the Dutch Reformed Church, but his governing board in Amsterdam opposed the policy as detrimental to commerce. Like Amsterdam itself, New Amsterdam did not enforce rules that prohibited worship to Jews, Catholics, and others. Thus, New Amsterdam flourished, and as New York City, it continues to be home to people of many different religious persuasions.

After the British captured New Netherland in 1664, Dutch immigration virtually ceased. England, however, imposed no severe restraints on the Dutch, and the vast majority remained in New York. By 1790 they numbered about 100,000 and, in addition to New York City, were clustered in towns and villages along the Hudson and Mohawk rivers. In New Jersey they established towns beside the Hackensack, Passaic, and Raritan rivers. In such places they dominated the local culture, spoke Dutch, and established both Reformed churches and day schools. After the American Revolution, the Dutch more rapidly assimilated into the dominant Anglo-American culture by adopting English for worship, attending public schools, and attaining social status within the general culture. Consequently, when a new wave of Dutch immigrants came to the United States in the 1840s, they found few people in New York or elsewhere who spoke Dutch.

Nineteenth-century Dutch immigration numbered about 200 people annually before 1845, when it increased to 800 and then averaged 1,150 annually over the next decade. That movement stemmed from religious and economic discontent in the Netherlands: a potato famine (1845–1846) and high unemployment combined with a division in the Reformed Church pitted conservative Calvinists against the increasingly liberal State Church and forced many Dutch to leave. At the same time, three clergymen organized colonies on the midwestern frontier. In 1848 Father Theodore J. Van den Broek (1783–1851) established a Catholic community in Little Chute, near Green Bay, Wisconsin. Two conservative Reformed pastors, Albertus Van Raalte

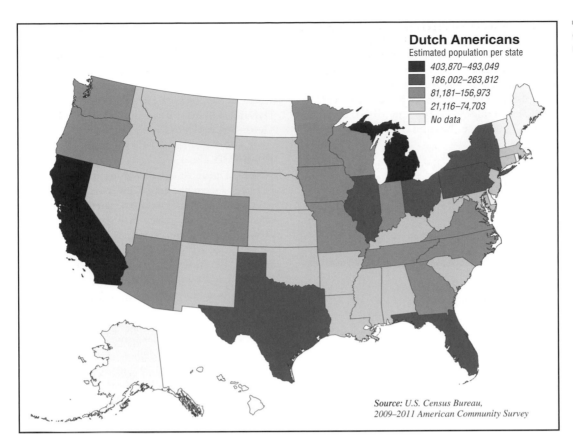

Dutch Americans
Estimated population per state

- *403,870–493,049*
- *186,002–263,812*
- *81,181–156,973*
- *21,116–74,703*
- *No data*

Source: U.S. Census Bureau,
2009–2011 American Community Survey

(1811–1876) and Hendrik P. Scholte (1805–1868), founded, respectively, Holland, Michigan (1847), and Pella, Iowa (1847). Once these communities were established, printed brochures and private correspondence triggered a persistent flow of newcomers until 1930, when immigration quotas and the Great Depression closed out that eighty-five-year period of migration. During that era, Dutch immigration followed typical northern European patterns, increasing or decreasing in response to economic prospects at home or in the United States. With peaks in the mid-1870s, the early 1880s, and 1890s, and again from 1904 to 1914, a total of about 400,000 Netherlanders immigrated to the United States between 1845 and 1930.

Of these immigrants, 75 to 80 percent originated from rural provinces surrounding the Netherlands' urban core. They settled mainly in the Midwest, clustering where the original colonies had been established in Wisconsin, Michigan, and Iowa. They also settled in and around Chicago, in Paterson, New Jersey, and in Grand Rapids, Michigan. Those with hopes of becoming independent farmers moved west and gained land under the Homestead Act, which encouraged settlement in northwestern Iowa, South Dakota, Minnesota, Montana, Washington, and California. In nearly every settlement, they organized and had prominent roles in local towns, establishing churches, private schools, and farm-related businesses of all sorts. After 1900, when the best homestead lands

were occupied, the Dutch selected urban industrial locations and formed solid ethnic enclaves in Grand Rapids, Chicago, and Paterson. By 1930, Dutch immigrant communities stretched from coast to coast across the northern tier of states, but they were concentrated most heavily around the southern half of Lake Michigan, from Muskegon, Michigan, through Chicago and north to Green Bay, Wisconsin.

After World War II, due to a war-ravaged economy and a severe housing shortage, a new wave of 80,000 Dutch immigrants came to the United States. The Dutch government encouraged emigration and sought to increase the annual U.S. immigration quota of 3,131. Consequently, under special provisions of the Walter-Pastori Refugee Relief Acts (1950–1956), about 18,000 Dutch Indonesians were admitted to the United States. These Dutch colonials, who had immigrated to the Netherlands after 1949 when Indonesia became independent, settled primarily in California, the destination of many other postwar Dutch immigrants. The 1970 U.S. Census recorded the highest number of foreign-born Dutch in California (28,000), while seven other states—Michigan, New York, New Jersey, Illinois, Washington, Florida, and Iowa—hosted nearly the whole 50,000 balance. These states, aside from Florida, retain relatively high populations of Dutch Americans. Most present-day Dutch Americans work in white-collar jobs, with over 22 percent employed in educational service, healthcare, and social services.

Dutch American Klompen dancers perform a circle dance in the street at the Tulip Festival in Holland, Michigan. © DENNIS MACDONALD / PHOTO EDIT. REPRODUCED BY PERMISSION.

LANGUAGE

In general, the Dutch language is no longer used by Dutch Americans. The vast majority of postwar immigrants have adopted English and the small number of immigrants who have arrived since the 1960s are bilingual because English is virtually a second language in the Netherlands. Still, some Dutch words and expressions have survived: *vies* ("fees") denotes filth and moral degradation; *benauwd* ("benout") refers to feelings of anxiety, both physical and emotional; *flauw* ("flou") describes foods that lack pepper or salt; a *flauw grap* is a bad or unfunny joke; and *gezellig* ("gezelik") is an adjective meaning cozy or comfortable. Typical Dutch greetings such as *dag* ("dag"), which means "good day," and *hoe gaat het* ("who gat het"), for "how are you doing," are no longer commonly used in the United States.

There are small groups of Dutch Americans who are descendants of nineteenth-century immigrants who have maintained provincial Dutch dialects (including dialects from Overijssel, Drenthe, and Zeeland) that are all but gone in the modern-day Netherlands. Consequently, some Dutch linguists have traveled to western Michigan and other Dutch American strongholds to record these antiquated dialects.

Formal Dutch remained vital among the immigrants until the 1930s, due partly to its use for worship services, but World War I patriotism, which prohibited the use of German, Dutch, and other languages, signaled the demise of Dutch usage in Reformed churches. Long before World War I, however, Dutch Americans, especially their American-born children, began to reject the ancestral language. It was well understood and frequently asserted among them that economic opportunities were greater for those who spoke English. Consequently, daily wage earners, business people, and even farm hands adopted English as quickly as possible. Formal Dutch is currently used only in commemorative worship services and in the language departments of several colleges founded by Dutch Americans. Calvin College in Grand Rapids, Michigan, offers a major in Dutch language and literature, while University of California Berkeley and University of Wisconsin-Madison offer majors in Dutch studies, including language. UC Berkeley and Harvard University boast the largest collections of Dutch-language books in the country.

RELIGION

Neither Dutch American Catholics or Jews have retained discernible ethnic practices in their religious exercises. Both groups are part of international organizations that, because they used either Latin or Hebrew in formal rituals, were not drawn into major controversies regarding vernacular language usage in worship. Furthermore, due to their general dispersion, Dutch American Catholics and Jews have had few opportunities to dominate either a parish or a synagogue. Instead, they have worshipped and intermarried readily within multi-ethnic religious communities. Dutch American Jews and Catholics have also not acted in concert to support particular branches of Judaism or specific viewpoints within the Roman Catholic Church. Even the Dutch Catholic stronghold around Green Bay, Wisconsin, has become ethnically diverse, featuring French, German, and Flemish Catholics. One village, Little Chute, Wisconsin, however, does continue to promote its Dutch ethnicity with a mid-September celebration (*kermis*) that has a Dutch costume parade, games, and craft exhibits. Meanwhile, Holland, Michigan, hosts an annual tulip festival in the spring. Dutch American Heritage Day is typically celebrated in mid-November in a number of American cities, most notably in Hudsonville, Michigan. Also, many Dutch ex-patriots living in the United States celebrate Queen's Day (*Koninginnedag*) on the last day in April to honor the birthday of the queen's mother.

By contrast, Dutch Protestants, most of whom affiliated with a cluster of Reformed churches, have spawned a long history of controversy regarding language usage, doctrinal interpretations, and liturgical expressions—all issues that were intimately related to cultural adaptation. In the colonial era, the Dutch Reformed Church experienced crippling divisions (1737–1771) due to conflicting views of ordination and theological education. One group favored continued interdependence with church authorities in the Netherlands (the Classis of Amsterdam), while the American party, led by Theodore Frelinghuysen (1692–1742), promoted education and clerical ordination at "home" in the colonies. Then, in 1792, the Dutch Reformed Church became an independent denomination that would later be known as the Reformed Church in America (RCA). The RCA moved toward mainline status by adopting English, cooperating with other major church groups (Presbyterian, Methodist, and Episcopal), and participating in interdenominational campaigns to establish churches on the midwestern frontier.

In the late 1840s, about 3,000 Dutch Protestant immigrants settled in Michigan, Illinois, and Wisconsin; by 1850 a large majority of these newcomers had become affiliated with the New York-based RCA. The immigrants' spiritual patriarch, Albertus Van Raalte, had contacted the RCA's leaders before coming, and because he found them both helpful and doctrinally compatible, he and his followers united with the RCA. Some midwestern immigrants, however, objected to this fusion and initiated a separatist movement in 1857 that became the Christian Reformed Church (CRC).

Throughout the next hundred years, the two denominations pursued different strategies for cultural adaptation. The RCA incorporated American church programs, including the revival, the Sunday school movement, and ecumenical cooperation, while neglecting its Netherlandic connections and traditions. The CRC, however, remained loyal to its religious cohorts in the Netherlands. That posture was marked by its general use of Dutch until the 1920s and by its efforts to recreate Calvinistic schools and other institutions on the Dutch model. In this practice, the CRC followed the views of Abraham Kuyper (1837–1920), the most prominent Reformed leader in the Netherlands. Consequently, the CRC attracted a majority of the Reformed immigrants who arrived between 1880 and 1920.

Since the 1960s, particularly the period from 1985 to 1995, the RCA and CRC have become more similar. Netherlandic theology and culture no longer influence the CRC significantly and the denomination increasingly emulates the liturgical and theological ethos of conservative evangelical groups affiliated with the National Association of Evangelicals. Although the RCA, with membership in the World Council of Churches, is more broadly ecumenical than the CRC, the two denominations have appointed a joint committee to encourage cooperation. At the same time, the growing tide of congregationalism has diminished denominational cohesion among them so that, like American political parties, the two groups contain a wide spectrum of viewpoints. Neither denomination, then, can be labeled exclusively liberal or conservative.

Current relations between the RCA and CRC are warm. Their respective clergymen, theological professors, and parishioners move freely across denominational boundaries, and their parishioners have a long history of acting jointly to establish nursing homes, retirement facilities, and mental health institutions. The two denominations proclaim identical confessions of faith, and no barriers restrict their mutual participation in sacramental rites. In 2011 the RCA and CRC held a joint session of their respective synods. While no formal efforts at reunification are currently in the works, the different traditions of the two

groups are becoming increasingly irrelevant due to a rapid assimilation of mainstream American religious attitudes and values.

The major strongholds of Dutch American separatism have been fragmenting rapidly. Reformed churches, schools, colleges, theological schools, and even retirement facilities for the aged are campaigning to gain a full spectrum of non-Dutch clients. Marriage outside of the ethnic group has become common, and media-driven popular culture has altered traditional behavior among all age groups. In short, mainstream culture has either attracted Dutch ethnics out of their enclaves or the surrounding culture has so altered the ethnic communities that they can no longer flourish on ethnic exclusivity.

CULTURE AND ASSIMILATION
During the chief era of Dutch immigration (1621–1970), religious and ideological viewpoints structured the character of public institutions in the Netherlands. In the Dutch Republic (1580–1795), Reformed Protestants controlled the government, schools, public charities, and most aspects of social behavior. Then, beginning in the 1850s, when the national constitution permitted a multiparty system, political parties grew from constituencies identified with specific churches or ideologies. The Reformed, Catholic, and socialist groups each organized one or more parties. In addition, each group established separate schools, labor unions, newspapers, recreational clubs, and even a schedule of television programs to serve its constituency. Dutch Americans re-created parts of that structure wherever they clustered in sufficient numbers to sustain ethnic churches, schools, and other institutions. Since the 1960s these enclaves have embraced mainstream American institutions more readily and have altered the goals of their private organizations to attract and serve a multicultural constituency.

Religious and cultural separation flourished primarily in the ethnically dense population centers of Reformed Protestants. Dutch Catholics, apart from those in the Green Bay, Wisconsin, area, were not concentrated in large numbers. Instead they joined other Catholic parishes in Cincinnati, Ohio; St. Louis, Missouri; New York City; and elsewhere. Even around Green Bay, Dutch Catholics intermarried readily with Catholics of other ethnicities. Lacking large and cohesive enclaves, Dutch Catholics were neither able nor inclined to re-establish ethnic institutions in the United States. Similarly, Dutch Jews settled mainly in cities such as New York, Philadelphia, and Boston, where they assimilated the social and religious patterns of much larger Jewish groups from Germany, Russia, and Poland. One prominent Dutch rabbi in New

York, Samuel Myer Isaacs (1804–1878), attempted to maintain a Dutch identity by founding a synagogue, a school, and the orthodox periodical *The Messenger*, but these institutions faltered after his death.

The 80,000 Dutch immigrants who arrived from 1946 to 1956 reinvigorated Dutch ethnicity across the continent. It is more from them than their nineteenth-century predecessors that ethnic foods and customs have been introduced to the Dutch American community.

The major strongholds of Dutch American separatism have been fragmenting rapidly. Reformed churches, schools, colleges, theological schools, and even retirement facilities for the aged are campaigning to gain a full spectrum of non-Dutch clients. Marriage outside of the ethnic group has become common, and media-driven popular culture has altered traditional behavior among all age groups. In short, mainstream culture has either attracted Dutch ethnics out of their enclaves or the surrounding culture has so altered the ethnic communities that they can no longer flourish on ethnic exclusivity.

There are no aggressively mean-spirited or demeaning stereotypes of Dutch Americans. They are correctly perceived as valuing property, being inclined to small business ventures, and being culturally conservative with enduring loyalties to their churches, colleges, and other institutions. The perception that they are exceptionally clannish is also accurate, but that characteristic is demonstrated primarily among Reformed Protestants. Other ethnic stereotypes—financial penury, a proclivity for liquor and tobacco, and a general humorlessness—reflect individual rather than group features. These stereotypes stem from the wars with Britain in the seventeenth and eighteenth centuries, during which the British waged a successful propaganda campaign against the Dutch. The following terms and phrases are remnants of that campaign and all connote negative ideas: "Dutch Uncle" is refers to someone who offers negative or severe comments; a "Dutch party" is an event where guests are expected to bring their own beverages or food; "to go Dutch" describes a meal or event where each participant is expected to pay for his or her own share.

Cuisine The earlier immigrants' plain diets (potatoes, cabbage, and pea soup with little meat beyond sausage and bacon) could not compete with America's meat-oriented menu. In general, Dutch foods are not rich or exotic. Potatoes and vegetables combined with meat in a Dutch oven, fish, and soups are typical. The Indonesian rice table, now widely popular in Dutch American kitchens, came from Dutch colonials. Holiday pastries flavored with almond paste are a major component of Dutch baked goods. Social gatherings thrive on coffee and cookies with brandy-soaked raisins during the Christmas season.

Traditional Dress In the Netherlands, traditional costumes vary by region, demonstrating local loyalties, once paramount, that still flavor Dutch life.

Men often dressed in baggy black pants and colorful, wide-brimmed hats, while women wore voluminous black dresses, colorfully embroidered bodices, and lace bonnets. Such traditional costumes, though, have almost entirely been replaced by modern clothes in the Netherlands. In the United States, traditional dress is reserved for special occasions. The Dutch are also renowned for their wooden shoes, which were better suited to the marshy terrain than typical leather shoes, though this footwear is worn only by farmers and is viewed by many as a cliché.

Holidays Dutch Jews and Christians generally celebrate the holidays associated with their particular religious affiliation. Many postwar immigrants, however, have preserved a distinctive pattern of Christmas observance that separates gift exchanges on St. Nicholas' Eve (December 5) from the religious celebrations of December 25.

Health Care Issues and Practices There are no specifically Dutch-related medical problems or conditions. Health and life insurance, either private or from institutional sources, long ago replaced the need for immigrant aid cooperatives that once provided modest death benefits. Reformed churches regularly assisted widows, orphans, and chronically dependent people prior to the Social Security system. In isolated cases, church funds are still used to supplement the incomes of especially needy persons or to assist those with catastrophic needs. For mental diseases, a cluster of Reformed denominations established the Pine Rest Psychiatric Hospital in 1910, but that institution now serves the general public. Other institutions, specifically the Bethany Christian Home adoption agency and the Bethesda tuberculosis sanatorium, have also been transformed to serve a multicultural clientele.

FAMILY AND COMMUNITY LIFE

Colonial New Netherland (New York), like Jamestown, Virginia, and other trading post colonies, attracted single men, few women, and even fewer families. Every account of New Amsterdam (New York City) refers to its rough and raucous social character—the products of an astonishing mixture of people, languages, and behavior that severely tested polite standards of social order. By the time of the British conquest in 1664, however, the arrival of immigrant women and the high colonial birth rate provided a population base for marriages and family life.

When the British took formal control of the colony, the Dutch populace, about 8,000 people, struggled to retain its cultural identity. Until about 1720, Dutch ethnics married within the group, worshipped together, and joined hands for economic and political objectives. Family cohesion was at the core of this ethnic vitality, but by 1800 Dutch ethnicity had weakened because economic and cultural bonds were established outside of the ethnic subculture. These bonds eventually led to marriages across ethnic lines.

Apart from in New York City, ethnic solidarity persisted well into the nineteenth century in the many towns founded by the Dutch (such as Albany and Kinderhoek in New York and Hackensack and New Brunswick in New Jersey). In such places Dutch families adhered to the values instilled by Reformed churches and their day schools. Men dominated all the public institutions, while women managed households that might have had six or seven children. Domestic life, including the education of girls, depended largely on Dutch homemakers. Girls and boys gained basic skills from part-time teachers who were also expected to indoctrinate their students into church membership. Formal education continued for boys who excelled academically, usually in the form of an apprentice relationship with lawyers, pastors, and business firms. Women received the bulk of their training from mothers and older female relatives. By 1800 most of the parochial schools were replaced by public instruction, which led to an increase in the level of formal education for girls.

In the nineteenth century most Dutch immigrants had family members who had preceded them. The newcomers came largely from rural areas and resettled in rural America, where extended families were frequently reconstituted. Siblings, parents, and even grandparents regularly joined the first settlers, contributing to the family-oriented character of that ethnic subculture. The original colonies in Michigan, Iowa, Illinois, and Wisconsin spawned more than one hundred similarly rural towns and villages, which attracted successive waves of farmers, farm hands, and craftspeople. When Dutch immigration shifted from rural to urban destinations (1890–1930), the newcomers clustered in enclaves that grew once again when extended families reunited in places like Paterson, New Jersey; Grand Rapids, Michigan; and the Chicago area. These Dutch American communities still exist, but the urban enclaves have regrouped in suburban areas, while many farmers have moved either to ethnic towns or suburban neighborhoods. Throughout its history, the Dutch subculture has been sustained by a complex institutional structure of churches, schools, homes for the aged, recreational organizations, and small businesses.

Private schools, which were especially attractive to devoted traditionalists, provided educational opportunities without a notable gender bias, but most women became housewives and supported the male-dominated institutions that served the ethnic subculture. Since the 1960s, Dutch American women have moved beyond the teaching, secretarial, nursing, and homemaking professions into medicine, law, business, and ecclesiastical positions.

Because the majority of Dutch immigrants moved to the United States over fifty years ago, they have come to largely conform to typical American household and community norms. Though not monolithic, most Dutch Americans are so assimilated and widely dispersed that little remains in the way of distinct ethnic characteristics in community life.

EMPLOYMENT AND ECONOMIC CONDITIONS

Free-enterprise capitalism was introduced to the United States by the joint stock companies that colonized the Eastern Seaboard. The New Netherland Colony (New York) exemplified that phenomenon just as obviously as Jamestown and the New England Company. Understandably, then, Dutch immigrants have never been seriously disoriented by economic procedures in the United States. Virtually the whole populace of New Amsterdam and its surrounding areas was defined by its relationship to the joint stock company. Early Dutch immigrants were stockholders, officers, and employees, or traders operating illegally on the fringes of the company's jurisdiction. In all these cases, including the farmers who provisioned the trading posts, small and large businesses dominated daily life in New Amsterdam.

Like others with roots in the colonial era, Dutch merchants, farmers, and land speculators benefited from being among the first to invest in the New World. Families such as the Van Rensselaers, Schuylers, and Roosevelts quickly joined the ranks of prominent Americans. By contrast, Cornelius Vanderbilt left a small farm to become a captain of great wealth 150 years after his ancestors immigrated to America in 1644. In fact, for all of the early Dutch Americans, as well as nineteenth-century immigrants, self-employment and economic security were major objectives.

Throughout most of the nineteenth century, Dutch immigrants preferred agriculture as the means to economic independence. Because 80 percent of them were farm hands, day laborers, small farmers, and village craftsmen, they readily became self-employed farmers either on inexpensive government land or, after 1862, on free homestead land until about 1900.

Dutch immigrants arriving in the twentieth century were frequently employed in factories, the construction trades, and garden farming. However, during the prosperous 1950s, many Dutch Americans developed small family businesses—construction, trucking, repair shops, and retailing. They ranged from door-to-door vendors of eggs and garden farm produce to developers of supermarket chains. Few were unionized shop workers. Supported by the G.I. Bill of Rights (1944), many Dutch American veterans acquired college and professional training to enter law, medicine, dentistry, and teaching so that today nearly every Dutch American family has postgraduate professionals among its children and grandchildren. Those who remain in agriculture (less than 10 percent) cultivate large farms. For non-professionals, incomes average about $30,000, and for the 50

Farmer Dave Van Ommering stands in a pen at the Van Ommering Dairy Farm in Lakeside, California, in 2013. The farm was established when Gerrit and Gerry Van Ommering emigrated from the Netherlands in 1960. Because land is limited in the Netherlands, many Dutch dairy farmers have immigrated to the U.S. SAM HODGSON / BLOOMBERG VIA GETTY IMAGES

percent who have attended college and professional schools, incomes are between $30,000 and $100,000. Home ownership, usually in suburbs or small towns, is a common feature of the Dutch American community. The economic downturn of the late 2000s did not disproportionately affect Dutch Americans. The unemployment rate for Dutch Americans was 5.3 percent in 2010 and their median household income was $52,791, both of which were significantly better than the national average.

POLITICS AND GOVERNMENT

Dutch Americans have traditionally tended to be Republicans. During the Anglo-Boer War (1899–1902), Dutch Americans organized to influence U.S. foreign policy in favor of the South African Boers. Because they distrusted Great Britain, the Dutch resisted Woodrow Wilson's pro-British policies prior to World War I. However, when war broke out, they did not resist the draft. Instead, to demonstrate their loyalty, they enlisted, bought war bonds, and adopted English. During that era, religious and educational leaders promoted patriotism, which has remained vibrant to the present day. In places where the Dutch are concentrated, especially in western Michigan and northwestern Iowa, they have elected Dutch Americans to local, state and national offices.

NOTABLE INDIVIDUALS

Academia Due largely to their abiding interest in Reformed religious perspectives, Dutch Americans have been prominent in theology, philosophy, and some facets of history. They have founded theological schools in Grand Rapids, Michigan (Calvin Theological Seminary, 1876), New Jersey (New Brunswick Theological Seminary, 1784), and Holland, Michigan (Western Theological Seminary, 1866). Graduates Lewis B. Smedes (1921–2002) and Richard Mouw (1941–) gained national acclaim from their publications and lectures. Robert Schuller (1926–) is the most widely known preacher with a Dutch Reformed heritage. Among theological school professors, Cornelius Plantinga (1946–) at Calvin, James Muilenburg (1896–) at Union, and Simon De Vries (1921–) at the Methodist Theological School in Delaware, Ohio, gained wide acclaim due to their classroom teachings and many publications. In philosophy,

Yale's Nicholas Wolterstorff (1932–) and Notre Dame's Alvin Plantinga (1932–) reinvigorated religious discussions throughout the international community of philosophers. Both William Bouwsma (1923–2004), in his re-examination of John Calvin (1509–1564), and Dale Van Kley (1941–), with revisionist studies of the French Revolution, rekindled and directed an interest in the historical significance of religion in Western history.

Art Willem De Kooning (1904–1997), who was born in Rotterdam and immigrated to the United States when he was twenty-two years old, was a widely celebrated artist. He was a founder of and creative force behind the artistic School of Abstract Expressionism, which came to prominence in the 1940s.

Business Major business leaders ranging from railroad builder Cornelius Vanderbilt (1794–1877) to Wayne Huizenga (1938–), cofounder of Waste Management Inc. and the Blockbuster Video chain, demonstrate that Dutch Americans have reached the highest levels of commercial success. Apart from its early engagement in establishing worldwide capitalism, however, Netherlandic culture has had little to do with the specific endeavors of its most prominent Dutch American entrepreneurs. Others in this category—Walter Chrysler (1875–1940) of auto fame, retail innovator Hendrik Meijer (1883–1964), and Amway Corporation cofounders Jay Van Andel (1924–2004) and Richard DeVos (1926–)—have created uniquely American institutions.

Charles Koch (1935–) and his brother David (1940–), owners of the conglomerate Koch Industries, whose annual revenues have exceeded $100 billion annually, became noted philanthropists and donors to conservative causes and institutions such as the Cato Institute.

Entertainment Dutch American entertainers include rock star Bruce Springsteen (1949–) and guitarist Eddie Van Halen (1955–), who was born in the eastern Dutch city of Nijmegen and immigrated to the United States as a child. The father of model and actress Rebecca Romijn (1972–) was born in the Netherlands.

Fashion Wealthy socialite Gloria Vanderbilt (1924–) dabbled in acting and writing, but she is best known as a fashion designer with her own eponymous label.

Journalism Greta Van Susteren (1954–) began her career as a legal analyst for CNN and went on to become a prominent news analyst on Fox News. Anderson Cooper (1967–), the son of Gloria Vanderbilt, became a high-profile journalist for CNN. He has won multiple Emmy Awards.

Literature Americans of Dutch descent have contributed significantly to American literature, but while firmly embedded in the literary canon, the works of notable individuals such as Walt Whitman (1819–1892), Herman Melville (1819–1891), and Van Wyck Brooks (1885–1963) demonstrate little or nothing that reflects a Dutch American ethos. Well-known authors whose Dutch ethnicity shaped and informed their works include Peter De Vries (1910–1993), David (1901–1967) and Meindert (1906–1991) De Jong, Frederick Manfred (1912–1994), and Arnold Mulder (1885–1959). Both De Vries's *The Blood of the Lamb* (1961) and Manfred's *Green Earth* (1977) draw deeply from the wells of ethnic experience. David De Jong's *With a Dutch Accent* (1944) highlights conflicts between settled and newly arriving immigrants within Dutch enclaves, while Meindert De Jong crafted his widely acclaimed children's literature from recollections of his Netherlandic (Frisian) boyhood. Prolific and award-winning author John Updike (1932–2009) was a descendant of Dutch immigrants who arrived in the United States in the seventeenth century.

Medicine Famed pediatrician Benjamin Spock (1903–1990) guided millions of young parents in the twentieth century with his baby books.

Politics Dutch American political activists such as Martin Van Buren (1782–1862), Theodore Roosevelt (1858–1919), Eleanor Roosevelt (1906–1975), and Franklin Delano Roosevelt (1882–1945), achieved national and historical prominence, though their accomplishments are not specifically attributed to their Netherlandic backgrounds.

Publishing Grand Rapids, Michigan, has become a center for the publication of religious books, led by the William B. Eerdmans Publishing Company. Eerdmans (1882–1966) and Louis Kregel (1890–1939) began by printing and reprinting Dutch and English books, catechisms, and pamphlets for the Reformed community. The Kregel firm continued to feature the republication of standard religious works, while Eerdmans issued an inventory of new studies in theology, literature, and history aimed at a wide spectrum of religious interest groups. The Baker Book House, founded by Louis Kregel's son-in-law, Herman Baker (1912–1991), became a publisher primarily for traditional religious groups. Peter J. Zondervan (1909–1993) left Eerdmans in 1931 to organize the Zondervan Corporation, which, with a chain of midwestern bookstores, created a market among Christian fundamentalists. Edward Bok (1863–1930) came to the United States from Holland as a small child; he became editor of *Ladies' Home Journal* and addressed it to U.S. homemakers—a move that sparked a revolution in publishing.

Sports Erik Spoelstra (1971–) is the head coach of the Miami Heat basketball team, which won the National Basketball Association championship in 2012. He is of Dutch, Irish, and Filipino descent.

MEDIA

Dutch-language journalism, vibrant between 1870 and 1920, included more than fifty periodicals, but none survived without adopting English. *De Wachter* (*Watchman*) persisted from 1868 to 1985 with subsidies from the Christian Reformed Church. Two bilingual periodicals, *D.I.S.*—published by the Dutch International Society—and the *Windmill Herald*, did retain an audience from among the postwar immigrants, but with the passing of that generation, even bilingual periodicals will probably cease to exist. *D.I.S.* continues to exist as an online publication, while the *Windmill Herald* announced in 2012 that it was ceasing publication.

URL: www.dutchinternationalsociety.org

ORGANIZATIONS AND ASSOCIATIONS

The Dutch International Society

With a North American and Netherlandic membership, the society maintains international relationships through travel tours, the publication *D.I.S.*, and sponsoring cultural programs and events.

2340 Woodcliff Avenue SE
Grand Rapids, Michigan 49546
URL: www.dutchinternationalsociety.org

Holland America Club of the Pacific Northwest

This organization aims to be a source of information for Dutch people or people of Dutch ancestry living in the Pacific Northwest.

Stefan Adelaar, Public Relations Officer
Holland America Club
15127 NE 274th Street
PMB 457
Redmond, Washington 98052
Phone: (206) 729-0214
Email: hollandamericaclubpnw@gmail.com
URL: www.holland-americaclub.com

The Holland Society of New York

This society is organized to collect and preserve information about the history of Colonial New Netherlands. Its membership consists primarily of Colonial Era descendants.

Rev. Everett L. Zabriskie, III, Secretary
20 West 44th Street
New York, New York 10036
Phone: (212) 758-1675
Fax: (212) 758-2232
Email: info@hollandsociety.org
URL: www.hollandsociety.org

Netherland-America Foundation (NAF)

The NAF works to advance educational, literary, artistic, scientific, historical, and cultural relationships between United States and the Netherlands.

Angela Molenaar, Executive Director
82 Wall Street
New York, New York 10005

Phone: (212) 825-1221
Fax: (212) 825-9105
URL: www.thenaf.org

The Netherlands-American Association of Minnesota

This is a non-profit cultural organization that organizes social events and provides resources for people interested in or connected to the language, culture, history, and heritage of the Netherlands.

Martin Weinans, Treasurer
3922 West 50th Street, #104
Edina, Minnesota 55424
Email: info@dutchclub.org
URL: www.dutchclub.org

Netherlands American Society of Southern California

This organization provides a social environment for people of Dutch descent.

Johanna Fitzgerald, President
10008 National Boulevard, Suite 349
Los Angeles, California 90034
URL: www.nassocal.org

MUSEUMS AND RESEARCH CENTERS

Association for the Advancement of Dutch-American Studies (AADAS)

The AADAS seeks to record the achievements and influence of North American Dutch and Americans of Dutch ancestry in government, industry, science, religion, education, and the arts. It analyzes North American-Netherlandic relations and maintains the Joint Archives of Holland, which contains the combined archival resources of Hope College, the Western Theological Seminary, and the Holland, Michigan, community. It also centers on the general history of Dutch Americans in the nineteenth and twentieth centuries.

Geoffrey Reynolds, Membership Secretary
Joint Archives of Holland
Hope College Campus
Holland, Michigan 49423
URL: www.aadas.nl

Calvin College and Theological Seminary Library Archives

These archives contain manuscripts, books, microfilm, and periodicals for the study of nineteenth- and twentieth-century Dutch American history, religion, and culture in the United States, Canada, and the Netherlands. Its publications include: *Origins*, a biannual historical journal; the annual *Newsletter*; and *Heritage Hall Publication Series*.

Lugene L. Schemper, Theological Librarian
3201 Burton Street SE
Grand Rapids, Michigan 49546
Phone: (616) 526-6121
Email: lschempe@calvin.edu
URL: library.calvin.edu

Van Namen Dutch Heritage Center

The center contains books, manuscripts, microfilm, and periodicals for the study of Dutch American history and culture in the greater Chicago area.

Marcille Fredrick, Director and Reference Librarian
Trinity Christian College
6601 West College Drive
Palos Heights, Illinois 60463
Phone: (708) 239-4797
URL: www.trnty.edu/lhome

Northwestern College Library Archives

The archives provide manuscripts, books, microfilm, and periodicals for the study of nineteenth- and twentieth-century Dutch American history in northwestern Iowa, including Orange City and Northwestern College.

Greta Grond, Reference and Systems Librarian
101 7th Street SW
Orange City, Iowa 51041
Phone: (712) 707-7238
Email: reflib@nwciowa.edu
URL: library.nwciowa.edu

SOURCES FOR ADDITIONAL STUDY

Balmer, Randall, H. *A Perfect Babel of Confusion: Dutch Religion and English Culture in the Middle Colonies.* New York: Oxford University Press, 1989.

Bratt, James H. *Dutch Calvinism in Modern America: A History of a Conservative Subculture.* Grand Rapids: Eerdmans Publishing Co., 1984.

Brinks, Herbert J. *Dutch Immigrant Voices, 1850–1930: Correspondence from the USA.* Ithaca: Cornell University Press, 1995.

Dutch Immigrant Memoirs and Related Writings, selected by Henry S. Lucas. Revised edition. Grand Rapids: W. B. Eerdmans Publishing Co., 1997.

Krabbendam, Hans, Cornelis A. Van Minnen, and Giles Scott-Smith, eds. *Four Centuries of Dutch-American Relations: 1609–2009.* Albany: State University of New York Press, 2009.

Kroes, Rob. *The Persistence of Ethnicity: Dutch Calvinist Pioneers in Amsterdam, Montana.* Chicago: University of Illinois Press, 1992.

Pegels, C. Carl *Prominent Dutch American Entrepreneurs: Their Contributions to American Society, Culture and Economy.* Charlotte: Information Age Publishing, 2011.

Shorto, Russell. *The Island at the Center of the World: The Epic Story of Dutch Manhattan and the Forgotten Colony that Shaped America.* New York: Vintage Books, 2005.

Swierenga, Robert P. ed. *The Dutch in America: Immigration Settlement and Cultural Change.* New Brunswick: Rutgers University Press, 1985.

———. *Faith and Family: Dutch Immigration and Settlement in the United States, 1820–1920.* New York: Holmes and Meier, 1999.

Van Hinte, Jacob. *Netherlanders in America: A Study of Emigration and Settlement in the Nineteenth and Twentieth Centuries of the United States of America.* Grand Rapids: Baker Book House, 1985.

ECUADORIAN AMERICANS

Jeremy Mumford

OVERVIEW

Ecuadorian Americans are immigrants or descendants of immigrants from Ecuador, a small country on the northwestern coast of South America. Ecuador is bordered by Colombia on the north, Peru on the south and east, and the Pacific Ocean on the west and is roughly the size of Colorado. The earth's equator, for which the country is named, runs through Ecuador only a few miles north of its capital, Quito. Ecuador measures 108,109 square miles (280,000 square kilometers) in area.

In 2012 the *CIA World Factbook* estimated Ecuador's population to be about 15.2 million, which is larger than the population of Illinois (12.8 million) but smaller than the population of New York state (19.6 million). Ecuadorians are about 95 percent Roman Catholic and 5 percent Protestant; however, the proportions of the two faiths are slightly more equal among Ecuadorian immigrants in the United States. The majority of Ecuadorians are descended from Spaniards and South American Indians, although there are also significant numbers of Ecuadorian Americans who are descended from Lebanese, Italians, Germans, Chinese, and Japanese. In addition, the Afro-Ecuadorian population numbers between 800,000 and 1.1 million people, making this segment about 1 percent of the total population. In 1999 Ecuador suffered a huge economic crisis, and the economy became destabilized. As a result, the poverty rate increased significantly. But since about 2002, Ecuador's economy has begun to move gradually but surely down the path of recovery. The unemployment rate as of 2011 was 4.2 percent (14.1 percent for workers younger than age twenty-four), and 28.6 percent of the country lives below the poverty line. This number has grown due to the increasing number of refugees who have fled to Ecuador, especially from Colombia. Ecuador's primary natural resource is petroleum and the source of its greatest wealth in recent times.

Prior to the 1960s, few Ecuadorians immigrated to the United States; however, certain factors caused this number to skyrocket after 1965, and over the last thirty years, between 200,000 and 500,000 Ecuadorians (between 2 and 5 percent of the national population) have immigrated to the United States. They settled primarily in New York, as well as in New Jersey and Connecticut, and they work in all levels of employment, from sweatshops and kitchens to entrepreneurial and professional positions. Since the start of the twenty-first century, Ecuadorian Americans have begun to claim dual citizenship by becoming naturalized U.S. citizens while still retaining their Ecuadorian citizenship and affiliation.

A total of 523,000 Ecuadorian Americans live in the United States (Pew Research Group, 2007); this group is approximately the size of the population of the state of Wyoming. Most Ecuadorian Americans live in the Northeast (around 67 percent), with about 42 percent living in New York and the rest mainly in New Jersey and Connecticut. Another sizable group lives in Los Angeles.

HISTORY OF THE PEOPLE

Early History A clearer understanding of the history of Ecuador can offer insight into the practices, pastimes, and preferences of modern Ecuadorian Americans. Many civilizations have inhabited Ecuador over the millennia, and because of this diversity in the population over an extended period of time, some segments of the modern population derive their historical origins from a broad spectrum of various groups. For example, many Ecuadorian indigenous groups have tracked their heritage and identified themselves as being linked to earlier groups such as the Cañari, Saraguro, and Otavalos. Coastal Ecuador has been called the cradle of South America because the earliest evidence of advanced human society was found there.

A shroud of mystery covers the first settlement of the continent. Most historians assume its first inhabitants were migrants from northeast Asia who crossed the Bering Strait to Alaska and worked their way south. In any case, the earliest South Americans whose artifacts have survived were coastal Ecuadorians—the Valdivian civilization in Manabí Province, whose pottery dates from 3500 BCE. Later Ecuadorians, known as *costeños* (people of the *costa*, or "coast"), produced finely worked gold and platinum ornaments; their descendants may have carried their pottery and metalworking skills into the Andean highlands and beyond.

While the earliest settled societies in Ecuador were on the coast, in later centuries, the most powerful and advanced societies were found in the mountains.

Various ethnolinguistic groups with varying degrees of political organization divided the highlands among them and were sometimes at war, sometimes at peace.

During the middle of the fifteenth century CE, the Incan state in what is now southern Peru began to expand rapidly under a series of gifted leaders. In the 1460s the Incan army penetrated the southern part of what is now Ecuador. The Inca were able to transform their conquered lands in a short time. They built excellent roads, leading to rapid and efficient communication within their empire. They forced whole villages to relocate, placing those who spoke their language (Quechua) on the conquered land while moving the conquered subjects to places where they had no roots or allies. In a short time, the Inca virtually obliterated the political entities that had preceded them in Ecuador. Incan rule in Ecuador was relatively brief; however, their legacy lingers on in the widespread use of Quichua (a derivative of Quechua), the most common Indian language in Ecuador. The circulation and adoption of this language was largely a result of Spanish colonization.

By the early sixteenth century, the Spanish conquistadors entered the picture. A minor nobleman named Francisco Pizarro, with an army of fewer than two thousand, was able to conquer an empire of half a million people within ten years. This conquest led to a three-hundred-year Spanish rule in South America. Until 1720 Ecuador was part of the viceroyalty of Peru; after that date, it was grouped with what is now Colombia in the viceroyalty of New Granada.

Modern Era At the time of South America's independence in the early nineteenth century, Ecuador was again a pivotal territory and was again contested by outside powers. Two great generals shared the glory of South America's liberation: Simón Bolívar, from Venezuela, and José de San Martín, a Spanish officer born in Buenos Aires, Argentina, who defected to fight for his native land. Starting at opposite ends of the continent, each achieved a series of stunning victories. After Bolívar had advanced as far as Quito in Ecuador, and San Martín had taken Peru from Spain, the two generals met in Quayaquil—the chief city of coastal Ecuador.

That meeting in 1822 between the continent's two greatest heroes has become legendary. Nobody knew how the great talents and plans of the two men would accommodate one another, and no one knows what they said to each other that day in Quayaquil. But after the meeting, San Martín left South America forever while Bolívar became known as the continent's liberator, and an Ecuadorian city was the point where the two movements of liberation met and the continent's destiny was decided.

After establishing its independence, Ecuador joined with what are now Colombia, Panama, and Venezuela to form a nation called Gran Colombia, and once again, Ecuador became a lesser section of a larger unit. This arrangement did not last long, however. When Bolívar's chosen successor, the Ecuadorian Antonio José de Sucre, was assassinated in 1830, the union collapsed, and Bolívar fled to Europe.

In modern times, the uncertainty of Ecuador's national identity with regard to its powerful neighbors has persisted. In 1941 Peru seized more than a third of Ecuadorian territory in the south and east. Most of this land was thinly inhabited Amazonian forest, and most of the people living there had little sense of being Ecuadorian.

Ecuador was governed by constitutional rule between 1947 and 1960, followed by a period of instability and military rule that lasted for almost twenty years and was particularly intense between 1972 and 1979. In 1973 Ecuador gained entry into the Organization of Petroleum Exporting Countries (OPEC). The cultivation and extraction of its petroleum reserves created a period of strong economic growth. Following the economic growth that had taken place from 1972 to 1979, the economy of Ecuador in general had stabilized and resulted in the nation being a more harmonious place to live.

In 1979 Ecuador became democratic with the election of Jaime Roldos Aguilera as president; however, Aguilera was killed in 1981 in a suspicious plane crash. In keeping with the terms of the country's constitution, the vice president, Osvaldo Hurtado, took over control of the government. His tenure faced extreme challenges by the end of the petroleum economic boom. An economic crisis arose during the early 1980s, and inflation soared. Hurtado strove to maintain Ecuador's financial security on an international basis. Despite his relative success in achieving this objective, however, the economic crisis continued through the tenure (1984–1988) of his successor, León Febres Cordero, who inaugurated free-market economic policies. Cordero also made attempts to crack down on drug trafficking and terrorist activities and maintained close ties with the United States.

Economic problems continued to plague the country through the 1980s, until the Ecuadorian people organized a successful protest movement that catalyzed a National Assembly designed to overhaul the constitution and reorganize the political infrastructure of Ecuador. This process lasted a year, and after an extended presidential election, the mayor of Quito, Jamil Mahuad, was elected president in 1998. His presidency was marked by peace agreements with Peru in 1998 and 1999. Mahuad also reorganized the currency of Ecuador by adopting the U.S. dollar as official currency. This move, however, proved extremely unpopular with Ecuador's financially challenged lower classes, who had difficulty converting their previous currency (sucres) into U.S. dollars, even while the upper classes became wealthier. Inflation again soared to record levels.

In the twenty-first century, demonstrations led Mahuad to resign in 2000, to be replaced by his vice president, Gustavo Noboa. One of Mahuad's final acts as president was to publicly announce his support of Noboa. The latter's presidency did not last long; in 2002 a new president was elected, military colonel Lucio Gutiérrez. Gutiérrez's tenure was also short-lived, however, as the public against protested his actions as political leader of the country. He was replaced in 2005 by his vice president, Alfredo Palacio, whose capacity to serve as president proved more effective than his predecessors'. Left-wing Economist Rafael Correa was took office in 2007 with promises to combat political corruption and increase social spending.

SETTLEMENT IN THE UNITED STATES

Before the 1960s very few Ecuadorians had immigrated to the United States. In the late 1960s, however, Ecuadorians began to immigrate in large numbers. Ecuadorian Americans come from every part of Ecuador. In the early period of immigration most came from the northern and central *sierra* (the mountainous central part of the country), a region that includes Quito and its environs. Later, large numbers of Ecuadorians came from the *costa*, or the coastal west.

This latter large wave of immigration was catalyzed by several factors. First, United States immigration law changed around this time. Before 1965 national quotas on immigrants strongly favored Europeans; after that, changes in the law made it easier for Latin Americans and other non-Europeans to immigrate to the United States. Furthermore, migration was physically easier, as air travel became affordable to ordinary people for the first time in history.

Another factor that impacted Ecuadorian migration was the Ecuadorian land reform of the mid-1960s. In 1964 Ecuador passed the Land Reform, Idle Lands, and Settlement Act. An attempt to end the feudal system that had existed in the *sierra* for centuries, the law redistributed land from absentee landlords to the peasants who farmed it. According to *Ecuador: A Country Study*, this act improved the lives of tens of thousands of poor Ecuadorians and brought a measure of social justice to the rural areas. At the same time, the act also unsettled what had been a stable society. Many of these new landowners ultimately were forced to sell their land because they went into debt due to a lack of understanding of how to manage it. In addition, many of these small plots of land (called *minifundios*) were virtually unusable. For these reasons, among others, large sections of the population left the *sierra* for the cities, the *costa*, and foreign lands such as Venezuela and the United States.

Once Ecuadorian immigration to the United States began, it snowballed. More than for any other reason, immigration becomes possible because people have contacts in the new country. As immigrants send money home and encourage others to join them, the immigrant community builds on itself. The 1990 U.S. Census counted 191,000 Ecuadorians in the United States, but there are so many undocumented Ecuadorian Americans that the true number was probably much larger. The Ecuadorian consulate in Manhattan estimated in the 1990s that there were 300,000 Ecuadorians in New York and New Jersey, and 500,000 in the United States altogether. During the early 1990s, the largest numbers came from the southern *sierra*, near the border with Peru. An estimated 5 percent of the Ecuadorian states of Cañar and Azuay have immigrated to the United States.

A majority of Ecuadorian immigrants have selected New York City as their destination of choice. The 2000 U.S. Census reported that 70 percent of the approximately 523,000 Ecuadorian Americans lived there. Ecuadorians in New York cluster in certain neighborhoods—usually the ones where other South Americans live. The greatest number live in the borough of Queens, especially in the northern neighborhoods of Astoria, Jackson Heights, and Flushing. Roosevelt Avenue in Jackson Heights is lined with Ecuadorian travel agencies, restaurants, and telephone and money-wiring services. Signs in local bars advertise South American soccer matches on cable television. Another group of Ecuadorians settled in the Bronx, in the Morris Hills and Highbridge neighborhoods north of Yankee Stadium. Still other Ecuadorian neighborhoods are found in Brooklyn, in Los Angeles, in New Jersey cities such as Newark and Jersey City, and in working-class towns in Connecticut.

One notable characteristic of Ecuadorians is their capacity to find their way to the United States through both traditional and undocumented channels. Many Ecuadorians arrive in the United States via legitimate paths; for example, a close relative or a prospective employer petitions for them, and they wait in Ecuador until a visa becomes available. This method, however, requires complex paperwork and can take years on a waiting list. Therefore, Ecuadorians sometimes employ other means of entering the United States. Some simply overstay their originally legitimate visas, until they can receive papers that allow them to remain as permanent U.S. residents. Other immigrants simply come and live in the United States for years without documentation. These Ecuadorians may smuggle themselves across the border without papers—either by foot from Mexico or by boat into Puerto Rico. Most often, they fly in with a limited-stay tourist visa and then never leave. One older study, reported in the *New York Times* (September 2, 1993) and conducted using a statistical formula applied to data from border crossings, airports, and the census, found that Ecuadorians were one of the three largest groups of undocumented aliens living in New York City at the time.

More recently, however, patterns of immigration from Ecuador to the United States have undergone a marked shift. In the first place, the decade of the

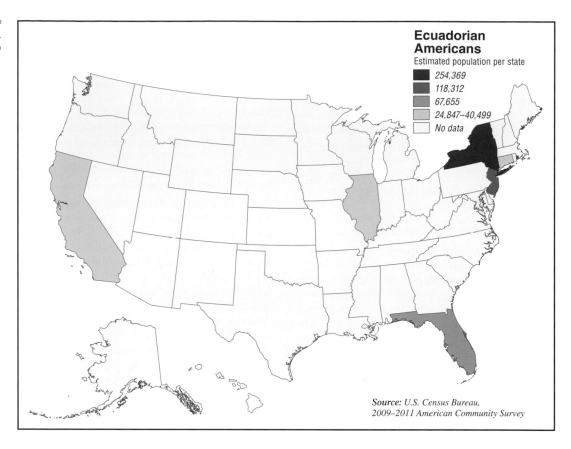

Ecuadorian Americans
Estimated population per state
- 254,369
- 118,312
- 67,655
- 24,847–40,499
- No data

Source: U.S. Census Bureau, 2009–2011 American Community Survey

1990s witnessed a huge increase in the number of individuals arriving from Ecuador. Possible reasons for this increase include slumping petroleum profits and skyrocketing inflation in Ecuador, which have negatively impacted its economy and elevated the poverty rate. As a means of dealing with these challenges, a number of Ecuadorian families have sent young male members of their clans to the United States not only to earn income to send back to Ecuador but also so that these young men might have a greater opportunity to become independent adults, as a struggling Ecuadorian economy has inhibited their capacity to do this at home.

Many of the undocumented Ecuadorian immigrants who arrive in the United States thus only do so as a means to an end; their migration is based on a desire to earn money from opportunities that might not be as available in their home country. Subsequently, as Jason Pribilsky notes in his book *La Chulla Vida: Gender, Migration, and the Family in Andean Ecuador and New York*, many of the undocumented Ecuadorian immigrants who arrived in the United States at the end of the twentieth century and in the early years of the twenty-first century have done so under the assumption that they will be able to earn more money than would be possible in Ecuador. As a whole, this group also harbors tentative plans to return to Ecuador after they have achieved greater financial stability.

As a result, a considerable gulf exists between the established community of Ecuadorian Americans whose families arrived in the United States years earlier and the population of undocumented Ecuadorians who arrived in the 1990s and later. Pribilsky observes that mention of undocumented workers in the *Ecuadoran News*, which is a popular periodical among Ecuadorian Americans, said virtually nothing about the challenges faced by the undocumented population. In addition, even the vibrant celebration of the Tenth of August Parade, which takes place in New York City and celebrates Ecuador's independence from Spain, effectively did not offer a means of support or an opportunity to foster a greater sense of community in the United States for undocumented immigrants. Instead, Ecuadorian undocumented immigrants might find some solace in attending Catholic masses offered in their language; however, as Pribilsky reports, this sense of connection to an established religious institution could just as likely cause undocumented Ecuadorians to miss their families back in Ecuador instead of giving them any sense of feeling at home.

A majority of documented or established Ecuadorian Americans are employed. They have only a 6.5 percent unemployment rate, as compared with a 7.3 percent unemployment rate among all Hispanics. Nevertheless, this number is still slightly higher than the national average of 6.3 percent (in 2009, according to a Pew Research report). They most frequently work in the information, finance, maintenance, and other service industries, finding employment in trade and transportation, sales and office support, and even in management and professional positions in industries in which Ecuadorian Americans are frequently employed. Undocumented Ecuadorians living in the United States pursue other types of occupations. As Pribilsky reports in his book, Ecuadorian workers in 1999–2000 were most frequently employed in restaurants or supermarkets, or they served as day laborers or worked in construction.

More-established Ecuadorian Americans, whose families arrived during the mid-1960s, were motivated to relocate by the land reform in Ecuador. Immigrants from later generations (the 1990s and later), however, sought economic opportunities abroad because of a lack of financial stability in their home country. For this reason among many others, a considerable gulf exists between the Ecuadorian Americans who have resided in the United States for a generation and those—frequently undocumented—who have come to the United States during the last couple of decades.

LANGUAGE

Ecuador is a bilingual country. Spanish is the country's primary language, but Quichua is also quite prevalent. In traditional Indian communities in the *sierra*, for example, the first language is Quichua, although they may also speak Spanish. Quichua (called Quechua in Peru) was the language of the Inca Empire and took root after the Inca conquered what is now Ecuador. Ironically, the Spaniards are responsible for the continued spread of Quichua; Spanish missionaries taught Christianity to the Indians in the Quichua language, thus prompting other Indian communities to learn it. In the *sierra*, Quichua is the only surviving Indian language. It has several dialects and is no longer understood by the Quechua speakers of Peru.

In the Amazonian *oriente*, or eastern region of Ecuador, about half the Indians speak Quichua. The rest of the Amazonian Indians, such as the Shuur and the Achuar, speak the languages of their tribes. These more traditional groups live mainly in the southern part of eastern Ecuador.

Nearly all Ecuadorians who immigrate to the United States speak Spanish. So few immigrants come from traditional Indian communities that they lack sufficient numbers to maintain a Quichua-speaking community in the United States. But while Ecuadorian immigrants cannot avoid speaking Spanish, the same does not hold true for English. The cohesiveness of the Ecuadorian American community allows many of its members to avoid learning fluent English, even after ten years or more in the United States. According to the U.S. Census Bureau's American Community Survey estimates for 2009–2011, only 51 percent of Ecuadorian Americans reported speaking English proficiently, and 90 percent reported speaking a language

other than English at home. (In contrast, the overall English-proficiency rate for U.S. Hispanics and Latinos was estimated at 65 percent.) Since the last several years of the twentieth century, the number of immigrants whose native tongue is Quichua has risen rapidly; this population of Quichua speakers is also largely female.

RELIGION

In Ecuador, the majority of people belong to the Roman Catholic Church (around 95 percent), with the remaining 5 percent being Protestant. Among Ecuadorian Americans, the proportion of Catholics to Protestants is more balanced. This is due to evangelical Christianity's recent spread in Ecuador. In the last few decades, evangelical Protestant missionaries have converted many in Ecuador, especially in the countryside and urban slums. These missionaries, mainly of North American origin, have experienced the most success in the southern *sierra*, including Cañar, Azuay, and Chimborazo Provinces. In Chimborazo Province, by 1980 nearly 40 percent of the population was evangelical Protestant.

Nearly all Ecuadorians who immigrate to the United States speak Spanish. So few immigrants come from traditional Indian communities that they lack sufficient numbers to maintain a Quichua-speaking community in the United States.

During the 1980s and 1990s, the largest number of Ecuadorian immigrants to the United States came from these provinces in the southern *sierra*. This fact has contributed to the greater number of Protestant Ecuadorian Americans in the United States. Since many Ecuadorians associate the United States with the Protestant missionaries who originate there, Protestant Ecuadorians are more likely to emigrate than Catholics are. In the United States they are not as small a minority as in Ecuador, and perhaps feel they can practice their religion more freely. There are no reliable statistics on this subject, but some community members estimate that one-third of Ecuadorian Americans are Protestant.

CULTURE AND ASSIMILATION

Like most immigrants today, Ecuadorian Americans are ambivalent about assimilation. It eases the difficulties of immigrant life, yet it steals what remains of home. New Ecuadorian immigrants tend not to embrace an American identity to the extent that some immigrant groups do, or did in the past. Many return home after a few years or intend to do so. For those who do stay, however, assimilation is difficult to resist. Older immigrants often complain that their grown-up children speak English better than Spanish, marry outside of the community, get divorced, abandon their religion, and ignore their parents.

A notable assimilation trend on the part of Ecuadorian Americans is their tendency to adopt not mainstream U.S. customs but rather practices that reflect the culture of the Latino American community in general. For instance, in Mexican American families, a girl's fifteenth birthday, or *quinceañera*, is an extremely important occasion, a coming-of-age celebration. This custom has never been a common one in Ecuador. Among Ecuadorian Americans, however, it has become the current custom, just as it has among other Latino Americans.

One difficult decision related to assimilation that many Ecuadorian American immigrants face is whether to become naturalized U.S. citizens. Only a minority of Ecuadorian Americans officially change their citizenship allegiance. Those who are undocumented aliens cannot become citizens, of course, and even those who have legally obtained a green card must wait five years before they are eligible for citizenship. Among Ecuadorian Americans, the 2011 American Community Survey administered by the U.S. Census Bureau reports that 46.1 percent of males and 53.9 percent of females are naturalized U.S. citizens.

Furthermore, many Ecuadorians view becoming a U.S. citizen as a betrayal of their own country. But as of September 2002, Ecuador began permitting expatriates to become citizens of other nations without losing their Ecuadorian citizenship. In addition, Ecuadorians who live abroad are allowed to vote in national elections. On an emotional level, however, many Ecuadorians feel uncomfortable swearing allegiance to the United States. Naturalization and assimilation, however, often helps lessen the discrimination that Ecuadorian Americans experience.

The primary means by which Ecuadorian Americans maintain the culture of their home country is via the regional association, unofficial groups established to unite immigrants from the same Ecuadorian province or town. Ecuadorians frequently maintain closer ties and greater loyalty to their home villages, cities, or regions than to Ecuador as a nation. For example, an Ecuadorian from Ambato may identify himself first as a resident of the city of Ambato, second as a *serrano* (someone from the *sierra*), and only third as an Ecuadorian. In New York, the area of greatest concentration of Ecuadorian Americans, an immigrant can join a group associated with his hometown or region. These associations, many of which have very little formal organization but join in loose federations with those from other regions, are a vital part of immigrant social life. Outside of New York, an immigrant may join an organization for Ecuadorians generally.

Regional associations allow immigrants to associate with others who not only share their homeland and language but also their cultural background, their regional accent, and perhaps even friends at home.

They provide an extended family to immigrants who may be homesick or lonely; they also offer a pool of credit for an immigrant to start a business, and they function as an informal channel for news and information as well as for sending and receiving gifts and money. The mail may be slow, and there may be no telephone at home, but at any given moment, someone from the regional association is about to visit Ecuador or has just returned.

Cuisine The cuisine of Ecuadorian Americans reflects their region of origin, as each of the different regions of Ecuador has its own cuisine. Perhaps the most distinctive and highly prized Ecuadorian dish, and what most closely approaches a national dish, is the ceviche of the *costa*. The dish is consumed in many regions of Latin America, but Ecuadorians claim to have invented it. Ceviche is raw seafood marinated in the juice of citrus fruits and served chilled. The acidic juice actually "cooks" the flesh, preserves it, and gives it a pleasing flavor. Ceviche can be made with many different kinds of fish, but shrimp is most commonly used. Lemon, lime, or even orange juice is used in the dish. Ceviche may also have vegetables such as onions, tomatoes, and peppers, and roasted peanuts may be sprinkled on top. The popularity of this dish can be demonstrated by its presence on the menu of any Ecuadorian American restaurant.

Besides fish, the other staple food of the *costa* is bananas. Ecuador was one of the original "banana republics," a country whose economy depended utterly on banana exports. Bananas have always been at the heart of lowland Ecuadorian agriculture and cuisine and are a major part of the diet both in the *costa* and the *oriente*. There are many *costeños* in New York, and these New Yorkers eat a lot of bananas.

A wide variety of bananas grow and are eaten in Ecuador: *guineos* (the large yellow bananas widely known in the United States), *magueños* (short, plump, red bananas), *oritas* (tiny yellow bananas), and *platanos* (green plantains, a starchier type of banana used in cooking) are the main varieties. These and others are all prepared by Ecuadorian Americans in many different ways—whole, sliced, and mashed; raw, boiled, fried, and baked.

Where *costeños* use bananas, *serranos*, who live in the colder mountain climates where bananas do not grow, use potatoes. The potato, which was first domesticated by ancient Andean farmers, has been a staple in the region for millennia. Like the banana, the potato has many forms in Ecuador and is prepared in many ways. Ecuadorian Americans from the *sierra*, therefore, use many different potatoes, as they are accustomed to a variety. Besides potatoes, *serranos* also love corn (maize), which can be eaten on the cob or in tamales. Much of *serrano* cooking takes the form of soups. Before the Spaniards came, Ecuadorians did not use ovens but mostly boiled their food. This custom has continued to influence their cuisine. The ordinary Ecuadorian meal will center on a *sopa* or *caldo*—soups made with potatoes and other vegetables and perhaps some meat.

The ordinary diet in Ecuador has very little meat. One traditional meat is the *cuy*, or guinea pig. Many Indian families in rural Ecuador keep guinea pigs, which they eat on special occasions. The meat is delicious, but there is very little of it. Ecuadorians in the United States have trouble getting *cuy* meat. But beef, chicken, and pork, which are more abundant and affordable in the United States than in Ecuador, have been more widely incorporated into Ecuadorian American cooking as a result.

In Ecuador one of the most popular drinks is *chicha*, a fermented liquor that is frequently referred to as "beer." In villages in the *costa*, the drink is still made with yucca tubers by the women, who first chew the yucca and spit it out before letting it ferment. Chemicals in the saliva help to ferment the yucca. In the United States, this drink is difficult to obtain. Most Ecuadorian Americans have adapted to this shortage by drinking wine or beer instead. Other types of liquors commonly consumed include *aguardient*, a liquor made from sugarcane, which is consumed in both Ecuador and abroad.

Ecuadorians also drink a lot of coffee, and often insist on making it in the traditional way that it is prepared in Ecuador. This method requires boiling the coffee down to a thick sludge known as *esencia* and bringing it to the table in a small pitcher or bottle. It is then blended in the cup with hot water, milk, and sugar. The final product has an unusual, rather bitter taste that is quite different from the coffee most Americans drink; however, Ecuadorian Americans prefer it.

Dances and Songs Music is an important part of Ecuadorian culture, and Ecuadorian Americans enjoy it in celebrations and as an everyday part of life. One of the most prominent musical styles in Ecuador is Andean music. Like all American musical forms, it has European and African influences, but musicologists believe that Andean music in its most basic form has remained the same since before the arrival of the Spaniards.

Andean music has become increasingly popular in the United States. Many Ecuadorian Americans of *serrano* Indian background perform this type of music in traditional groups in the United States, and they often perform with Peruvians and Bolivians. Some of these groups play on university campuses and in music halls, but many more play in the streets and subways of New York and other cities. With their long, straight hair; homburg (derby) hats; and brightly colored *serrano* ponchos, they create a spectacle anywhere they have not been seen before and may earn good money in spontaneous gifts from appreciative listeners. These musicians wear working clothes that emphasize their Indian background but that they would probably not wear at home, either in New York or in Ecuador.

The essential instruments of Andean music are winds and percussion. The wind instruments are flutes or panpipes—a row of pipes of various lengths attached together—while the percussion comprises various drums and rattles. Andean Indians also utilize stringed instruments such as violins, guitars, and ukulele-like instruments. The music's mood, carried by the winds and strings, is generally plaintive, even melancholy. The percussion carries the music forward at a steady pace, inviting dancing. The typical musical group is large (six or more different musicians) and is usually all male. To those unfamiliar with it, Andean music can sound monotonous, with slight variations on a theme by the flutes. But to those who understand it, the long Andean song is a hypnotic exploration of a musical idea.

In recent years, recordings of traditional music have become widely available, groups tour, and certain musical groups have become famous throughout the whole Andean region. For instance, the Bolivian group Los Kjarkas won a wide following throughout Ecuador when they toured there, and their songs are now played throughout Ecuador. Certain songs have become standards and are played throughout the region. Panpipes from the southern Andes, called *zampoñas*, are also becoming popular in Ecuador.

In addition to Andean music, Ecuadorian Americans enjoy listening to *musica nacional* (literally, "national music"), a style of music that uses amplified and electronic instruments and blends elements of traditional and popular Latin music. This music is played at weddings and other festivities and is also called *sanjuanitos*, after the festival of San Juan. Ecuadorian Americans utilize this type of music in their celebrations and family gatherings. Ecuadorians in the *costa* play a musical style closely related to the coastal Colombian *cumbia* style, with strong Afro-Caribbean influences. Nevertheless, despite the popularity of this type of music, and even though traditional Andean music is Ecuador's most distinctive cultural export, Ecuadorian Americans at home are more likely to listen to *sanjuanitos*, or the various other Latin styles that have come together in the Latino American community. This trend could reflect the tendency of some Ecuadorian Americans to appropriate Latino American culture over and above their assimilation of mainstream U.S. culture.

Other types of popular music include the *pasillo*, a style that shifts according to the village in which it is performed. As a dance, the *pasillo* resembles a waltz; the instruments that provide the accompaniment for this dance include guitars, mandolins, and other stringed instruments; a *rondin*, a type of flute, is also used to accompany the

ECUADORIAN PROVERBS

El bote que pertenece a muchos se agita y hierve mal aún peor.

> The pot that belongs to many is stirred poorly and boiled even worse.

Recuerden que manos que dan, reciben.

> Hands that give also receive.

Cada secreto es finalmente revelado.

> Every secret is eventually revealed.

La ira de la mente es veneno para el alma.

> Anger of the mind is poison to the soul.

Es un buen sermón sobre el ayuno cuando el predicador sólo tenía el almuerzo.

> It's a fine sermon about fasting when the preacher just had lunch.

No importa si el niño nace con una nariz chata, con tal de que el niño está respirando.

> No matter if the child is born with a flat nose, as long as it is breathing.

El diablo es más sabio por su edad no porque él es el diablo.

> The devil's wiser more on account of his age than on account of being the devil.

Gente fuerte perdonar a otros; personas débiles recordar transgresiones.

> The strong forgive; the weak remember.

COMMON ECUADORIAN PHRASES

Agringado

> Refers to a local trying to act like someone from the United States

Aló

> "Hello," used when answering the phone

A la johnny—

> Going to the United States

A precio de huevo—

> Cheap (literally, the price of an egg)

Chuta

> An exclamation of surprise

Estar con la luna

> Crazy (literally, "to be with the moon")

La familia pavoni

> Trying to get something for nothing, broke (literally, "turkey family")

Mantel largel

> Banquet in the house

Mucha

> Kiss (used in the *sierra*)

No sea mailto

> Expression used when a favor is needed

Palo grueso

> Influential person with a lot of power

Prenda el foco

> Think (literally, "turn the light on")

---

pasillo. Another popular type of song is practiced on Ecuador's coast—the *amor fino*, which is another example of a song that is danced to.

One of the most common occasions during which Ecuadorian Americans sing and dance are the fund-raising parties hosted by regional associations in order to acquire contributions to send to schools, libraries, and soup kitchens in Ecuador.

Holidays The most important holiday for Ecuadorians is August 10, the anniversary of the *primer grito*, or "first cry," of independence in Ecuador and South America. In New York, this day is designated as "Ecuador Day" and is marked by a parade on Thirty-Seventh Avenue in Queens. Ecuadorian New Yorkers also participate in the Desfile de Hispanidad, a parade of Latin American immigrants on the day before Columbus Day.

Many Ecuadorian Americans also celebrate the festivals of the Christian year, such as Christmas, Carnival, and Holy Week/Easter. In addition, individual saints have their festivals, which are associated with certain towns or regions of Ecuador. The feast of Saint John the Baptist (San Juan), celebrated on June 24, is of special importance to Otavaleños, and is celebrated by all-night music and dancing throughout the northern *sierra*. This festival is marked by three Catholic masses—a vigil (the evening before), a dawn, and a midday mass. In addition, flowers are collected and dried to make wreaths to be hung in the house over the following year. The feast of the Virgin of Carmen, on July 16, is observed by people from the town of Cuenca. Among Ecuadorian Americans, these religious holidays are generally celebrated in private, with family and friends, and not in public festivals as they are in Ecuador.

FAMILY AND COMMUNITY LIFE

Ecuadorians have two models of family life: the Spanish/mestizo (a mestizo is a person of "mixed" blood; i.e., both native and European descent) model and the Indian model. In the first model, the father rules the family. He has few responsibilities at home, spends much of his leisure time away from his family, and is tacitly permitted to see other women. The mother does the work within the family. Children are taught to be obedient to their parents. Daughters are allowed little freedom outside the house. In the Indian family, on the other hand, husband and wife have a more equal relationship. The wife plays a greater economic role and has more decision-making authority within the family. Extramarital affairs are socially unacceptable for either spouse.

Ecuadorian Americans are exposed to and frequently influenced by a third model of family life: that which exists in U.S. mainstream society and culture. In this model, the position of the two parents is relatively equal, there is more sexual freedom than in either style of Ecuadorian family, and children have greater freedom and independence. As do all immigrants, Ecuadorian Americans must grapple with the cultural differences in family life between their home and their adopted country, and they must decide whether to resist or to embrace American norms.

In terms of child rearing, the relationship between a child and a parent can be strongly impacted by gender, as Jason Pribilsky points out. Although children are expected to treat their parents with respect, the way that they interact with their mothers may contrast with their exchanges with their fathers. In Ecuador, many children experience a somewhat distant relationship with their fathers, based on a cultural expectation of *respeto* ("respect"), which produces rigid strictures in these relationships. Many Ecuadorian American fathers and children, however, find that they can relax this rigidity in their own relationships; through this structure, a sense of *cariño*, or affection, can enter into the equation. This development, in turn, also allows mothers to move into a slightly altered role, in the sense that they can help cultivate affection in their husbands' relationship with their children. Since many Ecuadorian American immigrants speak of having relocated for the sake of their children, as much as anything else, children are also a highly valued component of families for Ecuadorian Americans.

Immigration inevitably brings change to family life, whether one accepts or rejects the adopted culture. This is due not only to new cultural norms but also to the ways in which immigrating divides and rearranges families. Often Ecuadorian men immigrate alone, leaving their wives and children in Ecuador. In this respect, Ecuadorian immigrants differ from other South American immigrants, among whom women outnumber men. Such men may plan to get settled in the United States and then send for their families, or they may intend to return home after earning some money. Often such immigrants will first send for their older sons, and only later do their wives and other children join them. In working-class Ecuadorian neighborhoods in the United States, there is a predominance of men, which means that many Ecuadorian villages are currently made up mainly of women.

In general, Ecuadorian Americans tend to be married (51.1 percent); however, records show that more than one-third (34.5 percent) of Ecuadorian American women between the ages of fifteen and forty-four who gave birth around 2006 were not married. This rate is comparable to the average for U.S. women (33.4 percent). At the same time, however, some immigrants are young, single women who experience a level of freedom and independence they would not experience in Ecuador. Among the community of immigrant Indian street peddlers from the Otavalo region, for instance, there are many single women. Alone in an American city, they have a more independent life than they would have had at home.

One of the entities that greatly influences the type of life that Ecuadorian Americans live in the United States is the regional association. For example, not only do these associations provide a sense of community to immigrants, but they also offer services that would not otherwise be easily accessible. One major practice that these associations foster is the offering of charity. Individually, Ecuadorian immigrants send money to family and relatives. Through their membership in regional associations, however, they can extend this generosity beyond their families. Regional associations send large amounts of money to Ecuador every year—to schools, libraries, youth sports clubs, orphanages, and soup kitchens. One fund-raiser, for instance, may be held to renovate a hometown church, another to bring a sick child to the United States for an operation.

The associations use a variety of fund-raising techniques to garner contributions, including raffles, fund drives, and radio promotions; however, by far the most popular method of acquiring money to provide charity is the fund-raising party. Members will rent an appropriate space, perhaps a community center, dance club, or South American restaurant, or they will convince a community businessperson to let them use the space for free. They will advertise the event in community newspapers and with flyers in Ecuadorian neighborhoods and businesses. The party will have a modest admission price and will feature food, drink, music and disco-style lighting. The band will be Ecuadorian and will play a mix of traditional Ecuadorian folk music, romantic ballads, modern Ecuadorian dance music, and other Latino music.

Besides the regional associations, Ecuadorian Americans rely heavily on a range of services offered within the community. They depend on grocery stores, restaurants, travel agencies, and undertakers for services, and the buildings that house these service providers have even transformed sections of Queens into a little Quito, where one never has to feel like a foreigner. One of the most important of these services is Spanish-language banking. New York banks are notoriously unfriendly and will refuse to open accounts for those without much money, a job, or a Social Security number, so Hispanic banks are a crucial service for immigrants. Banks such as First Bank of the Americas, a Colombian-owned bank with branches in Queens, mean a great deal to Ecuadorian immigrants.

Whereas these communities and businesses offer options and connections to Ecuadorian Americans, their purpose is not to cover every aspect of life, to prevent Ecuadorian Americans from fully integrating into American society, or to replace American government in the lives of immigrants. Regional associations do not undertake to provide work or housing for new arrivals, as the institutions of some immigrants from other countries do. Ecuadorians are not insular, and they willingly seek out the benefits and services of society at large. The general average of Ecuadorian Americans who live below the poverty line is 14.8 percent; this number is higher than that of the general U.S. population (11.9 percent) but below the average of 19.5 percent of all Hispanic Americans.

Education In general, Ecuadorian Americans complete higher levels of educaion than do Hispanic Americans overall. Of all Ecuadorian Americans who are twenty-five years and older, 18.2 percent have earned a bachelor's degree (12.6 percent of all U.S. Hispanics have attained this educational level). Overall, 71 percent of Ecuadorian Americans have earned a high school diploma, and 38.95 percent have completed at least some college coursework (including the aforementioned 18.2 percent who have graduated with a four-year degree).

EMPLOYMENT AND ECONOMIC CONDITIONS

In general, Ecuadorian Americans occupy positions in a wide variety of industries, including construction and agriculture, manufacturing, trade and transportation, and information and finance. In fact, the greatest number of employed Ecuadorian Americans work in the information, finance, or service industries (50.9 percent). Almost half of employed Ecuadorian Americans work in this type of industry: other industries they work in include construction, agriculture, and mining (16.6 percent); manufacturing (12.2 percent); trade and transportation (21 percent). Within these industries, they occupy a wide variety of positions. The roles they occupy within the industries include the following breakdown: management and professional positions (18.4 percent),

service positions (23.5 percent), sales and office support (19.8 percent), construction and farming (15.8 percent), and maintenance, production, and transportation (22.5 percent).

More established Ecuadorian Americans who have been in the United States for a generation or longer have created a business organization, Profesionales Ecuatorianos en el Exterior (PRO-ECUA), which offers support and advocacy for trade issues, as discussed by Pribilsky in *La Chulla Vita*. This group of Ecuadorian Americans are financially stable, to the extent that they take part in groups that organize philanthropic fundraising for Ecuadorians. The organization La Casa de la Cultura Ecuatoriana (CCE) is one such group.

For other Ecuadorian Americans, however, the working conditions they encounter do not prove as dependable. Many of them pursue work as *esquineros* ("street corner men"), as described by Pribilsky. In this occupation, they frequently run the risk of inclement weather, prejudicial treatment by passers-by or business owners, and intense competition from other persons engaged in a similar pursuit. Likely the most challenging element of this occupation is the unpredictability of its success. Because they are frequently not protected by laws concerning work conditions, they risk their health and safety in their attempts to secure work and complete jobs. A somewhat more stable but still challenging position would be that of a *jornalero*, or a person who meets at a predetermined place to engage in day laboring work. Although this occupation provides flexibility and seems easier than that of the *esquineros*, they both prove difficult to pursue on an extended basis. Other than these positions, many Ecuadorian Americans also pursue employment in garment factories or restaurants, as Pribilsky notes. Both of these types of jobs prove more secure and offer more consistent work than that of the *esquineros* or *jornaleros*.

Another group of Ecuadorian Americans is the entrepreneurs. Many immigrants with initiative and capital start businesses catering to the Ecuadorian community. These include Ecuadorian restaurants, travel agencies, and telephone and money-wiring services. Such community-oriented businesses also provide jobs for other Ecuadorians.

A third group of Ecuadorians is the professionals. Of all the immigrants, the members of this group occupied the highest status in Ecuador, received the most education there, and are often the unhappiest in the United States. Immigrating with great ambitions, they meet great disappointments. To resume their profession in their new country, doctors, lawyers, architects, and social workers must receive new training and pass new tests, and they must become fluent in English even to begin this process. One group of Ecuadorian Americans who pursue professional positions has founded an association designed to help individuals form a sense of community and to benefit from their continued associations with each other. The Young Ecuadorian American Professionals Business Association (YEAP) is based in South Florida, and it serves its members by sustaining relations and network connections among them.

Overall, the median income for Ecuadorian Americans aged sixteen and older in 2007 was $21,655, according to Pew Research. This level is representative of the median earnings for U.S. Hispanics during the same period ($21,048). A considerable percentage of Ecuadorian Americans do own homes (41.8 percent), but this number is still lower than that of U.S. Hispanics in general (49.9 percent of whom own homes) and the U.S. population in general (67.2 percent).

Of particular note is one group of Ecuadorian immigrants to the United States whose close ties to their home community have not only maintained their sense of identity and purpose but have made them a success story in the United States: The Otavaleño Indians have made a unique contribution to the American economy and society. Living in the northern *sierra* near the modern town of Otavalo, this group has preserved its economic role—woven textile goods for sale to outsiders—since before the Incan conquest of their land.

Otavaleños are both weavers and farmers, and whereas the land redistribution created challenges for some Ecuadorians and caused them to immigrate to the United States, the Otavaleños actually benefited from the passage of this law. They left their workshops and took their weaving home. Otavaleños were determined to no longer allow others to reap the benefits of their skilled labor and traditions. Returning to a pre-Incan model, they sent members of their own community to other countries to market their woven goods. While other Indian communities practice traditional weaving, the Otavaleños are unique in their resourcefulness and success in selling their wares, without middlemen, on the international market.

In small factories in or near Otavalo, the Indians make heavy woolen sweaters, ponchos, hats, and blankets, all in bright colors with traditional designs. They send these items to Quito and other South American cities; to Mexico City, New York, and other North American cities; and to Europe and Asia to be sold by street vendors. At any given time six thousand Otavaleños, or 10 percent of the whole community, live abroad as itinerant vendors. The sellers may be the grown children of the manufacturer who are working in the family business and seeing the world at the same time. Even if they are not related, all the people involved are Otavaleño. The profits do not leave the community.

Otavaleño street vendors in New York, though relatively few in number (about three hundred by one estimate), are highly visible, with their traditional dress and appearance in outdoor shopping areas such as Canal Street. The men wear their long straight hair in braids and wear blue ponchos and white pants. The women wear embroidered white blouses, red wristbands, and heavy dark wraps around their shoulders and skirts. Otavaleño clothing is very traditional; in fact, the women's clothing has changed only slightly from the time of the Inca. The appearance that Otavaleño peddlers project helps them to sell their inventory, because it adds to the perceived authenticity of their products.

The outfit an Otavaleño peddler would wear in the streets of New York is not necessarily what he or she would wear at home. Furthermore, the product sold is not timeless and unchanging. Each year Otavaleño street vendors send home samples of the latest fashions, and the manufacturers make changes in style and color, even introducing new products, such as headbands. Many of the street vendors hold licenses from the city whereas others are unlicensed. Some sellers cannot afford the license fee whereas others only intend to stay in the city for a short time and so do not buy the license. Laws against unlicensed street selling are often only loosely enforced, but at times such street vendors must face having all their goods confiscated by the police. Furthermore, like all people who do business out of doors, Otavaleño merchants must operate within the complex and risky society of the street. They are subject to the whims of police, the maze of city regulations, the unwritten laws of those who sell clothes, food, stolen goods, sex, and drugs, and the extortionists and predators of the street. But the international marketing of their clothes has brought the Otavaleños great rewards.

Most Otavaleños abroad ultimately return home, often to attend university and enter a profession. Otavaleños have become wealthy and influential in their home province; indeed, the mestizo community of Otavalo is poorer than that of the Otavaleño Indians. The Otavaleños tend to convert their earnings into education and opportunities for their children.

Chinese Ecuadorians One small but significant segment of the Ecuadorian American community is that of Chinese Ecuadorians. People from southern China immigrated in the nineteenth century to every American country, including Ecuador. When Ecuadorians began immigrating to the United States in large numbers, after the mid-1960s, many Chinese Ecuadorians joined the migration—probably in greater numbers proportionate to their numbers in the general Ecuadorian population. This was partly because the Chinese Ecuadorians had shallower roots in Ecuador than others and had experienced discrimination there, and partly because New York, where most Ecuadorians went, had a large and established Chinese community. Today there are several thousand Chinese Ecuadorians in the United States, about 1 percent of the Ecuadorian American community. Chinese Ecuadorians are more likely to be in commerce or the professions than other Ecuadorians but in general are not demographically different from the rest of the community. Most have some familiarity with both Chinese and Spanish but are more fluent in Spanish. They typically live in Latino neighborhoods, not Chinese ones, and most live in New York City.

POLITICS AND GOVERNMENT

In general, Ecuadorian Americans are not very active politically, either at home or in their adopted country. Ecuador does not encourage its expatriates to cast absentee ballots in elections at home. While taking a keen interest in the news from home (Ecuadorian newspapers in the United States carried extensive news and analysis of the 1995 border hostilities between Ecuador and Peru, for example), this group of immigrants seldom organizes around specific policy issues at home. At the same time, few Ecuadorian Americans are U.S. citizens with the right to vote in the United States. This trend has limited their capacity to be influential in U.S. politics, but because many Ecuadorians plan to return home one day, they do not concern themselves much with U.S. politics.

One of the few legislative acts for which Ecuadorian Americans actively lobbied was the passage, in Ecuador, of a dual-citizenship law. The Ecuadorian congress passed the measure in response to vigorous and coordinated efforts by the Ecuadorian American organizations—in particular, by the New York umbrella group Comite Cívico Equatoriano. Because of the passage of this bill, Ecuadorian Americans no longer have to choose between being Ecuadorian citizens or American citizens but can embrace both sides of their identities.

Because Ecuadorian Americans are frequently more closely connected to their villages or cities of origin than they are to Ecuador as a nation, when Ecuadorian Americans do take a political stand, it is often linked to their region of origin. *Costeños* tend to be liberal while *serranos* are conservative. This difference can be seen in the different attitudes in *serrano* immigrant neighborhoods in Queens and *costeño* neighborhoods in the Bronx. Overall, however, Ecuadorians from all regions are socially conservative by U.S. standards. For instance, they are among the most outspoken proponents of the death penalty, long an topic of controversy in the state of New York.

One other notable area of political interest and activity for Ecuadorian Americans is labor unions. Because Ecuador itself fosters a more dynamic activist labor culture, Ecuadorian Americans who work under less than ideal conditions or who earn less than minimum wage frequently seek alternative avenues for ameliorating their undesirable working circumstances. These endeavors, however, sometimes fail, which can lead them to become disillusioned and apathetic.

In general, though, Ecuadorian Americans are a noncitizen, nonvoting community. Many Ecuadorian New Yorkers live in state legislative districts with Latino majorities, but politicians, tend to focus attention on the needs of Puerto Ricans and other voting Latinos. Noncitizens become ever more vulnerable as politicians across the nation advocate anti-immigrant measures. Concern over such measures is now prompting more Ecuadorians to file for citizenship, especially because they can do so without relinquishing their Ecuadorian citizenship and allegiances.

NOTABLE INDIVIDUALS

Because large-scale migration from Ecuador to the United States began only relatively recently, there are not many famous Ecuadorian Americans. There are, however, Ecuadorians who have made a mark on American society.

Art Oswaldo Guayasamín (1919–1999), born to an Indian father and a mestizo mother, forged a powerful art that addresses what it means to be Indian, to be mestizo, and to be Ecuadorian. His semiabstract paintings are generally figurative and feature the rugged faces and bodies of Indians at work or at home; they often illustrate scenes from Ecuadorian history and express his leftist views, his spirit of protest, and his sense of sadness at social injustice. His work is internationally acclaimed and has been exhibited all over the world.

In 1988 Guayasamín caused controversy in the United States by painting a mural in the Ecuadorian hall of Congress. One of the panels in the mural—intended to summarize Ecuador's history—showed a skull in a helmet, with the letters *CIA*. Despite his frustration with aspects of American policy, Guayasamín lived in the United States during the 1950s, when Nelson Rockefeller arranged an official invitation for him to come to the United States. He lived for several years with his family in the Bayside neighborhood of Queens, New York. In 1960, however, a visit to Communist China earned him official hostility in the United States, and he returned with his family to Ecuador.

Lady Pink (1964–) was born Sandra Fabara in Ambato, Ecuador. She grew up in Queens (New York City) and began expressing herself through graffiti around the age of fifteen after her boyfriend was exiled to Puerto Rico following an arrest. She integrated her boyfriend's name into her tagging label, and her nickname is derived from a number of influences, including her love of England, especially during the Victorian period, and her enthrallment with historical romances as well as the British aristocracy. A student of the High School of Art and Design in Manhattan, she soon made a name for herself as a renowned female artist in a field dominated by males. Lady Pink's work was featured in 1980 in the New York show "GAS: Graffiti Art Success," and her efforts in decorating subway trains from 1979 to 1985 earned her accolades that launched her film career (in the movie *Wild Style*, 1983). Her work is featured in museums across the world, and her works on canvas are now considered collectors' pieces.

Journalism Cecilia Alvear was born in the Ecuadorian village of Baquerizo Moreno, and she loved books from a young age. She immigrated to the United States in 1965 and as a journalist covered major wars in the 1980s, including military skirmishes in El Salvador and Nicaragua. She was one of twelve journalists awarded a prestigious Nieman Fellowship at Harvard University, where she spent the academic year of 1988–1989. She has had a long career in broadcast journalism, primarily working for NBC, and she is the former president of the National Association of Hispanic Journalists. Alvear became a U.S. citizen in 1984 but continued to frequently return to the Galapagos Islands to work on a project to benefit the public elementary school first started by her father, Alejandro Alvear, the former military governor of the islands. She is viewed as an inspiration to Latino Americans who wish to pursue a career in journalism or broadcasting.

Business One Ecuadorian American who made an important contribution to American business is Napoleon Barragan, founder of Dial-a-Mattress in Queens, New York. Recognizing that speed and convenience matter the most to some people, he sold mattresses over the telephone and delivered them immediately. In 1994 his business was the ninth largest minority-owned business in the New York area.

Music The pop singer Christina Aguilera (1980–) is of Ecuadorian descent. She gained prominence as a Star Search contestant in 1990 and was a member of The Mickey Mouse Club (1993–1994) with Justin Timberlake and Britney Spears. Her self-titled debut album had three number one singles: "Genie in a Bottle," "What a Girl Wants," and "Come on Over, Baby." She has currently released seven albums, all of which have been commercial successes and have solidified her international reputation. Along with her singing and other successes, she has been appointed as a United Nations ambassador and is extremely concerned with global human rights issues. She has earned a Golden Globe, four Grammy Awards, a Latin Grammy Award, and a star on the Hollywood Walk of Fame. She has also earned the George McGovern Leadership Award for her philanthropic efforts.

Politics In 1993 Ecuadorian immigrant Aida González (1962–) was named director of cultural

Ecuadorian American Andres Gomez plays during the French Open in Paris. DAN SMITH / GETTY IMAGES

affairs to Queens borough president Claire Shulman; she is one of a handful of Ecuadorian New Yorkers who are acquiring power and influence in the Democratic Party.

Sports Probably the most famous Ecuadorian athlete is Andrés Gómez (1960–), the world-class tennis player; many of his great matches have been played in the United States, and he has been a source of inspiration to Ecuadorian Americans and all lovers of tennis. He won the men's singles title at the French Open in 1990, and during his career from 1979 to 1992, he won twenty-one singles tournaments and thirty-three doubles titles.

Another important Ecuadorian tennis player is Francisco "Pancho" Segura (1921–), who has made the United States his home. An unorthodox but highly successful player in his youth, Segura surprised the professional tennis world with his powerful two-fisted forehand; the former tennis director at the La Costa Resort and Spa in Southern California, he retired from pro tennis and coached both Jimmy Connors and Andre Agassi.

MEDIA

PRINT

Various weekly, monthly, or occasional newspapers have been produced and distributed to the Ecuadorian American community in New York. Most do not last long. Magazines and daily and weekly newspapers from Quito and Quayaquil are also available at newsstands in Queens, with a lagtime of several days. These are rather expensive and do not contain local news or advertisements.

El Diario

For most of their local, national, and international news, Ecuadorian Americans rely on the general Spanish-speaking press, especially New York's *El Diario*. This paper was originally founded for a Puerto Rican readership, but in recent decades, the growing New York population of Ecuadorians, Colombians, Cubans, and Dominicans has forced the New York Spanish press to broaden its focus. This paper now contains news from various Latin American countries, as well as local news that is relevant to the new arrivals.

Susan DeCarava
One Metrotech Center
18th Floor
Brooklyn, New York 11201
Email: sdecarava@nyguild.org
URL: www.nyguild.org/el-diario.html

Ecuador News

One of the most prominent newspapers in the Ecuadorian American community.

Dr. Marcelo Arboleda Segovia, CEO and Editor in Chief
64-03 Roosevelt Avenue
2nd Floor
Woodside, New York 11377
Phone: (718) 205-7014
Fax: (718) 205-6580
Email: ecuanews@inch.com
URL: www.ecuadornews.com.ec

RADIO

There are several radio shows in the New York area geared toward Ecuadorian Americans.

WADO-AM (1280)

Broadcasts *Presencia Ecuatoriana(Ecuadorian Presence)*, a talk show discussing news, art, sports, and culture from Ecuador, hosted by Homero Melendez, president of the Tungurahua regional association on Sundays from 2:00 to 3:00 p.m. Its online address is:

URL: http://wado1280am.univision.com/quienes-somos/article/2010-02-01/quienes-somos.

ORGANIZATIONS AND ASSOCIATIONS

Alianza Ecuatoriana Tungurahua

M. Vargas
465 Forty-First Street
Brooklyn, New York 11232
Phone: (718) 854-1506

Comite Cívico Ecuatoriana

Oswaldo Guzman
41-42 102nd Street
2nd Floor
Corona, New York 11368
Phone: (718) 476-3832
Email: oswaldoguzman@yahoo.com
Email: info@ecuadorianciviccommitteeny.com
URL: www.ccecuatoriano.org
URL: www.ecuadorianciviccommitteeny.com

Young Ecuadorian American Professionals

A nonprofit based in South Florida that provides networking opportunities for Ecuadorian American professionals.

Jimmy Chang, President
Email: jimmy.chang@yeap.us
URL: www.yeap.us

MUSEUMS AND RESEARCH CENTERS

UCLA Institute of the Environment and Sustainability

Center for Tropical Research–Ecuador

Kelvin Fan, CTR Office Manager
La Kretz Hall
Suite 300 619 Charles E. Young Drive East
Los Angeles, California 90095-1496
Phone: (310) 206-6234
URL: www.environment.ucla.edu/ctr/irtc/index.html

Ecuador Field School

Valentina Martinez
416 Bellefield Hall
University of Pittsburgh
Pittsburgh, Pennsylvania 15260
Florida Atlantic University
Department of Anthropology
777 Glades Road
Boca Raton, Florida 33431
Phone: (561) 297-0084
Email: vmartine@fau.edu
URL: www.fau.edu/anthro/archfield.php

Latin American Network Information Center

The University of Texas at Austin

Carolyn Palaima, Project Director
LANIC Teresa Lozano Long Institute of Latin American Studies SRH 1.310
1 University Station D0800
Austin, Texas 78712
URL: http://lanic.utexas.edu/la/ecuador/

Latin American Studies Association, Ecuadorian Studies Section

Phone: (412) 648-7929
Fax: (412) 624-7145
Email: lasa@pitt.edu
URL: www.yachana.org/ecuatorianistas

SOURCES FOR ADDITIONAL STUDY

De la Torre, Carlos, and Steve Striffler. *The Ecuador Reader: History, Culture, and Politics.* Durham, NC: Duke University Press, 2009.

Handelsman, Michael. *Culture and Customs of Ecuador.* Westport, CT: Greenwood Press, 2000.

Perrottet, Tony, ed. *Insight Guide: Ecuador.* New York: Apa Publications, 1994.

Pineo, Ronn F. *Ecuador and the United States: Useful Strangers.* Athens: University of Georgia Press, 2007.

Pribilsky, Jason. *La Chulla Vida: Gender, Migration and the Family in Andean Ecuador and New York City.* Syracuse, NY: Syracuse University Press, 2007.

Egyptian Americans

Mona Mikhail

OVERVIEW

Egyptian Americans are immigrants or descendants of immigrants from Egypt, a country in northeast Africa. Egypt is bordered by the Mediterranean Sea to the north, Israel to the northeast, the Red Sea to the east, the Sudan to the south, and Libya to the west. With 90 percent of the land covered by desert, only 2.9 percent of the land area is arable. Approximately 95 percent of Egyptians live in this arable area, mainly along the Mediterranean Sea and the Nile River. The fact that Egypt controls both the Sinai land bridge that connects Africa to Asia and the Suez Canal, which provides access between the Indian Ocean and the Mediterranean Sea, adds to its international geopolitical clout. Egypt occupies an area of 386,488,261 square miles (1,001,450 square kilometers), approximately the same size as the state of New Mexico.

In July 2012 official census figures estimated the population of Egypt at 83,688,164. Approximately 90 percent of Egyptians are Muslim, and the majority of those are Sunni. Some 9 percent of Egyptians are Coptic Christians, and another 1 percent are Greek Orthodox, Catholic, or Jewish. According to a government census taken in 2006, 99.6 percent of Egyptians identified themselves as Egyptian, a group that includes Bedouins, Greeks, Nubians, Armenians, and Berbers. While Arabic is the official language, both English and French are generally understood by educated Egyptians due to the historical British and French colonial influence. Almost a third of the Egyptian workforce is engaged in the agricultural sector. At 12.2 percent in 2011, unemployment was considered unacceptably high by most Egyptians and was particularly problematic among young people. Egypt has a per capita income of $6,600, and a fifth of the population lives in poverty. The poor standard of living combined with widespread political discontent to oust President Mohamed Hosni Mubarak in 2011, with the result that the government drastically increased funding for social programs at the same time the economy slowed.

The first large wave of Egyptian immigrants to the United States followed the defeat of Egypt in 1967 in the Arab-Israeli War. By 1977, some 15,000 Egyptians had arrived in New York, New Jersey, California, Illinois, Florida, and Texas. Most of these immigrants were educated professionals who became assimilated into the American population. However, it was not until the 1990s that large numbers of Egyptians began immigrating to the United States. Between 1990 and 2000, the number of Egyptian Americans grew from 78,574 to 142,832. Most Egyptian immigrants come to the United States to pursue better educational opportunities, obtain better jobs, improve their standard of living, or to escape rampant bureaucratic corruption in Egypt.

In 2011 the U.S. Census Bureau estimated that there were 201,299 U.S. residents with Egyptian ancestry (American Community Survey three-year estimate for 2009–2011). This figure is comparable to the population of Tacoma, Washington. The largest single concentration of Egyptian Americans is found in the Little Egypt area of Queens, New York. According to the 2000 Census, the majority of Egyptian Americans live in California (30,959), New Jersey (25,170), New York (23,661), and Florida (6,759).

HISTORY OF THE PEOPLE

Early History Ancient Egypt was the cradle of Western Civilization. As early as 4000 BCE, people had come together to form an organized society. By 3100 BCE, the pharaoh Menes united the peoples of the Nile Delta into a single empire with those living southward along the river. During Egypt's height, its people thrived throughout the Nile valley, constructing massive pyramids, creating world-renowned art, establishing an advanced writing system, making advancements in science, building irrigation systems, and developing trade with Middle Eastern and Asian powers. By 1085 BCE, however, the Egyptian empire had begun to decay, again separating into Upper and Lower kingdoms—along the delta and the river. The Greeks, Romans, Aragians, North Africans, Turks, French, and British, came to Egypt seeking to conquer the Nile Valley and claim its riches.

For centuries, the majority of arable land in Egypt was possessed by a select few. This land was worked by the *fellahin*, who wielded two to three crops each season, usually keeping one-fourth to one-half of the harvest for themselves. Agricultural reform did not take place until the latter half of the nineteenth century when Egyptians began to grow cotton in an attempt to establish a market economy rather than simply growing food products. However, when other world markets began producing cotton as well, the market suffered and the well-being of the Egyptian rural class greatly deteriorated.

In 1882 the British assumed proxy control of the country and built roads, railways, telegraph systems, and canals. Egypt's royal family and the already wealthy landowners greatly benefitted from British occupation. Although the rural class was heavily taxed, many prospered as well, thus creating a middle class. It was this newly established middle class who joined the nation's armed forces and instigated Egypt's 1952 Revolution, which freed the country from British occupation and initiated land reform, thus altering the social, economic, and political power of Egypt's ruling families.

Modern Era In 1956 Egypt elected Gamal Abdal Nasser as its first president. In 1962 under Nasser's leadership, the newly established national charter limited the amount of land held by farm owners to 100 acres. The remaining land was confiscated by the government, divided into plots, and awarded to the middle and lower classes. Improved housing, transportation, and health care resulted in a significant increase in Egypt's population. Despite the modernization efforts of such leaders as Nasser and Anwar Sadat (making great strides in industrializing the country and establishing an open economy), inflation, overpopulation, and the general unrest in the Middle East continued to hinder national progress.

Efforts to modernize Egypt and grow the country's arable land led to the construction of the Aswan High Dam in 1960. In the late 1990s a project was launched to channel waters from Lake Nasser on the Nile River to the western desert to create a new fertile area conducive to agriculture and development. It was scheduled to be completed in 2017.

Modern Egypt is the most populous and most advanced of all Arab nations. Egypt serves as the seat of the League of Arab States and has also taken on a leadership role among African nations. During his tenure, Egyptian president Hosni Mubarak presided over the Organization of African Unity. Egypt's social order is partially composed of intellectuals, government officials, urban businessmen, and landowners. Egyptians from this segment of the population have been more likely than other Egyptians to immigrate to countries such as the United States, mostly for economic or educational purposes. While almost a third of the workforce is engaged in growing crops or fishing the waters of the Nile and its tributaries, 51 percent of the population now labors in the service sector. Only 17 percent of the workforce is involved in industry.

In December 2011 a young man in Tunisia immolated himself to draw attention to the country's lack of employment and freedom. Thereafter, pro-democracy protests were set in motion throughout the Middle East, resulting in what came to be known as the "Arab Spring." The following year, beginning on January 25, massive political demonstrations took place in Egypt, with protestors objecting to poor economic conditions, limits placed on suffrage rights and civil liberties, and widespread police brutality. President Mubarak's reform efforts failed to placate the general public, and he resigned on February 11, leaving the Supreme Council of Armed Forces to assume temporary control of Egypt. Egyptian Americans were outraged at Egyptian mistreatment of protestors and began lobbying the U.S. government to suspend military aid to Egypt. Democratic reforms within Egypt led to subsequent elections, and President Muhammad Mursi of the Muslim Brotherhood took office in June 2012.

SETTLEMENT IN THE UNITED STATES
Egyptian Americans are among the more recent groups to have immigrated to the United States. Unlike other peoples of Arab descent who settled in the Americas in large numbers as early as the mid-nineteenth century, Egyptians began to emigrate in significant numbers only during the latter part of the twentieth century. Although the majority left for economic or educational reasons, many Copts, Jews, and conservative Muslims emigrated because they were concerned about political developments in Egypt. Thousands of others left after Egypt's 1967 defeat in the Arab-Israeli War, with approximately 15,000 Egyptians immigrating to the United States from 1967 to 1977. The following three decades witnessed unprecedented movements of large Egyptian populations not only to the United States and Canada but also to Australia, Europe, and the Gulf Arab countries. Records from 2005 break down the immigration patterns by percentage: 11 percent of Egyptian Americans living in the United States at that time arrived before 1970. Another 18 percent immigrated in the 1970s, with the largest percentage—27 percent—arriving in the 1980s.

The majority of the first Egyptian immigrants to the United States comprised educated professionals and skilled workers. Their immigration was eased by the 1965 Immigration and Nationality Act, which welcomed certain professionals, especially scientists. According to 2011 estimates by the American Community Survey, of the 201,299 U.S. residents claiming Egyptian ancestry, 40 percent were born in the United States and 60 percent were immigrants. The largest concentration of Egyptian Americans are in New Jersey, New York, California, Illinois, Florida, and Texas.

LANGUAGE
Ancient Egyptians developed a pictographic and ideographic writing system known as hieroglyphics, which developed in several stages. Experts believe that pictographic communication evolved into a written

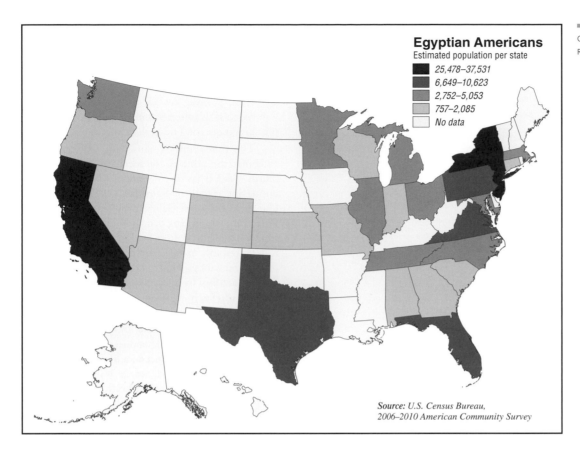

Egyptian Americans
Estimated population per state

- ▓ 25,478–37,531
- ▓ 6,649–10,623
- ▓ 2,752–5,053
- ▓ 757–2,085
- ▢ No data

Source: U.S. Census Bureau, 2006–2010 American Community Survey

language known as hieratic. In turn, hieratic evolved into a simplified language known as demotic. The Coptic language is viewed as a continuation of the traditional Egyptian language by some scholars and as a separate language by others. With the fall of the Egyptian empire and the eventual triumph of Islam over traditional modes of belief and a brief period in which Christianity predominated, the ancient language was lost altogether until the discovery of the Rosetta Stone, a tablet that included both demotic and ancient Greek translations of hieroglyphic text. The first writings were interpreted by Thomas Young, a British linguist, but it was not until 1822 that Jean-François Champollion fully deciphered the Rosetta Stone. Scientists have since concluded that this writing system, which functioned both vertically and horizontally in either long or abbreviated forms, has qualities similar to an alphabet.

Arabic has been the common language of all Egyptians since the eighth century. The dialect most often spoken in Egypt is Cairene Arabic, which is also the Arabic dialect most widely known throughout the Arabic-speaking world. Cairene Arabic is widely used by all Egyptian Americans at informal social gatherings. The great popularity of Egyptian singers and movies assists the dissemination of this dialect. Formal Arabic is used in religious services by Muslims and Copts. Recently, Copts have introduced English into their church services (usually in sermons) to maintain the participation of new generations of American-born Egyptians.

According to the 2011 American Community Survey estimates, 30 percent of Egyptian Americans speak only English in their homes, which represents a 13 percent increase from the 2000 Census. Although 70 percent speak their own language at home, they also speak English; 76 percent reported speaking English "very well."

Greetings and Popular Expressions

Hello / Peace upon you—*as-salam alaykum*

Response to hello—*wa alaykum e salam*

Goodbye when leaving—*ma'a salama*

Goodbye when staying—*alla ysalmak*

Good morning—*sabalt ala-kheir*

Goodnight—*tisbah ala-kheir*

Welcome—*ahlan wa sahlan*

Yes—*aiwa or na'am*

No—*la*

Please—*min fadhlik*

Thank you—*shukran*

You're welcome—*afwan*

What's your name?—*shismak?*

I don't understand—*ana atakallam*

EGYPTIAN PROVERBS

- What is written on the brow will inevitably be seen by the eye. (Meaning: One will inevitably meet one's destiny.)

- What is far from the eye is far from the heart. (Meaning: Out of sight, out of mind.)

- The one on shore is a master swimmer. (Meaning: Easier said than done.)

- Dressing up a stick turns it into a bride. (Meaning: Clothes make the man.)

- Winds do not blow as the ship wishes. (Meaning: You can't always get what you want.)

RELIGION

The majority of Egyptians are Muslim, while Copts (Orthodox Christians), the largest religious minority, are believed to form approximately nine percent of the religious community in Egypt. Both Egyptian Muslims and Egyptian Copts have settled in the United States. Within this immigrant community, the number of Egyptian Christians surpasses the number of Egyptian Muslims, although Egyptian Muslims in the United States have increased their numbers steadily since the 1990s.

Islam, which was introduced to Egypt in 641 CE, is a religious system that permeates Egyptian society at every level. "Islam" literally means submission to the will of God. A Muslim is one who has submitted to Allah (or God) and who acknowledges Muhammad as God's Prophet. Islamic tradition takes into account the doctrines of both Judaism and Christianity, and Muslims consider the Prophet Muhammad the last in a series of prophets that included Abraham, Moses, and Jesus.

Muslims believe in one God and in the afterlife as do Christians and Jews. Islam also acknowledges Jews and Christians as "people of the Book" or Bible (*ahl al-Kitab*) and has granted them privileged status from the early days of the Islamic Empire. For this reason, religious minorities throughout the Arab world have survived and flourished during periods of severe cultural and religious repression elsewhere.

Islamic acts of devotion and worship are expressed in the five Pillars of Islam. The first Pillar is the profession of faith, "There is no God but God, and Muhammad is his Prophet," or the *Shahada*, which requires the believer to profess the Unity of God and the mission of Muhammad. The assertion forms part of every prayer.

The second Pillar is prayer, or *Sala*, which is required five times a day: at dawn, noon, mid-afternoon,

sunset, and dusk. It may be performed in a state of ritual purity. The worshipper has the choice of praying privately in open air, in a house, with a group, outdoors, or in a mosque. Because Islam opposes the practice of withdrawing into ascetic life, there is no priesthood. There are, however, *Ulama*, or learned men who are well versed in Islamic law and tradition. Muslims also pray in mosques on Friday, their holy day of the week.

The third Pillar is almsgiving, or *Zakat*. This embodies the principle of social responsibility. The fourth Pillar is fasting, or *Saum*, which is observed during the month of Ramadan when God sent the Qur'an to the angel Gabriel who in turn revealed it to the Prophet. Fasting demands complete abstinence from food and drink from sunrise to sunset. Ramadan is followed by *Iftar*, a sumptuous banquet where friends and family gather to celebrate the break of fast. Dearly cherished by Egyptians in Egypt, this tradition is observed closely in America where it is celebrated with Christian Egyptians and American friends alike.

The fifth Pillar is the pilgrimage to Mecca, which is required of every able-bodied Muslim who can afford to do so at least once in a lifetime. Attached to the experience of the pilgrimage is an added status: the person will henceforth be addressed as *al-Haj* or *al-Hajjah*, a title which carries great prestige. Many Egyptian Muslims living in the United States go on a *Haj*, or pilgrimage, as well as an *Umrah*, a modified pilgrimage which can take place at different times of the year and not necessarily at the officially specified time.

The other significant group of Egyptian Americans are the Coptic Christians. The Copts are native to Egypt, having converted to Christianity as early as the first century CE. After the Arab conquest of Egypt in 642, the Coptic language began to give way to Arabic; however, Coptic is still used as the liturgical language in church services, is taught in Sunday schools, and is employed in some daily communications among *Ulama*.

Today, Coptic is still used in church services in the United States where large congregations of Egyptian Copts are found. There is an archdiocese in Jersey City, New Jersey, where one of the first American Coptic churches was founded in the early 1960s.

Among Muslim Egyptian Americans, the role of the mosque as a social center and as a religious gathering place is changing from what it was in Egypt. Today, for instance, women not only pray at the mosque but also participate in social activities there. The custom of women praying at the mosque has now become prevalent in Egypt, having been brought back there by returning Muslim Americans. Interaction between Egyptian Americans and other Muslim Americans has been enhanced by the increased prevalence of mosques in the United States in the twenty-first century.

There are well-developed cordial and reciprocal social relations between Egyptian Copts, Egyptian Muslims, and the general American public. In Egypt, many Copts have adopted a number of Islamic customs, just as some Egyptian Muslims have adopted certain Coptic customs, and this has carried over to the United States. Egyptian Copts sometimes share in the festivities of Ramadan, while Muslim Egyptians celebrate certain aspects of Christmas and the New Year.

In 2011 the ousting of President Mubarak and the suspension of the 1971 constitution ushered in a return to traditional Islamic laws and customs in Egypt, and some Christian Egyptian Americans and international women's groups have become concerned that religious beliefs have taken prominence over civil laws. Nevertheless, the majority of Egyptian Americans who continue to vote in Egyptian elections because of dual citizenship voted for the Islamist candidate in the 2012 presidential election.

CULTURE AND ASSIMILATION

Traditions and Customs Historically, Egyptian immigrants and their American-born children have had little difficulty adjusting to American culture, and this is particularly true of Christian Egyptian Americans. Leaders of early Egyptian immigrant groups lobbied the American government for Egyptian Americans to be counted as "White" in official accounts, believing that it would prevent discrimination against them. When the 2010 census was taken, however, Egyptian American groups joined other groups in urging Arab Americans to assert their identity independence and classify themselves as "Other Race" rather than "White."

The ease of assimilation has been largely due to the strong educational background of most Egyptian Americans. Numerous Egyptian Americans have also married outside their ethnic community, which has facilitated the assimilation process. Following World War II and the creation of Israel, however, conceptions of Egyptian Americans were often complicated by a pro-Israel and anti-Arab bias. That bias was considerably heightened by the terrorist attacks on the United States on September 11, 2001, conducted by members of the al-Qaeda organization. The subsequent War on Terror placed the civil rights of some Egyptian Americans in jeopardy. The American media has further contributed to the conception of all Arabs as being anti-American and all Muslims as repressive and violent.

Egyptian American organizations, including those that are professional, academic, and business-oriented, have served to unite Egyptian Americans and helped to preserve and promote pride in the Egyptian culture. Such organizations include the Egyptian American Professional Society, the Egyptian Physicians' Association, and the Egyptian Businessmen's Association. Several have also joined the numerous organizations of the more established Arab American community such as the Arab American University Graduates, the American-Arab Relations Committee, and the American-Arab Anti-Discrimination Committee (ADC).

Cuisine Egyptian cuisine is a mixture of Middle Eastern cuisine and a modified continental (French-style) cuisine. Considered Egypt's national dish, *kushari* provides a hearty meal of pasta, rice, lentils, garlic, and chickpeas cooked in a tomato sauce. Other traditional Egyptian dishes include *mullkhia*, a thick green soup made from chicken or meat broth (sometimes rabbit). *Squab* (stuffed pigeon) and *fatta*, a rice-and-bread dish, are among the many favorites. Traditionally, *fatta* is served to mark special occasions. What came to be known in the United States as *falafel* is also a favorite, as is the layered sweet baklava. Another popular food is *kahk*, a sweetbread baked for special feasts. To make *kahk*, a well-kneaded dough of flour and rarified butter is filled with honey or a mixed-nut filling. The dough is beautifully decorated by a special tool, a *minkash*, then is baked and sprinkled with powder sugar. *Kakh* can be purchased at bakeries.

During Lent and Advent, Egyptian Copts do not eat meat or dairy products, a practice that has given rise to many delicious nondairy and meatless grain-based meals that are a delight to the vegetarian and the health-conscious. Muslims are prohibited from eating pork and therefore buy their meats at *halal* or kosher butcher shops. In Brooklyn, on Atlantic Avenue, a large concentration of Arab and Muslim shops cater to the needs of the Middle Eastern community at large. Jersey City also has a growing community of Egyptians where one can find most of the specifically Egyptian ingredients to prepare native dishes. Middle Eastern specialty items can be found at grocery stores in almost every major U.S. city, and some staple items—such as pita bread—are found at supermarkets across North America.

Traditional Costumes Since the turn of the century, urbanized Egyptians have adopted Western-style clothing, and the vast majority who have come to the United States have retained this custom. Since the 1990s some Muslim women have chosen to dress in a traditional Islamic garment consisting of a floor-length, long-sleeved dress and a head covering. Many Muslim women adhere only to the tradition of covering the head, whereas the vast majority of Egyptian Americans wear the usual Western-style wardrobe. The men wear suits, though on rare occasions they wear a *gallabiyya*, a long white robe, for prayers or at home. When dressed casually, Egyptian males frequently wear Western clothing.

Traditional Arts and Crafts While decorating stone, plaster, wood, ceramic, glass and textiles with elaborate forms of calligraphy and other traditional crafts such as matting, carpet weaving, and silk weaving have seen a revival in modern Egypt, most Egyptian Americans have been assimilated into the workforce and no longer engage in such activities. On the other hand, Egyptian American organizations have made a concentrated effort to promote an appreciation of Egyptian art among their members.

Dances and Songs Egyptian Americans continue to promote their native culture at cultural festivals held throughout the United States. Egyptian American organizations also work with other cultural organizations to bring this culture to the attention of the American public. Egyptian belly dancing has been enjoying a revival in the United States, and belly dancers perform in traditional Egyptian costumes composed of scarves, veils, harem pants, and accessories. American dancer and choreographer Diana Calenti introduced Egyptian folkloric dance in the 1990s, blending both traditional and modern forms of dance to attract a wide audience while depicting expressions and emotions common to both the United States and Egypt.

Egyptian rap, which surfaced in the 1990s, has become popular among many Egyptian American young people. This music is available to an international audience via the Internet and social networking sites. It is considered a blend of African and Arabic rap. It is not widely accepted within Egypt because its themes are often considered anti-Muslim. Consequently, Egyptian rap artists such as MTM, Princess Emmanuelle, and Cairo City G'zz tend to operate underground. Oklahoma-bred Egyptian American country singer Kareem Salama has introduced his culture to mainstream audiences. A Muslim, Salama acknowledges that his faith is very much a part of the songs he writes.

Holidays Most Egyptian holidays are religious observances. There are two major Muslim holidays: Eid al Fitr, which falls at the end of Ramadan marking the end of the month-long fasting period, and Eid al-Adha (Feast of Sacrifice), which follows soon after, commemorating the willingness of Abraham to sacrifice his son Isaac to God and the substitution of the sacrificial lamb. Some Egyptian Americans, along with other Arab Americans, decorate their homes, exchange gifts, and hold festivals to celebrate these holidays. They may also be celebrated by a pilgrimage. Because these holidays are so important among Muslims, Arab American groups continue to lobby to have them accepted as legitimate holidays for Arab American students. The Islamic New Year as well as the birthday of the Prophet Muhammad are also important holidays for Muslims. Major holidays are celebrated at the mosques and among friends.

Christian Copts celebrate Christmas according to the Gregorian calendar, usually on January 6–7 of every year. Easter is a week-long observance of strict religious rituals culminating in Good Friday, a midnight mass on Holy Saturday, and a mass at dawn on Easter Sunday. A secular holiday, the New Year is celebrated by both Muslims and Christians.

Another important holiday is Sham al-Nassim, a rite of spring dating to ancient times that is celebrated on the Monday after Easter Sunday. Egyptians go out into the fields or onto the beaches and eat a specially prepared salted fish (*fisikh*), onions or shallots, colored hard-boiled eggs, fruits, and sweets. This tradition is dying out in the United States because Monday is a workday. Since Sham al-Nassim is a moveable feast, Egyptians sometimes celebrate it on Easter Sunday so that everyone can participate. It is an occasion when all Egyptians, irrespective of religious faith, can get together and enjoy themselves.

Health Issues Of the first wave of immigrants from Egypt to the United States, many were trained physicians who acquired additional fields of specialty in the United States. Many of these physicians serve people in their own communities, who turn to them for advice and medical care and who also find Egyptian American medical doctors a source of comfort, especially if they are still in the midst of overcoming the language barrier.

Within the general Egyptian American population, particularly among recent immigrants from Egypt, cultural issues that are common among Arabs may come into play. Reports from health care workers indicate that Egyptian Americans do not always consider nurses professionals and consequently may ignore their instructions or advice. Arab Americans may also have difficulty accepting help from social workers, as they typically believe that family life is private. Those who are ill may refuse to take medications or receive IV treatment while fasting during Ramadan. Mental illness carries a strong stigma within Arab culture, and as a result Arab Americans may refuse to seek help for such conditions. Because the American health system is so different from the subsidized health care with which most Egyptians are familiar, new immigrants may not understand how the American health care system works.

Death and Burial Rituals Some Egyptian Americans adhere to traditional Arab views and practices when dealing with death and burial. They tend to see death as being the will of God, but they do not usually feel comfortable when discussing death or dying. Because they believe that a body can continue to feel pain until it is buried, they do not approve of autopsies or cremation. When family and friends gather around a deathbed, they advise the dying to say a prayer that will allow them to enter Paradise. Burials generally take place within 24 hours.

Rituals call for a female's body to be washed by her husband or family members an odd number of times with soap and water. Perfumes are added to the water of the final washing. The body is then wrapped in five pieces of cloth, which are tied at the head and foot. During the burial, a body is placed facing Mecca. Only males are allowed to attend burials, and they each throw three handfuls of soil onto the grave. After being covered, the gravesite is usually marked by stones or by a simple marker.

Recreational Activities In Egypt, many recreational activities take place within private sporting clubs, which offer restaurants, swimming pools, sports facilities, and playgrounds. These clubs are open to both Egyptians and foreigners. In the United States, Egyptian Americans participate in the same activities enjoyed by other Americans. They may also participate in activities carried out at mosques and in those promoted by groups such as the Egyptian American Organization, which sponsors culture festivals, lectures, and exhibits.

FAMILY AND COMMUNITY LIFE

The nuclear family is the basic social unit of Egyptian society. Although the extended family also continues to play a dominant role in the intricate family grid, familial ties are beginning to loosen, even in Egypt. Some of these changes have become more accentuated in the United States. Wide distances may separate children from their parents, brothers, and sisters and from other members of the extended family. Traditionally, Egyptians grew up and spent their entire lives in the same neighborhood. Today, however, families of Egyptian Americans, like those of other Americans, are scattered throughout the fifty states.

The growing prevalence of intermarriage between Egyptians and Americans—most commonly between Egyptian-born men and American women—has challenged the family structure. A Muslim woman's husband is required by religion and law to convert to Islam, while a Muslim man's wife may retain her Christian or non-Muslim faith. In either case, the children must be raised as Muslims. In Egypt, women who marry non-Muslims may face arrest and possible loss of guardianship of their children to male family members. Christian Egyptians tend to be conservative and prefer that their children marry within the Coptic church. However, Egyptian Americans are less likely to adhere to this practice given their high level of assimilation within American culture.

Gender Roles Since the nineteenth century, women in Egypt have come to play a more prevalent role in improving their status and in increasing the degree of their participation within society. World War I and World War II brought radical change in the status of women in Egypt. By the 1920s women had begun to enroll in universities and entered the workforce as physicians, lawyers, and educators. Women further increased participation in the workforce after the 1952 Revolution and the implementation of the National Charter of 1962, which stipulated that "women must be regarded as equal to men, and must shed the remaining shackles that impede their free movement." Consequently, they have enjoyed a relatively long tradition of active participation in the public domain and have much more freedom to move about without male chaperonage than do women in many Arab countries. However, in 2012 only a fourth of Egyptian women worked outside the home, and women continued to face considerable discrimination

Egyptian Americans celebrate the ouster of Hosni Mubarak (1928–) in 2011. JIM WEST / ZUMAPRESS / NEWSCOM

because of the emphasis on traditional roles. A 2011 survey conducted by the World Economic Forum ranked Egypt 125 out of 134 countries on gender equality. However, when considered among Arab nations, Egypt is seen as relatively progressive, especially within its large urban populations. Educated and urbanized women are more likely than uneducated rural women living in traditional households to consider themselves equal to males. In a demonstration of their political and social power, Egyptian females took an active role in the Egyptian Revolution that ousted Mubarak in 2011.

Whether they immigrated to the United States or are American-born, most Egyptian women are active within American society on several levels. Women tend to participate within the workforce, even those who are raising families. This is especially true of the second wave of immigrants, some of whom have not acquired employment on a par with their college backgrounds. These underemployed immigrants labor as food stand operators, baby-sitters, or waitresses either in family-run restaurants or in the catering trade. Many Egyptian American women have created lucrative catering businesses that specialize in preparing foods for Egyptian households. Many others have successful careers in medicine and accounting, with a high number of them in academia.

Boys are often treated differently than girls and are given more leeway when it comes to curfews and dating. However, because education is highly esteemed by Egyptians, and because many members of the first generation of Egyptian Americans possess advanced college degrees, children—both boys and girls—are encouraged to attend college. Children who decide to attend school out of state generally obtain their parents' blessing, although some parents still prefer to have their children—especially their daughters—nearby. In some cases, mothers will move to another state just to live with their children. Some parents encourage their children to return to Egypt to obtain a degree, not only because it is less costly to do so (medical students receive free education in Egypt), but also because it ensures that their children will be supervised by members of the extended family.

Education According to the 2010 American Community Survey, 96 percent of Egyptian Americans had completed high school, 41 percent had attained a bachelor's degree, and 25 percent had completed a graduate or professional degree. Because the majority of first generation of Egyptian Americans are highly educated professionals, they have a tendency to apply to the best schools, private or public. In rare cases their children attend religious-affiliated schools such as those located in areas with large concentrations of Egyptian Americans. However, because of the emphasis on higher education, Muslims attending these schools tend to join regular school systems beyond the primary level.

Courtship and Weddings Among more traditional Egyptian families, many marriages are still arranged by relatives, and marriages are celebrated with great fanfare. Egyptian Americans—particularly Muslims—typically worry about their offspring's dating habits and urge their children to marry someone of Egyptian descent or to choose someone from the larger community of Arab peoples. Such families commonly send their children back to Egypt to immerse them within Egyptian society in the hope that they will choose a bride or groom there. Some Egyptian Americans encourage marriage between cousins, a practice common in Egypt.

Among more westernized Egyptian Americans, however, young people are allowed a good deal of control in their choice of marriage partners. Intermarriage with non-Egyptians is common among Egyptian American families who have lived in the United States for extended periods of time.

According to the 2010 American Community Survey, 59 percent of Egyptian Americans males and 60 percent of females are married. Some 33 percent of males and 27 percent of females have never married, and 8 percent of males and 13 percent of females are separated, widowed, or divorced. Egyptian American households tend to be made up of married couples, but a quarter of such households are made up of non-family members. Five percent of Egyptian American households are female-headed, and 5 percent are male-headed. Among traditional Egyptians, women may

obtain a divorce without the consent of their husbands if they are willing to cede all financial rights. Divorce is permissible among Coptic Christians only in the case of adultery or if a mate converts to another religion.

EMPLOYMENT AND ECONOMIC CONDITIONS

The first wave of immigrants consisted of individuals who either had obtained a professional degree or had come to the United States seeking further education. They pursued careers as doctors, accountants, engineers, and lawyers, and a good number joined the teaching faculties of major universities. The second wave held college degrees but had to accept menial jobs. When they first arrived, many drove taxicabs or waited on tables in restaurants. The economic recession and corporate downsizing undoubtedly have affected Egyptian Americans. Some enterprising citizens have gone into business for themselves. Because of the stigma attached to being unemployed or on welfare, Egyptian Americans have resisted receiving these benefits, but as time goes on their participation in social aid programs may become an increasing fact of life. According to the 2010 American Community Survey estimates, 12 percent of Egyptian American families live below the poverty line. The recession of the early twenty-first century led to an upswing in the number of multi-generational households within the Egyptian American community.

According to the 2010 American Community Survey, an estimated 68 percent of Egyptian Americans were in the labor force. Some 50 percent worked in management, professional, and other related occupations. Some 14 percent worked in service occupations, and 25 percent labored in sales and office jobs. Nine percent were engaged in production, transportation, and material moving. Economically, Egyptian Americans tended to do well economically, reporting a median family income of $62,812.

POLITICS AND GOVERNMENT

Egyptian Americans are only now beginning to show interest in municipal and national politics. As with every immigrant group, Egyptian Americans first had to establish themselves in society before venturing into the political arena. Unlike other groups of Arab Americans who have been in the United States for more than a century and who are only now coming into their own by being elected to positions in national and local government, Egyptian Americans only recently began to get involved politically, by exercising their right to vote and by supporting their preferred candidates. Because significant numbers do not belong to trade unions, they have had no perceptible influence on union politics. Since 9/11, Egyptian Americans have become instrumental in lobbying local legislatures on issues of civil liberties for Arab Americans. Lobbying efforts by Egyptian Americans and other

Arab groups led in 2012 to the California legislature passed the Workplace Religious Act, which addressed the issue of religious freedom for Arab Americans. It dealt specifically with the freedom to wear religious clothing and hairstyles in the workplace and prevented employers from segregating Arab Americans from customers or the public because of their appearance.

Up until the 1990s, Egyptian Americans tended to be politically conservative and were more likely to vote Republican than Democratic. Contrarily, in 1996, polls indicated that a majority of Arab Americans (29.6 percent) favored Democrat Bill Clinton over Republican Bob Dole (6.5 percent). In 2000, however, George W. Bush (42 percent) displayed a distinct advantage over Al Gore (36.5 percent) among Arab Americans as a whole. The following year proved to be a major turning point for Arab Americans, who shifted their allegiance to the Democratic Party in the wake of 9/11 and Bush's War on Terror. In 2008, for instance, more than half of all Arab Americans supported Barack Obama as compared to a third who expressed support for John McCain. The Arab American vote has become strategically important in key states such as Florida. Overall, a candidate's positions on issues involving the Middle East are a major factor in party support and voting patterns. Religion also plays an important political role. Among Muslims, 80 percent favored Obama over McCain in 2008, and more than half of Arab Christians also supported Obama.

Relations with Egypt As the number of Egyptian immigrants to the United States expanded after the 1990s, the Egyptian government began to express more interest in its citizens living in its expatriate communities and in maintaining good relations with them by encouraging them to invest in the Egyptian economy. For instance, in the past few years the Egyptian American Businessmen's Association has taken official tours to Egypt, meeting with officials and advising the country on various economic matters. The Union of Egyptians is a loosely structured organization that claims to meet Egyptian needs abroad by securing links with the homeland. Other organizations, such as the Egyptian American Professional Organization, prefer to avoid political matters, instead focusing on educational and cultural ties between Egyptian Americans and their home country.

Most Egyptian Americans have maintained close ties to their homeland, and large numbers of them hold dual citizenship. Thus, when a revolution broke out in Egypt in January 2011 in response to widespread public dissatisfaction, concern among Egyptian Americans continued to grow. Over 18 days of protesting, more than 300 people were killed. On October 9, twenty-seven Coptic Christians were killed in another demonstration in Cairo. Egyptian Americans joined their countrymen in blaming President Hosni Mubarak for the January deaths and the SCAF, which had been installed after Mubarak's resignation, for the latter deaths. They demanded that the United States suspend all military aid to Egypt.

Protests were held throughout the United States in cities containing large populations of Egyptian Americans such as San Francisco, California; Jersey City, New Jersey; Queens, New York; and Charlotte, North Carolina. Protestors waved Egyptian flags and carried protest signs. The votes of Egyptian Americans were instrumental in the election of President Muhammad Mursi, the Muslim Brotherhood candidate, in 2012.

NOTABLE INDIVIDUALS

Academia and Science In the fields of academia and science, significant contributions have been made by Egyptian Americans such as professor of women's studies and religion Leila Ahmed (1940–); professor of engineering Shihab S. Asfou microbiologist Ayaad Assaad, biochemist Rashad Khalifa (1935–1990); and chemist Ahmed Zewail (1946–). Major contributions in science have also been made by Egyptian-born Farouk El-Baz (1938), an archaeologist/geologist who is on faculty at Boston University's Center for Remote Sensing and has worked closely with NASA on American space exploration.

Business One of the world's wealthiest people, Houston financier Fayez Sarofim (1929–) is a venture capitalist and part owner of the pro football team the Houston Texans.

Entertainment Egyptian Americans have also played an important role in the field of entertainment. Within the world of music, composer and musician Halim El-Dabh (1921–) has written scores for Martha Graham ballets. Allen Adham is a cofounder of Silicon and Synapse, which became Blizzard Entertainment, the company that designed such popular video games as World of Warcraft and StarCraft. Egyptian-born Asaad Kelada is a producer/director who has been involved with television shows that have included *Rhoda, Family Ties, Who's the Boss, Everybody Loves Raymond, Two and a Half Men*, and *The Office*.

Government While still in her twenties, Dina Habib Powell (1973–) began making a name for herself in Republican political circles. She served as Director of Congressional Affairs and Senior Adviser to the Republican National Convention (1999–2001) before signing on as a Special Assistant to the President. By 2003 Powell was serving as George W. Bush's chief headhunter. In 2005 she began working with the State Department, serving as Assistant Secretary of State for Education and Cultural Affairs and as Deputy Undersecretary of State for Public Diplomacy and

Egyptian American Dina Habib Powell (1973–) is the former Assistant to the President and Director of Presidential Personnel for former U. S. President George W. Bush. PAUL J. RICHARDS / AFP / GETTY IMAGES

(1963–) signed with the Pittsburgh Pirates in 1982 as the seventh draft pick. When he left the team in 1987, he retired from the world of baseball.

Stage and Screen Sammy Sheik (1981–) has appeared in movies such as *Transformers*, *Dark of the Moon*, and *Charlie Wilson's War* and in television shows such as *The United States of Tara*, *24*, and *Nikita*. Although both an actor and a writer, Ronnie Khalil (1977–) is best known for his stand-up comedy routines that have been performed all over the world. Stephen Adly Guirgis has appeared as an actor in the movie *Meet Joe Black* and the television series *Law and Order*, but he is best known for writing for such series such as *NYPD Blue*, *UC: Undercover*, and *Big Apple*.

MEDIA

RADIO AND TELEVISION

More than 3,000 Egyptian radio stations are available online, allowing Egyptian Americans to instantly access the news, music, discussions, and culture of their homeland. WJPF AM (1340), based in Herrin, Illinois, and formerly owned by the Egyptian Broadcasting Company, was purchased by Max Media in 2003. Egyptian television can also be accessed online over the Internet.

PRINT

American Research Center in Egypt Newsletter

Reports quarterly on the Center's activities, plans, and projects. Covers archaeology, history, culture, and language of Egypt in all periods from pre-history to contemporary times.

Rachel Mauldin, Assistant Director for U.S. Operations
8700 Crownhill Boulevard
San Antonio, Texas 78209-1120
Phone: (210) 821-7000
Fax: (210) 821-7007
Email: info@arce.org

Public Affairs. In 2007 Powell left government to take on the position of president of Goldman Sach's Foundation, an organization that fosters global financial opportunities.

Journalism Award-winning journalist Mona Eltahawy (1967–) is an internationally respected expert on Arab and Muslim issues. Working from her New York base, her articles have appeared in newspapers around the world, including the *Washington Post*, the *Toronto Star*, and the *Jerusalem Report*. In September 2012 she received international attention of a different kind when she was arrested for spray painting over an anti-Jihad poster placed in a New York subway by the American Freedom Defense Initiative. She insisted that she had defaced the poster because as an Egyptian American, she refused to hate.

Sports After playing for Duke University (1986–1990), Alaa Abedelnaby (1968–) became the first Egyptian-born athlete to sign with the National Basketball Association. He spent five years with the Portland Trail Blazers and brief periods with other NBA teams such as the Boston Celtics and the Philadelphia 76ers. Omar Samhan (1988–), who played center for the St. Mary's Gaels, received national attention for scoring 61 points during championship games. He signed with a Lithuanian professional basketball club in 2010. The first and only Egyptian American to ever play with a major league baseball team, shortstop Sam Khalifa

ORGANIZATIONS AND ASSOCIATIONS

Egyptian Americans have come together to create a large number of organizations, which range from those specifically created to serve particular professions such as business and medicine to those that serve the Egyptian American community as a whole. Some of the more prominent of the latter type include the following.

American Egyptian Cooperation Foundation

Founded in 1987 and made up of companies, organizations, and individuals having an interest in promoting commercial, investment, tourism, and closer relations between Egypt and the United States. It focuses on efforts that increase international understanding.

A. F. Zaki, Founder, President, and COO
200 East 61ˢᵗ Street
Suite 12B
New York, New York 10065
Phone: (212) 867-2323
Fax: (212) 697-0465
Email: ecf32@gmail.com

Islamic Society of North America

Through the society's annual convention, Egyptian Americans are brought together with other North American Muslims.

Habibe Ali, Chief Operating Officer
P.O. Box 38
Plainfield, Indiana 46168
Phone: (317) 839-8157
Fax: (317) 839-1840
URL: www.isna.net

Muslim American Society

Established in 1993, the society promotes the religion, cultural, and educational aspects of Egyptian Americans along with that of other Muslim Americans through the work of 50 separate chapters.

1010 West 105ᵗʰ Street
Overland Park, Kansas 66212
Phone: (913) 888-444
Email: info@MuslimAmericanSociety.org
URL: http://muslimamericansociety.org

U.S. Copts Association

Established in 2010, the U.S. Copts Association is dedicated to bringing together information relevant to Egyptians living in both the United States and Egypt.

Michael Meunier, President
5116 Arlington Boulevard
Falls Church, Virginia 22042
Phone: (703) 379-7734
Email: mike@copts.com
URL: www.copts.com

MUSEUMS AND RESEARCH CENTERS

American Research Center in Egypt

Independent, nonprofit research organization operating in San Antonio, Texas, and in Cairo, Egypt, centering its attention on ancient and Islamic civilization in Egypt, including humanities and social studies in all periods.

Rachel Mauldin, Assistant Director for U.S. Operations
8700 Crownhill Boulevard
Suite 507
San Antonio, Texas 78209-1130
Phone: (210) 821-7000
Fax: (210) 821-7007
Email: info@arce.org
URL: www.arce.org

SOURCES FOR ADDITIONAL STUDY

Brewer, Douglas J., and Emily Teeter. *Egypt & the Egyptians.* New York: Cambridge University Press, 1999.

Brittingham, Angela, and G. Patricia de la Cruz. *We the People of Arab Ancestry in the United States.* Washington, D.C.: Government Printing Office, 2005.

Brugman, J. *An Introduction to the History of Modern Arabic Literature in Egypt.* Leiden: E. J. Brill, 1984.

Darwish, Nonie. *Now They Call Me Infidel: Why I Rejected the Jihad for America, Israel, and the War on Terror.* New York: Sentinel, 2006.

Marsot, Afaf Lutfi al-Sayyid. *A Short History of Modern Egypt.* London: Cambridge University Press, 1985.

Orfalea, Gregory. *Before the Flames: A Quest for the History of Arab Americans.* Austin: University of Texas Press, 1988.

Purnell, Larry, and Betty J. Paulanta. *Transcultural Health Care: A Culturally Competent Approach.* Philadelphia: F.A. Davis, 1998.

Stevens, Georgiana G. *Egypt Yesterday and Today.* New York: Holt, Rinehart and Winston, 1963.

Wolf, Bernard. *Coming to America: A Muslim Family's Story.* New York: Lee and Lou Books, 2003.

ENGLISH AMERICANS

Sheldon Hanft

OVERVIEW

English Americans are immigrants or descendants of immigrants from England, a country that is part of the United Kingdom. England occupies the southern end of the largest island off the Atlantic coast of Europe, sharing the island with Wales to the west and Scotland to the north. Its land area is 50,363 square miles (130,439 square kilometers), roughly the size of New York State, and it has 1,988 miles of coastline. No point in the country is more than 75 miles from the sea.

The 2011 census of England and Wales reported the population of England as 53 million, a 7.2 percent increase from the 2001 census. Approximately 80 percent of the English population is native born. Large communities of Scots, Irish, and Welsh live in its border counties, and more than two million Asian Indians, Pakistanis, West Indians, and other nonwhite peoples reside in its large cities. According to the British Social Attitudes Survey for 2009, just more than one-half of respondents in Great Britain described themselves as having no religious affiliation, while about one-fifth of the population belongs to the Church of England (Anglican Church). Almost 10 percent are Roman Catholics, and the remainder are divided among other Protestant denominations and non-Christian religions. Muslims are the largest non-Christian group, representing slightly more than 2 percent of inhabitants. One of the largest mixed-market economies in the world, England accounts for the bulk of the United Kingdom's economy, which had the eighteenth-highest gross domestic product (GDP) in the world as of 2009. England's capital, London, is the world's largest financial center and is home to 100 of the top 500 companies in Europe.

The English were among the first Europeans to explore and eventually settle the area now known as the United States. The Spanish had established St. Augustine (in present-day Florida) in 1565, but their efforts to colonize the mid-Atlantic Coast failed. After a small English colony on Roanoke Island disappeared in 1587, a permanent English settlement was finally constructed at Jamestown in 1606. A second settlement, Plymouth Colony, was founded in Massachusetts in 1620. By the end of the seventeenth century, more than 350,000 English had immigrated to the American colonies, with 60 percent settling in the New England colonies around Massachusetts Bay. Although English immigration to the United States has risen and fallen during the previous 200 years, the decade after World War II saw a noteworthy upturn in numbers, a trend fueled by the large disparity in standards of living between the two nations and by the vision of America as a land of economic opportunity. In the early twenty-first century, an increasing number of British have chosen to commute between England and the United States, particularly to such large Eastern financial and business centers as New York and Boston.

According to the U.S. Census Bureau's American Community Survey estimates for 2009–2011, over 26.3 million Americans are of English descent. The states with the highest populations of English Americans are California (2.3 million), Florida (1.5 million), New York (1.1 million), Ohio (over 1 million), Pennsylvania (over 1 million), and Texas (1.7 million).

HISTORY OF THE PEOPLE

Early History The English are descended from Celtic tribes who brought Iron Age technology from continental Europe to the British Isles during the first millennium BCE. England and Wales came under Roman control by the end of the first century CE, and during the next three centuries England developed as a typical Roman colony. The Romans promoted commerce, established social institutions, built roads, and introduced Christianity to the population. The collapse of Roman rule in the early fifth century marked the end of urban life there, and invading Germanic tribes such as the Angles, Jutes, and Saxons carved the country into competing enclaves. A diverse group of Anglo-Saxon kingdoms developed, vied for control of the island, and later resisted the waves of Viking intruders who assaulted the island from the eighth to the eleventh centuries. The most important Anglo-Saxon ruler was Alfred the Great, who defeated the Danish Vikings, founded the English navy, and made Roman Catholicism dominant in England.

In 1066 William of Normandy (a region in what is now France) conquered England, ending a century of instability, and during the next three centuries distinctively English institutions such as common law and parliamentary government were developed. The signing of the Magna Carta, or Great Charter of English Liberties, in 1215 imposed the first serious restraints on the power of the king. During the following centuries the country endured many social and political challenges, including its defeat in the Hundred Years' War (1337–1453) against France; depopulation caused by the Black Death (bubonic plague; 1348–1350); and, during the second half of the fifteenth century, the War of the Roses, which pitted two powerful families within the House of Plantagenet (the Yorks and the Lancasters) against each other and ended by bringing the Tudor dynasty to the throne in 1485.

The first Tudor king, Henry VII, restored a strong central government, developed fiscal reform, and reasserted the power of the crown. His successor, Henry VIII, gained renown not only for his eight marriages but also for his separation of England's church from the control of the Roman Catholic papacy. Despite his best efforts, Henry died without a surviving son and was succeeded by eldest daughter, Mary, who waged a bloody and ultimately unsuccessful battle to reinstate Roman Catholicism. Her sister Elizabeth restored the primacy of the Church of England and defended the British Isles from an attack by the Spanish Armada in 1588. Her prosperous reign supported such explorers as Sir Francis Drake and Sir Walter Raleigh, fostered a cultural revival led by William Shakespeare and Francis Bacon, and allowed merchant adventurers to settle England's first permanent colony on the American continent.

Elizabeth I died without an heir, and the throne of England passed to a new royal family, the Stuarts. Their rule did not prove popular, however, and between 1603 and 1714 a succession of Stuart rulers encountered parliamentary opposition to their religious, social, economic, and political policies. The result was a series of civil wars between 1642 and 1649 that ended with the public execution of King Charles I and the establishment of a republican commonwealth, led by Oliver Cromwell. Cromwell's militant Puritanism also proved unpopular, and the monarchy was restored in 1660, leading to a new period of political development that included the establishment of a bill of rights in 1689. During the seventeenth- to eighteenth-century Age of Enlightenment, English thinkers such as John Locke and Sir Isaac Newton made great contributions. In the eighteenth century England and Scotland established a union, and the monarchy passed to yet another royal family, the Hanoverian Windsors. During this century England created a vast empire, defeated the French in the Seven Years' War (1756–1763), and dominated international trade. After its defeat in the Revolutionary War, however, it lost thirteen of its mainland North American colonies.

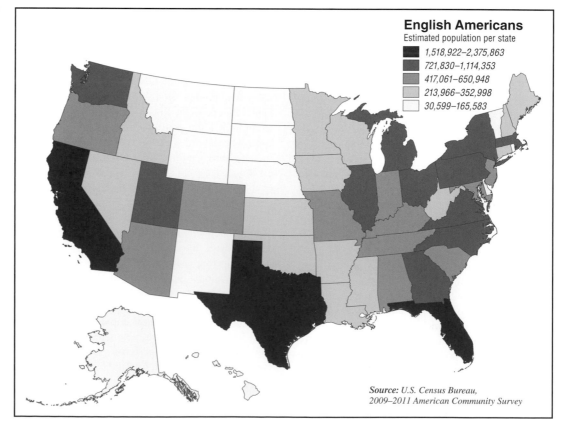

English Americans
Estimated population per state

- 1,518,922–2,375,863
- 721,830–1,114,353
- 417,061–650,948
- 213,966–352,998
- 30,599–165,583

Source: U.S. Census Bureau, 2009–2011 American Community Survey

Modern Era As the nineteenth century began, England led the alliance that defeated Napoleon I's attempt to control all of Europe. Later in the century, the Second Industrial Revolution introduced steam power and mechanized manufacturing, radically changing English society. Some sectors experienced great prosperity and an improved standard of living, but many others labored under severe conditions, and urban development began to erode the traditional life of rural England. The country's overall economic strength, however, fueled imperialistic expansion in Africa and Asia, and during the reign of Queen Victoria (1837–1901), the British Empire grew to encompass territories around the globe.

Victorian England also brought domestic social and economic reforms that made the government more democratic, but the nation still faced both internal and external challenges. The competition among European nations for power and territory reached a critical point early in the twentieth century, and although England was ultimately victorious in World War I, the nation sustained tremendous losses; the four years of brutal combat cost the nation 745,000 military dead and 1.7 million wounded. These costs, compounded by an outmoded industrial base, high unemployment, and negligible postwar growth, led to a decade of economic stagnation.

World War II took an even greater toll, leaving Great Britain financially distressed and, this time, with many of its urban centers partly turned to rubble. For the second time that century, the British were faced with rebuilding their nation. This enormous task was compounded by the massive social and geopolitical changes caused by the war. Long the world's premier colonial power, England lost many of its overseas possessions due to independence movements. This was not only a blow to its international power and prestige but also a disastrous loss of manpower, materials, and trading partners that further retarded its economic recovery. Still expected to play a major part in world politics, Britain was forced to ally itself more closely with the United States and, reluctantly, to increase its involvement in the European Common Market.

One of the most difficult challenges England faced at the end of the twentieth century was surrendering its historical independence and cooperating with the policies and obligations of Common Market membership. At the same time, however, the United Kingdom of Great Britain and Northern Ireland—which also includes Scotland, Wales, the Sea Islands, and the Channel Islands—retained many of its traditional institutions, including the constitutional monarchy. In 2012 Elizabeth II celebrated the sixtieth anniversary of her coronation, and despite occasional scandals the royal family remains popular with the majority of the British people. Executive power is still exercised by the prime minister and cabinet, whom the monarch appoints from among the members of the party winning a majority of seats in the House of Commons. Cabinet members must sit in Parliament, and they are responsible to both the Crown and Parliament, whose support they need in order to frame legislation, institute taxes, and determine domestic and foreign policy.

While no longer an economic superpower, England remains a major manufacturing, food-producing, and commercial nation and has one of the premier financial markets in the world. Its universities, museums, scientific institutions, and tourist attractions draw millions of visitors. Its population diversity continues to increase. In 2012 London successfully hosted the Summer Olympics, demonstrating once again the United Kingdom's vital role in the international community.

> We were put on a barge, jammed in so tight that I couldn't turn 'round, there were so many of us, you see, and the stench was terrible.
>
> Eleanor Kenderdine Lenhart in 1921, cited in *Ellis Island: An Illustrated History of the Immigrant Experience*, edited by Ivan Chermayeff et al. (New York: Macmillan, 1991).

SETTLEMENT IN THE UNITED STATES

After the Spanish established St. Augustine in 1565, the English were the next nonindigenous people to settle the area that became the United States of America. From the original permanent settlements established at Jamestown in the Colony of Virginia in 1607 and at Plymouth (now Plymouth, Massachusetts) in 1620 to the final Georgia colony founded by James Oglethorpe (near present-day Savannah) in 1732, English joint-stock companies, private proprietors, and Crown officials sought to create a modified version of their native society in American settlements. While many English came to the New World seeking liberation from religious intolerance in Europe, most of the early settlers were drawn by economic opportunities and by the desire to own land, then considered the only secure basis for wealth.

A group of single men sent by the Virginia Company in 1607 failed in their mission to find gold and create a profitable trade. The survival of the Colony of Virginia, even under royal proprietorship, was uncertain for two decades. It was not until the late 1620s—when a stable agricultural economy and lucrative tobacco export began attracting an annual influx of several thousand Englishmen and women, most of them indentured servants (their passage paid by a future employer)—that the success of Jamestown was assured. After the founding of colonies in Maryland (1632), Delaware (1682), and Pennsylvania (1682), larger numbers of indentured and working-class families immigrated, soon constituting a majority of the new English settlers to the area. The rate of English immigration to the Pennsylvania and Chesapeake colonies was fairly constant until the early part of the eighteenth century. At that point it swelled as a decade-long war between England and France demanded the exploitation of resources from British holdings abroad. Favorable immigration provisions made the prospect of relocating to the more recent U.S. colonies increasingly attractive for those seeking economic opportunity.

Further north, Pilgrim and Puritan settlements in the Massachusetts Bay region attracted more than 20,000 settlers from East Anglia and the counties west of London between 1620 and 1642. During these decades English settlements were begun in New Hampshire and Maine, and several English communities were established in Rhode Island and Connecticut by religious reformers whose dissenting views were not tolerated by the authorities in Massachusetts. Unlike those in the southern colonies, most of the settlers in New England were older and came with their families and friends. In some instances whole congregations immigrated to New England during this period. The influence of the clergy was strong throughout the region, and they successfully converted many Native Americans to Christianity. Conflicts with the indigenous peoples were sometimes fierce, however, especially during the Pequot War of 1637–1638, which devastated the Pequot tribe, and King Philip's War of 1675–1678, which destroyed many New England Puritan towns and killed a large number of settlers. The New England economy was based on fishing and seaborne trade, and much of the population was employed in industries—such as shipbuilding and lumber production—that supported this maritime economy.

When a British fleet captured the town of New Amsterdam from the Dutch in 1664, renaming it New York, English settlers already constituted a majority of the city's population and were well established in neighboring New Jersey. Pennsylvania, founded by English Quakers in 1681, attracted large numbers of German, French, Welsh, Scottish, and Scotch-Irish settlers, but the colony retained its English character throughout the colonial period. The majority of people immigrating to the thirteen colonies during the 1600s were from England.

From the colonies in Virginia and Massachusetts, the English presence expanded to other parts of the Atlantic coast. English settlers from Virginia migrated into North Carolina in the seventeenth century; in its middle decades, more English immigrants settled in all of the colonies between Connecticut and Maryland. The easy availability of African and Caribbean slaves beginning in the mid-1700s supported the region's labor-intensive cash crops—tobacco, cotton, and rice. Soon a plantation culture grew in the South, where slave-holding English immigrants became a landed gentry, dominating politics and society for decades to come.

In 1717 the British government began transporting felons to American colonies willing to accept them. More than 30,000 male and female prisoners convicted of serious felonies arrived in southern Pennsylvania, Delaware, and Virginia, increasing the number of unskilled workers. Although colonies as far south as Georgia received a stream of English prisoners and indentured servants until 1776, many were also successful in attracting merchant families and the younger sons and poorer cousins of the gentry. Clergymen, lawyers, government officials, and members of minor aristocratic families settled in the Chesapeake Basin, for example, developing large-scale plantations for the cultivation of tobacco, which soon became the area's main cash crop.

The majority of eighteenth-century English immigrants came from London and the northern counties. The proportion of female to male settlers increased from about 15 percent to nearly 25 percent during this time. English Americans began to intermarry with other nationalities more frequently than any other European group, partly because of greater numbers of mobile tradesmen, craftsmen, and merchants among the new group. England's economic and political troubles brought new spurts of English immigration in the 1720s and the following decades.

According to the first federal census in 1790, English settlers and their descendants constituted about 60 percent of the European settlers living from Maine to Georgia. More important, they had already ensured the dominance of English institutions and culture throughout the new republic. Since all but two of the original colonies were founded by the English, administered by English officials, protected by England's army and navy, and led by English-trained clergy, lawyers, and educators, the settlers adapted English models in their laws, constitutions, educational system, social structure, and cultural pursuits. From the colonial period it remained fashionable for wealthy Americans to send their sons to England for a year of college, and English styles in literature, poetry, music, architecture, industry, and clothing were the models to emulate until the twentieth century. English dominance persisted despite a growing influx of immigrants from other parts of Europe.

Throughout the colonial period Americans supported England's wars enthusiastically, and when resentment and resistance to British policies developed in the 1760s and 1770s, Americans looked to Parliament to redress their grievances, which they perceived as emanating from a tyrannical king and his corrupt ministers. After the Revolution English Americans led not only national and state governments but also the successful movement to add an English-style bill of rights to the new U.S. Constitution in 1789. Some loyalists left the United States for England and other colonies, but new English settlers arrived. While many assimilated easily, some friction inevitably developed. In states with

Dressed in period clothing, a volunteer stops and raises his hat as the flag "Cross of St George" is raised in 2007. The Jamestown settlement in Jamestown, Virginia, is a reproduction of the original homestead that was founded nearby in 1607 by a group of 104 English men and boys. MARK WILSON / GETTY IMAGES

large German, French, and Celtic communities such as Maryland, Pennsylvania, New York, and the Carolinas, English immigrants were rebuked for their "assumed superiority," their poverty, and their provincialism.

English immigration to the United States decreased sharply between 1780 and 1815, initially as a consequence of British involvement in India and Latin America as well as of events surrounding the French Revolution (1789–1799) and the ensuing Napoleonic Wars (1803–1815). In addition, tensions existed between Britain and the newly independent United States. When the United States declared itself at war with Britain in 1812, recent English immigrants—known as British Aliens, who often arrived with little or no documentation—were forced to register with local marshals; they were treated with suspicion and were severely restricted in their freedom of movement during nearly three years of war. Many English merchants, primarily in Charleston, South Carolina; Baltimore, Maryland; and New York, were relocated and prevented from conducting their business. Following the war—which ended with little change in relations between the two countries—new settlers found easy acceptance. Encouraged by a similar language, a familiar legal and political system, American variants of nearly every English religious denomination, and the popular admiration—especially in large U.S. cities and in the South—for "all things English," these immigrants had little inclination to establish their own churches, newspapers, or political organizations.

After 1815 German, Irish, Scandinavian, Mediterranean, and Slavic peoples dominated the new waves of U.S. immigration, but English settlers provided a steady and substantial influx throughout the nineteenth century. Most of the new arrivals were small farmers from depressed areas in the rural counties of southern and western England, although urban laborers continued to flee from economic difficulties and the massive social changes caused by the Industrial Revolution. Some English immigrants were drawn by dreams of creating model utopian societies in the United States, some based on religious tenets, such as the Shakers of Pennsylvania, and others, such as the transcendentalist-inspired Brook Farm in Massachusetts, on the liberal economic and political ideas then being formulated around Europe. The great majority of immigrants, however, were lured by the idea of new lands and the economic opportunities presented by a growing number of jobs in textile factories, railroads, and mining.

In the 1840s Chartism, a working-class movement for political reform, brought about massive urban protests in England and spurred another period of emigration. This wave peaked in 1854 and coincided with the arrival of Germans and central Europeans fleeing in the aftermath of the failed European revolutions of 1848. A preponderance of English immigrants traveled with one or more family members, and the number of industrial workers, tradesmen, and craftsmen outnumbered farmers by more than three to one. During the final years of 1860s, annual English immigration increased to more than 60,000, and by 1872 it had

BLUE LAWS

The majority of Puritan settlers came to New England with their families, as whole congregations and sizable groups of religious dissidents transferred their hopes of a "godly commonwealth" to America, where they established often strict religious customs. They created Sunday "blue laws" to sanctify the Sabbath by prohibiting public drinking, dancing, and work-related activities while encouraging prayer and charitable and missionary activities, especially among family members. Outside New England, however, modest displays of entertainment, especially dancing, singing, and athletic competitions among family groups, were common and often held under the auspices of the local Episcopal congregation. Certain blue laws are still in effect in the United States today. For instance, in Massachusetts and Connecticut, retail stores are prohibited from operating on Thanksgiving and Christmas. Many states, including Massachusetts, New York, and Mississippi, have laws restricting the sale of alcohol on Sundays. Other blue laws in the United States restrict horse racing, hunting, and selling cars on Sundays.

risen to more than 75,000 before experiencing a short decline. The final and most sustained wave of immigration began in 1879 and lasted until the depression of 1893. During this period English annual immigration averaged more than 80,000, with peaks in 1882 and 1888. The building of the U.S. transcontinental railroads, the settlement of the Great Plains, and the increasing pace of industrialization attracted many skilled and professional emigrants from England. Also, because cheaper steamship fares enabled ordinary workers to afford the journey to the United States, unskilled and semiskilled laborers, miners, and building tradesmen were increasingly represented among the new English immigrants. While most of the newcomers settled permanently in the United States, a number of skilled craftsmen remained itinerant, returning to England after a season or two of work.

Throughout the nineteenth century England was the largest investor in American land development, railroads, mining, cattle ranching, and heavy industry, although the English made up only 15 percent of the great nineteenth-century European immigration. Nevertheless, the new wave altered the distribution of English settlers in the United States: by the end of the century, the mid-Atlantic states had the largest number of English Americans, followed by the North-central states and New England. The growing number of English settling in the West and Pacific Coast regions left the South with the smallest percentage of English Americans.

In the twentieth century English immigration to the United States decreased, in part because Canada and Australia were offering English settlers increased economic opportunities and more favorable immigration policies. Throughout the first four decades of the century, the English made up an average of only 6 percent of the total number of European immigrants. Still, Americans prized English culture, literature, and family connections as a result of well-publicized marriages between wealthy Americans and the children of English aristocrats. The introduction of Western history and literature courses that stressed America's English heritage in colleges and in the public school curriculum after World War I also supported widespread Anglophilia.

During the course of the Great Depression of the 1930s, more English returned home than immigrated to the United States—and for the first time more English women than men arrived in the country. The general decline reversed itself during World War II, when more than 100,000 immigrants (18 percent of all European immigrants) came from England. This group contained a large contingent of war brides, who arrived between 1945 and 1948; the male–female English immigration ratio of the period was one to four. In the 1950s total English immigration increased to more than 150,000 (the level maintained in the 1920s) but remained less than 12 percent of the European influx. The next two decades saw the number of English immigrants rise to more than 15 percent of all incoming Europeans, in part because of a so-called "brain drain" in which multinational corporations lured English engineers, technicians, medical professionals, and other specialists to the United States.

From 1970 to 2000, English immigrants made up about 12 percent of the total number arriving from Europe and were usually unmarried, professionally trained men and women. While the average age of immigrants rose in the last decades of the twentieth century, the number of married people and children continued to decline. This may, in part, be attributed to the increasing number of English citizens who commute between homes in the United Kingdom and careers in the financial and political centers of the American East Coast. In 2011 the U.S. Census Bureau's American Community Survey reported that there were an estimated 26.3 million Americans of English descent. The states with over 1 million English Americans included California, Florida, New York, Ohio, Pennsylvania, and Texas; every state, however, has a substantial population of English Americans.

LANGUAGE

Although the United States and England share the same basic language, noteworthy differences exist in spelling, pronunciation, and accent. There are also differences in idiom, and the names of ordinary items may vary between the two countries. In England gasoline is called petrol, potato chips are crisps, sausages are bangers, and one rings off a phone call rather than hanging up. Many English expressions are well known in the United States, however, as a result of the popularity of British television programs, and although first-generation English immigrants are identifiable by their accents, their descendants rarely are.

RELIGION

The Church of England came to the United States with the earliest immigrants. Religious differences among the colonists contributed to the establishment of different settlements and the growth of various Protestant denominations. After the American Revolution, the Episcopal Church of America separated from the Church of England, and evangelical groups such as the Quakers and Methodists ended their affiliation with their English counterparts.

Throughout the nineteenth century most groups of English immigrants expressed their ethnic identity through their participation in the Episcopal Church or in the Methodist and Baptist Churches of the rural South. Such British groups as the Domestic and Foreign Missionary Society of the Episcopal Church of England, the Society for the Propagation of the Gospel, and the Salvation Army sent ministers and missionaries to English congregations in the United States. With funds raised in England and in English immigrant communities along the Atlantic seaboard, Kenyon College in Ohio and Jubilee College in Illinois were established to train Episcopal ministers for service in towns in the Midwest and far Western states, where numerous English immigrant communities of miners, craftsmen, and farmers had flourished. As American religious culture became increasingly diversified, newly arrived immigrants had a wide choice of churches—some very similar to what they had left behind in England, some very different—and no particular pattern of religious preference seems to have developed among English Americans.

English Presbyterian missionary John Eliot addresses a gathering of Algonquins in 1660. Known as "the Apostle of the Indians," Eliot established the first church for Native Americans in Massachusetts. MPI / GETTY IMAGES

ENGLISH PROVERBS

English proverbs show a characteristic combination of independence of mind and common sense along with a healthy dose of skepticism:

- Two is company; three is a crowd.

- An ounce of discretion is worth a pound of wit.

- Discretion is the better part of valor.

- Forewarned is forearmed.

- Good fences make good neighbors.

- Fool me once, shame on you. Fool me twice, shame on me.

CULTURE AND ASSIMILATION

In spite of a complicated beginning, the relationship between England and the United States has become increasingly close over the past 200 years, not only economically but also socially and politically. Britain's actions and policies throughout the twentieth century, represented in the American consciousness by heroism in the trenches of World War I, Prime Minister Winston Churchill's resistance to Adolf Hitler, and Prime Minister Margaret Thatcher's support of the United States in the Persian Gulf War, have strengthened the ties between the two countries. Similarly,

In this 2007 photo, historical interpreters in period dress enter James Fort at Jamestown settlement in Jamestown, Virginia. MANNIE GARCIA / AFP / GETTY IMAGES

British influences on popular culture—especially in the music and fashion trends of the 1960s and 1970s—have contributed to the "special relationship" enjoyed by the United States and England, an affiliation also reflected in the number of British commentators and journalists visible in American media. This cultural continuity enables English newcomers to feel welcome in the United States and to fit in quickly. In contemporary American society most English immigrants do not regard themselves as part of a distinctive cultural group. Because England itself has become increasingly multicultural, however, some of those leaving England for the United States may have been second-generation residents of England who retain ties (including traditions and customs, clothing, cuisine, and so on) to the cultural backgrounds of their parents.

Traditions and Customs In the nineteenth century England still had a thriving rural culture, with many unique traditions and customs. Social life was organized according to class, so the aristocracy and landed gentry had their own set of customs, while farmers and laborers lived very differently. Customs also varied by region, so it is difficult to point to typical English customs. Traditions observed in common by most groups—such as toasting the health of the monarch and holding county fairs—were very much tied to the land and politics of England and did not translate well to life in the United States.

While first-generation immigrants often confined their socializing to friends and relatives from their own county or region of England, their children soon merged into the general population. In comparison with other new immigrants, the English arrivals in the decades preceding the Civil War were more prone to separate from their own communities, more willing to intermarry, and more enthusiastic in embracing the culture of their new land. The English tendency to adapt and integrate increased in the second half of the nineteenth century. One study concluded that, at the turn of the twentieth century, less than 20 percent of children of English immigrants eventually married someone of English descent. By the mid-twentieth century urbanization and modernization had done away with most of the traditions and customs that had once been a part of English life, so newcomers to the United States generally experience little cultural displacement.

Cuisine Some English immigrants undoubtedly prepare traditional dishes from their homeland, such as fish and chips, Shepherd's pie (a meat stew topped with mashed potatoes), kippers (dried and salted fish), and steamed pudding (often made with beef fat). England adopted many foods from the countries it colonized, however, and considers the cuisines of India, China, and many other regions as part of the English national menu. On both sides of the Atlantic, tea and ale are favorite English beverages.

Traditional Dress Other than variations of style, there has been little significant difference in English dress and American dress from colonial times to the present. Although folk costumes were once worn for festivals in rural England, the practice had died out by the end of the nineteenth century and was never common among English immigrants to the United States. In the 1960s and 1970s, however, English fashion trends had a major influence on American fashion. The Swinging Sixties styles of Carnaby Street, for instance, were often brought to the States by such popular British bands as the Beatles and the Rolling Stones. English tailoring, as exemplified by the custom suits of Saville Row and the silk ties of Germyn Street, continues to influence American business dress for both men and women.

Dances and Songs Traditional folk songs and dances of the English countryside that survive in the early twenty-first century are not typically part of the English American experience. Contradancing is popular across ethnicities in the United States, however, especially in New England. Derived from sixteenth-century English country dances that were imported to the French court in the seventeenth century and to the United States with the early English settlers, contradancing is often accompanied by live traditional British music, with moves called out by a caller and elaborated on by dancers of all abilities. In the performance category, more than 100 teams of Morris dancers present the choreographed dance form, which dates from fifteenth-century England, at events around the United States.

Holidays Public holidays in England include traditional Christian observances such as Christmas and Easter; May Day (May 1); Armistice Day (November 11); and Boxing Day (December 26). May Day was long celebrated as a festive welcome to spring, featuring a maypole and folk dancing. Some English also observe May 1 as International Workers Day. Boxing Day was traditionally the day when servants and trades people received gifts from their employers and customers. Armistice Day commemorates the signing of the peace agreement between the Allies and Germany in 1918.

In the past English immigrants continued to celebrate unofficial holidays such as Guy Fawkes Day (November 5), which commemorates the deliverance of King James I and Parliament from a plot in 1605 to destroy them with gunpowder. Festivities included games, fireworks, and a large meal. Among some royalist families, St. Charles Day, marking the martyrdom of King Charles I on January 29, 1649, after the English Civil Wars, was celebrated with a somber ritual resembling a wake but featuring the imbibing of spirits, flag waving, and the reading of Charles's final speech from the gallows. Today, however, English Americans generally observe the same holidays as other Americans.

YORKSHIRE PUDDING

Ingredients

1½ cups all-purpose flour

1½ cups whole milk

3 large eggs

1¼ teaspoons salt

3 tablespoons butter, lard, or tallow

Preparation

Blend together flour, milk, eggs, and salt. Refrigerate until fully chilled.

When ready to make the pudding, preheat the oven to 450°F. Put butter, lard, or tallow into a 13 by 9 inch baking pan. Heat in oven until piping hot, 6 to 8 minutes. (If using butter, it will brown. Pull it from the oven when it becomes dark brown.)

Pour the batter into the hot baking pan and bake until pudding is puffed and center is golden brown, 26–28 minutes. Rotate the pan halfway through.

Serve immediately.

Death and Burial Rituals Customs associated with death and burial are no different in England than in the United States and other developed countries. Cremation has become more popular in England than in many parts of the United States, however, and this preference might be somewhat more prevalent among English Americans. As of 2012 physician-assisted suicide was illegal throughout England but legal in three American states.

Traditional Arts and Crafts The arts and crafts of England—such as spinning, weaving, pottery-making, basketry, and needlework—were brought to America by early settlers, so the artisans of both countries use similar methods, materials, and designs.

Recreational Activities English football (known in the United States as soccer) is extremely popular in most of the world, and many English Americans maintain an active interest in the sport. Cricket—a complicated bat-and-ball game—is another English favorite. Both games are played recreationally in the United States but not primarily by English Americans.

FAMILY AND COMMUNITY LIFE

As in other areas of American society, it was the English pattern of the nuclear family—focused on the husband, wife, and children with an occasional relative living in close proximity—that set the pattern of early life in the colonial era. While women were in short supply in the early decades of the colonial era, the majority of Puritan settlers came to New England with their families. English immigrants, especially those who were part of the larger waves of migration in the nineteenth century, usually settled in small towns with other English miners, metal workers, farmers, and skilled textile specialists and recreated English-style pubs, choral groups, sporting clubs, self-help societies, unions, and fraternal organization, few of which endured for very long beyond the lifetime of the founders.

Gender Roles The English concept of the nuclear family—focused on the husband, wife, and children and, occasionally, relatives living in close proximity—set the pattern of early life in the colonial era and became the template for American society. In all social classes, to differing degrees, English American women dominated the domestic and social life of the family as completely as men dominated the public aspects of family life and business. As in England, family celebrations and the maintenance of connections with relatives were left to women, especially in more affluent and socially prominent families. In the twentieth century, however, traditional gender roles began to break down in all Western countries, including England and the United States. Among contemporary English American families, gender roles reflect socioeconomic class, religious beliefs, and other factors, just as they do among most other American groups.

Education The New England Puritans and the English Quakers in Pennsylvania were among the earliest advocates of free public education at all levels, but the wealthy and professional classes of English settlers favored private schools and colleges, often affiliated with their particular religious denomination. Middle- and upper-class families took care to educate and discipline their older children and to encourage them to continue family businesses and social obligations. A large percentage of the early colleges in the country were founded and supported by English immigrants and their descendants, especially in New England and the Southeast. English American philanthropists also provided endowments to subsidize study in England for the children of English expatriates. The most famous of these programs is the Rhodes scholarship, named for the English financier and colonial official Cecil Rhodes.

Many colleges founded in the United States by English immigrants still support traditional English sports such as sculling (team rowing) and rugby, but the three English aristocratic pastimes that enjoy the greatest popularity in the United States—tennis, horse racing, and sailing—have largely shed their English identity. The same can be said for English football, known as soccer to young players across the country.

Although the American educational system was originally patterned after England's, significant differences have developed in teaching methods, curricula, division of the school year, the role of testing, and the requirements for academic advancement. In England, for example, test results may limit educational and career opportunities, and college is not accessible to all. Immigrants who transfer from English to American schools face some adjustments but soon adapt to a system that is in many ways less rigorous.

Courtship and Weddings Like most other American customs, rules for courtship were originally derived from the English model, and weddings were carried out the same way in both countries. Nineteenth-century English immigrants probably found that courting was less formal in the United States, but in contemporary life newcomers will notice no significant difference.

Social Organizations The only English social organizations to endure for several generations among English immigrants were the assorted groups of Odd Fellows, fraternal societies for the working class recreated in the United States by Thomas Wildey and John Welch in Baltimore in 1819. These lodges appealed to the more skilled immigrant tradesmen and craftsmen because they provided the companionship of English pubs, employment connections, and shelter from the criticism sometimes directed toward English immigration. Their appeal to the waves of English immigrants arriving between 1870 and 1893 was limited, however, and at the turn of the century fewer than three dozen chapters survived, mostly in New England and the northern states. Nevertheless, the organization has endured by opening its membership to all Americans and devoting its activities to civic affairs.

While a few other social organizations and some newspapers were established for English immigrants in the early nineteenth century, all failed to gain significant support. New York was the home of the first newspaper for English American readers, *Albion; or, the British and Colonial Foreign Gazette*. It began publication in 1827 and survived until 1863, outlasting its rivals, the *Old Countryman* (1830–1835), the *Emigrant* (1835–1838), and the *Anglo-American* (1843–1847). When inexpensive editions of British newspapers became available in the United States during the 1840s, their arrival undermined further efforts to publish dailies for the expanding communities of English residents of Massachusetts and New York.

A number of English immigrant groups—for example, textile workers in Lowell, Massachusetts; cutlery workers in Connecticut; and English miners in West Virginia—initially lived close together and established distinctly English denominational congregations. They were able to maintain some social cohesion and community identity. Self-help associations, buying cooperatives, fraternal lodges, and sporting associations could be found in some English communities in the late Victorian era (the turn of the twentieth century). Within a generation, however, they were absorbed into the mainstream of American life. Similarly, some communities of English miners, mill workers, and agricultural settlers in the Midwest established libraries, social clubs, and musical societies to provide English culture, but most, including the chapters of the St. George's Society in Madison, Wisconsin, and Clinton, Iowa, did not survive for more than a decade.

EMPLOYMENT AND ECONOMIC CONDITIONS

English Americans are not concentrated in any particular trades or professions, and they are subject to the same economic conditions as other Americans. Because they already speak English and come from a country with social and cultural values similar to those found in the United States, English immigrants face no special barriers to employment or to success in the workplace. Sometimes their accent even helps them, as it is often seen as a mark of intelligence.

POLITICS AND GOVERNMENT

Efforts among English immigrants to establish local labor unions, labor exchanges, and political pressure groups were unsuccessful. After Irish immigrants began to emerge as a political force in American politics, English American groups encouraged their reluctant countrymen to become citizens and actively engage in public life. The English often saw Irish religion and politics as foreign and dangerous, and they were unwilling to lose potential political influence to their Irish rivals. During the nineteenth century, however, fewer English renounced loyalty to their homeland than did immigrants from other parts of Europe. Their greater reliance on family, kinsmen, and contacts from their native regions of England already in America and the ease with which the new arrivals blended into American society with their assistance, compounded by the legal and social benefits of membership in the British Empire, may help explain why English immigrants were last among the new settlers to embrace American citizenship. The census of 1900 showed a significant increase in the percentage of English Americans becoming citizens of the United States, however, and this trend grew stronger in the twentieth century until the rate of English immigrant assimilation matched that of other European settlers.

One result of this trend was the organization of English American and British American political clubs in Philadelphia, Boston, and New York; in smaller industrial towns, including Elizabeth, New Jersey, and Stanford, Maine; and in Ohio, Iowa, and California, where communities of English miners, artisans, and industrial workers asserted their political muscle, predominantly on behalf of the Republican Party. These activities escalated after an 1887 banquet celebrating Queen Victoria's Golden Jubilee in Boston's Faneuil Hall was disrupted by thousands of angry Irish protesters, who tried to prevent the entry of the 400 ticket holders. When only a few British politicians condemned the demonstration, English and Scottish American leaders organized a federation of more than sixty political action clubs and launched a number of periodicals. Massachusetts, New York, Pennsylvania, and Illinois each had a dozen or more English communities that organized politically, with smaller groups emerging in New Hampshire, Connecticut, New Jersey, Ohio, Michigan, Iowa, and California. These clubs were often based on the racial and religious animosities that had unsettled Anglo-Irish relations for centuries. They had little impact on the elections of 1888 and 1892, however, and most were absorbed into a broader anti-Catholic confederation, the American

In Jamestown, Virginia, replicas of Powhatan Native American houses from the 17th century. MANNIE GARCIA / AFP / GETTY IMAGES

Protective Association, which itself was an offshoot of the nativist (anti-immigrant) and populist (antitrust) movements of the 1890s.

Three publications with more political aims that were launched in the late 1880s were the *British-American Citizen*, published in Boston from 1887 to 1913; the *Western British American*, published in Chicago from 1888 to 1922; and the *British-American*, published in New York and Philadelphia from 1887 to 1919. They attained a limited degree of success by appealing to immigrants from all parts of Britain. They did not manage to unite Americans of Scottish, English, Irish, and Welsh descent into a single effective political action group, but they served to sharpen the ethnic identity of their readers and underscore the importance of the British contribution to American society. The survival of these periodicals after the nativist frenzy of the 1890s cooled was in part a result of improved diplomatic relations between the United States and Britain after 1895, which led to an alliance in World War I.

There are no distinguishable patterns of political alignment or activism among contemporary English Americans, who are so widely distributed in the population that they cannot be statistically identified after the second generation. First-generation immigrants often retain an interest in British politics, but very few immigrants leave England for political reasons.

NOTABLE INDIVIDUALS

Art In the period before and after the American Revolution, artists of English descent and English decorative style dominated American creative life. Such artisans as Paul Revere (1734–1818) were highly influenced by English decorative designs in silver and porcelain, while English landscape and portraiture influenced artists like John Trumbull (1756–1843) and Gilbert Stuart (1755–1828). Painter Thomas Cole (1801–1848) was renowned for his ability to combine naturalism and romanticism in sweeping images of the American landscape. Born in England, Cole immigrated to the United States with his parents in 1818, and in 1825 he used proceeds from the first sales of his art to travel through the Hudson River Valley in upstate New York. The striking scenery became a lifelong inspiration for Cole, whose work not only attracted the attention of wealthy collectors but also became popular with general audiences. His influence lived on in the Hudson River School, an American art movement that included such noted painters as the German American Albert Bierstadt (1830–1902) and the American Frederic Edwin Church (1826–1900).

In the next century artists of English descent helped shape the American impressionist and realist movements, with noted impressionist Childe Hassam (1859–1935), landscape painter and printmaker Winslow Homer (1836–1910), illustrator N. C. Wyeth (1882–1945), and realist Andrew Wyeth (1917–2009) all claiming English descent.

In architecture Frank Lloyd Wright (1867–1959), whose prolific work in the Craftsman and Prairie styles helped define an original American sense of design, was also of English ancestry.

Activism Pamela Churchill Harriman (1920–1997), who was born into the privileged life of the English upper class in 1920, became one of the most celebrated socialites of her time. Her love affairs were notorious, and her husbands included Randolph Churchill (son of Winston Churchill) and Leland Hayward (a powerful Broadway producer). In 1971 she married Averell Harriman, an influential American politician and diplomat, and became a U.S. citizen. Building on her husband's connections in the Democratic Party, Harriman created a political action committee—nicknamed "PamPAC"—that raised funds for candidates in the 1980s and 1990s. Named Woman of the Year by the National Women's Democratic Club in 1980, Harriman became U.S. ambassador to France in 1993. She served in this capacity until her sudden death.

Journalism The fathers of American journalism, including printer, journalist, and annalist Benjamin Franklin (1707–1790) and pamphleteer Thomas Paine (1737–1809), were of English descent.

Journalist Ted Koppel (1940–) became well known to American viewers as the anchor of ABC's pioneering in-depth news program *Nightline*. Born to Jewish parents who had fled Germany for England, Koppel immigrated with his family to the United States in 1953 and began his broadcast career just ten years later. After establishing a reputation as a correspondent during the Vietnam War, Koppel began hosting the newly created *Nightline* in 1980 and remained in the anchor seat for twenty-five years. When he left the program in 2005, he took on a variety of roles with the Discovery Channel, National Public Radio, the BBC in the United States, and NBC's primetime news magazine *Rock Center*.

Literature Many of the most important and influential authors of the nation's first century, such

English American Pamela Harriman was a very influential supporter for the Democratic Party in the 1980s. LUKE FRAZZA / AFP / GETTY IMAGES

as Washington Irving (1783–1859), Stephen Crane (1871–1900), Walt Whitman (1819–1892), and Mark Twain (1835–1910), were of English descent.

Denise Levertov (1923–1997) was among the most noted poets of her generation, publishing twenty volumes of verse and receiving, among other honors, the Shelley Memorial Award and the Robert Frost Medal. Levertov grew up in England and began her writing career while still a teenager. Her work and life were significantly influenced by the spiritual journey of her father, a Russian Hasidic Jew who later became an Anglican priest. In 1947 Levertov married an American, and in 1955 she became a naturalized citizen. Her career included teaching at several prestigious universities as well as writing poetry that captured contemporary concerns about war, politics, and religion.

Politics Throughout American history English immigrants and their descendants have been prominent in every level of government and every aspect of American political life. Eight of the first ten American presidents and the preponderance of all presidents, as well as the majority of legislators, judges, and other members of the national government, have English ancestors. The same can be said of business, entertainment, and the arts—in fact, until the twenty-first century, the acronym WASP (White Anglo-Saxon Protestant) was used to describe the dominant political and cultural class in the United States. That dominance is rapidly changing, however, as ethnic diversity increases.

Stage and Screen Perhaps the best-known English American of the twentieth century, screen actor Cary Grant (1904–1986) became an icon of sophistication. Born Archibald Alexander Leach in Bristol, England, Grant joined a traveling theatrical troupe while still in his teens and decided to stay in the United States when the troupe returned to England. He became a naturalized citizen in 1942. Grant's urbane charm was showcased in such classic comedies as *Bringing Up Baby* (1938) and *The Philadelphia Story* (1940) and in romantic thrillers including *North by Northwest* (1959) and *Charade* (1963). During his long career Grant was paired onscreen with such famous actresses as Katharine Hepburn, Ingrid Bergman, Grace Kelly, and Audrey Hepburn. Grant is still viewed as the quintessential "leading man." Other notable English-born American entertainers include film star Elizabeth Taylor (1932–2011) and iconic stage and film comedian Bob Hope (1903–2003).

MEDIA

PRINT

Britain

A bimonthly magazine published by the British Tourist Authority that includes an abundance of pictures and special features on tourist attractions, festivals, and historical and architectural monuments. The publication is widely read in the United States, Canada, South Africa, and Australia.

Email: editor@britain-magazine.co.uk
URL: www.britain-magazine.com/

Guardian Weekly

The North American edition of the *Guardian* summarizes the news of the week in England and contains a variety of features, book reviews, international news articles, advertisements aimed at expatriates, and selections extracted from the Parisian *Le Monde* and the *Washington Post*. It has the largest circulation of any English newspaper in the United States.

19 West 44th Street
Suite 1613
New York, New York 10036
Phone: (212) 944-1179
URL: www.guardiannews.com

Journal of British Studies (JBS)

The official publication of the North American Conference on British Studies, *JBS* features book reviews and academic articles on British politics, society, economics, law, and the arts.

Brian Cowan, Editor
Elizabeth Elbourne, Editor
McGill University
Department of History
855 Sherbrooke West
Montreal, Quebec H3A 2T7
Canada
Email: jbs.history@mcgill.ca
URL: www.nacbs.org/index.php/journal-original/

Union Jack

This monthly newspaper brings news of Britain to the British community in the United States.

Ronald Choularton, Editor
P.O. Box 1823
La Mesa, California 91944
Phone: (619) 466-3129 or (800) 262-7305
URL: www.ujnews.com

RADIO AND TELEVISION

British Broadcasting Corporation (BBC)

The BBC publishes *London Calling*, a program guide for several shortwave radio programs that it broadcasts in the United States and other countries. The BBC also distributes some of its television series, such as *The East-Enders*, *Mystery Theatre*, and *Are You Being Served*, which are featured on the American Public Broadcasting System.

630 Fifth Avenue
New York, New York 10017
Phone: (212) 507-1500 or (212) 507-0033
URL: www.bbcamerica.com/

ORGANIZATIONS AND ASSOCIATIONS

Daughters of the British Empire in the United States of America National Society (DBE)

Founded during World War I, this charitable society maintains facilities for older British men and women.

URL: http://dbenational.org/

English-Speaking Union of the United States

Founded in 1920 to promote British-American friendship and understanding, the organization sponsors debates, lectures, and speakers. It provides scholarships and travel grants and has more than seventy branches throughout the United States. It publishes a quarterly newsletter.

144 East 39th Street
New York, New York 1001
Phone: (212) 818-1200
Fax: (212) 867-4177
Email: info@esuus.org
URL: www.esuus.org/esu/

International Society for British Genealogy and Family History (ISBGFH)

This group strives to foster interest in the genealogy and family history of persons of British descent, improve U.S.-British relations, increase the educational opportunities and knowledge of members and the public, and encourage preservation of historical records and access to these records.

P.O. Box 350459
Westminster, Colorado 80035
Email: president@isbgfh.org
URL: http://isbgfh.org/

North American Conference on British Studies

Founded in 1951, the national academic group promotes scholarly research and the discussion of British history and culture. It has seven regional branches, publishes the *Journal of British Studies*, and awards several prizes for the best new works in British studies.

Marjorie Levine Clark, Secretary
Email: marjorie.levine-clark@ucdenver.edu
URL: www.nacbs.org

St. George's Society of New York

Founded in 1770, the charitable organization limits membership to British citizens, their descendants, and members of Commonwealth nations. It provides assistance to needy British expatriates in the New York area.

John Shannon, Executive Director
216 East 45th Street
Suite 901
New York, New York 10017
Phone: (212) 682-6110
Fax: (212) 682-3465
Email: info@stgeorgessociety.org
URL: http://stgeorgessociety.org/

MUSEUMS AND RESEARCH CENTERS

Center for British and Irish Studies

An interdisciplinary unit of the University of Colorado at Boulder operating under its own board of directors, the center concentrates on British history, literature, and art. Research collections in the university's libraries include microfilmed sets of original manuscripts and early books and journals from the medieval, early modern, and modern periods.

Jeremy Smith, Executive Director
301 UCB
Boulder, Colorado 80309-0226
Phone: (303) 492-2723
Fax: (303) 492-1881
Email: jeremy.smith@colorado.edu
URL: www.colorado.edu/artssciences/british

Yale Center for British Art

Founded in 1968, the center is part of Yale University. It includes the Paul Mellon collection of British art and rare books, and it features a gallery, lecture and seminar rooms, and a library of more than 100,000 volumes. Affiliated with the undergraduate and graduate programs at the university, the center provides scholarships for research projects.

1080 Chapel Street
New Haven, Connecticut 06520
Phone: (877) BRIT ART or (203) 432-2800
Email: ycba.info@yale.edu
URL: http://britishart.yale.edu/

SOURCES FOR ADDITIONAL STUDY

Berthoff, Roland T. *British Immigrants in Industrial America, 1790-1950*. New York: Russell and Russell, 1968.

Bridenbaugh, Carl. *Vexed and Troubled Englishmen, 1590-1642*. London: Oxford University Press, 1976.

Bueltmann, Tanja, David T. Gleeson, and Donald M. MacRaild. *Locating the English Diaspora, 1500-2010*. Liverpool: Liverpool University Press, 2012.

Cohen, Robin. *Frontiers of Identity: The British and the Others*. London: Longmans, 1994.

Erickson, Charlotte. *Invisible Immigrants: The Adaptation of English and Scottish Immigrants in Nineteenth-Century America*. Coral Gables, FL: University of Miami Press, 1972.

Furer, Howard B., ed. *The British in America: 1578-1970*. Dobbs Ferry, NY: Oceana Publications, 1972.

Noble, Allen G., ed. *To Build a New Land: Ethnic Landscapes in North America*. Baltimore: Johns Hopkins University Press, 1992.

Tennenhouse, Leonard. *The Importance of Feeling English: American Literature and the British Diaspora, 1750-1850*. Princeton: Princeton University Press, 2007.

ERITREAN AMERICANS

Lolly Ockerstrom

OVERVIEW

Eritrean Americans are immigrants or descendants of people from Eritrea, a country that spans 670 miles of coastline along the Red Sea on the northeast Horn of Africa. Eritrea is bordered by Sudan to the north and west, and by Ethiopia to the south. The tiny country of Djibouti is located to Eritrea's southeast. A land of dramatically changing terrain, Eritrea comprises six Administrative Zones covering mountainous highlands and arid lowlands. Its land area totals more than 48,000 square miles, making it slightly larger than the state of Pennsylvania.

According to a July 2012 estimate by the *CIA World Factbook*, about 6 million people live in Eritrea. Equally divided between Christian and Muslim religions, Eritreans live a mostly agrarian life. Eritrea, independent since 1993, is a country with a struggling economy. As of 2010, 80 percent of the population was rural, with 50 percent working as farmers.

Eritreans began immigrating to the United States during the 1970s and 1980s in response to Eritrea's thirty-year war for independence from Ethiopia. Many of these immigrants, especially those who were older, lacked education and had a poor command of the English language. As a result, they sought out Eritrean communities, forming a large conclave in Washington, D.C., and not assimilating much to the wider American culture. In the early twenty-first century, younger immigrants with more education began arriving in the United States and worked hard to bridge their African culture with their new American home.

The 2010 U.S. Census estimated that there were roughly 30,000 Eritrean-born immigrants living in the United States; the Eritrean American population would only fill half the Mercedes-Benz Superdome in New Orleans. Washington, D.C., had the largest Eritrean community, though Columbus, Ohio; Atlanta, Georgia; Dallas, Texas; and Los Angeles and San Diego, California, also had significant Eritrean American communities.

HISTORY OF THE PEOPLE

Early History For centuries, peoples of diverse religions, traditions, and ways of life inhabited the area now known as Eritrea. The earliest reference to the name *Eritrea*, which is derived from the Greek word for "red," is found in *Fragment 67* of Aeschylus: "There the sacred waters of the Erythrean Sea break upon a bright red strand …"

Eritrea's history reaches back to about 4000 BCE, when people from the Nile Valley migrated to the Mereb-Setit lowlands. They are thought to be the first food-producing peoples in Eritrea. For several thousand years thereafter, migrations of Nilotic-, Cushitic-, and Semitic-speaking people entered Eritrea and were among the first in Africa to grow crops and domesticate livestock.

In the fourth century CE, Eritrea became part of the Ethiopian kingdom of Axum, though it remained a semi-independent state. Other powerful kingdoms were established in parts of Eritrea, but none controlled the entire area. Some of these kingdoms included that of the Ptolemic Egyptians of the third century BCE; the seven Beja kingdoms of the eighth to thirteenth centuries; and the Bellou kingdom of the thirteenth to sixteenth centuries. In the sixteenth century, the Ottoman Empire annexed Eritrea.

Modern Era The modern state of Eritrea was created by the decree of King Umberto I of Italy on January 1, 1890, at the height of European colonial expansion. An Italian priest, Father Guiseppe Sapeto, established a mission at Adua in 1840, and he later established one at Keren. In 1882, the Italian government purchased all the land near Assab, acquired earlier by a shipping company with the help of Father Sapeto. In 1889, the government also purchased land from the Sultan of Rahaita.

From 1890 to 1941, Italian plantation growers and industrialists settled in Eritrea. The Italian government established administrative oversight in Eritrea, creating transport services and a communications network. During World War II, Italian forces were defeated throughout Africa, and the British established a protectorate in Eritrea. It became a strategic regional center for the British and Americans during the war. In 1950, a United Nations resolution placed Eritrea under the Ethiopian federation. The resolution went into effect in 1952 despite Eritreans' desire for independence, although Eritrea retained limited democratic autonomy.

In 1961 Ethiopian emperor Haile Selassie annexed Eritrea using military force, ending Eritrean resistance to Ethiopian rule. Selassie was assassinated in 1974, and a ruling unit called the Derg took control in Ethiopia. The Derg received large amounts of military aid from the Soviet Union, and in 1978 it forced Eritrean troops to withdraw from cities they had controlled.

Between 1978 and 1990, border disputes between Eritrea and Ethiopia erupted in violent military struggle. By 1991, the Eritrean People's Liberation Front succeeded in establishing the Provisional Government of Eritrea. At the same time, an Ethiopian resistance group overthrew the Derg, and a transitional government was established in Ethiopia.

In April 1993, 99.8 percent of voting Eritreans passed a referendum for independence in an internationally monitored election. Independence was declared on May 24, 1993. The National Assembly was reorganized, and a four-year plan for drafting a democratic constitution was put into place.

When Eritrea's first constitution was ratified on May 23, 1997, a seventy-five-member legislative body was established. A repatriation program for 25,000 Eritrean refugees living in the Sudan also began. However, border disputes between Eritrea and Ethiopia continued to escalate during 1998 and 1999. In a statement to the United Nations Security Council in New York in March 1999, Eritrean Foreign Minister Haile Woldensae expressed Eritrea's willingness to abide by cease-fire proposals put forth by the United Nations and the Organization of African Unity. However, Ethiopia was reluctant to accept the terms of any cease-fire and skirmishes continued in the disputed border regions. In 2000, Eritrea and Ethiopia signed the Algiers Peace Agreement. As a result, in April 2002, the Eritrea-Ethiopia Boundary Commission (EEBC) attempted to maintain peace by issuing a border ruling awarding Badme to Eritrea. Ethiopia, however, disagreed with the terms presented, and Badme remains a source of conflict. As recently as 2010, tension remained between Eritrean and Ethiopian armies at the border.

In the twenty-first century, Eritrea found itself in more border conflicts. In 2008 Djibouti and Eritrea fought over the Ras Doumeira region on the Red Sea Coast, a conflict that dated to the 1930s, when Italy gave land to Eritrea. Following a violent standoff in June 2008, the United Nations intervened, demanding both nations withdraw their troops. The two countries agreed to refer to Qatar for mediation.

Following its thirty-year war with Ethiopia, Eritrea spent much of the 1990s rebuilding the country. The transportation infrastructure had all but collapsed, food was scarce as a result of drought and war, and Eritrea's industrial base was shattered. The economic system was also in ruins. By the time Eritrea gained independence in 1993, it was estimated that 75 percent of Eritreans depended on food aid for daily survival. Many Eritreans were forced to leave not only their homeland but also the African continent, relocating to the Arabian Peninsula and the United States.

SETTLEMENT IN THE UNITED STATES

Ethiopia annexed Eritrea in November 1962, and a resistance movement soon emerged. The militant Eritrean People's Liberation Front was supported by the great majority of Eritreans, who were willing to engage in combat for their country. Significant Eritrean immigration to the United States did not take place until the 1970s and 1980s, when drought and famine drained the resources of a country already devastated by war. Between one-fourth and one-third of Eritrea's population was forced to leave Eritrea; more than 750,000 left as refugees. Two-thirds of the refugees settled in neighboring Sudan, although many came to the United States. Metropolitan Washington, D.C., hosted the largest Eritrean community outside of Eritrea, but sizable communities also formed in Columbus, Ohio; Atlanta; Dallas; Los Angeles; and San Diego.

Eritrean family ties are very strong. Eritreans forced to leave their country seek out other family members and members of the larger Eritrean community. Although this is a common pattern among many immigrant groups, Eritreans feel a particularly close bond and move to areas where other Eritreans live. They are deeply loyal to their country and are always conscious of Eritrea's continued struggle for sovereignty. Most Eritreans living in the United States in the late 1990s expressed a desire to return to their homeland, and the majority of Eritreans identified themselves as displaced people.

As Eritrea struggles to maintain peaceful borders and to quiet civil unrest with its fledgling government in the twenty-first century, many Eritreans are still immigrating to the United States, and many current immigrants are choosing to stay due to their homeland's uncertain future.

LANGUAGE

The working languages of the Eritrean government are Tigrinya, Arabic, and English. Many older Eritreans speak some Italian. The government does not claim an official language. Generally, Tigrinya is common in the highlands, whereas Arabic is most often heard in the lowlands. According to the 2009 *Ethnologue: Languages of the World*, twelve distinct languages are known to exist in Eritrea, though most Eritreans claim only nine. Indigenous languages include Afar, Bedawiyet, Bilen, Kunama, Nara, Saho, and Tigré.

According to estimates provided by the *Ethnologue* online edition, the Tigrinya is spoken by about 2,540,000 people in Eritrea, out of a total of 5,790,000 speakers worldwide. Roughly half the people of Eritrea know or can speak Tigrinya. It has its own script of more than 200 characters, based on the ancient language Geez, and is used only in the Eritrean

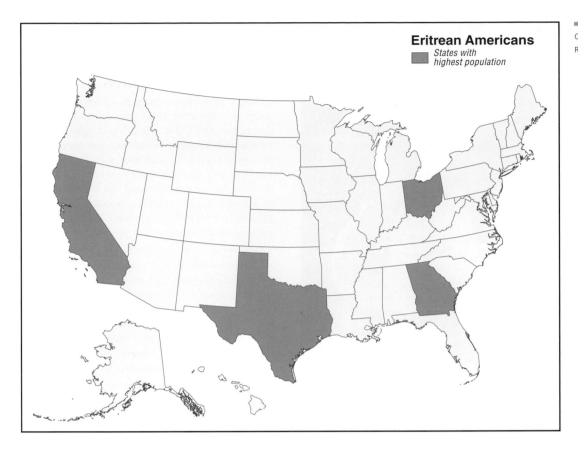

Eritrean Americans
States with highest population

Orthodox Church (also known as the Ethiopian Orthodox church). Each character represents a different sound. It is more of an oral than a written language, and is very difficult to learn.

Although there is no text offering phonetic instruction of Tigrinya, a few general characteristics can be observed. The sound of the letter *r* is always slightly rolled; the hard *k* is sounded in the back of the throat; and the *t* sound is pronounced with the tip of the tongue. Several other sounds originate in the back of the throat, often as a voiceless click rather than a voiced fricative. This includes the hard *g* and hard *h* sounds.

Eritrean American immigrants typically speak their native language when they are at home or within their close-knit Eritrean communities. There is a push within the community, however, for more Eritrean immigrants to learn English to further their educational and job prospects.

Greetings and Popular Expressions Typical greetings in Tigrinya, spelled phonetically include the following:

Selam—hello; *selamat* or *dehaan waal*—goodbye; *yekanyelay*—thank you; *uwauway*—yes; and *noaykonen*—no. Questions have different endings depending on whether you are addressing a single male, a single female, or several persons. For example, the greeting "How are you?" has several variants: *Kemayla-ha* (Kemey aleka)—male; *kemayla-hee* (kemey aleki)—female; *kemayla-hoom* (kemey alekum)—male or mixed plural; and *kemayla-hen* (kemey alekin)—female plural. The same is true when asking, "What is your name?": *Men shem-ka* (male); *Men shem-kee* (female); *Men shem-koom* (male or mixed plural); *Men shem ken* (female plural). Other phrases are: *Ayeteredanen*—I don't understand; *Shegur yelen* (shegr yelen)—no problem; and *Dehaan*—okay.

The most common exchange among Eritreans speaking Tigrinya is *selam*—hello; *keyayla-ha* (kemey aleka)—how are you?; *tsebuk*—I'm fine. In Arabic-speaking regions, the most common greeting is *keff*—hello.

RELIGION

Religion among Eritreans is equally divided between Christians, who live mostly in the highlands, and Muslims, who reside primarily in the lowlands. Large numbers of lowland Muslim groups were displaced during the 1970s and 1980s due to war and famine. This resulted in a greater number of Christian groups in Eritrea, at least temporarily. Among Christians, most follow the Eritrean Orthodox Church, though a significant number of the population adhere to Roman Catholicism. Less than 5 percent of the population are animists; this includes such ethnic groups as the Kunama.

Babies born to Eritrean Orthodox Christian families are christened at a ceremony performed by a priest,

where the Eritrean Orthodox Church is not available. Eritrean Muslims attend mosques with a variety of ethnic affiliations.

CULTURE AND ASSIMILATION

Through education, younger Eritreans tend to assimilate more easily than their older counterparts. Throughout the 1990s, the lack of English-language skills among Eritrean immigrants continued to prevent many from fully participating in American culture. This was especially true for Eritrean women. In 1999 the literacy rate in Eritrea was 20 percent overall, but just 10 percent among women. However, by 2010 the overall literacy rate was 67.8 percent, with women's literacy rising to 57.5 percent.

Many Eritrean immigrants settled where they could interact only in their native languages if they so chose. The strong sense of national identity felt among Eritreans, along with the fear of losing their culture, also contributed to the slow pace of acculturation. As families resettled in their new country and new generations were born in the United States, the young more successfully balanced the cultures of their past with the customs of their adopted country.

Traditions and Customs With nine distinct cultural identities, Eritrea is a country rich in traditions and religious beliefs. The major cultural group in Eritrea is the Tigrinya. The eight other ethnic groups are the Tigre, Nara, Afar, Bilen, Hedareb, Kunama, Rashaida, and Saho. Each group speaks its own language and observes its own customs.

About half the population is Muslim, and half is Christian. It is not uncommon to see older Eritreans with a tattoo of a cross on their forehead, identifying them as Christians. Dress can also denote religion. Muslim women wear scarves covering their entire heads, whereas Christian women wrap scarves about their heads for a distinctive headdress. Immigrants to the United States, particularly the older generation, will preserve this tradition, choosing to wear the headdress on holidays and other religious celebrations.

Eritreans follow both the Orthodox and the Roman calendars, though most businesses, as well as the younger generation, exclusively prefer the Roman. The older generation, which tends to be more religious, still follows the Orthodox Church calendar, which differs significantly from the Roman, with thirteen months rather than twelve. Twelve of the thirteen months have thirty days each; the thirteenth month has five days, or six in a leap year.

Cuisine Eritreans generally like spicy foods and are fond of bread. Two particular types of breads are staples in Eritrean diets. *Kitcha* is a thin pancake-type bread made from wheat. It is baked and unleavened. *Injera* is another type of pancake, more spongy and made from teff, wheat, or sorghum. It is fried on top of a special stove called a *mogogo*, which measures about 30 inches in diameter. Traditional *mogogo*s were fueled by wood

An Eritrean refugee takes part in a fashion show at the Refugee Youth Summer Academy on August 8, 2013, in New York City. The program aims to help young refugees acclimate to life in the United States and is sponsored by the International Rescue Committee. JOHN MOORE / GETTY IMAGES

which is attended by family and friends. Godparents are chosen for the baby, gifts are given, and generally the baby's parents offer a meal to those who attend the christening. Female babies are baptized eighty days after birth; boys are christened after forty days. Following the christening, the priest ties four strands of red and white thread around the infant's neck to signify that he or she has had a Christian baptism. The baby is then dressed in new clothes to begin his or her new life as a Christian. Eritrean Americans maintain their religious activities, including building churches specifically for the Eritrean community.

The Eritrean Orthodox Church (Tewahdo) North American Diocese is in Atlanta, and churches are being built all over the United States in large cities with significant Eritrean communities. Eritrean Americans also attend Greek Orthodox, Roman Catholic, and Lutheran churches in areas fires, though modern ones are electric. The dough is made from grains that are ground into a watery mixture and allowed to ferment for several days. Women usually cook enough bread to last from three days to one week. *Injera* is eaten with a stew, or *zigini*, in large pots set in the middle of a table. Family and friends gather at the table and eat out of the same plate, using pieces of bread to scoop up the stew. Another popular food is a bread into which whole eggs and large pieces of chicken are baked. Lamb, goat, and beef are also eaten frequently, as are lentils. A fava bean puree called *fool* is eaten at breakfast, as is a large cakelike bread called *basha (Himbasha)*. A legacy of Italian colonial days is the frittata, made by scrambling eggs with onion and peppers.

Eritrean cuisine is similar to Ethiopian food, and Eritrean Americans keep their traditions alive through the sharing of recipes and food from their homeland. Food is eaten communally with fingers. Those who share the meal often offer each other pieces of bread, putting it directly in the mouth of another. Meals tend to be noisy, joyous affairs, and no one is turned away.

The national drink is *suwa*, a bitter alcoholic beverage made of fermented barley. It is usually drunk from a special cup called a *wancha*. For holidays and important celebrations, a sweet honey wine, *mez*, is served. Eritrean Americans make these drinks at home using traditional techniques. The drink is considered a staple for everyday meals.

In Eritrea, coffee remains a delicacy outside the major cities. An invitation to drink coffee is a special occasion, and the guest is expected to spend at least an hour waiting for the coffee to be prepared. The coffee, presented in an elaborate ceremony, is often accompanied by burning incense. The common practice is to drink three cups. The experience of drinking coffee is surrounded by a great deal of ritual, which is communal in nature, and is as important as the coffee itself. This coffee-drinking tradition has not changed much as immigrants came over to the United States and remains an important part of Eritrean American culture.

Eritrean Americans have kept their traditional cuisine alive by opening Eritrean restaurants in cities with large Eritrean American communities. These restaurants feature the popular spices and dishes from Eritrea, as well as common Eritrean practices such as eating with the hands.

Traditional Dress Prior to Italian colonization, Eritrean costumes were very simple. Among the Tigrinya, leather kilts were widely worn by both genders. Some, including young girls, wore loincloths, which were baggy calico pants made of cotton that came just to the knee and were worn with loose cotton shirts. Tigrinya women wrapped themselves in *netsela*s, or cotton shawls embroidered at the edges. Sometimes more elaborate, multilayered shawls called *gabi* were worn.

As Italian influence spread, clothing began to change, particularly in villages and towns. Footwear, for example, was uncommon among the Tigrinya until the Italians arrived. Roughly made thonged sandals were worn only in lowland areas where the terrain was rocky. The Italians introduced rubber soles, and slowly shoes replaced traditional bare feet.

Traditional Tigrinya attire differed according to age and sex. Women were expected to cover their heads with *netsela*s, although young girls were not. Women wore long *jellebya*s, or gowns with long sleeves, which covered them almost completely. Young girls wore a short-sleeved *jellebya* reaching only to the knee. Men and boys wore long, tight-fitting cotton shirts slit at the sides that came to the knee. During periods of mourning, women wore black or black-spotted clothing; men in towns wore black ties or hats, similar to those worn in Ethiopia.

Among Tigrignya women, gold jewelry was worn, particularly on holidays or for special occasions. The more important the occasion, the more gold was worn. In earlier times, earrings, bracelets, necklaces, rings, and armbands were made of silver or wood, though gold is traditionally the metal of wealth and security.

Today, the colorful *jellbya* is considered the traditional dress of Eritrea, and it still seen worn by many women. Women choose to cover their heads based on religious beliefs; for example, some Muslims will cover their heads, particularly Arab Muslims, but not all will. Most people, particularly in the cities, will dress in Western clothing.

> I have come to like American food, but it took time, because the spices and texture of Ethiopian food are very different. After living here for two years, we have shifted our expectations and feel more comfortable being a part of this society.
>
> Citing Tesfai Gebrema in *New Americans: An Oral History: Immigrants and Refugees in the U.S. Today*, Al Santoli (New York: Viking Penguin, Inc., 1988).

Eritrean Americans typically dress similarly to their American counterparts, though they do dress in traditional attire for special occasions, particularly at community events.

Dances and Songs Music plays an integral part of daily life in Eritrea. Festivals are usually religious in nature and are always accompanied by singing and chanting. Families and community groups express their cultural and ethnic experiences through songs. Following religious ceremonies that last all night where religious songs are sung for hours, many Tigrinya continue their celebrations at home, eating, singing, and dancing. Drums called *koboro* are often used in nonreligious festivities. Women frequently

ERITREAN PROVERBS

Eritrean proverbs provide insight into Eritreans' worldview. Two typical proverbs of the Tigrinya people stress the importance of patience. One proclaims: "*Zurugay sava luchae yo-u-se*," or, "If you are patient, you'll get butter." Turning milk into butter takes a long time when churning, but the required patience and hard work are rewarded. A Tigrinya parent might say to a child, "*Kwakolo kus bekus bougru yehahid*," which means, "Little by little an egg will walk." The reference is to the process by which an egg is hatched and a chick emerges, gradually growing into an adult. The message is that a goal will be reached by working at it day by day.

Another common Tigrinya proverb has to do with possession and envy. "*Adgi zeybulu bakeali yenekeah*" can be roughly translated as, "You don't have a donkey, but you sneer at my horse." This means that those with nothing should not negatively comment on the possessions of others.

ululate, or make high-pitched trilling sounds with their tongues, to signify joy.

Drums used in Eritrean Orthodox Church festivals are called *negarit*. They are made of hollowed-out tree trunks with cows' skin stretched on either end and tied with rawhide strips; the tree trunks are of the *oule-eh*, a tree indigenous to Eritrea. *Koboro* used as an accompaniment for general, nonreligious singing are also made of cows' skin, though the skins are stretched over a metal cylinder.

The national song of Eritrea pays homage to the Eritrean struggle for independence. Roughly translated, the first lines evoke Eritrean strength: "Eritrea, Eritrea, Eritrea / Her arch-enemy destroyed wailingly / her sacrifices vindicated by freedom." Other songs are usually celebratory in nature and are sung on special occasions such as weddings, holidays, and religious festivals.

Hymns of praise to God are frequently sung. Singing is usually accompanied by clapping hands and the beating of the *koboro* while celebrants dance together in a circle. Everyone joins in the *guaila*, or circle dance, which often occurs spontaneously when a joyous event occurs. Dancing the *guaila* is a boisterous activity, which builds in momentum as the song rhythms increase in tempo and as the beating of the *koboro* grows faster. More and more family members and friends join in a large circle, which moves slowly around. Inside the circle are the drummers, sometimes two or three or more,

who jump up and down while beating the *koboro*. Singing and dancing is accompanied by a great deal of laughter and joking, and spirits remain high among the participants.

Church dancing, by contrast, occurs only in certain locations inside Orthodox churches, which have been designated for men. Women do not dance in church. Church dancing, which is referred to as either *zayma* or *mahalet*, consists of clapping hands and swaying back and forth while remaining in place. On special feast days, the men encircle the outside of the church building three times, but do not dance after they leave the building.

Tigrinya folk poetry, passed down through oral tradition, is usually sung from memory. Generally the poems are lamentations, in couplets. They may express grief over the loss of a loved one, disillusionment with life, longing for home, or the pain and sorrow of the poor. They are sung and accompanied by a guitarlike instrument called a *k'rar* or on a violinlike instrument called the *chira wata*. Both instruments are specific to Eritrea.

Holidays Eritrean American holidays reflect both Muslim and Christian traditions. The major Christian holidays include Christmas, on December 25; New Year's, January 1; Orthodox Christmas, January 7; and Timket, or the baptism of Christ, January 19. Women's Day is celebrated on March 8. Easter is known as Fasika. Meskel, or the Festival of the True Cross, is celebrated on moveable days in late September.

The dates of Muslim holidays, which follow the lunar calendar, change each year. Eid el-Fitr is a feast celebrated in the spring; another feast day is Eid el-Adha, which is summer's day. The Prophet's birthday, Eid Milad el-Nabi, is celebrated in autumn.

National holidays include Eritrean National Day, or Liberation Day, on May 24. Martyrs' Day is June 20. September 1 is celebrated as the Start of the Armed Struggle. January and February are popular months for weddings in Eritrea.

Eritrean Orthodox Church holidays are preceded by periods of fasting, sometimes as long as 40 days in observance of biblical example. When fasting, celebrants abstain from eating meat and certain dairy products. On the day of the holiday, Orthodox Eritreans attend an all-night church service that begins at sundown. Eritrean Orthodox Churches do not have pews or chairs; most churchgoers stand for the entire period unless they are elderly or sick. Many hold long staffs, which they can lean upon when tired. They sometimes pass them around during the service so another person can take a turn leaning on the staff.

Most traditional Christian singing, chanting, and praying takes place under the leadership of priests dressed in special black clothing and colorful vestments. Incense burners are lit. Men generally occupy one side of the church; women, usually dressed in traditional shawls and tunics, occupy another side. They remain on separate sides of the church throughout services, which sometimes last for hours. Children remain with the women.

The conclusion of the ceremony includes a procession in which church members go outside the building and encircle the church three times chanting and singing. Several traditional Eritrean drums and bell-like instruments accompany them. Finally, families return to their homes to eat. Women have spent days preparing for the feast, which includes breads, stews, and traditional *suwa*. The meal takes several hours, during which songs are sung and stories are told. Following the meal is more singing, dancing, and drum beating.

In the United States, the Eritrean Orthodox Church tries to maintain its traditions for its followers. Fasting is still an important ritual, as is the use of incense during worship services, especially during times of prayer. The church considers itself patriarchal and does not allow women to serve as priests or elders. The church services in the United States consider themselves part of the Coptic Church tradition and still practice separation of men and women during church services.

FAMILY AND COMMUNITY LIFE

Eritrean Americans celebrate major events with members of their community. Birthdays, marriages, graduations, and other events are commemorated with great fanfare. Traditional foods, songs, and music always play a major role. Many members of the community are included.

Lengthy, elaborate greetings are very important, especially on special occasions. Women greet each other by ululating, or making a high-pitched sound by trilling the tongue. They kiss each other on each cheek three times. It is customary to ask how the person is and also to inquire about one's spouse, children, and other family members. The happier one is to see a friend and the more important the occasion, the longer the list. Each greeting is accompanied by a great deal of genuine laughter and joyousness.

Care is taken to make guests feel welcome and included in all phases of the celebration. In the United States, Eritreans retain their cultural ways of celebrating life's milestones and are pleased when non-Eritreans show an interest in their customs.

Gender Roles Eritrean culture is patriarchal. As such, women in Eritrea generally experience less privilege, status, and economic security than men. Through efforts of groups such as the National Union of Eritrean Women this is changing, and women are enjoying the same educational and economic privileges as men.

In the United States, many Eritrean American women found opportunities to pursue higher education and careers outside the home. Even so, the Eritrean American community continued to be dominated by men, particularly in the community's efforts to reach out to the greater American cultural landscape. Although women enjoyed more freedom, maintaining the traditional gender roles within the family was still a number-one priority for many Eritrean Americans.

Eritrean Americans keep their traditions alive through the sharing of recipes and food from their homeland. Food is eaten communally with fingers. Those who share the meal often offer each other pieces of bread, putting it directly in the mouth of another.

Education In 2010 the overall literacy rate in Eritrea was nearly 70 percent; nearly 79 percent of males and 57 percent of females were literate. Children learn English beginning in the second grade, and classes are taught in English beginning in the sixth grade. After independence, more children attended school than ever before, but continued war and drought drastically impeded educational process. Prior to the defeat of the Italians by the British in 1941, the country had been administered by colonial rule, which barred Eritreans from occupying civil service positions. During the 1920s and 1930s, only twenty-four primary schools existed in Eritrea, and there were no secondary schools.

Following British rule, the first teacher training institution was established in 1943, and Eritreans were allowed to train for the civil service. Although some progress occurred after the British founded educational institutions in Eritrea, the country was subsequently beset by high unemployment. Military projects were closed down, and the workforce shrank from 30,000 in 1947 to barely more than 10,000 in 1962. During that time, little attention was given to education. After war broke out, the country remained in a state of emergency. Food, water, and medical attention preempted money that might have been used for building schools and supporting education.

Older Eritrean immigrants to the United States struggled with the English language and found that lack of education hindered their job prospects. As a result, education is a high priority among the younger generation of Eritrean Americans. These young men and women not only speak English well, but they also highly prize education. College education is encouraged by Eritrean American families and communities alike, and some Eritrean Americans have found a place in Ivy League schools.

Courtship and Weddings Marriage customs differ among Eritrea's nine ethnic groups and closely follow either Muslim or Christian traditions. Among the Tigre ethnic group, marriage is intimately connected to the financial and social well-being of families. Marriages may be arranged, even before birth, among affluent families strictly for the purpose of

Two immigrants from Eritrea attend classes at the Red Cross Center to get certification to be a home health aid and nurse assistant, on January 17, 2013 in Cambridge, Massachusetts. CHRISTIAN SCIENCE MONITOR / GETTY IMAGES

keeping wealth in the family or to strengthen the bond between the two families. For instance, if two families are experiencing a blood feud, they may settle their agreement through a marriage alliance. Also, if a poor man is able to marry off his daughter to a wealthy man to improve his family's financial circumstances, he will do so. Tigre parents have the final say in their children's marriage arrangements. Such agreements are preceded by many lengthy familial consultations, which include everyone's opinion except those who are to marry.

However, in many Tigre villages, practices are changing as a result of influences from both Catholic and Protestant churches. Ethnic border influences and geographical differences among Tigre communities have created variations in how marriages are arranged and conducted.

Among the Tigre, marriages between two closely related people may take place. This allows families to keep family wealth within a close circle. However, in some Tigrinya communities, people may not marry if they are blood-related within seven generations.

Nara families do not arrange marriages for their children. Both men and women can choose their own spouses. According to Tesfa G. Gebremedhin, in the book *Women, Tradition, and Development: A Case Study of Eritrea*, virginity among young brides has no value. Unmarried women who have previously given birth are in great demand, as they have already proved their ability to bear children.

Marriages in the United States are rarely arranged; however, Eritrean Americans tend to choose mates from within the Eritrean community. The younger generations are changing this notion a little, though. Weddings tend to follow religious traditions and are also a time to celebrate Eritrean culture with traditional food, dress, music, and dance.

Relations with Other Americans In the United States, Eritrean Americans remain fiercely loyal to their country. They have been able to put aside differences

with Ethiopians, however, and they sometimes socialize with each other, as they do with other immigrant Africans. Eritreans and Ethiopians share common cultural characteristics, which create a close bond. Eritrean Americans might have mixed feelings about Ethiopians being their closest cultural allies. As long as they avoid the topic of the war, the two groups are able to get along very well. In addition, many Eritreans had previously lived in Ethiopia or married Ethiopians.

EMPLOYMENT AND ECONOMIC CONDITIONS

Traditionally, Eritreans lived rural lifestyles as farmers or nomadic herdsmen and women. Farmers made up one-half of the population. Upon coming to the United States, Eritreans settled in urban communities, dramatically changing their way of life. Those who came to the United States had to develop new ways of earning a living. A number of Eritrean Americans became business owners, pharmacists, computer scientists, or entered other professions. Many Eritreans immigrants relied on their cultural traditions to start Eritrean restaurants.

During the 1990s, major efforts in Eritrea centered on rebuilding the country and repatriating refugees. Skilled carpenters, engineers, and city planners were in demand to help build roads, railways, ports, homes, and businesses. Equally important was the rebuilding of Eritrea's industries, which had either closed altogether or moved to Ethiopia during the war. Others tried to generate investment capital to restart dying industries.

The agricultural industry of Eritrea was particularly hard-hit during the war. Eighty percent of the population relied on agriculture for their livelihood at the end of the twentieth century. Drought and war almost wiped out agricultural businesses completely. The Eritrean government was determined to end dependency on other governments for food sources.

Many Eritreans who came to the United States as refugees first had to study English. Some went on to study engineering or business so they could to return to Eritrea and help in the rebuilding process. In 1987 the Eritrean government created the Commission for Eritrean Refugee Affairs (CERA) in response to the needs of Eritrean refugee communities. Although some refugees did return, many stayed in the country, finding employment in the service industries, working as janitors and public transportation workers. Many of these immigrants were uneducated, but Eritrean Americans have pursued education and have made sure the younger generation knows the importance of education. As a result, they now find a wide range of employment and often hold college and graduate degrees.

POLITICS AND GOVERNMENT

Most Eritrean immigrants were forced to leave their homeland, and many wished to return. Those who left Eritrea as adults, especially, maintained close contact with family members who remained behind. Because the border wars with Ethiopia continued after independence, Eritreans living in the United States followed political news closely well into the end of the twentieth century. First and second generations of Eritreans born in the United States also followed political developments closely, though with less urgency than older Eritreans. In the twenty-first century, Eritrean Americans have settled in the United States and do not necessarily consider themselves refugees who will one day return to Eritrea; however, they are still involved in the politics of Eritrea and often get involved in U.S. politics in order to help their home country. Groups such as the Organization of Eritrean-Americans (OEA) work to get immigrants together to campaign for U.S. and foreign diplomats to get involved in the political disputes of Eritrea.

NOTABLE INDIVIDUALS

Art Yegizaw "Yeggy" Michael (1968–), artist, was born in Ethiopia and grew up in Eritrea before immigrating to the United States in the 1990s. In 1997 he acted as director and organizer for an AIDS awareness campaign in his home country. His work has been displayed across the United States and included a mosaic for the Seattle Children's Art Museum.

Literature Selamawi "Mawi" Asgedom (1971–), public speaker and author, is of Ethiopian and Eritrean descent. From a family of refugees, Asgedom grew up in Chicago before studying history at Harvard University. His autobiography *Of Beetles and Angels* (2002) garnered much critical success, including attention from Oprah Winfrey.

Kassahun Checole (1947–) is the founder of Africa World Press and the Red Sea Press, two major publishers for books about Africa and issues surrounding the African American community. Born in Eritrea, Checole arrived in the United States in 1971 to pursue his educational goals at State University of New York at Binghamton. He joined the faculty at Rutgers University, though he later left academia to pursue publishing.

Bereket Habte Selassie is a scholar and writer focused on African government and law. Born in Eritrea, he has been a leading activist in Eritrean government and foreign policy. He has taught at the University of North Carolina, Howard University, and Georgetown University. In addition to his teachings, Selassie has published several books on Eritrea, including *Wounded Nation: How a Once Promising Eritrea was Betrayed and Its Future Compromised* (2010).

Music The EriAm Sisters are an Eritrean American pop and R&B musical group made up of three sisters, Haben Abraham, Salina Abraham, and Lianda Abraham, whose parents were from Eritrea. Their first success came with their appearance on the TV show *America's Got Talent* in 2009, where they were a top-ten finalist. They have toured across Europe, Africa, and the Middle East.

Sador "Sandman Ne" Fasehaye (1986–2012) was a rap singer, born in Bulgaria, but of Eritrean descent. Many of his lyrics reflected his childhood in South Los Angeles; he was also notable for mixing Tigrinya music with his English lyrics. In 2008 a gang-related shooting left him in a coma. He miraculously recovered only to be killed by a bullet in September 2012.

Nipsey Hussle (1985–) is a rapper of Eritrean descent. Based in Los Angeles, Hussle has worked with major recording artists such as Drake and Snoop Dogg. In 2007 he had a small part in Bone Thugs-N-Harmony's film *I Tried*.

Performance Luam Keflezgy was born in Eritrea before moving with her family to Seattle, Washington. At age seventeen, she left home to pursue dancing with African Rhythms Company at the University of Pennsylvania and Ballet Shango in Philadelphia. She then moved to New York and began a successful career as a choreographer, where she has worked on commercials for MTV and MasterCard and with such artists as Ludacris, Kanye West, Nelly Furtado, and Rihanna, among many others.

Sports Mebrahtom "Meb" Keflezighi (1975–) is an American athlete born in Eritrea. After immigrating to San Diego with his family at the age of twelve, Keflezighi began running in junior high school and high school. He won both the 1,600 meters and 3,200 meters in the CIF California State Championships in 1994. His career eventually took him to the 2004 summer Olympics, where he was awarded the silver medal in the men's marathon. In 2012 he finished fourth in the summer Olympics marathon.

Thomas Kelati (1982–) is a basketball player of Eritrean heritage. Kelati began his career in 2005 in the Belgian league. In 2012 he signed on with Valencia (Spain) Basket.

MEDIA

RADIO

WATB-AM (1420)

"Voices of Africa," a weekly radio program, is an Atlanta-area program broadcast Sundays between 3:00 p.m. and 10:00 p.m. and Saturdays from 2 p.m. to 9 p.m. Eritrea is one of the focuses of this program.

Benjamin F. Vannoy, Jr., General Manager
3589 North Decatur Road
Scottdale, Georgia 30079
Phone: (404) 292-1420
Fax: (404) 508-8930
Email: benv@mrbi.net
URL: www.watb1420.com

ORGANIZATIONS AND ASSOCIATIONS

Eritrean-American Community Association of Georgia

The EACGA is a nonprofit organization aimed at helping Eritrean immigrants assimilate and integrate into American culture and society. Its goal is to create a community for Eritrean Americans across the state of Georgia. Services offered include English conversation classes and job interview assistance.

3700 Market Street
Suite D-3
Clarkston, Georgia 30021
Phone: (877) 374-8732
Email: atleritrea@gmail.com
URL: www.atleritrea.com

The Eritrean Sports Federation in North America

The Eritrean Sports Federation in North America played a significant role in helping expatriate Eritreans maintain a strong sense of ethnic and national identity by founding an annual sports festival in 1986 in Atlanta.

Yosief Mebrahtu, President/Chairman
P.O. Box 1625
Lilburn, Georgia 30048-1625
Email: erfsna@gmail.com
URL: www.eritreansports.com

Organization of Eritrean-Americans

The organization's mission is to improve U.S.-Eritrea relations by providing information to the American public about Eritrea as well as encouraging Eritrean Americans to let their voice be heard in the American political realm.

URL: www.eritreanamerican.org

MUSEUMS AND RESEARCH CENTERS

African Studies Center, University of Pennsylvania

The African Studies Center aims to further the study of the culture and traditions of Africa, including Eritrea. The center offers Eritrean-specific resources including links to further research, an Eritrea fact sheet, and language courses in Tigrinya.

Dr. Ali B. Ali-Dinar, Associate Director
647 Williams Hall
255 S. 36th Street
Philadelphia, Pennsylvania 19104-6305
Phone: (215) 898-6971
Fax: (215) 573-7379
Email: aadinar@sas.upenn.edu
URL: www.africa.upenn.edu

SOURCES FOR ADDITIONAL STUDY

Doornbos, Martin et al, eds. *Beyond Conflict in the Horn: Prospects for Peace, Recovery, and Development in Ethiopia, Somalia, and the Sudan.* Lawrenceville, NJ: Red Sea Press, 1992.

Duffield, Mark, and John Prendergast. *Without Troops and Tanks: Humanitarian Intervention in Ethiopia and Eritrea.* Lawrenceville, NJ: Red Sea Press, 1994.

Grinker, Lori. "The Main Force: Women in Eritrea." *Ms. Magazine*, May/June 1992.

Hepner, Tricia Redeker. "Eritrean Immigrants." *Multicultural America: An Encyclopedia of the Newest Americans.* Ed. Ronald H. Bayor, 617–47. Santa Barbara, CA: Greenwood, 2001.

Moussa, Helena. *Storm and Sanctuary: The Journey of Ethiopian and Eritrean Women Refugees.* Dundas, Ontario: Artemis Enterprises, 1993.

Selassie, Bereket Habte. *Wounded Nation: How a Once Promising Eritrea Was Betrayed and Its Future Compromised.* Trenton, NJ: Red Sea Press, 2010.

Sorenson, John. "Discourses on Eritrean Nationalism and Identity." *Journal of Modern African Studies* 29, no. 2 (1991): 301–17.

Tesfagiorgis, Mussie G. *Eritrea (Africa in Focus).* Santa Barbara, CA: ABC-CLIO, 2011.

Wilson, Amrit. *The Challenge Road: Women and the Eritrean Revolution.* Lawrenceville NJ: Red Sea Press, 1991.

ESTONIAN AMERICANS

Mark A. Granquist

OVERVIEW

Estonian Americans are immigrants or descendants of people from what is today the Republic of Estonia, the northernmost of the three Baltic republics. Estonia is bordered on the north by the Gulf of Finland, on the east by Lake Peipus and Russia, on the south by Latvia, and on the west by the Baltic Sea, which contains some 1,500 islands that are part of the republic. The country measures 17,413 square miles (45,100 square kilometers), or slightly smaller than the central American nation of Costa Rica and slightly larger than the country of Denmark.

In 2011 the Estonian government census estimated the population of Estonia to be about 1,294,000. Approximately 72 percent is urban, with 400,000 living in or around the capital city of Tallinn. Lutherans constitute the largest religious group, with a significant number of other Protestant denominations (principally Baptist) represented, as well as a number of Eastern Orthodox Christians. In terms of ethnicity, 69 percent of the population is Estonian; 25 percent is Russian; and Ukrainians, Belarusians, and Finns each account for 1 to 2 percent. The official language is Estonian, with Russian also widely spoken. In 2004 Estonia became the seventeenth member of the European Union, and the country opted to adopt the euro as its currency in 2011. The World Bank considers Estonia a high-income economy, and the 2012 Index of Economic Freedom ranks it sixteenth in the world. Easily surpassing the economies of its two Baltic neighbors on the strength of its energy and machinery exports and booming financial sector, Estonia is sometimes referred to as the Baltic Tiger.

In the late nineteenth century a small number of Estonians entered the United States, forming small agricultural colonies in the Midwest; however, the two major waves of Estonian immigration occurred in the twentieth century. These two waves emigrated for differing political reasons: the first wave consisted of socialists that left Estonia following a failed Marxist revolution in 1905, while the second wave fled the country after World War II and the subsequent imposition of Soviet rule. By the early twenty-first century, few Estonians had entered the United States and few Estonian Americans had returned to their homeland.

According to the U.S. Census Bureau's American Community Survey estimates for 2009–2011, there were 29,381 Estonian Americans living in the United States. Estonian Americans easily accommodate mainstream U.S. culture. Most do not live in enclaves as such, but as a group they maintain an active network of cultural organizations, schools, and churches with which to preserve the language and culture of their homeland.

HISTORY OF THE PEOPLE

Early History The Estonians are a Baltic-Finnish group related to the Finno-Ugric peoples. Their first significant contact with an outside culture occurred during a series of battles with the Vikings in the ninth century. As their relationship became more peaceful, the Vikings and Estonians became trading partners, mutually influencing each other's culture. During the Middle Ages, Swedes, Danes, and Russians attempted to introduce elements of Christianity to the Estonians but failed to convert the population. In the thirteenth century Germans and Danes finally succeeded in imposing Christianity through military force. By 1346 the Teutonic Order, a German coterie of knights and priests, had purchased northern Estonia from Denmark and subjugated the native population. Centuries later, Germans dominated the Estonian Lutheran Church, monopolizing many aspects of Estonian national life. To many nineteenth-century Estonians, Lutheranism was felt as an oppressive foreign presence.

The Teutonic Order dissolved in 1561 and Sweden seized control. When Russia defeated Sweden in the Great Northern War in 1721, Estonia found itself under tsarist rule. Initially many Estonians viewed Russian rule as a means to free themselves from the German and Swedish domination, but under Russian governance they lost many of the traditional liberties that the Germans and Swedes had left in place. In 1819 serfdom ended and other social reforms followed, including permission in 1860 for Estonians to serve as pastors, however, the Russian government went on to enact a series of "Russification" policies in the 1880s, such as the banning of Estonian-language schools. Such actions initiated a grassroots patriotic movement that resulted in the ascendance of a new Estonian nationalism.

Modern Era In January 1905 Estonian revolutionary leaders demanded national autonomy from Moscow. The tsar's imperial forces crushed the rebellion, and many Estonian leaders fled abroad, and thousands of citizens followed. This proved to be a pivotal moment in Estonian history, resulting in the first serious emigration to the United States from the Estonian homeland. Twelve years after the Estonian rebellion, the Russian revolution brought down the imperial government, after which Estonia won autonomy and later independence. With help from Britain and Finland, Estonians fought for independence from Russia beginning in 1918 and ending in 1920, by which point Russian troops had been driven from Estonia and it became truly independent. Between the world wars the young state endured harassment from the Soviets while managing internal political and economic instability. In 1940 Soviet troops annexed Estonia with covert assistance from the Nazis, and Estonia became part of the Soviet Union. After war broke between Germany and the Soviet Union, Germany took control of Estonia in 1941. When Soviet troops reentered Estonia in 1944, roughly one-tenth of the Estonian populace fled the country, many to the United States. Estonia remained a Soviet republic until April 1990, when Estonia declared renewed independence and elected a national government. The Soviet Union came to an end in 1991, and Estonia was admitted to the United Nations that year.

After the collapse of Soviet rule in Estonia, the country entered a period of strong economic growth based on free market principles and trade with other European countries, particularly after Estonia joined the European Union in 2004. It enjoyed a robust economy and relative political calm, though relations with neighboring Russia remain unstable after negotiations over their shared border collapsed in 2005. The global financial crisis beginning in 2008 had a negative impact on the country's decade of financial growth, but emergency budget measures passed by parliament managed to reverse such damages and put Estonia back among the top-performing economies in Europe by 2010.

SETTLEMENT IN THE UNITED STATES

In the 1600s, when Estonia was under Swedish control, a small group of Estonians helped the Swedes establish a North American colony called New Sweden on the Delaware River. Other than that, Estonian immigration to the United States was quite limited until the late nineteenth century. The first Estonian immigrants to the United States were fortune hunters and sailors who jumped Russian sailing vessels in the 1880s and 1890s. Immigration records identified them as Russians rather than Estonians, a practice that continued until 1922. In 1894 one group settled near Fort Pierre, South Dakota, where the first Estonian Lutheran Church was founded in 1897. Others settled in New York and San Francisco, expanding their religious congregation as they went. The Estonian Lutheran Church became the first organization to support early Estonian immigrants, with Reverend

Hans Rebane, who arrived in the United States in 1896, publishing the first Estonian-language newspaper, *Eesti Amerika Postimees* (*Estonian American Courier*), in 1897.

The failed Marxist revolution in Estonia in 1905 resulted in the migration of Estonian socialists to the United States. Seeking jobs in labor and industry, a large majority of early Estonian immigrants settled in cities on the east and west coasts of the United States. A majority settled in New York City, while others moved to San Francisco and Oregon. Many Estonian men worked in the construction trades, and some rose to become independent contractors. Many women worked as domestics or in small retail or industrial operations. In the 1920s and 1930s, a number of Estonians worked as building attendants and superintendents in apartments and office buildings, especially in New York City. Other Estonians started small businesses, some of which were highly successful. However, communism created early conflicts within the Estonian American community. Many of the refugees from the failed 1905 revolution had become sympathizers, and they established a strong communist-oriented urban workers' movement within the community. Workers' societies formed in Estonian settlements, and in 1908 a central committee began to coordinate their activities. These organizations were often the only collective Estonian bodies in the community, and consequently they wielded influence. However, leaders of these organizations proved to be more radical than their American counterparts, as well as the majority of Estonian American workers. Between 1917 and 1920 the Estonian workers' movement split over the issue of whether to support the Soviet military takeover of the newly independent Republic of Estonia. Many of the movement's leaders adopted a communist platform that supported inclusion of Estonia within the Soviet Union, whereas the membership opposed the move. The split shattered the Estonian American workers' movement. The American Communist Party absorbed the Estonian communists soon after, dissipating their sense of ethnic identity. Prior to the split, the workers' movement had transformed many Estonian American institutions, causing turmoil within the community and friction with outside groups.

After 1945 a new wave of political refugees bolstered the economic status of the community. A strong emphasis on education and professionalism brought socioeconomic mobility to the Estonian American community, and most entered the middle class. The service of Estonian Americans during World War II, the Soviet annexation of Estonia, and the flood of refugees out of the country created a groundswell of American support, not only toward Estonia but toward its three Baltic neighbors, as well. (Estonian Americans are closely affiliated with immigrants from the Baltic countries of Latvia, Lithuania, and Finland. These groups share a common history in Europe and arrived in the United States at roughly

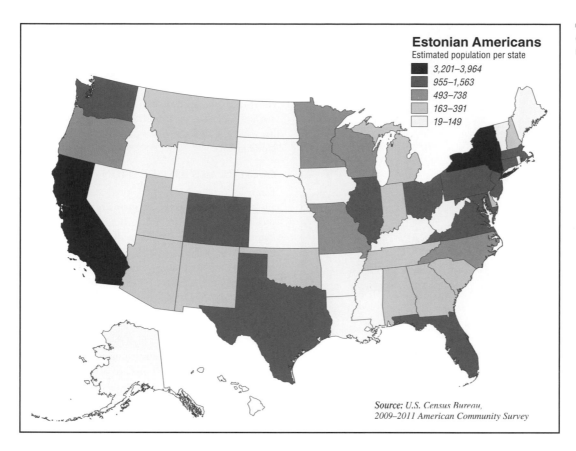

Estonian Americans
Estimated population per state

- 3,201–3,964
- 955–1,563
- 493–738
- 163–391
- 19–149

Source: U.S. Census Bureau,
2009–2011 American Community Survey

the same time.) Education, engineering, medicine, science, and the arts became professions of choice for Estonian immigrants, who were largely well-educated. In 1962 a study of young Estonian American professionals found that 43 percent worked in engineering and technology, 18 percent in the sciences, 16 percent in the humanities, 16 percent in the social sciences, and 7 percent in medicine. Others created small- to medium-sized businesses.

When Estonia gained its independence in 1991, there were an estimated 27,000 Estonians living in the United States. Many Estonian Americans saw Estonian independence as an opportunity to return to their home country, and about 2,000 Estonians left the United States throughout the 1990s.

LANGUAGE

The Estonian language is a branch of the Baltic-Finnish group of the Finno-Ugric family and is closely related to Finnish. Most ethnic Estonians speak Estonian, but ethnic Russians and others in Estonia continue to speak Russian with support of the Estonian government, which sponsors Russian-language schools and activities. Historically, a number of dialects have been spoken in Estonia, but the dialect spoken in the region around Tallinn, the capital, has come to dominate literary expression and thus influence the development of modern Estonian. Another form of Estonian, spoken by Estonian war refugees in Sweden, has unsurprisingly absorbed Swedish influences. The written language uses the Roman alphabet and consists of fourteen consonants and nine vowels (*a, ä, e, i, o, ö, õ, u,* and *ü*). The consonants *c, f, q, w, x, y,* and *z* are generally used only in names and words of foreign origin. The language has a musical quality and employs a number of diphthongs and other vowel combinations.

The Estonian American community has made strong attempts to maintain the language, but, as is often the case with such efforts, success has been mixed at best. A number of schools, publications, congregations, and learned societies within the community still use Estonian as a means of discourse. This is somewhat problematic within the larger community, as many non-Estonian spouses find Estonian difficult. Still, Estonian is taught at three midwestern universities (Indiana University, Kent State University, and Ohio State University), and a few U.S. public libraries have Estonian-language collections, including the Boston Public Library, New York Public Library, and Cleveland Public Library.

RELIGION

Estonia is predominantly Christian, with most Christians following the Lutheran tradition; Baptist and Orthodox faiths are also represented. In Estonian American communities, Lutheranism dominates as well. Headquartered in Stockholm, the Estonian

At the Estonian House, in New York, an Estonian American helps to stuff a blood sausage during a party. EVAN SUNG / REDUX

New York City in 1949. Estonian Orthodox parishes are active in Los Angeles, San Francisco, Chicago, and New York City.

Since 1945 religion has played a unifying role in maintaining a sense of group identity among Estonian Americans. Some Estonian Americans today, however, are ambivalent or even hostile toward religious belief because of its linkage with oppression in their homeland's history.

CULTURE AND ASSIMILATION

Estonian immigrants in the United States have generally assimilated well into the mainstream of American society, especially after 1945. Before World War II, Estonians in the United States did not push hard to become American citizens; in 1930 only 42 percent of immigrants had citizenship, placing them behind Finnish and other Baltic immigrants. By the late twentieth century, however, Estonian Americans had rapidly climbed the social and economic ladder, specializing in areas requiring technical expertise. A number of factors contributed to a high degree of assimilation among Estonian Americans: the size of the community, its rapid educational and social success, and the wide geographical dispersion of the immigrants.

Estonia quickly became an economic powerhouse after its independence in 1991, placing Estonian Americans in a positive light. The tensions inherent in acculturation were more visible in the lives of refugees who fled Estonia after World War II. Many created successful lives in the United States, but on the other hand, as with many political refugees from the Soviet system, they passionately supported the overthrow of communism in Estonia. Some maintained hope that they would someday return to their native land. This refugee status created internal tensions for some Estonian Americans as they balanced loyalty to their heritage with newfound patriotism toward the United States and a desire to assimilate into American society. Today, much of the Estonian American community is composed of these first- and second-generation immigrants. Their small numbers and similarities with their middle-class urban neighbors enable these Estonians to generate positive attention in the United States. Estonian immigrants, generally literate, skilled, and industrious, are considered an American success story.

Cuisine Estonian cooking blends culinary influences from Scandinavia, Germany, and Russia with native traditions. The raw ingredients come from the forests, farms, and coastal waters of Estonia: berries, pork, cabbage, sour cream, and seafood such as salmon, herring, eel, and sprat. From Scandinavia and Finland come the traditional foods of the smorgasbord; from Germany come sauerkraut and various cold potato salads. Russian influences also abound. Dark rye bread is among the most popular staples in the Estonian diet, and it is widely available in American grocery stores and bakeries. *Rossol* is a cold salad mixture of potatoes,

Evangelical Lutheran Church is the largest organized religious group among Estonian Americans, with 12 congregations and 3,500 members. Estonian American Baptists came to the United States before World War I to escape persecution in Estonia and have maintained a number of congregations. Estonian Pentecostal congregations also exist in the United States.

After 1945 the influx of Estonian war refugees produced a number new Lutheran congregations, all linked to the Estonian Evangelical Lutheran Church (EELC). Established in 1954, the EELC maintains Lutheran congregations in most major Estonian settlements in North America. The other religious presence to appear after 1945 was Estonian Orthodox Christianity, resulting in several regional parishes. Orthodoxy took root in Estonia during the nineteenth century, winning Estonian converts who were discontented with German-dominated Lutheranism. The first Estonian Orthodox parish was formed in vegetables, diced meat, and herring, with a sour cream and vinegar dressing. *Mulgikapsad* is a pork-and-sauerkraut dish that takes its name from an Estonian province. Other salads common to the Baltic region include a preserved mixed fruit salad and a sour cream and cucumber salad. Blood sausage, or *verivorst*, is also a favorite among Estonians and Estonian Americans, who often gather together around Christmas time to make this hearty mixture of cooked pig or cow blood with potatoes, onions, and spices wrapped in a sausage casing. Imported Estonian beers and liquors are often sold at community events. Today's Estonian Americans have fused native cuisine with traditional recipes, and the younger generation often prefers American fast food to its native cuisine, to the dismay of their parents.

Clothing As with many other European groups, Estonians have colorful regional costumes that immigrants sometimes brought with them to the United States, but these are worn only on special occasions, such as ethnic celebrations or festivals. Some Estonian Americans tend to favor the colors of the Estonian flag—blue, black, and white—when choosing a wardrobe.

Traditional costumes for women include a tunic shirt, a full colorful skirt, and an embroidered apron. The headdresses worn by women vary according to region and village. In southern Estonia, the traditional headdress for a married woman is a long embroidered linen kerchief worn around the head and down the back. In northern Estonia, small, intricately designed coifs (hats) adorn women's folk costumes. Heavy necklaces are also common. Men's costumes generally consist of wide-legged pants gathered at the knee and loose-fitting shirts. The principal headdress for men is a high, stiff felt hat or fur cap with earflaps, the latter of which is worn during the winter months. Both men's and women's traditional costumes include a decorative broach used to fasten shirts and blouses. During the winter, traditional Estonian costumes included high felt boots called *valenka*.

Holidays Along with the traditional Christian and American holidays, there are certain festival days that are of special significance to the Estonian American community. February 24 is celebrated as Estonia's Independence Day, marking the formal declaration of Estonian independence in 1918. A two-day holiday in June combines two separate celebrations, St. John's Eve (Jaanipäev, Midsummer) on June 23 and Victory Day on June 24. Reaching far back into history, Midsummer is a common festival in the Scandinavian and Baltic countries. Victory Day commemorates the defeat of the Soviet Armies in the Estonian War of Independence (1918–1920). In their celebration of Christmas, Estonians extend the holiday a day or two after December 25; the first few days after Christmas are devoted to visiting friends and family, while the major celebration of Christmas is usually held on Christmas Eve. Mother's Day is also very important to Estonians and Estonian Americans.

A feature of resurgent Estonian nationalism during the nineteenth and twentieth centuries was national song festivals, celebrated for a period of days during the summer. Estonians in Europe and North America continue to celebrate these festivals, organizing mass gatherings to honor Estonia and to maintain national identity. In North America, Estonians from Canada and the United States gathered in such celebrations from 1957 to 1968, twice in New York and twice in Canada.

Greetings and Popular Expressions Common Estonian greetings and other expressions (with pronunciation) include the following: *Tere hommikut* (tere hommikoot)—Good morning; *Tere õhtut* (tere erhtut)—Good evening; *Jumalaga* (yoomahlahgah)—Good-bye; *Kuidas käsi käib?* (kooydahs kasi kayb)—How are you?; *Tänan hästi* (tanahn haysti)—Fine, thanks; *Palun* (pahloon)—Please; *Tänan* (tanahn)—Thanks; *Vabandage* (vahbahndahge)—Excuse me; *Jah* (yah)—Yes; *Ei* (ey)—No; and *Nägemieseni* (nagesmiseni)—See you later.

Health Care Issues and Practices Estonian Americans have embraced medicine as it is practiced in the United States. Many have entered the medical profession. A 1975 survey by the *Väliseestlase kalender* ("Almanac for the Estonian Abroad") listed over one hundred Estonian American doctors or dentists, 25 percent of whom were women. The 2000 U.S. Census also indicated that there were over 1,400 Estonian Americans in the health care and social assistance fields, nearly 80 percent of which were women. The 2010 Census did not track ancestry, and although the Census Bureau's American Community Survey reported data for many ancestry groups, data for certain small groups, including Estonian Americans, were not released.

FAMILY AND COMMUNITY LIFE

Before 1920 the Estonian American community consisted for the most part of young single men and women who came either to look for work or to escape the religious and political repression of tsarist Russia. Because the majority lived in cities on the east or west coasts, a stable immigrant community of families and other social institutions was slow to develop. However, the 1920s and 1930s saw the emergence of a strong immigrant community, augmented after 1945 by the arrival of war refugees. Significant educational and economic advancement, a high rate of marriage outside the community, and gradual geographic dispersal moved the Estonians well into mainstream American life. At the same time, contemporary Estonian Americans have been able to retain a degree of ethnic consciousness that helps to hold the community together.

Festivals and events such as the West Coast Estonian Days festival, held annually in San Francisco, offer Estonian Americans a chance to congregate and share their traditional foods, songs, dances, and all other aspects of their culture with the larger American community. Another major Estonian cultural event, the

ESTO festival, has been held in different sites around the world every four years since 1972 and played an important role in garnering international support for a free and independent Estonia. An ESTO festival was held in New York City in 1992. The 2018 ESTO festival is scheduled to be held in Toronto, Ontario.

> After I got my citizenship, I sponsored two Estonian immigrant families. And a few years ago, I married a man from one of those families. So I have a new life. I feel that I have been blessed, really. This country has given me many things: a home, friendship, a chance to live again.
>
> Leida Sorro in 1951, cited in *American Mosaic: The Immigrant Experience in the Words of Those Who Lived It,* edited by Joan Morrison and Charlotte Fox Zabusky (New York: E. P. Dutton, 1980).

Gender Roles Whereas Estonian American men paralleled mainstream American gender roles in terms of acquiring education and working outside the home, Estonian American women transcended traditional gender roles in their pursuit of education and careers, beginning with the first migration. In 1932 an anonymous Estonian American writer commenting in his journal *Meie Tee* (quoted in *The Estonians in America, 1627–1975: A Chronology and Factbook*) remarked about his community: "Estonian women here have always worked, even though the husband might have a well-paying job." For example, a 1968 survey of young Estonian American women showed that, whereas 14 percent had ended their educations at the high school level, 61 percent had graduated from college. The 2000 U.S. Census also supported such findings, noting that 56 percent of Estonian American women held at least an associate's degree and 19 percent had attained a master's degree or higher. The above-average rate of women's educational levels and careers outside the home partly explains the swift rise in socioeconomic status of the Estonian American community. Estonian American women have also formed numerous local, national, and international women's organizations centered on educational and social concerns, which have banded with other Baltic-American women's groups to achieve common goals.

Education Education has played an important role in shaping the Estonian American community and in moving these immigrants into mainstream American life. Because Estonia in the nineteenth century had higher levels of literacy than many other parts of the Russian empire, many early immigrants were literate. Likewise, a significant number of the political refugees who fled Estonia after the abortive 1905 revolution were educated, and the socialist ferment within the community produced journals, newspapers, and reading rooms. Furthermore, a number of refugees who arrived in the United States after 1945 were members of Estonia's educational and political elite, and they increased the community's emphasis on education still more. The 2000 U.S. Census indicated that 95 percent of Estonian Americans were high school graduates or higher, and 51.5 percent held a bachelor's degree or higher. Also among the postwar immigrants were a number of Estonian intellectuals and academics who took positions in the American educational system. Estonian Americans have tended to specialize in science and technology, moving into fields such as engineering and architecture. The 2000 Census also showed growth in sales and management positions, and in teaching, particularly among Estonian American women. The Census Bureau did not release more recent statistics on smaller groups such as Estonian Americans.

The Estonian American community established a number of institutions to promote advancement in scholarship and education. These include Estonian academic fraternities and sororities, as well as an Estonian Students Association in the United States, which promotes knowledge of Estonian language and culture and Estonian study abroad. Learned societies, such as the Estonian Educational Society, sponsor publications and conferences. A number of other specialized educational groups have a broader membership that extends throughout North America and Europe.

Estonian schools, located in major centers of the Estonian American community, are designed to supplement the education of Estonian youth by teaching Estonian language, geography, history, and culture. The New York Estonian Educational Society, for example, sponsors the *New Yorgi Eesti Kool* (New York Estonian School), which has been in operation since 1950. These schools are linked through a regional and national network.

POLITICS AND GOVERNMENT

Political activity among Estonian Americans has been shaped in part by fluctuations in Estonia's status as an independent country. Because of Estonia's dependent circumstances in the nineteenth century, many Estonian immigrants lacked a clear consciousness of their national identity. The rise of Estonian nationalism, coupled with the communist struggle against the tsarist government, prompted Estonian Americans to become involved in their homeland's affairs. As political refugees streamed into the country after the unsuccessful revolution in 1905, leadership of the immigrant community and many of its institutions passed into communist hands. The Russian revolution and the struggle to free Estonia (1917–1920) divided Estonian Americans between those who supported a free Estonia and those who supported its inclusion within the Soviet Union. The Estonian nationalists prevailed as sense of national pride grew. In the wider sphere of American politics, the immigrant community was not particularly active unless the Republic of Estonia's affairs were directly involved. The number of immigrants seeking citizenship in the United States during this period was lower than for other Baltic nationalities.

The Soviet invasion of Estonia in 1940 along with the arrival of war refugees after 1945 dramatically increased the community's political involvement. The major concern became Estonian independence from Soviet control. Many Estonian and Baltic-American groups formed to support this goal, including the Joint Baltic American National Committee (1961) and the Baltic World Council (1972). There were also joint cultural and educational efforts and celebrations, and a Baltic Women's Council (1947). Their initial activities centered on lobbying both the U.S. government and the United Nations to prevent legal recognition of the Soviet conquest of Estonia. Because of their efforts (in concert with those of Latvian and Lithuanian Americans), the U.S. government never recognized the annexation of these three Baltic countries. Consequently, following World War II the three Baltic nations maintained consulates in the United States. Estonian Americans, as well as other Eastern European immigrant groups, were particularly outraged by the 1945 U.S.-Soviet agreement at Yalta, which they viewed as a betrayal of the nations under communist domination.

After 1945 most Estonian Americans supported the Republican Party, faulting the Democrats for the Yalta agreement and viewing the Republicans as more sympathetic to their concerns. In 1970 the Estonian American National Republic Committee was formed, with a network of Estonian American Republican clubs established in geographic centers of the immigrant community. This trend of support for the Republican Party continued until the collapse of the Soviet Union in 1991. Since that time, Estonian American political views have greatly diversified.

Estonian Americans served in the U.S. armed forces in every significant military conflict of the twentieth and early twenty-first centuries, including significant numbers in the Korean and Vietnam wars. In 1951 an Estonian American, Kalju Suitsev, received a Silver Star and Purple Heart for bravery in Korea. Many Estonian youth served in Vietnam, including a number who were killed or decorated for bravery. Given the fervent patriotic and anticommunist stance of the Estonian American community during this period, its support for military service was strong. The Estonian Defense Force also participated in the wars in Iraq and Afghanistan in the 2000s, continuing the tradition of military cooperation between Estonia and the United States.

NOTABLE INDIVIDUALS

Although small in number, the Estonian American community has produced a number of noteworthy people, particularly in the fields of architecture, education, engineering and technology, the applied arts, and music.

Architecture Perhaps the most prominent Estonian American architect was Anton Hanson, who was born in Estonia in 1879 and immigrated to the United States in 1906. Hanson was one of the architects of the Seattle World's Fair, for which he was awarded the grand prize.

Art The sculptor Woldemar Rannus (1880–1944) came to the United States in 1905. Rannus studied at the National Academy of Design in New York and later in Europe. He molded a bas-relief of Albert Beach, designer of the New York City subway, for the subway station near City Hall. Andrew Winter (1893–1958) painted winter scenes and seascapes in a realist style. Born in Estonia, he studied in the United States and eventually settled in Maine.

Commerce and Industry Carl Sundbach (1888–1950), born in Estonia, invented a freezer that greatly reduced the time required to bulk freeze fish. William Zimdin (1881–1951) was an international businessman and millionaire. Zimdin began his career in the United States in 1920 by arranging transactions between the United States and the Soviet Union. Otto Lellep (1884–1975), born in Estonia, was a metallurgical engineer who came to the United States in 1917. Working in the United States and Germany, he developed a cement baking oven and made advancements in the processing of steel, iron ore, and nickel. Lellep went into business manufacturing his ovens in the United States after World War II. John Kusik, born in Estonia in 1898, rose to become director and senior vice president of the Baltimore and Ohio Railroad and served on a number of other corporate boards.

Education Herrman Eduard von Holst (1841–1904) studied in Estonia and received his doctorate from the University of Heidelberg in Germany. He became the first chair of the history department at the University of Chicago and wrote a number of important works on American and European history. He also held academic positions in Germany and France. Theodore Alexis Wiel was born in Estonia in 1893 but attended college in the United States. After being decorated for service in France in World War I, Wiel earned a doctorate in international relations and taught at American International College, where he also served as dean. Ragnar Nursek (1907–1959) studied in Estonia and Britain before coming to the United States, where he taught economics at Columbia University. Nursek authored a number of works on international economics and also served on the League of Nations prior to World War II. Ants Oras (1900–1982) was an English professor at the University of Tartu in Estonia who came to the United States via England after World War II and then taught at the University of Florida. Arthur Vööbus (1909–1990) obtained his doctorate in Estonia in 1943 and came to the United States after the war. A biblical scholar and expert on early Syrian Christianity, Vööbus taught at the Lutheran School of Theology in Chicago.

Film Film director Bill Rebane (1937–) immigrated to the United States with his family in 1952. He is known for a number of horror films, including *Monster a-Go-Go* (1965) and *The Giant Spider Invasion* (1975).

Government William Leiserson (1883–1957), born in Estonia, received his PhD from Columbia University in 1911. A specialist in labor affairs, he was employed by the U.S. Department of Labor and appointed by President Franklin Roosevelt to the Labor Arbitration Commission in 1939.

Journalism Edmund Valtman (1914–2005) came to the United States in 1949. A political cartoonist with the *Hartford Times*, Valtman received the Pulitzer Prize for his drawings in 1961.

Music Ludvig Juht (1894–1957), an Estonian-born musician, specialized in the contrabass. Juht had an international career in Estonia, Finland, and Germany until Serge Koussevitzky brought him to the United States in 1934 to serve as principle contrabass with the Boston Symphony Orchestra. In addition, Juht taught at both the New England Conservatory of Music and Boston University and worked as a composer. Evi Liivak (1924–1996) was born in Estonia and studied the violin. In 1951 she joined her American husband in the United States and has enjoyed an international career.

Neeme Järvi (1937–) is an Estonian-born conductor who immigrated to the United States in 1980. He was the musical director of the Detroit Symphony Orchestra, New Jersey Symphony Orchestra, and Estonian National Symphony Orchestra, among others. His sons Paavo (1962–) and Kristjan (1972–) are both prominent conductors, and his daughter Maarika (1964–) is a flautist with a number of symphony orchestras around the world.

Performance Ballet dancer Tiit Helimets (1975–) was born in Estonia, where he performed with the Estonian National Ballet beginning in 1996. He became the principal dancer of the San Francisco Ballet in 2005.

Science and Technology Elmar Leppik, a biologist educated in Estonia and Europe, came to the United States in 1950. He taught at a number of American universities and then worked as a research scientist with the U.S. Department of Agriculture in Maryland. Igor Taum, born in Estonia in 1922, came to the United States in 1945 and served as a research physician at Rockefeller University in New York City, where he specialized in the study of viruses. Richard Härm (1909–1996) was educated in Estonia and Germany prior to coming to the United States after World War II. He taught mathematics at Princeton University. Rein Kilkson (1927–2011) was born in

Estonia and received his doctorate at Yale University in 1949. A physicist, he did research in the areas of biophysics and virology and taught at the University of Arizona. Lauri Vaska (1925–), a chemist, discovered a new chemical compound, which was eventually named the "Vaska compound." Vaska taught at Clarkson College of Technology in Potsdam, New York. Harald Oliver, Jyri Kork (1927–2001), and Rein Ise participated as scientists in the U.S. space program on the Apollo moon project and the Skylab space station.

Stage and Screen Miliza Korjus (1909–1980) was born in Estonia to Estonian and Polish parents. A soprano, Korjus performed the leading role in the film *The Great Waltz* (1938), a biography of the waltz king Johann Strauss. Korjus later settled in California to continue her singing career. Ivan (John) Triesault (1893–1980), born in Estonia, was a film actor who made over twenty-five films, from *Mission to Moscow* (1942) to *Von Ryan's Express* (1965). He specialized in playing character roles, including German military officers.

Actress Mena Suvari (1979–), known for her roles in such films as *American Beauty* (1999) and *American Pie* (2000) as well as her role on the HBO series *Six Feet Under* (2004), of Estonian descent.

MEDIA

Journal of Baltic Studies

Published by the Association for the Advancement of Baltic Studies, this quarterly provides a forum for scholarly discussion on topics regarding the Baltic republics and their peoples.

Terry Clark, Editor
Department of Political Science
Creighton University
Omaha, Nebraska 68178
Phone: (402) 280-4712
Fax: (402) 280-4731
Email: jbs@creighton.edu
URL: www.depts.washington.edu/aabs/publications-journal.html

Vaba Eesti Sõna (*Free Estonian Word*)

Estonian American weekly, established in 1949.

Kärt Ulman, Editor
Nordic Press, Inc.
243 East 34th Street
New York, New York 10016
Phone: (212) 686-3356
Fax: (212) 686-3356
Email: toimetus@vabaeestisona.com
URL: www.vabaeestisona.com

ORGANIZATIONS AND ASSOCIATIONS

Estonian American National Council

Founded in 1952, this umbrella organization represents all Estonian Americans and major Estonian American organizations. Coordinates the efforts of the member groups; supports political, cultural, and social activities; provides grants for study; and maintains a library and archives at its headquarters in New York City.

Marju Rink-Abel, President
243 East 34th Street
New York, New York 10016
Phone: (212) 685-0776
URL: www.estosite.org

Estonian Evangelical Lutheran Church (EELC)

The ecclesiastical structure for all Estonian Lutherans outside of Estonia, headquartered in Sweden. Promotes religious education and outreach in the immigrant communities, conducts religious services, and maintains congregations. The North American branch of the EELC consists of twelve congregations in the United States and eleven in Canada.

Rev. Udo Petersoo, Archbishop for North America
383 Jarvis Street
Toronto, Ontario M5B 2C7
Canada
Phone: (416) 925-5465
Fax: (416) 925-5465
Email: konsistoorium@eelk.ee
URL: www.eelk.ee

Estonian Heritage Society

Umbrella organization for over fifty Estonian cultural organizations. Promotes and seeks to preserve Estonian cultural heritage.

Mart Aru, Chair
Pikk 46
Tallinn 10133
Estonia
Phone: (372) 6412 522
Email: info@muinsuskaitse.ee
URL: www.muinsuskaitse.ee

New York Estonian Educational Society

Founded in 1929, this scholarly organization seeks to encourage Estonian studies, especially in English, and supports translation of Estonian literary works. Owns and operates the New York Estonian House, the largest Estonian cultural organization in New York.

Toomas Sõrra, President
243 East 34th Street
Estonian House, New York
New York 10016
Phone: (212) 684-0336
Fax: (212) 684-6588
URL: www.estonianhousenewyork.com

MUSEUMS AND RESEARCH CENTERS

Estonian Archives in the United States

The main archives for documents on the immigrant settlements and their development. Located in the Estonian American community of Lakewood, New Jersey, this institution is particularly valuable to the study of Estonian Americans.

607 East Seventh Street, Lakewood
New Jersey 08701
Phone: (732) 363-6523

Estonian Society of San Francisco

A cultural, educational, and social foundation for Estonian Americans on the West Coast. It sponsors ethnic scouting, dancing, and scholarship and maintains a library and reading room.

Ingrid Echter, President
255 King Street
Apt. 1609
San Francisco, California 94158
Phone: (917) 696-7888
Email: inxu24@yahoo.com
URL: www.ebtb.org

Immigration History Research Center

Located at the University of Minnesota, this center is a valuable archival resource for many of the immigrant groups from eastern and southern Europe, including the Estonians. In addition to newspapers and serials, the center also has a collection of books and monographs, along with the records of Estonian American groups in Minnesota and Chicago.

Dr. Rudolph Vecoli, Director
311 Elmer L. Andersen Library
222 21st Avenue S
Minneapolis, Minnesota 55455
Phone: (612) 627-4208
Fax: (612) 626-0018
Email: ihrc@umn.edu
URL: www.ihrc.umn.edu

Office of the Estonian Consulate General

Representing the Republic of Estonia in the United States, the consulate is a valuable resource for general information on Estonia and the Estonian American community.

3 Dag Hammarskjöld Plaza
305 East 47th Street
Suite 6B
New York, New York 10017-2001
Phone: (212) 883-0636
Fax: (212) 883-0648
Email: nyconsulate@mfa.ee
URL: www.nyc.estemb.org

SOURCES FOR ADDITIONAL STUDY

Balys, J., and Uno Teemant. "Estonian Bibliographies: A Selected List." *Lituanus: The Lithuanian Quarterly* 19, no. 3, (1973): 54–72.

Miljan, Toivo. *Historical Dictionary of Estonia*. Lanham, MD: Scarecrow Press, 2004.

Parming, Marju, and Tönu Parming. *A Bibliography of English-Language Sources on Estonia*. New York: Estonian Learned Society in America, 1974.

Pennar, Jaan, Tönu Parming, and P. Peter Rebane, eds. *The Estonians in America, 1627–1975: A Chronology and Factbook*. Ethnic Chronology Series, no. 17. Dobbs Ferry, NY: Oceana Publications, Inc., 1975.

Raun, Toivo. *Estonia and Estonians*. Studies in Nationalities. 2nd ed. Stanford, CA: Hoover Institution Press, 2001.

Tannberg, Kersti, and Tönu Parming. *Aspects of Cultural Life: Sources for the Study of Estonians in America*. New York: Estonian Learned Society in America, 1979.

Walko, M. Ann. *Rejecting the Second Generation Hypothesis: Maintaining Estonian Ethnicity in Lakewood, New Jersey*. New York: AMS Press, 1989.

ETHIOPIAN AMERICANS
Paul S. Kobel

OVERVIEW

Ethiopia is a landlocked country in eastern Africa located on the Horn of Africa. It is bordered by Eritrea to the north, Djibouti and Somalia to the east, Kenya to the south, and Sudan and South Sudan to the west. The topography of Ethiopia varies widely, its distinctive features including the rugged Western Highlands, the Great Rift Valley, and the arid Denakil Plain. The size of the country is 437,794 square miles (1,133,882 square kilometers), which is roughly twice the size of Texas.

According to the World Bank, Ethiopia had a population of about 87 million in 2012. There are many ethnic and linguistic groups that compose modern-day Ethiopia. The 2007 Ethiopian census identifies the largest group as the Oromo, who constitute roughly 34 percent of the population. The Amhara group makes up nearly 27 percent of the population and has been the most historically influential ethnic group in Ethiopian politics. The remaining population is mostly composed of the Somali, the Tigray, and the Sidama. There are three main religions practiced in Ethiopia; in 2007 approximately 43 percent of the population was Ethiopian Orthodox, 34 percent were Muslim, and 18 percent were Protestant, with a small minority practicing Catholicism or following other religious traditions (2007 Ethiopian census). Ethiopia's economy is primarily agricultural, and most Ethiopians are employed in this sector. In 2011 Ethiopia was ranked as the sixth poorest nation in the world by the World Bank, with a much lower per capita income than other sub-Saharan African nations and nearly 50 percent unemployment.

Ethiopians did not begin to arrive in the United States in large numbers until the 1980s. They settled mainly in large cities, including Washington, D.C., Los Angeles, and New York City. Many Ethiopians immigrated to the United States to escape the violent repression of Mengistu Haile Mariam's Marxist regime, which controlled Ethiopia from the mid-1970s through the early 1990s. Since 2000, a large percentage of Ethiopian immigrants arriving in the United States have been refugees seeking political asylum as a result of continuing ethnic conflict and human rights violations in Ethiopia. Between 2001 and 2010, more Ethiopians than any other African-origin group were granted asylum in the United States (Migration Policy Institute).

The U.S. Census Bureau's American Community Survey (ACS) for 2009–2011 estimated the Ethiopian American population at approximately 193,702 (a number comparable to the population of Mobile, Alabama, or Little Rock, Arkansas). The 2011 ACS documents that Ethiopian Americans were the second largest African-origin community in the United States by 2010, with Nigerians making up the largest group. The largest groups of Ethiopian Americans today are concentrated in Washington, D.C., and its outlying areas, New York City, Atlanta, and Los Angeles. The majority of Ethiopian Americans continue to live in immigrant communities that are populated by Africans from the same region.

HISTORY OF THE PEOPLE

Early History Ethiopia is one of the oldest kingdoms in the world. Among the first peoples to inhabit Ethiopia were Ge'ez-speaking agrarians, who settled in the Tigrayan highlands around 2000 BCE. In approximately the seventh century BCE, they formed the Da'amat Kingdom, which declined in the fifth or fourth century BCE. The inland Aksum Kingdom arose during the early Christian era. According to Ethiopian legend, it was founded by Menilek I, who is said to be the son of King Solomon and the Queen of Sheba. Aksum King Ezana made Christianity the official religion during his period of rule, which lasted from approximately 303 to 350 CE. When Muslims began to occupy much of Northern Africa and the Mediterranean, the Aksum Kingdom was crippled by poor external trade. The kingdom was subsequently replaced by the Zagwe' dynasty in Ethiopia between 1137 and 1270. Their most significant contribution was the creation of eleven churches carved out of stone in the city of Roha (today called Lalibela), which continued to stand at the start of the twenty-first century.

In the sixteenth century, several small kingdoms replaced the former Ethiopian empire, which would not be reunified until 1889, when Menilek II gained control. One of his most important accomplishments was the defeat of the Italians in 1896 at the Battle of Adwa. Menilek II then expanded the Ethiopian Empire to nearly twice its size. He also rebuilt the

Ethiopian infrastructure, including constructing a railway system and improving public health and education institutions.

In the early nineteenth century there was a brief period of internal strife brought on by the weakness of Menilek II's successor, Lij Iyasu, and Great Britain, France, and Italy were called upon to intervene to resolve the crisis. The modernization of Ethiopia then resumed under Emperor Haile Selassie in 1930. Haile Selassie introduced Ethiopia's first constitution in 1931. In 1935 Italy invaded Ethiopia in an effort to expand its influence in North Africa. Although Italian rule was coercive, many improvements to Ethiopia's infrastructure during this period were profitable to the country. With the help of Great Britain, Ethiopia drove out the Italians during World War II, and Haile Selassie was restored to power in 1941.

Modern Era In the early 1960s a civil war broke out in Ethiopia, instigated by the demands for independence by the Eritrean population who resided in the province of Eritrea in the northern region of Ethiopia. Eritrea had been taken over by the Italians in the late nineteenth century and was only reincorporated into Selassie's rule in the 1950s. Eritreans were incensed by the Ethiopian government's general lack of regard for their culture, which differed from the dominant Ethiopian culture, especially after Eritrean schools were mandated to teach Amharic as the primary language in lieu of the local Eritrean dialect. This unrest led to the emergence of an Eritrean independence movement in the early 1960s, which sparked a thirty-year war against the Ethiopian government that finally ended in 1991.

After a period of economic stabilization in the 1950s and 1960s following Italy's exit during World War II, the Ethiopian army overthrew the Selassie government in 1974. The provisional military government established that year was replaced shortly thereafter by a Marxist regime. The Provisional Military Administrative Council (PMAC), known as the Derg to native Ethiopians, was the military body that controlled Ethiopia between 1974 and 1991. Mengista Haile Mariam emerged as the leader of the Derg in 1977 and established a tyrannical regime that violently repressed any opposition to Marxist rule. In 1978 the Soviet Union and Cuba helped Mariam defeat a brief invasion attempt by neighboring Somalia. In 1984 the Ethiopian Socialist Party consolidated power and became the uncontested political party. Three years later the government adopted a new constitution, renamed the country the People's Republic of Ethiopia, and named Mariam its president.

The military dictatorship that governed Ethiopia between 1974 and 1991 had a tremendous impact on the social and economic development of modern day Ethiopia. The Derg was a Marxist regime modeled after the Soviet Union and ruled by military officers. Although a constitution was formally introduced in 1987, the Derg retained centralized power under Mariam. In 1991 a group of insurgents led by Eritreans and Tigrayans overthrew the Mariam regime. Eritrea subsequently seceded from Ethiopia, officially gaining independence in 1993. This ended the thirty-year war between Eritreans and the Ethiopian government that is generally referred to as the Ethiopian Civil War. In 1994 a new constitution was adopted in Ethiopia, and the following year the country enjoyed its first multiparty democratic election. The Ethiopian People's Democratic Revolutionary Front, which had essentially run the government since 1991, won the election.

The Ethiopian governmental structure is a parliamentary democracy with a bicameral legislature, a prime minister, and a president. The head of government is the prime minister, while the president, who is appointed by the legislature, is primarily a figurehead. The constitution of 1995 decentralized power, drew state borders along geographic ethnic divisions, and granted the states the right to secede.

Meles Zenawi was elected prime minister in 1995 in Ethiopia's first multiparty election. He was re-elected in 2000. General elections in 2005 generated suspicions of voting irregularities that favored Zenawi's party, the Ethiopian People's Revolutionary Democratic Front, resulting in widespread protests during which government forces were accused of murdering civilians. Human rights abuses remained high in Ethiopia into the early twenty-first century, and Zenawi's rule was widely criticized as increasingly oppressive. Zenawi served as prime minister of Ethiopia until his death in August 2012, which many saw as the end of an era of repression and an opportunity for restored stability and peace in the nation.

SETTLEMENT IN THE UNITED STATES

According to the U.S. Committee for Refugees (USCR), Africans have only recently begun immigrating to the United States and their numbers are rather small compared to groups from Asia and Europe. Ethiopians were among the first African immigrants to come to the United States voluntarily. In 1991 there were an estimated 50,000 to 75,000 Ethiopians living in the United States. Ethiopians began to immigrate in significant numbers after the passage of the 1980 Refugee Act, the United States' first formal policy regarding African refugees. Ethiopians were the most heavily represented group from Africa admitted between 1982 and 1994. In 2009, Nigerians exceeded the number of all other African origin immigrants entering the United States at 14 percent, with the numbers for Ethiopian immigration slightly lower at approximately 10 percent (Migration Policy Institute).

The 1980 Refugee Act set limits on the number of refugees allowed into the country in a given year. The ceiling for African refugees was initially set at 1,500 in 1980 and grew to 7,000 in 1995. The

An Ethiopian refugee works at Hertz rental cars while waiting to hear whether he will be granted political asylum. He had been jailed and tortured in Ethiopia for passing out political flyers. ANDY CROSS / THE DENVER POST / GETTY IMAGES

ceiling does not, however, reflect the actual number of African refugees admitted to the United States. Often the actual number of immigrants that come to the United States is lower than the ceiling. In 1986, for example, the limit on African refugees was 3,500 persons, but only 1,315 were admitted. Ethiopians who immigrated to the United States beginning in the early 1980s did so in large part to escape the repressive political tactics of the Mengistu Haile Mariam regime. Mariam's government, the Derg, or the "Committee," exercised violence against opposition groups and controlled the media in order to maintain power.

In relation to other continents, the number of refugees admitted from Africa has been consistently low. David Haines in *Refugees in America in the 1990s: A Reference Handbook* cites several reasons that account for the rather tenuous U.S. policy on the admission of African refugees. First, there is little political capital for U.S. public officials to earn by admitting African refugees. The number of politically active Ethiopians in the United States in comparison to other nationality groups is negligible. There is therefore little pressure among U.S. policymakers to admit Ethiopians in high numbers. Second, when Africans first began seeking asylum in the early 1980s, there was a desire among African governments, the Organization of African Unity, and the United Nations to relocate African refugees in other African countries. Lastly, the fear of uncommon diseases being introduced to the United States made politicians cautious about opening its doors to Africa.

During the 1980s famine in northern Africa and during the repressive Marxist rule of the Derg, many Ethiopians migrated to Sudan. The majority of Ethiopians that ultimately immigrated to the United States came from Khartoum, Sudan. The transitional resettlement period for Ethiopians in Sudan during this period was unpleasant for most. The majority of Ethiopians in Sudan were unemployed and lived in resettlement camps or relied on financial support from family members in Ethiopia. Given the poor economic status of Sudan at the time, Ethiopian refugees did not fare well in the region. When the opportunity to resettle to a third country emerged, most Ethiopians targeted the United States. They believed that they would receive the greatest opportunity to improve their condition, just as previous refugees to North America had done. When the nationalist wars in Ethiopia ended in 1991, much of the impetus for Ethiopian resettlement was eliminated. However, the defeat of the Derg led to violent upheaval in Southern Ethiopia, which caused the renewed displacement of some southern Ethiopian residents.

When Ethiopian refugees arrived in the United States, their first inclination was to settle in regions that were already heavily populated with Ethiopians, including Los Angeles, Washington, D.C., Dallas, and New York City. According to 1992 Office of Refugee Resettlement data, the majority of Ethiopians (62 percent) that were admitted to the United States up to that point were males. The primary reason that males outnumbered females was that men in Ethiopia had more educational opportunities than women,

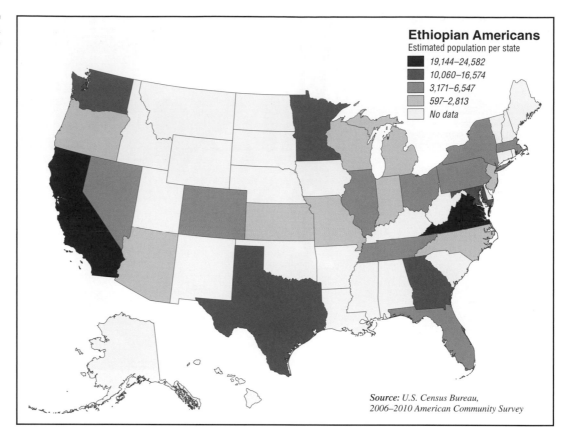

Ethiopian Americans
Estimated population per state

- 19,144–24,582
- 10,060–16,574
- 3,171–6,547
- 597–2,813
- No data

Source: U.S. Census Bureau, 2006–2010 American Community Survey

so Ethiopian women tended to lack the educational and occupational requirements for admittance into the United States. Another factor in admission was religion. The majority of Ethiopians initially admitted into the United States were Christian because they were considered the best candidates to assimilate easily into American culture. Educational background, however, was the main factor that determined whether an Ethiopian immigrant could enter the United States. Because the Amharic-speaking Ethiopians had the greatest access to education in Ethiopia, they were the most heavily represented group of Ethiopians admitted to the United States in the 1990s.

According to the U.S. Census Bureau, as of 2011 the number of Ethiopian immigrants to enter the United States prior to 1999 made up approximately 64 percent of the total population of native-born Ethiopians living in the United States, greatly outnumbering the group of Ethiopians that entered the country between 1999 and 2011. The female population of Ethiopian Americans has grown substantially since the 1990s, with the female population at 49.5 percent by 2007, only slightly outnumbered by the male population at 50.5 percent. The industry most dominated by Ethiopian Americans is the service sector. More Ethiopian Americans have been becoming small business owners in recent years, which is evidenced by the formation of such

organizations as the Ethiopian-American Chamber of Commerce and the Ethiopian American Retail Association.

LANGUAGE

Ge'ez is the classical Ethiopian language, but the most commonly spoken languages in Ethiopia are Amharic and Oromo. Amharic is the official language of the country. The majority of the languages spoken in Ethiopia derive from the Semitic languages of Abyssinia. *Amharic* has been called *lesana negus*, which means "language of the kings." It is predominantly spoken by Christians. The most idiosyncratic feature of Amharic pronunciation is the use of the pallet and the formation of sentences ending with a verb. The Amharic alphabet is made up of thirty-three letters and has seven vowels.

The most common language other than English spoken by Ethiopian Americans is Amharic, although some Ethiopian-origin individuals also speak Oromo or other less common dialects. While the older generation of native-born Ethiopians residing in the United States rely more heavily on their native language to communicate, the level of English-language fluency is quite high within the Ethiopian American community. Nonetheless, the native language continues to be spoken in the households most frequently, with 81 percent of Ethiopian American households speaking a language other than English at home, according to 2009-2011 ACS data. However, according to the Migration Policy Institute in 2007, the English proficiency rate for Ethiopian-origin individuals in the United States was 57 percent, which was above average for all immigrants to the country. There is an overall lack of native language preservation within the community, with second and third generation Ethiopian immigrants less likely to speak the language of their parents or grandparents. The fact that *Tadias*, the only successful Ethiopian American publication as of 2012, is an English-language magazine demonstrates the general lack of bilingualism within the community and may be reflective of the Ethiopian American community's general drive to learn English in order to succeed in the United States.

Common Amharic expressions include "*me'elkam edil*" (Good luck); "*melkam megeb*" (Bon appetit); "*Ïnen*" (a popular expression meaning "Let it be me instead of you," as in, "I wish I could have taken the fall instead of you"); and "*Seh-LAHM neh way?*" (male) / "*Seh-LAHM nesh way?*" (female) (a common greeting meaning "Are you in peace?").

RELIGION

The largest religious group in Ethiopia today is the Ethiopian Orthodox Church, or Ge'ez Tewahdo, with Islam as the second most practiced religious tradition in the country. The Ethiopian Orthodox Church is a derivation of the Coptic Church of Egypt. In the twelfth century Alexandria appointed an archbishop to Ethiopia whose title was *abuna*, meaning "our father." The bishop appointed was always of Egyptian origin. It was not until 1950 that a native Ethiopian was appointed the position of abuna. Ultimately, in 1959, Ethiopia formed an autonomous patriarchate. The Ethiopian Orthodox Church has historically been an integral part of Ethiopian political and social life. Emperor Haile Selassie used it to solidify his reign (1930-1974). The Marxist military regime that took control of Ethiopia in 1974 undermined religious practice, particularly the Ethiopian Orthodox Church, by seizing its land holdings. Despite these efforts to curb religious practice, many Ethiopians held to their religious beliefs during Ethiopia's Marxist period.

Islam is the religion practiced by the majority of the Somali, Argobba, Afar, and Harari ethnic groups in Ethiopia. The first Muslims in Ethiopia were followers of the Prophet Muhammad who migrated from Mecca to "Abyssinia" (modern-day Ethiopia)between 614 and 615 CE to escape the persecution of the ruling Quraysh tribe. While the first Muslims settled in the city of Axum, today the city of Harar is known as the principal center of Islamic culture in Ethiopia. In 2006 UNESCO recognized Harar as "the fourth holy city" of Islam due to its countless mosques and shrines, some of which date back to the tenth century.

A small but significant group of Ethiopian Jews, better known as Beta Israel, resided for centuries in the Gondar region of Ethiopia. The Israel Central Bureau of Statistics estimated that in total, there were approximately 150,000 Ethiopian Jews in 2011. This group faced growing persecution in Ethiopia, especially during the Mariam regime beginning in the 1970s. It was determined in 1977 that the Israeli Law of Return applied to Beta Israel, and attempts were soon made to relocate Ethiopian Jews to Israel. Beginning in 1979, aliyah activists and Israeli representatives sent word to Beta Israel from Sudan to cross into Sudan, and from there they were resettled in Israel. This movement, which lasted from 1979 to 1985, is known as Operation Brothers. During this period, more than 10,000 Ethiopian Jews were resettled in Israel. In 1990, an agreement between the Mariam government and Israel allowed the relocation of Ethiopian Jews to Israel, an exodus known as Operation Solomon, during which period approximately 14,000 Jews were resettled in Israel. As of 2012, the large majority of the Beta Israel population resided in Israel, approximately 130,000 Ethiopian Jews (Israel Central Bureau of Statistics). There are small numbers of Ethiopian Jews in the United States, and they have established cultural and community organizations such as the Beta Israel of North America (BINA) Cultural Foundation. BINA not only provides assistance to Ethiopian Jews who come to the United States, but also works to establish greater understanding between Ethiopian Jews and other ethnic groups within the Jewish community.

Today the vast majority of Ethiopians and Ethiopian Americans subscribe to either the Christian or Muslim faith. Over time, however, religious practice has waned for Ethiopian refugees in the United States. First generations of Ethiopian immigrants have had a difficult time passing on their linguistic and religious heritage to the next generation. Like many immigrants who are forced to adapt to American culture, Ethiopians have found it hard to compromise between the culture from which they came and the culture in which they must now live. One of the most common casualties resulting from the Americanization of Ethiopian refugees is the loss of religion in second and third generation refugees. Second generation Ethiopians must construct their own identity from the cultural heritage they inherit from their parents and the American culture to which they are exposed. Nevertheless, many Ethiopian Americans have joined or established religious centers that embrace their Ethiopian religious traditions and carry on their practice in the United States. In Atlanta, Georgia, one of the largest settlements of Ethiopian Americans in the country today, there are numerous Christian and Muslim institutions that play a significant role in Ethiopian community life.

CULTURE AND ASSIMILATION

According to a 1986 survey in *The Economic and Social Adjustment of Non-Southeast Asian Refugees*, assimilation into American culture has not been easy for Ethiopians. The study states that Ethiopians have not adapted well to the fast pace and "fend for yourself" attitude inherent in an advanced capitalist society. This has resulted in an unusually high rate of suicide and depression. Many Ethiopian refugees have managed to find support in areas where there are higher concentrations of Ethiopian Americans. Cities such as Washington, D.C., and Dallas, where previous generations of Ethiopians have established a social and economic foundation, facilitate the transition for incoming Ethiopians. There is also evidence in the same study to suggest that Ethiopians have greater success adapting to their new country when they gravitate to regions heavily populated with African Americans. Some of the activities Ethiopians engage in to strengthen their sense of belonging include playing soccer and joining social and economic support groups called *Ekub*. Traditionally, an *Ekub* was an Abyssinian financial group designed to make capital accessible and generate social activity. While some Ethiopians have penetrated middle-class American society with little difficulty, others have relied on social organizations modeled after the social structure in their native land.

Book Lakew, an Ethiopian scholar, suggested that even though there are now generations of educated Ethiopians in the United States, they still suffer social and economic resistance in American society. Part of the problem, according to Lakew, is that Ethiopians lack valuable exposure to the organized activities promoting teamwork and leadership that many

American children learn to thrive in at an early age. Lakew claimed that groups like the Boy Scouts and Girl Scouts, as well as activities such as grade school mock elections, provide American youth with the skills necessary to work in organizational settings later in life. The inability to flourish in an organizational setting, according to Lakew, prevents Ethiopian immigrants from making career advances in the United States. Lakew stated that this organizational handicap explains why Ethiopians rarely collaborate in business ventures in the United States, fail to form strong social and political organizations that promote the interests of Ethiopians in the United States, and lag behind other groups of immigrants who have graduated to the American middle class.

Cuisine Ethiopian cuisine is similar to Cajun and Middle Eastern food, which combine pepper spices with staples such as lentils, potatoes, green beans, and olive oil. Many Ethiopian dishes are made with *berbere*, or red pepper. Dishes are usually prepared warm rather than hot. A popular Ethiopian dessert is a drier version of the pastry baklava, which originated in the Ottoman Empire.

Most Ethiopian dishes are eaten without utensils. In place of a fork Ethiopians use bread called *injera* and their hands to deliver succulent entrees such as *fit-fit* (shredded bread and clarified butter) *kitfo* (marinated, minced raw beef), and *gored gored* (raw, cubed beef) to the mouth. *Injera* is similar to a Greek pita or a tortilla made from sourdough and soda water which makes for a chewy pancake-like

Ethiopian Americans cheer their female runners. THE WASHINGTON POST / GETTY IMAGES

texture. The conventional way of eating Ethiopian cuisine is to place a small portion of the entree on a torn piece of *injera* and rolling it up like a finger-sized tortilla. Many Ethiopian entrees are served in a stew called *wat*. Some common Ethiopian dishes include *alicha-sega wat*, consisting of beef cubes in purified butter; *doro wat*, chicken and egg cooked in red chili powder; *misir wat*, red split lentils cooked in spices; *tikil-gomen*, a combination of spiced cabbage, carrots, and potatoes; and *fosoli*, spiced string beans, carrots, onions, and garlic sautéed in olive oil.

Many Ethiopian Americans continue to incorporate much of this traditional Ethiopian cuisine into their diets in the United States. In addition, a number of Ethiopian Americans have opened restaurants that serve traditional Ethiopian cuisine. From larger cities such as Philadelphia to smaller towns like Ann Arbor, Michigan, Ethiopian restaurants have proliferated in recent years. As a result, Ethiopian cuisine has become more readily available not just to Ethiopian Americans but to all American diners.

Music One form of music popular among Ethiopians is a chant deriving from the Ethiopian Orthodox Christian Church. Ethiopian tradition holds that a series of chants was revealed to a man named Yared who subsequently transcribed the hymns in the sixth century. The Ethiopian Orthodox Christian Church trains chanters called *debtara*, who lead hymns for the congregation. They are not ordained but are considered part of the church's administration. The system of chants used by Ethiopians, which are written in the mother language of Ge'ez, is called *melekket*. Ge'ez is easily adapted to melody because each sign represents a syllable. Ethiopians use chants to accentuate different moods and occasions. *Araray* chants are used to punctuate a joyous occasion and *ezel* chants are performed during periods of fasting and mourning.

When Ethiopians began to immigrate to the United States in the 1970s, they concentrated in Washington, D.C. Thus, it is there that much of the substantial Ethiopian American music scene has been most prominent. In 1974 the important Ethiopian record producer Amha Eshete arrived in the city and laid the music scene's foundation by, among other things, opening Kilimanjaro, a nightclub where many Ethiopian musicians performed. In 1987 a number of Ethiopian musicians sought asylum in Washington, D.C., while on tour. Their arrival led to the formation of the Nile Ethiopian Ensemble and, later, the Orchestra Ethiopia, both of which played Ethiopian folk styles of music. Over time, both folk and modern Ethiopian music was being played live in Washington, D.C., and other large northeastern cities. In addition to these secular forms of Ethiopian music, Ethiopian Orthodox and Evangelical churches in the United States were also important sites for the growth of Ethiopian American music in the late twentieth and early twenty-first centuries.

Modern and popular forms of Ethiopian music have also grown in the United States since the influx of immigrants in the 1970s. Ethiopian artists such as the singer Chachi have recorded and released albums in the United States. This modern Ethiopian American music blends traditional Ethiopian styles of song with popular American genres such as rap and reggae. Despite this American influence, most Ethiopian American musicians sing in Ethiopian and maintain a distinctly Ethiopian vocal delivery.

Clothing The native Ethiopian dress is a white robe-like garment made of cotton called a *shamma*. Both men and women wore the *shamma*. Men traditionally wear tight-fitting white cotton pants beneath the shamma, while women wear colorful dresses that hang down to their ankles. During feast days, the shamma is adorned with a red stripe down the hem, which is called a *jano*. Men of distinguished heritage or rank wear an embroidered silk tunic called a *kamis*, which is color-coded in accordance with rank. In the evening, when it is cool, a shawl called a *barnos* is sometimes wrapped around the shoulders. A hood is usually attached to the *barnos*, though it is seldom worn. Few Ethiopian Americans dress in their native attire except on special occasions.

Health Care Issues and Practices Ethiopians generally receive superior health care services in the United States in comparison to their home country. In rural areas in Ethiopia health care is often inadequate, when available. A small percentage of Ethiopians have access to modern health care services. The infant mortality rate in Ethiopia is one of the highest in the world and the life expectancy is one of the lowest (fifty-seven years for men and sixty years for women in 2012). Because many Ethiopians have entered the service sector in the United States, few have comprehensive medical coverage. Fewer employers are providing health coverage in the United States and wages in the service industries are often insufficient for Ethiopian immigrants to pay for their own coverage. Consequently, many Ethiopian immigrants rely on subsidized health care assistance programs or holistic practices or go without coverage.

FAMILY AND COMMUNITY LIFE

Education Ethiopia suffers one of the highest illiteracy rates in the world, over 55 percent. Education is mandatory for six years (to the age of thirteen), but there is no federal law in Ethiopia requiring attendance. Very few Ethiopians have had an opportunity to expand their education beyond basic literacy. The primary higher education institution in Ethiopia is Addis Ababa University, which did not attain university status until 1961. Since the early 2000s, there has been an increased effort to expand higher education in Ethiopia, with the addition of nearly two dozen federal universities by 2010. Unfortunately, the regulation and quality assurance of the learning and curriculum delivered by private universities has since become an issue, which the government is struggling to address.

In the United States, second generation Ethiopians and beyond have access to the same educational services as other American children. The percentage of Ethiopian Americans attending institutions of higher learning has been steadily increasing, with approximately 28 percent of the Ethiopian-origin community in the United States having obtained a bachelor's degree or higher, according to the American Community Survey's estimates for 2006–2010. Although many Ethiopian immigrants have taken advantage of these services, some Ethiopian American youths have turned to drugs, crime, and gang membership in Los Angeles and Washington, D.C. Racism in the United States and the decline in influence of the Ethiopian Christian Church have been cited as primary reasons that some Ethiopian American youths have strayed. These issues are being addressed by a growing number of nonprofit organizations in recent years, including the Ethiopian Kids Community and the Ethiopian American Youth Initiative, with the goal of providing Ethiopian American youths with positive role models and extracurricular activities that offer alternatives to involvement in criminal activity.

Gender Roles Ethiopia is a patriarchal society, with status largely determined by one's class and ethnicity. Regardless of class and ethnicity, however, Ethiopians view women as subservient to men. Women generally have less access to education and fewer economic opportunities in Ethiopia. Coming from a patriarchal society often makes the transition to American culture more difficult, because the culture in the United States is more egalitarian. The social, political, and economic freedom granted to women in the United States often causes friction in Ethiopian marriages. Ethiopian men, who are accustomed to being dominant and exercising leadership in the family, often have difficulty accepting women as equals. The difference in attitude toward women has resulted in battery and divorce for many Ethiopian refugee households in the United States. Domestic violence against Ethiopian women has become a rising concern within the Ethiopian American community, although it is still an issue that is largely ignored or silenced by community members as a result of Ethiopians' deeply engrained patriarchal values.

In addition to the change in social status that an Ethiopian marriage must adapt to in the United States, married Ethiopian couples are disadvantaged by a general lack of family support through which marital guidance is often provided in their homeland. In the long run, however, female Ethiopian immigrants profit from the elevation in social status. Ethiopian American women are entering the workforce in increasingly higher numbers and playing a more active role in the public sphere outside of the home.

Weddings In Ethiopia marital arrangements are governed under a customary law called the *Fetha Nagast*. Polygamy is forbidden under civil law. There are three different types of marriages in Ethiopia: *damoz*, *kal kidan* or *serat*, and *bekwerban*. A *damoz* marriage is a temporary contractual arrangement between couples where a woman lives with a man for a period of time longer than one month. The *kal kidan* is the most common form of marriage among Ethiopians. Here, the parents of the bride and groom enter a civil contract in which the parents of the bride agree to offer their daughter for marriage sometime after puberty. Marriages are usually celebrated without the involvement of the church and are accompanied by days of elaborate feasting. The third type of Ethiopian marriage is the *kal kidan bekwerban*, or *bekwerban*, which is a civil marriage that is administered by the church. This type of marriage is usually entered into by older individuals, and the dissolution of a *bekwerban* marriage is not permitted. The religious ceremony involved in this type of marriage is the taking of communion by the newly joined couple. Divorces for the first two types of marriages, however, are relatively easy to obtain and can be requested by either the husband or wife. According to Ethiopian customary law, during a divorce property is divided between the couples in accordance with their individual contribution to the combined assets.

Although Ethiopian Americans must of course abide by American statutes regarding marriage and divorce, many Americans of Ethiopian descent incorporate aspects of their ethnic culture in their wedding ceremonies and celebrations. For example, groups of Ethiopian musicians are often hired to play traditional and contemporary music and Ethiopian cuisine is typically served. The traditional Ethiopian fabric *shemma* is also sometimes used in wedding attire, especially dresses.

Funerals Few events are celebrated with greater vigor among Ethiopians than death. Both men and women cry and sing dirges to the deceased. Shortly after death, the body of the deceased is washed, wrapped in cloth, and taken to a church to be blessed. It is buried in a shallow grave a few hours after the death. In place of headstones, Ethiopians usually mark a gravesite by piling stones shaped in a pyramid. Friends and relatives visit the home of the deceased throughout the first week after the death. On the twelfth, fourteenth, and eighteenth days after death, memorial services called *tezkar* are held.

EMPLOYMENT AND ECONOMIC CONDITIONS

Ethiopia itself functions primarily on an agricultural economy. Agriculture accounts for 90 percent of Ethiopian exports, and the vast majority of Ethiopians (80 percent) are employed by this industry. The bulk of the industrial sector, which

An Ethiopian immigrant participates at a "Save Darfur" rally in Washington, D.C., in 2006. CHIP SOMODEVILLA / GETTY IMAGES

includes food processing, beverages, textiles, chemicals, metals processing, and cement, is run by the state. This means that very few Ethiopians gain the industrial work experience necessary for gainful employment in advanced capitalist economies such as the United States. Only a small percentage of wealthy Ethiopians possess the skills necessary to forge a middle-class lifestyle in the United States. Many Ethiopians come to the United States under the impression that economic success is guaranteed. Unfortunately, few have realized their dream of blending into middle-class America. With the exception of professionals such as medical doctors and academics, the majority of Ethiopians have found work in the service sector of the U.S. economy.

Contrary to their expectations, many Ethiopian immigrants intent on escaping the poverty of their homeland find themselves underemployed after they arrive in the United States. Ethiopian immigrants earn their living in low-wage service jobs such as parking lot and gas station attendants, waiters and waitresses, and convenience store attendants. A minority of Ethiopian immigrants managed to open successful restaurants that feature Abyssinian cuisine. This opportunity usually only exists in larger U.S. cities such as Washington, D.C., Dallas, Atlanta, and Los Angeles. In these cities, where most Ethiopian immigrants are concentrated, the majority of Ethiopians have managed to secure some form of employment. The employment rate has increased in the 2000s, reflecting the higher level of education of many Ethiopian Americans

compared to other immigrant groups. The 2006-2010 American Community Survey documents that 79 percent of adult foreign-born Ethiopian immigrants were employed, versus 68 percent of immigrants overall and 65 percent of U.S.-born adults. Although these numbers are promising, many Ethiopians live below the poverty level and the unemployment rate among Ethiopian immigrants is much higher than it is for Americans in general.

Those who have been unable to secure gainful employment have participated in state and federal assistance programs when qualified. In Washington, D.C., and Los Angeles, roughly one half of Ethiopian immigrants have had to rely on federal and state assistance programs to survive. In the early 2000s, employment in the Washington, D.C., area seemed to be improving, with the Ethiopian community's establishment of its own ethnic zone in the metropolitan area, now unofficially named "Little Ethiopia," where Ethiopian business dominates and employs a large percentage of the Ethiopian population in the area. At this point it is difficult to determine how the Ethiopian American community was affected by the global economic recession that began in 2008, although the strength of community bonds within cities with large Ethiopian communities may have softened the blow slightly for some Ethiopian Americans. However, due to the lack of job security in the service sector, in which many Ethiopian Americans are employed, this immigrant community likely faced high levels of job loss.

POLITICS AND GOVERNMENT

Relatively little is known about the voting patterns of Ethiopian Americans since many do not participate in census counts or report their ancestry. Politicians in certain regions where the Ethiopian American community has gained particular prominence are beginning to cater to that population. This is especially true in the Washington, D.C., area, where Ethiopians control a significant sector of the local economy. Several politically oriented organizations associated with the Ethiopian community in the United States have been formed since the early 2000s. These include the Citizens League of Ethiopian Americans. Most notably, the Congressional Ethiopian and Ethiopian American Caucus was formed by Congressman Mike Honda in 2003. The Caucus released a statement on health care reform in October 2009 that overwhelmingly supported the passage of the health care reform bill proposed by President Barack Obama. Because a large sector of the Ethiopian American population relies on federal economic aid, many Ethiopian American organizations support continued social services for the entire American public. Ethiopian Americans also follow U.S. policy regarding Ethiopia very closely, and policy changes are likely to influence their political leanings during elections.

First generation Ethiopian refugees retain a strong sense of connection with their native land. Most refugees and immigrants have, at one point or another, visited their homeland and relatives, particularly after the nationalist civil war with Eritrea subsided in 1991. The major exception has been the Amharic-speaking Ethiopian refugees, who do not recognize the new Ethiopian government that was established in 1995. Amharic-speaking Ethiopians have initiated a political movement in the United States, with activities that include operating a radio station and forging ties with dissident groups in Ethiopia. Their goal is to discredit the Ethiopian People's Revolutionary Democratic Front (EPRDF), which assumed power in 1991.

Although most Ethiopians maintain positive sentiments toward their former country, very few opt to repatriate. The primary reason for this, according to a study by Mespadden and Moussa (1995), is that, upon revisiting Ethiopia, many Ethiopian refugees find that the people and places they left behind have changed beyond recognition. They therefore choose to resume the life they have established for themselves during their "transitional" period of residence in the United States.

NOTABLE INDIVIDUALS

Academia Teshome H. Gabriel (1939–2010) was an internationally recognized Ethiopian-born scholar and professor of film and Third World cinema who taught at the UCLA School of Theater, Film, and Television in Los Angeles. He was born in Ticho, Ethiopia, in 1939, and immigrated to the United States in 1962. Gabriel attended UCLA for his graduate studies, earning a master's degree in theater arts and a doctorate in film and television studies. He was considered an expert on cinema and film from Africa and the developing world. Gabriel began teaching at UCLA in 1974, becoming an assistant professor at the School of Theater, Film, and Television in 1981. He wrote and edited many books in his field, including *Third Cinema in the Third World: The Aesthetics of Liberation* (1982) and *Otherness and the Media: The Ethnography of the Imagined and the Imaged* (1993), which he coedited. Gabriel was also the founding director of several journals, including *Emergencies* and *Ethiopian Fine Arts Journal*.

Art Julie Mehretu, an artist who is recognized for her abstract paintings and prints, was born in Addis Ababa, Ethiopia, in 1970. Her family moved to the United States when she was a child. She received a master of fine arts degree from the Rhode Island School of Design in 1997 and has lived and worked in New York City since 1999. The artist is best known for her layering technique using different elements and media and for her large-scale drawings and paintings. Mehretu has participated in numerous exhibitions since the early 2000s, including *Painting at the Edge of the World* at the Walker Art Center in 2001, as well as being one of the artists featured in the Carnegie International exhibition of 2004-05. She received a MacArthur Fellowship (often referred to as the "genius grant") in 2005, and her work is in the permanent collection of the Museum of Modern Art in New York.

Journalism and Literature An award-winning American writer and journalist, Dinaw Mengestu was born in Addis Ababa, Ethiopia, in 1978. He left Ethiopia at the age of two and has spent the rest of his life residing in the United States. Mengestu has written critical pieces for *Rolling Stone* and *Jane* magazine on the conflicts in Uganda and Sudan. A 2012 MacArthur Fellow, Mengestu has also published the novels *The Beautiful Things that Heaven Bears* (2007) and *How to Read the Air* (2010). The author has also written for *Harper's* and the *Wall Street Journal* as well as numerous other publications. His 2007 novel narrates the story of an Ethiopian man who fled the Ethiopian Revolution decades earlier to begin anew in the United States, only to face countless adversities and challenges. The novel garnered Mengestu the 2007 Los Angeles Times Book Prize and the 2007 Guardian First Book Award.

Science Born in Ethiopia in 1966, Sossina M. Haile is a world-renowned U.S.-based scientist. Her family fled Ethiopia during the political upheaval of the mid-1970s, her historian father barely escaping death at the hands of Ethiopian soldiers. Internationally recognized for her creation of the world's first solid-acid fuel cell, Haile became a professor of materials science and of chemical engineering at the California Institute of Technology (Caltech) in 1996. Prior to her position at Caltech, Haile worked at the University of Washington, Seattle, as an assistant professor for three years. She has received numerous awards and accolades, including the AT&T Cooperative Research Fellowship (1986–92), the Fulbright Fellowship (1991–92), the 2000 Coble Award from the American Ceramics Society, and the 2001 J.B. Wagner Award of the High Temperature Materials Division of the Electrochemical Society.

MEDIA

The following publications are the most widely circulated Ethiopian and Ethiopian American periodicals. All are either solely English-language or are bilingual English and Amharic publications.

Addis Fortune

English-language weekly business newspaper published out of Addis Ababa.

> Hailu Teklehaimanot, Editor in Chief
> 259 Code 1110
> Addis Ababa, Ethiopia
> Phone: 251-11-416-3020
> Fax: 251-11-416-3039
> Email: Hailu_t@addisfortune.com
> URL: www.addisfortune.com

Ethiopian Review

An English-language Ethiopian online news and opinion journal based in the United States. It is the largest and most-visited Ethiopian news website.

> Elias Kifle, Editor
> 6412 Brandon Avenue, #252
> Springfield, Virginia 22150
> Phone: 202-656-5117
> Email: eliaskifle@gmail.com
> URL: www.ethiopianreview.net

Reporter/The Reporter

Two related publications: an Amharic-language newspaper published twice weekly, with an English-language newspaper published weekly. Both English and Amharic content is published online.

> Bruh Yihunbelay, Editor in Chief
> Bole Medhanialem Road, Addis Ababa
> Ethiopia
> Phone: 251-11-661-6185
> Fax: 251-11-661-6189
> Email: enquiry@ethiopianreporter.com
> URL: www.thereporterethiopia.com

Tadias

English-language Ethiopian American magazine published in the United States.

> Tseday Alehegn, Founder and Editor in Chief
> 555 Edgecombe Avenue
> New York , New York 10032

> Phone: 646-595-7344
> Email: info@tadias.com
> URL: www.tadias.com

ORGANIZATIONS AND ASSOCIATIONS

Citizens League of Ethiopian Americans (CLEA)

CLEA strives to enhance Ethiopian American political awareness and to promote the political participation of the Ethiopian American community in American politics.

> P.O. Box 404
> Los Gatos, California 95031
> Phone: (408) 806-7502
> Email: info@ethioamericans.com
> URL: www.ethioamericans.com

Ethiopian American Chamber of Commerce

Established in 2003, the organization provides advocacy, training and networking services to help business people of Ethiopian origin establish, run, and mature their businesses and companies.

> P.O. Box 88189
> Los Angeles, California 90009
> Phone: (213) 272-2262
> Fax: (213) 995-0900
> Email: info@eacoc.org
> URL: www.eacoc.org

The Ethiopian American Youth Initiative, Inc.

An association of Ethiopian and American youth with the intention of promoting Ethiopia in a new light and supporting youth-related efforts in America and Ethiopia.

> 812 Memorial Drive, Suite 614A
> Cambridge, MA 02139
> Phone: (617) 441-3140
> Email: info@ethusa.org
> URL: www.ethusa.org

The Ethiopian Community Association of Greater Philadelphia (ECAGP)

> 4534 Baltimore Avenue, 2nd floor
> Philadelphia, Pennsylvania 19143
> Phone: (215) 222-8917
> Fax: (215) 382-3608
> Email: ecagp@libertynet.org
> URL: www.ecagp.org

Ethiopian Community Development Council (ECDC)

ECDC is a federally funded refugee resettlement agency committed to working with refugees from Ethiopia and other African countries. Its public education program seeks to increase awareness within the wider community about issues of concern to African refugees and immigrants.

> 901 South Highland Street
> Arlington, Virginia 22204
> Phone: (703) 685-0510
> Fax: (703) 685-0529
> Email: contact_us@ecdcus.org
> URL: http://www.ecdcus.org/

Ethiopian Community Mutual Assistance Association

This organization aims to advance the economic and social welfare of the Ethiopian community in the United States as well as to preserve Ethiopian culture as a source of historical identity.

Mr. Binyam Tamene
552 Massachusetts Avenue Suite 209
Cambridge, Massachusetts 02139
Phone: (617) 492-4232
Fax: (617) 492-7685
Email: btamene@netscape.net
URL: www.krichevsky.com/maac-3/prof-Ethiopian.html

Ethiopian Kids Community

A nonprofit organization dedicated to nurturing connections and providing support for families with Ethiopian American children.

1889 29th Avenue NW
New Brighton, Minnesota 55112
Phone: (612) 636-7878
Email: stacy@bellward.com
URL: www.ethiopiankids.com

MUSEUMS AND RESEARCH CENTERS

The Ethiopian Community Association of Chicago

A nonprofit, charitable organization committed to promoting Ethiopian culture and traditions in Chicago. They have founded an Ethiopian Cultural Museum in Chicago.

1730 W. Greenleaf Avenue
Chicago, Illinois 60626
Phone: (773) 508-0303

Fax: (773) 508-0309
Email: eyimer@ecachicago.org
URL: www.ecachicago.org/home0.aspx

The Ethiopian Community and Cultural Center (ECCC)

The center's outreach program promotes Ethiopia and Ethiopian history and culture to communities around the San Francisco Bay Area.

353 Grand Avenue, Suite 1B
Oakland, California 94610
Phone: (510) 268-4770
Fax: (510) 268-4003
URL: http://ethiopianccc.org/index.php

SOURCES FOR ADDITIONAL STUDY

Bard, Mitchell G. *From Tragedy to Triumph: The Politics Behind the Rescue of Ethiopian Jewry.* Westport, CT: Greenwood Publishing Group, 2002.

Frazier, J.W., J.T. Darden, and N.F. Henry, eds. *The African Diaspora in the United States and Canada at the Dawn of the 21st Century.* New York: Global Academic Publishing, Binghamton University, 2009.

Getahun, Solomon Addis. *The History of Ethiopian Immigrants and Refugees in America, 1900-2000: Patterns of Migration, Survival, and Adjustment.* New York: LFB Scholarly Pub., 2007.

Marcus, Harold G. *A History of Ethiopia: Updated Edition.* Berkeley: University of California Press, 2002.

Metaferia, Getachew. *Ethiopia and the United States: History, Diplomacy, and Analysis.* New York: Algora Pub., 2009.

Ofcansky, Thomas P., and LaVerle Berry. *Ethiopia: A Country of Study.* Washington, D.C.: Library of Congress, 1993.

FILIPINO AMERICANS

H. Brett Melendy

OVERVIEW

Filipino Americans are immigrants or descendants of people from the Philippines, a country consisting of about 7,100 islands in the Pacific Ocean off the southeast coast of Asia. Set north of Indonesia, the islands form a north-south arc of 1,152 miles (1,854 kilometers) that at its widest point extends 682 miles (1,098 kilometers) from east to west. The Philippine archipelago is part of the Pacific Ocean's volcanic rim. Most of the islands, large and small, have high mountains, and many are surrounded by coral reefs. Eleven islands make up about 95 percent of the land mass of the Philippines, with the two largest, Luzon and Mindanao, accounting for 65 percent of the total land mass. The total land area of the Philippines is 115,831 square miles (300,001 square kilometers), slightly more than the state of Nevada.

According to the *CIA World Factbook*, the population of the Philippines in 2012 was about 104 million people, making it the twelfth-most populous nation in the world. The majority are Malays, and Chinese, Americans, and Spaniards form the largest minorities. The population is 83 percent Roman Catholic, 9 percent Protestant, and 5 percent Muslim.

The mountainous terrain of the Philippines permits cultivation of only 15 percent of the land. Nevertheless, agriculture—ranging from subsistence farming to export plantations—constitutes the country's economic base. The climate, which is tropical maritime, usually has high humidity and high temperatures, and monsoons and typhoons bring periods of heavy rain. These factors determine where and how Filipinos cultivate their land. (Although the country is spelled with an initial *Ph*, the people are referred to as Filipinos, spelled with an *F*.) Major domestic crops are rice and corn (maize); important export crops are *abaca* (Manila hemp), *copra* (dried coconut meat, from which coconut oil is made), pineapple, sugar, and tobacco. A persistent problem in the Philippines has been inequitable land distribution. A system of sharecropping, or tenant farming, has made most farmers virtual captives of landlords known as *caciques*. At the time of Philippine independence in 1946, over 70 percent of the crops went to *caciques*. Sharecropping has fomented considerable political unrest in the Philippines over the years.

Historically, limited economic opportunities due to the tenant-farming system and a high birthrate have stimulated immigration to Hawaii and the mainland United States.

According to the 2010 American Community Survey, U.S. immigrants from the Philippines number about 3.4 million—about the same as the population of Connecticut. According to the American Community Survey, Filipinos are the second-largest Pacific-Asian group in the United States after Chinese Americans. The first Filipino settlement in the United States was established in 1763 in southern Louisiana, but since that time, Filipinos in the United States have tended to settle in Hawaii, California, New York, Illinois, Texas, Florida, New Jersey, Nevada, and Washington.

HISTORY OF THE PEOPLE

Early History Perhaps the earliest inhabitants of the Philippine Islands were the dark-skinned, short-statured people who are under five feet tall and thought to have arrived about twenty-five thousand years ago. When the Spanish arrived in the sixteenth century, they named these people Negritos ("little black ones"). Over the centuries, the Philippines have seen the arrival of diverse groups, including Islamic Arab traders in the fourteenth century. Their descendants, the Moros, remain devout Muslims and live mostly in the southern islands. Trade between the Philippines and southern China has been existence since the fourteenth century, and Chinese and Japanese immigrants have settled in the islands. Japanese settlers rarely married persons from the local population, but the Chinese often did. Descendants of Filipino-Chinese marriages have dominated island businesses, achieving economic success that has led to political power. Their dominance has generated Filipino hostility toward the Chinese.

The first contact between Spain and the Philippines occurred in 1521 with the arrival of Ferdinand Magellan, who claimed the archipelago for Spain and the Catholic Church. Spain made his claim official in 1565. The islands were named the Philippines in the 1550s after King Philip II of Spain. In 1565 Philip sent a royal governor who imposed Spanish rule across much of the archipelago, using the same oppressive, often violent methods used in the Americas.

From 1565 to 1810 the galleon trade from Acapulco, Mexico, to Manila connected the Spanish Empire with the East Asian market via the Philippines. Manila served as the intermediary point between the two markets. The Spanish exchanged Latin American gold for Chinese silk, spices, and tea. As members of crews aboard Spanish ships, Filipinos had their first opportunities to emigrate, exploring the California coast and settling in Mexico and what is now Louisiana.

Embracing European practices of mercantilism and colonialism, Spanish monarchs exploited the Philippines to enrich themselves. Over the course of four centuries, Spanish settlers and their descendants acquired large estates and maintained control of the colonial government.

With the government's approval, the Catholic Church controlled large areas of land and used its monopoly on formal education to impose Catholic beliefs and the Spanish language on the natives. By 1898 the church had converted more than 80 percent of the population. Most Filipino immigrants to Hawaii and the U.S. mainland have been Catholic.

Colonialism's tiered society alienated Filipinos, but many suffered it quietly in order to survive. Spanish settlers began to marry Filipinos; the descendants of these marriages were known as *mestizos*, or "mixed bloods." By the nineteenth century, mestizos had inherited large tracts of agricultural land. This Filipino-Spanish upper class found that the lighter their skin color, the easier to mingle with Europeans and Americans. They also learned from the Spanish how to maintain power through force and corruption. This economic-political dominance came to be known as *caciquism*. It has been a contributing factor in the immigration of Filipinos to the United States, and it continues today.

Open revolts against Spanish control emerged in the nineteenth century. Initially the revolt leaders called for political and economic reform but not independence. An early opposition leader, José Rizal, formed *La Liga Filipina* (the Filipino League). The Spanish banished Rizal from the islands. When he returned, he was executed, which made him a national hero.

Twenty-seven-year-old Emilio Aguinaldo became the next leader of the insurrectionists. In 1898 Aguinaldo met with the American admiral George Dewey and U.S. consul general E. Spencer Pratt. Aguinaldo claimed that the three of them agreed that, if Filipinos would ally with the United States in a war against Spain, the Philippines would be given independence. Admiral Dewey and Consul General Pratt subsequently denied that they had agreed to this. Later that year the United States declared war on Spain, and the Spanish-American War ensued. The Philippine-American War soon followed. The United States attacked the Philippines, killing more than one million Filipinos and losing six thousand American lives.

The Treaty of Paris, ratified on February 6, 1899, gave the United States imperial authority over the islands.

Following Aguinaldo's lead, Filipinos turned their battle from Spain to the United States. The U.S. Army found itself continually suppressing uprisings throughout the islands. However, following his capture on March 23, 1901, Aguinaldo advised his followers to swear allegiance to the United States. On July 4, 1902, the army declared the insurrection over, even though the Moros, who had become largely independent under Spanish rule, fought until 1913.

William Howard Taft, president of the Philippine Commission, installed U.S. control on September 1, 1900 (although some areas still opposed that control). A year later, he became the first governor-general of the Philippines. Between 1901 and 1913, Americans centralized the government, creating an elected body, the Philippine Assembly. The judicial system and the civil service, modeled after American counterparts, replaced the Spanish system.

The greatest American impact occurred in education, with primary schools set up throughout the islands. Nationwide vocational schools and teachers colleges were established, as was the system's crown jewel, the University of the Philippines. Religious freedom was now guaranteed as governmental support of the Catholic Church ended, although most provincial colleges remained under Catholic control. Protestant denominations agreed to divide up the islands so as not to compete with one another for converts. A major cause of Filipino unrest under Spanish rule was the amount of Church-controlled land. To address that issue, the United States bought 400,000 acres (161,874 hectares) from the church and sold parcels of it to former tenant farmers for low prices and easy payment terms.

Modern Era Although American administrators tended to be benevolent, Filipinos still desired independence. Leaders of the Nacionalista (Nationalist) Party called for immediate independence. In 1907 the Nacionalistas gained control of elective offices in villages, provinces, and the Philippine Assembly, but wealthy, land-owning party members turned to *caciquism* to control the party. By 1917 two political leaders, Sergio Osmena and Manuel Quezon, had acquired national power. At this point most immigrants to the United States and the Territory of Hawaii were Nacionalistas who were fleeing *caciquism*.

In 1916 U.S. president Woodrow Wilson, who was committed to making the Philippines an independent nation, supported the Jones Act, which promised that the Philippines would become free when its government stabilized. The act, however, enabled Osmena's and Quezon's political machines to entrench themselves. In 1921 Republican administrations in both the United States and the Philippines insisted that the islands were not yet ready to govern themselves, and Philippine independence was tabled.

During the late 1920s, concerns over the influx of Filipinos into the West Coast of the United States, combined with falling agricultural prices for certain American commodities, prompted American farmers to agitate for ending free trade with the islands, while exclusionists called for ending Filipino immigration. Both groups argued for Philippine independence.

The Tydings-McDuffie Act of 1934 promised independence after ten years and created the Commonwealth of the Philippines. The Philippine legislature approved this act and in 1935 the Filipino people approved a constitution.

In the Philippines' first presidential election, in 1935, Quezon became president, and Osmena became vice president. With their inauguration, the Commonwealth of the Philippines came into being; however, many Filipinos remained ambivalent about independence. It appealed to their sense of nationalism, but the islands' economy depended on tariff-free American markets. Many felt that the imposition of tariffs would be disastrous.

According to the Tydings-McDuffie Act, the Philippines were to become independent in 1944, but when the Japanese took military control of the islands in 1942, the Quezon government fled to Australia and then to the United States, where Quezon continued as the commonwealth's president until his death in 1944.

U.S. president Harry Truman proclaimed the independence of the Philippines in 1946, and Manuel Roxas became the first president of the new republic. Meanwhile, Filipinos who had immigrated to the United States before Tydings-McDuffie or who had joined the U.S. military during World War II were granted eligibility for U.S. citizenship. The United States also imposed the Philippine Rehabilitation Act and the Philippine Trade Act, which favored American corporations to the detriment of the Philippine economy. These acts and the perceived threat of communism caused the United States to maintain military bases in the islands.

The new republic struggled to realize nationhood during the postwar years. The Huks, a communist group, waged war with Roxas's government until 1954. (*Huks* is a shortened term for *Hukbon Magpapalaya ng Bayan Laban sa Hapon*, or People's Anti-Japanese Liberation Army.) Since independence, violence has continued, and most election days in the Philippines are marred by violence.

In 1965 Ferdinand Marcos became president of the Philippines, prompting several opposition groups to adopt terrorist tactics. Marcos seized this development as the opportunity to declare martial law and appoint himself dictator. This state of affairs lasted for fourteen years. In 1973 Marcos proclaimed a new constitution, declaring himself president. In 1978

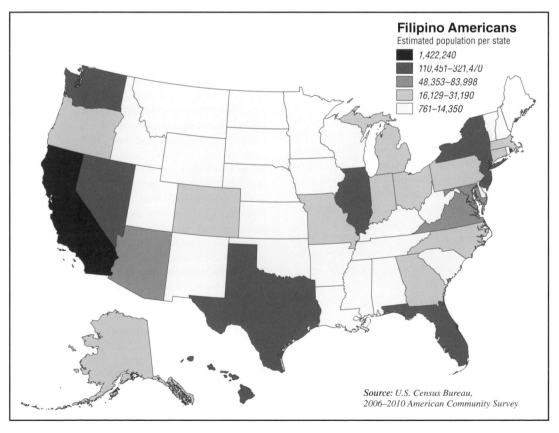

Filipino Americans
Estimated population per state

- 1,422,240
- 110,451–321,470
- 48,353–83,998
- 16,129–31,190
- 761–14,350

Source: U.S. Census Bureau, 2006–2010 American Community Survey

he gave his wife, Imelda, extensive political power. This heightened the level of political repression, and Marcos's political opponents began to leave the country, often for the United States and particularly Hawaii and California. In 1981 Marcos lifted martial law and turned political power over to the national legislature, enabling his reelection.

In 1983 Benigno S. Aquino Jr., a Filipino senator and the leading rival of Marcos, was assassinated, fomenting political unrest until 1986, when Marcos fled the country and Corazon Aquino, Benigno Aquino's widow, became the eleventh Philippine president. The end of the Marcos era did not bring calm, however. Unsuccessful coups against the government have continued, and the economy has remained weak. In additional, widespread poverty and communist opposition have posed threats to the unstable central government.

Benigno "Noynoy" Aquino III, the son of Benigno S. Aquino Jr. and Corazon Aquino in 2010 became the fifteenth president of the Philippines. In his state-of-the-nation address in July 2011, he acknowledged that the Philippines was struggling with hunger, poverty, and lack of opportunity. However, compared to its past, in the twenty-first century the Philippines has made significant progress in many ways. Rural areas have experienced job growth, child immunization programs have been initiated, the military has been modernized, and aid programs for the elderly and the physically challenged have been implemented. The Philippines' gross domestic product, which measures the country's national income and output, averaged $52.4 billion (U.S. dollars) from 1960 to 2011. In 2011 it reached a record high of $224.8 billion, reflecting the Philippines' dramatically increasing prosperity.

SETTLEMENT IN THE UNITED STATES

Filipino arrivals in the Territory of Hawaii and the United States mainland came in three waves. The earliest, from 1903 to 1935, brought many young men to enroll in American universities and colleges and then return to the Philippines. Also during this time, plantation workers arrived to work in Hawaii from 1906 to the 1930s, with a parallel movement occurring along the Pacific Coast during the 1920s—an immigration that lasted until enactment of the Tydings-McDuffie Act in 1934. A much smaller influx to American shores occurred following World War II. The third and largest immigration wave arrived after passage of the 1965 Immigration Act. Since 1970 Philippine immigration to the United States has been surpassed only by Mexican immigration.

The first wave of Filipino immigrants came to the United States seeking higher education. Governor-General Taft's administration prepared an educational plan, the Pensionado Act, to send promising young Filipinos to institutions of higher learning in the United States. Beginning in 1903, a group of one hundred students left for the United States, and by 1910 all had returned. These men came to play key roles in agriculture, business, education, engineering, and government.

Other students followed; a later estimate indicated that between 1910 and 1938 almost 14,000 Filipinos had enrolled in educational institutions throughout the United States. Most of them came as independent students and not part of the *pensionado* program. Many of these hopefuls became overwhelmed by the high cost of living, inadequate academic preparation, insufficient language skills, or an inability to determine what level of American education best suited their state of educational preparation. These Filipinos soon found themselves trapped in the world of unskilled laborers. Most who succeeded in graduating from major universities returned to the Philippines to take their places with other such graduates as provincial and national leaders.

A chance encounter in 1901 between a trustee of the Hawaiian Sugar Planters Association (HSPA) and a band of Filipino musicians en route to the United States led the planter to speculate about Filipinos as potential plantation workers, for he felt that these musicians had a "healthy physique and robust appearance." Even before 1907, Hawaii had begun looking for other pools of unskilled labor on the Philippine island of Luzon. During 1907 some 150 workers were sent to Hawaii. Two years later, with Chinese, Japanese, and Koreans now banned from immigrating to the United States, the HSPA returned to the Philippines, looking for workers. The U.S. Bureau of the Census reported 2,361 Filipinos in Hawaii in 1910. Recruiting efforts after 1909 centered on the Visayan Islands, Cebu in particular, and Luzon's Tagalogs.

In 1915 recruiters focused on Luzon's northwestern Ilocano provinces: Ilocos Norte, Ilocos Sur, and La Unión. The Ilocanos, suffering greatly from economic hardship and overpopulation, proved willing recruits. The HSPA awarded a three-year labor contract to Filipinos migrating to Hawaii that paid their passage to Hawaii and guaranteed free subsistence and clothing. If they worked a total of 720 days, they received money for their return passage. A worker was not penalized for violating his contract, but if he did, he forfeited all guarantees, including his return passage. Plantation owners found the Ilocanos to be excellent workers, and poverty in their provinces provided a stimulant for their emigration. By 1935 young, single Ilocano men were the largest Filipino ethnic group in Hawaii.

According to census figures, the Filipino population in Hawaii climbed from 21,031 in 1920 to 63,052 in 1930 but had dropped to 52,659 by 1940. The decline in the number of Filipinos during the late 1930s is attributable to the return of many to the Philippines during the Depression years and the departure of others to the U.S. West Coast. The high point of immigration to Hawaii occurred in 1925, when 11,621 Filipinos arrived in Honolulu. At that point, the HSPA closed active recruiting in the Philippines, relying upon the Filipinos' own desire to emigrate to maintain the influx of workers.

In 1910 only 406 Filipinos lived on the United States mainland. The largest group, 109, lived in New Orleans, the remnants of a nineteenth-century settlement of Filipino sailors who came ashore at that port city, married local women, found jobs, and settled down. The state of Washington had 17 and California had only 5. By 1920, 5,603 Filipinos were living along the West Coast and in Alaska. California then had 2,674 Filipinos while Washington had 958. The northeastern United States had the second-largest number: 1,844.

The 1920s saw dramatic changes in these numbers as California's Filipino population—mostly single, young men—increased by 91 percent as more than 31,000 Filipinos arrived at the ports of San Francisco and Los Angeles. In 1930, 108,260 Filipinos lived in the United States and the Territory of Hawaii. California had 30,470, and this number rose to 31,408 by 1940. Washington had 3,480 in 1930 and 2,222 in 1940. Apart from the West Coast and Hawaii, the next largest concentration was in New York, which in 1930 had 1,982 and 2,978 in 1940. Many of these Filipinos experienced significant racial discrimination.

Emigrants in the second wave left the Philippines in increasing numbers during the late 1940s and 1950s. This group included so-called war brides, the "1946 boys," and military recruits. War brides were mainly the spouses of American GIs who married Filipina women while stationed in the Philippines. After the passage of the War Brides Act of 1946, which exempted foreign spouses and children of American GIs from immigration quotas, it is estimated that 5,000 such brides came to the United States. Contracted workers called the "1946 boys," or *sakadas*, numbered 7,000 and were a major component of the second wave. They were the last large group of agricultural laborers brought to Hawaii by the sugar planters. Plantation owners brought them in an effort to break up the first interracial and territory-wide strike organized by the International Longshoremen and Warehousemen's Union (ILWU). The Philippine workers supported the ILWU strike, which resulted in the first major victory for Hawaii's agricultural workers. Filipinos who came to the United States through the U.S. military were another component of the second wave. During the Wilson administration the U.S. Navy had begun to replace African Americans with Filipinos for mess-hall labor and this trend continued after President Truman ended racial segregation in the military in 1946. By the 1970s more than 20,000 Filipinos had entered the United States through work with the navy.

After the Philippines became a republic, internal conditions in the country contributed to many Filipinos' moving to the United States. By 1960 Hawaii, which had become a state a year earlier, had 69,070 Filipinos, followed closely by California with 65,459. The two states together accounted for 76 percent of all Filipinos living in the United States.

The Pacific Coast states had 146,340 (83 percent of the total), while the East and the South had slightly more than 10,000 each, and the Great Lakes states had 8,600. Included in these census numbers were second-generation Filipino Americans.

Changes in American immigration law in 1965 significantly altered the type and number of immigrants coming to the United States. Unlike immigrants before World War II, who largely worked as unskilled laborers in West Coast and Hawaiian agriculture and in Alaska's salmon canneries, the third wave was composed of larger numbers of well-educated Filipinos between the ages of twenty and forty who came looking for better career opportunities than they could find in the Philippines. This highly skilled third-wave population spoke English, which allowed them to enter a wide range of professions.

Unlike earlier arrivals, most of the Filipino immigrants after 1970 came to the United States without intending to return to the Philippines. In 1970 Filipinos who lived in the United States numbered 343,060; by 2010 the number had reached 3.4 million. In 2011 the U.S. Department of State estimated the number at 4 million. According to the 2010 census, 1,474,707 people of Philippine descent (43 percent of all Filipino Americans) lived in California. Los Angeles alone was home to 374,285, and a section of the city became known as Filipinotown. Filipino Americans are the largest Asian American group in San Diego. A nearby portion of California State Highway 54 is named the Filipino-American Highway. The 2010 census lists Filipinos as Hawaii's largest Asian population. About 200,000 Filipino Americans live in the New York City area, mostly in the borough of Queens. The Philippine Independence Day parade marches down Madison Avenue annually on the first Sunday in June. Other states with substantial numbers of Filipinos include Illinois, Texas, Florida, New Jersey, Nevada, and Washington.

LANGUAGE

The official languages in the Philippines are Pilipino (a derivative of Tagalog) and English. Linguists have identified some eighty-seven different dialects throughout the country. At the time of Philippine independence, about 25 percent of Filipinos spoke Tagalog, the language of central Luzon. About 44 percent spoke Visayan; Visayans in the United States generally spoke Cebuano. The language most commonly spoken by Filipinos in Hawaii and the United States mainland is Ilocano, although only 15 percent of those in the Philippines speak this language. The coming of the fourth wave of Filipinos brought more Tagalog speakers; however, the high number of university graduates in this wave communicated easily in English. Others, however, did not know English or spoke it poorly. In Hawaii, social service centers taught English by showing Filipinos how to shop in supermarkets and how to order in restaurants. In 2011, according to the U.S. Office of Minority Health, 22 percent of Filipino Americans did not speak English.

Filipino Americans and other U.S. citizens in Manilla show their support for Barack Obama's presidential bid, 2008. LUIS LIWANAG / NEWSCOM

RELIGION

Because the majority of early Filipino immigrants to the United States were young single males, few Filipino Catholics attended church with any regularity. Once families began settling in the United States, however, religion became a central component of family and community life. According to a 2012 Pew Research Center survey, 65 percent of Filipino Americans are Catholic, 21 percent are Protestant, 8 percent are nonpracticing, and 1 percent are Buddhist. Filipino religious practices are unique in that influences of pre-Western Philippine tribal beliefs, such as the intervention of spirits, continue to have a presence. Although the Westernization of Filipino American religious practice is strong, some members of older generations still believe that barbequing on Good Friday will produce black freckles, bathing on Good Friday will cause deathly illness, and having sex on Good Friday will join a couple, literally, until they die.

CULTURE AND ASSIMILATION

From the outset of their arrival in Hawaii and the Pacific Coast, Filipinos, as a color-visible minority, encountered racial prejudice as they pursued their economic and educational goals. One major problem for Filipinos prior to 1946 was access to U.S. citizenship.

Beginning in 1898, Filipinos, classified as U.S. nationals, could travel abroad with U.S. passports and could enter and leave the United States at will. That ended in 1934 with the passage of the Tydings-McDuffie Act, which included making the Philippines independent. Thus Filipinos in the United States technically became immigrants and subject to current immigration laws, which limited the number entering as immigrants to fifty a year. The U.S. Supreme Court, in the 1925 decision *Toyota v. United States*, declared that only whites or persons of African descent were entitled to citizenship, thus closing the opportunity for Filipinos to become United States citizens. However, Filipinos who had enlisted and served three years in the U.S. Navy, Marine Corps, or Naval Auxiliary Service during World War I and who had received honorable discharges could apply for citizenship. In 1946 Congress passed a law that permitted Filipinos to qualify for American citizenship.

The inability to acquire citizenship was not only a social stigma but created serious economic and political problems. Since most states required citizenship in order to practice law, medicine, and other licensed professional occupations, Filipinos were prohibited from entering these fields. Unlike immigrants from other countries who had ambassadors and consuls, Filipinos had no recognized voice to speak for them or protest on their behalf. The Philippines had a resident commissioner in Washington, D.C., but this office generally proved ineffective in dealing with governmental bureaucracies.

Throughout the Great Depression of the 1930s, Filipinos encountered obstacles to qualifying for federal relief. Although the Works Progress Administration (WPA) in 1937 ruled that Filipinos were eligible for employment on WPA projects, they were often passed over because they were not citizens. During the 1920s and 1930s, Filipinos living on the Pacific Coast encountered severe prejudice and hostility, at times resulting in race riots. The sagging economy made assimilation difficult if not impossible.

In 1930, at the height of anti-Filipino discrimination in California, the state's Department of Industrial Relations published a racist study, *Facts about Filipino Immigration into California*, claiming that Filipinos posed economic and social threats. On the West Coast, restaurants and barbershops frequently denied service to Filipinos, and swimming pools, movie theaters, and tennis courts denied them admission. They found that their dark skin and imperfect English marked them, in the eyes of whites, as being inferior. White Californians presented several contradictions that confused Filipinos: Whereas farmers and certain urban enterprises welcomed them because they provided cheap labor, discriminatory attitudes relegated them to low-paying jobs and an inferior social existence. While denying them many kinds of employment, many Californians criticized the Filipinos for their substandard living conditions and attacked them for allegedly creating health problems and for lowering the American standard of living. Faced with discrimination in real estate, Filipinos were forced into ghettos known as "Little Manilas" in California cities. Filipinos in cities such as Chicago, New York, and Washington, D.C., also clustered together.

Discrimination against Filipinos continues in the twenty-first century, but civil rights legislation, affirmative action, and equal-opportunity laws have improved the conditions of most of those who have arrived in recent decades. An unexpected form of discrimination, however, has emerged for immigrants arriving after 1965: hostility from earlier-generation Filipino Americans. Some of the earlier immigrants see the later arrivals as benefiting from advances made by the earlier group without having paid the price. Conversely, more-recent Filipino arrivals at times perceive their older compatriots to be unsophisticated and backward, and if they cannot speak a Filipino language, they are not to be accepted as true Filipinos.

Many Filipino Americans today are firmly established members of the middle class, partly because of a steady stream of educated and skilled Filipino arrivals in the United States and partly because of the college-degree completion rate of second- and third-generation Filipino Americans. In 2011 Filipino American remittances to the Philippines reached over $20 billion—a 7 percent increase over 2010.

Traditions and Customs Cockfighting, a major source of entertainment and gambling in the Philippines, has been a common pastime among Filipino American men from the beginning of their U.S. immigration. Although cockfighting is now illegal, it continues to attract Filipinos in Hawaii and on the mainland.

Filipinos use the term *kuya* (literally, "big brother") as a term of respect for males older than the speaker. *Ate* (literally, "big sister") is the equivalent term for older females. *Mano po* refers to a gesture of respect toward elders that involves raising the elder's hand toward one's forehead. Filipinos use nonverbal communication more than most Americans. Two examples are their use of the eyebrows and the lips. Raised eyebrows mean yes. To indicate directions or locations, rather than voice them or point with their hands, Filipinos often simply pucker their lips and face the direction in question. As with many other Asian cultures, Filipinos customarily remove their shoes when entering a house. They also make a point of saying a hello when meeting and a good-bye when parting. Failure to do so is considered a slight.

Cuisine As with many Pacific Rim countries, rice is the staple food of the Philippines. Three popular dishes are *lumpia*, *kare kare*, and chicken and pork adobo. *Lumpia* are egg rolls—a *lumpia* wrapper filled with pork, shrimp, cabbage, beans, scallions, and bean sprouts, fried in peanut oil. *Kare kare* is a peanut-oil-flavored stewed mixture of oxtail and beef tripe mixed with onions and tomatoes. Chicken and pork adobo consists of these two meats boiled in vinegar and soy sauce and flavored with garlic and spices. This dish is then served over rice. Despite its appeal, Philippine cuisine is underrepresented among U.S. eating establishments. Those few Filipino restaurants that do exist often have American-influenced menus that are disdained by Philippine natives. Reasons given for this lack of representation are the lack of a clear Filipino identity, a preference for cooking traditional dishes in the home, and a tendency among young Filipino Americans to favor other cuisines, including American fast-food options.

Traditional Dress Philippine traditional dress encompasses tribal attire, which is worn in the United States only occasionally, typically at festivals. Filipino American men sometimes wear the official costume, the *barong tagalog*, to special events. The *barong tagalog* is a shirt jacket worn over a collarless Chinese shirt. Its design borrows from Chinese, Indo-Malay, Hindu, and European men's fashion. For formal occasions, Filipino American women sometimes wear the women's official costume, the *baro't saya*, or mestiza dress, which has sleeves shaped like butterfly wings. Sometimes it is called the Imelda dress after former First Lady Imelda Marcos. Muslim Filipinos wear traditional Muslim attire. In general, Filipino Americans have adopted Western clothing styles, and some young Filipinos even disdain the clothing of their heritage.

Dances and Songs *Tinikling* is a form of traditional dancing that uses bamboo poles to hit and slide against each other and drag on the ground as other dancers step over and between them. The *cariñosa* (meaning "loved one") is a dance in which dancers create romantic scenarios using fans and handkerchiefs. It is accompanied by Latin American music and Spanish lyrics.

Gongs, introduced to Southeast Asia by the Chinese before the tenth century CE, are a central instrument in the history of Philippine music. Later traditional Philippine music is a mixture of Asian, European, Latin American, American, and indigenous music. In the 1950s indigenous bands began to put Tagalog lyrics to American rock and roll. This led in the 1960s to a genre called Philippine rock. A Philippine rock band called the Rocky Fellers reached number sixteen on the U.S. charts with a song titled *Killer Joe*. A contemporary product of the Westernization of Filipino music is P-Pop (Philippine popular music), which exists alongside K-Pop (Korean popular music), J-Pop (Japanese popular music), and C-Pop (Chinese popular music). These and other forms of Filipino entertainment receive support from websites such as Philippine Entertainment Portal, Tagolog Lang, FilAm Creative, Adobo Nation, and Filipino Americans in Media Entertainment.

THE KARAOKE MACHINE AND THE YO-YO: FILIPINO INVENTIONS

In 1972 Philippine inventor Roberto del Rosario developed a prototype karaoke machine. It became popular enough that he began outsourcing its production to Japan. He soon noticed that similar machines were being sold in Japan. He filed a patent violation suit and won. By the 1990s Rosario's invention had been greatly improved and was known and used worldwide. It remains wildly popular today among Filipino Americans.

Although the yo-yo's roots reach to ancient Greece, the toy as we know it descends from a weapon that emerged in the Philippines in the 1500s. Consisting of a stone of about four pounds and a length of rope, hunters could throw it at running animals to entangle their legs. In the 1920s a Filipino named Pedro Flores moved to the United States and found employment at a hotel in Santa Monica, California. He would play with his yo-yo during his lunch break and found himself drawing crowds (*yo yo* means "come come" in Tagalog). Before long he was owner of the Flores Yo-Yo Company.

Holidays New Year's Day is a popular Filipino holiday. In the Philippines, celebrants open their doors and windows and make loud noises with *torotots* (small trumpetlike instruments made of cardboard), fireworks, drumming, coin clinking, and howling. This is thought to invite good luck into the home for the new year. These activities are not common among Filipino Americans, who find little support for them from their non-Filipino neighbors. The Lenten season is also important to Catholic Filipinos. Many attend masses in fourteen churches to represent Jesus's Fourteen Stations of the Cross. In the Philippines some devotees practice a custom called *Penitensya*, in which they are literally nailed to crosses to express their devotion to Jesus Christ. This practice is not done in the United States. Philippines Independence Day is celebrated on June 12 in honor of the Philippines' freedom from Spain. All Saints Day and All Souls Day occur on November 1 and 2, respectively. In the Philippines families celebrate by gathering in cemeteries to let their deceased relatives feel the love the living have for them. This custom is not as well observed in the United States. Roman Catholic Filipinos consider Christmas their most important holiday. They celebrate it much as other Christians do, with church services, family gatherings, and gift exchanges.

Art and Entertainment The Filipinos who came to Hawaii and the West Coast during the 1920s and 1930s sought a range of activities to relieve the monotony of long hours of unskilled labor. As a result of recruitment tactics of the agribusiness industry in Hawaii and the West Coast, the pre–World War II Filipino community consisted almost entirely of single, uneducated men, with few or no relatives in the United States. These men enjoyed betting on prizefights and wrestling matches, and gambling at poker, blackjack, and dice. During the 1930s they increased the profits of gambling operators and prostitution rings in Stockton, California, by about $2 million annually. These men's enthusiastic patronage of gambling, dance halls, and prostitution seemed to lend credence to white Americans' complaints that Filipinos were immoral and lawless. Many Filipino residents of California traveled to the casinos of Reno, Nevada, looking for the proverbial pot of gold. Pool halls in the "Little Manilas" provided both recreation and gambling. In recent years, a small but determined Philippine/Filipino movie industry has emerged. An edgy Filipino American art scene has established itself, with many of the artists linked by the Filipino American Artists Network. In 1972 Ferdinand Marcos created the National Artist of the Philippines Award, given for excellence in each of the respective arts.

Health Care Issues and Practices Second-wave Filipinos incurred severe health problems as they aged. One illness that seemed almost endemic was gouty arthritis, coupled with an excessive amount of uric acid in the blood. Doctors have speculated that a genetic characteristic makes these Filipinos unable to tolerate the American diet. One study conducted in Hawaii showed that Filipino women have a higher rate of heart disease and circulatory problems than the state's general population has. The same study noted that Filipino men suffered more from amyotrophic lateral sclerosis (Lou Gehrig's disease) than other men did. Other diseases of high incidence were liver cancer and diabetes. Recent immigrants are better educated and more likely to know the value of good health care. The U.S. Office of Minority Health reported in 2011 that 79 percent of Filipino Americans have health insurance coverage. Utilization of medical services has increased among Filipino Americans, and in fact this group is now well represented in the medical professions. The average life span of Filipino Americans today, at 81.5 years, is above the U.S. mean. However, societal factors such as language barriers and avoiding health services for fear of deportation pose threats to some Filipino Americans.

FAMILY AND COMMUNITY LIFE

Gender Roles Matrilinearity was common in the Philippines before the Spanish arrived, and its influences remain in the Filipino American community. Although patriarchy dominates Filipino culture, Filipino women fare better than those in many Asian cultures. Role models such as Imelda Marcos and former presidents Corazon Aquino and Gloria Macapalgal-Arroyo inspire Filipino women. In recent decades many women have come to the United States to be the family breadwinners in nursing careers. Husbands stay in the Philippines and raise the children. Divorce is not permitted in the Philippines. Men philander but disdain macho behavior. For example, manicures and pedicures often accompany haircuts. Transsexuals, both male-to-female and female-to-male, are more open than in the United States despite occasional violence against them. Filipino American families sometimes punish their women for wearing short hair or pants.

Education Of the fifty states, California is most successful in honoring Filipino culture. It teaches Tagalog in its public schools and has named October Filipino American History Month. Although numerically comparable to Chinese Americans nationally, according to the 2010 census, Filipinos lag behind them and other Asian American groups. They also have a smaller percentage in college and a smaller percentage of bachelor's degrees among the twenty-five-to- twenty-nine age group. A marked difference exists between Philippine-educated Filipinos and U.S.-educated ones, with the Philippine-educated (many of whom enter the medical profession) faring above the U.S. mean in most educational categories.

Courtship and Weddings Courtship among Filipino Americans tends to be of two quite different kinds. Courtship among Americanized families is much like courtship among mainstream Americans. This is becoming increasingly true even in the Philippines. However, courtship within traditional families can be a very different experience. A man contemplating a relationship with a Filipina woman probably will encounter a situation that is somewhere between these two extremes. First, traditional Filipino courtship is rooted in strict Catholicism. Men of other faiths or no faith might approach such a situation with caution because church is likely to play a major role in the marriage. The courtship is always initiated by the man because it is considered shameful for a woman to do so. It involves wooing the parents with small gifts, charm, and good manners when visiting the woman (and, initially, most or all visits will be at her home with the parents present). The one rule that most agree is written in stone is that propriety be observed in public to avoid bringing shame to the family. Having observed this in all instances, a suitor might find the rules a good deal more relaxed in private, sometimes even to the point where sex is condoned after the parents have given their daughter permission to marry. A potential suitor might also consider the fact that, traditionally, the bride's parents do not pay for the wedding; the groom does.

Traditional Filipino weddings have sponsors—older, adult friends and relatives of the family who confirm the couple's union and promise to support them over the years. Primary sponsors stand as principal witnesses to the taking of the vows. Secondary sponsors are involved in the veil-and-cord ceremony. With the bride and groom kneeling, they drape a large white veil over the bride's head and fasten it to the groom's shoulders. A cord is wrapped around them to symbolize the union's eternal nature. Then the bride and groom are each given a candle to light a unity candle. Three sets of sponsors are needed: two to "clothe us as one" (help with the veil), two to "bind us together" (handle the cord), and two to "light the way" (handle the candles). The wedding also includes memory sponsors who consist of the deceased, as well as living guests who could not attend. Finally the groom gives the bride the Arrhea, or the thirteen golden coins, which the priest has blessed for a prosperous and faithful marriage. Another tradition is the bride's wearing of her wedding ring on her right hand.

Relations with other Americans As second-wave Filipinos grew older and realized that they would not live to see acceptance by white America, they took matters into their own hands by forming various organizations to look after their welfare. These included Caballeros de Dimas-Alang, Legionairos del Trabajo, and Gran Oriente Filipino (Great Filipino Lodge). The first, organized in 1921, honored José Rizal, the Philippine national hero (his pen name when writing revolutionary tracts was Dimas-Alang). This fraternal lodge at one time during the 1930s had a hundred chapters throughout the United States and was one of many that commemorated Rizal's execution on José Rizal Day, December 30. Using federal and city agencies, Caballeros de Dimas-Alang built the Dimas-Alang House in San Francisco to care for elderly and low-income Filipinos. Legionairos del Trabajo, organized in San Francisco in 1920, originated in the Philippines. Centered in San Francisco, it had about 700 members, some of whom were women. Filipinos established Gran Oriente Filipino in San Francisco in 1924. At one time it had 3,000 members in forty-six states and the territories of Alaska and Hawaii. All lodges sponsored beauty pageants and dances in their various communities. Such pageants continue, and now often include a Mrs. Philippines pageant as well. The United Farm Workers Organizing Committee established the Paulo Agbayani Retirement Village near Delano for older Filipino field-workers. As younger Filipinos worried about the fate of these aging agricultural workers, the organization Pilipino Bayanihan in 1972 built the largest federally funded community, located in Stockton. Subsequently, branches were built in Tulare County, Coachella, Brawley, and Ventura. Pilipino Bayanihan hoped to fulfill the needs of the unemployed and underemployed, as well as of senior citizens.

Caught up in the broader struggle for racial equality, Filipino Americans today still find themselves experiencing at-times intense discrimination in schools, communities, and places of work. They have organized community groups representing a wide range of concerns, but a tendency toward fragmentation has made it difficult to present a common front on issues of mutual concern. Organizations may be based on professions or politics, but most have evolved from a common religion, city, barrio, language, school, or church in the Philippines. In 2011 California had more than four hundred cultural and social organizations representing Filipinos.

The distinct migration patterns of the Filipinos have led to unique community dynamics. The vast majority of the second wave of Filipinos migrating to Hawaii and the West Coast, as has been noted, were single young men. Few married and had families in the United States. The dream that most Filipinos had but never realized—returning to the Philippines—led to disillusionment as these young men grew old, still trapped in unskilled labor positions. Many of these men sent money to the Philippines to help their families pay taxes, buy land, finance the education of relatives, or meet other financial obligations.

Few of those who returned to the Philippines came from the West Coast. Most were from Hawaii's plantations. Those who did return were known as *Hawayanos*. Back in their home villages, the *Hawayanos* had a greater degree of affluence than that of their nonmigrant neighbors. Filipino Americans' philanthropy went mostly to benefit relatives in the Philippines. Filipinos sent funds to their families in Philippine barrios. Several mayors of villages in Ilocos Norte reported that about $35,000 a month was received through the pension checks of returned Ilocano workers and from remittances sent by fourth-wave immigrants. During the Marcos regime the Philippine government offered inexpensive airfares and incentives to foster return visits by recent immigrants, who in turn furnished information about life in the United States and, as had earlier immigrants, helped with family finances.

While some Americans in the 1930s believed that Filipinos of the second wave were head-hunting savages, others feared that they posed a health threat because of a meningitis outbreak at that time. The greatest concern, however, came from the attention that these young men lavished on American women. Given that in 1930 the ratio of Filipino males to Filipina females was fourteen to one, it was only natural that the men would seek companionship with non-Filipina women. During the 1920s and 1930s, young men frequented taxi-dance halls, where white girls, hired to dance with male customers, were paid ten cents for a one-minute dance. Many white citizens believed that meetings between the young Filipinos and the white women, whose morals were assumed to be questionable to begin with, led to inappropriate behavior by these men. In addition to these urban dance halls, "floating" taxi-dancers followed the Filipino migrant workers from California's Imperial Valley to the central and coastal valleys. Coupled with whites' fear of Filipino attention to white women was an economic motive—the fear of losing jobs to the migrant labor force.

In Filipino society the extended family, composed of paternal and maternal relatives, was traditionally the center of life. The family provided sustenance, social alliances, and political affiliations. Its social structure extended to include neighbors, fellow workers, and ritual or honorary kinsmen, called *compadres*. All of these people were welded together by this *compadrazgo* system, which emphasized group welfare and loyalty over individual concerns. Through this system, which stemmed from the Roman Catholic church's rituals of weddings and baptisms, parents of a newborn child selected godparents, and this in turn led to a lifelong association. This bound the community together while excluding outsiders. Given the tightly knit villages or barrios, the *compadrazgo* system created obligations that included sharing food, labor, and financial resources.

To offset the absence of kin in the Philippines or to compensate for the lack of female immigrants, Filipino Americans sought out male relatives and *compadres* from their barrios to cook, eat, and live together in bunkhouses. Thus they formed a surrogate family, known as a *kumpang*, with the eldest man serving as leader of the "household." In addition, Filipino Americans compensated for the lack of traditional families by observing "life-cycle celebrations" such as baptisms, birthdays, weddings, and funerals. These celebrations took on a greater importance than they would have in the Philippines, providing the single Filipino men without relatives in the United States the opportunity to become part of an extended family. Such new customs became an important part of the Filipino American strategy for adapting to a new life in the United States.

A few Filipinos in California married Filipinas or Mexicans, while those living in Hawaii married Filipinas, Hawaiians, Puerto Ricans, or Portuguese. Women from these groups came from cultures whose value systems were similar to those of the men; however, large weddings, common in the barrios, did not occur because of the lack of family members. The birth of a child saw the replication of the *compadrazgo* system. The rite of baptism presented an opportunity for those of the same barrio to come together for a time of socializing. As many as two hundred sponsors might appear to become godparents, but the sense of obligation found in the Philippines was not as strong in the United States. Marriages and funerals also brought Filipino Americans together to renew their common ties.

Recent immigrants, unlike the agricultural workers of the 1920s and 1930s, are likely to move to metropolitan areas because employment opportunities are better. Often wives will come to the United States by themselves because they are more employable as nurses, and send money home to their husbands. They bring their families later if they become sufficiently established. These recent arrivals also bring the barrio's familial and *compadrazgo* structures. Having complete families, they find traditional relationships easier to maintain. Those in the greater New York area settle in Queens and Westchester County in New York and in Jersey City, Riverdale, and Bergen County in New Jersey. A part of New York City's Ninth Avenue has become a center of Filipino culture, with restaurants and small shops catering to Filipinos' needs. Unlike on the West Coast, however, there is no identifiable ethnic enclave. Outsiders see these East Coast Filipinos merely as part of the larger Asian American community. They are largely professionals such as bankers, doctors, insurance salespeople, lawyers, nurses, secretaries, and travel agents.

EMPLOYMENT AND ECONOMIC CONDITIONS

Second-wave Filipinos came to the United States primarily "to get rich quick"—by Philippine standards—and return to their home provinces to live in affluence. Thus their goal was not to assimilate into life in the United States but to find high-paying jobs. They faced severe handicaps because of limited education and job skills, inadequate English, and racial prejudice. In 1901 the California legislature enacted a law forbidding whites to marry blacks, Mongolians, or mixed-race persons. In the early 1930s, California attorney general U. S. Webb ruled that Filipinos were Mongolians, but since his opinion did not have the force of law, it was up to each of the fifty-eight county clerks to determine the racial origins of Filipinos. By 1936 Nevada, Oregon, and Washington had enacted laws prohibiting marriages between Filipinos and whites. Consequently, white women could only become Filipino men's common-law wives. In 1948 the California Supreme Court ruled in *Perez v. Sharp* that the miscegenation law violated individual civil rights, which freed Filipinos to marry whomever they pleased.

Some found ready but low-paying employment as migrant field hands and cannery workers on the West Coast. Others were employed in the merchant marine or U.S. Navy. Compared with Philippine wages, agricultural workers' pay seemed high. The workers, however, became ensnared in these jobs due to the higher cost of living in the United States.

California agriculture, with its specialty crops, relied on migrant field-workers. From the Imperial Valley to the Sacramento Valley, farmers sought cheap field labor to harvest their crops. Filipino and Mexican workers dominated the throngs harvesting asparagus, cantaloupes, citrus fruits, cotton, lettuce, potatoes, strawberries, sugar beets, and tomatoes. Filipinos returned annually to work as members of an organized work gang headed by a *padrone* who negotiated contracts with growers. The *padrone* supervised the gang's work and provided housing and meals, charging a fee against wages. These gangs followed the harvest season north from California into Oregon's Hood River Valley and Washington's Wenatchee Valley. As late as the 1950s, Filipinos provided the largest number of migrant workers for western U.S. agriculture.

FILIPINO PROVERBS

Filipino proverbs are rich in wit and meaning. They include the following:

- A desperate person will even hold onto a knife blade.
- Working hard is better than not working, and working smart is better than working hard.
- A broom is sturdy because its strands are tightly bound.
- A dressed-up monkey is still a monkey.
- A year's care, a minute's ruin.
- All food is tasty in a famine.
- The fly on the water buffalo's back is taller than the water buffalo.
- The pain of study is less than the pain of ignorance.
- Find sugar, find ants.
- Don't empty the water jar until the rain falls.

Migrant jobs ended after the harvest season. Filipinos then moved to cities in the late fall and winter in search of employment. However, most usually had to return to the fields in the spring. By 1930 Los Angeles, San Francisco, Stockton, and Seattle each had "Little Manilas," resulting from discriminatory real estate covenants that restricted Filipinos to congested ghettos. The numbers living in these racial enclaves varied, depending on the time of year, with the population highest in the winter months. A few Filipinos catered to their countrymen's needs—barbershops, grocery stores, poolrooms, dance halls, restaurants, and auto-repair garages. Others found employment in hotel service jobs, working as dishwashers, bellhops, and elevator operators. Some worked in various unskilled restaurant jobs or as houseboys.

Second-generation Filipino Americans, descendants of immigrants of the 1920s and 1930s, worked in both skilled and unskilled jobs. California trade unions remained closed to them, keeping them out of many industrial jobs. Second-generation Filipinos in Hawaii found employment on plantations and in the islands' cities. Unions there became open to all Asians during the New Deal years. Many who immigrated to the United States after 1970 with limited education entered the unskilled labor market and soon found themselves joining second-generation Filipinos on welfare.

The Labor Movement Declining market prices for agricultural produce in the late 1920s and during the Great Depression of the 1930s seriously affected Filipino Americans. As migrant workers saw their wages fall lower and lower, they threatened strikes and boycotts. Given the American Federation of Labor's (AFL's) antipathy to nonwhite workers, minority workers, including Filipinos, sought to organize ethnic unions. In 1930 an Agricultural Workers Industrial League tried without success to organize all field-workers into a single union. California's Monterey County saw two short-lived unions emerge in 1933—the Filipino Labor Supply Association and the Filipino Labor Union.

Many Filipino Americans today are firmly established members of the middle class, partly because of a steady stream of educated and skilled Filipino arrivals in the United States and partly because of the college-degree completion rate of second- and third-generation Filipino Americans.

The Filipino Labor Union, utilizing the National Industry Recovery Act's collective bargaining clause, called on the Salinas Valley lettuce growers to recognize the union. The lettuce workers went on strike, leading to violence, white vigilante action, and defeat for the workers. The Filipino labor movement generally failed during the Depression years and well into the 1950s as growers used strikebreakers and court injunctions to quash union activities.

During the 1920s many Filipinos spent summer seasons in salmon canneries in the Pacific Northwest and Alaska. Again, Filipinos worked in labor gangs under contractors for seasonal work lasting three or four months. In 1928 about 4,000 Filipinos worked in Alaskan canneries for low wages. The wage issue was a flash point each season. This conflict continued until 1957 when Seattle's Local 37 of the International Longshoremen's and Warehousemen's Union (ILWU) became the sole bargaining voice for cannery workers in California, Oregon, and Washington.

In 1959 the AFL-CIO formed the Agricultural Workers Organizing Committee (AWOC) to organize grape pickers in California's lower San Joaquin Valley. At about the same time, Cesar Chavez founded the National Farm Workers Association (NFWA). Both unions were ethnically integrated, but Larry Itliong led the largely Filipino AWOC union. Itliong, born in the Philippines in 1914, campaigned during the 1960s to improve the lot of Filipinos and other minorities. Other Filipino union leaders of note included Philip Vera Cruz, Pete Velasco, and Andrew Imutan.

Both the AWOC and NFWA spent their initial energies recruiting members. In 1965 the unions protested the low wages being paid to grape pickers. On September 8, at the height of the picking season, the AWOC struck against thirty-five grape growers in the Delano area of Kern County, California. Domestic pickers, including Filipinos and Mexicans, demanded $1.40 an hour plus 20 cents a box. They argued that domestic pickers were receiving $1.20 an hour while *braceros* (Mexican migrant workers), under a United States Department of Labor order, received $1.40. Chavez's NFWA joined the strike, which lasted for seven months.

In August 1966 the AWOC and NFWA joined forces to end conflict between themselves. The merger resulted in the formation of the United Farm Workers Organizing Committee (UFWOC). Some major grape growers recognized this union as the bargaining agent for workers in the vineyards. Itliong was instrumental in securing three contracts with a $2.00 minimum wage for field-workers. The battle between the growers and their workers continued as the UFWOC challenged California's agricultural strongholds.

Filipinos were also instrumental in Hawaii's labor union movement. The key figure during the 1920s was Pablo Manlapit (1892–1969), who organized the Filipino Federation of Labor and the Filipino Higher Wage Movement. His organizations protested against the Hawaiian Sugar Planters Association (HSPA), which refused to meet the Filipinos' demands. This led to a 1920 sugar strike that lasted about six months. To rebuild his union, Manlapit organized Filipinos as they arrived from the Philippines. A second confrontation between Manlapit's followers and plantation owners caused a strike in 1924 that resulted in a bloodbath in Hanapepe, Kauai, where sixteen workers and four policemen were killed. During the 1930s the Filipinos' ethnic union, Vibora Luviminda, failed to make headway against the powerful HSPA. The ILWU started organizing dock and plantation workers in the 1930s and gained economic and political power after World War II. By 1980 Filipinos constituted 50 percent of the Hawaiian branch of the ILWU. Agricultural workers were not the only Filipino union members; Filipinos also formed 40 percent of the Hotel and Restaurant Workers' Union.

Many Filipinos arriving during and after the 1970s caused a "brain drain" in the Philippines. The country produced a higher number of college and university graduates per capita than any other country, and by 1980 the Philippines had replaced all European countries as the leading provider of immigrant accountants, engineers, nurses, physicians, teachers, and technical workers. In the early 1970s physicians, pharmacists, dentists, lawyers, and teachers ran into protective bureaucratic screens enacted by legislatures in western U.S. states. Filipino professionals who settled elsewhere in the United States found it easier to start careers because states in these areas had less-stringent laws or had reciprocity agreements that recognized and accepted the Philippine licenses.

In the past two decades, backed by affirmative action and equal opportunity legislation, the lot of Filipino American professionals has improved greatly.

They have begun to obtain employment in the professions for which they were trained. Doctors and nurses find ready employment after gaining certification. In 2011 Filipino physicians were numerically second only to Asian Indian physicians in the United States. In urban areas with high concentrations of Filipino businesspeople, Filipino chambers of commerce have organized. One purpose of such organizations is to encourage Filipino American small-business owners to be less conservative and think big. In 2012 only a handful of Filipino American entrepreneurs, such as Loida Nicolas Lewis, CEO of Beatrice International Holdings; the engineer and inventor Dado Banateo; Cecilia Pagkalinawan, of BoutiqueY3K; and Olivia Ongpin of fabric8, had achieved economic success that placed them among the wealthiest Americans.

POLITICS AND GOVERNMENT

During the Depression years, discrimination against Filipinos led to efforts by exclusionists to bar further immigration from the Philippines. Some Filipino organizations, concerned about the economic hardships confronting their countrymen, suggested a program of repatriation to the Philippines. Several members of Congress tried to enact a repatriation measure, but it did not gain much support until Representative Richard Welch of San Francisco introduced his repatriation bill. This bill provided for federal government payment of repatriation expenses for those wishing to return to the Philippines. These repatriates, however, could return to the United States only as one of the annual quota of fifty immigrants. When this program ended in 1940, only 2,190 of the 45,000 Filipinos living in the United States had elected to be repatriated. Many who took this opportunity for free transportation across the Pacific were university graduates who had already planned to return to assume leadership roles in the Philippines.

Repatriation did not satisfy California's exclusionists, who attempted to demonstrate that Filipinos were taking scarce jobs. Los Angeles County reported, however, that of the 12,000 Filipinos who lived in the county in 1933, 75 percent could not find work. At the time, they were not eligible for federal relief programs. During the Depression, not only did Filipinos face legal discrimination in obtaining licenses to practice their professions, but they also found that restrictive housing covenants prohibited them from living where they wished. During the New Deal era, Filipinos registered for relief projects only to be denied positions by the Civil Works Administration. In 1937 the United States attorney general restated that Filipinos were American nationals and thus eligible for employment on Works Progress Administration projects; however, they still could not receive preference because they were not citizens. Likewise, following World War II, 250,000 Filipino American veterans found themselves stripped of benefits when Congress passed the Rescission Act. In the more than sixty years

since then, the veterans have lobbied for reinstatement with only partial success and finally gave up in 2012, saying they would work instead to improve benefits in other areas. According to the National Asian American Survey, Filipino Americans tend to vote Republican, contrary to most Asian American groups. Recent research has also shown that naturalized Filipino Americans are more likely to register to vote than those who are born in the United States. In 2013 the Filipino Workers Center, a Filipino American advocacy group, spearheaded a lobbying effort for immigration reform, an issue that affects Filipinos in both the United States and the Philippines. Filipinos have the longest green card wait time of any immigrant group. According to exit polls in the 2012 election, the Filipino vote was split, with economically conservative Filipinos voting as Republicans and immigration-reform supporters voting as Democrats.

Military Service During World War I, some Filipinos enlisted in the U.S. Navy and the Marine Corps. Men who had served for three years and received an honorable discharge could apply for U.S. citizenship, and several did so. Following the Japanese attack on Pearl Harbor and the Philippines in 1941, which triggered the involvement of the United States in World War II, Filipinos tried to volunteer for military service or to obtain work in defense factories. Existing law had no provisions to enlist nationals, thus denying Filipinos employment in war industries. Given the need for army personnel, however, Secretary of War Henry Stimson on February 19, 1942, announced the formation of the First Filipino Infantry Battalion, which began training at Camp San Luis Obispo in California. It was activated on April 1, 1942, but in July the army reformed the unit as the First Filipino Regiment. A few weeks later, President Franklin D. Roosevelt issued an executive order that opened the way for Filipinos to work in government and in war industries. He also ordered a change in the draft law, reclassifying Filipinos from 4-C to 1-A, making them eligible for military service.

The First Filipino Regiment, after training at several California army posts, transferred to Camp Beale near Marysville, California. The citizenship of the troops remained a major issue. On February 20, 1943, army officers on Camp Beale's parade grounds administered the oath of allegiance, granting citizenship to a thousand Filipinos. Many in the First Regiment believed that citizenship gave them the right to marry their common-law wives, thus providing family allowances and making these women their federal insurance beneficiaries. An appeal to revoke the miscegenation law fell upon deaf ears, leading the regimental chaplain and the Red Cross to obtain emergency leaves for members so that couples could travel to New Mexico, where interracial marriages were legal, to marry before the regiment went overseas.

A second army unit, the Second Filipino Infantry Battalion, formed in October 1942 and reorganized

Filipino American designer Josie Natori. FAIRCHILD PHOTO SERVICE

The U.S. Navy began early to recruit Filipinos in the Philippines, Hawaii, and the mainland. By the end of World War I, about 6,000 Filipinos had served in the navy or the Marine Corps. During the 1920s and 1930s, enlistments totaled about 4,000. However, the only job open to these men was as mess stewards, for the navy had determined during World War I that this was the best assignment for Filipinos. During World War II, the navy continued its mess-boy policy and denied these men the opportunity to secure other ratings and privileges.

In 1970 more than 14,000 Filipinos were serving in the U.S. Navy. Most had sea duty as personal valets, cabin boys, and dishwashers. Captains and admirals had Filipino stewards assigned directly to them. Others worked at the White House, the Pentagon, the U.S. Naval Academy, and at naval bases. At the same time, the navy discovered that its ships' galleys had become "Filipino ghettos." The navy then provided opportunities for a few to train for other ratings. Some 1,600 Filipinos gained new assignments. The navy continued to recruit mess stewards in the Philippines. Of the some 17,000 Filipinos in the navy in 1970, 13,600 were stewards. Those in the navy did not complain as much as did outsiders. The steward's entry-level pay of $1,500 equaled the salary of a lieutenant colonel in the Philippine Army. Naval service was an important way for Philippine nationals to gain U.S. citizenship as well. During the Vietnam War, Filipino soldiers were not promoted above the rank of steward until the 1970s. As of 2012, of the 65,000 Asian Americans in the U.S. military, 23 percent were Filipino, with ten Filipino generals and flag officers.

NOTABLE INDIVIDUALS

Academia James Misajon was a prominent administrator at the University of Hawaii and served as the chair of the 1969 Governor's Statewide Conference on Immigration in Hawaii. Many other Filipinos are active in public and higher education. The University of California–Los Angeles Asian American Studies Center maintains a list of Filipino academics in the United States that, as of 2013, had eighty-one names.

Architecture In 2011 *i4Design* magazine named architect Lira Luis one of the top sixteen innovative design professionals in the Midwest. Luis is the first Filipino American to graduate from Frank Lloyd Wright's renowned Taliesin program.

Art and Music Noteworthy Filipino American artists include Alfredo Alcala (1925–2000), Linda Barry (1956–), Whilce Portacio (1963–), and Leo Valledor (1936–1989). Significant Filipino American musicians include Kirk Hammett (1962–), Enrique Iglesias (1975–), Mike Inez (1966–), Allan Pineda Lindo (1974–), and Nicole Scherzinger (1978–).

Fashion and Beauty Monique Lhuillier (1971–) and Josie Natori (1947–) are well-known fashion

in March 1944, training at Camp Cooke, California. This battalion and the First Infantry were sent to Australia and fought in New Guinea before landing in the Southern Philippines. The First Infantry Regiment also went to Australia and then to New Guinea. They fought in Mindanao, the Visayan Islands, and northern Luzon. From the First Infantry Regiment came the First Reconnaissance Battalion, organized in 1944, whose mission was to gather preinvasion intelligence in Luzon. Some 1,000 soldiers went ashore from submarines to work undercover as civilians.

The First Filipino Infantry Regiment earned the prestige of fighting bravely and with honor, closely paralleling the record of the more widely known Japanese American 442 Regimental Combat Team. At the war's end, 555 soldiers returned to the United States, 500 of whom reenlisted, while 800 of the regiment remained in the Philippines. Altogether, more than 7,000 Filipinos served in the United States Army.

designers. Angela Perez Baraquio (1975–) was Miss America in 2001.

Film and Theater Joan Almedilla (1973–), actress and singer, was cast in the musicals *Miss Saigon* and *Les Misérables* on Broadway. Deedee Magno (1975–), a former mouseketeer, was a cast member of the musical *Wicked*. Ruben Aquino (1953–) was on the animation team for Disney Studio's *Lion King* and *The Little Mermaid*. Pia Clemente was the first Filipino to be nominated for an Academy Award for the live-action short film *Our Time Is Up* in 2004.

Literature Peter Bacho (1951–) won the Washington Governor's Writers Award for his short story collection *Dark Blue Suit* (1996) and the American Book Award for the novel *Cebu* (1991). Carlos Bulosan (1913–1956) published the autobiography *America Is in the Heart* (1946). Tess Uriza Holthe (1966–) is a writer whose first novel, *When the Elephants Dance* (2002), became a U.S. best seller. Bienvenido N. Santos (1911–1996), author of the short story collection *Scent of Apples* (1979), won the Palanca Award for Philippine Literature in 1956, 1961, and 1965. Alex Tizon (1957–), a Knight International Journalism Fellow, won the Pulitzer Prize in 1997 and the Lukacs Book Prize in 2004 for his journalistic and literary contributions. José García Villa (1908–1997) was a poet whose works include the collection *Many Voices* (1939).

Politics and Law Several Filipinos have entered politics and won election to office. Those in Hawaii have had the most success, in part because of large Filipino enclaves and because of their strength in the ILWU, a strong arm of the Democratic Party in Hawaii. The Democratic Party gained control of the Hawaiian legislature in 1954 and won the governorship in 1962; Democrats have controlled Hawaii's politics ever since. Between 1954 and the winning of statehood in 1959, three Filipinos were elected to the Territorial House of Representatives. Peter Aduja (1920–2007), a lawyer, was elected to one term in 1954 but was defeated in his bid for a second term. After Hawaii won statehood, Aduja was elected to four terms, starting in 1966. Bernaldo D. Bicoy (1923–2013), another Filipino lawyer in the Territory of Hawaii, was elected in 1958. He was defeated in 1959 for a seat in the new State Senate, but he won election for one term to the House in 1968. The third pioneer Filipino legislator was Pedro de la Cruz, a longtime ILWU labor leader who was first elected to the House in 1958 and served for sixteen years until his defeat in 1974. In his later years in the House, he served as vice speaker.

Alfred Laureta (1924–) became Hawaii's first Filipino director of the Department of Labor and Industrial Relations. Governor John Burns appointed him to the directorship in 1963 and then in 1969 appointed him judge of Hawaii's Circuit Court One. He thus became the first federal judge of Filipino ancestry.

In 1974 Benjamin Menor (1922–) became the first Filipino appointed to the Hawaii State Supreme Court. Menor migrated to Hawaii in 1930. After practicing law in Hilo, he served for a time as a county attorney. In 1962 he was elected to the Hawaii State Senate, becoming the first Filipino in the United States to be elected a state senator.

In 2009 Steve Austria (1958–) became the first first-generation Filipino American to be elected to the U.S. Congress. He represented the 7th congressional district of Ohio 2009–2013 and was affiliated with the Republican Party.

Religion Oscar A. Solis (1953–) is the first Filipino American Roman Catholic bishop in the United States. Bruce Reyes-Chow (1969–) is the first Filipino American head of a major religious denomination in the United States. He was elected moderator of the 218th General Assembly of the Presbyterian Church (USA) in 2008.

Sports In 1948 Victoria Manalo Draves (1924–2010) became the first woman diver to win two gold medals in springboard diving in the Olympics. Many American sports enthusiasts remember Roman Gabriel (1940–), who gained national recognition as a quarterback for the Los Angeles Rams football team. Tedy Lacap Bruschi (1973–) was an All-Pro linebacker for the New England Patriots. Erik Spoelstra (1970–) is head coach for the NBA's Miami Heat. Jesus Salud (1963–) was WBA superbantamweight boxing champion in 1989. Tai Babilonia (1959–), Elizabeth Punsalan (1971–), and Amanda Evora (1984–) were U.S. Olympic figure skaters. J. R. Celski (1990–) won a bronze medal in short track speed skating in the 2010 Winter Olympics and is a five-time world champion. Paige McPherson (1990–) won a bronze medal in tae kwon do in the 2012 Summer Olympics. Kyla Ross (1996–) was on the U.S. gold medalist women's gymnastics team in the 2012 Summer Olympics.

MEDIA

PRINT

From the early 1920s to the late 1980s, several Filipino newspapers were published, although their existence was generally short-lived. In Hawaii the *Kauai Filipino News* became the *Filipino News* in 1931. In California, early papers were the *Philippine Herald* of 1920, the *Commonwealth Courier* of 1930, and the *Philippine Advocate* of 1934. In 1930 the *Philippine Mail* began publishing in Salinas, California. It succeeded the *Philippine Independent News*, started in Salinas in 1921. The *Philippine Mail* is still published in Salinas, making it the oldest Filipino newspaper in the United States. Over the years, it has reported news from the Philippines as well as news stories about Filipinos in the United States. In the 1990s Filipino publications included the *Philippine News*, printed in South San Francisco; *Filipinas Magazine*, published in San Francisco; and the *Philippine Review* out of Sacramento and Stockton, California.

FilAm Star

Bills itself as the newspaper for Filipinos in America.

> 1028 Mission Street
> San Francisco, California 94103
> Phone: (415) 593-5955
> Fax: (415) 946-6443
> Email: fastad@filamstar.net
> URL: www.filamstar.net

philSTAR

Serves the global Filipino community.

> 13th Corner Railroad Street
> Port Area
> Manila, Philippines 1016
> Phone: +63 2 527-6856
> Email: editor@philstar.com
> URL: www.philstar.com

ORGANIZATIONS AND ASSOCIATIONS

Filipino American National Historical Society

Gathers, maintains, and disseminates Filipino American history.

> Dorothy Cordova, Director
> 810 Eighteenth Avenue
> Suite 100
> Seattle, Washington 98122
> Phone: (206) 322-0203
> Email: fanhsnational@gmail.com
> URL: www.fanhs-national.org

Filipino Workers Center

The Filipino Workers Center supports the right of all people to a healthy, dignified quality of life. It provides resources that meet urgent short-term needs of low-income workers and their families.

> 2001 Beverly Boulevard
> Suite LI
> Los Angeles, California 90057
> Phone: (213) 250-4353
> URL: www.pwcsc.org

National Pinoy Archives

Photo and documentation repository for Philippine and Filipino history.

> 2001 Beverly Boulevard
> Suite LI
> Los Angeles, California 90057
> Phone: (206) 543-7946
> Fax: (206) 685-2146
> Email: hbcls@u.washington.edu
> URL: http://depts.washington.edu/labpics/repository/v/Filipino/fahns_collection_fred_and_dorothy_cordova/

Philippine American Educational Foundation

Provides scholarships for study in the Philippines.

> Philippine-American Educational Foundation
> 10/F Ayala Life-FGU Center-Makati

> 811 Ayala Avenue
> 226 Makati City, Philippines
> Phone: +63 2 812-0919
> Fax: +63 2 812-5890
> Email: fulbright@fulbright.org
> URL: www.fulbright.org.ph

Sistan C. Alhambra Filipino American Education Institute

Based at the University of Hawaii, gathers, maintains, and disseminates Filipino American history.

> Patricia Halagao, Director
> Phone: (808) 956-9295
> URL: http://filameducation.com

MUSEUMS AND RESEARCH CENTERS

Social Science Research Institute

Supports research that addresses problems in Hawaii and the Pacific Rim.

> Social Science Research Institute
> University of Hawai'i at Manoa
> Saunders Hall, Suite 704
> 2424 Maile Way
> Honolulu, Hawaii 96822
> Phone: (808) 956-8930
> Fax: (808) 956-8930
> Email: ssri@hawaii.edu
> URL: http://ssri.hawaii.edu

University of California–Davis Asian American Studies Center

Offers an interdisciplinary program that studies the experiences of Asian groups in the United States.

> University of California–Davis
> 3102 Hart Hall
> One Shields Avenue
> Davis, California 95616
> Phone: (530) 723-9767
> Fax: (530) 752-9260
> Email: asamstudies@ucdavis.edu
> URL: http://asa.ucdavis.edu

University of California–Los Angeles Asian American Studies Center

Maintains the Filipino American Scholars Directory, a list of university faculty of Filipino descent.

> David K. Yu, PhD
> 3230 Campbell Hall
> Box 951546
> Los Angeles, California 90015-1546
> Phone: (310) 825-2974
> Fax: (310) 206-9844
> Email: dkyu@ucla.edu
> URL: www.aasc.ucla.edu/aascresources/filam/directory.html

SOURCES FOR ADDITIONAL STUDY

Cabezas, Amado, et al. "New Inquiries into the Socioeconomic Status of Pilipino Americans in California" *Amerasia Journal* 13 (1986): 1–21.

Espiritu, Augusto. "Transnationalism and Filipino American Historiography." *Journal of Asian American Studies* 11, no. 2 (2008)

Espiritu, Yen Le. *Filipino American Lives*. Philadelphia: Temple University Press, 1995.

Francia, Luis, and Eric Gamalinda, eds. *Flippin': Filipinos on America*. New York: Asian American Writers' Workshop, 1996.

McWilliams, Carey. *Brothers under the Skin*. Rev. ed. Boston: Little, Brown, 1951.

Nadal, Kevin. *Filipino American Psychology*. Somerset, NJ: Garland, 2011.

———. Stephanie Pituc, Marc Johnston, and Theresa Esparrago. "Overcoming the Model Minority Myth: Experiences of Filipino American Graduate Students," *Journal of College Student Development* 51, no. 6 (2010): 694–706.

Okamura, Jonathan. *Imagining the Filipino American Diaspora: Transnational Relations, Identities and Communities*. New York: Garland, 1998.

Quinsaat, Jesse, ed. *Letters in Exile: An Introductory Reader on the History of Pilipinos in America*. Los Angeles: UCLA Asian Studies Center, 1976.

Root, Maria, ed. *Filipino Americans: Transformation and Identity*. Thousand Oaks, CA: Sage Publications, 1997.

San Juan, E., Jr. *From Exile to Diaspora: Versions of the Filipino Experience in the United States*. Boulder, CO: Westview Press, 1998.

FINNISH AMERICANS

K. Marianne Wargelin Brown

OVERVIEW

Finnish Americans are immigrants or descendants of people from Finland, a country located in the far northern reaches of Europe. It is bounded by Sweden to the west, Russia to the east, Norway to the north, and the Gulf of Finland to the south. Among the northernmost countries of the world, Finland is also one of the world's flattest countries due to the thick glaciers that formed there during the Ice Age and eroded the terrain underneath. The total land area of Finland is 130,128 square miles (337,030 square kilometers), making the country almost half the size of Texas.

According to the *CIA World Factbook*, the population of Finland was 5.26 million in 2011. The current population of Finland reflects the traditional groups that settled in the area centuries ago. The largest group consists of Finns who speak Finnish. The second-largest group, some 6 percent, consists of Finland Swedes (also known as Swede Finns) who speak Swedish. The most visible minority groups are the Sámi (about 4,400), who speak Sámi (or Lappish) and live in the north, and the Romani (about 5,500), who live in the south. About 83 percent of the people living in Finland are Lutheran, with the second-largest church, the Russian Orthodox Church, comprising just more than 1 percent of the population. Finland is considered a prosperous country with a standard of living similar to Germany's or France's. It derives most of its revenue from the engineering and manufacture of electronic goods.

Finnish immigration to the United States occurred primarily between 1864 and 1924. Early Finnish immigrants were familiar with agricultural work and unskilled labor; therefore, they were new to industrial work and urban life. Later, skilled workers such as carpenters, painters, tailors, and jewelers journeyed to the United States, but the number of professionals who immigrated remained small between 1924 through the end of World War II due in part to immigration quotas imposed by the United States. According to a study on Finnish emigration published by Elli Heikkilä and Elisabeth Uschanov, immigration from Finland to the United States resumed in small but steady numbers after the war. About 19,000 Finns immigrated to the United States in the latter half of

the twentieth century, and by 2001, 23,000 first-generation Finns were living in the United States.

According to 2009–2011 estimates from the U.S. Census Bureau's American Community Survey (ACS), there were 663,292 Finnish Americans living in the United States. Finnish American communities are clustered in three regions across the northern tier of the country: the East, Midwest, and West. Within these regions, Finland Swedes concentrated in California, Massachusetts, Michigan, Minnesota, Oregon, Washington, Wisconsin, and Florida. Sámi peoples settled predominantly in Michigan, Minnesota, the Dakotas, Oregon, and Washington.

HISTORY OF THE PEOPLE

Early History The ancestors of the Finnish people came under the domination of the Swedes in the twelfth century, when the area of present-day Finland became a province of Sweden. While the Swedish provinces operated independently for a time, efforts to centralize power in the kingdom in the sixteenth century made Finns citizens of Sweden. Sweden was the primary power in the Baltic region for more than a hundred years until challenged by Russia in the eighteenth century. By 1809 Sweden was so weakened that it was forced to cede its entire Baltic holdings, including Finland, to Russia.

Russia gave Finland special status as a grand duchy with the right to maintain the Lutheran religion, the Finnish language, and Finnish constitutional laws. This new status encouraged its leaders to promote a sense of Finnish spirit. Historically a farming nation, Finland did not begin to industrialize until the 1860s—later than its Nordic neighbors. Textile mills, forestry, and metalwork became the mainstays of the economy.

In the final days of the nineteenth century, Russia started a policy of Russification in the region, and a period of oppression began. Political unrest dominated the opening years of the twentieth century. Finland conducted a general strike in 1906, and the Russian tsar was forced to make various concessions, including universal suffrage (Finland was the first European nation to grant women the right to vote) and the right to maintain a parliament. Although oppressive conditions returned two years later, Finland remained part of Russia until

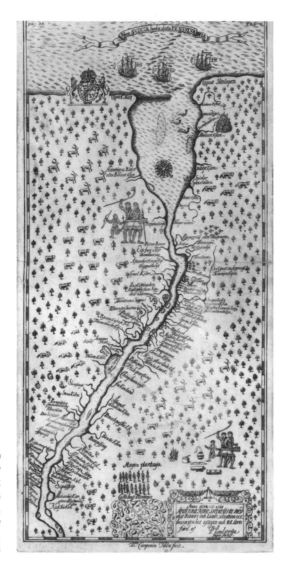

A 1654 map of New Sweden. Original artwork by Thomas Campanius Holm (c. 1670–1702), based on one drafted by Peter Lindestrom.
MPI / GETTY IMAGES

and 1930s emerged as a period of political conservatism and right-wing nationalism. On November 30, 1939, the Soviet Union invaded Finland, seeking complete conquest. This conflict, known as the Winter War, ended on March 13, 1940, with the Soviet army making significant territorial gains and taking control of almost a third of Finland's economic assets. Hostilities resumed in 1941, and for the next three years Finland and the Soviet Union engaged in the Continuation War. When the fighting ended in 1944, the Finns had lost 93,000 soldiers and had forfeited a fifth of their industrial capacity to the Soviet Union.

In the 1950s Finland continued its transformation from a predominantly agricultural economy into a modern industrial economy. By the 1960s it had established itself as a major design center in Europe, and by the end of the 1970s it maintained a postindustrial culture with a stable economy that continued to produce premier-quality works of art. By the 1980s Finland's GDP per capita ranked fifteenth in the world. The revitalization of Finland's economy occurred under the leadership of Urho Kekkonen (1900–1986), who served as prime minister from 1950 to 1956 and then as president from 1956 to 1982 when he retired from office due to illness. While in power, Kekkonen was able to maintain friendly trade relations with the Soviet Union, build a Western-style market economy, and establish Finland as a stable welfare state with an equitable distribution of wealth among its citizens. The key to his success was maintaining military neutrality between the hostile powers of the Soviet Union and the rest of Western Europe and the United States.

During the early 1990s, following the fall of the Soviet Union, Finland experienced an economic crisis. After the depression reached its low point in 1993, the Finnish economy rebounded for more than a decade before suffering another setback with the international financial crisis that began in late 2007. In the years following the crisis, Finland's economy has remained stable, as the country has avoided fiscal catastrophe that has struck other European countries such as Spain, Portugal, and Greece. Finland joined the European Union in 1995 and adopted the euro as its official currency in 2002.

SETTLEMENT IN THE UNITED STATES

The first Finns in North America came as colonists to New Sweden, a colony founded in 1638 along the Delaware River. Although the colony was abandoned to the Dutch in 1664, the Finns remained, working the forest in a slash-and-burn settlement pattern. By the end of the eighteenth century, their descendants had been absorbed into the dominant English and Dutch colonist groups. Few material signs—other than their distinctive log cabin design and place names—remain to mark their early presence. However, many Finnish Americans believe that John Morton (1725–1777), a signer of the Declaration of Independence, was a descendant of the Finnish pioneers.

declaring its independence in the midst of the Russian Revolution of 1917. As the newly independent nation struggled between the philosophies of the bourgeois conservatives and the working-class Social Democrats, a brief but bitter civil war broke out in 1918. Although the war spanned less than four months (January 27–May 15), approximately 37,000 Finns died with the nationalist forces (known in the west as the White Guard) taking control of Helsinki from the communist Red Guard in early April. The White Guard then ruthlessly executed and deported what remained of the weakening Red Guard and its sympathizers.

Modern Era In 1919 Finland began to govern itself under its own constitution and bill of rights. The following year the Treaty of Tartu reestablished the country's historic border with Russia, with the Finns receiving modest concessions in the northwest that expanded their territory and gave them control of the Barents Sea harbor. With basic democratic rights and privileges established and the threat of Soviet influence and aggression reasonably well contained, the 1920s

A second colonial effort involved Finns in the Russian fur-trading industry. In Sitka, Alaska, Finns mixed with Russian settlers in the 1840s and 1850s, working primarily as carpenters and other skilled craftsmen. Two of Alaska's governors were Finnish: Arvid Adolph Etholén (1799–1876) served from 1840 to 1845, and Johan H. Furuhjelm (1821–1909) held the office from 1859 to 1864. A Finnish pastor, Uno Cygnaeus (1810–1888), who later returned to Finland to establish the Finnish public school system, also served the Finnish American community. After 1867, when Alaska was transferred to the United States, some of the Sitka Finns moved down to communities developing along the Northwestern Coastline such as Seattle and San Francisco. Today this Finnish presence is represented in the Sitka Lutheran church, which dates from that period.

Finish colonial settlers were small in number. According to Reino Kero in *Migration from Finland to North America in the Years between the United States Civil War and the First World War* (1974), the Finnish sailors and sea captains who left their ships to enter the California Gold Rush or to establish new lives in American harbor cities like Baltimore, Galveston, San Francisco, and New York, numbered only several hundred. One sailor, Charles Linn (Carl Sjödahl, 1814–1883), became a wealthy Southern merchant who ran a large wholesale business in New Orleans and later established Alabama's National Bank of Birmingham and Linn Iron Works. He is credited with opening immigration from southern Finland to the United States when he brought fifty-three immigrants from Helsinki and Uusimaa in 1869 to work for his company.

Those from northern Norway and Finland who traveled as family groups were part of the Great Laestadian Migration of 1864–1895, which began shortly after the death of founder Lars Levi Laestadius (1800–1861). Looking for ways to maintain a separatist lifestyle and to improve their economic standing, Laestadian families began a migration that has continued to the present day. Finnish American Laestadian communities formed in the mining region of Michigan and in the homestead lands of western Minnesota, Oregon, South Dakota, and Washington. These Laestadians provided a sense of community and stability to new immigrants, mostly single men who had left their families in Finland and migrated from job to job in the United States. Some of these men returned to Finland; others eventually sent for their families.

After 1892 most emigrants from Finland were single and under the age of thirty. Women made up as much as 41.5 percent of this group. A large increase in the birthrate after 1875 added to the pool of laborers who left home to work in Finland's growing industrial communities, foreshadowing an exodus from Finland. Russification and a conscription for the draft added to the number of immigrants after 1898.

Twentieth-century emigration from Finland is divided into three periods: before the general strike, after the general strike and before World War I, and between World War I and the passage of the Immigration Restriction Act. Before the general strike, the immigrants who settled in the United States were more likely to be influenced by the concepts of Social Democracy. After the general strike, the immigrants were largely influenced by the use of direct force rather than political action to resolve social problems. Immigrants after World War I—now radicalized and disenchanted from the experience of the bloody civil war—brought a new sense of urgency about the progress of socialism.

Two immigration periods have occurred since the 1940s. After World War II a new wave of immigration, smaller but more intense, revitalized many Finnish American communities. These Finns were far more nationalistic and politically conservative than earlier immigrants. Beginning in the latter half of the 1970s, young English-speaking professionals came from Finland to work in high-tech American corporations. This trend continued through the early part of the twenty-first century. However, as has been the case since the end of World War II, the majority of Finns who emigrate move to Sweden or other countries in Europe. According to Heikkilä and Uschanov, more than 500,000 Finns immigrated to Sweden between 1945 and 2001. During that same time period, more Finns (23,500) immigrated to Canada than the United States (19,000).

Reverse immigration occurred in the nineteenth and twentieth centuries. In the nineteenth century many men came without families and worked for a while in the mining (especially copper and iron ore mining), lumber, fishing, and canning industries, as well as in stone quarries and textile mills and on railroads and docks. Many returned to the homeland. Others came and worked as domestics, returning to Finland to retire. The most significant reverse immigration occurred in the late 1920s and early 1930s, when ten thousand Finnish American immigrant radicals and their families sold their belongings and left to settle in the Finnish areas of the Soviet Union. They took their dreams of creating a workers' paradise with them, as well as solid American currency, American tools, and technical skills. There, they produced literary works, including novels and plays, which they published in Finnish American publications for much-needed cash. Most of these Finns were killed in Joseph Stalin's purges. Today reverse migration occurs primarily among the Laestadians, who may marry and then move to Finland.

Like the Swedes and Norwegians, Finns in the United States were tolerated and accepted into established American communities during the first wave of mass immigration. Early on they competed for work in the mines with the Irish and the Cornish, two groups with whom they had strained relations. Finnish

Miners work underground in the Calumet-Hecla copper mines, c. 1915 in northern Michigan. KEYSTONE-FRANCE / GAMMA-KEYSTONE VIA GETTY IMAGES

Americans soon developed a reputation for clannishness and hard work. Work crews of strictly Finnish laborers were formed. As documented in *Women Who Dared: The History of Finnish American Women* (1986), Finnish domestics were typically sought after because they worked hard and excelled at cooking and homemaking.

This reputation was tarnished, however, when the second wave of immigrants began to organize to fight poor wages and working conditions. As a result, Finns became known as troublemakers for organizing strikes and leading protests. They were blacklisted, and efforts were made to deport them. Racist slurs—epithets like "Finn-LAND-er" and "dumb Finn"—developed, and some Finns became victims of violent vigilantism. Efforts to single them out from other working-class immigrants as anti-American put them on the front pages of newspapers.

By the end of the twentieth century, Finnish Americans had largely assimilated into the American population. Many worked hard to be indistinguishable from other Euro-Americans. As descendants of white Europeans, they fit easily into the dominant culture. Today many do not visibly identify with their heritage. Key issues facing Finnish Americans relate to their position as a culture on the margin. Recent generations seem to be drawn more strongly to the hegemonic culture of the United States and, therefore, continue to move away from their unique heritage. The states with the highest population of Finnish Americans include Michigan, Minnesota, California, Washington, and Wisconsin. Other states with smaller but significant numbers of people of Swedish Finn descent are Florida, Massachusetts, and Oregon.

LANGUAGE

Late nineteenth- and early twentieth-century Finnish immigrants spoke either Finnish or Swedish. Those who spoke Swedish used a form known as Finland Swedish; those who spoke Finnish fell into the group of Finno-Ugric languages. Most nineteenth-century Finns spoke a northern rural form of Finnish, while later immigrants spoke a southern rural form. As Finnish Americans assimilated to U.S. culture, however, an entirely new language was born, dubbed "Finglish." Finns entering the United States at the close of the twentieth century tended to speak in a Helsinki dialect.

Issues of assimilation arose around the maintenance of the Finnish language in the United States, particularly in the early twentieth century. In the early 1920s the Finnish Socialist Federation was deeply divided over the issue of whether to Americanize its cultural practices, including the use of Finnish, in order to remain united with the Socialist Party of America. In 1927 Finnish American pastor John Wargelin (1881–1970), president of Suomi College in Michigan, resigned his presidency largely because of resistance to his advocacy of the use of English at the college. Although many churches vacillated on the language question, most finally gave in to using English after World War II. The Laestadians, however, have moved slower; some groups preach exclusively in Finnish, while others use simultaneous translation.

Greetings and Popular Expressions Typical greetings in Finnish (with pronunciation) include *Hyvä paivä* ("huv-vaeh pa-e-vaeh")—Good day; *Hyvä ilta* ("huv-vaeh ill-tah")—Good evening; *Tervetuloa* ("terr-veh-too-loh-ah")—Welcome; *Tervesiä* ("terr-veh-see-ah")—a general response to a greeting; *Näkemiin* ("nah-keh-mean")—Good-bye, Until we meet again; *Kiitos* ("key-tohs")—Thank you; *Hauska Joulua* ("how-skah yo-lu-ah")—Merry Christmas; *Onnellista Uutta Vuotta* ("own-nell-ee-stah oo-tah vu-oh-tah")—Happy New Year; *Mitä kuuluu* ("mi-taah koo-loo")—How are you?; *kyllä* ("kyl-lah")—yes; *Hyvä huomenta* ("huv-vaeh who-ow-men-tah")—Good morning; *Olkaa hyva* ("ol-kah huv-vaeh")—Please; and *Oma tupa, oma lupa*—Your own cottage, your own independence. All Finnish words are pronounced with an accent on the first syllable.

RELIGION

More than 90 percent of Finnish American immigrants are Lutherans—some more devout than others. Baptized into the church so that their births would be recorded, Finns traditionally sought confirmation so they could marry and be buried with official state records. During the nineteenth century a series of religious revivals deepened Finns' commitment to the Church of Finland. However, because socialism—a secular movement with all the fervor of a religion—developed around roughly the same time, many Finns left the church during the immigration process, participating only in socialist activities. Those who remained religious fell into three separate groups: Laestadians, Lutherans, and free-church Protestants.

The Laestadians, who were the first to arrive in the United States, called themselves Apostolic Lutherans and began to operate separately in the heady atmosphere of the free religious environment in the United States. However, they could not stay unified and therefore divided into five separate church groups. Laypeople lead these congregations, as ordained ministers trained in seminaries are not common to any of the groups.

The Finnish Evangelical Lutheran Church of America—also known as the Suomi Synod—was established in 1890. The Suomi Synod maintained the Church of Finland's divine worship service tradition and continued the practice of a clergy-led church. However, a new sense of power resting in the hands of the congregation developed, and the church evolved into a highly democratic decision-making institution. Although women were not granted the right to be ordained, they were given the right to vote in the affairs of the church in 1909. In addition, they were elected to high leadership positions on local,

regional, and national boards. Pastors' wives were known to preach sermons and conduct services whenever the pastor was serving another church within his multiple-congregation assignment. In the second half of the twentieth century, the Suomi Synod became part of an effort to create a unified Lutheran church in the United States, dubbed the Lutheran Church in America in 1963 and then the Evangelical Lutheran Church in America in 1984.

Other Finnish American churches include the Finnish National Evangelical Lutheran Church, organized in 1898 by former members of the Finnish Evangelical Lutheran Church of America. The Finland Swedes, excluded from these efforts, gradually formed churches that entered the Augustana Lutheran Synod, a Swedish American church group. Finnish immigrants also organized a variety of other free Protestant churches, including the Finnish Congregational Church (active mainly in New England, the Pacific Northwest, and California), the Finnish Methodist Church, Unitarian churches, and Pentecostal churches.

CULTURE AND ASSIMILATION

Finnish Americans are a multicultural society. The Finnish American hegemony is distinct from the Laestadian, Finland Swede, and Sámi minorities. Sociologists studying Finns in the 1920s and 1930s determined that the group had a tendency to be clannish—an impression that was echoed by other

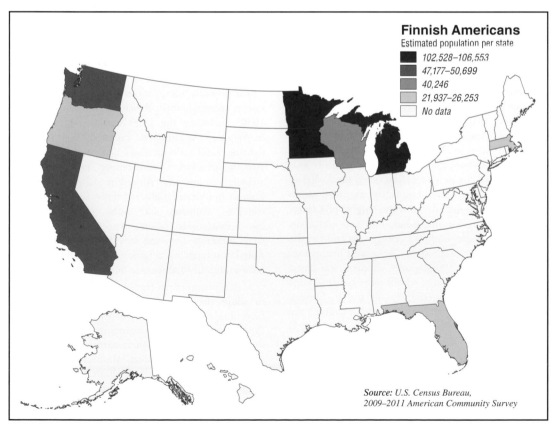

Finnish Americans
Estimated population per state

- 102,528–106,553
- 47,177–50,699
- 40,246
- 21,937–26,253
- No data

Source: U.S. Census Bureau, 2009–2011 American Community Survey

American citizens at the time. Finnish immigrants' unusual language, spoken only by a small population worldwide, reinforced this belief. Finnish immigrant children, who often spoke their native language in grade school, were marked as different. Because Finnish was difficult for English speakers to learn, American employers sometimes organized teams of Finnish-only workers. Further, the Finnish sauna ritual, an unheard of activity for most Americans, promoted a sense that Finns were both exotic and separatist.

Once in the United States, Finnish immigrants recreated institutions from their homeland including churches, temperance societies, workers' halls, benefit societies, and cooperatives. Within those institutions, Finnish Americans organized a broad spectrum of activities: weekly and festival programs, dances, worship services, theater productions, concerts, sports competitions, and summer festivals. They also created lending libraries, bands, choirs, self-education study groups, and drama troupes. Furthermore, they kept in touch with each other through the newspapers they published—more than 120 different papers since the first, *Amerikan Suomalainen Lehti*, appeared in 1876.

Finnish immigrants used these recreated Finnish institutions to confront, or ease their entrance into, American culture. For example, although Finnish American socialists created the Finnish Socialist Federation to organize Finns, the federation joined the Socialist Party of America, which connected them with other American socialists. Similarly, the Finnish Evangelical Lutheran Church in America wrote its Sunday school readers in Finnish but used the readers to teach American citizenship and history, combining stories of American role models such as Abraham Lincoln with Finnish cultural heroes.

To help maintain their cultural identities in the United States, early Finnish immigrants developed two institutions that had no counterpart in Finland. The first was a Masonic-type lodge called the Knights of Kaleva, founded in 1898, with secret rituals designed to preserve knowledge of the ancient Finnish epic *The Kalevala*. (A women's section called the Ladies of Kaleva followed in 1904.) Local chapters, called *majas*, meaning shed or log cabin, for the knights or a *tupas*, meaning home, for the ladies, provided education in Finnish culture, both for immigrants and for the larger American community. The second institution, directed toward the immigrants' children, was based on the American Sunday school movement. Groups published materials specifically for use in Sunday schools and summer camps, which taught children the ways of Finnish politics and religion in Finnish and later in English.

In big cities like Minneapolis, Detroit, and Chicago, immigrants created Finntowns, creating businesses and professional services to serve the Finnish community. In small cities such as Worcester and Fitchburg, Massachusetts, or Astoria, Oregon,

Finnish Americans often created separate institutions. In some cities—like those on the Iron Range in Minnesota—Finns became the largest foreign-born population group. For example, they made up more than 75 percent of the population of small towns such as Wakefield, Michigan, and Fairport Harbor, Ohio. Nevertheless, Finnish immigrants were quick to adopt American ways. Young women would discard the triangular cotton scarf worn over their hair (called a *huivi*) or the heavy woolen shawl wrapped around their bodies and begin to wear the large, wide hats and fancy puffed-sleeve dresses so popular in the United States at the end of the nineteenth century. Men donned bowler hats and stiff starched collars under their suit coats. Finnish immigrant women who began their lives in the United States as domestics quickly learned to make American-style pies and cakes. Even traditional Finnish log cabins, erected on barely cleared cutover lands, were covered with white clapboard siding as soon as finances permitted.

Despite assimilation, Finnish Americans became the victims of ethnic slurs, particularly after socialist-leaning Finnish immigrants began to settle in the United States at the turn of the twentieth century. Promoters of labor activism prompted racist responses directed at all Finnish Americans, which reached an apex in 1908 with the high-profile deportation trial of Finnish immigrant worker John Swan. According to Carl Ross in *The Finn Factor in American Labor, Culture, and Society* (1977), the unusual argument that Finns were actually of Mongolian descent—and therefore subject to the Asian Exclusion Act—polarized the Finnish American community into two camps. The conservative group identified itself as true Finns, while the socialist group promoted American citizenship to its membership. In spite of efforts on both sides, various vigilante activities continued against Finnish Americans even into the late 1930s, including the 1939 wrecking of Finn Hall in Aberdeen, Washington. *Finn-LAND-er* became a fighting word to both first- and second-generation Finnish Americans. Stereotyping hastened Finnish assimilation into the American mainstream. Some Finnish Americans anglicized their names and joined American churches and clubs. Others, identifying themselves as indelibly connected to America's racial minorities, entered into marriages with Native Americans, creating a group of people known in Minnesota and Michigan as "Finndians."

Recent emigrants from Finland have been quick to adopt the latest in American suburban living, becoming models of postmodern American culture. Privately, however, many maintain the conventions of their homeland: their houses contain the traditional sauna, they eat Finnish foods, they take frequent trips to Finland and instruct their children in the Finnish language, and their social calendar includes Finnish American events. In the process, they bring new blood into Finnish American culture, providing role models for Finnishness and reenergizing Finnish language usage among the third and fourth generations.

Traditions and Customs In the drive to assimilate, Finns in the United States maintained customs that could remain invisible to the outside world. Such diverse activities as berry picking, hunting, trapping, woodworking, knitting, and weaving can all be traced to the homeland. In addition, many Finnish Americans have not lost their love for the sauna. However, most institutions of the immigrants have gone. Except for the Laestadians, few Finnish Lutheran churches offer a glimpse into the rituals of the Church of Finland. Beginning in the 1950s, older institutions began to be replaced by a Finnish American club movement, which included such organizations as the Finlandia Foundation, the Finnish American Club, and the Finnish American Historical Society. Some of the older organizations, like the Saima Society of Fitchburg and the Knights of Kaleva in Red Lodge, Montana, have been revamped to serve a new generation's needs. Currently, there are nineteen Kaleva lodges in North America. In addition, large Finnish American populations such as the one in greater Detroit have created a new Finn Hall tradition that unifies various political and religious traditions.

Finnish cultural events and organizations have further strengthened Finnish traditions and customs in the United States. FinnFest USA, an annual national summer festival founded in 1983, brings together Finnish Americans from various political and religious camps for three days of seminars, lectures, concerts, sporting events, dances, and demonstrations. The festival's location revolves each year to a different region of the Finnish American geography. Salolampi, an educational institution founded in Minnesota in 1978, offers a summer program that allows young people to immerse themselves in Finnish language and culture. Part of the Concordia College Language Villages Program, the school serves children from throughout the United States.

In the 1960s a Finnish American renaissance began as third- and fourth-generation Finnish Americans looked to their past for models that could help solve the social crises in the United States. The renaissance, which included cultural revival, maintenance, and creativity, nurtured new networks between Finland and the United States and gave rise to a new generation of scholars and creative writers who focused on Finnish American history. By the 1970s, in response to the folk music movement, musicians turned to their Finnish American heritage for inspiration. While this collective renaissance activity can be found throughout the various regions of Finnish America, its center is in Minnesota—specifically the Twin Cities, where the University of Minnesota has provided a home at the Immigration History Research Center (IHRC) and Finnish Department. The IHRC helped to direct the Reunion of Sisters Project

Finnish Americans stand in line at a festival. © GARY CONNER / PHOTO EDIT. REPRODUCED BY PERMISSION.

(1984–1987), a unique cultural exchange program that brought together women and men from Finland and the United States to consider their common cultural heritage. In 1991 the IHRC cosponsored the *Making of Finnish America: A Culture in Transition*, the first conference to examine this renaissance.

Cuisine The Finnish diet is rich in root vegetables, such as carrots, beets, potatoes, rutabagas, and turnips, and fresh berries, such as blueberries, strawberries, and raspberries. Rye breads (*ruisleipa* and *rieska*) and cardamom-flavored coffee bread (*pulla* or *nisu*) are staples. Dairy products—cheeses, cream, and butter—enrich Finnish cakes, cookies, pancakes, and stews. Pork roasts, hams, meat stews, and fish—especially salmon, whitefish, herring, and trout—are served marinated, smoked, baked, or in soups. At Christmas, many Finnish Americans eat *lutefisk* (lye-soaked dried cod) and prune-filled tarts. The traditional, meatless meal on Shrove Tuesday (the day before Lent) centers on pea soup and rye bread or pancakes.

Plainness, simplicity, and an emphasis on natural flavors continue to dominate Finnish and Finnish American cooking even today. Spices, if used, include allspice, cardamom, cinnamon, and ginger. Coffee dominates all other beverages and is served in the morning, afternoon, and evening. "Coffee tables" are regular events featuring an assortment of baked goods. More recent Finnish immigrants favor foods that gained popularity after World War II—foods often associated with Karelia, the province lost to the Soviets in the Winter War. Among these are *karjalan piirakka*, an open-faced rye tart filled with potato or rice; *uunijuusto*, an oven-baked cheese, often called "squeaky cheese"; and pasties—meat, potato, and carrot or rutabaga pies adopted from Cornish miners in Michigan's Upper Peninsula.

Traditional Dress Finnish immigrants who landed on American soil in the nineteenth and early twentieth centuries as peasants or workers wore heavy woolen stockings, shirts, and skirts. Women wore a triangular scarf, called a *huivi*, over their heads. However, no traditional clothing was worn for special events and ceremonies. By the 1930s Finnish Americans became more affluent, and the popularity of Finnish national folk costumes increased as members of the middle class were in a position to travel to Finland and purchase traditional clothing.

Holidays Finnish Americans observe a number of holidays celebrated in Finland. On December 6 many communities commemorate Finnish Independence Day. Christmas parties known as Pikku Joulut are central to the holiday season, just as Laskiainen (sliding down the hill) is celebrated on Shrove Tuesday. Some communities also hold programs in honor of the Finnish epic *The Kalevala* on Kalevala Day each February 28. Festive midsummer celebrations, featuring a *kokko*, or large bonfire, occur every year.

In the 1950s Finnish Americans in Minnesota invented St. Urho's Day, a humorous takeoff on St. Patrick's Day, a traditional Irish holiday celebrated on March 17. St. Urho's Day, observed in Finnish American communities each March 16, purportedly commemorates the saint's success in driving the grasshoppers out of Finland. In 1999 Finnish Americans in Hancock, Michigan, located in the state's upper peninsula, invented another celebration called Heikinpäivä. Held on January 19, this midwinter festival borrows from the traditional Finnish celebration of St. Henrik's Day, a feast day that honors the patron saint of Finland and marks the halfway point of brutal Finnish winters. The event includes music, games, crafts, movies, and a polar bear dive, in which some members of the community take a brief dip in freezing lake waters. The festivities in Hancock also celebrate the tale of Heikki Lunta, a story from the 1970s that has acquired the status of legend in Hancock. As the story goes, there was a snowmobile race planned for the area on December 4, 1970, but when the day arrived there was no snow on the ground. David Riutta, a local salesman who worked at the radio station promoting the event, invented a character named Heikki Lunta and wrote a song called the "Heikki Lunta Snow Dance Song," using his pull to play the song on the air. Soon after the song was played, a storm hit—though the snowmobile race had to be postponed because of inclement weather.

Health Care Issues and Practices According to the *New England Journal of Medicine*, Finnish Americans have a high propensity for heart disease, high cholesterol, stroke, alcoholism, depression, and lactose intolerance. Many Finnish people believe in natural health care, and immigrants in the nineteenth and early twentieth centuries used such traditional healing methods as massage and cupping (or bloodletting). The sauna is a historic part of healing rituals. When Finns are sick, they take a sauna; even childbirth was handled by midwives in the sauna. A

Finnish proverb, *Jos ei sauna ja viina ja terva auta niin se tauti on kuolemaksi*, states that if a sauna, whiskey, and tar salve do not make you well, death is imminent. Saunas are used to treat respiratory and circulatory problems, relax stiff muscles, and cure aches and pains. Modern Finnish Americans often turn to chiropractors and acupuncturists for relief of some ailments, though the family sauna remains the place to go whenever one has a cold.

FAMILY AND COMMUNITY LIFE

Finnish immigrant families typically had a patriarchal structure. Rural Finnish families were usually large, while in urban areas, where both husband and wife worked, families often had only one child. (Today only the Laestadians continue the tradition of large families.) As immigrants were separated from their parents and extended families, immigrants tended to settle in with others from the same village or region.

Gender Roles Finnish women have played important roles in family affairs and community life. As in the old country, they ran and organized the household. In addition, immigrant women oversaw the farm while their husbands found work in the cities, mines, and lumber camps. The women also found daytime employment outside the home, working in laundries and textile manufacturing. In the evenings, they were active in choirs, theaters, politics, and the organization of religious events.

Education Education is highly valued by Finnish Americans, with self-education playing a central role in people's lives. Even early immigrants were largely literate, and they supported a rich immigrant publishing industry of newspapers, periodicals, and books. Immigrant institutions developed libraries and debate clubs, and Finnish American summer festivals included seminars, concerts, and plays. The tradition continues today through the three-day FinnFest USA, which features lectures, seminars, and concerts.

In spite of economic hardship, many immigrant children achieved a high school or college education. Two schools were founded by the Finns: the Työväenopisto, or Work People's College, in Duluth, Minnesota (1904–1941), where young people learned trades and politics in an educational environment that duplicated the folk school tradition in Finland, and Suomiopisto, or Suomi College, in Hancock, Michigan (1895), which began by duplicating the lyceum tradition of Finland. As the only higher-education institution founded by Finnish Americans, Suomi provides a Lutheran-centered general liberal arts curriculum and continues to honor its Finnish origins by maintaining a Finnish Heritage Center and the Finnish American Historical Archives. Started as an academy, Suomi added a junior college in 1923 and a four-year college in 1994, subsequently transforming into Finlandia University. The Finnish Evangelical

Lutheran Church in America (Suomi Synod) established and maintained a seminary at the college from 1904 to 1958.

Courtship and Weddings The 1920 U.S. Census Bureau records indicate that first- and second-generation Finnish Americans mostly married other Finnish Americans. By the 1990s, however, Finnish Americans of the third and fourth generations were marrying outside their ethnic group in somewhat greater numbers. However, the 2011 ACS indicates that only 3 percent of Finnish Americans report being of more than one race or ethnicity. Of all European immigrant groups, Finns are among the most likely to marry within their group. In a comparative study of Finnish and American weddings, Salla Hakulinen notes that Finnish and American courting and wedding rituals are, for the most part, similar, with the exception that American wedding ceremonies and receptions may be more grand or lavish, while Finnish weddings are likely to be simple. For example, most American weddings include a rehearsal dinner, which is not common among Finnish weddings. In addition, American brides are likely to have more bridesmaids than Finnish brides. One notable difference between Finnish and American receptions is that in Finland there is often at least one children's game, such as musical chairs, at the party, whereas American receptions usually consist of dinner, drinks, dancing, and socializing. However, Finnish American weddings are more likely to adhere to American cultural norms than Finnish traditions.

EMPLOYMENT AND ECONOMIC CONDITIONS

In the Midwest and the West early Finnish immigrant men worked as miners, timber workers, railroad workers, fishers, and dock hands. In New England they worked in quarries, fisheries, and textile and shoe factories. When single Finnish women began to settle in the United States, they went into domestic work as maids, cooks, and housekeepers. In the cutover lands across northern Michigan, Wisconsin, and Minnesota and in the farmlands of New England and upstate New York, immigrant families left industry to raise grain crops and potatoes and to run dairy and chicken farms. Finnish American immigrants living in cities worked in several crafts—as carpenters, painters, masons, tailors, and jewelers—as well as in factories and foundries.

Later generations that have had the advantage of an American education have chosen professions that expand on the working life of immigrants. Finnish American men frequently specialized in agriculture-related subjects, such as natural resources management, mining, engineering, and geology. A large percentage of Finnish American women studied nursing and home economics, working as researchers in industry or public managers in county extension agencies.

FINN CAMP

Although parochial education was not part of the Finnish tradition, Finnish Americans developed a program of summer schools and camps, such as the Detroit Finnish Cooperative Summer Camps (Finn Camp), where young people learned religion, Finnish culture, politics, and cooperative philosophies. Many of these camps became obsolete in the 1960s, but Finn Camp, which was founded in 1925, has continued to flourish through the turn of the twenty-first century. Finn Camp aims to develop sound moral character among Finnish American children and adolescents and offers a number of activities that build trust and create a spirit of cooperation, including a track meet and a stage production.

The fields of education, medical research, the arts, music, and law have also attracted Finnish American students. Finnish Americans have become so assimilated into American society that they can be found in every field and in all social classes. According to the 2011 ACS, nearly 43 percent of the 300,000 Finnish Americans employed in the United States hold white-collar jobs in management, science, or the arts. Another 24 percent work in sales. In addition, just more than 10 percent of employed Finnish Americans hold jobs in manufacturing and about 7 percent work in construction.

POLITICS AND GOVERNMENT

Finnish Americans are a politically active people. As voters, they overwhelmingly supported the Republican Party until the 1930s. However, after Franklin Delano Roosevelt became president in 1933, Finnish Americans became known as Democratic voters. Early immigrants emphasized temperance societies as a political action force. In 1888 Finnish immigrants organized the Suomalainen Kansallis Raittius Veljeysseura (Finnish National Temperance Brotherhood), which later had as many as ten thousand members. Many immigrants after 1892 had socialist leanings, and itinerant Finnish agitators found many converts in the United States. In 1906 the Amerikan Suomalaisten Sosialistiosastojen Järjestö (Finnish American Socialist Federation) was formed; two years later the organization became the first foreign-language affiliate of the Socialist Party of America. However, because of its increasing alignment with the Communist Party, the federation began to lose members over the next decade.

At the turn of the twentieth century, Finnish Americans worked to change U.S. national policy toward Finland. In 1899 a Finnish American delegation presented a petition to President William McKinley asking for aid to Finland in its fight against tsarist Russia. They also lobbied for early recognition of the Finnish Republic and for relief support to the homeland. Finnish American women organized feminist groups as early as 1895 for the purpose of self-education and the improvement of conditions for women. After 1906—when women in Finland were granted the right to vote—Finnish Americans became heavily involved in the American suffrage movement, passing petitions throughout the Finnish American community, participating in suffrage parades, and appearing at rallies. They organized into two wings: one aligned with the temperance movement, which promoted suffrage, and the other affiliated with the socialist movement, which promoted working women's issues. Both worked to improve conditions for all American women through political action.

Finns have been active in union organizing, often working as leaders of strikes in the mining and timber industries. Their workers' halls were centers of union activity and headquarters for strikes, notably the Copper Country Strike of 1913–1914 and the two Mesabi Range strikes of 1907 and 1916. After World War II Finnish Americans were central to the organizing of iron miners into the Steelworkers Union on the Marquette Range in Michigan. In addition, Detroit autoworkers used the Wilson Avenue Finn Hall to develop their union organizing. On the extreme, radical wing of Finnish American politics, Gus Hall (born Arvo Kusta Halberg, 1910–2000), longtime chairman of the Communist Party USA, was a four-time U.S. presidential candidate, although he never received even 1 percent of the popular vote.

Finns have been elected to political positions, mainly at the local and regional levels, serving as postmasters, clerks, sheriffs, and mayors. No Finn has been elected state governor, and only one Finn, O. J. Larson, had been a member of the U.S. Congress. (He was elected to the House of Representatives in 1920 and again in 1922.) However, Finnish Americans have served in state houses in Michigan, Minnesota, Wisconsin, and Alaska. The first woman elected to the office of mayor in Ohio—Amy Kaukonen—was a Finnish American medical doctor. She beat her opponent on a prohibition platform in 1922.

During the effort to win support for U.S. entry into World War I, the administration of President Woodrow Wilson orchestrated a loyalty movement among the Finns. In spite of their antidraft stance in World War I, Finns have readily served in the U.S. armed forces, beginning with the Civil War, when former Finnish sailors and recent immigrants signed on. Finns served in the Spanish-American War, World Wars I and II, and the Spanish Civil War. Finnish American nurses—mostly women—also have contributed to the American war effort.

Finnish Americans have long been involved in the political issues of Finland. The American Finnish Aid Committee gathered considerable funds for famine relief in 1902. After the general strike occurred in 1906, a number of Finnish agitators sought a safe haven in the Finnish American community. After Finland declared itself a republic, Finnish Americans worked with Herbert Hoover to provide food to famine-stricken Finland. Later, they lobbied effectively in Washington, D.C., for official recognition from the U.S. government for the new nation-state. Their most concerted effort on behalf of the Finns, however, occurred in 1939 and 1940, after the start of the Winter War. They mobilized efforts with Hoover's assistance to send four million dollars in aid to the war-torn country. Individual family efforts to collect food and clothing for relatives continued well into the end of the decade. In the 1990s Finnish Americans worked actively as volunteers and fund-raisers, promoting religion in the Finnish sections of the former Soviet Union.

NOTABLE INDIVIDUALS

Finnish Americans as a group tend to downplay the concept of individual merit. (*Oma kehu haisee*—a Finnish proverb often quoted by Finnish Americans—means "self-praise smells putrid.") Nevertheless, many Finnish Americans have risen to prominence. The following sections list their contributions.

Architecture The father-and-son architectural team of Eliel (1897–1950) and Eero (1910–1961) Saarinen was closely associated with Michigan's Cranbrook Institute, where Finnish design theory and practice were taught to several generations of Americans. Eero designed a number of important buildings, including the Gateway Arch in St. Louis; the General Motors Technical Center in Warren, Michigan; the TWA terminal at New York's Kennedy International Airport; and the Dulles International Airport near Washington, D.C.

Art Finnish American painters include Elmer Forsberg (1883–1950), longtime professor at the Art Institute of Chicago and a significant painter in his own right. Religious painter Warner Sallman (1892–1968), a Finland Swede, is most famous for his *Head of Christ* (1941), the mass-produced portrait of a Nordic-looking Jesus that became an icon of American Protestantism. Photojournalist Kosti Ruohomaa (1914–1961), a second-generation Finnish American from Maine, created a portfolio of photographs after working more than twenty years for *Life* and other national magazines. Rudy Autio (1926–2007), also a second-generation Finnish American, is a fellow of the American Crafts Council whose work is in the permanent collections of major museums. Minnesota-born sculptor Dale Eldred (1934–1993) became head of the Kansas City Institute of Arts and creator of monumental environmental sculptures that are displayed throughout the world.

Business The earliest successful Finnish American businessman was Carl Sjödahl (Charles Linn, 1814–1882), who began as a sailor and became a wealthy wholesaler, banker, and industrialist in New Orleans and Birmingham, Alabama. Another early Finnish seaman, captain Gustave Niebaum (1842–1908), established the Inglenook winery in California. Väinö Hoover (1905–1983), former president and chief executive officer of Hoover Electric Company, designed and manufactured electric actuators and power flight control system components for aircraft and deep-sea equipment. As an important figure in the American defense industry of the 1950s and 1960s, he was a member of President Dwight D. Eisenhower's National Defense Advisory Committee.

Yrjö Paloheimo (1899–1986) was a philanthropist and a rancher in New Mexico and southern California. He organized Help Finland activities in the 1940s, founded a farm and garden school for orphans in Finland in 1947, and established the Finlandia Foundation in 1952. In addition, he and his wife organized the Old Cienaga Village, a living history museum of early Hispanic life in New Mexico. Finnish American Armas Clifford "Mike" Markkula (1942–), a venture capitalist, was the second CEO of Apple Computer Inc.

Education Finnish Americans in education include Margaret Preska (1938–), one of the first women in the United States to head an institution of higher learning. She was president of Mankato State University from 1979 to 1992. Richard Ranta (1943–) was dean of the College of Communication and Fine Arts at the University of Memphis and also was a freelance producer of such television specials as the Grammy Awards.

Government Among the best-known Finnish Americans in government is Emil Hurja (1892–1953), the political pollster who orchestrated Franklin Delano Roosevelt's victorious presidential elections. Hurja became a member of the Democratic National Committee during the 1930s. O. J. Larson (1871–1957) was a U.S. representative from Minnesota in the early 1920s. Maggie Walz (1861–1927), publisher of the *Naisten Lehti* (*Women's Newspaper*), represented the Finnish American suffragists in the suffrage and temperance movements. Viena Pasanen Johnson, cofounder of the Minnesota Farmer Labor Party, was the first woman member of the Minnesota State Teachers' College board of directors. She later became a national leader in the Women's International League for Peace and Freedom. Gus Hall (1910–2000) was president of the Communist Party USA.

Literature Jean Auel (1936–), author of *Clan of the Cave Bear* and other best-selling novels dealing with prehistoric peoples, is a third-generation Finnish American. Less well known but still significant to American letters is Shirley (Waisanen) Schoonover (1936–2004), whose *Mountain of Winter* (1965) has been translated into eighteen languages. Anselm Hollo (1934–2013) was a renowned translator and writer with more than nineteen volumes of verse to his credit. Recent writers emerging from the small press movement include poets Judith Minty (1937–) and Sheila Packa (1956–), fiction writers/poets Suzanne Matson (1959–) and Jane Piirto (1941–); fiction

Eero Saarinen, who emigrated from Finland to the U.S. when he was 13, went on to design some of the most iconic modern furniture. Here is shown his Tulip-Chair inspired tables with his Womb Chairs. VIEW PICTURES / UIG VIA GETTY IMAGES

writers Mary Caraker (1929–), Joseph David Damrell (1944–), Kathryn A. Laity, Lauri Arvid Anderson (1942–), and G. K. Wuori; renowned autobiographer and poet Stephen Kuusisto (1955–); and award-winning science fiction writer Emil Petaja (1915–2000).

Music Composer Charles Wuorinen (1938–)—the youngest composer to win a Pulitzer Prize—was named a MacArthur Fellow in 1986. His music is performed by major symphony orchestras throughout the United States. Tauno Hannikainen (1896–1968) was the permanent director of the Duluth Symphony and an associate conductor of the Chicago Symphony Orchestra. Heimo Haitto (1925–1999) was a concert violinist who performed as a soloist with major philharmonics in Europe and the United States. Legendary virtuoso accordionist Viola Turpeinen (1909–1958) became a recording artist and professional musician. Jorma Kaukonen (1940–) played lead guitar for Jefferson Airplane.

Religion Finnish America's major contributor to American Lutheran theology was renowned professor of theology Taito Kantonen (1900–1993) of Wittenburg University. Melvin Johnson (1932–2012), an administrator at the Evangelical Lutheran Church in America headquarters in Chicago, and retired theologian Raymond W. Wargelin (1911–2003) were among the most prominent recent church leaders of Finnish descent in the United States.

Science and Medicine Olga Lakela (1890–1980), a former professor of biology at the Duluth campus of the University of Minnesota and the author of numerous scientific papers on plant and bird life in Minnesota, had her name inscribed on the Wall of Fame at the 1940 New York World's Fair as one of 630 Americans of foreign birth who contributed to the American way of life. Ilmari Salminen (1902–1986), a research chemist with Eastman Kodak, specialized in color photography. Verner E. Suomi (1915–1995), an emeritus professor at the University of Wisconsin-Madison, was responsible for several inventions currently used in the exploration of outer space. A younger generation of scientists includes Donald Saari (1940–), a Northwestern University mathematician in astronomy and economics; Marvin Makinen (1939–), a biophysicist at the University of Chicago; and Dennis G. Maki (1940–), a medical doctor who was an infectious disease specialist at the Medical School at the University of Wisconsin-Madison.

Sports Finnish American sports figures have achieved recognition in track, cross-country skiing, ski jumping, and ice hockey. The Finnish American Athletic Club was one of the strongest organizations in U.S. track and field competition. U.S. Olympic hockey and ski jumping teams have included Finnish Americans. Midwestern American sports teams in the 1930s were often called "Flying Finns," after legendary Finnish runner Paavo Nurmi (1897–1973), whose tour of the United States during the 1920s caused a sensation among American track and field enthusiasts. Waino Ketonen (1888–1974) was a world-champion middleweight wrestler from 1918 to 1927. Kevin Tapani (1964–), former pitcher for the Minnesota Twins, and sportscaster Dick Enberg (1935–) are both third-generation Finnish Americans.

Stage and Screen Stage actor Alfred Lunt (1892–1977), who teamed with his actress–wife Lynn Fontanne from the 1920s through the 1950s, was a second-generation Finnish American from Wisconsin. He showed his Finnish pride when he chose Robert Sherwood's poignant *There Shall Be No Night* (1940) as a touring vehicle and a significant way for the duo to present the plight of Finns fighting in the Winter War in Finland. Bruno Maine (1896–1962) was scenic art director for Radio City Music Hall, and Sointu Syrjälä (1904–1979) was theater designer for several Broadway shows. Movie actor Albert Salmi (1928–1990) began his career in the New York City Finnish immigrant theater, and Maila Nurmi (1922–2008), who once used the stage name Vampira, hosted horror movies on television in the late 1950s in Los Angeles. She also starred in Ed Wood's immortal alien flick *Plan 9 from Outer Space* (1959), considered by many critics to be the worst movie of all time. Other Finnish American actresses include Jessica Lange (1949–) and Christine Lahti (1950–), granddaughter of early Finnish American feminist Augusta Lahti.

MEDIA

PRINT

Amerikan Uutiset

A weekly newspaper in Finnish with some English. It has a long tradition of providing a national forum for nonpartisan political and general news from Finnish American communities across the country. Founded in 1932, the paper was later bought by Finland-born entrepreneurs interested in creating a more contemporary Finland news emphasis. It has the largest Finnish American readership in the nation.

Sakri Viklund, Editor
P.O. Box 8147
Lantana, Florida 33462
Phone: (407) 588-9770
Fax: (407) 588-3229
Email: amuutiset@aol.com
URL: www.amuutiset.com

Báiki: The North American Sámi Journal

A quarterly journal published since 1991 by descendants of Sámi peoples. It explores their own unique heritage.

Faith Fjeld, Editor
3548 Fourteenth Avenue South
Minneapolis, Minnesota 55407
Phone: (612) 722-0040
Fax: (612) 722-3844
Email: faithfjeld@q.com
URL: www.baiki.org

Finnish American Reporter

A newsprint journal featuring personal essays, Finnish American community news, and brief news articles reprinted from and about Finland. Founded in 1986, this monthly has gradually built itself into the leading publication for readers seeking an American-oriented presentation of Finnish American cultural life. It is published by the Työmies Society, the left-wing political movement of Finnish America.

Jim Kurtti, Editor
P.O. Box 479
Hancock, Michigan 49930
Phone: (906) 487-7549
Fax: (906) 487-7557
Email: editor@finnishamericanreporter.com
URL: www.finnishamericanreporter.com

Kippis!

The literary journal of the Finnish North American Literature Association, published biannually, has been in existence since 2005. Kippis! publishes high-quality literary works of fiction, nonfiction, and poetry, and features original art by Finnish American photographers and artists on its cover. Although originally published in print, it changed to an online version in 2012 with occasional commemorative print issues.

Beth L. Virtanen, Editor
P.O. Box 11
New Blaine, Arkansas 72851
Phone: (479) 938-1100
Email: admin@finnala.com
URL: www.finnala.com

New World Finn

New World Finn is a quarterly nonacademic journal that features poetry, fiction, and social commentary by Finnish Americans. The journal also publishes translations of Finnish poems and stories and reports on the happenings in Finnish cultural circles.

Gerry Henkel, Editor
P.O. Box 432
Cedar Grove, Wisconsin 53013
Phone: (218) 525-7609
Email: gerryhenkel@fatermac.net
URL: www.newworldfinn.com

New Yorkin Uutiset

A weekly independent newspaper featuring news from Finland and Finnish American communities. Founded in 1906 as a daily, the paper—written primarily in Finnish with some English articles—is now a weekly. New Yorkin Uutiset takes a nationalistic and politically conservative position on issues.

Leena Isbom, Editor
4422 Eighth Avenue
Brooklyn, New York 11220
Phone: (718) 435-0800
Fax: (718) 871-7230

Norden News

A weekly newspaper featuring news from Finland and Finland Swede American communities.

This Swedish-language paper provides the only current information on the Finland Swede community in the United States.

Erik R. Hermans, Editor
P.O. Box 2143
New York, New York 10185-0018
Phone: (212) 753-0880
Fax: (212) 944-0763

RADIO

KAXE-FM

The "Finnish Americana and Heritage Show," an English-language program presented the first Sunday of each month, includes Finnish folk and popular music and information about Finnish music events in Minnesota. It is broadcast in Bemidji on 94.7 FM, in Brainerd on 89.5 FM, and in Grand Rapids on 91.7 FM.

1841 East Highway 169
Grand Rapids, Minnesota 55744
Phone: (218) 326-1234
Fax: (218) 326-1235
Email: kaxe@kaxe.org
URL: www.kaxe.org

KUSF-FM (90.3)

The "Voice of Finland," a weekly one-hour program in the Finnish language, provides music, news, interviews, and information about Finnish activities occurring in the region.

2130 Fulton Street
San Francisco, California 94117-1080
Phone: (415) 386-5873
Email: kusf@usfca.edu
URL: web.usfca.edu/kusf

WCAR-AM (1090)

"Finn Focus," a light entertainment program in Finnish, provides music, news, notices about local activities, and interviews.

32500 Park Lane
Garden City, Michigan 48135
Phone: (313) 525-1111
Fax: (313) 525-3608

WLVS-AM (1380)

"Hyvät Uutiset" ("Good News"), sponsored by the Lake Worth Finnish Pentecostal Congregation, is a weekly half-hour broadcast in Finnish featuring religious music and talk. "American Finnish Evening Hour" provides light entertainment, music, and information about happenings in the listening area and in Finland. "Halls of Finland," a program broadcast in Finnish, includes news reports about local events and activities occurring in the United States and in Finland. "Religious Hour" is sponsored by the Apostolic Lutheran church.

1939 Seventh Avenue North
Lake Worth, Florida 33461-3898
Phone: (561) 585-5533
Fax: (561) 585-0131

WYMS-FM (88.9)

"Scandinavian Hour," broadcast once a month in two languages, provides news from Finland and the local region, interviews, and Finnish music. "Scenes from the Northern Lights" originates in Bloomington, Indiana, and is offered through syndication on National Public Radio. It features a wide variety of Finnish music, including rock, pop, classical, folk, and opera.

5225 West Vliet Street
Milwaukee, Wisconsin 53208
Phone: (414) 475-8890
Fax: (414) 475-8413
URL: www.wyms.org

TELEVISION

WLUC

"Suomi Kutsu" ("Finland Calling") is a weekly telecast on Sundays from 10 to 11 a.m. The first half hour is a newsmagazine about Finland and Finnish America featuring interviews, music, news, and video essays. The second half hour is a Finnish-language devotional worship service led by area Lutheran clergy.

Carl Pellonpaa, Host
177 U.S. Highway 41 East
Negaunee, Michigan 49866
Phone: (906) 475-4161
Fax: (906) 475-4824
Email: finland@wluctv6.com
URL: www.wluctv6.com

ORGANIZATIONS AND ASSOCIATIONS

Finlandia Foundation

Founded in 1953, this national philanthropic organization's mission is to cultivate and strengthen cultural relations between the United States and the Republic of Finland. Finlandia Foundation donates more than seventy thousand dollars annually for cultural programs, grants, and scholarships.

P.O. Box 92298
Pasadena, California 91109-2298
Phone: (626) 795-2081
Fax: (626) 795-6533
URL: www.finlandiafoundation.org

Finnish American League for Democracy (FALD)

This organization promotes the study of Finnish American history and culture.

Marita Cauthen, Executive Officer
P.O. Box 600
147 Elm Street
Fitchburg, Massachusetts 01420
Phone: (508) 343-3822

International Order of Runeberg

Promotes the preservation of pan-Scandinavian culture and traditions with special emphasis on Finland. It also conducts a student exchange program.

Deidre Meanley, Secretary
1138 Northeast 153rd Avenue
Portland, Oregon 97230
Phone: (503) 254-2054
Fax: (503) 261-9868
Email: dmeanley@worldacess.net
URL: www.orderofruneberg.org

MUSEUMS AND RESEARCH CENTERS

Finnish American Historical Archives

The Finnish American Heritage Center at Finlandia University features the best collection of materials that predate the twentieth century, as well as modern materials including records of the Help Finland Movement, the Finnish Evangelical Lutheran Church in America (Suomi Synod), and the celebration of the three hundredth anniversary of the Delaware Colony. The archives maintain a small, uncataloged, unsystematic collection of material objects, parts of which are usually on display. A large photograph collection, an oral history collection, and microfilm archives of newspapers and records stored in Finland round out the resources.

601 Quincy Street
Hancock, Michigan 49930
Phone: (906) 487-7347
Fax: (906) 487-7366
Email: archives@finlandia.edu
URL: www.finlandia.edu/index.php?id=620

Finnish–American Historical Society of the West

This organization of people of Finnish ancestry and friends of Finland focuses on discovering, collecting, and preserving material to establish and illustrate the history of persons of Finnish descent in the American West. The group maintains Lindgren Log Home, a museum of Finnish American artifacts from the 1920s.

Roy Schulbach
P.O. Box 5522
Portland, Oregon 97228-0552
Phone: (503) 654-0448
Fax: (503) 652-0558
Email: info@finamhsw.com
URL: www.finamhsw.com

Immigration History Research Center of the University of Minnesota

This collection—one of the largest available anywhere—is part of a larger collection of twenty-four late immigration groups. The Finnish section includes materials from the Finnish American radical and cooperative movements, theater, and music.

Erika Lee, Director
826 Berry Street
St. Paul, Minnesota 55114-1076
Phone: (612) 627-4208
Fax: (612) 627-4190
Email: ihrc@umn.edu
URL: www1.umn.edu/ihrc

Institute of Migration/Siirtolaisuusinstituutti

The institute was founded in 1974 with headquarters in Turku, Finland. It promotes the collection, storage, and documentation of research material relating to international and internal migration including immigrants and refugees. It also carries out and promotes migration research; publishes research reports, books, and articles on migration; and develops cooperation between universities and special organizations related to migration, both within Finland and abroad.

Ismo Söderling, Director
Eerikinkatu 34
Turku, Finland 20100
Phone: 358-2-2840 441
Email: ismo.soderling@utu.fi
URL: www.migrationinstitute.fi

Other archival collections of Finnish American materials are regional. For example, the Iron Range Research Center in Chisholm, Minnesota, has a rich northern Minnesota collection, and the Finnish Cultural Center at Fitchburg State College in Fitchburg, Massachusetts, has been trying to reconstitute materials from the New England region.

Finnish Americans have not developed any major museums. The most systematically catalogued collection of Finnish American materials can be found at Michigan State University Museum in East Lansing. The Nordic Heritage Museum in Seattle includes a display of Finnish culture, collected and organized by the local Finnish American community.

Finnish Americans also have preserved their cultural landscape history at two significant sites listed on the National Register of Historic Places. The Hanka Homestead in Arnheim, Michigan, provides an example of a small backwoods farmstead, and the town of Embarrass, Minnesota, is an excellent example of an entire Finnish American farming community.

SOURCES FOR ADDITIONAL STUDY

Hoglund, A. William. *Finnish Immigrants in America, 1880–1920*. Madison: University of Wisconsin Press, 1960.

Jalkanen, Ralph. *The Faith of the Finns: Historical Perspectives on the Finnish Lutheran Church in America*. East Lansing: Michigan State University Press, 1972.

Jarvenpa, Aili, and Michael G. Karni, eds. *Sampo: The Magic Mill: A Collection of Finnish American Writing*. Minneapolis: New Rivers, 1989.

Karni, Michael G., Matti E. Kaups, and Douglas J. Ollila Jr. *The Finnish Experience in the Western Great Lakes Region*. Turku, Finland: Institute for Migration, 1972.

Kivisto, Peter. "The Attenuated Ethnicity of Contemporary Finnish-Americans." In *The Ethnic Enigma: The Salience of Ethnicity for European-Origin Groups*, edited by Peter Kivisto. Cranbury, NJ: Associated University Presses, 1989.

Lainio, Jarmo, Annaliina Gynne, and Raija Kangassalo. *Transborder Contacts and the Maintenance of Finnishness in the Diaspora: Proceedings of FinnForum VIII, an Interdisciplinary Conference in Finnish, Finnish-North American, and Sweden Finnish Studies*. Eskilstuna, Sweden: Mälardalen University, 2009.

Ross, Carl. *The Finn Factor in American Labor, Culture, and Society*. New York Mills, MN: Parta, 1977.

———, and K. Marianne Wargelin Brown, eds. *Women Who Dared: The History of Finnish American Women*. St. Paul: University of Minnesota, 1986.

Taramaa, Raija. *Stubborn and Silent Finns with "Sisu" in Finnish-American Literature: An Imagological Study of Finnishness in the Literary Production of Finnish-American Authors*. Doctoral dissertation, Oulu University Press, 2007.

Virtanen, Beth L., ed. *Finnish-North American Literature in English: A Concise Anthology*. Lewiston, NY: Mellen, 2009.

FRENCH AMERICANS

Dennis Earl Fehr

OVERVIEW

French Americans, or Franco-Americans, are immigrants or descendants of people from France, a country in western Europe. Shaped roughly like a hexagon, France is bordered by the Atlantic Ocean to the west, the English Channel to the northwest, Belgium and Luxembourg to the north, Germany to the northeast, Switzerland to the east, Italy to the southeast, the Mediterranean Sea to the south, and Spain to the southwest. Half its borders, or 1,920 miles (3,090 kilometers), are coastline. The topography of France includes the Pyrenees mountains along the southern border and the Alps along the southeast border. The remaining terrain varies from mountain ranges to plains to forests, and includes four major river systems. France occupies 213,000 square miles (552,000 square kilometers), making it the largest country in Western Europe. It is slightly smaller than the state of Texas.

According to the World Bank, the population of France was approximately 65.5 million in 2011. The capital and major cultural center is Paris, where about one-fifth of the total population resides. In 2009, 64 percent of French people identified themselves as Catholic, compared to 81 percent in 1965. The decrease was larger among Catholics who described themselves as active: in 1952, 27 percent of the French claimed to attend Mass at least once a week; in 2006 only 4.5 percent did. A 2006 poll published by *Le Monde* found that 31 percent of the French population described themselves as atheist, 4 percent as Muslim, 3 percent as Protestant, and 1 percent as Jewish. In nominal figures, France has the fifth-largest economy in the world and the second-largest economy in Europe, behind its primary economic partner, Germany. In the late 2000s France entered the worldwide recession, emerging from it after only four quarters. Partly for this reason, Credit Suisse's 2010 *Global Wealth Report* ranked France the wealthiest European country (including 2.6 million millionaires), and the world's fourth-wealthiest nation in aggregate household wealth.

In 1682 Robert Cavalier de LaSalle, along with eighteen Native Americans, canoed the length of the Mississippi River, claiming the vast territory for France. French settlers quickly followed. Their settlements are today's Detroit, Michigan; St. Louis, Missouri; Memphis, Tennessee; and Mobile, Alabama. According to the U.S. Department of Homeland Security (2010), the United States has experienced little significant French immigration in the past 110 years, with the exception of a few thousand Jews during World War II.

According to the 2010 U.S. Census, the French American population was 11.8 million, (approximately the size of Ohio's entire population). French Americans have assimilated into the general population and do not live in distinctive ethnic communities with two exceptions: the Cajuns and the Creoles, both of whom live primarily in the state of Louisiana. Americans of French descent in New England continue to refer to themselves as Franco-Americans. According to the 2011 U.S. Census Bureau's American Community Survey estimates for 2009–2011, the states with the highest number of French Americans included California, Louisiana, Texas, Massachusetts, Florida, New York, and Michigan.

HISTORY OF THE PEOPLE

Early History The history of France dates to about 1000 BCE, when Celtic tribes moved into large areas of northern Europe. The Celts remaining in the area that became France were known as Gauls. Around 600 BCE, Greek colonists settled in the Mediterranean area of Marseilles, and their civilized ways influenced the Gauls. Led by Julius Caesar, Rome conquered the region in 59 BCE; it remained under Roman rule for more than 500 years. During this time the Romans built the foundations of many modern French roads and cities and established that Latin would form the basis of the French language. After the fall of the Roman Empire in 476 CE, France was ruled as an absolute monarchy by four successive dynasties. By the time King Henry IV established the Bourbon dynasty in 1589, France had developed a strict system of social hierarchy known as feudalism. Wealthy aristocrats owned the land and participated in government; poorer people worked the land and had few rights.

The stage was set for French immigration to North America in the early 1500s, during a religious movement known as the Reformation. At this time, many citizens of France and other European nations protested against some of the doctrines and corrupt practices then prevailing in the Roman Catholic Church. The Reformation caused conflict throughout Europe, eventually dividing the church into two separate factions, Catholics and Protestants. John Calvin, a French priest, was instrumental in the spread of Protestantism. His followers, called Huguenots, built 2,000 churches in France by the mid-1500s, though they also became the targets of persecution by French Catholics during thirty years of civil war. King Henry IV, who was born a Protestant but converted to Catholicism, stopped the conflict temporarily in the 1590s by enacting the Edict of Nantes. The edict granted political rights and religious freedom to French Protestants, and in so doing, suspended France's religious wars for ninety years. In 1685 King Louis XIV, after spending several years unsuccessfully pressuring Protestants to convert, revoked the Edict of Nantes. This sudden loss of rights drove thousands of Huguenots, the majority of whom were skilled, educated, and prosperous, to leave France for North America.

Another important event in French history that affected immigration to North America occurred in 1763, with the conclusion of the Seven Years' War (also known as the French and Indian War) between France and England. These traditional enemies had clashed repeatedly over expansionist policies and colonization in Europe, North America, and India. After losing this conflict, France relinquished control of its colonies to England through the Treaty of Paris. According to Jean-Baptiste Duroselle in *France and the United States: From Beginnings to Present* (1976), French Americans "nursed the knowledge that they had been abandoned by a country that was no longer their homeland, and of which they today retain nothing but the language." Duroselle says that this event marked the end of French political power in the land that would become the United States. The American Revolution began just twelve years later, however, and France was persuaded to provide invaluable military aid to the American side. In fact, many historians suggest that this support from France enabled the formation of the United States.

France became embroiled in its own revolution in 1789. As the French middle class, or bourgeoisie, became more prosperous and powerful, they began to resent the feudal system and demanded equal rights and tax reform. King Louis XVI accepted some of the people's demands but later brought troops into Paris to try to crush the rebellion. On July 14, crowds of armed protesters destroyed the Bastille, a fortress that was used to hold political prisoners and that gradually had become a symbol of oppression. This event marked the end of the old regime and the beginning of the French Republic, and it has been celebrated ever since as a national holiday—Bastille Day. France soon adopted a constitution that ensured equal rights for all citizens and

limited the powers of the monarchy and the church. The French Revolution continued, however, as conservative and radical forces vied for control of the new government. These factions staged reciprocal campaigns of violence against one another during what became known as the Reign of Terror.

In the meantime, France entered into war with a coalition of European nations determined to halt the revolution and its radical ideas. Napoleon Bonaparte gained prominence as a French military leader and then overthrew the government of France in 1799, granting himself dictatorial powers as Emperor Napoleon I. Although Napoleon scored many popular military victories and initiated lasting reforms to the French educational and legal systems, he also severely limited individual rights. His rules made it virtually impossible for French citizens to emigrate, for example, so only a few immigrants came to the United States during his reign, which ended in 1815.

Public opinion in the United States, which had been generally positive toward France since the American Revolution, gradually became negative during the Reign of Terror. The United States eventually claimed neutrality during the French Revolution and refused to provide assistance during the resulting war in Europe. Relations with France became the subject of intense debate among the leaders of the U.S. Congress and in the newly influential American press. Negative attitudes toward France peaked in 1797 with the XYZ Affair, when three unnamed French diplomats demanded a huge bribe before they would agree to speak with American delegates about a new treaty. This perceived insult caused the United States to prepare for a war with France.

During this time, French Americans—especially those who had come to the United States as refugees from the French Revolution—were viewed by some American leaders as a potential threat to national security. In 1798 the U.S. government passed the controversial Alien and Sedition Acts, which were intended to monitor and limit the power of immigrant groups. For example, the Acts increased the residency requirement from five to fourteen years before immigrants were allowed to vote, forced ships to compile dossiers on immigrant passengers, and granted the government the power to deport anyone it considered "dangerous." The Acts became the subject of considerable public outrage and were allowed to expire two years later. Shortly thereafter, the 1803 purchase of the Louisiana Territory from Napoleon helped relax the tension over immigration. This vast tract of land doubled the size of the United States and provided a new frontier for a large wave of new immigrants.

Modern Era After Napoleon was defeated at Waterloo in 1815, France was ruled first as a constitutional monarchy and then as a republic. In 1848 Napoleon's nephew Louis Napoleon Bonaparte was elected president of the republic, but he soon overthrew the government and proclaimed himself Emperor Napoleon III. He was soundly defeated in the Franco-Prussian War in 1870, however, which resulted in the loss of the French provinces Alsace and Lorraine to the German Empire. Thousands of Alsatians chose to immigrate to the United States at this time rather than live under German rule. France approved the democratic constitution of the Third Republic in 1875. The period ranging from 1871 to the start of World War I in 1914 was known as La Belle Époque. During this time, the arts and sciences flourished in France. Overseas France took control of northeastern Africa and French Indochina in southeastern Asia, which consists of present-day Vietnam, Cambodia, and Laos. While France's relations with other European countries and with the United States remained tense during this period, no major wars broke out, and many Western powers in addition to France experienced a time of economic prosperity during which they improved their infrastructure and expanded their overseas empires.

World War I (1914–1918), in which French and American soldiers fought side by side, helped improve relations between France and the United States. In the period between the World Wars, France endured a weak government and low birth rates. These conditions contributed to the fall of France in 1940, shortly after the beginning of World War II, and to its occupation by German troops for the next four years. After the war Alsace and Lorraine were returned to France, and the Fourth Republic was established in 1946. The government remained unstable and faced constant conflict with French colonies seeking independence. Charles de Gaulle became president of the Fifth Republic in 1958 and managed to bring some measure of peace and economic recovery to France.

During the early 1960s, France's colonial empire continued to disintegrate with de Gaulle signing the Evian Agreements ending war with Algeria and recognizing its sovereignty. By the end of the decade, France, much like the United States, was experiencing a period of social unrest with college-age students expressing sexual freedom and protesting the war in Vietnam. During the 1970s and 1980s, left-leaning political groups such as the Socialist Party and the Communist Party continued to attract followers in France.

Plans for the European Union had begun as far back as 1952, when the Inner Six (Belgium, France, West Germany, Italy, Luxembourg, and the Netherlands) formed the European Coal and Steel Community (ECSC), which unified the countries during the Cold War and the spread of Soviet Communism in Eastern Europe. In the decades that followed, France joined numerous other European communities and organizations until the formal establishment of the European Union in 1993. As of 2013 the European Union consisted of twenty-seven member states, with France, Germany, and United Kingdom considered the three most economically stable countries in the federation.

French American settlement patterns reflect the fact that French immigrants typically came to the United States as individuals or families seeking economic opportunity. Rather than joining groups of previous French settlers or establishing French American communities, these immigrants most often scattered to the areas where new opportunities seemed likely.

SETTLEMENT IN THE UNITED STATES

Many of the earliest French settlements in North America were mainly intended as trading outposts. Jean Ribaut, a French Huguenot sailor, established two of the first French colonies near Beaufort, South Carolina, and Jacksonville, Florida, in the 1550s. He settled in these locations in order to compete with the Spanish for control of trade in the Caribbean region.

Economic, religious, or political factors have caused several waves of French immigration to the United States; however, most French immigration has resulted from individual decisions rather than mass movements. The first significant flow of French immigrants began around 1538. It consisted of Huguenots who felt alienated from mainstream French society due to their Protestant faith. The Huguenots' emigration spiked after King Louis XIV revoked the Edict of Nantes in 1685, thus removing protection from Protestants. This forced the Huguenots to either convert to Catholicism or face death. According to Albert Robbins in *Coming to America: Immigrants from Northern Europe* (1981), the king's official decree gave orders to "kill the greatest part of the Protestants that can be overtaken, without sparing the women, to the end that this may intimidate them and prevent others from falling into a similar fault."

Many Huguenots fled France despite the fact that emigration was still illegal for Protestants. Those who managed to leave typically had to be wealthy enough to pay bribes or well-connected enough to acquire false passports. Consequently, a large percentage of the 15,000 Huguenots who arrived in North America were successful and skilled, and they eventually gained prominence as craftsmen and merchants. People of French descent created ethnic enclaves in early industrial cities in New England such as Lowell, Massachusetts; Lewiston, Maine; Woonsocket, Rhode Island; and Manchester, New Hampshire. These French ethnic neighborhoods were known as "Petits Canadas." They housed ethnic churches, schools, and business establishments where French was spoken. One can still hear French spoken on the street in some of these places. The Huguenots also established a strong presence in New York, with settlements in Harlem, Staten Island, New Rochelle, and New Paltz. Pennsylvania, Virginia, South Carolina, and Massachusetts also became the sites of successful Huguenot settlements. Because the Huguenots could not settle among French Catholics and felt alienated from France, most accepted North America as their new homeland and changed their names to sound more English.

Originally, French colonial policy allowed only Catholics to emigrate, but most French Catholics were reluctant to leave their homes. As a result, the few people who came to North America from France were mostly explorers, traders, or Jesuit missionaries seeking to convert the Native Americans. These individuals tended to spread out and travel far into the wilderness. In fact, by the time the Pilgrims arrived in New England in 1620, the French had already discovered three of the Great Lakes. This migration to the Midwest later led to French bases in Detroit and St. Louis. Robert Cavelier de La Salle traveled the length of the Mississippi River to the Gulf of Mexico in 1682. Upon completion of his journey he founded Louisiana by claiming the entire Mississippi Basin in the name of King Louis XIV of France. Jean-Baptiste Bienville followed by forming a successful French colony in New Orleans in 1717.

With the beginning of the French Revolution in 1789, a wave of Roman Catholic refugees emigrated from France to the United States. Many of these immigrants were either wealthy aristocrats or working-class people, such as chefs and hairdressers, who depended upon the aristocrats for their livelihood. Another important group of refugees to arrive at this time included one hundred French priests. Because there were only twenty-five priests in the American colonies prior to their arrival, these immigrants had a strong influence on the development of the Catholic Church in the United States. Missionary work carried the Roman Catholic refugees to far-ranging French colonial areas, such as Michigan, St. Louis, and Louisiana.

About 10,000 political refugees managed to leave France during the French Revolution, and many of these traveled through French colonies in the Caribbean to reach the United States. This group included about 3,000 people of mixed black and French ancestry who settled in Philadelphia. Following Napoleon's defeat in 1815, a large wave of French immigration began, which lasted through the start of the American Civil War. Napoleon's brother Jérome came to the United States at this time with several hundred former soldiers and tried unsuccessfully to establish settlements in Texas, Alabama, and Ohio.

The California Gold Rush, which began in 1848, convinced a record number of French immigrants to make their way to the United States. About 30,000 people arrived from France between 1849 and 1851, with an all-time high of 20,000 coming in 1851 alone.

Unfortunately they fared no better than other groups, with few ever finding the riches they sought.

In 1871 a group of Alsatian Jews settled in Los Angeles, after the Franco-Prussian War put the French provinces Alsace and Lorraine under German rule. Immigration slowed significantly during the American Civil War, and the years immediately following saw a larger percentage of unskilled workers from France moving to the United States. A number of French Jews immigrated after the fall of France to the Germans in 1940. However, from the end of World War II onward, a strong cultural and economic recovery in France caused the flow of French immigrants to slow considerably. Most French immigrants in the second half of the twentieth century came to the United States because they had married American citizens or simply wanted to try something different, rather than out of religious, economic, or political necessity.

The number of immigrants to the United States from France has always been smaller than from other European countries. In total, approximately 740,000 immigrants from France have settled in the United States since 1820, and between 30,000 and 40,000 came earlier. In 1990, 119,233 people living in the United States told the U.S. Census Bureau that they had been born in France; in 2011, the number was estimated to be 153,872 (American Community Survey).

Although these figures provide useful information about the trends of French immigration, demographers admit that counting French Americans has been problematic since U.S. colonial times. For many years U.S. officials tended to overestimate the number of French immigrants because they equated immigrants' nationality with their last place of domicile before arrival. This policy meant that many people who actually hailed from Germany or eastern Europe who had settled in France temporarily in order to facilitate their eventual passage to the United States were regarded as French Americans. Another problem in the U.S. immigration figures involves inconsistent treatment of the French-speaking people who came to the United States from Canada or the Caribbean. French Canadian Americans, Acadians (or Cajuns), and Creoles form distinct U.S. ethnic groups but are not always distinguished from French Americans in census figures. Compounding the problems with U.S. immigration figures is the fact that for many years French officials tended to underestimate the number of emigrants because they wished to downplay any outflow of French citizens. However, most sources agree that French immigration to the United States has been small over time.

French American settlement patterns reflect the fact that French immigrants typically came to the United States as individuals or families seeking economic opportunity. Rather than joining groups of previous French settlers or establishing French American communities, these immigrants most often scattered to the areas where new opportunities seemed likely. For example, the number of ethnic French living in Louisiana dropped from 15,000 in 1860 to half that number by 1930 as the prosperity of the South declined. In the meantime, the French population of California rose from 8,000 in 1860 to 22,000 by 1970 as immigrants pursued new opportunities in the West. According to *We the People: An Atlas of America's Ethnic Diversity*, in 1980 more immigrants directly from France lived in California, New York, New Jersey, and Pennsylvania than in any other states. Many of these French immigrants possessed professional skills that were most valuable in urban environments.

According to the U.S. Census Bureau's American Community Survey estimates for 2009–2011, the states with the largest numbers of French Americans were California and Louisiana. Other states with large French American populations included Texas, Massachusetts, Florida, New York, and Michigan.

LANGUAGE

French is a Romance language derived from Latin. It has enjoyed a prestigious position in world culture for more than three centuries. French was the official language of diplomatic negotiations and the preferred language among the upper classes of Western civilization, beginning around 1650. By about 1920, however, English began to gain popularity, and it eventually surpassed French in terms of international status. In 1975 the French National Assembly, reacting to what it viewed as an encroachment of English slang upon the French language (commonly called "franglais"), passed a law restricting the use of untranslated English words in advertising materials. They also hoped to discourage the French public from using English words when an equivalent French term existed.

As of 2010, an estimated 1.6 million people in the United States spoke French at home.

Greetings and Popular Expressions Common French greetings and other expressions include the following: *Bonjour*—Hello, Good morning, Good afternoon; *Comment allez-vous*—How do you do?; *Au revoir*—Good-bye; *Très bien*—Very good; *Oui, c'est ça*—Yes, that's right; *Merci beaucoup*—Thank you very much; *À votre service*—You're welcome, or Don't mention it.

RELIGION

The majority of French immigrants to the United States, including Cajuns and Creoles, have been Roman Catholic. This is partly because Catholics constitute a majority in France and partly because during colonial times only Catholics were allowed to emigrate.

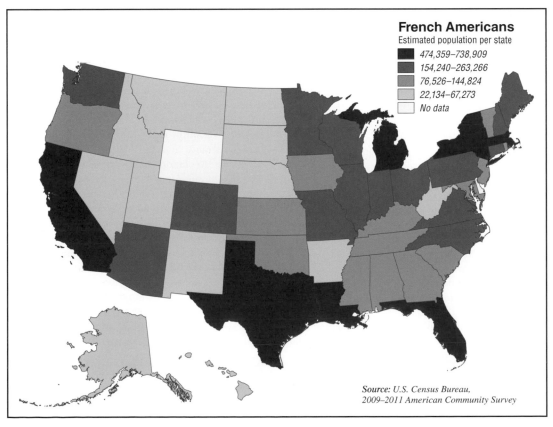

French Americans
Estimated population per state
- 474,359–738,909
- 154,240–263,266
- 76,526–144,824
- 22,134–67,273
- No data

Source: U.S. Census Bureau, 2009–2011 American Community Survey

THE FRENCH INFLUENCE ON AMERICAN ENGLISH

The influence of French is apparent in American English. For example, because French explorers often served as guides for other settlers after the United States purchased the Louisiana Territory, French words were used to describe many aspects of the frontier experience, including *portage, rapids, bayou, butte, peak, gopher, prairie, pass,* and *cache.* French explorers also left their mark on American place names; examples include Baton Rouge, Sault Ste. Marie, Detroit, Couer d'Alene, Marquette, Joliet, Lake Champlain, Lake Pontchartrain, Des Moines, Eau Claire, Fon du Lac, Charlevoix, and Terre Haute. Finally, numerous French words occur in everyday American usage, such as *croquet, poker, roulette, automobile, garage, lingerie, restaurant, crayon, bouquet,* and *boutique.*

Descendants of the 15,000 French Huguenots who came to the United States during Colonial times tend to be Anglican. In the 1800s emigrants from the French region of Switzerland escaped religious persecution by fleeing to the United States. During and after World War II, the United States became a refuge for French Jews. French Americans today assimilate more easily into the U.S. mainstream, including its religious practices, than any other non-English speaking group.

Mass in French was once common in ethnic enclaves. English-only masses did not become pervasive until the 1960s. Today mass in French is heard only irregularly in New England and Louisiana, usually for special occasions. With little difference between the two countries' Catholic and Anglican traditions, French Americans worship similarly to their compatriots in France.

CULTURE AND ASSIMILATION

Historically, the people who immigrated to the United States from northern Europe—including France— were more readily accepted than some other immigrant groups. For example, when the U.S. Congress passed a law restricting immigration in the 1920s, northern European groups received the most liberal quotas. This favored status allowed northern European immigrants to assimilate more easily into American culture. Moreover, the type of individual who was most likely to leave France for the United States had a particularly strong propensity toward assimilation. For instance, a high percentage of French immigrants were professionals or merchants who earned their livings among the greater population and within an urban environment. At the same time, very few French farmers— who would have lived in rural areas and been more isolated from the dominant culture—decided to emigrate. Typical French immigrants were also modernists who felt estranged from mainstream French culture

and viewed the United States as a progressive, classless, secular, and innovative society.

One early example of assimilation among French immigrants was when the Huguenots chose to join the less extreme Anglican Church in North America. In the modern era, despite the strong cultural nationalism found in France, French Americans have shown a higher rate of intermarriage than any other non-English-speaking immigrant group. In fact, French Americans tend to assimilate so quickly and completely that most sources can only cite their overall impact on American culture. Despite this, some cultural traces remain. French music, dance, and food are particularly relevant to Franco-Americans.

Traditions and Customs The rapid assimilation of French immigrants into American society ensured that few traditional customs were carried over and practiced by French Americans. Instead, Americans studied and emulated French culture, manners, cuisine, fashion, art, and literature. French Americans mainly disseminated information and acted as role models. French culture first gained widespread popularity in the United States in the early nineteenth century—shortly after the Revolutionary War—when Americans followed the events and supported the principles of the French Revolution. French chefs and restaurants bolstered the popularity of French cuisine, and the influence of French Impressionists on American art became apparent. Several U.S. presidents also ordered French furniture and silverware for use at the White House.

Cuisine French immigrants introduced a wide range of interesting foods to the United States. For example, French Americans made the first yeast breads in North America and brought technical farming skills that vastly improved American rice and wines. Huguenots grew and prepared the first okra, artichokes, and tomatoes. The popularity of French cuisine took off in the 1780s, following the alliance between France and the United States during the American Revolution. Many respected French chefs working in the United States have enjoyed celebrity status, including Alain Ducasse (of the restaurant Benoit), David Bouley (Bouley), Jean Georges (Trump Tower), all in New York; Joël Robuchon (Joël Robuchon, MGM Grand) and Guy Savoy (Guy Savoy, Caesar's Palace) in Las Vegas; and television chef Jacques Pépin. The absence of women in this list reflects a resistance throughout the entire culinary industry to admit women to the top echelon.

Tourtière, or French Canadian meat pie, and pea soup are still eaten in French ethnic neighborhoods during the holidays. Today many Americans, French and non-French alike, enjoy baguettes, omelettes, petit fours, croissants, and soufflés. French wines— Bordeaux, cabernet sauvignon, Chablis, merlot, pinots, sauvignon blanc, and Champagne—continue to set a standard for the U.S. wine industry. A number of French culinary terms—such as *bouillon, purée, fricassée, mayonnaise, pâté, hors d'oeuvres, bisque, fillet, sauté, casserole, au gratin*, and *à la mode*—are commonly used in American English.

Traditional Dress In the early nineteenth century, imported French attire, particularly items such as gloves and lace, gained popularity. Around 1850 the French even influenced men's fashion when their custom of wearing beards swept across the United States. In 1908, several American women wearing imported French skirts and fishnet stockings were arrested for indecent exposure. Names such as Louis Vuitton, Marc Jacobs, Coco Chanel, and Yves Saint Laurent have enabled France to maintain its influence on U.S. women's fashion.

Dances and Songs French Americans find many homeland influences in American music and dance. French dance forms that have come to the United States include the Can-can and ballet. French melodies that became popular in the United States when combined with English lyrics include Frank Sinatra's "My Way" and Elvis Presley's "Can't Help Falling in Love," "Yesterday When I Was Young," and "If You Go Away."

Contemporary French American performers such as Les Franco-Américains, Lucie Therrien, and Chanterelle have added French works such as "La Grain de Mil" ("The Millet Seed"), "Entre Moi" ("Between Me"), and "Le Bon Femme Robert" ("The Old Lady Robert") to the U.S. musical repertoire. Americans of all ethnic groups enjoy French classical works such as *Le Roi Lear* (King Lear), by Claude Debussy, and *Boléro*, by Maurice Ravel.

Josephine Baker, an American expatriate who performed in France for fifty years, became the toast of Paris with songs such as "J'ai Deux Amours." Following her example, an organization called the French American Fund for Contemporary Music offers performances, classes, commissions, and residencies that encourage cultural exchange in both directions between France and the United States.

Holidays French Americans observe many of the same religious holidays as Americans in general. At Christmas they sing *chants de Noël* (Christmas songs) such as "Dous Nuit" ("Silent Night") and "Mon Beau Sapin" ("O Christmas Tree"). French Americans also observe specifically French holidays such as Bastille Day. Bastille Day commemorates the destruction of the Bastille, a prison that had become a major symbol of the monarchy's oppression. This event led to the formation of the First Republic in 1792 and is celebrated in some communities throughout the United States on July 14. A popular song for Bastille Day is the "Marseillaise," France's national anthem.

The New Orleans tradition of Mardi Gras—a weeklong series of parades and parties usually held in February—was first organized in 1827 by French

FRENCH PROVERBS

Proverbs that French Americans have brought to the United States include the following:

A chaque oiseaux son nid est beau.

A bird loves its own nest. (Meaning: we often overestimate ourselves.)

A confesseurs, médicins, avocats, la vérité ne cèle de ton cas.

Conceal not the truth from thy physician and thy attorney.

Attente tourmente.

Those who live by hope die of hunger.

American students. Vermont celebrates Bennington Battle Day in honor of a battle that turned the tide of the American Revolution in favor of the Colonies and brought France into the conflict. The states of Connecticut, Maine, New Hampshire, and Vermont now hold Franco-American Day celebrations on June 24 to recognize French Canadians for their contributions to these states' cultures. Franco-Americans remember their French Canadian roots on June 24 in Lowell, Massachusetts.

Health Care Issues and Practices The average life expectancy in France is the same as in the United States—seventy years for men and seventy-eight years for women. Although no known congenital diseases are specific to French Americans, the French have shown a higher than average susceptibility to lung and throat cancers, mainly because they tend to smoke heavily. France also has one of the highest rates of alcoholism in the world, and French American alcohol consumption is above the U.S. norm.

FAMILY AND COMMUNITY LIFE

According to numerous studies, including a 1982 report published by Hervé Le Bras and Louis Roussel and a 2001 article in the *Journal of Sex Research*, the institution of marriage began to change drastically in France in the late 1960s. Before then, almost 90 percent of French people married by the age of fifty, but the percentage began to decrease in the 1970s. At first social scientists believed the diminishing marriage rates were due to the fact that adults in their twenties were putting off marriage until they had finished their educations and begun their careers. As it turned out, many of these people never married but instead chose to live alone, cohabitate with their sexual partners, or engage in non-cohabitating long-term relationships. By 1997 almost 40 percent of French children were born to unmarried parents.

Gender Roles Despite having a variety of socially acceptable options, aside from marriage, of living in long-term relationships, French men and women have tended to abide by age-old gender norms in which women are responsible for the majority of the domestic chores and child-care and men have more leisure time. Beginning in the 1970s more pressure was put on French women to get jobs to make ends meet, but throughout the end of the twentieth century French women were less likely to get hired than men, and those who did find work were less likely than men to end up in satisfying, long-term careers. As of 1996, over 80 percent of the part-time workers employed in France were women. Things have not changed in the new millennium. A 2010 report on gender equality issued by the World Economic Forum ranked France 46th among the nations of the world and noted that French women earn, on average, about 25 percent less than French men. The report also noted that in France women have more babies and buy more antidepressants per capita than women elsewhere in the European Union.

French American women tend to live in accord with American social and gender norms. For example, French American women who choose to maintain long-term relationships are likely to marry their partners. After age fifty, single French American women, like most other American women, are less likely than French women to date and seek a long-term sexual relationship. French American women have more opportunities in the American labor market than French women seeking employment in France. As is the case in France, French American women earn considerably less, on average, than French American men. According to the American Community Survey's estimates for 2011, the average annual salary among working French American males was almost $70,000 while employed French American women averaged just over $49,000 per year.

Education The French educational system, which was initiated during Napoleon's rule, has had a marked influence on schooling in the United States since the early 1800s. The French system features innovative nursery and primary schools, followed by *collèges*, the equivalent of American junior high schools. Students then must decide whether to complete their secondary education at an academic or a vocational *lycée*—a three-year preparatory school similar to American high schools. Admission to French universities is based upon a rigorous, competitive examination in a specific subject area. Only top students may attend the *grandes écoles*, or elite schools, that serve as a prerequisite for top jobs in business and government. Educators in the United States emulated the French system of progressive schooling culminating in admission to a private or municipal university. In France, however, the Ministry of National Education administrates the entire educational system, which differs from the United States, where individual states and local communities exercise more control over education than does the federal government. Proponents of the French methods claim that it is superior in that it demands students' best efforts and rewards exceptional performance. On the other hand, some detractors claim that the system works to maintain a social class system in France, since the vast majority of students at the *grandes écoles* hail from upper-class backgrounds.

EMPLOYMENT AND ECONOMIC CONDITIONS

Despite their relatively small numbers, French immigrants have tended to be more successful and influential than other groups in the United States. French immigrants are generally urban, middle class, skilled, and progressive, and they are most likely to be employed as artisans or merchants. The U.S. Census of 1910 showed that French Americans were more literate, more concentrated in liberal professions, and had fewer children and larger living spaces than other immigrant groups. In the 1930s, moreover, French Americans accounted for 10 percent of the entries in *Appleton's Encyclopedia of American Biography*, although they made up only 2 percent of the overall population.

Specific French immigration waves contributed different labor practices to American society. For example, the Huguenots introduced a number of skilled crafts to the United States, including sophisticated techniques of weaving, leather dressing, lace making, and felt manufacture. Some historians suggest that the Huguenots' stylish ways helped transform crude frontier settlements into civilized cities and towns. Refugees from the French Revolution and the fall of Napoleon who came to the United States tended to be former army officers or aristocrats. These educated individuals often taught the French language or such elite activities as fencing and dancing. A number of French chefs, hairdressers, dress designers, and perfumers accompanied the aristocrats and introduced French cuisine and fashion to the United States with great success.

POLITICS AND GOVERNMENT

Americans of French ancestry began to influence politics in the United States during colonial times. Most French immigrants rapidly became "Americanized," however, and participated in government as individuals rather than as a group. Changes in global politics have affected American views of the French, and hence of French Americans. Currently the right wing of American politics views France, and French Americans, unfavorably because of their perceived liberal views, although no data suggests that French Americans consistently vote either with the right or left. Most Americans seem to respect French Americans and France's contributions to American culture.

Military Service Many descendants of French Huguenots, including Paul Revere, were distinguished patriots during the American Revolution. In addition, the French government provided invaluable support to the American cause. One French army captain in particular, Gilbert du Motier, Marquis de Lafayette, had an important influence on the events at this time. Lafayette fought brilliantly as a major general in George Washington's army and later returned to France to convince King Louis XVI to formally recognize the independence of the United States and to provide military aid against the British. A number of cities, parks, and squares across the United States bear his name. French immigrants fought passionately on both sides of the American Civil War. For example, Brigadier General Benjamin Buisson, a veteran of the Napoleonic Wars, formed troops out of French volunteers to defend New Orleans for the Confederacy. A number of all-French American groups, known as Zouave units, fought for both the North and the South, wearing uniforms similar to those worn by the French in the American Revolution.

NOTABLE INDIVIDUALS

Art Pierre Charles L'Enfant (1754–1825), a civil engineer by training, fought with Lafayette during the American Revolution. He later became the architect of the U.S. capital city in Washington, D.C. His designs of majestic buildings and tree-lined squares were considered visionary. French artist Régis François Gignoux (1816–1882) came to the United States in 1844. He served as the first president of the Brooklyn Art Academy and had a vast influence on American landscape painting. In 1876 John La Farge (1835–1910) painted the first mural in the United States to decorate Trinity Church in Boston. He later developed techniques that allowed stained glass to be used on a large scale for decorative purposes. Frederic Remington (1861–1909) painted the American Wild West with great attention to details such as weaponry and clothing, but little to historical accuracy; his depiction honors the stereotypes of the heroic Caucasian cowboy and the Native American savage. Gaston Lachaise (1982–1935) was a figurative sculptor most known for his bronze depictions of his wife and muse Isabel Dutaud Nagle. Marcel Duchamp (1887–1968) was one of the giants of twentieth-century art. The provocative French Dadaist painter challenged traditional definitions of art and foreshadowed conceptualism by half a century. He became a U.S. citizen in 1955. Louise Bourgeois (1911–2010) pioneered a path for women artists with her avant-garde, autobiographical sculptures that suggested the human figure. In 2011 a work from her *Spider* series sold at auction for $10.7 million, a world record for a woman artist.

Education Thomas Gallaudet (1787–1851) founded the first American school for the deaf in Hartford, Connecticut, in 1817. He also established

Conceptual surrealist artist Marcel Duchamp (1887–1968) in his apartment behind a chessboard with pieces designed by fellow artist Max Ernst (1891–1976). New York, 1966. MARK KAUFFMAN / LIFE MAGAZINE / TIME & LIFE PICTURES / GETTY IMAGES

teachers' training schools and promoted advanced education for women. Gallaudet College, a national institute for the deaf, was established in Washington, D.C., in 1855. French American Edouard Seguin (1812–1880) was responsible for significant developments in the education of mentally challenged individuals. In 1842 Father Edward Sorin (1814–1893), a French priest, founded a seminary that later became the University of Notre Dame. James Bowdoin (1726–1790) served as governor of Massachusetts and first president of the American Academy of Arts and Letters. He also established the Massachusetts Humane Society. Jonathan Blanchard (1811–1892), pastor, educator, and abolitionist, served as Wheaton College's first president. Jean Mayer (1920–1993) was a renowned nutritionist and the tenth president of Tufts University.

Government Five U.S. presidents—John Tyler (1790–1862), James Garfield (1831–1881), Theodore Roosevelt (1858–1919), Franklin D. Roosevelt

(1882–1945), and Harry Truman (1884–1972)—were of French descent. Other notable French American political figures include Hillary Rodham Clinton (1947–), former vice president Al Gore (1948–), political consultant James Carville (1944–), labor organizer Eugene Debs (1855–1926), military officer and explorer John C. Frémont (1813–1890), and Founding Father Alexander Hamilton (1755 or 1757–1804). One of the most influential French Americans in the history of U.S. government was John Jay (1745–1829). Among his many contributions, Jay acted as president of the Continental Congress, negotiated the treaty with England that ensured American independence, and served as the first chief justice of the U.S. Supreme Court.

Industry Another famous French American, partly due to the variety of his contributions, is Paul Revere (1735–1818). The son of Huguenot Apollos Revoire de Romagnieu, Revere led several protests against British rule of the American colonies, including the Boston Tea Party. He also made the legendary "midnight ride" to warn Massachusetts residents that British soldiers were approaching at the start of the American Revolution. In his time, however, Revere was also known as a talented silversmith who developed a distinctly American style. He designed and engraved the plates for the first paper money in Massachusetts and established the first mill for rolling copper sheets. Peter Faneuil (1700–1743), who belonged to a wealthy and influential family of merchants, donated the public market and meeting place known as Faneuil Hall to the city of Boston.

Eleuthère Irénée Dupont de Nemours (1772–1834), who was considered a radical in France, came to the United States after losing his publishing business during the French Revolution. He opened a gunpowder mill in 1799, which grew rapidly during the War of 1812. Eventually, under the management of his heirs, his holdings grew into the Dupont Chemical-General Motors complex. In 1851, French American John Gorrie (1803–1855) invented an ice machine and received the first U.S. patent for mechanical refrigeration. Philip Danforth Armour (1832–1901), whose Armour brand meats are still sold in the United States, first entered the meat-packing business in 1863. His contributions to the industry included the development of advanced slaughtering methods and modern refrigeration techniques. Louis Chevrolet (1878–1941), along with William C. Durant (1861–1947), cofounded the Chevrolet Motor Car Company. Warren Buffett (1930–), of French Huguenot descent, became one of the wealthiest individuals in the world as a result of his widespread investment empire.

Literature Celebrated poet Henry Wadsworth Longfellow (1807–1882), of French descent, is perhaps best known for his epic *Song of Hiawatha*, published in 1855. John Greenleaf Whittier (1807–1892) became a prominent abolitionist as well as a poet. French American author and naturalist Henry David Thoreau (1817–1862) gained renown with the 1854 publication of *Walden*, a diary of his two years in the wilderness near Concord, Massachusetts. Two other respected French American writers were Edna St. Vincent Millay (1892–1950), who won the Pulitzer Prize in 1923 for *The Harp Weaver, and Other Poems*, and Stephen Vincent Benét (1898–1943), who won the 1929 Pulitzer Prize for his epic poem "John Brown's Body."

Science and Medicine Civil engineer Octave Chanute (1832–1910) came to the United States from France at the age of six. He conducted numerous experiments in aeronautics and created the wing design that became the basis for the Wright Brothers' successful airplane. John J. Audubon (1785–1851), the son of a French immigrant who fought in the American Revolution, is remembered as a premier naturalist. His comprehensive study *Birds in America*, which included more than 1,000 illustrations drawn or painted by Audubon, appeared beginning in 1827. Matthew Fontaine Maury (1806–1873) is credited as the founder of the modern science of hydrography. He was the first person to chart the flow of the Gulf Stream, to conduct deep-sea soundings, and to imagine the potential of a transoceanic cable. His best-known work, *The Physical Geography of the Sea*, was published in 1856. Marine explorer Jacques Cousteau (1910–1997) contributed to the invention of the aqualung in 1943 and won an Academy Award in 1957 for his documentary film feature *The Silent World*. Although Cousteau was a French citizen and not American, two of his grandchildren are prominent environmentalists with dual French and American citizenship: Alexandra Cousteau (1976–) and her brother Philippe Cousteau Jr. (1980–).

In medicine, surgeon François Marie Prevost (1771–1842) performed the first successful cesarean sections in Louisiana in 1809. Alexis Carrel (1873–1944) became famous during his tenure at the Rockefeller Institute as the first doctor to sew blood vessels together, transplant organs in animals, and keep human tissue alive in jars. He wrote the seminal work *Man, the Unknown* (1935), and won the Nobel Prize for Medicine in 1912.

Sports In sports, French American jockey Ron Turcotte (1941–) rode the most famous American racehorse of all time, Secretariat, to victory in the Triple Crown of horse racing. French American Baseball Hall of Famers include Lou Boudreau (1917–2001), Leo Durocher (1905–1991), Nap Lajoie (1874–1959), Rabbit Maranville (1891–1954), and Edd Roush (1893–1988). Andy Pettitte (1972–) was a starting pitcher for the New York Yankees. Bill Monbouquette (1936–) is a member of the Boston

Red Sox Hall of Fame. Charlie Manuel (1944–) managed the Philadelphia Phillies. Paul Arizin (1928–2006) and Bob Cousy (1928–) are in the Basketball Hall of Fame. Football Hall of Famers with French ancestry include Steve Largent (1954–), Darrell Royal (1924–2012), and athletic superstar Jim Thorpe (1888–1953), who was one-fourth French and an Olympic standout as well as an exceptional baseball player. Tom Landry (1924–2000) was a highly respected and successful coach of the Dallas Cowboys. French American hockey players of note include Brian Boucher (1977–), Francis Bouillon (1975–), Guy Hebert (1967–), John LeClair (1969–), Zach Parise (1984–), and Philippe Sauvé (1980–). Outstanding tennis players include Melanie Oudin (1991–) and Mary Pierce (1975–).

Stage and Screen Among the French American actors to gain prominence in the United States were Leslie Caron (1931–), Charles Boyer (1899–1978), and Claudette Colbert (1903–1996). After making her American debut in 1924, Colbert won an

Academy Award for best actress for her role in *It Happened One Night* in 1934. Actor Robert Goulet (1933–2007) made his debut in the Broadway production of *Camelot* in 1960 and went on to appear in many feature films and receive both Tony and Emmy Awards. Composer Maurice Jarre (1924–2009) won several Academy Awards for the musical scores he wrote for such classic American films as *Lawrence of Arabia*, *Dr. Zhivago*, *Grand Prix*, and *The Longest Day* in the 1960s. Ellen DeGeneres (1958–), a widely known television personality and businesswoman, was one of the first celebrities to publicly reveal her lesbianism.

MEDIA

PRINT

France-Amérique

This American publication, also known as *Le Journal Francais des États-Unis*, provides French-language coverage of news and culture. Its core readership is French expatriates and French-speaking Americans.

Louis F. Kyle, Publisher
FrancePress LLC
115 East 57th Street, 11th Floor
New York, New York 10022
Phone: (646) 202-9828
Fax: (646) 202-9847
Email: info@france-amerique.com
URL: www.france-amerique.com

ORGANIZATIONS AND ASSOCIATIONS

Le Cercle Jeanne Mance

Le Cercle Jeanne Mance is dedicated to the preservation of French faith and language and to the promotion of social, cultural, and civic activities in keeping with the French heritage.

Claudette Gagnon, President
Phone: (978) 452-7080
URL: http://ecommunity.uml.edu/francolowellma/organizations/JeanneMance.htm

French American Cultural Exchange

This cultural organization is dedicated to nurturing French-American relations through innovative international projects in the arts, education, and cultural exchange.

Oisin Muldowney
972 Fifth Avenue
New York, New York 10075
Phone: (212) 439-1449
Fax: (212) 439-1455
Email: info@facecouncil.org
URL: www.facecouncil.org

L'Institut des Femmes Franco-Américaines (Franco-American Women's Institute)

This organization's goal is to nurture Franco-American ethnic women's voices.

641 South Main Street
Brewer, Maine 04412
Phone: (207) 989-7059
Email: fawi2000@aol.com
URL: www.fawi.net

French Institute/Alliance Française (FIAF)

Formed in 1971 through the merger of Alliance Française de New York (founded 1898) and the French Institute in the United States (founded 1911), FIAF encourages the study of French language and culture among its 8,600 members and fosters friendly relations between French and American peoples. FIAF also offers a program of French lectures, films, concerts, theater, and art; operates a school of French for adults; and maintains a library of 40,000 volumes in French.

Jean Vallier, Director
22 East 60th Street
New York, New York 10022-1077
Phone: (212) 355-6100
Fax: (212) 935-4119
Email: reception@fiaf.org
URL: www.fiaf.org

Franco-American Heritage Center (AFA)

Founded in 2000, the Franco-American Heritage Center seeks to preserve Franco-American heritage in the performing arts while welcoming the cultures of its neighbors.

Louis Morin
46 Cedar Street
Lewiston, Maine 04240
Phone: (207) 783-1585
Email: lmorin@francocenter.org
URL: www.francocenter.org

MUSEUMS AND RESEARCH CENTERS

The American and French Research on the Treasury of the French Language (ARTFL) Project

The ARTFL is a cooperative effort of the University of Chicago and the Centre National de la Recherche Scientifique that is involved in the development of an online database covering French language and literature from the Middle Ages to the present, including more than 150 million words of major literary, technical, and philosophical texts.

Dr. Robert Morrissey, Director
Department of Romance Languages and Literature
1050 East 59th Street
Chicago, Illinois 60637
Phone: (773) 702-8488
Email: artfl@artfl.chicago.edu
URL: http://artfl-project.uchicago.edu

The Center for French and Francophone Studies

Located at Duke University, the center conducts research into French and francophone culture of the Southern United States and the Caribbean, including studies of mores and customs, work, law and commerce, the roles of women, Creole languages, and literature.

Laurent Dubois, Director
Center for French and Francophone Studies
Duke University
Box 90257
Durham, North Carolina 27708
Phone: (919) 660-3122
Fax: (919) 684-4029
Email: Djebar_Homer@forlang.lsl.edu
URL: sites.duke.edu/cffs/

Institute Francais, Assumption College

The institute is a leading site for the study of material relating to the more than one million French Canadians who immigrated to New England in the nineteenth and twentieth centuries. An active community of scholars engaged in ethnic studies, social history, and linguistic analysis currently utilizes the French Institute collection.

Leslie Choquette
Phone: (508) 767-7415
Fax: (508) 747-7374
Email: lchoquet@assumption.edu
URL: www.assumption.edu

Institute of French Studies, New York University

The Institute of French Studies brings together anthropologists, art historians, historians, literary scholars, political scientists, and sociologists from across NYU and from major French institutions to provide an overview of modern France and examine Franco-American relations, immigration and multiculturalism, the colonial past, the Francophone world, and the European Community.

15 Washington Mews
New York, New York 10003-6694
Phone: (212) 998-8740
Email: institute.french@nyu.edu
URL: http://ifs.as.nyu.edu

Society for French Historical Studies

The Society for French Historical Studies (SFHS) is an organization of North American historians of France. Its purpose is to promote scholarly study of all aspects of French history, chiefly through the publication of a journal, French Historical Studies, its prizes for scholarly excellence, and its annual conference.

Linda L. Clark
Duke University Press
905 West Main Street
Suite 18B
Durham, North Carolina 27701
Phone: (919) 687-3600
Fax: (919) 688-4574
Email: linda.l.clark@millersville.edu
URL: www.societyforfrenchhistoricalstudies.net

SOURCES FOR ADDITIONAL STUDY

Brasseaux, Carl A. *The "Foreign French": Nineteenth-Century French Immigration into Louisiana.* Lafayette: Center for Louisiana Studies, University of Southwestern Louisiana, 1990.

Duroselle, Jean-Baptiste. "The Hereditary Enemy." In *France and the United States: From Beginnings to Present*, translated by Derek Cotton. Chicago: University of Chicago Press, 1976.

Eccles, W. J. *The French in North America, 1500–1783.* Markham, ON: Fitzhenry & Whiteside, 2010.

Ekberg, Carl J. *French Roots in the Illinois Country: The Mississippi Frontier in Colonial Times.* Urbana: University of Illinois Press, 1998.

Gitlin, Jay. *The Bourgeois Frontier: French Towns, French Traders & American Expansion.* New Haven, CT: Yale University Press, 2010.

Hendricksen, Dyke. *Franco-Americans of Maine.* Mount Pleasant, SC: Arcadia, 2010.

Houde, Jean-Louis. *French Migration to North America, 1600–1900.* Chicago: Editions Houde, 1994.

Madore, Nelson, and Corinna Miller. *Voyages: A Maine Franco-American Reader.* Gardiner, ME: Tilbury House, 2007.

Nadeau, Jean-Benoit, and Julie Barlow. *The Story of French.* New York: St. Martin's Press, 2008.

Perreault, Robert B. *Franco-American Life & Culture in Manchester, New Hampshire: Vivre La Différence.* Charleston, SC: History Press, 2010.

FRENCH-CANADIAN AMERICANS

Marianne P. Fedunkiw

OVERVIEW

French-Canadian Americans are immigrants or descendants of people from Canada who descend, in turn, from seventeenth-century French settlers. The majority of French Canadians live in Quebec, which covers only one-sixteenth of Canada's land area but holds one-fourth of the country's total population. Commonly known as Quebecois (kay-beh-KWAH), these French Canadians are culturally distinct from Acadians, the mixed-race descendants of the native Wabanaki people and the French who settled in France's colony of Acadia, which spanned the eastern coast of Canada, including present-day New Brunswick, Prince Edward Island, and Nova Scotia. There are also small groups of French Canadians living throughout Canada, though they tend to identify more with their regional heritage (e.g., Franco-Ontarian) rather than with the more general term *French Canadian*, which is becoming less used as an ethnic identifier. Covering an area of approximately 3.9 million square miles (9,984,670 square kilometers), Canada is the second-largest country in the world, outranked only by Russia. Canada is bordered on three sides by oceans: the Pacific to the west, the Atlantic to the east, and the Arctic to the north. To the south lies the United States, and the two countries' border, 5,525 miles (8,893 kilometers) in length, is the longest undefended border in the world. The terrain of Canada varies between the plains of the west and the lowlands of the southeast. Converging air masses from the three oceans generate cyclonic storms east of the Rocky Mountains, and the northernmost area is covered with permafrost. As a result, 90 percent of Canada's population is concentrated within 100 miles (160 kilometers) of the Canadian/American border.

According to the *CIA World Factbook*, the population of Canada was estimated at 34.3 million in 2012. That same year, Quebec, Canada's largest province, recorded its population at 8.1 million. Some 28 percent of Canadians are of British origin, and 23 percent are of French origin. Another 15 percent are of other European origins, 2 percent are native peoples, 6 percent are of other ethnicities (mostly Asian, African, and Arab), and the remaining 26 percent report mixed ethnic backgrounds. Both English and French are official languages of Canada. English is spoken by 58.5 percent of the population, and 21.6 percent speak French. While many Canadians continue to be bilingual, the number of native French-speaking Canadians has declined slightly in recent years, dropping from 23.5 percent in 1996 to 21.6 percent in 2012. Almost one in five Canadians speaks a language other than English or French. Roman Catholicism is the majority religion of Canada (42.6 percent), followed by Protestantism (23.2 percent), other Christian religions (4.4 percent), and Islam (1.9 percent). Canada has the twentieth-highest standard of living in the world, with a per-capita income of $41,100 (2011). More than three-fourths of the workforce is engaged in service occupations. Canada's low income cut-off (LICO), which represents approximately the same measurement as a poverty level, was 9.4 percent in 2008.

The first and largest wave of Canadian immigrants swept into the United States in the last four decades of the nineteenth century, along with the Industrial Revolution. Those immigrants included both English- and French-speaking Canadians. By 1900 there were 1.2 million Canadian Americans living in the United States. In the 1920s another 920,000 arrived. Most French Canadian immigrants came to work in the mills, factories, and logging camps of New England. Because of the proximity of their homeland, these immigrants maintained strong cultural ties with Canada, frequently traveling back and forth between the two countries. French Canadians played a major role in shaping the cultures of factory towns such as Lowell and Fall River, Massachusetts; Lewiston, Maine; and Manchester, New Hampshire. So-called Little Canadas sprang up throughout the area. Predominantly Roman Catholic, this first wave of immigrants largely maintained their religious beliefs, which were in some ways different from American Catholicism, which had been largely shaped by Irish Catholic immigrants. Over time, however, French Canadian immigrants came to be integrated into the general American population. By the post-World War II era, the group had come to be known as Franco-Americans. Whereas some French Canadian women had worked in mills prior to World War II, the war forced more females to work outside the home than ever before, while the G.I. Bill allowed more males to partake of higher education. Because both academia and the workplace required them to speak English, many French Canadians stopped speaking French, and some converted to various Protestant religions. With greater assimilation, the economic status of the group soon mirrored that of other Americans. In the early twenty-first century, Canadian Americans were the fourth-largest group of American immigrants.

According to the U.S. Census Bureau, there were 2,138,601 persons of French Canadian heritage living in the United States in 2010, composing 0.7 percent of the total population. French was the fourth most spoken language in the country, following English, Spanish, and Chinese. Data from the 2000 Census reveals that the states with the largest French Canadian populations were New Hampshire, Vermont, Maine, Rhode Island, Massachusetts, Michigan, New York, California, and Louisiana. Despite the fact that French Canadian immigrants and their children tended to speak their native language far longer than most other immigrant groups had in U.S. history, assimilation had become so complete by this point that some historians were bemoaning the invisibility of French Canadians as a distinct group of American immigrants.

HISTORY OF THE PEOPLE

Early History The European credited with discovering the Canadian mainland is French explorer Jacques Cartier (1491–1557). Although seeking riches from the Far East via the famed (but never found) Northwest Passage, he instead reached Newfoundland in May 1534. He made another journey to Canada in 1535 and, unlike earlier explorers, continued west along the St. Lawrence River as far as modern-day Quebec City and eventually to the future site of Montreal. This first foray into the interior was difficult—particularly because of the harsh winter conditions in Quebec City and the rampant scurvy that killed many of his men. Others were said to have been saved from this disease of vitamin C deficiency by the native peoples, who advised them to drink a tea made from the bark of the native white spruce tree.

Permanent settlement of Canada did not occur until the burgeoning and lucrative fur trade provided added incentive for making the dangerous voyage. Samuel de Champlain (1567–1635) finally established the first trading post on the site of Quebec City in 1608. Champlain, too, had sought the Northwest Passage, but he soon realized that beaver pelts were potentially more important in enticing potential settlers. He set up a system of business monopolies to systematically hunt the animals and sell their pelts in exchange for 300 settlers coming to the new land annually from 1627 until 1642. Champlain's early settlement was attacked by English and native rivals.

In addition to founding Quebec, Champlain ventured into what is now northern New York, where in 1609 he discovered the lake now named for him. He also explored the Atlantic coast as far south as Massachusetts, including many of the larger rivers in Maine. Champlain's efforts to establish a successful French colony in the United States, however, were thwarted by bad weather, battles with the English and certain native groups, and limited support from France.

Despite all of the hardships, Louis XIV, the king of France, did not give up his colonization efforts. In 1665 he sent two ships to Quebec containing the first regular troops to be sent to Canada. Aboard was Alexandre de Prouville, the Marquis de Tracy (1596–1670), who was made lieutenant general for all French possessions in North America. The government changed from Champlain's business monopolies to a Sovereign Council composed of the governor of New France, a bishop, and an intendant (the chief representative of royal power in a French colony). France shipped boatloads of *demoiselles bien choisies* (young women of good health and upbringing), or *filles du roi* (king's girls), to raise the numbers and help settle New France. Jean Talon (1626–1694), the first intendant of New France, was instrumental in doubling the population, between 1666 and 1678, to 7,605 settlers. He was joined in his efforts by the first bishop, François de Montmorency-Laval (1623–1708), who established the seminary that became the University of Laval, and the governor of New France, Louis de Buade, the Comte de Frontenac (1622–1698).

Talon also successfully implemented the seigneurial system, in which feudal land tenures were granted to settlers (called seigneurs) free of charge in exchange for clearing the land and pledging loyalty to the king of France. The seigneur, in turn, subdivided his acreage to tenants who paid a nominal rent, cleared, and farmed the land. These settlers, called *habitants*, were the first French Canadians. Soon the settlements had, at their center, a parish church and an established *curé* (priest) to meet their religious needs. In addition to the *habitants*, there were the *coureurs des bois* (literally, "runners of the woods"), traders who negotiated for furs with the Indians in the upper reaches of the Ottawa River and around the Great Lakes.

The French settled in other parts of North America as well. In the Treaty of Utrecht (1713), France ceded Hudson Bay, Newfoundland, and Acadia to England, which had a much larger presence in North America due in large part to the fact that the French government allowed only Catholics to settle in the New World, while no such restrictions were imposed by the English. The French, however, retained control of present-day Cape Breton Island on the eastern end of Nova Scotia, where they built the fortress of Louisburg (1720–1740) to defend their remaining territory. In addition to Acadia (later to be known as the Maritime Provinces), the French could be found in the coastal region of northern Maine. The first Acadian settlement was established in 1604 by Pierre du Gua, Sieur de Monts, at St. Croix Island in the Bay of Fundy. Sixty-five hundred Acadians were deported to the American colonies in 1755 for having refused to take an oath to the king of England. Many of them later found their way to Louisiana where they came to be known as Cajuns, a derivation of the name *Acadian*. Other early French towns in the United States included Detroit, Michigan, founded in 1701 by Antoine de Lamothe Cadillac (1658–1730), who also served as colonial governor of the Louisiana territory.

Finally, the majority of French settlers outside of Quebec were concentrated in the areas that became the states of Louisiana, Mississippi, Missouri, and Illinois. The Louisiana Territory was claimed for France in 1682 and named for King Louis XIV by explorer René-Robert Cavelier, Sieur de la Salle (1643–1687). French forts along the Mississippi River spread northward from New Orleans. A pair of French Canadians founded and helped to colonize this southern French territory. Pierre le Moyne d'Iberville (1661–1706) established the city of Biloxi, Mississippi, in 1699, and Jean-Baptiste le Moyne de Bienville, established New Orleans in 1718. In 1803 the United States bought the Louisiana Territory, which spread from the Mississippi River to the Rocky Mountains,

from France for $15 million in what is known as the Louisiana Purchase.

There are many other place names in the United States that tell of French influence and settlement. The state of Maine is said to have been named for the province of Mayne in France, and Vermont comes from the French words *vert mont*, meaning "green mountain." Duluth, Minnesota, is named for Daniel Greysolon, Sieur Du Lhut (1636–1710), who claimed Lake Superior and the upper Mississippi region for France. Likewise, Dubuque, Iowa, is named for Julien Dubuque (1762–1810), a pioneer settler of Iowa. Vestiges of its French origins remain in Minnesota's state motto, *L'Étoile du Nord* (Star of the North).

The English, French, and Spanish all wanted to claim North America for their own. After a series of smaller skirmishes, the French and Indian Wars of 1689–1763 pitted the French against the English, finally leading to the fall of the French colonies. These battles, offshoots or extensions of various European wars, culminating in the Seven Years' War, saw the French and native peoples aligned against the British and their American colonists. In 1745 English forces captured the fort at Louisburg, which was returned to France in 1748. The most renowned battle, however, took place on the Plains of Abraham in 1759 in modern-day Quebec City. By the time the assault

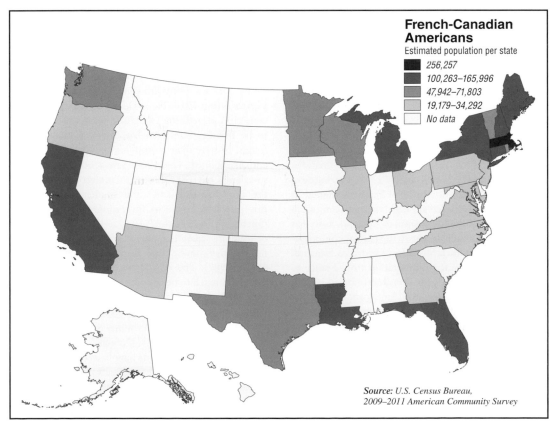

French-Canadian Americans

Estimated population per state

- 256,257
- 100,263–165,996
- 47,942–71,803
- 19,179–34,292
- No data

Source: U.S. Census Bureau, 2009–2011 American Community Survey

The grandmother of French Canadian potato farmer Patrick Dumond is depicted, c. 1940. THE LIBRARY OF CONGRESS.

had its own legislature, and French Canadians were allowed to practice their Roman Catholic religion. Nevertheless, tensions over the settlers' demands for a local government that was responsive to their needs culminated in a revolt in 1837. After the rebellion was quelled, the two halves were joined in 1840. A small number of the French rebels fled to the United States, particularly to New England. Finally, the Dominion of Canada was established in 1867.

The battle to maintain French Canadian culture and language under British rule also surfaced outside of Quebec. Resentful of the encroaching power of the English from the east, Louis Riel led a group of French Canadian Métis (individuals who are part French and part American Indian) in an attack on Upper Fort Garry, the main camp of the Hudson Bay Company, in 1869. Riel was one-eighth Native Canadian and seven-eighths French Canadian, and his Métis followers were of similarly mixed native and French ancestry. They captured the fort and used it as leverage to bargain for special rights for the French and the Métis in Manitoba.

Riel's actions—including the execution of Thomas Scott, a Protestant who fought the French Canadians and Métis—led to a growing hatred on the part of the English in the east. Although Manitoba entered the Canadian confederation in 1870, Riel was banished from Canada in 1875. He settled in Montana temporarily, but returned to Canada in 1884 to participate in the fight for French Canadian and Métis independence. He was charged with treason and later executed for his part in the Saskatchewan Rebellion of 1885.

Modern Era French Canadians' resentment of having to subordinate themselves to British rule continued into the twentieth century. When World War I broke out in 1914, French Canadians fought against conscription, refusing to fight in what they perceived to be Britain's war. French-speaking Canadians also fought to have their culture and language recognized and maintained. The 1960s saw a resurgence in the so-called Quiet Revolution to preserve "Québec for the French Canadians," and French Canadians in this province began to increasingly self-identify as Quebecois. In 1976 the Parti Québécois (PQ), a group of militant separatists, was elected to national office for the first time. Their leader was René Lévesque (1922–1987). The year after gaining power, the PQ declared French to be the official language of the province of Quebec. This was overturned by the Supreme Court of Canada in 1979, but French continues to be used as the language of government in Quebec and is the province's only official language.

A number of referenda have been taken in Quebec to gauge popular support for the idea of seceding from Canada. In 1980 the vote was against secession, but just two years later the province refused to acknowledge the new Canadian constitution. To address this

was over, both the French general, Louis-Joseph de Montcalm (1712–1759), and the British commander, Brigadier General James Wolfe (1727–1759), lay dead on the battlefield. The Treaty of Paris was signed in 1763, and France ceded its Canadian and American territories east of the Mississippi to England, as well as much of its Louisiana Territory to Spain as compensation for Florida, which Spain had yielded to England. This temporarily ended immigration from France to the Canadian colonies—the French numbered around 75,000 in 1763. During the American Revolution, some French Canadians moved to the United States to escape British rule, while many American Loyalists (British sympathizers) were granted land in Quebec and the Maritime Provinces.

In recognition of the differing interests of English and French Canadians, what are now the provinces of Ontario and Quebec became Upper Canada and Lower Canada, respectively, in 1791. Lower Canada issue, the premiers of the provinces met in 1987 and drew up the Meech Lake Accord (named for the site of the meetings). The accord recognized Quebec as a "distinct society," but changes to the constitution were not forthcoming since many English Canadians were opposed to special treatment for Quebec. The accord failed to be ratified by all the provinces. The Quebec electorate narrowly defeated a referendum that would have allowed Quebec to secede from Canada in 1995. In 2012 the Parti Québécois, which continues to be nominally separatist in nature, returned to power in the provincial government. During a victory speech, violence broke out, and one person was killed and another critically wounded. Such violence, however, is not indicative of a vibrant separatist movement in Quebec; while the Parti Québécois won election at the provincial level in 2012, the 2012 national election saw most of the province's seats in Parliament go to the pro-Canada New Democratic Party rather than the nationalist party Bloc Québécois.

SETTLEMENT IN THE UNITED STATES

The first French Canadians to arrive in the United States were fur traders and missionaries who came to the area that is now Michigan. Between 1755 and 1762, Acadians, the first large group of French Canadians (although they did not identify as French Canadian at the time since Acadia was separate from the rest of Canada) to immigrate to the United States, left the area that later became Nova Scotia to escape ethnic and religious harassment. Others fled Canada in the aftermath of the Patriote Rebellion of 1837, when hostility toward the French again intensified. The large number who crossed the border in the nineteenth century, particularly to the New England states, generally came seeking the opportunity for a better life. These immigrants were predominantly young adults, and many already had families. Traditionally, French Canadian Americans had large families, and these numbers, coupled with dismal economic conditions, drove them southward. Some estimates put the extent of the migration at 900,000 people between 1840 and 1930, which had the effect of draining Canada of a whole generation.

They were drawn to the work in textile mills and the logging industry—for some as a means of escaping the backbreaking farmwork that shaped their lives in Quebec, and for others as an opportunity to save money before returning to their lives on the farms. Six mills opened in Lewiston, Maine, between 1819 and 1869, drawing a large number of French Canadians to the area. Wherever they settled, French Canadian Americans sought to build a sense of community similar to those of French Canadian communities in Canada. For French Canadian Americans of this period, family life was centered on a parish church and school, thus combining both the nuclear family and the extended family of the ethnic community. By 1850 about 20,000 French Canadians had settled in the New England area, with the majority living in Vermont. By 1860 there were another 18,000, including clusters in Massachusetts, Rhode Island, and New Hampshire.

The influx of French Canadians in the years following the American Civil War resulted from the initiative of American businessmen to expand the textile and shoe industries. Although the French Canadian population was largest in Vermont throughout the 1850s and 1860s, Massachusetts claimed the majority after 1870. In *The French-Canadian Heritage in New England*, Gerard J. Brault notes that French Canadians "have the distinction of being the only major ethnic group to have immigrated to the United States in any significant number by train." Most French Canadians settled in a circular pattern radiating out from Boston—in towns such as Lewiston, Maine; Manchester, New Hampshire; and Lowell, Massachusetts, to the north; Worcester and Holyoke, Massachusetts, to the west; and Woonsocket, Rhode Island, and Fall River, Massachusetts, to the south. New York State also attracted some settlers, as did the midwestern states of Michigan, Illinois, and Minnesota. The majority of Franco-American settlements were established from the 1860s to the 1880s, though some areas of Vermont had high numbers of French Canadian Americans as early as 1815.

Quebec did not enjoy losing its youth. Starting in 1875, the Canadian government made fairly successful efforts to bring them back by offering either free or cheap land. In fact, up to half of those who had emigrated had returned to Canada by 1900. In the first two decades of the twentieth century, recessions in the United States and relative prosperity at home meant that immigration to the United States declined, and some French Canadian immigrants returned home.

French Canadian settlers in the United States maintained a high level of concentration and a low level of mobility. Census data for 1900 reveals that there were 1.2 million individuals of Canadian ancestry living in the United States, which was equal to one-fourth of Canada's total population. By that time, towns such as Woonsocket, Rhode Island (60 percent French Canadian American), and Biddeford, Maine (also 60 percent), were very much French Canadian. The most outstanding example is the area in Maine along the Canadian border, known as the St. John Valley, which was almost entirely Franco-American, populated both by French Canadians from Quebec and Acadians from New Brunswick. This level of concentration heightened the sense of community for the new immigrants and facilitated getting French Canadian priests to serve the thriving parishes. Spiritual guidance and a sense of community became all the more important because, for those who toiled in the mills, "home" was no longer fresh air and open land but crowded, dingy tenement houses.

According to *The Canadian Born in the United States* (1943), which used American census data, 47 percent of those reporting themselves as "French

Canadian born" had immigrated to the United States earlier than 1900. Almost 16 percent of those in the United States through the year 1930 had arrived between 1901 and 1910, while about 10 percent had arrived between 1920 and 1930.

The fact that French Canadians formed such large groups meant that they were able to set their own pace for assimilation. Many chose to retain their Canadian citizenship. Unmarried female immigrants, on the other hand, were more likely than other French Canadians to become naturalized U.S. citizens. The 1920s and 1930s were decades of strength for French Canadian Americans. By that time, French Canadian organizations had been established, French-language newspapers had begun to thrive, and there had been successful battles against attempts to abolish teaching in French within French Canadian schools. Mount Saint Charles Academy, a Franco-American diocesan high school in Woonsocket, Rhode Island, was established in 1924 and hailed as a strong academic school. Assumption College in Worcester, Massachusetts, continues to offer Franco-American studies as well as French-language instruction. Founded in 1904, it was built upon the model of the French Canadian *collège classique*, in which liberal arts were taught with traditional values and Catholic doctrine.

Elementary schools were set up in great numbers in the 1920s and 1930s. These were parochial schools, supported by the parishes, and they offered a half day of exposure to French language and culture. Such organizations, and the Franco-American community as a whole, came under increased scrutiny in the interwar period as extreme nativist groups such as the Ku Klux Klan decried the presence of French-speaking and Catholic institutions in the United States.

French speakers in Canada have retained the language in its more archaic form, while the language has evolved in France to include numerous idioms and entirely new words. In turn, Canadian French has been influenced by words from Native American languages as well as from English.

Maintaining French identity continued to be a challenge after World War II. The initial immigrants had established a tenuous community of French-language parishes, schools, press, and fraternal organizations, but the group was slowly assimilating or abandoning its French Canadian identity under pressure from nativist groups, and there was no large wave of immigration to keep up the enthusiasm. Immigration to the United States dropped off after the Great Depression of the 1930s. At the same time, many French Canadian Americans took advantage of the proximity of their home country, choosing to live in whichever country had the better economic conditions at the time.

The French were also regarded differently in Canada than in the United States—in Canada they represented one of the two founding nations, while in the United States they were just one of many ethnic groups within the American "melting pot." After World War II, the original incentives to maintain a tight community faded away. With the help of the GI Bill, more French Canadian Americans had the opportunity to get a higher education, for example, and their economic situations improved so that they no longer had to huddle in tenement houses while working long, hard hours in the textile and shoe mills. As a result, many began to drift outside of traditional Franco-American enclaves and into ethnically diverse suburbs. For example, most of the once-numerous French-speaking parochial schools near Albany, New York, had ceased to exist by the 1960s, having been demolished for urban renewal or sold to other denominations.

This trend reversed in the 1970s and 1980s, however, with a move toward reviving French Canadian traditions and language taking hold particularly among the educated elite. Many books have been written, in both English and French, on the Franco-American experience, and a number of historical centers, such as the French Institute at Assumption College in Worcester, Massachusetts, support Franco-American studies.

Historically, most of the French Canadian immigrants settled in the New England states, geographically closest to the province of Quebec, and most Franco-Americans continue to live in New England or in the Great Lakes area. Franco-American New England is often divided into three regions: (1) central and southeastern New England, which includes southern Maine; (2) western Vermont and upper New York State; and (3) northern Maine, particularly the area known as the St. John Valley. French Canadians make up from one-half to three-fourths of the populations of several cities in Maine, including Madawaska, Frenchville, Van Buren, Fort Kent, and Lewiston, and they compose 58 percent of the population of Berlin, New Hampshire. Massachusetts has fallen to fifth place in per-capita population among states that are home to large numbers of French Canadians, outranked by New Hampshire (25.2 percent), Vermont (23.3 percent), Maine (22.8 percent), and Rhode Island (17.2 percent).

It is interesting to note that the number of individuals citing their ancestry as French Canadian for the 1990 U.S. Census was substantially larger than for the census a decade earlier. One possible explanation given by census takers was that *French Canadian* was listed among sample response categories—intended to help those who were uncertain of their ethnic origin—in 1990, but had not been in 1980. Between 1990 and 2000, the number of Americans identifying themselves as French Canadians rose from 2,167,127 to 2,349,684, but by 2010, the number of French Canadian Americans had fallen slightly to 2,138,601.

Only 91,000 of that group had been born outside the United States, and only 47,000 were not American citizens, suggesting that most French Canadian Americans consider themselves permanent residents. However, these numbers are somewhat complicated by the fact that many people of French Canadian descent identify as French on census forms, while others identify as simply Canadian.

LANGUAGE

French belongs to the Romance, or Latin, subgroup of Indo-European languages. There are approximately 98 million people around the world who consider French their native tongue. In addition to France and Canada, those people generally live in Belgium, Switzerland, and parts of Africa. The biggest difference between the French spoken in France and in Canada is in accent, just as there are distinct differences in the English spoken in England and in the United States. Even within Canada, there are distinctions between the language of Acadians and other French-speaking Canadians. French speakers in Canada have retained the language in its more archaic form, while the language has evolved in France to include numerous idioms and entirely new words. In turn, Canadian French has been influenced by words from Native American languages as well as from English.

In addition to the people of Quebec, some 300,000 Canadians living in New Brunswick, Nova Scotia, and Prince Edward Island speak French as their first language. Because of the extent of both English and French speakers, Canada has evolved as a bilingual country. In 1867 the Parliament of Canada passed the British North America Act, now known as the Constitution Act, which legitimized parliamentary debates in French as well as in English. In 1969 Parliament passed the first in a series of Official Language Acts that recognized both English and French as official languages of Canada, cementing the country's bilingual nature. Today, everything from bank notes and postage stamps to street signs and legal documents are written in both English and French.

Greetings and Popular Expressions Some of the most common French Canadian sayings are similar to those of France. Greetings and popular expressions include: *bonjour* or *salut*—each of which can be translated as "hello" depending on what degree of formality is intended; *au revoir*—goodbye; *bonne chance*—good luck; *merci*—thank you; *de rien* or *il n'y a pas de quoi*—you're welcome, or (literally in the first case), it's nothing; *félicitations*—congratulations; *bonne fête* or *joyeux anniversaire*—happy birthday; *bonne année*—happy new year; *joyeux Noël*—merry Christmas; and *à votre santé*—to your health.

RELIGION

Religion is at the heart of French Canadian life. In Canada, French Canadians were staunch Roman Catholics, and this did not change when they immigrated

FRENCH CANADIAN PROVERBS

Many French Canadian proverbs are similar to those found today in English, although several are French Canadian in origin. Some well-known examples include: Each to his/her own taste; God dictates and women decide; Better to prevent than to heal; If the young knew and if the old could ...; To leave is to die a little; Speech is silver, but silence is golden; Better late than never; Slow but sure; After the storm comes good weather; Tell me with whom you associate, and I will tell you who you are; and, One you have is worth more than two you think you may get.

Mieux vaut manger un pan debout qu'un stak a genoux.

> It is better to eat a scrap of bread standing up than to dine on steak on your knees.

Ce qu'on laisse sur la table fait plus de bien que ce qu'on y prend.

> What you leave on the table may be better for you than what you take away.

Ça commence par un baiser, ça finit par un bébé.

> What begins with a kiss may finish with a baby.

L'amitié, c'est l'amour en habits de semaine.

> Friendship is love in weekday clothes.

to the United States. In fact, as was true in Canada, the church was an integral part of the early settlements—often the priest acted as counselor in secular matters in addition to serving as spiritual leader. Some of the earliest parishes were established in the 1830s and 1840s in rural northern Maine. By the turn of the century, there were eighty-nine Franco-American parishes.

In *Ethnic Diversity in Catholic America*, Harold J. Abramson states that the completeness with which French Canadian Americans transplanted their religion, especially to the New England area, was partly due to being close to Canada. Basically, the immigrants set up the same sort of parish-centered social organization that had existed in their home country. In his tale of Franco-American life in New England, *The Shadows of the Trees*, Jacques Ducharme writes, "The Franco-Americans are profoundly attached to their parish church, and there one may see them every Sunday.... From Maine to Connecticut these churches stand, forming a forest of steeples where men, women and children come to pray in French and listen to sermons in French. When the tabernacle bell rings, know that it proclaims the presence of *le bon dieu* [the good God]."

Despite their proximity to Canada, French Canadians in New England experienced many of the trials typical to new immigrants, including religious and linguistic discrimination. The church offered them a place where their language could be freely spoken and celebrated. But in the early days, parishes were often served by priests who spoke little or no French. Because of this, many attendees could not understand sermons, risked getting their fast days wrong, and gave little for special collections because they did not understand what they were for. To address this problem, a number of French Canadian nuns traveled to New England, where they became teachers in the newly built parochial schools and helped to kindle a sense of community among French Canadian immigrants.

The fight for French-speaking priests began in earnest in the late nineteenth century. For example, in October 1884 parishioners at the Notre-Dame-de-Lourdes Church in Fall River, Massachusetts, began a two-year struggle with the Irish American bishop of Providence, Rhode Island, in whose diocese they lived, to regain a French-speaking priest after the death of their French Canadian pastor. Their battle was finally successful, ending what became known as the Flint Affair.

Often it was the Irish Americans who opposed French-language services. In May 1897, for example, French Canadian Americans in North Brookfield, Massachusetts, wrote to the papal delegate to tell him that their Irish American priest would not allow religious services or teaching in French, but it was not until 1903 that a French priest and French services were permitted. Such fights also went on in communities in Rhode Island, Connecticut, and Maine. It was also some time before French Canadians assumed positions of power within the Catholic Church. The first Franco-American bishop was Georges-Albert Guertin (1869–1931), who was named bishop of Manchester, New Hampshire, in 1906. He was followed by, among others, Ernest J. Primeau (bishop from 1960 to 1974) and Odore Joseph Gendron (1975–1990).

These battles with Irish Americans over religious issues continued into the 1920s. One of the most notable was the Sentinelle Affair of 1924–1929. A group of French Canadian Americans, most from Woonsocket, Rhode Island, had been concerned about their religion, language, and culture surviving in the United States. They resented the hierarchy of the Catholic Church in the United States, which was mostly Irish, and militantly defended Franco-American parochial schools and the fragile autonomy of French-language parishes. While other French Canadian Americans in these regions supported assimilation efforts, militant Franco-Americans vocally opposed the construction of English-language schools in the area and were

subsequently excommunicated from the Catholic Church in 1928, although they would ultimately relent and be accepted back into the church.

Religion played another role in Franco-American communities through religiously affiliated fraternal organizations. Like other ethnic groups, French Canadian Americans set these up to offer insurance as well as language and cultural activities to new and recent immigrants. The older of the two most prominent mutual benefit and advocacy organizations is the Association Canado-Américaine, founded in 1896, followed by the Union St. Jean Baptiste in 1900. Both have been incorporated into parent companies, with the former affiliated with ACA Assurance and the latter affiliated with Catholic Financial Life (formerly Catholic Family Life Insurance).

Although French Canadian Americans have been assimilated into American society over time, there are still a handful of French Canadian churches in existence in the United States in areas that are home to large French Canadian populations, including some that have their services in French.

CULTURE AND ASSIMILATION

Traditions and Customs French Canadian life, in Canada and in the United States, centered on the community—first that of the family (which tended to be large), and then that of the larger French-speaking community, particularly the church and school. One thing French Canadian Americans had in common with their French Canadian ancestors was resistance to other ethnic influences. In Canada, French-speakers long opposed all things British, and in the United States, Irish or English Americans often viewed the newest immigrants as interlopers. This lack of acceptance helped to draw Franco-Americans closer together and resulted in the maintaining of traditions, customs, and language through the generations. Many of the traditions and beliefs are also tied to a strong sense of religion. To be a Franco-American immigrant was for most to be a strict Catholic, especially for the early settlers.

Because of the proximity of Canada—at least to the large pockets of French Canadian Americans in New England—many French Canadians in the United States still have strong ties to their home country. However, family ties have seemed to diminish with each passing generation: many third- and fourth-generation French Canadian Americans have lost touch with relatives who remained in Canada or who returned there. French-language newspapers and Franco-American studies programs continue to help French Canadian Americans keep abreast of what is going on in Quebec. There is also a major effort to preserve the French Canadian heritage in areas where it is an important part of state and local history, and Maine, New Hampshire, and Vermont all hold annual Franco-American Day festivals to keep that culture alive.

Cuisine French Canadian farmers ate hearty, simple meals. Breads and other baked goods were popular and readily available. Breakfast items included pancakes, fried eggs, salt pork spread on slices of bread, coffee, and tea. Soup, made from peas, cabbage, or barley, was a staple for lunch and dinner meals. Daily menus also frequently included potatoes, bread and butter covered in maple syrup, pork, and seasonal vegetables. In keeping with Roman Catholic tradition, no meat was served on Fridays.

More elaborate meals were prepared for special religious holidays and celebrations. *Tourtière* (pork and spice pie), *cretons* (pork terrine), *ragoût boulettes* (a stew of chicken, beef, or veal), *boudin* (blood sausage) and sugar pies are some of the dishes associated with French Canadians. In fact, one French Canadian dish, *poutine* (french fries covered with gravy and cheese curds) is now being served in some North American fast-food restaurants.

Traditional Dress Traditional French Canadian clothing harkens back to the days when the *coureurs des bois* hunted for beaver pelts and the *voyageurs* explored Canada. Most recognizable were the brightly colored woven sashes, or *ceintures fléchées.*

Early French Canadian settlers wore more common clothing, however, opting for flannel shirts over loose-fitting pants fashioned of *droguet*, or drugget, a durable, coarse woolen fabric. The pants were held up by suspenders or a broad leather belt. On his feet, a man wore stockings and moccasin-style boots. To combat the cold, the French Canadian farmer added a vest or sweater, a *tuque* (woolen cap), and an overcoat made of wool or animal skins fastened about his waist with a *ceinture fléchée.*

Women made many of these materials, such as the drugget. They too wore woolen stockings and moccasins in addition to a flannel skirt over a heavy slip, or *jupon*, as well as a long-sleeved bodice and sturdy apron. In the winter, women wore heavier blouses and skirts, shawls, and a cotton or woolen *capuche* (hood) on their heads to keep warm. Since most French Canadian Americans today live in towns or cities rather than on farms, these clothes are worn only for cultural festivals. Part of the assimilation process was to adopt "American" clothing.

Dances and Songs Rounds were a popular form of song for French Canadians. Round dances, in which the participants, often children, danced in a circle making certain actions as they sang, were also popular.

Among the most popular traditional folk songs were those that told stories of settlers, voyageurs, or kings, as well as courtships between maidens and young men. For example, "À Saint Malo" told the tale of ladies and sailors who argued over the price of grain until the women eventually won and got the grain for nothing. Perhaps the best-known song

Three French-Canadian farmers stand together outside a potato starch factory. CORBIS. REPRODUCED BY PERMISSION.

is "Alouette," which came from France but is identified with Quebec. Often sung by schoolchildren, the song, which tells the tale of a lark, can be sung as a round.

Traditional French Canadian dances include the quadrille and the gigue (jig). Square dancing, with many of the calls in French, also became popular in the twentieth century. All of these involved musical accompaniment—with fiddles, harmonicas, and, later, accordions. As part of the tight family and community structures in French Canadian life, music and dancing were featured at every celebration.

Holidays Some of the major French Canadian holidays are part of the Christmas season, from Advent (a time of fasting and prayer beginning four Sundays before Christmas) to Christmas Day with its midnight mass followed by a *réveille* (a repast designed to "wake you up"). There is also the feast of New Year's Day (a holy day of obligation for Catholics on which they must attend mass) that includes family visits and the *bénédiction paternelle*, in which the father blesses all of his children and grandchildren, and finally Epiphany (called *la Fête des Rois*) on January 6. For the evening meal on January 6 it is a French Canadian tradition to serve the Twelfth Night Cake (*le gâteau des Rois*—"the cake of the kings"). Inside the cake are a pea and a bean; whoever gets the slice with the bean is deemed king and whoever finds the pea is named queen. *La Chandeleur*, or Candlemas, another winter holiday, celebrated on February 2, included a candlelit mass and pancake parties in the evening.

In addition to the religious services of Holy Week and Easter in the spring, there is Saint Jean-Baptiste Day on June 24. John the Baptist was declared the patron saint of French Canadians by the pope in 1908, and a society was established in the saint's name in 1834 to promote patriotic celebrations. November features both All Saints' Day (on the first) and Saint

Catherine's Day (on the twenty-fifth); on the latter it is a French Canadian custom to pull taffy.

Although devout Franco-Americans still observe a number of these traditions and holidays, the French Canadian population in America, as in Canada, has become increasingly secular in recent years and tends only to observe the major religious holidays such as Christmas and Easter.

Health Issues In the early days of French Canadian immigration, there were no ailments specific to French Canadians in the United States, with the exception of occupational maladies related to the fact that many of the newly arrived immigrants worked in dusty, grimy mills or quarries. Dr. Paul Dufault (1894–1969) and Dr. Gabriel Nadeau (1900–1979), both French Canadian immigrants, were leaders in the treatment of tuberculosis, spending the better part of their careers at the Rutland Massachusetts State Hospital, the first state hospital for tuberculosis patients in the United States.

By the late twentieth century, physicians had begun diagnosing familial hypercholesterolemia (high cholesterol levels in the blood) among descendants of French Canadians living in the United States. There are two forms of the disease: the most common form is the heterozygous, which results in cholesterol rates two to three times the normal range, whereas the homozygous form results in rates six to eight times the normal range. In some areas of Quebec, the disease is occurring at six times the average rate elsewhere, whereas within the United States, physicians are most concerned about the Lewiston-Auburn area of Maine, where incidences are occurring at a rate of ten times that of the rest of the country. Physicians recommend that descendants of French Canadians begin testing for the disease at the age of five. Once diagnosed, many need to begin taking medication, often starting the medication in childhood. Without that medication, those suffering from familial hypercholesterolemia may suffer potentially fatal heart attacks.

Since modern-day French Canadian Americans often speak only English, they avoid the problems with American health care that is common among immigrant populations for whom language is a barrier. Likewise, the similarity of the cultures of the United States and Canada also preclude cultural problems involved in obtaining health care.

Death and Burial Rites Gerard J. Brault states that early French Canadian immigrants to the United States feared sudden death, or *la mort subité*, mostly because it meant there would be no time to prepare for death, particularly for the administering of the last rites by a priest. When a person died, the church sexton signaled the death by ringing the church bells to inform the town that there had been a death: one stroke signaled the death of a child; two, of a woman; and three, of a man.

The wake lasted for three days, during which visitors consoled the family at home. Until it became the practice to carry out wakes in "funeral parlors," the dead were laid out in the family home. Flowers were not part of the setting, although it was customary to shroud the room in white sheets so that it resembled a chapel and to hang a cross between a pair of candles at the person's head. Visitors came to pray with the family, gathering every hour to recite the rosary.

After the wake, a morning funeral was held, complete with a mass in church, and then the body was taken to the cemetery for burial. The priest accompanied the family and other mourners and said a prayer as the casket was lowered into the burial plot. Everyone then returned to the family's home for a meal in honor of the deceased.

In contemporary America, the assimilation of French Canadians means that there are few differences in death and burial rites between them and other Americans of the same religion.

FAMILY AND COMMUNITY LIFE

The family is at the center of the French-Canadian American's world. In previous decades this meant not only the nuclear family but also the extended clan who came together to eat, play cards, sing, drink, and dance.

Courtship and Weddings The tradition for French Canadian immigrants at the turn of the century was a conservative courtship where a potential suitor might visit a young woman's home on Sunday evenings to spend time with the entire family. As the relationship progressed, these visits might become more intimate, while still remaining public, including taking a buggy ride or sitting on the porch swing. Eventually, the young man, or *cavalier*, asked the father for the hand of his *blonde* in marriage (*blonde* being a French Canadian term for "girlfriend"). Often the young man was at least twenty-one years old, although his fiancée could be as young as sixteen.

The wedding itself was a festive affair marked by feasting and dancing. In parishes, the marriage banns (announcements) were read for three consecutive Sundays, proclaiming the intention of that particular couple to marry. With all parishioners being so informed, anyone who knew of any impediments to the upcoming marriage could reveal them during that time. In rural Quebec, the banns might only be read once because this procedure was viewed as embarrassing to the couple.

Much like today, the groom was given a stag party in his honor. In this case it was called the *enterrement de la vie de garçon*, or "burial of the bachelor (literally, 'boy') life," and was symbolized by a mock funeral in which the groom lay on planks while a eulogy, sincere or in fun, was read over him. The bride, in turn, was usually honored with a bridal shower.

Wedding attire was influenced by the fashion of the time. The elaborateness of the ceremony was dictated by the wealth of the participants. The church bells pealed for the morning nuptial mass, and a reception followed. Honeymoons often meant a few days' stay at a relative's home. After marriage, French Canadian women were often expected to dress more conservatively and in darker colors, while men displayed their marital status by growing a mustache or wearing a gold watch and chain. Today, many of the marriage practices reflect a greater assimilation into American culture as well as a move away from a predominantly rural way of life.

Baptisms Until recently, French Canadian Americans tended to have large families, often with ten or more children. Baptisms, as a religious rite, were an integral part of life. In cases where there was risk that the newborn might not survive, the priest was called immediately to baptize the baby. Otherwise the ceremony was performed within the first week. Traditionally, boys were given the name Joseph as part of their name, and girls' names included the name Marie. Often one of the other given names was that of a godparent.

The role of godparent, as in other cultures, was and still is filled by close relatives or friends. They are responsible for bringing up the child if the parents die, part of which includes ensuring that the child is brought up in the Catholic faith. After the baptismal ceremony, the parents, godparents, child, and guests returned to a family home for a celebratory meal. Godparents brought gifts for the child and, in the past, for the mother also. The church sexton rang the church bells to mark the occasion.

Interactions with Other Americans Some tension has existed historically between French immigrants, who were not particularly numerous in New England, and French Canadians because, while French immigrants tended to be well-educated, most of the first French Canadian immigrants were farmers and received little, if any, formal education.

Because French Canadians immigrated to the United States in such large numbers during the late nineteenth and early twentieth centuries, they became the majority group in towns such as Lowell, Massachusetts; Lewiston, Maine; and Manchester, New Hampshire. That majority status, coupled with the proximity to their homeland and the strength of tightly knit communities, eased the pain of assimilation faced by many other immigrant groups.

Although French Canadian Americans worked with Irish Americans in the mills and had religion in common, the language barrier and the sense that the Irish were established immigrants, having come a generation earlier, led to tension between them. In his 1943 account of New England immigrants, *The Shadows of the Trees*, Jacques Ducharme writes that "many were to feel the *caillou celtique*, or 'Kelly Biscuit,' for in the early days the Irish were not averse to violence by way of showing their distaste for the newcomers." There was opposition to lessons being taught in French in schools, and it spilled over into the workplace, where there was favoritism based upon background, and into the church, where it took years before American bishops brought French-speaking priests to Franco-American parishes.

There was also rampant prejudice against Catholics and Jews in New England in the 1920s. By 1925 the Ku Klux Klan numbered more than half a million members in New England alone. It supported the Protestants in the area and their efforts to "take back what was their own." This resulted in cross burnings and hooded klansmen fighting with French Canadian Americans throughout New England. Many French Canadian immigrants hid in their houses while the Klan stormed through the streets.

By the early twenty-first century, extensive assimilation, as well as a greater tolerance for diversity in American society, meant that little tension existed between French Canadians and their neighbors or between Protestants and Catholics. Second- and third-generation Franco-Americans often intermarried with Irish Americans, as their shared religions and similar experiences as immigrant groups gradually eased the initial tensions of the early and mid-twentieth century.

EMPLOYMENT AND ECONOMIC CONDITIONS

Immigration to the United States in the late nineteenth and early twentieth centuries effectively drained Quebec of a large number of its young adults. Economic times were tough in Canada, and the newly opened mills in New England offered employment for both women and men—although this was back-breaking, often unhealthy work. Many children joined the labor force in the mills as well. Women also earned money by taking in boarders. Another group of French Canadians settled near the forests of northern Maine to work in the logging industry.

While life improved economically for French Canadian immigrants after leaving their homeland, life in the rapidly industrializing United States tended to be harsh. Few French Canadians owned property, and almost none rose to supervisory positions in the mills and lumber camps in which they labored. They tended to live in overcrowded tenements. One study of the wages of cotton mill employees revealed that French Canadians earned an average of only $10.09 a week, less than the earnings of English, Irish, and Scottish immigrants doing the same jobs. In Lowell, Massachusetts, 52 percent of French Canadians in 1875 were considered impoverished. Poor health often accompanied poverty and overwork, making French Canadians susceptible to epidemics. In 1886, for instance, a diphtheria epidemic that swept through Brunswick, Maine, killed seventy-four French Canadians, mostly children. In Newburyport,

French Canadian lumberjack in the North Woods of New Hampshire. PHILIP SCALIA / ALAMY

ten years (1888–1898) in the Massachusetts House of Representatives. Another judge, Alfred J. Chretien, who was born in Fall River, Massachusetts, in 1900, attended Harvard University after spending his adolescence in Quebec. After graduating, he established a law practice in Manchester, New Hampshire, and went on to be named chief justice of the Manchester Municipal Court in 1940. He played an active role in the formation of the Legal Aid Society of New Hampshire and was a member of the National Council of Juvenile Court Judges.

A number of French Canadian Americans distinguished themselves in labor unions and syndicates. J. William Belanger (1902–1986), born in Newmarket, New Hampshire, began his working career at the age of fourteen in the Hamlet Mills. As an employee of the Hope Knitting Company in Central Falls, Rhode Island, he founded a union affiliated with the American Federation of Labor (AFL) during the Great Depression, and later became director of the Textile Union of Massachusetts, affiliated with the Congress of Industrial Organizations (CIO). In 1948 he was elected president of the Massachusetts CIO.

The first financial institution controlled by French Canadians in New England, the Banque Coopérative Lafayette, was set up in 1894 in Fall River, Massachusetts. Not long afterward, the first Franco-American Credit Union in the United States, La Caisse Populaire Sainte-Marie, opened in Manchester, New Hampshire, on November 24, 1908. Credit unions were founded in most of the important Franco-American centers of New England because Anglo banks in the area were hesitant to loan money to French Canadian immigrants. Initially parish-based, they later became independent entities that did much to support small businesses and to encourage home ownership. Today, credit unions are considered one of French Canadian Americans' most significant contributions to American life.

Because of the extensive assimilation of French Canadian Americans over time, the economic status and employment patterns of the group have come to mirror those of the general population. Some states, however, have continued to compile statistics on French Canadians. In 2010, for instance, Maine used federal census data to develop a profile of French Canadians who continued to cluster in the Saint John Valley of rural Aroostook County. With a total population of 321,994, French Canadian Americans were somewhat younger (at 39.1 years of age) than the state's general population (at 43.7 years). They were most likely to be employed in sales, production, natural resources, farming, and manufacturing than in other occupations. Their mean annual household income ($58,014) was only slightly lower than that of the general population ($61,648), indicating a high level of employment and economic assimilation.

Massachusetts, a study conducted in 1935 indicated that only 15.3 percent of French Canadians had achieved lower-middle-class status. Forty percent, on the other hand, ranked in the lowest economic group.

Although the first major wave of immigrants was made up predominantly of farmers, mill workers, and lumbermen with little education, there was also a select group of educated individuals, such as priests, doctors, and lawyers who came to serve the needs of their people. Of course, as Franco-Americans became more established, the numbers of professionals grew. There is a rich history of French-language journalism, particularly in the nineteenth and early twentieth centuries. For example, in the early 1870s, Hugo Dubuque (1854–1928) of Fall River, Massachusetts, led the way in refuting U.S. labor commissioner Carroll D. Wright's description of French Canadian Americans as "the Chinese of the Eastern States"; Dubuque became a Massachusetts Superior Court justice after serving

POLITICS AND GOVERNMENT

Historically, Franco-Americans supported the Democratic presidential candidate following the election of 1928 when the Catholic Al Smith was defeated by Herbert Hoover. Franco-Americans also voted for Franklin Delano Roosevelt in 1932, but by the elections of 1952 and 1956, most voted for the Republican Dwight D. Eisenhower. There are also regional trends: most today are Democrats, with the exception of French Canadian Americans in New Hampshire and Vermont, where many are "dyed-in-the-wool Republicans." The Franco-American elite have also supported Republican candidates in the past, and even the working class has voted the Republican ticket, as they did in Rhode Island in 1908, to elect one of their own, Aram Pothier, as governor or to distinguish themselves from the Irish who usually voted the Democratic ticket, as in Worcester, Massachusetts. In both 2008 and 2012, large numbers of French Canadians expressed support for Democrat Barack Obama. In 2012 polls indicated that most Canadians shared that view, indicating that 90 percent would cast their vote for Obama if allowed to vote in the American presidential elections. Voting patterns usually take into account religious and economic considerations, with French Canadian Americans choosing the candidate who is most supportive of their views.

In addition to being involved in local politics—Maine alone boasts of more than 500 Franco-American mayors and state legislators in the twentieth century. There were also a number of Franco-Americans elected to state and federal politics as well. Aram J. Pothier (1854–1928), a Republican, was chosen governor of Rhode Island in 1908 and served two terms, from 1909 to 1915 and from 1925 to 1928. Subsequent Franco-American governors also served in Rhode Island, including Democrats Emery J. San Souci (1857–1936) from 1921 to 1923 and Philip W. Noël (1931–) from 1973 to 1977. The current governor of Maine, Republican Paul LePage, is also of French Canadian descent and is a native French speaker.

On a federal level, Franco-American Félix Hébert (1874–1969), a Republican U.S. senator from Rhode Island, was elected in 1928 and served until 1934. Jean-Charles Boucher (1894–1960) was also a U.S. senator. Born in Rivière-Ouelle, Quebec, Boucher's family moved to Lewiston, Maine, around the turn of the century, and he was elected a U.S. senator from Maine in 1935. Journalist Antonio Prince (1894–1973) made a run for the U.S. Senate in 1935 as a Democratic candidate but was not successful. Georgette Berube (1928–2005) of Lewiston, Maine, a member of the state legislature, also made a run in the Democratic primary of June 1982, but was defeated.

French Canadians elected to the U.S. House of Representatives include three French Canadian Americans from Rhode Island (Louis Monast from 1927 to 1929; Aime J. Forand, 1937–1939 and 1941–1961; and Fernand J. St. Germain from 1961 to 1982) and two from New Hampshire (Alphonse Roy from 1938 to 1939 and Norman E. D'Amours from 1975 to 1984). Internationally, editor Elie Vézina (1869–1942) was named a special ambassador to Haiti by President Hoover as a member of a commission of inquiry in 1930. Vézina, born in Quebec, founded the newspaper Le Devoir in Michigan. Franco-Americans were also named to consular posts in France; Alphonse Gaulin Jr. (1874–1937) of Woonsocket, Rhode Island, was consul to LeHavre in 1905 and to Marseilles in 1909, and Eugene-Louis Belisle was named consul to Limoges in 1906.

Military Service Franco-Americans have served in all of the major wars, including the American Revolution; some 800 French Canadian Americans are believed to have fought for American independence. Rémi Tremblay (1847–1926) fought in the Civil War and wrote about his experiences in a novel titled Un Revenant (1884). There are also many tales of French Canadians being tricked into enlisting in the Union Army. After being offered jobs in the United States and given gifts of money, many signed a document they could not read and traveled south only to find themselves put in uniform and bullied into taking part in the Civil War. For many who survived, it was a natural decision to stay in the United States, and if they were married, they sent for their families as soon as they were able.

One of the most famous images of World War II features a Franco-American, Private René A. Gagnon (1924–1979) of Manchester, New Hampshire, one of three American soldiers raising the American flag on Mount Suribachi during the battle for Iwo Jima on February 19, 1945. It was captured on film by Associated Press photographer Joe Rosenthal. Gagnon survived the battle and returned from the war to settle in Hooksett, New Hampshire.

NOTABLE INDIVIDUALS

Academia Professor Gérard J. Brault (1929–) was born in Chicopee Falls, Massachusetts. A specialist on the Middle Ages, he is also interested in the language and culture of Franco-Americans. In 1986 he published The French-Canadian Heritage in New England, an important English-language work on Franco-American life in the United States.

Armand Chartier (1938–), born in New Bedford, Massachusetts, was a professor of French at the University of Rhode Island until he retired in 2000. He published Histoire des Franco-Américains de la Nouvelle-Angleterre in 1991, a thorough compendium of facts and figures on Franco-Americans in New England from 1775 to 1990.

Claire Quintal (1930–) was a professor of French at Assumption College in Worcester, Massachusetts, as well as the founding director of the college's French Institute and the director of the graduate school. A native of Central Falls, Rhode Island, she is a scholar of Franco-American, French, and French Canadian culture. Under her direction, the institute organized eleven colloquia, publishing the proceedings of these between 1980 and 1995.

Eloise Brière (1946–), born in Northampton, Massachusetts, has taught at Rutgers University and the State University of New York at Albany. Among her published work are *The North American French Language in New York State* (1982) and *Franco-American Profiles* (1984).

Leslie Choquette is a professor of history, L'Institut français Professor of Francophone Cultures, and the director of the French Institute at Assumption College in Worcester, Massachusetts. Her published works include *Frenchmen into Peasants: Modernity and Tradition in the Peopling of French Canada* (1997) and "Center and Periphery in French North America," in *Negotiated Empires: Centers and Peripheries in the New World, 1500–1820* (2002).

Mark Paul Richard is the associate director of the Center for the Study of Canada/Institute on Quebec Studies at the State University of New York College at Plattsburgh. His major publication is *Loyal but French: The Negotiation of Identity by French-Canadian Descendants in the United States* (2008).

Art Cartoonist Garry Trudeau (1948–), the creator of the popular *Doonesbury* comic strip, is of French Canadian descent.

Broadcasting Born to French Canadian American parents, stand-up comic Dave Coulier (1959–) is best known for his portrayal of Joey Gladstone in the television sitcom *Full House*. Television personality and singer Kathie Lee Gifford (1953–), known chiefly for her turn as cohost of *Live! With Regis and Kathie Lee* (1985–2000), is the daughter of a French Canadian mother. Actor Matt LeBlanc (1967–), whose father is French Canadian, played Joey Tribbiani on the long-running sit-com *Friends* and its short-term spin-off *Joey*. Master chef and cooking-show host Emeril Lagasse (1959–) is the son of a French Canadian father and a Portuguese mother.

Film Actor Brendan Fraser (1968–), who is known for films such as *The Mummy* series and *Journey to the Center of the Earth*, is the son of French Canadian parents. Onetime rapper and current actor Mark Wahlberg (1971–) has a French Canadian mother. Wahlberg is best known for films such as *The Perfect Storm* and *Planet of the Apes*. After beginning her career on teen television shows such as *The Secret World of Alex Max*, actress Jessica Alba (1981–) went on to star in the popular *Fantastic Four* series and other films. Her mother is Danish/French Canadian, and her father is Mexican American. Actress Kelly Le Brock (1960–), who starred in *Woman in Red* and *Weird Science*, has a French Canadian father. Also of French Canadian ancestry, actor Mark Ruffalo (1967–) has proved his versatility in romantic comedies such

as *Just Like Heaven* with Reese Witherspoon and action movies such as the 2012 remake of *The Hulk*, in which he plays physician-turned-monster David Banner.

Journalism Marthe Biron-Péloquin (1919–2012) came from a family of journalists. Her father, Louis-Alphonse Biron (1861–1947), was born in Saint-Louis-de-Lotbinière, Quebec, but after moving to Lowell, Massachusetts, he founded *L'Impartial* in 1898 and later acquired *L'Étoile* (1939–1957), a local daily. Marthe Biron-Péloquin wrote for *L'Étoile* and served as an editor for *Bulletin de la Fédération féminine franco-américaine* (*Bulletin of the Federation of Franco-American Women*) from 1973 to 1986. Wilfred Beaulieu (1900–1979) of Worcester, Massachusetts, was the longtime editor of the Franco-American newspaper *Le Travailleur*.

Literature Among the best-known Franco-American authors is "Beat Generation" novelist Jean-Louis "Jack" Kerouac (1922–1969). In addition to *On the Road*, he profiled his youth spent in the French-speaking community of Lowell, Massachusetts, in books such as *Doctor Sax* (1959), *Visions of Gerard* (1963), and *Vanity of Duluoz* (1968).

Annie Proulx (1935–) won the National Book Award (1993) and the Pulitzer Prize (1994) for *The Shipping News*. The novel also received the Heartland Prize from the *Chicago Tribune* and the Irish Times International Fiction Prize and was made into a major motion picture in 2001. She also wrote the short story "Brokeback Mountain," which was also made into an Oscar-nominated movie in 2005. Proulx was awarded a Pen/Faulkner Award in 1993 for her first novel *Postcards*. David Robert Plante (1940–), who was born in Providence, Rhode Island, is a prolific writer with nine novels to his credit. He regularly publishes in prestigious magazines such as the *New Yorker* and the *Paris Review*. Robert B. Perreault, the only Franco-American to publish a French-language novel since 1938, wrote *L'Heritage* (1983) and *Franco-American Life and Culture in Manchester, New Hampshire: Vivre la Différence* (2010). Playwright Grégoire Chabot serves as the director of the Franco-American theater group *Du Monde d'a Côté*.

Music Celebrated worldwide for her mezzo-soprano voice, Alanis Morissette (1974–) is the daughter of a French Canadian/Irish father. Since its 1995 release, her debut album, *Jagged Little Pill*, has sold 33 million units. Although retaining her Canadian citizenship, singer Celine Dion, who was born in Quebec in 1968, is one of the top-selling recording artists in the United States. She spent much of the first decade of the twenty-first century living in Las Vegas, Nevada, where she was a headliner at Caesar's Palace.

Politics Born to a mother of French Canadian ancestry, Hillary Rodham Clinton (1947–) is a former First Lady of the United States (1993–2001) and a former Democratic senator from New York (2001–2009). She was named U.S. secretary of state by President Barack Obama in 2009. Former United States senator Mike Gravel (1930–) represented Alaska from 1969 to 1981. He unsuccessfully sought the Democratic presidential nomination in 2008. Born to French Canadian parents in Lewiston, Maine, Paul LePage (1948–) was elected governor of Maine in 2011.

Sports In addition to such legends as Napoléon "Nap" Lajoie (1874–1959), who was among the first ten members of the Baseball Hall of Fame, and Leo Durocher (1905–1982), who led the Brooklyn Dodgers and then the New York Giants to three National League pennants in 1941, 1951, and 1954, and the Giants to a World Series victory in 1954, French Canadian Jeff Francoeur (1984–) has made a name for himself in the world of Major League Baseball. Francoeur began his career with the Atlanta Braves in 2005 and later played with the New York Mets and Texas Rangers before signing with the Kansas City Royals in 2010.

Joan Benoit Samuelson (1957–) is a marathon runner who won a gold medal in the 1984 Olympics and holds the record for fastest time in both the Olympic and Chicago marathons.

Martin Brodeur (1972–), goaltender for the New Jersey Devils professional ice hockey team, became an American citizen in 2009. He has the most wins of any National Hockey League goaltender in history. Other notable Franco-American hockey players include Mario Lemieux, John LeClair, and Brian Boucher.

MEDIA

PRINT
The first French Canadian newspaper published in the United States was *Le Patriote Canadien*, the first issue of which was printed in Burlington, Vermont, on August 7, 1839. The Franco-American press served not only to disseminate news, but also as a forum for ideas. French-language and bilingual papers flourished in the United States until the 1930s, when many were abandoned by readers in favor of English-language dailies. Others survived somewhat longer, including *Le Canado-Américaine*, which ceased publication in 1957, and *Le Travailleur*, which ceased publication in 1978. Raymond J. Barrette established *Le Journal de Lowell* in 1975 at a time when French-language newspapers had virtually died out in the United States. It survived until 2003 before shutting down. *Union Saint Jean-Baptiste* (formerly *L'Union Saint Jean-Baptist d'Amerique*) merged with Catholic Family Life Insurance in 1991. By the twenty-first century, French Canadian Americans had access to a plethora of newspapers, magazines, and television and radio stations in the French language via the Internet. Consequently, many venues have opted for providing a web format rather than print ones. For instance, Telévision de Radio-Canada, which is owned by the Canadian Broadcasting Company, regularly streams its programs on the web.

Le Forum (formerly *Le F.A.R.O.G. Forum*)
A bilingual quarterly first printed in 1972, it is published by the University of Maine's Center for Franco-American Studies with a circulation of more than 4,500. The journal offers articles on the activities of prominent Franco-Americans, book reviews, genealogy information, and scholarly pieces on Franco-American studies.

Yvon Labbé, Director
Franco-American Centre Franco-Américain
110 Crossland Hall
University of Maine
Orono, Maine 04469-5719
Phone: (202) 581-3764
Email: yvon_labbe@umit.maine.edu
URL: http://umaine.edu/francoamerican/le-forum

Le Soleil de la Floride
This monthly, founded in 1983 and with a circulation of 65,000, reaches French-speaking readers throughout Florida, Quebec, and parts of the Caribbean, especially French Canadian "snowbirds" who spend winter in warmer climates.

Louis S. St. Laurent, II, President and Coeditor
2117 Hollywood Boulevard
Hollywood, Florida 33020
Phone: (954) 922-1800
Fax: (954) 922-8965
Email: saint238@aol.com
URL: www.lesoleildelafloride.com

RADIO

WFEA-AM (1370)
"Chez Nous" with Roger Lacerte broadcasts from 9:00 a.m. to noon on Sundays.

Ray Garon, President/General Manager
500 Commercial Street
Manchester, New Hampshire 03101
Phone: (603) 669-5777
Fax: (603) 669-4641
Email: raydionh@wzid.com
URL: www.wfea1370.com/HomePage/2450903

WHTB-AM (1400)
Broadcasts every Sunday from 5:00 to 6:00 p.m.

Bernard Theroux
1 Home Street
Somerset, Massachusetts 02725
Phone: (508) 678-9727
Fax: (508) 673-0310
URL: www.wsar.com/

WNRI-AM (1380)
Broadcast on Saturdays and Sundays from 10:00 a.m. to noon.

Roger Laliberte
786 Diamond Hill Road
Woonsocket, Rhode Island 02895-1476
Phone: (401) 769-6925
Fax: (401) 762-0442
URL: www.wnri.com/

ORGANIZATIONS AND ASSOCIATIONS

In addition to the organizations listed below, there are many local historical societies and genealogical societies that target Franco-Americans.

American-French Genealogical Society (AFGS)

Formed in 1978, the AFGS helps members of French Canadian extraction to trace their lineage and discover aspects of Franco-American culture.

Normand T. Deragon, President
78 Earle Street
Woonsocket, Rhode Island 02895
Phone: (401) 765-6141
Fax: (401) 597-6290
Email: nderagon@afgs.org
URL: www.afgs.org

Union St. Jean-Baptiste (USJB)

USJB, which serves over 40,000 members, has local branches throughout New England. It is now a division of Catholic Financial Life (formerly Catholic Family Life Insurance).

259 Park Avenue
Woonsocket, Rhode Island 02895-9987
Phone: (401) 769-0520
Fax: (401) 766-3014
URL: www.catholicfinanciallife.org

MUSEUMS AND RESEARCH CENTERS

Alliance Française de Los Angeles Cultural Center (AFDELA)

A part of the Alliance Française global network, AFDELA promotes the Francophone cultures through language classes and cultural activities.

10390 Santa Monica Boulevard
Suite 120
Los Angeles, California 90025
Phone: (310) 652-0306
Email: admin@afdela.org
URL: www.afdela.org/index.php

Boston French Cultural Center

In association with the Alliance Française global network, the center is dedicated to promoting the French language and cultures in the New England area through language classes, cultural events, and an extensive library.

Catherine von der Branden, Executive Director
53 Marlborough Street
Boston, Massachusetts 02116
Phone: (617) 912-0400
URL: www.frenchculturalcenter.org

Centre Franco-Américain (Franco-American Center)

Established in 1991, the center is now part of St. Anselm College. It has been loosely affiliated with the fraternal organization Association Canado-Américaine. This resource center has an art gallery with featured exhibitions, a library, and offers French-language classes. The center is also affiliated with the Fédération Américaine Franco-American des Aînés/Francophone American Federation of the Elderly (FAFA), founded in 1981 to promote the interests of Franco-American seniors in both local affairs, as well as on a state and national scale.

Tina Dittrich, Executive Director
100 Saint Anselm Drive
#1798
Manchester, New Hampshire 03102-1310
Phone: (603) 641-7114
Fax: (603) 641-7229
Email: execdirector@facnh.com
URL: www.francoamericancentrenh.com/index.html

Centre Franco-Américain de l'Université du Maine (Franco-American Center).

As part of the University of Maine since 1972, the center's resources include library and video materials on Franco-Americans and their publications, *F.A.R.O.G. Forum* and *Maine Mosaic*.

Yvon A. Labbé, Director
Crossland Hall
University of Maine
Orono, Maine 04469-5719
Phone: (207) 581-3775
Email: labbe@maine.edu
URL: www.francoamerican.org/home.php

Conseil International d'Études Francophones

Founded in 1981, this research center conducts studies of Franco-American literature, history, culture, and language. There are approximately 300 individual members and twenty-five organizations.

Thierry Léger, Director General
Kennesaw State University
College of Humanities and Social Sciences
1000 Chastain Road
MD 2201
Kennesaw, Georgia 30339
Phone: (770) 423-6124
Email: directeur@cief.org
URL: www.cief.info/english.html

Franco-American Women's Institute

Established in 1996, the institute promotes the history and interest of French Canadian women as well as those of other French-speaking groups in the United States. It has an extensive archive of French Canadian history.

Rhea Côté Robbins, Founder and Director
641 South Main Street
Brewer, Maine 04412
Phone: (207) 989-7059
URL: www.fawi.net

The French Institute

Founded in 1979, the institute is associated with Assumption College. It has organized eleven colloquia and published twelve books dealing with the French experience in New England. These include *The Little Canadas of New England*, as well as books on schools, religion, literature, the press, women, and folklore. The center collects documents on Franco-Americans, and its holdings contain such archival materials as manuscripts, newspapers, and books. The archives include material on organizations such as Association Canado-Américaine and L'Union Saint Jean-Baptiste d'Amerique and videos of episodes of *Bonjour*.

Leslie Choquette, Director
Emmanuel D'Alzon Library
3rd Floor
Assumption College
500 Salisbury Street
Worcester, Massachusetts 01609
Phone: (508) 767-7415
Fax: (508) 767-7374
Email: instfran@assumption.edu
URL: www1.assumption.edu/frenchinstitute

Museum of Work and Culture

Maintained by the Rhode Island Historical Society, this museum is dedicated to the history of French Canadian immigrants in the Blackstone River Valley.

Ray Bacon and Anne Conway, Site Codirectors
42 South Main Street
Woonsocket, Rhode Island 02895
Phone: (401) 769-9675
Email: rbacon@rihs.org; aconway@rihs.org
URL: http://rihs.org/museums_mwc.html

SOURCES FOR ADDITIONAL STUDY

Brault, Gerard J. *The French-Canadian Heritage in New England*. Hanover, NH: University Press of New England, 1986.

Bumsted, J.M. *Canada's Diverse Peoples: A Reference Sourcebook*. Santa Barbara, CA: ABC-CLIO, 2003.

Je Parle Français: A Portrait of La Francophonie in Canada. Ottawa: Canadian Heritage, 1999.

Daniels, Roger. *Coming to America: A History of Immigration and Ethnicity in American Life*. New York: HarperPerennial, 2002.

Hamilton, Janice. *Canadians in America*. Minneapolis: Lerner, 2006.

Lee, Anthony W. *A Shoemaker's Story: Being Chiefly about French Canadian Immigrants, Enterprising Photographers, Rascal Yankees, and Chinese Cobblers in a Nineteenth-Century Factory Town*. Princeton, NJ: Princeton University Press, 2008.

Louder, Dean R., and Eric Waddell, eds. *French America: Mobility, Identity, and Minority Experience across the Continent*. Translated by Franklin Philip. Baton Rouge: Louisiana State University Press, 1993.

Purnell, Larry D., and Betty J. Paulanka, eds. *Transcultural Health Care: A Culturally Competent Approach*. Philadelphia: F.A. Davis, 2003.

Richard, Mark Paul. *Loyal but French: The Negotiation of Identity by French-Canadian Descendants in the United States*. East Lansing: Michigan State University Press, 2008.

Simpson, Jeffrey. *Star-Spangled Canadians: Canadians Living the American Dream*. New York: HarperCollins, 2000.

Takai, Yukari. *Gendered Passages: French Canadian Migration to Lowell, Massachusetts, 1900–1920*. New York: Peter Lang, 2008.

GARIFUNA AMERICANS

Liz Swain

OVERVIEW

Garifuna Americans are descendants of the Garifuna people, who share a common heritage and language rather than geographical boundaries. Their heritage can be traced to Africans who escaped slavery in the seventeenth century and intermarried with Caribs living in the eastern Caribbean. At the end of the eighteenth century, they settled along the Caribbean coastline of Central America, in what is now (from north to south) Belize, Guatemala, Honduras, and Nicaragua. Belize, the northernmost of the four countries, is bounded by Mexico to the north; Nicaragua, the southernmost of the four, is bounded by Costa Rica to the south.

According to the *CIA World Factbook* (2012), Honduras has an estimated total population of 8,296,693 that includes about 200,000 Garifuna people; Belize has 327,719 people with close to 20,000 Garifuna; Guatemala has 14.1 million people with approximately 17,000 Garifuna; and Nicaragua has 5.7 million people with about 8,000 Garifuna. The major ethnic group in these countries is "mestizo" (Amerindian-European), and Roman Catholicism is the primary religion. The Garifuna are a minority, descending from the Carib, Arawak, and West African peoples. Most Garifuna are Catholic, but religious syncretism prevails, with traditional African and Amerindian beliefs incorporated within their Catholic faith. The four countries are ranked as lower-middle-income economies by the World Bank, and their economic rankings in total GDP are as follows: Honduras 104, Guatemala 82, Belize 180, and Nicaragua 130. There is an unequal distribution of income in all four countries, and many Garifuna live in extreme poverty. Labor in these countries is distinctly divided by gender, with women tending to their families and farms and men working at banana plantations and in the fishing industry. Many Garifuna have migrated to the United States because of the region's poor economic conditions.

Statistics on Garifuna immigration to the United States are virtually nonexistent because admission records contain detailed country origins rather than ethnicity. Garifuna people began to arrive in the United States as merchant marines during World War II. Poor economic conditions in Central America and the Immigration Reform Act (1965) helped to increase immigration from the 1960s onward. Most Garifuna settled in big cities, particularly New York, Los Angeles, New Orleans, and Miami. First generation Garifuna Americans tend to work long hours at low-paying jobs such as housekeeping, home health care, construction, and outdoor maintenance. Many send money back to family members in Central America. Members of the second generation of Garifuna Americans have worked as teachers, police officers, and at other professional jobs. Garifuna immigration to the United States has continued to increase since the 1990s.

It is difficult to estimate the number of Garifuna Americans because they do not come from a single country and because they have had the sole option "other" when describing their ethnicity on U.S. Census forms. According to studies provided by organizations such as the Garifuna Coalition USA, Inc., in New York and the Garifuna American Heritage Foundation United (GAHFU) in Los Angeles, there were an estimated 300,000 Garifuna living in North America as of 2012. This number is comparable to the population of Cincinnati. Areas with significant numbers of Garifuna Americans include New York (which houses the largest population outside of Central America at an estimated 200,000), Los Angeles, New Orleans, Houston, and Miami.

HISTORY OF THE PEOPLE

Early History The nomadic Arawak people migrated along the South American coast and Caribbean islands as early as 4000 BCE, hunting, fishing, and farming cassava, a plant with a starchy root. They spread throughout the islands until about 1200 CE, when they encountered another nomadic tribe from South America called the Caribs, who killed and enslaved the Arawaks. Intermarriage between Carib males and Arawak females resulted in a new people known as the Island Caribs.

By the sixteenth century, much of Europe had political and economic interests in the New World. The land was annexed, and African slaves were used for labor. The Island Caribs fought to keep their islands, managing to keep two—Dominica and St. Vincent Island (then called Yolome or Yurume).

In 1635 two Spanish ships carried West African peoples captured from the Yoruba, Ibo, and Ashanti tribes of what is now Ghana, Nigeria, and Sierra Leone. Both vessels were shipwrecked near St. Vincent, located north of Venezuela in the Lesser Antilles, and the Africans escaped and swam to shore. The Island Caribs sheltered the refugees, resulting in a mingling of these two groups that blended their ancestry, traditions, and language. The new people called themselves "Garifuna" and continued the division of labor they had inherited from the Caribs, in which the men fished and hunted while the women raised the children and looked after the farms.

In the early eighteenth century, French settlers arrived at St. Vincent and lived alongside the Garifuna, who incorporated French words into their idiom, adopted French currency for trade, and formed an alliance against British colonization. In 1713 Britain tried unsuccessfully to gain control of the island. The British gave the Garifuna people the label "Garinagu," or "Black Caribs," and they referred to the Amerindians as the "Red and Yellow Caribs." This racial labeling would later be used as a means to discredit Garinagu claims to St. Vincent.

By 1750 the population of the Garifuna people had greatly increased; however, their way of life was threatened by the British, who hoped to use St. Vincent for the production of sugarcane. The British claimed that the island belonged to Red and Yellow Caribs (the Amerindians) and not to Black Caribs. This dispute escalated into war in 1772, with the French and Garinagu fighting against the British. Joseph Chatoyer, a respected Garifuna chief, signed a peace treaty in 1773 that shifted property boundaries and conceded land. The British continued to press for more territory, however, and by 1795 the Garinagu had decided to reclaim their land. Chatoyer led the revolt, going into battle on March 10, 1795, with Garifuna and French soldiers. This has become known as the Second Carib War. On March 12 he gave a speech in French titled "The 12th Day of March and the First Year of Our Liberty." Only two days later, he died in the war.

The French surrendered in 1796, but the Garinagu fought on until the following year. The British then exiled 4,338 Garinagu to Roatan— one of Honduras's Bay Islands—on April 12, 1797 (Settlement Day). Because the war and imprisonment had left the Black Caribs weakened and undernourished, only 2,026 people reached Roatan alive. The majority left the island within the year and sailed to Honduras. Those who remained on Roatan established Punta Gorda, which now stands as the oldest active Garinagu town.

Modern Era On September 23, 1797, the 1,465 Garinagu who left Roatan landed at Trujillo, Colon (Honduras). Over the following five years, the Garinagu dispersed along the Caribbean coastline of Central America, establishing villages in Nicaragua, Guatemala, and Belize. The arrival of the Garinagu in British Honduras in 1802 created racial tension. English colonists limited Garinagu access to labor markets by means of restrictive laws, which forced the Garinagu to develop autonomous ethnic communities through the nineteenth century. By the early twentieth century, however, many Garifuna traditions had been absorbed into the cultural mainstream. This prompted Thomas Vincent Ramos—a Honduran immigrant to Belize—to found two Garifuna community organizations and to advocate for the promotion and preservation of the Garifuna cultural heritage.

In the twentieth century, U.S. companies began growing and exporting bananas from Honduras. The Cuyamel Fruit Company made the first shipment in 1911, followed in 1913 by the United Fruit Company. Honduras soon became a world leader in banana exports and remained so for decades. Guatemala emerged as a major exporter, too. With their economies virtually controlled by the United Fruit Company, Guatemala and Honduras were transformed into what some called "banana republics." By the 1920s there were more than one hundred banana enterprises in Central America. Garifuna men worked for these companies, sowing bananas in the fields and loading them for export on the docks, and earned relatively good incomes.

In the 1930s and 1940s, some of the fruit companies were shut down because of plague, and World War II also hurt the trade. Consequently, many Garifuna men became unemployed. Hundreds of these men found work by signing on with the merchant marine of the United States, and the Garinagu in British Honduras received assignments to aid England during its war effort. With a stagnating economy in Central America and the implementation of the U.S. Immigration Reform Act (1965), immigration to the United States among Garifuna men and women increased significantly throughout the second half of the twentieth century.

In the twenty-first century, many Garifuna people in Central America continue subsistence farming, banana cultivation, and fishing. The Garifuna in Central America face extreme poverty, malnutrition, poor health care, and high rates of HIV/AIDS infection. Younger generations have frequently migrated to North America for better economic opportunities, and over half the Garifuna population now lives in North America. Nevertheless, the Garifuna culture remains vibrant. In 2001 UNESCO awarded the title "Masterpieces of the Oral and Intangible Heritage of Humanity" to the Garifuna language, dance, and music, and in 2005 the first Garifuna Summit was held on Corn Island in Nicaragua.

SETTLEMENT IN THE UNITED STATES

There is no official record of when the first Garinagu arrived in North America, but a clue can be found in an 1823 New York City theater playbill for *The Drama of King Shotaway*. The writer of the play, William Henry Brown, is believed to have been a Garifuna from St. Vincent. Thus, Garinagu may have been immigrating to the United States during the nineteenth century. Information on exactly how many Garinagu migrated to the United States is equally murky, because U.S. Immigration and Naturalization Service (INS) admissions records are based on country of birth. Ethnic origin is not listed in records prior to 1925. Forty-two people from Belize were admitted into the United States that year, and some perhaps were Garinagu. Each year through 1930, fifty-seven or fewer Belizeans were admitted to the country. Admission records from 1931 show twenty-eight people from Belize, 179 from Guatemala, 159 from Nicaragua, and 123 from Honduras.

Garinagu men came to the United States during or just after World War II to work as merchant marines. Sea duty took them to ports around the world, and they returned home to their native countries with stories that inspired other Garinagu men to enlist, some of whom settled in port cities such as Los Angeles, New York, and New Orleans. During the 1960s Garinagu women also began immigrating to the United Sates, often to work as nannies and domestics. In 1961 Hurricane Hattie's destruction in Central America opened the door to legal immigration, and the Immigration Reform Act of 1965 facilitated more immigration to the United States. In 1962,

according to INS admissions records, 191 Belizeans, 939 Guatemalans, 1,154 Hondurans, and 1,083 Nicaraguans immigrated to the United States; by comparison, in 1997 the INS admitted 664 Belizeans, 7,785 Guatemalans, 7,616 Hondurans, and 6,331 Nicaraguans.

Estimates of the number of Garifuna in the United States vary widely, but organizations such as the Garifuna Coalition USA and the Garifuna American Heritage Foundation United (GAHFU) have put the estimate at about 300,000 as of 2012. Garinagu from Belize have typically settled in Los Angeles, while those from Honduras and Guatemala have migrated to the East Coast, particularly in New York. (Garinagu from Nicaragua scarcely migrate.) According to the Garifuna Coalition USA, New York City has the largest Garifuna population in the United States—or anywhere outside Central America—with approximately 200,000 people. Houston, New Orleans, Chicago, and San Francisco are other notable Garifuna population centers. Many first generation Garifuna work as domestics, while second generation Garifuna hold professional jobs in fields such as education.

LANGUAGE

The Garifuna dialect is unique because it is spoken in multiple countries, each of which has its own national language, namely Spanish in Honduras, Guatemala, and Nicaragua and English in Belize and

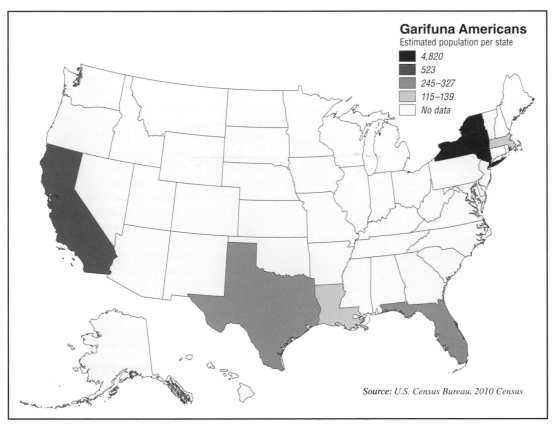

Garifuna Americans
Estimated population per state

- 4,820
- 523
- 245–327
- 115–139
- No data

Source: U.S. Census Bureau, 2010 Census

the United States. Garifuna is an Arawak language with many vocabulary words from the Carib dialect. French, English, and Spanish words are common in the Garifuna language (a testament to the diverse history of the Garifuna people), but it features almost no African vocabulary. Complex in nature, the Garifuna language has continued to evolve. Linguists estimate that the modern Garifuna language is about 70 percent Arawak, 5 percent Carib, 15 percent French, 5 percent Spanish, and 5 percent English.

Garifuna spellings vary because there is no common orthography (writing system) for the language. The name of the Garifuna leader Chatoyer, for example, is sometimes written as "Satuye." For years, Garifuna was an oral tradition, with history relayed to others through speech, dance, and song. Gender plays several roles in the Garifuna dialect. As with languages such as Spanish and French, there are masculine and feminine words. In addition, certain identify the gender of the speaker; a man, for example, would call the sea *barawa*, while a woman would use the word *barana*.

Some scholars have claimed that the Garinagu suffer from "invisibility" in the United States, because they are often assumed to be African American or Afro-Latino and are not recognized as a distinct ethnic group. It is also important to note that since the Garinagu come from different countries, many do not consider their national identities to be as significant as their transnational ethnic identity.

Pamela Munro, a linguistics professor at the University of California, Los Angeles, has provided pronunciation tips for speaking Garifuna. For example, most Garifuna consonants are pronounced as they would be in English. Additional consonants include *ch* (pronounced as in *church*, sometimes *sh* in *ship*). The *r* and *h* sounds are sometimes deleted by speakers. For vowels, *a* is pronounced as in *father* or *sofa*; *e* as in *bed* or *ego*; *i* as in *police* or *bit*; *o* as in *Ohio*; and *u* as in *Lulu*. The sixth Garifuna vowel, *ü* (u dieresis, u umlaut), is written as a slashed *i*. To approximate the pronunciation, *u* is pronounced with the lips spread wide (not rounded), as they would be when pronouncing *i*. Nasal vowels are pronounced like oral vowels, except that air is released through the nose rather than the mouth. The first vowel of a two-syllable word is stressed, as is the second vowel of a word with three or more syllables. Any word that does not follow these rules must have its stress marked. Stress is written if it falls on the second syllable of a two-syllable word or on the first syllable of any longer word, and is notated with an acute accent. Many organizations, such as the GAHFU in Los Angeles, strive to preserve the language of the Garifuna through education and outreach programs.

Greetings and Popular Expressions Common Garifuna greetings and expressions include the following: *Mábuiga*—Hello; *Buíti binafi*—Good morning; *Buíti amidi*—Good afternoon; *Buíti ranbá weyu*—Good evening; *Buíti gúyoun*—Good night; *Ayóu*—Goodbye; *Seremei*—Thank you; *Úwati mégeiti*—You're welcome; *Belú*—Come in (to the house, used in place of "Welcome"); *Buída lámuga lidi bin*—Good luck; *Adüga ba*—Congratulations (literally "You made it"); *Buídu lá buweyasu*—Have a good trip; *Bungíu bún*—God bless you (when someone sneezes); *Bungíu buma*—Go with God; *Bungíu buma súwan dán*—God be with you always; *Magadei bámuga*—Get well soon; *Buíti báüsteragüle*—Happy birthday; *Mábuiga Fedu*—Merry Christmas; *Búmagien láu sún ísieni*—Sincerely, as in the close of a letter; *Buídu lámuga básugurani ugúyen lábu súwan dán*—Best wishes today and always.

RELIGION

The majority of Garinagu in Central America and the United States are Roman Catholic, and a highlight of their worship is the Garifuna Mass. The Mass opens with a procession that symbolizes a welcome and that life acts as a journey to heaven. Another procession precedes the Gospel reading. During the offertory procession, worshippers give thanks by presenting gifts to God. The Mass ends with a final procession that is both a "great goodbye" and a reminder to return again for Mass.

A dramatic example of Mass is the Garifuna Settlement Day (Garifuna Thanksgiving) Mass on November 19, which celebrates when the Garifuna people arrived and settled in Belize after being exiled by the British from St. Vincent. Both Garinagu and non-Garinagu are welcome to attend. The service and songs are typically in the Garifuna language, and worshippers don traditional Garifuna garb. Liturgical dances during the processions serve as a form of prayer. In 2012 at the Our Lady of Mercy Church in Brooklyn, New York, Father Lawrence Nicasio from Belize presided over the service.

Another Garifuna tradition is a novena—the recitation of the rosary for nine days after someone dies—a tradition that was begun by Garifuna teacher Clifford Palacio in Los Angeles in 1979. Those gathered sing hymns in Garifuna, Spanish, English, and Latin, and it usually culminates in a *beluria*, an evening rite that includes punta dancing, choral singing, drumming, and storytelling. In addition, an abundance of Garifuna food is generally served.

Religious syncretism is notable among the Garifuna, who have incorporated African and Native American rituals into their Catholic faith. There are, for example, elements of voodoo and mysticism among the Garifuna in Central America that are not as prevalent in the United States. Occasionally, a shaman, or *buyei*, is consulted by Garifuna Americans. The *Dugu*—a funeral ceremony led by the *buyei*—has become increasingly popular among the Garifuna in Central America, particularly in Belize. The *Dugu* ritual, which reinforces cultural unity, is said to summon deceased ancestors.

CULTURE AND ASSIMILATION

Garinagu in Central America have long been valued as teachers and known for their flair for languages. These were important skills because Garinagu were dispersed to countries where their language was not the mother tongue. The Garinagu first migrated to Honduras, which was then controlled by Spain. Later Garinagu migrated to what was then British Honduras. The Garinagu spoke Garifuna and learned the official languages of the countries in which they resided. The Belizean Garinagu came to the United States as English speakers, giving them some advantages over the Spanish-speaking Garinagu from Honduras.

Not even fluency in English, however, could prepare Garinagu immigrants for what awaited them in the United States. For example, in his 1996 autobiography *My Life between the Cross and the Bars*, George Castillo, a retired prison chaplain, writes of the culture shock he experienced upon arriving in New York City as an immigrant. He had left Dangriga, Belize, in 1952 at the age of twenty-one and was astounded by New York's skyscrapers, traffic, and frenetic pace. "I had never used a telephone, radio, television or kitchen appliance, and wondered if I would ever be able to master them," Castillo writes. He eventually found an opportunity for advancement in the U.S. Air Force before fulfilling his dream of entering the seminary.

Castillo, like many Garinagu, encountered discrimination and segregation in the United States, notably on a bus ride from New York City to Texas when, in Mississippi, he was ordered to the back of the bus. Additionally, when the Castillo family wanted to rent a home in Maine in 1960, the landlady had doubts about them because of their race; only after a white tenant living next door gave permission for them to move in did the landlady consent.

Some scholars have claimed that the Garinagu suffer from "invisibility" in the United States, because they are often assumed to be African American or Afro-Latino and are not recognized as a distinct ethnic group. It is also important to note that since the Garinagu come from different countries, many do not consider their national identities to be as significant as their transnational ethnic identity. In other words, the Garinagu envision their "nation" as geographically dispersed but unified by culture and ethnicity. Anthropologists have debated how this has affected their assimilation process in the United States.

Traditions and Customs Many Garifuna traditions and customs have been brought to the United States by immigrants and largely reflect the vital bond of community. Several of these traditions and customs are evident at churches in the United States, particularly

Teofilo Colon Jr. (2nd from left) is the creator of the website beinggarifuna.com, which aims to provide a collective space for Garifunas to discuss culture. MARK NASSAL / ALAMY

on holidays such as Settlement Day in November, when Garifuna Americans dance to punta music, watch historical reenactments, and dress in traditional Garifuna costume. Since the Garifuna are transnational people who are united by a unique heritage, organizations and associations such as the Garifuna Settlement Day Group play an important role in the culture. Founded in Los Angeles in 1962, the group seeks to preserve Garifuna traditions, which include folklore, music, and dance.

Some customs have become increasingly popular in Central America but not in the United States. The *Dugu*, (the Feasting of the Dead), for example, is an elaborate and sacred Garifuna ancestral rite. A *Dugu* ceremony brings the deceased into the present time and can last up to two weeks. The ceremony is led by a shaman, or *buyei*, who, among other things, makes arrangements for food, beverages, and musicians. Other ancestral rites include the *Amuyadhani* (Bathing of the Spirit of the Dead) and the *Chugu* (Feeding of the Dead).

Cuisine Coconut is a popular Garifuna ingredient and is used frequently by Garifuna Americans in foods such as coconut candy, *pan de coco* (coconut bread), coconut water, *leche de coco* (coconut milk), coconut soup, *sere* (a stew of fish cooked with herbs in coconut cream), and a dessert featuring grated banana cooked in sweetened coconut milk. Marzipan is another popular dessert. Rhodel Castillo offers these and other popular choices on his menu at his restaurant Garifuna Flava in Chicago.

Also common in the Garifuna diet are vegetables such as sweet potatoes and yucca. The food associated most with Garinagu is *ereba*, or cassava bread, which is cracker-like and consists primarily of yucca and salt. Making cassava bread is a complex and time-consuming process. The basic steps are as follows: The yucca is peeled and washed with salt water and then grated with an *egi* (a wooden board with small quartz stones). The shredded yucca is packed into a *ruguma* (a palm-leaf strainer), which is then hung from the rafters and stretched in order to drain poisonous liquid from the plant. The yucca is removed from the ruguma, covered with a towel, and left to dry overnight. It is then sifted with a *jibise* (a large sieve) to produce a refined flour, that is spread on a grill in a circle. As the bread heats, it is flattened with a tool called a *garagu*, flipped, grilled on the other side, and then removed to cool.

Another popular Garifuna dish, particularly in Honduras, is *machuca* (*hudutu* in Garifuna). It is made by boiling green plantains that are mashed in a wooden mortar with pestle. *Machuca* is eaten with a soup consisting of coconut and fish.

Traditional Dress Particularly on holidays, Garifuna American women wear clothes featuring brilliant colors and patterns. The *arabutu* is a gown, the *douguo* is generally worn as a one-piece skirt and blouse, the *gafamelu* is colorful scarf for the neck, and the *manda* is a shawl. *Baramuda* is Garifuna daily wear for women. Men tend to dress in more subdued colors, such as khaki shirts and long dark pants. The guayabera (a button-up shirt worn by men throughout Mexico and Central America, distinguished by its patch pockets and two vertical rows of pleats) and T-shirts are especially popular among men, and some Garifuna men still prefer straw hats over, say, baseball caps. On holidays, sacred days, and during festivals, however, Garifuna Americans wear more traditional attire. Belize Settlement Day, for example, calls for more traditional.

Music The internationally acclaimed punta rock is a modern adaptation of the sacred Garifuna punta music. Belize is regarded as the "cradle of punta rock," and Belizean Andy Palacio is known as the "King of Punta Rock." He is a former teacher whose commitment to his culture led him to develop punta rock during the 1980s. He has performed in the United States, France, and other countries, and his album *Umalali: The Garifuna Women's Project* (2008) combines traditional Garifuna music with contemporary sounds. Other punta rock musicians known in the United States, Central America, and the Caribbean include Herman "Chico" Ramos, Aziatic, Horace "Mahobob" Flores, Paula Castillo, Peter "Titi-man" Flores, and Thamas "Bootsy" Lauriano. In 2001 Garifuna music was proclaimed by UNESCO to be a "masterpiece of oral and intangible heritage of humanity."

Dances and Songs Garifuna songs that are heard in the United States often have themes dealing with the loneliness of being far from loved ones. The most popular Garifuna dance in the United States is the punta dance, which is performed by couples who try to outdo each other with numerous lithe and virtuosic moves. A popular group dance is called the *hungu-hungu*, or circle dance. The *wanaragua*, also known as the John Canoe dance, is performed on Christmas and New Year's Day, as drummers, singers, and masked and costumed dancers travel household to household in a procession. There are varying accounts concerning its origins and import. Many Garifuna say it originated during the wars against the British on St. Vincent and that the men dressed as women in order to fool the British; others believe it was performed in the Caribbean when slaves were temporarily manumitted and allowed to dance and enjoy themselves for short periods of time. Popular in Honduras, Guatemala, and Belize, the *wanaragua* can be seen in the United States at performing arts centers, universities, and festivals. Flavio Alvarez and his apprentice Carlos Gonzales, participating in the Alliance for California Traditional Arts, lead the *wanaragua* procession each year in Los Angeles.

Holidays Garifuna Americans observe Christian holidays such as Christmas and Easter in the same manner as other Americans. They also celebrate two days related to their own history. April 12 is Garifuna Arrival Day, the anniversary of the Garifuna arrival in Honduras from Roatan. While the 1997 bicentennial of Garifuna Arrival Day attracted international attention, this day is observed more on the East Coast, where Honduran Garinagu migrated. Belize Settlement Day is observed with a daylong celebration on the weekend closest to November 19 (the arrival day of the Garinagu in Belize). The observance in Los Angeles starts with a Garifuna language Catholic Mass, in which the Garifuna Choir sings and dancers perform sacred dances. Celebrations in cities including Chicago and New York features speeches, dancing, music, and food.

Health Care Issues and Practices There were no documented physical and mental health problems for Garifuna Americans beyond those that other Americans also face. These include the lack of affordable health care, according to Jorge Bernardez, a Honduran Garifuna who was honored at the 2012 First Annual Garifuna Film Festival in Los Angeles for his dedication to the Garifuna community. According to Bernardez, there are some Garinagu that occasionally consult a *buyei*, a traditional healer, when modern medicine proves ineffective.

Garifuna American communities are active in helping the Garifuna in Central America. The AIDS crisis in Honduras prompted Mirtha Colon, a Garifuna New Yorker, to found Hondurans Against AIDS in 1992. The organization continues to focus on providing AIDS/HIV education to the Garifuna community in both Central America and New York. Colon was awarded the 2012 Outstanding Career Serving Humanity Award by Bronx assemblyman Eric Stevenson during the Night of Elegance Fundraising Gala on May 17, 2012.

FAMILY AND COMMUNITY LIFE

Garifuna American men and women continue to maintain strong community bonds. Their efforts have focused on maintaining the Garifuna heritage and assisting Garinagu in the United States. In Los Angeles during the 1970s, for example, Belizeans "Don Justo" Flores and Christola Ellis-Baker founded the Garifuna Sick Aid Association. The group provided financial assistance to members who were faced with costs associated with issues such as illness. The organization also worked to maintain Garifuna culture, traditions, and customs. Among its undertakings, it organized the first Garifuna Settlement Day celebrations during the 1960s to commemorate the 1832 arrival of the Garinagu in Belize.

The vibrancy of the Garifuna community is particularly evident in Los Angeles, where, as of 2012, a Garifuna-oriented art museum, choir, pageant, and language study group existed, as well as soccer clubs and dance groups. Garinagu have also worked with the American consul of Belize to sponsor trips to Belize for the Settlement Day celebration. Meanwhile, groups in cities such as Chicago have branched out to work on issues such as immigration and health care.

Gender Roles For more than two centuries, the mother was the focus of the home in Garifuna society, raising the children and taking care of the family farm while men hunted or fished. As the economy changed, men had to accept jobs that took them away from the village or sometimes even out of the country, and the woman became the head of the household. This situation gave women independence and also established them as the primary actors in the spiritual and emotional lives of family members and community. Other characteristics of this matrifocality include the remittance of money by immigrants to mothers back home, allocating the care of children to women relatives, and the formation of female-centered mutual aid societies. England writes that when Garifuna women immigrated to the United States, some of these practices continued. They banded together for support, and working women gave remittances to their mothers and sent their children back home to be cared for by female relatives.

The organization Mujeres Garinagu en Marcha (MUGAMA) illustrates this matrifocal Garifuna tradition. Founded in 1989, the group recognizes Garifuna women each March. MUGAMA helps to organize the celebration associated with Garifuna Arrival Day and provides educational and cultural programs for both men and women. MUGAMA's center in New York has been the site of forums on employment, education, immigration, domestic violence, and child abuse.

Education In New York the programs run by MUGAMA include an outreach to members of the Spanish-speaking community, among them Garifuna. English-as-a-second-language classes were started in 1990, and the implementation of Spanish-language GED in Spanish in 1996 made it easier for people to get their high school diplomas. Since 1996, MUGAMA has held summer cultural programs for children. Each June, MUGAMA sends letters of

GARIFUNA PROVERBS

Garifuna proverbs offer vivid images of Central American life. Some examples include the following:

The monkey believes in his own tail.
> You can't trust others to do things for you.

Don't say that you will never drink this water again.
> Never say never.

If someone hasn't touched your tail, don't turn around.
> Mind your own business.

Today for you, tomorrow for me.
> What goes around, comes around.

Just the same, not dying, not getting better.
> Still the same, no better, no worse.

If you don't get into the water, you don't get wet.
> If you don't try, you don't succeed.

congratulations to Garifuna graduates. The group also issues two scholarships to Garifuna American students annually.

The organization Garifuna American Heritage Foundation United (GAHFU) serves the Los Angeles community. Its goal is to preserve the Garifuna heritage through social and cultural awareness programs including youth mentoring and leadership.

Courtship and Weddings Marriage is established legally through a civil ceremony or a church service (particularly in a Catholic church) in the United States. Occasionally traditional Garifuna dress is worn.

A certain type of wedding ceremony used to be performed in Honduras and can still be seen on rare occasions. The *tatuniwa wuritagu* ("the drinking of coffee") brings together the couple and their parents, who are joined by family members and the elder. The bride's parents bring, or "give," her to the groom. After she is seated next to the groom, those in attendance drink coffee, and the families are thereafter bound together.

Relations with Other Americans Garifuna Americans identify with African Americans in various ways. They celebrate their culture during African American History month each February, and some museums and universities include Garifuna displays in exhibits related to African American history. Because of their unique Afro-Latin heritage, Garinagu also have a link with Hispanics. They attend Catholic services in which drums and dance are sometimes part of the proceedings. Furthermore, Garifuna Americans commonly live in Belizean, Guatemalan, Honduran, and Nicaraguan communities within major cities.

Surnames Garifuna, for the most part, have Spanish surnames. Some examples include Palacio, Martinez, Avaloy, Avila, Ariola, Beni, Blanco, Castillo, Cayetano, Paulino, and Zuniga.

EMPLOYMENT AND ECONOMIC CONDITIONS

First generation Garinagu tend to work long hours at low hourly wages in jobs such as home care, housekeeping, and construction. Some work legally, but others are in the United States illegally. The anthropology professor Sarah England found that first generation Garifuna women in New York worked in factories and as home attendants, while men continued to labor in the marine industries, including on cruise ships. Second generation Garinagu typically work professional jobs, gravitating toward the field of education. In Los Angeles many of these immigrants teach at Catholic elementary schools. In addition, the military draws both second and third generation Garinagu. Many Garinagu women work as nurses, and several practice medicine as doctors.

Garifuna Americans are also represented in religious groups. Sister Ruth Lambey, for example, is a Catholic nun belonging to the Holy Family order. Garifuna Americans ordained to the priesthood include Martin Avila in San Francisco and Milton Alvarez in Chicago.

POLITICS AND GOVERNMENT

The Garifuna are a transnational people, a group that identifies itself by its ethnicity. Thus, cultural awareness is vital to Garifuna Americans. This has led to the creation of organizations such as the New York–based Garifuna Coalition USA, which has become increasingly active in politics and voter registration. One of its goals is to better define Garifuna American demographics and to increase political representation. Although there are no definitive statistics, it is believed that the Garifuna Americans turned out at the polls in high numbers in 2008 and 2012, with about 75 percent voting for President Barack Obama, a Democrat.

Military service has long been a tradition for Garinagu, but it is difficult to determine how many Garifuna Americans have served in the military. Under the U.S. Department of Defense's statistics for the ethnic background of active-duty personnel, Garinagu are classified under the broad category of Latin American ancestry.

Garifuna Americans' strong ties to their former countries were best illustrated by the 1997 celebration that marked the 200th anniversary of the Garifuna arrival to Honduras from St. Vincent. People from

Central America, the United States, and other places planned and traveled to the celebration, which was held in Honduras. Among the festivities was a recreation of the Garifuna arrival to Roatan. Garinagu from different countries met together as the Garifuna Nation, a people bound by their common ancestry.

NOTABLE INDIVIDUALS

Cultural Promotion Jorge Bernardez (1958–), born in Manali, Honduras, and later based in California, is a physician board-certified in family medicine and well known for promoting the Garifuna language and culture. His children speak the Garifuna language. Bernardez was honored at the 2012 First Annual Garifuna Film Festival for his outstanding service to the Garifuna community in Los Angeles.

Clifford Palacio (1930–), a native of Seine Bight, Belize, was a prominent force in promoting the Garifuna culture in Los Angeles. Palacio joined the Garifuna Settlement Day celebration committee in 1973, holding the positions of both secretary and president over sixteen years. During the 1990s he conducted weekly Garifuna language study sessions, and he was a cofounder of the Garifuna Language and Culture Academy in 2005.

Ruben Reyes (1961–) was born in Honduras and immigrated to New York City. Among his accomplishments, he created *Lamumehan Garifuna*, a Garifuna radio program. After moving to Los Angeles, Reyes taught Garifuna language and culture in conjunction with the GAHFU. Reyes coproduced and codirected the movie *Garifuna in Peril* and wrote a trilingual dictionary (Garifuna-English-Spanish). In addition, he hosted the *Sasamu Show* on GariTV.com. Reyes won the Garifuna Heritage Award from the GAHFU in 2010.

Dance Manuela Sabio (1951–), a secondary education teacher in New York City, founded Wanichigu Dance Company in 1988 to teach Garifuna traditions and values to youths. The company's name means "Our Pride," and the troupe performed on August 17, 1997, at New York City's Lincoln Center Out of Doors Festival.

Anita Martinez (1951–) was born in Belize. In Los Angeles she cofounded the Wagiameme Performing Troupe with her daughter, Shantel Martinez (1980–). The troupe, whose name is a Garifuna word meaning "Still Us," consists of females between the ages of fourteen and twenty-one who perform dances and skits portraying Garifuna life. The group's performances have included the November 19 Settlement Day celebration in Los Angeles in 2004 and the 2004 Bob Marley Reggae Festival in Long Beach, California. Anita Martinez received the Garifuna Heritage Award from GAHFU in 2010.

Literature Justin Mejia Flores (1918–1994), a native of Dangriga, Belize, was known as "Don Justo." He was a member of the Honduras National Soccer

Team during the early 1950s. Also a renowned musician in both Central America and the United States, Don Justo made and played several instruments. He wrote, produced, and released several records with his band El Ritmo Caribe. In addition, he was a founding member of the annual November 19 Garifuna Settlement Day Celebration of Los Angeles during the early 1960s. While working as a machinist in Los Angeles, he wrote his first book, *Tumba Le* (1977), which is a fictional account of life, love, sports, and fun in a Garifuna village. His other books include *The Garifuna Story—Now and Then* (1979), the first Garifuna dictionary compiled and published by a Garifuna, the first Garifuna calendar, and *The Life and Obituary of Aunt Dominica* (1995).

Music Rhodel Castillo (1959–), born outside Dangriga, Belize, is a poet who has set many of his works to music. Castillo's poem "Our Children Must Know" is heard at the beginning of the 1998 documentary *The Garifuna Journey*, and his album *The Punta Rock Medley* was released in 1998. In 1991 he founded the Progressive Garifuna Alliance, an organization that preserves and promotes Garifuna culture. He is also the owner of Garifuna Flava, a restaurant in Chicago featuring Garifuna cuisine.

Belize native James Lovell (1991) is a recording artist who leads a New York performance group called the AfriGarifuna Youth Ensemble and teaches the Garifuna language and music at the BIKO Transformation Center in New York.

Toni Steelz (1978–) is a rapper of Garifuna descent born and raised in New York. She won an Underground Music Award in 2009 and was nominated for a 2012 Underground Music Award for Most Promising Female Artist.

Social Issues Reverend George Castillo (1932–) was born in Dangriga, Belize, and went on to become a United Church of Christ minister. In 1973 he began twenty years of service as a chaplain in the Federal Bureau of Prisons system. He wrote about that service in his 1996 book *My Life Between the Cross and Bars*. After retiring in 1993, he gave lectures and workshops on subjects such as the importance of marketable skills for prisoners, humane prison treatment, and support for families.

Mirtha Colon (1951–), born in Honduras, is a social worker who founded Hondurans Against AIDS in 1992. She served as president of the New York–based organization, which provided AIDS/HIV education and support in Central America and New York. She was presented with the 2012 Outstanding Career Serving Humanity Award by Bronx assemblyman Eric Stevenson.

Honduras native Dionisia Amaya (1933–) cofounded MUGAMA in 1989. She was a guidance counselor who became involved in Garifuna community activities in New York in 1974.

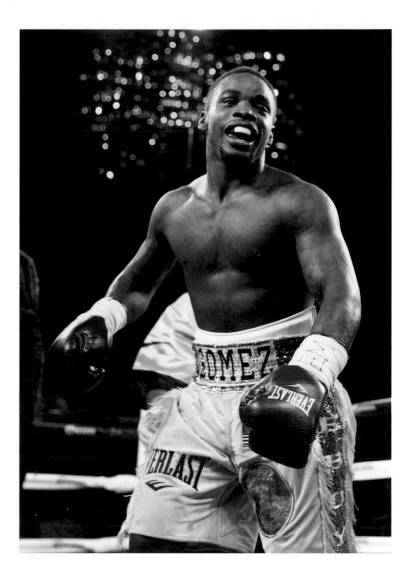

Garifuna American Eddie Gomez (1993–) celebrates after winning a Junior Middleweight fight in 2013. AL BELLO / GETTY IMAGES

Science and Technology Leonard Cayetano (1961–) was born in Cirque Arena, Toledo, Belize, and in 1999 he became the director of operations and production at Earthlink Internet service. In 2012 he delivered a series of workshops in Los Angeles on Garifuna cultural immersion.

Sports Eddie Gomez (1993–) is a Garifuna American professional boxer. In October 2012 at the Barclays Center in Brooklyn, New York, he scored his first knockout win. Two months later, he won a bout by unanimous decision under the bright lights at Madison Square Garden.

MEDIA

TELEVISION

GariTV (Garifuna Online Television)

Provides entertainment and news pertaining to Garifuna culture. Its offerings include music videos, interviews, performances, news, culture, and education.

P.O. Box 570402
Tarzana, California 91357
Phone: (800) 385-2910
Email: info@garitv.com
URL: www.garitv.com

RADIO

Garifuna Radio

An online radio station featuring live broadcasts from Sandy Bay, St. Vincent, as well as Garifuna news and music. Its mission statement is to entertain and inform listeners about Garifuna culture.

URL: www.garifunaradio.webs.com

WHPK-FM (88.5)

The station's *Belizean Melody Music Show* is broadcast from the University of Chicago. Featuring Garifuna music and news, it can be heard on Saturdays from 10 a.m. to 4 p.m. It is hosted by Randolph Coleman.

Theo Shure, Publicity Director
Reynolds Club
5706 University Avenue
Chicago, Illinois 60637
Phone: (773) 702-8289
Email: contact@whpk.org
URL: www.whpk.org

ORGANIZATIONS AND ASSOCIATIONS

Evangelical Garifuna

This Garifuna church in New York helps to gather together Garifuna Americans for worship.

344 Brook Avenue
Bronx, New York 10454
Phone: (718) 585-7253
Email: celsojaime@aol.com
URL: www.evangelicalgarifuna.ny.us.mennonite.net

Garifuna American Heritage Foundation United, Inc. (GAHFU)

Dedicated to the preservation of the Garifuna language, history, and culture. Its mission is to serve the Garifuna American community in Los Angeles and abroad by means of cultural and outreach programs. GAHFU provides mentor programs and scholarships and assists with providing health care, proper nutrition, clothing, and shelter.

2127 Atlantic Avenue
Long Beach, California 90806
Phone: (323) 898-6841
URL: www.garifunaheritagefoundation.org

Garifuna Coalition USA (GCU)

Founded in May 1998 as the umbrella group for Garifuna organizations in New York City, its purpose is to serve as a resource and forum for Garifuna issues and to help unite the Garifuna community. In 2009 GCU opened the Garifuna Advocacy Center in South Bronx, New York. The center provides information, educational services, and cultural events for the Garifuna community. GCU is actively involved in voter registration and partners with the U.S. Census to obtain accurate Garifuna demographics.

391 East 149 Street
215
Bronx, New York 10455
Phone: (718) 402-7700
Fax: (212) 202-7933
Email: info@garifunacoalition.org
URL: www.garifunacoalition.org

Garifuna Hope Foundation

Nonprofit organization that promotes cultural preservation of the Garifuna people through educational and performing arts programs. The Garifuna Museum of Los Angeles is under its auspices.

P.O. Box 570402
Tarzana, California 91357
URL: www.garifunahopefoundation.org

Garifuna Settlement Day Group

A nonprofit organization started in the 1960s in Los Angeles to celebrate Settlement Day. It protects and preserves Garifuna history and heritage through folklore, music, dance, and educational activities.

James Castillo, President
P.O. Box 11690
Los Angeles, California 90011
Phone: (323) 234-8202
Email: Castillo.james@sbcglobal.net
URL: www.settlementdaygroup.org

Mujeres Garinagu en Marcha (MUGAMA)

Founded in 1989, the group's name translates as "Garinagu Women Marching." Honduran Garinagu Dionisia Amaya, Lydia Hill, and Mirtha Sabio founded MUGAMA to recognize the accomplishments of Garifuna women in the New York tri-state area. The organization branched out, and its activities include awarding scholarships and offering classes in English as a second language.

Norma Guerrero, Secretary
420 Watkins Street
Brooklyn, New York 11212
Phone: (718) 485-6484

MUSEUMS AND RESEARCH CENTERS

Both public and university museums have held exhibits about the Garinagu. Sometimes the exhibits are tied into the February celebration of Black History Month. Generally, these exhibits have included cultural demonstrations that include dance and food.

The Garifuna Journey

A traveling exhibit centered on a forty-six-minute documentary of the same name produced by filmmakers Andrea Leland and Kathy Berger and released in 1998. The documentary was filmed in Belize and depicts Garinagu from that country and the United States. The documentary has been part of multimedia exhibits at museums and has won numerous awards. It was a finalist for Best Documentary in the Pan African Film Festival in Los Angeles and won an Award of Merit in the Latin American Studies Association Film Festival.

Andrea Leland
1200 Judson Avenue
Evanston, Illinois 60202
Phone: (847) 864-7752
URL: www.newday.com/films/GarifunaJourney/html

Garifuna Museum of Los Angeles (GAMOLA)

Opened in 2011, this museum focuses on the heritage and culture of the Garifuna people. There is a permanent collection of artifacts, models, and art. It is the only Garifuna museum in the United States.

1517 West 48ᵗʰ Street
Los Angeles, California
Phone: (424) 218-6212
URL: www.garifunamuseum.com

SOURCES FOR ADDITIONAL STUDY

Anderson, Mark. "The Significance of Blackness: Representations of Garifuna in St. Vincent and Central America, 1700–1900." *Transforming Anthropology: Journal of the Association of Black Anthropologists* 6, nos. 1–2 (1997).

Castillo, Reverend George. *My Life Between the Cross and the Bars.* Shalimar, FL: G&M Publications, 1996.

England, Sarah. *Afro-Central Americans in New York City: Garifuna Tales of Transnational Movements in Racialized Space.* Gainesville: University Press of Florida, 2006.

———. "Gender Ideologies and Domestic Structures within the Transnational Space of the Garifuna Diaspora." In *Diasporic Identity: Selected Papers on Refugees and Immigrant Issues,* edited by Carol A. Mortland. Arlington, VA: American Anthropological Association Committee on Refugees and Immigrants, 1998.

———. "Negotiating Race and Place in the Garifuna Diaspora: Identity Formation and Transnational Grassroots Politics in New York City and Honduras." *Identities: Global Studies in Culture and Power* 6, no. 1 (1999).

González, Nancie. "Garifuna Settlement in New York: A New Frontier." *International Migration Review* 13, no. 2 (1979).

Merrill, Tim, ed. *Guyana and Belize: Country Studies.* Library of Congress, Federal Research Division. Washington DC: Library of Congress, 1993.

Munro, Pamela. "The Garifuna Gender System." *Trends in Linguistics, Studies and Monographs* 108. Berlin: Walter de Gruyter and Company: 1997.

Palacio, Joseph. *The Garifuna, A Nation Across Borders: Essays in Social Anthropology.* Belize: Cubola, 2005.

Taylor, Chris. *The Black Carib Wars: Freedom, Survival, and the Making of the Garifuna.* Jackson: University Press of Mississippi, 2012.

GEORGIAN AMERICANS

Vladimir F. Wertsman

OVERVIEW

Georgian Americans are immigrants or descendants of people from Georgia, a country in the mountainous region of Transcaucasia. Georgia is bounded by Russia to the north and northeast, Azerbaijan to the east, the Black Sea to the west, and Armenia and Turkey to the south. The Caucasus Mountains form the country's northern border, and the landscape is rugged. Tbilisi is the capital of Georgia. The official language is Georgian, but Russian is used as a second language. Georgia, called Sakartvelo by Georgians, occupies about 27,000 square miles (69,700 square kilometers), making it almost half the size of Illinois.

According to a 2011 estimate by the World Bank, Georgia has a population of 4,486,000. Ethnic Georgians make up 71 percent of the population, but significant ethnic minorities include Armenians (8 percent), Russians (6.5 percent), Azeri (4.6 percent), Greeks (3 percent), Ossets (3 percent), and Abkhazians (2 percent). There are also smaller groups of Ukrainians, Turks, Persians, and Jews. Most Georgians belong to the Georgian Orthodox Church. Islam and Judaism, which are practiced by ethnic minorities, are tolerated. Agriculture and mining are the most prominent sectors of the national economy. With limited arable land and without oil or natural gas resources, in the early twenty-first century Georgia is one of the poorer of the former Soviet republics.

Georgians began to arrive in the United States in the early twentieth century, after the Russian Red Army invasion of Georgia in 1921 and the subsequent Soviet occupation of the country. They settled mainly in urban areas and took menial work. After World War II, most Georgian immigrants came to the United States fleeing the Soviet regime. They were aided by the passage of the Displaced Persons Act of 1948 and the Refugee Act of 1953. Since 1991, when the Soviet Union collapsed and Georgia gained independence, most Georgians immigrants have come to the United States in search of economic opportunity.

The Georgian American Foundation estimates that there are between 70,000 and 100,000 people of Georgian descent living in the United States in the early twenty-first century. Areas with significant Georgian American populations include New York, Boston, Washington, D.C., Chicago, Detroit, Seattle, Atlanta, and Los Angeles.

HISTORY OF THE PEOPLE

Early History According to traditional Georgian accounts, Georgians are descendants of Thargamos, the great-grandson of Japhet, son of the Biblical Noah. The ancient name of Georgia was Colchis, which was associated for centuries with the Greek myth of Jason and his fifty Argonauts, who sailed from Greece to Colchis to capture the Golden Fleece. The legend describes how Medea, the daughter of the king of Colchis, assisted Jason in his adventure but at the end was deserted by him. Colchis is historically recorded by Herodotus (484–425 BCE), Xenophon (ca. 430–354 BCE), and Josephus Flavius (37–95 CE).

Georgia was formed as a kingdom in the fourth century BCE, and for several centuries it was ruled by Romans, Persians, Byzantines, Arabs, and Turks. It regained full independence and unity under King David the Restorer (1089–1125) and reached the height of territorial expansion and cultural development under Queen Thamar (1183–1213). During the thirteenth and fourteenth centuries, invasions by the Mongolian conqueror Genghis Khan and the Turkic conqueror Tamerlane devastated the country and split its unity. In the fifteenth century Georgia was divided into the three kingdoms of Iberia, Imertia, and Kakhetia. In 1555 Turkey took over the rule of West Georgia, while East Georgia fell under Persian rule. In 1783 Georgia became a protectorate of Russia. At the beginning of the nineteenth century, the country was annexed and incorporated into Russia's tsarist empire. Georgia remained part of Russia until 1917, when the Bolsheviks overthrew the tsar and established a communist state.

Modern Era In 1918 Georgia became an independent state. However, three years later, the Russian Red Army invaded Georgia, and it was later forcibly incorporated into the Soviet Union. A rebellion designed to restore Georgian independence failed in 1924. In 1936 a new constitution was proclaimed, and Georgia became a Soviet Socialist Republic under the dictatorship of Joseph Stalin (1879–1953), who was born in Georgia as Iosef Dzhugashvili. Another Georgian, Lavrenti Beria (1899–1953), was a friend of Stalin's who became the chief of the NKVD, the Soviet secret police (precursor of the KGB). Beria was notorious for extending Stalin's regime of terror through executions, mass arrests, and deportations to vast labor camps known as gulags.

Following the collapse of the Soviet Union, Georgia again became an independent nation, in April 1991. During the first half of the 1990s, the country was forced to cope with difficult political, economic, and ethnic problems. Two secessionist movements, in the autonomous regions of Abkhazia and South Ossetia, required military intervention. Both conflicts ended in 1996 with the signing of a peace agreement. A bitter political struggle between various parties and factions brought Eduard Shevardnadze, a former foreign minister of the Soviet Union, to power. Shevardnadze quickly established a pro-Western government.

Shevardnadze left office in 2003 in the wake of the "Rose" revolution, and new elections in 2004 brought Mikheil Saakashvili to power. Russia's support of separatist forces within Abkhazia and South Ossetia culminated in a five-day armed conflict in 2008; the regions declared themselves independent, yet the Georgian government considered them as occupied territory. In 2012 billionaire Bidzina Ivanishvili became prime minister after his opposition bloc won elections.

SETTLEMENT IN THE UNITED STATES

The Georgian presence in the United States began in 1890 with the arrival of twelve Georgian horsemen hired by Buffalo Bill Cody and his Wild Congress of Rough Riders. The so-called Cossack horsemen successfully competed with talented horsemen from Mexico, Argentina, France, England, Spain, and the United States. The Georgians charmed audiences with their energy, style, and riding skills. In 1910 a second group of thirty Georgian male and female riders successfully performed in the United States with the Ringling Brothers Circus. A third group of nearly fifty Georgians was hired as laborers to work on railroads on the West Coast. Shortly before World War I, a few dozen Georgians returned to their native land, whereas those who decided to settle in the United States formed the nucleus around which the Georgian American community developed in later years.

The Georgian presence in the United States began in 1890 with the arrival of twelve Georgian horsemen hired by Buffalo Bill Cody and his Wild Congress of Rough Riders. The so-called Cossack horsemen successfully competed with talented horsemen from Mexico, Argentina, France, England, Spain, and the United States.

After the Russian invasion of Georgia in 1921, hundreds of families fled the country fearing repression by communist authorities. About two hundred Georgian refugees, including former political leaders, members of the aristocracy, and military officers, came to the United States. Unable to speak English and lacking financial resources or help from charitable organizations, many Georgian refugees had a hard time adjusting to their new lives in the United States. Some gave up their professional occupations to take menial jobs, while others with aristocratic titles married wealthy American women. Those who could not cope with life in the United States returned to Europe and joined other Georgian refugees who had established themselves in Germany, France, Poland, Turkey, and Belgium.

A second wave of Georgian refugees arrived after World War II. More than 250 men, women, and children came to the United States by virtue of the Displaced Persons Act of 1948 and the Refugee Act of 1953. Several were former prisoners of war who feared reprisals if they returned to the Soviet Union. There were also some Georgians who lived in Europe as refugees before the start of World War II. These new immigrants, unlike the first wave, received assistance from various charitable and nonprofit organizations, including the Georgian Association in the United States and the Tolstoy Foundation. Many immigrants from this second wave were skilled workers, professionals, military men, and clerical workers, and they found it relatively easy to adjust to their new homeland.

During the final decade of Soviet rule in Georgia, a third wave of immigrants—consisting of a few hundred men and women—came to the United States for economic, religious, educational, business, or family reasons. This wave consisted of both professionals and nonprofessionals and included persons from various ethnic groups within Georgia. By 1990 there were between 3,000 and 3,500 Georgian Americans in the United States, the majority of whom had settled in or around New York, Boston, Washington, D.C., Chicago, Detroit, Seattle, Atlanta, and Los Angeles.

Determining the size of the Georgian American community in the early twenty-first century is a complex issue. According to the Georgian American Foundation, which the Georgian government sponsors, between 70,000 and 100,000 people of Georgian descent lived in the United States in 2012. This figure has been called into question, however, by scholars who point to the low level of Georgian immigration to the United States. According to a study by the scholar Elene Medzmariashvili of Tbilisi State University, the number of Georgians who obtained American citizenship after 1991 was low: only 1,834 between 1991 and 1996; 325 in 1997; and 100 in 1998. The same study mentions difficulties in establishing Georgian identities because some have immigrated illegally and some families are of mixed ethnicity. Among immigrants from Georgia, there are also Abkhazians, Armenians, Jews, and others.

LANGUAGE

Karthli, the Georgian language, is part of the Ibero-Caucasian family of languages and is distinct from the Indo-European, Turkic, and Semitic languages. It is not

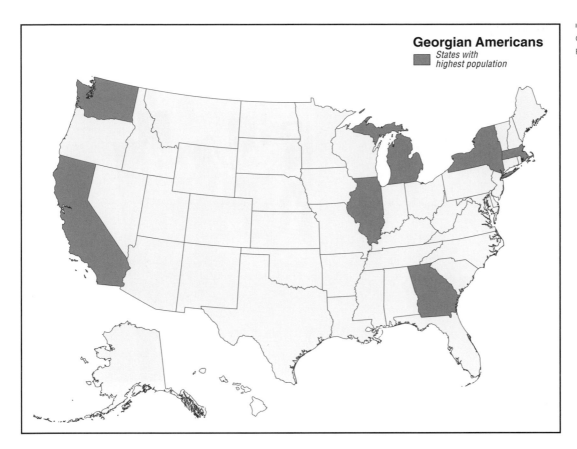

Georgian Americans
■ States with highest population

related to other Northern Caucasian language groups, even though it resembles them phonetically. Georgian is based on the Armenian alphabet, and its roots are attributed to St. Mesrop. The Georgian language features a frequent recurrence of the sounds "ts," "ds," "thz," "kh," "khh," and "gh." There are two systems of the Georgian alphabet. The first, Khutsuri, consists of thirty-eight letters and dates to the fifth century CE. It is used in the Bible and liturgical works. The second Georgian alphabet, Mkherduli, consists of forty letters and is used in ordinary writing; this alphabet is unique to Georgia.

The Georgian language is rich, flexible, and contains a complex grammar. High proportions of older Georgian Americans speak Georgian. Younger generations of Georgian Americans, many of whom were raised in the United States or immigrated for professional reasons, speak fluent English but also often know Russian or Georgian.

Greetings and Popular Expressions *Gamarjobat*—Hello; *Gmadlobt*—Thank you; *Inebet*—Please; *Nakhvamdis*—Good-bye; *Gauma... jobs*—Cheers" (when drinking wine).

RELIGION

Georgians were widely converted to Christianity in the fourth century CE under King Mirian (265–345), who erected the first Christian church, later renamed the Cathedral of Mtskhet. The Georgian Orthodox Church, a branch of the Eastern Orthodox Church, is headed by a Catholicos-Patriarch with its headquarters in Georgia. The Georgian Orthodox Church is the only religious denomination that is legally recognized by the country's government. A constitutional agreement passed in 2002 legally defines the relationship between the Georgian Orthodox Church and the state.

Georgian liturgy uses characteristic liturgical texts called *Kondaki* and various blessings for stated occasions called *Khurthkhevani*. Its system of chronology has its own order of ecclesiastical teachings and feasts. Mass is always accompanied by liturgical chants, which employ specific Georgian styles and forms. The Georgian cross is of a heraldic shape and different from the types of crosses used by other branches of the Eastern Orthodox Church.

By 2012 there were four Georgian churches in the United States: Saint Nino Georgian Orthodox Church in New York City; Saint Tamar Georgian Orthodox Church in Washington, D.C.; Saint George Orthodox Church in Philadelphia; and Saint Nicholas Georgian Orthodox Church in Los Angeles. There is also a Georgian monastery, St. King David Agmashenebeli Monastery, in Hanover Township, Pennsylvania. In communities without Georgian Orthodox churches, Georgian Americans typically attend Russian Orthodox, Ukrainian Orthodox, or Greek Orthodox churches.

CULTURE AND ASSIMILATION

Because Georgian Americans are small in number, less information is available about them than other ethnic groups. Despite this, Georgian Americans have preserved their heritage and culture through various organizations. As early as 1924, Georgian organizations were founded in San Francisco and New York City. These groups organized cultural activities and social gatherings and provided assistance to other immigrants. Between 1955 and 1975, the Georgian American press was very active. *Kartuli Azri* (*Georgian Opinion*) was the most popular newspaper and was heavily supported by donations from Georgian Americans. Over the years, Georgians have fully assimilated into American culture. However, Georgian Americans continue to proudly preserve many aspects of their unique culture, including their language, religion, food, and traditional celebrations.

Traditions and Customs In Georgia some tribes forbid women to have children until after they have been married for three years. Georgian custom allows a maximum of three children per couple. The birth of a boy is cause for great celebration, while the birth of a girl is often met with disappointment. Many Georgian Americans have long forsaken these customs. Other customs, however, are still observed. For example, formality and mutual respect guided the daily behavior of many Georgian Americans. From an early age, children are trained in etiquette and the social graces. The display of any sexual behavior in public was traditionally considered a source of great shame. Privacy and modesty are greatly cherished and women are treated with respect.

Cuisine Georgian Americans have a very rich, healthy, and tasty traditional cuisine. Other ethnic groups also enjoy Georgian cuisine, and it is typically featured on menus in Russian restaurants. There are also a number of Georgian restaurants in United States.

Georgian women often cook according to the traditions of their homeland. A typical first course in a Georgian-style meal might include fresh herbs, radishes, scallions, tiny cucumbers, quartered tomatoes sprinkled with dill, home-cured olives, pickled cabbage, red kidney beans dressed with walnut sauce, eggplant puree, cheese, and smoked sturgeon garnished with tarragon. *Khachapuri* (flatbread with cheese filling), *lobio* (kidney beans in plum sauce), and other types of appetizers are usually accompanied by *lavash* (thin white bread) and raki (a dry and strong liquor made from berries or grapes) or *chacha* (a grape vodka). *Sulguni*, a type of cheese, is served with fresh coriander and scallions. *Khmeli-suneli*, a very popular spice mix, consists of mixtures of dill, coriander, pepper, and other strongly scented spices. Melons and oranges are often added to goat or chicken that has been strongly spiced with peppers and heavily seasoned with garlic. A chicken soup called *kharcho* is also served with walnuts.

Second courses might consist of skewers of fried or broiled fish such as *khramuli* or *kogak*, a delicately flavored whitefish. Lamb or chicken stews (*chakhokh-bili*) are served with wine. *Shashlik* is made of chicken, onions, and other vegetables on a skewer. *Kotmis satsivi* is a roast chicken or roast suckling pig served with walnut sauce. *Mtsvadi* is grilled lamb, pig, or young goat, and *tabaka* is pressed fried chicken. Georgian cuisine also includes *pkhali* (vegetables and walnuts), *kinkali* (dumplings of beets), and pickled cabbage. Meals are served with excellent Georgian wines, especially *Kindzmarauli* and *Teliani*, both of which are prized for their aromatic flavors. Desserts include compotes, candied almonds or walnuts, various preserves, and *chuckella* (traditional candy made from grape juice and walnuts). Nonalcoholic beverages include yogurt, syrups, fruit juices, and Turkish coffee.

Traditional Clothing Traditional clothing is still found in the homes of some older Georgian Americans and is usually worn during Georgian folk festivals. Men wear black wool pants and a long-sleeved shirt that buttons halfway down the front. This shirt is usually black and often decorated around the edges with silver or gold thread. Soft, right-fitting leather boots that extend above the knee are also worn. These boots have a thin sole and no heels. A wool coat, usually black, brown, white, or gray in color, is worn over the shirt and pants. It has no collar and is cut with a long, narrow V-shaped opening from the neck halfway to the waist. Rows of narrow pockets, six or eight on each side of the coat, are sewn across the chest. A belt containing a dagger (*kinjal*) or sword is worn around the waist. The head is adorned with a *papakha*, a fur cap of sheep or goatskin with the fleece side out, which hangs over the forehead. During winter months a *bashlik*, a hood of finely woven woolen material that can be tied around the neck, is worn. A cape made of goat or sheep wool, called a *bourka*, is worn around the shoulders. It is usually black and semicircular in shape and fastened at the neck with thongs.

Traditional dress for Georgian women is a long, floor-length gown with a tight bodice and long sleeves ending at the waist. The gowns are made of silk and come in white or a variety of pastel colors. A long, flowing scarf is often wrapped around the head and shoulders. The hair is worn in at least two braids, which frequently extend past the waist. An ornamental gold belt covers the waist. A headdress, in gold or another bright color, covers the head. Older women wear similar dresses but in darker colors. They also wear a turbanlike headdress. Georgian women, like their male counterparts, also wear boots.

It should be noted that Georgian Americans, like those who live in contemporary urban Georgia, dress in Western-style clothes. Farmers also dress in European shirts and trousers that are conservative in color. Rural women typically wear blouses and long skirts.

Dances and Songs Georgian men and women love to dance. Men dance on the tip of their toes at increasing speeds, incorporating breathtaking leaps

GEORGIAN PROVERBS

Georgians, like many other ethnic groups from Transcaucasia, are known for their original proverbs.

- Low places are considered high when high places are lacking.

- That which one loses by laughing one does not find again by crying.

- There is always a dirty spoon in every family.

- He who does not seek friends is his own enemy.

- If you put your nose into water you will also wet your cheeks.

- The cock cannot profit by the friendship of the fox.

- One blames one's friend to his face and one's enemy to his back.

- Don't spit into a well; one day it may serve to quench your thirst.

- It is better to drink water from a small spring than salt water from a great sea.

- The cart is heavy, but it makes the load light.

- Catch the bird before you build a cage.

- Better your own copper than another man's gold.

- The world can be conquered with words but not with drawn swords.

- When three people say you are drunk, go to sleep.

- The cat that did not reach the sausage said: "Anyhow, it is Friday!"

and swift head movements. Female dances employ scarves, handkerchiefs and pitches, intricate arm movements, and simple, gliding steps. The most popular Georgian dances are *lezghinka*, in which men and women danced together; *partza*, a circular dance; *kartuli*, a dance of chivalry in which men are not permitted to touch the girls; and *samaya*, which is performed by three young girls to celebrate a wedding feast. Young women often dance the *narnari*, which features beautiful arm and hand movements.

Dances are accompanied by highly rhythmic music in which drumming plays a leading role.

LOBIO (KIDNEY BEAN SALAD)

Ingredients

1½ cups dried red kidney beans, soaked overnight in 5–6 cups of water

2 medium onions, diced

1½ cups of shelled raw walnuts

1 tablespoon of vegetable oil

2 cloves of garlic, pressed with a pinch of salt

¼ cup of red wine vinegar

1 teaspoon dried summer savory

1 teaspoon dried fenugreek leaves

⅓ cup of minced fresh herbs (such as basil, parsley, dill, and/or cilantro)

cayenne pepper

salt and black pepper, to taste

Garnish

1 cup pomegranate seeds

2 tablespoons minced herbs (see above)

Preparation

Simmer beans for about 2 hours until they begin to fall apart. Add more hot water as needed until they are done.

While the beans are simmering, heat the oil over medium and sauté the onions until softened and transparent. Grind walnuts finely, add salt, pepper, garlic and the dried herbs.

When the beans are ready, add onions and simmer for about 5 minutes. Then add the walnut sauce and correct the seasonings.

Remove from the heat and let the beans cool down slightly, then add the minced herbs and red wine vinegar a little at a time. The tartness of vinegar varies, so start by adding 2 tablespoons, taste, and add more if needed.

Serve lobio sprinkled with pomegranate seeds and herbs, salt and a pinch of sugar.

Serves 4

The characteristic feature of Georgian folk music is polyphony. As a rule, multivoice songs are performed by men. Women perform some solos and duets. Georgian folk music is also rich in lyrical songs honoring popular heroes. Georgian orchestras include flutes, lutes, drums, cymbals, bagpipes, and mandolins. Beginning in the 1950s, Georgian singers and dancers, trained in their homeland, performed in the United States and throughout the world. These groups are widely acclaimed for their exceptional artistic qualities.

Among Georgian Americans, traditional Georgian song and dance is typically reserved for special occasions such as weddings. There are also cultural groups, such as New York's Dancing Crane, that perform Georgian music and dance at festivals, celebrations, and other functions.

Holidays Dozens of religious holidays are celebrated in Georgia, depending on the region and locality. Several holidays are devoted to various saints, particularly St. George. Two religious holidays observed by Georgians and Georgian Americans are January 26 and May 19. Both of these days honor Saint Nino, the patron saint credited with bringing Christianity to the Georgians in the fourth century. Easter, Christmas, and New Years are also major holidays. Church services are followed by a meal and various festivities. Other important holidays include May 26, which celebrates the proclamation of Georgia's independence in 1918; and August 29, which marks Georgia's revolt against the Soviet Union in 1924. On April 9, 1991, Georgia declared its independence from the Soviet Union, and this date was added to the calendar of holidays. Among many Georgian Americans, these important Georgian national holidays are observed.

FAMILY AND COMMUNITY LIFE

Georgian American families are known for their strong ties. Women play an important role both in families and society, and divorce is frowned upon. Although the father is the head of the family, women might keep their own surnames when they marry, and there is no stigma when a husband lives with his wife's parents. Children are raised to value their family and respect older members. Young people are expected to become well-educated and encouraged to become professionals. Georgians enjoy gathering with family and close friends to gossip, praise traditions, and remember deceased family members. Georgians are also known for their hospitality.

Gender Roles In post-Soviet Georgia, despite democratic legislation, women continued to be marginalized and there was no mechanism to apply gender equality. For Georgian immigrants who arrived in the United States after 1991, the United States offered an opportunity for women to pursue new opportunities, especially economically. In addition to learning English, some Georgian American women completed their studies and moved into professional work. Many who are unable to complete advanced education work as home health aides, nannies, waitresses, and in other service positions. Working outside the home allowed Georgian American women to financially supplement or support their households and led to greater gender equality within the Georgian American community.

Courtship and Weddings Georgians usually marry at a young age, and married couples are expected to take care of their parents. In many cases, a marriage is arranged by the parents of the bride and groom, relatives, or close friends. Wedding receptions traditionally include a series of toasts. The *tamada*, or toastmaster, is chosen by the audience and leads toasts to the native land, parents, friends, the memory of the dead, women, life, children, and the guests. After the toasts are made, all the guests say *gauma … jobs* ("cheers"). No one except the *tamada* may make a toast without first asking permission. The couple then toasts the guests and thanks them for their good wishes. After each toast, the guests drink an entire glass of wine.

Weddings in the Georgian Orthodox Church are performed according to old customs. In the wedding ceremony, the groom is called *mepe* (king) and the bride *dedopali* (queen). The couple sipped wine from the same cup and put crowns on their heads as a symbol of their union. The priest blessed the couple, and they officially become husband and wife. The wedding ceremony is followed by a reception with music and dancing.

Birth and Baptisms During a baby's christening (*natloba*), the godfather (*natlia*) plays an important role. He first cuts the hair and nails of the newborn. It is believed that by doing this, godfather transmits his own qualities and talents to the child. When the child is placed in water during the christening, small coins are thrown in to bring the child good luck and happiness.

Funerals Following the death of a family member, church bells are rung three times a day until the funeral ceremony is completed. During the funeral ceremony the priest, assisted by a choir and deacon, sings prayers and hymns for the dead. In the name of the deceased, the priest asks for forgiveness of sins from family and friends. Prayers are recited at the cemetery, and the Gospel is read. The coffin is then lowered into the grave, and soil sprinkled with holy water is tossed on top of the coffin. Another recitation from the Gospel concludes the funeral. After the funeral, the family of the deceased shares a light meal and beverages to honor their loved one.

EMPLOYMENT AND ECONOMIC CONDITIONS

Unlike the first waves of Georgian Americans who were employed as taxi drivers or in manual labor jobs, succeeding generations have enjoyed greater opportunities. Many have become professionals (such as engineers, teachers, doctors, artists, and military officers), others have gone into business, and others became clerical workers. Most Georgian Americans belong to the middle class.

POLITICS AND GOVERNMENT

Georgian Americans are often extremely proud of their homeland, and they never accepted its forced incorporation into the Soviet Union. Georgian American organizations and newspapers lobbied constantly for the creation of an independent and democratic Georgia, a goal finally attained after the Soviet Union collapsed in 1991. New laws passed in Georgia sought to facilitate increased economic, cultural, and educational ties with Georgian Americans. However, Georgian Americans often remained dissatisfied with the poor economic situation and the political and ethnic conflicts that persisted in their homeland.

This dissatisfaction intensified in 2008, when Russian troops invaded the Georgian separatist regions of Abkhazia and South Ossetia, whose independence the Russians supported. Georgian Americans viewed the Russian invasion as a violation of their homeland's sovereignty and as a Russian attempt to reassert control over the former Soviet republic, which was aligned with the West. By and large, Georgian Americans approved of the United States' support of Georgia during and after the conflict. The conflict in 2008 increased demands from Georgian Americans, among many other groups, for Georgia's inclusion in the North Atlantic Treaty Organization (NATO).

NOTABLE INDIVIDUALS

Activism Prince Teymuraz Bagration (1913–1992), a descendant of Georgian royalty, became president of the Tolstoy Foundation in New York City after World War II and remained in this position until his death. He was known for his efforts to resettle Georgian, Russian, and other ethnic refugees from the Soviet Union and Eastern European countries. He was also involved in the resettlement of refugees from Vietnam, Cuba, Uganda, and other countries. As a member of Care and Interaction, a coalition of more than one hundred charitable organizations, Bagration was instrumental in assisting displaced persons who wanted to start a new life in the United States.

Business Artchil Gourieli-Tchkonia (1895–1955), who immigrated to the United States in 1937, and his wife Helena Rubinstein (1882–1965), known as the queen of cosmetic products, became a successful business couple. Georges V. Matchabelli (1885–1935), of Georgian aristocratic origin, fled Georgia in 1921 and immigrated to the United States. In 1924, he and his wife established the Prince Matchabelli Perfume Company, launching popular scents such as "Ave Maria," "Wind Song," and "Princess Norina."

Commerce and Industry Alexander Kartveli (born Kartvelishvili) (1896–1974) was one of the most important and innovative aircraft designers in U.S. history. Born in Georgia, he graduated from the Highest School of Aviation in Paris in 1922, came to the United States in 1927, and joined the Atlantic Aircraft Corporation (later Republic Aviation Company) during World War II. He and partner Alexander de Seversky produced new designs (P-35 and P-47) for the most effective U.S. fighter aircraft and later developed new designs for the F-84 Thunderjet, F-84F Thunderstreak, F-105 Thunderchief, and several other fighter jets.

Government Andrew Eristoff (1962–) is a Republican Party politician who served on New York City Council (1993–1999) and as commissioner of tax and finance (1999–2002). In January 2010, he became state treasurer of New Jersey. Andrew Eristoff's father, Constantine Sidamon-Eristoff (1930–2011), served as commissioner of New York City's Department of Highways under Mayor John V. Lindsay and later was a

Russian-born Georgian American ballet director and choreographer George Balanchine (1904–1983) sits on a stage surrounded by New York City Ballet dancers in 1969. BERNARD GOTFRYD / GETTY IMAGES

member of the Metropolitan Transit Authority of New York City (1974–1989) before becoming a regional director of the U.S. Environmental Protection Agency (1989–1993) under President George H. W. Bush.

General John Shalikashvili (1936–2011) served as chairman of the Joint Chiefs of Staff between 1992 and 1996. Shalikashvili immigrated to the United States from Georgia with his parents following World War II, completed a master's degree in international affairs at George Washington University, and joined the military in 1958. He is a decorated veteran of the Korean and Vietnam wars, and eventually became commander of U.S. troops in West Germany. Shalikashvili was also the commander-in-chief of American armed forces in Europe before President Bill Clinton named him chairman of the Joint Chiefs of Staff. It marked the first time that a Georgian American had been named to such a high position within the military.

Literature George Papashvily (1898–1978) was an author who married the American Helen White after immigrating to United States in the 1920s. Together they wrote *Anything Can Happen* (1944), which chronicled his immigrant experiences. The book was a bestseller, and it was made into a film released in 1952. Papashvily and his wife also wrote the novel *All the Happy Endings* (1956) and *Home and Home Again* (1973), which included their impressions of Georgia after a visit during the 1960s, as well as *Russian Cooking* (1970), which includes both Russian and Georgian recipes. Papashvily was also a sculptor; he created *Georgian Folk Singer*, which was featured in the documentary film *Beauty in Stone*.

Svetlana Alliluyeva (1926–2011), whose surname was originally Djugashvili, was the daughter of Joseph Stalin. She defected from the Soviet Union to the United States in 1967, but in the 1980s returned for several years, only to settle again in the United States. She wrote *Twenty Letters to a Friend* (1967) and *Only One Year* (1969), in Russian and English, which detail her experiences before and after her defection and her impressions about the United States.

Valery Chalidze (1938–), is an author, editor, and publisher who focused his writings on human rights violations in the former Soviet Union. He wrote *To Defend These Rights: Human Rights and the Soviet Union* (1975), *Criminal Russia: Essays on Crime in the Soviet Union* (1977), and *The Soviet Human Rights Movement: A Memoir* (1984).

David Chavchavadze (1924–), of Georgian aristocratic origin, served in the CIA before turning to a career as an author and teacher. He was born in London and raised in the United States after his parents immigrated in 1927. In 1943 he was called up for active duty in the U.S. Army and inducted into a military intelligence unit. He worked as a CIA interpreter for the next twenty-five years. His memoir *Crowns and Trenchcoats: A Russian Prince in the CIA* was published in 1989.

Performance George Balanchine (1904–1983), ne Balanchivadze, was a noted ballet master and choreographer who fled Russia in 1924 and immigrated to the United States in 1933. He was considered one of the most influential and finest choreographers of the twentieth century. Balanchine was the cofounder and artistic director of the New York City Ballet Company, worked for the New York Metropolitan Opera, created more than two hundred ballets, and choreographed several Broadway musicals and movies.

George Chavchavadze (1904–1962) was a noted pianist with international credits.

Alexander Toradze (1952–) is a noted classical concert pianist and professor at Indiana University in South Bend. Born in Georgia, he graduated from the Moscow Conservatory in 1978. In 1983, while on a foreign tour with the Bolshoi Symphony Orchestra of Moscow, he requested asylum in the United States, which was granted. He has performed with numerous international orchestras and is best known for his classical Russian repertoire.

MEDIA

PRINT

The Georgian American League published *Voice of Free Georgia* (1953–1958) in English; the American Council for Independent Georgia published *Chveni Gza/Our Path* (1953–1960s), in Georgian with English summaries; and the Georgian National Alliance sponsored the publication of *Georgian Opinion* (1951–1975). All three publications focused on events in Soviet Georgia, the fight for a democratic and independent Georgia, and events in the Georgian American community. By the 1990s there were no longer any Georgian American periodicals in publication.

ORGANIZATIONS AND ASSOCIATIONS

American Friends of Georgia

American Friends of Georgia provides practical humanitarian assistance to the children and families of the country of Georgia.

P.O. Box 1200
Truro, Massachusetts 02666
Phone: (508) 349-2180
Fax: (508) 349-0511
Email: afgeorgia@gis.net
URL: www.afgeorgia.org

Georgian Association in the United States of America

The Georgian Association works to strengthen and support the Georgian American community.

Irakly Zurab Kakabadze
2300 M Street NW
Suite 800
Washington, D.C. 20037
Phone: (202) 234-2441
Email: georgianassociation@gmail.com
URL: www.georgianassociation.org

U.S.-Georgia Foundation

Founded in 1992, this organization seeks to assist Georgia in becoming a more democratic society with a free market economy and a multiparty political system.

Eduard Gudava
1110 Vermont Avenue
Suite 600
Washington, D.C. 20005
Phone: (202) 429-0108
Fax: (202) 293-3419

MUSEUMS AND RESEARCH CENTERS

Harvard University (Houghton Library)

This collection includes archives of the Georgian government (1917–1921), the correspondence of its legation abroad, expenses made by the government, domestic and foreign press about Georgia, and other valuable documents.

Librarian of Houghton Library
Cambridge, Massachusetts 02138
Phone: (617) 495-2401
Fax: (617) 496-4750
Email: library_research@hks.harvard.edu
URL: hcl.harvard.edu

Indiana University Libraries

The university possesses a collection of rare materials about Georgia and the Caucasus region for the historical scholarly community. Access is restricted to those researchers that have permission to use the collection.

10th and Jordan Street
Bloomington, Indiana 47405
Phone: (812) 855-0100
Fax: (812) 855-3143
URL: libraries.iub.edu

Tolstoy Foundation

The foundation was founded in 1939 as a voluntary organization to help refugees who escaped from oppressive regimes around the world. Its archives include documents and other materials regarding Georgian refugees who were helped by the organization from the end of World War II until the fall of the Soviet Union.

Xenia Woyevodsky, Executive Director
104 Lake Road
Valley Cottage, New York 10989
Phone: (914) 268-6140; or (914) 268-6722
Fax: (914) 268-6937
Email: info@tolstoyfoundation.org
URL: www.tolstoyfoundation.org

SOURCES FOR ADDITIONAL STUDY

Chavchavadze, David. *Crowns and Trenchcoats: A Russian Prince in the CIA.* New York: Atlantic International, 1990.

Goldstein, Darra. *The Georgian Feast: The Vibrant Culture and Savory Food of the Republic of Georgia.* New York: Harper-Collins, 1992.

Lang, David Marshall. *The Georgians.* New York: Praeger, 1966.

Papashvily, George, and Helen Papashvily. *Anything Can Happen.* New York: St. Martin's Press, 1945.

Rosen, Roger, and Jeffrey J. Foxx. *Georgia: A Sovereign Country of the Caucasus.* 2nd edition. New York: Odyssey Publications, 2004.

Wertsman, Vladimir. "Georgians in America." *Multicultural Review* 4, no. 4 (1995), 28–31, 52–53.

GERMAN AMERICANS

LaVern J. Rippley

OVERVIEW

German Americans are immigrants or descendants of people from Germany, a country in Central Europe. Today Germany shares borders with nine countries: Denmark to the north; Poland and the Czech Republic to the east; Austria and Switzerland to the south; and the Netherlands, Belgium, Luxembourg, and France to the west. In the north, Germany borders the North Sea and the Baltic Sea. The country's geography is impressively diverse, from the peaks of the Alps in the south, through forested hills in central Germany, to broad valleys through which flow some of Europe's most important rivers, including the Rhine, Danube, and Elbe. Germany is 138,000 square miles (357,000 square kilometers) in size, approximately the combined size of Minnesota and Wisconsin.

The population of Germany was 81,857,000 in 2012. According to the *CIA World Factbook*, 34 percent consider themselves Protestant (*Evangelisch* or Lutheran), 34 percent Roman Catholic, and 28 percent unaffiliated. About 3.7 percent are Muslims, and 200,000 are Jewish. Berlin has the fastest growing Jewish community in the world. Germany's standard of living is among the highest in the world, and the distribution of wealth compares favorably with that of the other advanced countries. Incentives in the form of housing subsidies and tax concessions induce savings. Both workers and employers are assured adequate income, vacations, and broad health care coverage. Value-added tax revenues and balanced employer–employee incomes have boosted Germans' satisfaction with their living standards even in the face of the early twenty-first century economic crisis in Europe.

Although a few Germans arrived with the Jamestown settlers in 1608, the first significant group of German settlers were thirteen families of Quakers and Mennonites from Krefeld, who arrived in Philadelphia on October 6, 1683, aboard the *Concordia*, and founded the city of Germantown, now incorporated into Philadelphia. German immigration was particularly important in the early decades of the United States, and German-speaking districts of American cities were once common. Since the mid-twentieth century most German immigrants have been professionals coming for work reasons.

According to the 2010 U.S. Census, German is the leading ancestry group in the United States, with about 50 million people, or 17 percent of the U.S. population, declaring German heritage (of whom only 1.5 million still speak German at home). Another 337,000 identified as "Pennsylvania German" or "Pennsylvania Dutch," a specific group descended from immigrants from Southwest Germany who continue to live largely in Southeastern and South Central Pennsylvania. The states with two million or more Americans of German descent are Ohio, Pennsylvania, Michigan, Illinois, New York, Texas, California, Florida, and Wisconsin. More than half of the nation's 3,143 counties reported a plurality of people describing themselves as German American. Today many German Americans are fully assimilated into U.S. culture and may not identify themselves with their ancestral group.

HISTORY OF THE PEOPLE

Early History Germany is derived from *Germania*, a region of Central Europe first mentioned by the Roman historian Tacitus about 98 CE, from which the English appellation *Germany* developed. The people have referred to themselves throughout history variously as Saxons, Burgundians, Bavarians, or simply as *Deutsch*, the latter meaning roughly "the people," hence the country's contemporary name, Deutschland. Recorded German history begins with Tacitus, who recounted a battle involving Arminius, a prince of the Germanic tribe the Cherusci, who vanquished three Roman legions in the Teutoburg Forest in 9 CE near the town of Kalkriese (Oldenburg). The name *Deutschland* came into use in the eighth century when Charlemagne incorporated German and French speakers into a common nation. As cohesion among the population of the eastern realm increased, the term *Deutsch* became applicable to all German speakers. Once confined west of the Elbe River, Germans gradually penetrated farther east into former Slavic territory, often peacefully but sometimes by force.

Germany bore versions of the name Holy Roman Empire of the German Nation, beginning with the Salian dynasty and proceeding with rule by Hohenstaufens, Habsburgs, and Hohenzollerns. When a Wittenberg Catholic priest named Martin Luther proposed religious reforms in 1517, he initiated the

Protestant Reformation, which led to pillaging of the country (and many other parts of Europe) by those who profited from the weakened central political, religious, and social ruling structures. The religiously motivated Thirty Years War (1618–1648) that erupted a century after Luther's death devastated both Germany's territory and its moral fiber until the age of French absolutism. During the Age of Enlightenment, Prussian King Frederick the Great (1740–1786) became a patron of the American Revolution. Frederick sent Baron von Steuben, Nikolaus Herchheimer, Johannes DeKalb, and others to train American military novices at Valley Forge, Pennsylvania, and elsewhere.

During the Napoleonic period the Holy Roman Empire dissolved and was replaced by the Deutscher Bund (German Confederation), a loose federation of individual sovereign states that functioned with a single central participatory government unit—the *Bundestag*—a non-elected but delegated parliament in Frankfurt. Often the *Bundestag* behaved like a monarchical oligarchy, suppressing freedom, enforcing censorship, and controlling the universities and political activity.

Arguments among the liberals arose over whether to establish a "greater Germany" along the lines of Great Britain or a "smaller Germany" that would include only the more traditionally German principalities and leave out Austria. Because Austria wanted to bring its different ethnic groups into the union, the National Assembly opted for the smaller Germany. They offered a constitution to King Friedrich Wilhelm IV of Prussia, but his rejection of it triggered popular uprisings in the German states, which were met with military suppression. At this time a significant number of German intellectual liberals, known as Forty-eighters, immigrated to the United States to escape persecution. The contemporary flag of Germany, with its black, red, and gold stripes, derives from the flag used by this Forty-eighter parliament.

Despite reactionary forces at the higher levels of government, an economic entity called the *Deutscher Zollverein*, or German Customs Union (occasionally considered the precursor of the current European Community), came into being in 1834. It was an inland unitary market system for the whole of Germany, which was facilitated in 1835 by the opening of the first German railway lines. This event was due in part to a return emigrant from the United States, Friedrich List (1789–1846). Exiled to the United States in 1825 for attempting to abolish tariffs and tithes in his native Württemberg, List worked hard to streamline the U.S. economy by offering free trade between the states and also by founding various railroads in Pennsylvania.

In 1870 the new Prussian Chancellor Otto von Bismarck united the remaining German states into the "smaller German" Reich, which lasted until World War I, but its military bluster in foreign affairs led to Germany's downfall in world affairs. Coupled with domestic unrest that erupted when Kaiser Wilhelm II attempted to suppress the domestic socialist working class, Germany in the early twentieth century struck up alliances with Austria and Ottoman Turkey that triggered fear abroad and ultimately the alliance between France, England, and Russia, which concluded with Germany's World War I defeat in November 1918.

Modern Era After the war the German Social Democrats and the Catholic Center Party wrote a constitution that instituted the Weimar Republic. From its outset, burdensome war reparations, inflation, foreign military occupation west of the Rhine, and heavy losses of territory doomed the republic. In 1925 Field Marshal von Hindenburg, a hero during World War I, was elected president. Following the onset of the worldwide economic depression in 1929, Hindenburg appointed Adolf Hitler to be chancellor in 1933. Hitler promptly banned all political parties, expelled Communists from the government, and restructured the military. Hitler's goals were to purify Germany by removing anyone without pure Teutonic blood and to expand German territory throughout Europe. By 1939 Germany had conquered Poland and was occupying Czechoslovakia and Austria. Germany took France the following year, along with Norway and whole regions of western Russia. In the process the policy was to exterminate unwanted peoples, including Jews, the Roma people, and others.

Hitler's death squads rounded up Jews in Germany and the occupied countries and sent them, along with Communists, clergy, disabled people, homosexuals, and political prisoners from Belgium, France, Greece, Italy, Holland, and the Soviet Union, to a series of work camps and death camps where many starved to death and many more were murdered outright. About six million Jews perished, but if Catholic clergy, prisoners of war, and forced work details are included, the figure is at least double that of Jews alone. Germany finally fell to the Allies in 1945, with Hitler dying in his Berlin bunker.

Following the war the Allies occupied the country. The western zones were then consolidated as the Federal Republic of Germany in 1948, and the Soviet-occupied eastern zones became a Russian satellite called the German Democratic Republic. For nearly 40 years distrust between East Germans and West Germans was encouraged by the Soviet Union on the one hand and by the West on the other. Both feared a united Germany. In 1989 demonstrations in East Germany caused the Communist regime to relent, and the Berlin Wall, which isolated West Berlin from East Berlin and Eastern Germany, was opened on November 9. On October 3, 1990, Germany was officially reunited, and Berlin became the nation's capital. In the decades of separation, West Germany had become a modern economic and industrial powerhouse, while East Germany had suffered from economic stagnation and cultural malaise.

Chancellor Helmut Kohl shepherded the united nation through its first few years, when economic matters were precarious; former West Germans blamed the former East Germans for the problems associated with addressing their aging infrastructure, lack of modernization, and high unemployment rate. Gerhard Schroeder became chancellor in 1998, leading a coalition government of the Social Democratic Party and the Green Party. He instituted the Agenda 2010 program, which sought to curtail the country's broad social welfare policies, lower taxes, and reform employment regulations. This program was decidedly unpopular. In 2002 Germany replaced the Deutsche Mark with the Euro and, as one of the stronger economies in Europe, took a leading role in the European Union.

In 2005 Angela Merkel, leader of the Christian Democratic Union, became chancellor, following a stalemate election that led to a coalition government between the CDU, the Christian Social Union, and the Social Democratic Party of Germany; Merkel was reelected in 2009. During her chancellorship, Merkel became the president of the European Council and was considered the leader of the European Union. Her negotiations during the debt crisis spawned by the global recession of 2008 proved key in keeping Greece from seceding from the European Union. Her leadership in the subsequent sovereign debt crisis led to calls for new austerity measures, which would upset decades of generous government support for most European citizens. While this resulted in her popularity plummeting, Merkel's deft negotiations during the fiscal crisis gained her the reputation as the most powerful woman in the world, according to *Forbes* magazine, and the second most powerful person in the world. Germany's economic state remained strong as the rest of the eurozone endured a period of austerity and uncertainty.

SETTLEMENT IN THE UNITED STATES

With their arrival at Jamestown in 1608 and for four centuries thereafter, Germans have been one of the three largest ethnic groups in American society. When Christopher Columbus discovered the Americas in 1492, he did so in the name of Ferdinand and Isabella of Spain—that is, with the entitlement of the Habsburgs, who also ruled Germany as part of the Holy Roman Empire. It was a German cartographer, Martin Waldseemüller, who suggested the New World be designated America.

Between 1671 and 1677 Pennsylvania founder William Penn made trips to Germany on behalf of his Quaker faith. His recruiting attracted the Mennonite settlers who founded Germantown in 1683, as well numerous others who created communities that were symbolic in two ways: they were specifically German-speaking and they were comprised of religious dissenters. Pennsylvania has remained the heartland for the various branches of Anabaptists (Old Order

Mennonites, Ephrata Cloisters, Brethren, and Amish), but it also became home for many Lutheran refugees from Catholic provinces (e.g., Salzburg), as well as Catholics who had been discriminated against in Protestant provinces.

Significant numbers of Germans immigrated to flee war and poverty. For example, in 1709, 15,000 Palatines fleeing a French invasion of the southwest German region called the Pfalz departed for England at the invitation of Queen Anne, who offered them money and land in the New World. Arriving on ten ships to New York harbor, 850 families settled in the Hudson River Valley, others went to Little Falls on the Mohawk River, and some to the Schoharie Valley. In 1734 another group of religiously persecuted emigrants, around 300 Protestants from the province of Salzburg, accepted Governor Oglethorpe's invitation to Georgia in 1734.

On balance, though, most of the immigration from Germany resulted not from religious persecution but economic conditions, as industrialization and urbanization resulted in widespread social and demographic changes. By the time of the first U.S. census in 1790, over 8.5 percent of the U.S. population was German, although in Pennsylvania it was more than 33 percent. During the Revolutionary War, the German Americans were numerically strengthened by the arrival of about 30,000 Hessian mercenaries who fought for England during the hostilities, of whom some 5,000 choose to remain in the New World after the war.

Until about 1815 Americans and some foreign shippers brought many Germans to the United States under the redemptioner system. The scheme was that a German peasant traveled on a sailing vessel without charge and upon arrival at an Atlantic port was sold to an American businessman to work from four to seven years to redeem his passage and win his freedom. For some of the early sectarians, including the Baptist Dunkers, the Schwenkfelders, and the Moravian Brethren, this was the only way to reach the United States.

Populous as German immigrants to America were by the end of the eighteenth century, the major waves of immigration awaited the conclusion of Napoleonic wars in 1815. Germany's economy began to suffer in several ways: Too many goods were imported, especially cloth, from an industrialized England. Antiquated inheritance laws in southwestern Germany caused land holdings to be subdivided continuously, rendering farms too miniscule for subsistence. Cottage industries collapsed when faced by a flood of foreign products. Finally, the population had skyrocketed and many were dependent on the potato crops. As in Ireland, rural Germany in the 1840s was suddenly hit by famine precipitated by a potato blight.

When the 1848 revolutions Europe failed to bring democracy to Germany, several thousand fugitives left for America in addition to nearly 750,000 more who immigrated in the following years. While a mere 6,000 Germans had entered the United States in the decade of the 1820s, nearly one million did so in the decade of the 1850s, the first great influx from Germany. Despite annual fluctuations, especially during the Civil War period when the decadal figure dropped to 723,000, the tide swelled again to 751,000 in the 1870s and peaked at 1,445,000 in the 1880s.

In the nineteenth century religious and political refugees were numerous. During the 1820s, for example, Prussia had forced a union of the Reformed and Lutheran congregations, which by the late 1830s caused many Old Lutherans to emigrate. Saxon followers of Martin Stephan came in 1839 to escape the "wickedness" of the Old World. Other refugees were the Pietists who founded communal societies in Harmony and Economy, Pennsylvania; Zoar, Ohio; St. Nazianz, Wisconsin; and Amana, Iowa.

Societies sponsored by German princes used emigration as a solution to social problems at home. For example, the Giessener Emigration Society (1833) and the Adelsverein of Texas (1843) operated on the principle that a one-way ticket for the downtrodden was cheaper than a long-term subsidy. Also influential in unleashing a tidal wave of German emigration were writers like Gottfried Duden whose 1829 book *Bericht über eine Reise nach den westlichen Staaten Nordamerika's* (Report of a Journey to the Western States of North America) was a bestseller and compared the Mississippi region to the Rhine region in Germany.

During the 1850s small farmers and their families dominated the first major wave of immigrants, who often came from southwest Germany. Soon after, artisans and household manufacturers were the main arrivals from the more central states of Germany, while day laborers and agricultural workers from the rural northeast states characterized subsequent waves of German immigrants. Not until Germany's industrialization process caught up with the English in the late nineteenth century did Germans no longer have to leave the country to improve their lives. Beginning in the late 1880s and for several decades thereafter, migration from depressed agricultural regions was destined less for America and more for the manufacturing regions of Berlin, the Ruhr, and the Rhine in Germany itself.

Interspersed among these waves of economic emigrants were also those fleeing a variety of oppression, including German Jews who left because of economic and social discrimination. Young men sometimes fled to avoid serving in the Prussian military service. Organized industrial laborers also fled the antisocialist laws enacted when a would-be assassin threatened the life of Germany's Kaiser Wilhelm I, who blamed Socialist labor leaders for the attempt. Catholics, too, were oppressed by Bismarck's infamous May Laws of the 1870s, sometimes called the *Kulturkampf*, which suppressed the Catholic Center Party and its drive for greater democracy during the first decade of the emperor's reign.

Also during the latter half of the nineteenth century, agents fanned out across Germany to drum up emigration. Some were outright recruiters operating against the law. Others were agencies that took the form of aid societies working to better the lot of the emigrés in Germany, such as the Catholic Raphael Society, the Bavarian *Ludwigmissionsverein*, the Leopoldinen *Stiftung* in Vienna, the Pietist society of Herrnhut in Saxony, and the Lutheran support groups of Neuendettelsau in Franconia in northern Bavaria. Frankenmuth, Michigan, for example, traces its roots to such Lutheran groups. Aiding the immigrants on this side of the Atlantic were the Catholic Leo House in New York and the Central-Verein in St. Louis. Much better funded promoters were those established by the North Central states (most prominently Michigan, Wisconsin, and Minnesota) as they joined the Union, many of which had ample support from legislatures for their Immigration Commissioners. Even more influential were the transcontinental railroads that sent agents to the ports of debarkation along the Atlantic and Germany to recruit immigrants either to take up their land grants or to supply freight activity for their lines. Especially active was the Northern Pacific during the time when German immigrant Henry Villard headed the corporation and sought to populate his land grant with industrious German farmers.

In the latter phases of German immigration newcomers joined established countrymen in a phenomenon called chain migration. Chain migration is defined as the movement of families or individuals to join friends and family members already established in a given place. Chain migration strengthened already existing German regions of the United States. One such concentrated settlement pattern gave rise to the so-called "German triangle," defined by St. Paul, Minnesota; St. Louis, Missouri; and Cincinnati, Ohio, with lines stretching between them so that the triangle incorporated Chicago, Indianapolis, Fort Wayne, Milwaukee, Davenport, and other strongly German cities. Other descriptors include the more accurate "German parallelogram," which stretches from Albany, New York, westward along the Erie Canal to Buffalo and farther westward through Detroit to St. Paul and the Dakotas, then south to Nebraska and Kansas, back to Missouri and eastward along the Ohio River to Baltimore. Except for large settlements in Texas, San Francisco, and Florida, German settlement is still largely contained within this German belt.

Data collected by the U.S. Census Bureau shows that German, Irish, and English are the most frequently reported ancestry groups. According to the Census Bureau's American Community Survey estimates for 2009–2011, about 49 million persons claim German ancestry, many more than the second-place group, the Irish, with 35 million. In terms of distribution, the 2000 census data confirm

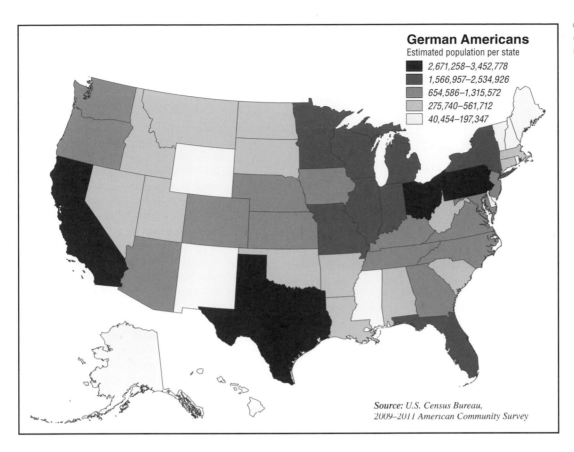

German Americans
Estimated population per state
■ 2,671,258–3,452,778
■ 1,566,957–2,534,926
■ 654,586–1,315,572
■ 275,740–561,712
□ 40,454–197,347

*Source: U.S. Census Bureau,
2009–2011 American Community Survey*

that those of German heritage predominate in the northern half of the country, as well as Florida and Alaska. Those of German heritage form the plurality of the population from Pennsylvania in the east to Oregon and Washington in the West, with every Midwestern and Western state in between (the exceptions being Utah, California, Arizona, New Mexico, and Texas). States with the highest total population of German Americans include California (3.3 million), Pennsylvania (3.4 million), Ohio (over 3 million), Wisconsin (2.4 million), New York (2.1 million), Michigan (2.1 million), Texas (2.6 million), Florida (2.1 million), and Illinois (2.5 million).

LANGUAGE

The German language is related to Danish, Norwegian, Swedish, Icelandic, and English—the so-called Germanic languages. High German, the dialect spoken in the east-west central geographic elevation, differs linguistically from the language spoken in the lower-lying topographical regions of northern Germany, where Low German was once in everyday usage. It is also different from Bavarian and Swiss German that is typically spoken in the southern, more Alpine regions.

According to 2011 American Community Survey estimates, about 1.1 million people speak German at home in the United States; this was down from 1.38 million in the 2000 Census. Of these, only about

188,000 spoke English less than "very well." Among the Pennsylvania Dutch, roughly 18 percent speak a language other than English at home—for many, a dialect of German known as *Deitsch*.

German was widely spoken by millions of U.S. immigrants, and many American communities had German-language newspapers until the outbreak of World War I, at which time speaking German fell out of favor (and was sometimes outlawed) in many communities as anti-German sentiments rose. Such sentiments declined following World War II amid increasing American interests in Germany and Germany's increasing economic importance. German is now taught in many American schools as an elective and is the third most popular foreign language to study after Spanish and French.

RELIGION

Religious differences have characterized the German people since 1517, when Martin Luther challenged Catholic papal authority. In the first wave of the nineteenth century, German immigrants to the United States largely came from the conservative Reformed and Old Lutheran denominations. They founded several synods throughout the country, including the Missouri Synod in Chicago in 1847. In 2013 the Missouri Synod had 2.3 million members, most of whom were concentrated in the upper Midwest. Many smaller Lutheran denominations formed by

During World War I, German "aliens" living in New York City's "Little Germany" (Yorkville) line up to be fingerprinted and registered at the East 68th Street police station, in 1918. BETTMANN / CORBIS

German and Scandinavian immigrants merged into the Evangelical Lutheran Church in America (ELCA) in 1988. Headquartered in Chicago, the relatively liberal synod (as opposed to the Missouri Synod) has about 4 million members. The Wisconsin Synod, most conservative of the three major Lutheran groups, was founded in 1850 in Milwaukee and has roughly 380,000 members. Other Protestant German immigrants, namely Calvinists, formed what later became the United Church of Christ, and some immigrants joined Methodist churches. Mennonite and Quaker groups were among the first encouraged to immigrate to the United States at the behest of William Penn. A number of such families founded Germantown, Pennsylvania, in 1683; the Pennsylvania Dutch followed in the eighteenth century and settled in Lancaster, Pennsylvania.

In the nineteenth century, many German immigrants to the United States were Roman Catholic. German churches that used the German language exclusively featured a liturgy rich with ritual and music and offered its parishioners a variety of associations and societies. They also addressed numerous social needs by supporting and operating orphanages and hospitals. By the late twentieth century, however, many German American Catholic parishes experienced attrition, following the national trend for most Catholic parishes and mainline Protestant congregations.

German Americans' views toward religion today reflect those of Americans overall. Most continue to identify as Protestant but do not necessarily practice as devoutly as their ancestors did. For instance, while its membership includes many Scandinavian Americans and people of other ethnicities, the ELCA—the nation's largest Lutheran sect—reported a 21 percent decline in church attendance from 2001 to 2008. Declines were also reported in the more German American-dominated LCMS and Wisconsin Synod sects of the Lutheran Church. Many German

Americans were following religious trends among Americans overall, including larger numbers gravitating toward large nondenominational Christian churches, and many were also abandoning religious practice altogether.

CULTURE AND ASSIMILATION

In many respects Germans were slower to assimilate than their fellow immigrants from other countries. This was due in part to their size and percentage of the population. With most of their needs provided by their own ethnic communities, assimilation was not urgent. Germans had their own professionals, businesses, churches, and schools. However, second generation German immigrants were drawn more quickly into the mainstream, and the survival of German communities depended upon immigration. Assimilation hastened during World War I, when some communities passed laws that prevented people from speaking German in public.

In the post–World War II era, the days of mass immigration from Germany were long over, and German Americans' perception of their heritage became associated with certain icons and costumes, notably Oktoberfest celebrations, high-quality sports cars, sausage and sauerkraut, and Bavarian folk music. In the United States, Bavarian culture is regarded as synonymous with all of German culture, even though Bavarian customs and language are confined to the southeastern regional state of Bavaria and its capital, Munich. German Day festivals almost always feature Bavarian dance and clothing such as *lederhosen* (men's leather shorts with suspenders) and the *dirndl* (women's full skirt). Replicas of German cities—such as Leavenworth, Washington, or Frankenmuth, Michigan—assume an air of Alpine Bavaria.

Traditions and Customs In addition to customs discussed elsewhere, one of German Americans' most enduring customs has been a tradition of social beer drinking. In the nineteenth century many American cities had great numbers of German pubs, and the brewing industry was dominated by German Americans. At that time, many German Americans also would imbibe at German societies, clubs, or family-friendly beer gardens, where they could speak German and mingle with fellow immigrants. Though the tradition of German clubs largely died by World War I, the tradition of saluting one's host or guests with a toast of "*Prost!*" endures. However, although German American culture, especially for men, is still often associated with heavy beer drinking and attendant rowdiness—and Germany continues to have one of the highest rates of alcohol consumption in the world—there is little evidence that German Americans consume more alcohol than other ethnic groups in the United States today.

German Americans also have strong traditions of physical activity, particularly in the outdoors. Activities like skiing, skating, shooting, and hiking have long been popular among German Americans as they are in Germany, with whole families often enjoying such activities together. Some claim that the concept of a picnic was brought to the United States by Germans.

Cuisine German American cuisine has been called a "forgotten cuisine" in American culture. This is not because its dishes are no longer enjoyed, but because they have become so ubiquitous in American culture—and in many cases global culture—that they are no longer recognized as being of German origin. Such dishes, introduced to this continent by German Americans, include hamburgers, frankfurters (hot dogs), jelly doughnuts, cheesecake, and potato salad. Other German American-introduced foods and drinks include lager beer (America's most heavily-consumed beer), pretzels, sauerkraut, and several kinds of sausages and breads. To varying extent, these foods have been so Americanized that they bear only a passing resemblance to dishes still eaten in Germany.

German American restaurants are common in most major American cities as well and can also be found in rural areas with a large German American population like the Pennsylvania Dutch Country, Wisconsin, or Iowa. Typically, their menus are heavy on meat dishes, including *schnitzels* (fried pork and chicken), sausages, and *sauerbraten*, a German pot roast that is typically marinated for several days in vinegar with seasonings. Common sides at these restaurants include *spätzle*, a soft egg and flour noodle; boiled potatoes; and potato pancakes—the latter of which is rarely seen in Germany. Also common at these restaurants are *biergartens*, or beer gardens, outdoor drinking areas with a wide selection of beers from Germany and other European nations. German American cuisine is especially common at Oktoberfest celebrations in communities of all sizes, and "sausage feeds," or sausage dinners, are common in many rural communities as well.

Traditional Dress Being a nation of many distinct regional customs, Germany has a wide array of traditional dress and costumes. Most German Americans do not wear any traditional clothing, except during festivals like Oktoberfest, when Bavarian clothing is common. This includes *lederhosen* for men, which are shorts and suspenders often made of leather, and *dirndl* for women, an outfit featuring a bodice, blouse, skirt, and apron, usually in bright colors.

Dances and Songs German-produced instruments that remain popular in the United States include the Chemnitzer concertina, which looks like a small accordion, and the accordion itself, first as made by Hohner and today made by Weltmeister. While the waltz and the polka might have had their origins in Austria and Bohemia respectively, other eastern European immigrants are likewise fond of these dances performed to their regional folk tunes. Especially folkloric for Germans are the oompa bands of the upper Plains and the industrial heartland, from Chicago,

Illinois, to Philadelphia, Pennsylvania. Germans in the United States continued the tradition of the Sängerfest, a gathering of competitive choirs (called a Sängerbund) who performed competitively in events that sometimes lasted for days. These events reached their zenith at the turn of the twentieth century and waned after World War I. Today Sängerfests are still held in areas with high number of people of German heritage, such as Pennsylvania and Wisconsin.

Holidays In addition to traditional American holidays, many German American Catholic communities celebrate Corpus Christi, which includes outdoor processions to altars decorated with flowers. On Epiphany (January 6), children dressed as the three wise men, adorned with paper crowns, carry a star on a short pole and sing traditional songs in exchange for treats as they go door to door. Catholic Christmas traditions served as the basis for American celebrations—the exchange of gifts, as well as the Christmas tree, a custom deriving from early modern Germany and sometimes still illuminated by real candles as widely practiced in Germany. December 6 was the traditional visit of St. Nicholas, a custom that evolved into the Americanized jolly form of Santa Claus. Similarly, the Easter Bunny (*Osterhase*) originated in German folklore, though like the Christmas traditions, it is so well absorbed into general American holiday celebrations that it is not typically recognized as a German American contribution.

In the United States, Bavarian culture is regarded as synonymous with all of German culture, even though Bavarian customs and language are confined to the southeastern regional state of Bavaria and its capital, Munich.

Groundhog Day, February 2, is a custom carried on by the Pennsylvania Dutch immigrants who brought it with them from the Palantinate region, where Candlemas Day was held to brighten the dark days of winter. Many immigrants, who were farmers, looked for signs of spring on this day and took stock of the supplies that had to last the rest of the winter. Looking for an animal's shadow—initially a bear or a hedgehog, which became standardized as a groundhog in the United States—became a tell-tale sign of six more weeks of winter.

October 6 was declared German American Day by President Reagan in 1983, the three hundredth anniversary of the arrival of the first Germantown settlers. Congress made the designation permanent in 1987. Several American cities feature German American parades on or around this date. Often called a "Von Steuben Parade" in honor of Friedrich Wilhelm Von Steuben, a general in the Revolutionary

THE AMERICAN TURNERS

Gymnastics are another popular activity that German immigrants brought to the United States. In Germany in the nineteenth century, athletic clubs called *turnvereine* (from *turnen*, meaning to perform gymnastics, and *verein*, meaning club) were popular. German immigrants in the United States established their own societies, which became known as "Turners," and some cities built large facilities to host games and practice. The Turners had a slight political bent to them, and many were active in labor causes and hosted large festivals for gymnastic competitions. Their slogan *frisch, fromm, frölich, frei* (fresh, pious, happy, free) promoted the idea of maintaining a sound body and mind. Like many other German traditions, the turnvereine declined in popularity after World War I, but several dozen Turner groups are still active in the United States in the early twenty-first century.

War, the parades typically feature traditional German music and dress, dancing, and associated banquets and galas. New York, Philadelphia, and Chicago have the nation's largest Von Steuben parades. The tradition of the parades began in New York in 1957.

Oktoberfest is also a very popular German American festival. Originating in 1810 in Munich as a wedding party for Crown Prince Ludwig, Oktoberfest is still Germany's largest annual festival. German American immigrants brought the Oktoberfest tradition to the United States in the nineteenth century, and today Oktoberfests are celebrated in many American cities in late September or early October. Though the original was a two-week festival, most in the United States last for a weekend at most. They are an opportunity for German Americans and Americans generally to celebrate German culture and feature a wide selection of beers, typically in German styles if not of German origin; German music, usually from the Bavaria region; and some German costumes, as noted above. The largest Oktoberfests in the United States are in Cincinnati (about 500,000 annual attendees) and Denver (about 450,000 attendees), but they are common in communities large and small; by some counts, there several hundred annual Oktoberfest celebrations in the United States.

Death and Burial In the nineteenth century many German American cemeteries were quite elaborate, including Prospect Hill Cemetery in Washington, D.C., the German Lutheran Cemetery in Philadelphia, and Union Cemetery in Milwaukee. Use of cast iron grave markers was once common. Traditional German American headstone epitaphs included *Hier Liegt* ("Here Lies") and *Hier Ruht* ("Here Rests"). Markers also long included symbols intended to ward off evil spirits, like rosettes, stars, and pentagrams, though

these are less common today. At one time the deceased was dressed by the family; today this is generally handled by funeral home professionals. For some conservative German Americans, particularly Mennonites, cremation is still viewed as inappropriate. In earlier times, German Americans visited the burial sites of their relatives frequently, often at least monthly. This is less common today.

FAMILY AND COMMUNITY LIFE

Early German immigrants who were farmers tried to purchase land and homes as soon as they were able. As a result, few were tenant farmers. German Americans placed a high value on home ownership and often constructed their houses of brick or stone. Such an attitude about financial security persists among German Americans today, though many aspects of their culture are hard to separate from American culture generally.

Gender Roles The traditional German American family was patriarchal, with women taking care of the home and children. Farm families were large, and wives and daughters worked with the sons and fathers to manage the harvest and livestock. Children frequently left school early to help with farm work full-time. According to the 1880 U.S. Census figures, a smaller proportion of German American women were part of the work force than women in other immigrant groups. Some who worked outside the home worked in factories or in jobs where knowledge of English was necessary.

Many nineteenth-century German Americans held fairly rigid attitudes toward gender roles, with adult males working outside the home and women rearing children and looking after household affairs. Fathers were considered the stricter parent, and families were considered to be more emotionally reserved than other ethnic groups. Today gender roles among German Americans reflect those of American society at large.

According to American Community Survey estimates from 2010, a majority of German American households with children and two parents had both parents working—66 percent in households with children under 6 years of age, rising to 74 percent in households with older children. German American women were about five times as likely to be a single parent than German American men, reflecting the fact that childrearing still falls predominantly on women; this difference between women and men was true for Americans overall. German American women participated in the labor force at roughly the same rates as men and had roughly the same educational attainment, though they were more likely to work in business or service occupations than men, who were more evenly spread across industries, including manual occupations.

Education German Americans in the eighteenth and nineteenth centuries maintained their own German-language schools, first by establishing their own institutions and later by pressuring school districts to offer curriculum in German. Additionally, parochial schools operated by Catholics and Lutherans enrolled thousands of the children of German immigrants. Some German-language schools were sponsored by non-religious organizations, such as a local German school society. Sometimes these schools offered new pedagogical principles that had a lasting impact on the American school system. For example, they introduced the German concept of kindergarten as a transition year between home and full-time school, and at higher grades they instituted sports programs that stemmed from the German Turner societies. The German immigrants of the Moravian Protestant denomination founded Salem College in Winston-Salem, North Carolina, in 1772, which was the first institution of higher education devoted exclusively to girls and women. Many religious colleges, including Wartburg, Wittenberg, and Capital University, were founded by German immigrants.

In 1890 the Wisconsin legislature passed the Bennett Law. This required that children attend school more regularly and added the stipulation that at least some subjects be taught in English. In Illinois a similar measure surfaced as the Edwards Law. As a result, the Lutheran and Catholic constituents of these states campaigned to defeat Wisconsin's governor William Dempster Hoard and to free the German language schools of state intervention. Over time, despite their efforts, German faded in favor of English instruction. To supply teachers for these many schools, German Americans maintained a teachers' college, while Turner gymnastic societies developed their own teacher preparation institute. After the turn of the twentieth century, the German American Alliance promoted teaching German in part to preserve their culture and to maintain an audience for German-language newspapers and books.

Elementary German language school enrollments reached their zenith between 1880 and 1900. In 1881 more than 160,000 pupils were attending German Catholic schools, and almost 50,000 were in Missouri Synod Lutheran schools. Of the roughly half million people attending school with a curriculum partly or all in German, 42 percent were attending public schools, more than a third were in Catholic schools, and 16 percent were in Lutheran private schools. However, when World War I broke out, legal action was brought against some organizations not only to dampen considerable German cultural activities but also to eliminate the German language from American schools. The flagship case was the Mockett Law in Nebraska, which anti-German enthusiasts repealed. Eventually 26 other states followed suit, banning instruction in German and of German. On June 4, 1923, the Supreme Court ruled that a mere knowledge of German could not be regarded as harmful to the state, and the majority opinion added that the right of parents to have their children taught in a language other than English was within the liberties guaranteed by the Fourteenth Amendment. Nevertheless, as a language of instruction in schools, during church service, and at home, German was gradually overshadowed by English as assimilation accelerated.

Today most German American children attend public schools and learn in English. They continue to have high levels of academic achievement. According to American Community Survey estimates from 2011, 90 percent—both male and female—earn high school diplomas, about 7 percent points higher than the general population. About 34 percent of German Americans earn college degrees, higher than the national average of roughly 28 percent.

Courtship and Weddings Except in more closed religious or rural communities, German Americans have intermarried with other ethnic groups fairly frequently since the eighteenth century. Weddings among Lutheran or Catholic German Americans generally follow American customs: couples generally marry for love, choosing their own partners, although the groom may formally ask permission from the bride's father first. Weddings are often held in churches, followed by lively celebrations with dancing, drinking, and a formal dinner.

Until the mid-twentieth century, some Mennonite and other conservative German American religious communities practiced a more secretive form of courtship, wherein a couple's plans to marry were kept secret until a few weeks before the wedding, when the plans were announced or "published" in church. Sexual relations before marriage were strictly forbidden, and divorce was very rarely allowed. Wedding ceremonies often did not include many elements that have long been common among Protestants: rings were not used until the 1950s, hymns were sung by a choir in place of more common wedding music, and even kissing at the end of the ceremony remained uncommon until the twentieth century. After World War II, however, these differences largely disappeared. Still, among Mennonites and other Anabaptist groups today, wedding attire is often simpler, but the ceremony and reception are very similar—except the absence of alcohol, which is often forbidden among these groups.

EMPLOYMENT AND ECONOMIC CONDITIONS

Many German immigrants of the eighteenth and nineteenth centuries, in addition to being farmers, were skilled in trades such as baking, carpentry, brewing, and machinery. Others were musicians, merchants, and builders. According to the 1870 census figures, 27 percent of German Americans were employed in agriculture, 23 percent in the professions, and 13 percent in trades and transportation. By 1890, however, around 45 percent reportedly were laborers or servants, perhaps as a result of recent immigration by industrial workers rather than farmers. This may explain why the labor movement in the United States gained considerable impetus from German immigrants. The mid-nineteenth century witnessed the introduction of the Communist ideologies of Wilhelm Weitling (1808–1871) and Joseph Weydemeyer (1818–1866), which gave rise to early struggles for social and economic reform. The International Workingmen's Association in America was founded in 1869 as the first of the Communist and socialist groups in the United States, and its membership was predominately German American. In 1886 German American anarchists were also instrumental in the labor movement implicated in the Chicago Haymarket bombing during the labor strikes of that period.

Had it not been for the greater need for workers to unite against their employers and join the American Federation of Labor (AFL), German trade unions might have been consolidated in the late 1880s. In future years many leaders of American labor were German American, including Walter Reuther, who fought on the picket lines during the 1930s before becoming president of the AFL-CIO following World War II. For German immigrants, labor union membership led to improved working conditions and helped them form solidarity with workers from other ethnic backgrounds as well. In the twenty-first century only a minority of workers belong to labor unions, and many German-owned companies operating in the United States, including Daimler AG, Siemens, BASF, and BMW of North America, have followed the trend in declining union membership among its employees.

Reflecting their size within the American populace, in 2011 German Americans' economic and employment conditions closely mirrored those of Americans overall. According to the American Community Survey's estimates from that year, German Americans were split among occupations and industries almost exactly along the same percentages as Americans overall, and their median household income was very close to the national average. Significantly fewer German Americans received supplemental food assistance or food stamps—about 5.4 percent versus 10.2 percent for the country overall. Similarly, poverty rates were roughly half those of the American average.

POLITICS AND GOVERNMENT

As the German American population swelled in the nineteenth century, both the Democratic and Republican parties made overtures to them, through such policies as allowing German language schools, ease of naturalization, and lower fees and taxes for German-dominated industries such as brewing. Although the Democratic Party had generally been more successful at attracting German Americans and other immigrant groups before the Civil War, loyalty to Abraham Lincoln and the Union brought many Northern German Americans to the Republican Party in the late nineteenth century.

Throughout the nineteenth century, many German Americans maintained distinct love for their

In Amana, Iowa, a worker makes furniture at the Amana Furniture & Clock Shop. The shop was opened when German immigrants established the communal Amana Colonies in 1855. JIM WEST / ALAMY

German homeland in addition to their allegiance to the United States. As German American politician Carl Schurz put it, it was like loving one's mother along with one's wife: the two are not incompatible. But as World War I erupted, such a dual loyalty was suddenly called into question. Many leading German Americans opposed the United States' entry into the war, though after Congress declared war, most German Americans expressed uncompromised loyalty to the United States. This was not enough to satisfy many nativists, who persecuted German Americans regardless of their position on the war and renamed streets, stores, and even sauerkraut ("liberty cabbage") in an attempt to erase German Americans' considerable influence on American society.

After the war these tensions abated for the most part, but it signaled the end of German language politics and education. Stunned and perhaps resentful of the bitter treatment they had received, German Americans helped oust Democrat Woodrow Wilson and then shunned major leaders in both parties for a time, supporting third-party candidates for Congress and the presidency in elections during the 1920s. During this period, fearing threats to their success in the brewing industry (as well as their culture of consuming beer), German Americans also fiercely protested Prohibition and temperance reforms as they swept the country. The Democratic Party also opposed Prohibition, and by the 1930s many German Americans had returned to the party, with great numbers supporting Franklin Delano Roosevelt, who campaigned for repeal of Prohibition. Yet some German Americans continued to be thoroughly isolationist, as it appeared that the country was headed toward another European war. When the United States declared war against the Axis powers in 1941, the vast majority of German Americans supported this choice.

After the war German American political allegiances were less cohesive than they had been in the past. Many supported Harry Truman in 1948, resulting in Truman's surprise upset of Thomas E. Dewey. Truman had taken a stand against Joseph Stalin at the Potsdam Conference in 1945, implemented the Marshall Plan to rebuild Europe (including Germany) in 1946, steadily opposed Communism in Europe, and initiated the Berlin Airlift in May 1948, all of which endeared Truman to the German Americans. Later in the twentieth century, however, some German Americans supported liberal candidates, while others supported conservative candidates. By the late twentieth century, German Americans had ceased to be a significantly visible voting bloc.

NOTABLE INDIVIDUALS

Academia Hannah Arendt (1906–1975) was a Jewish, German-born writer and professor. Her most notable publication is *The Origins of Totalitarianism* (1951). She taught at University of California Berkeley, Princeton University, and the University of Chicago.

Franz Boas (1858–1942) has been called the "father of modern anthropology." Trained as a geographer in Germany, he became known for detailed studies of the Inuit and other native peoples of Canada and became a professor at Columbia University in 1896. As an organizer of the American Anthropological Association, he was instrumental in shaping the discipline.

Architecture Walter Gropius (1883–1969) was a German architect and founder of the Bauhaus School who immigrated to the United States in 1934 and influenced post-war architecture by popularizing International Modernism. He taught at the Harvard Graduate School of Design.

Ludwig Mies van der Rohe (1886–1969) was an architect and guided the Bauhaus movement after its move to Chicago and Boston. In Chicago he was head of the school of architecture at the Armour Institute of Technology and ushered in the International Style that became omnipresent in the 1950s.

Helmut Jahn (1940–), born in Nuremberg, is an architect whose works include the Citigroup Center tower in Chicago, terminals at Chicago's O'Hare International Airport, and the Veer Towers in Las Vegas. He is also famous for the Kemper Center in Kansas City and the Auraria Library in Denver, in addition to the Potsdam Platz structures in Berlin, the Weser Tower in Bremen, and Munich Airport.

Art Albert Bierstadt (1830–1902) immigrated to the United States as a child and later founded the Hudson River School and painted dramatic scenes of the American West.

Josef Albers (1888–1976) was a graphic artist and member of Germany's Bauhaus school of architecture and design who immigrated to the United States to teach at North Carolina's Black Mountain College when the Nazis closed down the Bauhaus in 1933. Later he taught design at Yale.

Thomas Nast (1840–1902) was an artist who created both the donkey and the elephant mascots that have long symbolized the American Democratic Party and the Republican Party, respectively.

Alfred Stieglitz (1864–1946) was a pioneering photographer in New York City at the turn of the twentieth century. He was born in New Jersey to German Jewish immigrants.

Hilla Von Rebay (1890–1967) was born in Germany and became a notable abstract painter in the early twentieth century. She immigrated to the United States in 1927 and helped her friend Solomon Guggenheim collect the works of art that created the Guggenheim Museum in New York.

Anni Albers (born Annelise Fleischmann, 1899–1994) was one of the twentieth century's most notable textile artists, known especially for her weaving. Born in Berlin, she married famous glass artist Josef Albers (1888–1976) in 1925, and the two immigrated to the

United States in 1933. She and her husband became important collectors and teachers of art, and her books on textiles and design were highly acclaimed. In 1980 she was awarded the American Craft Council's Gold Medal for "uncompromising excellence." Her life's work elevated the field of fiber and textile arts considerably in the United States.

Business Eberhard Anheuser (1805–1880), a candle maker born in Germany, was the founder of what became the Anheuser-Busch Company, one of the world's largest breweries.

Adolphus Busch (1839–1913) was a German-born businessman and cofounder of the Anheuser-Busch Company with his father-in-law.

Adolph Kohrs (1847–1929), also spelled Coors, was born in Barmen, Germany, and immigrated to the United States in 1868, moving to Denver in 1872. In 1873 he cofounded the Golden Brewery and by 1880 was its sole owner, changing its name to Coors Brewing.

John D. Rockefeller (1839–1937) was the founder of the Standard Oil Company and a philanthropist who founded the Rockefeller University and the University of Chicago. He was born in New York to parents with German ancestry.

Peter Thiel (1967–) is a venture capitalist and hedge fund manager who was an early investor in Facebook. He was born in Germany but raised in California.

Donald Trump (1946–) is a real estate developer and television personality. As head of the Trump Organization, he has engaged in real estate ventures around the world. His paternal grandparents were German immigrants.

Commerce and Industry Eric Schmidt (1955–) was the CEO of Google from 2001 to 2011, during which time he worked closely with founders Larry Page and Sergey Brin to turn the Internet search company from an upstart into one of the most successful companies in the world.

Walter P. Chrysler (1875–1940) founded the Chrysler Corporation in 1925, soon becoming one of the world's most successful automobile companies.

John Roebling (1806–1869) was a German-born civil engineer. He and his son Washington built the Brooklyn Bridge based on a revolutionary new design for building bridges that incorporated wire suspensions.

Levi Strauss (1829–1902) was born in Bavaria and immigrated to America at the age of 18, where he joined his brothers' dry goods business. In 1853 he opened a West Coast branch of the company in San Francisco and in 1872 began manufacturing his signature jeans.

John Jacob Astor (1763–1848) immigrated to the newly independent United States from Germany after the Revolutionary War. He became the young country's first millionaire due to his business ventures in fur trading and real estate.

Friedrich Weyerhauser (1834–1914) was the country's most powerful timber baron in the nineteenth century, creating an empire that controlled timber production in much of the upper Mississippi basin and the Pacific Northwest. His company remains the largest seller of timber in the world. Born to a farming family in Germany, he immigrated to western Pennsylvania at the age of 18, joining family members there before branching out on his own.

Culinary Arts Irma Rombauer (1877–1962), who lived her entire life in St. Louis, is credited with shaping American home cooking to a greater extent than almost any other American. Her *Joy of Cooking* cookbook, originally self-published in 1931, went on to become one of the world's most-published cookbooks, passing through several editions and still in print today. The first edition was illustrated by Rombauer's daughter, Marion Rombauer Becker (1903–1976), who was credited as a coauthor for later editions.

Education Maria Kraus-Boelté (1836–1918) was a major proponent of formalized kindergartens in the United States. Born in Germany, she moved to New York in 1872 and established a model kindergarten while also promoting the concept through widely read books.

Ruth Westheimer (1928–) is a German-born psychologist and sex therapist who escaped Nazi Germany at the outbreak of World War II. She immigrated to the United States in 1956, where she received several degrees in sociology, education, and human sexuality. In the 1980s, she gained renown as a radio personality through her syndicated talk show, *Sexually Speaking*.

Fashion Heidi Klum (1973–) is a model, designer, and television personality. After rising to prominence in the 1990s as a Victoria's Secret model, she appeared in a wide range of advertisements well beyond the fashion industry, and by 2011 she was ranked second on *Forbes'* list of top-earning models. She was also a host and judge on the popular reality television show *Project Runway*. Born and raised near Cologne, Germany, she became an American citizen in 2008.

Government Carl Schurz (1829–1906) served as ambassador to Spain, became a general in the Civil War, was elected U.S. senator from Missouri, and finally was appointed Secretary of the Interior under Rutherford Hayes.

John P. Altgeld (1847–1902), a German who became a Progressive Democrat, was elected in 1893 governor of Illinois, where he favored labor activists and other progressive causes.

Herbert Hoover (1874–1964), born to Quaker parents in Iowa, was the first American president (1929–1933) of German descent (on his father's side).

Dwight D. "Ike" Eisenhower (1890–1969) was the first American president with a German surname. His ancestors originally settled in Pennsylvania but later moved to Texas and then Kansas. Eisenhower did not necessarily identify with his German heritage; during World War II he served as the Supreme Commander of the Allied Forces in Europe and was instrumental in defeating the German-led Axis Powers.

Richard Milhous Nixon (1913–1994) served as U.S. president from 1969 to 1974. He began his political career as a Republican representative and then senator from California.

Chester W. Nimitz (1885–1966) was a five-star admiral of the U.S. Navy and the commander in chief of the Pacific Fleet during World War II.

Norman Schwarzkopf (1934–2012), commander of the coalition forces in the Persian Gulf War, was of German lineage.

John Boehner (1949–) was elected to U.S. Congress in 1991 and served as speaker of the U.S. House of Representatives beginning in 2011.

Henry Kissinger (1923–) was born in Bavaria and immigrated with his family to New York in 1938. A noted diplomat and the Secretary of State under President Nixon and President Ford, Kissinger received the Nobel Peace Prize in 1973 for his work in bringing peace to Vietnam.

Literature Theodore Dreiser (1871–1945) was an American novelist known especially for *Sister Carrie* (1900) and *An American Tragedy* (1925). His father was a German immigrant.

John Steinbeck (1902–1968) was the author of the novels *Of Mice and Men* (1937) and *The Grapes of Wrath* (1939) and received the Nobel Prize for Literature in 1962.

Kurt Vonnegut (1922–2007) was the author of many well-regarded novels, including *Slaughterhouse-Five* (1969), which was influenced by his experience as a prisoner of war in World War II.

Theodor Seuss Geisel (1904–1991), better known as the children's writer Dr. Seuss, was a second-generation German American who worked in advertising and as a cartoonist for the U.S. Army during World War II before he wrote such classics as *Green Eggs and Ham* and *The Cat in the Hat*.

Charles Bukowski (born Heinrich Karl Bukowski, 1920–1994) was born in Germany shortly after World War I; his father, whose parents had immigrated to the United States in the 1880s, had returned to Germany as a soldier in the U.S. Army, while his mother was from the local community. Raised in Los Angeles, Bukowski became a noted countercultural poet and novelist who published prolifically and remains a cult favorite.

Gertrude Stein (1874–1946) was born in Pennsylvania to German-Jewish parents but lived for much of her life in France, where she led a group of vanguard expatriate American writers and artists. She published her most famous work, *The Autobiography of Alice B. Toklas*, in 1933; Toklas was her partner for much of her life. She was also a major collector of art.

Sylvia Plath (1932–1963) was born in Boston to an Austrian American mother and a German father. She published a number of highly acclaimed collections of poetry and short stories exploring themes of nature, death, resurrection, and mental illness. She was awarded a posthumous Pulitzer Prize in 1982.

Kathy Acker (1947–1997) was a noted feminist novelist, playwright, critic, and literary theorist who explored themes of sex, punk culture, and gender. Among her most famous works was *Blood and Guts in High School* (1984), an explicit novel that was banned in Germany.

Music Walter Johannes Damrosch (1862–1950) was a conductor and composer born in Breslau, Germany (now Wroclaw, Poland), who was the conductor of the NBC symphony orchestra from 1928 to 1942. His father Leopold and brother Frank were also prominent musicians.

Oscar Hammerstein (1847–1919) was born in Stettin, Pomerania (now part of Poland). He arrived in New York during the Civil War in 1864. Best known as an opera promoter, Hammerstein was also an inventor, writer, editor, publisher, composer, and showman, whose nickname is the "Father of Times Square."

Oscar Hammerstein II (1895–1960) was born in New York in 1895 and later became famous as half of the Broadway musical production team of Rodgers and Hammerstein. The duo created a string of popular musicals, including *Oklahoma!*, *South Pacific*, and *The Sound of Music*.

John Denver (born Henry Deutschendorf, Jr., 1943–1997) was a folk singer-songwriter popular in the 1970s and 1980s. He adopted his stage name in honor of his favorite state, Colorado. Among his most famous songs were "Country Roads, Take Me Home" (1971), "Sunshine On My Shoulders" (1972), and "Rocky Mountain High" (1972).

Alison Krauss (1971–) is a bluegrass and country singer-songwriter. Performing with the band Union Station since the late 1980s, she is well known for her performances on the soundtracks of *Oh Brother, Where Art Thou?* and *Cold Mountain*. By 2012 she had won 27 Grammy Awards. Her father was a German immigrant and language teacher who came to the United States in 1952.

Religion Reinhold Niehbur (1892–1971) was among the most important Protestant theologians of the twentieth century. Beginning as a pastor in a German-speaking church in Detroit, he became a significant figure in American public affairs from the 1930s through the 1960s, introducing Christian Realism, articulating the concept of "just war," and supporting the fight for equal opportunity regardless of race or religion. He received the Presidential Medal of Freedom in 1964.

Paul Tillich (1886–1965) was also one of the most important Protestant theologians of the twentieth century. He was born in Germany and lived much of his life there, immigrating to the United States in 1933 on the invitation of Reinhold Niehbur. He is best known for his work on the idea of Christian existentialism, a personal approach to understanding how belief works and humans' place in the universe. *The Courage to Be* (1957) was his most popular book and had major influence even for non-Christians.

Science and Medicine George Westinghouse (1864–1914) invented electrical equipment and air brakes for trains and trucks.

Albert Einstein (1879–1955) was a German-born physicist who immigrated to the United States as World War II loomed in Europe. He developed the general theory of relativity, upon which modern physics is based. He received the 1921 Nobel Prize in Physics.

Julius Robert Oppenheimer (1904–1967), known as the "father of the atom bomb," was born to German immigrants, who sent their son back to Germany to earn his Ph.D. at the University of Göttingen. During World War II Oppenheimer was the top ranking scientist of the Manhattan Project, which designed and built the atom bombs that were dropped on Japan in 1945. After the war he directed the Institute for Advanced Study at Princeton University.

Wernher von Braun (1912–1977) was a German rocket scientist who surrendered to the Allies near the end of World War II. He began the second half of his career working for the United States, designing rockets for the newly formed NASA that enabled the United States to land the first human on the moon.

Maria Goeppert-Mayer (1906–1972) was a pioneering German American scientist, the second woman to win a Nobel Prize for Physics in 1963 for her work modeling the nucleus of a cell. She followed her husband, German American physicist Joseph Edward Mayer (1904–1983), to the University of Chicago.

Sports Lou Gehrig (1903–1941) was born Ludwig Heinrich Gehrig in New York City. Gehrig, known as "The Iron Horse," played first base for the New York Yankees from 1923 to 1939.

George Hermann (1895–1948), better known as Babe Ruth, was known as the "Sultan of Swat" and was in 1927 the first player to hit 60 home runs in one season. He began his major league career with the Boston Red Sox in 1914 and retired in 1934 after many years with the New York Yankees.

Jack Nicklaus (1940–), known as "the Golden Bear," is a professional golfer who has won 18 major championships and designed many prestigious golf courses.

Steffi Graf (1969–) is believed by many to be the best female tennis player of all time. Her 22 Grand Slam titles are the most won by any tennis player since the 1960s, and she was ranked Number 1 among women for a record 377 weeks in a row. Born in Mannheim, Germany, she moved to Las Vegas, Nevada, with her husband, tennis champ Andre Agassi, and their two children.

Abby Wambach (1980–) is a two-time Olympic gold medalist soccer player. She grew up in New York State and attended the University of Florida, where she helped the Gators win the NCAA championship in 1998. A forward, she joined the U.S. National Team in 2003; her header goal gave the U.S. National Team a gold medal against Brazil at the 2004 Summer Olympics in Athens. Although an injury prevented her from playing in the 2008 Olympics, she returned for another gold medal in 2012 in London. Also in 2012, she was named the FIFA World Player of the Year.

Stage and Screen Fred Astaire (born Frederick Austerlitz, 1899–1987) was one of the most famous dancers and musical actors of the twentieth century, making a total of 31 musical films. Born in Nebraska to second-generation German Americans, he grew up in New York and first became famous on stage in several Gershwin operettas on Broadway and in London in the 1920s. With Ginger Rogers, he achieved movie fame at RKO Pictures in the 1930s. In 1960 he received the Cecil DeMille Lifetime Achievement award at the Golden Globes, and he was named the Fifth Greatest Male Star of All Time by the American Film Institute.

Jon Voight (1938–) is an actor who won an Academy Award for his portrayal of a paraplegic Vietnam War veteran in *Coming Home* (1978). He was also nominated for Academy Awards for his work in *Midnight Cowboy* (1969), *Runaway Train* (1985), and *Ali* (2001). His other notable films include *Deliverance* (1972), *Mission: Impossible* (1996), and *Varsity Blues* (1999). His maternal grandparents were German immigrants.

Meryl Streep (1949–) is one of the most successful actors of her generation. Some of her most notable films are *The Deer Hunter* (1978) *Sophie's Choice* (1982), and *The Iron Lady* (2011). She has been nominated for seventeen Academy Awards and won three.

Sandra Bullock (1964–) is an actor whose mother was a German opera singer. Her best-known films include *The Blind Side* (2009), for which she won an Academy Award for Best Actress.

Marlene Dietrich (1901–1992) was born in Berlin and became a U.S. citizen in 1939. She was one of the most famous actors of her day, beginning her career during the silent era. She was best known for her roles in Josef von Sternberg's *The Blue Angel* (1930), *Blonde Venus* (1932), and *Destry Rides Again* (1939).

Leonardo DiCaprio (1974–) is an actor best known for his roles in *Titanic* (1997), *Catch Me if*

You Can (2002), *Gangs of New York* (2002), *Inception* (2010), *J. Edgar* (2011), and *The Great Gatsby* (2013). His mother immigrated to the United States from Germany, and his father is of German descent.

Kirsten Dunst (1982–) holds dual citizenship in the United States and Germany. She is an actor best known for her work in the *Spider-Man* trilogy (2002–2004). Other notable films include *Marie Antoinette* (2006), *Interview with a Vampire* (1994), and *Melancholia* (2011).

Katherine Heigl (1978–) is an actress who played Dr. Stevens on the television show *Grey's Anatomy*, for which she won an Emmy Award in 2007. She also starred in *Knocked Up* (2006), and produced and starred in *Life As We Know It* (2010).

MEDIA

PRINT

German American newspapers were common beginning in the mid-nineteenth century in communities large and small; many rural counties with a population of one or two thousand German Americans had their own German-language newspaper. For example, in Iowa in the 1880s at least one German-language paper was published in fifteen of sixteen counties with more than 2,000 German American residents. New York had four German language dailies in 1850, more than Berlin. Weekly circulation nationwide was in the millions, and German language publications made up as much as 80 percent of the nation's immigrant press. After the 1890s, however, the German American press declined rapidly, as the group became more assimilated and as World War I led to suppression of German language activities in the United States. Few German language papers remain.

Amerika Woche

Newspaper with text in English and German.

ONA Publishing Corp
P.O. Box 391
Gladwyne, Pennsylvania 19035
Phone: (516) 771-3181
Fax: (516) 771-3184
Email: info@amerikawoche.com
URL: www.amerikawoche.com

Atlantic Times

This monthly "newspaper from Germany" is devoted to issues of German American national relations and business ties, as well as culture and politics for an American audience. The main publishing office is in Germany, but it also maintains editorial offices in Washington and New York.

Rüdinger Lentz
2000 M Street NW
Suite 335
Washington, D.C. 20036
Phone: (703) 981-2215
Email: info@atlantic-times.com
URL: www.atlantic-times.com

Das Fenster

German- and English-language magazine that has been published in Athens, Georgia, since 1904.

Susanne Petermann, Chief Editor
103 E. Meadow Dr.
Athens, Georgia 30605
Phone: 1-800-398-7753
Fax: (706) 548-8856
Email: info@dasfenster.com
URL: www.dasfenster.com

German Life

Bimonthly magazine on German culture, history, and travel, which also focuses on the German American experience.

Mark Slider, Editor
P.O. Box 3000
Denville, New Jersey 07834-9723
Phone: 1-866-867-0251
Email: comments@germanlife.com
URL: www.GermanLife.com

German World

Billing itself as the only bilingual German American magazine, *German World* has been published bimonthly to a national audience from Los Angeles since 2002. The magazine focuses on events, business, and news for German, Swiss, and Austrian Americans. Total paper circulation is around 100,000.

Petra Schürmann, Publisher
PO Box 3541
Los Angeles, California 90078
Phone: (323) 876-5843
Email: office@german-world.com
URL: www.german-world.com

IGAR News

Monthly publication of the Institute for German American Relations that promotes friendly German American relations through education.

Marianne Bouvier, Executive Director
9380 McKnight Road
Suite 102
Pittsburgh, Pennsylvania 15237-5951
Phone: (412) 364-6554
Email: mbouvier@igar-usa.org
URL: www.igar-usa.org/newletter.html

Nordamerikanische Wochen-Post

This weekly carries a front page directly from Germany, reports on many German American organizations, and includes coverage of business activity in Germany. It is the most widely distributed such publication in America.

Knuth Beth, Publisher
1300 W. Long Lake Road
Troy, Michigan 48098
Phone: (248) 641-9944
Fax: (248) 641-9946
Email: info@wochenpostusa.com
URL: www.wochenpostusa.com

Society for German-American Studies—Newsletter

Quarterly publication of the society that focuses on German immigration and settlements in the United States and on German American history and culture.

Email: MKGAC@iupui.edu
URL: http://sgas.org/publications/newsletter

RADIO AND TELEVISION

DW-TV North America

A branch of Germany's international broadcasting service, DW-TV is available on American cable and satellite networks. The channel features programming in both English and German, including news, documentaries, serials, and children's shows.

Deutsche Welle
Kurt-Schumacher-Strausse 3
Bonn, 53113 Germany
Phone: +49 228-429-0
Email: press@dw.de
URL: www.dw.de

WNWI AM Chicago

Broadcasting at 1080 AM, this mostly Polish language station broadcasts the "Deutschland Echo" program on Saturday and Sunday mornings from 9:00 until 11:00 am, hosted by Armin Homann and featuring German music. The program may also be streamed online.

Mr. Sima Birach, Operations Manager
934 W 138th Street
Riverdale, Illinois 60827
Phone: (708) 201-9600
URL: www.birach.com/wnwi.html

"Continental Showcase" WJYI AM Milwaukee

This long-running German music program, on the air for nearly 60 years, broadcasts on 1340 AM in the Milwaukee area on Saturdays from 1:00 to 4:30 pm. It may also be streamed online.

Robert Deglau, Host
JOY 1340
5407 W. McKinley Ave.
Milwaukee, Wisconsin 53208
Phone: (414) 761-9402
Email: rdeglau@continentalshowcase.com
URL: www.continentalshowcase.com

ORGANIZATIONS AND ASSOCIATIONS

German-American Heritage Foundation of the USA

The organization was founded in 1977 in Philadelphia by Hans R. Haug and is now based in Washington, D.C. It is the first national organization, as opposed to local community organization, dedicated to representing German Americans and protecting their common heritage.

Ruediger Lentz, Executive Director
719 Sixth St. NW
Washington, D.C. 20001

Phone: (202) 467-5000
Fax: (202) 467-5440
Email: info@gahmusa.org
URL: http://gahmusa.org

Max Kade Foundation, Inc.

The foundation, which Kade founded in 1944, promotes Germanic studies in the United States and the exchange of information between the United States and German-speaking countries through undergraduate, graduate, and faculty exchange programs. Max Kade Houses exist at 30 locations in the United States and at 17 in Germany. The foundation also bestows grants on nonprofit organizations.

Lya Friedrich Pfeifer, President
6 E 87th Street, Floor 5
New York, New York 10128
URL: http://maxkadefoundation.org

German American National Congress (Deutsch Amerikander National Kongress, DANK)

Founded in 1959 in Chicago, DANK aims "to inspire people with Germanic heritage and those interested in Germanic cultures and language to recognize and celebrate that culture." The organization publishes the *German-American Journal* six times yearly, maintains a blog on issues of interest to German Americans, facilitates genealogy research, and organizes language classes. Local chapters are primarily clustered in Illinois, but others can be found across the Midwest and North Atlantic states and in Phoenix, Arizona.

Eva Timmerhaus, Executive Secretary
4740 N. Western Ave.
Suite 206
Chicago, Illinois 60625
Phone: (773) 275-1100
Email: office@dank.org
URL: www.dank.org

German American Citizens League of Greater Cincinnati (GACL)

Founded in 1895, GACL is an umbrella organization for 33 German American groups in the Ohio Valley. It organizes social events, cultural activities, and advocacy for German American groups in the area and is an example of German American collaborative organizations that exist in many American metropolitan areas.

Dr. Heinrich Tolzmann, President
Phone: (513) 574-1741
Email: dhtolzmann@yahoo.com
URL: www.gacl.org

Society for German-American Studies (SGAS)

This professional organization promotes the study of German language, history, and literature in the United States. The society organizes an annual symposium and publishes the annual *Yearbook for German-American Studies*.

Randall P. Donaldson
Email: rdonaldson@loyola.edu
URL: http://sgas.org

MUSEUMS AND RESEARCH CENTERS

German-American Heritage Museum

The German-American Heritage Foundation, which boasts a membership of 18,000 nationwide, is headquartered in Washington, D.C. The organization runs the museum, which opened in 2010.

Ruediger Lentz, Executive Director
719 Sixth Street NW
Washington, D.C. 20001
Phone: 1-866-868-8422
Email: info@gahmusa.org
URL: http://gahmusa.org/gahm/gahm.html

DANK Haus German American Cultural Center

Located in Chicago and operated by DANK, the DANK Haus offers classes and lectures in German culture and language, historical exhibits, and exhibitions by German and German American artists.

4740 North Western Ave.
Chicago, Illinois 60625
Phone: (773) 561-9181
Email: dank@dankhaus.com
URL: www.dankhaus.com

SOURCES FOR ADDITIONAL STUDY

Adams, Willi Paul. *The German-Americans: An Ethnic Experience*. Translated by LaVern J. Rippley and Eberhard Reichmann. Indianapolis: Max Kade German-American Center, 1993.

Bank, Michaela. *Women of Two Countries: German-American Women, Women's Rights, and Nativism, 1848–1890*. New York: Berghahn Books, 2012.

Fogelman, Aaron Spencer. *Hopeful Journeys: German Immigration, Settlement, and Political Culture in Colonial America, 1717–1775*. Philadelphia: University of Pennsylvania Press, 1996.

Fox, Stephen. *America's Invisible Gulag: A Biography of German American Internment and Exclusion in World War II*. New York: Peter Lang, 2000.

Haller, Charles. *Across the Atlantic and Beyond: The Migration of German and Swiss Immigrants to America*. Bowie, MD: Heritage Books, 1993.

Honck, Mischa. *We Are the Revolutionists: German-Speaking Immigrants and American Abolitionists after 1848*. Athens, GA: University of Georgia Press, 2011.

Kamphoefner, Walter D., Wolfgang Helbich, and Ulrike Sommer, eds. *News from the Land of Freedom: German Immigrants* Write Home. Ithaca, NY: Cornell University Press, 1991.

Miller, Judith. *A Bond Never Broken: A Novel*. Minneapolis: Bethany House, 2011.

Rippley, LaVern J. *The German-Americans*. Lanham: MD: University Press of America, 1984.

Tolzmann, Don Heinrich. *The German-American Experience*. Amherst, NY: Humanity Books, 2000.

GHANAIAN AMERICANS

Drew Walker

OVERVIEW

Ghanaian Americans are immigrants or descendants of people from the Republic of Ghana, a western African nation on the Atlantic Ocean's Gulf of Guinea. Ghana is bordered by Burkina Faso to the north, Ivory Coast to the west, and Togo to the east. Just a few degrees north of the equator and with the prime meridian passing through it, Ghana is closer to being the geographic "center" of the earth than any other country. The country mostly consists of flat tropical plains, low hills, and some forested plateaus; its highest point is about 3,000 feet (900 meters). The Volta River Basin runs through its central region, and the eastern part of the country is dominated by Lake Volta, the largest artificial lake in the world. With an area of 92,098 square miles (238,533 square kilometers), Ghana is slightly larger than the state of Minnesota.

A 2011 census estimated Ghana's population at 25 million, according to the Ghanaian Embassy in the United States. The majority of Ghanaians self-identify as Christians, though there are also sizable populations practicing traditional religions and Islam. Within Ghana there are more than fifty distinct ethnic groups, all of which affect the cultural identity of Ghanaian Americans. Major groups include the Akan, Ewe, Guan, Mole-Dagbane, and Ga-Adangbe, which differ in history, language, and cultural practices. Many others differ in language and regional characteristics, making Ghana's diverse population difficult to categorize into one shared cultural identity. Although Ghana is a relatively small nation, it is rich in natural resources, and its economy and production statistics are among the highest in Africa. In 2011, however, the United Nations ranked Ghana number 135 (out of 185 members) on its Human Development Index, a list measuring life expectancy, literacy, education, standard of living, and quality of life for countries worldwide. According to the World Bank, 27 percent of Ghana's population lives on less than $1.25 per day.

Ghana (known as the Gold Coast until gaining its independence in 1957) was the area of origin for many Africans who were shipped to the United States as slaves between the seventeenth and nineteenth centuries. As of the 1790s the majority lived in the American south, where until 1863 they worked in forced labor supporting the agrarian economy.

In modern times Ghanaians began immigrating to the United States in noteworthy numbers during the late 1950s and early 1960s after Ghana gained its independence from England in 1957. Most of these early arrivals moved to the United States to pursue education or business opportunities. During the 1970s and 1980s economic hardships, military coups, and a succession of undemocratic governments led an increasing number of Ghanaians to immigrate to the United States. Many of the Ghanaian Americans who have arrived during more recent years are family members of those who immigrated between the 1950s and 1980s.

As of 2011 the U.S. Census reported that there were 130,399 Ghanaian Americans living in the United States, though an estimate including undocumented immigrants by Georgetown University researchers put the number closer to 300,000. Significant communities of Ghanaian Americans exist in cities such as Atlanta, Chicago, Detroit, New York City, Los Angeles, and Washington, D.C.

HISTORY OF THE PEOPLE

Early History Archeological evidence suggests that the area of present-day Ghana was first inhabited during the Bronze Age, and that the earliest settlers were likely nomadic fishers and hunters. From the eleventh to mid-fourteenth centuries, distinct states arose around the ever-growing trade networks to the north. Within these networks gold was the most valuable commodity, and by the thirteenth century mines were operating in central Ghana to supply gold as the key indirect export to Europe and Asia. Direct contact with European traders, starting with the arrival of the Portuguese in 1471, began to diminish the importance of North African trade routes, and the majority of gold trafficking began moving south to the Atlantic coast. Around this time the lands of modern-day Ghana first became known as the Gold Coast, as traders from Great Britain, Denmark, France, Portugal, Spain, and Germany built trading posts, forts, and even castles there to solidify their positions within the resource-rich region.

During the 1500s Europeans began to establish plantations and colonial settlements across the Atlantic Ocean in the New World, rapidly and vastly expanding the demand for slaves in the newly settled

Americas. Their primary source was Africa's west coast and, with a seemingly insatiable market and substantial profits to be made, slaves quickly eclipsed precious metals as the Gold Coast's primary export. Profiteers came from all over Europe, and conflict flared among colonial European powers, traders, and competing African kingdoms as they battled for a piece of the slave trade. Access to much of the land and resources of the Gold Coast was controlled by Portugal until the nation abandoned its permanent settlements there in 1642. Afterward a revolving door of European nations, African chiefs, and chartered companies such as the Dutch West India Company and British African Company of Merchants continued to control the slave trade.

While slave trading was already firmly embedded in many African cultures before the arrival of Europeans, the institution of commercial slavery as constituted in the New World was vastly different than the kind common between the indigenous peoples of the Gold Coast region. In Africa men and women captured during local warfare often became slaves but were typically treated as junior members of society with some specific rights, and many were ultimately accepted as full members of their masters' families. By comparison slaves sent to the Americas were denied basic human rights, faced the harshest living conditions, and had little to no chance of gaining their freedom.

Along with the growth of the slave trade, indigenous groups from the Ghanaian interior grew in wealth and power, now using firearms and gunpowder against their adversaries. Local chiefs of the Asante, Fante, and Ahanta peoples were known to have engaged in the slave trade, and the names of individual African slave merchants such as John Kabes, John Konny, and Thomas Ewusi are still known today. The slave trade peaked during the eighteenth century, and historians estimate that some 6.3 million slaves were shipped from western Africa to North and South America. During the trade's heyday perhaps 5,000 each year came from the Gold Coast alone. While slavery boomed the coastal regions of present-day Ghana boasted nearly forty separate active forts controlled by European slave and gold traders.

As the power of these forts grew, southern coastal peoples such as the Asante built ever-stronger relations with the European traders, establishing themselves as middlemen between the Europeans and the indigenous peoples of the north. By the eighteenth century the Asante came to control the supply of slaves and other goods from the region. They also further secured their power through a series of successful conquests against coastal tribes. By the early nineteenth century, however, the slave trade was losing strength. The importation of slaves into the United States was outlawed in 1807, and by 1814 the British, Dutch, and Danes had banned slavery altogether. In the following decades the British asserted their power over the Asante by forging alliances with various rival indigenous groups. Great Britain also began buying out the interests of other remaining European nations and, after a decisive victory over the Asante in 1874, declared the Gold Coast a colony of the British Empire.

Modern Era The introduction of the cocoa trade in 1878 hastened British efforts to build and maintain an infrastructure in Ghana, including European educational institutions unique in western Africa at the time. Despite these developments, divisions between English colonialists and indigenous peoples as well as long-standing resentment between northern and southern Ghanaian peoples led to political unrest throughout the early part of the twentieth century. Efforts by locals to secure a free and independent Gold Coast intensified after World War II, when African war veterans were denied the pensions and jobs they were promised for serving alongside British troops. When ex-servicemen attempted to organize a peaceful demonstration in Accra on February 28, 1948, they were violently put down by colonial police. This incident sparked the five-day Accra riots, an ugly and high-profile incident historians view as the catalyst for Ghana winning its independence.

Among those arrested during the Accra riots was future Ghanaian president Kwame Nkrumah, who had spent some years living in the United States as a student and whose political activism had been partly shaped by his experiences there. After his release Nkrumah formed the leftist Convention People's Party (CPP) under the slogan "self-government now." The CPP led a campaign of strikes, demonstrations, and "positive action" that won support among rural and working-class people. In the elections of 1951 the CPP secured nearly every seat in the legislative assembly, and the British governor of the Gold Coast invited Nkrumah and his cabinet to lead a new administration. The CPP soon came to hold power almost entirely independent of British rule. In 1957 Nkrumah renamed the country Ghana and obtained recognition from the United Nations as a sovereign member of the British Commonwealth, making it the first African colony to win independence.

During nine years in power, Nkrumah established a one-party system and attempted to anoint himself leader for life of both the government and the CPP. Facing a decline in living standards, corruption, and massive debt, however, he was removed from power in a 1966 coup. Nkrumah's ouster signaled the beginning of a fifteen-year period of political upheaval in Ghana, culminating when military leader Jerry Rawlings seized control in 1981. Rawlings initially ruled as a dictator, suspending Ghana's constitution, outlawing political parties, and prompting a severe economic decline that caused many citizens to flee the country for the United States and Europe during the 1980s. After more than a decade with unchecked powers, Rawlings succumbed to sustained political and economic pressure to institute sweeping reforms. A new constitution was ratified in 1992, and during the next eight years Rawlings twice won re-election as Ghana's democratic president, stepping down due to term limits in 2000.

Although political corruption still exists in Ghana, the reforms of the 1990s led to "a quarter century of relatively sound management, a competitive business environment, and sustained reductions in poverty levels," according to the *CIA World Factbook*. Today Ghana's government is considered one of the region's more stable governments, and the country has even begun to market itself as a tourist destination for Ghanaian Americans. Still classified as a developing nation, Ghana struggles with poverty and unemployment, but its economy continues to profit from its wealth of natural resources. It is considered a major exporter of oil, cocoa, natural gas, and timber.

SETTLEMENT IN THE UNITED STATES

Because of Ghana's proximity to the sea, many Ghanaians became sailors after their first contact with Europeans, and it is probable that some of the first to arrive in the New World worked on trade ships. The vast majority, however, were taken as slaves; historians estimate that more than 15 percent of slaves sent to the early United States came from the Gold Coast. Little specific documentation was kept from this time, but in the instances in which records still exist some Ghanaian Americans can trace their ancestry back to these original arrivals. After the abolition of slavery in the United States in 1863 very few Ghanaians immigrated (and those who did were typically grouped into the larger category of "African immigrants") until after Ghana gained independence from Great Britain in 1957.

During the civil rights movement of the late 1950s and 1960s, influential African American leaders such as W. E. B. Du Bois (himself a Ghanaian American) and Malcolm X cited newly independent Ghana as a symbol of black achievement and possibility. At the same time Ghanaians were beginning to immigrate to the United States in search of educational and work opportunities as well as a respite from the political turmoil that surrounded Ghana's formative years as a sovereign nation. The trickle of Ghanaians entering the United States during the 1960s and 1970s turned into a steady stream during the 1980s and 1990s due to the steep economic recession suffered in Ghana during the early days of the Rawlings regime. Many of the immigrants of this period sought business opportunities as well as specialized experience and training.

Ghanaian Americans historically endured the same racial prejudice and stereotypes faced by all African Americans, though class and economic status were also factors. Ghanaians who migrated during the 1950s and 1960s were often professionals or government-sponsored students who thought of themselves as members of the educated elite. This group was largely eager to adopt the culture and etiquette of the United States, and societal pressures often encouraged them to maintain only weak links to their African roots. The second generation of migrants, who left Ghana during the 1980s and 1990s, included more blue-collar workers who hoped for employment in labor and service industries. The U.S. Census reported that the Ghanaian American population jumped from 20,889 to 65,570 between 1990 and 2000. These new arrivals hoped to join family members who had immigrated earlier and to take advantage of strong economic conditions in the United States at the time. As the situation in Ghana began to stabilize around the turn of the century, numbers of Ghanaian American immigrants returned to steady but comparatively small levels. During the years 2006 through 2011, 49,800 Ghanaians legally immigrated to the United States, averaging about 8,300 new arrivals each year, according to the U.S. Department of Homeland Security. Most of the immigrants from Ghana during this period arrived via the Diversity Immigrant Visa Program, a government-mandated service offering visas to people from countries with comparatively small immigration rates to the United States. This program awards visas through a lottery system.

In 2002 Ghana became the first African country to enact a "right to abode" law that offers dual citizenship to those with Ghanaian ancestry, including Ghanaian Americans, if they spend several years living in Ghana.

Notable communities of Ghanaian Americans can be found in large cities such as Atlanta; Boston; Chicago; Detroit; Washington, D.C.; New York City; Newark, New Jersey; and Los Angeles. The largest single neighborhood community likely exists in New York City, where since 2001 the Mount Hope section in the Bronx has been nicknamed "Little Ghana." In 2012 the Census Bureau reported there were around 22,000 Ghanaian Americans living in New York City. Chicago's Uptown neighborhood and the Chicago suburb of Bolingbrook, Illinois, have also become popular destinations for Ghanaian Americans.

Because so many Ghanaians fled the country during the 1980s and 1990s, it is often said that every family residing in modern Ghana has at least one relative living outside the country. Many of these emigrants disembarked for neighboring African nations, but the most popular overseas destinations were the United States and England. During the two decades since this migration began, Ghanaians have expanded their concept of traditional family to include those living abroad, and governmental policy has evolved to become more hospitable to the relatives of those who moved away. In 2002 Ghana became the first African country to enact a "right to

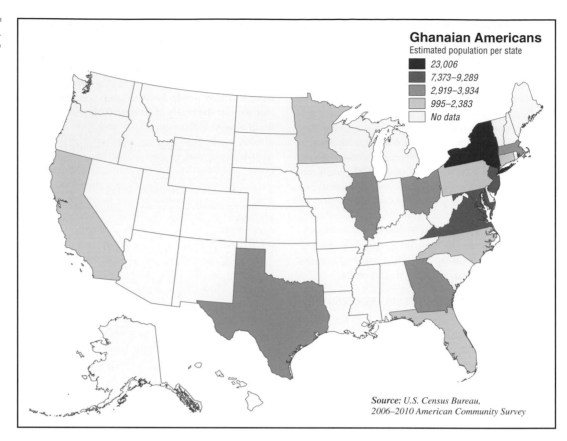

Ghanaian Americans
Estimated population per state

- 23,006
- 7,373–9,289
- 2,919–3,934
- 995–2,383
- No data

*Source: U.S. Census Bureau,
2006–2010 American Community Survey*

abode" law that offers dual citizenship to those with Ghanaian ancestry, including Ghanaian Americans, if they spend several years living in Ghana.

LANGUAGE

Language can be a divisive topic among Africans living abroad. Historically, many African families living in the United States for more than one or two generations have elected not to teach their American-born children native languages. In more recent times, however, movements among African Americans to preserve traditional African culture and language have been growing in popularity. Ghanaian Americans who learn native languages may speak any one or more of 100 distinct dialects. Linguists categorize the languages of Ghanaians into two subfamilies of the greater family of Niger-Congo languages found throughout Africa. These two language groups are referred to as the Kwa group and the Gur group.

The Kwa group of languages comprises the most common indigenous languages among Ghanaian Americans, which are spoken by 75 percent of the population of Ghana as well. This group includes major languages such as Akan, Ga-Adangbe, and Ewe. Further subdivisions are made within these groups, including Asante, Bono, Akwapim, Akyem, Fante, Akwamu, Kwahu, Ahanta, Nzema, and Safwi (all belonging to the Akan subgroup); Ga, Adangbe, Ada,

and Krobo or Kloli (belonging to the Ga-Adangbe subgroup); and Nkonya, Tafi, Logba, Lolobi, Likpe, and Sontrokofi (belonging to the Ewe subgroup). The Gur group of languages is primarily spoken in Ghana's northern region and includes subgroups known as Gurma, Mole-Dagbane, and Grusi, within which further subgroups can also be classified.

Since the period of European colonialism, systems of writing based on the same Latin alphabet as English have been developed for many of these languages. In Ghana and in the United States, Ghanaians typically use English to communicate with countrymen outside of their own ethnic group. According to a 2007 study of African immigrants living in the United States sponsored by the Migration Policy Institute, 20 percent of Ghanaian Americans reported speaking English as the primary language in their home. Of those who did not speak English at home, 59 percent of Ghanaian Americans reported speaking English "very well," while another 17 percent said they spoke English "well." Just 3 percent of Ghanaian Americans responded that they "did not speak English very well."

RELIGION

The diverse religious affiliations of Ghanaian Americans for the most part reflect the affiliations of Ghanaians. According to a 2011 report from the Ghana Embassy in the United States, 40 percent of the Ghanaian population identify themselves as Christians, including Roman Catholics, Baptists, and Protestants; 40 percent also report practicing traditional indigenous religions, while another 12 percent, mostly living in the less-populated northern parts of the country, are Muslims.

Among Ghanaian Americans church attendance and devotion at mosques are regular features of life. Overall, Ghanaian Americans are tolerant of different Christian and Islamic religious practices, and they are also inclusive of traditional Ghanaian religious practices. In this community one religious interest and commitment rarely rules out another.

CULTURE AND ASSIMILATION

Slaves brought to the New World between the sixteenth and nineteenth centuries were typically denied the most basic human rights, and any connection they nurtured to the customs and traditions of their African cultures were often done in secret. In the United States some slave owners publicly sought to "civilize" slaves by forcing them to become indoctrinated into Western culture, religion, and education. They believed that religion and some rudimentary education would help pacify slaves and make them more malleable workers. Families were often separated, and mental and sexual abuses were commonplace. Out of these hardships the culture that slaves fashioned for themselves was a blend of European and western African traditions. After all slaves in the United States were freed in 1865, most African Americans stayed in the United States and worked diligently to assimilate and be accepted as American citizens in the face of decades of prejudice and unfair treatment.

Because of these and other factors, many long-standing Ghanaian American families did not foster strong connections to their African heritage. Due to a lack of family records, some may not have even known they were descendants of Ghana. During the U.S. civil rights movement, many African Americans began to research and rediscover their African roots, resulting in a revival of traditional culture and traditional dress. More recently DNA testing has allowed some African Americans to more accurately pinpoint the origins of their ancestors, even leading a small percentage to seek dual citizenship in countries that offer it, such as Ghana.

Immigrants who arrived in the United States from Ghana during the middle part of the twentieth century were largely professionals or college students who were desirous of assimilating quickly into American culture. In addition, social pressures often encouraged them to at least publicly separate themselves from traditional African culture in favor of falling in line with more "normal" Western mores. During the 1980s and 1990s more blue-collar workers began to join professionals and students in migrating from Ghana to the United States. Though they also assimilated into American culture, these newer arrivals tended to feel a closer relationship with Ghana.

Some joined or founded cultural organizations and maintained a connection to family members still living in Ghana by making trips home or by remitting a portion of their incomes each year. In 2005 alone remittances from Ghanaian Americans to relatives in Ghana totaled nearly $100 million, according to the Institute for the Study of International Migration and Inter-American Dialogue.

Today mainstream media acknowledgment of the Ghanaian American community continues to be sparse, except in instances when it coincides with some culturally meaningful event. For example, major American media outlets, such as *Time* magazine, the *New York Times*, and the *Wall Street Journal*, spotlighted Ghanaian American culture before and after Ghana's 2–1 victory over the United States in the 2010 World Cup of soccer. Ghanaian culture is kept alive in neighborhoods such as New York City's Little Ghana in the Bronx, where Ghanaian Americans can join cultural organizations, restaurants serve Ghanaian food, and social events often feature traditional dress, music, and dance. People of Ashanti descent living in the Bronx, for example, sponsor cultural and religious gatherings and elect a regional chief as their ceremonial leader.

According to a 2012 report by Kirk Semple in the *New York Times*, however, even as the Ghanaian American population in New York City continued to increase, membership in traditional groups has been dwindling. When the political and economic situation in Ghana began to stabilize during the early 2000s, many original members of Ghanaian American cultural associations moved back to Ghana and have not been replaced by their assimilated offspring born in the United States, Semple reported. He explained, "This is a pattern familiar to many immigrant diasporas. Organizations formed by early waves of immigrants struggle to remain relevant as the needs and desires of later generations and more recent newcomers shift." In 2009 President Barack Obama and the first family stopped in Ghana during a visit to Africa, generating considerable national and international publicity and coverage. The *New York Times* referred to Obama's African trip as having "enormous historic and symbolic resonance."

Traditions and Customs The traditions and customs of Ghanaian Americans can be roughly divided in terms of the major Ghanaian ethnic groups that have settled in the United States. Major groups include the Akan, Ewe, and Ga-Adangbe from southern Ghana as well as the Mole-Dagbane, Guan, Grusi, and Gurma from the north.

The Akan people occupy the greatest part of the areas south and west of the Black Volta River. The primary form of social organization among the Akan is the extended family, or the *abusua*. The Akan are a matrilineal society, which means that a child's family and group membership is determined by the child's

A Ghanaian American electrical engineer from St. Petersburg, Florida. ZUMA PRESS, INC. / ALAMY

regarding the ancestors of the group. In addition to honoring their ancestors, the Ewe participate in group and village rituals involving local spirits and gods. Many Ewes also practice Christianity.

The Guan are thought to have originated north of Ghana in what is Burkina Faso today. The settlement of the Guan moved down the Black Volta, eventually reaching the coastal plains. Today the Guan form enclaves in or near areas settled by other groups, such as the Akan, Ewe, and Ga-Adangbe. Guan culture has often been eclectic, as they have taken customs and practices from their neighbors and adapted them for their own purposes.

Although many groups inhabit the northern parts of Ghana, the three most prominent groups are the Mole-Dagbane (also referred to as the Mossi-Grunshi), Gurma, and Grusi. Of these three subfamilies of the Gur language group, Mole-Dagbane make up 15 percent of Ghana's population and are by far the largest group in their region. Being quite varied culturally, the Mole-Dagbane group includes subgroups such as the Dagomba, Wala, Mamprusi, Frafra, Talensi, Nanumba, and Kusase. Known for their diversity of political structure, Gur-speaking peoples traditionally lived in small, self-governed communities that maintained relations among themselves through intermarriage and trade. In many of these communities a traditional religious leader would sometimes be summoned to settle disputes. This was not, however, the rule in all Mole-Dagbane communities. Some, such as the Dagomba, Mamprusi, and Gonja, lived in societies of a larger scale and had kings.

The Ga-Adangbe live in the Accra Plains along Ghana's southern coastal area. They are two distinct yet culturally similar groups, the Ga and the Adangbe. Their languages stem from the same root but are today unintelligible to each other. Today the Adangbe include a number of subgroups all speaking different dialects, such as the Shai, Ningi, Kpone, La, Gbugle, Krobo, and Ada. Among the Ga are groups such as the Ga-Mashie, who are found in the neighborhoods of central Accra, as well as those who have immigrated to this area from Akwamu, Akwapim, Anecho (in neighboring Togo), and other areas surrounding Accra. Ga communities are prominent within the capital city of Accra, and much of Ga culture is still practiced in such urban settings.

Cuisine Where once Ghanaian Americans may have struggled to find the ingredients necessary to make traditional Ghanaian dishes, stores specializing in African foods can now be found in most major cities in the United States. The many traditional foods prepared by Ghanaian Americans vary from group to group. The traditional foods of Ghanaian Americans who are from Ghana's forested regions typically feature maize, coco yam, plantain, and cassava, while groups from the savanna typically prepare dishes from cereals such as millet, rice, Guinea corn, and maize. Common

mother's lineage. Every member of the Akan becomes a member of a corporate group that has its own symbols, property, and individual identity. Each corporate group has its own symbolic, carved stool or chair. This chair is often named after the female founder of the group. Such stools or chairs are seen as a group's most important possessions. Each group also shares a belief in certain spirits and gods around whom many traditions and beliefs are centered. The Akan are exogamous, which means that each person is obligated to marry outside of his or her own corporate group.

The Ewe live in southeastern Ghana as well as the southern regions of neighboring countries Togo and Benin. The majority of the Ewe make their living as farmers, although fishing is also a common profession in some areas. The Ewe are also known as traders and makers of textiles and pottery. They are a patrilineal society that regards children as descending from the family of their father. The head of the patrilineal family or group is often the oldest man; he is responsible for keeping the peace, representing his group in political affairs with other groups, and heading rituals staple foods are the yam and pounded yam (known as *fufu*). Wet and dry vegetables as well as beans are also prepared and eaten with yams and other foods. Meat of all sorts is also commonly consumed. Traditional alcoholic beverages include palm wine and a drink known as *pito*, which is brewed from Guinea corn, or sorghum of maize.

Though restaurants that specialize in Ghanaian food are less common in the United States than those serving traditional foods from African countries such as Nigeria and Ethiopia, some major American cities do boast Ghanaian cafes and eateries. New York City restaurants include Papaye Restaurant in the Bronx and Meytex Enterprises in Brooklyn, while Chicago has the Palace Gate Restaurant and Philadelphia is home to Naana Xtra O Restaurant. Their menus typically offer traditional fare such as dried fish, meat kabobs, *jollof* (rice and vegetable dishes spiced with cumin and curry), fufu, soups, and stews.

Traditional Dress In the United States, Ghanaian Americans sometimes opt to wear traditional dress during festivals or cultural gatherings. Traditional dress for Ghanaian Americans can be divided according to the geographic origins of their ancestors, and these divisions, like many others in Ghanaian society, are drawn between north and south.

In southern Ghanaian, men's traditional dress includes a garment called "the cloth," which is a piece of fabric hanging over the shoulder and wrapped around the body. Of the cloths, Kente cloth is the most popular. Kente cloth dates from twelfth-century Ghana and was traditionally worn by kings, queens, and other great figures of state during ceremonial events and functions. The name *Kente* comes from the word *kenten*, which means "basket," because of the cloth's resemblance to the woven design of a basket. Traditionally each pattern of Kente was unique and had its own name and meaning. Men of the north typically wear a similar garment that resembles a smock. Like the Kente, certain traditional smock designs are also associated with certain ethnic groups. Among the traditional outfits of Ghanaian American women, the slit (long skirt) and *kaba* (blouse) is the best known.

Dances and Songs Ghanaian music and dance, which vary among ethnic groups, are performed in the United States at festivals, funerals, weddings, ceremonies where children are named, and other occasions. Such performances often feature traditional instruments, usually the ensemble performance of multiple percussion instruments. The complex drumming techniques of many African cultures are said to speak an intricate language. A *gangkogui*, a double iron bell, is one of the most important instruments in many ensembles and is used to anchor tempo and timing. The drum is also a key instrument. The *atsimewu* is a lead drum. Standing four and a half feet tall, the drum is open at the bottom, and the bottom is smaller in diameter than the top head. Played by striking it on the head as well as the rim and sides, this lead drum is a "talking drum" and a powerful speaker of song in rhythm, often reciting syllables of prose with drum strokes.

Other instruments include the *sogo* and the *kidi*, barrel drums that are closed at the bottom; the *agboba*, a large-barrel bass drum, three feet high, with a closed bottom; and the *kloboto* and *totodzi*, which are short open-bottom barrel drums. The *kaganu* is a narrow barrel drum that is played with light sticks and is of similar proportions to the *atsimewu* but built to the height of the *kidi*. The *atoken* is a small single boat-shaped bell laid in the open palm and played by striking it with piece of metal. The *axatse* is a gourd rattle that is usually shaken and struck with the hand and thigh.

Dances, which are often unique to the celebrated occasion, also vary along ethnic lines. One prominent dance is the *adowa*, a graceful dance that borrows from other traditional Ghanaian dances, including the *kete* and the *denesewu*. The *adowa*, which was originally a funeral dance, is characterized by a dignified walking movement and is usually preceded by a chorus of voices accompanied at first by two boat-shaped bells and later joined by two drums. When the singing and drumming have set the mood in song, the *atumpan* drums enter with parts of the drum rhythms being picked up by different parts of their bodies. This is accompanied by a spinning and bowing that the melody of the song suggests to the dancer. This dance is popular among the Twi, the Fante (who call it *adzewa*), and the Ga.

Adzohu was originally a cult dance associated with a war god of Benin. In the first part of this dance, called *kadodo*, only women dance. Gathering in a group as a chorus, the women sing and perform rituals, while the young men are spiritually prepared for war. Then in the second part, called *atsia*, the young men preparing for war begin to dance. Here many of its movements imitate the various positions of battle, from moving in formation to hand-to-hand combat to reconnaissance.

A number of Ghanaian American groups, such as California's Zadonu, also perform innovative and traditional dances within the United States.

Holidays In accordance with their diverse ethnic heritage, Ghanaian Americans celebrate a wide range of traditional festivals and holidays. The most common include Adae Kese, a festival held to mark a number of specific milestones in the history the Asante people; Odwira, celebrated by the Asante and Akuapim to mark an important military victory dating back to 1826; Akwambo, a summertime festival held each year in August by the Fantes of Agona and Gomoa; Homowo, celebrated each May by the Ga people to coincide with the planting of crops; Hogbetsotso, celebrated on the first Saturday in November by the Ewe

GHANAIAN PROVERBS

Anomuto ne nam nye fan

The toothless man's meat is cabbage.

Bubulo yo bu we ba

Even a pauper manages to cover his nakedness with cloth instead of leaves.

Bosompo botoo abotam

The rocks existed long before the sea.

Dam wobo kyere aman

An insane person's behavior does not escape the notice of the community.

Akan-Abowa apatabi se de "Adze woye no nano nano."

The squirrel sings "things must be done in the proper way."

Adangbe-Ateplee ke efi nge mi ne ake yahe na

The cockroach says it gave its excrement as its contribution toward the purchase of a cow.

Krakpahe ke enyuwumi nge enane mi ne kee su pa mi loko emaafo, se kpo no lohwehu tsuo ke eza we.

The duck says its activity rests in its feet and that it can run only when it is in the water, but all other animals accuse it of sluggishness.

people of Anlo and calling for the forgiveness of all disagreements among the people; Damba, celebrated by the people of the northern and upper regions of Ghana each July or August; Bugum, a fire festival celebrated by the Dagombas of the northern region during the first month of their lunar calendar; Kwafie, celebrated by the Dorma in the Brong Ahafo region during November and December; Aboakyer, a ceremonial antelope hunt by the Effutu people of Winneba; and Oguaaa Fetu Afahye, a traditional parade held by the people of the Cape Coast.

In the United States these festivals are often sponsored by ethnic associations within the Ghanaian American community. They include traditional dancing, music and drumming, storytelling, and the display of traditional costumes. For example, the Homowo festival celebrated in New York City annually is one of the most popular festivals in the greater New York area. There is also a well-known Homowo festival in Philadelphia. This celebration includes a pilgrimage to the city's Amugi Naa shrine, where participants pour libations and give thanks to ancestors and spirits.

For many Ghanaian Americans these ceremonies are important to maintaining links between the living and the dead by paying tribute to the departed and their memory. It is also not uncommon for Ghanaian Americans, when possible, to return to the homeland, town, or village of their ancestors during one of the many such festivals to maintain links with their heritage and tradition.

Odwira is a traditional Akan festival, observed in Ghana and in the United States, that functions as a thanksgiving, dedication, purification, and reunion. Sponsored by the Okuapeman Association in the United States, it is one of the festivals observed by different groups of Ghanaian Americans. This festival is traditionally religious, reflecting and displaying many of the long-held cultural practices of the Akan people. It is considered key to maintaining a strong and respectful link between the living and the dead and is therefore dedicated to the honor of ancestors and their spirits. This festival is usually celebrated on the ninth Sunday of the year according to the traditional Akan calendar. The main ritual activity in this festival is the purification of the sacred royal black stools, called the *nkonnwa tuntum*, and the calling for blessings of the ancestors.

Birth and Birthdays Ghanaians within and outside of the Akan group have a custom of deriving names from the seven days of the week. Children born on a given day of the week are given a name, called the *kra din*, that is derived from that day's name. According to this custom, a child born on Tuesday whose parents speak the Twi language would have a name derived from *Benada*, the Twi word for Tuesday. A boy would have the name Kwabena, and a girl, Abena. If born on Friday (*Fiada*) a boy would be named Kofi and a girl, Afua, and so on. In addition it is common among the Fante that nicknames or pet names, such as Siisi and Fiifi, are derived from these names. People from the northern and upper regions of Ghana practice a variation of this tradition by using the Hausa names of the week as their base for naming. Among these, names such as Teni, Lariba, Alamisa, Azuma, and Atlata are common. Although different groups have their own variations on these names, this practice is a special element of Ghanaian and Ghanaian American culture.

Death and Burial Rituals Among Ghanaian Americans there is no more critical and profound time than the death of a loved one. After services are performed in the United States according to the family's religious orientation, it is not uncommon for the ethnic association of the family of the deceased to hold a memorial service and to aid the family in returning the deceased to Ghana for burial, as Ghanaians believe the deceased must be returned to their ancestral homeland. Such memorial services are one of the major functions of Ghanaian American associations.

FAMILY AND COMMUNITY LIFE

Ghanaian American family and community dynamics vary greatly from group to group. For most, extended family ties are strong and often represent ongoing financial or social commitments. For example, many affluent Ghanaian Americans financially support relatives in Ghana or in the United States. The numerous ethnic associations found in cities where large numbers of Ghanaian Americans live have their roots in the urban centers of Ghana. Most Ghanaian American ethnic and cultural associations were founded in the 1980s, and many were created as support organizations for Ghanaian immigrants of a particular ethnic origin, such as Asante, Ewe, Guan, Mole-Dagbane, and Ga-Adangbe.

In 2007 there were eleven major Ghanaian ethnic associations in New York City alone, including Akyem, Asanteman, Brong-Ahafo, Ga-Adamgme, United Volta, and Yankasa organizations. Similar organizations can be found in most major cities where Ghanaian Americans have congregated. While membership is usually not restricted to persons of a particular ethnicity, most of the members of these organizations can claim common roots in one of Ghana's ethnic groups. It is also not uncommon for Ghanaian Americans living in non-urban communities where there is no ethnic association to be members of an ethnic association in the nearest large city.

Ghanaian American ethnic associations are dedicated to cultural issues and charitable causes. Most associations operate as nonprofit entities, channeling the excess from dues and fundraising into cultural education, group events, and aiding the families of members in the United States and Ghana. For the most part these associations, unlike their earlier counterparts in Ghana, are not devoted to economic or political concerns. Of the many benevolent roles played by these associations, the provision of help for newly arrived immigrants and the families of members in times of distress are the most prominent. Most associations are run by volunteers and are headed and staffed by officials elected by the membership as a whole.

According to a 2012 report in the *New York Times*, however, membership may be declining in these cultural associations. Many original members have either died or returned to Ghana and have not been replaced by their more assimilated American-born offspring. Dues-paying membership in the New York Asante Association was down to about 70, as compared to about 1,000 members during the 1990s.

Gender Roles Gender roles among Ghanaian Americans can often depend on multiple factors, including social class, specific ethnic traditions, length of time spent in the United States, and level of assimilation into mainstream American culture. Because Ghana was the first African country to win independence from Europe, in 1957, and because its educational systems and infrastructure were some

of the best in the region at the time, the first wave of modern Ghanaian women to arrive in the United States during the 1950s and 1960s were often professionals who were able to find jobs working in fields such as teaching, nursing, and office management. Their desire to quickly assimilate into the culture of the United States influenced many to adopt the gender roles of American society and to pass them on to their American-born offspring.

Ghanaian Americans who have immigrated more recently often feel a stronger connection to the traditions of Ghana, where gender roles differ greatly across various ethnic groups. In most Ghanaian traditions women assume basic domestic roles, including caring for children, though responsibilities outside the home can be dictated by geographic and ethnic factors. Among the Akan, for example, the matrilineal culture traditionally allows women to attain considerable political and economic status. Akan men and women both work and are responsible for providing financially for the family. Among the Ga and Adangme it is more common that women do not hold formal jobs, but many are involved in petty trade. In the rural north, Ewe women have fewer formal commercial opportunities but often work alongside men in agricultural settings in addition to their domestic duties.

In traditional Ghanaian society, motherhood has been particularly emphasized in the lives of women due to various cultural pressures. A 2007 study by the Ghanaian government revealed that the size of the average Ghanaian household was 5.1 members and that families in rural areas were producing more offspring than families in urban areas. In the United States, and in some urban centers of Ghana, lower rates of infant mortality, the costs of child rearing, and the constraints of time and career are affecting Ghanaians' traditional views of women's roles. Many Ghanaian American women have found successful careers in addition to or in lieu of their traditional family roles, and many others have also begun to seek training and pursue careers as entrepreneurs and in business.

Education On the whole, Ghanaian Americans are a well-educated group, and many work in professions that require advanced degrees. According to a 2007 study conducted by the Migration Policy Institute, 51 percent of Ghanaian Americans aged twenty-five or older reported having attained a four-year college degree or having attended some college. Another 14 percent had earned master's, doctorate, or professional degrees. Many earlier Ghanaian immigrants first arrived in the United States as foreign students and decided to stay. It is also not uncommon for Ghanaian Americans to continue their studies while in the workforce, with the hope of advancing their careers.

Courtship and Weddings Traditional courtship practices vary among the ethnic groups of Ghanaian Americans, and many younger Ghanaians find it

A Ghanaian-born businessman stands in front of his Ghana Homes business in the Bronx, New York. Ghana Homes sells houses in Ghana to Ghanaian Americans. NANCY SIESEL / THE NEW YORK TIMES / REDUX

difficult to carry on the courting traditions of their parents in the urban centers where most live. Nevertheless, many Ghanaian Americans are aware of the traditional practices that many older members of the community followed before immigrating to the United States. It is not uncommon for Ghanaian Americans, especially when marrying within the group, to be married in a Christian ceremony as well as in a ceremony reflecting the traditions of their specific Ghanaian ethnic group. Ghanaian marriage traditions involve many preliminary steps in which the man gains the grace of his prospective wife's family. During the ceremony the families come together, and gifts are bartered and exchanged according to local customs. When an agreement is reached and all are satisfied, the couple is considered married. Afterward a long-running feast is usually held in which songs are sung (most often by women) and music is played, often accompanied by dancing.

Relations with Other Americans Outside of their ethnic groups Ghanaian Americans often interact with other African immigrants with whom they often share common sentiments, traditions, and experiences as immigrants. To a lesser extent Ghanaian Americans interact with African Americans. Interaction with and assimilation into African American culture is more pronounced in younger Ghanaian Americans, who share many of the same experiences as other African Americans.

EMPLOYMENT AND ECONOMIC CONDITIONS

According to a 2007 study by the Migration Policy Institute, Ghanaian Americans reported high employment rates and a median income similar to that of immigrants from other African countries. Of those surveyed, 84 percent of Ghanaian American men aged eighteen to sixty-four reported being employed, while 73 percent of Ghanaian American women aged eighteen to sixty-four were employed. Median income was listed at $30,000 per year. Ghanaian Americans are employed in many different jobs found in the urban United States. There is a strong sense of entrepreneurship that stems from long traditions of trade within Ghana. A significant number of women work in health care professions and business. As a group, Ghanaian Americans are upwardly mobile, pursuing advanced degrees in practical areas of study and using networks to compete in the global economy. There are also many Ghanaian Americans in the arts, art education, the social and natural sciences, and the humanities.

POLITICS AND GOVERNMENT

Ghanaian Americans have gained few notable positions in United States government, but many are politically active, keep themselves abreast of politics and government, and, when necessary, are outspoken and eloquent critics. While many of their concerns relate to the politics of Ghana and other African nations, Ghanaian Americans are also active in issues of immigration, racism, and economic concerns. The most prominent Ghanaian American politician in the United States is Kwame Raoul, a Democratic member of the Illinois state senate. In 2004 he was elected to represent the state's thirteenth district, a seat vacated by future U.S. president Barack Obama.

The government of Ghana has begun to reach out to the members of the Ghanaian diaspora, including Ghanaian Americans. The country was among the first in Africa to enact a "right to abode" law offering dual citizenship for people of Ghanaian descent, and it has begun to market itself as a tourist destination for Ghanaian Americans. With so many Ghanaians living abroad, it is a stated goal of the Ghanaian government to try to mobilize its diverse worldwide diaspora around domestic Ghanaian issues. Extended family ties, village allegiances, and other cultural ties continually influence events among groups in Ghana and their related groups in the United States. Ghanaian Americans often act as connections between the Ghanaian and U.S. economies, whether through investment or the wealth of international connections found in the major urban centers of the United States.

It is common for Ghanaian Americans to visit their homelands frequently and to sponsor relatives and other Ghanaians for visits, immigration, or study stays in the United States. The relations between Ghanaian Americans and Ghanaians are generally strong and beneficial to both groups.

NOTABLE INDIVIDUALS

Academia James Emman Kwegyir Aggrey (1875–1927) was a Ghanaian-born scholar whose first major contribution was translating the Bible into the Fante language. Working as an editor at the *Gold Coast Methodist Times*, Aggrey rallied a successful campaign against the Lands Bill of 1897, thus stopping the colonial government from seizing all land that was not in visible use. In 1898 Aggrey went to the United States to study at Livingstone College in Salisbury, North Carolina. During the next two decades he engaged in ministerial work and studied theology at Columbia University and the Hood Theological School, where he received his doctorate in 1912. Serving in various posts, including as a board member of the commission on education for the prestigious Phelps-Stokes Fund, Aggrey spent years working for the promotion of education and social transformation of African people. After cofounding Achimota College in Ghana in 1924, he returned to the United States in 1927. Shortly afterward he died in New York.

Another Ghanaian American scholar is Kwame Anthony Appiah, who has been a professor of philosophy at numerous American universities, including Harvard, Yale, and Princeton. Born in London to a Ghanaian father and English mother in 1954, Appiah made a name for himself working with diversity, cultural identity, and community building in areas as diverse as metaphysics, anthropology, history, and sociology. His many published works include *In My Father's House: Africa in the Philosophy of Culture* (1992), a collection of essays on race and culture that was named a *New York Times* Notable Book of the Year in 1992 and was the winner of the African Studies Association's Herskovits Award in 1993. With Henry Louis Gates Jr. he coedited numerous volumes of critical perspectives on different African American writers, including Langston Hughes and Toni Morrison. In 2002 Appiah was appointed the Laurance S. Rockefeller University Professor of Philosophy at Princeton University.

Music Zadonu, a California-based group specializing in traditional Ghanaian music and dance, has had a wide range of successes. The group was founded by married couple Kobla and Dzidzorgbel Ladzekpo, longtime performers and instructors who taught at the University of California, Los Angeles, and the Naropa Institute. They were both on the faculty of the California Institute of the Arts, with Kobla serving as chair of the music department. Zadonu became known throughout the world for its workshops, seminars, and performances, which were successful at bringing together African cultural groups in the United States. Zadonu performed for the president of Ghana and at the Super Bowl. Among the group's credits are the score for the Hollywood film *Mississippi Masala* (1991).

Science Edward Ayensu (1935–), scientist and economist, is widely known as a policymaker on international environmental issues. Born in Ghana, Ayensu was first educated at Achimota College, received bachelor's and master's degrees in the United States, and earned a doctorate from the University of London. After receiving his degree in London, Ayensu returned to the United States, where he served as an associate curator of botany at the Smithsonian Institution before serving as chair and curator from 1970 to 1989. While at the Smithsonian, Ayensu also served as director of the institution's Endangered Species Project from 1976 to 1980. During this time Ayensu served on many prominent international boards for the environment. His publications include *Tropical Forest Ecosystems in Africa and South America* (1973) and *Medicinal Plants of West Africa* (1978).

Sports Several Ghanaian American professional football players have become noteworthy contributors to the National Football League (NFL). Most notable among them is Pro-Bowl running back Joseph Addai (1983–), who won an NCAA national championship playing for Louisiana State University before beginning a career in the NFL that included a Super Bowl victory with the Indianapolis Colts in 2007. Other Ghanaian Americans who have played in the NFL include Charlie Peprah (1983–), the grandson of a former military leader of Ghana; Visanthe Shiancoe (1980–); and Jon Asamoah (1988–).

Other standout Ghanaian American professional athletes include soccer players Freddy Adu (1989–) and C. J. Sapong (1988–), basketball player Nazr Mohammed (1977–), and professional wrestler Kofi Kingston (1981–), whose real name is Kofi Nahaje Sarkodie-Mensah. Boxer Jack Johnson (1878–1946), who became a central figure in early African American struggles for equal rights by winning the heavyweight championship in 1908, was of Ghanaian descent.

MEDIA

GhanaWeb

An English-language website aggregating news about Ghana and Ghanaian Americans.

Daalwijkdreef 47
1103 AD Amsterdam, Netherlands
Phone: +31 20 6977764
Email: info@ghanaweb.com
URL: www.ghanaweb.com

ORGANIZATIONS AND ASSOCIATIONS

African-American Association of Ghana (AAAG)

An association of African Americans who have repatriated to Ghana, the AAAG strives to be the premier cultural, social, spiritual, and economic organization for African Americans and other people of African descent returning from the diaspora into Ghanaian society.

PMB CT 34 Cantonments
Accra, Ghana
Phone: +233 24 076 5199
Email: TheAAAG@yahoo.com
URL: www.africanamericanassociationofghana.com

National Council of Ghanaian Associations

An umbrella organization encompassing various associations for Ghanaians living abroad. Includes numerous contacts in the United States.

Ofori Anor, Executive Secretary General
Phone: (718) 690-6873
Email: esg.ncoga@gmail.com
URL: www.ncoga.org

SOURCES FOR ADDITIONAL STUDY

Attah-Poku, Agyemang. *The Socio-Cultural Adjustment Question: The Role of Ghanaian Immigrant Ethnic Associations in America.* Brookfield, VT: Avebury, 1996.

Capps, Randy, Michael Fix, and Kristen McCabe. *New Streams: Black African Migration to the United States.* Washington, D.C.: Migration Policy Institute, 2011.

Hollander, Sophia. "In Little Ghana, a Big Celebration." *Wall Street Journal,* June 27, 2010.

Kondor, Daniel. *Ghanaian Culture in Perspective.* Accra: Presbyterian Press, 1993.

Mensah, Ishmael. "Marketing Ghana as a Mecca for the African-American Tourist," *Modern Ghana,* June 10, 2004. http://www.modernghana.com/news/114445/1/marketing-ghana-as-a-mecca-for-the-african-america.html.

Semple, Kirk. "With Fanfare, Ashanti People from Ghana Install Their New York Chief." *New York Times,* June 3, 2012.

GREEK AMERICANS

Jane Jurgens

OVERVIEW

Greek Americans are immigrants or descendants of people from Greece, which is officially known as the Hellenic Republic. Greece is a mountainous peninsula located in southeastern Europe between the Aegean and Mediterranean seas. It is bordered to the north by Bulgaria and Macedonia. Nearly 2,000 islands surround its eastern, southern, and western borders. The nine major land areas that constitute Greece include Central Pindus, Thessaly, the Salonika Plain, Macedonia/Thrace, Peloponnesus, the Southeastern Uplands, the Ionian Islands, the Aegean Islands, and Crete. With a landmass of 51,000 square miles (132,100 square kilometers), Greece is slightly smaller than the state of Alabama.

According to a 2012 estimate from the CIA World Factbook, Greece's population was around 10,767,827, making it the seventy-eighth most populous country in the world. The capital city, Athens, and the city of Thessaloniki (Salonika) have the largest populations in Greece. The ethnically and linguistically homogeneous nation is predominantly Greek speaking; 97 percent of the populace speaks Greek, whereas only 1 percent speaks Turkish. The Eastern Orthodox church is the dominant religion; only about 1.5 percent of the population is Muslim, and a small percentage is Roman Catholic, Greek Catholic, or Jewish. The Greek census does not ask about ethnicity, distinguishing only between Greeks and foreign-born citizens. Greece has a capitalist economy that hit crisis levels in 2009 due to large amounts of debt and the global financial crisis. These financial troubles led Greece to accept history's two largest bailouts (2010, 2011) from the International Monetary Fund. In exchange, Greece promised intense reforms and austerity measures that were highly unpopular with the general public. Quality of life declined significantly in Greece, and in 2011 the country had a 17.4 percent unemployment rate.

The first significant wave of Greek immigration to the United States began in the 1880s. Many of these immigrants were young men seeking to improve their financial circumstances. Greeks settled all over the United States but most often chose major metropolitan areas, frequently in the Midwest and Northeast, where they engaged in factory work or other unskilled labor. A substantial number also opened businesses such as restaurants, candy manufacturing plants, and dry cleaners, which were typically staffed by newly arrived Greeks. Greek immigration to the United States was significantly slowed by the anti-immigration measures of the 1920s through 1960s. From the 1960s through the 1980s, Greek Americans—along with other minority groups—benefited from a sociopolitical trend that caused women and ethnic groups to advocate for their rights. They established organizations focused on the Greek American experience and felt free expressing their opinions on political issues both in the United States and in Greece. Since immigration quotas came to an end in 1965, Greek immigration to the United States has remained slow but steady.

According the 2007 census, there were 1.3 million Greek Americans in the United States, a number slightly higher than the population of Rhode Island, though some estimate the number to be as high as 3 million. In an effort to improve these numbers and celebrate Greek American culture, the Hellenic American Census Committee also pushed for a "Greek" designation to be added to the 2010 census and, in lieu of that happening, encouraged Greek Americans to write in their ethnicity as Greek. This movement reflected Greek Americans' connection to their ethnic heritage as well as their engagement in contemporary American life. By the end of the twentieth century and the turn to the twenty-first, Greek Americans were an established and assimilated group in the United States, frequently proud of their heritage but living by mainstream American standards in terms of education, career, and family. Greek Americans now live all over the United States, though the largest populations are in the places that saw the most early immigration, including New York, Boston, Chicago, and Detroit, with sizable populations in Florida, Georgia, California, and Utah as well.

HISTORY OF THE PEOPLE

Early History Traditionally, Greeks referred to themselves as "Hellenes" and to the country of Greece as "Hellas." The word "Greek" comes from the Latin *Graeci*, a name given to the people of this region by the Romans. Greece is an ancient country that has been continuously occupied from 6000 BCE, the beginning of its Neolithic period, until the present. The Bronze Age, traditionally divided into early, middle, and late phases, dated from 2800 BCE to 1000 BCE. It was during this period that the Minoan civilization of Crete and the Mycenaean civilization of mainland Greece flourished. These civilizations were destroyed around 1000 BCE just as the individual city-state or "polis" was beginning to experience rapid growth. In 479 BCE the city-states united to defeat Persia, a common enemy, but national unity proved to be short-lived. The power struggle between Athens and Sparta, the principal city-states, dominated the period.

Athens reached its zenith during the fifth century BCE, a period known as its Golden Age. At this time Athens experimented with a form of internal democracy unique in the ancient world, achieved a singular culture, and left enduring literary and architectural legacies. Socrates, Plato, Xenophon, Herodotus, Sophocles, Euripides, and Aeschylus came into prominence, and in 432 BCE the Parthenon on the Acropolis was completed. The Peloponnesian War, fought between Athens and Sparta from 431 to 404 BCE, and a plague that raged through Athens in 430 brought the Golden Age to an end. For a time Sparta dominated the Greek world, but war and severe economic troubles hastened the decline of all of the city-states.

Greece came under Macedonian domination between 338 and 200 BCE. The Macedonian king, Alexander the Great, conquered Greece, Persia, and Egypt to create an empire, and he carried the idea of Hellenism to places as far away as India. The Hellenistic Age that followed Alexander's rule lasted until 146 BCE. As a Roman state from 127 BCE to CE 330, Greece and its city-states had no political or military power. When the Roman Empire was divided in CE 395, Greece became part of the Eastern Empire, which continued as the Byzantine Empire until 1453. That year the Turks captured Constantinople, the capital of Byzantium, and Greece became part of the Ottoman Empire.

Modern Era Greece's declaration of independence from the Ottoman Empire on March 25, 1821, resulted in the Greek War of Independence, which lasted until 1829, and began the history of independent modern Greece. Great Britain, France, and Russia assisted Greece in its struggle for independence, and Greece came under the protection of these powers by the London Protocol of 1830. In 1832 the Bavarian Otto I became the first king of Greece, and in 1844 a conservative revolutionary force established a constitutional monarchy. George I, who succeeded Otto I, created a more democratic form of government with a new constitution in 1864.

During the 1880s and 1890s, transportation, education, and social services rapidly improved. Then in 1897 a revolt against the Turks in Crete led to war between Greece and the Ottoman Empire and to eventual self-governance for Crete. A revolt by the Military League in 1909 prompted the appointment of Eleuthérios Venizélos as prime minister of Greece. Between 1910 and 1933 Venizélos enacted major financial reforms.

During World War I Greece joined the Allied forces in opposing Germany. After the war Greece regained much of the territory it had lost to the Ottoman Empire. But in 1921 Greece began a war against the Turks in Asia Minor and suffered a crushing defeat in 1922. In 1923, under the Treaty of Lausanne, more than 1.25 million Greeks moved from Turkey to Greece, and more than 400,000 Turks in Greece moved to Turkey.

Between the World Wars, the Greek population vacillated between the establishment of a republican form of government and the restoration of monarchy. In 1936 Greece became a military dictatorship under General Ioannis Metaxas, who remained in power until 1944. The Germans occupied Greece during World War II, and the country did not recover until the 1950s, when it slowly began to regain economic and political stability. In 1952 Greece joined the North Atlantic Treaty Organization and also granted women the right to vote and to hold political office. Alexander Papagos acted as prime minister from 1952 to 1955, and Konstantinos Karamanlis held the office from 1955 to 1963 and again from 1974 to 1980.

On April 27, 1967, Colonel George Papadopoulos led a military coup, resulting in the suspension of constitutionally guaranteed rights and the imposition of harsh social controls. Papadopoulos declared Greece a republic in 1973 and put an end to the monarchy before his government was overthrown. In November 1974 Greece held its first free elections in more than a decade. Parliament adopted a new constitution in 1975, and a civilian government was established.

The first Socialist government in Greece gained control in 1981, the year Andreas Papandreou—the son of George Papandreou and a member of the Panhellenic Socialist movement—succeeded conservative Georgios Rallis as prime minister. In this same year, Greece joined the European Union. In 1989 a conservative-communist coalition formed a new government, and Papandreou, pledging that Greece would be an active participant in the greater European community, was reelected. Under a largely socialist government, Greece thrived, strengthening ties to Europe and the global community, increasing quality of life for its citizens, and hosting the summer Olympic Games in 2004. However, Greece was hard-hit by the economic recession of 2007, which caused its sizable debt to balloon, leading to multiple downgrades in Greece's credit rating. The problems in Greece's economy rippled across the European Union, inciting fears of other economic catastrophes and endangering the strength of the Euro as a global currency. In 2012, Greece's financial woes and its people's dislike of extreme austerity measures led some to question whether Greece should or would leave the eurozone.

SETTLEMENT IN THE UNITED STATES

According to official records, the Greek sailor Don Teodoro or Theodoros, who sailed with the Spanish explorer Pánfilo de Narváez in 1528, was the first Greek to land in America. John Griego and Petros the Cretan are other Greek sailors who may have come to America during this period. There is some speculation that Juan De Fuca, who discovered the straits south of Vancouver Island, may actually have been a Greek named Ionnis Phocas.

One of the first Greek colonies was at New Smyrna near Saint Augustine, Florida. Andrew Turnbull and his wife, Maria Rubini, daughter of a wealthy Greek merchant, persuaded approximately 450 colonists to journey to America and settle. With the promise of land, Greek colonists, primarily from Mani in the south of Greece, as well as Italians, Minorcans, and Corsicans, began arriving in Florida on June 26, 1768. The colony was an overwhelming failure and was officially disbanded on July 17, 1777, but many of the colonists had already moved to neighboring Saint Augustine, where they were becoming successful as merchants and small businessmen. A small community of Greeks also built a chapel and school there.

The first significant wave of Greek immigrants included about forty orphans who had survived the Greek Revolution of 1821 and who were brought to the United States by American missionaries; survivors of the 1822 massacre of Chios by the Turks; and merchant sailors who settled in the Americas. Most of these Greeks were from islands such as Chios, and others came from Asia Minor, Epirus, and Macedonia. By 1860 about 328 Greeks were living in the United States, with the majority residing in California, Arkansas, New York, and Massachusetts.

The Greek American population remained small until the 1880s, when poor economic conditions in Greece prompted many Greeks to immigrate to the United States. During the 1880s most who came were from Laconia (notably, from the city of Sparta), a province of the Peloponnesus in southern Greece. Beginning in the 1890s, Greeks began arriving from other parts of Greece, principally from Arcadia, another province in the Peloponnesus. The largest numbers arrived between 1900 and 1910 (686) and 1911 and 1920 (385). In the late teens and early 1920s there was a substantial influx of Greeks forced by Turks from their ancestral homes in Asia Minor. Most were young single males who came to the United States to seek their fortunes and wished to return to Greece as soon as possible. About 30 percent of those who came before 1930 did return, including some who went to fight in the Balkan Wars of 1912–1913.

Many males returned to Greece after establishing themselves in the United States and then returned to the United States with brides. This was a typical pattern for unmarried males.

> **I felt grateful the Statue of Liberty was a woman. I felt she would understand a woman's heart.**
>
> Stella Petrakis in 1916, cited in *Ellis Island: An Illustrated History of the Immigrant Experience*, edited by Ivan Chermayeff et al. (New York: Macmillan, 1991).

During the 1890s Greeks began settling in major urban areas, including the industrial cities of the Northeast and Midwest. The first immigrants settled in Massachusetts and southern New Hampshire. The city of Lowell, Massachusetts, attracted the majority of Greeks, and by 1920 it had the third largest Greek community in the United States. In eastern Pennsylvania, Philadelphia-Reading also boasted a substantial Greek community in the 1920s. Greeks also settled in the New England towns of Haverhill, Lynn, Boston, Peabody, and Manchester. The largest Greek settlement in the twentieth century was in New York. Greeks also settled in western Pennsylvania, particularly Pittsburgh, and in the Midwestern cities of Detroit, Milwaukee, Cleveland, Youngstown, and Chicago.

Small Greek communities existed in Galveston, Texas, and Atlanta, Georgia, but the largest concentration of Greeks in the South was at Tarpon Springs, Florida. In the first half of the twentieth century, this unique settlement of Greeks made its living by sponge diving.

Attracted to mining and railroad work, Greeks also settled in Salt Lake City in large numbers, with smaller concentrations inhabiting Colorado, Wyoming, Idaho, and Nevada. The heaviest early concentration on the Pacific Coast was in San Francisco. Today, Greeks live primarily in urban areas and are increasingly moving to the South and West. The 2010 U.S. Census revealed that New York State still had the largest population of Greeks. The next largest populations were in California, Illinois, Massachusetts, and Florida.

The Immigration Acts of 1921 and 1924 reversed the open-door policy of immigration and established quotas. The Act of 1921 limited the number of Greek admittants to 3,063; the Act of 1924 limited the number to 100. Legal petition increased the quota, and between 1925 and 1929 about 10,883 Greeks were admitted. Another 17,000 Greeks were admitted under the Refugee Relief Act of 1953, and 1,504 were accepted as a result of further legislation in 1957.

The Immigration Act of 1965 abandoned the quota system and gave preference to immigrants

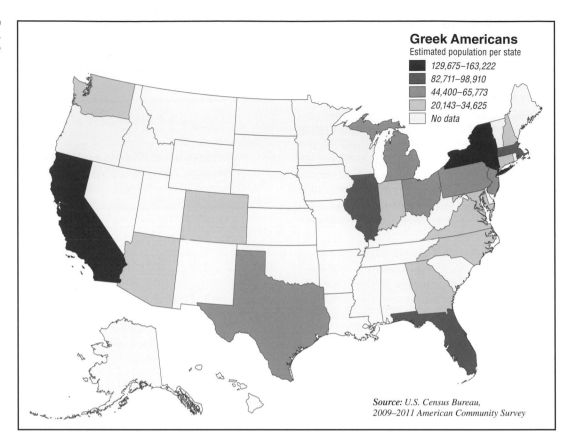

Greek Americans
Estimated population per state

- 129,675–163,222
- 82,711–98,910
- 44,400–65,773
- 20,143–34,625
- No data

Source: U.S. Census Bureau, 2009–2011 American Community Survey

with families already established in the United States. The new Greek arrivals usually were better educated than their predecessors and included men and women in equal numbers, as well as family groups. From 1820 to 1982 a total of 673,360 Greeks immigrated to the United States. After 1982 immigration slowed but remained consistent with less than 10,000 Greeks immigrating to the United States over the next three decades.

LANGUAGE

Greek is a conservative language that has retained much of its original integrity. Modern Greek is derived from the Attic Koine of the first century CE. During Byzantine times, the language underwent modifications and also incorporated many French, Turkish, and Italian words. Modern Greek retained the ancient alphabet and orthography of the more ancient language, but many changes have taken place in the phonetic value of letters and in the spelling. Although about 75 percent of the old words remain from the ancient language, words often have taken on new meanings. Modern Greek also retains from the ancient language a system of three-pitch accents (acute, circumflex, grave). In 1982, a monotonic accent (one-stress accent) was officially adopted by the Greek government.

Greeks are fiercely proud of the continuity and relative stability of their language, and much

confusion and debate persists about "correct Greek." Language traditionalists in Greece and the United States lament the "bastardization" of the language by foreign influences and by the late-twentieth century influx of immigrants and guest workers to Greece. Two separate languages were once widely written and spoken in Greece: demotic Greek (*Demotiki*), the more popular language of the people, and *Katharevousa*, the "pure" archaic language of administration, religion, education, and literature. In 1967 demotic Greek was recognized as the official spoken and written language of Greece; this is the language adopted for liturgical services by the Greek Orthodox church in the United States.

Modern Greek contains twenty-four characters with seven vowels and five vowel sounds. It is traditionally written in Attic characters; the letters, their names, transliterations, and pronunciations are: "Αα"—alpha/a ("ah"); "Ββ"—beta/b ("b"); "Γγ"—gamma/g ("gh," "y"); "Δδ"—delta/d, dh ("th"); "Εε"—epsilon/e ("eh"); "Ζζ"—zeta/z ("z"); "Ηη"—eta/e ("ee"); "Θθ"—theta/th ("th"); "Ιι"—yiota/i ("ee"); "Κκ"—kappa/k, c ("k"); "Λλ"—lambda/l ("l"); "Μμ"—mu/m ("m"); "Νν"—nee/n ("n"); "Ξξ"—kse/x ("ks"); "Οο"—omicron/o ("oh"); "Ππ"—pi/p ("p"); "Ρρ"—rho/r ("r"); "Σσ"—sigma/s ("s"); "Ττ"—taf/t ("t"); "Υυ"—upsilon/y ("u"); "Φφ"—Phi/ph ("f"); "Χχ"—Chi/h ("ch" [as in "ach"]); "Ψψ"—psee/ps ("ps" [as in "lapse"]); "Ωω"—omega/o ("oh").

Greek language schools can be found throughout the United States. These are often the product of Greek Orthodox churches intent on passing the language along to American-born children. These schools teach modern Greek language and, often, traditional Greek culture—including dance, music, and history. Because so many Greek Americans feel connected to their cultural heritage, new generations are often encouraged to discover Greek's rich rewards. Further, because of the importance of Greek history to Western civilization, many American universities offer courses in ancient Greek language and history.

Greetings and Popular Expressions Some of the more common expressions in the Greek language (with pronunciation) include:

Οχι ("ohchi")—No

Ναι ("neh")—Yes

Ευχαριστο (Efcharisto)—Thank you

Καλημερα ("kahleemera")—Good morning

Καλησπερα ("kahleespehrah")—Good afternoon/evening

Γεια σωυσασ ("yah soo"/"yah sahs")—Hello/Good-bye (informal)

Χαιρετε ("chehrehteh")—Greetings/Hello (formal)

Ωπα! ("ohpah")—Hooray!

Toasts may include Για χαρα ("yah chahrah")—For joy and Καλη τυχη ("kahlee teechee")—Good luck. Other popular expressions are Χρωνια πωλλα ("chrohnyah pohllah")—Many years/Happy birthday; Χαλη χρωνια ("kahlee chrohnyah")—Good year; Καλη Σαρακωστη ("kahlee sahrahkohstee")—Good Lent; Κuλu Χριστωυγεννα ("kahlah chris tooghehnna")—Merry Christmas. Expressions used at Easter are Καλω Πασχα ("kahloh pahschah")—Happy Easter (used before Easter); Καλω Ανασταση ("kahlee ahnahstahsee")—Good Resurrection (said after the Good Friday service); Χριστωσ ανεστη ("christohs ahnehstee")—Christ has risen (said after the Good Friday service) and its response, Αλη θωσ ανεστη ("ahleethohs ahnehstee")—Truly he has risen.

RELIGION

Theodore Salutos in *The Greeks in the United States* wrote: "Hellenism and Greek Orthodoxy—the one intertwined with the other—served as the cord that kept the immigrant attached to the mother country, nourished his patriotic appetites and helped him preserve the faith and language of his parents." The Greek Orthodox church helped to meet the emotional and spiritual needs of the immigrant. The early churches grew out of the *kinotitos* (community) where a *symvoulion* (board of directors) raised the money to build the church. The first Greek Orthodox church in the United States was founded in New Orleans in 1864. As Greek communities grew, other churches were established in New York (1892); Chicago (1893); Lowell, Massachusetts

(1903); and Boston (1903). By 1923, there were 140 Greek churches in the United States.

Today, the liturgy and spirit of the Greek Orthodox church help to keep alive Greek ethnic cultural traditions in the United States. According to Gary Kunkelman in *The Religion of Ethnicity*, to a Greek American, "ethnicity is synonymous with the church. One is a Greek not because he is a Hellene by birth; indeed many of Greek parentage have abandoned their identities and disappeared into the American mainstream. Rather one is Greek because he elects to remain part of the Greek community and an individual is a member of the Greek community by virtue of his attachment to the Greek Orthodox church, the framework on which the community rests." A Greek Orthodox seminary in the United States, Hellenic College/Holy Cross Greek Orthodox School of Theology in Massachusetts provides a supply of mostly U.S.-born priests. This has lessened dependence on clergymen from Greece, who often arrive with scant understanding of the American way of life.

For many the Greek Orthodox church is the center of community life. In the United States all dioceses, parishes, and churches are under the ecclesiastical jurisdiction of the Archdiocese of America, an autonomous self-governing church within the sphere of influence of the Ecumenical Patriarch of Constantinople and New Rome. The Ecumenical Patriarch has the power to elect the archbishop and the bishops, directs all church matters outside the American church, and remains the guiding force in all matters of faith. Founded in 1922, the Archdiocese is located in New York City. It supports 540 parishes across the United States.

"Orthodox" comes from the Greek *orthos* (correct) and *doxa* (teaching or worship). The Greek Orthodox churches share a common liturgy, worship, and tradition. In its fundamental beliefs, the church is conservative, resistant to change, and allows little flexibility. The Orthodox tradition is an Eastern tradition with the official center of Orthodoxy at Constantinople. After the tenth century Eastern and Western traditions grew apart on matters of faith, dogma, customs, and politics. East and West finally divided on the issue of papal authority.

The basic beliefs of the Orthodox are summarized in the Nicene Creed dating back to the fourth century. The Orthodox believe that one can achieve complete identification with God (*theosis*). All activities and services in the church are to assist the individual in achieving that end. The most important service is the Divine Liturgy in which there are four distinct liturgies: St. John Chrysostom (the one most frequently followed), St. Basil (followed ten times a year), St. James (October 23), and the Liturgy of the Presanctified Gifts (Wednesdays and Fridays of Lent and the first three days of Easter Holy Week). The church uses Greek Koine, the language of New

Testament Greek, as its liturgical language. The seven sacraments in the church are Baptism, Chrismation, Confession, Communion, Marriage, Holy Unction (Anointing of the Sick), and Holy Orders. The Greek Orthodox calendar has many feast days, fast days, and name days. The most important feast day ("the feast of feasts") is Holy Pascha (Easter Sunday). In addition to Easter, the "twelve great feasts" are the Nativity of the Mother of God, the Exaltation of the Holy Cross, the Presentation of the Mother of God in the Temple, Christmas, Epiphany, the Presentation of Jesus Christ in the Temple, Palm Sunday, Ascension of Jesus Christ, Pentecost, the Transfiguration of Jesus Christ, and the Dormition (death) of the Mother of God.

The Greek Orthodox church also follows the Byzantine tradition in its architecture. The church is divided into the vestibule (the front of the church representing the world), the nave (the main area where people assemble), and the sanctuary. The sanctuary is separated from the nave by an iconostasis, a screenlike partition. Only the priests enter the sanctuary. Icons (images of saints) decorate the iconostasis in prescribed tiers. The service takes place in the sanctuary, which contains an altar table and an oblation (preparation) table. The Greek Orthodox church is filled with symbols, including crosses and icons, which create an aura of heaven on earth.

The church continues to face the process of Americanization. The American Orthodox church has many American elements: an American-trained clergy, the introduction of English into the service, modern music written for organ, and modern architecture and architectural features (pews, choir lofts, and separate social halls). Churches also often serve as sites for outreach and heritage building, running Greek language schools and hosting festivals of Greek food and culture. The limited role of women in the church is being questioned. Until the second century, women fully participated in the church as teachers, preachers, and deacons. After that period, however, their roles were limited by official decree. Today women are taking more active leadership roles, and some have discussed reviving the role of deacon for women; however, the question of ordaining women to the priesthood has not been seriously considered, and questions about women's roles continue to be debated. As a response to the increasing "Americanization" of the church that took place between the 1960s and the 1980s, the Greek Orthodox hierarchy has become increasingly conservative, and debate over issues such as women's roles has not been robust.

Baptisms and Chrismations The *koumbari* who act as wedding sponsors usually also act as godparents for a couple's first child. The baptism begins at the narthex of the church, where the godparents speak for the child, renouncing Satan by blowing three times in the air and spitting three times on the floor. They then recite the Nicene Creed. The priest uses the child's baptismal name for the first time and asks God to cleanse away sin. The priest, the godparents, and the child go to the baptismal font at the front of the church, where the priest consecrates the water, adding olive oil to it as a symbol of reconciliation. The child is undressed, and the priest makes the sign of the cross on various parts of the child's body. The godparents rub olive oil over the child's body, and the priest thrice immerses the child in the water of the baptismal font to symbolize the three days Christ spent in the tomb. The godparents then receive the child and wrap him or her in a new white sheet. During chrismation, immediately following baptism, the child is anointed with a special oil, (*miron*), which has been blessed by the Ecumenical Patriarch of Constantinople. The child is dressed in new clothing, and a cross is placed around his or her neck. After the baptismal candle is lighted, the priest and godparents hold the child, and a few children walk around the font in a dance of joy. Finally, scriptures are read, and communion is given to the child. This ceremony is typically followed by a festive dinner celebration sponsored by the parents.

CULTURE AND ASSIMILATION

Few negative Greek stereotypes persist. Greeks share the American work ethic and desire for success and are largely perceived as hardworking and family-oriented. They are also said to possess a "Zorba"-like spirit and love of life. However, many Greek Americans perceive more recent Greek immigrants as "foreign" and often consider them a source of embarrassment. Conversely, many recent immigrants, who are thoroughly modernized Europeans, find the emphasis that Greek Americans place on traditional elements such as Greek

In the Greek Orthodox Epiphany Ceremonies, the Archbishop throws a cross into the water and a group of boys dive in to try to find it first. AP IMAGES / CHRIS O'MEARA

dancing, costumes, and music to be "old-fashioned" and even humorous.

Traditions and Customs Greeks have an assortment of traditional customs, beliefs, and superstitions to ensure success and ward off evil and misfortune. Old beliefs persist in some communities in the United States. For example, belief in the "evil eye" is still strong and is supported by the Greek Orthodox church as a generalized concept of evil. Precautions against the evil eye (*not* endorsed by the church) include wearing garlic; making the sign of the cross behind the ear of a child with dirt or soot; placing an image of an eye over the lintel; wearing the *mati*, a blue amulet with an eye in the center; and recitation of a ritual prayer, the *ksematiasma*. Greeks may also respond to a compliment with the expression *ptou, ptou* to keep the evil eye from harming the person receiving the compliment. Greeks also "knock wood" to guard against misfortune, and reading one's fortunes in the patterns of coffee dregs remains popular. Although not an official practice of the Greek Orthodox faith, many Greek Americans expect the priest to annually bless their homes.

Cuisine Greek food is extremely popular in the United States, where Greek American restaurants flourish, and many communities host yearly Greek food festivals. In Greek restaurants and in the home, many of the traditional recipes have been adapted (and sometimes improved upon) to suit American tastes. In Greece, meals are great social occasions where friends and family come together, and the quantity of food is often impressive. Olive oil is a key ingredient in Greek cooking and is used prodigiously. Traditional herbs include parsley, mint, dill, oregano (especially the wild oregano *rigani*), and garlic. You will find on most Greek tables olives, sliced cheese (such as feta, *kasseri*, and *kefalotiri*), tomato, and lemon wedges, along with bread. Feta has become so popular in the United States that it is used widely by modern restaurants and home cooks for a variety of dishes—not necessarily Greek. Fish, vegetables, chicken, beef, and especially lamb are all found on the Greek menu and are prepared in a variety of ways. Soup, salad, and yogurt are served as side dishes. Sheets of dough called *phillo* are layered and filled with spinach, cheese, eggs, and nuts. Greeks create such masterpieces as *moussaka*, a layered dish of eggplant, meat, cheese, and bread crumbs sometimes served with a white sauce. Other popular Greek dishes in the United States include *souvlakia*, a shish kebob of lamb, vegetables, and onions; *keftedes*, Greek meatballs; *saganaki*, a mixture of fried cheese, milk, egg, and flour; *dolmathes yalantzi*, grape leaves stuffed with rice, pine nuts, onion, and spices; and gyros, slices of beef, pork, and lamb prepared on a skewer, served with tomatoes, onion, and cucumber yogurt sauces on pita bread.

Soups include *psarosoupa me avgolemono*, a rich fish soup made with egg and lemon sauce; *spanaki soupa*, spinach soup; *mayeritsa*, an Easter soup made with tripe or lamb parts and rice; and *fasolatha*, a white

The original Mama Maria Koursiotis is depicted here. Mrs. Koursiotis opened The Original Mama Maria's Greek Cuisine restaurant in Tarpon Springs, Florida. JEFF GREENBERG / ALAMY

bean Lenten soup made with tomatoes, garlic, and spices. Salads always accompany a meal. The traditional Greek salad (*salata a la greque*) is made with feta cheese, tomatoes, onion, cucumbers, olives, oregano, and olive oil. Greek American restaurants frequently modify this salad by adding lettuce to it, in keeping with traditional American ideas about what constitutes salad.

The national drink of Greece is *ouzo* ("oozoh"), an anise-flavored liquor that tastes like licorice and that remains popular with Greek Americans. Traditionally, it is served with appetizers (*mezethes*) such as olives, cheese, tomato, and lemon wedges. A popular Greek wine, *retsina*, is produced only in Greece and is imported to the United States.

Traditional Dress Greek traditional costumes come in a variety of styles, some dating back to ancient times. Women's clothing is heavy, with many layers and accessories, designed to cover the entire body. The undergarments include the floor-length *poukamiso* (shirt) made of linen or cotton and the *mesofori* (underskirt) and *vraka* (panties), usually of muslin. The outer garments consist of the forema-palto, a coatdress of embroidered linen; the *fousta* (skirt) of wool or silk; the *sigouni*, a sleeveless jacket of embroidered wool worn outside the *forema-palto*; the *kontogourni* or *zipouni*, a short vest worn over the fousta; the podia, an apron of embroidered wool or linen; and finally the *zonari*, a long belt wrapped many times around the waist. Buckles on these belts can be very ornate.

The popular movie *My Big Fat Greek Wedding* humorously depicted a typical Greek American wedding. IFC FILMS / THE KOBAL COLLECTION / GIRAUD, SOPHIE

are placed on the bride's and groom's right hands, and then the official wedding sponsors (*koumbari*) exchange the rings three times. Many things in Greek Orthodox ceremonies are repeated three times because of the importance of the Holy Trinity to the religion. During the wedding ceremony the bride and groom each hold a lighted white candle and join right hands while the priest prays over them. Crowns (*stephana*) joined with a ribbon are placed on their heads, and the *koumbaros* (male) or *koumbara* (female) is responsible for exchanging the wedding crowns three times above the heads of the couple during the service. The crowns traditionally are preserved and buried with the individuals. Often read at the ceremony are the Epistle of Saint Paul to the Ephesians and the second chapter of the Gospel of Saint John, which stress the mutual respect and love the couple now owe each other and the sanctity of the married state. After the couple shares a common cup of wine, they are led around the table by the priest in the Dance of Isaiah, which symbolizes the joy of the church in the new marriage. The *koumbaros* follows, holding the ribbon that joins the crowns. With the blessing of the priest, the couple is proclaimed married, and the crowns are removed. The Orthodox church will not conduct marriages between Orthodox Christians and non-Christians, but they make provisions for marriages between Orthodox Christians and Christians of other denominations.

The wedding reception reflects the influence of both Greek and American tradition, and is notable for its abundance of food, dancing, and singing. The wedding cake is served along with an assortment of Greek sweets that may include baklava, and *koufeta*—traditional wedding candy—is often distributed in candy dishes or in *bombonieries* (small favors given to guests after the wedding).

Death and Burial Rituals The funeral service in the Greek Orthodox church is called *kithia*. Traditionally, the *trisayion* (the three holies) is recited at the time of death or at any time during a forty-day mourning period. In the United States the *trisayion* is repeated at the funeral service. At the beginning of the service, the priest greets the mourners at the entrance of the church. An open casket is arranged so that the deceased faces the altar. During the service mourners recite scriptures, prayers, and hymns, and they are invited by the priest to pay their last respects to the deceased by filing past the casket and kissing the icon that has been placed within. The family gathers around the casket for a last farewell, and the priest sprinkles oil on the body in the form of the cross and says a concluding prayer. After the priest, friends, or family members deliver a brief eulogy, the body is taken immediately for burial (*endaphiasmos*). At the cemetery the priest recites the *trisayion* for the last time and sprinkles dirt on the casket while reciting a prayer. After the funeral guests and family share a funeral meal (*makaria*), which traditionally consists of brandy, coffee, and *paximathia* (hard, dry toast). A full meal may also be served, with fish as the main course.

EMPLOYMENT AND ECONOMIC CONDITIONS

The first immigrants were for the most part young single men who had no intention of remaining permanently in the United States. They came to work in the large industrial cities of the Northeast and Midwest as factory laborers, peddlers, busboys, and bootblacks. Those who went to the mill towns of New England worked in textile and shoe factories, whereas the Greeks who went West worked in mines and on the railroads. These Greeks often were subject to the *padrone* system, a form of exploitative indentured servitude employed in many of the larger industrial cities of the North and in the large mining corporations of the West.

Greeks in the United States have stressed individual efforts and talent and have had a long tradition of entrepreneurship. Many who were peddlers and street merchants in the United States became owners of small businesses—first-generation Greeks who were fruit and vegetable peddlers became owners of grocery stores; flower vendors opened florist shops. Greeks in Lowell, Massachusetts, became successful in numerous businesses. By 1912, according to *Lowell: The Story of an Industrial City*, they owned "seven restaurants, twenty coffee houses, twelve barber shops, two drug stores, six fruit stores, eight shoeshine parlors, one dry-goods store, four ticket agencies, seven bakeries, four candy stores [and] twenty-two grocery stores."

In the 1920s Greeks owned thousands of confectionery stores across the country and usually owned the candy-manufacturing businesses that supplied the stores. When the candy businesses collapsed, Greeks became restaurant owners. By the late 1920s several thousand Greek restaurants were scattered across the country. Many immigrants of the 1950s and 1960s went into the fast-food restaurant business.

The Greek professional class remained small until the 1940s. During the first quarter of the twentieth century, most Greek professionals were doctors. The next largest group comprised lawyers, dentists, pharmacists, and chemists. A few became professors of literature, philosophy, and the classics. Although the Greeks were slow to develop an academic tradition in this country in part because of low economic incentive, a new professional class began to emerge after World War I. Today Greek Americans engage in many professional academic endeavors. Instead of remaining in family-held businesses, third- and fourth-generation Greek Americans increasingly are pursuing professional careers. Currently, Greeks are found in almost every occupation and enterprise, and constitute one of the wealthier economic groups in the United States.

POLITICS AND GOVERNMENT

Numerous Greek American political and social organizations have existed since the 1880s. These organizations often were made up of Greeks who had come from the same region in Greece. They had a shared sense of Hellenism and a common religion and language, often aligning themselves with native Greek concerns. The *kinotitos* (community) was an organization similar to the village government in Greece. Although the *kinotitos* helped to preserve Greek traditions, it sometimes hindered assimilation.

In 1907 the Pan-Hellenic Union was founded with several intended goals, including to coordinate and incorporate local organizations, to provide a means of helping Greece obtain more territory from the Ottoman Empire, and to support the return of Constantinople to Greece and the consolidation of all Greek colonies in the Eastern Mediterranean under Greek authority. It also helped Greeks to adapt to their new home in the United States. Many Greek immigrants were slowly beginning to accept the fact that they would not be returning to Greece and that the United States was their permanent home. In 1922 the American Hellenic Educational Progressive Association (AHEPA) was founded. Although the AHEPA supported the assimilation of Greeks to the American way of life, it did not relinquish its strong attachments to Greece. During World War II, the AHEPA was a major contributor to the Greek War Relief Association.

The one issue that mobilized the Greek American community to political action was the Turkish invasion of Cyprus on July 15, 1974. The efforts of well-organized lobby groups to effect an arms embargo against Turkey were impressive. The AHEPA played a leading role in these activities, along with other lobby groups—the American Hellenic Institute and its public affairs committee, the influential United Hellenic American Congress, and the Hellenic Council of America. The Greek Orthodox church and local community organizations also assisted. Primarily because of the successful lobbying of these groups, the United States imposed an arms embargo on Turkey on February 5, 1975, which lasted until 1978.

Greek American politicians were also instrumental in shaping U.S. policy toward the Republic of Macedonia, established after the breakup of the communist Yugoslav federation in the early 1990s. Greece strenuously objected to Macedonia's use of a name that also refers to a region in Greece and announced a trade embargo against the new country. When, on February 9, 1994, President Clinton announced that the United States would officially recognize Macedonia, Greek American politicians launched an intensive campaign to reverse this policy, gathering 30,000 signatures on a protest petition. Clinton succumbed to this pressure and announced that the United States would withhold diplomatic relations until an envoy could resolve Greece's objections.

Greek political figures are almost overwhelmingly Democratic. They include Michael Dukakis, Paul Tsongas, John Brademas, Paul Spyros Sarbanes, Michael Bilirakis, Andrew Manatos, and George Stephanopoulos. Although Greek Americans traditionally have voted Democratic, their increasing wealth and status have led to an even division within the Greek American community between Republicans and Democrats. Owing largely to the wedge issue of abortion, many shifted to the Republican Party in the early 2000s. Greek Americans have also participated in large numbers in all major wars fought by the United States.

NOTABLE INDIVIDUALS

Greek Americans have made significant contributions in virtually all of the arts, sciences, and humanities, as well as in politics and business. Following is a sample of their achievements.

Academia Aristides Phoutrides (1887–1923), a distinguished professor at Harvard and Yale universities, established Helikon, the first Greek student organization, in 1911 in Boston. George Mylonas (1898–1988) had a distinguished career in the fields of Classical and Bronze Age art and archaeology. His numerous books include *Mycenae, the Capital City of Agamemnon* (1956), *Aghios Kosmos* (1959), *Eleusis and the Eleusinian Mysteries* (1961), *Mycenae and the Mycenaean Age* (1966), *Mycenae's Last Century of Greatness* (1968), *Grave Circle B of Mycenae* (1972), *The Cult Center of Mycenae* (1972), and *The West Cemetery of Eleusis* (1975).

Theodore Saloutos (1910–1980) was a professor of history at the University of California, Los Angeles, well-known for his studies of the Greek immigration experience. His most important work, *Greeks in the United States* (1964), became a model for other works on this topic.

Education John Celivergos Zachos (1820–1898), one of forty orphans who came to the United States during the Greek Revolution of 1821, was associate principal of the Cooper Female Seminary in Dayton, Ohio (1851–1854), principal and teacher of literature in the grammar school of Antioch College in Yellow Springs, Ohio (1854–1857), a surgeon during the Civil War, a teacher at Meadville Theological School (1866–1867), and a teacher and curator at Cooper Union in New York until 1898. Michael Anagnos (1837–1906) became the director of the famous Perkins Institute for the Blind in Boston, where he promoted vocational training and self-help.

Stage and Screen John Cassavetes (1929–1989) was a well-known stage, screen, and television actor, director, playwright, and screenwriter. His many film appearances include *Fourteen* (1951), *The Killers* (1964), *The Dirty Dozen* (1967), and *Rosemary's Baby* (1968). He directed and produced many films including *Too Late Blues* (1962), *A Child Is Waiting* (1963), *A Woman Under the Influence* (1974), and *Big Trouble* (1986).

Elia Kazan (1909–2003) was born Elias Kazantzoglou in Constantinople. He was well-known as a director, producer, actor, and writer. His best-known productions include *A Streetcar Named Desire* (1951), *A Face in the Crowd* (1957), *Splendor in the Grass* (1961), *America, America* (1963), and *The Arrangement* (1969). He directed such films as *A Tree Grows in Brooklyn* (1945), *Gentlemen's Agreement* (1947), *On the Waterfront* (1953), and *East of Eden* (1954). His writings include *America, America* (1962), *The Arrangement* (1969), *The Assassins* (1972), *The Understudy* (1974), *Acts of Love* (1978), and *The Anatolian* (1982).

Katina Paxinou (1900–1973), born Katina Constantopoulos, was a popular actress who starred in many films, including *For Whom the Bell Tolls* (1943), *Confidential Agent* (1945), *Mourning Becomes Electra* (1947), *The Inheritance* (1947), and *Prince of Foxes* (1945).

Telly Savalas (1923–1994), a popular film and television actor, was best known for his role as Theo Kojack in the National Broadcasting Corporation's television series *Kojack* (1973). Born in Garden City, New York, Savalas starred in several films, including *The Young Savages* (1961), *Birdman of Alcatraz* (1962), *The Greatest Story Ever Told* (1965), and *The Dirty Dozen* (1967).

George Chakiris (1934–), a singer, dancer, and actor, has been in films since the 1940s. He starred in roles in *Gentlemen Prefer Blondes* (1953); *White Christmas* (1954); *West Side Story* (1961), for which he won a Golden Globe Award and an Academy Award for Best Supporting Actor; *Diamond Head* (1962); and *Is Paris Burning?* (1963).

Olympia Dukakis (1931–), a well-known film actress and the cousin of politician Michael Dukakis, appeared in a number of roles since the 1960s. Selected films include *Lilith* (1964), *Twice a Man* (1964), *John and Mary* (1969), *Made for Each Other* (1971), and *The Idolmaker* (1980). More recent films include *Steel Magnolias* (1989) and *Moonstruck* (1987)—for which she won an Academy Award for Best Supporting Actress—and the critically acclaimed *Away from Her* (2006).

Jennifer Aniston (1969–), an actress, lived a year of her childhood with family in Greece and is best known for her portrayal of "Rachel" on the television series *Friends* (1994–2004) and various film roles, including *Office Space* (1999), *The Good Girl* (2002), and *Marley and Me* (2008).

Tina Fey (1970–) is a writer, actress, producer, and comedian. She got her big break as a writer for *Saturday Night Live*, where she also performed on the recurring segment "Weekend Update." She returned to SNL several times between 2008 and 2011 to portray Governor Sarah Palin, the 2008 Republican vice presidential candidate. She drew on her experience as an SNL writer for the television series *30 Rock* (2006–2012), which she created and in which she had a starring role. Fey acted in the films *Mean Girls* (2004), which she also wrote; *Baby Mama* (2008); and *Date Night* (2010).

Amy Sedaris (1961–) is an actress, comedian, and writer, best known for her work on the television series *Strangers with Candy* (1999–2000) and the spoof hospitality books *I Like You: Hospitality Under the Influence* (2006) and *Simple Times: Crafts for Poor People* (2010). She also regularly collaborates with her brother, writer David Sedaris (1956–). Michael Constantine (1927–) is an actor best known for his role as the Greek father in *My Big Fat Greek Wedding* (2002). He won an Emmy award for Outstanding Supporting Actor for his role on the 1970s television series *Room 222.*

Fine Arts Christos G. Bastis (1904–1999), born in Trikala, Greece, established the Sea Fare restaurant in New York City and became a notable collector of ancient sculpture. He donated several works from his collection to the Metropolitan Museum of Art and was an honorary trustee of that institution and a member of the board of trustees of the Brooklyn Museum. Painter William Baziotes (1912–1963) was a notable painter who contributed to the abstract expressionism movement. He taught at the Brooklyn Museum Art School, the Museum of Modern Art, Hunter College, and New York University.

Journalism Constantine Phasoularides published the first Greek American newspaper in New York in 1892, the *Neos Kosmos* (*New World*).

Nicholas Gage (1939–), born in Lia, is a journalist and writer associated with the *Worcester Telegram and Evening Gazette, Boston Herald Traveler, Associated Press, Wall Street Journal,* and the *New York Times.* He left the *New York Times* in 1980 to write *Eleni,* a work detailing the events surrounding the execution of his mother by communist guerrillas in Greece in the 1940s; in 1985 the book was made into a movie. Gage also wrote *Greek Fire: The Story of Maria Callas and Aristotle Onassis* about the affair of two fellow Greeks.

Another biographer of Maria Callas, Arianna Huffington (1950–) is a writer, politician, and political commentator. She shook up political circles when she switched her allegiance from conservative to liberal politics. She is best known for her news Web site and content aggregator, *The Huffington Post.* Robert Quinlan "Bob" Costas (1952–) is a sportscaster for NBC Sports television. The recipient of eight National Sportscaster of the Year awards from the National Sportscasters and Sportswriters Association (NSSA), he was inducted into the organization's Hall of Fame in 2012. Television journalist George Stephanopoulos (1961–) is the chief political correspondent for ABC News, host of ABC Sunday morning *This Week,* and coanchor of ABC News' *Good Morning America.* He also served as a political adviser to Bill Clinton as well as other Democratic candidates.

Literature In 1906 Mary Vardoulakis wrote *Gold in the Streets,* the first Greek American novel.

Olga Broumas (1949–), born in Syros, is a feminist poet who writes a poetry of the "body" with distinct lesbian-erotic motifs. Many of her poems capture the spirit of the Greek homeland. Her works include *Beginning with O* (1977), *Sole Savage* (1980), *Pastoral Jazz* (1983), *Perpetua* (1985), and a collection, *Rave: Poems, 1975–1999* (1999).

Kostantinos Lardas (1927–) writes both poetry and fiction. His major works are *The Devil Child* (1961) and *And in Him Too; In Us* (1964), which was nominated for a Pulitzer Prize in 1964.

Henry Mark Petrakis (1923–) is a major figure in Greek American fiction. His novels include *Lion of My Heart* (1959), *The Odyssey of Kostas Volakis* (1963), *The Dream of Kings* (1966), *In the Land of Morning* (1973), and *Hour of the Bell* (1976). The sequel to *Hour of the Bell, The Shepherds of Shadows*—second in a planned trilogy—came out in 2009. Petrakis writes of the immigrant experience, detailing the conflict between the old and new generations.

Jeffrey Eugenides (1960–) is a highly celebrated contemporary American author. His debut novel *The Virgin Suicides* (1993) was made into a film by Sofia Coppola in 1999. His novel *The Marriage Plot* (2011) updates the traditional love plot for the modern era. He is best known for *Middlesex* (2002), for which he won the Pulitzer Prize in 2002. *Middlesex* tells the story of three generations of Greek Americans, focusing on the experiences of Cal Stephanides, an intersex person (or, to use the Greek as Eugenides does, a hermaphrodite) raised as a girl who ultimately chooses to live as a man.

David Sedaris (1956–) writes memoirs, fiction, and quirky works that defy genre and is a popular speaker and contributor to radio programs such as NPR's *This American Life.* His best-known works are *The Santaland Diaries* (1992), *Naked* (1997), *Me Talk Pretty One Day* (2000), *When You Are Engulfed in Flames* (2008), and *Squirrel Seeks Chipmunk: A Modest Bestiary* (2010).

> *Greeks have an assortment of traditional customs, beliefs, and superstitions to ensure success and ward off evil and misfortune. Old beliefs persist in some communities in the United States. For example, belief in the "evil eye" is still strong and is supported by the Greek Orthodox church as a generalized concept of evil.*

Military Captain George Partridge Colvocoresses (1816–1872) distinguished himself as commander of the *Saratoga* in the Civil War. His son Rear Admiral George P. Colvocoresses fought in the Spanish-American War and was appointed the commandant of midshipmen at the U.S. Naval Academy.

Music Dimitri Mitropoulos (1896–1960), a well-known composer-conductor, conducted the among Grenadian Americans is growing. In fact, many Grenadians are in the United States to receive postsecondary education. After graduation, many choose to remain in the United States, marry, and raise a family. Some, however, return to Grenada to help others there.

EMPLOYMENT AND ECONOMIC CONDITIONS

Emigration from Grenada increased in the latter half of the twentieth century, with many Grenadians seeking employment in the United States. Female immigrants often found work in the service industry as domestic workers and nurses. This era also saw an influx of Grenadians who lost work in Aruba and Curaçao after the decline of the oil industry there. In response, the United States opened some migration channels, allowing for immigrants to work in the growing number of oil refineries in the United States. The children of these immigrants were sent to American schools. Once able to find jobs and sponsors, these children usually applied for their parents' permanent residence in the United States.

Because it offers a path to better work and citizenship, education is highly valued, and Grenadian Americans maintain a reputation of being good students with high attendance rates in the American public school system. Many children of immigrants have obtained higher-education degrees and gone on to find a range of jobs across the country. According to the 2010 Census, the median household income of Grenadian Americans was $49,097 a year, placing the average Grenadian American family solidly within the middle class. The 2010 Census also reported that the most common occupation for Grenadian Americans was in the service industry, followed closely by management, business, science, and arts occupations. Other common jobs included sales, office, construction, and maintenance occupations.

POLITICS AND GOVERNMENT

Americans from Grenada maintain close ties with their former country. News concerning political and governmental activities comes to the United States from radio, newspapers, and television. Radio stations and newspapers are readily available on the Internet to help keep Grenadian Americans up-to-date with their home country. Phone conversations with friends and family also help Grenadian Americans keep abreast of current affairs in Grenada.

Grenadian American participation in American politics is felt most strongly in New York City. In 2009, for example, Jumaane Williams became the first Grenadian American elected to the New York City Council. Upon Williams's election, Grenadian prime minister Tillman Thomas stated his hope that the two men could "work together to help attract to Grenada those of us in the Diaspora who are willing and able to assist in Grenada's development."

NOTABLE INDIVIDUALS

Activism Human rights activist Malcolm X was born Malcolm Little in Nebraska in 1925 to a Grenadian-born mother. After joining the religious movement the Nation of Islam, Malcolm X began preaching black

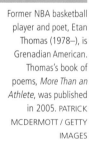

Former NBA basketball player and poet, Etan Thomas (1978–), is Grenadian American. Thomas's book of poems, *More Than an Athlete*, was published in 2005. PATRICK MCDERMOTT / GETTY IMAGES

self-reliance and power and attracted new members across the country. Following his departure from the Nation of Islam, Malcolm X continued to speak publicly at college campuses and other organizations' meetings, spreading his political ideas, many of them controversial, which gained him a number of enemies. On February 21, 1965, Malcolm X was assassinated by members of the Nation of Islam.

Literature Audre Lorde, born in New York City in 1934 to a Grenadian immigrant, became known for her poetry in the 1960s, which was published in Langston Hughes's *New Negro Poets* in 1962. Her first volume of poetry, *The First Cities*, was published in 1968. She left New York during the 1970s to teach at Tougaloo College in Mississippi, where she wrote her second volume of poetry, *Cables to Rage*. She is notable for her political agendas, including fighting for civil rights for people of color as well as of women and gays and lesbians. In 1991 she was named poet laureate of the state of New York. She died in 1992.

Politics Basil Alexander Paterson (1926–) and David Paterson (1954–), his son, both of Grenadian descent, were members of New York state government. Basil Paterson was a member of the "Gang of Four," an African American political coalition based in Harlem in the 1950s and 1960s. He was later elected to the New York State Senate and then served as the first black secretary of state of New York. His son David Paterson served as the governor of New York from 2008 to 2010.

MEDIA

PRINT

The Barnacle

Weekly print newspaper and business journal for Grenadians founded by Ian M. B. George in 1991.

> Mt. Parnassus
> St. George's 3530, Grenada West Indies
> Phone: (473) 435-0981
> Email: barnacle@spiceisle.com
> URL: www.barnaclegrenada.com

Grenada Broadcasting Network

Sports, news, and music from Grenada's Klassic AM and HOTT FM. Available online.

> Observatory Road
> P.O. Box 535
> St. George's, Grenada
> Phone: 1 (473) 555-5521
> Fax: (473) 440-4180
> Email: gbn@spiceisle.com
> URL: www.klassicgrenada.com

WEB

Grenada Broadcast

A live-streaming Internet broadcast that airs every Sunday. George Grant, of Grant Communications, delivers

The American political activist and civil rights leader Malcolm X (1925–1965) was of Grenadian descent. FPG / HULTON ARCHIVE / GETTY IMAGES

programs surrounding the current affairs of the island of Grenada.

> George Grant
> P.O. Box 553
> Tanteen
> St. George's, Grenada
> Phone: (473) 440-7764
> Email: gg@grenadabroadcast.com
> URL: www.grenadabroadcast.com

Grenada News Day

A website that features news from around the Caribbean, with a particular emphasis on Grenadian politics and sports.

> URL: www.grenadanewsday.com

ORGANIZATIONS AND ASSOCIATIONS

Friends of Grenada

An online community that allows users to connect with others of Grenadian descent.

> URL: friendsofgrenada.ning.com

The Grenadian-American Young Women's Association

A Brooklyn, New York–based group that aims to promote youth enrichment, enhancement, and empowerment.

> Email: GAYWA2010@gmail.com
> URL: www.facebook.com/GAYWA2010

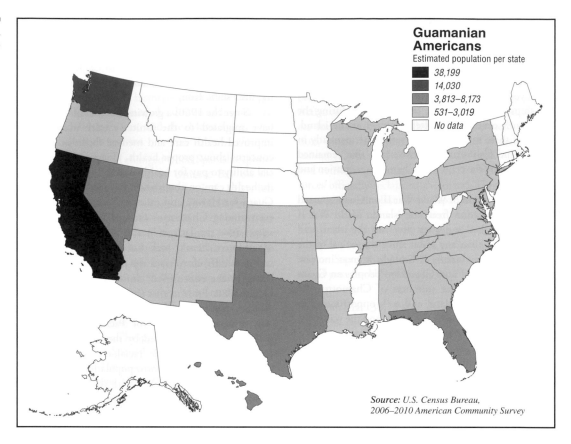

Guamanian Americans
Estimated population per state

- 38,199
- 14,030
- 3,813–8,173
- 531–3,019
- No data

*Source: U.S. Census Bureau,
2006–2010 American Community Survey*

The Chamorro population is not large, so the steady loss of natives from the island to the continental United States and Hawaii initially raised concerns about the effect on traditional Chamorro language, customs, and culture. But even though large numbers of young, educated Chamorros have left the island, many migrants have continued their cultural practices.

LANGUAGE

Chamorro, the ancient language of the Chamorros, and English are both official languages in Guam. English is prevalent as a result of decades of U.S. political and military control as well as American policies instituted in the 1920s that included banning the native language and burning dictionaries. Since the 1950s the majority of Chamorros have grown up as U.S. citizens speaking English as their first language. To combat the decline in Chamorro language fluency, educational and cultural organizations have made vigilant efforts to ensure the survival of the language. On the island itself, groups such as the University of Guam's Micronesian Language Institute work to study and spread the native Chamorro language. In the United States the Guam Society of America is responsible for heightening awareness of the language domestically. At least 5,000 years old, Chamorro belongs to the western group of the Austronesian language family, which includes the languages of Indonesia,

Malaysia, the Philippines, and Palau. Since Spanish and American influences merged on the island, the Chamorro language has evolved to include many Spanish and English words. In addition, other immigrants to Guam brought their own languages, including Filipino, Japanese, and many other Asian and Pacific Islander tongues. One of the most important Chamorro expressions is *Hafa Adai*, which is translated as "Welcome." For the hospitable Chamorros, nothing is as important as welcoming friends and strangers to their country and to their homes.

RELIGION

About four-fifths of the Guamanian population, both on the island and in the United States, are Roman Catholic. The Chamorros began converting to Catholicism—usually involuntarily—in the seventeenth century, when the first Spanish missionaries arrived on the island. As with other indigenous cultures that were converted to Catholicism, the Chamorros often incorporated their native religious practices, such as ancestor veneration, into their practice of Catholicism.

Congregationalists arrived on Guam in 1902 and established their own mission, but they were forced to abandon it in 1910 for lack of financial support. The following year, Americans with the General Baptist Foreign Missionary Society moved into the abandoned

Congregationalist mission. In 1921 the Baptists built Guam's first modern Protestant church, on a grander scale than the previous missions. A Baptist church constructed in 1925 in Inarajan was still in use in the mid-1960s. After World War II, the Seventh-Day Adventists established missions in Guam, led by a U.S. Navy chief, Harry Metzker. The Seventh-Day Adventists, who were well known in the twentieth century for their attention to health and well-being, also set up a clinic in Agana Heights. The Adventists soon became the second-largest denomination on the island, representing approximately one-fifth of the island's population.

CULTURE AND ASSIMILATION

Under Spanish rule, the native Chamorros were expected to adopt Spanish customs and religion. Yet despite the best efforts of Spanish officials and Jesuit missionaries, the islanders managed to maintain their own identity, even as the population diminished throughout the years of struggle with their Spanish conquerors. What emerged during the years of Spanish control was a unique hybrid, combining elements of Catholic Spanish culture with native traditions. This hybridization was extended in the twentieth century to encompass American culture. Throughout this process of adoption and adaptation, native Chamorro culture and traditions have remained at the core of Chamorro identity, both on and off the island.

The philosophy of *inafa'maolek*, entailing striving for the ideal of harmony and interdependence among humans and with nature, shapes Chamorro behavior. A strong system of reciprocity, known as *chenchule*, also guides Chamorro society.

Traditions and Customs Ancient Chamorro legends reveal the heart and soul of native Guamanian identity. Chamorros believe they were born of the island itself. The name of the city of Agana, known as Hagåtña in the Chamorro language, is taken from the tale of the formation of the islands. This ancient Chamorro legend tells of the island's beginnings, when Fu'una used parts from the body of her dying brother, Puntan, to create the world. His eyes were the sun and moon, his eyebrows were rainbows, his chest the sky, and his back the earth. Then Fu'una turned herself into a rock, from which all human beings originated. *Agana*, or *Hagåtña*, means blood, and the name represents the lifeblood of the larger body called *Guahan*, or Guam. In fact, most names for places on the island refer to the human body: *Urunao*, the head; *Tuyan*, the belly; and *Barrigada*, the flank.

Kostumbren Chamorro, the core of traditional Chamorro society, was centered on the idea of respect—respect that extended to elders, to people in authority, to members of one's clan, to nature, and to the supernatural. Accordingly, customs included kissing the hands of elders, fishing conservatively from the ocean so as to not deplete its resources, and requesting permission from spiritual ancestors upon entering a jungle. Activities such as canoe-making and preparation of herbal medicines were prized because they could be handed down from generation to generation.

Another traditional activity is the chewing of betelnut, also known in Chamorro as *pugua* or *mama'on*. The seed commonly referred to as "betelnut" is actually the seed of a palm tree called *areca catechu*, which is chewed wrapped in the leaf of the betel vine. Both substances are stimulants. Chamorros and other Pacific Islanders chew betelnuts like Americans chew gum. Each island has its own species of betelnut tree, and each species has a different taste. Chamorros prefer the hard red-colored nut variety called *ugam*, due to its fine, granular texture. When that is out of season, the coarse white *changnga* is chewed instead. This practice, which was traditionally passed from grandparent to grandchild, is included as a part of any social event, and friends and strangers alike are invited to partake. The changes produced in tooth enamel by chewing betelnut helps to prevent cavities, and archaeological investigations of prehistoric skeletons show that ancient Chamorros had betel-stained teeth. Chamorros usually chew betelnut—at times mixed with powdered lime and wrapped in the peppery leaves—after a meal.

While betelnut chewing continues in Guam and has increased in other Asian nations, use by Chamorros has decreased because of a lack of domestic availability, changing ideals of beauty and hygiene, and a greater knowledge of the health risks associated with its use. Studies have shown that consistent use can be linked to higher risk of several forms of cancer as well as prenatal complications, similar to those reported for mothers who consume alcohol or tobacco during pregnancy.

Cuisine The original diet of the Chamorros was simple: fresh fish, shrimp patties, rice, coconut, *ahu* (a dessert soup made with young coconuts), bananas, breadfruit, taro, and other tropical fruits and vegetables. With the arrival of the Spanish in the sixteenth century, many staples of Latin American cuisine, such as tamales and empanadas, were adapted to include native ingredients and flavors, and these remain staples of Chamorro cuisine. As Asians settled on the island in the twentieth century, Chinese and Japanese food combined with the existing native ingredients, as well as with newly introduced ethnic cuisines like Filipino, to provide a variety of foods that are unique to the island. A popular example of this fusion is lumpia, a combination of beef, pork, and shrimp fried in a pastry, which reflects the influence of Chinese and Filipino cuisine.

Modern staples of Chamorro cuisine include grilled fish such as tuna, barbequed meats, and many varieties of *kelaguen*, a dish made from chopped broiled chicken, lemon juice, grated coconut, and hot peppers. A hot sauce native to Guam, *finadene*, made with soy sauce, lemon juice or vinegar, hot peppers, and onions, is a favorite accompaniment to any savory dish. In addition, the coconut has remained a major element in Chamorro cuisine, which uses coconut milk as a cooking agent for braising meats and coconut meat as a basis for many of the island's most popular desserts and sweets, including cookies, puddings, and candies.

Many of these dishes, particularly *kelaguen*, have also become staples of Chamorro celebrations, both on the island and in the continental United States and Hawaii. Served with fish, barbecued ribs and chicken, and the Filipino noodle dish *pancit*, these dishes are often seen alongside traditional American fairground staples such as hot dogs, popcorn, and nachos at festivals and celebrations.

Traditional Costumes Early Spanish explorers who met the indigenous Chamorros described them as tall and somewhat fair, with long straight black hair often reaching the waist. Men, who were often bearded, wore no clothing at all, except in battle, where warriors wore a vest of matted pandanus, a palm-like tree common to the Pacific Islands. Women did not cover their upper bodies, but after reaching the age of eight or ten, wore a thin strip of bark called a *tifi* to cover their pubic area. Both sexes wore large pandanus hats, called *batya*, and covered their skin in coconut oil as protection against the sun. Inexplicably from the Spanish point of view, native women dyed their teeth black and red with the juice of the betel nut—something seen as a sign of beauty among the islanders. On special occasions native women often wore grass skirts with pandanus belts adorned with shells and inscribed baby coconuts. Both sexes also wore garlands of fragrant flowers on ceremonial occasions.

With the arrival of the Spanish, several changes occurred among the natives, including the limited adoption of European dress, the adoption of a top-knot by men, and the bleaching of women's hair by prolonged exposure to the sun. Beyond this, little changed in the style and type of native dress. The Spanish-influenced *mestiza*, a style of dress consisting of a blouse with butterfly sleeves and a long skirt, was adopted in the nineteenth century. Today it is considered a traditional Chamorro costume and is worn for ceremonial occasions; *mestizas* made of lace are often used as wedding dresses.

While most modern Chamorros of both sexes have adopted Western styles of dress, some native traditions, including wearing garlands of flowers, have remained a part of ceremonial life. Crafting and wearing traditional jewelry has not only remained a part of native culture but has also become a major part of the island's tourism industry, serving as an important source of income for Chamorro craftspeople, who market their creations to the island's visitors.

Dances and Songs The simple, rhythmic music of the Chamorro culture tells the stories and legends of the island's history. Native instruments include the *belembautuyan*, made from a hollow gourd and strung with taut wire, and the ancient nose flute, which made a return at the end of the twentieth century. The Chamorros' style of singing was born from their workday. One popular form, the *kantan*, starts with one person giving a four-line chant, often a teasing verse directed at another person in the group of workers. That person picks up the song and continues in the same fashion, creating a musical dialogue that sometimes lasts for hours. The folk dances of the Chamorros portrayed legends about the ancient spirits, such as the doomed lovers who leaped to their death off Two Lovers' Point (*Puntan Dos Amantes*) or Sirena, the beautiful young girl who became a mermaid.

The official song of Guam, written in the twentieth century by Ramon Sablan in English and translated into Chamorro by Lagrimas Untalan, speaks of Guamanians' faith and perseverance:

> Stand ye Guamanians, for your country
> And sing her praise from shore to shore
>
> For her honor, for her glory
> Exalt our Island forever more
>
> May everlasting peace reign o'er us
> May heaven's blessing to us come
>
> Against all perils, do not forsake us
> God protect our Isle of Guam
>
> Against all perils, do not forsake us
> God protect our Isle of Guam.

More than three hundred years of colonial rule and Christian interventions against native culture caused a decline of traditional dance. However, since the 1980s the re-creation of traditional native dances has become an important element in the effort to restore and protect native Chamorro culture. In Guam's public schools, classes and extracurricular activities involving traditional dance have become popular among all students, regardless of ethnic background. Additionally, groups specializing in traditional dance are popular and much sought-after elements of the tourism industry.

Traditional dance has remained one of the major elements in the festivals and celebrations of Chamorros living in the continental United States and Hawaii—especially among Chamorro students at American colleges and universities, who use native costumes, songs, and dances to celebrate their cultural heritage. Francisco B. Rabon, who founded the Taotao Tan'o Cultural Dancers in the 1980s, was awarded the title of "Master of Chamorro Dance" by the governor of Guam in the early 1990s in recognition of his work reviving native Chamorro dance. Rabon has noted that he was not exposed to indigenous forms of dance on Guam but rather encountered them, particularly Hawaiian hula, when he attended college in the United States. This inspired him to re-create dance as ancient Chamorros might have practiced it.

Holidays Guamanians are U.S. citizens and therefore celebrate all of the major U.S. holidays, especially patriotic holidays such as July 4. Liberation Day, July 21, observes the American landing on Guam during World War II, which marked an end to Japanese occupation. The first Monday in March is celebrated as Guam Discovery Day, and in addition there are many civic and regional festivals each year. The official festival season is from April to October, when many villages in the southern part of the island hold their annual festivals. One of the most popular, the Malojloj Fiesta in the town of Inarajan, involves three days of celebrations featuring native Chamorro food, beer, music, and dancing. In a unique blend that illustrates the complex culture of modern Guam, native foods such as fried lumpia and coconut are served alongside traditional American fairground food like popcorn and nachos, and American fairground contests, like climbing a greased pole, occur alongside traditional Chamorro competitions and games such as coconut husking and grating.

The feasts of Catholic saints and other church holy days are observed by Chamorro Catholics. Each of the nineteen villages on Guam has its own patron saint, and each holds a fiesta, or festival, to honor the saint's feast day. The entire village celebrates with a mass, a procession, dancing, and food. The continuation of these religious festivals has become a hallmark of many Chamorro communities in the United States, where celebrations such as Sacramento's San Roke Fiesta and San Diego's Santa Rita Festival carry on the tradition.

Health Care Issues and Practices Access to quality health care, particularly for cancer treatment, has long been a concern of many Chamorros, and in the last few decades of the twentieth century, it became a major impetus for the migration of natives to the continental United States and Hawaii. The lack of modern medical facilities on the island in the years following World War II severely limited islanders' ability to seek medical treatment and general healthcare. Even Chamorros covered by military or government benefits often had to travel to Hawaii for treatment during this time, and the cost of travel and accommodations frequently caused severe financial hardships. Many Chamorros chose to migrate—initially to Hawaii, and later to other states—in order to gain access to healthcare. This trend has continued in the new century as increasing numbers of natives, still limited by the lack of healthcare on the island and now with the financial ability to afford quality healthcare, have chosen to leave the islands for Hawaii and the mainland.

A specific health issue for Chamorros is amyotrophic lateral sclerosis, or ALS, also known as Lou Gehrig's disease. *Lytico-bodig* is the native term for the condition, which affects muscle control and is inevitably fatal. The incidence of ALS among Chamorros is disproportionately high when compared to other cultural groups, and natives of Guam share a specific strain of the disease that is now called "Guamanian ALS." Although one hypothesis has connected ALS among the island-dwelling Chamorros with specific environmental factors, no definitive explanation has been identified. Guamanian ALS has increasingly attracted scientific attention, in part because there are possible connections between this form of ALS and more prevalent diseases, including Parkinson's disease, Alzheimer's, and other types of dementia.

FAMILY AND COMMUNITY LIFE

Chamorros in the United States and on the island have traditionally viewed the family as the center of cultural life, and they have extended that idea to encompass the surrounding community, emphasizing interdependence (the Chamorro concept of *inafa'maolek*) and cooperation among everyone in the community. Because Chamorro culture was traditionally matrilineal, women remain central to the organization and survival of the group. Since ancient times, women have exerted great authority over the household, including managing the family purse strings. In modern culture, especially in the United States, where education has offered Chamorros a greater opportunity to improve their economic status, these lines have blurred. Contemporary Chamorro women and men work together to support and manage the family.

The influence of American society, with its focus on the individual and the nuclear family, has begun to erode the traditional Chamorro concepts of kinship and interdependence—a process accelerated by the increase in economic opportunity available to both native and migrant Chamorros. Despite these pressures, Chamorros have maintained the time-honored practice of demonstrating respect for elders.

Gender Roles Precontact Chamorro culture had a balance in gender roles, with authority inside the clan vested in both the oldest son and the oldest daughter. Women traditionally held power in the household, while men were responsible for hunting, fishing, and public duties. The influence of the Spanish and the Catholic Church during three centuries of colonial rule slowly changed this system, particularly in the public sphere, where a clearer division of responsibility emerged, with men dominating political offices and women leading social, religious, and cultural organizations.

This trend continued under American influence, as men were selected over women to hold positions in any public capacity, whether in government, business, or the church. Women have retained control over the household through their control of resources, including the salaries and labor of family members and control of land tenure, which was passed through the female line until the militarization of the island after World War II removed much of Guam's land from public use and ended the agricultural basis of the island's economy. In recent times Chamorro women have found greater acceptance as elected officials and leaders of government and civic organizations, although men still outnumber women in positions of political leadership.

Education The public school system on Guam is modeled on the American educational system, with a single unified school district, the Guam Department of Education, operating elementary schools, middle schools, high schools, and an alternative school. The combined institutions serve more than 30,000 students. All of these schools are accredited by the Western Association of Schools and Colleges, with classroom teachers certified by the Guam Department of Education. Primary instruction is in English, but the curriculum includes classes in Chamorro language and culture.

While these schools often share the same problems as mainland American schools, including high drop-out rates, violence, and gang activity, the main problem has been funding. The public school system depends on income taxes and revenues gained from the travel industry, making school finance dependent on fluctuating cycles of tourism and changing economic conditions that can negatively affect wages. This instability makes long-term planning for the school system difficult.

Higher education institutions on the island include the Guam Community College, a two-year school providing undergraduate transfer courses, adult education courses, and vocational training, and the University of Guam, a four-year university offering bachelor's degrees and a limited number of graduate programs leading to a master's degree. Like the public school system, the University of Guam is accredited by the Western Association of Schools and Colleges.

Access to mainland schools and universities has long been a cause of migration for Chamorros, who see education as an avenue to better career opportunities. Several universities in the Western United States and Hawaii, including the University of Hawaii, Chaminade University, and the University of Washington, have traditionally hosted significant numbers of Chamorro students. These students' efforts are often actively supported by their communities through organizations that award grants and scholarships to Chamorro students.

Courtship and Weddings In traditional Chamorro society there were a large number of traditions, rituals, and ceremonies surrounding courtship and weddings. Arranged by clan elders, marriages were an opportunity to increase social and economic status through the binding together of clans. As a result, young women from good families and girls who already had children commanded a larger

A Guamanian American family gathers in a courtyard. BLEND IMAGES / ALAMY

dowry than others. If the prospective groom's gifts were acceptable to the clan, then the marriage could go forward. Children were no bar to marriage and were an accepted occurrence in pre-Catholic Guam, where a small population based on extended family groups produced a different cultural climate than that found among Western cultures. These attitudes persist today, despite more than 300 years of Catholic influence.

Once the marriage was agreed to in theory, both families began a series of rituals leading up to the actual wedding. These rituals included *mamaisen saina*, the formal visit of the groom and his family to the home of the bride, the *fandånggo*, or groom's party, where the family of the groom welcomed the arrival of a new daughter, and the *komplimentu*, a return visit to the bride's home to express appreciation for the family of the bride's presence at the *fandånggo*. Only after these rituals had been completed could the *inakkamo'*, or wedding ceremony (expenses of which were shouldered by the groom's family) occur. Once the ceremony was completed, both families returned to the home of the bride's family for the formal *amotsan nobia*, or bride's breakfast, a solemn affair attended by the couple's parents and godparents.

While some of these traditions have been maintained among modern Chamorros, those wishing to marry have increasingly begun to opt for civic ceremonies or American-style weddings. Increasingly, the primary responsibility for developing and carrying out the wedding plans has shifted from the clan elders and parents to the bride and bridegroom themselves, and the traditional rituals of *mamaisen saina* and *komplimentu* have become increasingly rare. These have generally been replaced by bridal showers and joint receptions, often held at a hotel or other public space. Wedding expenses also are being divided evenly, rather than the groom's side shouldering the financial burden.

EMPLOYMENT AND ECONOMIC CONDITIONS

Half of the modern economy on the island of Guam has emerged from American military establishments and related government services on the island. For years a majority of Guamanians have been employed by the U.S. government and military, serving as cooks, office personnel, and in other administrative positions, with many advancing to the upper levels of government salary tracks following years of service. Since the 1960s the tourism industry has been the second largest employer on the island, creating a substantial number of jobs in travel- and tourism-related industries, including airlines, hotels, and restaurants. Between them, these two employment categories account for 64 percent of the Guamanian workforce. Other industries that contribute to the domestic economy include

A Guamanian American during basic training for the United States Army at Fort Jackson in 2007. SCOTT OLSON / GETTY IMAGES

agriculture (mostly for local consumption), which employs approximately 26 percent of the workforce, with the remainder employed in commercial poultry farming and in small assembly plants for watches, textiles, and light machinery.

At the beginning of the twenty-first century, unemployment in Guam was relatively high (about 11 percent), and roughly one quarter of the population lived below the U.S. poverty line. In 2005 the per capita income in Guam was about $15,000, and in 2007 the total labor force on the island was approximately 83,000. Although there is little statistical data on Chamorros living in the continental United States or Hawaii, it is generally believed these groups are only slightly better off than their island counterparts. Chamorros, like other Pacific Islanders, tend to have slightly higher levels of unemployment than the general population and a larger percentage of families in poverty.

POLITICS AND GOVERNMENT

Because of its history as a U.S. territory, Guam has a complex political story, the dominant theme of which has been a quest for self-determination. Ceded to the United States by Spain after the latter's defeat in the Spanish-American War, the island was deemed to be unincorporated territory of the United States—a nebulous status that gave the U.S. Congress unlimited authority over the island. This privilege was upheld by several Supreme Court decisions. As a result, the development of native political institutions was sacrificed in favor of U.S. strategic and national security interests. This continued after the liberation of the island from the Japanese in 1944, fueling local dissatisfaction and agitation. The desire for Guamanian self-determination was partially recognized in 1950, when jurisdiction over the island was transferred from the U.S. Navy to the Department of the Interior, and a new political system was authorized. Under this structure, the island would have a governor appointed by the president of the United States, a popularly elected unicameral (single-body) legislature, a locally elected judiciary, and, perhaps most importantly, U.S. citizenship for all residents of Guam. The right of citizenship had previously been reserved for Guamanians naturalized in the United States or who had served in the United States military. A further step toward self-determination came in 1968, when the Elective Governor Act allowed for popular election of the island's governor.

Despite these changes, Guam remained in a unique and somewhat undefined political state. Throughout the 1980s and 1990s, support grew among Guamanians for an enhanced political status that would make the island either a state or a commonwealth. The idea of enhanced status became the central focus of Guamanian politics, both domestic and national. Those in favor of such a status for the island maintained that the political status of Guam had not significantly changed since the ceding of the island to the United States over a century ago. Successive U.S. administrations, however, actively opposed any changes to Guam's legal status, arguing that Guam lacked the economic self-sufficiency to deserve enhanced status, especially in view of the island's economic dependence on federal and defense spending.

Notwithstanding these setbacks, many Guamanians continue to work for an enhanced status for the island, and various groups advocate for formal statehood, union with the state of Hawaii, union with the Northern Mariana Islands as a single territory, or independence.

Military Because of their long relationship with the American military, Chamorros are well represented in all branches of the military as enlisted men, officers, and support personnel. Currently 14 out of every 1,000 Guamanians join the U.S. military, the highest enlistment rate of any state or territory. One native Guamanian, Peter A. Gumataotao, achieved the rank of rear admiral in the United States Navy and command of an aircraft carrier strike group and its attendant ships. In addition to those in the services, many Guamanians have also worked for the United States military and diplomatic services in civilian roles.

NOTABLE INDIVIDUALS

Military Rear Admiral Peter A. Gumataotao is a senior United States naval officer who was commander of the U.S. Navy's Carrier Strike Group Eleven, an aircraft carrier battle group built around the USS *Nimitz*.

Politics Manuel Flores (Carson) Leon Guerrero (1914–1985) was both secretary of Guam and acting governor of the island. In 1963 U.S. president John F. Kennedy appointed Guerrero the governor of Guam, a position he retained until 1969. In 1967 Guerrero established the Guam Tourist Commission, paving the way for the growth of the tourism industry, which has become the basis of the island's economy.

MEDIA

Marianas Variety Guam Edition

One of the island's two daily newspapers.

Jon A. Anderson, Editor in Chief
215 Rojas Street, Suite 204
Tamuning, Guam 96913
Phone: (671) 649-4950
Email: editor@mvguam.com
URL: www.mvguam.com

Pacific Daily News

One of the island's two daily newspapers. Also publishes the online publication *Joint Region Edge*, an authorized publication for U.S. Service personnel and their families.

David Crisostomo, Editor
P.O. Box DN
Hagatna, Guam 96932
Phone: (671) 472-1736
Fax: (671) 472-1512
Email: dcrisost@guampdn.com
URL: www.guampdn.com

UNO Magazine

A lifestyle magazine focusing on Guam, launched in 2010.

Lana Lozano Denight, Editor in Chief
P.O. Box 192
Hagatna, Guam 96932
Phone: (671) 635-2379
Fax: (671) 637-5832
Email: sales@unoguam.com
URL: www.unoguam.com

ORGANIZATIONS AND ASSOCIATIONS

Guam Humanities Council

Founded in 1991, the Guam Humanities Council (GHC or the Council) is an affiliate of the National

Endowment for the Humanities (NEH). It is a
nonprofit organization committed to promoting
public humanities programming for the people
of Guam.

Kimberlee Kihleng, Executive Director
222 Chalan Santo Papa
Reflection Center, Suite 106
Hagåtña, Guam 96910
Phone: (671) 472-4460/1
Fax: (671) 472-4465
Email: info_ghc@teleguam.net
URL: www.guamhumanitiescouncil.org

Guam Society of America

A nonprofit organization founded in 1952 and based
in Washington, D.C. Its purposes are to foster and
encourage educational, cultural, civic, and social
programs and activities among its members; and
to foster and perpetuate the Chamorro language,
culture, and traditions. Any Chamorro (a native of
Guam, Saipan, or any Marian Islands) or any person
who has a bona fide interest in the purposes of
the society is eligible for membership. The society
sponsors events and activities throughout the year
that include Chamorro language classes in the D.C.
metropolitan area, a Golf Classic, the Cherry Blossom
Princess Ball, and Chamorro Night.

Mike Blas, President
P.O. Box 1515
Washington, D.C., 20013
Phone: (571) 209-7185
Email: info@guamsociety.org
URL: www.guamsociety.org

The Guam Women's Club

Founded in 1952, the Guam Women's Club is the oldest
women's civic organization in Guam. A volunteer
nonprofit organization, the club's stated mission is
to investigate, discuss, and seek improvement of
conditions within the Territory of Guam that affect
the general welfare, education, and health of the
population.

P.O. Box 454
Hagatna, Guam 96932
Phone: (671) 647-2351
Email: reveksler@gmail.com
URL: http://guamwomensclub.com

MUSEUMS AND RESEARCH CENTERS

University of Guam Richard Flores Taitano Micronesia Area Research Center (MARC)

Multifaceted research arm of the University of Guam that
includes the Micronesian Language Institute and the
Chamorro Language and Cultural Center.

John A. Peterson, Director
University of Guam
UOG Station
Mangilao, Guam 96923
Phone: (671) 735-2150
Fax: (671) 734-7403
Email: lavonneg@uguam.uog.edu
URL: www.uog.edu/dynamicdata/
MicroAreaResearchCenter.aspx

SOURCES FOR ADDITIONAL STUDY

Gailey, Harry. *The Liberation of Guam*. Novato, CA: Presidio Press, 1998.

Cunningham, Lawrence J. *Ancient Chamorro Society*. Honolulu: Bess Press, 1992.

Kerley, Barbara. *Songs of Papa's Island*. Boston: Houghton Mifflin, 1995.

Maga, Timothy P. *Defending Paradise: The United States and Guam, 1898–1950*. New York: Garland Pub., 1988.

Quinene, Paula A. Lujan. *Remember Guam*. West Conshohocken, PA: Infinity Publishing, 2009.

Rogers, Robert F. *Destiny's Landfall: A History of Guam*. Honolulu: University of Hawaii Press, 1995.

Rottman, Gordon L. *Guam 1941 & 1944: Loss and Reconquest*. Oxford: Osprey Publishing, 2004.

Sacks, Oliver. *The Island of the Colorblind*. New York: Vintage, 1998.

Souder-Jaffery, Laura M. T., and Robert A. Underwood. *Chamorro Self-Determination: The Right of a People = I Derechon I Taotao*. Agana, Guam: Chamorro Studies Association, 1987.

Goetzfridt, Nicholas J. *Guahan: A Bibliographic History*. Honolulu: The University of Hawaii Press, 2011.

DeLisle, C.T. "'Guamanian-Chamorro by Birth but American Patriotic by Choice': Subjectivity and Performance in the Life of Agueda Iglesias Johnston". *Amerasia Journal* 37, no. 3 (2011): 61–75.

GUATEMALAN AMERICANS

Maria Hong

OVERVIEW

Guatemalan Americans are immigrants or descendants of people from Guatemala. Guatemala is located in the northern part of Central America and is bordered by Mexico to the north and west, El Salvador and Honduras to the south and east, the Pacific Ocean along its West Coast, and Belize and the Caribbean Sea to the north and east. The southern half of the Republic of Guatemala—where the majority of the nation's population resides—mainly consists of mountain highlands and plateaus, which are susceptible to earthquakes. Guatemala's total land mass encompasses 42,042 square miles (108,889 square kilometers), which is slightly larger than the state of Maine.

Guatemala had a population of just over 14 million people in 2012, the largest population of any nation in Central America. According to the Guatemalan government's 2002 census, mestizos or "ladinos" (mixed indigenous-Spanish ancestry) made up the majority of the population at 60 percent, with the remaining 40 percent made up of several different indigenous groups. The largest indigenous groups in Guatemala are Mayan, including the Maya Quiché at 11 percent, the Maya K'ekchi at 7.6 percent, the Cakchiquel at 7.4 percent, the Mam at 5.5 percent, with small tribal groups making up the remainder. The country's thirty-six year civil war from 1960 to 1996 had a crippling effect on the economy, from which it began a slow recovery at the end of the twentieth century.

Guatemalans began to arrive in large numbers in the United States beginning in the late 1970s as a result of its violent civil war. Early immigrants began to settle in the Southwest states of California and Texas and many found employment as seasonal migrant workers in the agricultural industry. Many of these immigrants were men who were fleeing the immediate danger of kidnapping, politically motivated violence, or forced service in the military they would face if they remained in their homeland. While Guatemalan immigration has waned somewhat since the beginning of the twenty-first century, many families and individuals continue to emigrate in search of better economic opportunities.

The U.S. Census Bureau's American Community Survey documents that there were approximately 1.2 million individuals of Guatemalan descent residing in the United States in 2011, which is roughly population of Dallas, Texas. Guatemalan Americans are the sixth largest Hispanic group in the United States. Areas with a large population of Guatemalan Americans include Los Angeles, California; Houston, Texas; Miami, Florida; New York City; and northern New Jersey.

HISTORY OF THE PEOPLE

Early History Guatemala's roots lie in the great Mayan civilization, which was concentrated in separate city-states established throughout what is now southern Mexico and Central America. From 2000 BCE through 900 CE, Mayan civilization accomplished much in the areas of astronomy, written language, architecture, the arts, and religion. Some of their massive structures from their ancient cities remain today, such as the immense stone temples and pyramids at Tikal in the Petén.

The Mayan city-states were militaristic, and they devoted much of their energy and resources toward conducting wars with each other. By 900 CE, various factors, probably including sustained crop failure, environmental degradation, and frequent war, had led to a precipitous decline of the Mayan civilization. By the time the Spanish arrived in the early sixteenth century, about one million indigenous people remained and were easily conquered. Two events that paved the way for the conquest of the region of modern-day Guatemala were Hernán Cortés' conquest of Tenochtitlán in modern-day Mexico in 1521, and the Spaniards' exploration and conquest of the area now known as Panama, led by Vasco Núñez de Balboa, which began as early as 1510. From 1523 to 1524, the Spanish, led by Pedro de Alvarado, colonized many former Mayan city-states located to the south of the former Aztec empire in Mexico. De Alvarado became the first captain general of Guatemala, which then encompassed most of Central America. The Spanish settlements in the Central American region facilitated travel and trade with Spain's island colonies in the Caribbean and served as a rich source of raw materials, including minerals, crops, and timber for export to Spain. By 1650 a large percentage of these indigenous people had been wiped out by disease, war, and exploitation, and the Mayan population dwindled to about 200,000.

In 1821, Guatemala gained independence from Spain, and in 1824 it joined the Central American Federation. In 1838 the Federation disbanded, due mostly to a revolt against it led by an indigenous general, Rafael Carrera, who then seized control of the newly independent nation of Guatemala.

The efforts of activists such as Guatemalan Nobel Peace Laureate Rigoberta Menchú have focused international attention on the oppression of indigenous people in Guatemala. However, an apartheid-type of oligarchic system remains entrenched with the government and other power centers controlled by a small European-descended minority.

Modern Era In 1871 a liberal *caudillo* (military dictator), Justo Rufino Barrios, took power and ruled as president from 1873 to 1885. Barrios enacted anti-clerical legislation, began to establish a national education system, and fostered the inception of Guatemala's coffee industry. Guatemala was ruled by a succession of military dictators until the last *caudillo*, Jorge Ubico, was overthrown in 1944, and Juan José Arevalo was elected president in 1945. Arevalo instituted political democracy in Guatemala, encouraging organized labor, the formation of a social security system, and industrialization.

Arevalo's successor, Colonel Jacobo Arbenz Guzmán, redistributed land from wealthy landowners and the U.S.-based United Fruit Company, which had exploited workers for decades. Arbenz's challenge to United Fruit and his support of Guatemala's Communist Party led to conflict with the Eisenhower Administration. In mid-1954, Arbenz was overthrown by a U.S.-supported, largely CIA-directed revolt, led by Colonel Carlos Castillo Armas.

For the next thirty years, most of the agrarian and labor reforms achieved under Arevalo and Arbenz were undone by a succession of mostly military rulers. Leftist guerrillas attempted to undermine these military regimes, while right-wing paramilitary death squads fought back against the guerrillas by brutally repressing the civilian population. According to Amnesty International, at least 20,000 civilians were killed by the death squads from 1966 to 1976.

During the late 1970s, a popular resistance movement to the military governments began to operate through a collaboration among *ladinos, indígenas* (indigenous peoples), peasants, labor leaders, students, journalists, politicians, and Catholic priests. In response the army and paramilitary counterinsurgency units stepped up their repression efforts. From 1980 to 1981 guerrilla forces encouraged and sometimes coerced large numbers of highland *indígenas* to join them in their armed revolutionary efforts. The army retaliated by massacring whole indigenous villages;

kidnapping, torturing, and murdering people suspected of supporting the guerrillas; and scorching peasant crops and homes.

The Commission for Historical Clarification convened by the Oslo Peace Accords of 1994 called the military efforts an ethnic genocide campaign, stemming from pervasive discrimination against *indígenas* in Guatemalan society. In addition to destroying indigenous villages, the government army forced more than one million *indígenas* into military-controlled "model villages" and "reeducation camps," and conscripted men into the army's civil defense patrols.

Violence in the villages peaked under Efraín Ríos Montt, a Pentecostal Protestant, who became president through a military coup in 1982. By the army's own count, the counterinsurgency movement destroyed 440 villages and damaged numerous others between 1980 and 1984. Widespread terrorism continued under Ríos Montt's successor Brigadier General Óscar Humberto Mejía Victores, who became president in 1983. In 1984 the Guatemalan Supreme Court reported that around 100,000 children had lost at least one parent during the decades-long civil war.

Facing mounting international pressures—many as a result of the international publicity received by Guatemalan indigenous activist Rigoberta Menchú's *testimonio* revealing the horrors of the civil war that was published in 1983—General Mejía allowed a gradual return to democracy. This transition began with the 1984 election of a Constituent Assembly, which then drafted a democratic constitution. The new constitution took effect in May 1985, after which Marco Vinicio Cerezo Arévalo, a Christian Democratic party leader, won the first election held under the new constitution, receiving nearly 70 percent of the vote.

As President Cerezo struggled to lead the transition from a military to a civilian government, and many of the reforms he attempted to institute ultimately failed. In the meantime, political killings by the right-wing death squads continued. Cerezo was succeeded in 1991 by Jorge Serrano Elías, who two years later attempted to dissolve Guatemala's Congress and suspend the constitution. After a short period of political turmoil, the Congress elected Ramiro de León Carpio, a former human rights ombudsman, as president. On March 29, 1994, the government and the Guatemalan National Revolutionary Unity (URNG) signed three peace agreements brokered by the United Nations. In December 1996 the long civil war finally ended when rebels and the government announced a peace treaty.

The CIA declassified thousands of pages of reports in May 1997 regarding its participation in the orchestration of the 1954 coup that overthrew President Jacobo Arbenz. These reports reveal that the United States's role in distributing guns and money to rebel forces and training mercenaries through the nearly four decades of the Guatemalan civil war. In 1999 the Commission for Historical Clarification, backed by the United Nations, released a report documenting that Guatemalan security forces were responsible for 93 percent of all human rights violations committed during the civil war, which claimed approximately 200,000 lives. Nearly 24,000 innocent Guatemalans were executed, about 80 percent of whom were Mayans from the Quiché area. Despite the achievements of the peace accords, however, widespread violence, including abductions, torture, and executions by army and paramilitary men, continued into the early twenty-first century.

In 2003, in response to the Guatemalan Supreme Court's ruling that Efraín Ríos Montt was constitutionally barred from running for president, the "jueves negro" (Black Thursday) riots occurred. Thousands of masked FRG supporters swarmed the streets of Guatemala City, wreaking havoc with machetes, clubs, and guns, shooting out windows and setting buildings and cars on fire. The Supreme Court decision was overturned and Montt was allowed to run for president. This situation is just one example of the persistence of political and governmental corruption and coercion in modern-day Guatemala. That same year, former Guatemala City mayor, Óscar Berger, was elected president.

In Guatemala 63 percent of the population lives in extreme poverty. In this mostly rural, agrarian country, 2 percent of the population owns over 64 percent of the arable land. Peasants survive by subsistence farming land or by doing seasonal migratory work on coastal coffee, sugar, and cotton plantations. Among Central American nations, Guatemala has the highest infant and child mortality rates, the lowest life expectancy, and most malnourished population, with rampant severe hunger. In his 2006 article "The Limits on Pro-Poor Agricultural Trade in Guatemala: Land, Labour and Political Power," published in the *Journal of Human Development*, Roman Krznaric blames globalization and the domination of Guatemala's elite for the persistently large income gap in Guatemala between the affluent and impoverished classes. While the elite benefits directly from foreign investment and neoliberal economics, these benefits do not reach Guatemala's large impoverished sector, much of which is made up of indigenous peoples.

The efforts of activists such as Guatemalan Nobel Peace Laureate Rigoberta Menchú have focused international attention on the oppression of indigenous people in Guatemala. However, an apartheid-type of oligarchic system remains entrenched with the government and other power centers controlled by a small European-descended minority. Although several hundred thousand Guatemalans remain uprooted within Guatemala, hundreds of thousands have fled to the United States and Mexico to escape the violence since the late 1970s.

SETTLEMENT IN THE UNITED STATES

Until 1960 the United States did not keep separate statistics on the number of immigrants from Guatemala, and figures reflect migration from the entire Central American region. During the 1830s only 44 arrivals of Central Americans were recorded. Between 1890 and 1900, 500 Central Americans immigrated to the United States according to records of legal migration. The numbers increased during the next two decades, with 8,000 arriving from 1900 to 1910 and 17,000 migrating between 1910 and 1920. Emigrants from Guatemala may have been seeking a better life following a devastating earthquake in 1917.

During the 1930s the number of Central American immigrants fell to fewer than 6,000 for the whole decade, due in part to quotas on immigration from Western Hemisphere nations enacted in the 1920s. However, since the mid-1950s the annual number of legally admitted Central Americans has steadily risen, with 45,000 arriving between 1951 to 1960.

Due to political upheavals and related economic crises throughout the region, large numbers of undocumented Guatemalans and other Central Americans have been coming to the United States since the late 1970s. During the early 1970s, inflation, political turmoil and violence, unemployment, low wages, and land scarcity due to inequitable land allocation precipitated the mass internal and external displacement of Guatemalan *campesino* peasants, *indígenas*, and professionals. In February of 1976 an earthquake destroyed much of Guatemala City, causing some residents to emigrate. From 1967 to 1976, 19,683 Guatemalans immigrated to the United States, and the 1970 U.S. Census recorded a Guatemalan American population of 26,865 persons. The 1980 U.S. Census recorded 62,098 Guatemalan Americans, with 46 percent arriving between 1975 and 1980.

However, the majority of Guatemalan Americans have arrived in the United States since 1980. Official immigration statistics do not reflect the true number of immigrants from Guatemala, because most arrivals are undocumented. In 1984 hundreds of thousands of Guatemalans fled to Mexico and the United States. Thousands also escaped to neighboring Belize, Costa Rica, Nicaragua, and Honduras.

Since the early twentieth century, Mayan Guatemalans had traveled annually to southern Mexico to work on seasonal coffee harvests, attracted by the wages and low cost of living. By the late 1950s, 10,000 to 15,000 men and women were crossing the border into Mexico and back every year. In the 1960s and 1970s, the number increased to around 60,000 annually; some of these settled in the Mayan communities of the state of Chiapas in southern Mexico. After the massacres of Mayan villages in Guatemala, *indígenas* from the departments of Quiché, Alta Verapaz, Huehuetenango, Itzabal, and the Petén fled to this region, and many seasonal workers remained in Mexico. Refugee camps were established in the Mexican states of Chiapas, Campeche, and Quintana Roo. Due to the dismal economic and health conditions in these camps, many Guatemalan refugees moved on to the United States, often enduring great hardships on the way.

Because they must cross the border illegally, many immigrants hire guides called *coyotes*, who facilitate the crossings for fees as high as several thousand dollars per person. During the trips many experience robbery, rape, kidnapping, or imprisonment by people who exploit their vulnerability. Some are smuggled to the United States by religious workers who also give them sanctuary once they arrive. Due to the expense of the trip, those who migrate to the United States are not generally the poorest of the poor.

According to the 1970 U.S. Census, 90 percent of Guatemalans in the United States were classified as white because they were mostly of Spanish or European heritage. These immigrants tended also to be middle class. Before the 1980s most Guatemalan political emigrants were *ladino* activists and politicians from urban centers. After 1980 large numbers of indigenous people and *campesinos* fled to the United States from counter-insurgency campaigns in the western highland areas. Significant numbers of schoolteachers, student activists, journalists, and other professionals accused of being guerrilla sympathizers also immigrated for political reasons. In March 2006 the Pew Hispanic Center estimated that there were more than 300,000 undocumented Guatemalan immigrants living in the United States.

A large portion of the Guatemalan American population in the United States works in the service sector, while many others work in the construction, transportation and agricultural industries. Undocumented immigrants tend to work in the informal job sector, often finding temporary labor in construction or as domestic workers, such as nannies and maids.

The United States has not recognized Guatemalans as political refugees. Most recent immigrants from Guatemala are considered economic immigrants, and only one to two percent of Guatemalan requests for political asylum are granted. Many sources state that immigration officials view Guatemalan asylum cases less favorably than those from applicants from other countries where human rights abuses are common, because U.S. refugee policy is politicized. They say that the United States has historically granted asylum to people fleeing communist regimes rather than those from countries the United States is friendly with. For over a decade, immigration officials denied bias in assessing asylum cases, asserting that Central American asylum seekers, especially Guatemalans and Salvadorans, fell "outside of the category of political asylum on the grounds that these migrants were fleeing economic conditions and generalized conditions of violence rather than targeted political persecution, and that they could therefore safely remain within their countries of origin or the Central American region," criminologist Susan Coutin documents in her 2009 American Sociological Association report "Falling Outside: Lawyering, Central Americans, and the Boundaries of Political Asylum."

This denial of bias was largely proven false, however, by the U.S. Justice Department's 1990 settlement of a lawsuit filed by organizations including the Immigrants' Rights Project of American Civil Liberties Union on behalf of more than 150,000 Guatemalan and Salvadoran undocumented immigrants who were denied political asylum or were still awaiting decisions on their applications. The government's decision basically admitted that U.S. authorities had violated the law in their refusal to grant political asylum in a nonpolitical manner. Many of these immigrants did have their original sentences reversed and were granted amnesty by the courts.

Illegal immigrants who are caught by the Immigration and Customs Enforcement (ICE) are usually deported back to Guatemala, where they may face dangerous situations as repatriates. Some Guatemalan emigrants travel to Canada, where they can receive refugee status. Despite the threat of deportation, the difficulty of the trip to the United States, and problems here as undocumented persons, Guatemalans have continued to arrive in the United States and are one of the fastest-growing American immigrant groups.

According to the U.S. Census Bureau's American Community Survey, approximately 1.2 million persons of Guatemalan origin resided in the United States in 2011. Of these, 787,000 were born in Guatemala, reflecting the large portion of recent immigrants among the Guatemalan American population. However, the actual number of Guatemalan Americans is higher, owing to those who have immigrated illegally and are not part of the official count. Guatemalan Americans are the second-largest immigrant group from Central America after Salvadoran Americans.

Guatemalan Americans have settled primarily in cities with large existing Latino communities. The greatest number—probably over 400,000—are in Los Angeles, which has the largest concentration of Central Americans in the United States. Significant numbers of Guatemalan Americans also reside in Houston, Chicago, New York City, Washington, D.C., Southern Florida, and San Francisco. Smaller enclaves are found in Miami, New Orleans, Phoenix/Tucson, and other cities in Texas and North Carolina.

During the early 1980s, Phoenix/Tucson became an important center for the Sanctuary Movement, a group of mostly Christian religious organizations that provided sanctuary to illegal migrants from Guatemala and El Salvador. These groups supported immigrants in their efforts to gain legal status and helped them obtain work and housing. Since then, most of those Guatemalans have moved on to areas outside of Arizona.

The Latino communities in Chicago and New York expanded considerably during the mid- to late-1980s. In these cities Guatemalan Americans tend to be inconspicuous, blending in with the more established Mexican or Cuban American populations, in hopes of eluding Immigration and Customs Enforcement (ICE). In the San Francisco Bay Area and Washington,

D.C., Central Americans predominate among Latinos. A number of wealthy Guatemalan Americans live in Miami, the commerce gateway to Latin America.

Many of the Guatemalan Americans in Los Angeles live in or near the Central American-dominated Pico-Union district. Once primarily a Mexican American area, Pico-Union is now characterized by businesses that cater to Central Americans, including bakeries, restaurants, grocery stores, and social service organizations. A substantial portion of the Guatemalan Americans in Los Angeles and in southern Florida are Kanjobal Mayans. In Houston, there are over a thousand Mayans from the provinces of Totonicapán and Quiché. These indigenous communities represent the best-documented Guatemalan American populations.

Guatemalan Americans have met with both hostility and empathy from the general American public. Many of the negative reactions from "established" Americans have focused on immigration issues. During the recession of 2008 and concurrent waves of anti-immigrant sentiment, Guatemalans and other Central Americans have been depicted as overwhelming government social services and undermining American employment by taking low-paying jobs. Others have described newly arrived Central Americans as resourceful contributors to the economy, many of whom take jobs that other Americans presumably do not want.

The U.S. government's refusal to designate Guatemalan immigrants as political refugees and its persecution of Sanctuary Movement workers can be interpreted as an unsympathetic stance toward Guatemalan Americans. On the other hand, grassroots supporters and many major city governments have defended Guatemalan immigrants. In the mid-1980s some members of Congress and at least a dozen cities, including Los Angeles, St. Paul, and Chicago, criticized President Reagan and his administration's federal policy concerning illegal Central Americans and limited city cooperation with Immigration and Naturalization Services officials.

Guatemalan Americans' relations with other Latino groups have been similarly mixed. The more established Chicano communities have expressed both resentment and support for the newer residents. Sometimes Central American and Mexican groups vie for jobs, and cultural differences can preclude social interaction among people of different national origins. A number of Native American groups have been supportive of indigenous Guatemalan immigrants to the United States and empathize with their struggle against genocide.

Although many Guatemalan Americans have ancestors who came to the United States generations ago, the key issues facing the group in the near future are still linked with their immigration status, since the

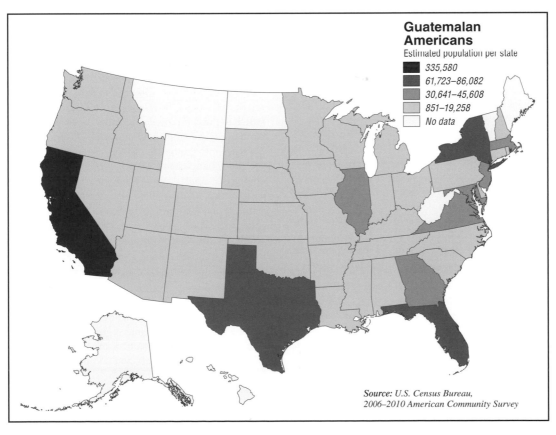

Guatemalan Americans

Estimated population per state

- 335,580
- 61,723–86,082
- 30,641–45,608
- 851–19,258
- No data

Source: U.S. Census Bureau, 2006–2010 American Community Survey

majority of Guatemalan Americans have arrived since the mid-1980s. Most Guatemalan Americans face a host of challenges in the areas of work, health, and cultural preservation due to their undocumented status and the adverse economic and political situations they left behind.

LANGUAGE

Spanish is the official language of Guatemala and is spoken by most first-generation Guatemalan Americans. However, some indigenous immigrants, especially women from the rural areas, speak Mayan exclusively and are unfamiliar with Spanish. Many first- and second-generation Mayan Americans are trilingual, and can communicate in Spanish, English, and a Mayan dialect. The U.S. Census Bureau's 2011 American Community Survey reported that nearly 90 percent of Guatemalan Americans spoke a language other than English. The Mayan languages spoken by Guatemalans in the United States include Kanjobal, Quiché, Mam, Cakchiquel, Chuj, Jacaltec, and Acatec. In Los Angeles, several dialects of Kanjobal are spoken, according to what area the person originates from.

The Mayan Americans in Houston speak both Quiché and Spanish. However, in her book *Deciding to Be Legal: A Maya Community in Houston* (1994), Jacqueline Maria Hagan noted that the Quiché language is diminishing both in Houston and in Guatemala, due to the predominance of Spanish in both areas. Children in Latino communities in Houston and Los Angeles learn Spanish in school and in their neighborhoods. Since Spanish is the language of access in Guatemala and in Latino areas, parents may encourage children to learn Spanish so they can interpret for them in various situations.

Language issues are intimately linked with assimilation, as children of immigrants sometimes reject both their Mayan language and customs. In Los Angeles some second-generation Kanjobal Americans attend a Spanish-language church rather than one that holds services in Kanjobal. Guatemalan Americans sometimes learn to speak Mexican Spanish to disguise their national origin. By passing for Mexican, they may be able to evade detection by the immigration authorities. For example, they may use Mexican terms such as *lana* instead of the Guatemalan term *pisto* for money. In some cities Guatemalan immigrants learn to speak Puerto Rican Spanish for the same reasons.

Greetings and Popular Expressions Popular Spanish-language Guatemalan greetings and expressions include: *Buenos días* ("bwenos deas") meaning "good morning," "good day," or "hello" and *buenas noches* ("bwenas noches"), meaning "good night." *Gracias* ("grasyas") means "thank you"; *con mucho gusto* ("kon mucho gusto") means "with much pleasure," which is used to mean "you're welcome" or "it's a pleasure to meet you." *Sí pues* ("se pwes") can mean either "it's okay" or "you're right"; con permiso ("kon per meso") means "excuse me"; *que rico, que riquíssimo* ("ke re ko, ke rekesemo") is an exclamation meaning "how rich," or "delicious," or "great!"; ¡*Salu!* means "to your health" or "cheers"; and ¡*Buen provecho!* ("bwen pro ve cho") means literally "good digestion" and is exclaimed before a meal.

In Kaqchikel, the Mayan language spoken by the Kaqchikel people in central Guatemala, *Raxnek, seker, xseker* means "good morning"; *xocok'a', xok'a* means "good night"; *nuch' ocob'a'* means "I'm sorry"; *matiox* means "thank you"; *ja'e* means "with pleasure" (like *con gusto*); and *rutzil, ruwech* means "hello."

RELIGION

Organized religion has greatly influenced the lives of Guatemalans and Guatemalan Americans. Since the time of the Spanish conquest, Guatemalans have practiced Roman Catholicism, while also maintaining Mayan religious customs and beliefs. The Roman Catholic church is still dominant in Guatemala and has been involved with all aspects of life there, including politics, community development, social services, and internal refugee relief.

During the early 1980s, when two Evangelical Pentecostal Protestant presidents ruled the nation, the Catholic clergy were associated with rebel forces and became targets for violence. In some areas it was dangerous to identify with Catholicism. Evangelical Protestantism grew dramatically during this time, as American churches sent missionaries to convert people. Thus, many recent Guatemalan Americans are Evangelical Protestants, in contrast to the majority in the Latino community, who are Roman Catholic.

Norita Vlach, who interviewed Guatemalan refugee families in San Francisco, observed in her book *The Quetzal in Flight: Guatemalan Refugee Families in the United States* (1989), that many Catholic families switch to the Pentecostal church during their first years in that city because those churches offered women's groups, youth groups, and Spanish language classes. In Houston, La Iglesia de Dios, a Protestant Evangelical church, is similarly active among the Totonicapán community, holding Bible readings for women and multiple services during the week, and hosting cultural events such as *quinceñeras* for church members and non-church members alike.

In *Seeking Community in a Global City: Guatemalans and Salvadorans in Los Angeles* (2001), Nora Hamilton and Norma Stoltz Chinchilla documented that in the Los Angeles area, 43 percent of Guatemalans and Salvadorans belonged to a church or were involved in a religious organization. They note that for many Central American refugees, religion "is a source of community and commitment." Many Guatemalan Americans in Los Angeles belong to charismatic Catholic congregations as well as Evangelical Protestant churches, including the Centro Cristiana Pentecostal in Hollywood.

Other Protestant religions and Catholicism are practiced by the majority of Guatemalan Americans in Houston. In Indiantown, Florida, and Los Angeles, the Kanjobal are Catholics, Seventh Day Adventists, Catholic Charismatics, and Protestants; many do not practice any religion although they may be nominally Catholic. A few practice traditional Mayan rituals of *costumbre*. Some *cofradías*, or indigenous village elders who interpreted Catholicism in villages, mixing Mayan and Catholic customs, have immigrated to the United States, but they often have a diminished role in their new environments. It is difficult for some Guatemalans to maintain their Mayan religious practices in the United States because some of these practices revolve around sacred places in Guatemala. *Catequistas*, or followers of the Catholic Action Movement, seek to remove indigenous practices from Catholicism.

The Catholic Church has provided shelter and many social services for Guatemalan American refugees. In Indiantown, Holy Cross Church funded a social service center that helped process asylum and immigration papers and supplied emergency relief, health referrals, and organizational help. Services are in Spanish and Kanjobal, and the annual festival for Guatemala's patron saint is held there. The Presbyterian Church's Office of World Service and World Hunger has also the supported the formation of local cultural groups in Indiantown.

CULTURE AND ASSIMILATION

Guatemalan Americans are a culturally diverse group of people. Within Guatemala 23 distinct ethnic groups speak different languages and maintain unique cultural traditions. The majority of these groups are Mayan; and *ladinos*, or Hispanic Guatemalans, constitute a separate population that adheres to the Spanish language and culture. Given this diversity, it is impossible to generalize about the group as a whole.

Immigrant Mayan American communities have maintained their traditional practices the most visibly. Hispanic Guatemalans have tended to blend in more with other Latino cultures and little information about them or third-, fourth-, and fifth-generation Guatemalan Americans exists. For instance, no studies have been conducted on how traditions are being passed on beyond the second generation. Further inquiry into these areas is needed and will probably occur as the recent wave of immigrants gives rise to second- and third-generation adults.

Certain practices like the celebration of *quinceñeras*, the formation of soccer leagues, and the organization of patronal fiestas have been maintained in most of the newer Guatemalan American neighborhoods. Specific Guatemalan American groups in Los Angeles, Houston, and southern Florida have received the most attention from sociologists and the media. The following sections on these three communities illustrate how some Guatemalan traditions are being preserved or transformed through the process of acculturation.

Guatemalan Americans in Los Angeles Until the late 1970s Los Angeles's Pico-Union district was populated by Mexican immigrants, Chicanos, African Americans, and European Americans. Some Central and South Americans began arriving in the mid-1950s, and after 1980 an influx of Central Americans settled the neighborhood. These Central American immigrants, including university students, teachers, clergy, and *campesinos*, came from all classes and political persuasions. New residents could shop at Latino-owned businesses such as grocery stores, botánicas selling religious articles and herbs, and informal vendors.

Among the Guatemalan immigrants were Mayan Chujes, Quichés, and Kanjobals. The Kanjobals from the highlands of Huehuetenango near the Mexican border constitute the largest Mayan group in Los Angeles, with a population of more than 5,000 in 1999, according to the UN Refugee Agency. Many call themselves *Migueleños* after their hometown of San Miguel Acatán. The first Kanjobal immigrants to Los Angeles came during the late 1970s in search of work, and more followed during the early 1980s, when Kanjobals were targeted as guerrilla sympathizers, and both guerrillas and the army pressured men and boys to fight on their sides during the civil war.

Coming from an agrarian society, the Kanjobals have made many adjustments to living in urban Los Angeles. Many had not used electricity or cars before. Women who had washed their clothes by hand in rivers became accustomed to laundromats. Both men and women encountered unfamiliar appliances such as refrigerators and unfamiliar foods like hot dogs.

To avoid deportation to Guatemala, many have tried to pass for Mexican American. For example, women generally do not wear the brightly embroidered blouses called *huipils* outside the home, and they have dispensed with carrying their infants on their backs in colorful cloth *rebozos*. In general, Guatemalans prefer deportation to Mexico versus their home country. Compared to their homeland, the economic opportunities for Guatemalan migrants are much greater in Mexico, and there is actually a large population of Guatemalan migrants who live and work in Mexico without ever making it to the United States. Additionally, Guatemalan immigrants tend to face more discrimination within the Latino/Chicano population in the United States because of the stark differences between their indigenous culture and traditions and those of the dominant mestizo culture, and thus passing as Mexican American helps them to avoid stigmatization based on their country of origin.

Deeper forms of integration into American society may be more elusive. Jacqueline Maria Hagan, who researched Houston's Mayan community, noted that assimilation can be intimately tied to legalization. Legal status affords the opportunity to join

The proprietor of Rinconcito Guatemalteco stands inside the authentic Guatemalan restaurant in Los Angeles, California. KAYTE DEIOMA / PHOTOEDIT

traditional social and cultural customs, and *indígenas* from Totonicapan can depend on a well-developed community for support upon arrival.

Some traditions have been lost upon settlement in the United States. Totonicapán is known as the capital of artisan production in Guatemala, and most of the male immigrants to Houston were previously tailors, weavers, or bakers. Since those skills were not transferable to the Houston workplace, many have transitioned from cottage industry production to wage labor. Women, however, still buy traditional garments from Totonicapán immigrants for special events.

Close relations between Guatemalan home villages and Mayan American communities also sustain cultural practices on both ends. Many Guatemalan Americans have close family members remaining in Guatemala. As they have achieved temporary or permanent residency status, some Guatemalans in Houston have been able to make the trips themselves. Items typically transported include traditional clothing, Guatemalan foods and spices, and occasionally things like wedding bands or other special items.

Some families have moved out of the Houston Totonicapán community after gaining legal status and saving enough money. Researcher Hagan saw this as part of a shift toward adopting American Texan culture, which included buying newer cars and women updating their hairstyles and clothes.

Kanjobals in Southern Florida A small farming town 25 miles inland from the east coast of Florida called Indiantown is home to approximately 4,000 to 5,000 Maya refugees from Guatemala, notes Allan Burns in *Maya in Exile: Guatemalans in Florida* (1993). Along with migrant workers from other countries, Guatemalan Americans here harvest sugar, oranges, cucumbers, and other crops during the winter growing season. Indiantown derived its name from the Seminole Native Americans who used to inhabit the area; now it is the center of the Guatemalan American population of southern Florida, which extends to other small towns like Immokalee.

Most of the Guatemalans in Indiantown are Kanjobals, although there is a small non-Kanjobal speaking group from the mostly *ladino* town of Cuilco. The Kanjobals first arrived in late 1982, when a Mexican American crew boss brought some refugees from Arizona to Indiantown to pick crops. These workers subsequently led family and friends from Kanjobal communities in Los Angeles and Guatemala to the area, and the town became a refuge from both the civil war and urban environments. As in other Mayan American communities, the tradition of going to the weekly market to exchange news and gossip and buy fresh fruit, meat, and vegetables has been supplanted by going to supermarkets. However, other customs remain intact and the Kanjobals maintain a visible ethnic presence.

established institutions, such as banks, and become active in higher education and community sports and other activities. As undocumented immigrants, many Guatemalan Americans refrain from interacting with mainstream society.

A nonprofit group called the Guatemala Unity Information Agency (GUIA) provides Guatemalan immigrants in the Los Angeles area with assistance related to immigration, education and social services.

Guatemalan Americans in Texas Fifteen percent of the total Guatemalan American population resides in Texas, according to the 2010 U.S. Census. As in Los Angeles, most Guatemalans emigrated after 1980 to escape political violence and economic repression. Both Hispanics and *indígenas* migrated to Houston, including Mayans from Quiché and Totonicapán in the Southwestern Highlands. The thousand or so Mayans have maintained many of their

Kanjobal marimba players from Indiantown played at the U.S. Folk Festival in 1985 and they also received a grant to teach Kanjobal American teenagers traditional music. The local Catholic church and Mayan American associations sponsor an annual fiesta in honor of the patron saint of San Miguel Acatán. Committees of men and women organize entertainment, sports, and the election of festival queens who give speeches in Kanjobal, Spanish, and English. Participants wear traditional clothing and teach children how to dance to marimba music. The dances involve costumed performances with masks made from paper maché. The patronal fiesta functions as an important gathering of Kanjobals, who must work and live outside of Indiantown, and as an affirmation of their ethnic identity.

Although many Mayan Americans have strived to preserve traditions such as these, others eschew their native customs. Since acculturation is ultimately a personal choice, degrees of assimilation vary from individual to individual. As in every other ethnic group, there are many like Mateo Andres, a first-generation Kanjobal American farmworker who told *New York Times* reporter Larry Rohter that he sees no need to pass on Mayan languages or practices to subsequent generations and hopes that his newborn son grows up to be "100 percent American."

Cuisine Savory and sometimes spicy Guatemalan cuisine has its origins in Mayan foods. Staples such as corn, beans, hot chili peppers, and tomatoes are still the staples of Guatemalan cooking. During the Spanish conquest, rice and other European and Asian ingredients were introduced into the cuisine. Guatemalan cooking falls into three categories: the highland indigenous cuisine; the Spanish colonial style cultivated by *ladinos*; and the food of the Caribbean coast town of Livingston. The last style of cooking developed with the culinary input of indentured laborers from India and Africa and resembles the cuisine of neighboring Belize. Unlike the other two kinds of Guatemalan cooking, this type is tropical and uses a lot of seafood, coconut, and bananas in its recipes.

The indigenous and Spanish styles are much more prevalent and somewhat intermixed. They make use of many of the vegetables and fruits native to the region. Some of the most popular ingredients include *chayote* or *huisquil*, a pear-shaped vegetable with firm, deep to pale green skin, which can be boiled, fried, mashed, baked, or used in salads and desserts; cilantro or *culantro*, a green, leafy herb otherwise known as coriander; and *cacao*, a chocolate made from local cacao beans sold in small cakes or tablets, which are used in cooking and to make hot chocolate.

Tortillas and black beans are among the most common foods in Guatemala. In indigenous villages, women often make the tortillas by grinding corn with a rounded pestle on a flat lava stone called a *piedra* or *metate* and baking the flat corn disks on a dry, clay platter known as a *comal*. This process is very time-consuming and is generally not used in the United States. Black beans are prepared whole, pureed, as soup, or paste and can be eaten at all meals. On the Caribbean coast and in cities, beans may be eaten with rice.

There are many varieties of tamales, which are essentially dough with meat and/or vegetables wrapped and steamed in a corn husk, leaf, or other wrapping. The dough can be made from cornmeal, flour, potatoes, or green bananas. In Guatemalan towns, women sell homemade tamales in markets. *Chuchitos* are a type of cornmeal tamales made with chicken, pork, or turkey, tomatoes, and chiles.

Chilaquiles consist of tortillas stuffed with cheese or other ingredients dipped in a batter and then fried or baked. They can be served with a savory tomato sauce. In the chilly Guatemalan highlands, *caldos*, or soups, are a frequent meal. Soup ingredients can include beef, chicken, lamb, potatoes, carrots, *chayotes*, onions, mint, eggs, tomatoes, beans, garlic, cilantro, and *epazote*, a mildly antiseptic herb that also has medicinal purposes.

Turkeys are native to the Americas and were raised, eaten, and sacrificed as a ceremonial bird in Mayan times. In Guatemala, turkey is still prepared and eaten during fiestas and national holidays. Another festive meat dish is *pepián*, which is eaten on Corpus Christi Day in June. *Pepián* consists of beef stewed with rice, spices, and vegetables such as tomatoes, green snap beans, chiles, and black peppercorns.

Plantains or *plátanos* are commonly eaten in the cities and in the more tropical areas. This very versatile fruit is similar to the banana but is higher in starch and lower in sugar content. Thus, it is always cooked, usually while it is green. It can be boiled, mashed, pan-fried, and deep-fried. Some varieties of ripe plantains are sweeter and can be prepared as a dessert with chocolate, cinnamon, or honey.

Sweets are quite popular in Guatemala and there is a wide variety of desserts like *pan dulce*, a sweet corn bread. *Hojuelas* are fried flour crisps drizzled with honey, which are sold in cities and in village markets. There are also prepared drinks like *boj*, a fermented sugar cane liquor drunk by Kekchi *indígenas* in Cobán. *Atol de maíz tierno* is a popular beverage made by boiling the paste of young corn, water, cinnamon, sugar, and salt.

Traditional Dress Since the 1930s most Guatemalan men have worn European-style clothing, but women of the highlands still wear the brightly colored garments distinct to each Mayan village. The wearing of traditional clothing, or *traje típico*, has evolved into a way to preserve ethnic identity and pride in both Guatemala and in the United States. Mayan American women may wear *traje* at home and especially at cultural events like fiestas, church meetings, and weddings. The *huipil* is a multicolored, intricately embroidered blouse. The *corte* is an ankle-length brightly woven skirt that may also be embroidered. Traditionally, hair is kept long and worn in a braid or ponytail. On festive occasions women may also wear colorful beaded or silver necklaces and sparkly earrings. The cloth for *traje típico* is traditionally hand-woven on a loom, but today machine-produced cloth is widely available in Guatemala, although the hand-woven fabric might be preferred for special occasions.

Holidays Guatemalan Americans celebrate American and Christian holidays as well as Guatemalan holidays, such as *Semana Santa* (the holy week of Easter) and patronal festivals. Totonicapán immigrants in Houston sometimes travel to San Cristóbal to celebrate their town's patron saint fiesta *La Fiesta de Santiago*, Christmas, and *Semana Santa*. The week-long festivities of Semana Santa reflect the blending of Mayan and Catholic rites and include costumed allegorical dramas that depict the Spanish conquest. During the week, participants cover the streets with *alfombras*, or "carpets," made of colored sawdust arranged in intricate patterns. The celebration reaches its climax on the last day when the parish priest leads a procession of the townspeople across the *alfombras*.

Although they are not national holidays, preparations for fiestas that honor a town's patron saint are elaborate, and many Guatemalan Americans maintain these traditions. Kanjobals in both Los Angeles and

Pastries from Guatemalteca Bakery in Los Angeles, California. KAYTE DEIOMA / PHOTOEDIT

southern Florida celebrate the fiesta of the patron saint of San Miguel Acatán on September 29 every year.

In 1990 more than 900 people attended the patronal festival in Los Angeles, which involved the coronation of festival queens, traditional Guatemalan food, trophies for athletes, and a Deer Dance. The ancestral Deer Dance is performed by people dressed as animals and different types of people. In Guatemala 60 to 80 dancers participate in the dance. The costumes have religious meaning and prayers are said before the dance commences. Celebrants set off firecrackers and rockets and play music on the marimba and on a drum made of wood and deer skin during the dance.

Health Care Issues and Practices The theory of health and illness common in Mesoamerica is based on a humoral dichotomy of hot and cold, which should be in balance. In her study of the health practices of Mayan Americans in Florida, *A Matter of Life and Death: Health-Seeking Behavior of Guatemalan Refugees in South Florida* (1989), Maria Miralles observed that they sometimes attributed their illnesses to an imbalance in hot and cold or to the weather and heat.

Many of the indigenous and rural immigrants are not accustomed to relying on modern American medicine to cure their health problems. In rural Guatemala and in some cities, *curanderos*, or traditional curers, use teas, herbs, and other natural remedies to heal the sick. *Curanderos* are also consulted as spiritual diviners and healers. Some *curanderos* are specialists trained in bone setting or the treatment of tumors. In Los Angeles the Kanjobals can go to local *curanderos* for problems like stress or depression. However, *curanderos* have been mostly supplanted by U.S. doctors, because they cannot get licenses to practice medicine in the United States. *Promotores de salud* or health promoters trained by Catholic Action missionaries to know first aid and preventative medicine also work in Guatemalan villages.

In many Mayan cultures, birth ceremonies are extremely important and the infant is received as a part of the community. Babies are traditionally delivered by midwives, and it is considered scandalous to go to a hospital to give birth. However, in the United States women may go to hospitals to deliver in order to obtain birth certificates for their newborns, despite their preferences.

Curative herbs are often consumed or used in medicinal steam baths. In Guatemala the herbs can be bought from herb vendors; in the United States some can be found at *botánicas*. Some of the herbs used are *manzanilla* or chamomile and *hierba buena*, a mixture from Mexico. These can be taken for stomach disorders or headaches. Guatemalan immigrants who relied on traditional curative practices may prefer them to those of the American medical establishment. However, many also go to clinics and hospitals to cure their ailments.

The journey from Guatemala to the United States can be traumatic for emigrants escaping persecution or extreme poverty. Traveling by foot for up to thousands of miles with little money and few possessions, many become dehydrated, malnourished, and exhausted. Many travel through Mexico, where they may stay in overcrowded refugee camps that provide little food and shelter and have poor sanitary conditions. Under these circumstances, they are susceptible to serious diseases such as malaria and tuberculosis as well as parasites, gastrointestinal disorders, severe malnutrition, cracked and damaged feet, and skin infections.

Many are survivors of extreme violence and subsequently suffer from mental health problems, which often go untreated. Physical and psychological problems from conditions in Guatemala and the journey are compounded by the precariousness of the immigrants' positions once they settle in the United States. Poor housing, underemployment, fear of deportation, and drastic cultural changes can induce stress-related ailments such as ulcers and high blood pressure. Anxiety, depression, and alcohol abuse have also afflicted immigrants.

Undocumented immigrants usually do not receive insurance from employers, Medicaid, or other government health-care benefits, and they often do not have access to affordable health care. However, in Los Angeles and Indiantown, health clinics have been established for Guatemalan and other immigrants without papers. In Indiantown a county-sponsored health clinic known as *el corte* operates a Woman, Infant, and Child program for family planning and gives vaccinations to migrant workers' children. A privately run clinic known as *la clínica* provides screening, acute episode care, chronic disease management, and laboratory and x-ray services on a sliding-fee basis. Kanjobal immigrants use both clinics, although they may also use traditional remedies at home.

In 1983 several social service and ecumenical religious groups created the Clínica Monseñor Oscar A. Romero, a free health care center for Central Americans in Los Angeles. It was formed to address the special needs of refugees who cannot go to public medical facilities due to the risk of deportation and who contend with language and financial barriers that keep them from going to other clinics.

FAMILY AND COMMUNITY LIFE

For many Guatemalan Americans, large extended kinship groups maintain close bonds of loyalty, obligation, and social support. The family group traditionally includes grandparents and fictive kin such as *comadres*, or godmothers.

However, many immigrants are separated from their families, because it is nearly impossible for everyone to immigrate at the same time. Many men were forced to flee without their families because they were

in immediate danger of being conscripted or killed in the civil war. Undocumented immigrants usually travel to the United States alone, because they cannot afford to pay the *coyotes* for everyone at once, and because their chances of making the crossing and surviving in the new environment are better if they go alone.

After establishing their lives in the United States, immigrants generally try to bring the rest of their families over. Spouses, children, and siblings are frequently reunited. However, elderly parents and grandparents often do not make the trip, which can require withstanding physical dangers and hardships. Children are sometimes left with grandparents in Guatemala, because both parents must work long hours and cannot afford day care or similar services.

Separation and reunification after long periods of living apart can strain family relations. Housing conditions may also change family dynamics. In immigrant

Two young girls wear traditional, handwoven Guatemalan dresses as they participate in a Central American ethnic pride parade in Chicago, 1995. PHOTOGRAPH BY SANDY FELSENTHAL. CORBIS. REPRODUCED BY PERMISSION.

enclaves like Indiantown, families live in crowded tenement apartments. In these situations, a family may share a one-room apartment with other families. Because of the lack of privacy and the pressures these conditions create, many families move out of the community when they save enough money to do so.

Despite the difficulty of finding work and making a living as undocumented persons, most Guatemalan Americans do not receive public assistance. Illegal aliens are not eligible for public assistance and are usually wary of government institutions. Children who are U.S. citizens may be eligible for welfare and food stamps, but undocumented parents are often afraid to apply for such benefits. In 2011 20 percent of the Guatemalan American population documented by the U.S. Census Bureau received food stamps or SNAP benefits.

As in many immigrant communities, younger family members adjust more quickly to American life. In urban Latino neighborhoods, adolescents may face conflict with their parents if they assume *cholo* identities. *Cholo* refers to an originally Chicano teenage subculture that involves the use of slang, a street-wise pose and walk, low-rider cars, marijuana, and a specific style of dress—pressed khaki pants, plaid shirts, and tattoos for boys, and lots of make-up for girls.

Attitudes toward marriage have also changed in several Guatemalan American communities. Divorce and couples living together without being married are more common in the United States than they are in Guatemala. The absence of older generations in some communities may lead to a decline in the observance of traditional customs. In general, there is little intermarriage with other ethnic groups among the first-generation. Immigrant men are more likely to date or marry non-Guatemalans than women immigrants are, and second-generation girls may be encouraged more than boys to date only Guatemalan Americans.

Gender Roles As in Latino families, Guatemalan American women occupy complex and important positions within their families and communities. Guatemalan society is patriarchal and patrilineal, with men controlling most of the major institutions. However, within the past four decades women have garnered more leadership roles in all areas of society and they have led and played crucial parts in many of the popular resistance movements. During the 1980s, organizations such as CONAVIGUA, composed mostly of indigenous widows of murdered or disappeared men, formed and fought for women's and human rights. With the absence of male figures in the community as a result of the civil war, women assumed more responsibility in the public sphere in order to preserve their communities.

In many cases women take on a larger economic role in the family when they immigrate to the United States. In migrant worker communities, both women and men do wage field work. In addition, women are often expected to do all the domestic labor—child-rearing, cooking, and cleaning. Given the large size of households in some neighborhoods, this can involve an enormous amount of work, cooking and cleaning for 10 to 20 people. Men are more likely to be involved in social organizations such as soccer clubs that allow interaction with other men from the community in the public sphere.

Immigrant women tend to transmit and sustain traditional culture more readily than the men, especially among Mayan immigrants. By maintaining religious practices and their native language, preparing traditional foods, and wearing traditional clothes and hairstyles, women preserve the cultural fabric of their ethnicity. Women also frequently organize church-related or community-oriented events like fiestas.

Education Education is a high priority for many Guatemalan American parents. In urban areas such as Los Angeles and Houston the available public schools often have poor reputations, and parents prefer to send their children to Catholic schools if they can afford it. Guatemalan American parents whose children remain in Guatemala will often pay for their children's education through remittances.

Children who were previously educated in Guatemalan schools in which the curricula are rigorous generally adjust easily to American schools once they learn English. However, many immigrant students have not had much prior education, due to decades of war, violence, and poverty. In southern Florida, two schools have been set up to address the needs of the migrant workers' children, who may not yet speak English and must deal with other challenges. The Migrant Head Start Program and the Hope Rural School are attended by Guatemalan American and many other children from Indiantown's diverse community.

No statistics on the number of Guatemalan Americans who go to four-year universities and graduate schools are available. Since many colleges or universities do not distribute financial aid (they are not eligible for federal financial aid, but can potentially receive state and local aid) to undocumented students, it is difficult for them to attend institutions of higher learning. However, it is not impossible, and some institutions do offer aid to undocumented youth. In 2010 about 13 percent of all Hispanics had obtained at least a bachelor's degree, versus 8 percent of individuals of Guatemalan descent. Advocacy for children of undocumented immigrants led to the creation and passage of the DREAM Act by Congress. This legislation, enacted in 2012, provides a path toward legal immigration that entails a college education and in some cases, military service.

Relations with Other Americans Guatemalan Americans face the stereotypes that have historically plagued almost all immigrant groups in the United States. Like other Latino groups, not to mention the Irish, Eastern Europeans, and Asians that have preceded them, Guatemalan Americans have been scapegoated by nativists as docile, ignorant workers who do not mind being exploited, who overwhelm American economic and social resources, and who are of little value except as workers in undesirable jobs. During economic recessions, politicians have exploited this anti-immigrant bias to curry favor with constituents who want to blame their own financial woes on vulnerable targets rather than coming to terms with the real sources of the problem.

Guatemalan Americans are also generally lumped together with other Central American and Latino groups as indistinguishable from one another. Although there is great diversity within and among the different Central American and Latino groups, many Americans tend to perceive them as one entity, subjecting Guatemalan, Nicaraguan, Salvadoran, Honduran, Mexican, Cuban, and Puerto Rican Americans to the same stereotypes.

EMPLOYMENT AND ECONOMIC CONDITIONS

Although Guatemalan Americans with legal resident or citizen status work in any number of professional fields such as law, teaching, and medicine, the large percentage of recently arrived undocumented immigrants have little access to decently paying jobs. These Guatemalan Americans generally take low-paying jobs in the service sector, manufacturing, and agriculture. These are the same jobs that have historically been held by other new immigrant groups upon arrival in the United States. In rural areas throughout the United States, Guatemalan immigrants work as migrant harvesters, picking fruit, flowers, vegetables, and commodities such as tobacco in places like the San Joaquin Valley in California. In 2010 the median annual income of Guatemalan Americans ages 16 and older was approximately $17,000, versus $28,500 for the general U.S. population.

Field work of this type is often dangerous because of accidents and exposure to pesticides that can cause rashes and burns, and it demands long hours of physical exertion and a lifestyle of constant mobility. Exploitation of migrant workers is also common, as it is easy for agricultural contractors to pocket their Social Security payments or refuse to pay them altogether. If legal status is obtained, Guatemalan Americans usually move on to other types of work such as construction, or jobs where they can apply their professional skills in areas like education or social services. Many Guatemalan immigrants worked as trained professionals in Guatemala but cannot obtain the same type of work here because of their undocumented status.

The Mayan Americans of southern Florida and Los Angeles sometimes work in garment factories during the migrant workers' off-season. Very few undocumented garment workers in Los Angeles belong to unions, although they legally have a right to unionize to demand better working conditions and wages.

However, the building maintenance industry has a more active history of Central American involvement. Chinchilla and Hamilton document that in the early 1990s, Guatemalan women represented 5 percent of the women working as janitors in Los Angeles, and they were pivotal to the earlier success of the Service Employees International Union's (SEIU) campaign for higher wages in the mid-1980s. The vice president of SEIU, Eliseo Medina, as quoted by Chinchilla and Hamilton, praised their dedication to the cause observing that "immigrants from Central America have a much more militant history as unionists … and the more militant they are, the more the union can do." Nevertheless, the difficulty of organizing itinerant laborers, language barriers, lack of experience with unions, and fear of being deported contribute to the lack of union activity among most undocumented Guatemalan Americans.

Other Guatemalan Americans in Los Angeles and Florida work as gardeners in nurseries, landscapers on golf courses, and in restaurants and hotels. During the early 1990s, a textile cooperative was developed in Indiantown to create safe, year-round work in the Kanjobal neighborhood. The cooperative produces women's clothing that incorporates Mayan-style weaving.

Men may also do odd jobs as carpenters, roofers, or as informal vendors. Women often work as domestics throughout the United States, cooking, cleaning, or looking after children for individual families with whom they live. Women may also earn money by babysitting, doing laundry by hand, or cooking for people within their community.

In an unusual situation, many of the Totonicapán American men in Houston work as maintenance or stock workers in one retail chain. The employers who hired the original migrants from Totonicapán think of the Mayans as hard-working, responsible, and loyal. As more Totonicapán immigrants arrived, they obtained jobs with the same company, creating a steady labor supply for the chain. This situation and the legalization of community members has made the acculturation process relatively smooth for this group.

Undocumented Guatemalan American workers are vulnerable to exploitation by employers since they are not afforded the same benefits as U.S. citizens, as well as to immigration raids and deportation that could involve criminal charges and/or lead to the separation of their families. A poignant example of this is the U.S. Immigration and Customs Enforcement's (ICE) 2008 raid on an Agriprocessors kosher meatpacking plant in Postville, Iowa. ICE agents detained 389 undocumented immigrant workers in the plant, 293 (75 percent) of whom were Guatemalan. The most notable part of this case was the fact that several hundred of the detainees were accused of a criminal violation of the law, "aggravated identity theft," which was a felony rather than the more common charge of an administrative or civil violation. As Susanne Jonas explains, "the Postville raid was emblematic of the excesses of U.S. 'enforcement-only' immigration policies of the early 2000s, with its mass criminalization and deportation of undocumented workers." For Guatemalan Americans, Jonas notes, the raid demonstrated the potentially devastating disadvantages of immigration in the twenty-first century. While legislation introduced by Barack Obama in his second presidential term may finally open up a viable path for the amnesty of millions of undocumented immigrants in the country, it will undoubtedly face vehement opposition by anti-immigration politicians and activists.

Most of the work available to immigrants without legal papers is sporadic, and underemployment is a problem for many. However, the same people who have limited access to nonexploitative work are also ineligible for unemployment benefits. In 2011 almost 9 percent of the adult Guatemalan American population was unemployed, according to the U.S. Census Bureau. While it is difficult to discern the impact of the recession of 2007–2008 on this specific community, it is likely that they faced increasing financial difficulties as did many other minority ethnic groups during that period. The need for reliable, fairly paid employment continues to be the most pressing issue in many Guatemalan American communities. The Guatemalan population's poverty status in 2010 continued to be much higher at 26 percent than that of the general population.

POLITICS AND GOVERNMENT

Because immigration in general and refugee status in particular are at the heart of the issues affecting many Guatemalan Americans, changes in federal immigration law have influenced the group. Since the 1980s, there have been several key pieces of federal legislation in this regard.

The 1980 Refugee Act mandates that immigration officials judge political asylum cases individually, rather than by national origin, and that the rulings be independent of the government's relations with the country the applicant has come from. However, critics of asylum processes during the Reagan era claimed that the INS continued to base asylum decisions on national origin. This criticism was borne out by the fact that fewer than two percent of Guatemalan applicants received asylum in the 1980s. This number is substantially less compared with applicants from countries the United States did support like Nicaragua or the former Eastern Bloc countries. Although the act did not immediately change the way asylum decisions are made, it paved the way for later legislation and court decisions. The complex Immigration Reform and Control Act (IRCA) of 1986 enabled immigrants living in the United States continuously since January 1, 1982, and arriving before that date to apply for legalization status. This provision helped the small percentage of Guatemalan emigrants who arrived before then. Another provision of IRCA called for employer sanctions that penalize employers who hired unauthorized workers after November 6, 1986.

Immigration has been one of the hardest issues confronted by legislators in the past twenty years or so, mostly as a result of the competing demands of powerful interest groups. These included the trade unions who were concerned about the depression of wages due to the unhindered flow of immigrant labor. An immigration measure offering a path to citizenship to a wide cross-section of the undocumented immigrant community was introduced to Congress in 2007 but was quickly discarded by legislators who disagreed over the weight placed on border-enforcement measures versus the attention given to granting citizenship to millions of undocumented immigrants.

In February 2013, both the White House and a bipartisan group of congressman known as the "Gang of Eight," including Republican Senator Marco Rubio, drafted preliminary immigration reform legislation. President Obama's plan would potentially pave the way for citizenship for approximately 11 million undocumented immigrants in the country through the proposed "Lawful Prospective Immigrant" visa, while also increasing border enforcement measures. The proposal made by the "Gang of Eight" places more emphasis on a guest worker program and increased border security than granting citizenship to currently undocumented immigrants. However, until a bill makes it through Congress, the status of undocumented individuals—including that of many Guatemalan Americans—remains tenuous.

Because Guatemalan Americans form a small minority group, their involvement with American politics has been minor. A number of grass-roots refugee advocacy groups, however, have lobbied for immigrant rights. There are no statistics on Guatemalan American voting patterns, the number of elected officials of Guatemalan heritage, or Guatemalan Americans' participation in the armed forces. The National Association of Latino Elected and Appointed Officials in Houston does not categorize their listing of Latino politicians by national origin. However, several Guatemalan American politicians are active across the country.

Jim Gonzalez was appointed to city and county supervisor on the San Francisco Board of Supervisors in 1988 and served until 1992; more recently he has worked as a political consultant. He also worked as a special assistant to Senator Dianne Feinstein from 1981 to 1986. Ed Lopez was active in the Republican Party and served as the National Vice Chairman of the Republican Liberty Caucus beginning in 2011; although Lopez was born in Puerto Rico, he identifies his heritage as Guatemalan. Norma Torres, who was born in Guatemala and immigrated to the United States in 1970, is a Democratic politician who served as a member of the California State Assembly, representing the 52nd district, which includes cities in Orange County, beginning in 2012.

Relations with Guatemala Most Guatemalan Americans have family or close friends remaining in Guatemala, and the majority remain concerned about the state of affairs there. While many Guatemalan Americans do not have the resources or time to address the conditions they fled from, several Guatemalan American organizations actively strive for an end to violence and corruption in Guatemala. These groups include refugee aid organizations.

NOTABLE INDIVIDUALS

The following subsections list some notable Guatemalan Americans and their accomplishments.

Business Luis Alfredo Vasquez-Ajmac (1961–) serves as the president of MAYA, a marketing communications firm targeting Latinos in Washington, D.C., which he established in 1990. He also served as an advisory member to the Corporation for Public Broadcasting.

Luis von Ahn (1979–), an entrepreneur and associate professor in computer science at Carnegie Mellon University, is known for his pioneering work in crowdsourcing. Von Ahn also founded the company reCAPTCHA, which was bought by Google in 2009.

Marta Ortiz-Buonafina (1933–) is an associate professor of marketing at Florida International University. She has published many articles and books, including the second edition of *Profitable Export Marketing* in 1992.

Film Daphne Eurydice Zuniga (1962–) is an actress known for playing Jo Reynolds on the Fox soap opera *Melrose Place* and Victoria Davis on the CW drama *One Tree Hill*.

Benito Martinez (1971–) is an actor best known for playing police captain David Aceveda in the FX crime drama *The Shield*. Martinez studied at the London Academy of Music and Dramatic Art (LAMDA) in London, England. He also appeared on the television program *Saving Grace*.

Literature Arturo Arias (1950–) cowrote the screenplay for *El Norte* with Gregory Nava and Anna Thomas, which won the Montreal Prize and was nominated for an Academy Award for best screenplay in 1982. The film portrays the experiences of a Kanjobal brother and sister who flee from persecution in Guatemala and make the arduous journey to Los Angeles. The realistic depiction of their struggles on the way and in the United States was well received by the Kanjobal American community in Los Angeles, on which it is based. Arias has also written several novels, including *Jaguar en llamas* in 1989, and he served as a professor of humanities at Stanford University, San Francisco State University, and the University of Texas at Austin.

Francisco Goldman (1954–) is a journalist and author whose first novel *The Long Night of White Chickens* was published in 1992 to critical acclaim. The book evokes contemporary Guatemala and is narrated by a Guatemalan American character who travels to Guatemala in search of a friend who was murdered under mysterious circumstances. An Allen K. Smith Professor of Literature and Creative Writing at Trinity College, Goldman received the Mary Ellen von der Heyden fellowship for Fiction, and was a 2010 Fellow at the American Academy and a Guggenheim Fellow.

Donald Kenneth Gutierrez (1932–) is a writer and professor emeritus of English at Western New Mexico University. He has published numerous essays and scholarly books, including *Breaking Through to the Other Side: Essays on Realization in Modern Literature* in 1994.

Hector Tobar (1963–) is a journalist for the *Los Angeles Times* who won a Pulitzer Prize in 1992 for his coverage of the Los Angeles riots. His novel *The Tattooed Soldier* concerns both the neighborhood affected by the riots and the violence in Guatemala during the civil war. His nonfiction work, *Translation Nation*, explores the up-and-coming Latino and Hispanic communities outside of the American southwest.

David Unger (1950–) is a writer, translator, and former codirector of the Latin American Writers' Institute. His published works include *The Price of Escape* (2011) and *Life in the Damn Tropics* (2004). He has received awards for his translation work from the New York State Council on the Arts.

Music Aida Doninelli (1898–1996) was the daughter of Italian immigrants to Guatemala and was both born and raised in Guatemala. She made her American debut as an opera singer in Chicago in 1927. A dramatic soprano, she performed on the major concert stages of the United States and Latin America and sang with New York's prestigious Metropolitan Opera from 1928 to 1933. During her tenure at the Met, Doninelli performed in many operatic roles, including Micaela in *Carmen*, Mimi in *La Bohème*, and Cio-Cio San in *Madame Butterfly*. She also appeared in some of the earliest musical films, such as *La Traviata* and *Tosca*, and introduced Latin American music to a wide U.S. audience by singing in radio shows broadcast from New York.

Manny Marroquin (1971–) was born in Guatemala and moved to Los Angeles when he was nine. He has won several Grammy Awards for his sound production work with Alicia Keys, John Legend, Usher, and Kanye West. He has also worked with Rihanna, Linkin Park, Nelly Furtado, Mariah Carey, and Santana.

Lorena Pinot (1981–) is a recording artist and songwriter who gained fame in 2001 as a lead singer in the Latin/pop girl group MSM (Miami Sound Machine), a new incarnation of the 1980s outfit led by Gloria Estefan.

Karl Cameron (K.C.) Porter (1962–) is a record producer, songwriter, musician, and singer who has won three Grammys and Latin Grammys. Porter is best known for helping produce Carlos Santana's best-selling and award-winning album *Supernatural.*

Science and Medicine Julio Alfredo Molina (1948–) is a psychiatrist and the founder and director of the Anxiety Disorders Institute of Atlanta.

Carmen Carrillo (1943–) is a psychologist and the director of Adult Acute Services at San Francisco's Department of Public Health. She has earned many awards for her work in education, psychology, mental health, and Latino issues, including the City and Council of San Francisco Distinction and Merit Award in 1988, the National Women's Political Caucus Public Service Award in 1989, and the California School Boards Association Service Award in 1991.

Jorge Huascar del Pinal (1945–) is a statistician and the chief of the U.S. Bureau of the Census's Ethnic and Spanish Statistics Branch.

Hermann Mendez (1949–) is an associate professor of pediatrics at the State University of New York Health Science Center at Brooklyn and has received awards from the Department of Health and Human Services and the assistant secretary of health for his outstanding contributions to the fight against AIDS. He was also named as one of the best doctors in New York by *New York Magazine* in 1991 and as one of the best doctors in America by Woodward/White Inc. in 1992.

John Joaquin Munoz (1918–1999) was a scientist emeritus at the National Institute of Health's Rocky Mountain Laboratories. He served as chairman of the immunology section of the American Society of Microbiology and received an NIH Director's Award in 1979. He has also published many papers.

Victor Perez-Mendez (1923–2005) edited two books, wrote over 300 articles, and was a professor of physics and faculty senior scientist at the University of California at Berkeley.

Sergio Ramiro Aragón (1949–) is a professor of chemistry at San Francisco State University and established a supercomputer center at California State University in 1989.

Sports Ted Hendricks (1947–) was a linebacker who played NFL football with the Baltimore Colts, the Green Bay Packers, and the Oakland Raiders from 1969 to 1983.

MEDIA

La Opinión

A Spanish-language daily newspaper popular among Central Americans in Pico-Union.

700 S. Flower
Suite 3000
Los Angeles, California 90017
URL: www.laopinion.com

El Quetzal

Quarterly publication from the Guatemalan Human Rights Commission that provides information on the human rights situation in Guatemala.

Kelsey Alford-Jones, Director
3321 12th Street NE
Washington, D.C. 20017
Phone: (202) 529-6599
Fax: (202) 526-4611
URL: www.ghrc-usa.org/index.htm

Revue: Guatemala's English-language Magazine

Bilingual Spanish and English publication published by the Guatemalan Education Action Project. Features articles on the political situation in Guatemala and Chiapas.

John, Editor
Terry Kovick Biskovich, Editor
3a Avenida Sur No. 4-A
La Antigua, Guatemala
Phone: (502) 7931-4500
URL: www.revuemag.com

ORGANIZATIONS AND ASSOCIATIONS

Guatemala Education Action Project

Formed in 1986 by Guatemalan refugees in the United States to build awareness, response, and respect for the people of Guatemala.

8124 West Third
Suite 105
Los Angeles, California 90048-4328
Phone: (323) 782-0953
Email: greview@igc.org
URL: www.geaplosangeles.com

Guatemala Human Rights Commission/USA

Monitors and provides current information about human rights in Guatemala, and runs a frequently updated blog outlining new developments and issues.

Kelsey Alford-Jones, Director
3321 12th Street NE
Washington, D.C. 20017-4008
Phone: (202) 529-6599
Fax: (202) 526-4611
Email: ghrc-usa@ghrc-usa.org
URL: www.ghrc-usa.org

Network in Solidarity with the People of Guatemala (NISGUA)

Founded in 1981, NISGUA acts as an umbrella organization for groups that support human rights in Guatemala. Collects and disseminates information about the political, military, and economic situation there.

P.O. Box 70494
Oakland, California 94612

Phone: (510) 763-1403
Email: info@nisgua.org
URL: www.nisgua.org

MUSEUMS AND RESEARCH CENTERS

Dallas Museum of Art

The museum displays an extensive collection of pre-Columbian and eighteenth- to twentieth-century textiles, censers, and other art objects from Guatemala.

1717 North Harwood
Dallas, Texas 75201
Phone: (214) 922-1200
URL: www.dm-art.org

Human Rights Documentation Exchange

Formerly known as the Central America Resource Center, maintains a library of information on human rights and social conditions in many countries, including Guatemala, as well as some information on Guatemalan Americans.

Rebecca Hall, Executive Director
PO Box 2327
Austin, Texas 78768
Phone: (512) 476-9841
Fax: (512) 476-0130
Email: mail@hrde.org
URL: www.handplant.com/mockups/hrde

Middle American Research Institute (MARI)

Part of Tulane University, this institute features a collection of pre-Hispanic, Mayan textiles and archeological artifacts from Guatemala.

Middle American Research Institute
Tulane University
6823 St. Charles Avenue
New Orleans, Louisiana 70118
Phone: (504) 865-5110
Fax: (504) 862-8778
Email: mari@tulane.edu
URL: www.tulane.edu/~mari

Nettie Lee Benson Latin American Collection at the University of Texas at Austin

This internationally renowned library of books and periodicals on Latin America maintains a good collection on Guatemalan Americans and Guatemala.

Margo Gutierrez, Head Librarian
Sid Richardson Hall 1.108
General Libraries
University of Texas at Austin
Austin, Texas 78713-8916
Phone: (512) 495-4520
Fax: (512) 495-4568
Email: blac@lib.utexas.edu
URL: www.lib.utexas.edu/benson

San Antonio Museum of Art

Features a variety of textiles and sculpture from Guatemala.

Marion Oettinger, Jr., Curator, Latin American Folk Art
200 West Jones Avenue
San Antonio, Texas 78215
Phone: (210) 978-8100
Fax: (210) 978-8118
URL: www.samuseum.org

The Textile Museum

Displays a collection of handmade historic and ethnographic textiles from Guatemala and other Latin American countries.

William J. Conklin, Research Associate, Pre-Columbian Textiles
2320 South Street NW
Washington, D.C. 20008
Phone: (202) 667-0441
Fax: (202) 483-0994
URL: www.textilemuseum.org

The University of Texas Institute of Texan Cultures at San Antonio

The multicultural museum and educational resource center maintains a library of books, files, and photographs of 90 ethnic groups in Texas, including Guatemalan Americans.

801 East Cesar E. Chavez Boulevard
San Antonio, Texas 78233
Phone: (210) 458-2300
URL: www.texancultures.com

SOURCES FOR ADDITIONAL STUDY

Ashabranner, Brent. *Children of the Maya: A Guatemalan Indian Odyssey.* New York: Dodd, Mead & Company, 1986.

Burns, Allan. *Maya in Exile: Guatemalans in Florida.* Philadelphia: Temple University Press, 1993.

Chinchilla, Norma S., and Nora Hamilton, eds. *Seeking Community in a Global City: Guatemalans and Salvadorans in Los Angeles.* Philadelphia: Temple University Press, 2001.

Hagan, Jacqueline Maria. *Deciding to Be Legal: A Maya Community in Houston.* Philadelphia: Temple University Press, 1994.

Hernandez, Marita. "Kanjobal Indians: Guatemala to L.A.—Bid for Survival," *Los Angeles Times,* Sept. 24, 1984, Part 1.

Loucky, James, and Marilyn Moors, eds. *Maya Diaspora: Guatemalan Roots, New American Lives.* Philadelphia: Temple University Press, 2000.

Miralles, Andrea Maria. *A Matter of Life and Death: Health-Seeking Behavior of Guatemalan Refugees in South Florida.* New York: AMS Press, Inc, 1989.

Rohter, Larry. "In a Florida Haven for Guatemalans, Seven Deaths Bring New Mourning," *New York Times,* Oct. 24, 1991.

Vlach, Norita. *The Quetzal in Flight: Guatemalan Refugee Families in the United States.* Westport, CT: Praeger, 1989.

GUYANESE AMERICANS

Jacqueline A. McLeod

OVERVIEW

Guyanese Americans are immigrants or descendents of people from the Cooperative Republic of Guyana—formerly the colony of British Guiana—a country larger than the rest of the English-speaking Caribbean put together. It sprawls across 83,000 square miles of the northeastern coast of South America, bounded on the west by Venezuela, on the southwest by Brazil, and on the east by Suriname. As one of many Caribbean nations, Guyana is often assumed to be an island rather than a continental country. Its northern boundary consists of 250 miles of coastline on the Atlantic Ocean, and as a nation, it is slightly bigger than the state of Kansas.

According to a 2012 U.S. State Department report, Guyana has a population of about 751,000. Around 52 percent of Guyanese are Christian, with 65 percent of Christians identifying themselves as Protestant, and the other 35 percent self-identifying as Roman Catholic. As a result of ambitious missionary activities during the nineteenth century, the Afro-Guyanese are mostly Christian. Of the non-Christian Guyanese, 34 percent are Hindu, 9 percent are Muslim, and 5 percent are an unknown denomination. The 2002 Guyana census reported that 43.5 percent of the population was of East Indian ethnicity, 30.2 percent were of African descent, 16.7 percent were of mixed ethnicity, 9.1 percent were Amerindian, and the remaining 0.5 percent reported being of other ethnicities. Chinese, Portuguese, and British peoples have also contributed to the cultural heritage of the land. The standard of living in Guyana is relatively high due largely to its natural resources (specifically, oil, tropical rain forests, and the sugar industry). Still, approximately 35 percent of the population lives below the poverty line.

Guyanese immigration to the United States occurred in two major waves, the first of which took place during the first two decades of the twentieth century. These immigrants were typically single males who had left their families and possibly a fiancée behind in the hopes of sending for them later. They tended to work around the clock and supplement their educations in the evenings, typically settling in the northeastern cities of the United States. During the 1960s and 1970s, more Guyanese women than men settled in the United States, and they became the family members primarily responsible for securing immigrant status for their families. By 1990 more than 80 percent of Guyanese Americans lived in the Northeast.

According to the U.S. Census Bureau's American Community Survey estimates, 209,680 people of Guyanese ancestry resided in the United States during the time period between 2009 and 2011. The heaviest concentration of Guyanese Americans can be found in New York, New Jersey, and Maryland, though a significant portion of the population also settled in Florida, California, Texas, and Pennsylvania. About 18 percent of the total population of Guyana moved to New York City—particularly the East Flatbush, Flatbush, and Crown Heights sections of Brooklyn—in the 1980s.

HISTORY OF THE PEOPLE

Early History Guyana is an Amerindian word that means "land of [many] waters." The Europeans first used the name to refer to the triangle formed by the Orinoco, Amazon, and Negro rivers. The British used "Guiana"—an English spelling of the same Amerindian name—to refer to their New World colony. Before the arrival of the Europeans, Guyana was inhabited by several native groups. The largest group was the Caribs, who lived in the upper reaches of the Essequibo River, as well as near the Mazaruni, Cuyuni, Pomeroon, and Barima rivers. Between the Corentyne and Waini rivers lived the Arawaks, a friendly, peace-loving native group whose people were the first to greet Christopher Columbus in other areas of the Caribbean. Another native group, the Warrau, inhabited the swampland near the mouth of the Orinoco in present-day Venezuela but eventually moved east into Guyanese territory.

Christopher Columbus was the first European known to have sailed along the coast of Guyana. But during his voyage to the New World in 1498, Columbus only viewed the land's low-lying tropical shore. It was not until 1499 that Alonso de Ojeda became the first Spaniard to actually set foot on the land that would later be known as Guyana. No settlement, however, resulted from this early exploration. Between 1595 and 1616, English explorer Sir Walter Raleigh—who dreamed of "El Dorado" (the mythical land of gold)—led three expeditions to the Guyanese territory. Although Raleigh failed to locate any gold, his efforts resulted in the earliest mapping of the Guyanese coastline.

The Dutch were the first Europeans to gain a real foothold in Guyana. In Europe, the Dutch States-General (governing the provinces of present-day Holland) granted the Dutch West India Company a charter over the Guyana territory in 1621. The charter gave the company complete political and economic authority, the privilege to undertake pirate raids against Spanish shipping, and the right to carry slaves from West Africa to the New World. By 1770 more than 15,000 Africans were enslaved in Guyana. With this slave labor force at work, the farms began to grow in size and in yield. The success of the Dutch venture encouraged the development of sugar plantations in other inland regions of Guyana.

In 1781 war broke out between the Dutch and the British over ownership of the colony; the conflict resulted in a year of British control over Guyana. In 1782 the French seized power and governed for two years, during which time they created the new town of Longchamps at the mouth of the Demerara River. The Dutch regained power in 1784 and maintained control over the Berbice, Essequibo, and Demerara settlements until 1796, when a British fleet from the Caribbean island of Barbados conquered the country. The British governed until 1802, at which time Guyana was restored to the Dutch under a truce established by the Treaty of Amiens. The next year the British once again conquered the colony, which was finally ceded to them in 1814 under agreements contained in the Treaty of Paris and the Congress of Vienna. In 1831, three years before slavery ended in the region, the British merged Berbice, Essequibo, and Demerara to form British Guiana. After slavery was abolished throughout the British colonies on August 1, 1834, former slaves were subjected to a four-year apprenticeship to facilitate their transition to a wage labor system. However, after emancipation, few former slaves chose to work—even for wages—for the plantation owners who had once enslaved them.

Faced with a critical shortage of workers, planters decided to import workers under a system of indentured servitude. By 1844 indentured servitude in Guyana was almost solely the domain of East Indian laborers. After a five-year indenture period, the East Indians were "free" to return to India at their own expense. This indenture system, which satisfied the planter aristocracy's demand for workers, was abolished in British Guiana in 1917. But no matter how much headway was achieved by the former slaves or by former indentured laborers, the reins of political power remained in the firm grasp of a European elite.

Modern Era Guyana's road to independence was a rocky one. In 1953 a new constitution granted universal adult voting rights and established a two-house legislature. But political turmoil followed the first general election. The British government feared the communist leanings of the winning People's Progressive Party (PPP), which was led by Cheddi Berret Jagan (1918–1997). Consequently, the British suspended the new constitution and the elected government, and Guyana's constitution did not go into effect until 1961.

In addition to its communist stance, the PPP also advocated independence from Great Britain. From 1954 until the time that new elections were held in 1957, an interim government ruled British Guiana. Meanwhile, Jagan, an East Indian, and his fellow PPP cofounder, Linden Forbes Sampson Burnham (1923–1985), an African, had a major disagreement that ended their collaboration. This dissolution caused a chasm in the PPP—a division that fell largely (though not exclusively) along lines demarcated by ethnicity. Jagan's supporters were more Afro-Guyanese, whereas many Indo-Guyanese dedicated themselves to Burnham. Burnham left the PPP in 1957 and formed the People's National Congress (PNC), which eventually became an opposition party to the PPP. The split weakened the party's majority, but the PPP still won the most legislative seats in 1957 and again in 1961.

As head of the PPP, Jagan was elected prime minister of the colonial Guyanese government in 1957. Following the election, Burnham decided he needed greater support among the middle-class Afro-Guyanese; subsequently, he catered to this group—specifically those who had membership in the United Democratic Party. Ultimately, his segment of the PPP formed a new coalition with the UDP, named the People's National Congress (PNC). In response to these developments, Jagan cultivated greater ties with the Indo-Guyanese community. Although Jagan was named prime minister in the elections of 1961, the PNC posed challenges to him during his continued tenure in office.

Jagan also faced conflict with the United Force, a political party connected to the business section, and with the organization of the American Institute for Free Labor Development (AIFLD). This group was reputedly funded by the CIA, and it catalyzed riots in the early 1960s, many of which led to widespread destruction. In March 1964, Jagan's administration passed an unpopular Labour Relations Bill that was decried as a heavy-handed demonstration of political power. The nation erupted in riots on April 5, followed by a general strike on April 18. These events resulted in an extended period of violence so considerable that a state of emergency was declared. On July 7, the bill lapsed without going into effect, and the government pledged it would consult with union officials before trying to enact legislation of a similar nature.

Meanwhile, a sugar workers' strike led to another riot that produced escalations of violence, resulting in a state of emergency in May 1964. The ensuing hostilities led to widespread destruction and 160 deaths. As a result, the political parties of Guyana requested that the British government change the constitution to allow for proportional representation. In October 1964, elections were held, and the PPP was defeated. The colonial governor declared Burnham the victor by virtue of his ability to lead a coalition of the PNC and the United Force (UF), a third party led by Portuguese businessman Peter Stanislaus d'Aguiar. Under Burnham's leadership, the nation's long struggle for independence ended on May 26, 1966, when he assumed the office of prime minister of an independent Guyana.

In an attempt to put an end to foreign meddling in Guyanese affairs, Burnham steadfastly positioned Guyana among the world's nonaligned nations in world affairs. With Burnham at the helm, Guyana declared itself a "Cooperative Republic" in 1970. The change meant that Guyana became a socialist nation—a country committed to achieving prosperity by pooling its material and human resources. The Guyanese government also nationalized its industries, including foreign-owned bauxite companies (bauxite is used in the production of aluminum), which produced much of the country's wealth. By 1985, the end of Burnham's twenty-year tenure as chief executive and the year of his death, more than three-quarters of the country's economy had been brought under government control.

Immediately following Burnham's death, Vice President Hugh Desmond Hoyt was sworn into office. Regularly scheduled elections, criticized as fraudulent, were held in December 1985. Hoyt and the PNC won a solid but questionable victory. However, in national elections held in October 1992 under the watchful eye of the international community, the Jagan-led PPP won, bringing the tenure of the PNC as ruling party to a close after almost three decades.

SETTLEMENT IN THE UNITED STATES

The Guyanese people immigrated to the United States as part of two major waves of British West Indian immigration. The earlier wave took place roughly between the years 1900 to 1920; during this time, the number of immigrants steadily increased until the Immigration Act of 1924 was passed. This act placed race and ethnicity restrictions on entry to the United States and included the English-speaking Caribbean in the quota allotted to Great Britain. It also introduced a visa limit of 800 per year, with a preference system for skilled workers and relatives of U.S. citizens. In 1952 the McCarran-Walter Act imposed a quota system for immigrants arriving from West Indian colonies including Guyana; this act halted the migration of Guyanese to the United States. The second wave of immigration began in 1965, with the passage of the Hart-Celler Act, which removed this quota system.

From the 1960s onward, political disputes and racial struggles created conflict between Afro-Guyanese and Indo-Guyanese. The ensuing violence led to considerable unrest in the country. Subsequently, people from both these groups immigrated to the United States to escape the problems of their home nation. Like many immigrant groups, they also sought to take advantage of job opportunities available in the United States.

In addition to the patterns described above, Guyanese immigration to the United States also increased sharply with the passage of Britain's 1962 Commonwealth Immigration Act, which overturned the British Nationality Act of 1948. The earlier act allowed citizens of Guyana to claim citizenship in the United Kingdom and granted all Commonwealth citizens the same legal rights accorded to British citizens. Many Guyanese took advantage of this opportunity to further their education and improve their economic status. However, the concentration of nonwhite manual workers and their families in British cities stimulated an outcry against unregulated immigration, culminating in the 1962 act, which restricted their entry. With the doors of their "mother country" virtually closed to them, many Guyanese, mostly of the professional and technical classes, began to turn to the United States as their new land of opportunity.

The McCarran-Walter Act was amended in 1965 with the intention of protecting American workers and simultaneously restricting Western Hemispheric immigration to the United States. However, in 1968 an annual ceiling of 120,000 immigrant visas from the Western Hemisphere was introduced, and the purpose of the 1965 amendment was undermined. During this time, skilled laborers from Western Hemisphere countries journeyed to the United States in record numbers, including Guyanese applicants whose employment status fell into the categories of "professional," "technical," and "kindred" (or skilled) workers.

During the 1970s and 1980s, the number of immigrants from Guyana increased dramatically as Guyana underwent drastic economic and political changes. The country declared itself a "Cooperative Republic" in 1970 and then promptly began taking steps to nationalize available resources. This period witnessed a considerable increase in the number of stresses and strains experienced by Guyana: these conditions produced declining productivity, massive unemployment, and skyrocketing inflation. The Burnham regime was also denounced for its repression of political opposition.

Between 1960 and 1970, more Guyanese entered the United States than ever before. Around this time, the United States experienced labor shortages—particularly within the health industry and in private households employing domestic servants. These were traditional areas of employment for women, so Guyanese women, like other Caribbean women, met demands in the United States for workers in the health and domestic fields. The first Guyanese to arrive in 1968, either as "private household workers" or as nurses' aides, were of African descent.

According to Monica Gordon in *In Search of a Better Life: Perspectives on Migration from the Caribbean*, more Guyanese women than men settled in the United States in the 1960s and 1970s, making them primarily responsible for securing immigrant status for their families. These women, Gordon concludes, tended to see migration as a means to improve their economic and social status as well as to attain

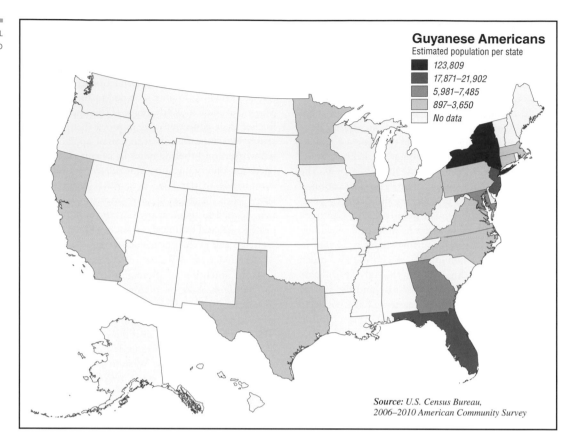

Guyanese Americans
Estimated population per state

- 123,809
- 17,871–21,902
- 5,981–7,485
- 897–3,650
- No data

*Source: U.S. Census Bureau,
2006–2010 American Community Survey*

educational opportunities for their children. U.S. Census Bureau records indicate that of the 48,608 people of Guyanese ancestry living in the United States in 1980, 26,046 were female. Based on this pattern, Guyanese immigrants no longer fit the traditional immigration pattern, in which the men settle in a new country first and send for their families later. Since the 1960s, female immigrants have assumed the status of "principal alien," the term given to an immigrant worker within a specific or delineated labor force capacity, whose status activates other provisions in the migration process of family members. By 1990 approximately 81,665 people of Guyanese ancestry were living in the United States. According to the 2000 U.S. Census, there were more than 161,000 Guyanese Americans. By 2011 the Census Bureau estimated the population to be closer to 209,680 (American Community Survey estimates for 2009–2011).

LANGUAGE

Guyanese generally speak and understand Creole or Creolese, which is a linguistic fusion of African dialects and English. Standard English is used for formal communication, though it is spoken in a definite Guyanese vernacular. As was common for many Caribbean immigrants, the first generation of Guyanese to travel to the United States settled among other Caribbean enclaves. Because people in their immediate communities could understand their oral communication,

these immigrants made no real attempt to alter their speech patterns. Many who moved away from their Caribbean neighbors and integrated socially into more mainstream U.S. society gradually lost their distinctive Guyanese speech pattern. Some immigrants, however, chose to hold onto their speech pattern as a way of maintaining their identity.

As English is a language commonly used in Guyana, Guyanese Americans typically do not encounter the same type of language barriers and challenges as other immigrant populations. Guyanese American children, however, are sometimes taught in schools how to speak English without their Guyanese accents. In such cases, parents may feel that their children are "losing" their Guyanese heritage. Often, however, children retain the capacity to speak English both with and without their accent. Speaking without an accent has been characterized as an effort to use "proper" English, though whether such a shift actually represents an incarnation of "proper" English over "improper" English remains an unsettled issue. The ability to shift between different types of speaking patterns allows Guyanese American children to preserve their heritage as well as to interact in different types of settings and situations. The 2009 to 2011 American Community Survey, conducted by the U.S. Census Bureau, showed that 96 percent of Guyanese Americans spoke only English at home. Only 1.1 percent spoke English less than "very well."

RELIGION

Guyanese Americans generally maintain an affiliation with the religious denomination of their homeland. The vast majority of Guyanese American churchgoers are Episcopalian. Priests from Guyana who immigrate to the United States frequently take on leadership positions in Guyanese American churches. These churches also serve as network centers for newly arrived immigrants. Many Caribbean-led Episcopalian churches in the New York City area have established schools that cater to the educational demands of Caribbean parents; frequently, these schools are staffed by former Caribbean schoolteachers.

Beginning in the 1970s, the Guyanese established a surge of nondenominational churches in the New York and New Jersey areas. These "churches," which were more like teaching centers, attracted many newly settled Guyanese Americans. These so-called Unity Centers continue to serve as community centers, teaching positive thinking and ways to cultivate a closer relationship with God. The congregation reflects the many faces of the nations in the Caribbean, although Guyanese usually predominate at Unity Centers run by Guyanese priests and priestesses. Another notable trend in religious practices is the number of practicing Hindus among Guyanese Americans. This religion is especially dominant among the Indo-Guyanese, and more than 200,000 Hindu Guyanese Americans reside in New York and practice their religion faithfully.

Baptism is one religious practice that has retained its significance among Guyanese Americans. Family members may live hundreds of miles from an infant, but they often still travel to attend a baptismal celebration. According to Guyanese tradition, a female child will have two godmothers and one godfather, and a male child will have two godfathers and one godmother. The godparents are responsible for purchasing the baptismal gown for the child; however, if the mother still has her wedding dress, she may choose to use it to make a baptismal dress for her firstborn. The godparents take the child to church; the priest then confers the grace of God by placing his hand on the child's head. The godparents promise to lead the child in the way of the Lord. Then the priest blesses the child in the name of the Holy Trinity while rubbing incense on the forehead and chest, pours holy water over the forehead, and finally offers the child up to God.

After the baptism, it is customary to have a large gathering with lots of music, dancing, and food. Family members and friends shower the child with gifts, and money is pinned on the child for good luck and prosperity. Guyanese custom dictates that the child be given a piece of gold jewelry for good luck soon after birth. Typically, girls are given a pair of gold bangles (bracelets) and a pair of gold earrings, and boys are given a gold ring and a gold bracelet.

CULTURE AND ASSIMILATION

Many immigration studies on the Caribbean focus on other island nations, including Jamaica, Haiti, Barbados, Tobago, and Trinidad, in addition to Guyana, because a large number of their population resides abroad. Despite this migratory pattern, however, Guyanese Americans have typically settled in neighborhoods with other people of Caribbean origin. This pattern is especially predominant in New York City, which is one of the population centers for Guyanese Americans and has an immigration pool drawn primarily from the Caribbean. Of the top five source countries, four were Caribbean nations—the Dominican Republic, Jamaica, Haiti, and Guyana. Between 1982 and 1989, 70 percent of all Guyanese immigrants moved to New York.

Guyanese American immigrants first attracted international attention in 1978, after an incident at People's Temple in Guyana in which more than 900 Americans committed mass suicide by ingesting poison. The People's Temple, a cult that originated in California, consisted of U.S. citizens under the leadership of Reverend Jim Jones. Members of the Guyanese government found Jones's credentials sound and granted him permission to construct a religious center in Guyana's western region, near Port Kaituma. The enterprise, however, ended in tragedy when Jones—under scrutiny by the U.S. government for his questionable dealings—incited his followers to commit suicide. For years after, the country of Guyana was associated with this tragedy, which precipitated a noticeable increase in the Guyana immigrant population in the United States during the 1980s.

Traditions and Customs Much Guyanese folklore and tradition dates back centuries, and the practices and customs of Guyanese Americans are based on these elements of their heritage. Notable among these customs are habits retained based on a deeply ingrained belief in and respect for Guyanese superstitions. Guyanese Americans who sustain these belief systems frequently identify with some Caribbean enclave. The following are some examples of Guyanese customs based on such superstitions: Good Friday is considered a very unlucky day to be involved in outdoor activities if they are not related to church. When entering a house late at night, a person should go in backward in order to keep evil spirits out. To cure a fever, a sliced potato should be placed on the ill person's forehead. To cure the effects of a stroke (such as a twisted mouth), a whole nutmeg should be placed inside the mouth on the affected side. A black cat crossing in front of a pedestrian will bring bad luck. A dog howling at a particular house is a sign that death will soon come to someone in that household. A pond fly in the house is a sign of news or correspondence. Stepping over someone's leg will stunt their growth. All references to the dead must be prefaced with the words: "God rest the dead in the living and the

BLACK EYED PEAS COOK-UP RICE

Ingredients

2 cups long grain rice

1 cup of black eyed peas (soaked overnight)

1 pound smoked turkey

3 cups water

2 cups coconut milk

1 tablespoon thyme, finely chopped

1 medium onion, minced

1 scotch bonnet pepper, minced

¼ teaspoon ground black pepper

1 tablespoon cassareep or soy sauce (optional)

2 small or 1 large bouillon cubes

1 teaspoon ground allspice

½ teaspoon salt

2 tablespoons oil

Preparation

In a soup pot, heat 1 tablespoon oil and add black eyed peas. Cook until slightly brown. Add 1 tablespoon of cassareep or soy sauce and allspice to taste. Continue to cook until it's absorbed. Pour in 2 cups of water. Bring to a rapid boil and reduce to a simmer. Cook black eyed peas for 30 minutes, or until cooked but firm. Transfer to a bowl and set aside.

Add to pot 1 tablespoon oil and chopped onion. Sauté until softened. Add turkey and sauté for 5 minutes. Add rice, scotch bonnet pepper, thyme, black pepper, bouillon, salt, coconut milk, cooked black eyed peas, and the additional water. Stir and bring to a rapid boil. Reduce heat and simmer for 20 minutes.

Fluff with a fork and transfer to a serving platter.

looking." The fact that Guyanese Americans continue to keep these traditions alive exemplifies the strength of these customs as well as the power of the beliefs that underlie and perpetuate them.

Cuisine Guyanese Americans have retained the diverse flavors that combine to form their distinctive cuisine, which is appetizing, spicy, and delicious. Spices and herbs are used in abundance, and one-dish meals occupy an important place in Guyanese cuisine. These dishes—sometimes called "poor man food"—are nourishing, inexpensive, and very easy to prepare. Guyanese men and women both enjoy cooking, and each gender tries to outdo the other in the excellence of the meals they prepare.

Pepperpot, one of the most popular dishes and considered representative nationally of Guyanese American cuisine, is a combination of different meats (beef, pork), spices, a dash of sugar, lots of onion, and *cassareep* (a sauce made using the fermented juice from the bitter cassava plant); it is eaten with rice or bread. *Cook-up rice*, another national dish, is a blend of rice, split peas or black-eyed peas, spices, onion, coconut milk, and meats. Also central to the repertoire of Guyanese recipes is the array of Indian curried dishes, made with curry powder, an East Indian spice with a distinctive flavor. *African Metemgee*, an inexpensive dish that is very filling, is made from coconut milk, meat or fish, onion, spices, plantains, and dumplings. Other popular dishes include *souse*, a very spicy and tangy dish made from boiled pig ears and pig feet, and flavored with cucumber, hot pepper, scallions, and lemon juice. Portuguese garlic pork is highly spiced pork pickled in garlic and vinegar. It is served fried and is eaten with bread. *Dahl* is a blend of boiled split peas, onion, garlic, curry powder, and cumin. It can be served over rice or eaten with *roti*, a pancake-like bread. Guyanese cuisine is not complete without Chinese noodles and chow mein, and black pudding, also called blood pudding, which is served with a tangy hot sauce.

Another culinary trend practiced by Guyanese Americans is to make dishes that blend together ingredients from different types of cuisine. The cuisine of Guyana has been impacted by the different ethnic groups that have lived in Guyana, and the dishes typically prepared by Guyanese Americans reflect this diversity. *Konkee* is a sweet dish made from corn flour, sugar, spices, grated coconut, and raisins. The mixture is then wrapped in a banana leaf and boiled. *Foofoo*, one of several substitutes for rice, is simply boiled plantains pounded in a mortar with a pestle. This is usually served with some type of stew. *Coocoo*, another substitute for rice, is a corn meal mush blended with seasoned boiled okra. *Cutty Cutty soup*, a "poor man" dish, is made with okra, salted beef, pig tail, tripe (stomach tissue, usually from a cow), onion, green plantains, and dumplings. *Salt fish cakes*, also called codfish cakes, are made from shredded salted codfish mashed together with boiled potatoes, onion, and pepper, then placed in a batter and fried. Black cake is Guyanese fruit cake, usually made at Christmas or for weddings. It is a very dark and very rich fruit cake made with rum. Ginger beer is a nonalcoholic homemade drink made from grated ginger and sweetened water.

Traditional Dress People of Indo-Guyanese descent represent one of the largest groups within the Guyanese American population, and many Indo-Guyanese women wear their traditional *sari* for special occasions such as weddings or East Indian holidays. *Saris* are garments made from long pieces of light cloth: one end is wrapped around the waist to form a skirt and the other is draped over the shoulder or the head. Some Afro-Guyanese wear the African *booboo* and *head wrap*.

Dances and Songs Guyana's National Dance Company—a multiethnic troupe—performs East Indian and African dances during national holidays,

GUYANESE PROVERBS

A wealth of proverbs from Guyanese culture have survived through the generations.

Hint at Quashiba mek Beneba tek notice.

Pay attention to the hints someone drops.

Wuh is fun fuh school boy is dead fuh crappo.

One man's meat is another man's poison.

Bush gat ears, goobie gat hole.

When you least expect it, people are eavesdropping.

Mouth open, story jump out.

Some people can't keep a secret.

Show me yuh company, I'll tell you who you be.

People judge you by the friends you keep.

Moon run til day ketch he.

Your deeds usually catch up with you.

Greedy man y'eye does yalla twice, fuh he own and he mattie own.

Some people are never satisfied.

Monkey mek he pickney til he spoil'um.

Similar to "Too many cooks spoil the broth."

Wuh fall from head drop pun shoulder.

Sins of the parents fall on the children.

If yuh guh to crab dance, yuh mus get mud.

What you sow you reap.

Who lif yuh up doan put yuh dung.

Those who get you into trouble don't get you out.

It's a lazy horse that can't carry its own oats.

Your burden is yours to carry.

Hand wash hand mek hand come clean.

More is accomplished through cooperation.

Mocking is ketching.

Don't laugh at another's situation, it might be yours.

Monkey know wuh limb to jump pun.

Bullies know exactly on whom to pick.

Donkey ears long, but he doan hear he own story.

Some people mind other people's business.

Do suh nuh like suh.

Treat others as you would like to be treated.

If yuh nuh gat muhma suck granny.

Make do with what you have.

Every rope got two ends.

Every story has two sides.

Cat a ketch rat but he a teef he massa fish.

Good and evil frequently come from the same source.

Big tree fall down, goat bite he leaf.

When the mighty fall on hard times, they are disrespected by all.

All cassava get same skin but all nah taste same way.

People may look the same, but that they all still act in unique ways.

including Independence Day; *Deepavali*, the Hindu celebration of lights; *Phagwah*, the Hindu festival to welcome spring; and the republic celebrations. In addition to these practices and rituals, many Guyanese Americans keep their artistic traditions strong by listening to chutney music, a dance-based genre that integrates calypso with more traditional Indian folk songs to form a style frequently heard in Guyana. Because of the dominance of Indo-Guyanese people within the Guyanese American population, music and dances made popular by Bollywood films are also a notable element of Guyanese culture in the United States.

Holidays In addition to Christmas Day, New Year's Day, and Easter Sunday, Guyanese Americans celebrate Guyana's Independence on May 26 and, to a lesser degree, "August Monday," the first Monday in August, symbolizing Emancipation Day. At Independence Day celebrations, the national anthem, "Dear Land of Guyana," is sung. Many of these holidays are celebrated with great verve in Little Guyana in New York City. Many Guyanese Americans—especially those living in Little Guyana—also celebrate Holi, an event commonly called Phagwah (a "festival of colors"), which is associated with the Hindu religion. Another holiday observed by Guyanese Americans is Pitri Paksh (commonly called Peter Pak in the Caribbean): this is a two-week period in mid-October during which Guyanese Americans can reflect on their heritage and honor their ancestors by making daily offerings, sometimes of the preferred dish of a deceased family member. In the Hindu tradition, these practices please the deity. In more recent years, an event called Guyanese-American Family Fun Day has taken place in New York City. In 2007 organizers had difficulty agreeing with officials about how to control attendance at the event; it was subsequently canceled. Other Guyanese-American Family Fun Days have since taken place in other areas of the country (including in Orlando, Florida, in 2010), and people have attended these events in high numbers.

FAMILY AND COMMUNITY LIFE

During the two major waves of immigration from Guyana over the last century or so, family practices, dynamics, and structures have shifted as different behavioral trends emerged and became dominant. During the early decades of the twentieth century, the first wave of Guyanese immigrants typically consisted of single males who had left their families and possibly a fiancée behind temporarily in the hopes of sending for them later; in the interim, they supplemented the income of the family back home. Many married men did not immigrate ahead of their families because their jobs at home provided the only source of income. In the case of the Indo-Guyanese, some husbands and wives came together, leaving children with grandparents or other relatives. Within the past few decades, there has been an increase in the number of Indo-Guyanese women who have immigrated without their families. In fact, in many cases, Indo-Guyanese women have had to travel without their spouses and children, and they have become the primary breadwinners in their families. However, their numbers are still minuscule in comparison to Afro-Guyanese women, who began moving to the United States alone in the 1960s. Typically, these newcomers first stayed for a short time with friends or relatives. After finding work, however, they usually rented rooms in crowded boarding houses (often occupied by other Guyanese and Caribbean immigrants).

Like typical first-generation immigrants, the Guyanese worked hard and saved most of their earnings, doing without the simplest of pleasures. Their primary goal was to facilitate the passage of their family members to the United States. Many of the males worked around the clock and went to night classes to better themselves educationally; women typically performed "sleep in" work—living six days per week at their place of employment and returning to the boarding house for one day, usually beginning Saturday night and ending Sunday night. That one day off was spent in church and at stores shopping for things to "pack a barrel" for their kin back home.

After acquiring permanent resident status and securing their family's passage to the United States, Guyanese immigrants then concentrated on improving their economic and educational status. Many women pursued nursing degrees part-time while holding multiple jobs.

Gender Roles Traditionally, Guyanese society has been relatively patriarchal, sometimes to the extent that women might encounter not only dominance by their partners or husbands, but occasionally even situations involving domestic abuse. In the United States,

this trend is not nearly as dominant, as the genders interact in a more balanced manner. In addition, women can often gain greater access to educational opportunities in the United States and thereby secure more stable and advanced employment positions. In New York City, Guyanese American females are typically more involved in the workforce than they are in Guyana. Many Guyanese American women also participate actively in their communities, serving as visible leaders in various roles. For these reasons, among others, gender dynamics function slightly differently among Guyanese Americans than they do in Guyana. It is not uncommon for Guyanese American women to be the primary breadwinners for their families.

Family is at the core of the Guyanese social network. Other Guyanese are preferred as marriage partners, but many Guyanese marry persons from other Caribbean nations or Americans of Caribbean parentage. The percentage of marriages between Guyanese and Americans—black or white—is low.

Education Guyanese parents view education as a combination of learning and discipline; many opt to pay for private schooling as a means of assuring that their children will receive a solid education. Guyanese Americans have typically taken advantage of the educational opportunities available in the United States. The men who were part of the first wave of migration worked long hours, yet still found the motivation and perseverance to complete night classes to better their positions and themselves.

Courtship and Weddings Among Guyanese Americans, as in Guyana, weddings are a time of extended celebration and enjoyment not only for the couple, but also for their friends and family. As a preparatory ritual, the bridal shower is a social custom practiced in Guyana among many Christians and non-Christians alike. For Christian weddings, banns are usually announced in the church for three consecutive Sundays so that impediments to the marriage—if any exist—can be brought to the attention of the priest. During this period, the priest counsels the couple on the duties of marriage. As in the United States, the couple selects a best man, maid (or matron) of honor, bridesmaids, and attendants. In most cases, the best man and maid/matron of honor serve as godparents to the couple's first child. The godmother then becomes the couple's *mac mae* ("mac may") and the godfather the *com pae* ("com pay").

One tradition common in Guyana involves an act that takes place the night before the wedding in which the bride is feted by the older women of her family in a celebration of song and dance called a *kweh kweh*. The actual wedding ceremony mirrors the traditional American church wedding, with some exceptions. For instance, silver coins are blessed by the priest and given to the bride and groom for good luck and prosperity. The priest wraps a robe around the bride and groom, symbolizing their union, and blesses them before concluding the ceremony. These traditions, though an important part of Guyanese culture are not prevalent among Guyanese Americans and are in danger of fading from their cultural traditions.

Most Guyanese American weddings are held at a private home or at a Caribbean catering hall to ensure a Guyanese menu. Gifts are usually delivered before the day of the wedding. Toasting or paying respects to the newlyweds is the focal point of the reception. The best man gives his blessings and advice first; he then directs the parents of the couple to speak before he offers the opportunity to elders in the audience. The bridegroom then speaks, thanking everyone for attending. The reception is accompanied by Caribbean music and dancing. Two weeks after the wedding, the couple entertains family and friends at a gala called a "Second Sunday."

In contrast to Guyanese Americans of Afro-Guyanese descent, Indo-Guyanese Americans tend to view marriage in a more utilitarian manner. They commonly participate in arranged marriages, even among different classes, as is sometimes still practiced in India. Any examination of how this group as a whole has adapted to life in the United States must necessarily encompass the complexity of both of these groups, with a particular focus on their courtship and marriage rituals.

Relations with Other Americans From their first arrival, the Guyanese began to interact with other ethnic groups, particularly Jamaicans, Trinidadians, Barbadians, Grenadians, and people from other English-speaking Caribbean nations. Guyanese Americans frequently reside in communities that do not have distinct spatial boundaries from other groups, especially other peoples of Caribbean island nation descent. This nurturing of a Caribbeanness contributes to the resistance to marry outside of the Caribbean group.

EMPLOYMENT AND ECONOMIC CONDITIONS

Many early Guyanese immigrants settled in the northeastern region of the United States, particularly in New York. These individuals found work in health care, domestic labor, banking, clerical, and physical security fields. During this earlier period, they were often paid the lowest wages and—like members of other immigrant groups—typically worked several jobs at a time. After accumulating work experience and permanent resident status, many Guyanese advanced to better paying positions.

Some Guyanese Americans established their own small, family-run businesses, such as bakeries and takeout restaurants catering to the tastes of a Caribbean community. Others who could not afford to rent business space in Caribbean neighborhoods sold Guyanese food out of their homes on weekends.

As the Guyanese immigrants became more established, they opened real estate offices, guard services, small grocery stores (specializing in food products from home, such as *cassareep*), neighborhood law offices (specializing in immigration and real estate law), beauty salons, and travel agencies. According to the 2009–2011 American Community Survey, 30.7 percent of Guyanese Americans sixteen years of age and older worked in management, business, sciences, or arts; 26.1 percent worked in sales and office occupations; and 25.3 percent worked in service industries.

Education is highly valued in Guyana, and teachers are highly respected. Even during the first wave of immigration, Guyanese Americans actively sought out educational opportunities and chances to "better" themselves. Many Guyanese Americans and Guyanese immigrants to the United States were already certified or licensed in professions, and this trend also impacted their employment possibilities and economic practices.

POLITICS AND GOVERNMENT

Guyanese are active in the organizations of the larger Caribbean region. There are many Guyanese nurses' and police associations. Although Guyanese Americans are interested in acquiring information about the world, including information about political developments, their actual engagement in political discussions, or in political matters, is low when they are considered collectively. Thus, Guyanese Americans have not yet made a collective impact on national political activity. Locally, however, they have started to engage in organized movements designed to improve conditions in their neighborhoods. In more recent years, Guyanese Americans have taken an active interest in U.S. politics at the local, state, and federal levels. As a group, they have become aware that their capacity to engender change lies in their right to vote, and that this power can help them protect their rights (for example, in securing low-interest student loans). The active status of the Guyanese American media has contributed to this increased awareness of the importance of engaging in political activism. Subsequently, Guyanese Americans have formed organizations and coalitions that are designed to protect the rights of Guyanese Americans as a group.

Relations with Guyana Guyanese Americans maintain close ties to their homeland and its people, and they provide significant financial support to their native country. During the late 1970s and 1980s—when Guyana was experiencing a terrible economic crisis owing to the further devaluation of the Guyanese dollar, skyrocketing prices for consumer goods, and shortages of basic necessities—Guyanese organizations pooled their fund-raising resources and made generous donations of money, food, clothing, and equipment to Guyanese hostels, orphans, almshouses, schools, and hospitals. High school alumni associations furnished their alma maters and other schools with chairs, desks, books, and office supplies. Nurses'

Congresswoman Shirley Chisholm (1924–2005) was the first black American elected to Congress. She was also the first woman to run for the Democratic Presidential nomination in 1972. DENNIS BRACK BS20 / NEWSCOM

Literature and the Arts Guyana has long provided a theme for literary expression. Popular Guyanese American authors include Jan Carew (1920–2012), Gordon Rohlehr (1942–), and E. R. Braithwaite (1920–). Braithwaite's memoir *To Sir, with Love* (1959) details his experiences as a black high school teacher in a white London slum. The work was praised for its hopeful view of difficult race relations and was adapted for a 1967 film of the same name. The works of Jan Carew include *Black Midas* (1958), a picaresque novel acclaimed for its vivid portrayal of raw and roguish types in the diamond fields of Guyana; *The Wild Coast* (1958), a sensitive study of a young man's difficult passage from puberty to manhood; and *The Last Barbarian* (1961), a study of West Indian and African life in Harlem.

Miramy, a full-length Guyanese comedy by Frank Pilgrim, is set on an imaginary island in the West Indies. It became the first locally written play to be performed outside of Guyana.

Music Rihanna (1988–) (given name Robyn Rihanna Fenty) was born in Barbados to a Guyanese mother and a Barbadian/Irish father. She is one of the most successful young female singers and performers of the early twenty-first century, and her music has sold more than 25 million albums and 60 million digital singles worldwide. She has had thirty-five Number 1 hits in thirty-five countries, and she has won five Grammy Awards.

Politics Shirley Anita St. Hill Chisholm (1924–2005) served as an American politician, teacher, and writer. She was the first African American woman elected to Congress in 1968, and she represented New York's 12th Congressional District for seven terms (1969–1983). During her political career, she also broke through barriers by running to be a presidential nominee for the Democratic Party in 1972. She was born in Brooklyn, New York, and her father was an immigrant from Guyana.

Sports Maritza Correia (1981–) was born to parents who immigrated to San Juan, Puerto Rico, from Guyana. Correia qualified for the U.S. Olympic swim team in 2004 and was the first Puerto Rican of African descent to make the team. She also set both a U.S. and a world swimming record, becoming the first African American U.S. swimmer to set such a precedent.

Rycklon Stephens, stage name Ezekiel Jackson (1978–), performs with the World Wrestling Entertainment company (WWE): he joined the organization in 2007 and won the 2010 championship of a specific program televised by the WWE. He holds a degree from the State University of New York, University at Buffalo.

Stage and Screen Sean Patrick Thomas (1970–) was born in Wilmington, Delaware, to Guyanese parents. He studied at the University of

organizations donated syringes, bed sheets, thermometers, penicillin, and other scarce supplies to hospitals.

There is a steady flow of scholarly exchange between Guyana and the United States in the form of academic conferences. There are Caribbean associations in almost every college or university with a sizable Caribbean student body that encourage the connections with home through guest lecturers, trips, and networking. In the United States, academic organizations such as the Association of Caribbean Historians, the Caribbean Studies Association, and the Caribbean Writers Association cater to scholars from the Caribbean.

NOTABLE INDIVIDUALS

Guyanese Americans represent a minuscule percentage of the United States' total population, but they have made significant contributions to American popular culture, the arts, academia, and politics.

Virginia before earning a master's degree in drama from New York University in 1995. He is best known for his film roles in *Save the Last Dance* (2001) and *Barbershop* (2002), and for his television role on *Lie to Me*.

MEDIA

Caribbean Journal LLC

The *Caribbean Journal* was founded in 2011 to offer news and political observations in a new and innovative manner. It is the first to offer all Caribbean-related news in one periodical. The publication serves as a central news source for islanders.

ORGANIZATIONS AND ASSOCIATIONS

The Guyana Association of Georgia

This organization was designed to provide Guyanese Americans with a venue through which they could interact to sustain and keep their culture alive, as well as to stay connected with events taking place back in Guyana.

Orrin Marshall
P.O. Box 360744
Decatur, Georgia 30036
Email: Information@gaog.org
URL: www.gaog.org/historical.html

Guyana Friends Association of Massachusetts, Inc.

Guyana Friends Association of Massachusetts, Inc., expresses and fosters Guyanese culture through art, music, and education.

Ronald H. Lammy, President
21 Dewey Street
Roxbury, Massachusetts 02119
Email: rlammy@guyanafriendsofmass.org
URL: http://guyanafriendsofmass.org/

Guyana Republican Party (GRP)

P.O. Box 260185
Brooklyn, New York 11226-0185
Phone: (718) 756-7500
Fax: (973) 484-1615
Email: 103203.652@compuserve.com

Guyanese American Association of Schenectady

The Guyanese American Association of Schenectady is dedicated to promoting empowerment of people, protection of the environment, and respect for cultural diversity. This organization is designed to provide Guyanese Americans with a sense of family and community, and to offer them services on which they can rely.

Punema Singh, President
P.O. Box 80
Schenectady, New York 12301
URL: http://guyamerica.org/

MUSEUMS AND RESEARCH CENTERS

Harvard University David Rockefeller Center for Latin American Studies

Founded in 1994, Harvard's David Rockefeller Center for Latin American Studies (DRCLAS) works to increase knowledge of the cultures, economies, histories, environment, and contemporary affairs of past and present Latin America.

Center for Government and International Studies
1730 Cambridge Street
Cambridge, Massachusetts
Phone: (617) 495-3366
Fax: (617) 496-2802
URL: http://www.drclas.harvard.edu/taxonomy/term/23

SOURCES FOR ADDITIONAL STUDY

Dindayal, Vidur. *Guyanese Achievers USA & Canada: A Celebration.* New York: Trafford, 2011.

Levine, Barry B., ed. *The Caribbean Exodus.* New York: Praeger, 1987.

Palmer, Ransford W. *In Search of a Better Life: Perspectives on Migration from the Caribbean.* New York: Praeger, 1990.

Ramsaroop, Yuvraj. *Realizing the American Dream: The Personal Triumph of a Guyanese Immigrant.* New York: XLibris, 2010.

Udeogalanya, Veronica. *Demographic and Socio-Economic Characteristics of Caribbean Immigrants and Non-Immigrant Population in the United States.* Brooklyn: Caribbean Research Center, Medgar Evers College, 1989.

HAITIAN AMERICANS

Felix Eme Unaeze and Richard E. Perrin

OVERVIEW

Haitian Americans are immigrants or descendants of immigrants from Haiti (officially the Republic of Haiti), which occupies the western third of the island of Hispaniola. The Dominican Republic occupies the eastern two-thirds of the island. Hispaniola forms part of the West Indies, and lies between Cuba and Puerto Rico. Haiti's terrain is mostly rough and mountainous. With a total area of 10,714 square miles (27,750 square kilometers), Haiti is slightly larger than the state of Maryland.

Haiti's fourth national census, conducted in 2006, estimated the population at about 8.4 million. Although the vast majority of Haitians are Roman Catholic—roughly 80 percent—Haiti is the only country that officially recognizes vodou, or voodoo, as a religion. About one-half the population practices vodou to some extent. Haiti is the poorest country in the Western Hemisphere, ranking 145th of the 182 countries worldwide tracked by the UN 2010 Human Development index. As of the country's 2006 census, Haiti was experiencing steady unemployment rates of approximately 33 percent, with a large portion of the population being dependent on subsistence farming.

Haitians began immigrating to the United States to escape harm during the slave revolt of the 1790s, and they settled primarily in New Orleans, Philadelphia, New York City, and Boston. Major immigration waves from Haiti have tended to coincide with times of political hardship, especially during the rule of the dictators Francois "Papa Doc" Duvalier (1957–1971) and his son, Jean-Claude "Bebe Doc" Duvalier (1971–1986). From 1972 to 1981, during Jean-Claude's years in power, the United States Immigration and Naturalization Service (INS) estimated that over 55,000 refugees fled to Miami, Florida, in old, crudely made boats, settling an area that has since become known as "Little Haiti."

The 2010 U.S. Census estimated the number of documented Haitians living in the United States—and Americans with Haitian heritage—to be around 830,000, roughly equal to the population of San Francisco, California, or the entire state of South Dakota. Including undocumented immigrants, the number of Haitian Americans is estimated to be much higher, with a significant increase from immigration following a devastating earthquake in Haiti in 2010. A large Haitian population still exists in the Boston area, but the majority of Haitian Americans reside in immigrant communities in the New York City and Miami metropolitan areas. Other states with significant numbers of Haitian Americans include New Jersey, Georgia, Pennsylvania, and Connecticut.

HISTORY OF THE PEOPLE

Early History The island, which was first inhabited by Indian tribes—the Arawaks, the Tainos, and lastly the Caraibes—called their country "Quisqueya" and later "Haiti," which means "the body of land." The island has had a turbulent and bitter history. When Christopher Columbus landed at the Mole St. Nicholas Bay on December 5, 1492, he claimed the island in the interest of the Spanish rulers who had financed the expedition—Ferdinand and Isabella—and called it "Hispaniola," which means "Little Spain."

Although the Indians welcomed the new settlers, the discovery of gold in the riverbeds sent the Spaniards into a frenzied search for the coveted nuggets. The Indians died by the thousands from diseases introduced by the Spaniards, who also enslaved the natives, treated them with extreme cruelty, and massacred them. The Indian population was reduced from about 300,000 to less than 500. In 1510 the Spaniards began to import their first African slaves from the West Coast of Africa to work in the gold mines. The French, who came in 1625 and changed the name of the island to Saint Domingue, fought the Spaniards to keep a hold on part of the territory. After Spain signed a treaty in 1697 in which it conceded the western part of the island to France, the colony developed rapidly under French rule. The 700,000 slaves who worked cotton, sugar cane, and coffee plantations generated great wealth for the plantation owners; Saint Domingue became a prosperous colony in the New World and was called "the Pearl of the Caribbean."

After the French Revolution in 1789, the slaves revolted against the colonists. Under the leadership of such generals as Toussaint L'Ouverture, the slaves made significant progress in their struggle. Self-educated, Toussaint served first in the Spanish army and then in the French army. He was one of the main instruments of Haiti's independence, defeating the

English who had invaded Saint Domingue. He also administered and divided the country into districts without the approval of the mainland "Metropole." The French later grew angry with General Toussaint and placed him in a French prison where he died on April 7, 1803, from hunger and lack of medical care. Although disheartened, the rebel army fought under Generals Dessalines and Petion and beat the French army at every turn. French General Leclerc died of yellow fever on November 2, 1803; his successor, General Rochambeau, took refuge. Dessalines surrounded his officers and proclaimed the independence of Saint Domingue in Gonaives on January 1, 1804, restoring the former name of Haiti. Independence was won and the country became the second independent republic in the Western Hemisphere (after the United States), and the first independent black republic in the world. It is from these self-emancipated African slaves that roughly 95 percent of modern Haitians and Haitian Americans are descended.

Modern Era Dessalines became Haiti's first head of state. Following the elaboration and ratification of a constitution, full powers were given to Dessalines on September 2, 1804. He proclaimed himself Emperor and took the name Jacques the First. He redistributed the country's wealth and converted most of the colonist plantations to state property. He made many political enemies who later resented his manner of governing. Ambushed on his way to Port-au-Prince, he was killed on October 17, 1806. After his death a constituent assembly amended the Constitution and limited the powers of the president. General Henri Christophe, who had started a power struggle with General Alexandre Petion, withdrew to the northern part of the country and formed a new government; Petion was elected president in March of 1807, thus dividing the new nation. Petion governed the West and South while Christophe ruled the North. In March of 1811, Christophe proclaimed himself king and took the name of Henri the First. Because of his strict regulations, the Kingdom of the North became prosperous, and he erected monuments, which became symbols of power and authority. For example, the Citadel Laferriere, a monument to human endurance, was constructed by the labor of 20,000 men between 1805 and 1814 as a center of resistance against any attempt by foreigners to conquer the island. His ornate palace at Sans Souci near Cap Haitien and his vast citadel, though in ruins, are likewise marvels of massive masonry. When Christophe died in an apparent suicide in 1820, the North and South were reunited, with Jean-Pierre Boyer succeeding Petion.

Twenty different presidents headed the Haitian government from 1867 to 1915, and Haiti's unstable political and economic conditions made it vulnerable to outside intervention. Haiti's rising external debt caused European countries to threaten force to collect. At this time World War I was at its peak in Europe and in July of 1915, the United States Marines landed on Haiti's coast and occupied the country. Under the Monroe Doctrine—a document stating U.S. opposition to European involvement in the Western Hemisphere—the U.S. Marines remained in Haiti for 19 years from 1915 until 1934. The Haitian people resented American occupation and wanted to restore their national sovereignty. Guerrilla resistance movements were in place but were crushed. In 1946 a popular movement brought forth a rising middle class whose members asked for the sharing of power and liberalization of governmental institutions. The movement was aborted, which contributed to the fall of then-President Elie Lescot (1941–1946), and Dumarsais Estime was elected president. From that period on, almost all Haitian presidents have been deposed by military coups d'état.

In 1957 François Duvalier was elected president. He became a dictator, enforcing a reign of terror with his secret police, sometimes referred to as *tonton macoute*. Duvalier proclaimed himself President-for-Life in 1964 and his reign of terror continued. The Haitian economy began to deteriorate and the people suffered greatly in the 1960s. Duvalier died in 1971 and his son, Jean-Claude "Bebe Doc" Duvalier, who was only 19 years old, succeeded his father. The Duvaliers ruled for nearly 30 years. It was during this period that many Haitians fled. Jean-Claude followed in his father's footsteps, maintaining the same policies of repression. Following a period of widespread public demonstrations, Jean-Claude gave in to additional pressure from the U.S. government and stepped down as president, leaving Haiti for France aboard a U.S. Air Force plane on February 7, 1986. A period of instability followed with several transitional governments and military coups.

Free elections were held on December 16, 1990; and, although Jean-Bertrand Aristide was elected by a majority of 67 percent, he was overthrown by the army on September 30, 1991, and took refuge in the United States. In 1994, backed by a force of 20,000 U.S. marines, he returned to Haiti and was restored to the presidency peacefully through last-minute negotiations with the ruling military junta. However, he was ousted again in a 2004 coup d'état, which some suspect was orchestrated by the U.S. government.

In January 2010 a magnitude 7.0 earthquake further destabilized Haiti, leaving more than 300,000 dead and more than one million homeless. The government's inability to address the large-scale displacement led to a 2010–2011 cholera epidemic that infected more than 100,000 people and claimed more than 3,000 lives. General elections scheduled for January 2010 were postponed until November. Following a run-off election, President Michel Martelly took office March 2011. As of 2012 much of the homelessness and displacement resulting from the earthquake had still not been addressed.

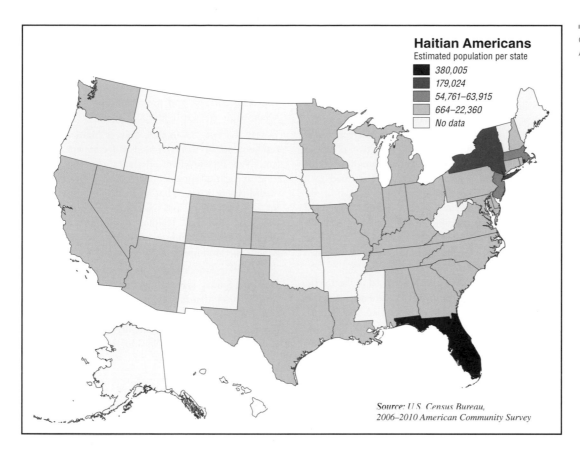

Haitian Americans
Estimated population per state

- 380,005
- 179,024
- 54,761–63,915
- 664–22,360
- No data

*Source: U.S. Census Bureau,
2006–2010 American Community Survey*

SETTLEMENT IN THE UNITED STATES

During the 1790s Haiti was the most affluent of the French colonies. It was then that the African slave populace of the island revolted, causing some to flee in a panicked exodus. Thousands of whites, free blacks, and slaves fled to American seaports, culminating in large French-speaking communities in New Orleans, Philadelphia, Baltimore, New York City, and Boston.

These early immigrants from Haiti subsisted by whatever means they could muster. Jean-Baptiste Point du Sable, a trapper who settled on the shore of Lake Michigan was an early Haitian arrival; he established a trading post on the Chicago River at a point that would later become the city of Chicago. Pierre Toussaint, a devout Catholic who came to New York as a slave of a French family in 1787, became a prominent hair dresser to wealthy New York patrons and later raised funds for destitute Haitians both back home and in the United States. With France providing the most significant haven for educated Haitians, most working middle-class Haitians have chosen to immigrate to the United States.

According to the U.S. Census Bureau's 2009 Community Survey, there were about 830,000 people who claimed Haitian ancestry; however, this figure did not include the tens (or hundreds) of thousands of undocumented Haitians who were living in the United States. Moreover, there are second- and third-generation Haitian Americans who simply identify themselves as black; and some legal immigrants find it difficult to claim a heritage so often associated with superstition and poverty. Speculating on the number of people who fall into these categories, but not counting immigrants who have arrived following the 2010 Haitian earthquake, researchers have estimated the number of people in the United States of Haitian ancestry to be about 1.3–1.4 million. With more than 380,000, Florida is the state with the largest concentration of Haitian Americans. New York (179,024), Massachusetts (63,915), and New Jersey (54,761) also boast large numbers. Other states with significant Haitian American populations include Georgia (22,360), Pennsylvania (19,433), and Connecticut (18,345).

There are several major periods of Haitian immigration to the United States, each coinciding with a period of instability in Haiti: the period of French colonization; the Haitian revolution (1791–1803); the United States occupation of Haiti (1915–1934); the rule of the Duvaliers (1957–1986); the overthrow of President Aristide (1991); and the 2010 earthquake. For almost three decades, from 1957 to 1986, when François "Papa Doc" and Jean-Claude "Baby Doc" Duvalier were in power, political persecution caused Haitian professionals, the middle class, and students to leave the island in large numbers. Haitians emigrated in search of political asylum or permanent residence status in other Caribbean countries, North and South America, Europe, and Africa.

In the 1980s more than 55,000 Haitian immigrants arrived in the United States by boat on the shores of Florida and were known as the "boat people." Although President Carter gave such refugees a legal status similar to that granted by him to Cubans in 1980 with his Cuban-Haitian entrant program, eighteen months later President Reagan subscribed to a policy of interdiction and indefinite detention for Haitian refugees. In June 1982 a federal court ruled against such detention and several thousand refugees were released. In 1986, 40,000 Haitians who came to the United States seeking political asylum were given permanent resident status.

A similar pattern of events occurred in the 1990s. When Aristide was removed by military coup in 1991, there was another wave of Haitian boat people. Under the administrations of both President Bush and President Clinton, many were not allowed to reach the shores of the United States. Instead, they were stopped at sea and returned to Haiti. Others were put in detention camps at the U.S. Naval Station at Guantánamo Bay, Cuba. Between 1995 and 1998, 50,000 Haitians were given asylum and temporary legal status but were denied the permanent resident status extended to many of their Nicaraguan and Cuban counterparts. The National Coalition for Haitian Rights pushed for legislation to address this issue. In 1998, the Haitian Refugee Immigration Fairness Act was adopted, and immigrants were given the opportunity to apply for permanent resident status.

Michel S. Laguerre has also documented that volunteer lawyers and local activists have helped many refugees remain in their adopted country, through the generosity of various humanitarian organizations. However, in his book *American Odyssey: The Haitians in New York City*, Laguerre has also recorded that some refugees attempted suicide while in detention. Despite the odds, the Haitian refugees had the energy and determination to survive in the United States. In her book, *Demele: "Making It,"* social anthropologist Rose-Marie Chierici, herself a Haitian American, has used the Creole word *demele* to describe how Haitian immigrants manage life in the face of hardship.

Nearly every wave of migration from Haiti has come during political turmoil; however, economic malaise has always accompanied such turmoil, making it difficult to distinguish political from economic migrants during these periods. Early Haitian immigrants stayed in cities in the United States where they could work and maintain contact with their homeland. The greatest concentrations of immigrants are found in New York City, Miami, Chicago, New Orleans, Los Angeles, and Boston. Until 1977 Brooklyn was the heart of Haitian America; however, between 1977 and 1981 the nearly 60,000 Haitian boat people who landed in and around Miami shifted the center of the Haitian Diaspora south. Now the largest Haitian population in the United States centers around a community of stucco cottages and mom-and-pop businesses in Miami dubbed "Little Haiti."

In the early 1980s thousands of Haitian doctors, teachers, social workers, and entrepreneurs moved from New York to Miami. Restaurants serving Haitian food specialties such as conch and goat meat and record shops blaring Haitian meringue music sprang up on 54th Street and Northeast Second Avenue, with the Tap Tap Haitian Restaurant in Miami Beach becoming a hub of interaction for the Haitian American community.

Haitian Americans are employed in various fields. Deborah Sontag reported in the *New York Times* on June 3, 1994, that Haitian workers comprise not only migrant general laborers in Florida but also wealthy doctors on Long Island, taxi drivers in Manhattan, and college professors in Washington, D.C.

LANGUAGE

Both Haitian Kreyòl (anglicized as Creole) and French are recognized as official languages in Haiti. However, French is often considered the language of the educated elite, while virtually all Haitians (the educated included) speak Creole.

The term *Creole* derives from the Portuguese word *crioulo*, meaning an individual of European ancestry who was born and reared abroad. Haitian Creole developed when slaves who were taken to the Caribbean island of Saint Domingue from various areas of the west coast of Africa interacted with each other and with Europeans. Although derived primarily from an amalgamation of French and African dialects, some Spanish and Amerindian (Carib and Arawak) words have entered the language. Haitian Creole is distinct from both its French and African root languages, adopting its own unique grammar, morphology, and syntax.

Greetings and Popular Expressions

Allo ("ah-low")

Hi!

Bonjou ("bohn-ZHEW")

Good morning/day

Bonswa ("bohn-SWA")

Good afternoon/evening

Ki jan ou rele? ("kee jan oo ray lay")

What is your name?

M'rele … ("m ray lay …")

My name is …

Kote ou rete? ("ko TAY oo ray TAY")

Where do you live?

A Haitian man next to an altar. AP PHOTO / LYNSEY ADDARIO

Ki numewo telefon ou? ("kee new meh-wo tele FON OO")

What is your telephone number

Suple ("soo-PLAY")

Please

Mesi ("MAY-see")

Thank you

Orevwa ("oh-ray-VWAH")

Goodbye

Na wè demen si Bondyé vlé ("nah weh day-MAYN see BOHN dyeh vleh")

See you tomorrow if God is willing

Haitian immigrants to the United States, especially more recent immigrants, communicate best in Creole. This causes problems in interaction with Americans who have little knowledge of Creole and believe that all Haitians speak French. Working first-generation adults are affected most noticeably, while children are encouraged to work toward fluency in both Creole and English to ease their assimilation into American culture and significantly increase their opportunities in the future.

RELIGION

Religion is at the center of home life for Haitian Americans and is typically carried over from family practices back in Haiti. As such, the vast majority of Haitian Americans practice Roman Catholicism. Much as they would have in Haiti, children of legal immigrants are baptized early and typically attend Catholic schools. Also in keeping with Haitian tradition, roughly half of all Haitian American households practice vodou to some degree.

Vodou, which blends elements of Catholicism with those of diverse African beliefs, plays a central role in the spiritual lives of those who practice it. A key to understanding the relationship and interplay between Catholicism and vodou is the fusion of the two belief systems. Children born into rural families are generally baptized twice, once into the vodou religion and once in the Catholic Church. Vodou means many things. It means an attitude toward life and death, a concept of ancestors and the afterworld, and a recognition of the forces which control individuals and their activities.

Those who practice vodou believe in a pantheon of gods who represent and control the laws and forces of the universe. Foremost in the pantheon is *Bondyé* (pronounced "bohn dyeh"), a monogod roughly equivalent to the Judeo-Christian conception of God, but who is unreachable and does not intercede in human affairs. There are also the *loa* (pronounced "lwa"), a large group of lesser deities—analogous to the Catholic saints and several African deities—to whom most prayers are directed, and the twins known as *marassas*, who are believed to be the divine first children of Bondyé. The loa are believed not only to protect people but also to accord special favors through their representatives on earth, which are called *hougans* (priests) and *mambos* (priestesses). Owing to the prominence of the *marassas*, twins are believed to have special powers and are honored in special services once a year.

Vodou worship centers in family and community groups headed by a hougan or mambo. These leaders are primarily responsible conducting ceremonies for such events as Christmas and the harvest, and also for specials occasions such as initiations and funeral services. They are also looked to for daily spiritual guidance and, in most cases, health care. The duties of the hougan or mambo in these ceremonies can include drumming and dancing, the leading of Roman Catholic prayers, and the preparation of feasts. Each group of worshipers is independent and there is no central organization, religious leader, or set of beliefs. As such, individual beliefs and practices can vary significantly from group to group.

Fearing discrimination, most Haitian Americans practice vodou only in the privacy of their own homes and talk about it as little as possible outside of Haitian immigrant communities. For much the same reason, second- and third-generation Haitian Americans are less likely to practice vodou at all.

Haitian cooking is a unique blend of many cultural influences. It is a mixture of the traditions of Europeans, West African slaves, and indigenous people of the island. The most common ingredients used in Haitian cuisine are black-eyed peas, squash, pumpkin, cassava, rice, cornmeal, and plantain.

CULTURE AND ASSIMILATION

Like most immigrants in the United States, Haitian Americans are preternaturally concerned with social status and financial security. This idea is implicit in the Creole saying, *Se vagabon ki loue kay* ("respectable people don't rent"). However, behind the facade of pride and achievement, there is a litany of social problems—domestic abuse, homelessness, and economic exploitation are particularly prevalent in Haitian communities. Contributing significantly to these issues are the stress-related emotional disorders common among undocumented immigrants, who live in constant fear of being deported or imprisoned. Similar anxieties frequently keep them from using such facilities as public hospitals. Instead, they rely on folk medicine to cure ordinary ailments, or they seek a private clinic with exclusively Haitian medical personnel. Marc Abraham, a Haitian who has lived on Long Island for over 40 years, has posited that, as a result of the aforementioned social issues, "Americans see Haitians as desperate people, instead of decent people who struggle."

According to Thomas Wenski (now archbishop of Miami and formerly director of the Pierre Toussaint Haitian Catholic Center in Miami), Haitians have been specifically and harshly excluded in part because of "America's endemic 'negrophobia' and inherent racism." Wenski adds that, given the prejudice with which African American citizens are treated, "one must ask: will the Haitians be able to assimilate into American society as other immigrant groups […] and can Haitians hope for a 'piece of the American pie' while native-born American blacks still fight for crumbs? Many would see an eventual amalgamation into the African American community, but does such a view give too much importance to race as a determinant and underrate such values as religion and culture?" (Fr. Thomas Wenski, "Haitians in South Florida," unpublished research done in Miami, Florida, July 1991.)

Since the early 1980s Haitian Americans have also been stigmatized by a stereotype that Haitians are disproportionately affected by HIV/AIDS. The tide seemed to be changing in 1998, when Universal Studios agreed to remove inflammatory lines from their black-oriented hit movie, *How Stella Got Her Groove Back*, following protests led by the National Coalition for Haitian Rights. But the stigma persists. In December 2010, New York hip-hop disc jockey Cipha Sounds made remarks on his Hot 97 morning show, *The Cipha Sounds and Rosenberg Show*, that the main reason he is HIV negative is "because he doesn't mess with Haitian girls."

Cuisine Haitian cooking is a unique blend of many cultural influences. It is a mixture of the traditions of Europeans, West African slaves, and indigenous people of the island. The most common ingredients used in Haitian cuisine are black-eyed peas, squash, pumpkin, cassava, rice, cornmeal, and plantain. The meat served tends to be spicy and high in salt and fat. In the United States, Sunday dinners often consist of spicy chicken and goat, rice, and djondjon (a dried mushroom).

Kabrit boukannen ak bon piman, barbecued goat with hot pepper, is a traditional favorite both in Haiti and the United States, and it is often served with *Pois et ris*, a combination of kidney beans and rice that is typically considered the national dish of Haiti. *Soup joumou* is a pumpkin soup. *Kasav ak manba* is homemade peanut butter, made with or

HAITIAN PROVERBS

Dye mon, gen mon.

Beyond the mountains, more mountains.

Li pale franse.

He speaks French–said of someone who is likely deceiving you.

Piti, piti, wazo fe nich li.

Little by little the bird makes its nest.

Konstitisyon se papie, bayonet se fe.

The constitution is paper, bayonets are steel.

Bourik swe pou chwal dekore ak dentel.

The donkey sweats so that the horse can be decorated with lace.

Fanm pou you tan, manman pou tout tan.

Wife for a time, mother for all time.

Sak vid pa kanp.

An empty sack cannot stand up.

Neg di san fe.

People talk and don't act.

Bondye fe san di.

God acts and doesn't talk.

without spices and hot peppers and often eaten with cassava bread. *Griyo ak bannan* is deep-fried pork and fried plantain. *Pwason fri* is fried fish, often sold with fried plantain and fried sweet potatoes. *Accra* or *calas* are black-eyed pea patties, and the tradition of eating them on New Year's Eve means luck for the coming year.

Holidays Mostly Roman Catholics, Haitian Americans celebrate many of the same holidays as the rest of the western world, including Christmas Day, New Year's Day, Carnival or Mardi Gras, All Saints' Day, and All Souls' Day. One distinct holiday carried over from Haitian custom is *Jour des Aleux* (Ancestors' Day), a memorial celebration of the individuals who sacrificed their lives during the struggle for Haitian independence in the late eighteenth and early nineteenth centuries. Celebrated on January 2nd each year, the occasion is often marked by community festivals culminating in large traditional meals in the evening.

Health Care Issues and Practices Health care beliefs vary widely among Haitian Americans. First-generation immigrants from rural areas typically prefer traditional medicine—relying heavily on recommendations from family elders, folk healers, and

vodou priests—while immigrants from Haitian urban centers are more likely to seek the services of licensed health care providers. Social class and education also influence the type of medical help sought, with those from a lower social class or who have not attained legal status in the United States again turning to traditional medicine. In the United States, folk and vodou healers' capabilities are often restricted by the limited availability of traditional ingredients. Only in cases where traditional treatments are unavailable or unsuccessful are individuals encouraged to seek the services of licensed medical professionals.

Licensed pharmacies in Haitian American communities often specialize in herbal remedies and French medications. They typically employ only Haitian personnel and, when available, stock ingredients and preparations familiar to practitioners of traditional Haitian folk medicine. Typical home remedies and herbal preparations include *Asorousi*, a tea boiled from leaves that will restore a person's appetite; *Fey korosol*, an herbal preparation used to bathe a child's head to cure insomnia; a variety of leaves used to treat gas or if a child's stomach is swollen; and warm oils used in combination with massage to solve a number of problems from aches and sprains to displaced organs.

Immigrants from rural areas believe that illness can be of either natural or supernatural origin. Natural illnesses are called *maladi pei* (country diseases) or *maladi bon die* (diseases of the Lord). Natural illnesses last for only a short time. Supernatural illnesses appear suddenly, are more persistent, and are typically attributed to angry vodou spirits—the spirits could be angered, for instance, if a person offends the family's vodou spirit protector in some manner. A vodou priest is consulted to help in diagnosing such illnesses and is tasked with contacting the spirit to ascertain the reason for its unhappiness, what the person must do to appease the spirit, and what medications will properly treat the person's symptoms.

Haitian American culture, like most cultures, places great value on nutrition, personal hygiene, and consistent sleep schedules. However, they maintain vastly different body image standards when compared to mainstream Americans and Europeans. Individuals Americans might consider overweight are considered by Haitian Americans to be healthy and happy, whereas thin people are believed to be afflicted with psychological and emotional problems affecting their appetite and digestion.

Haitian Americans often believe that only traditional healers have the knowledge and skills to treat particular illnesses and will avoid interactions with the American medical profession in all but the most extreme cases. Haitian Americans often take issue with American physicians' conduct during office visits; they typically expect the physician to receive them with a few moments of general conversation before commencing a hands-on examination. They also expect

Two Haitian American friends who were originally migrant workers and then became volunteers who packed free meals for the elderly. ACEY HARPER / TIME LIFE PICTURES / GETTY IMAGES

that the examination should not include a long list of questions by the doctor—it is the doctor, not the patient, who is supposed to determine what is wrong. However, physicians who make an effort to learn and be sensitive to the patient's cultural needs can establish positive working relationships with entire Haitian American communities.

Death and Burial Rituals Burial ceremonies vary according to local tradition and the status of the deceased. Relatives and friends expend considerable effort to be present when death is near. Upon the death of a friend or family member, grief among Haitians often manifests itself in physical and vocal emotional outbursts. Persons who are knowledgeable in the funeral customs wash, dress, and place the body in a coffin. Mourners wear white clothing which, in contrast to American and European custom, represents death. A priest may be summoned to conduct the burial service, which usually takes place within 24 hours of passing.

Some Haitian Americans maintain the traditional vodou belief that the spirits of the dead live in close proximity to the loa, in a place called "Under the Water," while others believe that they become loa. Restless spirits, for one reason or another unfulfilled in their first life, are sometimes believed not to pass to another realm at all but instead continue to wander the earth. These disembodied souls may be used in magic or reincarnated in new-born members of the deceased's immediate family. Elaborate burial customs have been established to ensure that these restless dead remain buried, as it is believed that their corpses, when removed from their tombs, may be turned into zombies, who then serve the will of their master.

FAMILY AND COMMUNITY LIFE

The family is the nucleus of Haitian society, both in Haiti and in the United States; within it, individuals are dependent upon each other. The immediate family—typically extending at least as far as grandparents, aunts, and uncles—is involved in all decision-making for its members.

Family honor is of utmost importance. Family reputation is so important that the actions of a single member of the family are considered to bring either honor or shame to the entire family. A family's reputation in society is based on both current conduct and family history.

Haitian American parents are generally strict with their children, as is customary in Haiti. The children are monitored by the adults of the family. Adult rules are to be respected and obeyed without question. Children are expected to live at home until they are married. Haitian American children seem to accept these customs and values despite the freer attitudes and lifestyles they see in their American counterparts. Haitian parents have immigrated to seek a better standard of life for their children and they want to obtain a good formal education for them. They want their children to grow up to be obedient, responsible, and close to the family.

Treatment of the elderly in Haiti differs from that in the United States. Senior citizens are highly respected because they have wisdom that can only come from living a long life. Sending an aged parent to a nursing home is unthinkable for Haitians. Children vie with each other for the privilege of caring for the parents.

Gender Roles Though marital dynamics are more egalitarian among Haitian immigrants in the United States, elements of traditional patriarchal structures persist. By tradition, the father is the breadwinner and authority figure, while the mother manages the household, finances, and childcare. In fact, many women rear children without the consistent presence of the father.

From birth, males are granted more freedom and educational opportunities than females. Transgressions in behavior are more readily overlooked in males, and the "macho" image is admired, as men are expected to fill dominant roles in society. Young females often lead a sheltered and protected life, and social mobility outside the home is typically limited.

These traditionally clear distinctions in gender roles are slowly dissolving as a result of both economic necessity and gradual assimilation. More urban women are working outside the home, enjoying some degree of freedom and social mobility. As a result they are less willing to play a subservient role to their male partners and family members.

Courtship and Weddings The most common domestic relationship in Haiti has traditionally been the *plasaj*, an arrangement roughly equivalent to common-law marriage but lacking legal status in Haiti. Although the *plasaj* also lacks legal status in the United States, many undocumented Haitian couples living in the United States continue to follow the tradition.

Relations with Other Americans Haitian Americans often struggle with both individual and cultural identity. The general American public has typically seen them as indistinguishable from any other black American populace, which is a major source of tension for two reasons. First, cultural and linguistic differences make assimilation into mainstream black American society difficult, particularly for first-generation immigrants. Second, first-generation parents often intentionally isolate themselves and their children from mainstream black American culture because they believe stereotypes about violent music, squalid housing projects, and gang affiliation. Most families and communities have begun to seek a middle ground between being merged with the rest of the black population and complete isolation, in part by making efforts to establish a distinct Haitian American identity in the public eye.

EMPLOYMENT AND ECONOMIC CONDITIONS

With a cultural emphasis on social status and financial security, Haitian Americans are hard-working and use menial entry level jobs as springboards to better paying, more permanent positions. For many years Haitian-owned U.S. businesses dependent on trade with Haiti were hurt by the various international embargoes against the country. This is especially true in Little Haiti in Miami, where neighborhood unemployment has consistently reached 30 percent.

Haitian Americans are accustomed to using rotating-credit associations as an avenue of saving. Such associations are called "sangue," "min," or "assosie" in Creole. They rotate money to members of the association from a lump-sum fund into which each member has contributed an amount of money. It is assumed that the Haitians adapted this system of contribution from their West African friends who call it "esusu." Haitian immigrants, especially those who are undocumented and therefore have no bank accounts, use the sangue to buy homes and finance various business ventures.

POLITICS AND GOVERNMENT

New York City has traditionally been the center for Haitian opposition politics. During the dictatorship of François Duvalier, more than thirty opposition political groups were in existence there. However, direct action involving Haitian politics tapered significantly after the ouster of Jean-Claude Duvalier in 1986, and twenty-first-century activist groups in the United States have focused their efforts more on immigration policy, public access, and cultural preservation.

Involvement in the American political process began in earnest in 1968 when Haitian Americans formed the Haitian American Political Organization. This organization was formed to lobby on behalf of the Haitian American community. Haitian Americans

Haitian American immigrants at a Miami, Florida Democratic Party presidential election rally. JEFF GREENBERG / ALAMY

have worked in various elections to increase their presence as a political force to obtain public services.

On April 20, 1990, more than 50,000 Haitian Americans marched across the Brooklyn Bridge to City Hall to protest the action of the Centers for Disease Control and the American Red Cross. These organizations had ruled that no Haitian could donate blood because Haitians in general were considered significant AIDS risks. This was one of the largest demonstrations of its type, and it encouraged local leaders to find a Haitian candidate for the city council from Brooklyn.

Since the late 1990s Haitian Americans have also risen to positions of power within the mainstream American political system. In 1999 Representative Marie St. Fleur (a Democrat from Massachusetts) became the first Haitian American elected to a state-level office. In 2009 the National Haitian American Elected Officials Network was formed, comprising 22 elected officials nationwide. The organization meets to discuss immigration legislation and U.S. policy toward Haiti. Its membership includes state lawmakers, mayors, city-council members, and a handful of federal politicians—most notably, President Barack Obama's Haiti-born director of the White House Office of Political Affairs, Patrick Gaspard.

Military The American Revolution saw the participation of freedmen from Saint Domingue who fought under General Lafayette at Savannah in 1779. From 1814 to 1815, Joseph Savary headed the Second Battalion of Freemen of Color—a group of over 200 Haitian soldiers who had fought with Savary against the French during the Haitian Revolution. Fighting under General Andrew Jackson's command, Savary became the first black man to reach the rank of major in the U.S. Army.

Since the majority of Haitian immigrants arrived in the United States after World War II, their involvement with U.S. participation in the war was limited.

However, many Haitian Americans served in the Vietnam War, and Haitian Americans continue to serve in the U.S. armed forces. Some of them played a special role as Creole interpreters in Haiti during the efforts to reinstate President Jean-Bertrand Aristide in the 1990s and during relief efforts following the 2010 earthquake.

NOTABLE INDIVIDUALS

Academia Michel S. Laguerre, professor and director of the Berkeley Center for Globalization and Information Technology at the University of California at Berkeley, has researched many aspects of Haitian American life and has published numerous books and articles. Carole M. Berotte Joseph, who was born in Port-au-Prince and came to the United States in 1957, became the fifth president of Bronx Community College/CUNY in July 2011 after previously serving in a number of other academic administrative positions. She is an authority on bilingual and foreign-language education, a founder of the International Alliance for Haiti, Inc., and coeditor of the landmark book *The Haitian Creole Language: History, Structure, Use and Education* (2010).

Art Jean-Michel Basquiat (1960–1988) was born in Brooklyn, New York, to Haitian parents. He struggled as an underground graffiti artist before rising to national renown as a neo-expressionist and primitivist painter.

Edouard Duval-Carrié (1954–) was born in Haiti. An acclaimed painter and sculptor, he is well known for evocative works that draw on Haitian imagery and themes, including African fables.

Journalism and Broadcasting Joel Dreyfuss, a journalist, editor, and writer, emigrated from Haiti in the 1950s. Dreyfuss has served as managing editor of *The Root* and maintained a *Huffington Post* blog about Haiti. He has also worked as a *PC Magazine* editor and *USA Today* New York bureau chief. Ricot Dupuy is the director and station manager of Radio Soleil, which was created after the 1991 coup in Haiti.

Literature Edwidge Danticat (1969–) is a Haitian-born American author. She is a two-time National Book Award nominee (*Krik? Krak!*, 1996; *Brother, I'm Dying*, 2007) and the recipient of a MacArthur Foundation "genius" grant (2009).

Music The migration of Haitians to the United States has caused a boom in its music. Haitian music serves as an anchor connecting individuals with their country, one another, and themselves. Music functions as a sanctioned means of social protest. Wyclef Jean, solo hip-hop artist and one-third of the hip-hop group, the Fugees, is a source of pride for Haitians and Haitian Americans alike. Not only does he incorporate his country's music in his songs but he also has regularly given back to his fellow countrymen through benefit concerts.

Science John James Audubon (1785–1851) was born in Cayes, Haiti. His drawings of birds in America are an invaluable source of information for naturalists and anthropologists.

Sports Jozy Altidore (1989–), born to Haitian parents in Livingston, New Jersey, has played at the striker position in professional soccer for AZ Alkmaar in the Netherlands and for the U.S. National team in international competitions.

MEDIA

PRINT

Haiti en Marche

Published weekly in French. There is a section in Creole for Creole speakers.

Miami, Florida

Haiti Observateur

Published weekly in French, Creole, and English.

50 Court Street
Brooklyn, New York 11201

Haiti Progress

Published weekly in French.

1398 Flatbush Avenue
Brooklyn, New York 11210

RADIO

Radio Tropical and Radio Soleil d'Haiti are subcarrier stations that broadcast 24 hours a day over special radios sold to listeners. They broadcast talk, call-in shows, news, gossip, and social announcements.

WNYE-FM (91.5)

Broadcasts various daily programs aimed at the Haitian American audience.

112 Tillary Street
Brooklyn, New York 11201

TELEVISION

Several cable companies offer programs aimed at their local Haitian American communities. Programs air political debates and instructions on coping with life in the United States.

ORGANIZATIONS AND ASSOCIATIONS

Haitian American Leadership Organization (HALO)

Aims to improve the lives of Haitian Americans by "promoting education, fostering unity, promoting networking, and improving the image of Haitians throughout South Florida."

Beatrice Cazeau, Executive Director
P.O. Box 827832
Pembroke Pines, Florida 33082
Phone: (888) 759-0085
Fax: (888) 759-3161
Email: halo@halohaiti.org
URL: www.halohaiti.org

Haitian-American Historical Society (HAHS)

Dedicated to discovering, disseminating, and highlighting the contributions of Haitians and other black individuals to American culture.

Daniel Fils-Aimé, Chairman
645 NE 127th Street
North Miami, Florida 33161
Phone: (786) 621-0035
Fax: (305) 759-0800
Email: haitianhistory@bellsouth.net
URL: www.haitianhistory.org

Haitian Studies Association

"Provides a forum for the exchange and dissemination of ideas and knowledge in order to inform pedagogy, practice, and policy about Haiti in a global context."

Charlene Desir, President
University of Massachusetts Boston
100 Morrissey Boulevard
McCormack Hall, Room 2-211
Boston, Massachusetts 02125
Email: hsa@umb.edu

MUSEUMS AND RESEARCH CENTERS

Many museums of African American history contain Haitian collections or substantial exhibits of Haitian culture items, including the Afro-American Historical and Cultural Museum in Philadelphia, the Black Heritage Museum in Miami, the Museum for African Art in New York City, the Museum of African American Art in Los Angeles, and the National Museum of African Art at the Smithsonian Institute in Washington, D.C.

Amistad Research Center

The center contains material relating to ethnic history and race relations in the United States, with concentration on blacks, Native Americans, Chicanos, Asian Americans, Puerto Ricans, and Haitians.

Lee Hampton, Executive Director
Tulane University
Tilton Hall
6823 St. Charles Avenue
New Orleans, Louisiana 70118
Phone: (504) 862-3222
Fax: (504) 862-8961
Email: reference@amistadresearchcenter.org
URL: www.amistadresearchcenter.org

Haitian American Museum of Chicago (HAMOC)

Aims to reclaim and highlight Haitian Americans', and particularly Jean-Baptiste Point Du Sable's, contributions to the founding and cultural heritage of the city of Chicago.

Elsie Hernandez, Founder and Director
4654 North Racine Avenue
Chicago, Illinois 60640
Phone: (773) 213-1869
URL: www.hamoc.org

Schomburg Center for Research in Black Culture (Harlem)

Reference library devoted to material by and about blacks throughout the world, with major emphasis on Afro-America, Africa, and the Caribbean, especially Haiti. Among its Haitian holdings is the Kurt Fisher and Eugene Maximilien Collection of Haitian manuscripts.

Khalil Gibran Muhammad, Director
135 Malcolm X Boulevard
New York, New York 10037
Phone: (212) 491-2200
Email: scgenref@nypl.org
URL: www.nypl.org/locations/schomburg

SOURCES FOR ADDITIONAL STUDY

Chierici, Rose-Marie Cassagnol. *Demele: "Making It": Migration and Adaptation among Haitian Boat People in the United States*. New York: AMS, 1980: 1–12.

Clark, Mary. "Domestic Violence in the Haitian Culture and the American Legal Response: Fanm Ayisyen ki Gen Kouraj." *The University of Miami Inter-American Law Review*, 37, no. 2 (Winter 2006): 297–317.

Danticat, Edwidge. *The Butterfly's Way: Voices from the Haitian Dyaspora* [sic] *in the United States*. New York: Soho, 2001.

Dreyfuss, Joel. "The Invisible Immigrants: Haitians in America Are Industrious, Upwardly Mobile and Vastly Misunderstood." *New York Times Magazine*, May 23, 1993: 20–21, 80–82.

East, Georgia. "Haitian Americans Seek Greater Political Clout in South Florida." *SunSentinel*, June 3, 2012, http://articles.sun-sentinel.com/2012-06-03/.

Laguerre, Michel S. *American Odyssey: Haitians in New York City*. New York: Cornell University Press, 1984.

———. *The Complete Haitiana: A Bibliographic Guide to the Scholarly Literature, 1900–1980*. Millwood, NY: Kraus International Publications, 1982.

Nicolas, Guerda, Angela DeSilva, and Kelly Rabenstein. "Educational Attainment of Haitian Immigrants." *Urban Education* 44, no. 6 (2009): 664–86.

Philogene, Jerry. "Visual Narratives of Cultural Memory and Diasporic Identities: Two Contemporary Haitian American Artists." *Small Axe: A Caribbean Journal of Criticism* 16 (2004): 84–99.

Stepick, Alex. *Pride against Prejudice: Haitians in the United States*. Boston: Allyn and Bacon, 1998.

Zéphir, Flore. *The Haitian Americans*. Westport, CT: Greenwood, 2004.

HAWAIIANS

Elaine Winters and Mark Swartz

OVERVIEW

Native Hawaiians are the indigenous people of the Hawaiian Islands, an archipelago in the Pacific Ocean. There are 8 major and 124 minor islands, volcanic in origin, with a total landmass of 6,425 square miles (16,641 square kilometers). The 8 major islands are Niihau, Kauai, Oahu, Molokai, Maui, Kahoolawe, Lanai, and Hawaii. Honolulu, the capital, is located on Oahu and is 2,394 miles (3,853 kilometers) southwest of San Francisco. The islands' topography includes such diverse features as active volcanoes, grassy pastures, and long stretches of beach. The exact etymology of the name *Hawaii* is debated by scholars; some claim the word's origin lies with the word *Hawaiki*, which means "place of the gods," while others believe comes from the Polynesian word *Sawaiki*, meaning "homeland."

Scholars are divided on how to determine the exact population of the Hawaiian Islands prior to European contact in 1778, and estimates range from 200,000 to 1 million. The first Hawaiians were dependent upon the land, revering their relationship with the natural world. They had a complex social system, called *kapu*, which set up the social and government structure and laws of the land. The native society was an agricultural one, and the land provided well for the Hawaiians, who lived a comfortable life.

Descendants of the first Hawaiians still live in the islands today, though many have also moved to the mainland United States, especially California, Nevada, and Washington state. The migration from the Hawaiian Islands was largely motivated by economic and educational concerns. Once Hawaii gained statehood in 1959, it focused on growing its tourism business.

At the time of the 2010 U.S. Census, the entire population of the state of Hawaii was 1.36 million. Of these, 289,850, or 21.3 percent, identified themselves as having native Hawaiian ancestry. There has been a widespread diaspora of native Hawaiians, largely to the West Coast of the United States—mostly California—and also to other Pacific Island nations. According to the 2010 U.S. Census, 527,000 Americans reported having some amount of native Hawaiian ancestry.

HISTORY OF THE PEOPLE

Early History The islands in the triangle formed (roughly) by Tahiti, New Zealand, and Hawaii are inhabited by people who possess common prominent genealogical traits, speak related languages, and, historically, have lived similar lifestyles. They are descendants of Polynesians (Polynesia is Greek for "many islands"), who began settling in the South Pacific islands around 1100 BCE. The Polynesians are believed to have reached the Hawaiian Islands sometime between 300 CE and 500 CE. They called the largest island *Havaiki* after one of the major islands of their former home. Dogs, pigs, chickens, tuber (taro), coconuts, bananas, breadfruit, yams, and sugarcane made up much of the traditional Polynesian diet. The mulberry plant called *wauke* was pounded and bleached to make *kapa*, or bark-cloth. *Ti*, a lily, provided leaves for *hula* skirts and roots to weave into matting or brew into a liquor called *okolehao*.

The first Western contact with native Hawaiians is usually dated to January 18, 1778, when the English seaman Captain James Cook arrived at the island Kauai with the crews of his two ships, H.M.S. *Resolution* and H.M.S. *Discovery*. The British visitors recorded trading iron nails for fresh water, pigs, and sweet potatoes. Captain Cook named the archipelago the "Sandwich Islands," after his patron, the Earl of Sandwich. Cook was killed by natives on the island of Hawaii one year after his arrival in a skirmish over a small boat that had been stolen from him.

In 1780 Kamehameha (1758?–1819), the first and mightiest of four leaders with the name, began a campaign to unite the islands under a single chiefdom. Hawaiian chiefs had traditionally clashed over land and the resources of the sea, but many of their disputes were settled in ritualized combat, which resulted in relatively few casualties. Kamehameha, however, adapted the modern weapons and armaments of the British visitors to suit his own purposes and hired two of Cook's seamen as war advisers. By 1795 he had obtained complete power over the eight main islands.

With the new weaponry and ammunition introduced by foreigners, called *haoles* (a term that later came to apply exclusively to white people), Kamehameha was able to take advantage of political and economic opportunities. He established a trade advantage and created a personal monopoly over foreign commerce. He used *kapu*, the existing system of religious and social customs, to exclude both commoners and lesser chiefs from engaging in commerce with ships that passed by, and brought fresh provisions to these ships personally. As soon as he realized the value that foreigners placed on pearls, he reserved pearling in Pearl Harbor for himself and employed commoners to dive. Furthermore, he exacted tolls for the privilege of using Honolulu's harbor. In these ways, Kamehameha gained power over the Hawaiian people and accumulated enormous wealth.

Westerners ventured to the Sandwich Islands in large numbers. Missionaries from various Protestant sects, particularly Calvinists, were the first major group of haoles, followed by Norwegian whalers, Mormons, diplomatic representatives from various countries, plantation owners, and Filipino, Japanese, and Chinese workers.

Sandalwood became a trading commodity as soon as people realized that the Chinese held it in high regard and were willing to pay virtually any price for it. Kamehameha incorporated sandalwood into his tribute demands from commoners and left the collection process to lesser chiefs. The sandalwood trade, however, required substantial labor, thus drawing workers away from food production. Demand for provisions by ships stopping in Hawaii further diminished local food supplies, leading to a famine in 1810 that significantly weakened the small nation. Hawaii's position further degenerated when all the sandalwood was sold and trade ceased altogether.

In 1794 George Vancouver, a British navigator, drafted an agreement with island chiefs to transfer ownership of the islands to Great Britain. He believed the chiefs had formally granted the islands to Great Britain, while the chiefs thought they had a defense agreement. Although Britain did not ratify the agreement, the British Empire, which held sway over lands in Asia, the Middle East, and Africa, established a dominant presence in Hawaii.

In 1819 the kapu system was abandoned following the death of Kamehameha. During the mourning period, the kapus were temporarily removed. Kamehameha's son Liholiho was to reinstate the kapus upon his coronation, but he failed to do so. In the ensuing chaos, many temples and works of sacred art were destroyed. As Christianity, fueled by the influx of missionaries, supplanted kapu, such cultural practices as hula dancing, surfing, and kite flying were forbidden along with other so-called pagan practices.

The population of native Hawaiians diminished considerably after Western contact, falling from an estimated 300,000 in 1778, when Cook arrived, to 71,019 in 1853. This dramatic decrease was largely due to the introduction of various diseases (including cholera, chicken pox, influenza, measles, mumps, and syphilis), for which the immune systems and medical expertise of the natives were completely unprepared. In addition, the introduction of firearms to the archipelago had made tribal conflicts much deadlier.

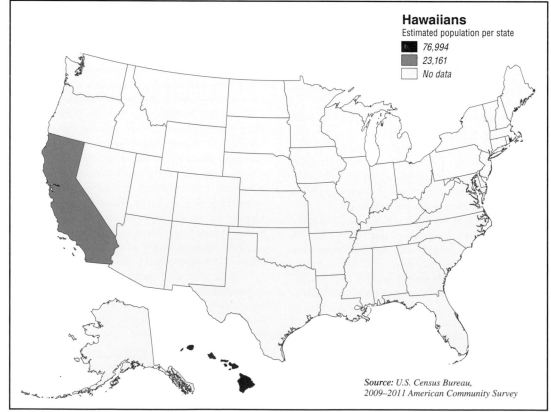

Hawaiians
Estimated population per state
- 76,994
- 23,161
- No data

Source: U.S. Census Bureau, 2009–2011 American Community Survey

In 1893 the Hawaiian monarch, Queen Liliuokalani, was overthrown in an unofficial coup d'état led by resident American and European businessmen and enforced by U.S. Marines. They established a republic, but their ultimate goal was to be annexed by the United States. President Grover Cleveland (in office 1893–1897) opposed annexation, but his successor, William McKinley (in office 1897–1901), supported a policy of amplified political, military, and economic activity in the Pacific. Citing such reasons as resolving racial unrest on the islands, arresting the influence of Japan, and boosting American shipping and commerce, the United States officially annexed Hawaii in 1898. For her refusal to go along with annexation and her support of an attempted uprising against American domination, Liliuokalani is remembered by politically liberal native Hawaiians as a freedom fighter.

U.S. involvement with Hawaii reached a new plateau after Japan bombed Pearl Harbor on December 7, 1941. The islands were placed under martial law for the duration of the war and were used extensively as bases, bombing practice sites, and rest and recreation spots for soldiers and sailors. The memorial at the site of the sunken battleship *Arizona* attracts many visitors each year, as does the national cemetery at Punchbowl (an extinct volcanic crater), with its spectacular view of Honolulu and the harbor. Hawaii joined the union in 1959, thus becoming the fiftieth state.

SETTLEMENT IN THE UNITED STATES

Native Hawaiians are descendants of the Polynesians who initially settled the Hawaiian islands, sometime around the third century. Prior to European settlement in the eighteenth century, native Hawaiians viewed land as the common property of everyone. The economic interests of the common people, the king, and the chiefs were collaborative, mutually beneficial, and intertwined. The native government was akin to a feudal system, with a chief lording over workers. However, lack of true land ownership did not mean an absence of conflicts. Neighboring chiefs would challenge other chiefs for land and its resources. The arrival of settlers and their Western ideas of title and ownership terminated that approach to government.

With the arrival of European settlers, many young Hawaiian men began to work on ships to take advantage of the newly opened trade routes. Beginning around the 1850s, during the California gold rush, native Hawaiians began migrating off the Hawaiian Islands, moving to the mainland United States and Canada to mine for gold. Hawaiian communities were set up in Sutter County, California, and Iosepa in Tooele Couñaty, Utah Utah, as well as places in and around Oregon and Canada, specifically British Columbia. These immigrants participated mostly in manual labor, mining for gold (and diving for gold off the coast of California), until the communities no longer needed miners. For example, when the

Utah gold-mining towns began to close, many native Hawaiians returned to the Hawaiian Islands.

California boasted the largest native Hawaiian community in the nineteenth and early twentieth centuries, and it is still the mainland state with the largest population of Hawaiians. Even once the gold mining began to wane, native Hawaiians tended to stay in California, first fishing and selling their catch to locals and then learning to farm. In Sutter County, California, the Hawaiians intermarried with the Maidu Native Americans, and their descendent still celebrate both ancestries.

In the 1950s the first large migration of Hawaiians took place. The rising cost of living and decreasing job opportunities on the Hawaiian Islands led many native Hawaiians to move to the mainland United States in search of better jobs and education.

LANGUAGE

The Hawaiian language is dying out as a spoken language. Today it survives mostly on the island of Niihau, in some religious services, and in words and phrases used by English speakers, rather than as a language of everyday use. Traditionally unwritten, Hawaiian had no alphabet until the arrival of the *haoles*. The Hawaiian alphabet was Romanized and first written by early missionaries. It contains twelve letters: *a, e, i, o, u, h, k, l, m, n, p,* and *w*. In general, vowels are pronounced separately, except for diphthongs such as *ai* ("eye"), *au* ("ow"), and *ei* ("ay"). Thus, the name *Kamehameha* is pronounced "kah may hah MAY hah." Less than 0.1 percent of the state's population speaks Hawaiian as their mother tongue, most of them older people. Scholars consider Hawaiian an endangered language, and they project that it will survive only in isolated phrases and in place names throughout the islands, though efforts are being made to rectify this. Programs aimed at revitalizing the Hawaiian language, like the Punana Leo program, are bringing Hawaiian language classes to public schools as well as establishing language schools. Classes, from preschool to master's degree courses, are now being offered in the native tongue, making these programs among the leading native-language revitalization programs in the United States.

All the languages of Oceania, and particularly those of Polynesia, are linguistically related. New Zealand, Tahiti, Fiji, Samoa, and Hawaii share many words, with slight variations. Some representative words in Hawaiian are *ali'i* (chief or royalty); *kahuna* (priest and/or expert healer); *kapu* (taboo or sacred); *mahalo* (thank you); *mana* (energy or spiritual power); and *ohana* (extended family).

RELIGION

The ancient religion of Hawaii incorporates hundreds of deities as well as animist beliefs. Hawaiians worshipped both in their homes and in open-air temples called *heiau*. Ruins of these temples are still visible on all the islands. The largest were *heiau waikaua*, or war temples, at which sacrifices occurred. Chief gods were Ku (god of war and male fertility), Kane (the creator and chief god), *Lono* (god of thunder and agriculture), and Kanaloa (god of the ocean and winds). With the arrival of other groups, particularly early explorers in the early 1800s, ancient Hawaiian religious practices disappeared completely. Today many Hawaiians practice Buddhism, Shinto, and Christianity.

Remnants of the traditional religious practices still exist today. Makahiki, a series of festivals celebrating the Hawaiian New Year, was recognized as a Native Hawaiian Religious Ceremony by the government in 2004. On the Kona Coast, a National Historical Park was established in 1955 to preserve the Pu'uhonua o Honaunau, or place of refuge, which was once an ancient religious sanctuary.

CULTURE AND ASSIMILATION

Writing in 1916, British novelist W. Somerset Maugham described Honolulu, in a story of the same name: "It is the meeting of East and West. The very new rubs shoulders with the immeasurably old." The ethnic variety of immigrants since the arrival of Captain Cook has created many opportunities for cultural exchange and hybridization. According to the 2010 U.S. Census, of the 1.36 million people living in Hawaii in 2010, 24.7 percent described themselves as white, 14.5 percent as Filipino, 13.6 percent as Japanese, 5.9 percent as pure native Hawaiian, 4 percent as Chinese, 1.6 percent as black, 1.8 percent as Korean, and 0.3 percent Native American; the remainder identified as another Asian race, other

Pacific Islander, and mixed race (23.6 percent). Only 21.3 percent of the state's residents reported having native Hawaiian ancestry.

Hawaiian culture greatly affected the attitudes and perspectives of many immigrant groups. The most striking example is the spirit of *aloha*, which is found on all the islands and among all ethnic groups. Although many consider the term to have been corrupted by colonialist opportunism and the tourist industry, it remains an important aspect of the culture of the state of Hawaii. The word *aloha* means many things: hello, good-bye, peace, and, perhaps most importantly, a sense of welcome and identity within the larger community.

Traditions and Customs Storytelling is a great Hawaiian tradition. Before the Hawaiian language was written, the literature of Hawaii was spoken. The Hawaiian legend of the daughter of the king of Ku-ai-he-lani is similar to the Western tale of Cinderella, as it tells the story of a young girl who journeys from rags to riches to claim her royal birthright; and the legend of Au-ke-le is akin to the ancient Greek epic the *Odyssey*, as it recounts the journey of the young chief Au-ke-le, who ventures into unknown lands and fights monsters as he undertakes a quest. Legends of the *menehunes* (small forest dwellers with supernatural powers, rather like Irish leprechauns) abound. For example, menehunes are believed to be responsible when something is misplaced. In various locations, on all the islands, there are elaborate fish ponds that do not appear to have been formed naturally. There is

A Hawaiian group sings at a luau, accompanied by a woman playing ukulele. Milolii, Hawaii, 1969. PHOTOGRAPH BY JAMES L. AMOS. CORBIS. REPRODUCED BY PERMISSION.

a traditional native Hawaiian belief that menehunes built them, and there are strict rules about these ponds. Nothing must be removed, or the menehunes will come at night and take it back. The implication is that the retrieval will be unpleasant.

Many traditional beliefs and customs in Hawaii are still observed in modern form. Ti leaves, for example, which were once worn by kahuna priests in ancient rituals, are still reputed to ward off evil spirits. Many homeowners keep a ti leaf plant on each corner of their house for good luck and decorate entries and windows with ti leaves when they think there is an evil spirit afoot. Hawaiians bring ti leaves to football games and wave them like pom-poms to keep bad spirits away from a favorite team. Wearing ti leaves is still considered good luck. Feasts, or *luaus*, are a native Hawaiian tradition still held on every important occasion. The traditional practice involves roasting a pig in an *imo*, a large oven dug into the ground. Weddings, childbirth, the completion of a canoe or a house, and a good catch or an abundant harvest are typical occasions for a native Hawaiian luau. Today, luaus are held everywhere in Hawaii and by Hawaiians elsewhere. Churches frequently hold luaus as fundraising events, and the entire community joins in the festivities and the eating. Tourists expect to enjoy a luau before leaving the islands.

Marine Culture Fish has traditionally supplied most of the protein in the Hawaiian diet. Fishing is also a crucial and highly developed trade. Early Hawaiian fishermen were often accompanied by an individual responsible for actually finding the fish—the fish watchman. This skill involved understanding the sea floor, both inside and outside of the reef; the shape of the reef, including where the fish liked to hide; and what kind of net, hook, and bait were appropriate for each fish. Various traps were also devised for catching fish and other marine animals that lived in streams. Many fishermen today forego modern technology such as sonar, preferring to keep ancient Hawaiian traditions alive; a walk along a Hawaiian beach might bring a sight of a fisherman using nets or traps. Some will even use a kayak or surfboard to go into the ocean before casting nets.

Not everyone was allowed to eat every species of fish; certain types of fish were for special events and then only for royalty. Priests were consulted every step of the way when it came to consumption of various foods. Rarely did women consume fish; rather, they were permitted shrimp and other shellfish.

Nautical culture was an important aspect of early Hawaiian life. There were freshwater ponds and shore ponds. The shore ponds were enclosures built of stone that encompassed both shallow and deep water; some ponds were as large as 60 acres. The walls had sluice gates made of wood. Native Hawaiians have long believed in the conservation of fresh water. In early times, the pond water was used to irrigate crops. Waste

from ponds, a rich source of calcium, was an excellent fertilizer. (Hawaiian soil is low in calcium.) Some of these early conservation traditions have been revived and are practiced by native Hawaiians today.

Canoes were built for either transportation or racing. Racing is believed to have been reserved for royalty, and the large double canoes are thought to have been used for major inter-island travel and trading. The elaborate process of building a canoe began with a priest selecting the appropriate lumber. Suitable animal sacrifices (pigs or chickens) were offered, and incantations and ceremonies accompanied each step of the process. For example, ti leaves were wrapped around the tree at various stages of the carving and building to ward off evil spirits. Canoe racing remains an active sport in modern Hawaii. One organization devoted to revitalizing the tradition of building and racing canoes is the Hawaiian Canoe Racing Association in Honolulu. Outrigger canoe racing, which employs a special type of canoe made with one or more floating supports, is growing in popularity across the Pacific Islands, including Hawaii. Used now for sport rather than true transportation, this type of canoeing has been reviving canoe traditions in Hawaii since the 1970s.

Native Hawaiians have expressed a mix of determination and apprehension as they face the beleaguered state of their centuries-old culture. The Hawaiian language, considered a crucial aspect of cultural identity, has been the object of renewed attention. In 1978 Hawaiian won recognition as an official state language.

Cuisine Hawaii's patchwork past is most apparent in its varied cuisine. Japanese *manju* (sweet black-bean pastry), Portuguese sweet bread, Chinese noodles or crispy duck, and spicy Korean *kimchi* are as easy to find as Hawaiian *poi*, which is served as the traditional island staple. Hawaiians eat about twice as much fish as residents of any other state, as well as more fresh fruit. Mangoes, papayas, bananas, pineapples, oranges, and avocados are grown locally. Different areas are famed for specialty crops: open-air markets on Oahu overflow with Kahuku watermelons, Maui onions, Waimanalo corn, Manoa lettuce, and Puna papayas. Many Hawaiian dishes feature coconut; for instance, a pudding called *haupia* is made by mixing coconut with sugar and *pia* (arrowroot); modern recipes call for cornstarch when arrowroot is not available. Haupia is served at most luaus and has also become a popular topping for wedding cakes.

One of the best-known foods in modern Hawaiian cuisine is Spam, a canned ham product. The product was first brought to Hawaii by American soldiers stationed on the islands during World War II. Because

A Hawaiian dancer and musician plays the ukulele. JERRY GINSBERG / DANITADELIMONT.COM "DANITA DELIMONT PHOTOGRAPHY" / NEWSCOM

Chinese brought chicken, and Norwegian whalers brought salmon marinated with onion and tomato (lomi salmon). All are now standard luau dishes.

About three hundred varieties of taro are known to have existed in Hawaii. The entire taro plant was traditionally used. The leaves were steamed alone or wrapped around potatoes or fish. The root was steamed in an *imo* and then peeled and pounded into a stiff paste called *pa'i 'ai* that could be taken traveling when wrapped in pandanus leaves. Adding water to this paste produces *poi*, a starchy thick paste sometimes allowed to ferment. The entire coconut was used as well. Unripe coconuts provided nourishing liquid for journeys when no fresh water was available. The flesh of the mature nut was grated and pressed to produce a cream; subsequent presses would produce coconut milk. The husks were halved when the mature coconut was harvested and, when empty, were used as drinking or baking cups. The fibers on the outside of the husks were pounded and then woven into rope. The leaves of the plant were sometimes used for thatching houses.

Traditional Dress Because of Hawaii's tropical climate, early natives usually wore no more than a strip or two of barkcloth (*kapa*). Many Hawaiians also covered much of their bodies with tattoos. Warriors ornamented themselves with spectacular yellow and gold capes and helmets of woven feathers. Today, Hawaiians continue to dress casually. Some Hawaiian women wear the *muumuu*, a voluminous dress originally designed by modest missionaries for Hawaiian women. Today these dresses are printed in bright and colorful cotton or silk. More firmly grounded in Hawaiian culture is the *lei*, a colorful wreath of fresh flowers or other decorative objects worn around the neck. Originally an artful offering to the gods, leis have become an emblem of Hawaiian hospitality and warmth.

Dances and Songs Although it has long been associated with Hawaii, the ukulele originated in Portugal. "Aloha Oe," a song written by Queen Liliuokalani in 1878, is a perennial favorite on this small, four-stringed, guitar-like instrument. Hawaiian musicians have also developed the distinctive slack-key style (a type of open tuning) for guitar, an instrument introduced to the islands from Spain. Instruments native to Hawaii include beating sticks, bamboo pipes, and rattles and drums of various kinds. According to historians, native Hawaiians also played a bamboo nose flute, a whistle made from a gourd, and an instrument having one string that was played with a bow. A variety of jaw harp was also used.

Singing, drumming, and the hula dance are sacred forms of worship and remain integral to the daily life of some native Hawaiians. Hula traditionally tells the story of the volcano goddess Pele, but the dance can tell many other ancient myths and stories. It has been described as a convergence of poetry, dance, and song. Christian missionaries attempted to ban the practice

of Hawaii's tropical climate, a meat that did not need refrigeration was immediately popular. Dishes made with Spam, such as stir-fry and Spam *musubi* (in which the meat is served like sushi, atop a rice ball wrapped with dried *nori* seaweed), are common in Hawaiian homes and restaurants. Hawaiians even host festivals to celebrate their favorite meat product; every year, Spam connoisseurs attend the Spam Jam in Waikiki. According to the Spam Jam website, nearly seven million cans of the meat are consumed each year in Hawaii.

During a luau, a pig is roasted in a pit lined with wood, lava rocks, and banana stumps. The pig is stuffed with hot rocks, wrapped in leaves, and buried along with pieces of fish, taro, yams, and breadfruit. A festive banquet for friends and extended family, the luau has absorbed many non-Hawaiian elements. In the nineteenth century missionaries brought cakes, of hula in the nineteenth century, but the tradition survived. In the twentieth and twenty-first centuries, the hula culture has been preserved by dance troupes who perform traditional dances, mainly for tourists.

Certain superstitions continue to be observed with regard to modern hula; for example, while black can be used to ornament a costume, a dancer never dresses totally in black for hula, since black is the traditional color of mourning. It is believed that ancient Hawaiians blackened their faces and limbs when in mourning.

Holidays Ancient religious holidays are not known, owing to the determination on the part of missionaries to enforce the celebration of only the Christian holidays. In addition to federal holidays observed by the entire United States, Hawaii also celebrates Kuhio Day (Kuhio was a prince) on March 26 and Kamehameha Day on June 11.

Health Care Issues and Practices Religion and medicine were closely related in traditional native Hawaiian life. People expected prayer to heal most things. There were several classes of *kahuna lapa'au* (medical priest/healer) who treated physical and mental ailments according to a variety of traditions now mostly lost to history.

Drinking seawater followed by fresh water was considered a universal remedy. Various native plants were used as compresses for relieving pain or injury, and the leaves of plants were brewed in teas and used for healing purposes. *Piper methysticum* (the source of the intoxicating *awa* or *kava*) was used in many ways. Today, this species is a sedative given in mild form to infants during teething and is used in commercial diuretics. Seasonal changes and extremes of humidity and dryness produced many respiratory problems among native Hawaiians. There were as many as fifty-eight herbal remedies for asthma, many of which have been studied or adapted by modern medical science.

In addition to the diseases brought by the first wave of immigrants to Hawaii, leprosy, whose origin is not known and for which there has never been a cure, had a profound effect on the health of native Hawaiians. Because of the social stigma attached to the disease (it was mistakenly thought to be a venereal disease) as well as its extreme contagiousness, lepers were isolated on the island of Molokai beginning in 1886. For sixteen years, a Belgian priest named Father Damien Joseph de Veuster provided medical care for these patients, whom the medical community refused to treat, before succumbing to the illness himself in 1889.

Compared with Hawaiians of European and Asian ancestry, native Hawaiians have continued to bear the brunt of the archipelago's health problems. According to a 2006 study by I. Anderson et al., whereas Hawaii as a whole boasts the longest average life span of any state (males live an average of

SPAM FRIED RICE

Ingredients

3 tablespoons low-sodium soy sauce

1 tablespoon toasted sesame oil

1 teaspoon hot sauce (like Tapatio or Sriracha), more or less to taste

1 tablespoon vegetable oil

2 cups chopped Spam

1 red bell pepper, stemmed, seeded and chopped

6 green onions, chopped, white and green parts separated

3 garlic cloves, minced

½ tablespoon minced fresh ginger

5 cups day-old cooked rice, white or brown, cold

3 large eggs

1–2 cups fresh pineapple, coarsely chopped

Preparation

In a small bowl, whisk together the soy sauce, sesame oil and hot sauce. Set aside.

In a large nonstick skillet, heat 1 teaspoon of vegetable oil until hot and shimmering. Add the Spam, red bell pepper, and the chopped white parts of the green onions. Cook, stirring often, until lightly browned and the red pepper is just tender, about 5–7 minutes. Stir in the garlic and ginger and cook another minute. Scrape the mixture onto a plate and set aside.

Heat another teaspoon of oil in the skillet until hot. Add the cold rice and cook, breaking up large clumps, until the rice is heated through, 5–6 minutes.

Push the rice to one side of the skillet and heat the last teaspoon of oil on the empty side of the skillet. Crack the eggs into the hot oil and stir lightly with a spatula or wooden spoon, cooking until the eggs are lightly scrambled and set. Stir the eggs and the ham mixture into the rice. Pour the soy sauce mixture into the rice and cook, stirring, until thoroughly combined and hot.

Off the heat, stir in the pineapple and green parts of the onions.

Serve immediately.

Serves 6

75.9 years; females, 82.1 years), the life span of native Hawaiians (71.5 years for males and 77.2 for females) is lower than the U.S. average (75 years for males and 80 years for women). The U.S. Office of Minority Health lists the 2002 infant mortality rate for native Hawaiians as 9.6 per 1,000 live births, higher than the U.S. rate of 7.0 per 1,000 live births. In addition, native Hawaiians experience high rates of diabetes and hypertension. Health care workers consider poor diet a major factor, and economic problems undoubtedly contribute to this situation.

Young hula dancers wearing plumeria leis perform at the Lei Day celebration at Hilton Hawaiian Village in Honolulu, HI. JENNIFER CRITES / PHOTO RESOURCE HAWAII / ALAMY

Death and Burial Rituals Traditionally, when someone died, the *kahuna aumakau* (priest of the appropriate ancestral deity) of the dead person came and ritually sacrificed a pig or a chicken to ensure that the soul would live with its ancestors. There were several ways of disposing of the dead. Burial in the ground was the most common method; there are ancient graveyards on all the major islands. In another disposal ritual, the corpse was eviscerated, filled with salt, and burned. Sometimes the flesh was scraped off the bones, and the skull, femur, and humerus were saved, though this usually only occurred with a special corpse, like the body of a king or chief. The bones were thought to bring prosperity to the owner. The rest of the body was taken by boat far out to sea and dumped. Those in the boats were not permitted to look back once the remains were deposited into the sea, or the soul would follow them back to the land and thus not rest properly. Remnants of woven caskets, unique to Hawaii, have been found, and it is believed they were used to hold the bones of kings. Such caskets are considered extraordinary works of art.

The bones of the dead are still revered among native Hawaiians today. Water is ceremoniously sprinkled in the house of the deceased so the soul will not return. After attending a funeral, mourners sprinkle their bodies with water so that the soul will not follow them home. While modern customs like caskets have become common in Hawaiian burials, many Hawaiians still participate in traditional sea burials, usually by cremating the body before scattering the ashes.

FAMILY AND COMMUNITY LIFE

In the past, children were raised by the entire extended family, a practice called *hanai*. Grandparents usually had more to say in the upbringing of children than parents did. When the first child was a boy, it was taken by the father's parents and raised by them and the father's siblings—the child's aunts and uncles. If the first child was a girl, it was raised by the mother's parents and her extended family. Childless couples were unheard of in the social sense; there were always children who needed attention and instruction. Hawaiian chiefs created political alliances by marrying both commoners and other royalty. Most chiefs had many wives and provided for adopted as well as biological children.

Among native Hawaiians today, many of the old ways, while fragmented, are still observed. For example, in neighborhoods that are predominantly

Hawaiian, children move in and out of houses freely, and adults are clearly watching out for all the children in view. The concept of children belonging to and being the responsibility of the larger extended family remains vital.

Gender Roles Traditionally, the differences in raising native Hawaiian boys and girls center on their eventual roles as adults. Boys learn to plant, cultivate, cook, and fish; girls learn to cook and to prepare *tapa*, a cloth made from the bark of trees and painted, for decoration or clothing.

The traditional *kapu* system, which set up laws and a code of conduct, separated men and women at times, including during meal times. Women found some autonomy in this system. They led their own lives, cooked food for themselves, had their own deities, and had their own function in matters of royal inheritance and social stature. Women's status depended on social position and birth order. Older sisters were respected and generally wielded greater authority than junior siblings, including males. Older women continue to command respect in the community, relative to younger men and women.

While many modern gender roles are still influenced by the strict laws of the past, as well as by the morals passed down from Christian missionaries, many twenty-first-century Hawaiians are working to bring back ancient gender roles. One example is the third gender, or *mahu*, which is a term used to describe a man living and dressing as a woman. While this is a common tradition among Polynesian cultures, the concept of the third gender was suppressed as Hawaiians assimilated to the Christian culture. Progressive scholars and advocacy groups are working to restore mahus' acceptance within Hawaiian society.

Education Bilingual programs exist to accommodate children for whom English is not a first language. Many classes are given in Hawaiian, which is the second official language of the state of Hawaii. For native Hawaiian children there are the well-endowed Kamehameha Schools, which were established in perpetuity by the estate of Bernice Pauahi Bishop, the last descendant of Kamehameha. The schools were intended to provide native Hawaiian children with a place where they could learn together.

The University of Hawaii has two major campuses (Manoa and Hilo) and several smaller ones, which provide both education and employment to various strata of the native Hawaiian population. There are also several community colleges.

Courtship and Weddings In traditional Hawaiian culture, engagements were arranged by the parents of the prospective bride and groom during their late childhood or early adolescence. When arrangements were settled by the parents, the young people were consulted, and once agreement to the match was

TRADITIONAL HAWAIIAN AGRICULTURE

The Hawaiian farmers of ancient times were superior cultivators who systematically identified and named plants—both those cultivated as well as the wild species gathered for use when crops failed. The farmers developed procedures for cultivation at every arable location on an island (approximately 15 percent of the land), taking into account the variety of altitudes, exposures, and weather conditions. Elaborate systems of aqueducts and ditches brought water from dammed springs to planted terraces, demonstrating engineering and building skills as well as planning and organizing abilities. The remnants of these systems can still be seen from the air. Plants cultivated for food included such staples as taro, breadfruit, and yam, as well as foods that offered variety and additional nutrients, including banana, sugarcane, coconut, candlenut (*kukui*), arrowroot, and ti.

obtained from all parties, the engagement became binding. Hawaiian weddings were traditionally, and continue to be, associated with flowers. Both the bride and groom wear elaborate *leis*—necklaces of flowers, nuts, seeds, and other plant material woven together. Traditional Hawaiian weddings are still performed with the addition of whatever civil or religious sanction is necessary for legal purposes.

There are also superstitions linked with weddings. The bride and groom are not wished good luck on their wedding day, as this can result in bad luck. The only way this situation can be reversed is if the individual who was offered the wish crosses his or her fingers immediately after it is offered, thus counteracting the curse. In addition, pearls should not be worn on the wedding day, as they resemble tears and will cause the marriage to be filled with sorrow.

EMPLOYMENT AND ECONOMIC CONDITIONS

Before tourism and the establishment of the U.S. military on the islands, agriculture was the biggest source of employment in Hawaii. Sugar, coconut, and pineapple cultivation formed the core of the plantation system. When the large plantations were established in the 1820s and 1830s, native Hawaiian men were employed as farm workers while Hawaiian women processed sugarcane or worked in the houses of white immigrants as maids and washerwomen.

Wage labor first developed to meet foreign demand and was centered in Honolulu and Lahaina. Beginning around 1820, commoners were enticed to work for wages (although records show that such payment was usually practiced to avoid taxation). By the mid-1840s there existed a group of landless native Hawaiian laborers in Honolulu; these people were paid about a dollar a day in 1847, less than half of what *haoles* earned. Plantation owners, in fact, set wages at different levels for each of the different racial groups, in order to maintain distrust among them and thereby prevent workers from organizing.

At a planter's convention in the 1880s, the plantation kingpin Sanford B. Dole (1844–1926)—who also served for a time as president of the Hawaiian Republic—criticized the planter system, which often abused its contract labor: "I cannot help feeling that the chief end of this meeting is plantation profits, and the prosperity of the country, the demands of society … the future of the Hawaiian race only comes secondarily if at all." Even to those commoners who were conscious of their exploitation, however, working for wages on plantations seemed a better way of life than working to pay tribute to chiefs. Plantation workers, for example, had taxes paid for them by plantation owners, and an early strike forced plantations to pay workers directly rather than through the chief.

Emigration of male native Hawaiians to the west coast of the United States occurred during the California gold rush. The growing absence of local labor resulting from this exodus, as well as from the dwindling native Hawaiian population, encouraged the importation of Chinese, Japanese, and Portuguese farm workers; a total of 400,000 came between 1850 and 1880. Smaller numbers of European workers came from Germany, Norway, and other countries.

From the time of the missionaries until the beginning of World War II, Hawaii was economically controlled by five powerful companies: Castle and Cooke, Alexander and Baldwin, Theodore Davies, C. Brewer, and American Factors (Amfac). About one-third of the directors of these five companies were direct descendants of missionary families or immediately related to them by marriage. Collectively, these companies formed an alliance that, by 1930, controlled 96 percent of the islands' sugar industry and every business associated with that crop. They therefore manipulated virtually all the sizable businesses and institutions on the islands: banking, insurance, utilities, transportation, wholesale and retail sales, marketing, and inter-island and mainland shipping. In 1932 the Big Five gained control of the pineapple industry, Hawaii's second most important agricultural crop prior to World War II. After the war, in which many Japanese Americans served with great distinction, the Japanese vote broke the political power of the

A native Hawaiian fisherman mends a net on the island of Kauai, Hawaii. DAVID R. FRAZIER PHOTOLIBRARY, INC. / ALAMY

planter elite. With the Big Five essentially in control of agriculture, the plantation culture of Hawaii began to decline, which in turn caused an overall decline in the islands' agricultural economy, beginning in the 1920s and continuing throughout the twentieth century.

Beginning in the 1980s, the economy of the state of Hawaii was based on tourism. Visitors to Hawaii spent almost $14.3 billion in 2012 alone. The second largest employer was the U.S. Department of Defense, which spent more than $12.2 billion in 2009. As agriculture diminished in magnitude and economic importance, opportunities became scarce for native Hawaiians who had traditionally worked in the fields and canneries. Native Hawaiians often took jobs as domestic servants or served in other, often menial, capacities to meet the needs of visitors to the islands. According to the U.S. Bureau of Labor Statistics, unemployment in Hawaii was about 7.0 percent in 2010, which was still below the national average of 9.6 percent, and the cost of living remains high, with average four-bedroom home prices over $700,000, making it much more expensive than the majority of the country. These economic factors have caused many native Hawaiians to leave the islands for better opportunities on the mainland.

POLITICS AND GOVERNMENT

For a long time after annexation, Hawaii's politics were dominated by conservative men of European descent who served the interests of the plantations. In the wake of World War II and Hawaiian statehood, labor unions—especially the International Longshoremen's and Warehousemen's Union—exerted a strong political influence, creating a tradition of support for the Democratic Party and a politically liberal climate. The presence of Hawaiians of Japanese descent in the political arena has created the impression of progressive attitudes regarding race. Nevertheless, native Hawaiians have not always benefited from liberal politics.

Native Hawaiians have expressed a mix of determination and apprehension as they face the beleaguered state of their centuries-old culture. The Hawaiian language, considered a crucial aspect of cultural identity, has been the object of renewed attention. In 1978 Hawaiian won recognition as an official state language. For many, cultural survival is inextricably linked to having a political voice. More than a century after the overthrow of the last Hawaiian monarch, the issue of sovereignty resurfaced. The organization Ka Lahui Hawai'i (the Nation of Hawaii), founded in 1987, is dedicated to mobilizing support for this objective. Chief among their complaints is that native Hawaiians are the only indigenous people living within the borders of the United States who are not recognized as a separate nation by the federal government. Rather, they are regarded as "wards" of the state of Hawaii. Informed by the civil rights movement of the 1960s and encouraged by sovereignty movements around the globe, Ka Lahui Hawai'i asks that native Hawaiians be treated as other Native Americans and

be given their own protected native lands (in addition to homestead lands, or lands that they legally own) as well as rights of self-governance.

The sovereignty movement maintains that the independent and internationally recognized government of the Hawaiian Islands was illegally overthrown by the government of the United States. It is further argued that acculturation—produced by intermarriage and lack of attention to native traditions, customs, and language—is a form of racial genocide. Because native Hawaiian religion, traditions, and values are closely associated with 'aina (the land) and respect for the environment, many native Hawaiians feel that American desecration of the environment, resulting from military and commercial exploitation, constitutes a grievous crime. The island of Kahoolawe, which was rendered uninhabitable after its use for target practice by the U.S. military, is cited as a prime example of these destructive policies—as are the crowds of tourists.

In 1993 sovereignty activists picketed President Clinton while he attended fund-raising activities on Waikiki Beach. Four months later, Clinton issued a formal apology for the United States' overthrow of the Hawaiian monarchy and for "the deprivation of the rights of native Hawaiians to self-determination." In 1994 activists delivered a Proclamation of Restoration of the Independence of the Sovereign Nation State of Hawaii and began work on a new constitution, which was signed and ratified on January 16, 1995. This document called for the restoration of the inherent sovereignty of the native Hawaiian people and guaranteed equal rights to all citizens regardless of race. In 1999 a Native Hawaiian Convention convened in Honolulu to begin the process of forming a native Hawaiian government. In 2012 the process continued with Senator Daniel Akaka lobbying for the Hawaiian Government Reorganization Act, which, according to the act, would "recognize a Native Hawaiian Governing entity under the Indian Reorganization Act."

The sovereignty movement, however, is far from unified. Ka Lahui Hawai'i is but the largest of some 100 organizations working for native Hawaiian issues, and members disagree on what form sovereignty should take. For some, secession from the United States is the goal; others envision a status similar to that of American Indian reservations, or one that designates certain areas in Hawaii as zones for traditional lifestyles.

Supporters of the movement for a native Hawaiian government often point to the race relation issues that have historically plagued native Hawaiians. The circumstances surrounding the alleged rape of Thalia Massie in 1931 represent for many native Hawaiians the racial injustice of the present as well as the past. Massie testified that two Japanese, two Hawaiians, and a Chinese Hawaiian had attacked her near Waikiki, but the trial resulted in a hung jury. Massie's husband took matters into his own hands and killed one of the Hawaiians—a crime that brought him a sentence of only one hour.

NOTABLE INDIVIDUALS

Academia Haunani-Kay Trask, a political theorist, is professor of political science at the University of Hawaii and author of *From a Native Daughter: Colonialism and Sovereignty in Hawaii* (1993). Trask is also the author of the poetry collections *Light in the Crevice Never Seen* (1994) and *Night Is a Sharkskin Drum* (2002).

Art The artist Palani Vaughan has produced a work of his photos and verse called *Na leo*.

Literature John Dominis Holt (1919–1993) is an author of fiction and nonfiction. In 1964 he published the essay "On Being Hawaiian," which many consider an impetus for the Hawaiian artistic renaissance. A second edition of Holt's *The Art of Featherwork in Old Hawaii* was published in 1997.

Dana Naone Hall is a poet and the editor of *Malama: Hawaiian Land and Water* (1985).

Music Don Ho (1930–2007), Hawaii's beloved singer, achieved fame for his recording "Tiny Bubbles" (1967). On April 14, 2007, Ho passed away from cardiac failure, following a long battle with a heart condition. Singer and ukulele player Israel "Iz" Ka'ano'i Kamakawiwo'ole (1959–1997) is famous for his tender medley of the songs "Somewhere Over the Rainbow" and "What a Wonderful World," which was released on his 1993 album *Facing Future* and gained popularity when it was later used in a number of Hollywood films. Keola (Keolamaikalani Breckenridge) Beamer (1951–), a descendant of Queen Ahiakumai Ki'eki'e and Kamehameha I, has played a central role in integrating traditional chants and instruments into contemporary music. He is also an expert in slack-key guitar. He tours widely, has recorded several slack-key albums, and has won numerous Hoku Awards.

Politics Congressman Daniel Akaka (1924–) represented Hawaii first in the House of Representatives (1977–1990) and then in the Senate (1990–2013). John Waihee (1946–), governor of the state of Hawaii from 1986 to 1994, was the first person of native Hawaiian descent to serve in that office.

Stage and Screen The actor Keanu Reeves (1964–), whose film credits include *Bill and Ted's Excellent Adventure* (1989), *My Own Private Idaho* (1991), *Point Break* (1991), *Speed* (1994), and *The Matrix* trilogy (1999, 2001, 2003), is part Hawaiian.

MEDIA

RADIO

KPOA-FM (93.5)

Plays ethnic Hawaiian music.

Alaka'i Paleka, Program Director
311 Anno Street
Kahului, Hawaii 96732
Phone: (808) 877-5566
Fax: (808) 877-2888
Email: studio@kpoa.com
URL: www.kpoa.com

ORGANIZATIONS AND ASSOCIATIONS

Daughters of Hawaii

An organization of native Hawaiian women working to perpetuate the memory and spirit of old Hawaii; preserves the nomenclature and pronunciations of the Hawaiian language. Offers classes in Hawaiian.

Dale Bachman, Regent
2913 Pali Highway
Honolulu, Hawaii 96817
Phone: (808) 595-3167
Fax: (808) 595-4395
Email: info@daughtersofhawaii.org
URL: www.daughtersofhawaii.org

Halau Mohala Ilima

A group of professional dancers offering instruction in *hula* and traditional Hawaiian culture.

Mapuana de Silva
1110 'A'alapapa Drive
Kailua, Hawaii 96734
Phone: (808) 261-0689

Hana Cultural Center

Community facility that mounts exhibits about Hana history.

Esse Sinenci, President
4974 Uakea Road
Hana, Hawaii 96713
Phone: (808) 248-8622
Email: hccm@aloha.net
Email: mail@hanaculturalcenter.org
URL: www.hanaculturalcenter.org

Nation of Hawaii

Organization working toward renewed Hawaiian sovereignty, including a model of a sustainable village called Pu'uhonua o Waimanalo.

Aloha First
P.O. Box 701
Waimanalo, Hawaii 96795
Phone: (808) 259-6309 or (808) 259-9018
Email: exec@hawaii-nation.org
URL: http://hawaii-nation.org/index.html

State Council on Hawaiian Heritage

State-funded agency that sponsors seminars in dance and presents the annual King Kamehameha Hula Competition. Also sponsors conferences and seminars on traditional storytelling and ancient legends of Native Hawaiians.

P.O. Box 25142
Honolulu, Hawaii 96825
Phone: (808) 536-6540
Fax: (808) 536-6540
Email: niele2@aol.com
URL: http://hotspotshawaii.com/scohh.html

MUSEUMS AND RESEARCH CENTERS

Bernice P. Bishop Museum

Founded by Charles Bishop in memory of his wife, Bernice (the last known surviving member of the Kamehameha family), it is one of the most significant scientific and cultural facilities in the Pacific region. The collection of ancient Hawaiian artifacts is world famous. The museum owns extensive collections and mounts frequent exhibits related to the cultural and natural history of Hawaii. There is also an Immigrant Preservation Center that houses collections and permits scholarly research of immigrant artifacts from all the major ethnic groups.

Blair D. Collis, President
1525 Bernice Street
Honolulu, Hawaii 96817-0916
Phone: (808) 847-3511
Fax: (808) 848-4147
Email: museum@bishopmuseum.org
URL: www.bishop.hawaii.org

Hawaiian Historical Society

Founded in 1892, the society maintains historical documents from Hawaii and the Pacific region. Publishes scholarly works on Hawaiian history. Offers free programs to the public.

Barbara Dunn, Administrative Director and Librarian
560 Kawaiahao
Honolulu, Hawaii 96813
Phone: (808) 537-6271
Fax: (808)537-6271
Email: hhsbarb@lava.net
URL: www.hawaiianhistory.org

Lyman Museum and Mission House

Historical residence containing historical artifacts as well as information about native flora and fauna, geology, and local family genealogies.

Jill Maruyama, Curator of Collections and Exhibits
276 Haili Street
Hilo, Hawaii 96720
Phone: (808) 935-5021
Fax: (808) 969-7685
URL: www.lymanmuseum.org

Polynesian Cultural Center

Presents, preserves, and perpetuates the arts, crafts, culture, and lore of Fijian, Hawaiian, Maori, Marquesan, Tahitian, Tongan, Samoan, and other Polynesian peoples.

Von D. Orgill, President
55-370 Kamehameha Highway
Laie, Hawaii 96762
Phone: (800) 367-7060
Fax: (808) 293-3022
Email: culturalexpert@polynesia.com
URL: www.polynesia.com

Queen Emma Summer Palace

Historical building that houses ancient Hawaiiana, including tapa, quilts, furniture, and other artifacts belonging to Queen Emma, who was the royal consort of King Kamehameha IV in the nineteenth century, and her family.

Dale Bachman, Regent
2913 Pali Highway
Honolulu, Hawaii 96817
Phone: (808) 595-3167
Fax: (808) 595-4395
Email: info@daughtersofhawaii.org
URL: www.daughtersofhawaii.org

University of Hawaii at Manoa: Kamakakuokalani Center for Hawaiian Studies

The University of Hawaii at Manoa's Hawaiian studies program seeks to further the study of Hawaiian culture, history, language, and politics.

Professor Lilikala Kame'eleihiwa, Director
2645 Dole Street
University of Hawaii
Honolulu, Hawaii 96822
Phone: (808) 973-0989
Fax: (808) 973-0988
Email: chsuhm@hawaii.edu
URL: http://manoa.hawaii.edu/hshk/index.php/site/acad_studies/en/

SOURCES FOR ADDITIONAL STUDY

Buck, Elizabeth. *Paradise Remade: The Politics of Culture and History in Hawai'i*. Philadelphia: Temple University Press, 1993.

Clarke, Joan, with photography by Michael A. Uno. *Family Traditions in Hawai'i: Birthday, Marriage, Funeral, and Cultural Customs in Hawai'i*. Honolulu: Namkoong Pub., 1994.

Fuchs, Lawrence H. *Hawaii Pono: An Ethnic and Political History*. Honolulu: Bess Press, 1992.

Gray, Francine Du Plessix. *Hawaii: The Sugar-Coated Fortress*. New York: Random House, 1972.

Kame'eleihiwa, Lilikalā. *Native Lands and Foreign Desires: Pehea Lā E Pono Ai?* Honolulu: Bishop Museum Press, 1992.

Kane, Herbert Kawainui. *Ancient Hawai'i: Words and Images*. Captain Cook, HI: Kawainui Press, 1997.

McGregor, Davianna. *N Kua'ina: Living Hawaiian Culture*. Honolulu: University of Hawaii Press, 2006.

Nordyke, Eleanor C. *The Peopling of Hawai'i*. 2nd ed. Honolulu: University of Hawaii Press, 1989.

Osorio, Jonathan Kay Kamakawiwo'ole. *Dismembering Lāhui: A History of the Hawaiian Nation to 1887*. Honolulu: University of Hawaii Press, 2002.

Silva, Noenoe K. *Aloha Betrayed: The Hawaiian Resistance to American Colonialism*. Durham, NC: Duke University Press, 2004.

Stannard, David E. *Before the Horror: The Population of Hawai'i on the Eve of Western Contact*. Honolulu: Social Science Research Institute, University of Hawaii, 1989.

HMONG AMERICANS

Carl L. Bankston III

OVERVIEW

Hmong Americans are immigrants or descendants of people from the mountainous regions of Laos, a nation in Southeast Asia. Laos is bordered by Thailand in the southwest, Cambodia in the south, Myanmar (Burma) in the west, China in the north, and Vietnam in the east. Laos has a tropical climate, with a rainy season that lasts from May to November and a dry season that extends from December to April. Most of the lowland population is ethnic Lao, while various minority groups, including the Hmong, live in the highlands. Laos measures approximately 91,400 square miles (236,800 square kilometers), making it slightly larger than the state of Utah.

According to the *CIA World Factbook*, Laos had an estimated population of 6,586,266 as of 2012. The Hmong made up 8 percent of the total population, meaning there were about 527,000. About 67 percent of the people in Laos are identified as Buddhist and 1.5 percent as Christian, and 31.5 percent adhere to religions unspecified in any official estimates. Shamanism, ancestor worship, and animism (spirit worship) are common, and many Buddhists also hold animist beliefs. Although traditional Hmong religion consists of shamanism and worship of spirits and ancestors, Christianity is much more common among the Hmong than among the ethnic Lao. Indeed, the Hmong most likely make up the majority of the Christian population in Laos. According *CIA World Factbook* population estimates for 2012, the ethnic Lao accounted for a slight majority (55 percent) of the country's population, the Khmou made up 11 percent, and 26 percent of the population was divided among more than one hundred small ethnic groups. Although Laos has experienced economic growth in recent years—reducing its official poverty rate from 46 percent of the population in 1992 to 26 percent by 2012—it continues to be one of the poorest countries in Southeast Asia, despite a plethora of natural resources, such as minerals, timber, and rubber. Three-quarters of the country's labor force works in agriculture.

The Hmong began arriving in the United States as refugees in late 1975, after communist forces came to power in their native country, but they did not immigrate in large numbers until the 1980s. By 2010, according to U.S. Census data, about one-third of Hmong Americans lived in California, one-fourth in Minnesota, and one-fifth in Wisconsin. Coming from a dramatically different society, Hmong Americans have had relatively high rates of unemployment and have found jobs most often in service and lower-level manufacturing sectors. Hmong workers were more seriously affected than their American counterparts by the decline in U.S. manufacturing in the late twentieth and early twenty-first centuries and by the economic recession that began in 2008. They did, however, experience an increase in employment in health care occupations.

The 2010 Current Population Survey of the U.S. Census reported 247,545 Hmong in the United States, plus 12,478 people who identified themselves as Hmong in addition to another ethnic or racial category. The Hmong are most heavily concentrated in the Minneapolis–St. Paul–Bloomington region in eastern Minnesota and western Wisconsin and in the Sacramento-Arden-Arcade-Roseville area in inland northern California.

HISTORY OF THE PEOPLE

Early History The Hmong can be grouped in many ways, including by the typical color or design of their clothing. According to Hmong legend, these divisions developed as a result of ancient Chinese conquerors who forced the Hmong to split into different groups and to identify themselves by wearing distinctive clothing. White, Black, Flowery, Red, Striped, and Cowry Shell are some of these divisions. Another method of identifying subgroups is by their dialect. Most Hmong Americans are speakers of either *Hmoob Dawb* ("White Hmong") or *Moob Leeg* (no English translation). Though the *Moob Leeg* do not identify themselves as such, the White Hmong call them the Blue Hmong or the Green Hmong. This does not mean that most Hmong Americans are members of the White or Blue/Green color group, because the linguistic and color distinctions overlap and cut across groups. The kin group is a more important identifier than language or color affiliation.

Chinese historical sources indicate that the Hmong have lived in China since 2000 BCE. Many scholars believe that they may have dwelled in Siberia prior to this date because blond hair and blue eyes are occasionally found among the Hmong. For centuries, the Hmong, who lived in the mountainous regions of southern China, struggled against the Chinese government to maintain their distinctive ethnic identity. In the 1700s Chinese generals convinced Sonom, the last Hmong king, to surrender, promising him that his people would be treated well and that his surrender would bring an honorable peace to the mountains. Instead, Sonom was taken to Beijing, where he, his officers, and his advisors were tortured to death in the presence of the Chinese emperor.

After China was defeated by the British in the first Opium War (1842), the imperial Chinese government was forced to pay indemnities to the victors. To raise money, the government of China levied heavy taxes on its subjects, thus increasing tension between Chinese authorities and the Hmong minority. Between 1850 and 1880, the Hmong waged a series of wars against the Chinese. Unsuccessful in their rebellion, the Hmong fled southward; the majority settled in Laos, although many migrated to Vietnam and Thailand.

Modern Era In Laos the Hmong met new oppressors—the French—who had claimed Vietnam, Laos, and Cambodia as part of their vast Indochinese empire. French taxation led to two major revolts against the French by the Hmong, one in 1896 and another in the 1920s. (The second revolt was initiated by Pa Chay, who called for the establishment of an independent Hmong kingdom and remains a hero to many Hmong today.)

> Being an American is really espousing the founding principles of freedom, no matter whether you speak the language or not. ... And I think the Hmong. ... know in their hearts that these principles are what they have fought for, even in Laos—the basic principles of freedom.
>
> Mouachou Mouanoutoua in 1988, cited in *Hmong Means Free: Life in Laos and America*, edited by Sucheng Chan (Philadelphia: Temple University Press, 1994).

In an effort to pacify the Hmong, the French established an autonomous Hmong district that was allowed to partake in self-government. This created competition, however, between the heads of two prominent families in the district, one headed by Fong and the other by Bliayao. In 1922 a feud broke out between them over which group would rule the district. To defuse the perilous situation, the French organized a democratic election for chief of the district in 1938. Touby Lyfong, the son of Fong, won the election, defeating his cousin Faydag Lobliayao, the son of Bliayao. The subsequent rivalry between these two men and their followers led to the permanent political separation of the Hmong in Laos. Touby Lyfong made common cause with the French and later allied himself with the Americans in their fight against the North Vietnamese. Faydang Lobliayao, on the other hand, joined forces with the Lao nationalists, who favored total independence from France; he later became an important leader of the Lao communist forces.

The United States became involved in Southeast Asia to preserve a noncommunist regime in South Vietnam. Because the *Pathet Lao*, the communist guerrillas of Laos, were allied with North Vietnam's *Viet Minh* (later known as the *Viet Cong*), the United States provided economic and tactical support to the royal Lao government to fight the guerrillas as well as North Vietnamese troops. Many of the individuals recruited by the U.S. government were Hmong, led by Vang Pao, an anticommunist Hmong military leader who had earlier assisted the French. According to many sources, the Central Intelligence Agency (CIA) officials who organized the Hmong army promised the soldiers, who numbered 40,000 by 1969, that the United States would resettle the Hmong if they were defeated.

After American troops were withdrawn from Indochina in 1973, the Lao government was forced to negotiate with its enemies and to bring the pro-North Vietnamese leftists into a coalition government. Following the fall of South Vietnam in April 1975, the leftists in Laos consolidated their political power, the royal government crumbled, the king abdicated his throne, and the Lao People's Democratic Republic was declared. Despite General Vang Pao's insistence that the United States resettle all of the Hmong soldiers, the U.S. government evacuated only about one thousand Hmong in the first year.

The new Laotian government sent many Hmong to harsh reeducation camps. Others fled deep into the jungle, and some continued to fight against the Lao government. Still other Hmong made their way across the border into Thailand, where they stayed in refugee camps for months, sometimes even years. The Thai government has often seen these refugees as a burden. Following talks among the governments of Laos and Thailand and the United Nations' High Commission for Refugees, in the early 1990s the Lao government agreed to take back all of the 50,000 to 60,000 Hmong refugees in Thailand. However, few Hmong agreed to return. Thailand has provoked controversy on several occasions for attempting to forcibly return the Hmong to Laos. At the end of 2009, the *New York Times* reported that the Thai military was preparing to forcibly return 4,000 Hmong refugees.

SETTLEMENT IN THE UNITED STATES

The first wave of Hmong immigration to the United States took place in the late 1970s. In December 1975 the United States agreed to begin resettling

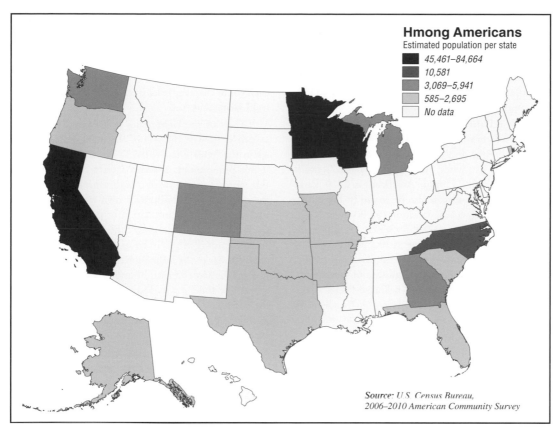

Hmong Americans
Estimated population per state

- 45,461–84,664
- 10,581
- 3,069–5,941
- 585–2,695
- No data

Source: U.S. Census Bureau, 2006–2010 American Community Survey

the Hmong in America and Congress admitted 3,466 individuals. In 1976, 10,200 refugees from Laos (who had fled across the border into Thailand) were admitted to the United States, The number of Laotian immigrants then dipped to only 400 in 1977 before climbing to 8,000 in 1978, when an estimated 30,000 Hmong lived in the United States. The second wave began after the U.S. Congress passed the Refugee Act of 1980, which established policies and programs for the entry and resettlement of refugees. By the early 1980s, about 58,000 Hmong were living in the United States, and this second wave grew throughout the decade. By the time of the 1990 U.S. Census, estimates of Hmong living in the United States had increased to 94,439 people. The U.S. Hmong population doubled again in the 1990s, reaching a census count of 186,310 in 2000, although some Hmong spokespeople maintained that this was an undercount.

The second wave had largely ended by 1995. Most of the population growth since then has been through Hmong children born in the United States, though a small number of refugees have continued to be admitted to the United States. In 2003, following controversy over one of Thailand's efforts at forcible repatriation of Hmong in Thai refugee camps, the United States agreed to accept an additional 15,000 Hmong refugees. By 2010, according to estimates from the American Community Survey of the

U.S. Census, about 56 percent of Hmong Americans had been born in the United States. Among those younger than eighteen, an estimated 87 percent were American-born. In a very short period of time, the Hmong had become a new native-born American minority.

American refugee resettlement agencies dispersed the twelve traditional Hmong groups all over the country, placing clusters in fifty-three different cities and twenty-five different states, where voluntary agencies such as churches could be found to sponsor the refugees. Between 1981 and 1985, Hmong who were scattered around the nation reassembled through a massive secondary migration, making their way across the country in small family groups. Drawn by the lure of reforming their kin-based society and by the moderate climate of the Pacific Coast, many of these internal migrants congregated in farming towns and small cities in California.

The Minneapolis–St. Paul area in Minnesota was the center of Hmong America in the 1980s because of the great involvement of volunteer agencies, and it has retained this status. According to the 2010 U.S. Census, the region was home to more than 53,000 Hmong Americans, or one-quarter of the total immigrant group in the United States. Milwaukee, Wisconsin, also has a large Hmong concentration. The 2010 U.S. Census estimated that 6 percent, or about 12,000, of the nation's Hmong resided in the area. According to the 2010 census data, other midwestern metropolitan regions with notable Hmong populations included Appleton-Oshkosh-Neenah in Wisconsin (about 5,500); Wausau, Wisconsin (5,300); Detroit, Michigan (3,700); Sheboygan, Wisconsin (3,600); Lacrosse, Wisconsin (3,600); and Madison, Wisconsin (3,500).

Beyond the Midwest, northern California has become another focus of Hmong settlement, particularly Fresno and Sacramento, which, based on U.S. Census estimates, were each home to between 24,000 and 26,000 Hmong Americans in 2010. Large Hmong populations can also be found in the northern California towns of Stockton (6,900 as of 2010), Merced (6,300), and Chico (3,300). Additionally, North Carolina (9,700 as of 2010, including 5,200 in the Hickory-Morgantown area), Georgia (3,600, including 2,700 in the Atlanta area), and Washington state (3,200, including 2,400 in Seattle-Everett area). At least some Hmong Americans live in virtually every state in the United States.

Among the motivations for moving to northern California and other less-urban areas was to recover some of the traditional way of life through farming. The Hmong met with little success in this effort, though. By 2010 their most common occupations, as listed in the American Community Survey data, were as assemblers of electrical equipment, cashiers, machine operators, nursing aides and attendants, cooks, and laborers. The occupational distribution of American-born and younger Hmong was similar to that of immigrants and older people. The Hmong also had very high rates of nonparticipation in the labor force. About 28 percent of working-age people (twenty-five to sixty-five years old) were not in the labor force.

LANGUAGE

The primary dialect spoken by the Hmong in the United States is either *Hmoob Dawb* ("White Hmong") or *Moob Leeg* (no English translation). *Hmoob Dawb* speakers refer to *Moob Leeg* speakers as *Hmoob Ntsaub*, Blue/Green Hmong. Hmong is monosyllabic and tonal, meaning that it consists mainly of one-syllable words and that the sound of a word affects meaning. Hmong uses eight different tones, more than the average of other Asian tonal languages.

According to Hmong oral tradition, the Hmong lost their original writing system after joining the Chinese Empire, and any Hmong caught using that system was punished with death. Women of the tribes tried to keep the alphabet alive by sewing the letters into the patterns of their traditional clothes. Portions of this alphabet can be found on Hmong clothing today, but few people are capable of reading these carefully preserved designs.

Prior to the mid-twentieth century, those Hmong who could write their language usually did so with Chinese characters. In the 1950s, American and French missionaries in Laos developed the Romanized Popular Alphabet (RPA), a means of writing Hmong with a version of the alphabet used by English and other Western European languages. Because Hmong is substantially different from European languages, however, some characteristics of the RPA are not familiar to English speakers.

Each of the eight tones is indicated by a consonant written at the end of the word. For example, when the letter *b* is written at the end of a word, it is not pronounced; it serves merely to indicate that this word is spoken with a high tone. The letter *j* at the end of a word indicates a high-falling tone, a bit like the descending intonation or pitch of "day-o" in the popular Caribbean song "The Banana Boat Song." A word ending in *v* is to be spoken with a mid-rising tone, similar to the intonation at the end of a question in English. Moreover, at the end of a word, *s* indicates a mid-low tone, *g* a mid-low, breathy tone, and *m* at the end of a word a low, glottalized tone that is vocalized through a tensing of the throat. Words ending in *d* have a low-rising tone.

Most of the vowels and consonants that do not occur at the ends of words have pronunciations similar to those of Western European languages, but there are some differences. The consonant *x* is pronounced like the English *s*, while *s* is pronounced like the English *sh*. Likewise, *z* in the RPA has the sound of the *s* in "leisure." The Hmong *r* has no equivalent in English, but is closer to the English *t* or *d* than to the English *r*. The consonant *c* in this writing system has a sound similar to those of *t* and *y* if the phrase "quit you" is pronounced very rapidly. The consonant *q* is like the English *k* or *g* but is pronounced farther back in the throat. Finally, *w* has a tone that linguists call the "schwa," the vowel sound in the word "but," and *aw* is a longer version of this, somewhat like the vowel resonance in "mud."

Because Hmong Americans are so new to the United States, their ability to speak their ancestral language is still common. According to U.S. Census data, in 2010 over 90 percent of Hmong reported that they spoke a Hmong language at home, while only 8 percent said they spoke English at home (most of the others reported using Thai or Lao). Most Hmong today are bilingual. Only 11 percent of Hmong under the age of eighteen said that they spoke English exclusively. However, traditional Hmong culture is largely oral, and most Hmong have only limited reading and writing abilities in their own language. While there are efforts to teach reading in Hmong at community centers in regions such as Minneapolis–St. Paul, younger Hmong are attaining most of their literacy in American schools in English.

Greetings and Popular Expressions The White Hmong phrases below are written in the RPA. Therefore, in words that end in consonants, the final consonant is not pronounced. It indicates the tone with which the word should be spoken.

Koj tuaj los?

> You've come?

Kuv tuaj.

> I've come.

Mus ho tuaj.

> Come again.

Tus no yog leej twg tub?

> Whose son is this?

Tus no yog leej tus ntxhais?

> Whose daughter is this?

Tus no yog leej tus pojniam?

> Whose wife is this?

Tus no yog leej tus txiv?

> Whose husband is this?

Koj nyob qhov twg?

> Where do you live?

Nyob. Wb tham mentsis tso maj.

> Stay, and we'll chat a little first.

Qhov no yog dabtsi?

> What's this?

RELIGION

The cult of spirits, shamanism, and ancestor worship compose the three major parts of traditional Hmong religion. It is a pantheistic religion, teaching that there are spirits residing in all things. According to Hmong religious beliefs, the world consists of two parts: the invisible world of *yeeb ceeb*, which holds the spirits, and the visible world of *yaj ceeb*, which holds human beings, material objects, and nature.

The shaman is important because he can make contact with the world of the spirits. Each shaman has a set of spirits that serve as his allies in intervening with the unseen world on behalf of others. Certain spirits, particularly those of ancestors, also make themselves accessible to people who are not shamans. Some households, for example, place spoonfuls of rice and pork in the center of the table at family get-togethers, thereby inviting the spirits to share in the feast. Because women are most often in charge of medicinal herbs, they are responsible for propitiating the spirits of healing on special altars.

Some Hmong Americans adhere to the *Chao Fa* (in Lao, literally "Lord of the Sky") religion. It is said to have begun in Laos in the 1960s when a Hmong prophet, Yang Chong Leu (sometimes written as Shang Lue Yang), announced that the Hmong would be sent a king who would lead them to salvation from their enemies, provided they rejected lowland Laotian and Western ways and returned to the traditions of their ancestors. Yang Chong Leu also taught an original system of writing known as *Pahawh Hmong*, which

A Hmong American couple enjoys the Hmong Sports Festival at McMurray Field in St. Paul, Minnesota. STEVE SKJOLD / ALAMY

is still used by adherents to *Chao Fa*. The prophet was killed in 1971, but his followers continued to grow in numbers and were active in the fight against the new Laotian government after 1975.

Missionaries from a wide variety of Christian denominations converted many Hmong in Laos. Even more Hmong converted to Christianity after arriving in the United States. Baptists, Catholics, Presbyterians, members of the Church of Christ, Mormons, and Jehovah's Witnesses have all been energetic in seeking converts among the Hmong in the United States. Although it is difficult to say exactly how many Hmong Americans are Christian, estimates by Hmong organizations and agencies suggest that about half professed Christianity by 2010. Since religion is regarded as the foundation of life among the Hmong, conversion has been among the most drastic social changes. In many cases, conversion to Christianity has split families, with some members taking up the new faith and others adhering to traditional beliefs. Marriage, in particular, has been affected by religious conversion since many traditional Hmong practices, such as the bridal price, arranged marriage, and the marriage of girls, are strongly discouraged by Christian churches.

CULTURE AND ASSIMILATION

Hmong Americans generally view their new country positively, and younger generations tend to understand both cultures quite well. However, there is a general ignorance of the Hmong on the part of most Americans, who find it difficult to distinguish them from the Vietnamese or other Asian groups. Insofar as stereotypes have arisen, the Hmong are often seen as hardworking but also extremely foreign. Many Americans are also perplexed by the rituals of the Hmong and by the music that often accompanies them. Nonetheless, Hmong Americans tend to be friendly to members of other groups and welcome attempts on the part of outsiders to learn more about their culture. The Hmong themselves are rapidly becoming an American minority, rather than an alien group, in American society. As of 2010, about one-third of the Hmong in the United States were born in this country, according to U.S. Census data. Thus, the number of Hmong Americans who have personal memories of Laos is decreasing rapidly.

Many Hmong customs are not practiced in the United States, especially by those who have converted to Christianity. As might be expected in a group that has experienced such rapid social change, Hmong Americans are still trying to sort out which traditions may be retained in the new land and which must be left behind.

Traditions and Customs The Hmong have a primarily oral culture in which ancient traditions are conveyed through tales. In recent years, efforts have been made to record and preserve the Hmong's ancient stories as younger members of the ethnic group are drawn into the media offerings of American culture. One of the most comprehensive collections is the large, bilingual volume *Myths, Legends, and Folktales from the Hmong of Laos* (1985), edited by Charles Johnson.

The stories told by the Hmong date back to before the group became part of the Chinese Empire. Magic, supernatural events, and spirits occupy a prominent place in these stories. As in the folktales of other nations, animals can often talk, and people are occasionally transformed into animals and vice versa. Reincarnation is common, with characters sometimes reappearing after their deaths. Many Hmong stories convey moral lessons, relaying happy outcomes for honest, hardworking, and virtuous individuals and unfortunate endings for the evil, lazy, or selfish.

These stories express the Hmong tradition of a reality divided into material and spirit worlds. Shamans act as intermediaries between these two realms, performing important rituals to promote benefits and counteract evils coming from the spirit world. Hmong men or women are often identified as shamans when they exhibit signs of physical or mental illness. Thus, behavior that other Americans might identify as insanity may be seen by the Hmong as indicating special spiritual gifts. Shamanism is often inherited through family lines.

Mus Thawj thiab ("go become again," or more simply "reincarnation") is a traditional Hmong belief. Thus, every newborn is seen as a reincarnated soul. Children officially have a soul and, therefore, join human society three days after they are born. If a child dies before the three days pass, no funeral ceremonies are held. After three days of life, a shaman evokes a soul to be reincarnated in the baby's body. The family's ancestors are called upon to join the living family members in blessing the incarnation and in protecting the baby. The baby is then given a silver necklace that is supposed to keep the newly reincarnated soul from wandering. Some Hmong Americans still follow this custom.

Hmong society is organized by clans. Every family belongs to the clan of its father, and women join the clan of the men they marry. The ties among clan members are strong and require mutual support and help. Clan leaders are key figures, providing direction and helping to resolve quarrels. The clan structure continues to be important for Hmong Americans, but it is weakening among those born in the United States.

Cuisine White rice is the staple food of the Hmong. The dishes eaten with rice are often spiced with peppers in a manner similar to Thai food. The Hmong also eat noodle dishes that resemble a Vietnamese noodle soup known as *pho*, which has become popular in the United States. Common meat dishes include broiled chicken, lemongrass marinated pork, and sautéed chicken. The Hmong Americans often grow their own vegetables in gardens, including bitter melon, bok choi, eggplant, and turnips. Traditional foods are especially popular among Hmong Americans at the annual New Year festival.

Traditional Dress The Hmong's *Paj Ntaub*, or flowered clothes, are famous for their embroidery. Though heavily embroidered dresses and turbans characterize traditional dress among all the female Hmong, their clothing generally differs according to region and group. Striped Hmong women traditionally wear black or blue stripes on their sleeves; they may also wear black pants with aprons in front and back and a silver necklace. Green or Blue Hmong women often wear black aprons with blue center panels, and their turbans or headdresses often have pom-poms. Green Hmong women often wear short embroidered skirts with leggings, an apron, and silver necklaces. White Hmong women may wear a white or pleated skirt with a black apron. The attire of Hmong men also differs according to group and location, but it typically involves pajama-like pants that vary in length and bagginess. Hmong men also wear sashes around the waist as part of their traditional dress. In the United States, the Hmong usually wear their traditional clothes only on special occasions.

Traditional Arts and Crafts For centuries, Hmong women have practiced an elaborate needlecraft known as *paj ntaub* (also frequently spelled *pa ndau*). This art combines the techniques of embroidery and applique to produce colorful, abstract, geometric designs. The needlecraft is done entirely by hand, without the use of instruments even for measurement. After arriving in the refugee camps in Thailand, the Hmong began to put this ancient craft to a new and more explicitly representational use, drawing scenes of the life they had left behind them in Laos and sewing them into tapestries. Often known as "story cloths," these tapestries have become symbols of Hmong identity. *Paj ntaub* is commonly practiced among Hmong American women, and their work has become popular in the United States, especially in areas with significant Hmong populations.

The Hmong also make musical instruments. Chief among these is the *keej*, an L-shaped wind instrument with a reed made of bamboo pipes. The musicians dance while they play ancient ceremonial songs on these instruments. Other instruments made by the Hmong include the *raj*, or flute, and the *ncas*, which is a type of jaw harp. These instruments are still made and used in Hmong American communities.

Dances and Songs Dancing is an important part of Hmong culture. Among Hmong Americans, festive occasions such as the New Year celebration invariably include traditional dances. These involve using the feet and hips and, especially, the hands and wrists. The dances, usually performed by younger women, are interpretive. Some tell stories about Hmong life, using hand gestures to depict activities such as farming, digging, or picking flowers. In dances that accompany love songs, the performers may bring their hands to the chest and then move them forward before finally forming a circle with them to indicate togetherness.

Hmong poetry is typically sung and is part of many rituals, including courtship and funerals. Since it is a way of singing chanted words, traditional Hmong poetry is often referred to as "poetry chanting." Some younger Hmong Americans have combined the style of the poetry chant with popular American musical forms such as hip hop.

Holidays The New Year Festival (*noj peb caug*) is the most important Hmong American holiday. In Laos, this holiday begins with the crowing of the first rooster on the first day of the new moon in the twelfth month, or harvest time, and lasts four to seven days. The scheduling is somewhat more flexible in the United States—though it takes place at least around the time of the new moon in December—and the holiday does not usually last as long. The only holiday shared by the entire Hmong American community, the New Year Festival brings different families together.

The purpose of the New Year ceremonies is to banish the evil influences of the old year and to invoke good fortune for the new one. The "world renewal ritual" is central to the holiday. It involves a small tree that is traditionally brought in from the forest (although Hmong Americans may use a green stick as a symbolic tree) and is placed in the ground at the celebration site. One end of a rope is tied to the top of the tree and the other is held by a participant or tied to a rock. Holding a live chicken, an elder stands near the tree and chants; everyone else circles the tree three times clockwise and four times counter-clockwise. The chanting during the clockwise movement is intended to remove the accumulated bad fortune of the previous year, while the chanting during the counter-clockwise movement brings out good fortune. The evil fortune, in the traditional perspective, is believed to accumulate in the blood of the chicken. After the participants have finished circling the tree, the elder is supposed to take the chicken to a remote place in the forest and cut its throat to take away the evil influences. This practice, however, is frequently not carried out in the United States.

Other rituals associated with the New Year ceremonies involve calling home the ancestral spirits to enjoy the festivities with the living and offering sacrifices to the guardian spirits of each house. For Hmong Americans, the New Year serves as an opportunity to reaffirm their culture and to teach their children about their traditions. Therefore, New Year celebrations in the United States usually involve displays of traditional cultural practices, such as dances, that are intended to educate American-born Hmong children. Aspects of Western culture, such as performances by rock bands, have been integrated into the ceremonies. Many New Year exhibitions feature a merging of new and old, as when young Hmong women participate in beauty pageants wearing their elaborate traditional dresses.

Because the New Year holiday brings together people from different clans, it is considered an important occasion for young men and women to meet each other. A game called *pov pob*, in which long lines of prospective couples toss a ball back and forth, is a colorful tradition that has survived in the United States. A player who drops the ball must give a token to a player of the opposite sex in the other line. The token can be reclaimed by singing a love song to the other player.

Health Care and Practices Traditional Hmong methods for healing, including the use of herbal medicines and massage, are based on shamanism. Shamanistic health practices stem from the belief that illness is essentially spiritual in nature. For this reason, some Western students of Hmong shamanism have characterized it as a form of psychotherapy.

members may be able to perform the rituals. If a baby cries during the night, for example, an adult family member may go to the door and swing a burning stick back and forth in order to light a path back for the child's soul. In more serious illnesses, a shaman is needed to perform rituals that typically include animal sacrifices.

Lost souls may also be found by someone who has a *neng*, a healing spirit in his own body. The *neng* and the healing skills that accompany it must be inherited from a clan member. A healer who has a *neng* is not only capable of finding a lost soul but can also cure an illness caused by an evil spirit, frequently by engaging in battle with that spirit.

The Hmong, particular women, have a great knowledge of curative herbs, and most Hmong households in the United States have small herbal gardens. Herbs and massages are often combined to treat ailments such as stomach aches.

While the Hmong are, generally speaking, a healthy people, Hmong Americans attracted nationwide attention during the late 1970s and 1980s as victims of Sudden Unexpected Nocturnal Death Syndrome. Similar to Sudden Infant Death Syndrome, the illness strikes during sleep. The mysterious fatalities occurred almost exclusively among males, most of whom showed no prior signs of illness. Physicians have connected the disease to breathing difficulties, but many Hmong ascribe it to an evil spirit that sits on the chests of victims during slumber.

Western-style health care professionals often have difficulty winning the confidence of Hmong patients because their concepts of illness are so different. Experts on the subject contend that doctors, nurses, and other health care providers who work with the Hmong must try to better understand the group's approach to healing. Some of these experts have also pointed out that the Hmong, with their intimate knowledge of herbal medicines, have much to teach American doctors.

Death and Burial Rituals Before the Hmong came to the United States, the death of a family member was announced by firing three shots into the air. This action was thought to frighten away evil spirits. Today, this tradition is rarely followed by Hmong Americans because of U.S. laws regulating the use of guns in populated areas.

The body of the deceased is washed, dressed in new clothes, and left to lie in state. Mourners bearing gifts visit the deceased's home, where they are fed by family members. A shaman makes an offering of a cup of alcohol to the dead person and tells the soul that the body has died. Colorful bits of paper, representing money for use in the spirit world, are burned, and the shaman tells the soul the route it must follow to reach ancestors and how to avoid dangers during the journey.

Recreational Activities Many Hmong American men enjoy recreational activities with origins in their

Hmong teens at the Hmong Sports Festival at McMurray Field in St. Paul, MN. STEVE SKJOLD / ALAMY

In shamanism, the world is composed of two parts: the visible and invisible. The visible is the material reality we see around us; the invisible is the realm of spirits, such as the souls of the living, the spirits of the dead, and caretaker and malevolent spirits. The shaman is capable of making contact with the spirit world and dealing with it on the behalf of others.

The Hmong recognize that illnesses come from many sources, so the method of treatment depends on the cause. For example, an illness may derive from the loss of one's spirit or soul. Fear, loneliness, separation from loved ones, and other emotional stresses can rip the soul away from the body, leading to a variety of physical symptoms, such as loss of weight and appetite, that usually reflect a more serious disease.

The "soul-caller" is among the most important roles in traditional Hmong health care. There are many methods of calling a wandering soul back to its body. In less serious illnesses, parents or other family ancestral lands in Laos, such as hunting and fishing. Hmong people also participate in sports that are popular all over the world, including soccer. Since 1980 Hmong Americans have held an Annual Hmong Freedom Celebration Sports Festival on July 4 in St. Paul, Minnesota.

FAMILY AND COMMUNITY LIFE

While the extended family is the basic unit of social organization for the Hmong in Asia, it is more difficult to maintain this structure in the United States. Large numbers of people cannot live together under one roof in the United States due to fire and housing codes. Hmong Americans, therefore, have had to break up into nuclear-style families. However, extended family members almost always live near each other and assist newcomers with living expenses, child care, and adaptation to American society.

Kinship groups, though still recognized, have become less important to Hmong living in the United States. Respected elders previously took their functions from the rituals they performed in traditional ceremonies. Since the conversion of some Hmong to Christianity, however, these ceremonies have become less common. Furthermore, many of the ceremonies require the sacrifice of animals, which is often illegal— or, at the very least, frowned upon—in the United States. Many elders are gradually being replaced by newer and younger leaders who are well educated and fluent in English and are, therefore, better able to help their families and other Hmong understand the nuances of American society. Newer leaders, however, rely on the moral authority and blessings of the elders, who are still held in high regard.

The ways in which Hmong American parents raise their children reflect their situation as new immigrants. They do not want the enculturation of their children taken completely out of their hands, and the language and ways of their ancestors are viewed as worthy social attributes. Young Hmong Americans, however, sometimes have difficulty comprehending the relevance of the cultural values that their parents hold so dear. As a result of this generation gap, some social workers say that the rising rate of teenage runaways has become a major issue among Hmong Americans and other refugee groups from Southeast Asia.

By American standards, Hmong families are large. The average Hmong family in 2010 contained six family members, according to U.S. Census figures. With such large families, the Hmong American population has grown rapidly and has skewed young. In 2010 half the Hmong population of the United States was younger than twenty.

Gender Roles Among Hmong Americans, men are generally regarded as the head of the family. Nonetheless, women often wield a great deal of power, primarily because many of their duties revolve around the household, where small children are regarded as

HMONG PROVERBS

Hlais nqaij ntshaw zoo riam; ua neej nyob ntshaw zoo pojniam.

> To slice meat, you need a good knife; to have a good life, you need a good wife.

Ib koog hav zoov muaj ib tug ntoo ntev; ib cuab kwvtij muaj ib tug ntse.

> Each jungle has one tree that's tallest; each group of clanmates has one who's smartest.

Ib koog hav zoov muaj ib tug ntoo loj; ib cuab kwvtij muaj ib tug coj.

> Each jungle has one tree that's biggest; each group of clanmates has one who's the leader.

Niam tshuab ntuag; txiv qaiv (khaiv) ntxaiv.

> The wife is the loom; the husband hangs the thread.

Niam mloog txiv qhuab; txiv mloog niam hais.

> The wife listens to the husband's lessons; the husband listens to the wife's opinions.

Noj txiv yuav saib noob; yuav tabzag saib caj Hmoob

> Eat fruit, watch out for the seed; marry spouse, look at the lineage.

Noj nqaij yuav saib txha; yuav tabzag saib neejtsa

> Eat meat, watch out for the bone; marry spouse, look at the relatives.

Txawj ntos tsis qeg txia; Txawj hais tsis qeg lus.

> Able to weave, don't waste thread; able to speak, don't waste words.

Pos ntse tsis yuav hliav; neeg ntse tsis yuav piav.

> No need to sharpen a thorn; no need to explain to a smart person.

Tsuas muaj tus ntses lawv tus dej; tsis muaj tus dej lawv tus ntses.

> There are only fish that follow the river; there are no rivers that follow the fish.

Plaub hau ntxhov thiaj yuav zuag los ntsis; plaub ntug ntxhov thiaj yuav txwj laus los lis.

> Tangled hair, use a comb to unsnarl it; complicated dispute, use an elder to solve it.

treasures. As the chief providers of care for children, Hmong American women can be extremely influential in their communities.

In Laos the Hmong recognized divorce, but it was a rare occurrence. In the United States divorce has become more common, as influences from American society and the entry of women into the labor force have created pressures on traditional gender roles, especially between husbands and wives.

Education In Laos formal education played a small part in the lives of most Hmong, who lived in a mainly oral culture and supported themselves through farming, hunting, and fishing. Children learned their life skills from their elders, who also passed on cultural knowledge.

Given this tradition, many of the difficulties faced by Hmong Americans result from inadequate educational preparation. Nearly one-third of Hmong Americans over the age of twenty-five and had less than a fifth-grade education in 2010, according to U.S. Census data, and about 40 percent were not high school graduates. This did, however, represent a substantial educational gain from 1990, when nearly 55 percent of Hmong Americans over the age of twenty-five had less than a fifth-grade education and nearly 70 percent were not high school graduates. Ironically, Hmong born or raised in the United States have shown surprisingly high rates of college attendance. By 2010, according to the U.S. Census, an estimated 40 percent of Hmong Americans ages eighteen to twenty-four were in college, a percentage higher than those of white and black Americans.

Courtships and Weddings Traditionally, young people in Laos most often met potential mates during the New Year celebration, which brought together people from different villages. Young women wore their most colorful skirts and showed off their sewing and embroidery skills, while young men displayed their horse-riding and other abilities, sometimes even playing musical instruments to serenade their love interests. Men generally married between the ages of eighteen and thirty, while women were between fourteen and eighteen.

Traditional Hmong marriages required the prospective groom to secure a go-between, most often a relative, who bargained with the young woman's family for a bridal price, usually paid in silver bars. Marriages were made public by a two-day feast that featured a roasted pig. This feast symbolically joined the clans of the bride and groom, as well as the bride and groom themselves.

When a suitor could not reach an agreement on bridal price with a woman's family, the couple sometimes eloped. This practice became especially common after World War II when the social disruptions of war loosened parental control. Following the elopement, outside arbitrators helped to find an acceptable bridal price to pay in settlement.

Though always regarded as a serious transgression by the Hmong, young men with poor marriage prospects might have attempted to abduct a woman and force her into marriage. Families without formidable kin groups to back them could not always prevent this from happening to their daughters. Usually the abductor and his relatives would offer the unwilling bride's family some form of payment in hopes of mollification. The government in Laos did not intervene in such situations, but the U.S. government does. Naturally, the practice has become extremely rare in the United States.

Although most Hmong men had just one wife, polygyny was an accepted practice. During the war in Laos in the 1960s and early 1970s, polygyny became common due to a custom that required Hmong men to marry the widows of their dead brothers in order to provide a means of support for the brothers' families. Wealthy men often had several wives as symbols of affluence. Moreover, leaders sometimes used polygyny to establish many political alliances.

U.S. culture and laws have made it necessary for the Hmong to change many of their attitudes and practices regarding marriage. There have, however, been rare instances of young Hmong American men kidnapping and sexually assaulting young females. The use of negotiators to arrange marriages remains fairly common among Hmong Americans, though many women now wait until their late teens or early twenties to marry. Surveys of Hmong Americans indicate that the majority believe it is best for women to delay marriage until they are at least eighteen years old. Polygyny is rare among Hmong Americans.

Relations with Other Americans Hmong Americans interact most closely with ethnic Laotian Americans, with whom they work in a number of Southeast Asian refugee assistance organizations. Most Hmong who grew up in Laos or had some schooling there speak Laotian, which facilitates interaction with Laotian Americans. The Hmong also maintain friendly relationships with members of most other groups, but intermarriage is relatively rare because of the continued importance of kinship groups. According to the 2010 U.S. Census, the wives of over 97 percent of married Hmong men were also Hmong, as were the husbands of over 94 percent of married Hmong women.

Conflicts that exist between Hmong Americans and other Americans are often rooted in cultural differences. In 2004, for example, a Hmong American truck driver named Chai Soua Vang made national news when he shot eight people, killing six of them. Vang had been hunting deer on private land and apparently got into an argument with other hunters who asked him to leave. Some accounts suggest that he did not understand that hunting can be forbidden on open land and that he saw the other hunters as threatening and disrespectful.

Negative attitudes toward Hmong youth have arisen in some parts of California, Wisconsin, and Minnesota because of gang activity. Although Hmong gangs usually fight amongst themselves, they have been viewed as a criminal element by other residents in these regions.

Philanthropy As relatively recent settlers in the United States, the Hmong have focused on supporting each other. The Hmong Community Foundation, associated with the Minnesota Council on Foundations, collects contributions from Hmong Americans to address challenges facing members of the group. The Hmong Women's Giving Circle, started by a group of women in Minnesota in 2004, collects funds for distribution to Hmong community groups and is especially interested in efforts to improve the situations of Hmong girls and women.

Surnames Hmong surnames are based on clan membership and are passed on from fathers to children. Although women join the clans of their husbands at marriage, they retain the surnames of their own fathers. Some common clan surnames are: Lis (usually spelled "Ly" in English), Xyooj ("Xiong"), Vaaj ("Vang"), Tsab ("Chang"), Koo ("Kong"), Faaj ("Fang"), Muas ("Moua"), and Yaaj ("Yang").

EMPLOYMENT AND ECONOMIC CONDITIONS

Adjusting to life in a highly industrialized society has not been easy for the Hmong, but they have made notable advances. In 1990, according to the U.S. Census, almost two-thirds of Hmong Americans (63.6 percent) lived below the poverty level. By 2010 an estimated 30 percent of Hmong lived below the poverty level, a rate that, though still high, had declined sharply.

The traditional Hmong occupation of farming led some immigrants to settle as clans on farmland. However, they met with little success in these efforts. By 2010, according to the U.S. Census, under 2 percent of Hmong in the labor force were working in agricultural production in crops or livestock. Instead, they had become concentrated in manufacturing, service, and retail occupations. The most common occupations among Hmong American men in 2010 were (in order) assemblers of electrical equipment, machine operators, cooks, manual laborers, cashiers, wood lathe and planning machine operators, truck and tractor drivers, stock and inventory clerks, and retail sales clerks. Among women the most common occupations were assemblers of electrical equipment, cashiers, nursing aides, waitresses, machine operators, retail sales clerks, customer service representatives, hand packers and packagers, and food preparation workers.

Reports from agencies concerned with the Hmong indicate that the group was hit hard by the recession that began in 2008 because of its concentration in manufacturing occupations. Nevertheless, Hmong Americans had an unemployment rate similar to that of other Americans in 2010: a little over 8 percent. However, Hmong Americans had somewhat high rates of nonparticipation in the labor force, meaning that they were neither employed nor seeking employment. About 17 percent of working-age men and 33 percent of working-age women were outside the labor force. The large proportion of women was probably due primarily to the continuing influence of traditional gender roles on Hmong culture.

Part of the Hmong adaptation to the American economy is rooted in the demand for their traditional handicrafts. For centuries Hmong women have practiced the elaborate needlecraft known as *paj ntaub* (also frequently spelled *pa ndau*), which combines the techniques of embroidery and applique to produce colorful, abstract, and geometric designs. During the 1980s, the cottage industry of *paj ntaub*—which had been forged in the Thailand refugee camps—emerged in large Hmong American communities, especially in California. Responding to the American marketplace, Hmong artisans began to produce bedspreads, pillowcases, wall hangings, and other items. This growing industry confirms the cultural value of the Hmong while also demonstrating the economic importance of women to their families and communities. Today, consumers can find Hmong embroidery for sale in all areas with sizeable Hmong populations, and their embroidered works are readily available on websites.

POLITICS AND GOVERNMENT

Since Hmong Americans are so new to the United States, they have only recently begun to become involved in American politics. Those who vote or are politically engaged tend to support the Democratic Party. Mee Moua and Cy Thao, both Democrats, became the first Hmong to be elected to the Minnesota state legislature, in 2002. Understandably, they were strongly supported by the Hmong voters in their districts in and around St. Paul.

Hmong Americans are also passionately concerned with political events in their native land, where the communist party that overthrew the Laotian government has remained in power. Although the government of Laos appears to have moderated its position toward political opponents in recent years, most Hmong remain strongly opposed to the regime. In fact, some American Hmong communities provide economic aid for small groups of Hmong in Laos that are fighting the government. It has been suggested that Hmong Americans have been coerced into making contributions to anticommunist forces in their homelands by groups operating in the United States, but this has not been definitively established.

NOTABLE INDIVIDUALS

Government General Vang Pao (1929–2011) was the leader of the Hmong army in Laos before coming to the United States. In World War II, he joined the French army in Laos and fought against invading Japanese forces. After Laos became independent from France, he continued his military career in the Royal Lao Army. In the 1960s and 1970s, he commanded the Hmong Secret Army, cooperating with the American Central Intelligence Agency in the fight against communists in Laos. He became the most visible political leader of the Hmong in the United States. In 2007 the U.S. government brought charges against him for allegedly plotting to overthrow the government of Laos, a violation of the Neutrality Act. Many Hmong Americans protested the arrest, and the American government dropped its charges against him in 2009. When he died, more than 10,000 Hmong mourned him in a traditional funeral in Glendale, California. He was denied burial at Arlington National Cemetery, but mourners nevertheless held a memorial service for him at the Laos Memorial there.

Mee Moua (1969–) became the first Hmong woman to be elected to a state legislature, in Minnesota in 2002. Born in Xieng Khouang, Laos, Moua arrived in the United States with her family as a refugee when she was five years old, earned a bachelor's degree from Brown University, a master's degree in public health from the University of Texas, and a law degree from the University of Minnesota. During her time on the Minnesota legislature, Moua chaired the judiciary committee. In addition to her work on the state legislature, she served as president and executive director of the Asian American Justice Center.

Medicine Bruce "Thow Pao" Bliatout (1948–) was born in Laos and first came to the United States in 1966 as an exchange student. Among his many achievements, he was director of the TB Prevention and Treatment Center of the Multnomah County Health Department in Oregon. He also served for many years on the board of directors of the Hmong American Association of Oregon. Bliatout is an authority on Sudden Death Syndrome and has written numerous books and articles, including *Hmong Sudden Unexpected Death Syndrome: A Cultural Study* (1982).

Xoua Thao (1962–) arrived in the United States in 1976 at the age of fourteen. Thao's mother is a traditional herbalist, and his father is a shaman. As a result of this family background in healing, Thao developed an interest in medicine and attended medical school at Brown University. He went on to found the Xoua Thao Medical Center in St. Paul, Minnesota, and was cofounder of the Hmong Minnesota Bar Association and the Hmong Chamber of Commerce.

Anthropologist Dia Cha (1962–) is considered one of the nation's foremost authorities on Hmong folkways and culture. She authored the book *Dia's Story Cloth: The Hmong People's Journey of Freedom* (1996) and compiled *Folk Stories of the Hmong* (1991) with Norma Livo.

Zha Blong Xiong (1967–), an associate professor of family social science at the University of Minnesota, became the first Hmong professor in the United States to receive tenure, in 2006. Xiong arrived in the United States in 1982 after three years in a Thai refugee camp. He specialized in bicultural parent-adolescent relations among Southeast Asian immigrant families and in delinquency among immigrant youth.

Stage and Screen Actor Bee Vang (1991–) was born in Fresno, California, to refugee parents. In 2008 he costarred with Clint Eastwood in *Gran Torino*, the first major American film to deal extensively with the issues facing Hmong Americans.

Whitney Cua Her (1992–), also known as Ahney Her, grew up in Lansing, Michigan. She, too, had a major role in the film *Gran Torino*, as the sister of Vang's character.

MEDIA

BROADCAST

KFXN-AM 690, Hmong Radio

This Minnesota-based radio station is geared toward Hmong Americans, offering news, business information, and discussion of public issues. It also has programs devoted Hmong arts and poetry.

1088 Payne Avenue
St. Paul, Minnesota 55130
Phone: (612) 810-6412
URL: www.hmongradioam690.com

Hmong Wisconsin Radio

Broadcasting in the Hmong language twenty-four hours per day, the station provides educational, cultural, and historical information.

337 West Wisconsin Avenue
Suite 6
Appleton, Wisconsin 54911
Phone: (920) 882-2940
URL: www.hmongwisconsinradio.com

Suab Hmong International Broadcasting Company

Based in Milwaukee, Wisconsin, this radio company broadcasts to audiences in a wide range of locations on issues of concern to the Hmong people.

P.O. Box 250886
Milwaukee, Wisconsin 53225
Phone: (224) 333-1132
URL: http://shrdo.com

PRINT

Hmong Times

A newspaper for the Hmong American community, based in St. Paul, Minnesota.

P.O. Box 9068
St. Paul, Minnesota 55109
Phone: (651) 224-9395
URL: www.hmongtimes.com

ORGANIZATIONS AND ASSOCIATIONS

Hmong American Partnership

This organization provides a wide variety of support services to Hmong Americans in the Minneapolis–St. Paul metropolitan area and elsewhere.

Bao Vang, President
1975 Arcade Street
St. Paul, Minnesota 55105
Phone: (651) 495-9160
Fax: (651) 495-1699
Email: hapmail@hmong.org
URL: www.hmong.org

Hmong Council

A community organization serving America's largest Hmong population, the Hmong Council assists with housing problems, language barriers, health and social services, and conflict resolution.

Houa Yang, President
4753 East Olive Avenue
Suite 102
Fresno, California 93702
Phone: (209) 456-1220

Hmong National Development, Inc. (HND)

A national nonprofit organization that promotes the interests of Hmong Americans, the HND facilitates communication among local Hmong organizations and advocates for increased resources to Hmong organizations and communities.

Bao Vang, President
1628 16th Street NW
Washington, D.C. 20009
Phone: (202) 588-1661
Email: bvang@hndinc.org
URL: www.hndinc.org

Lao Family Community of Minnesota

A nonprofit mutual assistance association founded in 1977 as the Hmong Association of Minnesota, it strives to help the Hmong community strike a balance between traditional Hmong culture and modern American life.

Chupheng Lee, President
320 West University Avenue
St. Paul, Minnesota 55103
Phone: (651) 221-0069
Fax: (651) 221-0276
Email: admin@laofamily.org
URL: www.laofamily.org

Lao Family Community Empowerment, Inc.

Provides service and advocacy programs and activities for community engagement and outreach.

Ger Vang, CEO
8338 North West Lane
Suite 101
Stockton, California 95210
Phone: (209) 466-0721
Fax: (209) 466-6567
Email: info@lfcempowerment.org
URL: http://lfcempowerment.org

MUSEUMS AND RESEARCH CENTERS

Hmong Cultural Heritage Center and Museum

The first museum in the United States dedicated to gathering, preserving, and sharing works relating to the history, culture, and art of the Hmong.

550 Shaw Avenue
Fresno, California 93710
Phone: (559) 241-6534
Email: paodirector@hmongnationalmuseum.org

Hmong Cultural Center

The center offers community outreach and cultural education for teaching the Hmong about their history and culture. It has an extensive collection of materials relating to the Hmong and also partners with Hmong Archives to maintain a virtual museum of Hmong embroidery on the website www. HmongEmbroidery.org

995 University Avenue West
Suite 214
St. Paul, Minnesota 55104
Phone: (651) 917-9937
Fax: (651) 917-9978
Email: txong@hmongcc.org
URL: www.hmongcc.org

Southeast Asian Resource Action Center (SEARAC)

SEARAC is a national organization aimed at advancing the interests of Cambodian, Laotian, and Vietnamese Americans. The organization's resource center is one of the best sources of information on these groups.

1626 16th Street NW
Washington, D.C. 20009
Phone: (202) 667-4690
Email: searac@searac.org
URL: www.searac.org

SOURCES FOR ADDITIONAL STUDY

Chan, Sucheng, ed. *Hmong Means Free: Life in Laos and America*. Philadelphia: Temple University Press, 1994.

Hein, Jeremy. *Ethnic Origins: The Adaptation of Cambodian and Hmong Refugees in Four American Cities*. New York: Russell Sage Foundation, 2006.

Her, Vincent K., and Mary Louise Buley-Messner, eds. *Hmong and American: From Refugees to Citizens*. St. Paul: Minnesota Historical Society, 2012.

Keown-Bomar, Julie *Kinship Networks among Hmong American Refugees*. New York: LFB Scholarly Pub., 2004.

Vang, Chia Youvee *Hmong America: Reconstructing Community in Diaspora*. Urbana: University of Illinois Press, 2010.

Vang, Pao. *Against All Odds: The Laotian Freedom Fighters*. Washington, D.C.: Heritage Foundation, 1987.

HONDURAN AMERICANS

William Maxwell

OVERVIEW

Honduran Americans are immigrants or descendants of people from Honduras, a country in the center of Central America. Honduras is bordered to the north by the Caribbean Sea, to the west by Guatemala, to the southwest by El Salvador, to the southeast by Nicaragua, and to the south by the Pacific Ocean. More than three-fourths of the land area of Honduras is mountainous. The total land area of the country is 43,278 square miles (112,090 square kilometers), making it slightly larger than the state of Tennessee.

According to official United States government statistics, as of July 2012 the population of Honduras was 8,296,693. Roman Catholics make up 97 percent of the population, and 3 percent belong to various Protestant denominations. The vast majority of Hondurans, 90 percent, are mestizo (mixed indigenous and European). The next largest group is indigenous peoples (Pueblos Indigenas) at 7 percent, with smaller populations of Afro-descendant (2 percent) and white (1 percent). With 60 percent of the population living below the poverty level, Honduras is the second poorest country in Central America. Exports to the United States account for 30 percent of the country's GDP and remittances for another 20 percent, tying about half of Honduras's economic activity to the United States.

The first wave of Honduran immigrants entered the United States beginning in the early twentieth century in two groups: artists and writers, most of whom were sponsored by institutions or corporations and went to large cities, primarily New York; and working-class immigrants who were employees of Honduran banana companies and settled mostly in New Orleans. After a political coup in 1963 left the livelihood and lives of Liberal Party members in danger, many of the immigrants were male political exiles. A small but significant number of women also immigrated to work in the service industries. When Hurricane Mitch devastated Honduras in 1998, tens of thousands of Honduran immigrants entered the United States under the temporary protection status policy. In November 2011 the policy was extended until July 5, 2013.

According to the U.S. Census Bureau, in 2010 there were 633,401 people of Honduran descent living in the United States, making Honduran Americans the eighth largest Hispanic group in the country. Six in ten Hondurans live in the South, mostly in Florida and Texas. California, New York, and the city of New Orleans also have significant Honduran populations.

HISTORY OF THE PEOPLE

Early History It is not known when the area that is now Honduras was originally settled by humans, but archaeologists have found evidence of a complex society that is at least 3,000 years old. Over the millennia, city-states gradually developed in the vast geographical area that includes large parts of present-day southern Mexico, Guatemala, western El Salvador, and western Honduras. These city-states had many shared cultural characteristics, including a common spoken and written language, and they are collectively referred to as the Maya civilization.

Long before Columbus arrived in 1502 and named the country after the deep water off the Caribbean coast, Honduras was populated by a mixture of indigenous peoples representing various cultures and linguistic groups. The best known and most advanced of these groups, the Maya, developed Copán, a city near what is now the town of Danta Rosa de Copán. The city was a major ceremonial center of the Mayan culture. Scholars believe it was likely of particular importance as a center for astronomical studies and art. Mayan civilization was at its height in the ninth century when the priests and rulers abandoned Copán and the city fell into ruin. Descendants of the Maya remained in western Honduras, calling themselves the Chorti Maya, or simply Chorti, and speaking a language descended from the one that appears on the ancient glyphs in Copán. Other indigenous groups included the Lencas in western-central Honduras; the Tol on the central north coast; the Pech (or Paya), who originally occupied the Bay Island of Roatan; and the Miskito on the Mosquito Coast in northeastern Honduras.

In 1524 Hernan Cortés, conquistador (conqueror) of the Mexican Aztecs, sent Cristóbal de Olid to conquer and rule Honduras in the name of the Spanish crown. When Olid arrived in the region, he seized power for himself and declared independence from Spain. Cortés sent an army to take it back, but Olid was assassinated by rivals before the army arrived.

In the meantime Cortés decided to go to Honduras himself with another army. He consolidated Spanish power over Honduras before returning to Mexico. Shortly thereafter Spain appointed Diego López de Salcedo as the first royal governor of Honduras.

In the eighteenth century, gold and other mineral deposits were found in the central mountains and near the Caribbean coast, and the Spanish colonists employed nearby indigenous people in the mines. As mining expanded, larger numbers of workers had to be found to work in them. Forced labor, forced migration, and severe working conditions resulted in the deaths of large numbers of these indigenous workers. Revolts by these groups then led to massacres at the hands of the armies of the Spanish colonists. Mistreatment and violence against the indigenous peoples remain a problem in Honduras today.

During the seventeenth century Spanish control of Honduras was limited by attacks from pirates, mostly British along with some Dutch and French, who attacked Spanish fleets and in 1643 destroyed the city of Trujillo, then the main shipping port of Honduras. The British found allies in the Miskitu people, to whom they supplied arms to challenge the Spanish. According to some accounts, the Miskito gained their name from the muskets given to them by the British. In 1786 Britain recognized Spanish sovereignty over the Caribbean coast of Honduras, but just over fifty years later, Britain reasserted control over the Bay Islands, an authority Britain retained until 1859.

In the eighteenth century most colonists settled in cities in the highlands near the Pacific coast, including Tegucigalpa and Comayagua. The Caribbean coast was inhabited by the Miskito and Black Carib (and later by banana plantation workers, managers, and owners as well). The Bay Islands were also settled by the Black Caribs, a people created by the mixing of indigenous people with descendants of African runaway or emancipated slaves. Two slave ships wrecked off the island of St. Vincent in 1635. Survivors found sanctuary with the island's Carib Indians, who were themselves immigrants from Guyana, Surinam, and Venezuela. The two groups intermarried. In 1797, after the British colonizers defeated a revolt on St. Vincent, they loaded several thousand slaves onto ships and sent them to Roatan, one of the Bay Islands. More than a thousand slaves died on the journey, but those who survived mixed with the indigenous tribe on the island and became the Garifuna, or Black Caribs of Honduras. A second Afro-Honduran group migrated to the Bay Islands in the 1840s, mostly English-speaking Afro-Caribbean Creoles, with later additions by other Creoles from Jamaica.

In 1823 the Central American provinces of Mexico broke away to form the United Provinces of Central America. Then, after years of interstate tension, squabbling, rewriting of the constitution, and moving of the capital, the Central American states decided to form independent, sovereign nations. Honduras declared independence on October 26, 1838, and adopted a constitution as the Republic of Honduras in January 1839. The constitution of 1839 provided a single legislative body, a president elected by a majority of the registered male population, and a supreme court whose justices are appointed by the president. It was a constitution inspired in part by the U.S. model.

Modern Era During the early twentieth century Honduras's Caribbean coast developed into a vast network of giant plantations owned by U.S. companies. La Ceiba, Trujillo, and Puerto Cortez became huge ports where the fruit was, and still is, loaded onto ships bound for the United States and other countries around the world. Honduras charges American companies very low taxes for the export of fruit and charges no taxes at all on profits from sales.

The fruit companies built schools, hospitals, and housing for their workers and connected cities in the region to a railroad network. The Caribbean coast has been the region with the country's best infrastructure and standard of living, even for the peasants. However, not all of the fruit companies' activities have been so benevolent. When the companies began to return some of the land to the government in the 1960s, they continued to market the bananas grown by small farmers or peasant cooperatives on the returned land. The new arrangement allowed the companies to avoid the political problems of land ownership, and, at the same time, placed all the risk of crop failure on the small growers while keeping disproportionate profits for the companies. They also introduced environmental destruction due to monocropping (growing a single crop year after year), deforestation, draining swamps, and pesticide use.

In 1956 the problems with political instability that Honduras had had since its foundation came to a head. The 1954 presidential election was inconclusive; no candidate won a majority of votes. The Honduran congress, the arbiter of such dilemmas, was not able to reach a decision on any of the candidates. Lozano Díaz, the vice president, assumed power after the president had a heart attack and was flown to Miami. Díaz unconstitutionally proclaimed himself president and arrested the leaders of principal parties, labor unions, and farmers' unions. As the political situation became more and more repressive in Honduras under Díaz, the military seized power in a bloodless coup and replaced him with a *junta*, a governing council of military officers. The next forty years would see a revolving-door leadership between the military and civilian-elected governments. The last half of the twentieth century was a period of political turmoil as a series of military and civilian leaders displaced one another.

The succession of military leaders plunged Honduras into a period of largely ineffective government and widespread corruption that included charges of bribery, drug trafficking, and murder. Although Honduras was more stable than the rest of the region, it was not unaffected by the civil unrest that rocked neighboring countries. When Sandinista rebels in Nicaragua overthrew the Somoza dictatorship in 1979, many members of the Nicaraguan military fled to Honduras. At the same time refugees from the war raging in El Salvador were entering Honduras in large numbers. United States military aid, which was $3.3 million in 1980, jumped to $31.3 million in 1982, and the country became one of the top ten recipients of U.S. military and economic aid. Nicaraguan refugee camps in the Honduras served as bases for the U.S.-sponsored Contra War, an undeclared, covert operation against the Sandinista government. The United States was also training Salvadoran military forces in Salvadoran refugee camps inside Honduras. (These were banned in 1984.)

When thousands of Hondurans protested, hundreds of opposition and student leaders were kidnapped and killed. It was not until 1988, two years after it was revealed that the Reagan administration in the United States had covertly and illegally used money from the sale of arms to Iraq to support the Contras, that the Honduran government refused to sign a new military agreement with the United States and promised the Contras would leave Honduras. During the 1990s Honduras made a gradual transition to true democracy. The Central American civil wars ended, the United States became a critic of the military, and civilian politicians more boldly addressed the issue of military privileges. The military lost much of its political influence, and three consecutive free elections (1989, 1993, and 1997) resulted in transition between competing parties without interference.

Panamanian-born Ricardo Manduro Joest, who was inaugurated president in of Honduras in 2001, concentrated on the country's massive crime and gang problem. His successor, Jose Manuel "Mel" Zelaya Rosales, who won the 2005 presidential election with the smallest margin in Honduran electoral history (less than 4 percent), was removed from office in a military coup on June 28, 2009. Soldiers arrested Zelaya and flew him, still in his pajamas, into exile in Costa Rica. The military insisted they were acting under the orders of the Supreme Court of Honduras, who viewed as illegal a constitutional referendum proposed by Zelaya that could have allowed him to extend his presidency. Despite condemnation of the coup from many countries, including the United States and Venezuela, Roberto Micheletti, with the backing of the Honduran Congress, courts, and army, became president.

By the time Porfirio Lobo won the November 2009 election, Honduras had endured months of political turmoil, had been isolated by the international community, and had been stripped of aid and investment. Honduras was excluded from the Organization of American States after the coup and not readmitted

A Honduran immigrant reads to his daughter in their home in Nashville, Tennessee. AP IMAGES / MARK HUMPHREY

until June 2011. The readmission did not end internal problems in Honduras, which in 2012 had the highest homicide rate in the world. It was also considered one of the world's most dangerous countries for members of the media. Twenty-two journalists were murdered between 2009 and 2012, and human rights activists routinely have been threatened and harassed by gangs and local political groups. Poverty and crime pushed thousands of Hondurans into emigration. According to some counts, in 2012 a Honduran left the country every five minutes.

The rise of gang violence in Honduras has been attributed to U.S. policy. Many of the Salvadorans and Guatemalans who fled to the United States in the wake of civil warfare in their own countries in the 1980s settled as illegal immigrants in poor neighborhoods of Los Angeles where gang activity was rampant; in reaction, they formed their own gangs. In the 1990s the United States began focusing on mass deportations of these gang members (as well as illegal immigrants with even minor criminal records). Back in El Salvador and Guatemala, the gangs took hold and spread to Honduras. In the four-year period between 2000 and 2004 alone, the United States deported more than 20,000 felons to Central America. The increase in gang violence in Honduras has been accompanied by new drug routes through Central American countries, including Honduras, into Mexico. The violence in combination with the high rate of poverty have in turn increased the number of Hondurans entering the United States, many of them illegally.

SETTLEMENT IN THE UNITED STATES

The United States Census Bureau did not count immigrants from individual Central American countries before 1930, so little is known about early Honduran immigration to the United States. The employees of the banana companies accounted for the first influx of Honduran immigrants. Most of them settled in New Orleans, their port of entry, where many of their descendants still live. Between 1930 and 1939, only 679 Hondurans entered the United States legally. There was no significant increase in that number until the 1960s. During that decade more than 15,000 Hondurans were granted legal permanent resident status. By 1999 the number had increased to 7,100 each year. The first decade of the twenty-first century saw an 81 percent increase in the number of Hondurans entering the United states - the largest increase of any immigrant group. An estimated one million Hondurans were living in the United States in 2008, but up to 70 percent of that number was thought to be illegal immigrants. According to the 2010 U.S. Census, the Honduran American population increased 180 percent between 2000 and 2010.

The majority of Honduran Americans who have entered the United States since 1960 have done so to seek better economic opportunities and to escape political turmoil or oppression in Honduras. During the 1980s Hondurans migrated in substantial numbers, but their entry into the United States frequently was obscured by the larger number of Guatemalans and Salvadorans who fled their war-torn nations during the same time. As many as 80,000 Hondurans entered the United States under temporary protected status in 1998 after Hurricane Mitch left 20 percent of the population homeless and destroyed much of the country's infrastructure and 70 percent of its crops. Many multinational fruit companies, the country's major employers, left Honduras. Significant numbers of Hondurans are dependent upon remittances sent by relatives who work in the United States. According to the Honduran foreign ministry, in 2007 remittances totaling $2.8 billion were sent to Honduras by workers in the United States. This money allows many of the receiving families to live above the poverty level and to keep children in school. Additionally, Honduran residents of the United States who return to their native country for visits account for 40 percent of all tourism revenue in Honduras.

Central American immigrants traditionally have settled in the Southwestern states and Illinois, but since 1990, substantial communities of Central American immigrants have been established in seventeen states. It is estimated that 65 percent of Hondurans have settled in five states; more than half of these have settled in Texas (19 percent) and Florida (18 percent), while 13 percent have settled in California, 9 percent in New York, and 6 percent in North Carolina. Before the 1990s most Honduran immigrants were agricultural workers, but the range of occupations has widened to include building maintenance, construction, food service, manufacturing, and transportation. For men, construction, extraction, transportation, and service occupations accounted for more than 60 percent of

those employed in 2008. During the same period, 54 percent of female Honduran immigrants were employed, most in the service industry.

The proliferation of young, low-skilled immigrants with limited proficiency in English has contributed to anti-immigrant sentiments, particularly in states unaccustomed to substantial immigrant populations. During difficult economic times, such as the economic recession of the late 2000s, immigrants are often a target for fiscal and employment concerns. Such concerns are intensified when a high proportion of immigration is illegal. Although Honduran Americans are rarely targeted as a specific group, anti-immigration sentiment makes little distinction among immigrant groups from Latin American nations, including Honduras.

Honduran Americans are a diverse group that includes people of Spanish, indigenous, Garifuna, African, Palestinian, and Chinese ancestry, among many others. They have made important improvements in their own standards of living, major educational and professional achievements, and important cultural contributions to American society.

LANGUAGE

Besides English, the almost universally spoken language of Honduran Americans is Spanish. Most Honduran indigenous peoples also speak it. In addition, most Maya speak Chorti, and the Black Caribs speak Garifuna. More than 90 percent of Hondurans in the United States speak Spanish as their household language. Because Honduran Garifuna immigrants are so easily assimilated into African American communities, the Garifuna language is a primary means of maintaining cultural identity. Since the late 1990s there has been a concentrated effort to revitalize the language, and some Garifuna parents in the United States send their children to relatives in Honduras during school breaks to reinforce language and other cultural ties.

According to a Pew Research Center study conducted in 2007, fewer than four in ten Honduran immigrants speak English proficiently. A year later a report from the Migration Policy Institute confirmed the Pew study, finding that 72 percent of Hondurans in the United States reported limited English proficiency, a rate considerably higher than the average of 52 percent for all foreign-born persons. ("Limited English proficiency" means that the individuals self-identified as speaking English less than "very well.") The significant decrease in high school dropout rates for Honduran Americans—from almost 40 percent among first-generation immigrants to 6 percent for the second generation—suggests a comparable increase in English proficiency.

The following are some Garifuna expressions (with pronunciations): *Jin!* (hing)—"Hey, you!"; *Buiti binafi illawuritei* (booitey binaffy illawoorittay)—"Good morning, Uncle." *Abau isilledu eiguini, fulesei* (ab-bow eeseelaydoo aiguiny, foolasay)—"A plate of food, please."

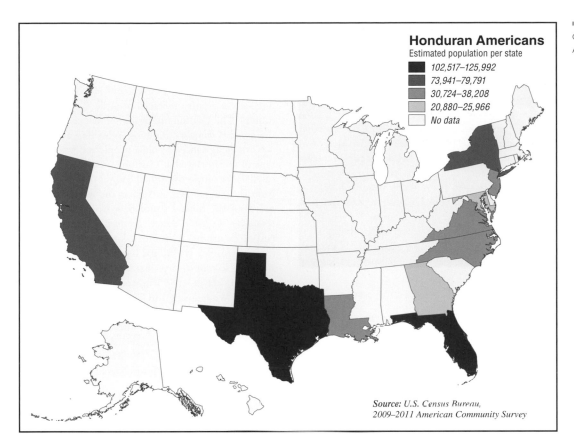

Honduran Americans
Estimated population per state

- 102,517–125,992
- 73,941–79,791
- 30,724–38,208
- 20,880–25,966
- No data

Source: U.S. Census Bureau,
2009–2011 American Community Survey

RELIGION

An overwhelming majority of Hondurans are Roman Catholic. The church exerts less influence than in the past but remains central in the lives of many Honduran Americans who are active in their church communities. Women take major responsibility for church affairs, such as attending Sunday church suppers and helping to organize parish charity drives. Rituals such as baptism, confirmation, and funeral prayers continue to be observed. The religious celebration most identified with Honduran Catholics is the February 3 the Feast and Mass of Our Lady of Suyapa, who was declared the patron saint of Honduras by Pope Pius XI in 1925. This feast day is celebrated at most churches in the United States that serve congregations of Honduran immigrants.

A wave of evangelical conversions, mostly Pentecostal, swept Honduras in the 1960s, and a second wave followed in the 1990s. Not only have some immigrants brought their Protestant evangelical identity with them, but also, more and more Honduran Americans are exploring Protestant religions, with a sizeable number converting. Evangelical denominations actively proselytize among Hispanic groups, offering services in Spanish and classes in English as a second language.

In an unusual reversal, many Garifuna immigrants, most of whom live in New York City, identify with their religion more strongly in the United States than they did in Honduras. The Garifuna religion they practice is not a syncretism but an innovation that reshapes the traditions and rituals of their native religion within the context of the African diaspora. This religion is strongly influenced by Cuban Santería and West African Yoruba symbols.

CULTURE AND ASSIMILATION

Foreign-born Hondurans in the United States identify themselves as Hondurans. Hondurans born in the United States commonly identify themselves as Honduran Americans. The dominant American culture demonstrates little awareness of Hondurans as a separate ethnic group, categorizing them more often as Central Americans or even more broadly as Hispanics, which in many sections of the country is assumed to be synonymous with Mexican. The Garifuna self-identify as Garifuna from Honduras rather than Hondurans. There appears to be almost no interaction between Garifuna and the larger mestizo Honduran immigrant populations.

Cuisine Serving traditional foods provides a way for Honduran Americans to maintain a connection to their heritage. Unlike some other Latin American foods, Honduran food does not customarily use hot

Honduran immigrants participate in a pro-immigration rally at the U.S. Capitol in Washington, D.C. in 2013. Supporters want Congress to pass a number of immigration reform laws that include a direct path to citizenship for the nation's 11 million undocumented immigrants. THE WASHINGTON POST / GETTY IMAGES

spices. Cumin, curry, allspice, coriander, oregano, and lime juice are the most commonly used seasonings. Honduran dishes also use more coconut than other Central American cuisines. Beans, rice, tortillas, cheese, *mantequilla* (Honduran sour cream), eggs, and fried plantains are the typical *cena* (dinner plate). *Anafres*, a refried black bean and cheese fondue served in a clay pot accompanied by tortilla chips, is the favorite appetizer in the country. Like tacos in Mexico or *pupusas* in El Salvador, the *baleada*—a folded wheat flour tortilla filled with beans, crumbled cheese, sour cream, and sometimes beef, chicken, or pork—is a popular snack food.

Social events that involve drinks and dancing call for more elaborate dishes. The preparation and cooking of *carne asada* (also called *carneada*) is a tradition that is passed on from one generation to another. Large cuts of beef are marinated in sour orange juice, salt, pepper, and other spices and then grilled. The *carneada* is usually accompanied with *chimol* sauce (chopped tomatoes, onion, and cilantro with lemon and spices), roasted plantains, *chorizo* (sausage), cheese, tortillas, guacamole, and beans. Food is also connected with religious observances. *Sopa de pescado*, a very rich fish soup, is served on Good Friday. Garifuna celebrations often include *ereba*, a tortilla-like bread made from pounded cassava root, and *sopa de caracol*, or conch soup cooked in coconut milk and the conch's broth and served with *machuca*, or pounded plantain. Coconut bread is also a Garifuna favorite.

Dances and Songs The blend of Spanish colonial, African, and Native American history in Honduras is reflected in its music and dance styles and in the country's most common musical instruments. The *siqueis*, a typical folk dance, is similar to the *jota*, a dance common throughout Spain, and to the waltz. Although local differences can be observed in the steps of the *siqueis*, it is danced in unison by couples who separate at intervals to carry out individual steps and

clap hands. Many traditional dances are tied to agricultural or religious traditions. One dance depicts a machete fight between the male dancers in which the women intercede.

The *punta*, the best-known Honduran dance outside the country, emerged from the Garifuna community. The Garifuna term for the dance portion of the *punta* is *banguity*, meaning "new life," although it was originally danced by older people and was the only type of music played at Garifuna wakes. The complicated dance moves use only the lower part of the body, from the waist down, as well as the feet. Traditional moves of the funeral dance have been adapted to a seductive courtship dance. *Punta* can be sung at the end of mourning ceremonies, known as *fin de novenario*. Men play traditional instruments that include first and second drums, maracas, a conch shell, and sometimes claves—two hardwood sticks that are beat together. Women sing in Garifuna with a soloist and chorus similar to African music or gospel call-and-response singing. Although the sounds are joyous, the lyrics are often somber, focusing on loss and the ephemeral quality of life. The improvisations of the musicians are similar to those characteristic of jazz.

Garifuna music is the Honduran music that has become best-known in the United States. Geoffrey Himes described this music in the *Washington Post*: "Legend has it that the Garifuna culture sprang from the survivors of a shipwrecked slave vessel who swam ashore on St. Vincent Island in the sixteenth century. There they intermarried with the local Carib and Arawak Indians and created a music that blended West African drumming and Caribbean Indian group singing. The culture then spread to Belize and Honduras." Punta is described as an astonishingly melodic and intricate music. The beat is usually carried by two to four large tuba (or hollow log) drums. The tercera drum provides the booming bass notes that establish the foundation rhythm. The primera drum supplies the melodic lead pattern, and the segunda drum shadows the primera with a counter rhythm. These three main patterns are amplified by turtle shells, claves, timbales, bongos, congas, maracas, and tambourines. Himes noted: "Because each drum has its own pitch and timbre and because the vocals are woven inextricably into the drumming, the music has a richness you'd never expect from just percussion and voice."

Health Care Issues and Practices Honduran immigrants have limited access to health care in the United States. A large percentage of Honduran immigrants (as many as seven in ten) are undocumented. Historically, undocumented immigrants have been denied access to government-funded health care. Legal immigrants' access to health care was also limited with the passage of two Congressional acts in 1996, the Personal Responsibility and Work Opportunity Reconciliation Act and the Illegal Immigration Reform and Immigrant Responsibility

Act. Under this legislation, legal immigrants arriving in the United States after August 1996 were denied access to the Supplemental Nutrition Assistance Program (SNAP), Medicaid, and the Children's Health Insurance Program (CHIP) for the first five years they were in the country. In addition, many documented Honduran immigrants work at low-paying jobs that do not provide health insurance. Often those who qualify for Medicaid and other programs are too suspicious of the system to participate. American-born children of the undocumented (nationally estimated at three out of every four children in immigrant families) are eligible for benefits, but participation is low because parents fear that using the services for their children will expose their illegal status. Slightly more than half (52 percent) of Hondurans legally in the United States have no health insurance, compared to 31 percent of all Hispanics and 15 percent of the general U.S. population. Language differences can also present barriers to health services. All of these factors combine to place Hondurans among the immigrant groups who delay seeking health care, mental health services, and dental care as long as possible, most often until emergency situations arise.

Research suggests that despite the limited health services available, most Honduran immigrants are likely to use conventional sources of health care more often than folk sources. When folk sources are used, they typically begin with a home remedy such as tea made from various herbs, spices, or fruits and prepared in a specific and prescribed manner. Hondurans may consult a relative or neighbor for advice, and only when these methods fail to bring relief is a *yerbero* (herbalist) or *sobador* (massage therapist) consulted. If all these measures fail, an individual may then visit a *curandero* (lay healer) who uses a combination of physical and spiritual treatment. Sometimes a *curandero* may be consulted at the same time a patient is receiving attention from a primary care physician. *Curanderos* are consulted far less frequently in the United States than in Honduras, where conventional health care is in short supply, particularly in isolated communities.

Psychiatry presents another area in which Honduran Americans, particularly new arrivals, have felt alienated. This is due less to neglect than to different cultural attitudes toward psychiatry in Latin America and in the United States. Older, traditional therapy in Honduras for psychological problems has included Santería, a Caribbean-based faith that combines elements of African ritual with Catholicism, and *espiritualismo* (spiritualism). Both therapies see the psychological problem as a spiritual problem, an imbalance of supernatural forces. Therapy can then take the form of an attempt to reach a transcendent consciousness by using meditation, concentrating on specific personal objects, or consulting a medium. It can also take the form of an

SOPA DE PESCADO

Ingredients

2 cups chicken broth

2 cups bottled clam juice

2 cloves of garlic, crushed

1 sweet pepper, diced

salt to taste

1 jalepeño

1 yucca (or potato), cubed

1 onion, sliced

1 cup coconut milk

1 whole red snapper or yellowtail fish, cleaned and cut in cubes.

Preparation

Put both broths in pan with garlic and simmer for 15 minutes.

To the stock add onions, sweet pepper, and salt. Give it a little kick with jalapeño peppers. Add yucca (or potatoes), sliced onions, and coconut milk. Cook until the yucca is tender.

Fry the fish or boil it in the stock for 7 minutes.

If the fish is fried, place in a bowl and pour the liquid over it. Serve with mashed plantains on the side with a few slices of lemon.

exorcism, in which the treatment is meant to drive out an evil spirit or devil from the victim.

Psychiatrists and clinical psychologists in some urban medical centers around the United States are seeking to break down cultural barriers to clinical therapy and begin addressing the psychological traumas that affect Latin American immigrants in particular. Especially acute is post-traumatic stress disorder, caused by witnessing horrors such as death squads, political assassinations, and massacres of peasants.

Another difference between Hondurans and Americans involves a congenital condition among certain Hondurans that affords them a specific medical immunity. The Garifuna, whose ancestors include black Africans and Caribbean Indians, have an African-component sickle-cell genetic adaptation that makes them immune to malaria.

FAMILY AND COMMUNITY LIFE

Family structure in Honduras has been affected by increasing numbers of women entering the work force, but the greatest change in the twenty-first century has been the prevalence of the transnational family, with one or two family members working in the United States and sending a portion of their income to family members who remain in Honduras. In 2010 Hondurans remitted a total of $2.67 billion, or 19 percent of the gross domestic product of Honduras, an amount substantially greater than development aid and foreign investment combined. The transnational family is a survival strategy and a mobility strategy.

The typical Honduran migration narrative has focused on men who leave their homes during tough economic times in order to support their families or to save money to build a home in Honduras. The idea is that the man will spend two to five years working in the United States and then return to live with his family. The practice has created communities in Honduras filled with new homes, financed through remittances, whose owners remain in the United States. Although males outnumbered females immigrating to the United States (53 percent to 47 percent in 2010) feminization of migration has increased as women have left their homes not merely as dependents accompanying a spouse but as autonomous workers who leave to provide for their families. Research shows that women tend to remit a higher percentage of their incomes than do men and to remit to a larger number of family members and over a longer period of time, despite making on average 62 percent of what their male counterparts make. Frequently the female immigrant is a woman who has experienced domestic violence, divorce, or abandonment that has left her sole provider for her children.

Separation from family is difficult for men and women, and most participate in weekly telephone calls to maintain contact with their families and to attempt to provide a degree of parental guidance despite the distance. The problems of separation are compounded for migrant mothers who are forced to deal with stigma, guilt, and criticism for the "unnatural" choice of separating from their children, homes, and sometimes husbands. Studies also found that children experience more emotional problems when mothers migrate because of traditional gender norms related to child care. The degree of difficulty experienced by children was related to the quality of care provided by parental substitutes. Children left to care for themselves were three times as likely to experience psychological problems as were those left in the care of another family member.

Some Honduran immigrants do return to Honduras, but others find reintegration into Honduran society difficult and may move back and forth between the two cultures or settle permanently in the United States. Women particularly may become reluctant to surrender the greater freedom and opportunities they have gained. Unlike other immigrant groups, Hondurans rarely dominate a city or even a neighborhood but tend toward a greater dispersion. Family reunification is a goal for many who send for children left in Honduras. Social gatherings, usually associated with birthday parties, weddings, baptisms, confirmations, or wakes, are important to maintaining extended familial, community, and cultural identity. Often such events are videotaped and sent to family members in Honduras. Events of national significance such as Independence Day and the annual mass for the Virgin of Suyapa draw together larger crowds of Hondurans, as do Honduran soccer clubs in cities such as New York and New Orleans.

Education It has been easier for Honduran American girls to stay in school than for Honduran American boys. Especially in working-class families, there is tremendous pressure for boys, once they turn twelve or fourteen, to start working full-time. This pressure is not as strong on the girls. The 2010 census educational attainment statistic provides numbers for Central Americans as a group. Fifty percent of males over twenty-five had less than a high school education, but the number dropped to around 47 percent for women. The pattern continues with post-secondary education. Almost 12 percent of Central American women hold a bachelor's degree or higher, whereas only 9.7 percent of males do. Regardless of gender, the younger a child is when entering the United States, the greater the likelihood of secondary and postsecondary education.

As related in *The Hispanic Outlook in Higher Education*, the story of Bonilla, a Honduran American immigrant, is typical of young Hondurans who are proving exceptions to the pattern of their countrymen as the least-educated among the top eight groups of the growing Hispanic population in the United States. Her early education was in her native village in Honduras, but she immigrated with thirteen family members and graduated from an American high school in 2002. Her dream of attending college was frustrated by the rejections she received because she lacked proper documentation. Eventually she was admitted to a community college near her home, and in 2012 she earned her associate's degree with a 4.0 grade point average. She sometimes worked as many as three jobs to pay tuition, but she is the first member of her family to hold a postsecondary degree. She plans to continue her education at a four-year school and go on to law school. Because community colleges offer more affordable tuition, a stronger support system, and an open admissions policy that includes accepting undocumented immigrants, Hispanics generally have favored these institutions, making up 16 percent of the 7.4 million students enrolled. Significantly, 52 percent of Hispanics who pursue higher education begin at a community college.

EMPLOYMENT AND ECONOMIC CONDITIONS

While new arrivals have traditionally entered fields involving basic labor, established Honduran American immigrants have shown impressive success in moving into more lucrative professions. Of the 34,220 Honduran Americans who immigrated to the United

States between 1980 and 1990, according to the U.S. Census, 33.7 percent described themselves as being in service occupations, which include working as waiters, other restaurant work, janitorial work, and work in laundries and retail stores. Only 24.2 percent of the immigrants who arrived before 1980 are in that industry. Of those who immigrated during the 1980s, 27.3 percent were operators, fabricators, and laborers; for those who arrived before, only 18.7 percent fit into that category. Those who immigrated before 1980 are more heavily represented in managerial and professional specialty occupations: 14.6 percent as opposed to 5.6 percent for the newer arrivals. The contrast in public administration is similar, with a ratio of 3 percent for established Honduran Americans to 1 percent for newer arrivals; the same is true of educational services, the ratio being 4.9 percent to 2.4 percent. These figures demonstrate the trend toward self-improvement as Honduran Americans establish themselves in the United States.

Honduran Americans have high workforce participation. According to the 2009 and 2010 Current Population Survey compiled by the U.S. Census Bureau and the Bureau of Labor Statistics, 81 percent of Honduran men ages sixteen to sixty-four were employed in the civilian labor force, mostly in low-skilled jobs including construction, extraction, transportation, and service occupations. The employment rate is much lower for second-generation males: 67 percent compared to 91.4 percent of first-generation males. The rate of employment for both generations of women is about 60 percent. Unemployed males are in school, disabled, or seeking employment. Most unemployed women take care of households or family members. The generational gap can be explained in large part by the reverse gap in school attendance. Less than 30 percent of first-generation Hondurans ages sixteen to twenty-four are enrolled in school, but more than 73 percent of the same age group of second generation are in school.

Even within low-wage sectors, Hondurans, along with Mexicans and other immigrants from Central America, are employed in the lowest-paying jobs. The median annual personal earnings for Hondurans ages sixteen and older was $18,000 in 2010; the median earnings for all U.S. Hispanics was $20,000. About a quarter of Hondurans live below the poverty line, more than other foreign-born groups and a significantly higher proportion than the 14.3 percent of the general U.S. population. Rates fall among second-generation Hondurans, who meet the national median.

The youth of Honduran workers, whose average age is twenty-seven, along with their low levels of education and recent entry into the workforce, has made them vulnerable to the recession of the 2000s. They also tend to be concentrated in construction, manufacturing, hospitality, and other industries that have been heavily affected by the economic downturn. Undocumented immigrants and recent arrivals also lack access to social services that provide a safety net for other population groups and thus are more likely to experience abject poverty in case of long-term unemployment. Between the end of 2007 and the end of 2008, the percentage of working-age Hispanics with jobs fell at almost twice the rate for the overall population. The loss of employment has a ripple effect since it also results in a reduction in remittances sent to family in Honduras. One 2009 study reported that as many as 74 percent of Hondurans receiving remittances had experienced a decrease over the prior year. Job loss of a relative living in the United States was the most frequent reason.

POLITICS AND GOVERNMENT

Being a relatively new immigrant group from a country that has seen its share of political turmoil, Honduran Americans have not been conspicuous in American politics or unions, nor has there been much overt action on the part of Honduran Americans to influence politics in the mother country. Only about one in five Hondurans is a U.S. citizen. Despite a steady increase in population, Honduran participation in U.S. politics is not significant. Several factors contribute to this low political profile. Ethnic and class differences that exist in Honduras carry over into the immigrant population in the United States. Thus, Hondurans lack a sense of themselves as a single, coherent group with common needs and purposes. The residential dispersal has made organization at local levels rarer. Since many Honduran immigrants view their stay in the United States as temporary, their focus tends to be on their home communities in Honduras. Finally, the large number of Hondurans who entered the United States illegally makes the group reluctant to attract the attention of authorities.

Politically active groups within the Honduran community have been regional and focused. To address problems of the undocumented alien community, a group of Honduran American and other Central American undocumented aliens formed the Aliens for Better Immigration Laws in February 1994. At that time the group filed a class-action lawsuit in federal court to allow undocumented aliens to work while they are on a decade-long waiting list for green cards. This grassroots lobbying organization has fought to bring the issues of undocumented immigrants to the forefront, not only in the courts but also in the consciousness of the American public. Unidad Hondurena in Miami has protested fee hikes for temporary work permits and citizenship applications. Hondurans have also been active in the Central American Resource Center in Washington, D.C.

Honduran Americans have taken an active role in defending the United States. Of all the native (U.S.) Honduran American males sixteen years old and over, 13.7 percent are military veterans. More than 700 Honduran American male noncitizens are veterans. The percentage of naturalized Honduran American male civilians sixteen years old and over who have served in the armed forces is 13.2 percent. For those who arrived in the United States before 1980, this number jumps to 18.4 percent, almost one-fifth.

NOTABLE INDIVIDUALS

Art American artist Andres Serrano (1950–), whose father was from Honduras, is known for his controversial photographs of bodily fluids and corpses. His most notorious work is *Immersion (Piss Christ)*, a 1987 photograph of a crucifix submerged in the artist's urine; it sparked debates worldwide about issues of censorship.

Julian Albert Touceda is a New Orleans artist and supporter of Latin art who was born and lived the first years of his life in Honduras. Born in the early 1940s, Touceda has been instrumental in preserving Latin American culture and exposing the community to Latin artists. Touceda's main influences are the Spanish painters Francisco Goya and Diego Balasca, Mexican muralist Diego Rivera, and Mexican painter Rufino Tamayo. Since 1976 Touceda has had exhibits in Louisiana, Mississippi, Florida, and New York. Among more than fifty prominent artists, he was the only Hispanic artist selected to exhibit his works at the Louisiana World Exposition in 1984.

Music David Archuleta, born December 28, 1990, was runner-up on the seventh season of the TV show *American Idol*. The son of Lupe Marie (née Mayorga), a Honduran salsa singer and dancer, and Jeff Archeluta, a jazz trumpet player of Spanish-Basque descent, Archuleta released his first album in 2008. It debuted at number two on the Billboard 200 chart. He has also appeared on television shows *iCarly* and *Hannah Montana*. He released his fifth album, *Begin*, in 2012, the same year he took a two-year break from his career to serve as a missionary in Chile for the Church of Jesus Christ of Latter-Day Saints.

Publishing Motivational speaker Julio Melara, a second-generation Honduran American, grew up in Louisiana. He was only twenty-eight years old when he became the top sales executive at WWL radio in New Orleans and the only million-dollar producer in the radio industry in Louisiana. Two years later he became the publisher of *New Orleans Magazine*. He is the author of the books *Do You Have Time for Success?*, *It Only Takes Everything You've Got!*, and *Keys to Performance*. President and co-owner of the *Baton Rouge Business Report*, Melara owns Time for Action, a sales- and skills-building training firm.

Stage and Screen Born the sixth child of Honduran immigrant parents in 1984 and raised in the San Fernando Valley of California by a single mother, America Ferrera made her film debut in *Real Women Have Curves*, a performance that won her the Jury Award for Best Actress at the Sundance Film Festival. She also starred in *The Sisterhood of the Traveling Pants* (2005) and its sequel (2008). From 2006 to 2010 she played the title role in *Ugly Betty*, a television series based on the Colombian telenovela *Yo Soy Betty Le Fea*, a role that earned her multiple awards, including a Golden Globe, an Emmy, an American Latino Media Arts Award, and praise from Congress as a Latina role model.

MEDIA

Honduran Americans can access radio broadcasts and current newspapers directly from their native country through the Internet. Media that is specifically Honduran is rare because the Honduran American community is relatively small and new. Honduran Americans make up part of the audience for general Hispanic media, which is abundant in all formats.

Honduras New York

This one-hour weekly program airs on Cable Channel 69, also known as BronxNet, a New York City public access cable channel. It can also be viewed on the BronxNet website.

David Jenkins, Jr., Public Access Programming Manager
BronxNet Television
Lehman College Campus
Carman Hall Room C4
Bronx, New York 10468
Phone: (718) 960-1183
Fax: (718) 960-8354
Email: david@bronxnet.org
URL: www.bronxnet.org

Honduras Weekly

International weekly newspaper in English. Covers news in Honduras as well as items of interest to Hondurans abroad.

Stanley Marrder, Publisher
Email: editor@hondurasweekly.com
URL: www.hondurasweekly.com

ORGANIZATIONS AND ASSOCIATIONS

There are no large, national organizations specifically for Honduran Americans, with the exception of Garifuna organizations, which are transnational. Instead Hondurans come together in associations that are connected to a particular town, city, or region in their homeland. The associations provide a means of cultural identification in the new setting, a link to those who remain in Honduras, and assistance to those in need. Some groups have a political purpose as well. In 2009 there were around thirty of these groups within Honduran communities, each consisting of from fifteen to one hundred members that meet on a regular basis. The total number of affiliated volunteers could be substantially larger. Most of these groups raise less than $10,000 a year. Some organizations exist for short periods and disappear.

Garifuna American Heritage Foundation United

Founded to preserve and disseminate Garifuna culture and to foster Garifuna Americans' awareness of their heritage.

Cheryl Noralez, CEO and Founder
2127 Atlantic Avenue
Long Beach, California 90806
Phone: (323) 898-6841
Email: gahfuinc@garifunaheritagefoundation.org
URL: www.garifunaheritagefoundation.org/243.html

Honduran Organization of Palm Beach

Founded to support the Honduran community in Florida and to organize assistance projects for the community in San Pedro Sula, Honduras.

José Cerrato, President
114 Urquhart Street
Lake Worth, Florida 33461
Phone: (561) 856-0028
Email: jfracerrato@yahoo.com

La Casa del Hondureno

Supports the Hispanic community generally and promotes Honduran artists, folklore, and cultural events.

Xiomara Fields, President
3580 Wilshire Boulevard #1280
Los Angeles, California 90010
Phone: (213) 389-9295
Email: xfields@lacasadelhondureno.org
URL: www.lacasadelhondureno.org/home-english.html

MUSEUMS AND RESEARCH CENTERS

Florida Museum of Natural History

The Honduras Ceramic Collection—The collection, which includes more than five thousand shards from a wide geographical area, was donated to the museum in 1929 and 1930 by G. W. Van Hyning, the museum's first director, and the N. Geraci Fruit Company, a banana company operating in Honduras in the 1930s.

Douglas S. Jones, Director
Dickinson Hall
1659 Museum Road
University of Florida
Gainesville, Florida 32611
Phone: (352) 392-1721
Fax: (352) 846-0287
Email: dsjones@flmnh.ufl.edu
URL: www.flmnh.ufl.edu/latinarch/honduras/honduras.htm

Roger Thayer Stone Center for Latin American Studies

The center's Latin American Resource Center (LARC), one of the largest and most comprehensive centers of its kind in the United States, offers specialized services to schools and colleges across the nation to promote the study of all subject matter relating to Latin America at both the K–12 and university levels. LARC provides services such as a lending library that holds more than three thousand videos, slide packets, culture kits, curriculum units, games, and miscellaneous print items; consulting; and professional development for educators. Activities connected to Honduras have included lectures on Honduran politics, soccer tournaments, expeditions to study Honduran architecture, and fundraising to build two health clinics in the mountains of Honduras.

Tom Reese, Executive Director
Tulane University
100 Jones Hall
New Orleans, Louisiana 70118
Phone: (504) 865-5164
Email: rtsclas@tulane.edu
URL: http://stonecenter.tulane.edu/search/

SOURCES FOR ADDITIONAL STUDY

Brick, Kate, A. E. Challinor, and Marc R. Rosenblum. *Mexican and Central American Immigrants in the United States*. Washington, D.C.: Migration Policy Institute, 2011.

England, Sarah. *Afro Central Americans in New York City: Garifuna Tales of Transnational Movements in Racialized Space*. Gainesville: University Press of Florida, 2006.

Fash, William L. *Warriors and Kings: The City of Copán and the Ancient Maya*. London: Thames and Hudson, 1991.

González, Nancie. "Garifuna Settlement in New York: A New Frontier." *International Migration Review* 13, no. 2 (1975).

Himes, Geoffrey. "Chatuye: Upholding the Garifuna Beat." *Washington Post*, April 2, 1993.

Johnson, Paul C. *Diaspora Conversions: Black Carib Religion and the Recovery of Africa*. Berkeley: University of California Press, 2007.

Nazario, Sonia. *Enrique's Journey*. New York: Random House, 2007.

Orozco, Manuel, and Eugenia Garcia-Zanello. "Hometown Associations, Philanthropy, and Development." *Brown Journal of World Affairs* 15, no. 2 (2009).

River, Elaine. "Erasing a Stigma—Mental Health Center Deals with Latinos' Special Needs." *Newsday*, August 24, 1994.

Schmalzbauer, Leah. "Family Divided: The Class Formation of Honduran Transnational Families." *Global Networks* 8, no. 3 (2008): 329–46.

HOPIS

Ellen French and Richard C. Hanes

OVERVIEW

The westernmost of the several Pueblo Indian tribes, the independent Hopi (HO-pee) Nation is situated on historical Hopi land in the southwestern United States, east of the Grand Canyon near what is commonly referred to as the Four Corners region, where Colorado, New Mexico, Arizona, and Utah meet. Hopi Indians hold that their ancestral lands extend from the Grand Canyon north to Navajo Mountain in San Juan County, Utah; east through the Black Mesa region of Arizona to the Lukachukai borderlands; and south to the Mogollan Rim near the border of New Mexico. In spite of the arid land, the Hopi were able to grow a variety of vegetables, including corn, through a practice known as "dry farming." "Hopi" is a shortened form of the original term *Hopituh-Shi-nu-mu*, for which the most common meaning is "peaceful people."

According to the *Encyclopedia of Native American Economic History* (1999), archeologists, historians, and ethnographers estimate that the Hopi numbered close to 50,000 in 1583. They inhabit twelve villages, most of which are situated atop three rocky mesas that rise 600 feet from the desert floor. First Mesa supports the villages of Waalpi (in Hopi orthography; Walpi in English), Hanoki (Hano or Tewa), and Sitsomovi (Sichomovi); Second Mesa includes the Songoopavi (Shungopavi), Musungnuvi (Mishongnovi), and Supawlavi (Shipaulovi) villages; and the Hotvela (Hotevilla), Paaqavi (Bacavi), Kiqotsmovi (Kykotsmovi), and Orayvi (Oraibi) villages occupy Third Mesa. Atkya Munqapi (Lower Moenkopi) and Ooveq Munqapi (Upper Moenkopi) are 45 miles away, on Hopi land near Tuba City (on the Navajo Reservation). Thirty-four clans live in the villages. Clan membership—made up of those with a matrilineally traced common ancestor—impacts a variety of social and political aspects of Hopi life, including tribal offices, ceremonial responsibilities, and familial relationships. Prior to interaction with Spanish conquistadors in the sixteenth century, the Hopi were villagers and subsistence farmers. Afterwards they also grazed small herds of sheep and cattle. Additionally, they made jewelry, rugs, cotton cloth, and pottery and traded with neighboring and nomadic tribes.

The Hopi are ancient, having lived continuously in the same place for a thousand years, and are a federally recognized Indian tribe. Their reservation is located in Navajo and Coconino counties, occupying 2,532 square miles in northeastern Arizona. It is completely surrounded by the reservation of the Navajo Nation. President Chester A. Arthur established the Hopi Reservation by executive order on December 16, 1882, in an attempt to curb Navajo encroachment. The boundaries set by President Arthur omitted much of the Hopi's traditional land and their sacred and ceremonial landmarks. The Hopi Reservation is considerably rich in minerals, including coal, copper, zinc, lead, gold, silver, and uranium. Much of the tribe's income is derived through mining permits, which accounted for approximately $13 million of the tribe's income in 2010.

According to the 2011 American Community Survey, the total Hopi population was 18,050, with approximately 6,836 people living within the Hopi Reservation. Many of the Hopi continue to live around the four corners area, with the majority of the population residing in Arizona. Hopi continue to practice farming. Although the tribe relies on tourism for some of its income, some Hopi villages choose to close selected ceremonies to the public. Land disputes with the Navajo are a constant issue, and the Hopi are divided on providing access to outsiders, such as the Peabody Coal Company, to conduct business on the reservation. As is the case with other Native American tribes, the Hopi fear that their culture is diminishing and are attempting to revitalize it through organizations such as the Hopi Cultural Preservation Office, which supports traditional artisans, language teachers, excavation of historical artifacts, and the collection of tribal stories and oral histories from Hopi elders.

HISTORY OF THE PEOPLE

Early History According to Suzanne and Jake Page's book *Hopi* (1994), the Hopi are called "the oldest of the people" by other Native Americans. Frank Waters writes in *The Book of the Hopi* (1963) that they "regard themselves as the first inhabitants of America. Their village of Oraibi (settled around 1150) is indisputably the oldest continuously occupied settlement in the United States." While Hopi oral history traces the tribes' origin to a Creator and the subsequent emergence from previous worlds, scientists place them in their present location for the last thousand years, perhaps longer. In her book *The Wind Won't Know Me* (1992), Emily Benedek argues, "Anthropologists have shown that the cultural remains present a clear, uninterrupted, logical development culminating in the life, general technology, architecture, and agriculture and ceremonial practices to be seen on the three Hopi mesas today." Archaeologists definitively place the Hopi on the Black Mesa of the Colorado Plateau by 1350.

In 2007 E. Charles Adams prepared a report for the Hopi Tribe, providing an archeological perspective on Hopi water use in the Lower Colorado River drainage. Adams marks the period from 1275 to 1540 as the Hopi "ancestral period," characterized primarily by the augmentation of the villages. A need for greater social organization arose from increased village size and from the agricultural needs of the tribe. Kivas, the underground ceremonial chambers found in every village, also grew in size and developed further as a prominent space for communal worship. Additionally, coal was mined from mesa outcroppings, which required unprecedented coordination. The Hopi were among the world's first people to use coal for firing pottery.

The complex Hopi culture, much as it exists today, was firmly in place by the 1500s, including the ceremonial cycle, the kinship clan and chieftain social system, and agricultural methods that utilized every possible source of moisture in an extremely arid environment. The Hopi's "historical period" began in 1540, when first contact with Europeans occurred. In that year a group of Spanish soldiers led by the explorer Francisco Vásquez de Coronado arrived, looking for the legendary Seven Cities of Gold. After a brief, confrontational search produced no gold, the Spanish destroyed part of a village and left.

The Hopi were left in peace until 1629, when the first Spanish missionaries reached them, building missions in the villages of Awatovi, Oraibi, and Shungopavi. Historians speculate that the Hopi pretended to adopt the new religion while practicing their own in secret. Hopi oral history confirms this interpretation. Rebelling finally against the Spanish yoke of religious oppression, the Hopi joined the rest of the Pueblo people in the unified Pueblo Revolt of 1680. During this uprising, the Indians killed Franciscan priests and Spanish soldiers and then besieged Santa Fe for several days. When the Hopi finally returned to their villages, they executed the missionaries.

The Hopi then moved three of their villages, Walpi, Mishongnovi, and Shungopavi, from the foothills to the mesa tops as a defensive measure against possible retaliation. The Spanish returned to reconquer the Rio Grande area in 1692. Many Rio Grande Pueblo Indians fled west to Hopi, where they were welcomed. Over the next few years, a group of inhabitants of Awatovi invited the Spanish priests back, causing a serious rift between those who wanted to preserve the old ways and those who embraced Christianity. Finally, in 1700, the Hopi killed all Christian men

in the settlement of Awatovi and then destroyed the village. The destruction of Awatovi ended Spanish interference in Hopi life, although contact between the groups continued. Hester Harris indicates in *Remembering Awatovi: The Story of an Archeological Expedition in Northern Arizona 1935–1939* (2008) that the obliteration of Awatovi served as a symbolic gesture that allowed the Hopi to move beyond the shadow of Spanish colonialism.

Modern Era In an effort to protect their sovereignty, the Hopi never signed a land treaty with the United States. When President Chester A. Arthur established the Hopi Reservation in 1882, he set aside 2,472,254 acres in northeastern Arizona for "Moqui [the Spanish name for Hopi] and other such Indians as the Secretary of the Interior may see fit to settle thereon." The Hopi Reservation was centered within a larger area (considered by the Hopi to be their ancestral land also) that was designated as the Navajo Reservation, however. As populations increased, the Navajo expanded their settlements well beyond their own borders, encroaching more and more on the Hopi Reservation. Despite the executive order setting the reservation boundaries, this situation continued for many decades. By 1934 the Navajo Reservation had increased from 3.5 million acres to approximately 16 million acres, continuing to intrude upon the smaller Hopi Reservation. The Hopi petitioned the government, which failed to act, and the Navajo continued to overrun Hopi lands until they had taken over 1,800,000 acres of the original Hopi designation. The Hopi were left with only about 600,000 acres.

While confining Native Americans to reservations, the U.S. government carried on the policy of Americanization it had begun in 1790. In 1910, under President William Howard Taft, the government had attempted to subdivide the Hopi Reservation, assigning small parcels to individual Hopi. The effort failed, and the reservation remained intact. The Indian Reorganization Act of 1934 forced tribes to abandon traditional forms of government and establish constitutional governments similar to that of the United States. In 1936 the federal government officially recognized the Hopi Tribal Council and its adopted constitution. Tensions developed between the federal government and the tribal council, however, and in 1943 the government disbanded the council. The discovery of large coal deposits on Hopi land and the need to negotiate the complex mineral and water rights shared by the Hopi and Navajo caused the government to reinstate the council in 1951. That year, Congress passed the Navajo-Hopi Long Range Rehabilitation Act, allocating approximately $90 million to improve reservation roads, schools, utilities, and health facilities. The Hopi Tribe received federal recognition again in 1955, making available a further range of social services and funding opportunities.

In an attempt to settle their claim to their original reservation lands, the Hopi Council sued the Navajo

Tribe in 1962. The Arizona District Court found that both tribes had valid claims to the land. The federal government answered appeals in 1970 by declaring some of the lands as the Navajo-Hopi Joint Use Area. In 1966 both the Hopi and Navajo tribes had entered into agreements with the Peabody Western Coal Company, leasing to the company the mineral rights for nearly 65,000 acres in the Black Mesa region. Peabody began strip-mining the area in 1970. Some Hopi elders attempted to block the mining through the federal courts but failed; the case went all the way to the U.S. Supreme Court, which backed the decision of the lower courts.

Although the tribes entered formal negotiations to reconcile the dispute over lands, Navajo families continued to encroach and trespass on Hopi lands. Officially recognizing the problem, Congress finally passed the Navajo-Hopi Settlement Act in 1974, which returned 900,000 acres to the Hopi. The act divided the Joint Use Area into distinct Hopi and Navajo zones, with the tribes possessing equal shares of subsurface mineral rights. The act also provided funds for relocating Navajo who were currently living within the exclusive Hopi area. Congress set a deadline of 1986 for resettlement, but a number of Navajo families refused to leave, claiming ancestral ties to the land, and the dispute over relocation and the remaining 900,000 acres treated in the Settlement Act continued. In 1980 Congress granted some Navajo the right to remain on the land if they could prove their ancestral ties did not interfere with previous Hopi claims.

In 1998 the Hopi won a $6 million judgment that ordered the Navajo to share with the Hopi the taxes collected from the Peabody coal mining operation in the Joint Use Area. That year the Hopi signed an agreement with the federal government providing almost $3 million in funds for water and wastewater construction for the villages of First Mesa. Although both tribes have profited from the Peabody enterprise, the area has suffered from air and water pollution, soil erosion, and loss of cultural artifacts. Their coal, natural gas, oil, and uranium mineral resources grant the Hopi membership in the Council of Energy Resource Tribes. Founded in 1975, the council is the recognized political authority in dealings with the federal government on mineral exploration and development policies and provides technical information to the member tribes.

By the end of the twentieth century, most of the Navajo families had relocated. Seeking an amicable compromise, the Hopi government approved seventy-five-year leases to Navajo who stayed on the land. In 2000 the two tribes reached a settlement for past trespassing and overgrazing, with the Navajo agreeing to pay $29 million in damages. Throughout the first decade of the twenty-first century, the Hopi continued to wage legal battles against the Navajo, the U.S. government, and the Peabody Western Coal Company.

A Hopi girl in Arizona, c. 1920s. BUYENLARGE / GETTY IMAGES

Perhaps the most successful litigation, brought jointly by the Hopi and Navajo tribes, pressured Peabody to shut down its Black Mesa Mine. Condemning the company's overuse of water, the tribes argued that the operation contributed to the contamination of the limited water supply, which had religious and cultural as well as practical significance. The Black Mesa Mine closed at the end of 2005 and failed to gain approval to resume mining activities in 2010 because of environmental concerns. Also in 2005 the Hopi secured water rights to the Colorado River in the Cibola Basin and began work on a pipeline to bring water to the reservation from the Coconino Aquifer.

Today, many Hopi continue to farm and tend livestock, but the majority of tribal members earn income either through labor or selling crafts. The Hopi government continues to seek a balance between the lucrative mineral and tourist industries and retaining the intimacy and sacredness of its spiritual artifacts and ceremonies. Modern-day concerns have applied pressure to tribal culture, dividing opinions among the Hopi. The tribe attempts a delicate balance, protecting and celebrating Hopi traditions while adopting some aspects of modern American culture in order to survive and grow economically.

SETTLEMENT IN THE UNITED STATES

By the end of the twentieth century, the Hopi Tribe was considered one of the more traditional Indian societies in the continental United States. The degree of their cultural preservation is a remarkable achievement, facilitated by isolation, secrecy, and a community that remains essentially closed to outsiders. As far back as archeologists can reliably traced their history (to the period called Pueblo II, between 900 and 1100), the Hopi have been sedentary, living in traditional native sandstone buildings. Their villages consisted of houses arranged around a central plaza containing one or more kivas. Hopi villages are arranged in much the same way today. During the Pueblo III Period (1100 to 1300), the population in the villages grew as the climate became more arid, making farming more difficult. The village buildings grew in size as well as number, some containing hundreds of rooms. According to Page and Page, during the Pueblo IV Period—the Hopi ancestral period that lasted from 1350 to 1540—the houses, made "of stone cemented with adobe and then plastered inside were virtually indistinguishable from the older houses of present-day Hopi, except that they were often multistoried." They add that the houses of that period contained rooms with specific functions, such as storage or grinding corn, and that kiva design was "nearly identical" to that of today. The houses and kivas of this period were heated with coal, which was also used for firing pottery.

Today the Hopi occupy the older masonry dwellings as well as modern houses. The kivas remain largely as they were in earlier times: rectangular rooms built of native stone, mostly below ground. (The very ancient kivas were circular.) "Sometimes," writes Waters in *The Book of the Hopi*, "the kiva is widened at one end, forming the same shape as the T-shaped doorways found in all ancient Hopi ruins." This design is intended to echo the hairstyle of Hopi men. The kiva contains an altar and central fire pit below the roof opening. A ladder extends above the edge of the roof. When not in use for ceremonies, kivas are also used as meeting rooms.

Many Hopi still live on or around the Hopi Reservation, continuing to live in small sandstone homes and participating in religious ceremonies. The Hopi Tribe has embraced a cash based economy, but they continue to infuse spiritual meaning to their work

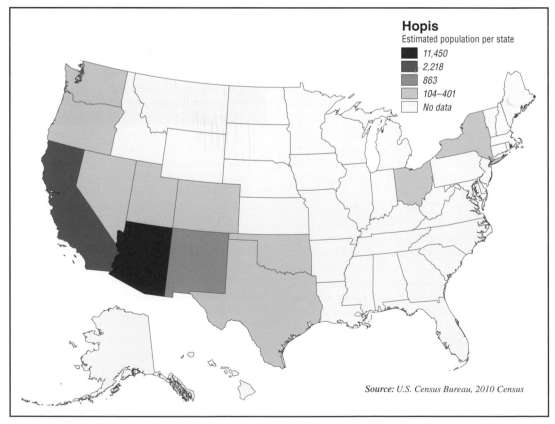

Hopis
Estimated population per state
- 11,450
- 2,218
- 863
- 104–401
- No data

Source: U.S. Census Bureau, 2010 Census

and crafts. Economic challenges, however, have forced many Hopi to leave the reservation, seeking employment in cities like Durango, Colorado, Albuquerque, New Mexico, and Phoenix and Flagstaff, Arizona. After the 2005 closure of the Black Mesa mine, the tribe lost a substantial source of royalties. Unlike other tribes, the Hopi have continually rejected gambling and casinos on the reservation. The declining revenues have left the tribe without the means to develop an infrastructure. With virtually no industry and inadequate community services, the Hopi Reservation faces a complex set of issues. Although nearly 60 percent of the community is unemployed, Hopi continue to sustain themselves through subsistence farming. Tribal officials, however, are attempting to establish Hopi enterprises, such as mineral mining and small businesses, that will draw back members of the tribe to the reservation.

LANGUAGE

The Hopi are the only Pueblo tribe that speaks a Shoshonean-derived language of the Uto-Aztecan linguistic family. They use several dialects of a single language, Hopi, with the exception of the residents of the village of Hano, who speak Tewa, which is derived from the Azteco-Tanoan linguistic family. Waters notes in 1963 that "Hopi is not yet a commonly written language, perhaps because of the extreme difficulty in translation, as pointed out by Benjamin Lee Whorf, who has made a profound analysis of the language." Despite being unwritten and untranslated, the language has been preserved and passed down by the strong Hopi oral tradition.

The Hopi today, including the younger generations, speak both Hopi and English. The 2011 American Community Survey estimated that 6,634 people spoke the Hopi language. Schools on the Hopi Reservation routinely teach the language to elementary and secondary students, contributing to a culture that continues to retain much of its heritage. Both the University of Arizona (Tucson) and Northern Arizona University (Flagstaff) began developing a Hopi writing system with a dictionary so far containing over 30,000 words. The survey indicates, however, that an increasing number of American Indians only speak English, and the Hopi Cultural Preservation Office states that some of the ancient language has been lost.

Common Words and Expressions Some Hopi words and phrases are: *tiva* (tee-vah)—"dance"; *kahopi* (kah-ho-pee)—"not Hopi"; *kachada* (kah-chah-dah)—"white man"; *Hotomkam* (ho-tom-kahm)—"Three Stars in Line" (Orion's Belt); *kachinki* (kah-cheen-kee)—"kachina house"; *Hakomi?* (hah-ko-mee)—"Who are you?"; and *Haliksa'I* (hah-leek-sah)—"Listen, this is how it is."

RELIGION

The Hopi religion is a complex, highly developed belief system incorporating many gods and spirits, such as Taiowa (the sun-father), Kokyangwuti (spider woman), and the various kachinas, or invisible spirits of life, which embody forces of nature, both benevolent and malevolent, as well as historical moments and aspects of human nature. Waters describes this religion as "a mytho-religious system of year-long ceremonies, rituals, dances, songs, recitations, and prayers as complex, abstract, and esoteric as any in the world." The Hopi identity centers on this belief system. Waters explains their devotion, writing, "The Hopis […] have never faltered in the belief that their secular pattern of existence must be predicated upon the religious, the universal plan of Creation. They are still faithful to their own premise." Page and Page state that 95 percent of the Hopi people continue to adhere to these beliefs.

According to oral tradition, the Hopi originated in the first of four worlds, not as people but as fractious, insectlike creatures. Displeased with these creatures' grasp of the meaning of life, the Creator, the Sun spirit *Tawa*, sent the spirit Spider Woman to guide them on an evolutionary migration. By the time they reached the Third World, they had become people. They reached the Fourth, or Upper, World by climbing up from the underworld through a hollow reed. Upon reaching this world, they were given four stone tablets by Masaw, the world's guardian spirit. Masaw described the migrations they were to take to the ends of the land in each of the four directions and how they would identify the place where they were intended to finally settle. And so the migrations began, with various clans starting out in each direction. Their routes formed a cross, and their destined permanent home turned out to be at the center—their starting point—which was the Center of the Universe. This story of the Hopi Creation holds that their completed journeys finally led them to the plateau that lies between the Colorado and Rio Grande Rivers, in the Four Corners region. As Waters explains, the Hopi "know that they were led here so that they would have to depend upon the scanty rainfall which they must evoke with their power and prayer," preserving their faith in the Creator who brought them to this place. The Hopi are thus connected in a deeply religious way to their land with its agricultural cycles and the constant quest for rainfall.

CULTURE AND ASSIMILATION

The U.S. government subjected the Hopi Tribe to multiple means of forced assimilation, including the removal of Hopi children from the reservation to boarding schools. Faced with the generational loss of their language, Hopi elders sought to preserve their culture through its oral tradition. The Hopi tradition of oral literature has been crucial to the survival of the Hopi Way, a term that refers to a code of behavior and ethics involving traditional principles and emphasizing the value of kinship systems. Since the language was unwritten until recent years, the oral tradition has made it possible to foster Hopi pride during modern

times and to continue customs, rituals, and ceremonies, sustaining the religious beliefs that are the essence of the Hopi Way. The body of Hopi oral literature is huge.

Like many tribes, the Hopi face numerous cultural challenges, such as consumerism and colonization by religious denominations. In spite of the challenges, the Hopi have shown themselves to be resilient, maintaining their spiritual beliefs and ceremonies. The Hopi Cultural Preservation Office has established a variety of programs targeting educational and community development and has also launched a series of media campaigns designed to maintain traditional Hopi values in modern times.

Traditions and Customs Benedek writes that "in spirit and in ceremony, the Hopi maintain a connection with the center of the earth, for they believe that they are the earth's caretakers, and with the successful performance of their ceremonial cycle, the world will remain in balance, the gods will be appeased, and rain will come." Central to the ceremonies are the kiva, the *paho* (a prayer feather, usually that of an eagle), and the creator, Corn Mother, who is somewhat synonymous with Mother Earth. The kiva symbolizes the ancients' emergence into this world, with a small hole in the floor leading to the underworld and a ladder extending above the roof opening, which represents the way to the upper world. Kivas are found in various numbers in Hopi villages, always on an east-west axis, sunk into the central plaza of a village. The paho is used to send prayers to the Creator. Pahos are prepared for all kiva ceremonies. Corn has sustained the Hopi for centuries, and it plays a large role in Hopi ceremonies; for example, cornmeal is sprinkled to welcome the kachinas to the Corn Mother. Waters describes the Corn Mother as "a perfect ear of corn whose tip ends in four full kernels." It is saved for rituals.

The number four has great significance in the Hopi religion, so community rituals often call for repetitions of four. In accordance with Hopi tradition, both boys and girls were initiated into the kachina cult between the ages of eight and ten. Barbara Leitch writes in *A Concise Dictionary of Indian Tribes of North America* (1979) that the rite included "fasting, praying, and being whipped with a yucca whip. Each child had a ceremonial mother (girls) or father (boys) who saw them through the ordeal." She also noted, "All boys were initiated into one of the four men's societies, Kwan, Ahl, Tao, or Wuwutcimi, usually joining the society of their ceremonial father. These rites commonly occurred in conjunction with the Powama ceremony, a four-day tribal initiation rite for young men, usually held at planting time." A tradition no longer observed is the prepuberty ceremony for ten-year-old girls, which involved grinding corn for an entire day at the girl's paternal grandmother's house. "At the onset of menses," Elsie Clews Parsons records in *Hopi and Zuñi Ceremonialism* (1950), "Girls of the more conservative families go through a puberty ceremony marked by a four-day grinding ordeal." These girls would also receive a new name and would then occasionally wear the traditional Hopi squash blossom hairstyle, the sign of marriageability.

Cuisine Subsistence farming and small game have always provided the basis of the Hopi diet. In the ancestral period wild game was more plentiful, and Hopi men hunted deer, antelope, and elk with bows and arrows and also by corralling animals into a fenced-in area. They also hunted rabbit with a boomerang. Besides meat, Page and Page list corn, squash, beans, and some wild and semicultivated plants—such as Indian millet, wild potato, piñon, and dropseed—as staples of the period. The authors also noted that salt was obtained with considerable effort by making long excursions to the Grand Canyon area. Leitch records that the women gathered "pinenuts, prickly pear, yucca, berries, currants, nuts, and various seeds" to supplement their cuisine. In the sixteenth century the Spanish introduced wheat, onions, peaches and other fruits, chiles, and mutton to the Hopi diet.

The Hopi continue to depend on the land. Wild game had dwindled significantly in the region by 1950, leaving only rabbit and a few quail and deer. Modern Hopi farmers still use the old methods, raising mainly corn, melons, gourds, and many varieties of beans. Corn is the main crop, and the six traditional Hopi varieties are yellow, blue, red, white, purple, and sweet. All have symbolic meaning stemming from the Creation story. A corn roast is an annual ritual, and corn is ground for use in ceremonies as well as to make *piki*, a traditional bread baked in layers on hot stones. The 1983 film *Corn Is Life* documents the importance of corn and its religious significance to Hopi culture. The film portrays traditional methods of planting, cultivating, harvesting, and preparing corn, including the baking of piki bread on hot, polished stones.

Traditional Dress In earlier times Hopi men wore fur or buckskin loincloths. Some loincloths were painted and decorated with tassels, which symbolized falling rain. The men raised cotton in addition to the edible crops and spun and wove it into cloth, robes, blankets, ceremonial garments, and textiles. The hand-woven cotton blankets were worn regularly as clothing. In 1861 Mormon and Catholic missionaries described the Hopi as being wrapped in blankets with broad white and dark stripes. At that time women commonly wore loose black gowns with a gold stripe around the waist and at the hem. Men wore shirts and loose cotton pants, covered with a blanket wrap. During the ritual ceremonies and dances, Hopi men have always worn elaborate costumes that include special headdresses, masks, and body paints. These costumes vary according to clan and ceremony.

Married women wore their hair long or braided, but marriageable girls twisted theirs up into large whorls on either side of their head. These whorls represent the squash blossom, which is a symbol of fertility. The hairstyle is still worn by unmarried Hopi girls, but because of the amount of time required to create it, it is reserved for ceremonial occasions. Traditionally, Hopi men wore their hair in a T-style, after which kiva design was sometimes patterned: straight bangs hung over the forehead, the sides were worn long, covering the ears, and the hair in the back was knotted. The same style of bangs is still seen among traditional Hopi men.

Hopi women and girls today wear a traditional black dress embroidered with bright red and green trim. As in early days a bride's uncles weave white cotton cloth to be made into robes for the ceremony. The bridal costume consists of a large robe decorated with tassels that symbolize falling rain and a second, smaller robe, also with tassels, rolled up and carried in a reed scroll called a "suitcase" in English. When the woman dies, she is wrapped in the suitcase robe.

The traditional ceremonies that constitute Hopi holidays are performed as instructed in sacred stories and relate to most aspects of daily Hopi life. Such occasions commemorate important times in an individual's life and important times of the year; ceremonies are also conducted for healing, spiritual renewal, bringing rain, initiating people into respected positions, and giving thanks.

Dances and Songs The Hopi ceremonial cycle continues all year. Rituals are conducted within the kivas in secrecy and are followed by ceremonial dances in the plaza These dances are rhythmic, mystical, and full of pageantry. Outsiders are sometimes allowed to watch the dances. Hopi men dressed and masked as the spirits perform kachina dances, which are tied to the growing season. One of the most important ceremonies, Soyal, is held at the winter solstice. The first ceremony of the year, it features the first kachina dance and represents the second phase of Creation. The Niman ceremony, or the Home Dance, is held at the summer solstice in late July. At that point the last of the crops have been planted and the first corn has been harvested. The Home Dance is the last kachina dance of the year.

Although other ceremonial dances are also religious, they are less so than the kachina rituals. These other dances include the Buffalo Dance, held in January to commemorate the days when the buffalo were plentiful and Hopi men went out to the Eastern Plains to hunt them; the Bean Dance, held in February to petition the kachinas for the next planting; and the Navajo Dance, celebrating the Navajo tribe. While the well-known Snake Dance is preceded by eight days of secret preparation, the dance itself is relatively short, lasting only about an hour. During this rite the priests handle and even put in their mouths unresisting snakes gathered from the desert. Non-Hopi experts have tried to discover how the priests can handle snakes without being bitten, but the secret has not been revealed. At the conclusion of the dance, the snakes are released back into the desert, bearing messages for rain. The Snake and Flute Dances are held alternately, every other year. The Flute Dance glorifies the spirits of those who have passed away during the preceding two years. Women's dances, including the Basket Dance, are held near the end of the year.

Holidays The traditional ceremonies that constitute Hopi holidays are performed as instructed in sacred stories and relate to most aspects of daily Hopi life. Such occasions commemorate important times in an individual's life and important times of the year; ceremonies are also conducted for healing, spiritual renewal, bringing rain, initiating people into respected positions, and giving thanks. Hopi observances included the Flute, New Fire, Niman Kachina, Pachavu, Powamu, Snake-Antelope, and Wuwuchim ceremonies and Soyal.

Health Care Issues and Practices Page and Page state that although the Hopi utilize many herbal remedies and are quite knowledgeable about the various medicinal properties of certain plants and herbs, much of Hopi healing is psychic. Ritual curing is done by several societies, including the kachina society. Parsons writes, "The Kachina cult is generally conceived as a rain-making, crop-bringing cult; but it has also curing or health-bringing functions." She adds that "On First Mesa kachina dances (including the Horned [W]ater [S]erpent and the Buffalo Dance) may be planned for afflicted persons." Cures for some illnesses are administered by specific societies. For example, according to Parsons, snakebite is treated by the Snake society on First Mesa, and rheumatism is treated by the Powamu society, which then inducts the afflicted into the

society. Other cures are less logical to an outsider. "On First Mesa," Parsons continues, "lightning-shocked persons and persons whose fields have been lightning-struck join the Flute society. A lightning-shocked man is called in to cure earache in babies." Other rituals include the practice of "sucking out" the disease, usually when dealing with sick infants and children. The curer holds cornmeal in his mouth during this procedure and then "spits away" the disease. In Hopi culture both men and women served as healers and continue to do so in the twenty-first century.

The Hopi also utilize modern medical science, doctors, and hospitals. A government hospital was established in 1913 in Kearns Canyon, Arizona, on the Hopi Reservation. An Office of Native Healing Services is located in nearby Window Rock, Arizona. In 2000 the Hopi Health Care Center, serving approximately 16,000 people from the Hopi and Navajo reservations, was constructed on First Mesa.

FAMILY AND COMMUNITY LIFE
The Hopi have traditionally practiced monogamy, and their families were matrilineal in nature, with the husband joining his mother-in-law's household. The social organization of traditional Hopi society is based on kinship clans determined through the woman's side of the family. Clan membership shapes Hopi identity. The clans influence various kinds of social relations of individuals throughout their lives, including possible marriage partners and their place of residence. In the late 1990s approximately thirty Hopi clans existed.

Education Hopi children pursue their education at a variety of local public schools, federal government schools, local village schools, and private schools and are exposed to traditional educational activities in such places as kivas. Between 1894 and 1912 the U.S. government established schools near Hopi villages. Until the late twentieth century children had to leave home to attend secondary level government-sponsored or private off-reservation boarding schools. In 1985 new Hopi middle and high schools were opened for all tribal students. The on-reservation schools have facilitated traditional education by allowing students to live at home so that they may participate in year-round village rituals and ceremonies. Traditional education begins in earnest around the age of eight with a series of initiation rites into the Hopi Way.

Since 2005 the Hopi government has developed high school programs with Northern Arizona University that prepare students for college classes and allow them to earn up to thirty college credits that will transfer from high school to the university. The programs also fund research and resources that enable elementary and secondary teachers to include Hopi language and culture as part of the curriculum. In 2012, according to the Arizona State Department of Education, Hopi High School in Kearns Canyon had the highest high school graduation rate in the

state, with close to 80 percent of the students graduating, compared to the state average of 63 percent. In October 2011 the Four Corners Sustainable Futures Initiative reported that more than 68 percent of members over the age of eighteen had received a high school diploma from either a reservation high school or from a public school, nearly 19 percent had completed a college or university degree program, and more than 12 percent had received vocational training.

As of 2012 seven universities and colleges operate within 250 miles of the reservation. Northland Pioneer College in Holbrook, Arizona, provides education on the reservation and also has campus in Winslow, Arizona. A number of Hopi tribal members attend the Southwestern Indian Polytechnic Institute (SIPI) or the University of New Mexico (UNM), both in Albuquerque. Fort Lewis College in Durango, Colorado, provides tuition waivers for Native American students. Diné College, with its main campus in Tsaile, Arizona, and several satellite campuses in Chinle, Cronpoint, Ganado, Kayenta, Shiprock, and Tuba City, caters to Hopi students. Partnerships between the Hopi Education Endowment Fund, Northern Arizona University, and the University of New Mexico have created scholarships and distance learning programs to further assist Hopi educational pursuits.

Gender Roles Because Hopi society is matrilineal, women owned the farming and garden plots, though men were responsible for the work of cultivating and harvesting the crops as well as grazing the sheep and other livestock. Corn planting was a community event involving men and women. Women are centrally involved in Hopi arts and crafts. By tradition the women's products are specialized and determined by their residence. On First Mesa, women make ceramics, including the fine pottery they have created for centuries. Second Mesa women make coiled basketry, and those on Third Mesa make wicker basketry. Hopi men, however, were traditionally the weavers and kachina doll carvers. Originally toys for children, the dolls now sell at handsome prices to tourists.

Contemporary Hopi society maintains many of the traditional gender roles; however, economic pressures have afforded Hopi women greater opportunities than they have had in the past. While the matrilineal aspect of the culture still supplies Hopi women with some power, they have enjoyed additional success in education and employment. The Hopi Cultural Preservation Office and the Hopi Foundation have sponsored a variety of projects, from craft cooperatives to job training programs, that help Hopi women find work. These organizations have also jointly established the Hopi Leadership Program. Although not all services cater exclusively to women, Hopi cultural centers have sought out women as mentors, and many leaders of the Preservation Office and Hopi Foundation are women.

Courtship and Weddings Many traditional Hopi marriage customs are still observed, but others have fallen into disuse. Fifty years ago, for example, courtship was an elaborate procedure involving

NAMING CEREMONY

In their book *Hopi* (1994), Suzanne and Jake Page explain the special rituals observed by Hopi when naming a new baby. A newborn is kept from direct view of the sun for its first nineteen days. The child's Corn Mother, symbolized by an ear of corn with four kernels at the tip, is placed with the newborn. A few days prior to the naming, the traditional Hopi stew is prepared at the home of the maternal grandmother, who figures prominently in the custom. Babies belong to their mother's clan but are named for their father's. In the naming ritual the grandmother kneels and washes the mother's hair then bathes the baby. The baby is wrapped snugly in a blanket, with only its head visible. With the baby's Corn Mother, the grandmother rubs a mixture of water and cornmeal on the baby's hair, applying it four times. Each of the baby's paternal aunts then repeats this application, and each gives a gift and suggests a name. The grandmother chooses one of these names and then introduces the baby to the sun god just as the sun comes up. A feast follows.

a rabbit hunt, corn grinding, and family approval of the marriage. The bride was married in traditional white robes woven for the occasion by her uncles. The couple lived with the bride's mother for the first year. Today the courtship is much less formal. The couple often marry in a church or registry office and then return to the reservation. Page and Page point out that because not all men know how to weave now, it may take years for the uncles to produce the traditional robes. Marriage customs still in practice include a four-day stay by the bride with her intended in-laws. During this time she grinds corn all day and prepares all the family's meals to demonstrate her culinary competence. Prior to the wedding the aunts of both the bride and groom engage in a good-natured free-for-all that involves throwing mud and trading insults, each side suggesting the other's relative is no good. The groom's parents wash the couple's hair with a shampoo of yucca, a ritual that occurs in other ceremonies as well. A huge feast follows at the bride's mother's house. Once married, the bride wears her hair loose or in braids.

Clan membership plays a role in partner selection. A rule against marrying another member of the same clan has kept genetic lines strong. Although in the past, marriage into an associated clan was forbidden as well, Page and Page suggest that this tradition is changing. Marriage to nontribal members is rare, a fact that has helped preserve Hopi culture. Clan membership is passed down through the mother, and, traditionally, members were required to have a clan of birth; thus, if the mother was not Hopi, her children were not Hopi either. In modern times, persons of one-fourth or more Hopi "blood," as documented through ancestry, are eligible for tribal enrollment. Adoption into the tribe is extremely rare.

Funerals To the Hopi old age is desirable because it indicates that the journey of life is almost complete. They have a strong respect for the rituals of honoring and burying the dead. Their religion holds that the soul's journey to the land of the dead begins on the fourth day after death. It is customary, therefore, to bury the dead as quickly as possible to avoid interfering with the soul's ability to reach the underworld. Traditionally, the hair of the deceased was washed with yucca shampoo by a paternal aunt. Leitch adds that the hair was then decorated with prayer feathers and the face covered with a mask of raw cotton, symbolizing clouds. The body was then wrapped—a man in a deerskin robe, a woman in her wedding robe—and buried by the oldest son, preferably on the day or night of death. As Leitch explains, "The body was buried in a sitting position along with food and water. Cornmeal and prayer-sticks were later placed in the grave." A stick was inserted into the soil of a grave as an exit for the soul. If rain followed, it signified the soul's successful journey. These traditions are still practiced by some Hopi.

Interactions with Other Tribes The Hopi have maintained historical relations with the Zuñi, Hano, and Tewa groups of Pueblo peoples in the Rio Grande River valley to the east. Extensive trading networks existed among the groups prior to the Pueblo Revolt of 1680, when they united to drive Spanish influence out of the region. The Hopi preserved their ties with the Pueblo, but the Navajo, who were also retreating from European expansion, encroached upon Hopi land, initiating a period of fighting that lasted until 1864. The complex land issues with the Navajo have problematized relations between the two tribes. The Hopi elective government have fought for defense of their original reservation, while other tribal members support the Navajo families' efforts to remain on the disputed lands.

EMPLOYMENT AND ECONOMIC CONDITIONS

For more than three thousand years, the Hopi have been sedentary agriculturalists. A great drought occurred from 1279 to 1299, requiring them to adopt inventive farming methods in an arid desert climate that are still in use today. Every possible source of moisture is utilized. The wind blows sand up against the sides of the mesas, forming dunes that trap moisture. Crops are then planted in these dunes. The Hopi also dry farm in washes that occasionally flood, as well as in the mouths of arroyos, and they construct irrigated terraces on the mesas, often irrigating by hand. They supplement their subsistence economy by hunting small game.

By the 1970s farming income was declining and wage labor was gaining importance in the Hopi economy. An undergarment factory was established in Winslow, Arizona, in partnership with the Hopi in 1971 but failed in only a few years. In the late twentieth century, the Hopi had a diverse economy that included small-scale farming and livestock grazing, various small businesses, mineral development royalty payments, government subsidies for community improvements, and wage-labor incomes. Many traditional Hopi objects were transformed from utilitarian and sacred items to works of art. Commercial art includes the making of kachina dolls, silver jewelry, woven baskets, and pottery. Cooperative marketing organizations and various enterprises for Hopi craftspeople, including Hopicrafts and Artist Hopid, exist both on and off the reservation. In addition to arts and crafts shops, small businesses on the reservation include two motels, a museum, and several dining facilities and gas stations. The early twenty-first century brought no additional employment opportunities to the reservation. As of 2011, 46 percent of tribal jobs were associated with federal or tribal entities such as the Bureau of Indian Affairs, the Hopi Tribal Government, and the Indian Health Service.

The median household income for Hopi residents is $23,446; the figure is considerably lower than Arizona's statewide median of $44,261. More than 40 percent of the reservation population and close to 70 percent of the total Hopi population live below the federal poverty line. Hopi tribal members have an unemployment rate of 11.7 percent, nearly three times the statewide rate of 4.2 percent.

POLITICS AND GOVERNMENT

The Hopi Tribal Council's function is representative; it does not govern the tribe. Several villages continue to refuse to recognize the political authority of the tribal council over village affairs. The Hopi government divides its authority between the fourteen-member elected tribal council and the village representatives from Upper Moenkopi, Bacavi, Kykotsmovi, and Sipaulovi. Since the 2011 elections, the villages of Mishongnovi, Shungopavi, Oraibi, Hotevilla, and Lower Moenkopi and the First Mesa Consolidated Village have not had representatives on the council. This central tribal government makes decision by majority rule.

Continuing in the traditional Hopi system, each village maintains an autonomous government led by a *kikmongwi*, or village chief, who also interprets the religious and cultural aspects of the clan. Village governments retain all authority concerning land use, business development, and housing. Villages select their own governmental structures, and most villages tend to be democratic, relying on consensus decision making. Page and Page describe this system as "a loose confederation of politically independent villages, rather like the city-states of ancient Greece,

knit together by basically similar views of their history, [and] by similar religious beliefs and ceremonial practices." The authors also note that the clan system is "one of the main forms of social glue that has historically held the separate Hopi villages together."

NOTABLE INDIVIDUALS

Academia Elizabeth Q. White (ca. 1892–1990), also known as Polingaysi Qoyawayma, was born at the traditional village of Old Oraibi. She graduated from Bethel College in Newton, Kansas, after studying to be a Mennonite missionary at the Hopi Reservation. She became a noted educator on the reservation, eventually earning the U.S. Department of Interior's Distinguished Service Award. White wrote several books on Hopi traditional life and founded the Hopi Student Scholarship Fund at Northern Arizona University.

Emory Sekequaptewa (1928–2007) was a Native American scholar who served on the editorial board that compiled the first dictionary of the Hopi language. The project to create *Hopi Dictionary: Hopìikwa Lavàytutuveni: A Hopi-English Dictionary of the Third Mesa Dialect with an English-Hopi Finder List and a Sketch of Hopi Grammar* ran from 1985 to 1998 and was conducted under the auspices of the Bureau of Applied Anthropology at the University of Arizona.

An enrolled Hopi tribal member, Matthew Sakiestewa Gilbert grew up in Upper Moenkopi, Arizona. He earned a PhD in Native American history from the University of California, Riverside and is currently teaches American Indian studies at the University of Illinois at Urbana-Champaign. Gilbert has written numerous articles, produced the documentary, *Beyond the Mesas*, and wrote *Education beyond the Mesas: Hopi Students at Sherman Institute, 1902–1929* (2010).

From the village of Shungopavi on Second Mesa, Hopi tribal member Sheilah Nicholas is an assistant professor at University of Arizona in the College of Education, working in several areas: the department of Teaching, Learning and Sociocultural Studies (TLSS), the program in Language, Reading and Culture (LRC), the American Indian Studies Program (AISP), and Second Language Acquisition Teaching (SLAT). Her academic pursuits focus on Hopi language. Nicholas serves as a consultant for the Hopi Tribe and local schools and has established the Hopi Language Summer Institute.

Also an enrolled Hopi tribal member from Shungopavi, Angela Gonzales is an associate professor of Development Sociology and Indigenous Studies at Cornell University and a community-based health researcher. Her work focuses on Native American access to healthcare, in particular American Indian women's access to preventive, diagnostic, and curative treatments for cancer and human papillomavirus (HPV).

Art Traditional Hopi anonymity changed in the twentieth century as many individuals began to be recognized for their work.

Nampeyo (1859–1942), born in Hano on First Mesa, helped revive Hopi arts by reintroducing ancient forms and designs from archaeological remains into her pottery. Her work became uniquely artistic. She appeared in promotional photographs used by the Santa Fe Railway and others, and her pots were added to the collection of the National Museum in Washington, D.C. Nampeyo's daughters, granddaughters, and great-granddaughters carried on her artistry in ceramics. Granddaughter Hooee Daisy Nampeyo (1905?–1994) studied in Paris and made pottery influenced by archeological finds created in the ancient Zuni tradition. Dextra Quotskuyva (1928–), another granddaughter of Nampeyo, is a renowned potter and artist, known for using traditional Hopi methods and designs. In 1995 she was awarded the Arizona Indian Living Treasure prize, and in 1998 she received the first Arizona State Museum Lifetime Achievement Award.

> She knew it was the duty of the youngest member of a Hopi family to feed the family gods and she was the youngest present, but she was in a hurry to be off and would have neglected the duty had not her grandmother reminded her.
>
> Polingaysi Qoyawayma, *No Turning Back: A True Account of a Hopi Girl's Struggle* (Albuquerque: University of New Mexico Press, 1964).

Fred Kabotie (1900–1986) was born in the traditional village of Shungopavi on Second Mesa and attended the Santa Fe Indian School as a teenager, where his talent for painting was recognized. Kabotie became especially well known for his depictions of kachinas, which vividly portrayed supernatural powers. In 1922 he won the first annual Rose Dugan art prize of the Museum of New Mexico, and by 1930 his paintings were on permanent exhibit in the museum. Earning international recognition, his work was exhibited at such major museums as the Museum of Modern Art in New York, the Peabody Museum of Harvard University, and the Corcoran Gallery in Washington, D.C., and toured internationally in Europe and Asia. He received a Guggenheim Foundation fellowship in 1945 and he was elected to the French Academy of Arts in 1954. In the 1940s, Kabotie founded the Hopi Silvercraft Cooperative Guild, teaching unemployed World War II veterans the art of silverworking. Charles Loloma was a noted student. From 1937 to 1959 Kabotie taught art back home in Oraibi, Arizona, furthering a tribal artistic tradition. In 1958 he was awarded the U.S. Indian Arts and Crafts Board's Certificate of Merit. His son, Michael, cofounded Artist Hopid to promote Hopi artists.

Charles Loloma's (1921–1991) jewelry is among the most distinctive in the world. The originality of his designs stems from the combination of nontraditional materials, such as gold and diamonds, with such typical Indian materials as turquoise. He also received great recognition as a potter, silversmith, and designer. Loloma was born in Hotevilla on the Hopi Reservation and attended the Hopi High School in Oraibi and the Phoenix Indian High School in Phoenix, Arizona. In 1939 he painted the murals for the Federal Building on Treasure Island in San Francisco Bay as part of the Golden Gate International Exposition. The following year the Indian Arts and Crafts Board commissioned him to paint the murals for the Museum of Modern Art in New York. In 1940 Loloma was drafted into the army, where he spent four years working as a camouflage expert in the Aleutian Islands off the Alaskan coast. After his discharge he attended the School for American Craftsmen at Alfred University in New York, a well-known center for ceramic arts. This choice was unprecedented on Loloma's part, since ceramics was traditionally a women's art form among the Hopi. After receiving a 1949 Whitney Foundation Fellowship to study the clays of the Hopi area, he and his wife, Otellie, worked out of the newly opened Kiva Craft Center in Scottsdale, Arizona. From 1954 to 1958 he taught at Arizona State University, and in 1962 he became head of the Plastic Arts and Sales Departments at the newly established Institute of American Indian Arts in Santa Fe, New Mexico. In 1963 Loloma's work was exhibited in Paris. After 1965 he spent the rest of his years on the Hopi Reservation, where he continued working and taught several apprentices. By the mid-1970s his jewelry had been exhibited throughout the country and in Europe, and his pieces had won numerous first prizes in arts competitions. Loloma was one of the first prominent Indian craftsmen who had a widely recognized unique personal style.

Otellie Loloma (1922–1992), born at Shipaulovi on Second Mesa, received a three-year scholarship to the School of the American Craftsmen at Alfred University in New York, where she specialized in ceramics. At Alfred she met and later married Charles Loloma, an internationally famous Hopi artist. Otellie herself received world acclaim for her ceramics and was considered the most influential Indian woman in the field. Loloma taught at Arizona State University, at the Southwest Indian Art Project at the University of Arizona, and at the Institute of American Indian Arts (IAIA). She also mastered traditional dance, performing at the 1968 Olympics in Mexico and at a White House special program. Her work has been shown internationally and is exhibited at a number of museums, including New York's Museum of the American Indian, the Heard Museum in Pheonix, and Blair House in Washington, D.C. One of her last awards was an Outstanding Achievement in the Visual Arts award from the 1991 National Women's Caucus for Art.

Thomas Nahsonhoya (1928–), a member of the Roadrunner Clan and resident of Sitsomovi, is a traditional textile weaver. He was selected to receive the 2010–2011 Arizona Indian Living Treasures Award and was also recognized by the Pu'Tavi Project as a Hopi Living Treasure.

Weaver Ramona Sakiestewa (1949–) was born in Albuquerque, New Mexico, to a Hopi father. She attended New York's School of Visual Arts and specialized in the treadle loom. Sakiestewa combines ancient design elements with contemporary weaving techniques, establishing a unique tradition in Native American arts. She cofounded ATLATL, a national Native American arts organization. Her tapestries have been shown at the Heard Museum of Phoenix and the Wheelwright Museum of American Indian in Santa Fe, among other venues.

Award-winning artist and teacher Linda Lomahaftewa (1947–) was born in Phoenix, Arizona. She attended the Institute of American Indian Arts in Santa Fe and earned an MA in fine arts in 1971 from the San Francisco Art Institute. Lomahaftewa's drawings and paintings reflecting Hopi spirituality and storytelling have been exhibited throughout the United States. She has received numerous awards and has taught at various colleges and universities, including the University of California, Berkeley and at the Art Institute.

Education Eugene Sekaquaptewa (1925) was born on the Hopi Reservation at Hotevilla. He earned an MA from Arizona State University before joining the U.S. Marines in 1941. He survived the U.S. invasion of Iwo Jima and other intense battles. Sekaquaptewa returned to Arizona State University to teach education courses and participate in the university's Indian Community Action Project, in addition to teaching at the Indian boarding school in Riverside, California, the Sherman Institute. He has published a number of professional papers on Hopi education.

LuAnn Leonard (1961–) of the Alwungwa (Deer) Clan from the village of Sichomovi is the executive director of the Hopi Education Endowment Fund (HEEF). In 2008 she became the first Native American to be appointed to the Arizona Board of Regents.

Film, Television, and Theater Maggi Banner, a Hopi independent filmmaker documenting experiences of the native peoples of the Southwest, produced *Coyote Goes Underground* (1989) and *Tiwa Tales* (1991).

The prolific independent filmmaker Victor Masayesva Jr. (1951–) produced the documentaries *Hopiit* (1982), *Itam Hakim Hopiit* (1984), *Siskyavi: A Place of Chasms* (1991), and *Imagining Indians* (1992) among others.

Journalism An influential periodical publisher and editor, Rose Robinson (1932–) was born in Winslow, Arizona and earned degrees from the Haskell Indian Nations Institute in Lawrence, Kansas, and American University in Washington, D.C., in journalism studies. Robinson was a founding board member of the American Indian Press Association (later renamed Native American Journalist Association) before becoming its executive director. She also served as a member of the U.S. Department of the Interior's Indian Arts and Crafts Board, as information officer for the Bureau of Indian Affairs' Office of Public Instruction, as vice president and director of the Phelps-Stokes Fund's American Indian Program, and in various leadership roles with the North American Indian Women's Association. Robinson guided the publication of periodicals for the Native American-Philanthropic News Service, including the *Exchange* and the *Roundup*. In 1980 she received the Indian Media Woman of the Year award.

Literature Don C. Talayesva (1890–?) was born on the Hopi Reservation in Oraibi and was raised in the traditional Hopi Way for the early part of his life. After attending the Sherman School for Indians in Riverside, California, and living among whites for several years, Talayesva returned to the reservation to resume the traditional Hopi lifestyle. He became the subject of study by anthropologist Leo Simmons in 1938, which led to the noted 1942 publication *Sun Chief: The Autobiography of a Hopi Indian*. The book has remained a popular account of Hopi life.

Poet Wendy Rose (1948–), of Hopi, Miwok, and European ancestry, was born Bronwen Elizabeth Edwards in Oakland, California, and grew up in the San Francisco Bay area. She studied at Contra Costa College and earned an MA in anthropology at the University of California, Berkeley. Some of her early poems were published under the name Chiron Khanshendel. Her work, which focuses on modern urban Indian issues, has been included in numerous anthologies, in feminist collections such as *In Her Own Image* (1980), and in more general collections, among them *Women Poets of the World* (1983). Her own published collections include *Hopi Roadrunner Dancing* (1973), *Lost Copper* (1980), *What Happened When the Hopi Hit New York* (1982), *The Halfbreed Chronicles and Other Poems* (1985), *Now Poof She Is Gone* (1994), and *Bone Dance: New and Selected Poems, 1965–1993* (1994). Rose has also served as editor for the scholarly journal *American Indian Quarterly* and has taught at Fresno City College, where she was director of the American Indian Studies Program.

Music Casper Lomayesva (1967–) performs Hopi Reggae and has released three albums on his own label, Third Mesa Music. Lomayesva's success pushed touring acts, such as Steel Pulse, to include the Hopi mesas on their routes. In 2001 he was honored at the

Native American Music Awards, winning the prize for Best World Music. From 2009 to 2011 he served as an advisor for Native Music Rocks.

Public Service Chief Tuvi (also Tuba or Toova) (ca. 1810–1887), leader of Moenkopi Hopi village, was the first Hopi converted to the Church of Jesus Christ of Latter-Day Saints. The city of Tuba, Arizona, is named after him.

Lori Ann Piestewa (1979–2003), a Hopi from Tuba City, Arizona, was a U.S. Army Quartermaster Corps soldier killed during the Iraq War; she was the first Native American woman to die while serving in the U.S. military.

Hopi tribal member Diane J. Humetewa (1964–) served as the U.S. Attorney for the District of Arizona from 2007 to 2009. The first female Native American U.S. Attorney, Humetewa also served on the Hopi Tribal Appellate Court and the Native American Subcommittee of the U.S. Sentencing Commission. She has been the Special Advisor to Arizona State University's President on American Indian Affairs, Special Counsel in the ASU General Counsel's Office and Professor of Practice at the ASU Sandra Day O'Connor College of Law.

Science and Technology Al Qoyawayma (c.1938–), a prominent Hopi engineer, became a noted ceramic artist. Born in Los Angeles, he earned an MS in mechanical engineering from the University of California, Berkeley in 1966. Working for Litton Systems, Inc., Qoyawayma developed high-tech airborne guidance systems. He moved to Arizona to take the position of manager for environmental services for the Salt River Project. As an understudy of his aunt, renowned potter Polingaysi Qoyawayma (Elizabeth White), he has accomplished much as a ceramicist, with his works displayed at the Smithsonian Institute and the Kennedy Art Center in Washington, D.C.

A geneticist and the first Hopi to receive a doctorate in sciences, Frank C. Dukapoo (1943–) founded the National Native American Honor Society in 1982. Born on the Mohave Indian Reservation in Arizona, Dukapoo has specialized in investigating factors contributing to birth defects in Indians, among other research topics. He is also an accomplished saxophone player. He earned a PhD from Arizona State University and has taught at Arizona State, San Diego State University, and Northern State University in Aberdeen, South Dakota. Besides holding an executive position with the National Science Foundation from 1976 to 1979, Dukapoo was also director of Indian Education at Northern Arizona University in Flagstaff, Arizona, and executive secretary for the National Cancer Institute.

Sports Hopi Louis Tewanima (1879–1969) established world records in long-distance running. Born at Shungopovi, Second Mesa, Tewanima was on the track team of the Carlisle Indian School in Pennsylvania under legendary coach Glenn "Pop" Warner, along with famous teammate Jim Thorpe of the Sac and Fox tribes. The U.S. Olympic Team selected him and Thorpe without requiring them to undergo trials—a rare honor. In 1912 the two runners sailed to Stockholm, where they became U.S. heroes. Thorpe was proclaimed "the greatest athlete in the world" by the king of Sweden, and Tewanima won a silver medal in the 10,000-meter race. His performance set a U.S. record that lasted more than fifty years, until Billy Mills, a Sioux distance runner, surpassed it in the 1964 Tokyo Olympics. Tewanima returned home to Second Mesa, where he tended sheep and raised crops, sometimes running to Winslow, eighty miles away, for fun. In 1954 he was named to the All-Time United States Olympic Track and Field Team and in 1957 was the first person inducted, to a standing ovation, into the Arizona Sports Hall of Fame at a dinner given in his honor. The Tewanima Foot Race is run every September at Kykotsmovi Village. The tribe established a 2002 Winter Olympic Committee to mark a return of the Hopi to the Olympics and showcase Hopi arts and crafts.

Stage and Screen Actor Anthony Nukena (1942–), of Hopi and California Karok ancestry, appeared in *Pony Soldier* (1952) and *Westward Ho the Wagons!* (1957).

MEDIA

Hopi Tutuvehni

After sixteen years of being out of print, the bimonthly newspaper was restarted in 2010. The paper circulates throughout all Hopi villages and serves as the Hopi Tribe's official newspaper.

Mihio Manus, Managing Editor
URL: www.hopi-nsn.gov

KUYI-FM (88.1)

Launched in 2000, Hopi public radio station KUYI provides news, commentary, and music to the Hopi reservation.

Richard Alun Davis, Station Manager
P.O. Box 1500
Keams Canyon, Arizona 86034
Phone: (928) 738-5505
Email: info@kuyi.net
URL: www.kuyi.net

Navajo-Hopi Observer

This weekly newspaper covers issues on the Navajo and Hopi reservations and in the Flagstaff area.

Doug Wells, Publisher
2717 North Fourth Street
Suite 110
Flagstaff, Arizona 86001
Phone: (800) 408-4726
Fax: (928) 635-4887
Email: nhoeditorial@nhonews.com
URL: www.navajohopiobserver.com

ORGANIZATIONS AND ASSOCIATIONS

Hopi Cultural Center

Opened in 1970, the on-reservation facility houses various collections of Hopi arts and crafts and the Hononi crafts shop.

P.O. Box 67
Second Mesa, Arizona 86043
Phone: (928) 734-2401
Fax: (928) 734-6651
Email: info@hopiculturalcenter.com
URL: www.hopiculturalcenter.com

The Hopi Education Endowment Fund

This organization provides educational funding and services to Hopi tribal members who wish to pursue postsecondary education.

LuAnn Leonard, Executive Director
P.O. Box 605
Kykotsmovi, Arizona 86039
Phone: (928) 734-2275
Fax: (928) 734-2273
Email: heef@hopieducationfund.org
URL: www.hopieducationfund.org

The Hopi Foundation

The nongovernmental foundation has its base on Third Mesa, promoting cultural preservation led by Hopi professionals and laypersons

P.O. Box 301
Kykotsmovi, Arizona 86039
Phone: (928) 734-2380
Fax: (928) 734-9520
Email: info@hopifoundation.org
URL: www.hopifoundation.org

Silvercraft Cooperative Guild

Supports and sponsors Hopi artists.

P.O. Box 37
Second Mesa, Arizona 86043
Phone: (602) 734-2463

MUSEUMS AND RESEARCH CENTERS

Hopi Cultural Preservation Office

Established in 1989 to implement a 1987 tribal historic preservation plan protecting important Hopi sacred and cultural sites, including traditional subsistence gathering areas.

Leigh Kuwanwisiwma, Director
P.O. Box 123
1 Main Street
Kykotsmovi, Arizona 86039
Phone: (520) 734-2244
Email: lkuwanwisiwma@hopi.nsn.us
URL: www8.nau.edu/hcpo-p

Heard Museum

Originally founded in 1929, the museum focuses on the arts and traditions of Native Americans, with an emphasis on tribes of the Southwest.

2301 North Central Avenue
Phoenix, Arizona 85004
Phone: (602) 252-8848
Fax: (602) 252-9757
Email: contact@heard.org
URL: www.heard.org

Museum of Northern Arizona

Originally founded in 1928, the museum campus serves as a regional center with collections, exhibits, educational programs, publications, and research projects on the tribes of the Colorado Plateau.

Robert G. Breunig, Director
3101 North Fort Valley Road
Flagstaff, Arizona 86001
Phone: (928) 774-5213
Email: info@mna.mus.az.us
URL: www.musnaz.org

SOURCES FOR ADDITIONAL STUDY

Benally, Malcolm D. *Bitter Water: Diné Oral Histories of the Navajo-Hopi Land Dispute*. Tucson: University of Arizona Press, 2011.

Benedek, Emily. *The Wind Won't Know Me: A History of the Navajo-Hopi Land Dispute*. New York: Knopf, 1992.

Gilbert, Matthew Sakiestewa. *Education Beyond the Mesas: Hopi Students at Sherman Institute, 1902–1929*. Lincoln: University of Nebraska Press, 2010.

Glenn, Edna, John R. Wunder, Willard Hughes Rollings, and C. L. Martin. *Hopi Nation: Essays on Indigenous Art, Culture, History, and Law*. Lincoln: University of Nebraska Press, 2008.

Ishii, Lomayumtewa C. "Western Science Comes to the Hopis: Critically Deconstructing the Origins of an Imperialist Canon." *Wicazo Sa Review* 24, no. 2 (Fall 2010): 65–88.

Leitch, Barbara A. *A Concise Dictionary of Indian Tribes of North America*. Algonac, MI: Reference Publications, 1979.

Loftin, John D. *Religion and Hopi Life in the Twentieth Century*. Bloomington: Indiana University Press, 1991.

Lyons, Patrick D. *Ancestral Hopi Migrations*. Tucson: University of Arizona Press, 2003.

Nicholas, Sheilah E. "Language, Epistemology, and Cultural Identity: 'Hopiqatsit Aw Unanguakiwyungwa' ('They Have Their Heart in the Hopi Way of Life')." *American Indian Culture and Research Journal* 34, no. 2 (2010): 125–44.

Page, Susanne, and Jake Page. *Hopi*. New York: Harry Abrams, 1994.

Parsons, Elsie Clews. *Hopi and Zuñi Ceremonialism*. New York: Harper and Bros., 1950. Reprint. Millwood, NY: Kraus Reprint, 1976.

Secakuku, Alph. *Hopi Kachina Tradition: Following the Sun and Moon*. Flagstaff, AZ: Northland, 1995.

Trafzer, Clifford, Matthew Sakiestewa Gilbert, and Lorene Sisquoc, eds. *The Indian School on Magnolia Avenue: Voices and Images from Sherman Institute*. Corvallis, OR: Oregon State University Press, 2012.

Waters, Frank. *Book of the Hopi*. New York: Viking Press, 1963.

HUNGARIAN AMERICANS

Steven Béla Várdy and Thomas Szendrey

OVERVIEW

Hungarian Americans are immigrants or descendants of people from Hungary, a small, landlocked country in the Carpathian Basin of Central Europe. Hungary is bounded by Slovakia in the north, Ukraine in the northeast, Romania in the east, the former Yugoslavia (Serbia, Croatia, and Slovenia) in the south, and Austria in the west. Hungary's strategic location—along main land routes between western Europe and the Balkan Peninsula, as well as between the Ukraine and Mediterranean basin—has greatly influenced its history. Budapest is the country's largest city and also its capital. The total area of Hungary is 35,919 square miles (93,030 square kilometers).

According to 2011 census data from the Hungarian Central Statistical Office, Hungary had a population of 9,982,000, and Hungarians (Magyars) constituted 96.1 percent of its population. The remaining 3.9 percent was made up of Germans, Slovaks, South Slavs, Roma (Gypsies), and Romanians. The census indicated that 67.8 percent of Hungarians were Catholic, 20.9 percent Calvinist (Reformed), and 4.2 percent Lutheran (Evangelical). Of the remaining population, 2.3 percent belonged to minor denominations (Greek or Byzantine Catholic, Orthodox Christian, Baptist, and Adventist), while 4.8 percent claimed no religious affiliation. Jews—who in 1941 had constituted 6.2 percent of Hungary's population—numbered only 12,800 (0.1 percent of the population) in the 2011 Hungarian census. Other estimates place the number at around 100,000, or about 1 percent of the Hungarian population, making it the largest Jewish community in east-central Europe. This discrepancy stems in part from the reluctance of many Jews to identify themselves as such in the census. After World War II, many Hungarian Jews who survived the Holocaust taught their children to downplay their Jewish heritage. It should also be noted that, like the Jews, the Roma population has been heavily persecuted in Hungary, and its numbers are thought to be potentially much greater than the 2 percent indicated in the 2011 census, perhaps as high as 10 percent. Hungary, which joined the European Union in 2004, was hit hard by the recession of the late 2000s due to its heavy dependence on foreign capital.

The first large wave of Hungarian immigration to the United States occurred in 1849 and 1850, when many people fled from Austrian authorities after the failed Hungarian Revolution of 1848. During World War II, Hungarian immigrants were mainly Jews fleeing the horrific circumstances of the Holocaust. Some 40,000 immigrants came to the United States in 1956 and 1957 after a failed Hungarian revolution against the Soviet Union, which governed Hungary at the time. Like the groups that had fled Hungary a century earlier, these people, sometimes referred to as "Fifty-sixers," were motivated by fear of political persecution.

According to the U.S. Census Bureau's American Community Survey, there were an estimated 1,415,187 people of Hungarian descent living in the United States in 2011. States with significant Hungarian American populations at that time included Ohio, New York, California, Pennsylvania, New Jersey, Michigan, and Florida.

HISTORY OF THE PEOPLE

Early History In the year 896 CE, under the leadership of Prince Arpád, seven Hungarian/Magyar tribes conquered and settled the geographic area that now makes up modern Hungary, gradually extending their rule over the entire Carpathian Basin. One of Arpád's successors, Stephen I, king of Hungary from 1000 to 1038 (and referred to as Saint Stephen because he was canonized in 1083), Christianized his people and made the country part of the Western Christian world.

During the next four centuries, the Hungarians continued to expand beyond the Carpathian Basin, especially into the northern Balkans. At the end of the eleventh century, they conquered and annexed Croatia as an autonomous kingdom, while in the twelfth and thirteenth centuries they extended their influence over Bosnia, Dalmatia, and northern Serbia, largely at the expense of the declining Byzantine Empire. Moreover, in the fourteenth century, under the Angevin rulers Charles Robert (reigned 1308–1342) and Louis the Great (reigned 1342–1382), the Hungarians expanded their control over the newly formed Vlach (Romanian) principalities of Wallachia and Moldavia and, for a brief period (1370–1382), even over Poland.

With the expansion of the Ottoman Turkish Empire into the Balkans in the late fourteenth and fifteenth centuries, Hungarian influence over the northern Balkans declined and was usurped by that of the Turks. Even so, Hungary still experienced

A Hungarian immigrant family out for a walk in Long Island, New York, c. 1956. VECCHIO / GETTY IMAGES

moments of greatness, particularly under Regent John Hunyadi (ruled 1444–1456) and his son King Matthias Corvinus (ruled 1458–1490). Matthias even conquered Moravia and eastern Austria and also established a Renaissance royal court at Buda (now part of Budapest).

Medieval Hungary's greatness ended with its defeat at the hands of the Ottoman Turks at the Battle of Mohács in 1526. Turkish conquest was followed by the country's trisection, which lasted for nearly two centuries. Western and northwestern Hungary ("Royal Hungary") became part of the Habsburg Empire, which ruled from Vienna; central Hungary was integrated into the Ottoman Turkish Empire; and eastern Hungary evolved into the autonomous principality of Transylvania, whose semi-independence under Turkish suzerainty ended with the country's reconquest and reunification by the Hapsburgs in the late seventeenth and early eighteenth centuries.

Hungary retained considerable autonomy within the Hapsburg Empire. In the mid-nineteenth century the Habsburgs and the Hungarians clashed in the Hungarian Revolution and War of Independence (1848–1849), and two decades later they united in the Austro-Hungarian Compromise of 1867. This compromise—engineered by Francis Deák (1803–1876) and Emperor Franz Joseph (reigned 1848–1916)—resulted in the dual state of Austria-Hungary, which played a significant role in European politics until nationality problems and involvement in World War I on the German side resulted in its dissolution in 1918–1919.

The demise of Austria-Hungary was accompanied by the dismemberment of historic Hungary, codified in the Peace Treaty of Trianon in 1920. This treaty turned Hungary into a small truncated country, with only 28.5 percent of its former territory (35,900 square miles versus 125,600 square miles) and 36.5 percent of its former population (7.6 million versus 20.9 million). Trianon Hungary became "a kingdom without a king" under the regency of Admiral Nicholas Horthy, who ruled from 1920 to 1944 and devoted most of the country's resources to regaining at least some of its territorial losses. These efforts did result in temporary territorial gains from 1938 to 1941, but because the expansion was achieved with German and Italian help, Hungary wound up in an unfortunate alliance with Germany during World War II.

Modern Era After World War II, Hungary was again reduced in size and became one of the communist-dominated Soviet satellite states under the leadership of Stalinist dictator Mátyás Rákosi, who ruled from 1948 to 1956. Communist excesses and the relaxation that followed Joseph Stalin's death in 1953 led to the Hungarian Revolution of 1956, the most significant anti-Soviet uprising of the postwar period. Put down by Soviet military intervention, it was followed by a brief period of retribution and then by a new communist regime under János Kádár, who ruled from 1956 to 1988 and initiated a policy of political liberalization (1962) and economic reform (known as the New Economic Mechanism of 1968). By the 1970s these reforms—supported by generous Western loans—had made Hungary the envy of the communist world.

Even though Hungary experienced some persistent economic changes and a degree of political liberalization throughout the 1980s, its most important development involved the replacement of Kádár in 1988, which signaled the end of communist rule in the People's Republic of Hungary. At this time, the parliament implemented a "democracy package" that incorporated trade union diversity, electoral law, a major revision of the constitution, and freedom of assembly, association, and the press.

On August 19, 1989, a peace demonstration known as the Pan-European Picnic took place near the town of Sopron on the Austrian-Hungarian border. It was an important moment in the political developments that led to the collapse of the Iron Curtain and to Germany's reunification. From October 16 through 20 of that same year, the Communist Party held its final congress and renamed itself the Hungarian Socialist Party. During the session, the parliament approved legislation that paved the way for multiparty parliamentary and presidential elections determined by a majority vote of the citizenry. The new legislation assured human and civil rights, converted the country from the People's Republic of Hungary to the Republic of Hungary, and established an institutional framework that safeguarded a governmental separation of judicial, legislative, and executive powers.

The Hungarian Democratic Forum (HDF), headed initially by József Antall, led the country from 1990 to 1994. The HDF regime immediately began to transform Hungary from a communist to a democratic state, but the economic and social problems it encountered—such as rapid social polarization, the collapse of the protective social welfare system, and the pauperization of a large segment of the society— proved to be too much. Voted out of office in 1994, the HDF was replaced by a coalition of the Hungarian Socialist Party and the Federation of Free Democrats. Former communist Gyula Horn (1932–), who had been Hungary's foreign minister during the peaceful transition from communism to democracy in 1989–1990, became the country's new prime minister in 1994, serving until 1998.

In 2004 Ferenc Gyurcsány succeeded Péter Medgyessy as prime minister. Two years later, antigovernment protests were triggered by the release of a private speech by Gyurcsány in which he confessed that his Hungarian Socialist Party had lied to win the 2006 election. Gyurcsány's lack of accomplishments while in office exacerbated matters. Taking place mostly in Budapest and other major cities between September 17 and October 23, it was the first sustained protest in Hungary since 1989.

SETTLEMENT IN THE UNITED STATES

According to Hungarian tradition, the first Hungarian to reach American shores was a certain Tyrker who arrived with the Viking chief Eric the Red in around 1000 CE. This is said to have happened concurrently with Stephen I's transformation of Hungary into a Christian kingdom. If the Tyrker story is discounted, the first documented Hungarian to land in America was the learned scholar Stephen Parmenius of Buda (c. 1555–1583), who participated in Sir Humphrey Gilbert's expedition in 1583 and later drowned off the coast of Newfoundland.

Over the next two and a half centuries, increasing numbers of Hungarian explorers, missionaries, and adventurers came to North America. The most noted among the latter was Colonel Michael de Kováts (1724–1779), a member of the Pulaski Legion during the Revolutionary War who is generally credited with being one of the founders of the American cavalry. The late eighteenth and early nineteenth centuries saw the arrival of the first sporadic settlers, most of whom came from the middle and upper classes and often immigrated for personal reasons, usually winding up in coastal cities such as Boston; New York; Philadelphia; Charleston, South Carolina; and New Orleans, Louisiana.

In 1849–1850, the first mass Hungarian immigration to the United States occurred. These immigrants, called "Forty-niners," came to escape

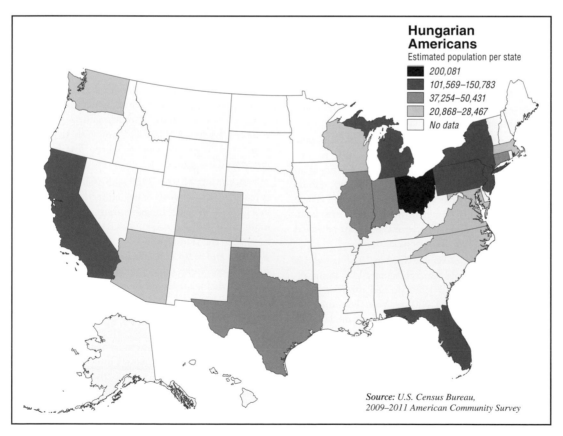

Hungarian Americans

Estimated population per state

- 200,081
- 101,569–150,783
- 37,254–50,431
- 20,868–28,467
- No data

Source: U.S. Census Bureau, 2009–2011 American Community Survey

SHIFTING PERCEPTIONS OF HUNGARIAN IMMIGRANTS

The relationships of Hungarians with Anglo-American society varied according to the diverse waves of immigrants. The Forty-niners, also known as the "Kossuth immigrants" (after the leader of the revolution, Lajos Kossuth), had been received with awe and respect. Because of their gentry-based background and education, they established the image of Hungary as a "nation of nobles." However, this perception was undermined by the turn-of-the-century economic immigrants, most of whom were poor and uneducated. They unwittingly created the negative "Hunky" image of Hungarians, which then was transferred to all of the east and southeast European immigrants. The stereotype persisted well into the post–World War II period, even though by that time the intellectual immigrants of the 1930s and the political immigrants of the 1950s had begun to diversify the ethnic group's social composition. Although far fewer in number, these newer immigrants were the ones who gave birth to the revised image of Hungarians that Laura Fermi defines as the "mystery of the Hungarian talent" in her highly praised study *Illustrious Immigrants* (1968). This was a natural by-product of the measureable impact these intellectual and political immigrants made on American society with their achievements.

retribution by Austrian authorities after the defeat of the Hungarian Revolution of 1848. Several thousand strong, the wave included mainly educated men, many of whom were from the gentry class (middle nobility). A large number of these immigrants joined the Union Army during the Civil War, and some returned to Hungary during the 1860s and 1870s. Most, however, became part of American society.

The next wave, known as the "Great Economic Immigration," took place at the turn of the twentieth century and brought some 1.7 million Hungarian citizens, including 650,000 to 700,000 ethnic Hungarians (Magyars), to American shores. These immigrants sought greater prosperity in a new land, and they represented the poorest and least-educated segment of the Hungarian population.

The outbreak of World War I in 1914 halted this mass migration, while the exclusionary U.S. immigration laws of 1921 and 1924 pushed the Hungarian quota down to under 1,000 per year. This situation did not change until another immigration law, the Hart-Celler Act of 1965, ended the quota system. Yet during the intervening four decades, there were a number of nonquota admissions that brought completely different types of Hungarian immigrants to the United States. These included the refugee intellectuals (2,000 to 3,000) of the 1930s who were fleeing the spread of Nazism; the post–World War II displaced

persons, or DPs (17,000), who came under the Displaced Persons Act of 1948; and the "Fifty-sixers," or Freedom Fighters (38,000), who left Hungary after the failed revolution of 1956. The combined number of these last three groups (60,000) was less than 10 percent of that of the turn-of-the-century economic immigrants, but their impact on American society was much more significant.

Although the turn-of-the-century economic immigrants were from rural areas, almost all of them settled in the industrial cities and mining regions of the northeastern United States. Fewer than 0.2 percent of all the Magyars who lived in the United States in 1920 were engaged in agriculture. Virtually all of these Hungarians worked in mining and industry, most in the unskilled and semiskilled categories. This was primarily because the majority came to the United States not as immigrants but as migrant workers who intended to repatriate to Hungary. Their goal was to return with enough accumulated capital to be able to buy land and become prosperous farmers. To do this, however, they had to work in industry, where work was readily available because the rapidly expanding American industrial establishment of the Gilded Age was in great need of cheap immigrant labor.

Most of the immigrants were never able to fulfill their original goal of repatriation, although up to 25 percent did return to Hungary permanently. Among the factors that kept them in the United States were their inability to accumulate the capital to buy sufficient land; the difficulties they encountered in readjusting to Hungary's class-conscious society; the influence of their American-born children, who viewed Hungary as an alien land; and, most important, Hungary's post–World War I dismemberment, which transferred the homelands of most of the immigrants to such newly created states as Czechoslovakia and Yugoslavia and to the much-enlarged Romania. They did not wish to join the ranks of Hungarians who had been forcibly transferred to these states.

According to the 1920 U.S. Census, 945,801 persons in the United States either had been born in Hungary or had Hungarian-born parents; slightly more than half of these (495,845) were Magyars. In 1922 the Hungarian-born Magyars numbered 474,000 and were concentrated in ten northeastern states: New York, Ohio, Pennsylvania, New Jersey, Illinois, Michigan, Connecticut, Wisconsin, Indiana, and West Virginia. They migrated to these regions to work in coal mines, steel mills, textile mills, and machine factories.

This settlement pattern remained unchanged until the 1960s, when many Hungarian Americans began to move to the West and the South, partially because of the arrival of the more mobile political immigrants and also because of a general population shift in previous decades.

Despite renewed contacts with the homeland, Hungarian Americans are losing their struggle to survive as a separate ethnic group in the United States. This is evident both in their declining numbers and in the disappearances of their ethnic institutions, churches, cultural organizations, and fraternal organizations. The 1980 U.S. Census reported that 1.78 million people claimed to be fully or primarily Hungarian; by 2011 that number had dropped to 1.42 million, according to estimates by the U.S. Census Bureau's American Community Survey. In the past thirty years, Greater Pittsburgh alone has lost about a half-dozen Hungarian churches, and those that remain are struggling to survive. The same fate has befallen Hungarian cultural and social organizations in western Pennsylvania, few of which are active today. This trend appears to be equally true in the entire Northeast, though it is not as evident in California and Florida, which experienced rapid growth in their Hungarian populations from the 1960s through the 1990s. However, from the turn of the twenty-first century to 2011, even California experienced a decline in its Hungarian population (from 164,903 to 120,189), whereas Florida saw a marginal increase (from 89,587 to 102,994), largely due to its popularity with retirees. According to the American Community Survey estimates for 2009–2011, Ohio was the state with the highest population of Americans of Hungarian descent. Other states where large numbers of Hungarian Americans reside are Pennsylvania, California, Florida, Michigan, New Jersey, and New York.

LANGUAGE

Hungarian is classified as a Finno-Ugric language and is part of the larger Uralic linguistic family. The most distinctive characteristic of these languages is that they are agglutinative—that is, words are extended into complex expressions through the use of prefixes and suffixes. For example, the meaning of a single word, *szent* (saint), can be changed by adding numerous prefixes and suffixes as follows (hyphens indicate the additions): *szent-ség* (sanctity), *szent-ség-ed* (your sanctity), *szent-ség-ed-del* (with your sanctity), *szent-ség-eid-del* (with your sanctities), *meg-szent-ségel-és-ed* (your sanctification), *meg-szent-ség-telenít-hetetlen-ség-ed-del* (with your ability to withstand desanctification).

The closest linguistic relatives of the Hungarians are the Voguls from western Siberia. Hungarians are also distantly related to the Turkic peoples, and there is a substratum of Turkish words in the Hungarian language (which is not, however, related to Turkic languages). This is due both to their common roots and to the renewal of contacts through the mixing of Finno-Ugric and Turkic tribes during the first nine centuries of the Common Era.

Before the conquest of Hungary, Hungarians had their own runic script. After their conversion to Christianity, they borrowed the Latin liturgical language and alphabet and adapted this alphabet to the phonetic properties of the Hungarian dialect. This was done by doubling up letters to represent a single sound—*cs* ("ch"), *gy* ("dy"), *ly* ("y"), *ny* (soft "n"), *sz* ("s"), *ty* (soft "t"), *zs* ("zh"), *dzs* ("dzh")—or by adding diacritical marks (*á, é, í, ö, ő, ü, u*). In many instances the accent marks not only signify the pronunciation but also alter the meaning of the word, such as with *sor* (row), *sör* (beer); *bor* (wine), *bőr* (skin); *sas* (eagle), *sás* (sedge); *szar* (excrement), *szár* (stem). The meaning of a single word can be changed several times simply by adding or subtracting a diacritical mark, such as with *kerek* (round), *kerék* (wheel), *kérek* (I am requesting).

The English language has had an impact on how Hungarian Americans speak Hungarian. This was particularly true for the less-educated immigrants, who readily mixed their simple Hungarian with working-class English. Thus, they developed a language of their own known as "Hunglish" (Hungarian English), which introduced English words into the Hungarian but transformed them to fit Hungarian pronunciation and orthography: *trén* (train), *plész* (place), *szalon* (saloon), *bedróm* (bedroom), *atrec* (address), *tájm* (time), *szendsztón* (sandstone), *gud báj* (goodbye), *foriner* (foreigner), *fandri* (foundry), *fanesz* (furnace), *bakszi* (box), *burdos* (boarder), *burdosház* (boarding house), *görl* (girl), *groszeri* (grocery).

There was also a reverse version of Hunglish that may be called "Engarian" (English Hungarian), which adjusted the primitive English to the ears of the immigrants. The result was two hodgepodge languages that were barely comprehensible to Hungarians or Americans who did not speak both languages, with phrases such as *Szé, miszter, gimi order, maj hen trók brók!* (Say, Mister, give me the order. My hand truck broke!) Such usage is no longer common, largely because the Americanized offspring of the turn-of-the-century immigrants have switched to English but also because the more educated post–World War II immigrants never really acquired it.

Greetings and Popular Expressions Common greetings are as follows (all words are pronounced with the accent on the first syllable): *Jó reggelt* ("yo reggelt")—Good morning; *Jó napot* ("yo nahpote")—Good day; *Jó estét* ("yo eshtayt")—Good evening; *Jó éjszakát* ("yo aysahkaht")—Good night; *Kezitcsókolom* ("kezeet choakholohm")—I kiss your hand; *Szervusz* or *Szerbusz* ("servoos, serboos")—Hello, Hi; *Szia* ("seeyah")—Hi, Hello; *Viszontlátásra* ("veesoantlahtahshrah")—Goodbye, See you again; and *Isten áldjon meg* ("eeshten ahldyoan meg")—God bless you.

Other popular expressions include: *Boldog Új Évet* ("bohldogh ooy-ayveth")—Happy New Year; *Kellemes húsvétot* ("kellehmesh hooshvaytoth")—Happy Easter; *Kellemes karácsonyi ünnepeket* ("kellehmesh karahcho-anyi ünnepeketh")—Merry Christmas; *Boldog ünnepeket* ("bohldogh ünnepeketh")—Happy holidays; and *Egészségedre* ("eggayshaygedreh")—To your health (spoken when toasting).

RELIGION

Hungary has been a Roman Catholic country since its conversion to Christianity in the late tenth and early eleventh centuries. This religious uniformity was shattered only in the sixteenth century, when Protestantism entered the country and spread, especially in its Calvinist form. After a century of intense struggle, Catholicism remained strong in the country's western and central areas, while Calvinism came to dominate its eastern regions. This Catholic-Calvinist rivalry was complicated somewhat by the presence of a significant minority of Lutherans (Evangelicals), Jews, Greek/Byzantine Catholics, and Unitarians, as well as by a few other small Christian sects. Yet in spite of its losses to rival faiths, Roman Catholicism retained its dominant position as Hungary's only official "state religion" until the communist takeover in 1948.

The religious divisions in Hungary also came to be reflected in Hungarian American society. The Calvinists were the first to establish their pioneer congregations in 1891 in Cleveland and in Pittsburgh, to be followed in 1892 by the Roman Catholics (St. Elizabeth of Hungary Church, Cleveland) and in 1907 by the Lutherans (Cleveland). These early congregations soon spawned scores of other Hungarian churches throughout the northeastern United States. Although the Calvinists had the greatest number of churches, their congregations were small, and as such they represented only one-third as many faithful as did the Roman Catholic churches.

Roman Catholics, Calvinists, and Lutherans together constituted slightly over 90 percent of all religious affiliations of Hungarian Americans. The other 8 to 10 percent was made up of smaller denominations, including the Byzantine Catholics, Jews, Baptists, and Adventists. Because of their slight numbers, however, none of the latter had more than a limited and passing influence on Hungarian American life.

The religious practices of Hungarian Roman Catholics and Protestants in the United States are basically identical to those of their coreligionists in Hungary and are also similar to those of their American counterparts. Although religious practices did not change after immigration, the social significance of the congregations and the position and the role of the parish priests and pastors underwent major alterations. In Hungary religious congregations and their priests or ministers were supported by their respective mother churches through an obligatory religious tax. As a result, these congregations were centrally controlled, with little or no input from the congregation members. This was particularly true of the Roman Catholic Church, which had retained its monarchical structure from the Middle Ages. Although Calvinist and Lutheran congregations did elect their pastors even in Hungary, the powers of the presbytery (church council) were much more limited than in the United States. This was true not only because of the somewhat authoritarian nature of traditional Hungarian society

but also because the pastors did not depend on the financial support of their parishioners. In Hungary, therefore, it was the priests and the ministers who controlled the congregation, not vice versa.

After immigration, this relationship changed significantly, as much of the control over church affairs fell to the members of the church council. This shift in the power dynamic was due both to the lack of state support for religion and to the fact that now the members of the congregations were paying for the upkeep of their churches and for their pastors.

The function of the church itself has also changed. Traditionally, American churches have always combined religious and social functions, a phenomenon that was largely unknown in Europe. This American practice was accepted by the immigrant churches, which consequently ceased to function solely as houses of prayer. They now also assumed the role of social clubs and thus lost some of the sanctity of their Old World counterparts.

The pinnacle of Hungarian religious life in the United States occurred from the 1920s to the 1960s. By the 1970s, however, a process of slow decay had set in, and it accelerated to a point in the 1980s where several Hungarian ethnic churches were closing their doors every year.

During the past century, all Hungarian American denominations have been plagued by dissension, but none more so than the Hungarian Calvinist (Reformed) Church. Within a quarter-century of taking root in the United States, the church experienced dissension that led to the establishment of several competing Calvinist denominations, a process that resulted in a new sub-denomination as late as 1982. While some of these conflicts and fragmentations were of an ideological and administrative nature (e.g., the relationship with the mother church in Hungary), most were really the result of personal animosity among the clergy. American social practices make it easy for anyone to establish a new church, so personality conflicts and group squabbles have often resulted in institutional divorces. Hungarian Calvinists are still divided into a half-dozen rival and competing churches that are held together only by the awareness of their common roots and by their membership in the Hungarian Reformed Federation (HRF). Founded in 1898 as a fraternal association, the HRF serves as a force of unity among Hungarian Calvinists.

CULTURE AND ASSIMILATION

The Hungarian presence in the United States was established primarily by the large mass of rural immigrants in the three decades before World War I. These immigrants held on to their Hungarian identity and sense of community because of their social, cultural, and psychological needs and also because of Anglo American society's unwillingness to accept them. The same cannot be said of their U.S.-born children, who tended to assimilate at a rapid pace. They were driven by the socioeconomic drawing power of American society, as well as by their own conscious desire to separate themselves from their simpler immigrant parents. Most managed to move up a notch or two in social status, but the result was that many left the ethnic communities founded by their parents. Their efforts to assimilate, however, were not fully successful, for although they were born in the United States, they were still viewed as outsiders by the Anglo American majority.

The situation changed significantly with the second U.S.-born generation, whose maturation into adulthood coincided with the beginning of the "ethnic revolution" in the 1960s. Their embrace of this revolution led to the rediscovery of their ethnic roots. However, it was impeded by their inability to speak Hungarian and by the gradual disintegration of viable Hungarian ethnic communities, a process that began precisely at the start of this ethnic revolution. At present, most self-contained Hungarian American communities are in the process of final dissolution. A few of their cultural and religious institutions still exist, but they serve only the needs of the older generation and, very briefly, some of the new arrivals. An example of this decay can be found at the oldest and largest Hungarian Catholic parish in the United States, St. Elizabeth of Cleveland (founded in 1892), where the ratio of burials to baptisms is nearly twenty-to-one.

Early-twentieth-century immigrants and their descendants provided the foundations of Hungarian American life, but their role and influence were much more limited than those of the later waves, which brought a high level of education and a strong sense of historical and national consciousness. Most first-generation Hungarian Americans retained a large degree of dual identity that they passed on to their second- and third-generation descendants.

American-born offspring of the various immigrant waves still practice some Hungarian folk traditions, sometimes during social events held at their churches and social clubs but mostly during major festivals. One such festival is Hungarian Days, which is celebrated in large centers of Hungarian life, such as New Brunswick, New Jersey; Pittsburgh; and Cleveland.

Misconceptions about Hungarians abound in the United States, although this is much less the case now than in the early part of the twentieth century when they were often misidentified as Mongols or Gypsies. This was due in part to American society's minimal knowledge about central and eastern Europe and also to conscious distortions by politically motivated propagandists. Today, the situation has improved significantly because of the impact of the Hungarian Revolution of 1956 and the greater number and enhanced quality of publications about Hungary, which are produced mostly by the American-educated offspring of political immigrants.

Cuisine Much modern Hungarian cuisine reflects the historically nomadic lifestyle of the Magyar people, Hungary's primary ethnic group. This in part explains the prominence of meat dishes that were once cooked over an open fire in a *bogrács* (or cauldron), such as goulash (*gulyás*, literally "herdsman's [meal]"), *pörkölt* stew, and a spicy fisherman's soup called *halászlé*. Various kinds of noodles and dumplings,

A Hungarian American man wears an Uncle Sam suit to express both his patriotism and Hungarian ancestry. Ellis Island, New York. JOSEPH SOHM / AGE FOTOSTOCK

HUNGARIAN PROVERBS

Addig nyújtózkodj, amíg a takaród ér.

Only stretch as far as your blanket reaches.

Aki két nyulat hajt egyet se ver.

Grasp all, lose all.

Egy fecske nem csinál nyarat.

One swallow does not make a summer.

Festi az ördögöt a falra.

Painting the devil onto the wall.

Lónak négy a lába, mégis megbotlik.

A good marksman may miss.

Mindenki a maga szerencséjének kovácsa.

Everyone's the blacksmith of their own fate.

Nem zörög a haraszt, ha a szél nem fújja.

The bushes don't rattle if there's no wind.

Olcsó húsnak híg a leve.

Cheap meat produces thin broth.

Sokat hallj lass keveset szólj.

Keep your mouth shut and your ears open.

Üres hasnak nem elég a szep szó, hanem a czo.

Fine words butter no parsnips.

Vak tyúk is talál szemet.

Even the blind chicken finds grains.

Jó bornak nem kell cégér.

Good wine needs no label.

potatoes, and rice are commonly served as side dishes. Hungarian cuisine employs both spices (especially paprika) and a large variety of cheeses, such as *túró*, *trappista*, and *pálpusztai*. Modern Hungarian cuisine draws from ancient Asiatic—as well as Germanic, Italian, and Slavic—foods. Today in the United States, many Hungarian Americans prepare a variety of traditional Hungarian dishes at home. Additionally, Hungarian restaurants can be found throughout the country, especially in areas with large Hungarian American populations.

Traditional Dress Hungarian folk dress is colorful and often richly embroidered. It may feature sashes, laces, boots, or embroidered shoes. Women's garments are often characterized by puffed sleeves, while a vest and long sleeves are often worn as a part of male attire.

Holidays Hungarian Americans generally celebrate three major national holidays: the Revolution of 1848 (March 15), Saint Stephen's Day (August 20), and the Revolution of 1956 (October 23). These celebrations might combine patriotic and religious elements. There is no specific Hungarian American holiday, perhaps because the attention of most unassimilated Hungarian Americans is focused on the mother country.

Health Care Issues and Practices Hungary has the highest suicide rate in the world (45 to 48 per 100,000). The factors connected with this suicide rate, however, appear to be limited to Hungarian society, and Hungarian Americans are no more prone to mental health issues than are other ethnic groups in the United States.

FAMILY AND COMMUNITY LIFE

After the early and predominantly male phases of economic immigration abated, Hungarian American communities assumed a traditional and stable family structure. By the 1920s most Hungarian immigrants had resolved to stay permanently in the United States. They established families and became intimately involved in the social lives of their churches, fraternal societies, and cultural institutions that served as their extended families. The structure survived almost intact into the 1960s, although with only limited participation by the political immigrants of the interwar and postwar periods. Unable to agree on a common platform with the earlier economic immigrants, the latter group usually founded its own organizations, which were more politically oriented.

With the exception of the relatively few immigrants who came during the 1960s through the 1980s—many of whom were from the Hungarian-inhabited regions surrounding Hungary—Hungarian Americans have generally not relied on public assistance. Traditionally in Hungarian society, accepting "handouts" was perceived as an admission of failure. Recent immigrants, however, became accustomed to state assistance under Hungary's communist system, so this view is less prevalent than it once was.

The immigrant experience transformed basic traditional patterns of family life for Hungarian Americans, resulting in a hybrid set of customs. In terms of everyday existence, Hungarian Americans conform to U.S. patterns, but with a greater emphasis on education. The role of women has been enhanced compared with the male-dominated Hungarian model, largely due to the desire of Hungarian American women to work rather than stay at home. The adoption of American customs is also evident in dating, marriage, and divorce. Until a generation ago, dating practices were very strict and circumscribed, but they have loosened, as has the commitment to marriage. Whereas a generation ago divorce among Hungarian immigrants was rare, today it is almost as common as it is within American society as a whole.

EMPLOYMENT AND ECONOMIC CONDITIONS

Hungarian immigrants have been involved in all facets of American economic life, with their type of employment generally depending on their social backgrounds. Hungarians who came before the mid-nineteenth century were individual adventurers who were well prepared for all eventualities in the New World. Although these immigrants were not great in numbers, most who stayed often proved to be successful. Some became well-known merchants in Philadelphia; Baltimore, Maryland; and New Orleans, Louisiana, while others emerged as well-respected professors at American universities. Whatever their profession, they typically did it well, because they had arrived in the United States equipped with a good education.

To a large degree, this was also true for the 3,000 to 4,000 Forty-niners who immigrated to the United States after the defeat of the Hungarian Revolution of 1848. Belonging mostly to the gentry, they had no intention of becoming farmers or laborers in the United States. They easily adjusted to American pioneer society. Some became involved in the establishment of Hungarian colonies in the West, such as László Ujházy (1795–1870), a high-ranking official of the revolutionary government who founded New Buda in Iowa in 1852. One thousand of the Forty-niners joined the Union Army in the Civil War, after which a good number of them went into diplomatic service or into various major business ventures in the West.

The next wave of immigrants, during the late nineteenth and early twentieth centuries, came with the intention of repatriating after four or five years with enough capital to become prosperous farmers. Few immigrants achieved this goal, and virtually all of them took jobs as unskilled or semiskilled workers in the United States' bustling industries. They were the peons of America's Gilded Age, contributing their brawn to coal mines and steel mills and creating the mythical Hungarian American hero Joe Magarac, who could bend steel bars with his bare hands.

The next four immigration waves consisted of the interwar "intellectual immigrants"; the post–World War II "political immigrants"; the Fifty-sixers; and finally the political-economic immigrants of the past several decades. Given their achievements in Europe, the

Hungarian-born American fashion designer Adrienne Vittadini (center front) is shown with models dressed in her 1984 fall designs on the grounds of the Cathedral of St. John the Divine, New York, New York, 1984. SUSAN WOOD / GETTY IMAGES

intellectual immigrants moved immediately into the most esteemed American intellectual and scientific circles and almost overnight created the myth of the uniqueness of Hungarian talent. The political immigrants, or DPs, represented the military-legal-administrative leadership of interwar Hungary and had few transferable skills; thus, many were forced to engage in physical labor. Many eventually did manage to transfer to white-collar work, although it was largely their American-educated children who rapidly moved up the professional ladder.

The Fifty-sixers differed from the DPs in their relative youth, orientation toward transferable technical and practical skills, and diminished cultural background (the product of a decade of communist restructuring of Hungarian society). Yet they and the American-educated children of the DPs produced a class of professionals that permeated all aspects of American scientific, scholarly, artistic, literary, and business life.

The final immigration wave began during the 1960s and is still going on today. It is characterized by a slow but gradual influx of professionally oriented individuals. During the 1960s through the 1980s, political persecution was the ostensible motive for immigration. Since the collapse of communism, however, they have come as needed professionals.

By the 1920s most Hungarian immigrants had resolved to stay permanently in the United States. They established families, had children, and became intimately involved in the social lives of their churches, fraternal societies, and cultural institutions that served as their extended families.

POLITICS AND GOVERNMENT
Hungarian Americans established several mutual aid societies in the second half of the nineteenth century, but it was not until 1906 that they created the first successful political organization, the American Hungarian Federation (AHF), which is still in existence. The mission of the AHF was to protect the interests of the Hungarian immigrants and to promote the cause of Hungary in the United States. During its first decade of existence, the AHF worked toward these goals in close cooperation with Hungary. During World War I, particularly after the United States entered the war on the opposite side, this task became impossible.

The darkest and most difficult period in Hungarian political activism came during World War II, when the AHF and the major fraternal organizations were forced to defend Hungary's territorial gains while maintaining their support for the U.S. war effort. To prove their loyalty to the United States, more than 50,000 Hungarian Americans served in the U.S. armed forces, and all Hungarian American organizations bought U.S. defense bonds and made repeated declarations of allegiance. Toward the end of the war, they organized

the American-Hungarian Relief Committee, whose members undertook a major effort to send aid to their devastated homeland, as well as to hundreds of thousands of Hungarians who had been trapped in German and Austrian refugee camps. Moreover, the AHF and the major Hungarian fraternal societies supported the Displaced Persons Act (passed in 1948, amended in 1950), which brought almost 18,000 Hungarian political refugees to the United States.

The appearance of the post–World War II political immigrants—the DPs during the early 1950s and the Fifty-sixers after the Hungarian Revolution of 1956—created a completely new situation. Much better educated and more involved politically than most of their predecessors, the newcomers devoted themselves to their own organizations.

From the late 1950s through the early 1980s, most of the nonminority-oriented organizations were concerned primarily with the liberation of Hungary and then with soliciting U.S. government help to undermine the nation's communist regime. Throughout this period the politically active new immigrants had little concern for American domestic politics; their attention was focused on Hungary. Thus, after becoming citizens, they usually voted with the Republican Party, which they perceived to be tougher on communism. On the other hand, the turn-of-the-century economic immigrants and their American-born descendants paid only lip service to Hungary. They were much more concerned with domestic politics than with the problems of communism. These people voted mostly Democratic.

The rise of a new generation among the political immigrants during the 1970s and 1980s produced notable changes. On the one hand, the American-born or American-educated members of the younger generations became involved in U.S. domestic politics in both political parties. On the other hand, they began to assume a much more realistic approach toward Hungary and its "goulash communism." Some of these people assumed positions of leadership in the AHF and carried their pragmatism into its politics. This approach split the AHF and brought about the foundation of the National Federation of Hungarian Americans (NFHA) in 1984 and then several rival organizations, including the very active and influential Hungarian American Coalition (HAC) in 1992.

The collapse of communism and the rise of a nationalist government in Hungary under the Hungarian Democratic Forum (1989–1990) produced a general euphoria among Hungarian Americans and also a surge in their desire to help their homeland. This coincided with Hungary's unprecedented popularity internationally for its role in undermining communism. However, the positive feelings did not last. The country's social and economic problems produced general disillusionment that extended to Hungarian Americans.

At present, most Hungarian Americans are heavily involved in both U.S. political parties while still displaying considerable interest in the goings-on in Hungary. Despite their disillusionment with the situation in Hungary, they continue to pursue pro-Hungarian lobbying efforts through several umbrella organizations as well as through their presence in the U.S. Congress. The most visible and active among the Hungarian congressional representatives was Fifty-sixer Tom Lantos (1928–2008) from California, who became increasingly involved in Hungarian-related political activities after taking office in 1981.

Military Relative to their size as an ethnic group, more Hungarian Americans served in the Civil War than any other nationality. Of the approximately 4,000 Hungarians in the United States (including women and children) at the outbreak of the war in 1861, more than 800—at least three-fourths of the adult male population—were in the Union Army. Among them were two major generals, five brigadier generals, fifteen colonels and lieutenant colonels, thirteen majors, twelve captains, about four dozen first and second lieutenants, and scores of noncommissioned officers.

The most prominent of the officers was Major General Julius H. Stahel (1825–1912), who was known in Hungary as Gyula Számvald before his emigration. General Stahel became a confidant of President Abraham Lincoln and the first Hungarian recipient of the Congressional Medal of Honor. Among the nearly 1,000 Hungarians in the Union Army was the young Joseph Pulitzer (1817–1911), who subsequently became a titan in American journalism and the founder of the famous literary prize that bears his name.

NOTABLE INDIVIDUALS

Academia George Pólya (1887–1985) and Gábor Szegő (1895–1985) were responsible for making Stanford University one of the world's leading mathematics institutions. Another Hungarian American exponent of finite mathematics and its applications, John George Kemény (1926–1992), served as president of Dartmouth College from 1970 to 1981.

Nicholas Nagy-Talavera (1929–2000) survived the Holocaust in World War II and immigrated to the United States, where he taught Russian and Eastern European history at California State University, Chico, from 1967 to 1991. He also wrote prolifically, including the book *The Green Shirts and Others: A History of Fascism in Hungary and Romania* (1970).

Commerce and Industry Since the late nineteenth century, Hungarians have made important contributions to U.S. industry and finance. Two of the earliest entrepreneurs were the Black (Schwartz) and Kundtz families. The Black family founded a series of garment factories and department stores, while Tivador Kundtz (1852–1937) established the White

A Hungarian American physicist at a meeting of the Nobel Prize laureates in Lindau, Ge. INTERFOTO / ALAMY

Machine factory. These two families employed and aided thousands of fellow immigrant Hungarians.

Modern entrepreneurs include the billionaire financier George Soros (1930–), who has played a significant role in the transformation of the former Soviet world through philanthropic efforts such as the establishment of the Budapest- and Prague-based Central European University; and Andrew Grove (born András Gróf; 1936–), who, as the founder and president of Intel Corporation, created the world's largest manufacturer of computer chips.

Film Two Hungarians were influential in the development of the Hollywood film industry: Adolph Zukor (1873–1976), the founder of Paramount Pictures, and William Fox (1879–1952), the founder of Twentieth Century-Fox. Zukor and Fox transformed the stylish Biedermeier culture of the Austro-Hungarian Empire into the glamorous society portrayed in Hollywood film.

Other film pioneers of Hungarian descent include directors/producers Michael Curtiz (born Kertész; 1888–1962), Sir Alexander Korda (1893–1956), George Cukor (1899–1983), and Joseph Pasternak (1901–1991); screenwriter Joe Eszterhas (1944–); art director William S. Darling (1882–1964); and directors Sam Raimi (1959–) and Steven Spielberg (1946–).

Music By the time internationally known composers Béla Bartók (1881–1945) and Ernő Dohnányi (1877–1960) immigrated to the United States in the 1940s, the American cultural scene already featured a number of prominent Hungarian composers, including Fritz Reiner (1888–1963), George Szell (1897–1970), Eugene Ormandy (1899–1985), Antal Dorati (1906–1988), and Sir Georg Solti (1912–1997). Hungarians were also present on Broadway in popular American musicals. The best-loved among them was Sigmund Romberg (1887–1951), who was perhaps the most successful transplanter of the Viennese and the Budapest operetta. Also significant were the contributions of Miklós Rózsa (1907–1995), who worked with Sir Alexander Korda and wrote the music for classic American films such as *Spellbound* (1945) and *Ben-Hur* (1959).

More recently, Paul Simon (1941–) is an American singer and songwriter who first earned fame in the 1960s as part of the duo Simon & Garfunkel and went on to a successful career as a solo artist; Gene Simmons (1949–) was the bassist and a vocalist for the popular rock band Kiss; and Michael Peter Balzary (1962–), commonly known as Flea, was the bassist for the rock band the Red Hot Chili Peppers, who were inducted into the Rock and Roll Hall of Fame in 2012.

Science and Medicine Three Hungarians assisted Enrico Fermi with the breakthroughs in atomic fission that resulted in the development of the atomic bomb in the 1940s: Leo Szilard (1898–1964); Eugene Wigner (1902–1995), a quantum physicist who won a Nobel Prize in 1963; and Edward Teller (1908–). Other Hungarian contributors were Theodore von Kármán (1881–1963), father of the heat and quantum theory; Johann von Neumann (1903–1957), father of the computer; and Zoltán Bay (1900–1992), a pioneer in radar astronomy.

A number of other Hungarian American scientists achieved prominence, including Nobel laureates Georg Karl Hevesy (1855–1966), Albert Szent-Györgyi (1893–1986), Georg von Békésy (1899–1972), and Dennis Gabor (1900–1979). The list also includes several members of the Polányi family: social philosopher Karl Polányi (1886–1964), physicist-philosopher Michael Polányi (1891–1976), and the latter's son, John Charles Polányi (1926–), who won the Nobel Prize in Chemistry in 1986. In addition, George Andrew Olah (1927–) received the Nobel Prize in Chemistry in 1994.

Sports Larry Csonka (1946–), a running back for the Miami Dolphins and New York Giants from 1968 to 1979, was inducted into the Pro Football Hall of Fame in 1987. George Halas (1895–1983) was a founder of the National Football League and the long-time owner and coach of the Chicago Bears. He was also a generous philanthropist. Don Shula (1930–) was head coach of the Baltimore Colts (1963–1969) and the Miami Dolphins (1970–1995). He led the Dolphins to Super Bowl titles in the 1972 and 1973 seasons. Joe Namath (1943–), a quarterback for the New York Jets (1965–1976) and Los Angeles Rams (1977), is a member of the Pro Football Hall of Fame.

Monica Seles (1973–), once the top-ranked female tennis player in the world, won nine Grand Slam singles titles.

Rebecca Soni (1987–), Olympic swimmer, set world records in the 100- and 200-meter breaststroke.

Stage and Screen Film and television stars of Hungarian descent include Leslie Howard (born Arpád

Steiner; 1893–1943), Bela Lugosi (1883–1956), Tony Curtis (born Bernard Schwartz; 1925–2010), Adrien Brody (1973–), Goldie Hawn (1945–), Jerry Seinfeld (1954–), Joaquin Phoenix (1974–), Freddie Prinze (born Freddie Preutzel; 1954–1977), and the Gabor sisters, Zsa Zsa (1917–), Eva (1919–1995), and Magda (1915–1997). Magician Harry Houdini (born Erich Weisz; 1874–1926) was also of Hungarian descent.

MEDIA

PRINT

Amerikai Magyar Népszava & Szabadság (The Hungarian American People's Voice & Liberty)

Amerikai Magyar Népszava & Szabadság is the oldest and largest Hungarian weekly newspaper printed in the United States. Established in 1891, it is headquartered in New York City.

192 Lexington Avenue
Suite 218
New York, New York 10016
Phone: (443) 921-8321
Email: admin@nepszava.com
URL: www.nepszava.com

Amerikai Magyar Szó (*American Hungarian Word*)

Founded in 1952 as a successor to several earlier socialist newspapers, this is a Hungarian-language independent weekly currently published in New York by the American Hungarian Federation, a nonprofit organization based in Washington, D.C.

130 East 16th Street
New York, New York 10003
Phone: (212) 254-0397
Fax: (202) 737-8406
Email: info@americanhungarianfederation.org
URL: www.americanhungarianfederation.org

Californiai Magyarság (*California Hungarians*)

Founded in 1924 as a moderate regional newspaper, it is now a national paper that has retained its middle-of-the-road stance.

207 South Western Avenue
Suite 201
Los Angeles, California 90004
Phone: (213) 463-3473
Fax: (213) 384-7642
Email: editor@californiaimagyarsag.com
URL: www.magyarsajto.com

Kanadai/Amerikai Magyarság (Canadian/American Hungarians)

This is the Western world's largest weekly newspaper in Hungarian.

747 St. Clair Avenue West #103
Toronto, Ontario, Canada
Phone: (416) 656-8361
Fax: (416) 651-2442
Email: info@kanadaimagyarsag.ca
URL: www.kekujsag.com

Magyar Elet (*Hungarian Life*)

Circulated throughout Canada and the United States, this is an independent weekly newspaper published in Hungarian.

390 Concession 7
R.R. #5
Claremont, Ontario L1Y 1A2
Phone: (289) 200-6772
Email: info@magyarelet.ca
URL: www.magyarelet.ca
Canada

TELEVISION

The Nationality Broadcasting Network

Located in Cleveland, Ohio, this network broadcasts Hungarian programs every day via satellite throughout North America.

Miklós Kossányi, President
11906 Madison Avenue
Cleveland, Ohio 44107-5027
Phone: (216) 221-0331

ORGANIZATIONS AND ASSOCIATIONS

American Hungarian Federation (AHF) (Amerikai Magyar Szövetség [AMSZ])

Founded in Cleveland in 1906, the AHF is the oldest and largest umbrella organization of Hungarian Americans. It represents the interests of its members and the Hungarian American community in general. After being based in Washington, D.C., from the 1940s to the 1970s, it transferred its office to Akron, Ohio, in the early 1980s.

Frank Koszorús, Jr., President
2631 Copley Road
Akron, Ohio 44321
Phone: (330) 666-1313
Fax: (330) 666-2637
Email: info@americanhungarianfederation.org
URL: www.americanhungarianfederation.org

American Hungarian Folklore Centrum (AHFC)

This organization supports and promotes Hungarian studies and folk culture within the scholarly and public life of the United States.

Kalman Magyar, Director
P.O. Box 262
Bogota, New Jersey 07603
Phone: (201) 836-4869
Fax: (201) 836-1590
Email: magyar@magyar.org
URL: www.magyar.org

American Hungarian Reformed Federation (AHRF) (Amerikai Magyar Református Egyesület [AMRE])

Founded in 1898, the AHRF is the second-largest and only religiously based Hungarian American fraternal association in existence. It has about 20,000 members, and although it is now primarily an insurance company, it continues to support Hungarian cultural activities and also engages in some lobbying efforts on behalf of Hungarian causes.

Gyula Balogh, Co-President
2001 Massachusetts Avenue NW
Washington, D.C. 20036-1011
Phone: (202) 328-2630

Hungarian American Coalition (Magyar-Amerikai Koalíció)

Founded in 1992, the coalition is a relatively recent Hungarian umbrella organization. Politically, it has a moderate-centrist, pragmatic orientation. It attempts to carry out an effective lobbying effort on behalf of Hungarian causes in Washington, D.C.

1120 Connecticut Avenue NW
Suite 280
Washington, D.C. 20036
Phone: (202) 296-9505
Fax: (202) 775-5175
Email: hac@hacusa.org
URL: www.hacusa.org

William Penn Association (WPA)

Founded in 1886, as the Verhovay Aid Association, the WPA is the largest Hungarian fraternal association in North America. It assumed its present name in 1955, when it absorbed its largest rival, the Rákóczi Federation of Bridgeport, Connecticut. Although primarily an insurance company, the WPA still sponsors certain Hungarian cultural functions. In the early 2000s the WPA transferred much of its archives and library to the Hungarian Heritage Center of New Brunswick, New Jersey.

709 Brighton Road
Pittsburgh, Pennsylvania 15233-1821
Phone: (412) 231-2979 or (800) 848-7366
URL: www.williampennassociation.org

MUSEUMS AND RESEARCH CENTERS

American Hungarian Foundation (AHF), Hungarian Heritage Center

Founded in 1955, the AHF is a major Hungarian cultural foundation that operates the Hungarian Heritage Center in New Brunswick, New Jersey. The Hungarian Heritage Center possesses one of the largest collections of archival materials relating to Hungarian Americans as well as one of the largest Hungarica libraries in the United States (40,000 volumes).

August J. Molnar, President
300 Somerset Street
New Brunswick, New Jersey 08903-1084
Phone: (732) 846-5777
Fax: (732) 249-7033
Email: info@ahfoundation.org
URL: www.ahfoundation.org

Hungarian Institute, Rutgers University

Founded in 1992 with the financial support of the Hungarian government, the Hungarian Institute at Rutgers draws heavily on the intellectual and library resources of Rutgers University (Hungarica, 2,000 volumes), as well as on the library of the nearby American Hungarian Foundation (Hungarica, 40,000 volumes).

Paul Hanebrink
102 Nichol Avenue
New Brunswick, New Jersey 08901
Phone: (732) 932-7129
Email: hanebrin@history.rutgers.edu
URL: http://hungarian.rutgers.edu

Institute of Hungarian Studies

An integral part of Indiana University, the institute focuses on Hungarian society and civilization, including contemporary economic and cultural affairs.

Gustav Bayerle, Director
Goodbody 233
Bloomington, Indiana 47405
Phone: (812) 855-2233
Email: hca@indiana.edu
URL: www.indiana.edu/~rugs/ctrdir/ihs.html

SOURCES FOR ADDITIONAL STUDY

Lengyel, Emil. *Americans from Hungary*. Philadelphia; New York: J. B. Lippincott, 1948.

McGuire, James Patrick. *The Hungarian Texans*. San Antonio: University of Texas, Institute of Texan Culture, 1993.

Papp, Susan M. *Hungarian Americans and Their Communities in Cleveland*. Cleveland, OH: Cleveland Ethnic Heritage Studies, Cleveland State University, 1981.

Tezla, Albert. *The Hazardous Quest: Hungarian Immigrants in the United States, 1895–1920*. Budapest: Corvina, 1993.

Várdy, Steven Béla. *Clio's Art in Hungary and in Hungarian-America*. New York: Columbia University Press, 1985.

———. *The Hungarian-Americans*. Boston: Twayne, 1985.

———. *The Hungarian Americans: The Hungarian Experience in North America*. New York; Philadelphia: Chelsea House, 1990.

Várdy, Steven Béla, and Agnes Huszár Várdy. *The Austro-Hungarian Mind: At Home and Abroad*. New York: Columbia University Press, 1989.

———. *Hungarian Americans in the Current of History*. New Columbia University Press, 2010.

Vida, Istvan Kornel. *Hungarian Émigrés in the American Civil War: A History and Biographical Dictionary*. Jefferson, NC: McFarland, 2011.

ICELANDIC AMERICANS

Lolly Ockerstrom

OVERVIEW

Icelandic Americans are immigrants or descendants of immigrants from Iceland, a volcanic island in the North Atlantic Ocean and the most westerly nation of Europe. It is also the least populated and was the last to be settled. Located between Greenland, the United Kingdom, and Norway, it is about 500 miles northwest of the outer islands of Scotland. Iceland touches the Arctic Circle with its northernmost edge, but the Gulf Stream brings mild winters and cool summer temperatures to the island. The country is predominately a plateau with a coastline of bays and fjords. Because of its glaciers and active volcanoes, it is often referred to as "the Land of Fire and Ice." The island is approximately 40,000 square miles (103,000) square kilometers in size, slightly smaller than the state of Colorado.

According to the *CIA World Factbook*, 313,183 people lived in Iceland in 2012, residing mainly in towns located on its 3,000-mile (5,000-kilometer) coastline. More than half of the total population resides in Reykjavik, the northernmost national capital city in the world. The *Factbook* also records that roughly 80 percent of Icelanders belong to the Lutheran Church of Iceland, that 94 percent have a combined Norse and Celtic ancestry, and that the country has one of the highest standards of living in Europe, with an especially high quality of housing. Education, including university, is provided free for all of its citizens, as are health care and retirement pensions. Iceland's fishing industry supplies more than 70 percent of the country's exports, aluminum accounts for about 11 percent, and geothermal and hydropower provide two other major economic resources.

The first Icelandic immigrants to United States settled in Utah in 1855. During the next half century, thousands also migrated to northern Wisconsin, Minnesota, the Dakotas, and Alaska. They worked in the areas of agriculture, building, and fishing in their new locale, all trades familiar to them from home. As the United States became more industrialized in the early twentieth century, the economy changed in character from agrarian to more urban. This change affected many small Icelandic American farming communities, and many immigrants began relocating to larger urban areas such as New York City, Seattle, Chicago, and San Francisco. While some still live in rural immigrant communities in the Midwest, many have been absorbed into a broader populace over the course of the last half-century.

The U.S. Census Bureau's American Community Survey estimated in 2010 that the total number of people of Icelandic descent in the United States was 51,234 (roughly enough people to fill New York's Yankee Stadium). At the time more than half of Icelandic Americans lived in the West and the Midwest. According to the American Community Survey, the states with the largest populations of Icelandic Americans included California (7,372), Washington (6,800), Minnesota (3,875), and Utah (3,861). A smaller number of Icelanders reside in Florida (2,368) and North Dakota (2,840).

HISTORY OF THE PEOPLE

Early History In 825 CE the Irish monk Dicuil recorded the earliest firsthand accounts of settlers on the island of Thule, which later became known as Iceland. Sometime between 850 and 875, a Swede named Garðar Svavarsson is thought to have arrived on the island, followed by an influx of pagan Norse from 874 to 930. The first man to settle permanently in Iceland was Ingólfur Arnarson. According to the *Landnamabok*, or Book of Settlements, written in the twelfth century, Arnarson was a chieftain from Norway. Bringing his family and dependents to Iceland, he built a farm on the site of the later capital city of Reykjavik. Like many of the first settlers in Iceland, Arnarson had fled Norway to avoid oppression under the tyrannical ruler Harald Fairhair. Harald was attempting to unify Norway by conquering all of the other lords and kings of Norway. Many early settlers of this period were seafarers, including Erik the Red (Eirikur Rauði), who discovered Greenland in 982. In the year 1000 his son, Leif Eriksson, became the first person to travel to North America, predating Columbus by 500 years.

Iceland's central parliament, the Althingi, was established in 930, along with a constitutional law code. It is considered to be the oldest parliament in the world. In the tenth century small numbers of Irish and Scots settlers brought Christianity, specifically Catholicism, to Iceland, and the parliament adopted the religion in the year 1000, about one hundred years after Christianity had made its way to mainland Scandinavia. Bishoprics, or dioceses, were quickly established in the town of Skálholt in 1056 and in Hólar in 1106. Both places became centers of learning, typical of medieval universities throughout Europe, which were established for training clerics.

Feuds and civil war came to Iceland between 1262 and 1264, weakening the island's unity, and by 1397 Iceland was under the dominion of Denmark. Danish kings took control of the church, forcing Icelanders to abandon Catholicism for Danish Lutheranism. The Danes also established a monopoly over Icelandic trade, devastating the island's economy. By 1662 Denmark had taken complete control of Iceland.

The first census of the island, taken in 1703, revealed a population of 50,000. After a smallpox epidemic that lasted from 1707 to 1709, that number plunged to a low of 35,000. A series of famines and natural disasters plagued Iceland that century, keeping the population below 40,000. By 1800 there were only half the number of Icelanders there had been in 1100. In addition, the Danish dissolved the Althingi at the end of the eighteenth century, causing further distress for the Icelanders.

Modern Era Iceland began to develop a national identity during the nineteenth century. The National Library of Iceland was established in 1818, followed by the Icelandic National Museum in 1863 and the National Archives in 1882. In 1843 the Althingi was reestablished, although it was only used as a consultative assembly. Statesman and scholar Jón Sigurðsson led a political struggle for national independence, and Denmark granted Iceland home rule in 1874, allowing Icelanders to write their own constitution. In 1904 Hannes Hafstein was appointed as the first Icelandic government minister. Iceland gained control of almost all its domestic affairs in 1918, although the Danish king remained the official head of state.

In 1940 British forces invaded and occupied Iceland as a place from which to fight Germany. Promised favorable compensation, Iceland submitted but officially maintained its neutrality throughout World War II. American forces took over the defense of the North Atlantic island in 1941. One American stationed in Iceland was David "The Zink" Zinkoff, a famous sports announcer in Philadelphia known for twenty years as the "Voice of the 76ers." After the war Zinkoff celebrated his military service by founding the Icelandic-American Veterans, informally called the FBI—"Forgotten Bastards of Iceland"—in 1950. It lasted until his death in 1985.

On June 17, 1944, a national referendum established the modern Republic of Iceland with 97 percent voter approval. After achieving its independence, the country quickly joined four important international organizations, beginning with the United Nations in 1946. It was a founding member of the Organization for Economic Cooperation and Development (OECD)

in 1947 and of the North Atlantic Treaty Organization (NATO) in 1949. In 1950 it joined the Council of Europe (COE). Turning its attentions homeward, it inaugurated a national theater and symphony orchestra, also in 1950.

Iceland's strategic location in the North Atlantic made the country attractive to Western allies. Iceland had no military of its own, so in 1951 it signed a defense agreement with the United States, creating the Iceland Defense Force, which was based at Naval Air Station Keflavik. The group included members of the U.S. Air Force, Marine Corps, and Navy as well as Icelandic civilians. Throughout the second half of the twentieth century, Iceland continued to fortify its position in Europe, joining the Nordic Council, a forum for political and economic cooperation, in 1952. The Iceland Defense Force disbanded in 2006, and the U.S. military withdrew its last troops in September of that year.

Beginning in the 1950s and over the course of the next several decades, Iceland concentrated on strengthening its vitally important fishing industry. Fishery limits, which had been set at 3 miles off the coast through agreements with competitors in neighboring countries, were extended to 4 miles in 1952. Two years later the boundaries were expanded again to 12 miles from the coast. The struggle between Iceland and Great Britain over fishing rights during this period is referred to as the Cod Wars. By the mid-1970s fishing limits had been extended to 200 miles, causing a sudden boom in the Icelandic economy. Through negotiations within NATO, Britain, Norway, and other countries conceded to the extensions as a preventive measure to keep the Soviet Union from gaining more control in the Atlantic Ocean. In the twenty-first century, even with these broad limits, Icelandic fisheries have become depleted, leading to a decline in the economy.

Iceland joined the European Free Trade Association (EFTA) in 1970. Denmark returned ancient Icelandic manuscripts to Iceland in 1971, a final gesture of the restoration of Icelandic culture. In 1974 the country marked the 1,100[th] anniversary of its original settlement. Reykjavik celebrated its bicentennial in 1986 and also hosted the Reagan-Gorbachev Summit, a milestone of the Cold War era, and in 1994 Icelanders commemorated the fiftieth anniversary of the modern Icelandic Republic. In 2008, during the global financial crisis, the Landsbanki (the national bank of Iceland) collapsed. Although the bank continued to honor the accounts of Iceland's citizens, foreign investors suffered losses, and the failure greatly affected Iceland's economy. The country was absorbed into the European Union (EU) in 2009, which boosted its economy and national credit rating, and unemployment declined from 9 percent in 2010 to 6 percent in 2011.

Iceland has always been considered progressive in the realm of women's rights. The country retained its first female president, Vigdís Finnbogadóttir, for four consecutive terms (1980–1996). In 2009 Jóhanna Sigurðardottir was elected as the first female prime minister, a position that holds more power than the president's in Iceland's democratic republican government. Prime Minister Sigurðardottir was also the first openly gay public official in Iceland, a testament to the country's acceptance of the Lesbian, Gay, Bisexual, and Transgender (LGBT) community.

During the latter part of the twentieth century and into the twenty-first, several volcanic eruptions affected the country. The tourism industry suffered because volcanic ash disrupted air travel and because fears of future eruptions deterred visitors. Many Icelanders had to be evacuated as a result of massive flooding from snowmelt. Three major eruptions stand out in the modern era. In 1973 the Heimaey volcano erupted on the only inhabited island in the Westmann Islands. In 2010 Eyjafjallajökull on the Eyjafjöll glacier suspended much of the air travel in northern Europe for weeks. The eruption of Grímsvötn on the Vatnajökull Glacier interrupted European travel again, though not to the extent of the previous year's blast.

SETTLEMENT IN THE UNITED STATES

Among the first to leave predominately Presbyterian Iceland for North America were Thorarinn Haflidason Thorason and Gudmund Gudmundsson, who had converted to Mormonism in Denmark, moved to Westmann Island, and started the first Icelandic Mormon Mission. They arrived in Utah in 1855, seeking a religious freedom denied them in Iceland. In all, eleven Mormon converts left Iceland for North America between 1854 and 1857, eventually settling in the town of Spanish Fork, Utah, along with other Scandinavians. For the next twenty years, small groups of Icelanders joined the settlement from time to time. Most of these immigrants were artisans, tradespersons, and farmers, and they brought useful skills for the frontier with them, although it was some time before they could use those skills in gainful employment.

The last three decades of the nineteenth century saw the largest wave of Icelandic immigration. Between 1870 and 1900, about 15,000 Icelanders resettled in North America. The majority of these immigrants found a home on the west shore of Lake Winnipeg in the town of Gimli, located in Manitoba, Canada. They called this colony New Iceland. In addition to the significant community in Utah, those coming to the United States settled primarily in the upper Midwest, especially in Wisconsin, Minnesota, and the Dakota Territories. William Wickmann, a Danish immigrant who had worked for a time in Eyrarbakki on the southern coast of Iceland before arriving in Milwaukee in 1856, wrote letters to Iceland describing his new home. His reports of the plentiful life in Wisconsin were circulated among his Icelandic friends. In particular, Wickmann's accounts of the abundance of coffee, of which Icelanders were especially fond, proved irresistible. In 1870 more Icelanders left for Milwaukee, eventually settling on Washington Island in Lake Michigan, just off the Green Bay peninsula.

In Washington Island, Wisconsin, an Icelandic American woman prepares lake chub to be smoked over maple fire in smokehouse. VOLKMAR K. WENTZEL / NATIONAL GEOGRAPHIC / GETTY IMAGES

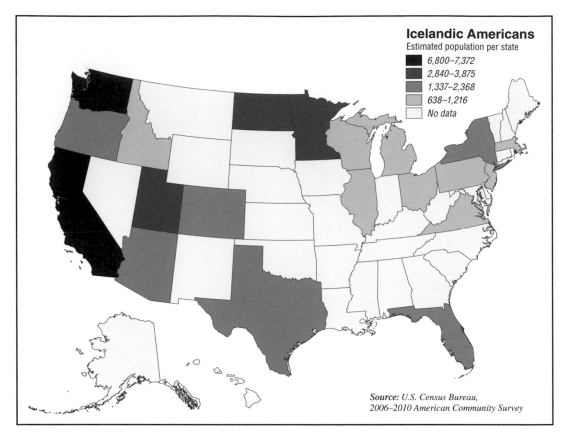

Icelandic Americans
Estimated population per state

- 6,800–7,372
- 2,840–3,875
- 1,337–2,368
- 638–1,216
- No data

*Source: U.S. Census Bureau,
2006–2010 American Community Survey*

In 1874 a group of Icelandic immigrants proposed a settlement in Alaska, which they felt would provide a climate and terrain similar to that of Iceland. Jón Ólafsson went so far as to meet with President Ulysses S. Grant to secure Alaskan land for a massive Icelandic settlement. They managed to convince the U.S. government to assist them in visiting the proposed Alaskan site. Many Icelanders (and several of the U.S. governmental representatives) apparently lost interest in the project because of the inhospitable Alaskan climate and terrain, and plans for the new colony were abandoned.

In the mid-1870s the United States suffered an economic depression, and jobs were scarce. For newly arrived Icelanders who knew little if any English, employment was even harder to find. Many men took laboring jobs as unskilled factory workers and woodcutters in various places or as dockworkers in Milwaukee when they first arrived. Preparing to start farms, these early immigrants built up capital and learned farming techniques suitable for their new land. Their communities became largely agricultural or related to the fishing industry; drawing from their customary lifestyle in their home country, they thus maintained their ties to their Icelandic heritage.

By 1878 severe weather conditions, outbreaks of smallpox, and religious disputes had forced more than one hundred Icelanders from the Canadian colony of

New Iceland to relocate south to the United States, where they joined more recent Icelandic immigrants in the northeastern section of the Dakota Territory. With the help of more established Norwegian and German immigrant groups, they formed what later became the largest Icelandic community in America. Whereas the first generation were mostly farmers and laborers, second- and third-generation Icelanders were drawn into other fields of employment, including journalism, academia, and politics. A large group of Icelandic Americans also settled in the Puget Sound, predominantly in the Ballard neighborhood of Seattle, to work in the fishing and boat-building industries.

By 1900 new immigration from Iceland had almost completely ceased. It is estimated that about 5,000 Icelanders had taken up residency in the United States by 1910. The exact number is difficult to determine, because until 1930 the U.S. Census, unlike the census in Canada, did not differentiate between Icelanders and Danes, sometimes going as far to list them all as Northern Europeans. In 1910, however, the census did report that 5,105 U.S. residents had grown up in a home where Icelandic was spoken. Not until after the end of World War II did Icelanders again immigrate to the United States in any substantial numbers. The post–World War II immigration wave was made up predominantly of war brides of American servicemen who had been stationed in Iceland.

Early-twentieth-century industrialization transformed the United States from an agrarian culture into an urban one, affecting traditionally agrarian-based Icelandic American communities. By the end of the century, new Icelandic immigration had shifted from rural to urban communities. In addition, by 1970 more than half of second- and third-generation Icelandic Americans had taken up residence in urban areas.

The 1990 U.S. Department of Commerce Census reported a total count of 40,529 Icelandic Americans and Icelandic nationals living in the United States. According to the American Community Survey estimates, by 2010 this number had increased to 51,234. The largest populations of Icelandic Americans can be found in California, Washington, Minnesota, and Utah, as well as North Dakota and Florida.

In the late twentieth century, Americans of Icelandic descent showed great interest in tracing their ancestors. Most amateur genealogists of Icelandic heritage were interested in the settlements in Winnipeg and Utah. Several websites began offering help with mapping Icelandic lines of descent. *Islendingabok* (*The Book of Icelanders*), although it dates from 1200, still serves as a valuable tool today in tracing ancestry.

LANGUAGE

Icelandic is the national language of Iceland, although many Icelanders also understand and speak both English and Danish. The country has no indigenous linguistic minorities. Icelandic is a Germanic language and a member of the Scandinavian language family. Two letters of the Icelandic alphabet resemble Old English: *thorn* (þ), pronounced like the *th* in *thing*, and *eth* (ð), pronounced like the *th* in *them*. The language is thought to have changed very little in the thousand years since the first Nordic settlers arrived on Iceland. Icelandic speakers still read and appreciate many songs and epic poems dating from the twelfth century in their original forms. The relative purity of the language is largely the result of Iceland's isolation as an island nation.

In 1959 the Althingi passed a bill barring the adoption of names not Icelandic in origin for public establishments, a reflection of the nation's pride in its language. Only one vote was cast in opposition to the bill. While some Icelandic Americans still speak Icelandic in their homes or community circles, most have assimilated into the larger American population through their jobs in urban centers.

Greetings and Popular Expressions Typical Icelandic greetings and expressions and their approximate pronunciations include the following: *góðan dag* ("gothan dag")—good day; *gott kvöld* ("goht kwvold")—good evening; *Komið pér saelie*? ("komith pearr sauleuh")—How do you do?; *Hallo. Hvaðer um að vera*? ("hallo. kwath aer uem ath verra")—Hi. What's going on?; *Hvað heitir pú*? ("kwath hayterr

peu")—What is your name?; *Ég heiti…* ("ag haete")—My name is…; *sjáumst* ("syoymst")—bye; *góða nótt* ("gotha noht")—good night; *Gleður mig að kynnast pér* ("glathur may ad kednast pear")—Glad to meet you; *Já eða nei*? ("yaah aytha nay")—Yes or no?; *Ég skil ekki* ("ag skeel ahhki")—I don't understand; *Gleðileg jól* ("glathelay yawl")—Merry Christmas; and *Gleðileg nyár* ("glathelay nyarr")—Happy New Year.

Iceland's language, customs, and historical background link it ethnically to Scandinavia, though Icelanders have always perceived themselves as having a distinct culture. The differences have seldom been clear to non-Icelanders, who have conflated the Icelandic culture with those of Denmark, Sweden, and Norway.

RELIGION

The *CIA World Factbook* reported that in 2006, 80.7 percent of the population of Iceland belonged to the Evangelical Lutheran Church of Iceland; 2.5 percent were Roman Catholic; 7.6 percent attended institutions representing other indigenous religions, such as the Reykjavik Free Church and the Hafnarfjörður Free Church; and 9.2 percent were unaffiliated or unspecified. Early Icelandic immigrants to North America did not remain dogmatically Lutheran. They were happy to be relieved of the heavy tax burden the Icelandic church imposed. Some of the early Icelandic immigrants who settled in Utah rejected Lutheranism altogether and embraced Mormonism. Churches continued to fill important social, spiritual, and community functions for Icelanders as they established settlements in their new land, however. Two early immigrants, Pall Thorlaksson and Jon Bjarnason, were leaders among Icelandic Lutherans in North America. Both men trained in the ministry, but they represented different philosophies, and this led to a temporary split in the Icelandic American Lutheran Church.

As Icelandic immigrants assimilated into the general American culture, some branched into subsects of Lutheranism. In the 1880s the Unitarian movement drew a number of Icelanders, and the competition strengthened the commitment of the remaining Lutherans. The Icelandic Evangelical Lutheran Synod of America was established in 1885. In 1942 the synod was absorbed into the United Lutheran Church of America, which became part of the Evangelical Lutheran Church of America in 1988.

Icelandic Americans who have remained in the Lutheran Church have continued the practice of christening newborns as part of a community, if not spiritual, expression of welcome. Christenings follow the principles set down by the Lutheran Church of Iceland: the parents of the child choose godparents, and the baby is brought to the christening font,

THE MYTH OF GRYLA

For centuries the myth of Gryla, a troll who was thought to live in the mountains and to appear in the lowlands at Christmas, was a staple of holiday lore. Icelandic immigrants handed down the story to younger generations, and the myth has continued to play an important role in Christmas festivities in United States. Gryla's characteristics have changed over the centuries since her first appearance in Icelandic literature in the ninth century. Hjorleifur Rafn Jonsson argued in a 1990 article in *Nord Nytt*, a Nordic journal of ethnology and folklore, that the myth was adapted according to changing social and economic developments. Like the Icelandic Americans who brought the myth with them to North America, Gryla's character changed but remained rooted in Icelandic culture.

usually at the age of two or three months. A celebration follows. Christening gowns are treasured items, often handed down through the generations.

CULTURE AND ASSIMILATION

Iceland's language, customs, and historical background link it ethnically to Scandinavia, though Icelanders have always perceived themselves as having a distinct culture. The differences have seldom been clear to non-Icelanders, who have conflated the Icelandic culture with those of Denmark, Sweden, and Norway. Few studies in English have concentrated on Icelanders, and many reference books have omitted them altogether from general accounts of ethnic or national cultural variations.

Icelandic immigrants have eagerly adopted new customs in the United States, learning English, holding public office, and integrating into the general culture. At the same time they have retained a strong sense of ethnic pride, as evidenced by the large number of Icelandic American organizations that have been established throughout the United States since the founding of the Icelandic National League in 1919. The league promotes Icelandic culture, customs, and traditions. It spans both Canada and the United States, with U.S. chapters in Washington D.C., New York, Illinois, and Minnesota. Near the end of the twentieth century, widespread attention to multiculturalism spurred many Icelandic Americans to reclaim their heritage.

Traditions and Customs Like other Scandinavians, Icelanders take great delight in stories of trolls, elves, and fairies. Fairies and elves are said to exist everywhere, beneath rocks and mushrooms. Often, good luck is attributed to the work of elves. In contrast, prior to the twentieth century, trolls were always associated with danger. Icelandic folklore is still cherished as a cultural treasure.

Icelandic sagas are also a highly prized literary tradition and are admired throughout the world. Consisting of medieval mythology, the sagas describe events involving the Norse and Celtic inhabitants of Iceland from the tenth and eleventh centuries, focusing on genealogy, family history, and the conquests of early Norse generations. Beginning as oral folktales, the sagas are thought to have been written in the thirteenth and fourteenth centuries. The Icelandic Saga Database (www.sagadb.org) digitally publishes sagas translated into English.

In earlier times Tuesday was a day on which meat was eaten, a custom handed down from Iceland's Catholic days. Some Icclanders (often children and servants) played a game called *ad sitja i fastunni* ("to sit in the fast"). It consisted of wordplay in which common terms for meat, drippings, and gravy were replaced by other words. Children tried to see if they could get through the entire day without being tricked into using the usual language for meats, even as they tried to get others to slip into saying the forbidden words. This practice has slipped into obscurity in Icelandic American households.

Cuisine Typical Icelandic fare includes many types of fish (including shark and skate, particularly on special occasions), lamb, and dark breads. The many variations of basic recipes suggest regional as well as individual differences. Women have traditionally done the cooking; each family treasures its own recipes, and each claims that its mother and grandmother produced the finest version. Icelandic Americans bring many of these traditional foods to summer festivals and Christmas feasts. A prevalent one is *vinarterta* (which translates as "Vienna Cake"), a layered cake made with cardamom, cinnamon, and ground, boiled prunes and served with whipped cream during the winter holidays and at weddings.

Icelandic brown bread, made with molasses and wheat germ, differs from Icelandic black bread, which contains rye. Both are staples of the diet. Icelandic pancakes, or *ponnukokur*, are similar to the flat, crêpelike Swedish pancakes. They are savory and are served with meat fillings. A *flatbroud*, or rye pancake, is another traditional food. Pastries include *kleinur*, Icelandic donuts made with sour cream, buttermilk, vanilla, and nutmeg; and *Astarbollur*, raisin donut balls rolled in granulated sugar and cinnamon.

Seasonal variation is common. Traditional foods associated with the autumn slaughtering season and the limited methods for preserving meat in earlier times include dried fish (*hardfiskur*); blood pudding (*slatur*); and smoked lamb (*hangikjot*). Eating Icelandic fruitcake at Christmas is a special holiday ritual.

Pylsa—Icelandic hot dogs—became popular in Iceland during the latter part of the twentieth century. Similar to American hot dogs but longer and thinner, they are eaten with ketchup, onions, mustard, and a mayonnaise-based topping called *remoladi*. *Brennivin*, the Icelandic national drink, is a type of schnapps, with the consistency of syrup and without flavor. Often drunk with herring or shark, it is consumed in small quantities in much the same way as the Danish drink *aquavit*. Aside from holidays and special occasions, most Icelandic Americans have adopted the typical American diet in their process of assimilation.

Traditional Dress Traditional Icelandic women's dress includes several distinct garments, usually of fine material that has been embroidered. A sweater suit, or *peysufot*, was used for everyday wear well into the twentieth century, particularly in the countryside. The hair was covered with a *faldur*, secured with a scarf or scarves wrapped around the head. Other elements of this headdress included a *skotthufa*, or tail cap. The tail was made of numerous small strands of material. Just below its top, the tail was enfolded in a sleeve, richly ornamented in gold or silver threads. A more formal headdress was called a *faldbuningur*.

On special days women also wore an ornamental vest called an *upphlutur* ("upper part"), abundantly embroidered with gold thread. It was worn with a skirt and apron, both of which were sewn of very good material. While some higher-quality costumes were worn only for certain festivities, others served for Sundays and traveling.

Confirmation in the Lutheran Church required special dress and headgear. Children were confirmed at the age of fourteen. On this occasion girls wore a headdress called *skautbuningur*, which was a small white cap with a veil trailing down the back. A golden coronet was positioned at the forehead. The traditional white dress was called a *kyrtill*. Confirmation marked a girl's transition into adulthood, which included wearing adult attire, an exciting change. In writing of her confirmation day in her autobiography *When I Was a Girl in Iceland* (1919), Holmfridur Arnadottir exclaimed, "How grand, that from that day I should be dressed as the grownup women!" After confirmation a woman wore a black skirt appliqued with velvet and a bodice embroidered in silver thread. Both younger and older women wore a special belt. The belt for the older woman was embroidered and had a buckle of filigree, while that of the young girl was completely handmade of filigree.

Icelandic Americans' assimilation into popular culture has extended to their dress habits. They may wear traditional dress during religious ceremonies or on certain holidays, but overall they wear the same clothing as other Americans.

Dances and Songs Icelanders are fond of music and poetry. Their national anthem, originally a hymn written in 1874 for the millennial celebration of Iceland's first settlement, is called "Ó Guð vors lands" ("Our Country's God") and expresses a national sentiment of submission to God. The final lines defer to a deity who can offer guidance: "O, prosper our people, diminish our tears / And guide, in

Thy wisdom, through life!" It is sung at the opening of state and national events. It was authored by Matthias Jochumsson (1835–1920), a clergyman who was also a journalist, a dramatist, and the national poet. Included among his other work are translations into Icelandic of Shakespearean tragedies.

Choral singing is among the most popular of Iceland's arts. Icelandic settlers cultivated traditional songs on the American frontier in all areas of existence—religious, social, and domestic. While no longer practiced in everyday life, choral singing is still a popular tradition during festivals and holidays. Particularly at Christmas, Icelanders participate in choirs and bands. Iceland's most prominent musical genre is the *rimur*, an epic song form that dates back to the thirteenth century. Because the Icelandic language has changed little since that time, some of the oldest songs are still performed and enjoyed in their original form.

Icelandic pancakes, served at the Norwegian-Icelandic-run Sunset Resort on Washington Island, Wisconsin, are filled with frothy yogurt cream sauce and cherries. LAUREN VIERA / CHICAGO TRIBUNE / MCT / GETTY IMAGES

The Christmas and New Year's holidays are marked by joyous singing and dancing around bonfires. Some celebrants dress up as elves. In her autobiography Arnadottir describes Twelfth Night dances, when white and black fairies "with all kinds of headdresses" come down from high cliffs carrying torches. A procession of celebrants parade to a bonfire, where the fairies sing and dance in a circle and recite poetry. When the bonfire has burned out, everyone moves to a dance hall, where they continue dancing. In general these traditional songs and dances are reserved for religious holidays and special cultural occasions.

Holidays Icelandic Americans continued to celebrate Icelandic holidays well after they settled into Americanized routines. Early immigrants commemorated August 2, 1874, a date significant on two counts: on the day of the millennium of Iceland's first settlement, the Danish king granted the country its autonomy. June 17, the day on which Iceland became a republic in 1944, later became the major holiday observed by Icelandic immigrants.

Iceland's holidays are typical of those celebrated in other Western, Christian nations, although with some differences. The Christmas season lasts several days and is traditionally celebrated with bonfires, dancing, and stories of elves and trolls.

On New Year's Eve people customarily invited elves into their home. Lights, or candles, were lit throughout the house in order to drive out the shadows. The mistress of the house walked around the outside of the house three times, chanting an invitation to the elves to come, stay, or go. At least one light remained burning throughout the night. Also on New Year's Eve, the pantry window was left open and a pot was placed on the pantry floor in an attempt to capture hoarfrost (the ephemeral frozen dew that forms a white coating on surfaces). The mistress of the house remained in the pantry all night. In the morning a cover was placed over the pot to keep the hoarfrost in, known as the "pantry drift." Capturing it in this way was thought to bring prosperity to the household. While Icelandic Americans still observe these holidays, celebrations have come to resemble traditional American ones, both in the church and in homes and communities.

Twelfth Night, celebrated twelve days after Christmas on January 5, is often called the "Great Night of Dreams" in Iceland. This refers to the night when the Kings of the Orient are thought to have dreamed of the birth of Jesus. In some parts of Iceland, Twelfth Night was referred to as "The Old Christmas" or "The Old Christmas Eve." Twelfth Day is celebrated on January 6 with bonfires and dancing.

Lent traditionally takes place during the six-week period before Easter Sunday, and in Iceland the first three days are filled with festive games. Lenten (or Shrove) Monday is known in Icelandic as *Bolludagur* ("the day of muffins" or "bun day") or *Flengingardagur*

("the day of whipping"). The holiday is believed to have been transported to Iceland by Danish and Norwegian bakers who immigrated to Iceland in the late nineteenth century. The day begins with early risers "beating" those who are still in bed with small whips or wands that the children have made of colored paper. Those who are whipped provide the children with a bun or muffin. The whipping is done mainly by the children, and is done good-naturedly. Bolludagur is usually a school holiday, allowing for family visits to friends and neighbors, who invariably provide muffins served with coffee. In the United States the Icelandic traditions surrounding Lent have faded over time.

Ash Wednesday, or *Oskudagur*, was celebrated by playing a teasing game related to the tradition of repentance and involving ashes or stones. On the days prior to Ash Wednesday, women and girls made small bags into which ashes or small stones were placed. Constructed with drawstrings, the bags were fastened to people's backs with pins. Bags containing ashes were intended for men and boys; bags with stones were for women and girls. (Stones likely symbolized the old punishment of tying bags of stones around the necks of adulterous women in order to drown them.) People carried the bags a certain distance, sometimes three steps or across three thresholds. As many as thirty bags might be attached to back of a person's clothing. Much like the traditions surrounding Lent and other religious holidays, these practices have all but vanished in Iceland, and the holiday is now similar to American Halloween in that young children dress up in costumes and go door to door collecting candy.

Like people in other Nordic countries, Icelanders view the first day of summer as the second most significant holiday of the year (Christmas being the first). As early as 1545, gifts were exchanged among family members on this holiday, and food played a prominent role in the festivities. Although food was scarce after the long winter, Icelanders saved all they could so they could serve their best food and drink during First Day of Summer festivals. Often the amount of food saved indicated the degree of a family's wealth. In the western fjords many Icelanders stored food in a special barrel during the autumn that was not to be opened until the following summer. Special summer-day cakes made of rye were served to each person. The large cakes measured one foot in diameter and were three-quarters of an inch thick. Each cake was topped with one day's portion of food, which included *hangiket*, or butter; *lundabaggar*, or flanks (sheep's internal organs boiled and then soaked in whey); hard fish; halibut fins; and the like.

First Day of Summer celebrations included a religious service with special hymns and a sermon, after which children played such games as blind man's bluff. The hard winter over, Icelanders stayed outdoors for most of the day, celebrating the coming of long days filled with sunlight. Prior to 1900 the First Day of Summer was a day for socializing among family and friends, eating, and marking the end of winter. Public performances were gradually integrated into the holiday. Young people in particular began to give speeches and recite poetry. Sports, singing, and dancing became important activities, as well as plays and other theatrical productions. While these practices may be revived at traditional celebrations of Iceland's heritage, they are not common practices among Icelandic American families.

Two holidays unique to Iceland are *Krossmessa* ("Crossmas") and St. Thorlak's Day, both popular during the nineteenth and early twentieth centuries, Krossmessa, observed on May 14, was the day when domestic servants moved on to new jobs. Servants were usually hired for a one-year period, although many stayed with their employers for several years before moving on. St. Thorlak's Day was celebrated on December 23 to honor Thorlak Thorhalli, who became the bishop of Skalholt in 1177. On this day the Christmas *hangiket*, or smoked mutton, is cooked, clothes are washed, and the house is cleaned. Both of these holidays fell into obscurity in Iceland during the early twentieth century and are not usually observed by Icelandic Americans.

The 1960s brought the revival of another holiday specific to Iceland, an ancient pagan festival called the *Thorrablot*. It was originally observed in midwinter, when sacrifices to the Norse god Thorri were made. The holiday predates Christian Iceland and died out when Christianity was adopted. It regained popularity in 1873 when revived by Icelandic students in Copenhagen and in 1881 when a group of archaeologists in Reykjavik toasted each other using Viking horns on that day. Icelandic Americans now celebrate the holiday with festivals in several major cities, including Seattle, Chicago, Atlanta, San Francisco, and Washington D.C., as well as in Spanish Fork, Utah. This holiday, along with the cultural associations that promote it, serves to bring the Icelandic American community together.

Another major festival, observed by Icelandic immigrants in North Dakota, is called the Deuce of August. Icelanders congregate in Mountain, North Dakota, on the first weekend before the first Monday in August to celebrate Iceland's constitution, originally ratified on August 2, 1874. The oldest ethnic festival in North Dakota, the Deuce of August marked its 114th annual celebration in 2013. The festival brings together immigrants and visitors alike to celebrate Icelandic culture and heritage.

Health Issues Icelanders are known for their generally good physical health. The average life expectancy in Iceland is 80.9 years for women and 75.7 years for men. There do not appear to be medical conditions specific to Icelandic Americans. As Icelandic Americans change their diets and living habits to assimilate into American culture, their general health may vary with current trends of the general population.

ICELANDIC PROVERBS

Proverbs are common among Icelanders; they are fond of saying that "sometimes we speak only in proverbs." One typical Icelandic saying, "Even though you are small, you can be clever," expresses the Icelandic respect for the individual. Another, "It is difficult to teach a dog to sit," is a typical response to a request to change, similar to the English saying, "You can't teach an old dog new tricks." The slogan once used in promoting an Icelandic festival in North Dakota was *"Hvad er svo glatt sem godra vina fundur?"* ("What is as joyful as a gathering of friends?") Although they may be perceived by non-Icelanders as serious and quiet, Icelanders and Icelandic Americans often show a sense of humor that includes joking at their own expense: they are often the first to laugh at themselves.

FAMILY AND COMMUNITY LIFE

The 1992 Icelandic census showed that the most common family configuration was two parents and a child. This trend toward small family units mirrors those in other Western nations and is reflected in the size of Icelandic American families. Icelanders show strong familial and ethnic identification.

Gender Roles Iceland is largely egalitarian and has an economy more evenly distributed by gender than many other countries. The country is politically progressive, with a woman president from 1980 to 1996 and a woman prime minister from 2009 to 2013. Icelandic American women have joined all aspects of the American workforce, gaining the same status as men in their respective fields.

Education Since the end of the eighteenth century, Iceland has provided education for all its citizens, and literacy among Icelanders has been universal. In 1907 school attendance in Iceland was made obligatory for all children between the ages of ten and fourteen. Children younger than ten years of age were usually taught at home. In 1946 the age for compulsory attendance was extended, and by the 1990s, the law covered all children between the ages of seven and seventeen. A theological seminary, the first institution of higher learning in Iceland, was founded in 1847. A medical school followed in 1876 and a school of law in 1908. In 1911 all three merged and became the University of Iceland. Later a fourth division was added, the Faculty of Philosophy, which offers study in philology, history, and literature.

Immigrant Icelanders in the Dakota Territory set up their first school district in 1881, and more districts soon followed. The value Icelanders placed on education on the American frontier had been instilled in them in their native land. With an unbroken literary history dating from the thirteenth century, the new immigrants continued to cherish literary activity. Books were among the household goods most brought with them to the United States. Many had books sent to them from Iceland once they were settled in their new homes. New immigrant communities organized reading circles and quickly established newspapers. Icelandic immigrants' focus on education is one of the strongest factors contributing to their high rate of assimilation into the American workforce. According to the U.S. Census Bureau's American Community Survey estimates for 2009–2011, 95 percent of Icelandic Americans have a high school diploma or the equivalent, 42 percent have a bachelor's degree or higher, and 16 percent have a graduate or professional degree.

Courtship and Weddings The *Islendingabok* has always been considered a viable resource for Icelanders to ensure that they were not dating or marrying their relatives—a concern in such a small country. Icelandic Americans are less affected by this phenomenon as they assimilate more fully into the larger American society. Icelandic weddings generally follow the forms established by the Icelandic Lutheran Church. When they marry, women do not change their names.

The institution of marriage does not carry the same importance for Icelanders as it does for Americans. As a result, in Iceland women have never been stigmatized for giving birth outside of marriage. The rate of births by unmarried mothers has varied from 13 percent in the nineteenth century to 36 percent in 1977. One result of single parenthood is that many women in Iceland work fewer hours outside of the home than men. Coupled with the already lower pay scales for women, this further limits single mothers' income levels.

Family Names The Icelandic system of handing down family names is unique in the region and the world. Generally it observes the ancient patriarchal tradition of using the father's first name as a last name. For example, Leifur Eiriksson's name indicates that he is the son of Eirik. The last name of Leifur's son would be Leifursson—son of Leifur. Maria, the daughter of Hermann Jakobsson, would be called Maria Hermannsdottir. After her marriage to Haraldur Jonsson, her name would not change, although her daughter Margret would be known as Margret Haraldursdottir. Family members living in the same household, therefore, do not share a common family name. Directories in Iceland are organized alphabetically by first names.

Legislation dating from 1925 regulates Icelandic names and preserves the Icelandic naming tradition. Members of the clergy are vested with veto power over names of infants. The Faculty of Arts at the University of Iceland serves as the court of appeal. A 1958 case brought before the faculty by a German immigrant upheld the Icelandic tradition. Upon becoming a citizen of Iceland, the man changed his name from Lorenz to the Icelandic Larus. When his son was born, however, he wanted his son to be known as Lorenz. The pastor of his church refused to conduct the christening, and the case went to the Faculty of Arts, which supported the minister. The Icelandic naming tradition is still practiced by some Icelandic immigrants in the United States, although the high rate of absorption into the general population and the adoption of American Lutheran religions have lessened the degree to which it is observed.

Relations with Other Americans Because of the relatively small numbers of Icelanders in the United States, Icelandic immigrants have always interacted with those of other national backgrounds. As a matter of survival, early immigrants were eager to learn from the experiences of other immigrants, particularly the Norwegians, with whom they felt a kinship. In areas inhabited by few other persons of Icelandic descent, Icelanders gladly worked with Norwegians, Swedes, Danes, and Finns to develop communities. Although Icelandic American societies exist throughout the United States and Canada, many Icelanders join Scandinavian clubs. Icelandic Americans are still active in these clubs and organizations as a means of preserving their cultural heritage, but as they have assimilated, they have easily become part of broader communities.

EMPLOYMENT AND ECONOMIC CONDITIONS

The economic base of modern Iceland lies in the fishing industry: fish and fish products account for more than 70 percent of the country's exports. The waters around Iceland are rich fishing grounds. The Gulf Stream and cold nutrient currents of the Arctic meet at the continental shelf that surrounds the island. These conditions are favorable for many kinds of marine life. Icelandic fishing techniques, using the most up-to-date computers and other technologies, are among most innovative and advanced in the world. Sheep and dairy cattle are the main livestock in Iceland; agricultural land is used mostly for growing grass to feed the livestock. Aluminum accounts for about 11 percent of the country's exports. Iceland imports almost all of its consumer items.

Their agricultural, building, and fishing skills stood Icelandic immigrants to North America in good stead. In modern times the loss of the agrarian economic base in the United States, combined with the high rate of education among Icelandic Americans, has led them to seek jobs in business, education, medicine, entertainment, the arts, and a variety of other white-collar fields.

POLITICS AND GOVERNMENT

Iceland is a representative democratic republic with a multiparty system, a parliament, and an elected president who appoints a prime minister. The Althingi (parliament)—the legislative body—has sixty-three members who are elected by popular vote. They serve for terms of four years, as do the president and prime minister. There are no term limits. Any eligible voter can run for a seat in the Althingi, except the president and judges of the Supreme Court. Following the election of each new parliament, the president calls together the leaders of the political parties for discussions, and together they choose a cabinet made up of members of parliament. Cabinet ministers remain in power until the next general election.

The three largest political parties in Iceland are the Independence Party, the Progressive Party, and the Social Democratic Alliance. Together, these parties represented 73 percent of the vote in the 1991 elections. The remaining 27 percent of the vote was divided among the People's Alliance, the Citizens/Liberal Party, and others. In 1983 feminists formed a national political party known as the Women's List that won some parliamentary elections and, in 1987, claimed six seats in the Althingi and 10.1 percent of the total vote. In 1991, however, the Women's List lost ground, winning five parliamentary seats with 8.3 percent of the vote, and in 1998 the party split, some members merging with the People's Alliance and the National Awakening to form the Social Democratic Alliance, and others joining the Left-Green Movement.

Icelandic Americans have adapted easily to the system of democracy practiced in the United States. A number of Icelandic Americans have entered local and state politics. In North Dakota alone, there have been several state attorneys general, state supreme court judges, and state legislators of Icelandic heritage.

Military Service Iceland entered into a defense agreement with the United States in 1951, and it does not maintain its own army or navy. The Icelandic Defense Force, located at the Keflavik base, is maintained by members from all branches of the U.S. Armed Forces, as well as military personnel from the Netherlands, Norway, and Denmark. Icelandic civilians also work at the base. By the late 1990s twenty-five different units of various sizes were attached to the Icelandic Defense Force. The base published an online newsletter in the late 1990s called the *White Falconline* and also maintained a webpage. U.S. forces left the Keflavik base in 2006, turning it over to the Icelandic Defense Agency, which closed it in 2011. While Iceland does maintain a coast guard that patrols the country's shores and airspace, they have no standing army, although they do serve with N.A.T.O. forces.

NOTABLE INDIVIDUALS

Art Holger Cahill (1887–1960) was born in Iceland and immigrated to North Dakota as a homesteader with his family around the turn of the twentieth century. He served as the director for the Federal Art Project during Franklin D. Roosevelt's New Deal era of the Great Depression. In the early 1930s he was acting director of the Museum of Modern Art in New York City. He also authored two books: *Look South to the Polar Star* (1947) and *The Shadow of My Hand* (1956).

The abstract painter Nina Tryggvadottir (1913–1968) made a name for herself as an Icelandic artist in the United States. She immigrated to New York in 1942 and her work was reviewed favorably in the influential publication *Art News*. Tryggvadottir also designed scenery and costumes. Despite a promising career, Tryggvadottir was blacklisted during the McCarthy era and accused of being a Communist sympathizer. She is best known for the nature abstractions she produced between 1957 and 1967.

Another notable Icelandic American in the art world was H. Harvard Arnason (1909–1986), an art historian who served as the director of Minneapolis's Walker Art Center from 1951 to 1961. Arnason also served as vice president for art administration at the Guggenheim Foundation during the 1960s and authored *A History of Modern Art* (1968). Charles Gustav Thorson (1890–1966), born in Canada with Icelandic ancestry, lived in California in the 1930s and 1940s and worked in animation at Walt Disney Studios and Warner Brothers. He is credited as the creator of early Bugs Bunny prototypes and developed the characters of Snow White and Elmer Fudd.

Broadcasting Dori Monson (1961–), a radio producer, broadcaster, and sports reporter of Icelandic descent, was born in Seattle. He attended the University of Washington and served as a radio announcer for the school's football team, the Washington Huskies. In 1995 he began hosting his own politically oriented talk radio show, *The Dori Monson Show*, on KIRO-FM radio. Since 2002 he has hosted *Hawk Talk* on Seattle Seahawks Radio for the city's National Football League team.

Film Actor Gunnar Hansen (1947–) is an Icelandic American immigrant best known for his role as Leatherface in the original *Texas Chainsaw Massacre* (1974). His family moved from Reykjavik to Maine when he was five years old and later relocated to Texas, where he attended the University of Texas at Austin. He has acted in more than twenty films, taught at the collegiate level, and authored *Islands at the Edge of Time: A Journey to America's Barrier Islands* (1996).

Leslie Stefanson (1971–) is an Icelandic American actress born in Fargo, North Dakota. Known for her roles in *The General's Daughter* (1999), *Unbreakable* (2000), and *The Hunted* (2003), Stefanson is also an accomplished sculptor.

Journalism Jon Olafsson (1850–1916) served as founding editor of the first Icelandic newspaper in North America, the *Heimskringla*. The paper is named after medieval Icelandic epic poet and politician Snorri Sturluson's historical and mythological book about Norwegian kings (*heimer* translates as "the world" and *kringla* as "globe"). Founded in September 1886 in Winnepeg, the paper was published completely in Icelandic with the exception of some advertisements written wholly or partially in English. Olafsson left the paper in the 1890s and worked as a librarian in Chicago before returning to Iceland in 1897. Another journalist of Icelandic descent, Kristjan Valdimar "Val" Bjornson (1906–1987), was part-owner of the newspaper the *Minneota Mascot* and served as associate editor of the St. Paul *Pioneer Press*. The Val Bjornson Icelandic Exchange Scholarship between his alma mater, the University of Minnesota, and the University of Iceland commemorates his work.

Literature Poet Helga Steinvor Baldvinsdottir (1858–1941) wrote poetry in Iceland before she immigrated with her family to Canada. Under the pen name Undma Undina, she published her work in the *Heimskringla* and other Icelandic American periodicals and translated others' works from English to Icelandic. Her only complete volume of verse appeared posthumously in Iceland in 1952. She spent the last decade of her life in Washington State.

Stephan G. Stephanson (1853–1927) was an Icelandic American poet who immigrated to Wisconsin in 1873 and published a volume of poetry called *Andvökur* (1909; *Sleepless Nights*). He later moved to Canada, and he returned to Iceland in his mid-sixties. Kristjan Niels Julius (1860–1936), an Icelandic satirical poet, lived in Minnesota and North Dakota. Richard Beck (1897–1980) was an Icelandic American poet and critical author who wrote *History of Icelandic Poets: 1800–1940* (1950). Icelandic American poet and essayist Bill Holm (1943–2009) wrote twelve books over the course of his life. He split his time between Minnesota, where he taught literature and poetry at Southwest Minnesota State University, and Iceland.

Music Peter Steele, born Peter Thomas Ratajczyk (1962–2010), was an American rock musician with Icelandic heritage on his mother's side. Born in Brooklyn, he sang and played guitar and bass in a series of heavy metal bands, including Type O Negative, Carnivore, and Fallout. In 1995 he appeared as a centerfold model in *Playgirl* magazine. Steele died of heart failure in 2010 at age forty-eight.

Science and Technology Icelandic immigrant Vilhjalmur Stefansson (1879–1962) was educated in North Dakota and Iowa before attending and later teaching at Harvard University. He became known for his archaeological work and Arctic explorations. Chester Hjortur Thordarson (1867–1945) immigrated to the United States in 1873, founding a manufacturing company in Chicago and making a name for himself as an inventor and entrepreneur in the field of electricity. He designed the first million-volt transformer, which won a gold medal at the 1904 St. Louis World's Fair.

Sports Rob Morris (1975–) is an Icelandic American born in Nampa, Idaho, and raised in the Mormon faith. He attended Brigham Young University in Provo, Utah, where he was named a First Team All-American by the Associated Press. From 2000 to 2008 he played football as a linebacker for the Indianapolis Colts and was a starter in the 2006 Super Bowl. His career ended after a serious knee injury.

MEDIA

Islandica

A series of volumes in Icelandic and Norse studies begun in 1908 as a yearly publication, the books are now published less regularly. Since 2003 works have been published electronically by Cornell University Library.

Patrick J. Stevens, Managing Editor
Cornell University, Kroch Library
Willard J. Fiske Islandic Collection
Ithaca, New York 14853
Phone: (607) 255-3530
Email: fiskeref@cornell.edu
URL: http://cip.cornell.edu/islandica

ORGANIZATIONS AND ASSOCIATIONS

The American-Scandinavian Foundation/ Scandinavia House

This foundation promotes relations between the United States and the Nordic countries of Denmark, Finland, Iceland, Norway, and Sweden through educational and cultural exchange.

58 Park Avenue
New York, New York 10016
Phone: (212) 779-3587
URL: www.scandinaviahouse.org
Email: info@amscan.org

Icelandic American Chamber of Commerce (IACC)

Founded in 1986, the Icelandic American Chamber of Commerce has eighty members. It is a multinational organization that meets several times a year and publishes a monthly newsletter.

Ólafur Jóhann Ólafsson, Chairman
c/o Consulate General of Iceland
800 Third Avenue, 36th Floor
New York , New York 10022
Phone: (212) 593-2700
Fax: (212) 593-6269
Email: icecon.ny@mfa.is
URL: www.icelandtrade.com

The Icelandic Association of Washington, D.C.

This association brings Icelandic Americans living in the greater Washington, D.C., area together for cultural meetings and events, including a Thorrablot (Thorri Banquet), summer picnic, holiday bazaar, and Independence Day celebration.

Anna Bjarnadottir Wahoske, President
P.O. Box 1616

Woodbridge, Virginia 22195
Phone: (325) 370-3324
Email: icelanddc@hotmail.com
URL: http://icelanddc.com

The Icelandic Club of Greater Seattle

A nonprofit organization whose mission is to promote Icelandic heritage, culture, and language and to strengthen relationships within the Icelandic American community.

Sonna Somerville Ghilarducci, President
P.O. Box 70102
Seattle, Washington 98127
URL: www.icelandseattle.com

Icelandic National League of North America

Formed in 1919, the league promotes Icelandic culture, customs, and traditions. The organization spans both Canada and the United States, with U.S. chapters in Washington, D.C., New York, Illinois, Washington, and Minnesota.

103-94 1st Avenue
Gimli, Manitoba ROC 1B1 Canada
Phone: (204) 642-5897
Fax: (204) 642-9382
Email: office@inlofna.org
URL: http://inlofna.org

Icelandic Roots

A website that promotes Icelandic heritage, genealogy, and travel for Icelanders and Icelandic American immigrants. The site has links to other Icelandic clubs and organizations around the United States and Canada.

Hjálmar Stefán Brynjólfsson, Website Manager
URL: http://icelandicroots.com

MUSEUMS AND RESEARCH CENTERS

Fiske Icelandic Collection

A division of the Rare Manuscript Collections in the Kroch Library at Cornell University. Holdings include books, journals, and other serial literature on Islandica with an emphasis on Icelandic language, literature, and history.

Patrick Stevens
Level 2B, Carl A. Kroch Library
Cornell University
Ithaca, New York 14853
Phone: (607) 255-3530
Fax: (607) 255-9524
Email: fiskeref@cornell.edu
URL: http://guides.library.cornell.edu/icenorse

Nordic Heritage Museum

The Nordic immigrants (Danish, Finnish, Norwegian, Swedish, and Icelandic Americans) of Seattle are represented in this museum founded in 1980.

3014 NW 67th Street
Seattle, Washington 98117
Phone: (206) 789-5707
Email: michaelo@nordicmuseum.org
URL: www.nordicmuseum.org

SOURCES FOR ADDITIONAL STUDY

Arnason, David, and Michael Olito. *The Icelanders*. Winnipeg, Manitoba: Turnstone Press, 1981.

Bjornson, Valdimar. "Icelanders in the United States." *Scandinavian Review* 64 (1976): 39–41.

Bjornsson, Arni. *Icelandic Feasts and Holidays: Celebrations, Past and Present*. Trans. May and Hallberg Hallmundson. Reykjavik: Iceland Review History Series, 1980.

Houser, George J. *Pioneer Icelandic Pastor: The Life of the Reverend Paul Thorlaksson*. Ed. Paul A. Sigurdson. Winnipeg, Manitoba: Manitoba Historical Society, 1990.

Jonsson, Hjorleifur Rafn. "Trolls, Chiefs and Children: Changing Perspectives on an Icelandic Christmas Myth." *Nord Nytt: Nordisk Tidsskrift for Folkelivsforskning* 41 (1990): 55–63.

Karlsson, Gunnar. *The History of Iceland*. Minneapolis: University of Minnesota Press, 2000.

Krakauer, Jon, and David Roberts. *Iceland: Land of the Sagas*. New York: Villard Publishing, 1998.

Walters, Thorstina Jackson. *Modern Sagas: The Story of Icelanders in North America*. Fargo, ND: Institute for Regional Studies, 1953.

Wolf, Kirsten. *Writings by Western Icelandic Women*. Winnipeg: University of Manitoba Press, 1996.

INDONESIAN AMERICANS

Eveline Yang

OVERVIEW

Indonesian Americans are immigrants or descendants of people from Indonesia, a Southeast Asian archipelago of more than 17,508 islands. The Republic of Indonesia consists of an array of island stepping-stones scattered in the sea between the Malay Peninsula and Australia, astride the equator, and spanning about an eighth of the world's circumference. By comparison, the continental United States stretches across about a sixth of the world's circumference. The islands and island groups are located at the confluence of the Pacific and Indian Oceans. The western side of the archipelago includes the islands of Sumatra, Java, Bali, and the Lesser Sundas, or, in Indonesian, *Sumatera, Jawa, Bali*, and *Nusa Tenggara*. The islands of Borneo, Celebes, and the Moluccas, or *Kalimantan, Sulawesi,* and *Malukus,* comprise the eastern side. The total land area is 782,665 square miles, and the sea area covers 1,222,466 square miles; altogether, the nation is approximately the size of Mexico.

According to the U.S. Department of State in 2011, Indonesia had a population of approximately 246 million people who belong to more than 300 distinct ethnic groups. The vast majority of Indonesians, about 90 percent, are Muslim, making it the most populous Muslim country in the world, with more than 204 million adherents. Distinctly smaller percentages of Indonesians practice Buddhism, Hinduism, Roman Catholicism, and Protestantism. In 2012 Indonesia had the sixteenth-largest economy in the world. Its rapid growth, fueled by a relatively young population and rapid urbanization of its cities, has Indonesia on pace to be the world's seventh-largest economy by 2030.

Indonesians first began to immigrate to the United States in sizable numbers during the 1950s. Many of these early immigrants—the majority of whom settled in California—were not indigenous Indonesians but were descendants of Dutch settlers. They came to the United States as refugees after Indonesia declared its independence from the Netherlands in 1945. Today the United States is a popular choice for young Indonesians looking to further their educational attainment. Beginning in 2008 President Barack Obama's administration has attempted to increase higher education exchanges between the United States and Indonesia.

According to the U.S. Census Bureau's American Community Survey (ACS) estimates for 2011, there were nearly 107,000 people of Indonesian descent living in the United States. States with a significant number of Indonesian Americans include California, Texas, Washington, Pennsylvania, Florida, Maryland, Oregon, Virginia, and New York. Although Indonesian Americans have largely assimilated and have not established any notable ethnic enclaves in the United States, Indonesian-owned restaurants and coffee shops have become unofficial gathering places in many cities with large Indonesian communities, such as San Francisco, Los Angeles, and New York City. The Indonesian Consulate General also organizes cultural events and festivals aimed at fostering a sense of community among Indonesian Americans and their neighbors.

HISTORY OF THE PEOPLE

Early History By the fifteenth century, when the Renaissance was just pulling Europe from the Middle Ages, the islands of Java and Sumatra already had a thousand-year heritage of advanced civilization, spanning two major empires. From the seventh to the fourteenth century, the Buddhist kingdom of Srivijaya flourished on Sumatra. At its peak the Srivijaya Empire reached as far as western Java and the Malay Peninsula and had established mercantile and diplomatic relationships with China and other nations. By the fourteenth century the Hindu kingdom of Majapahit had risen in eastern Java. Gadjah Mada, the chief minister who ruled the empire from 1331 to 1364, succeeded in gaining allegiance from most of what is now known as modern Indonesia as well as much of the Malay archipelago.

Islam arrived in Indonesia in the twelfth century and had almost wholly supplanted Hinduism as the dominant religion in Java and Sumatra by the end of the sixteenth century. The island of Bali, however, has retained its Hindu heritage to this day. In the eastern archipelago, both Christian and Islamic proselytizing took place in the sixteenth and seventeenth centuries; currently, there are large communities of both religions on these islands.

Because of Indonesia's longstanding prominence in the spice trade—particularly in the Moluccas, which came to be known as the "Spice Islands"—several

European empires gained interest in the region. The first Europeans to arrive were the Portuguese, who established a trading post on the island of Ambon in 1512. The Dutch followed with expeditions in 1596 and again in 1598, establishing the *Vereenigde Oost-Indische Compagnie* (United East India Company, commonly known as the Dutch East India Company) in 1602. In the early seventeenth century Indonesia's many kingdoms had become fragmented, and the Dutch gradually established themselves on almost all of the islands of present-day Indonesia, controlling the islands' social, political, and economic institutions. The eastern half of the island of Timor was likewise occupied by the Portuguese until 1975. During the 300-year Dutch rule, the region then known as Netherlands East Indies became one of the world's richest colonial territories.

Modern Era Much of Indonesia's history in the modern era revolves around Sukarno (born Kusnasosro; 1901–1970). The Indonesian independence movement began during the first decade of the twentieth century and continued throughout both World Wars. The Japanese occupied Indonesia for three years during World War II. Then, on August 17, 1945, after Japan had agreed to surrender to the Allied Powers, Sukarno and other nationalists declared national independence and established the Republic of Indonesia. Despite several attempts the Dutch failed to recapture the territory lost to Japan. The victory over the Dutch strengthened Indonesia's sense of national identity. In 1950 the country became a member of the United Nations.

During the following decade Sukarno revised the 1945 constitution and became "President for Life." The Communist Party—known as the *Partai Komunis Indonesia*, or PKI, in Indonesia—began to grow during the early 1960s, with Sukarno's encouragement. In 1965 a group of Indonesian army officers, calling themselves the September 30th Movement, killed six generals and other officers whom they accused of plotting to overthrow President Sukarno. Suharto, a general in the Indonesian military, claimed control of the army and halted the coup, accusing the PKI of orchestrating the event. Suharto and the Indonesian army then embarked on an anticommunist purge, killing between 200,000 and 300,000 people throughout Indonesia. Sukarno's affiliation with the PKI severely hampered his reputation and ability to lead, and in 1967 the Indonesian parliament replaced him with General Suharto as president.

Under Suharto's rule, from 1966 through the mid-1990s, Indonesia experienced significant economic expansion. However, the 1997 Asian economic crisis exposed deep flaws in the Indonesian economy, which saw a rapid devaluation of its currency. The Suharto regime, including his family, was accused of corruption, and there were widespread student protests calling for an ousting of the president. When four

student protesters were shot by the military, massive rioting ensued. The ethnic Chinese were particularly targeted by these riots. They had lived in Indonesia in large numbers for centuries but were often viewed as suspicious outsiders, tolerated only for their contribution to the national economy and their ability to attract foreign investment by Chinese conglomerates. As the Indonesian economy collapsed in early 1998, the relatively wealthy ethnic Chinese were scapegoated by indigenous Indonesians and faced widespread violence, looting, and sexual assault, leading to a mass exodus of Chinese Indonesians to neighboring countries such as Hong Kong, Singapore, and Australia. The United States also became a destination for many of these refugees, with more than 7,300 Chinese Indonesians receiving refugee status in the decade after the 1998 riots.

Suharto, who was only the second president of Indonesia since its independence, resigned on May 21, 1998. In 1999 Muslim cleric Abdurrahman Wahid was named president of Indonesia by the People's Consultative Assembly. He was forced out of office in 2001 amid scandals and political unrest and was replaced by his vice president and Sukarno's daughter, Megawati Sukarnoputri. In 2004 Susilo Bambang Yudhoyono became the first popularly elected president of Indonesia.

In recent years the country has been afflicted by religious tensions and terrorist attacks, such as the 2002 bombing in a Bali nightclub that killed 202 people and the 2009 bombings of the Jakarta Ritz-Carlton and Marriott hotels that killed seven. Because of this, most Indonesians who choose to leave their country for other countries are part of a religious or ethnic minority, such as Chinese Indonesians or Christian Indonesians. Noted for their diverse cultural and religious backgrounds and geographical origins, Indonesians who live in the United States tend to split their affection and loyalty between their newfound country and whatever part of their homeland they or their ancestors once inhabited.

SETTLEMENT IN THE UNITED STATES

Few Indonesians immigrated to the United States prior to the 1950s. In 1952 an advisor to the Indonesian Ministry of Religion named Hamka embarked on a four-month tour of the United States, visiting academic, political, and religious institutions throughout the country. He praised the educational climate he found there in two volumes titled *Empat bulan di Amerika* (*Four Months in America*, 1954). Subsequently, in the mid-1950s many Indonesian students came to the United States to study at American universities and colleges. In 1953 the International Cooperation Administration (ICA), now the United States Agency for International Development (USAID), started offering scholarships for medical faculty members of the University of Indonesia to study at the University of California, Berkeley. In

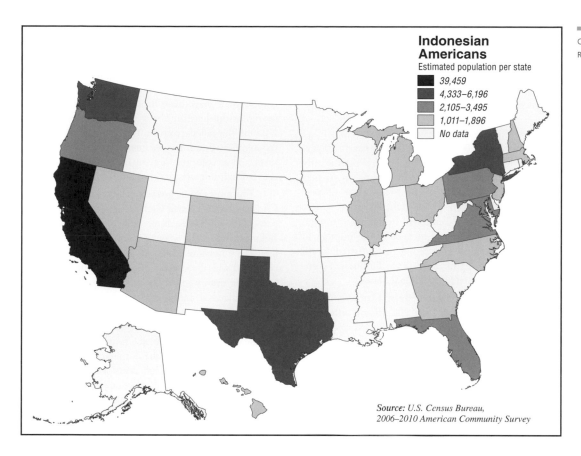

Indonesian Americans
Estimated population per state
- 39,459
- 4,333–6,196
- 2,105–3,495
- 1,011–1,896
- No data

Source: U.S. Census Bureau,
2006–2010 American Community Survey

1956 the ICA likewise provided scholarships for the teaching staff of the Bandung Institute of Technology to study at the University of Kentucky.

During the 1960s, when a number of political and ethnic skirmishes arose in Indonesia, several thousand Indonesians, the majority of whom were Chinese Indonesian, came to the United States. This immigration wave was short lived, however, due to the rapid reestablishment of peace in Indonesia and the limitations imposed by U.S. immigration quotas. The economic collapse of 1998 and the subsequent unrest sparked another wave of Indonesian immigration and asylum seeking, primarily by Chinese Indonesians and Christian Indonesians. These groups fled the country during or shortly after the 1998 riots and settled primarily in the Los Angeles area, as well as in east coast cities in New York and New Jersey. According to the 2011 ACS, 51 percent of Indonesian Americans have entered the country since 2000, and approximately 7,000 to 10,000 Indonesians immigrate to the United States each year.

The number of Indonesians residing in the United States is relatively low compared to overall Asian immigration figures. The 2011 ACS reports that, of the 17.6 million Americans who claim all or partial Asian ancestry, only 106,995 are of Indonesian descent, making them a mere .6 percent of the Asian American population. The majority of Indonesian Americans reside in large cities such as Los Angeles, San Francisco, Houston, New York, and Chicago. This is partly due to the improved employment opportunities of these areas and to the fact that these cities have established Asian American communities. Besides New York, Texas and California, states with large numbers of Indonesian Americans include Washington, Pennsylvania, Florida, Maryland, Virginia, and Oregon.

LANGUAGE

According to the 2011 ACS, 33.2 percent of Indonesian Americans speak only English in their homes, while 66.8 percent speak a language other than English. Further, 30.2 percent of Indonesian Americans indicate that they speak English "less than very well." Although second- and third-generation Indonesian Americans tend to speak English as their primary language, a 2009 study by the Modern Language Association notes that there were 297 students enrolled in Indonesian language studies programs throughout the United States, up from 225 in 2002. The Indonesian Embassy in Washington, D.C., also offers free twenty-two-week language courses for those interested in learning or maintaining Indonesian language skills.

With more than 300 regional languages and dialects, there is considerable diversity in the languages used in Indonesia. Austronesian, which includes Malay, Polynesian, and Formosan, is the country's major language family. Bahasa Indonesia, a modified form of Malay, was named by Indonesian nationalists in 1928 as the official language. The majority of educated Indonesians in urban areas speak at least two languages. Spoken Indonesian varies depending on the rank or status of the speaking partner. Respected elders are usually addressed in a kinship term—*bapak* (father or elder) or *ibu* (mother). Indirect references are usually preferred in conversation.

RELIGION

According the 2000 Indonesian census, nearly 90 percent of Indonesians observe Islam, with significantly smaller populations observing Protestantism (6 percent), Catholicism (3 percent), Hinduism (2 percent), and Buddhism (1 percent). Many Chinese Indonesians follow Buddhist teachings, though there has recently been an increase in the number of Chinese Indonesians converting to Christianity. All five religions play significant roles in Indonesian communities in and outside the United States.

Indonesia is among the largest Islamic countries in the world, with more than 204 million adherents. Historically, Indonesians have practiced a less strict interpretation of Islam than the one followed in the Middle East, though there has been a turn toward conservatism in the twenty-first century. The constant interaction between Muslims and the Hindu-Buddhist population in Java, ever since the initial introduction of Islam by traders from India between the twelfth and fifteenth centuries, has created over time a loosely organized belief system called Javanism, or *agama Jawa*. It was officially recognized as a religion in the 1945 constitution.

Hinduism is perceived to enforce a rigid caste structure, dividing people into classes: priests, ruler-warriors, and commoners-servants. However, the caste system has never been rigidly applied in Indonesia. The majority of the Hindus in the country are in Bali, and they express their beliefs through art and ritual instead of scripture and law. Ceremonies at puberty, marriage, and, most notably, death are closely associated with the Balinese version of Hinduism. Buddhism is thought to have been brought to Indonesia in the second or third century by travelers from India. In the wake of the failed coup in 1965, many Indonesians registered as Buddhists—some simply to avoid being suspected as communist sympathizers and others sincere enough to construct monasteries.

The most rapidly growing religions in Indonesia are Christian based: Roman Catholicism and Protestantism, particularly Pentecostalism, which was brought to Indonesia in the early twentieth century by Dutch evangelists. The number of Christians in Indonesia is very small compared with the number of Muslims, but Christianity has a long history in the country and its numbers have steadily increased since the late 1900s. It was introduced by Portuguese Jesuits and Dominicans in the sixteenth century. When the Dutch defeated Portugal in 1605, the Calvinist Dutch Reformed Church expelled Catholic missionaries and became the dominant Christian influence on the islands for 300 years. Because Calvinism was a strict, austere, and intellectually uncompromising variety of Christianity that demanded a thorough understanding of scripture, Christianity gained few converts in Indonesia until the nineteenth century, when German Lutherans introduced evangelical freedom and Jesuits established successful missions, schools, and hospitals on some of the islands, including Timor and Flores.

Membership in Christian churches surged after the 1965 coup attempt, when all nonreligious persons were labeled atheists and were suspected to be

After orders for deportation were issued, a group of Indonesian immigrants, including five-year-old Christa Pangemanan and her mother Maryana Pangemanan, were given sanctuary by the Reformed Church of Highland Park in New Jersey in 2012. AP IMAGES / MEL EVANS

communists. By the 1990s the majority of Christians in Indonesia were Protestants, with Pentecostalism being the most prominent sect. In 2001 the *Gereja Pentekosta di Indonesia* (Pentecostal Church of Indonesia) claimed two million members, and a number of Pentecostal "mega churches," such as the 6,300-seat Katedral Mesias in Jakarta, have recently been constructed. Catholic congregations have grown less rapidly, due to the Church's heavy reliance on Europeans in positions of leadership. Nevertheless, the increase in Christianity since 1965 has led to significant tensions between the country's Muslim majority and its growing Christian population, which is predominantly made up of ethnic Chinese.

Many of the Chinese Indonesians who fled the country after the 1998 riots were also Christian. In 2006 a group of around seventy Chinese-Indonesian Christians who were living in the Northeastern United States on expired tourist visas were ordered to leave the country under threat of deportation. They took sanctuary in New Jersey's Highland Park Church, citing their fear of religious persecution in Indonesia. While some of the refugees eventually returned to Indonesia or sought refuge elsewhere, five continued to live in the church until they were granted a reprieve by the U.S. government in 2013.

Because of fear of persecution in Indonesia, a significant number of Indonesian Americans have become Protestant or Roman Catholic. Some Christian churches sponsor Indonesian families, which helps to facilitate their immigration to the United States. Despite the fact that Indonesia is the world's most populous Muslim country, Indonesian Muslims constitute a small percentage of the Muslim American community. Indonesian Muslim Community Inc., founded in 1989, was instrumental in establishing Masjid Al-Hikmah in Astoria, New York. "The Wisdom Mosque" serves as a cultural and worship center for both Indonesian and non-Indonesian Muslims.

CULTURE AND ASSIMILATION

Assimilation for Indonesian American immigrants has been difficult, often causing them to become more attached to the traditions of their homeland. Particularly after the attacks of September 11, 2001, Indonesian Americans have faced suspicion from other Americans, who often unfairly associate immigrants from predominantly Muslim countries with Muslim extremists. Furthermore, unlike other immigrant groups, there are no established Indonesian American ethnic enclaves. This may be attributed to the fact that Indonesia has one of the most ethnically diverse populations in the world; their diversity in social classes, language, religion, ethnic and cultural backgrounds, and geographic location has lessened the possibility of forming a community of common traditions. However, there are numerous organizations, clubs, and religious groups in cities where a relatively large concentration of Indonesians exists,

including the United States–Indonesia Society, the Indonesian American Association, and the Indonesian Community Heritage Foundation.

Traditions and Customs Indonesians' sense of art is closely related to their mystic sense of identity with nature and with God. Humanity, nature, and art constitute an unbroken continuity. Artistic expression in Indonesian art is particularly evident in the group's

Wayang golek puppets are central to the shadow theater that is traditionally associated with Indonesian culture. The show is often accompanied by an Indonesian gamelan orchestra. AGMIT / ISTOCKPHOTO.COM

Unlike other immigrant groups, there are no established Indonesian American ethnic enclaves. This may be attributed to the fact that Indonesia has one of the most ethnically diverse populations in the world; their diversity in social classes, language, religion, ethnic and cultural backgrounds, and geographic location has lessened the possibility of forming a community of common traditions.

A Balinese dancer in full costume. CORBIS / DAVID CUMMING; UBIQUITOUS. REPRODUCED BY PERMISSION.

traditional dress, which includes the wearing of batik—hand-printed fabric designed using one of two techniques: The older method is called *canting* because a crucible of that name is used along with hot wax to make a design directly on the fabric. When cooled, the wax resists the dye into which the cloth is immersed so that all of the cloth except the area bearing the design accepts the dye. The wax is then removed, and the dyeing process is repeated. The second technique is regarded by some as inferior because the batik it produces is perceived to be machine-made. Actually, the design is made by a *tjap*, a printing stamp that is applied by hand to the cloth. The Yale University Art Gallery houses a collection of more than 600 pieces of Indonesian textiles that constitute one of the largest and most popular exhibits of Indonesian art in the United States.

Other distinctive arts of the Indonesian people are the dance dramas of Bali and the Mataram court tradition. Both are essentially religious in character, though some Balinese dance is frivolous, flirtatious, or playful. Puppet dramas, or *wayang kulit*, have been popular for many years. The most popular puppets are flat and made of leather, but wooden puppets are also used. The puppeteer sits behind a white screen and moves the puppets to act out stories. A palm-oil lamp throws the shadows of the puppets onto the screen. The plots usually involve a virtuous hero who triumphs over evil by means of supernatural powers and self-discipline. In 2012 the U.S. State Department invited the Papermoon Puppet Theater, a popular Indonesian wayang company, to tour the United States. They performed a work called *Mwathirika*, which tells the story of the 1965 coup and subsequent unrest, in theaters throughout the United States.

Many Indonesians practice Western arts, from oil painting to metal sculpture, the subjects of which are often inspired by Indonesian life and traditions. The literary arts are also popular. Early Indonesian literature consisted largely of local folk tales and traditional religious stories. The works of classical Indonesian authors, such as Prapanca, are still read today, though modern literature in the Indonesian language began in the 1890s. Indonesia's all-time best-selling author as of early 2013, Andrea Hirata, sold more than five million official copies of his debut novel, *Laskar pelangi* (2005; *The Rainbow Troops*, 2013), and an estimated fifteen million more pirated copies in Indonesia alone. Hirata attended Iowa University's International Writing Program in 2010.

Cuisine Rice is a central ingredient to the Indonesian diet. Indonesians boil or fry rice in several ways and serve it with a variety of other foods. Foods are usually cooked in coconut milk and oil and sometimes wrapped in banana or coconut leaves. Fish, chicken, and beef are prepared with spices and served with rice. Indonesians eat little pork, since most of them practice Islam, which forbids it. However, since many Indonesian immigrants are not Muslim, pork is sometimes eaten by the Indonesian American community. Tea and coffee are favorite beverages.

At ceremonial occasions, including modern weddings, funerals, or state functions, foods such as *sate* (small pieces of meat roasted on a skewer), *krupuk* (fried shrimp or fish-flavored chips made with rice flour), and highly spiced curries of chicken and goat are commonly served. These foods are often served buffet style and at room temperature. Food is eaten with fingertips or with a spoon and fork. Water is served after the meal. These dietary customs are usually observed by Indonesian Americans during holidays and special events in the United States. For everyday meals, some Indonesians adapt readily to American food, while others prefer Indonesian or Chinese cuisine.

A number of Indonesian restaurants in the United States cater to the Indonesian American community. New York City's Upi Jaya, for example, is a popular meeting place for residents of the Elmhurst neighborhood, which is home to a majority of the city's Indonesian immigrants. In 2012 Upi Jaya hosted Indonesian President Yudhoyono and a number of Indonesian delegates who were attending the General Assembly of the United Nations.

Traditional Dress Although Indonesian Americans have largely adapted to the typical American style of dress, both Indonesian American men and women sometimes wear sarongs, traditional Indonesian garments with batik designs. Men generally wear sarongs only in the home or during informal occasions. Women wear sarongs on formal occasions, along with the *kebaya*, a tight, low-cut, long-sleeved blouse, and often tie their hair into a bun or attach a hairpiece. Men may also don batik shirts that are worn outside their trousers and a black felt cap, called a *peci*, an item once associated with Muslims or Malays that has acquired a more secular, national meaning in the postindependence period.

Dances and Songs The most popular forms of dance in Indonesia are the Balinese dance and the *wayang wong*, also known as the *wayang orang*, which is a human recreation of the popular *wayang kulit* shadow puppet performances. In *wayang wong*, male and female dancers imitate the movements of the *wayang* shadow puppets, often performing shortened versions of classic wayang plays.

There are a number of dance troupes in the United States that feature Indonesian dances, including Indonesian Dance of Illinois, Saung Budaya Indonesian Dance Group of New York, and Santi Budaya Performing Arts Group of Washington, D.C. Festivals such as the annual Los Angeles Indonesian Festival also feature Indonesian dance groups.

Holidays Because of their ethnic and religious diversity, Indonesian Americans observe a variety of major holidays. Muslim Indonesian Americans, for example, celebrate Eid al-Fitr, also known as Hari Raya or Lebaran (in Indonesian), which marks the end of Muslims' obligatory thirty-day fast during Ramadan. Many Indonesian Americans celebrate Eid al-Fitr with a traditional Muslim feast. The date of this holiday is determined by the lunar calendar, so it varies from year to year. Christian holidays such as Christmas and Easter are celebrated by Christian Indonesian Americans. One holiday that virtually all Indonesian Americans celebrate is Indonesian Independence Day on August 17. On this day, Indonesians in the United States are invited to celebrate along with Indonesian officials in a flag-raising ceremony and reception held at the Indonesian consulates in Los Angeles, New York, Chicago, San Francisco, and Houston and at the Indonesian Embassy in Washington, D.C.

FAMILY AND COMMUNITY LIFE

Indonesians and Indonesian Americans are very family oriented, with most young Indonesians choosing to live with their parents or other family members until they are married. According to the 2011 ACS, nearly 55 percent of adult Indonesian Americans are married. Of those who were not married, almost 35 percent have never been married, while only 6 percent are divorced. The survey estimates that almost 70 percent of Indonesian Americans live in a family household, and 43 percent live in a family household with children under the age of eighteen. Indonesians typically respect the extended family, and it is not atypical to find more than two generations of Indonesian Americans living in the same household. The average family size is 3.49. The ACS reports that almost 38 percent of Indonesian grandparents are responsible for caring for their grandchildren.

Gender Roles In traditional Indonesian society, women still occupy a lower social status than men, though the degree of this difference can vary depending on the region. In general, women in Indonesian American households have adapted to more modern

Two Balinese dancers. PHOTOGRAPH BY DENNIS DEGNAN. CORBIS. REPRODUCED BY PERMISSION.

views of gender roles. The 2011 ACS estimates that Indonesian American women participated in the labor force at a rate of 59.5 percent, which is slightly higher than the percentage of American women in general, who participated at a rate of 58.1 percent. Indonesian American women work in a variety of occupations, though only a small fraction are employed in what would typically be considered blue-collar jobs. According to the study, among Indonesian American women, more than 44 percent attained a bachelor's degree or higher, compared to 47 percent of their male counterparts who attained bachelor's degrees.

Education In recent years Indonesians have immigrated to the United States to attend American colleges or graduate schools. After earning their degree, many choose to apply for permanent residency or for citizenship. In 2010 President Obama announced programs totaling 165 million dollars that would boost education exchanges and academic partnerships with Indonesia, and in 2011 representatives from both countries participated in a U.S.–Indonesia Higher Education Summit in Washington, D.C. According to 2011 ACS estimates, 41.5 percent of the Indonesian American population was enrolled in college or graduate school. Of Indonesian Americans

INDONESIAN NAMING CONVENTIONS

Some Indonesians, particularly those from Java, use only one name; for instance, the former president Suharto used only his given name and had no surname. However, most Indonesian names have two parts, and some, such as Suharto's successor, Susilo Bambang Yudhoyono, have three or more names. Muslim Indonesians typically have two names, with the second one being the father's given name; an example is Megawati Sukarnoputri (literally, "Megawati, daughter of Sukarno"). The second name does not function like a surname or family name. Instead, the person is typically referred to by his or her first name—in this case, "Megawati" or "Mrs. Megawati." When Indonesians with only one name travel or immigrate to the United States, it is common for their given name to be listed as their surname and "FNU" (first name unknown) to be listed as their first name on official documents. This convention has been a source of frustration among Indonesian Americans, as it often causes confusion and mistakes when dealing with government agencies.

twenty-five and older, nearly 46 percent currently hold bachelor's degrees or higher.

The attitudes of Indonesian graduate students at selected universities in the United States were reported in Rustam Amir Effendi's doctoral dissertation of 1983. Students attending the University of Illinois at Urbana-Champaign, the University of Michigan, Michigan State University, the University of Minnesota, Ohio University, the Ohio State University, and the University of Wisconsin were polled about their success with academic adjustment and their overall satisfaction with American education. The study disclosed that approximately 80 percent of Indonesian students were male and that 50 percent of them were between the ages of thirty-one and thirty-five. Slightly more than 50 percent of them had worked as professionals for several years after they acquired their undergraduate degrees in Indonesia and before they came to the United States. Most of them were university faculty or government officials. Most studied engineering and the social sciences.

The successful personal adjustments and academic achievements of Indonesian American students are decided by mainly two factors: language efficiency and the ability to adjust to American society. While some of them return to Indonesia, many choose to remain in the United States to continue their professional pursuits.

Courtship and Weddings The type of wedding ceremonies Indonesian Americans celebrate depend largely on the ethnicity, region of origin, and religion of the bride and groom. Some features common to most Indonesian American weddings are gamelan music, which consists primarily of percussion instruments, and traditional Indonesian dances and foods. Typically, Indonesian Christians will celebrate their nuptials in a Western church, and Indonesian Muslims will celebrate weddings in their local mosque.

Intermarriage is not uncommon between Indonesians and Americans from other ethnic groups, especially for the younger generation, though elder-generation Indonesians prefer that their offspring marry others of Indonesian heritage. According to the ACS, in 2011 more than 53 percent of adult Indonesians reside in a married-couple household.

EMPLOYMENT AND ECONOMIC CONDITIONS

According to the ACS estimates for 2011, 36 percent of employed Indonesian adults in the United States held jobs in management, business, science, and arts; almost 27 percent work in service occupations; nearly 22 percent work in sales and office positions; less than 4 percent work in natural resources, construction, and maintenance jobs; and nearly 12 percent are employed in production, transportation, and moving material occupations. Because so few Indonesian Americans were employed in the construction sector, which was deeply impacted by the financial crisis of 2008, Indonesians did not experience a disproportionate impact on their economic well-being. According to the survey, the median household income for Indonesian Americans in 2011 was $55,085, which was higher than the overall U.S. median household income of $51,413.

A large number of Indonesians make their living in the importing and exporting business. The United States is Indonesia's third-largest export market, receiving $16.5 billion worth of goods in 2010. In turn, Indonesia imported $6.9 billion worth of U.S. goods that year. Trade between the two countries has increased greatly over the past several years. Organizations working to facilitate commercial trade include the American-ASEAN (Association of Southeast Asian Nations) Trade Council, the American Indonesian Chamber of Commerce, the Central Indonesian Trading Company, the Indonesian Investment Promotion Office, and the Indonesian Trade Promotion Center, all located in New York City. Recently, branches of these and other similar organization have been established in other cities, including Los Angeles and Houston.

POLITICS AND GOVERNMENT

Since the resignation of President Suharto in 1998, Indonesia has undergone rapid transformation and has emerged not only as an economic powerhouse but also as a strong democracy. In 2004, for the country's first direct presidential election, voter turnout was nearly 75 percent, with Indonesian Americans who retained their Indonesian citizenship participating via polling stations at their local consulate general. Accordingly, the United States has increasingly sought out Indonesia as an ally in the region. Former Secretary of State Condoleezza Rice and former President George W. Bush visited Indonesia in 2007 and sought the country's help in the global War on Terrorism. Yet many Indonesians viewed the Bush administration's fight against terror as a thinly veiled attack on Islam itself.

The U.S. presidential election of 2008 held particular significance for Indonesian Americans. Then-candidate Obama had, between the ages of six and ten, lived in Jakarta, Indonesia, and had a half-sister of Indonesian descent. These facts spurred a unique interest in the candidate among Indonesians and Indonesian Americans. Upon Obama's election to the presidency in 2008, Indonesian President Yudhoyono congratulated him and noted that Indonesia had a "special affection" for the president-elect and that "he knows our people and culture." President Obama and First Lady Michelle Obama visited Indonesia in November 2010. When President Obama was reelected in 2012, President Yudhoyono again expressed congratulations, stating that he hoped for "continued strategic cooperation based on mutual respect and on an equal footing." According to a 2008 Pew Research poll, 37 percent of Indonesians viewed the United States favorably. That number rose dramatically to 63 percent in 2009.

NOTABLE INDIVIDUALS

Activism Maya Soetoro-Ng (1970–) is a teacher and children's book author who is perhaps best known for being the maternal half-sister of President Obama. In 2008 she participated in the Democratic National Convention. She was born in Indonesia and, as of early 2013, was living in Hawaii.

Art Sunny Bak (1960–) is a world-renowned photographer who first started taking pictures in Manhattan. During the 1980s she photographed numerous entertainers, including Madonna, Philippe Saisse, and the band 10,000 Maniacs. Her images of the Beastie Boys were featured on their multiplatinum album *Licensed to Ill* (1986).

Journalism Atika Shubert is a CNN journalist who first joined the network in 2000. She initially worked out of the network's Jakarta bureau before becoming a Tokyo correspondent in 2004. Shubert was one of the first journalists to report firsthand on the 2004 Indian Ocean earthquake and resulting tsunami. Since 2008 she has been based in CNN's London bureau.

Literature Greg Van Eekhout is the author of young adult novels, including *Norse Code* (2009), *Kid vs. Squid* (2010), and *The Boy at the End of the World* (2011). He has also written several short stories. His parents are both Dutch-Indonesian.

Music Michelle Branch (1983–) was born in Arizona to an Irish father and a mother who is of Dutch-Indonesian descent. She began singing and playing guitar at a young age. Her first album, *The Spirit Room* (2001), was released when she was eighteen and went on to be certified double platinum. Since then she has continued to enjoyed artistic and commercial success as a singer and songwriter.

Noted guitarist Eddie Van Halen (1955–) was born in the Netherlands, though his mother was half Indonesian. He moved to the United States in 1962. Founder of the eponymous band Van Halen, he is considered by many to be one of the greatest rock guitarists of all time.

Sports Tony Gunawan (1975–) is a highly decorated badminton player, considered by many to be the best doubles player to play the game. He has won numerous titles, including an Olympic gold medal in 2000 when he competed for his native Indonesia. He moved to the United States in 2002, and in 2005 he won the United States' first world championship medal. In 2011 he became a U.S. citizen, and he competed for his adopted country at the 2012 Olympics in London.

Johnson "John" Juanda (1971–) is a professional poker player who held five World Series of Poker bracelets. In 2011 his total lifetime winnings at live poker were more than $11.7 million. He was born in Indonesia and moved to the United States to attend Oklahoma State University in 1990.

Stage and Screen Mark-Paul Gosselaar (1974–) is an American actor who has starred in the television programs *Saved by the Bell*, *NYPD Blue*, *Raising the Bar*, and *Franklin & Bash*. His mother is of Dutch-Indonesian extraction and was born in Bali, Indonesia.

Tania Gunadi (1983–), actress was born in Bodung, West Java, Indonesia, and immigrated to the United States when she was a teenager. She has appeared in the television programs *Aaron Stone*, *It's Always Sunny in Philadelphia*, and *Boston Public*. She has also acted in the films *Pixel Perfect*, *Go Figure*, *Bob Funk*, and *Possessions*.

MEDIA

PRINT

Indonesia Journal

Indonesia Journal is a semiannual journal dedicated to the study of Indonesian culture, history, economy, and society. It has been published since 1966 by Cornell University's Southeast Asia Program.

Joshua Barker, Contributing Editor
180 Uris Hall
Cornell University
Ithaca, New York 14853
Phone: (607) 255-8038
Fax: (607) 254-5000
Email: SEAP-Pubs@cornell.edu
URL: http://seap.einaudi.cornell.edu/ indonesia_journal

Indonesia Media

Indonesia Media bills itself as the world's largest international Indonesian media company. It produces a biweekly journal and website that covers culture, politics, and news.

505 East Arrow Highway
Suite C
Glendora, California 91740
Phone: (626) 335-9833
Fax: (626) 335-3892
URL: www.indonesiamedia.com

ORGANIZATIONS AND ASSOCIATIONS

American Indonesian Chamber of Commerce (AICC)

This unofficial and nonpolitical organization was incorporated in the United States in 1949, before Indonesia received full independence—a fact that signified the willingness of U.S. firms to trade directly with the emerging Republic of Indonesia. Since then its mission has been to foster and promote trade and investment between the United States and Indonesia. The AICC works closely with both Indonesians and Americans who are interested in doing export and import business from the United States or from Indonesia.

Allan Harari, Chairman
317 Madison Avenue
Suite 1619
New York, New York 10017
Phone: (212) 687-4505
URL: www.aiccusa.org

Indonesian American Association (IAA)

The Indonesian American Association aims to strengthen the bonds of friendship among Indonesians living in the Washington, D.C., area. Its activities include organizing social, cultural, and sporting events.

Tony Sumartono, Chairman
Email: warta.iki@indonesianamerican.org
URL: www.indonesianamerican.org

Indonesian Community Heritage Foundation (ICHF)

A nonprofit organization founded by Indonesian immigrants in 1998 to establish a sense of community for displaced Indonesians and to educate other Americans about Indonesian culture.

Daniel Fu, President
4329 Nobleman Point
Duluth, Georgia 30097
Phone: (770) 447-6304
Email: info@ichf.us
URL: www.ichf.us

United States–Indonesia Society (USINDO)

USINDO was founded in 1994 by Indonesians and Americans who agreed on the need for an organization to focus on expanding mutual understanding between the two countries. They foster this by organizing a regular forum series, a speakers' bureau, and a summer language study and by sponsoring grants and fellowships.

David Merrill, President
1625 Massachusetts Avenue NW
Suite 550
Washington, D.C. 20036
Phone: (202) 232-1400
Fax: (202) 232-7300
Email: usindo@usindo.org
URL: www.usindo.org

MUSEUMS AND RESEARCH CENTERS

Asian American Arts Centre (AAAC)

AAAC supports the exhibition of traditional and contemporary Asian American, Chinese, Japanese, Indonesian, Indian, Korean, and Filipino arts, including dance, music, performance art, and poetry.

111 Norfolk Street
New York, New York 10002
Phone: (212) 233-2154
Fax: (360) 283-2154
Email: aaacinfo@artspiral.org
URL: www.artspiral.org

Cornell Modern Indonesia Project

The Center for International Studies at Cornell University conducts research activities in the United States on Indonesia's social and political development. The research efforts have resulted in the publication of monographs, bibliographies, and biographies of Indonesian historical figures. The research scope also includes cultural, military, and foreign affairs of Indonesia.

Eric Tagliacozzo, Director
Southeast Asia Program
180 Uris Hall
Ithaca, New York 14853
Phone: (607) 255-2378
Fax: (607) 254-5000
Email: seappubs@cornell.edu
URL: http://seap.einaudi.cornell.edu/cmip

Indonesia/East Timor Documentation Project

This project seeks to identify and release classified government documents regarding U.S. policy toward East Timor from 1965 to 1999. It aims to assist East Timorese and Indonesian official and nongovernmental efforts to document and seek accountability for more than three decades of human rights abuses committed during the rule of Indonesian President Suharto.

Brad Simpson, Director
Phone: (609) 751-8206
Email: bsimpson@princeton.edu

UCLA Center for Southeast Asian Studies— Department of Indonesian Studies

Founded in 2008, this extension of the UCLA Center for Southeast Asian Studies stages Indonesian cultural events, hosts scholars and presenters from Indonesia, and provides grants for students who want to study in Indonesia.

Geoffrey Robinson, Faculty Chair
11274 Bunche Hall
Box 951487
Los Angeles, California 90095-1487
Phone: (310) 206-9163
Fax: (310) 206-3555
Email: cseas@international.ucla.edu
URL: www.international.ucla.edu/cseas/
indonesia/

Yale University Art Gallery—Department of Indo-Pacific Art

This extensive collection of Southeast Asian art includes an array of Indonesian art and artifacts, some stemming from prehistoric times.

Ruth Barnes, Curator
1111 Chapel Street
New Haven, Connecticut 06510
Phone: (203) 432-0600
Email: artgalleryinfo@yale.edu
URL: http://artgallery.yale.edu/

SOURCES FOR ADDITIONAL STUDY

Aznam, Suhaini. "Passport Control: New Immigration Law Can Render Citizens Stateless," *Far Eastern Economic Review*, March 26, 1992, 18–19.

Cunningham, Clark E. "Unity and Diversity among Indonesian Migrants to the United States." In *Emerging Voices: Experiences of Underrepresented Asian Americans*, edited by Huping Ling, 90–108. New Brunswick, NJ: Rutgers University Press, 2008.

Gardner, Paul F. *Shared Hopes, Separate Fears: Fifty Years of U.S.-Indonesian Relations.* Boulder, CO: Westview Press, 1997.

Frederick, William H., and Robert L. Worden, eds. *Indonesia: A Country Study*, fifth edition. Washington, D.C.: Federal Research Division, Library of Congress, 1992.

Obama, Barack. *Dreams from My Father: A Story of Race and Inheritance.* New York: Crown Publishing Group, 1995.

Steenbrink, Karel. "Indonesian Muslims and the North-American West." In *Fullness of Life for All: Challenges for Mission in Early 21ˢᵗ Century*, edited by Inus Daneel, Charles van Engen, and Hendrik Vroom, 261–78. Amsterdam: Rodopi, 2003.

INDOS

Anthony Ruzicka

OVERVIEW

Indos, also known as Indonesian-Dutch, Dutch-Indonesians, "Indische Nederlander" (in Dutch), or more broadly Indo-Europeans and Eurasians, immigrated to the United States from Europe after having moved there from the Dutch East Indies (modern-day Indonesia) following World War II. They are descendants of Europeans, as well as some Middle Eastern and Asian peoples, who intermarried with indigenous Indonesian people. Indonesia is a chain of approximately 17,508 islands in Southeast Asia; Australia is to the south, and the Asian mainland is to the northeast. The total land area of Indonesia is 735,358 square miles (1,904,569 square kilometers), roughly 100,000 square miles larger than Alaska.

The Dutch East Indies (DEI), also called the Netherlands East Indies, Dutch Nederlands Oost-Indië, or Nederlandsch-Indië, was a colonial society governed by the Netherlands from 1818 to 1945. It included the islands of present-day Indonesia, including Java, Sumatra, Suriname, and Borneo. Before World War II (1939–1945) the population of the DEI had reached roughly 6.5 million, including 60,000 white Dutch and other Europeans, 200,000 Indos, 1.2 million Chinese, and 60 million native Indonesians. The majority of Europeans and Indos were Christian, while most of the native Indonesians were Muslim. The Chinese population practiced either Buddhism or Confucianism, and a small part of the population was Hindu. The Dutch government colonized the East Indies in part because of its prime location for trade and its spices, which were in great demand throughout Europe. Later the government introduced nonindigenous crops, such as rubber, tobacco, tea, sugar, and coffee, to the islands, which all became important exports. When the Japanese invaded the DEI during World War II, they saw the rubber plantations and oil fields as essential to their war effort. On August 17, 1945, as World War II was ending, what is now Indonesia declared its independence from the Netherlands.

After the Netherlands finally recognized Indonesia's independence in 1949, many Indos fled Indonesia, and more than 300,000 of them immigrated to the Netherlands. From there, beginning in the early 1950s through the mid-1960s, roughly 60,000 Indos moved to the United States. They settled throughout the United States, with many choosing southern California as their new home. Indos entering the United States from the Netherlands were typically sponsored by religious and national relief organizations, often folding into the communities of their host families. Today, while small groups dedicated to Indo culture exist in Southern California, some are concerned that Indos successfully assimilated into American culture to the detriment of their culture of origin.

Reliable numbers for the Indo population living in the United States are unavailable. The U.S Census does not track their population, but some unofficial estimates place the number at around 200,000. Based on a survey by the Indo Project, a nonprofit organization dedicated to creating awareness about Indos, the states with large numbers of Indos include California, Washington, Oregon, Florida, New York, Massachusetts, Connecticut, Maryland, Pennsylvania, and New Jersey. However, the Indo Project also stresses that this information is incomplete because there are many Indos living in the United States who were not surveyed. Indos in the United States have attempted to organize a cultural renaissance by establishing a globally cohesive group largely facilitated through Internet interaction.

HISTORY OF THE PEOPLE

Early History The origin of Indo people can be traced back to the sixteenth century, when Portuguese traders arrived in Southeast Asia and began to intermarry with the native Indonesian population. The community, known as *Mestiço* in the sixteenth through eighteenth centuries, grew with the arrival of the Dutch East India Company, or *Verenigde Oostindische Compagnie* (VOC), in the seventeenth and eighteenth centuries. Often working as intermediaries between the local traders and the Portuguese, Indos, or *Mestiços*, were familiar with the native languages spoken and the culture and customs of the native Indonesians. They continued to serve as intermediaries when Dutch colonists arrived. The Dutch government encouraged its colonists to intermarry with the native people, a colonial strategy of assimilation that allowed the Dutch government to establish itself as a dominant presence in the territory. However, the strong hybrid culture and Malay language (which included both indigenous and Portuguese languages) worked against the VOC's efforts to enforce the use of the Dutch language and encourage Dutch cultural activities.

After the VOC went bankrupt and was formally dissolved in 1800, the Dutch government assumed colonial control of the VOC's former territories, which became the Dutch East Indies, now Indonesia. By 1818 the Dutch East Indies had become an official colony of the Dutch government. Many military personnel and businessmen flooded into the region, mainly from the Netherlands but also from England, Germany, Spain, and Belgium. Their relationships with native women resulted in a large population of Indo-Europeans. Affairs outside of marriage were unspeakable in the Netherlands, but in the colonies this was a common experience that helped create the Indo European population. The arrival of Dutch women in what was a largely male European colony accelerated assimilation of Dutch culture. The colony was atypical in that it was not a plantation colony relying on the importation of slaves but rather functioned primarily as a large trading outpost that controlled existing governing bodies through military force. In this system Indos were treated like second-class citizens because the Dutch colonial government favored white Dutch citizens. At the same time, many Indos, whose fathers were affluent and acknowledged their children, were educated in Dutch schools and learned Dutch. After Napoleon's defeat in Europe and the return of power to the Dutch in 1813, a string of military campaigns across the Indonesian archipelago ensued. The Dutch granted Indos born of European men and indigenous women European citizenship in order to recruit more cost effectively soldiers to the Royal Netherlands East Indies Army (Koninklijk Nederlands Indisch Leger, or KNIL) for Dutch colonial wars. A mandatory conscription act ensued, creating a ratio of one European soldier to every three Indo soldiers. German and Belgian mercenaries also served in the KNIL and intermarried with the local population, increasing the number of Indos.

In the mid-nineteenth century the Dutch colonial government implemented the Cultivation System, which required native Indonesians to devote part of their land to growing export crops, such as sugar and coffee rather than staples such as rice. The government also developed a system by which tax collection officers were paid by commission, resulting in widespread abuses of colonial power. The 1860 novel *Max Havelaar: Or the Coffee Auctions of the Dutch Trading Company* was writen by Eduard Douwes Dekker, pen name Multatuli, to protest these policies. Dekker was a Dutch civil servant working in the Dutch East Indies and quickly became disgusted with the way Indonesians were treated by the colonial government. He began writing newspaper articles and pamphlets to expose government corruption and abuses of the native people. The Dutch government tried to suppress the publication *Max Havelaar* but did not succeed.

By 1870, when the Dutch colonials put a ban on Indonesian land ownership, Indonesians were forced to organize for the first time in order to dispel the effort. *Max Havelaar* was widely read in European circles, helping raise awareness that European wealth derived from the suffering of other individuals. This awareness forced the Dutch government to abandon the Cultivation System and in 1901 to create the Ethical Policy. The Ethical Policy was an attempt to "repay" Indonesians for their work and cooperation with education. However, only natives who were part of the elite and loyal to the colonial government benefited from such education reforms.

In the twentieth century Indonesian political groups such as the "Indo European Alliance" championed Indonesian independence from the Netherlands, but these efforts were restrained during World War II. Indos were drafted into the KNIL, but many also volunteered to serve in the KNIL and branches of the Dutch armed forces, including the Royal Dutch Navy. In 1940 the Netherlands was occupied by the Nazis, and on January 10, 1942, Japan invaded the Dutch East Indies. Many Indos, particularly those of Dutch descent, were sent to Japanese concentration camps set up on the islands. The Japanese saw the Dutch as oppressors of native Indonesians and mainly targeted the Dutch and Indos of Dutch descent. According to estimates, between 100,000 and 120,000 Dutch and Dutch Indos—about 60,000 children and 40,000 adults—were imprisoned in Japanese internment camps set up in Indonesia. The living conditions of the concentration camps were brutal. Prisoners were subject to torture, starvation, inhumane working conditions, and poor sanitation, which led to disease and death. Survivors recount stories of seeing men beaten to death and being given a spoonful of rice as a day's rations. In one camp almost 3,000 women and children were interned, but by the end of the war, only 800 of them had survived.

Almost 40,000 Dutch and Indo soldiers and militia volunteers were captured by the Japanese and sent to POW camps. Along with British and Australian POWs, many were forced to build the Burma Railway that crossed the River Kwai. Although a small number of Indos and Dutch were allowed to live independently in their homes, they lived in constant fear of being killed by Japanese soldiers. Because the Japanese destroyed all evidence of their internment camps, including paperwork, it is not known exactly how many prisoners survived. Researchers must rely on personal narratives and first-hand accounts to attempt an estimate. Estimates of the number of survivors of the camps range from half to three-quarters.

Modern Era The end of World War II marked the beginning of the Bersiap era in Indonesia. Days after Japanese capitulation on August 17, 1945, Sukarno (leader of the Indonesian struggle for independence and later the first president of Indonesia) declared

Indonesia's independence from the Netherlands, and the Indonesian National Revolution began. Young Indonesian militants, known as *pemudas*, began a genocide of Indos, Dutch citizens, Chinese, and anyone else who were sympathetic to the Dutch government. The Japanese had turned over many of their weapons to the *pemudas* before leaving Indonesia, and even Sukarno was unable to control the violence. Brutal killings and executions were carried out on Indo children, women, and men. Many were also physically beaten and maimed, as well as imprisoned with no apparent criminal charges against them. The new Indonesian government sent around 46,000 Dutch and Indos back to World War II internment camps, mostly in Java, primarily to protect them from being further targeted by the *pemudas*. Indos were given a choice either to leave Indonesia or to give up their Dutch citizenship and cultural identities. Visas and documents needed to exit the country were difficult to access for Indos, and many had to wait several years before being granted permission to leave. The estimated number of Dutch and Indos who were killed during the Bersiap era range from 3,500 to 20,000. Because the increasingly hostile attitudes toward Dutch and Indos in the area and a tumultuous political environment, many fled to the only remaining Dutch colony in the Dutch East Indies, Dutch New Guinea, while most left the East Indies entirely for the Netherlands.

Between 1945 and 1963 approximately 300,000 Indos immigrated to the Netherlands. The relocation is commonly referred to as "repatriation," because many Indos were Dutch citizens, had lived Dutch cultural lives, and were Christians. The Indos arriving in the Netherlands experienced a cold, wet climate, and although they were Dutch citizens, their different skin color set them apart from other native Dutch. Indos generally made every attempt to assimilate as quickly as possible, often marrying into Dutch families.

The Dutch were unprepared for the influx of citizens from the former Dutch colonies, and most did not know the distinction between native Indonesians and Indos. While many Indos had been educated in Dutch schools and spoke Dutch, most Indos found it difficult to adjust to life in the Netherlands. Holland had endured significant bombing during World War II and was in the process of rebuilding, so there was still a shortage of housing. With a focus on the reconstruction of the Netherlands itself, little economic priority was given to the new wave of immigrants. The Dutch government gave most Indos who repatriated contract pensions, which allowed the government to decide where Indos could live and how much food and other resources they could have. Indos were subject to poor housing conditions and given thin blankets and few supplies. They also faced a great deal of racial prejudice and hostility, mostly the result of postwar economic tensions. Some Indo Americans recall being called names like *Pinda Chang*, which means "peanut Chinese."

Tired of the limited opportunities, discrimination, and shortage of basic supplies and housing, many Indos in the Netherlands chose to emigrate further to the United States and other countries, including Brazil. Those who remained in the Netherlands successfully integrated despite movements that promoted Indo culture. Approximately 50 percent of first-generation Indos in the Netherlands married Dutch-born citizens, and that number rose to 80 percent in the second generation. There have been some attempts made by third-generation Indos, especially in the world of academia, to affirm Indo roots and reclaim Indo heritage. Nora Iburg, a Dutch scholar of Indo descent, claimed that there is no separate, distinct Indo cultural heritage; rather, she describes it as simply a hybrid of many other cultures. During the early twenty-first century, attempts to reconnect Indos worldwide have become aided by growing curiosity about Indo culture and by the proliferation of websites and social media.

SETTLEMENT IN THE UNITED STATES

After World War II Indos were forced from Indonesia to various locations abroad, including Australia, Canada, and the United States, but most went to the Netherlands. Although many Indos had immigrated to the Netherlands because it was their ancestral homeland, few of them felt like they fit in. Because there were food and housing shortages in the Netherlands after the war, the Dutch government decided where Indos could live and how much food and other necessities they could have. Indos were also subject to discrimination and racial slurs. From the early 1950s through the mid-1960s, nearly 60,000 Indos immigrated to the United States from the Netherlands. Dutch foreign officials asserted the refugee status of Indos in the hope of surpassing stringent U.S. immigration policies, designed in particular to bar Asian ethnic groups. Both the Refugee Relief Act of 1953 (which took place after a disastrous flood in the Netherlands and expanded acceptance of Indo-Dutch visas) and the World Refugee Year Law of 1960 resulted in a large wave of immigration.

Indos entered the United States through the initiative of two major organizations: Church World Services and Catholic Relief Services. These organizations provided an array of sponsors for new citizens across the United States. Many Indos settled in the Pacific Northwest and places with warm climates, such as Hawaii, Arizona, and southern California. (According to some estimates, Los Angeles is now the home to approximately 100,000 Americans of Indo descent, making it the area with the majority of Indos in the United States.) Stricter immigration laws in 1963 reduced the number of Indos immigrating to the United States. Indos spread throughout the country and attempted to assimilate quickly.

According to a 2012 Indo Project survey, the states with the largest numbers of Indo Americans

Indos

States with highest population

included California, New York, Massachusetts, Florida, Maryland, and Washington. Other states where smaller populations reside were Connecticut, New Jersey, Pennsylvania, and Oregon. Many second- and third-generation Indos in America have begun to research their family history and are learning more about Indo culture in order to save it.

LANGUAGE

During the colonial period, many young Indos attended Dutch schools. They were knowledgeable about Dutch culture and history, and they were fluent in Dutch. First-generation Indos generally spoke Dutch as their first language and also knew Austronesian, known before as Malayo-Polynesian, which was the dominant language in Indonesia. The children of wealthy first-generation Indos often learned Indonesian, generally known as Malay, as tool to communicate with servants and nannies. When first-generation Indos moved to the United States, they learned English as quickly as possible in an effort to assimilate. Second-generation Indos often grew up in the United States with English as their primary language and Dutch spoken around the household. First-generation Indos intermarried into their new communities, and second-generation Indos intermarried even more frequently. Many third-generation Indos know English as their sole language.

Though most of the Austronesian language is completely dissimilar from English, "hi" is actually

pronounced and spelled similarly: *hai*. Other common phrases include Good morning (*selamat pagi*), good evening (*selamat malam*), thank you (*terima kasih*), and you're welcome (*kembali*). *Opa* is the term for grandfather (in Dutch) and *Oma* is the term for grandmother. *Tempo doeloe* is a phrase that denotes the time of colonialism in Dutch Indonesia, and it connotes a sense of nostalgia, or "good times," of the colonial period.

RELIGION

Although the majority of Indonesians have been Muslim since the late sixteenth century, Indos were predominantly Christian and lived peacefully alongside Muslims, Hindus, Buddhists, and Confucianists during the colonial period. Many Indos in the United States continue to identify as Christians and practice Christianity in some form.

CULTURE AND ASSIMILATION

Traditions and Customs Occasionally in areas such as Seattle or Los Angeles, where there are larger groups of Indos, Indos will assemble for *koempoelans*, or traditional line dances, and eat traditional Indo cuisine. Many first- and second-generation Indos remember the horrors of WWII and the Bersiap period and avoid talking about their experiences. However, many Indos have recognized the dying out of their culture and are using the Internet and social media to raise awareness. An example of this is the Insulinde Club, which is located in Portland, Oregon, but maintains a Facebook page so Indos can connect regardless of their location. Other groups, including the Indo Project, aim to collect and share information about the culture and history of the Indos. *De Indo*, a monthly magazine published and distributed by René Creutzburg, includes stories of Indo history, culture, and events, as well as poetry, photographs, and personal narratives.

Cuisine While most Indos living in the United States eat food typically sold in U.S. grocery stores, many of them continue to cook and serve traditional Indo dishes. Most Indo cuisine is a fusion of Dutch, or other European, and Indonesian culinary practices. Central to the Indo diet is rice, often prepared by boiling or frying. It is commonly served with coconut milk or coconut oil, and occasionally the food is wrapped in banana leaves or coconut leaves. Meats in Indo cuisine include beef, chicken, goat, and fish and are often cooked in a variety of spices. Traditional Indonesian dishes that remain part of Indo tradition include satay, which is a skewer with mostly meat, and *krupuk*, which are fried rice flour chips with fish or shrimp flavors. Other dishes include *Spekkoek*, a layered cake; *Semur Daging*, a stewed beef dish; and Beef Rendang, beef simmered in coconut milk and spices. Tea and coffee are particularly popular drinks because both were grown and exported in the Dutch East Indies.

Common items in traditional cuisine include *sambal oelek* (chili paste), *nasi goreng* (fried rice), *pisang goreng* (fried bananas), *lumpia goring* (fried spring rolls), and *bami* (fried noodles). Nutmeg was one of the first popular exports in the early colonial period and continues to be a part of the Indo diet. Also common are curry leaves, bean sprouts, ginger, and lemongrass. Dutch foods include sausage bread, called *worstenbroodje* if it is made with bread dough, or *saucijzenbroodje* when made with puff pastry. One of the traditional foods served for Sinterklaas (St. Nicholas Day) by both Dutch Americans and Indo Americans is *boterkoek*, or Dutch buttercake. *Huzaren salade*, or Hussar's Salad, composed of cold beef, cold boiled potatoes, pineapple, pickles, hardboiled eggs, beets, and a mayonnaise-based dressing is typically served on New Year's Eve.

Traditional Dress Traditionally Indos often wore a sarong featuring a traditional Indonesian design known as batik. Along with the sarong, women wore *kebayas*, which are tighter long-sleeved blouses, and men often wore batik shirts over their trousers. Many of them also wore traditional European clothing. In the United States Indos wear typical Western clothing, although they will sometimes don a sarong or a *kebaaya* for special occasions.

Dances and Songs There are two popular types of music in Indo culture: Kroncong and Indorock. Kroncong began around the area of Jakarta and has at its core Portuguese Fado music. This music usually

BABI KETJAP

Ingredients

1 pound, 2 ounces pork tenderloin, cut into strips

1 large onion, finely diced

2 garlic cloves, minced

1 inch fresh ginger, peeled and minced

7 tablespoons dark sugar

3 tablespoons soy sauce

2 tablespoons oil

2 cups water

juice from 1 lemon

1 boullion cube

salt and pepper to taste

Preparation

Combine pork, onion, garlic, ginger, sugar, pepper, and salt.

Heat oil in small saucepan and cook meat mixture until onion is soft and pork is dark. Add the soy sauce, water, lemon juice, and bouillion cube. Simmer for 30 minutes.

Serve with basmati rice.

consists of a variety of instruments, including a string bass, guitar, violin, flute, and cello, and chief among them is the ukulele. The guitar and ukulele parts are melodic and often appear to be speaking to one another. Usually the instrumental part is delivered quickly, while the vocals are slower (it is often compared to Hawaiian music by people who are not familiar with it). Indos engage in a form of line dancing, often to Kroncong music. Indorock, begun during the fifties in the Netherlands, borrowed from Kroncong and mimicked American rock and roll, often covering electric hits from the United States. The genre became popularized by The Tielman Brothers, Indo-Dutch brothers living in the Netherlands who played in a variety of stage antics and wild styles, including playing guitar with their teeth. Dutch DJs, most popularly Tiesto, have featured remixes of popular Indorock music. Although Indo musicians are not well known in the United States, Internet radio, YouTube, and services such as iTunes have made both types of music available to Indos in the country. Many traditional Indonesian songs from the colonial period are still frequently sung by Indos at *koempoelans* or special Indo events.

A colonial tradition that combined elements of Chinese, European, Indo, and native Indonesian cultures was *Komedie Stamboel*, a form of theater featuring the Malay language, Chinese opera, Javanese musicians, and stories from both Eastern and Western

TJALIE ROBINSON

Jan Boon, alias Tjalie Robinson, is considered the most influential Indo writer of the twentieth century. Most of his books were written in Petjok, a Dutch-based creole language used mainly by Indos. His best-known works, *Tjies* (1960) and *Tjoek* (1961), were critically acclaimed in the Netherlands.

Robinson was born on January 10, 1911, in the Netherlands to a Dutch father and an Indo mother. The family moved back to the Dutch East Indies when Robinson was a baby, and he lived there for more than forty years. During the Japanese occupation of the Dutch East Indies (1942–1945), he spent time in several concentration camps.

Robinson worked tirelessly to define Indos as a distinct ethnic and cultural group and to revive Indo pride. Robinson organized the annual Tong Tong Fair in The Hague, formerly known as Pasar Malam Besar, which is a popular festival celebrating Indo food, music, dance, and culture. In 1958 he started *Tong Tong*, a Dutch language magazine whose target audience is Indos in the diaspora and is now published under the title *Moesson*. He also founded the short-lived magazine *American Tong Tong* when he immigrated to the United States in the 1960s. Before his death in 1974, he moved back to the Netherlands. His ashes were scattered in the Java Sea in Jakarta, Indonesia.

traditions, such as Ali Baba and the Forty Thieves, Hamlet, and Snow White. It mainly included Indo actors, making it a uniquely Indo tradition. However, this tradition, which flourished during the era of Dutch colonialism, was not brought to the United States when Indos migrated.

Holidays Because most Indos are Christian, they celebrate the traditional Christian holidays, such as Easter and Christmas. They also observe typical American holidays, including Thanksgiving and the Fourth of July. Additionally, many Indos of Dutch descent observe Sinterklaas, or Saint Nicholas Day, on December 5. Sinterklaas, or Saint Nicholas, is similar

There have been some attempts made by third-generation Indos, especially in the world of academia, to affirm Indo roots and reclaim Indo heritage. Nora Iburg, a Dutch scholar of Indo descent, claimed that there is no separate, distinct Indo cultural heritage; rather, she describes it as simply a hybrid of many other cultures.

to Santa Claus in the United States. According to tradition, Sinterklaas keeps a list of all the children, noting who's been good and who's been bad. On the eve of December 5, children place their shoes next to the fireplace and wake up the following morning to find candy or a small gift inside their shoes. Queen's Day, which honors the head of the Dutch monarchy, is another holiday that many Indos observe. Some Indos also consider advancement in Dutch soccer tournaments as holidays.

FAMILY AND COMMUNITY LIFE

During the colonial era many European men married or lived with native Indonesian women. As a result, Indos have typically had Dutch, German (Schwartzman), Portuguese (Simao, De Fretes, Perera, and Henriques), and French surnames.

Despite the fact that the Dutch government encouraged racial integration as a tool of assimilation, there was also a stigma attached to marrying a native or Indo woman. Many Dutch men chose not to marry and instead fathered illegitimate children whom they could recognize or ignore. Although Indos were not treated as well as the full-blooded Dutch colonists, they were still treated better than native Indonesians. This meant when the father acknowledged his illegitimate, Indo offspring (*voorkinderen*), they were afforded economic and social advantages, such as education at a Dutch school. Many Dutch men rejected their native wife or mistress (*nyais*), along with their children, and would marry a Dutch woman with whom he could have legitimate, white children (*nakinderen*). The terms *nakinderen* and *voorkinderen* were used to denote illegitimate children of a mixed union. State orphanages had to be established in order to care for the large numbers of neglected *voorkinderen*. Indos in the Dutch East Indies became a marginalized group, similar to mulattoes in the United States. Technically they did not fit into either culture, Indonesian or Dutch. Although many young Indo men worked as Dutch civil servants, they were often denied promotions in favor of young Dutch men who were increasingly arriving from the Netherlands.

After World War II the majority of refugee immigrants who repatriated to the Netherlands or immigrated to the United States were married. While both Indo men and women preferred to marry another Indo, they were also concerned with assimilation. In the Netherlands many chose to marry Dutch partners, and in the United States they often married Americans. Marriage was often the way to integrate themselves quickly into society.

EMPLOYMENT AND ECONOMIC CONDITIONS

The early Indo immigrants in the United States, arriving from the early 1950s to the mid-1960s, were educated, learned English, and integrated well into American culture, and many married Americans. This rapid assimilation was an important reason for the group's economic success in the United States.

POLITICS AND GOVERNMENT

Because of their small population in the United States, Indos have had little participation in American politics and government. Notable exceptions are Das Williams

(1974–), elected to the Santa Barbara City Council in 2003 and the California Assembly and 2010, and Joyce Luther Kennard (1941–), who in 1989 became the second woman appointed to the California Supreme Court.

NOTABLE INDIVIDUALS

Scholars Greta Kwik was an American of Dutch Indonesian ancestry who wrote the comprehensive ethnography *The Indos in Southern California* (1989).

Journalism Atika Shubert was an American of Dutch Indonesian descent who became a CNN journalist based out of London and interviewed Wikileaks founder Julian Assange.

Literature Greg Van Eekhout is a Dutch-Indo American author of young adult science fiction, as well as of the adult fantasy novel *Norse Code* (2009) and award-winning short stories.

Jan Boon (1911–1974), who is best known under the pseudonyms Tjalie Robinson and Vincent Mahieu, was an Indo author and advocate for the Indo community first in Indonesia, then in the Netherlands, and then in the United States. He was the founder of the Indo magazine *Tong Tong*.

Music Eddie and Alex Van Halen (1955–and 1953–) were born in the Netherlands to an Indo mother and a Dutch father. They became extremely popular figures as members of Van Halen, a rock and roll group formed in 1972.

Michelle Branch (1983–), an Irish and Dutch-Indonesian singer and songwriter, grew up in Phoenix, Arizona, and won a Grammy for her collaboration with Carlos Santana.

Patrick Kerger is the founding member of Tjendol Sunrise, a revolutionary Indorock band in the 1960s.

James Intveld (1959–) is a musician, singer, songwriter, and performer born in Los Angeles. He was the singing voice of Johnny Depp's character in the movie *Cry-Baby*.

Armand Van Helden (1970–) is an American DJ of Dutch Indonesian descent. A producer of electro house music, he had done remixes of Daft Punk, Katy Perry, the Rolling Stones, and Britney Spears.

Television and Film Mark-Paul Harry Gosselaar (1974–) played the lead role of Zack Morris in the popular teen show *Saved by the Bell* in the 1990s. He also appeared in other television programs and movies. He had a father of Dutch descent and a mother of Indonesian descent.

Politics Das Williams (1974–) is an Indo American member of the California State Assembly.

Joyce Luther Kennard (1941–) is an Indo of Dutch Indonesian descent born in Bandung, Indonesia. She was appointed to the California Supreme Court in

1989, making her the first Indo and second female justice ever to serve on the highest court in California.

Religion Frederick J. Eikerenkoetter II (1935–2009), or Reverend Ike, was born in South Carolina and is of African-American and Dutch-Indonesian descent. One of the first televangelists, he taught about achieving material wealth, a message that appealed to the middle class.

Indo musician Michelle Branch (1983–) performs in San Francisco, California, in 2012. C FLANIGAN / FILMMAGIC / GETTY IMAGES

ORGANIZATIONS AND ASSOCIATIONS

The Indo Project

The Indo Project is a nonprofit organization dedicated to historical education and preservation of Indo culture.

Priscilla Kluge McMullen, Chairwoman
19 Chestnut Square
Boston, Massachusetts 02130
Email: pmcmullen@theindoproject.org
URL: www.theindoproject.org

MUSEUMS AND RESEARCH CENTERS

Indo Library

The Indo Library collects books about the Dutch East Indies.

19830 Calle Senita
Walnut, California 91789
Phone: (909) 598-2996

SOURCES FOR ADDITIONAL STUDY

Bosma, Ulbe, and Remco Raben. *Being "Dutch" in the Indies: A History of Creolisation and Empire 1500–1920*. Athens: Ohio University Press, 2008.

Crul, Maurice, Flip Lindo, and Ching Lin Pang. *Culture, Structure and Beyond: Changing Identities and Social Positions of Immigrants and Their Children*. Amsterdam: Het Spinhuis Publishers, 1999.

Gouda, Frances. *American Visions of the Netherlands East Indies/Indonesia*. Amsterdam: Amsterdam University Press, 2002.

Hollander, Inez. *Silenced Voices: Uncovering a Family's Colonial History in Indonesia*. Athens: Ohio University Press, 2009.

Krancher, Jan A. *The Defining Years of the Dutch East Indies, 1942–1949*. Jefferson, NC: McFarland & Company, 1996.

Kwik, Greta. *The Indos in Southern California*. AMS Press, 1989.

Schenkhuizen, Marguérite. *Memoires of an Indo Woman*. Trans. by Lizelot Stout van Balgooy. Athens: Ohio University Press, 1993.

Taylor, Jean Gelman. *Indonesia: Peoples and Histories*. New Haven: Yale University Press, 2003.

———. *The Social World of Batavia: European and Eurasian in Dutch Asia*. Madison: University of Wisconsin Press, 1983.

INUPIAT

J. Sydney Jones

OVERVIEW

Once known as Eskimos, the Inuit are an indigenous people who inhabit the Arctic region, one of the most forbidding territories on earth. Occupying lands that stretch from parts of Siberia, along the Alaskan coast, across Canada, and on to Greenland, the Inuit are one of the most widely dispersed people in the world. There are competing theories as to the meaning of the word *Eskimo*. It was long thought to be a name given to these people by neighboring Abenaki Indians meaning "eaters of raw flesh." However, more recent anthropologists, such as Ives Goddard with the Smithsonian Institution, theorize that it means "snow-shoe netter." The name they call themselves is *Inuit*, or "the people."

Because of their dispersion across four separate countries and the ruggedness of the land they inhabit, exact figures for early Inuit populations are subject to debate, though James Mooney estimated in 1928 that the pre-European Inuit population was about 40,000. Alaskan Inuit typically comprise the Alutiiq, Yup'ik (or Yupiat), and Inupiat tribes. As the first two tribes are dealt with separately, this essay will focus on that group regionally known as Inupiat, and formerly known as Bering Strait or Kotzebue Sound Eskimos, and even sometimes West Alaskan and North Alaskan Eskimos. Before contact with Europeans, the Inupiat maintained subsistence lifestyles, depending solely on hunting and fishing for survival. They also established intricate trading routes throughout their lands in order to disperse goods.

The Inupiat predominantly reside in territories in the west, southwest, and far north and northwest of Alaska. It is estimated that the Inupiat arrived on the North American continent some 4,000 years ago, thus coming much later than other indigenous peoples. Many aspects of modernity have been absorbed into Inuit life. Hunts are now conducted with rifles instead of the traditional spears or bows and arrows. Additionally, many Inupiat now travel on snowmobiles instead of dog sleds. In recent years, climate change has posed a threat to the Inupiat way of life. In addition to disrupting traditional animal migrations and populations, it has altered the physical landscape of the arctic region, making navigation for the Inupiat more treacherous.

According to the Canadian Council for Aboriginal Business, in the 2006 census, 50,485 Inuit resided in Canada. According to a U.S. Census Bureau estimate, in 2010 there were more than 24,859 Inupiat people living in the United States, roughly equivalent to the number of people who annually run the Boston Marathon. Most Inupiat in the United States live in Alaska, but other states with significant numbers include California, Washington, Oregon, Arizona, Colorado, Florida, and Texas.

HISTORY OF THE PEOPLE

Early History Among the last Native groups to come into North America, the Inuit crossed the Bering land bridge sometime between 6000 BCE and 2000 BCE, according to various sources. Anthropologists have discerned several different cultural epochs that began around the Bering crossing. The *Denbigh*, also known as the Arctic Small Tool culture, began in around 3000 BCE, and over the course of the next millennium it spread westward through Arctic Alaska and Canada. Oriented to the sea and to living with snow, the Denbigh most likely originated the snow house. Characterized by the use of flint blades, skin-covered boats, and bows and arrows, the Denbigh was transformed further east into the Dorset Tradition by about 1000 BCE.

Signs of both the Denbigh and Dorset cultures have been unearthed at the well-known *Ipiutak* site, located near the Inupiat settlement of Point Hope, approximately 125 miles north of the Arctic Circle. Point Hope, still a small Inupiaq village at the mouth of the Kukpuk River, appears to have been continuously inhabited for 2,000 years, making it the oldest known Inupiat settlement. The population of the historical Ipiutak was probably larger than that of the modern village of Point Hope, with a population of about 2,000 people. Houses at Ipiutak were small, about twelve by fifteen feet square, with sod-covered walls and roofs. Benches against the walls were used for sleeping, while the fire was kept in a small central depression in the main room. Artifacts from the site indicate that the people of Ipiutak hunted sea and land mammals, as do modern Inuit. Seals, walruses, and caribou provided the basis of their diet. Although the tools of whale hunting, including harpoons, floats, and sleds, were missing from this site, bone and ivory carvings of a rare delicacy—reminiscent of some ancient Siberian art—were found.

Other Inuit settled in part-time villages during the same epoch. The continuous development of these peoples is demonstrated by the similarities in both ancient and modern Inuit cultures. Called by some the *Old Bering Sea Cultures*, these early inhabitants traveled by kayak and *umiak* skin boats in the warmer months, and by sled in the winter. Living near the coast, they hunted sea and land mammals, lived in tiny semi-subterranean dwellings, and developed a high degree of artistic skill.

The Dorset culture was later superseded by the Norton culture, which was in turn followed by the Thule. The Thule already had characteristics of culture common to Inuit culture: the use of dogs, sleds, kayaks, and whale hunting with harpoons. They spread westward through Canada and ultimately on to Greenland. However, it appears that some of the Thule backtracked, returning to set up village sites in both Alaska and Siberia.

Anthropologically classified as central-based wanderers, the Inuit spent part of the year on the move, searching for food, and then part of the year at a central, more permanent camp. Anywhere from a dozen to fifty people traveled in a hunting group. The hunting seasons were seal, caribou, and whale. They hunted seals in the winter, when the ice was solid; in the spring, when the ice began to break up, they hunted for whales, and caribou hunting took place in the summer. A caribou hunt was also mounted in the fall, and in the southern areas the Inuit fished for salmon in the autumn. The year was marked by occasional feasts after the seal and caribou hunts and by summer trade fairs that groups from miles around attended.

There is some dispute whether the Arctic peoples were originally organized into tribes; however, those of present-day Alaska are to a certain extent. One reason for such organization is the whaling occupation of the northwestern Alaska natives. These people settled north of the Brooks Range and along the coast from Kotzebue in the southwest, up to Point Hope and north and east to Barrow, the mouth of the Colville River, and on to the present-day Canadian border at Demarcation Point. These areas provided rich feeding grounds for bowhead whale. Strong leaders were needed for whaling expeditions; thus, older men with experience who knew how to handle an *umiak*, the large wooden-framed boat, took part in whale hunts.

For thousands of years the Inuit lived lives unrecorded by history. This changed with their first contact with Europeans. The Vikings under Erik the Red encountered Inuit in Greenland in 984. Almost six hundred years later, the British explorer Martin Frobisher made contact with the Central Inuit of northern Canada. In 1741 the Russian explorer Vitus Bering met the Inupiat of Alaska. It is estimated that there were about 40,000 Inupiat living in Alaska at the time, with half of them living in the north, both in the interior and in the far northwest. The Inuit, Aleut, and Native Americans living below the Arctic Circle were the most heavily affected by this early contact, occasioned by Russian fur traders. However, northern Inuit were not greatly affected until the second round of European incursions in the area, brought on by an expanded whale trade.

Russian expeditions in the south led to the near destruction of Unangan and Sugpiat culture. This was the result of both the spread of disease by whites as well as outright murder. The first white explorers to reach Arctic Alaska were the Englishmen Sir John Franklin and Captain F. W. Beechey, both in the 1820s. Both noted the extensive trade carried on between Inupiat and other Indian groups. Other early explorers noted this intricate trading system, in which goods were moved from Siberia to Barrow and back again through a network of regularly held trade fairs. All of this changed, however, with the arrival of European whalers by the mid-nineteenth century. Formerly hunters of Pacific sperm whale, these whaling fleets came to Arctic regions following the bowhead whale migration to the Beaufort Sea for summer feeding. Unlike the Inuit, who used all parts of the whale for their subsistence, the whaling fleets from New England and California were interested primarily in baleen, the long and flexible strips of keratin that served as a filtering system for the bowhead whale. This material was used for the manufacture of corsets and umbrellas, and it fetched high prices. One bowhead could yield many pounds and was valued at $8,000, a substantial amount of money for that time.

In 1867 the United States purchased Alaska, and whaling operations increased. The advent of steam-powered vessels further increased the number of ships in the region. Soon, whaling ships from the south were a regular feature in Arctic waters. Their immediate effect was the destruction of the intricate trading network built up over centuries. With the whalers to pick up and deliver goods, Inuit traders were no longer needed. A second effect, due to contact between the whalers and the Inuit, was the introduction of new diseases and alcohol. This, in conjunction with an obvious consequence of the whaling industry, the reduction of the whale population, made life difficult for the Inuit. Dependence on wage drew the Inuit out of their millennia-long hunting and trading existence as they signed on as deckhands or guides. Village life became demoralized because of the trade in whiskey. Small settlements disappeared entirely; others were greatly impacted by diseases brought by the whalers. Point Hope lost 12 percent of its population in one year. In 1900, 200 Inupiat died in Point Barrow from a flu epidemic brought by a whaler, and in 1902, 100 more were lost to measles.

Although relatively unaffected by the whaling operations, the Inuit of the inland areas, known as *Nuunamiut*, also saw a sharp decline in their population from the mid-nineteenth century. Their independence had not protected them from the declining caribou herds nor from increasing epidemics. As a result, these people almost totally disappeared from their inland settlements, moving instead to coastal areas.

Modern Era A number of actions were undertaken in attempts to improve the conditions of the Inuit at the end of the nineteenth century and the early years of the twentieth century. The U.S. government intervened, ostensibly, to ameliorate the situation with improved education. However, the motivations behind this strategy by the U.S. government are the subject of much debate by many Natives and scholars of Inupiat culture and history. Schools were established at Barrow and Point Hope in the 1890s, and new communities were only recognized once they established schools. The government also tried to make up for depleted resources, because the whaling trade had died out in the early years of the twentieth century due to depleted resources as well as the discovery of substitutes for baleen. The U.S. Bureau of Education, the office given responsibility for the Inupiat at the time, imported reindeer from Siberia. They planned to turn the Inupiat, traditionally semisedentary hunters, into nomadic herders. However, after an early peak in the reindeer population in 1932, their numbers dwindled, and the reindeer experiment ultimately proved a failure. Game was no longer plentiful, and the Inupiat themselves changed, seeking more than a subsistence way of life. For a time, beginning in the 1920s, fox fur trading served as a supplement to subsistence. Trapping, however, led to an increased breakdown of traditional cooperative ways of life. Fox fur trading lasted only a decade, and by the 1930s the U.S. government was pouring more money into the area, setting up post offices and aid relief agencies. Christian missions were also establishing schools in the region. Concurrent with these problems was an increase in mortality rates from tuberculosis.

The search for petroleum also greatly affected the region. Since the 1968 discovery of oil in the North Slope (Alaska's northernmost region), the culture as well as the ecology of the region has changed in ways never imagined by nineteenth-century Inupiat. Other wage economies developed in the region. The Cold War brought jobs to the far north, and native artwork became a source of income, especially for carvers. In the 1950s the construction of a chain of radar sites such as the Distant Early Warning system (DEW) employed Inupiat laborers, and many more were later employed to maintain the facilities. In 1959 Alaska became the forty-ninth state, thus extending U.S. citizenship rights and privileges to all of the state's population.

During the mid-1970s, the International Whaling Commission (IWC), responding to concerns over dwindling bowhead whale populations, enacted a moratorium on all bowhead-whaling activities. This ban had a negative impact on the coastal

An Inuit boy enjoys an ice cream cone in Katovik, Alaska. LOETSCHER CHLAUS / ALAMY

Inupiat's subsistence lifestyle, as bowhead whale made up a significant percentage of their diets. In response, the Inupiat formed the Alaska Eskimo Whaling Commission (AEWC), which proposed managed hunts that emphasized sustainability of the bowhead species. The proposal was accepted and the Inupiat managed to preserve their traditional whale hunt.

As the twenty-first century unfolds, the largest challenges facing the Inupiat revolve around changes in the global climate. In 2012 the amount of Arctic sea ice reached an all-time low of 1.3 million square miles, which represented a 50 percent decrease in coverage from the 1979-to-2000 average. The decrease in Arctic sea ice has hindered the Inupiat's traditional hunting seasons and disrupted historic wildlife migratory patterns. It has also made the Arctic region more accessible to outside groups such as mining and oil companies, scientists, environmentalists, and military ships. As the sea ice diminishes, these groups have begun to encroach more and more on traditional Inupiat lands. For a people whose existence has, over millennia, been so tied to the land and environment, these changes pose a threat to their traditional way of life.

SETTLEMENT IN THE UNITED STATES

Residing in some three dozen villages and towns—including Kotzebue, Point Hope, Wainwright, Barrow, and Prudhoe Bay—between the Bering Strait and the McKenzie Delta to the east, and occupying some 40,000 square miles above the Arctic Circle, the Inuit group has been divided differently by various anthropologists. Some classify the Inuit into two main groups, the inland people or Nunamiut, and the coastal people, the Tagiugmiut. Ernest S. Burch Jr., however, in his book *The Inupiaq Eskimo Nations of Northwestern Alaska*, divides the heartland, or original southerly Inupiat, who settled around Kotzebue Sound and the Chukchi Sea, into twelve distinct tribes or nations. This early "homeland" of the Inupiat, around Kotzebue Sound, was extended as the tribes eventually moved farther north. Within Inupiat territory, the main population centers are Barrow and Kotzebue. While some Inupiat have ventured beyond these areas, the vast majority still reside in this region. Other states where small, but significant, numbers of Inupiat reside are Texas, Washington, California, Oregon, Florida, Colorado, and Arizona.

LANGUAGE

The Inupiat communities of northern Alaska speak Inupiaq, part of the Eskaleut family of languages. All Inupiat bands speak very closely related dialects of this language family. Alaskan Eskaleut languages include Aleut, Yup'ik, and Inupiaq.

Many Inuit words have become common in English and other languages of the world. Words such as *kayak*, *husky*, *igloo*, and *parka* all have come from the Inuit.

The future of Inupiaq-speaking Alaska is optimistic. Language instruction in school was for many years solely in English, with native languages discouraged. Literacy projects have been started at Barrow schools to encourage the preservation of the language. However, English is the primary language of the region.

RELIGION

A central tenet of Inupiat religion is that the forces of nature are essentially malevolent. Inhabiting a ruthless climatological zone, the Inupiat believed that the spirits of the weather and of the animals must be placated to avoid harm. As a result, there was strict observance of various taboos as well as dances and ceremonies in honor of such spirits. These spirit entities found in nature included game animals in particular. Inupiat hunters would, for example, always open the skull of a freshly killed animal to release its spirit. Personal spirit songs were essential among whale hunters. Much of this religious tradition was directed and passed on by shamans, both male and female. These shamans could call upon a *tuunsaq*, or helping spirit, in times of trouble or crisis. This spirit often took the shape of a land animal, into whose shape the shaman would change himself or herself. Traditional Native religious practices, as well as the power of the shamans, decreased with the Inupiat's increased contact with European missionaries, who viewed such practices as evil. Attempts to impose Christianity on the Inupiat were largely successful, and today most Inupiat are Christian.

CULTURE AND ASSIMILATION

As with the rest of Native Americans, the Inupiat acculturation and assimilation patterns were more the result of coercion than choice. A main tool of assimilation was education. Schools, set up by the state or by missions, discouraged the learning of native languages; English became the primary language for students, who were often transported hundreds of miles from their homes. Students who spoke their native Inupiaq language were punished and made to stand with their faces to the corner or by having their mouths washed out with soap. Returning to their home villages after being sent away for four years to the Bureau of Indian Affairs high schools, these Inupiat no longer had a connection to their language or culture. They were ill equipped to pass traditions on to their own children.

By the 1970s, however, this trend was reversed, as the Inupiat began organizing, demanding, and winning more local autonomy. More local schools opened that honored the ancient ways of the Inupiat. For many this was too little, too late, though old dances and festivals have returned, and the language is studied by the young.

Traditions and Customs Inupiat social organization was largely based on bilateral kinship relations, which calls for each individual to identify all others as cross-cousins or parallel cousins. While there were disagreements, there were no blood feuds between clans. Parallel cousins were to be polite under all circumstances. Disputes were worked out through cross-cousins, who presented disputes on behalf of their cross-cousins in ceremonies and festivals. Hunting or trading provided other opportunities for cooperative endeavors, in which different kinship groups teamed up for mutual benefit.

Wintertime was a period for the village to come together; men gathered in the common houses called *kashims* or *karigi*, also used for dancing. Games, song contests, wrestling, and storytelling brought the people of small villages together after hunts and during the long, dark winter months. Much of Inupiat life was adapted to the extremes of summer and winter night lengths. The Inupiat formerly lived in semi-excavated winter dwellings, made of driftwood and sod built into a dome. Moss functioned as insulation in these crude shelters. A separate kitchen had a smoke hole, and there were storage areas and a meat cellar. These dwellings could house eight to twelve people. Temporary snow houses were also used, though the legendary igloo was a structure used more by Canadian Inuit.

Cuisine Subsistence food for the Inupiat of Alaska included whale meat, caribou, moose, walrus, seal, fish, fowl, mountain sheep, bear, hares, squirrels, and foxes. Plant food included wild herbs and roots, as well as berries. Meat is dried or kept frozen in ice cellars dug into the tundra. As more Inupiat move to towns and villages with supermarkets and modern conveniences such as refrigerators, traditional foods now supplement a more typical American diet.

Traditional Dress Traditionally, Inupiat women tanned seal and caribou skins to make clothing, much of it with fur trim. Two suits of such fur clothing were worn in the colder months, the inner one with the fur turned inward. Waterproof jackets were also made from the intestines of various sea mammals, while shoes were constructed from seal and caribou hide that had been toughened by chewing. Such clothing, however, has been replaced by manufactured clothing. Down parkas have replaced the caribou skins, and insulated rubber boots have replaced chewed sealskin ones. However, such clothing has become a major source of income for some individuals and groups. Traditional clothing, from mukluks to fur parkas, has become valued as art and artifact outside the Inupiat.

Dances and Songs The Inupiat danced at traditional feast times in ritual dance houses called *karigi*. These dances were accompanied by drums and the recitation of verse stories. Some of these dances represented the caribou hunt; others might portray a flight of birds or a battle with the weather. Both poetry and dance were important to the Inupiat; storytelling was vital for people who spent the long winter months indoors and in darkness. The word for "poetry" in Inupiaq is the same as the word "to breathe," and both derive from *anerca*, "the soul." Such poems were sung and often accompanied by dancers who moved in imitation of the forces of nature. Many of the traditional singers were also shamans and had the power to cast spells with their words. Thus, dance took on both a secular and a religious significance to the Inupiat. The Inupiat created songs for dancing, for hunting, for entertaining children, for weather, for healing, for sarcasm, and for derision. Some dance and song festivals would last for days, with the entire community participating, their voices accompanied by huge hoop drums. These dance traditions have been resurrected among Inupiat communities. For example, the Northern Lights Dancers have pioneered this venture.

Holidays Major feasts for the Inupiat took place in the winter and in spring. In December came the Messenger Feast, held inside the community building. This potlatch demonstrated social status and wealth. A messenger would be sent to a neighboring community

Inuit dancer and drummers in Nome, Alaska, c. 1910. MICHAEL MASLAN / HISTORICAL / CORBIS

to invite its members to be guests at a feast. Invitations were usually the result of a wish for continued or improved trading relations with the community in question. Gifts were exchanged at such feasts. Some southern groups also held Messenger Feasts in the fall.

The spring whaling festival, or *nalukataq*, was held after the whale hunt as a thanksgiving for success and to ask for continued good fortune with whale hunting. It was held also to appease the spirit of the killed whales. Similar to other Bladder Dances or Festivals of non-Alaskan Inuit groups, these ceremonies intended to set free the spirits of sea mammals killed during the year. At the *nalukataq*, a blanket toss would take place, in which members of the community were bounced high from a walrus-skin "trampoline." Another spring festival marked the coming of the sun. Dressed in costumes that were a mixture of male and female symbols to denote creation, the Inupiat danced to welcome the sun's return.

Trading fairs took place throughout the year. The summer Kotzebue fair was one of the largest. In 1991 it was revived, held just after the Fourth of July. For the first time in a century, Russian Inuit came to celebrate the fair with their Alaskan relatives. The Messenger Feast has also been reinstituted, held in January in Barrow.

Health Care Issues and Practices In traditional Inupiat society the healing of the sick was the responsibility of the shaman or *angakok* (*angakkuq*), who contacted spirits by singing, dancing, and drum beating. He would take on the evil spirit of the sick. The *angakok* also knew how to use plants to cure many ailments. They were, however, helpless against the diseases brought by the Europeans and Americans. Tuberculosis was an early scourge of the Inupiat, wiping out entire villages. Alcohol proved equally as lethal, and though it was outlawed, traders were able to bring it in as contraband to trade for furs. Alcohol dependency continues

BIRTH AND BIRTHDAYS

Among the Inupiat birth and pregnancy were traditionally surrounded by many taboos. For example, it was thought that if a pregnant woman walked out of a house backward, she would have a breech delivery, and if a pregnant mother slept at irregular times during the day, this would result in a lazy baby. Also, there were special birthing houses or *aanigutyaks*, where the woman went through labor alone in a kneeling (or squatting) position. These postures have been recognized by Western culture as often preferable to the hospital bed.

Most children are baptized within a month of birth and given an English name along with an Inupiat one. Chosen by their parents, these names are usually of a recently departed relative or of some respected person. Siblings help care for children after the first few months, and babies soon become accustomed to being carried about in packs or under parkas. There is no preference shown for either girls or boys; both are seen as a gift from nature. While moss and soft caribou skin have been replaced with cotton and disposable diapers, the Inupiat's attitude toward their children has not changed. They are loved and given much latitude by both parents, and fathers participate actively in raising their children.

to be a major problem among Inupiat villages and has resulted in a high occurrence of fetal alcohol syndrome. Thus, ten villages in the Northwest Arctic Borough have banned the importation and sale of alcohol, while Kotzebue has made the sale of liquor illegal but allows the importation of it for individual consumption. Nonetheless, alcohol continues to be a source of major problems despite the implementation of "dry" towns and boroughs. Rates of accident, homicide, and suicide among the Inupiat are far higher than among the general Alaskan population. Moreover, there are high rates of infant mortality, sudden infant death syndrome (SIDS), and infant spinal disorders.

Another health issue, particularly for the Inupiat of the Cape Thompson region, is cancer, brought on by the disposal of 15,000 pounds of nuclear waste by the Atomic Energy Commission (AEC) between 1959 and 1962. The waste was left over from experiments related to "Project Chariot," which studied the feasibility of using nuclear explosions to construct an artificial harbor in the Ogoturuk Valley. Also, radiation experiments on flora and fauna of the region as well as Russian nuclear waste dumping offshore have contaminated many areas of northwestern Alaska, putting the native population at risk.

FAMILY AND COMMUNITY LIFE

Local groups were formed by nuclear and small extended families led by an *umialik*, or family head, usually an older man. The umialik might lead hunting expeditions, and he and his wife would be responsible for the

distribution of food. Beyond that, however, there was little control exerted on proper behavior in traditional Inupiat society. Villages throughout northern Alaska have replaced hunting bands, thus preserving to some extent the fluid network of their traditional society.

Gender Roles There is still a recognized division of labor by gender, but it is a fluid one. In traditional societies the men hunted, while the women tanned skins and made clothing and generally took care of domestic activities, and this occurred under the aegis of the extended family. In the modern era much of this has changed, but in general, outside employment is still the obligation of the male, as are any ancillary hunting activities necessary to help make ends meet. However, since the twentieth century women have headed ANCSA corporations and tribal units and have sought higher education at Ilisagvik College in Barrow, Alaska.

Education Education for the Inupiat is still problematic. Each village has its own school, funded by the state with extra funds from the federal government. Yet the dropout rate is still high among their youth. There was a 30 percent dropout rate in grade school in 1965, a rate that climbed to 50 to 80 percent in high school. And for those few who reached college at that same time, some 97 percent dropped out. Ten years later, in 1975, the rates had gone down considerably, in part due to a revival of teaching in Inupiaq, as opposed to English-only instruction. Most Inupiat under the age of fifteen are minimally literate in English. Ilisagvik College is the only tribally controlled college in Alaska and is the northernmost accredited community college in the United States.

Courtship and Weddings In the past, marriages were often arranged by parents; however, today dating openly occurs between teens. Group activities take precedence over individual dating. In traditional times, the most successful hunter could take more than one wife, though this was uncommon. Also in the past, temporary marriages served to bond non-kin allegiances formed for hunting or warfare. Married couples traditionally set up their home with the man's parents for a time. Plumpness in a wife was considered a virtue, a sign of a family's health and wealth. While divorce was and is practiced in both traditional and modern Inupiat societies, its incidence is not as high as in mainstream American society.

EMPLOYMENT AND ECONOMIC CONDITIONS

Traditionally, the Inupiat economy revolved around the changing seasons and the animals that could be successfully hunted during these periods. The Inupiat world was so closely linked to its subsistence economy that many of the calendar months were named after game prey. For example, March was the moon for hanging up seal and caribou skins to bleach them; April was the moon for the onset of whaling; and October was the moon of rutting caribou. Whaling season began in the spring with the first break up of the ice. At this time bowhead whales, some weighing

An Inuit from Barrow, Alaska, sits with his gun awaiting the whale call. ACCENT ALASKA.COM / ALAMY

as much as 60 tons, passed by northern Alaska to feeding grounds offshore, which were rich in plankton. Harpooners would strike deep into the huge mammal, and heavy sealskin floats would help keep the animal immobilized as lances were sunk into it. Hauling the whale ashore, a section of blubber would be immediately cut off and boiled as a thanksgiving. Meat, blubber, bone, and baleen were all taken from the animal by parties of hunters under the head of an *umialik*, or boss. Such meat would help support families for months.

Caribou, another highly prized food source, was hunted in the summer and fall. In addition to the meat, the Inupiat used the caribou's skin and antlers. Even the sinew was saved and used for thread. Baleen nets were also used for fishing at the mouths of rivers and streams. Walrus and seal were other staples of the traditional Inupiat subsistence economy.

These practices changed with the arrival of the Europeans. Many attempts were made to replace diminished natural resources, including the importation of reindeer and the trapping of foxes for fur. These were unsuccessful, and modern Inupiat now blend a wage economy with hunting and fishing. A major employer is the state and federal government.

The Red Dog Mine, which produces zinc and lead, as well as the oil industry on the North Slope, also provide employment opportunities. Smaller urban centers such as Barrow and Kotzebue offer a wider variety of employment opportunities, as does the Chukchi Sea Trading Company, a Point Hope arts and crafts cooperative that sells native arts online. Other Inupiat must rely on assistance programs; and most continue to depend on both wage and subsistence economies.

In general, living costs are greater in the rural areas of the north than in the rest of Alaska. For example, as David Maas points out in *The Native North American Almanac* (1994), a family living in Kotzebue could pay 62 percent more per week for food than a family in Anchorage, and 165 percent more for electricity. The incidence of poverty is also higher among Alaskan Inupiat than for others in the state.

POLITICS AND GOVERNMENT
Although traditional Inupiat society depended greatly on cooperative behavior for survival, the Inupiat also maintained a large degree of individual freedom. Partnerships and non-kin alliances became crucial

during hunting seasons and during wars and feuds, but it was mostly based on the nuclear or extended family unit. When bands came together, they were more geographical than political in nature, and while leaders or *umialik* were important in hunting, their power was not absolute. The social fabric of Inupiat society changed forever in the twentieth century. The Inupiat of Barrow and Shungnak voted against establishing the reservations that formed all over the United States in the 1930s.

During the mid-twentieth century, there was a great deal of competition for once-native lands, from both the private and the public sector. In 1932 a petroleum reserve in the north was set aside and then developed by the Navy and later by private companies. The Atomic Energy Commission (AEC) also wanted Inupiat land. In 1958 the AEC requested some 1,600 square miles of land near Point Hope to create a deep-water port using an atomic explosion many times more powerful than the one that decimated the Japanese city of Hiroshima in World War II. Some of the first political action taken by the Inupiat was in opposition to this experiment. As a result, the plan, Project Chariot, was called off.

The decrease in Arctic sea ice has hindered the Inupiat's traditional hunting seasons and disrupted historic wildlife migratory patterns. It has also made the Arctic region more accessible to outside groups such as mining and oil companies, scientists, environmentalists, and military ships. As the sea ice diminishes, these groups have begun to encroach more and more on traditional Inupiat lands.

After their success against Project Chariot, Natives began to organize in a concerted way to protect their lands. In 1961 various village leaders formed the Inupiat Paitot (The People's Heritage Movement) to protect Inupiat lands. In 1963 the Northwest Alaska Native Association was formed under the leadership of Willie Hensley, later a state senator. The Arctic Slope Association was formed in 1966. Both associations mirrored the activities of the statewide Alaska Federation of Natives (AFN), which lobbied for Native rights and claims. Local villages and organizations throughout the state were filing claims for land not yet ceded to the government. In 1968, with Congress beginning to review the situation, oil was discovered on the North Slope. Oil companies wanted to pipe the oil out via the port of Valdez, and negotiations were soon underway to settle Inupiat and other Native claims.

The result was the 1971 Alaska Native Claims Settlement Act (ANCSA), which created twelve regional for-profit corporations throughout the state. These corporations held title to surface and mineral

rights of some 44 million acres. Additionally, Natives would receive $962.5 million in compensation for the 335 million acres of the state that they no longer claimed. Thus, the way was paved for the construction of the Alaska pipeline.

As a result of ANCSA, all Alaskans with at least one-quarter Native blood would receive settlement money that would be managed by regional and village corporations. Alaskan Inupiat villages then organized into several corporations in hopes of taking advantage of the opportunities of this legislation. Amendments in 1980 to the Alaska National Interests Lands Conservation Act restoring Native rights to subsistence hunting and fishing, and, in 1988, ensuring Native control of corporations in perpetuity, helped equalize ANCSA legislation. In the four decades since the passage of ANCSA, the Alaska Native Regional Corporations have emerged as an economic force in Alaska, allowing businesses to flourish within the state while improving the social and cultural well-being of Alaskan Native peoples.

Inupiat groups organized in the 1970s to see that high schools were built in their villages. In the Barrow region, local schools broke away from the Bureau of Indian Affairs administration and formed local boards of education more amenable to the teaching of Inupiaq language, history, and customs. The North Slope Borough, formed in 1972, took over school administration in 1975, and the Northwest Arctic Borough, formed in 1986, did the same. These regional political structures are further subdivided into villages with elected mayors and city councils. Slowly, through the work of advocacy groups, the Inupiat of northern Alaska are reclaiming their heritage in the modern world.

The North Slope Borough is the only regional governing unit almost entirely run by indigenous people in the state of Alaska. This accomplishment gives the Inupiat more political and economic clout than other indigenous Alaskans have.

NOTABLE INDIVIDUALS

Academia Martha Aiken (1926–2009) was an educator born in Barrow, Alaska, of Inupiat descent. Aiken authored seventeen bilingual books for the North Slope Borough School District, translated eighty hymns for the Presbyterian Church, and was a major contributor to an Inupiaq dictionary. She also served on the board of the Arctic Slope Regional Corporation.

Sadie Brower Neakok (1916–2006) was an educator, community activist, and magistrate from Barrow. A full-time teacher for the Bureau of Indian Affairs, Neakok was appointed magistrate by the state of Alaska and was instrumental in introducing the American legal system to the Inupiat.

Tikasuk "Emily" Brown (1904–1982) was born in Unalakleet, Alaska. She became a grade school teacher and an early advocate for bilingual education. She later received two bachelor's degrees from the University of Alaska. Her master's thesis from the University of Alaska was published as a book called *The Roots of Ticasuk: An Eskimo Woman's Family Story* (1981). She received numerous awards throughout her lifetime, including a presidential citation from Richard Nixon. In 2009 she was posthumously inducted into the Alaska Women's Hall of Fame.

Art Larry Ahvakana (1946–), Inupiat sculptor and mixed-media artist, trained at the Institute of American Indian Art in Santa Fe and at the Cooper Union School of Arts in New York. Ahvakana is known for blending modern sculptural techniques with his Native heritage to create lasting pieces in stone and wood. His interpretations of Alaskan myth often appear in his art.

Sylvester Ayek (1940–), an Inupiat native, grew up on King Island, a tiny island far north of Anchorage in the Bering Sea. He found success as a successful sculptor, and his work has been shown in museums and placed in permanent collections in Alaska and the Smithsonian Museum in Washington, D.C.

Susie Qimmiqsaq Bevins-Ericsen (1941–) is an Inupiat carver and mask maker. In 1994 President Clinton displayed one of her pieces in a White House garden exhibit. Her masks often speak of the split personality of Natives growing up in two cultures.

Melvin Olanna (1941–1991) was an Inupiat sculptor and jewelry designer born in Shishmaref, Alaska. Educated in Oregon and at the University of Alaska, Fairbanks, Olanna had numerous individual and group exhibitions of his work, and also won a number of Alaskan awards for the arts. A practitioner of the ancient carving traditions of the Inupiat, Olanna brought this older design form together with modern forms. He and his wife helped found the Melvin Olanna Carving Center, dedicated to training young Inupiat in their ancient traditions.

Joseph Senungetuk (1940–) is a printmaker and carver of Inupiat descent from Wales, Alaska. An activist as well as artist, writer, and teacher, Senungetuk has devoted his life to Native issues and the revitalization of Alaskan arts. He grew up in Nome, where an uncle first taught him to carve, then attended the University of Alaska in Fairbanks. Senungetuk also wrote an autobiographical and historical book, *Give or Take a Century: An Eskimo Chronicle* (1971).

Journalism Howard Rock (1911–1976) was born in Point Hope, where in the 1960s he joined Inupiat Paitot to stop the government from using the locale as a nuclear test site. Rock became the editor of a newsletter formed to educate other Inupiat about the dangers. In 1962 this newsletter became the *Tundra Times*, with Rock serving as its editor until his death in 1976. In 1965 he helped organize the first Alaska Federated Natives meeting in Anchorage.

Literature Alootook Ipellie (1951–2007) was a writer and artist who also contributed articles to the

Nunavut and *Nunatsiaq News*. His story collection *Arctic Dreams and Nightmares* (1993) blends written and visual imagery to interpret the mythological world of the Inuit.

Politics William L. Hensley (1941–), also known as Iggiagruk or "Big Hill," is an Inupiat leader recognized as one of the primary architects of the Alaskan Federation of Natives. He also served as an Alaskan state senator. Born in Kotzebue to a family of hunters and fishermen, Hensley left home for his education, attending a boarding school in Tennessee. He earned a bachelor's degree from George Washington University in Washington, D.C., where he first became politicized about the conditions of his people in Alaska. Returning to Alaska, he studied constitutional law at the University of Alaska. In 1966 Hensley became one of the founders of the AFN, which was instrumental in lobbying Washington for Native claims. Since that time he has played an active role in Alaskan politics and has been an untiring spokesperson for the rights of the Inupiat. He founded the Northwest Alaska Native Association and was instrumental in the development of the Red Dog Lead and Zinc Mine in northwest Alaska, the second-largest zinc mine in the world. He was Visiting Distinguished Professor at the University of Alaska Anchorage College of Business and Public Policy, where he taught Alaska Policy Frontiers. In 2008 he published *Fifty Miles from Tomorrow: A Memoir of Alaska and the Real People*.

MEDIA

PRINT

Alaska Native News

Describes itself as "news for the people of the last frontier."

P.O. Box 2996
Homer, Alaska 99603
Phone: (907) 756-1142
URL: alaska-native-news.com

The Arctic Sounder

Billing itself as Alaska's rural news leader, the *Arctic Sounder* serves the Northwest Arctic and the North Slope.

Jason Evans, Publisher and President
Alaska Media LLC
500 West International Airport Road
Suite F
Anchorage, Alaska 99518
Phone: (907) 770-0820
Email: ads@reportalaska.com
URL: www.thearcticsounder.com

RADIO

KBRW-AM (680) and KBRW-FM (91.9)

Isaac Tuckfield, Program Director
Skakkuagvik Communications
1695 Okpik Street

Barrow, Alaska 99723
Phone: (907) 852-6811
Fax: (504) 889-9898
Email: info@kbrw.org
URL: www.kbrw.org

KOTZ-AM (720) and KOTZ-FM (89.9)

Johnson Greene, Program Director
P.O. Box 78
Kotzebue, Alaska 99752
Phone: (907) 442-3434
Fax: (907) 442-2292
Email: message@kotz.org
URL: www.kotz.org

ORGANIZATIONS AND ASSOCIATIONS

Alaska Federation of Natives (AFN)

Founded in 1966, this group serves as an advocate for Inupiat, Native Americans, and Aleut at the state and federal level. It publishes an AFN newsletter.

1577 C Street
Suite 300
Anchorage, Alaska 99501
Phone: (907) 274-3611
Fax: (907) 276-7989
Email: AFNInfo@nativefederation.org
URL: www.nativefederation.org

First Alaskans Institute

Helps develop the capacities of Alaska native people and their communities to meet the social, economic, and educational challenges of the future. Also home to the Alaska Native Policy Center.

606 E Street
Suite 200
Anchorage, Alaska 99501
Phone: (907) 677-1700
Fax: (907) 677-1780
URL: www.firstalaskans.org

Inuit Circumpolar Council Alaska

Nonprofit corporation that represents and advocates for the Inupiat of the Arctic Slope, Northwest, and Bering Straits.

Jim Stotts, President
3003 Minnesota Drive
Suite 204
Anchorage, Alaska 99503
Phone: (907) 274-9058
Fax: (907) 274-3861
Email: icc@iccalaska.org
URL: www.iccalaska.org

Maniilaq Association

Provides health and social services to residents of Northwest Alaska.

Ian Erlich, President
P.O. Box 256
#773 5th Avenue
Kotzebue, Alaska 99752
Phone: (907) 442-3311
URL: www.maniilaq.org

MUSEUMS AND RESEARCH CENTERS

Alaska Native Heritage Center

A cultural center and museum dedicated to expanding understanding of Alaska's indigenous people.

Annette Evans Smith, President
8800 Heritage Center Drive
Anchorage, Alaska 99504
Phone: (907) 330-8000
Fax: (907) 330-8030
Email: info@alaskanative.net
URL: www.alaskanative.net

Alaska State Museum

Collections represent the diverse cultures and rich historical record of Alaska.

395 Whittier Street
Juneau, Alaska 99801-1718
Phone: (907) 465-2901
Fax: (907) 465-2976
URL: www.museums.state.ak.us

Anchorage Museum

Featuring art, history, and science, the Anchorage Museum aims to create a rich, deep understanding of the human experience.

625 C Street
Anchorage, Alaska 99501
Phone: (907) 929-9200
Fax: (907) 929-9290
Email: museum@anchoragemuseum.org
URL: www.anchoragemuseum.org

Northwest Arctic Heritage Center

Operated by the National Parks Service; its collection contains Inuit artifacts and arts and crafts.

P.O. Box 1029
Kotzebue, Alaska 99752
Phone: (907) 442-3890
Fax: (907) 442-8316
URL: www.nps.gov/kova

Simon Paneak Memorial Museum

Contains a collection of Nunamiut Inuit history and traditions.

P.O. Box 21085
Anaktuvuk, Pass Alaska 99721
Phone: (907) 661-3413
Fax: (907) 661-3414

SOURCES FOR ADDITIONAL STUDY

Anderson, Wanni. *Dall Sheep Dinner Guest: Inupiaq Narratives of Northwest Alaska.* Fairbanks: University of Alaska Press, 2005.

Burch, Ernest. *Social Life in Northwest Alaska: The Structure of Inupiaq Eskimo Nations.* Fairbanks: University of Alaska Press, 2006.

Chance, Norman A. *The Eskimo of North Alaska.* New York: Holt, Rinehart and Winston, 1966.

———. *The Inupiat and Arctic Alaska.* Forth Worth, TX: Harcourt Brace, 1990.

Craig, Rachel. "Inupiat." *Native America in the Twentieth Century: An Encyclopedia*, edited by Mary B. Davis. New York: Garland Publishing, 1994.

Damas, David, ed. *Handbook of North American Indians.* Vol. 5, *Arctic*. Washington, D.C.: Smithsonian Institution, 1984.

Langdon, Steve. *The Native People of Alaska.* 3rd edition, revised. Anchorage: Greenland Graphics, 1993.

Sprott, Julie E. *Raising Young Children in an Alaskan Iñupiaq Village: The Family, Cultural, and Village Environment of Rearing*. Santa Barbara, CA: Praeger, 2003.

IRANIAN AMERICANS

Mary Gillis

OVERVIEW

Iranian Americans are immigrants or descendants of people from the country now known as the Islamic Republic of Iran in the Middle East region of Asia. The country is bounded on the north by the Transcaucasian and Turkistan territories of the former Soviet Union, along with the Caspian Sea; on the east by Afghanistan and Pakistan; on the west by Iraq and Turkey; and on the south by the Persian Gulf and the Indian Ocean. Most of Iran is an arid geographic plateau located about 4,000 feet above sea level; the plateau is spotted with mountains where the annual snowfall provides much of the water needed for irrigation during the hot spring and summer months. The country occupies 635,932 square miles (1,648,000 square kilometers), an area slightly smaller than the state of Alaska.

According to the *CIA World Factbook*, in 2012 Iran was the eighteenth most populous nation in the world, with almost 79 million people. The majority of Iran's population converted to the Islamic religion after invasion by Arab tribes in the seventh century CE. Of the 98 percent of the present-day population that is Muslim, 89 percent are members of the Shiite sect and 9 percent belong to the Sunni order. There are minority Christian, Jewish, Zoroastrian, Mandaean, and Baha'i populations as well. While 61 percent of the population is Persian, there are smaller populations of Azeris (16 percent), Kurds (10 percent), Lurs (6 percent), Balochs (2 percent), Arabs (2 percent), and Turkmen and Turkic tribes (2 percent). Iran's gross domestic product ranks just outside the top 8 percent of the countries ranked as of 2012. Approximately 45 percent of the population works in the service sector, 31 percent in industry, and about 25 percent in agriculture. The state's control of the economy—and the inefficiency of the state—hampers the growth of the private sector, which is limited to small workshops, agriculture, and services. Oil constitutes a major part of the government's revenue.

Between 1950 and 1977, about 1,500 Iranian immigrants (along with about 17,000 nonimmigrants) per year entered the United States, but the vast majority of Iran's emigrants left their homeland immediately before or during the Iranian Revolution in 1979. For the period 1978 to 1980, the average number of Iranians annually entering the United States as nonimmigrants increased to more than 100,000. Because many immigrated to the United States for social, political, and religious reasons rather than for financial opportunity, and many came with assets and education, Iranian Americans tend to be highly successful. A great number have advanced levels of education, earn substantial incomes, and work in prestigious occupations.

According to the U.S. Census Bureau's American Community Survey estimates for 2009–2011, the number of U.S. residents of Iranian descent was 464,691. Estimates by other groups are even higher. While the largest segment of Iranian Americans—48 percent—lived in California, especially in the Los Angeles metropolitan area, 7 percent lived in New York; 8 percent resided in Greater Washington, D.C., including Virginia and Maryland; and almost 7 percent lived in Texas.

HISTORY OF THE PEOPLE

Early History The ancient Persian empire, founded by Cyrus the Great in 546 BCE and carried on by Darius the Great from 522 to 486 BCE, became the largest, most powerful kingdom in the history of civilization to that point. At its peak, it encompassed lands that have since become Iraq, Pakistan, Afghanistan, Turkmenistan, Uzbekistan, Tajikistan, Turkey, Jordan, Cyprus, Syria, Lebanon, Israel, Egypt, and the Caucasus region. For the most part, Persian rulers led with love rather than fear. Cyrus issued the first declaration of human rights, banned slavery in all conquered territories, and established tolerance of other cultures and religions, and his successor, Darius, instituted a building program that resulted in a canal between the Nile River and the Red Sea and an improved road system. The superpower fell in the fourth century BCE when Alexander the Great swept through the region on his way to India. Still, the advanced Persian sciences, literature, and learning seduced the leaders of more than one invading army in the years to come.

After having a vision at the age of thirty, the Persian prophet Zarathushtra (called Zoroaster by those in the West) founded the religion of Zoroastrianism in the sixth century BCE. Unlike other religions in Iran at the time, which worshiped many gods and promoted an oppressive class structure in which princes and priests controlled the people, Zoroastrianism advocated for one supreme power and forwarded the concepts of good, evil, and judgment day. Influential to the history and culture of Persia, the ancient religion also served as the basis for the development of Judaism, and by extension, Christianity and Islam. Arabs began invading Iran during the seventh century CE, however, imposing the Islamic religion over the Iranian people. By the eleventh century the religion of Islam dominated the plateau.

Iran's strategic location, bridging the Middle East and India, has determined its history as one of invasion by foreign armies. The Mongolian emperor Genghis Khan invaded in the thirteenth century and the Turkic conqueror Timur in the fourteenth. Various native rulers controlled the region over the next centuries. The Safavids ruled from the early sixteenth century until 1736. Their founder and first ruler, Shah Ismail, tried to unify the conglomeration of loosely united tribes scattered through the land by converting them to Shiism as the state religion. During this era theologians laid the basis of Shiite theology as it is currently practiced in Iran; also, since then, Shiism has been a badge of Persian identity in the Islamic world. By the end of the eighteenth century a Turco-Iranian tribe called the Qajars ruled the area known today as Iran.

Modern Era The Qajars governed Iran until the 1920s, when Reza Shah (1878–1944) took over the government and established the Pahlavi monarchy. In 1935 he changed the country's name from *Persia* to *Iran* because *Persia* (*Pars*) was technically the name of only a single part of the entire country, while the historical name for the whole country had been *Iran*. In 1941 Reza Shah, whose sympathies leaned toward the Nazis at the start of World War II, was forced to abdicate to his son, Mohammed Reza Pahlavi (1919–1980), by Britain and the Soviet Union, which had established a presence in the country in order to block Nazi influence in the region. Some consider the first episode of the Cold War to be the Soviets' refusal to remove their troops from Iran until forced to do so by the United States and the newly formed United Nations (UN) in 1946.

Iran, which possesses as much as 10 percent of the world's oil reserves, became an even more significant player on the political scene worldwide as oil began to dominate the postwar world market. It was through its oil contacts that Iran gradually became Westernized, a process consciously accelerated during the "white revolution" of 1962–1963, when various reforms were enacted (including giving women the right to vote and to hold public office) and opposition—increasingly centered on the religious community—was suppressed.

Although Iran was officially a constitutional monarchy, in practice the shahs ruled as absolute monarchs. After 1962 Mohammad Reza Shah Pahlavi's rule became even more autocratic. The Iranian Revolution of 1979, however, toppled the Western-backed government of this second Pahlavi Shah, who had led the country for nearly four decades. At this point Iran officially became an Islamic republic governed by the laws of the Quran and the traditions of the Shiite religion as interpreted by the Ayatollah Ruhollah Khomeini (1902–1989). Khomeini was the nation's official spiritual guide (*faghi*) and leader (*rehbar*) until his death a decade after the revolution, when he was replaced by Ayatollah Ali Khamenei (1939–).

Iran experienced severe economic, social, and cultural turmoil throughout the twentieth century, particularly in the years leading up to the 1979 revolution. Since that time the country has restricted its people's freedom of religion and struggled to work out the details of its dedication to the teachings of the prophet Muhammad in everyday life and in specific government policies. The country fought an expensive border war with Iraq from 1980 to 1988 and saw several million of its wealthiest and most highly educated citizenry, who did not support the new regime or suffered persecution under its policies, immigrate to the West.

The rift between conservatives and reformists in Iran widened upon the 2009 reelection of conservative president Mahmoud Ahmadinejad (1956–). Suspecting voter fraud, supporters of reform candidate Mir-Hossein Mousavi took to the streets to protest in Iran and around the world. Although the protests in what came to be known as the Green Movement started peaceably on June 13, they grew in violence over the next few days. The government conducted a partial recount but did not annul the vote.

Iran's suspected nuclear program has led to external tensions as well. Iran started building its first nuclear reactor with Russian help in the southern Bushehr province in 1975. In 2002 U.S. president George W. Bush proclaimed Iran part of the "axis of evil" (along with Iraq and North Korea), accusing the country of developing nuclear weapons for terrorist activity. When Barack Obama succeeded President Bush in 2009, he softened the rhetoric around Iran's nuclear activities, although Washington continued to suspect Iran of developing weapons of mass destruction. President Ahmadinejad claimed that the country's nuclear ambitions were peaceful and intended for energy production only. Just two months after the UN voted to impose a fourth round of sanctions on Iran in 2010, Tehran began loading the Bushehr reactor with fuel, citing huge advances in its crusade to create nuclear energy. Tensions between Iran and the UN escalated into a UN ban of Iranian oil imports in July 2012. Although the European Union buys 20 percent of Iran's oil exports, the ban did little to slow the country's nuclear program.

SETTLEMENT IN THE UNITED STATES

The bulk of Iranian immigration to the United States occurred in two back-to-back phases: before the 1979 Iranian Revolution and after. The first phase, which

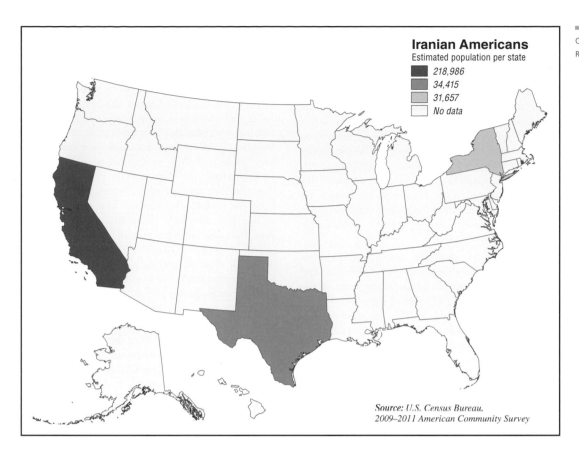

Iranian Americans
Estimated population per state

- 218,986
- 34,415
- 31,657
- No data

*Source: U.S. Census Bureau,
2009–2011 American Community Survey*

started around 1950, consisted mainly of supporters of the monarchy and college students coming to the United States to equip themselves for the oil-rich industrializing Iran. The second phase, from 1978 to the present, has been primarily exiles, political refugees, and asylum seekers, including a disproportionate number of religious and ethnic minorities such as Jews, Zoroastrians, Armenians, Assyrians, and Baha'is, all of whom suffered persecution under the Islamic regime. Young men avoiding service in the Iran-Iraq War (1980–1988) are also included in this group, as are women and families emigrating for political and educational reasons. The first phase consisted of 34,000 people; the second, 330,000, according to the Migration Policy Institute. According to the U.S. Census Bureau's American Community Survey estimates for 2006–2010, the states with the highest numbers of Iranian Americans are California, New York, Texas, Maryland, and Virginia.

The number of Iranian-born immigrants admitted to the United States peaked in 1990, when 24,977 received permission for permanent residence, according the U.S. Department of Homeland Security's *Yearbook of Immigration Statistics*. The majority settled in California, especially in Los Angeles but also in the San Francisco metropolitan area. Others moved to New York and Washington, D.C., as well as Dallas, Houston, Chicago, Boston, and Seattle. The relationship between Iranian Americans and the surrounding population since the 1979 revolution appears to be one characterized by fear and prejudice on the one side and anger and sadness on the other. Those adhering to the Islam religion in particular are often subjected to a kind of nationwide backlash that identifies all Muslims as violent fanatics or terrorists. A 2008 national public opinion survey of Iranian Americans commissioned by the Public Affairs Alliance of Iranian Americans (PAAIA) and conducted by Zogby International revealed that almost half of the Iranian Americans surveyed had either experienced or knew someone who had experienced discrimination because of their ethnicity or country of origin. Discrimination came from airport security officials and immigration officials, as well as in social and business contexts. Most Iranian Americans—85 percent—thought there needed to be greater understanding between Americans and Iranians. Despite the discrimination, foreign-born Iranian Americans are among the most highly educated and well-paid immigrant groups in the United States.

LANGUAGE

The official language of Iran is Farsi, known in the West as Persian, which combines the ancient Persian language with many Arabic words and is written with Arabic characters and script. Turkish and Turkic dialects are also spoken in several areas of Iran. The nomadic tribes that migrate vertically every spring and fall from the Zagros mountain range to the surrounding lowland plains speak a variety of other languages and dialects.

The prestige accorded those fluent in a second language—especially French or English—in Iran meant that conversations held in public or on social occasions were rarely conducted in Persian; prior to the 1979 revolution, this attitude was carried over to the American context, reflecting the long-standing Iranian fascination with Western culture. As a result, most Iranians speak English with some degree of fluency upon arrival in the United States. In fact, 80 percent of Iranian American households speak both English and Persian, and 20 percent speak exclusively English.

Anthropology professor Diane Hoffman has noted, however, that since the 1979 revolution, and thus for the majority of Iranian immigrants in the United States, the attitude toward use of the Persian language has reversed itself. This has resulted in a resurgence of interest among immigrants in traditional Persian culture and literature. Hoffman has argued that the resistance to speaking English among Iranians living in the United States indicates a renewed pride in their own cultural heritage as "a response to the twin threat to cultural identity posed by the revolutionary changes in Iran itself and the stresses of living in the United States."

Although Iranian immigrants have taken more pride in their native heritage since the revolution, their children are assimilating steadily into American society. English is becoming the main medium of communication and, although Persian remains a spoken language at home and within community settings, generations born and raised in the United States read and write it less and less even while retaining spoken fluency and cultural mores associated with the language.

Greetings and Popular Expressions Common Farsi greetings and other expressions include the following:

Salam (or, more informally, *Cheh*)—Greetings; *Khabar?*—What's new?; *Cheh khabareh?*—What's happening?; *Khoda Hafez*—Good-bye; *Loftan*—Please; *Mamnoon am*—Thank you; *Khabeli nadereh*—You're welcome; *Inshallah*—If God be willing; and *Maashallah*—May God preserve (often used with expressions of admiration or by itself to express admiration of someone).

Other expressions of admiration include: *Cheghadr ghashangeh!*—How beautiful!; *Kheili jaleheh*—Very interesting; and *Aliyeh!*—Great!

RELIGION

As in Iran, most Iranians in the United States are Muslims, the great majority associating with the Shiite rather than the Sunni faction. According to PAAIA, 40 percent of Iranian Americans identify with Islam; 20 percent identify with Christianity, Judaism, Zoroastrianism, and Baha'ism, in equal proportions; and the remaining 40 percent identify with no religion in particular. Minority religious groups in Iran often establish new religious organizations once they arrive in the United States. While some Muslims do as well, most take up practice at neighborhood mosques with Muslims from other parts of the world. Assyrian Christians from Iran and their descendants have established their own churches or share those with Assyrians from Iraq and Syria. Zoroastrians from Iran share fire temples with Zoroastrian immigrants from the Indian subcontinent. The same holds for Iranian Jews who have settled in Los Angeles, New York, Houston, and other major U.S. cities near other Jewish immigrants. Many Iranians, though, tend to be secular, while identifying with Islam for the way it has shaped the values and worldview of most everyone in their home country.

While many Shiite Iranian Americans do not necessarily attend communal religious events or services in the United States, they often do respect the Islamic creed and follow Muslim traditions during ceremonies such as wedding and funerals. On the other hand, Iranian Baha'is, Zoroastrians, Jews, and Christians tend to be more culturally and religiously conservative than their coreligionists in the United States.

CULTURE AND ASSIMILATION

Because of hostilities between the United States and Iran and the economic and social opportunities available in the United States, Iranian Americans have varying responses to their new country. Some try to assimilate to the new culture completely, aided by the fact that they tend to be educated and economically advanced, while others try to withdraw, doing their best to associate only with other Iranian Americans. Whereas foreign-born Iranian immigrants sometimes resent American pop culture, their children, born on U.S. soil, typically embrace it with much more ease and sometimes have trouble relating to the culture and memories of their parents.

Despite their tendency to assimilate, many Iranian Americans maintain strong ties to their homeland, often idealizing it and feeling a deep sense of nostalgia for it. Most consider their ethnic heritage very important, and many still have immediate family in Iran with whom they communicate several times a week or month, according to a 2009 survey by the Public Affairs Alliance of Iranian Americans. In addition, the second generation of Iranian Americans has shown a renewed interest in Iranian language and culture and has set about creating identities that incorporate both their American and Iranian heritages.

Cuisine Iranian cuisine draws heavily from the culinary traditions of ancient Persia but also includes influences from ancient Greece and Rome along with numerous other Asian and Mediterranean cultures. Traditional Iranian cooking adheres to the principles of balance and contrast. Compared with many other Middle Eastern cuisines, Iranian food contains less salt and oil and is less aggressively spiced so that no single taste dominates. It is thought that a harmonious arrangement of colors, spices, aromas, and textures strengthens the body and mind.

Rice is the staple of the Iranian diet and may be prepared simply by boiling the grains in water with salt and oil or by steaming them in such a way that a golden crust (tahdig) forms at the bottom of the pot. The tahdig is typically garnished with saffron and perhaps barberries, an acidic berry, or orange peels along with almonds or pistachios. This combination is then added to the top of the servings of rice. *Tahchin*, another of the more complex rice dishes, consists of rice, yogurt, beaten eggs, and saffron steamed with meat and either eggplant or spinach.

The main meal of the day often consists of rice with lamb and an assortment of garnishes. Chicken may be substituted for lamb, as may fish, which is especially popular in the northwestern villages by the Caspian Sea. The meat may be steamed with the rice or grilled on a skewer and served as a kabab alongside the rice. Plain white rice with skewered meat, known as *chelo kabab*, is perhaps the most common meal in the country. A more elaborate meal may include a serving of herbs and greens, known as *sabzi khordan*, or "edible greens." Sabzi khordan may include a combination of mint leaves, chives, parsley, and dill and may come with walnuts, feta cheese, and naan, a round, flat bread cooked over a bed of heated stones. Iranians also eat a thick bread called *barbari*, as well as *n-é shirm* (dough mixed with milk) and a crispier form of this bread called *n-é rhani* (dough mixed with butter). In addition to *sabzi khordan*, *dolma*, or grapes leaves stuffed with a mixture of meat and rice, is another popular side dish.

Iran is famous for *khoresh* (a word that derives from the Persian verb meaning "to eat" and refers generically to stew), the composition of which often varies according to the season. For example, *khoresh na'najafari* is a spring stew that may be seasoned with chopped mint, parsley, rhubarb, almonds, and sour grape juice. Perhaps the most famous of these stews is *khoresh fesenjan*, a fall stew consisting of a thick, dark sauce made from ground walnuts and pomegranate juice usually served with duck. In winter, eggplant and apricots may be added to this base. A plain yogurt is likely to be served with these stews.

For dessert Iranians eat a wide variety of ice creams, which may be seasoned with saffron and rosewater, and confections, which are usually moist and delicate and may be topped with glazed fruits. As with many other people in this part of the world, Iranians are fond of baklava, a pastry made from phyllo dough, sugar, and ground nuts, topped with a light syrup.

Iranian Americans tend to prefer the more carefully prepared meals of their homeland to American fare, which they often find to be bland and uninspiring. However, many Iranian Americans, especially those who arrived before the 1990s, have experienced difficulty finding the ingredients required to make an elaborate Iranian meal. With the proliferation of specialty food stores, the required ingredients are now available in many midsized and small American cities. Even so, many traditional Iranian dishes take a long time to prepare, and Iranian Americans who prefer Iranian cuisine to American food are more likely to have simple rice and kabab dishes than seasonal stews. Iranian restaurants are common in major metropolitan areas, such as New York, Los Angeles, and Washington, D.C. However, because U.S.-Iranian relations have been acrimonious since the Iranian Revolution in 1979, Iranian American restaurant and shop owners are likely to call their establishments Persian rather than Iranian.

Traditional Dress Women in Iran are required to dress extremely modestly, covering their heads and bodies with fabric as a symbol of modesty, privacy, and morality. The *hijab*—the scarf that covers a woman's hair and neck—is a controversial aspect of Islamic culture, and public conformity is often considered a signal of fluctuations in the political atmosphere. During the reign of the Westernized Pahlavi monarchy, women were discouraged from wearing the *chador* (the enveloping robe that ensures women's hair and skin are hidden from view), and among the upper and middle classes the garment came to be associated with oppression. After the revolution, although the *chador* itself was not mandated, it was required that all women appearing in public obey the dictates of modesty in covering themselves completely, including wearing the *hijab*.

Upon arrival in the United States, most Iranian women cease wearing the chadors and hijabs they wore in their home country, adopting more American ways of dressing, which offer much more freedom and choice. While most embrace a more Westernized style of dress, many maintain a sense of modesty, opting for clothes that offer more coverage than typical American styles. Their children, however, often in reaction to the more modest practices of their immigrant parents, are embracing Western clothing.

Holidays The most significant Iranian holiday is the holy month of Muharram. Muharram focuses on the seventh-century martyrdom of Hussein ibn Ali, the grandson of the prophet Muhammad, who is considered the rightful heir to the caliphate (religious leadership) by Shiite Muslims. Muharram is a period of mourning and penitence as all Shiite grieve the murder of Hussein, his family, and his followers at Karbala. The first eight days represent the period they were besieged in the desert; the eighth and ninth days of Muharram are thus the most intense days of this holiday. The tenth day, *Ashura*, is the height of the Muharram festival. Muharram is the first month

An Iranian American woman dances at the Fourth Annual Persian Parade in New York City. The parade celebrates Nowruz which means New Year in the Farsi language. The holiday symbolizes the purification of the soul and dates back to the-pre Islamic religion of Zoroastrianism. RICHARD LEVINE / ALAMY

play, reinforcing the communal feeling among the audience, and the audience interacts with the players onstage by singing along, crying, and beating their breasts in sorrow or penitence. Many Iranian immigrants to the United States observe the Muharram rites modestly and without the passion plays of their counterparts in Iran.

Held on the spring equinox in March, Nawruz—the Persian New Year—is another holiday many Iranian Americans celebrate. In Iran, Iranians cook, clean, and buy new clothes in preparation for the thirteen-day festival. They set their tables with decorations and flowers and mark certain occasions during the celebratory period with ceremonies such as jumping over a bonfire. Even if Iranians in the United States do not have the means for full-fledged Nawruz celebrations, they often take time out to remember their native country, tune in to Iranian radio and television stations, and contact loved ones from home. Nawruz remains the most cherished and widely celebrated of all holidays among Iranian Americans, irrespective of creed, background, and outlook.

FAMILY AND COMMUNITY LIFE

Although most of the Iranian population is not of Arab ethnicity, all Muslim Iranians—the vast majority of the population—share a common religious tradition with other Muslims of the Middle East, Arab and non-Arab. Muslim society in general is centered on extended family networks headed by the father. Traditionally, business and political life as well as social life have been determined by the family network. According to Helen Chapin Metz in *Iran: A Country Study*, "Historically, an influential family was one that had its members strategically distributed throughout the most vital sectors of society, each prepared to support the others in order to ensure family prestige and family status." Thus the family is at the center of the individual's economic and political as well as social and emotional life. The extended family is enlarged through marriage with other Muslims and continues through a strong tradition of family inheritance. "On the whole," says Metz, "this heritage of social grouping and family values characterized the value system of immigrant Muslims."

Iranian American families have undergone change, however, as they have become more and more assimilated in the United States. The extended family network, which traditionally provided one's social identity as well as the all-important comforts of the private domain, is often not possible for immigrants, some of whom have left most or all of their family behind. In addition, the values of the new country, where women enjoy much more freedom and equality, have undermined the male dominance in the traditional Iranian culture.

Changes in the characteristic Middle Eastern family structure in the North American context have resulted in part from the loss of power that had

of the Islamic calendar, which is a lunar calendar; so with respect to the Western Gregorian calendar, the month shifts from year to year.

Muharram festivities include processions during which banners or commemorative tombs are displayed; narrative readings are performed; and, most importantly, *ta'ziyeh* (mourning songs)—traditional plays in honor of the martyrs of Karbala—are enacted in every village. Despite the essentially religious subject matter of the ta'ziyeh plays—which traditionally depict the death of Hussein and his family or related events, such as the awful fate that awaits their assassins in the afterlife—"they are political as well as religious ceremonies during which a community reaffirms its commitment to the shared set of social values inherent in communally held religious beliefs," according to Milla C. Riggio in her 1994 essay *Ta'ziyeh in Exile: Transformations in a Persian Tradition*. Food is often shared throughout the performance of the been accorded to elders as purveyors of important cultural knowledge and to the father as head of the family. The knowledge elders possess may not be considered relevant in the context of immigration. Power relations are sometimes reversed when the second generation finds it necessary to instruct the first on various aspects of the new culture or to represent the family to the outside world due to their greater knowledge of English. Furthermore, influenced by the culture around them, members of the second generation often desire greater freedom to determine their own lives, while their elders struggle to maintain control over the family. One area that has not changed is adherence to the Islamic law to take care of the elderly when they cannot take care of themselves.

Gender Roles Women of the middle and upper classes—many of whom had adopted secular, Westernized values—were among those most affected when the conservative Islamic government came to power with the revolution in 1979. Strict enforcement of the traditional dress code might extend to flogging for violations such as wearing makeup or nail polish, even if covered by sunglasses and gloves. Throughout the 1980s the official attitude toward Iranian women, as indicated by police enforcement of the dress code through patrols and roadblocks, varied somewhat by region (women are more severely restricted in rural areas than in Teheran, the capital city) and with fluctuations in the political realm. Although Iranian women believe they are allowed more independence than women in other Middle Eastern countries, this is still far less than was accorded them before the revolution, and the inconsistency with which the laws have been applied is nerve-wracking.

Still, social change in Iran is coming about in spite of the state, according to Iranian American feminist scholar Valentine Moghadam. Although the legal and economic systems in Iran still favor men over women, Moghadam describes patriarchy in the country as "in crisis," as a feminist press proliferates and more Iranian women attend university and work outside the home (albeit at nongovernmental jobs).

In the United States, Iranian women enjoy many freedoms not accessible to them in their home country. Most Iranian American women hold more liberal views about gender roles than their counterparts in Iran, supporting equality on both the familial and societal levels, according to sociology professor Ali Akbar Mahdi ("Perceptions of Gender Roles among Female Iranian Immigrants in the United States"). They do not see gender distinctions—related to work, property ownership, childcare, decision making, and power sharing, both inside and outside their homes—as relevant to their lives, and they do not support outside forces, be they political, religious, or familial in nature, that restrict their relationships with their spouses.

A *TA'ZIYEH* FOR AMERICAN AUDIENCES

The *ta'ziyeh* is an epic religious pageant, often centered on mourning, performed in the Middle East, but most elaborately in Iran. Iranian American director Mohammed Ghaffari, however, has staged traditional ta'ziyeh plays in Europe and the United States. In her study of his adaptation, Milla C. Riggio discusses the ways in which Ghaffari has altered the plays because of the differences between American and Iranian audiences. Because his American audience could not—or would not, given the constraints of Western theater-going—verbally respond to the spectacle onstage, the play's traditional "call for vengeance against the cultural as well as religious enemies of Shi'ism" was not available to Ghaffari. Instead, the director transformed the community-affirming message of the play into a personal expression of his feelings about his own exile. This was achieved in part by altering the traditional costuming, action, and theme of the play, "which abstracted and universalized the idea of cruelty rather than localizing it in Shi'i martyrdom," argues Riggio. "Replacing the call to martyrdom with a mystical dance which affirms the beauty of his life while recognizing human cruelty, Ghaffari displaced the communal values of the *ta'ziyeh* tradition in favor of the existential experience of the isolated individual," Riggio concludes. Essentially, rather than the ta'ziyeh being represented as a passionate martyrology of Shiites versus Sunnis, Muslim Iranian Americans seek to view it as a link to their past, to their lost country, and to their Islamic faith.

The father, as head of the family, is considered responsible for the family's social, material, and spiritual welfare, and in return expects respect and obedience from his wife and children. Many women help support their families by working outside the home, and those who worship tend to do so in the mosque instead of in the privacy of their homes. "This has meant that the essentially separate worlds of Muslim men and women in the public spheres have now become fused," Azim A. Nanji remarks in his 1994 essay "The Muslim Family in North America." However, even within the Islamic Republic of Iran, women are ever-present in the workplace alongside men—albeit often, but not always, wearing the hijab—and those practices that entered Iranian society under the Pahlavi dynasty remain strong within the Muslim Iranian American community. Separation based on gender was not present in Iran for Jews, Christians, Zoroastrians, Baha'is, or Mandaeans, however, and so Iranian immigrants from those communities have no taboos against interactions between men and women.

In 1990 about 48 percent of Iranian American women living in Los Angeles worked outside the home. By 1997 even more women led more Western-style lives: they had pursued college educations and careers as professors, businesspeople, and doctors and specialists in hospitals. Sometimes traditionalists shunned these women. Still, Iranian American girls, especially of the second generation, saw the possibilities of life in the United States and wanted to take advantage of them. Some protested family rules that decreed more freedom for their brothers. For example, many Iranian American families prevented their daughters from attending college outside of their home city or state. The family pressure had the potential of being psychologically damaging. Yet some families embraced Western ways for their daughters, arguing that her potential lifetime earnings could take the place of a dowry.

Groups have sprung up to help first-generation Iranian American women with the transition to American life, especially those in a problematic marriage. Organizations such as the Coalition of Women from Asia and the Middle East offer help by providing shelters, counseling, and legal assistance to victims of domestic violence and others.

Courtship and Weddings In Iran marriage, often within the extended family network, is encouraged at a young age both officially and unofficially, and although multiple wives (as many as four) are allowed for men by Islamic law, it has often been discouraged both by the government and by the family. In addition, the Shiite religion, the predominant sect of Islam in Iran, allows the practice of temporary marriage, or *muta*. Muta is not practiced by Shiites in the United States. Iranian Muslim women are forbidden to marry non-Muslims, as it is feared the woman and her children will most certainly be lost to Islam, but Muslim men may marry non-Muslims if they are Jewish or Christian, on the assumption that the woman will convert to Islam and raise the children according to Islamic law. Iranian Americans are increasingly marrying outside their faiths and communities, and immigrant parents are finding it less likely that they will be permitted to choose the partners their children wed in the United States.

The relationship between the Iranian American population and the surrounding population since the 1979 revolution appears to be one characterized by fear and prejudice on the one side and anger and sadness on the other.

Relations with Other Americans Due to the oil shortage experienced in the United States in the 1970s, the romanticized or exotic image of the Middle East, cultivated by such fairy tales as *Aladdin and the Magic Lamp* and *Ali Baba and the Forty Thieves*, was replaced by a negative stereotype of greedy oilmen and of terrorists driven by Islamic fundamentalism, as noted in "Media Blitz" (*Scholastic Update*, October 22, 1993). When Iranian political radicals

kidnapped fifty-two Americans in 1979 and held them hostage for more than a year in the American Embassy in Teheran, Iran's capital city, anti-Iranian sentiment in the United States grew, and Americans began to associate Iranians with hate and destruction. The arrest of four Muslim immigrants for the bombing of New York City's World Trade Center in 1993 and the devastating attacks in New York City and Washington, D.C., by Islamic terrorists in 2001 further reinforced the negative stereotypes of Islamic cultures—though none of the perpetrators were Iranian. Iranian Americans by and large have little sympathy for Islamic fundamentalism of either the Sunni or the Shiite varieties.

Some Muslims blame the American media and popular culture for propagating negative stereotypes about their culture and religion. For example, Disney's popular film *Aladdin* (1992) features a Middle Eastern character who sings about cutting off ears as legal punishment and calls his homeland "barbaric." The 1984 book *Not Without My Daughter* and its 1991 movie adaptation, about an American woman and her daughter escaping from Iran, reinforce negative stereotypes by portraying Iranians as demonic. Middle Eastern critics of American popular culture point to the preponderance of Arabs or Muslims in the role of villain in movies and television shows in the late twentieth and early twenty-first centuries. Furthermore, in "Media Blitz," these critics contend that through the media's reliance on such terms as "Islamic terrorists" and "Islamic fundamentalists," Americans are encouraged to confuse the few Islamic radicals who espouse violence with the majority of the adherents of the Islamic religion, who reject violence.

EMPLOYMENT AND ECONOMIC CONDITIONS

It is common for Iranian Americans to achieve notable success both academically and professionally. According to the American Community Survey's estimates for 2009–2011, 92.2 percent of Iranian Americans over the age of twenty-five were high school graduates, and 58.7 percent reported having a bachelor's degree or higher. These figures are higher than the national average (85.6 percent and 28.2 percent, respectively). In addition, the American Community Survey indicated that Iranian Americans had higher earnings than the overall U.S. population. Iranian American men working full-time earned an average of $93,242 (while the national average was $64,502), and Iranian American women with similar employment situations earned $69,008 (while the national average was $46,560). Finally, 54.3 percent of Iranian Americans worked in management or professional occupations (compared with 35.9 percent for all Americans). Many Iranian Americans have excelled in the fields of law, medicine, education, art, the media, and sports.

POLITICS AND GOVERNMENT

Shiism has traditionally shown a disdain for both secular authority and direct involvement in political life. Iranian leaders of Twelver Shiism (*Ithna 'Ashariyah*), the dominant form of Shiism, have followed the ancient tradition of remaining separate from the world's political concerns, avoiding the ministering of justice, and seeking a spiritual victory in defeat. There is also a tradition of revolt against injustice within Shiism, however, and an inability to suffer the corruption of political figures except when to protest would put one's life in danger. This stance is known as *taqiyah* ("necessary dissimulation") and is traced back to Ali, Muhammad's son-in-law, who quietly accepted the promotion of three others to the caliphate before him in order to avoid civil war. In *The Shiites: Ritual and Popular Piety in a Muslim Community* (1992), David Pinault identifies *taqiyah* as a "guiding principle for any Shiite living under a tyrannous government too powerful to be safely resisted; one may give an external show of acquiescence while preserving resistance in one's interior, in one's heart."

Iranian Americans generally participated little in U.S. politics for more than two decades after their arrival, but in the twenty-first century they have become more and more involved in American politics, running increasingly for public office at both state and national levels. Of the 80 percent of Iranian Americans registered to vote in 2008, 50 percent were registered as Democrats, 12.5 percent as Republicans, and 25 percent as independents, according to the 2008 national public opinion survey of Iranian Americans commissioned by PAAIA and conducted by Zogby International.

Iranian Americans have become more involved in the electoral process in the twenty-first century as well. The Iranian American Political Action Committee raises money for the federal, state, and local campaigns of candidates attuned to domestic issues affecting Iranian Americans, regardless of party.

NOTABLE INDIVIDUALS

Academia Vartan Gregorian (1934–), a former university professor and president of the New York Public Library, served as president of Brown University from 1989 to 1997 before leaving to head the Carnegie Corporation of New York. He has received honorary degrees from seventy universities in the United States and received the National Humanities Medal and the Presidential Medal of Freedom, among other honors. His 2003 autobiography is titled *The Road to Home: My Life and Times.*

Business Pierre Omidyar (1967–), the founder and chairman of the eBay online auction site, was born in France to Iranian immigrants and raised in Maryland. He wrote his first computer program at the age of fourteen, graduated from Tufts University in 1988 with a degree in computer science, and worked at Claris, an Apple Computer subsidiary before starting eBay, a service that revolutionized online commerce.

Fashion Bijan Pakzad (1940–2011) was a fashion designer of exclusive men's apparel and perfumes who ran an exclusive, by-appointment boutique on

Rodeo Drive in Beverly Hills, California. He dressed a number of extremely influential people, including many heads of state.

Film Bob Yari (1961–), born in Iran and raised in New York City, produced Hollywood movies including *Where the Red Fern Grows* (2003), *Laws of Attraction* (2004), and *The Illusionist* (2006). His 2004 film *Crash* won the Academy Award for Best Picture.

Journalism Roxana Saberi (1977–), born in New Jersey to an Iranian father and a Japanese mother, is a photojournalist who made headlines when she was arrested in Iran in 2009 and charged with espionage and possessing classified information, both which she denied. She was held for five months before being released. Her 2010 book *Between Two Worlds* tells her story.

Literature Sadeq Chubak (1916–1998), considered one of the foremost modern Iranian writers, is the author of short stories, novels, and dramatic works frequently involving characters from the lowest strata of society.

Sports Andre Agassi (1970–) was a dominant professional tennis player for two decades during the 1990s and 2000s. He won his first competition in 1987 and won Wimbledon in 1992. He won numerous other Grand Slam competitions, including the U.S. Open in 1994 and the Australian Open in 1995, and he won a gold medal in the 1996 Summer Olympics. He hit a career slump in 1997, later citing a drug problem, but then made a comeback in 1999, winning the U.S. Open that year and the Australian Open numerous times. He retired from tennis in 2006.

Stage and Screen Comic actress Nasim Pedrad (1981–) joined the cast of *Saturday Night Live* in 2009. She was born in Tehran, Iran, but immigrated to the United States with her parents at the age of two. She graduated from the UCLA School of Theater in 2003 and has had roles in various movies and television shows.

MEDIA

PRINT

Asre Emrooz

An Iranian daily newspaper published in the United States.

16661 Ventura Boulevard
#112
Encino, California 91205
Phone: (818) 783-0000 or (818) 783-2829
URL: www.asreemrooz.com/Newspaper.html

Iran Nameh

A quarterly academic journal published by the Foundation for Iranian Studies.

Hormoz Hekmat, Managing Editor
4343 Montgomery Avenue
Suite 200

Bethesda, Maryland 20814
Phone: (301) 657-1990
Fax: (301) 657-1983
Email: FIS@fis-iran.org
URL: fis-iran.org

Iran Times International

A weekly newspaper in English and Farsi.

Javad Khakbaz, Editor and Publisher
2727 Wisconsin Avenue NW
Washington, D.C. 20007
Phone: (202) 659-9869
Fax: (202) 337-7449
Email: news@iran-times.com or khakbaz@iran-times.com
URL: www.iran-times.com

Iranian

A magazine focusing on art, science, philosophy, history, and cultural issues.

Jahanshah Javid, Publisher
2220 Avenue of the Stars #2301
Los Angeles, California 90067
URL: www.iranian.com

Par Monthly Journal

A monthly publication in Persian by the Par Cultural Society.

P.O. Box 703
Falls Church, Virginia 22040
Phone: (703) 533-1727
Email: Par@erols.com

Persian Heritage

Quarterly magazine published by Persian Heritage, Inc.

Shahrokh Ahkami, Editor in Chief
110 Passaic Avenue
Passaic, New Jersey 07055
Phone: (973) 471-4283
Fax: (973) 471-8534
Email: mirassiran@aol.com
URL: persian-heritage.com

RADIO

Radio Iran 670AM KIRN

Los Angeles–based Iranian radio station, with live streaming online.

Jim Kalmenson, General Manager
3301 Barham Boulevard
Suite 300
Los Angeles, California 90068
Phone: (323) 851-5476
Email: jimk@670amkirn.com
URL: www.670amkirn.com

ORGANIZATIONS AND ASSOCIATIONS

American Institute of Iranian Studies (AIIrS)

Nonprofit, nongovernmental consortium of U.S. universities and museums founded in 1967 to promote the interdisciplinary study of Iranian civilization and United States-Iran cultural dialogue.

Erica Ehrenberg, Executive Director
118 Riverside Drive
New York, New York 10024
Email: aiis@nyc.rr.com
URL: simorgh-aiis.org

Iran Freedom Foundation

The Iran Freedom Foundation (IFF) is a nonprofit
organization founded in August 1979 by Ali A.
Tabatabai and organized under the laws of the state
of Maryland. The fundamental purpose of the IFF is
to protect and enhance the human and civil rights
of Iranians and to promote the establishment of a
secular constitutional democracy in Iran.

M. R. Tabatabai, President
P.O. Box 34422
Bethesda, Maryland 20827
Phone: (301) 215-6677
or

Phone: (301) 335-7717
Fax: (301) 907-8877
Email: mrtabatabai@iffmrt.org
or

Email: mrtabatabai@comcast.net
URL: www.iffmrt.org

National Council of Resistance of Iran

A coalition of democratic Iranian organizations opposed
to the dictatorship in Iran. It organizes opposition
worldwide through diplomatic efforts and
demonstrations and strikes in Iran.

Maryam Rajavi, President-elect
URL: www.ncr-iran.org/en

Public Affairs Alliance of Iranian Americans, Inc. (PAAIA)

PAAIA is a nonprofit, nonpartisan, nonreligious
organization that advocates for Iranian Americans
on domestic issues in front of lawmakers and the
American public. It strives to promote intercultural
understanding and involve Iranians in the democratic
process at all levels.

Adrienne M. Varkiani
1614 20th Street NW
Washington, D.C. 20009
Phone: (202) 828-8370
Email: info@paaia.org
URL: www.paaia.org

MUSEUMS AND RESEARCH CENTERS

American Institute of Iranian Studies

Founded in 1967, the American Institute of Iranian
Studies is a nonprofit consortium of universities and
museums to promote the interdisciplinary study
of Iranian cultures and Iran-U.S. relations. It is the
sole organization in the United States committed to
funding Iranian studies research.

Dr. Erica Ehrenberg, Executive Director
18 Riverside Drive
New York, New York 10024

Email: aiis@nyc.rr.com
URL: www.simorgh-aiis.org

Center for Iranian Studies

Academic research center with an active publication
program. Founded in 1968 by Professor Ehsan
Yarshater, the Center sponsors or arranges art
exhibitions, film screenings, musical performances,
and occasional lectures for students, staff, and the
community, but the main focus of its activities is
an extensive program of scholarly publications and
several related projects.

Ehsan Yarshater, Director
Center for Iranian Studies
Columbia University
450 West 116th Street
New York, New York 10027
Phone: (212) 851-9150
URL: cfis.columbia.edu

Iranian Studies Group at MIT

The Iranian Studies Group at MIT conducts research on
cultural, social, economic, and political issues related
to Iranians and Iranian immigrants. The nonprofit
academic organization publishes its work to inform
public dialogue and policy regarding Iran.

Salome Siavoshi, President of the Executive Board
Iranian Studies Group
Massachusetts Institute for Technology
77 Massachusetts Avenue
Cambridge, Massachusetts 02139
Email: salome@isgmit.org
URL: isgmit.org

SOURCES FOR ADDITIONAL STUDY

Ansari, Maboud. *The Making of the Iranian Community in America*. New York: Pardis, 1992.

Hoffman, Diane M. "Language and Culture Acquisition among Iranians in the United States." *Anthropology and Education Quarterly* 20, no. 2 (1989): 118–32.

Katouzian, Homa, and Hossein Shahid, eds. *Iran in the 21st Century: Politics, Economics & Conflict*. New York: Routledge, 2008.

Kelley, Ron, ed. *Irangeles: Iranians in Los Angeles*. Berkeley: University of California Press, 1993.

Mahdi, Ali Akbar. "Perceptions of Gender Roles among Female Iranian Immigrants in the United States." In *Women, Religion and Culture in Iran*, edited by Sarah Ansari and Vanessa Martin, 185–210. London: Curzon, 2001.

Metz, Helen Chapin, ed. *Iran: A Country Study*. Washington, D.C.: U.S. Government, 1989.

Moossavi, Homayoon. "Teheran Calling." *Progressive* 52, no. 4 (1988): 34.

Nanji, Azim A. "The Muslim Family in North America." In *Family Ethnicity: Strength in Diversity*, edited by H. P. McAdoo, 229–42. Newbury Park, CA: Sage, 1993.

Pinault, David. *The Shiites: Ritual and Popular Piety in a Muslim Community*. New York: St. Martin's, 1992.

IRAQI AMERICANS

Mary C. Sengstock and Sanaa Al Harahsheh

OVERVIEW

Iraqi Americans are immigrants or descendants of people from the nation of Iraq, which is a member of the League of Arab States. Iraq was founded in 1920 by the League of Nations and includes territories of the former Ottoman Empire. On the west, Iraq is bordered by Jordan and Syria; on the south, by Kuwait and Saudi Arabia; on the east, by Iran; and on the north, by Turkey. At 166,859 square miles (432,160 square kilometers), the area of Iraq is approximately the size of the state of California.

According to the *CIA World Factbook*, the population of Iraq in 2012 was 31.1 million. Most Iraqis are Muslim, with about 60 percent belonging to the Shia branch of Islam and about 35 percent belonging to the Sunni branch. The majority of the population is Arab, but Kurds make up a large ethnic minority in the northern part of country. The Kurds trace their origins to the ancient Medes, whose original homeland was in Persia (now Iran), and as a result Kurds generally do not identify themselves either as Arabs or Iraqis. Iraq's economy is largely dependent upon the petroleum industry. Agriculture and textiles are also important in the economy, even though much of the terrain is arid and only about 13 percent of the land is available for agriculture. The economy was negatively impacted by the Gulf Wars, and according to the *CIA World Factbook* about one-fourth of the Iraqi population is believed to be living below the poverty line.

Iraqis have been immigrating to the United States since the early twentieth century, with many of the earliest immigrants settling in the area of Detroit, Michigan, in communities where others from the Middle East had already settled. Although the predominant religion in Iraq is Islam, the majority of early Iraqi immigrants were Chaldean Christians, who sought opportunities for economic advancement and a setting more conducive to practicing their Christian faith. There was a substantial increase in the number of Iraqi immigrants in the last decade of the twentieth century and the first decade of the twenty-first century, largely because of the turmoil in Iraq due to the Gulf Wars.

According to the 2010 U.S. Census, there were 105,981 people in the United States who reported having Iraqi ancestry, a number comparable to the population of Green Bay, Wisconsin. However, the Arab American Institute (AAI) estimates the actual Iraqi American population to be significantly larger—possibly up to 60 percent higher than this number, as U.S. Census data has historically not accounted for the entire Arab American population. Areas with a significant number of Iraqi Americans include Detroit and Dearborn, Michigan; Turlock and San Diego, California; Phoenix, Arizona; and Chicago. Other states with small, but significant, populations of Iraqi Americans are Texas and New York.

HISTORY OF THE PEOPLE

Early History Iraq lies in a region sometimes referred to as Mesopotamia, which refers to the area between the Tigris and Euphrates rivers. The region is also known as the "cradle of civilization," because it was home to early civilizations of antiquity. Prior to the Common Era, Mesopotamia was occupied at various times by Sumerians, Babylonians, Assyrians, Chaldeans, Akkadians, and Jews. The Bible reports that Abraham was from Ur, a city settled by the Chaldean people. In the first century after the death of Christ, the area was reportedly visited by his apostles and disciples, converting many of its inhabitants to the new religion. In the seventh century CE, most residents of the area were converted to Islam by the Prophet Muhammad. After Muhammad's death, there were disputes concerning who would be the key leaders of Islam. Followers of Muhammad known as the Sunni believed that caliphs (Arabic for "successors") should be elected to succeed him. Another group of Muhammad's followers, the Shia, believed that the leadership should be drawn from the family of Muhammad. In 680 CE, the two groups came to blows in the battle of Karbala, a city in what is now southern Iraq. The leader of the Shia (Hussein ibn Ali, grandson of Muhammad) and several of his followers were killed. Today they are viewed as martyrs by the Shia, who observe a period of intense grieving each year on the anniversary of the battle.

In the sixteenth and seventeenth centuries, the area that is now Iraq was part of the Ottoman Empire, which covered an extensive area in eastern and southern Europe as well as the Middle East. In the mid-nineteenth century, the Ottoman Empire faced a considerable loss of its power. During this period, there was increased European interest, particularly

THE NEW IRAQI FLAG

Following the establishment of the new Iraqi government, there was considerable controversy over the character of the Iraqi flag. Since 1963 the flag had consisted of four colors: red, black, white, and green, the colors of the pan-Arab movement. Following the second phase of the Iraq War, there was a movement to change the flag in radical ways, replacing the colors with blue, yellow, and white; there was general public dissatisfaction with this plan. In 2008 a new flag was developed. Largely a modification of previous flags, it consists of three horizontal bands of red, white, and black. In the white band, the *takbir*, a phrase meaning "God is great," appears in green Arabic letters.

by the British Empire, in exerting economic and political influence in the area. Britain encouraged British Christian missionaries to attempt to convert the Muslims in the area to Christianity. After World War I, following the defeat of the Ottoman Empire, the area became a protectorate of the British government. At that time, the British government estimated the population at about three million. Most of the population was Muslim, divided between Sunni and Shia. About 15 to 20 percent were Kurdish, and Christians, Jews, and other religions together constituted about 5 percent.

Modern Era Iraq became an independent nation by action of the League of Nations in 1932. In 1948, after World War II, Israel was created from portions of Palestine—an action that had a dramatic impact on the Arab Middle East. Non-Jewish Palestinians were displaced, which caused anger and resentment in the Arab world. The Ba'th Party, which promoted unifying the Arab world, grew in prominence in Syria and eventually other places in the Middle East, including Iraq. Saddam Hussein, representing the Ba'th Party, came to power in Iraq in 1968. In the early 1970s he fought against Kurdish rebels, who for a time received aid from Iran. In 1980 Iraq went to war against Iran, and the ensuing eight-year conflict produced little gain for either country.

In 1990 Iraq invaded the petroleum-rich country of Kuwait to its south. Western countries, including the United States, felt compelled to support Kuwait and, in a conflict known as the First Gulf War, succeeded in expelling Iraq from Kuwait. The conflict's aftermath for Iraq was severe. The United Nations Security Council imposed trade and financial restrictions against Iraq, which led to extreme poverty, food shortages, and inadequate health services, as well as increased tensions among Iraqi ethnic minorities. With the onset of the Second Gulf War, in 2003, the crisis only increased. The West, led by the United States, sought to ensure

that Iraq had no weapons of mass destruction or any other mechanisms that might support terrorism. Although no weapons of mass destruction were found, Saddam Hussein and the Iraqi military were defeated, destabilizing the country. Saddam Hussein was arrested in 2004 for crimes against humanity and, following his conviction, executed in 2006.

Refugees from Iraq reported severe limits on food and medicine and a lack of clean water. Death rates increased dramatically, particularly in children. Although a degree of stability was achieved in 2010 when a new Iraqi government was established, the importance of adequately representing Iraq's three major religious and ethnic groups—Sunni, Shia, and Kurds—in the government continued to be a concern. Some segments of the Iraqi Parliament believed that religious and ethnic divisions would remain a problem, in part because there were no provisions for the smaller minorities, particularly Christians, Jews, and Turkomen. From the invasion of Iraq on March 20, 2003 to Iraq's reconstruction, declared December 21, 2010, Kurds had hoped for the establishment of a separate Kurdish state, a dream that was never realized.

SETTLEMENT IN THE UNITED STATES

Iraqi immigration to the United States began in the earliest decades of the twentieth century, when residents from Telkaif, a village near the city of Mosul in the northern province of Ninewah, made their way to the United States. This northern area of Iraq differs from other segments of the country in that it is populated primarily by members of two Iraqi minorities: the Kurdish ethnic group and Christians. The village of Telkaif is predominantly Christian—specifically of a specific ritual group of the Catholic Church called the Chaldean rite. This group also differs from the majority of Iraqis in that their ancestral language is Chaldean rather than Arabic. Thus, uncharacteristic of the greater Iraqi population, the initial wave of Iraqi immigrants was predominantly Christian.

U.S. Census data for 2010 lists 105,981 persons reporting Iraqi ancestry, an increase of 16,089 over the 89,892 listed in the 2000 census. The 2010 population was more than double the number reported in the 1990 U.S. Census (44,916). This jump was largely a result of the turmoil in Iraq following the two Gulf Wars, but it also reflects the impact of the 1965 changes in U.S. immigration law that eliminated the national-origins quota system. It should be noted, however, that accurate data on the number of Iraqis in the United States is difficult to obtain, because the U.S. Census categories are not worded in a manner likely to elicit a response from all Iraqis. These include primarily Chaldean and Assyrian Christians, as well as Jews and Kurds, most of whom do not identify either as Iraqis or as Arabs. Making use of numbers from the individual Iraqi communities provides a much larger figure for the number of Iraqis in the United States. For example, in 2009 the largest Iraqi immigrant community, the Chaldeans, estimated their total numbers (including both immigrants and American-born) at 150,000, while the entire Iraqi American population in the United States has been estimated at 245,000 to 265,000.

The earliest immigrants from Iraq originally settled in Detroit around 1910. Others from the Middle East—Catholic immigrants from Lebanon, called Maronites—had already begun to settle there. Chaldean Iraqis continued to move into the Detroit area during the early years of the twentieth century. However, once the United States government imposed the quota system on immigration in the 1920s, the number of immigrants from Iraq who could be admitted was limited to one hundred a year; consequently, Iraqi immigration was slow. During this period, some members of Iraq's dominant Muslim group immigrated to the United States, but their number was less than that of Iraqi Christians because the quota system favored people who had relatives in the United States.

Migration from Iraq largely ceased during World War II. It increased after the war and Iraqis could come to the United States with a student visa. Again, Chaldeans continued to have an advantage because of their existing ties in the United States. Many Chaldean immigrants were able to marry members of the Chaldean community and remain as permanent residents. Other Iraqis did not have this advantage. By the early 1960s the Chaldean community contained about three thousand members.

The most dramatic increase in immigration from Iraq occurred following the passage of the Immigration and Nationality Act of 1965. This law made immigration easier, particularly for nations that had exceptionally small quotas, such as Iraq, and had not yet established a sizable presence in the United States. Immigration from Iraq increased, which led to major growth in Detroit's Chaldean community. Many Muslim Iraqis came to the United States at this time as well. In the late twentieth century and early twenty-first century, the unrest in Iraq led other Iraqi religious and ethnic groups to seek emigration. This was particularly true of the Shia and Kurdish populations, both of which reported suffering discrimination at the hand of Iraq's dominant Sunni leadership.

Once in the United States, Iraqi immigrants tend to move into the areas where others from their religious groups have settled. Chaldean Iraqis tend to move into the Detroit Chaldean community or other Chaldean communities, primarily in Turlock and San Diego, California; Phoenix, Arizona; and Chicago. Muslim Iraqis are often attracted to Detroit area as well, thanks to the large Middle Eastern Islamic community in Dearborn, a suburb of Detroit. The few Jewish Iraqis who have immigrated tend to move into Jewish communities, primarily in New York and California. Texas is another state in which a significant population of Iraqi Americans exists.

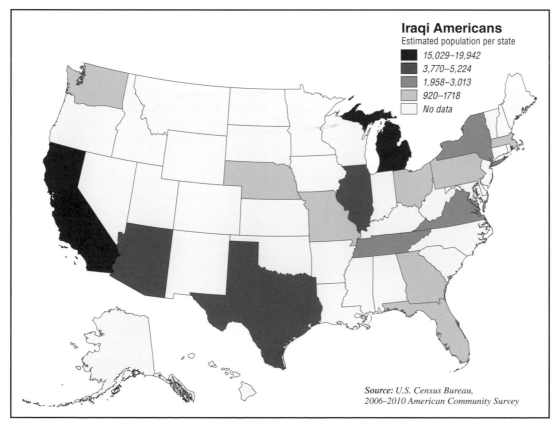

Iraqi Americans
Estimated population per state

- 15,029–19,942
- 3,770–5,224
- 1,958–3,013
- 920–1718
- No data

Source: U.S. Census Bureau, 2006–2010 American Community Survey

LANGUAGE

Most Iraqi immigrants speak Arabic, the national language of Iraq, and for Muslim Iraqi Americans this is usually the language of choice. However, the Christian minorities also speak a dialect of Aramaic that they call Chaldean or Assyrian. This is the language Jesus spoke during his life, a matter of great pride to the group. If Christian Iraqi Americans wish to teach their children their ethnic language, it is likely to be Chaldean or Assyrian, not Arabic. Similarly, since Jewish Iraqi Americans generally merge into the broader American Jewish community, they tend to use English rather than Arabic and would consider Hebrew their historic language.

English is becoming the language of choice for the children born in the United States to Iraqi immigrants, and its use is increasing in most Iraqi homes. Iraqi immigrants, particularly male immigrants, tend to learn English quickly in order to work in American society. Immigrant married women who stay at home may take longer to learn English but most soon learn to speak it to communicate with their children. However, in predominantly Arabic communities, such as Dearborn, Michigan, and other sections of the Detroit area with large Arabic-speaking populations, numerous business and public enterprises, including health and social service facilities, provide signs and other information in Arabic. Local schools offer classes in English as a second language for children whose first language is Arabic. Local universities and community colleges have also introduced the Arabic language as a subject for study.

RELIGION

The vast majority of Iraq's population is Muslim, most of whom (about 60 percent) belong to the Shia sect. Although members of the Sunni sect constitute only about 35 percent of Iraqis, they are the group that has typically held power in the public sphere. The remaining 5 percent of the population is made up of other religious denominations, including Christians and Jews. Iraqi Americans of each religious group tend to congregate with members of their respective religions rather than congregating together as a distinct Iraqi settlement. Thus the religious traditions of Iraqi Americans must be discussed within each of the respective religious subgroups.

The Islamic tradition established by Muhammad in the seventh century is based on the belief in one God, with Muhammad as his prophet. Followers of Islam believe they are descended from the Prophet Abraham, through Ishmael, his son by Hagar. Muslims have recorded the teachings of Muhammad in their holy book, the Quran. There are five major tenets, known as the Five Pillars of Islam: belief in the One God; need to pray often; requirement to fast; giving alms to the poor; and making a pilgrimage, called the *hajj*, to the Holy City of Mecca. Muslims pray five times each day. Fasts in the Islamic religion are particularly rigorous, requiring complete abstention from food and drink, even water, from sunup to sundown during the holy month of Ramadan. According to Muslim tradition, religion is not to be separated from other aspects of life but should permeate all of human activity.

Muslim Iraqi immigrants tend to move into heavily Islamic communities, such as Dearborn, Michigan, which has a number of mosques and other Islamic community organizations, several of them established specifically for Iraqi Muslims. The Sunni and Shia sects of Islam are not clearly distinct, so observant Muslims can practice their faith in any mosque. This is true in both Iraq and the United States.

Although Islam is the major religion in Iraq by far, the largest group of Iraqi American immigrants has been those who follow the Roman Catholic Chaldean rite. Chaldeans were among the earliest immigrants from Iraq to the United States. They sought economic advancement and freedom to practice their Christian faith. Chaldeans have established a Detroit-area Chaldean diocese that has seven churches. Most are located in the northern section of Detroit and in nearby Oakland and Macomb counties. Other Christian Iraqis have moved into communities in New York, California, and Illinois. Their presence in the western United States has led to the development of an additional diocese, located in San Diego, for the western states. Iraqi American Chaldean church leaders estimate their group's membership at approximately 150,000, based on requests for church membership and for church services such as weddings and funerals.

Chaldean religious traditions and beliefs are similar to those of other Catholics. They consider the Pope of Rome to be the head of their church. Mass is their basic religious ceremony, and they follow the same rituals for baptism, Holy Communion, weddings, and funerals. A major difference is the language used in the rituals. Most ritual services of the Chaldean rite make use of the Chaldean (Assyrian) language, a modern-day variant of Aramaic. In recent years, some services have been translated into Arabic and English to make them more understandable to Arab-speaking and English-speaking Chaldeans. Chaldean Iraqi Americans have established several churches to provide the community with the special Chaldean services. However, for routine religious services, such as weekly Mass, many Chaldean Iraqi Americans often go to services at the nearest Catholic church.

Many Iraqi Jews who fled Iraq moved to Israel, but there are an estimated 15,000 Jewish Iraqi Americans. Jewish Iraqis moving into the United States have largely settled into Jewish communities scattered throughout the country, but the majority live New York and California. Three specific congregations have been established to honor Iraqi Jews' historical ties to the ancient settlement of Jews in Babylon; these congregations conduct services according to ancient Babylonian Jewish practice. Many would consider

An Iraqi American woman, with her brother (center) and husband, prepare a fish for a picnic in Anthem, Arizona, in 2013. THE WASHINGTON POST / GETTY IMAGES

them to belong to the Sephardic branch of Jewry. Like other Iraqi Americans, Jewish Iraqi Americans have largely merged into the larger population of their religious tradition in the United States.

CULTURE AND ASSIMILATION

Iraqi American traditions and practices vary along religious lines and must be reviewed within each of these groups: Muslim, Christian, and Jewish. However, it should also be noted that members of some of these groups do not generally identify with Iraq, the Iraqi people, or the Arabic culture. Arab Muslims from Iraq, both Sunni and Shia, generally identify themselves as Iraqis. Christians from Iraq are more likely to identify themselves by means of their religious denomination or with the ancient Babylonian or Chaldean culture. Iraqi American Jews identify with the Jews of the Babylonian period in the sixth century BCE. And Iraqi immigrants of Kurdish ancestry are more likely to identify with the Kurdish language and culture, which crosses the borders of several nations in western Asia and the Middle East, including Iraq. Some customs appear to be common to all Iraqis, however. For example, some of the favorite dishes prepared by Iraqis, such as *dolma* and *kibbeh*, are enjoyed by members of each of the religious groups, with modifications to eliminate pork for Muslims and Jews, and alcohol for Muslims. The traditional dress formerly worn by Iraqis is common to Muslims, Christians, and Jews. Also, brides in all subgroups seem to share a common tradition of *Lilat al-henna*, or decorating their bodies with henna dye prior to the wedding.

Traditions and Customs The extended family is the central dimension of life for all Iraqis. Life revolves around the family, and protection of the family and its honor is essential. Equally important to most Iraqis is their respective religious tradition. Hence the most important events in life are carried out in the context of the family and the specific group's religion. In all religious groups, weddings and the birth or education of children are important events calling for great celebration.

In the Islamic community, the first religious tradition a male child will experience is circumcision, which occurs as soon as possible after birth. An important tradition for both boys and girls focuses on imparting knowledge of the Quran, the Islamic holy book, to the children. The training process, called *al-Khitma*, begins when the child is between nine and twelve years old. The child in the class who learns to read the text most effectively is honored with the title *hafiz*, which means "memorizer," and the family usually holds a celebration to recognize the child's achievement.

Other important Islamic traditions accompany the holy month of Ramadan, a month of prayer and repentance to draw believers closer to God. Ramadan occurs in the ninth month of the Islamic calendar. During this month Muslims are required to abstain from all food and drink from sunup to sundown.

Iraqi Christians follow the customs of the Christian churches. Shortly after birth, babies are baptized, and the event involves a great family and community celebration. Chaldean Catholic children receive their first communion around seven or eight years of age—this is another cause for a large family celebration. Weddings are substantial affairs, with a large church ceremony and a subsequent celebration for the extended family and community as a whole. Often, hundreds of family and community members attend these events.

Similarly, the important traditions of Iraqi Jews focus on religious events. Weddings follow traditional Jewish patterns. As with Muslims, the circumcision of a baby boy is an occasion of great celebration. In the Jewish faith, circumcision takes place eight days after birth. Jewish children become adults in the eyes of God when they become bar mitzvahs (in the case of boys) or bat mitzvahs (in the case of girls) at age thirteen. One of the requirements for becoming a bar mitzvah is learning to read Hebrew and reading from the Torah during a synagogue service. Their presentation at the synagogue is an occasion of great celebration in the family and community.

On a more secular level, Iraqi men often gather at coffeehouses or tea houses in Iraq, where they share beverages, smoke the hookah (water pipe), and share conversation. This tradition has been carried over to U.S. communities as well. In both countries these social groups tend to be divided along religious lines. Hospitality and generosity are also important Iraqi traditions. Visitors must be welcomed and treated royally. Islamic tradition actually states that guests must be allowed to stay for three days before they can be questioned about their long-range plans. When visitors are invited, they are expected to view this as a great honor; refusals are considered an insult. Throughout the year, but especially during the holy month of Ramadan, Muslims are required to exhibit generosity to those less fortunate by giving alms, or *zakat*.

Cuisine There are certain types of dishes that are recognized as distinctively Middle Eastern, and among these there are some that are distinctively Iraqi. These dishes are typically made by all of the various religious groups, with certain alterations made to adapt them to use by Muslims, Christians, and Jews. For instance, Muslims and Jews make the same dishes as Christian Iraqis, but they ensure that the animals are slaughtered and their meat prepared in the proper manner (called *halal* by Muslims, *kosher* by Jews), and they do not use any pig products. Muslims abstain from alcohol, while Christians and Jews typically do not.

Rice is served with most dishes. Lamb and beef are popular. Many vegetables are used, such as green beans, peas, okra, cauliflower, and eggplant. Chickpeas are also popular, particularly in the form of *hummus*, a dish in which the chickpeas are ground into a smooth paste and mixed with olive oil, *tahini* (made with sesame seeds), and lemon juice. The *hummus* is served as a dip for pita bread or sometimes spread on sandwiches. *Dolma* is a dish made with grape leaves, which

are stuffed with a meat and spice mixture. Cabbage and green peppers can be stuffed with the same mixture. *Kibbeh* is another popular dish among Iraqis. It is made with ground beef or lamb mixed with bulgur wheat and spices. Typical Arabic *kibbeh* is formed into balls or triangles and fried, whereas Iraqi *kibbeh* is formed into a flat pie before cooking. A similar dish, called *kubbeh*, is made by Iraqi Jews. The Arab shish-kebab dish, made with cubes of meat and vegetables and grilled on a skewer, is also enjoyed in Iraq. Iraqis make various desserts from phyllo dough and honey, often containing dates and pistachios or other nuts. *Caleche* is a cookie made with dates or walnuts and formed into a crescent or diamond shape.

Each Iraqi religious group serves special foods at their respective religious holidays. Muslims serve special foods for use in breaking the rigorous fast followed during the holy month of Ramadan. Typically these are high in carbohydrates to counter the low blood sugar that may accompany fasting. Dates are particularly important during Ramadan, not only due to their high carbohydrate content but also because Muhammad is said to have used dates to break his fast. For Christmas, some Iraqi Christians prepare a special dish, called *pacha*, made with tripe and intestines. Jews ensure that meals prepared during Passover have no traces of wheat or other grains.

In the United States, even second- and third-generation Iraqi Americans consume many of these traditional foods, but all have also adopted a wide variety of American foods as well. Additionally, Iraqi cuisine has become popular to American tastes. Numerous restaurants all over the country provide Iraqi or other Middle Eastern food. A restaurant in southeast Michigan has even introduced an annual event each spring, honoring Iraqi Jewry and serving Iraqi Jewish food.

Traditional Dress Traditional clothing in Iraq reaches across religious and ethnic lines, with similar items being worn by Muslims, Jews, Kurds, and Christians. Traditional garb for Iraqi men is a long robe, reaching to the ankles, called a caftan. It is worn with a cloth wrapped around the head similar to a turban or tied with a cord. Today, most men in urban areas of Iraq have adopted Western dress. Iraqi women wear long robes that cover them from head to toe. For Muslim women, the long robe, called an *abaya*, is still worn with a *hijab* (veil) that covers the head and face to abide by the Islamic requirement that women exhibit modesty when outside the home. Beneath their robes and veils, they wear normal dress. Veils are removed when at home or in female-only settings. Muslim women are more likely to continue the traditional dress patterns, but Iraqi women from other religions—and some Muslim women—have largely discarded the traditional style of dress.

In the United States, men wear Western-style clothing, and nearly all Christian and Jewish Iraqi American women have adopted Western-style clothes.

The pattern among Muslim Iraqi American women is mixed; some continue to wear traditional clothing, particularly the *hijab*, while others have adopted Western clothing styles.

Traditional Arts and Crafts Iraqi art is based on Islamic tradition and has been known for its beauty since before the creation of Iraq as a nation. Achievements have been made in ceramics, carpets, panting, calligraphy, glass, and Islamic-style fashion design. Since Islamic custom prohibits the visual depiction of human or animal forms, Islamic art has developed along the lines of calligraphy (decorative lettering) and the presentation of intricate geometric and floral patterns. The Arabic language, in its written form, is particularly well adapted to artistic presentations. Iraqi artisanship is particularly notable in the architecture of the Iraqi mosques, which are beautifully decorated. Iraqi artistic work can also be seen in its handicrafts, including jewelry, rugs, blankets, leather, and pottery. There is some indication that Iraqi arts and crafts are also being carried out by Iraqi American immigrants. However, such instances are few and far between, due to the pressures of adapting to a new environment.

Dances and Songs Music and dance are important customs in the culture of Iraq and often are present at weddings, parties, and other social events. Iraqis are known in the Middle East for their unusual music, including a fiddle-like instrument called a *rebab* and a wind instrument called an *oud*. Performers base their work on one of several melodic patterns, or *maqams*, many of which are derived from Arabic poetry, particularly poetry of the Abbasid Empire in Baghdad in the sixth through thirteenth centuries CE. Iraqi songs are usually performed in Arabic, although some of the traditional songs use lyrics from other languages of the area, including Aramaic, Armenian, Hebrew, Kurdish, Persian, or Turkish. Chaldeans and other Iraqi Christians may perform them in their historic Aramaic language. Many songs focus on either love or war and tell of the history of Iraq and its people. The *pesteh*, a kind of light song in the *maqam* pattern, gained popularity in the late twentieth century with the rise of recorded music and radio broadcasts. Performance arts, such as music festivals including the Babylon International Music and Arts Festival, have been important in Iraq. However, economic conditions following the Gulf Wars have made such festivals scarce.

A line dance (called *chobi*, or *dabke* in Arabic) is the most popular dance among Iraqi Muslims and in Iraq as a whole. Chaldeans also perform a line dance, called *khiga*, as do Iraqi Jews—the *horah*—although the horah's origins are in eastern Europe and Israel rather than Iraq. Today English dance music and songs and Western musical instruments have been adopted and are a part of many Iraqi parties, weddings, and other functions in Iraq and the United States. Although many Iraqi Americans now prefer Western music, the traditional Iraqi line dances, songs, and instruments are still used by some Iraqi Americans of all religions.

Holidays Holidays for Iraqis, both in Iraq and in the United States, tend to be centered around the faith traditions of each specific religion. There are two major holidays (referred to as *Eid*) for Iraqi Muslims, both tied to the Islamic faith. Eid al-Fitr is the celebration that brings the month-long fast of Ramadan to a close. The celebration continues for three days. The other major holiday is Eid al-Adha (the Festival of Sacrifice), which occurs at the end of the month in which Muslims traditionally make the *hajj*, or pilgrimage to the holy city of Mecca. In both festivals, families hold feasts and may share the food with the poor, one of the major requirements of Islam. Other Islamic commemorations are the Islamic New Year, which occurs at the beginning of the month of Muharram and is typically recognized with quiet prayer and reflection; Mawlid al-nabi, the Prophet Muhammad's birthday (the twelfth day of the Islamic month of Rabi I); and Eid al-Isra wa al-Miraj, the commemoration of the Prophet Muhammad's visit to heaven, occurring on Rijab 27 (in July). Another important commemoration, observed only by Shia Muslims, is Ashura, which gives believers the opportunity to recall the massacre of Muhammad's grandson Hussayn and his followers in 680 CE; Ashura occurs on Muharram 10 (in January). Muslim Iraqi Americans generally continue to commemorate these festivals.

Like other Christians, Iraqi Christians celebrate Christmas and Easter. These holidays are celebrated with religious services in the church and large feasts for the extended family, with numerous traditional foods. Iraqi Christians also observe the penitential season of Lent, which precedes the feast of Easter. Lenten fasts for Iraqi Christians tend to be more rigorous than the traditional fasts for American Christians. Major holidays for Iraqi Jews are similar to those of Jews as a whole, primarily Rosh Hashanah (the Jewish new year) and Yom Kippur in the fall; and Pesach (Passover) in the spring. Both religions also have numerous minor holidays as well.

Health Care Issues and Practices Iraq had a highly advanced system of health care in 1970s and 1980s. Because it was established on a system of socialized medicine, Iraqi health care was generally free. However, sanctions imposed on the nation after the First Gulf War—sanctions that restricted the import of any commodities that might be used in the production of weapons—prevented Iraqi hospitals and physicians from getting necessary equipment and medicine. This radically changed the medical situation. Sanctions also limited the import of chemicals and equipment needed to purify Iraq's water supply. In the early 1990s the number and types of diseases began to rise dramatically due to the residue from radioactive chemicals introduced to the area during the First Gulf War. The frequency of cancer, hypertension, birth defects, and other diseases increased. The cost of medicine rose as a consequence of the conflict, and as medicine became more expensive to make, the quality declined. As a result, some Iraqis turned to herbal medicine.

Iraqi immigrants often suffer from conditions that could not be treated under the conditions existing in Iraq. They may also suffer from various mental health conditions, such as post-traumatic stress disorder, as a result of the wars and their aftermath. Numerous immigrants have also lived in refugee camps under extremely brutal conditions.

Iraqi immigrants face a dramatic change in the health care system when they come to the United States. In Iraq they were used to going to the doctor or hospital and being taken care of—they are not familiar with the U.S. requirement for physician prescriptions for medications, problems of waiting for care, the need for insurance, and other complications of American health care. They are not used to the idea that insurance is necessary or commonly tied to one's employment, and many do not gain immediate employment. Therefore many Iraqi Americans lack proper health care in the United States.

Death and Burial Rituals Death rituals among Iraqis follow the traditions of each respective religious group. Islamic funerals, which are called *janazah* in Arabic, follow specific rites. Funerals are generally the same for everyone, rich or poor. When a Muslim passes away, the death is announced to relatives and friends by the deceased's immediate relative. Family gathers for a last farewell before the deceased is taken to the mosque. According to *sharia* (Islamic religious law), Muslims are supposed to be buried on the day following their death. The burial is preceded by a simple ritual involving bathing and shrouding the body, followed by a prayer, or *salah*. Cremation is forbidden in Islamic tradition. Neither do Muslims believe in viewing the body. Muslim Iraqi American follow the same rites. However, in the United States, funeral directors who follow Islamic tradition typically provide the services the family would have provided in Iraq. During the funeral, female family members dress in black, without makeup. After the burial, relatives, neighbors, and friends gather to console the family of the deceased, offering ritual expressions of sorrow and sympathy. Usually, friends and relatives help provide breakfast, lunch, and dinner for everyone. This mourning period usually lasts for three days.

Christian burials are similar to those of other Christians in the United States. The death is announced to relatives and friends by the next of kin. In the Chaldean liturgy, the body is washed and prepared for burial while priests and deacons prepare for the church service. In the United States, funeral homes generally handle the preparation that would be provided by the family in Iraq. The Chaldean funeral service takes place in church. It includes a Mass and goes on for an extended period. The body is then taken to the cemetery, where an additional religious service usually takes place. Following the services, family and friends gather to console the family. Mourning usually lasts for three days. Women traditionally wear black clothing and engage in loud wailing. Additional memorial services usually are held on the fortieth day after the death as well as on the first anniversary following the death.

Iraqis Jews follow the traditional patterns for Jewish funerals. Those present at the death immediately say the traditional prayer for the dead, known as the mourner's prayer (*kaddish*), and relatives rend their garments (*keriah*). Burial takes place as soon as possible, preferably on the actual day of death, although modern-day logistics mean that rarely happens. Cremation, autopsy, embalming, and public viewing are considered violations of the body and are forbidden. Rather than being held in a synagogue, funerals were formerly were held at home. In the United States, funeral homes that follow Jewish practice generally fulfill the rites. Following the funeral, family members gather at home for a formal period of mourning (*shivah*) that lasts seven days. Visitors come to express their sympathy.

Recreational Activities Iraqi Americans generally participate in the same recreational activities as other Americans: baseball, basketball, football, and other sports and games played in the United States. School sport teams in the Dearborn, Michigan, area, where many Muslim Iraqis live, have even adopted modified schedules for practices to accommodate the rigors of the Ramadan fast for Muslim youth. Some immigrants retain recreational activities brought from Iraq. First-generation immigrants play *tawlee*, a board game similar to backgammon, but this tradition does not seem to have been passed down to subsequent generations. Smoking the hookah, a water pipe, is another recreational practice brought from Iraq.

FAMILY AND COMMUNITY LIFE

For all Iraqis, regardless of religion, the family is the most important social institution. Loyalty to the family is critical, and family honor must be preserved at all cost. It is highly improper to speak ill of the family or reveal negative family matters to outsiders. Family is understood in a broad sense; it consists of all relatives, including parents, grandparents, children, grandchildren, siblings, aunts and uncles, and cousins. In Iraq the strength of family was often displayed in the traditional family household, in which a man, his wife, and their children shared a home with grandparents, unmarried sisters, and often the eldest son and his family. In the United States, it is less common for the extended family to live together in one house. However, frequent contact with extended family members, as well as shared

IRAQI PROVERBS

Proverbs tend to be characteristic of the different cultural subgroups in Iraq. The following are examples of Iraqi proverbs in (phonetic) Arabic:

Min shaf ahbaba, nisa ashaba.

When he sees his lovers, he forgets about friends.

Yigtil il mayit, w yimshi bjanaztu.

He kills the victim and attends his funeral.

Illi faat maat.

The thing that has passed is dead.

Sabi'a Sanaayi'a, wil bakhit dhaayi'a.

Seven jobs but no fortune.

Huwa naayim, w rijleih bil shamis.

Sleeping but his legs are in sun.

Lmbal lil ma ykhaaf mnil matar.

The soaked do not fear rain.

Lbaab illi yijiik mina lriih, sida w istariih.

Close the window that the wind comes through.

Maa ilna biiha laa naaqa wala jamal.

We do not have a male or female camel.

Kalaam il leil yimhii il nahaar.

Day erases whatever was said at night.

---

financial responsibility, continue to be important. Family members assist each other even across national lines, with Iraqi Americans often sending money to family members remaining in Iraq. Respect for the elderly is an important component of Iraqi culture. The elderly are believed to be the repository of community wisdom. This tradition has been brought to the United States, where many Iraqi elders still live with their children. To place them in senior residences is considered unacceptable, although the Chaldean Iraqi American community has attempted to provide senior living facilities for elderly members of the community.

Gender Roles Gender roles are very clearly defined in Iraq, a pattern that prevails throughout the Arabic world in general. This tradition remains, particularly in the rural areas, and involves a clear segregation between the sexes except when eating and sleeping. Men work outside the home and are the head of the household. Women are expected to take care of the home and bear children, who are considered members of their father's lineage. Boys and girls are indoctrinated into their respective gender roles practically from birth.

These strict gender patterns were brought to the United States by the earliest Iraqi immigrants in the first quarter of the twentieth century. However, gender patterns are changing for Iraqis, not only in the United States but also in Iraq. Increasingly, girls are becoming educated and moving into roles outside the home. They continue to be responsible for care of the household and children, however. Many Iraqi American girls continue to complain that they have more household responsibilities than their brothers, and some even indicate they are responsible for caring for their brothers' rooms. Some Iraqi males, on the other hand, complain about the increased freedom of the women in their families.

These traditional gender patterns can be found among Iraqis of all religious groups. The birth of a son is cause for much greater celebration than the birth of a daughter. Especially great celebrations are held for the birth of the firstborn son on the thirtieth day after his birth.

Education Education was not a priority in Iraq until the second half of the twentieth century. The earliest emigrants from Iraq were poorly educated, most having only a few years of schooling, if any. They generally moved into jobs requiring a low level of skill. The earliest Chaldean Iraqi Americans were grocers, and many reported learning to read English by studying the cans as they stocked the shelves in the store. Today, higher education is a goal for most Iraqis, both in Iraq and in the United States. The most recent immigrants often have a college education, and Iraqi Americans born in the United States—from all religious groups—usually pursue a college education. This pattern is encouraged by Iraqi organizations such as the Chaldean Federation, which provides scholarships to assist its youth in attending college and holds a ceremony to honor their achievements when they graduate.

Courtship and Weddings According to Middle Eastern tradition, marriage is a contract between families, with the views and the needs of the families considered more important than those of the individuals to be married. The idea of a couple falling in love was not relevant; rather, it was considered more important for the couple to share the same culture, and the family was considered more capable of making a wise choice than the couple themselves. Marriages nearly always occurred within the same ethnic group, and marriage between cousins was common. Men were married when they were old enough to support a family, typically around twenty to twenty-five years of age, whereas brides were usually much younger, often as young as twelve or fourteen.

By tradition, the women in the prospective groom's family would visit the family of the girl they had in mind, and they would have a conversation about a possible arrangement between their respective families. It was critical that the discussion be held in vague terms. A direct request was dangerous; in the event the girl's family did not agree, this would be a great embarrassment for both families. Should the initial contact indicate that an arrangement was acceptable, a formal, more public request for the girl's hand in marriage would be made by the groom himself and his family. Once an agreement was reached, it was followed by a formal announcement and engagement party. These marriage patterns persisted among Iraqis of all religions, even into the mid-twentieth century. In the Islamic community, the initial section of the Quran, called *al-Fatihah*, is read for the couple. This prayer, which honors Allah and asks for guidance, is an important part of all Islamic prayer life.

The extended family is the central dimension of life for all Iraqis. Life revolves around the family, and protection of the family and its honor is essential. Equally important to most Iraqis is their respective religious tradition.

In the Islamic community, a special party is held the night before the wedding, called *Lilat al-henna*. This is a relatively small party for the couple, including immediate family, aunts and uncles, and cousins. During the party, the bride's mother or aunt prepares a bowl with the reddish-brown dye from the henna plant and dances around the guests. The groom and bride place their little fingers in the bowl of henna, and their fingers are connected by a ribbon. Henna is often distributed to the women and girls to decorate themselves. Jewish, Kurdish, and some Christian brides may also have prewedding ceremonies using henna.

Weddings remain the most important festivals in Iraq. In the Islamic religion, the actual marriage ceremony is relatively brief and is held in the home of the groom. Christian ceremonies formerly followed the same pattern, but today they are more elaborate, especially in the Chaldean community, with a long Catholic Mass and numerous bridesmaids and groomsmen. Wedding traditions of Iraqi Jews are similar to those of other Jews. The bride and groom sign a *ketubah* (marriage contract). They take their vows under a *chupah* (canopy), and the ceremony concludes with the groom shattering a glass with his foot. In all three religious groups, the ceremony is followed by a celebration for the extended family and the community as a whole. In Iraq the celebration may extend for two or three days. Traditionally, Iraqi brides wore brightly colored clothing with gold jewelry, but today they are more likely to wear Western-style white bridal gowns. Members of the groom's family often give gifts of gold to the bride, such that she can support herself and her children in the event of widowhood. Divorce is rare among all Iraqi religious groups, even though Islamic Sharia law (the moral code and religious law of Muslims) makes it relatively easy to obtain.

Many of these traditions continue in some form in Iraqi American communities. However, there have been modifications to adapt to American culture. In particular, the increased liberty in the gender sphere is evidenced in the greater freedom of choice of marriage partners. Marriage between cousins has become rare, both in Iraq and the United States. In traditional Iraqi society, bride and groom did not meet before the ceremony. Today, dating before marriage and allowing the couple more involvement in the choice of a mate are more common. Weddings of Iraqi Americans, in all religions, tend to follow American bridal customs. Brides wear long white gowns and veils and have numerous bridesmaids; grooms and groomsmen wear tuxedos. Receptions are elaborate and last well into the night, often hosting hundreds of guests.

Relations with Other Americans Relations between Iraqi immigrants and other Americans changed dramatically in the century since the first Iraqis settled in the United States. The earliest Iraqi immigrants devoted most of their efforts to developing their businesses and making arrangements to bring relatives from Iraq to the United States. Their focus was on growth of the Iraqi Chaldean community itself, and they spent little effort developing relationships with other Americans. This is not an unusual pattern among newly developing ethnic groups. Like other immigrant groups, as the Iraqi American population grew and became more adapted to the new environment, they became more active in civic and political affairs and began to develop ties to the broad American community. The various Iraqi religious groups have become more involved in the broader community, mainly within the boundaries of their own religious groups but increasingly with other groups as well. Muslim Iraqis have moved into the larger Islamic communities, both of their particular denomination of Islam and of the Islamic community as a whole. Some Muslim imams have represented their religious community to outside groups. Iraqi Jews have largely become a part of the broader Jewish community. Chaldeans are becoming more recognized as part of the larger Catholic community, although they have also made moves to work with the Jewish community, because Chaldeans and Jews often live in nearby suburban areas, and both recognize their common origins in the Middle East. At the dawn of the twenty-first century, a few Iraqi Americans became active in civic groups and ran successfully for public office.

Philanthropy Iraqi Americans have developed a variety of philanthropic organizations to deal with the problems of their communities. As is true with most Iraqi customs, these activities tend to develop along religious lines. The Chaldean community has developed numerous philanthropic organizations. One of the earliest was the Chaldean Ladies of Charity, founded in the1950s to provide aid for Chaldean families. This group currently assists Chaldean refugees as well. Several Chaldean organizations have banded together under the auspices of the Chaldean Federation, which helps Chaldean refugees and provides financial aid to Chaldean students who want to attend college. Muslim Iraqi Americans participate in philanthropic organizations such as ACCESS (Arab Community Center for Economic and Social Services) that serve the Muslim and Arabic-speaking community in general. Because of their very small numbers, Jewish Iraqi Americans tend to work within broader Jewish organizations. However, they have formed a few specific Iraqi Jewish organizations, such as the American Aid Society (formerly the Iraqi Aid Society). This group assists Iraqi Jews in adapting to American society and also serves as a burial society. The Adopt-a-Refugee Family Program, founded to assist refugees from the Gulf Wars, helps Iraqi immigrants regardless their religious or ethnic origins.

Surnames Iraqi surnames vary among the different religious groups, largely because each has a long-term connection to a different linguistic and religious tradition, each with its preferred naming tradition. Thus, Muslim names are based in Arabic and may honor traditional Islamic leaders. Chaldean names are derived from Aramaic and tend to favor Christian saints. Jewish names are often derived from Hebrew and commemorate ancient Jewish leaders. The following are common Iraqi surnames:

Iraqi Muslim: Al-Alousi, Al-Asadi, Al-Baghdadi, Al-Basri, Al-Bayati, Al-Dujaili, Al-Hassani, Al-Husseini, Al-jbori, Al Karbalai, Al-Musawi, Al-Rawy, Al-Saadi, Al Shamari, Al Shirazi, Al Soraifi, Al-Tamimi, Al-Tikriti, Al-Zahawi, Al-Zuhairi, Ali, Aljohari, Jaffari, Zerjawy.

Iraqi Chaldean/Assyrian: Acho, Binno, Bidiwid, Garmo, George, Hakim, Kashat, Khami, Kherkher, Konja, Lossia, Mansour, Matti, Najor, Namo, Roumayah, Sarafa, Sesi, Shammamy, Shamoun, Sitto, Yaldo, Yasso, Yono, Yousif, Zeabari.

Iraqi Jewish: Akerib, Anwarzadeh, Bakhash, Ben-Josef, Bessel, Dabby, Darwish, Ezra, Jiji, Nassim, Pishanidar, Rabbie, Shamash, Shohet, Yadgar, Yadoo, Yahuda, Zadka.

EMPLOYMENT AND ECONOMIC CONDITIONS

In the Middle East, Iraqis were known for obtaining an education and moving into a variety of professions. During the rule of Saddam Hussein, many Iraqis were educated in Great Britain and became medical doctors, engineers, and professors. This pattern of a wide diversity of occupations is true of Iraqi Americans as well.

Economic patterns among Iraqi Americans vary between the different religious groups. Christian Iraqis, the earliest arrivals, are typically the most established.

By the 1990s Chaldean Iraqi Americans owned more than one thousand grocery stores in the Detroit metropolitan area. They continue to be active in this field but have also moved into a variety of other occupations, including fields that serve the grocery business, such as wholesale grocery distributorships; services to stores, such as providing butcher equipment and burglar alarm systems; and real estate development. A common occupation for Muslim Iraqi Americans in the Detroit metropolitan area is the combination gas station and convenience store. Many Chaldeans, and Iraqis of other religions as well, have moved into a variety of professions, such as law, dentistry, medicine, and pharmacy.

POLITICS AND GOVERNMENT

Members of the Iraqi American communities are relative newcomers in the United States, and their participation in U.S. politics and government has been limited. Adam Benjamin Jr., an Assyrian Iraqi American from Indiana, was the first Iraqi American to be elected (1977) to the U.S. House of Representatives. With the U.S. involvement in Iraq in the Second Gulf War and its aftermath, however, some Iraqi Americans have begun to see the need to become more involved in American political affairs, especially to influence American Middle Eastern policies.

NOTABLE INDIVIDUALS

Academia Majid Khadduri (1909–2007) was an expert on the politics of the Middle East and the founder of the Paul H. Nitze School of Advanced International Studies Middle East Studies program. Professor Khadduri served at Indiana University as well as the University of Chicago before accepting a position at Johns Hopkins University. During his tenure there, he founded the SAIS Middle Eastern Studies program and directed the Center of Middle East Studies. Throughout his distinguished career Khadduri wrote more than thirty-five books in English and Arabic.

Thomas L. Saaty (1926–) was a professor in the Joseph M. Katz Graduate School of Business at the University of Pittsburgh. In the 1970s Saaty developed the Analytic Hierarchy Process (AHP), a complex rubric based on a combination of mathematical and psychological principles that enables large groups, such as corporations, schools, and hospitals, to evaluate data and make decisions. Saaty also developed a less complex version of this decision-making tool called the Analytic Network Process (ANP).

Donny George Youkhanna (1950–2011) was a respected scholar and curator. Recognized by his contemporaries as "the man who saved the Iraqi National Museum," Youkhanna has also written numerous books and made contributions to the fields of archaeology and anthropology.

Activism Dave Nona (1948–) has been active in community and civic organizations for many

years. He was a founding member of the Chaldean American Chamber of Commerce and served as its chairman for several years. Joseph Kassab (1952–), executive director of the Chaldean Federation of America, was responsible for refugee assistance programs. Iraqi American social activist and writer Zainab Salbi (1970–) cofounded Women for Women International, an organization based in Washington, D.C. Dahlia Wasfi (1971–) is an Iraqi American physician and peace activist.

Business Sam Attisha (1966–) is the vice president of business development and external affairs for Cox Communications in San Diego. He was named one of San Diego's "Top Influentials" by the *Daily Transcript* in 2010.

Shakir al Khafaji (1955–), a Detroit-based Iraqi American businessman, is a senior executive with more than thirty years of business experience. He also served as chairman of the Iraqi Expatriate Conference.

Journalism Ayad Rahim (1962–) is a journalist who was praised for his work on a series of articles on the Operation Iraqi Freedom documents. Rahim hosts a radio show on WJCU in Cleveland.

Literature Sinan Antoon (1967–) is an associate professor at New York University's Gallatin School of Individualized Study. An acclaimed novelist and poet, Antoon codirected the 2003 documentary *About*

Baghdad, which chronicles the lives of people who lived under the tyranny of Saddam Hussein.

Mahmoud Saeed (1939–) teaches courses on Iraqi political history at DePaul University (Chicago) and is the author of *Saddam City* (2004), an autobiographical novel about Saeed's experiences in the Iraqi prison system during Hussein's rule. Saeed has published numerous other works, including short-story collections and scholarly articles.

Military Ahmed Kousay al-Taie (1965–2007) was an Iraqi American U.S. Army soldier who was captured in Baghdad in October 2006 and executed by his captors.

Music Rahim AlHaj (1968–) is an Iraqi American composer whose work has been called a mix of old-style Iraqi *maqams* (poems that are sung in an ancient Iraqi dialect) and contemporary music styles. Ashur Bet Sargis (1949–) is an Assyrian American composer and singer. He became famous in Assyrian communities worldwide for his nationalistic songs in the 1970s. Janan Sawa (1956–) is a famous Chaldean musician. To date, Sawa has released twenty-three albums. His brother, Esam Sawa, is also a singer.

Performance Christopher Lee (Chris) Kattan (1970–) is an Iraqi American actor/comedian best known for his work on *Saturday Night Live*. Remy Munasifi (1980–) is an Iraqi American standup comedian, parody musician, and video artist.

Politics Adam Benjamin Jr. (1935–1982) was the first Iraqi American to be elected to the U.S. House of Representatives. He represented Indiana's First Congressional District from 1977 until his death in 1982. Iraqi American Anna Eshoo (1942–) was elected to the U.S. House of Representatives for California's Eighteenth Congressional District in 1992. Iraqi American John J. Nimrod (1922–2009) was a minority rights activist and Illinois state senator.

Religion Ibrahim Ibrahim (1937–) is bishop of the Chaldean Church in Eastern North America, based at Mother of God Church in Southfield, Michigan. Sarhad Jammo (1941–) is bishop of the Chaldean Church in the Western United States, based at St. Peter's Chaldean Catholic Cathedral in El Cajon, California. Hassan Al-Qazwini (1964–) is the leader of the Islamic Center of America in Dearborn, Michigan, the largest mosque in North America, representing the Twelver Shia branch of Islam.

Stage and Screen F. Murray Abraham (1939–) is an Assyrian American actor known for his roles in film, television, and theater. He won the Academy Award for Best Actor for his role as Antonio Salieri in *Amadeus* (1984). Ashley Sawdaye (1974–) is an Iraqi American actor best known for his role as Sergeant Bridges in the 2007 film *The Ungodly*. Alia Martine Shawkat (1989–) is an Iraqi American actress who has appeared in a number of films and television programs, including *Amreeka*, *State of Grace*, and *Arrested Development*.

MEDIA

Iraqi Americans operate several media sources directed mainly to their ethnic communities. Some media outlets, however, are aimed at other Arabic, Iraqi, or Middle Eastern groups as well.

NEWSPAPERS

The Arab American News.com

A national online newspaper with coverage on issues of importance to the American Arabic-speaking population.

URL: www.arabamericannews.com

Betha Kaldaya

A community newspaper published by the Chaldean American Institute.

269 East Lexington Avenue
Suite B
El Cajon, California 92020
Phone: (619) 500-3224
URL: www.bethakaldaya.com

Michigan Arab Times Alhadath Newspaper

Newspaper offering articles for the Arabic-speaking community in Michigan, including some materials on the Chaldeans.

Email: michiganarabtimes@gmail.com
URL: www.michiganarabtimes.com

Nineveh

A quarterly magazine published by the Assyrian Foundation of America, *Nineveh* contains articles in English as well as in Assyrian (Aramaic/Chaldean).

P.O. Box 2600
Berkeley, California 94702
URL: www.assyrianfoundation.org

RADIO

The Arab American Radio Network

AARN reaches out to immigrants from the Middle East and North Africa living in major cities in the United States. These broadcasts cover the U.S. cities with the largest Arab American communities.

648 Live Oak Drive
McLean, Virginia 22101
Phone: (703) 333-2008
Fax: (888) 747-0957
Email: Contact@allied-media.com
URL: www.allied-media.com/Arab-American/Arab_radio.htm

Arab Detroit Radio

Arab Detroit Radio was founded with the purpose of promoting an accurate image about the Arab American community and the Arab world.

14628 West Warren Avenue
Dearborn, Michigan 48126
URL: streema.com/radios/Arab_Detroit_Radio

KBES-FM 89.5

The first Assyrian radio station owned and operated by Assyrians in Northern California.

P.O. Box 4116
Modesto, California 95352
Phone: (209) 537-0933
URL: www.betnahrain.org/kbes/kbes.htm

ORGANIZATIONS AND ASSOCIATIONS

American Kurdish Society (KAS)

A Kurdish cultural organization based in New York City that promotes and highlights Kurdish culture. Some KAS responsibilities are to make contact with other Kurdish organizations, to promote good relationships, to develop policies to improve the situation of Kurds in the United States, and to strengthen the relations with American friends in many areas, such as art, science, sport, and education.

Phone: (718) 635-0064
Email: info@usakurds.org
URL: www.usakurds.org

Arab American and Chaldean Social Services Council (ACC)

A nonprofit organization that assists the Middle Eastern communities in the United States. Services focus on education, employment and training, youth recreation, self-enrichment, cultural activities, immigration, and health.

26400 Lahser
Suite 330
Southfield, Michigan 48033
Phone: (248) 354-8460
URL: www.myacc.org

Iraqi-American Council

IAC is a nonprofit, nongovernmental organization that advocates for Iraqi Americans regardless their religious, political, or ethnic backgrounds. The council promotes, coordinates, and conducts various activities and programs for the advancement of the civil rights and social, economic, educational, cultural, and ethnic interests of Iraqi Americans.

7263 Maple Place
Suite 210
Annandale, Virginia 22003
Phone: (877) 807-8700
Fax: (877) 803-1800
Email: iraq@al-iraq.org
URL: dir.groups.yahoo.com

MUSEUMS AND RESEARCH CENTERS

Arab American National Museum (AANM)

The first and only museum in the United States devoted to Arab American history and culture. A section of its space is devoted to the Iraqi Chaldean community.

13624 Michigan Avenue
Dearborn, Michigan 48126
Phone: (313) 582-2266
Fax: (313) 582-1086
URL: www.arabamericanmuseum.org

Chaldean Cultural Center

Features historical data and artifacts relating to Chaldeans.

5600 Walnut Lake Road
West Bloomfield Township, Michigan 48323
Phone: (248) 681-5050
Email: info@chaldeanculturalcenter.org
URL: www.chaldeanculturalcenter.org

Hoover Institution, Stanford University: Middle East Collection

Formally established in 1948, the collection concentrates on twentieth-century history, politics, economics, military affairs, and U.S. national security affairs, and it includes materials from and about the Arab countries of western Asia and North Africa, Turkey, Israel, Iran, and Afghanistan.

Carol Leadenham, Archives reference
Hoover Institution
Stanford University
434 Galvez Mall
Stanford, California 94305-6010
Phone: (650) 723-3563
Email: carol.leadenham@stanford.edu
URL: www.hoover.org/library-and-archives/collections/middle-east

SOURCES FOR ADDITIONAL STUDY

Brown, Matthew Hay. "U.S. Slow to Meet Needs, Refugees Say." *Baltimore Sun*, December 29, 2008.

Hanna-Fatuhi, Amer. *The Untold Story of Native Iraqis: Chaldean Mesopotamians 5300 BC–Present.* Bloomington, IN: Xlibris, 2012.

Hassig, Susan M. *Cultures of the World: Iraq.* New York: Marshall Cavendish, 1993.

Levy, L. Review of *Babylonian Jewish Customs*, by Abraham Ben-Yaacob. *The Scribe: Journal of Babylonion Jewry* 71 (April 1999). http://www.dangoor.com/71frame.htm.

Najor, Julia. *Babylonian Cuisine: Chaldean Cookbook from the Middle East.* Detroit: National Books, 1981.

Schopmeyer, Kim. "A Demographic Portrait of Arab Detroit." In *Arab Detroit: From Margin to Mainstream*, edited by Nabeel Abraham and Andrew Shryock, 61–92. Detroit: Wayne State University Press, 2000.

Sengstock, Mary C. *Chaldean-Americans: Changing Conceptions of Ethnic Identity.* Staten Island: Center for Migration Studies, 1999.

———. *Chaldeans in Michigan.* Lansing: Michigan State University Press, 2005.

Wiswell, Joyce. "A New Life: First Iraqi Refugees Arrive." *Chaldean News*, September 1, 2007.

IRISH AMERICANS

Brendan A. Rapple and Jane Stewart Cook

OVERVIEW

Irish Americans are immigrants or descendants of immigrants from Ireland, an island west of Great Britain across the Irish Sea and St. George's Channel. The island is divided into two separate political entities: the independent Republic of Ireland, which occupies nearly five-sixths of the island, and Northern Ireland, which is part of the United Kingdom but is chiefly self-governing. Known as the Emerald Isle, Ireland is the third-largest island in Europe after Great Britain and Iceland. With a total area of 32,595 square miles, the entire island is a little larger than the state of Maine.

According to 2011 estimates by their respective governments, the population of the Republic of Ireland was nearly 4.6 million and that of Northern Ireland was about 1.8 million. The Republic of Ireland's population is overwhelmingly Roman Catholic; about 87 percent claimed Catholicism as their religion in 2011, down from 95 percent twenty years earlier. Northern Ireland, by contrast, is made up of about 40 percent Roman Catholics, followed by Presbyterian (18 percent), Church of Ireland (14 percent), and nonreligious (10 percent). After a period of rapid economic growth in the early twenty-first century, the Republic of Ireland experienced a recession and economic uncertainty during the late 2000s global financial crisis, suffering much greater declines than the rest of Europe and having to undergo serious austerity measures to cope with its collapsing banking sector. The country has a very service- and export-dependent economy, with its once-dominant agriculture sector in decline. Northern Ireland, similarly, has seen its once-industrial economy grow more dependent on services and financials in recent decades.

The Irish were among the earliest European immigrants to the American colonies. Their numbers swelled during the nineteenth century, when famine and political unrest drove more than two million Irish to immigrate to the United States, most of them settling in such major metropolitan areas as New York, Chicago, and San Francisco. Suffering from discrimination and poverty, many Irish Americans remained poor laborers well into the twentieth century. From the mid-twentieth century to today, however, Irish Americans have emerged as a well-educated, prosperous ethnic group, with considerable representation all over the nation. Recent economic troubles in Ireland caused a resurgence of Irish immigration to the United States, but as a whole this has been small relative to the total number of Irish Americans.

According to the U.S. Census Bureau's American Community Survey (2011) estimates, more than 34.5 million Americans claim Irish ancestry—only about 3 million less than the 2011 population of the state of California. Irish Americans are the nation's second largest ethnic group after German Americans. Roughly 260,000 of all Irish immigrants are foreign-born. Another 3.5 million Americans consider themselves Scotch-Irish; these are largely descendants of immigrants from the province of Ulster, which is partially in the Republic of Ireland and partially in Northern Ireland. Irish Americans are well distributed around the nation, but northeastern cities (particularly Boston, New York, and Philadelphia), Chicago, New Orleans, and San Francisco—all major destinations during the primary period of Irish immigration—still retain particularly large populations of Irish Americans. They have generally been absorbed into the larger population, though some urban neighborhoods, such as South Boston and Woodlawn in the Bronx, retain considerable Irish character.

HISTORY OF THE PEOPLE

Early History Sometime between 600 and 400 BCE, Ireland was occupied by Celtic peoples, who came to be known as Gaels. Because the Romans never invaded Ireland, the Gaels remained isolated and were able to develop a distinct culture. In the fifth century St. Patrick came to Ireland from Britain and introduced the Gaels to Christianity, initiating a new religious and cultural period. Irish monasteries—preserving the Greek and Latin of the ancient world—not only became great centers of learning but also sent many famous missionaries to the European continent. Towards the end of the eighth century, the Vikings invaded Ireland, fighting for sovereignty for more than two centuries. Finally, at the 1014 Battle of Clontarf, the Irish under King Brian Boru soundly defeated the Viking forces. An important legacy of the Viking invasion was the establishment of such cities as Dublin, Cork, Waterford, Limerick, and Wexford. In 1167 a local Irish king turned to King Henry II of England for help in fighting a rival. A series of Anglo-Norman conquests commenced, leading to the English Lordship of Ireland. By the close of the medieval period, many of the Anglo-Norman invaders had been absorbed into the Gaelic population.

English kings traveled to Ireland on several occasions to impose order and rally allegiance to the Crown. The English were generally too occupied with the Hundred Years War (1337–1453) against France and the War of the Roses (1455–1485) within England to adequately rule the Irish, however. By the sixteenth century English control over Ireland was limited to a small area of land surrounding Dublin. Consequently, Henry VIII (who ruled England from 1509 to 1547) and his successors endeavored to force the Irish to submit through military incursions and by "planting" large areas of Ireland with settlers loyal to England. At the end of the sixteenth century, the northern Irish chieftain Hugh O'Neill led a strong resistance movement against the English reconquest. Following O'Neill's defeat in 1603 and his subsequent flight to the Continent, the Crown commenced the large-scale plantation of Ulster with English; Scottish Presbyterians soon followed. During the seventeenth century Ireland came increasingly under English rule. In 1641 the Irish allied themselves with King Charles I, supporting the Stuart cause in the impending civil war between the monarchy and the republicans. After the defeat and execution of Charles in 1649, Cromwell and his Puritans devastated much of Ireland, massacred thousands, and rewarded his soldiers and followers with vast tracts of Irish land. Hoping to regain some of their property, the Catholic Irish sided with James II of England, a Catholic, but their fortunes further declined when James was defeated by William of Orange, the Protestant contender for the thrones of England, Scotland, and Ireland, at the Battle of the Boyne in 1690. Viewing the Irish as an inferior race and themselves as civilizers, the English enacted a series of brutal penal laws to keep the Irish subservient and powerless. These succeeded so well that eighteenth-century Catholic Ireland was economically and socially shattered.

In 1798 the English defeated a United Irish (Protestants and Catholics) rebellion led by revolutionary Wolfe Tone. Two years later Parliament passed the Act of Union, combining Great Britain and Ireland into one United Kingdom, and, in 1829 (chiefly as a result of the activities of the Irish politician Daniel O'Connell), the Catholic Emancipation (or Relief) Act, which lifted general civil and political limitations and the Irish penal laws. During the 1830s and 1840s, a new nationalist movement arose: Young Ireland. The rebellion it launched in 1848 was easily defeated, however. The second half of the 1840s was one of the grimmest periods in Irish history: the crop failure of Ireland's staple food—the potato—led to the Great Famine. Millions died or emigrated, mainly to the United States. The second half of the nineteenth century brought increased nationalistic demands for self-government and land reform, most notably in the activities of the Home Rule Movement under the leadership of Charles Stewart Parnell. Although the Government of Ireland Act 1914 was finally passed, its implementation was deferred because of the onset of World War I, and it never took effect. On Easter Monday 1916 a small force of Irish nationalists rebelled in Dublin against British rule. The rising was a military failure and had little support among the public. The harsh response of the British government, however, and particularly its execution of the rising's leaders, won many over to the independence cause.

Modern Era In 1921 the United Kingdom of Great Britain and Ireland signed the Anglo-Irish Treaty with the secessionist Irish Republic, creating the Irish Free State. Although it was self-governing, it was tied to the British Commonwealth and its constitution and required allegiance to the Crown. The Free State was composed of twenty-six of Ireland's thirty-two counties; the other six chose to remain part of Britain as Northern Ireland. Ultimately, in 1949 the twenty-six counties left the British Commonwealth and became the Republic of Ireland, an independent nation, spurring a period of modernization and economic expansion throughout the Republic. The surge was interrupted by periods of stagnation in the late 1970s. Ireland joined the European Economic Community (later the European Union) in 1973 and was one of the original states to adopt the Euro in 1999. Earning the nickname "The Celtic Tiger," the nation underwent a period of particularly strong economic growth in the 1990s and early 2000s as property values and foreign investment soared, infrastructure was modernized, and new immigrants arrived from throughout Europe. One of Western Europe's poorest nations became one of its wealthiest. This growth came to a rapid end in 2008, however, as the global economy collapsed and Ireland's economy, dependent on real estate and banking, followed suit. By 2012 the nation was crippled by debt, its gross domestic product had contracted, and its rate of unemployment was among Western Europe's highest. Leaders enacted a series of austerity measures to try to bring the nation's spending into balance.

Despite the establishment of an independent Ireland in 1949, the island's six northern counties remained part of United Kingdom, while the Republic consistently maintained its claim over them. Violence erupted frequently over this issue throughout the twentieth century in what came to be known as "The Troubles." Such rival groups as the Irish Republican Army (which fought for unification) and the Ulster Defence Association (enforcing loyalty to the United Kingdom) carried out retributive attacks that sometimes spilled over into the Republic of Ireland and England, resulting in the deaths of more than 3,000 people. Hostilities diminished in the late twentieth and early twenty-first centuries, following the Good Friday Agreement of 1998 (between the British and

Irish governments and the political parties of Northern Ireland), the disarmament of paramilitary groups, and moves toward power-sharing in the Northern Irish government. By 2007 bloodshed had decreased to a point that the United Kingdom allowed Northern Ireland greater control over its own affairs. Although disputes still exist, violent confrontation over this issue is far less frequent.

SETTLEMENT IN THE UNITED STATES

The Irish like to boast that an early Irish monk, St. Brendan, sailed to the Americas almost a millennium before Christopher Columbus. There is no physical evidence of such an event, but the Irish were still among the first Europeans in the New World. Galway-born William Ayers was one of Columbus's crew in 1492. During the seventeenth century the majority of the Irish immigrants to North America were Catholics. Most were poor, many coming as indentured servants; others, called redemptioners, arrived under agreements to reimburse their fare sometime after arrival. A minority paid their own passage. A small number came seeking adventure, while others were among the thousands whom Cromwell exiled to the West Indies during the 1640s and who later made their way to North America.

There was an increase in Irish immigration during the eighteenth century, though the numbers were still relatively small. Most of the century's arrivals were Presbyterians from the northern province of Ulster who had originally been sent there from Scotland as colonists by the British Crown. Many of these, dissenters from the established Protestant Church in their homeland, were fleeing religious discrimination. In later years, especially in the second half of the nineteenth century, it was common to assign the term Scotch-Irish to these Ulster Protestant immigrants, although they thought of themselves as strictly Irish.

There were also numerous Irish Quaker immigrants, as well as some Protestants from southern Ireland. A significant minority of eighteenth-century immigrants were southern Catholics. Most of these were escaping the appalling social and economic conditions and the draconian penal laws enacted by the British to annihilate the Celtic heritage and the religion of the Catholic majority. In time, some of these Catholic arrivals converted to Protestantism, after encountering severe antipapist discrimination as well as an absence of Catholic churches and priests. The preferred destinations of most of the eighteenth-century Irish immigrants were New England, Maryland, Pennsylvania, the Carolinas, and Virginia.

In the first decades of the nineteenth century, Protestants continued to account for the majority of Irish immigrants to the United States, many them skilled tradesmen. There were also numerous political refugees, especially after the abortive United Irishmen uprising of 1798. Because the passage to eastern Canada was substantially cheaper than that to the United States, many Irish immigrants landed there first, at Quebec, Montreal, or Halifax, and then sailed or even walked down into the United States.

By the 1820s and 1830s, however, the overwhelming majority of those fleeing the country were unskilled, Catholic, peasant laborers. Ireland had become Europe's most densely populated country, the

> The first time I saw the Statue of Liberty all the people were rushing to the side of the boat. 'Look at her, look at her,' and in all kinds of tongues. 'There she is, there she is,' like it was somebody who was greeting them.
>
> Elizabeth Phillips in 1920, cited in *Ellis Island: An Illustrated History of the Immigrant Experience*, edited by Ivan Chermayeff et al. (New York: Macmillan, 1991).

population having increased from about three million in 1725 to more than eight million in 1841. The land could not support such a number. One of the main problems was the absence of the practice of primogeniture (with the first-born inheriting all) among the Irish. Family farms or plots were divided again and again until individual allotments were often so small—perhaps only one or two acres in size—that they were of little use in raising a family. Conditions worsened after the Napoleonic Wars (1803–1815), when an agricultural depression led many Irish landlords to evict their tenants, wanting to use the land for grazing. Meanwhile, increased industrialization had all but ended the modest amount of domestic weaving and spinning that had helped to supplement the income of some families. In addition, famine was never distant—a number of severe potato failures occurred during the 1820s and 1830s, before the Great Famine of the 1840s. The concurrent steep rise in population left thousands of discontented, hungry, landless Irish eager to seek new horizons.

Whereas most of the Irish Catholic immigrants during the eighteenth century had taken up farming in their new country, those arriving in the first decades of the nineteenth century tended to sail from Ireland directly to an American port and to remain in such urban centers as Boston, New York, and Philadelphia or in the textile towns where their unskilled labor could be readily utilized amid the rapidly industrializing (and urbanizing) American economy of the 1820s and 1830s Market Revolution. Some found jobs building roads or canals (such as the Erie) as the nation's infrastructure expanded for domestic and international trade. These immigrants were impoverished but usually not as destitute as those who came later, beginning in the 1840s. Still, times were difficult for most of them, especially the Catholics, who frequently found themselves in the minority and were targets of discrimination in an overwhelmingly Protestant nation.

Mrs. Bridget Casey, of County Cork, Ireland, is photographed with her nine children right after arriving in New York. 1929 BETTMANN / CORBIS

It was the cataclysmic Potato Famine of 1845–1851, one of the most severe disasters in Irish history, that initiated the greatest departure of Irish immigrants to the United States. The potato constituted the main dietary staple for most Irish and when blight struck a number of successive harvests, social and economic disintegration ensued. As many as 1.5 million individuals perished of starvation and the diverse epidemics that accompanied the famine. A great number of the survivors emigrated, many of them to the United States. From the beginning of the famine in the mid-1840s until 1860 about 1.7 million Irish immigrated to the United States, mainly from the provinces of Connaught and Munster. In the latter part of the century, though the numbers fell from the highs of the famine years, the influx from Ireland continued to be large. While families predominated during the famine exodus, single people now accounted for a far higher proportion of the immigrants. By 1880 more single women than single men were immigrating, creating one of America's only major immigration waves consisting of more women than men. It has been estimated that from 1820 to 1900 about four million Irish immigrated to the United States.

The majority of Irish immigrants continued to inhabit urban centers, principally in the northeast but also in such cities as Chicago, New Orleans, and San Francisco. Only a small number engaged in farming. Most Irish immigrants were indeed peasants with experience working on small farms, but few had the money to purchase land or had sufficient skill and experience to make a success of large-scale American agriculture. Despite suffering exploitation, oppression, and hardships, most nineteenth-century Irish immigrants endured, and their work-related mobility slowly improved. Their prowess and patriotic fervor during

the Civil War helped to diminish anti-Irish bigotry and discrimination. As the years went by, the occupational caliber of Irish immigrants gradually improved in line with the slow amelioration of conditions in Ireland. By the end of the century, a high proportion were skilled or semiskilled laborers or had trades. Moreover, these immigrants were greatly aided by the Irish American infrastructure that awaited them: the parochial schools, charitable societies, workers' organizations, and social clubs smoothed their entry into a society that still frequently discriminated against Irish Catholics. Furthermore, the influx of even poorer southern and eastern European immigrants helped the Irish attain increased status.

Emigration continued apace through additional economic troubles of the late nineteenth and early twentieth century, with Ireland consistently being among the top five countries of origin for American immigrants. Increasing American concern about immigration, particularly about rising numbers of unskilled immigrants from Italy and Eastern Europe, led to the tightening of immigration laws in the 1920s. In particular, the Emergency Quota Act of 1921 and the Immigration Act of 1924 limited the number of new immigrants from any particular country to a small percentage of its immigrant population already in the United States. In 1929 a total quota of 150,000 unskilled immigrants, regardless of national origin, was instituted. Although not as severely affected as immigration from southern and Eastern Europe and Asia, Irish immigration dropped 19 percent almost immediately after the initial quota came into effect, and the decline continued through the Great Depression of the 1930s.

After World War II the number of Irish immigrating to the United States picked up again but remained lower than numbers of those arriving from other European nations more directly affected by the war, including Germany, Britain, and Italy. The 1960s saw immigration from Ireland falling further as a result the Immigration and Nationality Act of 1965. Passed during the years of the civil rights movement, the act repealed the inherently racist quota system established forty years prior and opened immigration to all nations with a per-nation quota of 20,000. Furthermore, criteria for visas paid more attention to family connections and certain skills. An overall annual cap of 120,000 immigrants from the Western Hemisphere limited western European immigration somewhat by opening up more immigration from the rest of the world.

Legal immigration from Ireland thus slowed, but economic stagnation in that country in the 1970s and 1980s contributed to an unprecedented influx of undocumented Irish immigrants, especially to such traditionally Irish centers as New York, Boston, Chicago, and San Francisco. Many of these immigrants were young and well educated. They left a country with one of the highest rates of unemployment in

Western Europe to work largely in Irish American–owned businesses as bartenders, construction workers, nannies, and food servers. This influx slowed during the "Celtic Tiger" years of economic growth in Ireland but picked up again after the financial crisis struck Ireland in 2008. In 2012 Irish authorities reported that emigration had reached the highest level since the mid-nineteenth century. While the United Kingdom received the largest number of Irish emigrants, the United States was a major destination as well, for both legal and illegal immigration. By 2013 advocacy groups estimated that about 50,000 undocumented Irish lived in the United States. Legal Irish immigration remained much lower than in the past; the U.S. Department of Homeland Security estimated that just under 19,000 new permanent residents arrived from Ireland between 2000 and 2011.

LANGUAGE

Irish is a Celtic language of Indo-European origin, related to the ancient language of the Gauls. Linguistic scholars usually identify at least four distinct stages in the development of Irish: Old Irish (ca. 600–900); Middle Irish (ca. 900–1400); Early Modern Irish (ca. 1400–1600); and Modern Irish (ca. 1600–present). Three fairly discrete dialects developed through this history: those of Ulster, Munster, and Connaught. Beginning in the nineteenth century, the Irish language—until then widely spoken throughout the

country—began a rapid decline, mainly because of the Anglicization policies of the British government. Since the founding of the Irish Free State in 1921, however, the authorities have made great efforts to promote the widespread usage of Irish. The Constitution of the Republic of Ireland names Irish as the official language (though it recognizes English as prevalent), and the native language is still taught in most schools. The result is that competence in Irish language—as well as general interest in the language—is higher today than at any time in the republic's history. Nevertheless, despite all efforts to render Irish a living national language, it is used in daily communication by only about twenty or thirty thousand Irish, most them living in the northern, western, and southern fringes of the island, known collectively as the *Gaeltacht*, which includes Counties Donegal, Connemara, and the Dingle Peninsula. Only a tiny number of Northern Ireland's population speaks Irish.

Although it was a great loss for nationalistic and cultural reasons, the decline in the usage of Irish and the triumph of English as the first language of Ireland throughout the nineteenth century proved to be a boon to Irish immigrants to the United States. Along with the English and Scottish, most Irish spoke the language of their adopted country, unlike the majority of immigrants. Today, there is a resurgence of interest in the Irish language among many Irish Americans. In cities such as New York, Chicago, Boston, and San

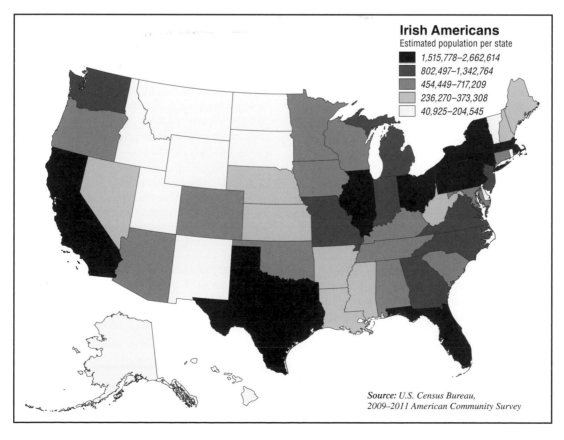

Irish Americans
Estimated population per state

- 1,515,778–2,662,614
- 802,497–1,342,764
- 454,449–717,209
- 236,270–373,308
- 40,925–204,545

Source: U.S. Census Bureau,
2009–2011 American Community Survey

Francisco, classes in Irish are extremely popular. A growing number of American colleges and universities now offer Irish language courses.

Greetings and Popular Expressions *Dia dhuit* ("dee-ah guit")—Hello; *Conas atá tú*? ("kunus ah-thaw thoo")—How are you?; *Fáilte romhat*! ("fawilteh rowth")—Welcome; *Cad as duit*? ("kawd oss dit")—Where are you from?; *Gabh mo leithscéal* ("gauw muh leshgale")—Excuse me; *Le do thoil* ("leh duh hull")—Please; *Tá dhá thaobh ar an scéa* ("thaw gaw hayv air un shgale")—There's something to be said on both sides; *Más toil le Dia* ("maws tule leh dee-ah")—God willing; *Tá sé ceart to leor* ("thaw shay k-yarth guh lore")—It's all right; *Beidh lá eile ag an bPaorach*! ("beg law eleh egg un fairoch")   Better luck next time!; *Buíochas le Dia* ("bu-ee-kus leh dee-ah")—Thank God; *Is fusa a rá ná a dhéanamh* ("iss fusa ah raw naw ah yea-anav")—Easier said than done; *Go raibh míle maith agat* ("guh row meela moh ugut")—Thank you very much; *Slán agat go fóill* ("slawn ugut guh fowil")—Good-bye for the present.

RELIGION

Many, if not most, Irish Protestant immigrants found the transition into mainstream Protestantism in the United States relatively easy. The vast majority of subsequent Catholic immigrants, however, many of whom considered their religion to be an intrinsic part of their Irish heritage as well as a safeguard against the Anglo establishment, held steadfastly to their faith and, in so doing, helped Roman Catholicism grow into one of the country's most populous religions. Since the late eighteenth century, many aspects of American Catholicism have possessed a distinctly Irish character. Past and present American Catholic clergy comprise a disproportionate number of Irish names. Scores of Irish laymen have been at the forefront of American Catholic affairs. The Irish have been particularly energetic supporters of the more concrete manifestations of their church and have established great numbers of Catholic schools, colleges, universities, hospitals, community centers, and orphanages, as well as churches, cathedrals, convents, and seminaries throughout United States.

Until the mid-twentieth century, Catholic Irish American life revolved around the parish. Many children went to parochial schools, and the clergy organized such activities as sports, dances, and community services. Local politics almost always involved the participation of the priests. The clergy knew all the families in the community, and pressure to conform to the norms of the tightly knit parish was considerable. The parish priest, generally the best-educated member of the congregation, was usually the dominant community leader. At a time when there were far fewer social workers, guidance counselors, and psychologists, parishioners flocked to their priest in times of trouble. Religious practice and devotion have declined in the late twentieth and early

twenty-first centuries as Irish Americans assimilate more fully into American culture. Although the typical religious community is more loosely organized, many Catholic Irish still identify strongly with their parishes, which can remain considerably distinct from Italian Catholic and other Catholic immigrant groups' parishes.

The American Catholic Church has undergone great changes since the 1960s, largely because of the innovations introduced by the Second Vatican Council (1962–1965), which aimed to bring the church into the modern era. Some Catholic Irish Americans, wishing to preserve their inherited church practices, have been dismayed by the transformation. Some, alienated by the modernization of the liturgy—with respect to the introduction of the vernacular, new hymns, and guitar playing at services—have been offended by what they consider a diminution of the mystery and venerability of church ritual. Some have attempted to preserve the traditional liturgy by joining conservative breakaway sects such as the Slaves of the Immaculate Heart of Mary, founded by Father Leonard Feeney in Boston.

Most Irish American Catholics have embraced these recent developments, however. Many are now far more inclined than non-Irish Catholics to question doctrine and take issue with teachings on such subjects as abortion, contraception, divorce, priestly celibacy, and female priests. The number of Irish Americans entering the clergy has also declined, and, overall, the number of Catholic priests in the United States has dropped by as much as 10 percent in the last decade. Like other European American Catholics, the numbers of Irish Americans receiving the sacraments and attending mass have also substantially dropped, and many have abandoned traditional attitudes toward lifestyle issues, especially sex. Nevertheless, most Irish American Catholics are still faithful to many teachings of their church and continue to identify as Catholics despite some disagreements with Vatican teachings.

Although Catholicism is the denomination most commonly associated with Irish Americans, surveys in the late twentieth century found that just over half of Irish Americans identify as Protestant. The early Irish Protestant immigrants came from Northern Ireland and belonged to the Methodist or Presbyterian churches. Unlike their Catholic counterparts, Irish American Protestants have largely melded into the mainstream of American Protestantism; thus their religious practices are less visible overall.

CULTURE AND ASSIMILATION

Because the Irish have been present in the United States for hundreds of years, Irish Americans have had more opportunity than many other ethnic groups to assimilate into the wider society. Each successive generation has become more integrated with the dominant culture.

Although the eighteenth-century Protestant Irish became acculturated and were socially accepted relatively easily, the vast numbers of Catholic Irish who flooded into the United States in the postfamine decades had far more difficulty coalescing with the mainstream. Common negative stereotypes, many imported from England, characterized the Irish as pugnacious, drunken semisavages. Cartoons depicting them as small, ugly, simian creatures armed with liquor and a shillelagh (a cudgel) pervaded the press; and such terms as "paddy-wagons," "shenanigans," and "shanty Irish" gained popularity. The prejudices endured for at least the rest of the nineteenth century.

Despite the effects of these offensive images, compounded by poverty and the lack of formal education, the Irish Catholic immigrants possessed important advantages. They arrived in great numbers, most were able to speak English, and their Western European culture was similar to American culture. These factors allowed them to blend in far more easily than some other ethnic groups. Their Catholicism still aroused hostility amid the dominant culture as late as 1960, however, when it was a major issue during John F. Kennedy's presidential campaign. Over the decades it has been accepted and has became an important part of American culture.

It is now more difficult to define Irish American ethnic identity. Particularly in younger generations, intermarriage has played a major role in the blurring of ethnic lines. In recent decades a great Irish American migration from their ethnic enclaves in the cities to the suburbs and rural regions has facilitated the process of assimilation. Greater participation in the multicultural public school system and a corresponding decline in parochial school attendance has played a significant role as well. Another major factor has been the great decrease of immigrants from Ireland as a result of immigration laws disfavoring Europeans.

Today, with more than 34 million Americans claiming Irish ancestry, American society as a whole associates few connotations—positive or negative—with this group. Irish immigrants and many of their descendants still take great pride and feel a certain prestige in being Irish. Nevertheless, some non-Irish persist in the belief that the Irish are less cultured, less advanced intellectually, and more politically reactionary and even bigoted than some other ethnic groups. Particularly around such major festivals as Saint Patrick's Day, the image of Irish Americans as heavy drinkers persists. The results of numerous polls show, however, that Catholic Irish Americans are among the best educated and most liberal in the United States. Moreover, they are well represented in law, medicine, academia, and other prestigious professions, and they continue to be upwardly socially mobile. Traditionally prominent in the Democratic ranks of city and local politics, many, especially since the John F. Kennedy presidency, have now attained high positions in the federal government. Countless more have become top civil servants. Irish acceptability has also grown in line with the greater respect many Americans accord the economic advances made by the "Celtic Tiger."

Dances and Songs Ireland's cultural heritage, with its diverse customs, traditions, folklore, mythology, music, and dance, is one of the richest and most distinctive in Europe. Rapid modernization and the extensive homogenization of Western societies, however, have rendered much of this heritage obsolete or, at best, only vaguely evoked in contemporary Ireland. With Irish Americans' widespread assimilation into American culture, the continuity and appreciation of the domestic cultural heritage has waned. Nevertheless, many elements in Irish American culture are truly unique and lend the group a distinct cultural character.

Irish music and song brought to the United States by generations of immigrants have played a seminal role in the development of American folk and country music. Elements of traditional Irish ballads introduced during the seventeenth and eighteenth centuries are easily discernible in many American folk songs. Irish fiddle music of this period is an important root of American country music. This earlier music became part of an American rural tradition. Much of what was carried to the United States by the great waves of Irish immigration during the nineteenth century, on the other hand, became an important facet of the American urban folk scene. With the folk music revival of the 1960s came a heightened appreciation of Irish music in both its American and indigenous forms.

Today, Irish music is extremely popular not only among Irish Americans but among large sectors of the general American public. Many learn to play such Irish instruments as the pipes, tin whistle, flute, fiddle, concertina, harp, and the bodhrán. Many also attend Irish *céilithe* (festive gatherings) and dance traditional reels and jigs to hornpipes. In the 1990s Riverdance, an Irish step dance performance created in Ireland by Michael Flatly, drew huge crowds of Irish Americans and Americans in general, playing to sold-out audiences at Radio City Music Hall and on national tours. Irish music has also influenced other musical genres. Some musical groups, such as Flogging Molly and the Dropkick Murphys, have become popular in the United States with an energetic, Irish-influenced punk rock.

Holidays One of most important holidays of the year for Irish Americans is the feast of St. Patrick, the patron saint of Ireland, on March 17. Little is known about his life except that he was a Romano-Briton missionary, perhaps from Wales, who spread Christianity throughout Ireland in the fifth century. Although Irish Americans of all creeds are particularly prominent on St. Patrick's Day, the holiday is now so ubiquitous that individuals of many other ethnic groups participate in the festivities. Many cities and towns hold St. Patrick's Day celebrations, parties, and, above all, parades. One of the first major observances of the holiday in the United States was organized in

1737 by Protestant Irish in Boston under the auspices of the Charitable Irish Society. Boston, especially the districts of South Boston, still holds great celebrations each year, though the holiday is now more closely identified with Catholic Irish. The largest and most famous parade is in New York City, which held its first St. Patrick's Day parade in 1762. In the early years the Friendly Sons of St. Patrick organized the event; in 1838 the Ancient Order of Hibernians took over and still holds the sponsorship today. New York's main cathedral is dedicated to St. Patrick.

Most people celebrating St. Patrick's Day wear green, Ireland's national color. Green dye is often put in food and drink. The mayor of Chicago regularly has the Chicago River dyed green for the day. If people cannot find a shamrock to wear, they carry representations of the plant. According to legend, the shamrock, with its three leaves on the single stalk, was used by St. Patrick to explain the mystery of the Christian Trinity to the pagan Irish. In Ireland, however, while St. Patrick's Day is celebrated with enthusiasm, festivities tend to be more subdued than in the United States because of a greater appreciation of the feast's religious significance.

Cuisine Although distinctive Irish cuisine is not prominent in Irish Americans' daily diet, many cook Irish dishes at home or eat them in Irish pubs and restaurants, which are common and serve a large clientele in American metropolitan areas. American shops that sell such Irish favorites as rashers (bacon), bangers (sausages), black and white pudding (whole or sliced sausage traditionally made with and without

pig's blood), and soda bread (made from flour, soda, buttermilk, salt, and sometimes currants or raisins) find a thriving market. Potatoes are still a staple of the Irish American diet, as well as butter, milk, and cheese in large quantities. Many eat oatmeal stirabout or porridge for breakfast. Irish stew is a favorite, and smoked Irish salmon, imported from Ireland, is a popular delicacy. Other traditional foods include coddle, a dish originating in Dublin that is prepared with bacon, sausages, onions, and potatoes; and *drisheens*, made from sheep's blood, milk, bread crumbs, and chopped mutton suet. Corned beef and cabbage, sometimes served with juniper berries, is a traditional Easter Sunday meal in many parts of Ireland and is consumed by many Irish Americans on this and other days, including Saint Patrick's Day.

Boxty bread, a potato bread marked with a cross, is served on Halloween or the eve of All Saint's Day. Also on the table at Halloween is colcannon, a mixture of cabbage or kale and mashed potatoes with a lucky coin placed inside; and barmbrack, an unleavened cake abundant with raisins, sultanas, and currants with a ring inside. It is said that whoever receives the slice containing the ring will be married within the year. Tea, served at all times of the day and night, is probably the most popular Irish beverage. Irish coffee—whiskey mixed into coffee—is an Irish American invention not drunk much in Ireland. Although scotch and whiskey are made in many other countries, the Irish believe that their whiskey, *uisce beatha* (the water of life), is a finer drink. Irish stout, particularly the Guinness variety, is well known and distributed throughout the United States and the world.

Irish step dancers perform at New York City's 251st Annual St. Patrick's Day parade. KEVIN DOWNS / DEMOTIX / CORBIS

Traditional Dress True folk costume is rarely worn in Ireland nor by Irish Americans. The *brat*, a black hooded woolen cloak, is sometimes seen on old women in County Cork. During the nineteenth century many women found the shawl to be a cheaper substitute for the cloak, and even today older rural women may be shawled. The heavy white *báinín* pullovers, traditionally worn in the west and northwest of Ireland by fishermen whose sweaters each bore a unique and identifiable cable pattern, are now frequently seen throughout the nation and have been popular at times in the United States. Aran Islander men still sometimes wear traditional homespun tweed trousers flecked with colors found in the Irish landscape, and the weave has been consistently used in American fashion. Although assimilated in their daily dress habits, modern-day Irish Americans make an exception for the kilt, which members of *céilí* bands and traditional Irish dancers sometimes wear. This plaid skirt is actually Scottish, however, and was adopted in the early twentieth century during a period of resurging interest in Irish culture and language known as the Gaelic Revival.

Health Care Issues and Practices The health of Irish Americans is influenced by the same factors affecting other ethnic groups in the Western world: old age, pollution, stress, excessive use of tobacco and alcohol, an unhealthy diet, employment and other economic problems, discord in marriage and personal relationships, and so on. Heart-related diseases, a chief cause of death, are exacerbated by the Irish fondness for a rich diet traditionally high in fat and caloric content. Alcohol plays a strong role in Irish American social life, and alcohol related illnesses are common. The rate of alcoholism in Irish Americans is relatively high; a 1997 survey found that 40 percent of Irish Americans reported that alcoholism had existed in their homes when they were children. George Vaillant, a Harvard medical professional and alcoholism expert, wrote in 1995 that Irish Americans in his research were seven times more likely to be alcoholic than Italian Americans. Other researchers have suggested that heavy drinking amid Irish Americans remains a stereotype, and still others believe it is the result of a self-fulfilling prophecy. They note that the alcoholism rate in Ireland is moderate. Irish Americans also have an above-average rate of mental health diseases, with organic psychosis and schizophrenia being particularly prevalent. In the twentieth century Irish males were found to have a 4 percent chance of being schizophrenic, roughly four times the rate among the general American population, a prevalence that persists in the twenty-first century. Irish American Patrick Tracey explored these trends among Irish Americans and his own family tree in *Stalking Irish Madness*, published in 2008.

In the earlier days of immigration the Irish, like numerous other groups, brought their folk medical remedies with them. Most of these, especially the

IRISH STEW

Ingredients

3 pounds lamb, cubed

2 pounds russet potatoes, thickly sliced

½ bunch parsley, finely chopped

1 pound onions, thinly sliced

salt and pepper to taste

water

Preparation

Preheat oven to 250°F.

Layer lamb into a heavy oven-proof casserole with potatoes, parsley, and onions. Season generously with salt and pepper. Add 2 cups water. Heat to a simmer over low heat (do not boil). Cover, put in oven. Cook 2½–3 hours. Add water if needed.

Serves 6

preparations involving herbs, are unknown to the majority of contemporary Irish Americans; however, a number of traditional medical beliefs survive. In order to maintain good health and prevent illness, Irish Americans may recommend wearing holy medals and scapulars, blessing the throat, never going to bed with wet hair, never sitting in a draft, taking laxatives regularly, wearing camphor about the neck during influenza season, taking tonics and extra vitamins, enjoying bountiful exercise and fresh air, and avoiding physicians except when quite ill. Some traditional treatments are still used, such as painting a sore throat with iodine or soothing it with lemon and honey, putting a poultice of sugar and bread or soap on a boil, drinking hot whiskey with cloves and honey for coughs or colds, and rubbing Vicks on the chest or breathing in hot balsam vapors, also for coughs and colds.

Death and Burial Rituals Traditionally, the Irish generally treated death in a boisterous and playful manner. The two or three days during which the dead person was laid out prior to burial were filled with storytelling, music, singing, dancing, feasting, and playing of games specific to wakes, such as Hide the Gulley. These activities may owe something to pre-Christian funeral games and may also have stemmed in part from a welcoming of death by an exploited and destitute people. Today, Irish Americans wakes are much more sedate and respectable and generally last only one night. The main purpose of a wake is for relatives, neighbors, and friends to visit and pay their respects to the dead person and to offer condolences to the family. Although food and drink are still invariably provided to visitors, the once-customary overindulgence rarely occurs. Also traditionally, the body was

IRISH PROVERBS

Sceitheann fíon fírinne

Wine reveals the truth.

Níl aon tinteán mar do thinteán féin

There's no fireside like your own fireside.

Más maith leat tú a cháineadh, pós

Marry, if you wish to be criticized.

Mol an óige agus tiocfaidh sí

Give praise to the young and they will flourish.

An té a bhíos fial roinneann Dia lei

God shares with the generous.

Is maith an scáthán súil charad

The eye of a friend is a good mirror.

Is fada an bóthar nach mbíonn casadh ann

It's a long road that has no turn.

Giorraíonn beirt bother

Two people shorten the road.

laid out on a bed in the person's home, whereas today the wake often takes place in a funeral home with the body in a casket. Catholic dead frequently have rosary beads entwined in their crossed hands. Flowers and candles usually surround the casket. A constant watcher stands beside the dead person, these days out of respect but traditionally to guard bodies from the predations of "body-snatchers"; in the eighteenth and nineteenth centuries, the theft of dead bodies for use in medical schools was rife in Ireland. Women no longer practice the *caoine* or keening over the corpse in this country or in Ireland except on rare occasions. Visitors at a wake commonly offer a short silent prayer for the soul of the dead person.

FAMILY AND COMMUNITY LIFE

It is difficult to discuss the Irish American family in isolation from the broader society. Irish assimilation into American culture has been occurring over a long period and has been quite comprehensive. That said, aspects of Irish American life remain distinct for some, particularly in regards to marriage, gender roles, child rearing, and education. Even in these respects, however, most Irish Americans are generally indistinguishable from the greater American society.

Marriage During the nineteenth and much of the twentieth centuries, Irish Americans married later than their counterparts in many other ethnic groups. People delayed getting married, wishing first to attain a sufficient economic level. Many men did not marry until their mid-thirties; women often waited until their late twenties, well behind women in other immigrant groups. Large numbers did not marry at all, deciding to remain celibate, respecting strict Irish Catholic teachings that celibacy was a higher moral calling than even marriage. Today delayed marriages are less common, and there is probably less sexual dysfunction both within and outside marriage than before. Furthermore, those Irish whose families have long been established in the United States tend to have a more accepting attitude towards divorce than do the more recently arrived Irish. Many young Irish Americans are more inclined than their elders to look favorably on divorce. The negative attitude of the Catholic Church on the topic still affects perceptions, however. Many Irish Americans, even those who obtain a civil divorce, seek to procure a church annulment of their marriages so that they may remarry within Catholicism. Although Irish Americans frequently intermarry with other ethnic groups, a strong leaning toward marrying within the same religion remains.

Gender Roles The traditional Irish American mother remained at home to take care of the household. Female dominance of domestic life was common, and mothers generally played a dominant role in raising children. Not all Irish women were tied to the house, however. Many were also active in community-oriented projects, such as charity activities, parochial work, and caring for the old and sick. In addition, many women fleeing the famine and terrible conditions in Ireland in the nineteenth-century immigrated to the United States alone, displaying particular independence and resolve for women of the period. This boldness and determination remains one of the most dominant character traits of contemporary Irish American women. Few today are content to devote their lives to traditional housework, with the majority working in either part-time or full-time jobs. Great numbers have thrived in such professional spheres as academia, law, business, politics, and a variety of other occupations.

Children Irish American families have traditionally been large. This is partly a result of the continued adherence of many to the Catholic Church's teachings against contraception. Yet, like most Americans, Irish Americans have had considerably smaller families in recent years. A family's socioeconomic background largely determines its child-rearing practices. As in many Western cultures, the mother often cares for the children and imparts foundational values while the father is frequently a distant figure. Overt parental affection is not as prevalent as in some other ethnic groups, perhaps because of stricter views on authority rooted in the Catholic hierarchy. Negative reinforcement, such as shaming, can be as common as positive reinforcement. There has always been a tendency to imbue children with a strong sense of public respectability, and some have even argued that the desire to be thought respectable has deterred many Irish Americans from taking chances and has impeded their success.

Education In earlier generations of Irish Americans, more attention was paid to the education of sons than of daughters. Girls were generally expected to become homemakers, and if some did have a job, such work would be considered secondary to their household duties. Today, while some Irish American parents—particularly mothers—still indulge their sons, the education of daughters is a major focus.

Irish American families encourage achievement in school. The traditional respect of the Irish for education dates back to the fifth through eighth centuries, when Ireland attained the name of "Island of Saints and Scholars"; Irish monks helped preserve Latin and Greek learning in Europe, as well as the English language itself, by copying manuscripts. In addition, Irish Americans well understand that academic success facilitates achievement in wider social and economic spheres. The result is that Irish American Catholics are among the highest-achieving groups in the United States in terms of education. They are more likely than any other white gentile ethnic group to go to college and are also more likely than most other ethnic groups to pursue graduate academic and professional degrees.

While many Irish Americans attend public schools, colleges, and universities, numerous others attend Catholic educational institutions. During the nineteenth century, Irish parochial schools provided a route for Irish Americans to "protect" their children from being seduced by what many felt to be the Protestant ethos of the public schools. There is strong evidence that attendance at today's Catholic educational institutions, many of which have high standards, facilitates elevated levels of educational achievement and upward social mobility. Contrary to some beliefs, a Catholic education is not a deterrent to either academic or economic success. Among the most renowned Catholic universities are Boston College and the University of Notre Dame.

EMPLOYMENT AND ECONOMIC CONDITIONS

In the eighteenth and the first half of the nineteenth centuries, the great majority of Catholic Irish immigrants languished at the bottom of the U.S. economic ladder as unskilled laborers. Although some were farm workers, many more worked in such areas as mining, quarrying, bridge and canal building, and railway construction. So many Irish were killed building railroads that a common saying was "there is an Irishman buried under every tie." Others were dockworkers, ironworkers, factory-hands, bartenders, carters, street cleaners, hod-carriers, and waiters. Irish women generally worked in menial occupations. Multitudes were employed as domestic servants in Anglo-Protestant households, while others worked as unskilled laborers in New England textile mills. Some Irish became quite successful, but their numbers were few. The handful who attained white-collar status were frequently shopkeepers and small businessmen. An exceedingly meager number of Irish Americans were professionals. Those Irish who made the long trip to the Western States tended to have somewhat more prestigious jobs than their compatriots in the East and North, in part because of the large numbers of Chinese in the West who did much of the manual labor. Many Irish participated in the California Gold Rush.

In the years after the Civil War, the occupational lot of Irish Americans began to improve. More entered skilled trades; many moved into managerial positions in the railroad, iron, construction, and other industries; and some went into business for themselves, especially in the building and contracting sectors. Numerous others became police officers, firefighters, streetcar conductors, clerks, and post-office workers. Irish Americans held many leadership positions in the trade union movement. They also began to achieve greater recognition in the entertainment industry and in athletics. Far fewer opportunities existed for women in general at the time; still, many Irish American women attained upward occupational mobility by becoming teachers, nurses, and secretaries. Many Irish American nuns held positions of responsibility in hospitals, schools, and other Catholic social institutions.

By the beginning of the twentieth century, Catholic Irish Americans were clearly ascending the occupational ladder. Although most remained members of the working class, large numbers moved into the ranks of the lower middle classes. This improvement in socioeconomic status has continued. Today, Irish Americans are well represented in academia, medicine, law, government service, politics, finance, banking, insurance, journalism, the entertainment industry, the Catholic clergy, and most other professions.

POLITICS AND GOVERNMENT

The vast majority of Irish Catholic immigrants to the United States during the eighteenth and nineteenth centuries were politically progressive, a stance instilled by years of oppression at the hands of the British. Not surprisingly, most favored the policies of Thomas Jefferson, and their vote greatly assisted his election over the federalist John Adams to the presidency in 1800. They demonstrated their political inclinations again in 1829, supporting the populist politics of Democrat Andrew Jackson, the seventh American president and the nation's first of Irish descent (though a Protestant).

The clear understanding that they would be unable to match the Anglo-Protestant establishment in the world of business and economics, Irish American Catholics, many of whom entered the United States with fundamental political experience gained through mass agitation movements at home, realized that politics would provide them with a potent vehicle for attaining influence and power. In the years after the Civil War, the Irish American talent for political activity was increasingly evident. Irish American control of New York's Tammany Hall, the center of the city's Democratic Party in the nineteenth century, remains a resolute symbol of their powerful and sometimes dubious involvement in American urban politics. Although graft, cronyism, and corruption were once an integral part of many of their political "machines" in New York and other cities, Irish American politicians were frequently more successful than their Anglo-Protestant counterparts in reaching the people, feeding the poor, helping the more unfortunate obtain jobs, and organizing other practical social welfare activities. The Irish American political machine generally had a strong democratic, reformist, and pragmatic agenda, and it often included American Jews, Italians, Germans, Poles, and other immigrant groups.

Despite the notable twentieth-century presence of such influential Catholic Irish American reactionaries as the demagogue Father Charles Coughlin and the communist-baiter Senator Joseph McCarthy, members of the group are among the most likely to advocate the right of free speech. They also tend to be more supportive of liberal issues than many other white ethnic groups. For example, they have traditionally promoted such causes as racial equality, welfare programs, environmental issues, and gun control. Irish Americans, including the Kennedys and Presidents Bill Clinton and Barack Obama, have been and still are among the most stalwart supporters of the Democratic Party. Beginning in the late twentieth century, however, there has been a movement by some toward the Republican Party, particularly among more socially conservative Irish Catholics for whom abortion is a major concern.

Armed Forces Either as regulars or as volunteers, Irish Americans have served in all U.S. military involvements. They fought with distinction in the Revolutionary War, most siding with Washington. It is estimated that as many as 38 percent of Washington's army was composed of Irish Americans, even though they made up only 10 percent of the population. Of his generals, twenty-six were Irish, fifteen of them born in Ireland. In the Civil War most Irish Americans sided with the Union, and great numbers of them fought in Union armies. "The Fighting 69th" was probably the most famous Irish regimental unit, though thirty-eight Union regiments actually had "Irish" in their names. The contribution of the Irish to the Confederate cause was also significant. As many as 40,000 Confederate soldiers were born in Ireland, and numerous others were of Irish ancestry. Irish Americans continued to fight in the U.S. armies in subsequent wars and were particularly prominent, with many gaining decorations, in the two World Wars, the Korean War, and the Vietnam War. Their ready and distinguished participation in U.S. military conflicts has helped the Irish to gain respectability in the eyes of generations of other Americans and to assimilate into mainstream American life.

Labor Movement The Irish have contributed greatly to the labor movement in the United States. Their struggle for American workers' rights began as an outgrowth of their fight against oppression in Ireland. American capitalist injustice in industry was not much different in principle from persecution by English landlords at home. Even in the antebellum years, Irish Americans were active in workers' organizations, many of which were clandestine, but it was during the second half of the nineteenth century that their involvement in labor activities became especially prominent. Particularly well known are the activities of the "Molly Maguires," anthracite coal miners of Pennsylvania who in the 1860s and 1870s violently resisted the mostly English, Scottish, and Welsh mine bosses. Found guilty of nine murders, ten Mollies were hanged in 1876. This did not deter Irish involvement in American labor activities, however. Terence V. Powderly (1849–1924), the son of an Irish immigrant, was for years leader of the Knights of Labor, the first national labor organization, which was founded in 1869. He later became commissioner general of immigration under President William McKinley. Peter James McGuire (1852–1906), a carpenter, was another leading union activist. A founder of the American Federation of Labor, he was its secretary and first vice president. He is perhaps best known today as the "Father of Labor Day."

Irish women have also been prominent in the American labor movement. The Cork-born Mary Harris ("Mother") Jones (1830–1930), after losing all her possessions in the Chicago fire of 1871, began a fifty-year involvement in organizing labor unions and in striving to improve workers' conditions and wages throughout the United States. Today, a nationally circulated magazine devoted to liberal issues bears her name. Another famous Irish woman in the labor movement was Elizabeth Gurley Flynn (1890–1964), who cofounded the American Civil Liberties Union in 1920 and later became head of the United States Communist Party.

Kerry-born Michael Joseph Quill (1905–1966) founded the Transport Workers Union of America in 1934 and was its first president. In 1937 Irish American Joe Curran became the National Maritime Union's first president. George Meany (1894–1979), grandson of an Irish immigrant, was president of the combined American Federation of Labor and Congress of Industrial Organizations (AFL-CIO) from 1955 to 1979. Irish American participation in the U.S. union and labor movement has been and continues to be of vital importance and benefit to the well-being of American society.

Northern Ireland The attention of many Irish Americans from all generations has been sharply focused on Irish political affairs since the creation of Northern Ireland as part of the United Kingdom in 1921 and especially since the Catholic civil rights movement began in the late 1960s. The movement responded to decades of institutionalized and private discrimination against Catholics by the Protestant majority in the region in such spheres as voting, housing, and employment. Throughout the late twentieth century, Northern Ireland was convulsed by political upheaval, the frequently controversial tactics of an occupying force of British soldiers, Protestant and Catholic paramilitary activity, riots, killings, bombings, hunger strikes, internment without trial, and patent violations of human rights. The reactions of numerous Irish Americans have been forceful.

In 1970 the Irish Northern Ireland Aid Committee (NORAID), an American-based organization, was formed to provide material help to Catholics in Northern Ireland. The Irish National Caucus, a Washington-based lobbying group, has been vociferous in its call for a British withdrawal from Northern Ireland and for a reunification of the nation. Many Irish American politicians and lobbying groups have campaigned intensively to demand a solution to Northern Ireland's problems, consistently exerting pressure on successive administrations to use their influence with London, Belfast, and Dublin to help amend human rights abuses in Northern Ireland and to aid in the provision of social and economic justice in that region. Even after the Good Friday agreements of 1998, Irish Americans continue to be deeply concerned about the status of Northern Ireland and of the potential for further conflict there.

NOTABLE INDIVIDUALS

A vast number of Irish Americans have attained distinction over the past few centuries. The following sections list only a fraction of them and their achievements.

Art Many Irish Americans have achieved prominence in the arts. In the fine arts, for example, the following three achieved particular fame: Mathew Brady (1823–1896), Civil War photographer; James E. Kelly (1855–1933), sculptor; and Georgia O'Keeffe (1887–1986), painter.

Commerce and Industry Numerous Irish Americans have made their mark in the world of business and finance. Among them are William Russell (1812–1872), founder of the Pony Express; William Russell Grace (1832–1904), entrepreneur and first Roman Catholic mayor of New York; Andrew Mellon (1855–1937), banker, art collector, and philanthropist; Samuel S. McClure (1857–1949), leading journalist and newspaper publisher; Henry Ford (1863–1947), auto manufacturer; Howard Hughes (1905–1976), wealthy and eccentric industrialist, aerospace manufacturer, and moviemaker; and Jack Welch (1935–), noted General Electric CEO from 1981 to 2001.

Education John R. Gregg (1867–1948), inventor of the Gregg system of shorthand, and William Heard Kilpatrick (1871–1965), philosopher and leader in the progressive education movement, are among prominent Irish American educators.

Irish American author Frank McCourt is best known for his memoir, *Angela's Ashes.* JAMES LEYNSE / CORBIS

Literature Irish Americans have made a major impact in American literature since the early nineteenth century. Among the most notable Irish American literary personalities are Mathew Carey (1760–1839), author, book publisher, and political economist; Edgar Allan Poe (1809–1849), one of the greatest figures in American literature; Eugene O'Neill (1888–1953), one of the most eminent American playwrights; F. Scott Fitzgerald (1896–1940), internationally popular novelist and short story writer; James T. Farrell (1904–1979), an author whose work, notably his Studs Lonigan trilogy, centers on working-class Irish American families on Chicago's South Side; Mary McCarthy (1912–1989), novelist and critic; Flannery O'Connor (1925–1964), novelist and short story writer of the American South; William F. Buckley (1925–2008), editor, critic, commentator, and novelist; Frank McCourt (1930–2009), whose memoir *Angela's Ashes* is a classic of Irish American experience; Cormac McCarthy (1933–), Pulitzer Prize–winning novelist; and Billy Collins (1941–), U.S. poet laureate from 2001 to 2003.

Music Irish Americans have found success in both traditional and popular musical arenas. Well-known Irish American music groups include the punk bands Dropkick Murphys, founded in Massachusetts in 1996 and led by Ken Casey (1969–); and Flogging Molly, founded in Los Angeles in 1997 and led by Dublin-born Dave King (1961–). Popular American musicians of Irish descent who play non-Celtic music include singer-songwriter Tori Amos (1963–); John

Fogerty (1945–), lead singer of Creedence Clearwater Revival; Mandy Moore (1984–), singer-songwriter and actress; Christina Aguilera (1980–), popular singer; and Bruce Springsteen (1949–).

Government The fields of politics and law have featured more than their share of eminent Irish Americans. Among the earliest prominent immigrants was Sir Thomas Dongan (1634–1715), Irish-born governor of New York in 1682. Two extremely influential and powerful figures were James Michael Curley (1874–1958), mayor of Boston for four terms, and Richard J. Daley (1902–1976), mayor of Chicago from 1954 to 1976. Irish American involvement in both state and national politics also gained prominence in the twentieth century. Alfred Emanuel Smith (1873–1944), the grandson of Irish immigrants, was the first Irish American Catholic to receive the nomination of a major party (Democratic) in a presidential election; he was defeated by Herbert Hoover in 1928. An Irish American Catholic finally reached the White House in 1960 with the election of John F. Kennedy (1917–1963), who was assassinated in 1963. His brother, Senator Robert F. Kennedy (1925–1968), another prominent Democratic politician (he had served as attorney general in the Kennedy administration), was assassinated in 1968 while campaigning for president. A third brother, Edward (Ted) (1932–2009), was one of the most liberal and effective champions of social reform in the history of the U.S. Senate until his death in 2009 from natural causes.

Numerous other Irish American politicians have gained national attention in recent decades. Two twentieth-century presidents, Richard M. Nixon (1913–1994) and Ronald Reagan (1911–2004), both Republicans, were of Irish Protestant background. President Clinton (1946–) also claimed Irish descent, though no firm evidence surfaced. President Obama (1961–) has Irish Protestant roots on his mother's side; he visited his ancestral village in County Moneygall in 2011. Vice President Joe Biden (1942–) strongly identifies with his Irish Catholic roots. In addition, Irish Americans are well represented in the U.S. Congress. The Republican candidate for President in 2008, Senator John McCain (1936–), is of Scotch-Irish descent. Thomas "Tip" O'Neill (1912–1994) and Thomas S. Foley (1929–2013). Speakers of the House of Representatives, and Supreme Court Justices William J. Brennan (1906–1997) and Sandra Day O'Connor (1930–) the first woman on the court, all came from an Irish background.

Religion Famous Irish American religious leaders include Archbishop John Joseph Hughes (1797–1864), first Roman Catholic archbishop of New York; John McCloskey (1810–1885), first American cardinal of the Roman Catholic Church; James Gibbons (1834–1921), Francis Joseph Spellman (1889–1967), Richard J. Cushing (1895–1970), and Terence Cooke (1921–1983), all Roman Catholic cardinals; Archbishop Fulton John Sheen (1895–1979),

charismatic Roman Catholic Church leader; and Father Andrew Greeley (1928–), priest, sociologist, and novelist. Two famous humanitarians are Father Edward Joseph Flanagan (1886–1948), a Roman Catholic priest who worked with homeless boys and founded Boys Town in Nebraska; and Thomas A. Dooley (1927–1961), a medical doctor who performed great humanitarian work in Southeast Asia.

Sports Many Irish Americans have been eminent in sports, among them John L. Sullivan (1858–1918), James John "Gentleman Jim" Corbett (1866–1933), Jack Dempsey (1895–1983), and Gene Tunney (1898–1978), all heavyweight boxing champions; Babe Ruth (1895–1948), baseball player; Ben Hogan (1912–1997), golfer; Maureen "Little Mo" Connolly (1934–1969), a tennis star who won the U.S. women's singles championship three times; John Elway (1960–), two-time Super Bowl–winning quarterback; and Jason Kidd (1973–), talented National Basketball Association point guard.

Stage and Screen A great number of Irish Americans have attained distinction in the entertainment industry, including Will Rogers (1879–1935), humorist and actor; Buster Keaton (1895–1966), famous silent film comedian; James Cagney (1899–1986), movie actor; film director John Ford (born Sean Aloysius O'Feeny; 1895–1973); Spencer Tracy (1900–1967), movie actor; Ed Sullivan (1901–1974), television personality; Bing Crosby (1901–1977), singer and movie and radio actor; John Huston (1906–1987), film director; John Wayne (1907–1979), movie actor; Errol Flynn (1909–1959), movie actor; Maureen O'Sullivan (1911–), movie actor; Gene Kelly (1912–1996), dancer, actor, and singer; Tyrone Power (1913–1958), movie actor; Mickey Rooney (1920–1998), movie actor; Maureen O'Hara (1920–), movie actor; Carroll O'Connor (1924–2001), television actor; Grace Kelly (1929–1982), movie actor and later princess of Monaco; Jack Nicholson (1937–), movie actor; Mia Farrow (1945–), movie actor; Alec Baldwin (1958–), movie and television actor; Sean Penn (1960–), actor, director, and screenwriter; Ben Affleck (1972–), actor, director, and screenwriter; Jennifer Connelly (1970–), movie actor; and Macaulay Culkin (1980–), movie actor. Irish Americans have also been particularly successful as comedians and comedic actors. Examples from the late twentieth and early twenty-first centuries include George Carlin (1937–2008), Bill Murray (1950–), Will Ferrell (1967–), Conan O'Brien (1963–), Denis Leary (1957–), Bill Maher (1956–), Kathy Griffin (1960–), and Janeane Garofalo (1964–).

MEDIA

PRINT

Boston Irish Reporter

Founded in 1990, this monthly newspaper is sold at newsstands in Boston and eastern New England. The paper includes profiles of Irish Americans and news and culture items of interest to the Irish American community.

William P. Forry, Managing Editor
150 Mt. Vernon Street
Suite 120
Dorchester, Massachusetts 02125
Phone: (617) 436-1222
Fax: (617) 825-5516
Email: news@dotnews.com
URL: www.bostonirish.com

Irish America Magazine

Established in 1985, this bimonthly magazine publishes information about Ireland and Irish Americans, including interviews and book, play, and film reviews.

875 Avenue of the Americas
Suite 201
New York, New York 10001
Email: info@irishamerica.com
URL: www.irishamerica.com

Irish Echo

Established in 1928, this nationally distributed weekly periodical bills itself as the oldest and most widely read Irish American newspaper. It contains articles of interest to the Irish American community.

Ray O'Hanlon, Editor
11 Hanover Square
New York, New York 10005
Phone: (212) 482-4818
Fax: (212) 482-6569
Email: rohanlon@irishecho.com
URL: www.irishecho.com

Irish Herald

Established in 1962 and reestablished in 1996, this free monthly newspaper covers Irish American interests from a west coast perspective. The paper is distributed to metropolitan areas from Seattle to San Diego.

John J. Gallagher, Managing Editor
1201 Howard Avenue
Suite 203
Burlingame, California 94010
Phone: (650) 344-3765
Fax: (650) 344-3056
Email: editor@irish-herald.com
URL: www.irish-herald.com

IrishCentral.com

This website, launched in 2009, bills itself as the largest Irish American media site on the Internet and features news about Irish Americans, Ireland, and Irish culture throughout the nation. The site is also home to *Irish America* and *Irish Voice* magazines.

Kate Hickey, Editor
875 Sixth Avenue
New York, New York 10001
Phone: (212) 871-0111
Email: info@irishcentral.com
URL: www.irishcentral.com

RADIO

WFUV-FM (90.7)

This public radio station, based at Fordham University in the Bronx, New York, features three popular shows for Irish Americans and others of Celtic descent, including *Míle Fáilte*, a show about Irish language and culture presented by Séamus Blake; *A Thousand Welcomes*, a Celtic music show presented by Kathleen Biggins; and *Ceol na nGael Music of the Irish*, an Irish music, news, and sports program presented by Tara Cuzzi and Megan Scully. Shows are available online for download.

Chuck Singleton, General Manager
Fordham University
Bronx, New York 10458-9993
Phone: (718) 817-4550
URL: www.wfuv.org

WGBH-FM (89.7)

This Boston-based public radio station broadcasts *The Celtic Sojourn*, a Celtic music program presented by Brian O'Donovan. The station also maintains a permanent online Celtic music stream.

Marita Rivero, General Manager
One Guest Street
Boston, Massachusetts 02135
Phone: (617) 300-5400
URL: www.wgbh.org

WPNA-AM (1490)

This Chicago-based international music station carries programs of interest to the Irish American community, including the *Hagerty Irish* Hour and the *Mike O'Connor Show*. Both of these long-running shows feature music, news, and culture from Ireland and Chicago's Irish American community.

Phone: (708) 848-8980
Fax: (708) 848-9220
Email: email@wpna1490am.com
URL: www.wpna1490am.com

Find information about the *Hagerty Irish Hour* at

URL: www.irishhour.com

and the *Mike O'Connor* Show at

408 South Oak Park Avenue
Oak Park, Illinois 60302
URL: www.chicagoirishradio.com

ORGANIZATIONS AND ASSOCIATIONS

Ancient Order of Hibernians in America (AOH)

AOH is the oldest Irish Catholic fraternal organization in the United States. It was founded in Pennsylvania's coal mining regions and New York City in 1836. With more than 80,000 members throughout the United States, Canada, and Ireland, AOH is the largest Irish American organization, with divisions throughout the country. Originally founded to protect the Catholic faith of its members, the AOH works today to assist Irish immigrants to the United States with social programs and advocacy. Membership is confined to men over the age of sixteen. The organization also seeks to promote awareness throughout the United States of all aspects of Irish life and culture. It publishes a bimonthly newspaper, the *National Hibernian Digest*.

Thomas D. McNabb, Secretary
31 Logan Street
Auburn, New York 13021
Phone: (315) 252-3895
Email: thomas.mcnabb@aoh.org
URL: www.aoh.org

Irish American Cultural Institute (IACI)

Founded in 1962, this membership-driven nonprofit foundation, whose purposes are apolitical and nonreligious, fosters the exploration of the Irish experience in Ireland and the United States. Among its programs are the Irish Way, which takes American high school students on a summer educational tour of Ireland; lectures featuring Irish and Irish American writers and scholars; grants and fellowships for Irish American researchers; and traveling exhibits about Irish American history and experience. IACI publishes *Éire-Ireland*, a semiannual scholarly journal of Irish studies. The organization has fifteen chapters throughout the United States.

Carol Buck, Director of Operations
1 Lackawanna Place
Morristown, New Jersey 07960
Phone: (973) 605-1991
Fax: (973) 605-8875
Email: info@iaci-usa.org
URL: www.iaci-usa.org

Irish American Partnership

This nonprofit organization was founded in 1986 with seed money from the Irish Parliament to promote stronger cultural ties between the United States and the Republic of Ireland. The partnership encourages Irish Americans to participate in exploring their Irish heritage and supporting education and economic development in Ireland.

Joseph Leary, President
33 Broad Street
Boston, Massachusetts 02109
Phone: (617) 723-2707
Fax: (617) 723-5478
Email: jfl@irishap.org
URL: www.irishap.org

MUSEUMS AND RESEARCH CENTERS

American Conference for Irish Studies (ACIS)

Founded in 1962, ACIS is a multidisciplinary scholarly organization with more than 800 members in the United States, Canada, and abroad, who do research in a wide variety of Irish Studies. ACIS organizes a national annual conference as well as regional conferences at which scholars share their work with each other and the general public, alongside literary readings, performances, and Irish films. ACIS also organizes fellowships in Irish Studies and administers a grant program.

Sean Farrell, President
Department of History
Northern Illinois University
DeKalb, Illinois 60115
Phone: (815) 753-0131
Fax: (215) 545-3015
Email: sfarrel1@niu.edu
URL: www.acisweb.com

American Irish Historical Society (AIHS)

Founded in New York in 1897, the AIHS promotes awareness among Americans of Irish descent of their history, culture, and heritage and "inform[s] the world of the achievements of the Irish in America." The society presents lectures, readings, musical events, and art exhibitions at its headquarters in New York. Members make an annual contribution to the organization to support its programs. Each year the AIHS awards a gold medal to an Irish American or Irish individual who best reflects the society's ideals. Its annual journal, the *Recorder*, contains articles on a wide range of Irish American and Irish topics with a primary focus on the contribution of the Irish in American history. The AIHS library contains more than 10,000 volumes together with major manuscript and archival collections, including an extensive collection of historical newspapers documenting the Irish American experience, personal papers of leading Irish Americans, and works by Irish American artists. The library is open to the public by appointment.

Christopher Cahill
991 Fifth Avenue
New York, New York 10028
Phone: (212) 288-2263
Fax: (212) 628-7927
Email: aihs@aihs.org
URL: www.aihs.org

The Celtic Arts Center of Southern California

Founded in the mid-1980s, the center organizes events, classes, and workshops to celebrate and deepen understanding of Celtic and Gaelic—as well as Irish American—cultures. Offerings include Irish language classes and dance workshops, the Los Angeles County Irish Fair, and an annual Samhain (Celtic New Year) festival.

Douglas R. Dean, President
5062 Lankershim Blvd. #3003
North Hollywood, California 91601
Phone: (818) 760-8322
Email: celt@celticartscenter.com
URL: www.celticartscenter.com

Irish American Heritage Museum

For more than twenty years, the Irish American Heritage Museum has featured exhibits and programs to "preserve and tell the story of the contributions of the Irish people and their culture in America." Its new building opened in January 2012 in downtown Albany, New York, and features year-round exhibits, special programs, and the Paul O'Dwyer Library.

Jeff Cleary, Executive Director
370 Broadway
Albany, New York 12207-2969
Phone: (518) 427-1916
URL: www.irishamericanheritagemuseum.org

John J. Burns Library, Boston College, Special Collections and Archives

The Irish collection at Boston College's Burns Library is considered one of the most comprehensive collections of its kind outside of Ireland. The library also administers the Burns Library Visiting Scholar in Irish Studies Chair and maintains a significant Irish music collection.

Robert K. O'Neill, Burns Librarian
140 Commonwealth Avenue
Chestnut Hill, Massachusetts 02467
Phone: (617) 552-3282
Fax: (617) 552-2465
Email: robert.oneill.1@bc.edu
URL: www.bc.edu/content/bc/libraries/collections/burns.html

SOURCES FOR ADDITIONAL STUDY

Barrett, James R. *The Irish Way: Becoming American in the Multiethnic City*. New York: Penguin Press, 2012.

Dezell, Maureen. *Irish America: Coming Into Clover*. Norwell, MA: Anchor Press, 2002.

Dolan, Jay P. *The Irish Americans: A History*. New York: Bloomsbury Press, 2010.

McCourt, Frank. *Angela's Ashes: A Memoir*. New York: New York University Press, 2007.

Meagher, Timothy J. *Columbia Guide to Irish History*. New York: Columbia University Press, 2005.

Miller, Kerby A. *Emigrants and Exiles: Ireland and the Irish Exodus to North America*. New York: Oxford University Press, 1996.

Smith, Betty. *A Tree Grows in Brooklyn: A Novel*. New York: Harper, 1943.

Tracey, Patrick. *Stalking Irish Madness: Searching for the Roots of My Family's Schizophrenia*. New York: Bantam, 2008.

Waters, Maureen. *Crossing Highbridge: A Memoir of Irish America*. Syracuse, NY: Syracuse University Press, 1991.

IROQUOIS CONFEDERACY

Loretta Hall

OVERVIEW

Prior to contact with Europeans, the peoples that constitute what is today called the Iroquois Confederacy were a league of five culturally and linguistically related tribes that lived in the plains of the Schoharie Valley, a 93-mile stretch of land along the Schoharie Creek, which runs from the foot of the Catskill Mountains to the Mohawk River in present-day Upstate New York. The name *Iroquois* was given to the people by French colonists, who adapted the term from the word *Iroqu,* or "rattlesnake," the name given to the five tribes by enemy Algonquian people who also occupied the region. The members of the Iroquois Confederacy prefer to call themselves *Haudenosaunee,* their original name, which means "People of the Longhouse."

The Iroquois were farmers and formed their confederacy, which consisted of the Cayuga, Mohawk, Oneida, Onondaga, and Seneca peoples, sometime between 1450 and 1600 to stop fighting among the tribes. According to Gary Warrick's *A Population History of the Huron Petun, A.D. 500–1600,* the Iroquois people were a sophisticated society of some 5,500 people when the first white explorers encountered them sometime around 1630. A sixth tribe, the Tuscarora, was added to the group in 1722.

The Iroquoian tribes own seven reservations in New York State, one in Wisconsin, and two in Canada, but the majority of the people live off the reservations. Although much of their homeland was taken away from them following the American Revolution, the Iroquois Confederacy largely avoided forced relocation, and as a result, the nation was able to stay near traditional lands in the state of New York. Some Oneida, however, moved to Wisconsin, where they maintain reservation lands near Green Bay. As a rule, the Iroquois Confederacy are not averse to adapting to new circumstances and using new technologies when such changes are beneficial, but they also strive to maintain their own traditional identity and work hard to preserve their culture.

According to the 2010 U.S. Census, there were 48,365 Iroquois living in the United States. The Iroquois are the country's eighth-largest Native American group. Most of the population lives in New York state, but Wisconsin, Oklahoma, Texas, North Carolina, Michigan, Florida, and California also boast significant numbers.

HISTORY OF THE PEOPLE

Early History The names of each of the tribes in the Iroquois Confederacy references either a characteristic of the group or denotes something about the land that tribe inhabits. The Mohawk called themselves *Ganiengehaka,* or "people of the flint country." Their warriors, armed with flint arrows, were known to be overpowering; their enemies called them *Mowak,* meaning "man eaters." The name *Oneida* means "people of the standing stone," referring to a large rock that, according to legend, appeared wherever the people moved, to give them directions. The Onondaga ("people of the hills"), Cayuga ("where they land the boats"), and Seneca ("people of the big hill") named themselves by describing their homelands. The last group to join the Iroquois, the Tuscarora, who migrated to the region from the Carolina area in the early eighteenth century, took their name from their original tribal name *ska-ru-ren,* which translates as "hemp gatherers" or "shirt-wearing people," a reference to the Indian hemp, sometimes called milkweed, that they used to make rope and clothing.

Although Iroquois tribes settled for centuries in close proximity to Algonquian tribes, who lived on both sides of the Iroquois, the groups have distinct cultural and linguistic heritages. Archaeological evidence suggests that the Iroquois migrated into the New York area around 1000 CE from some other place, but no evidence has been found to indicate where they came from. The Cherokee people, whose historic homeland was in the southeastern United States, belong to the same linguistic group as the Iroquois and share some other links with them. It is not known, however, where and when they may have lived near each other. Iroquois creation myths attempt to explain the linguistic differences in the New York area. According to one popular tale, the daughter of the Great Spirit became pregnant and had twin sons: one good and one evil. The evil brother, angered by the good brother's sympathy for the earth's humans, engaged his brother in a years-long battle, in which the good brother died. Legend says that the tones of their voices, as they passed through different areas of the land during their strife, determined the language that the people there

groups in the area. They repeatedly sought battle against tribes in the Midwest, along the Atlantic seaboard, in the south, and eventually against the French.

Modern Era The French had established a presence in Canada for over fifty years before they met the Iroquois in or about 1630. Beginning in 1609, the Iroquois began to acquire European weapons and goods through raids on other Indian tribes. The recurring raids prompted the French to help their Indian allies attack the Iroquois, which had the effect of providing the Iroquois with even more weapons: after defeating their opponent, the Iroquois would take their French wares. The French would replenish the defeated tribes, and the Iroquois would strike again seeking products that the Iroquois had come to prefer to their own materials. The French fought with firearms, while traditional Iroquois weapons were bows and arrows, stone tomahawks, and wooden warclubs. The Iroquois found other implements such as metal axes, knives, hoes, and kettles far superior to their implements of stone, bone, shell, and wood. Woven cloth began to replace the animal skins usually used for clothing materials.

In response to European influence, the Iroquois gradually changed their military tactics to incorporate stealth, surprise, and ambush. Their motives for fighting also changed. In the past, they had fought for prestige or revenge, or to obtain goods or captives; now they fought for economic advantage, seeking control over bountiful beaver-hunting grounds or perhaps a stash of beaver skins to trade for European goods. The more they raided and conquered, the more dependent the Iroquois became on European goods. The cycle continued through the end of the century as the raids that had begun in 1609 escalated into a series of conflicts known as the Beaver Wars, which saw the Iroquois wrest control of the fur trade from the French.

Although it provided the Indians with better tools, European incursion into the territory was disastrous for the indigenous people. In the 1690s alone, the Iroquois lost between 1,600 and 2,000 people through fighting with other Indian tribes. In addition, European diseases such as smallpox, measles, influenza, lung infections, and even the common cold took a heavy toll on them since they had developed no immunity and knew no cures.

These seventeenth-century population devastations prompted the Iroquois people to turn increasingly to their traditional practice of taking outsiders into their tribes to replace members who had died from violence or illness. While some captives were unmercifully tortured to death, others were adopted into Iroquois families. The adopted person was treated with the same affection, given the same rights, and expected to fulfill the same duties as the person he replaced.

Early in the eighteenth century the Tuscarora, another Iroquoian-speaking tribe living in North

would speak. Thus, the Iroquois tribes share a common tongue, but the tribes and nations surrounding them do not.

Archaeologists are also unsure when the Iroquois Confederacy was formed, with some arguing for a date as far back as 1150 CE but most agreeing that the five tribes united sometime between 1350 and 1600. According to Iroquois legend, two men, the Great Peacemaker Deganawidah (also spelled Dekanawida) from the Huron area and his disciple Hiawatha, formed the nation in order to stop infighting among the tribes because their squabbling had left them vulnerable to attacks from the surrounding Algonquin people. The legend says that all the other leaders readily accepted this call for peace, except Tadadaho, the cannibalistic ruler of the Onondagas. After enduring a set of brutal trials, Hiawatha, whose name means "he who combs," finally converted Tadadaho by removing snakes from his hair. Once united, the five Iroquois tribes became one of the most feared and respected

Carolina, moved into the territory occupied by the Confederacy. They had rebelled against the encroachment of colonial settlers, against continual fraudulent treatment by traders, and against repeated raids that took their people for the slave trade. However, they had suffered a terrible defeat in this war, with hundreds of their people killed and hundreds more enslaved. The survivors made their way north and became the sixth nation of the Iroquois Confederacy. The first half of the eighteenth century was a period of rebuilding. The Iroquois made peace with the French and established themselves in a neutral position between the French and the English. This strategy lasted until the French and Indian War erupted in 1754; although the Confederacy was officially neutral, the Mohawk sided with the English, and the Seneca with the French.

The French and Indian War ended in 1764. Eleven years later, in 1775, the onset of the American Revolution presented the Iroquois Confederacy with a similar dilemma. Again, the various tribes failed to agree on which side to support. Without unanimous agreement on a common position, each nation in the Confederacy was free to pursue its own course. The Oneida fought on the side of the colonists; a major faction of the Mohawk sided with the British and recruited other Iroquois warriors to their cause. The Confederacy as a political entity was severely damaged by the conflict, and the war itself brought death and devastation to the member tribes. After the war, American retaliatory raids destroyed Iroquois towns and crops and drove the people from their homelands.

In 1798 a Quaker delegation worked among the Seneca, teaching them to read and write. They also instructed the Seneca in modern farming, selling them European tools, often at no profit to the Quakers. Though not all welcomed the assimilation, Christianity and the English language began to take hold on the Seneca lands. More Iroquois began to accept the concept of private ownership of land (historically, tribal lands were held in common).

In 1799, amidst the Christian missionary efforts, a revival of the ancient religion developed, combined with Christian beliefs. A Seneca known as Handsome Lake had spent much of his life in dissolute living and fell gravely ill when he was about sixty-five years old. He expected to die, but instead, he experienced a profound vision and recovered. Inspired, he began to spread the Good Word among his fellow Iroquois. The new religion (which came to be known as the Longhouse Religion) was essentially a revitalization of the ancient Iroquoian beliefs, although some Quaker influence can be detected.

The Iroquois Confederacy, which had been divided by two wars among white people, remained fragmented in political, social, and religious ways throughout the nineteenth century. Shortly after the end of Revolutionary War in 1783, a series of treaties resulted in Iroquois land being turned over to New York State, furthering fragmenting the Six Nations. As part

of these treaties, the Iroquois sold large amounts of land in exchange for useful trade goods. Leading chiefs were sometimes induced to support such sales by the offer of lifetime pensions. Families were encouraged to leave the longhouses and live separately on small farms. In 1807 the Cayuga sold their New York lands, choosing to move to Ohio. While some, including the Seneca, Tuscarora, and Onondaga, avoided the mass forced removals of the 1830s, other tribes moved from their ancestral lands. In 1838 the Oneida relocated to reservation lands near Green Bay, Wisconsin. Further government interference caused more tribal division. The Canadian government established the Indian Acts of 1869 and 1876, which in part attempted to relegate how chiefs were elected, a decision that caused political strife among the Six Nations in both Canada and the United States.

The twentieth century saw further legal battles, which began to bring the Iroquois together as a people. Beginning in the 1950s, the Mohawk, Seneca, and Tuscarora became involved in major land disputes over power-production and flood-control projects proposed by the New York State Power Authority and the United States Army Corps of Engineers. Paired with the social climate favoring ethnic assertion in the mid-twentieth century, these land disputes helped foster resurgence in Iroquois solidarity. In what became known as the Oka Crisis of 1990, Mohawks on both sides of the border protested the building of a golf course on Indian land in Oka, Quebec. Following a battle with the SWAT team involving tear gas and gunfire, the golf course expansion was cancelled. In 2010 the Iroquois once again banded together to fight the U.S. law regarding the use of tribal passports as international travel documents.

Iroquois steel workers at a construction site in the 1920s. Historical / CORBIS

SETTLEMENT IN THE UNITED STATES

The Iroquois lived in what is now New York state for most of their existence; their ancestral lands, however, were threatened as the European settlers began to move into the area. By the nineteenth century, through a series of land-claim treaties with the United States, the Iroquois land was reduced to a small number of reservations. The Oneida land decreased from 6 million acres in New York to just 32 acres (in Madison County); most Oneida moved on to Wisconsin. Other Iroquois chose to stay close to their cultural lands. The Onondaga settled a 7,300-acre reservation south of Syracuse, while the Seneca occupied three reservations in New York. The St. Regis Mohawk tribe was given 14,640 acres on the U.S.-Canada border. Other reservation lands were established in Erie County and Niagara County, as well as one in Ontario and one in Oklahoma. According to the U.S. Census Bureau's American Community Survey estimates for 2006–2010, the largest population of Iroquois reside in New York (21,078). Other states with smaller numbers include Wisconsin (7,843), Oklahoma (2,278), Texas (1,278), North Carolina (1,496), Michigan (1,167), Florida (1,384), and California (1,472).

Various Iroquois communities see themselves as sovereign nations, not as merely another ethnic group within the U.S. population, and gaining further recognition of that status is a major objective.

They have asserted their position in interesting ways. For example, when the United States declared war on Germany in 1917, the Iroquois Confederacy issued its own independent declaration and claimed status as an Allied nation in the war effort. In 1949 a Haudenosaunee delegation attended groundbreaking ceremonies for the United Nations building in New York City. Iroquois statesmen and athletes use Haudenosaunee passports as they travel around the world. The use of Iroquois passports became national news in 2010 when the Iroquois national lacrosse team could not travel to the world competition because the British government would not recognize their tribal passport. Although Secretary of State Hillary Clinton made a one-time allowance for the lacrosse players (who were still denied entry to Britain), the U.S. government has maintained a strict law that Native Americans carry the proper United States–issued documentation for international travel, including an official U.S. passport.

Protecting the land is another priority for the Iroquois. As was the case with other Native Americans, much of the friction between the Iroquois and non-Indians has been rooted in different attitudes toward land. During the 1950s and 1960s the long-standing disparity was brought into sharp focus during the planning and construction of the Kinzua Dam, which flooded over 9,000 acres of Seneca Land. The Indians

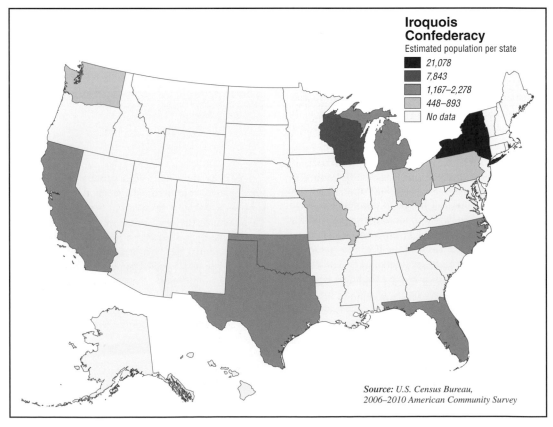

Iroquois Confederacy
Estimated population per state
- 21,078
- 7,843
- 1,167–2,278
- 448–893
- No data

Source: U.S. Census Bureau, 2006–2010 American Community Survey

fought the dam, claiming it violated the treaty between the Six Nations and the United States. The government reimbursed the tribe financially, but the reservation was disrupted. The grave of the revered warrior Cornplanter had to be moved to accommodate the dam; his descendant Harriett Pierce commented, "The White man views land for its money value. We Indians have a spiritual tie with the earth, a reverence for it that Whites don't share and can hardly understand" (Alvin M. Josephy Jr., *Now That the Buffalo's Gone: A Study of Today's American Indians*, 1982).

After New York state attempted to condemn a portion of the Seneca's land for use in building a highway, a federal court ruled in the 1970s that the state would have to negotiate with the Iroquois as equal sovereigns. In another land issue, the St. Regis (Akwesasne) Mohawk Reservation has been affected by off-reservation pollution sources, including a neighboring toxic-waste dump and nearby air-fouling industrial plants. In the 1990s struggles over land rights and protection of the land also included the extension of leases on property and towns in western New York, as well as ongoing conflicts over pollution and the environment. The land-rights conflicts continued into the twenty-first century as the Iroquois fought for control over land in New York State. Among those claims included a 250,000-acre plot of land between Syracuse and Utica, filed by the Oneida people, and another 64,000 acres at Cayuga Lake, claimed by the Cayugas. Both claims were dismissed, though the legal battles over the land persist.

LANGUAGE

The Iroquois language is rich in words for tangible things but lacking in abstract expressions. A 1901 treatise noted, "for the varieties, sexes, and ages of a single animal they would have a multitude of terms, but no general word for animal. Or they would have words for good man, good woman, good dog, but no word for goodness" (Lewis H. Morgan, *League of the Ho-de-no-sau-nee or Iroquois*). The six Iroquoian dialects are similar enough to allow easy conversation. The Mohawk and Oneida dialects are quite similar, as are the Cayuga and Seneca; the Onondaga and Tuscarora dialects are each different from the five others. One characteristic common to all six dialects is the absence of labial consonants (formed by bringing the lips together).

Historically, the Iroquois language was oral, though stories were passed down through a kind of language using colored beads woven into what was known as a wampum belt. Designs were woven into the belts, making symbols that represented ideas. These could be read by anyone familiar with the language of the wampum. The wampum also recorded public records, like marriages, or told legends and stories. In the mid-1800s a Congregational missionary named Asher Wright devised a written version of the Iroquois language using the English alphabet and

edited a Seneca newspaper. During the latter half of the twentieth century, written dictionaries and grammar texts were developed for teaching five of the dialects of the Iroquois language on the reservations.

Greetings and Popular Expressions Some basic Mohawk expressions include the following: *shé:kon* ("SHAY kohn") or *kwé kwé* ("KWAY KWAY")—hello; *hén* ("hun")—yes; *iáh* ("yah")—no; *nia:wen* ("nee AH wun")—thank you.

RELIGION

From ancient times the Haudenosaunee believed that a powerful spirit called Orenda permeated the universe. He created everything that is good and useful. The Evil Spirit made things that are poisonous, but the Great Spirit gained control of the world. From this belief emerged the myth of the twin brothers who brought the many languages to the Iroquois people's world. The idea of Orenda, and the continuous battle of good versus evil, is central to much of the early mythology.

The use of masks, or "false faces," was a major component of Iroquois rituals. They symbolized spirit forces that were represented by the person wearing the mask at festivals or healing ceremonies. One group of spirits was depicted by masks carved from living trees, while another group was represented by masks made from braided corn husks. Miniature corn husk masks, three inches across or less, were kept as personal charms; in ancient times the miniatures were also made of clay or stone.

As a rule, the Iroquois Confederacy are not averse to adapting to new circumstances and using new technologies when such changes are beneficial, but they also strive to maintain their own traditional identity and work hard to preserve their culture.

During the seventeenth century, French Jesuit missionaries converted many of the Iroquois to Catholicism. Kateri Tekakwitha, who was baptized in 1676, became the first Native American nun. She was extraordinarily devout; since her death many visions and miraculous cures have been attributed to her intervention. She was beatified by the Catholic Church in 1980 and canonized by Pope Benedict XVI in 2012. The "Blessed Kateri" is revered at the feasts and celebrations of many Native American nations, particularly those who have incorporated Catholicism into their spiritual belief systems. St. Kateri Tekakwitha's feast day is July 14.

An intense rivalry developed between the pagan and Christian factions of the Iroquois, and in 1823 a group of Oneidas led by Eleazar Williams, a Mohawk from Canada who had become an Episcopalian minister, left their New York homeland and moved to Wisconsin, where they established a reservation.

In 1799 a Seneca called Handsome Lake initiated a religious movement that combined Christianity with traditional religion, which eventually became known as the Code of Handsome Lake. It is also called the Longhouse Religion because the traditional longhouse was used as the place of worship. Major tenets of the Handsome Lake Code include shunning alcoholic beverages, abandoning beliefs in witchcraft and love potions, and denunciating abortion. The fact that Handsome Lake's message had come to him in a dream gave it a profound impact among the Haudenosaunee. The religion was instrumental in showing many Iroquois how to retain their own culture while adapting to a world dominated by non-Indians. The Handsome Lake Code continues to be a major spiritual focus among the Iroquois people. Some adhere solely to its practice, while others maintain a parallel membership in a Christian church.

CULTURE AND ASSIMILATION

The Iroquois have been willing to adapt to a changing world, but they have resisted efforts to substitute a European culture for their own heritage. For example, in 1745 the Reverend David Brainerd proposed to live among them for two years to help them build a Christian church and become accustomed to the weekly worship cycle. They were direct in declining his offer: "We are Indians and don't wish to be transformed into white men. The English are our Brethren, but we never promised to become what they are." (James Axtell, *The European and the Indian: Essays in the Ethnohistory of Colonial North America*.)

Traditional values are sustained on the various Iroquois reservations. The ancient languages are spoken and taught, traditional ceremonies are observed, and baskets are woven. Material wealth is not characteristic of reservation Indians, but Tonawanda Seneca Chief Corbett Sundown, keeper of the Iroquois "spiritual fire," disputes the assessment that the people are poor. He told a *National Geographic* writer: "We're rich people without any money, that's all. You say we ought to set up industries and factories. Well, we just don't want them. How're you going to grow potatoes and sweet corn on concrete? You call that progress? To me 'progress' is a dirty word" (Arden Harvey, "The Fire that Never Dies," *National Geographic*, September 1987).

Traditions and Customs The longhouses in which the Iroquois lived were constructed with a vestibule at each end that was available for use by all residents. Within the body of the house, a central corridor 8 feet wide separated two banks of compartments. Each compartment, measuring about 13 feet by 6 feet, was occupied by a nuclear family. A wooden platform about a foot above the ground served as a bed by night and chair by day; some compartments included small bunks for children. An overhead shelf held personal belongings. Every 20 feet along the central corridor, a fire pit served the two families living on its opposite sides. Bark or hide doors at the ends of the buildings were attached at the top; these openings and the smoke holes in the roof 15 to 20 feet above each hearth provided the only ventilation. Today, longhouses are used only for religious and ceremonial purposes.

Villages of 300 to 600 people were protected by a triple-walled stockade of wooden stakes 15 to 20 feet tall. About every fifteen years the nearby supplies of wild game and firewood would become depleted, and the farmed soil would become exhausted. During a period of two years or so, the men would find and clear an alternate site for the village, which would then be completely rebuilt.

The primary crops, revered as gifts from the Creator, were called the "Three Sisters": Corn provided stalks for climbing bean vines, while squash plants controlled weeds by covering the soil. The complementary nutrient needs and soil-replenishing characteristics of the three crops extended the useful life of each set of fields. In addition to providing food, the corn plants were used to make a variety of other goods. From the stalks were made medicine-storing tubes, corn syrup, toy warclubs and spears, and straws for teaching children to count. Corn husks were fashioned into lamps, kindling, mattresses, clotheslines, baskets, shoes, and dolls. Animal skins were smoked over corn-cob fires.

Although bows and arrows tipped with flint or bone were the primary hunting weapons, blow guns were used for smaller prey. Made from the hollowed stem of swamp alder, blow guns were about six feet long and one inch thick, with a half-inch bore; the arrows were two and a half feet long.

Cuisine Corn is the traditional staple of the Iroquois diet. It was baked or boiled and eaten on or off the cob; the kernels were mashed and either fried, baked in a kettle, or spread on corn leaves that were folded and boiled like tamales. Some varieties of corn were processed into hominy by boiling the kernels in a weak lye solution of hardwood ashes and water. Bread, pudding, dumplings, and cooked cereal were made from cornmeal. A parched-corn beverage, served hot, was brewed by mixing roasted corn with boiling water.

Besides corn, and the beans and squash they raised with it, the Iroquois people ate a wide variety of other plant foods. Wild fruits, nuts, and roots were gathered to supplement the cultivated crops. Berries were dried for year-round use. Maple sap was used for sweetening, but salt was not commonly used.

The traditional diet featured over thirty types of meat, including deer, bear, beaver, rabbit, and squirrel. Fresh meat was enjoyed during the hunting season, and some was smoked or dried and used to embellish corn dishes during the rest of the year. The Iroquois used the region's waterways extensively for transportation, but fish was relatively unimportant as food. Today the Iroquois attempt to combine their traditional heritage with twenty-first century life, including their diet. While they enjoy the modern amenities available at the local supermarket, many tribes continue to grow their own food, particularly those with ceremonial uses, such as corn and tobacco. Ancestral recipes are passed down to the next generation as a way of preserving the Iroquois culture.

Traditional Dress The fundamental item of Iroquois men's clothing was a breechcloth made of a strip of deerskin or fabric. Passing between the legs, it was secured by a waist belt, and decorated flaps of the breechcloth hung in the front and back. The belt, or sash, was a favorite article; sometimes worn only around the waist, and sometimes also over the left shoulder, it was woven on a loom or on the fingers and might be decorated with beadwork, a practice that became popular after the beginning of the fur trade era as the Iroquois craftsmen gained access to more fabrics and beads.

The basic item of women's clothing was a short petticoat. Other items that were worn by both sexes included a fringed, sleeveless tunic, separate sleeves (connected to each other by thongs, but not connected to the tunic), leggings, moccasins, and a robe or blanket. Clothing was adorned with moose-hair embroidery featuring curved line figures with coiled ends. Decorated pouches for carrying personal items completed the costumes. Women used burden straps, worn across the forehead, to support bundles or baskets carried on their backs.

By the end of the eighteenth century, trade cloth replaced deerskin as the basic clothing material. Imported glass beads replaced porcupine quills as decorative elements. In the twenty-first century, traditional dress is still worn in ceremonies and dances in order to preserve cultural heritage.

Traditional Arts and Crafts The Iroquois put elm bark to many useful purposes, including constructing houses, building canoes, and fashioning containers. Baskets were woven of various materials, including black ash splints. Pottery vessels were decorated with angular combinations of parallel lines.

Wampum (cylindrical beads about one-fourth inch long and one-eighth inch in diameter) was very important in the Iroquois culture. The beads were made of quahog, large clam shells, and could only be obtained through trading or as tribute payments from coastal tribes. White and purple beads were made from the different sections of the shells. Although the beads were used as ornamentation on clothing, wampum had several more important uses. Strings of the beads were used in mourning rituals or to identify a messenger as an official representative of his nation. Wampum belts served as symbols of authority or of contract. Patterns or figures woven into wampum belts recorded the terms of treaties; duplicate belts were given to each of the contracting parties. Because of its important uses, wampum became a valuable commodity and was sometimes used as a form of currency in trading.

In the mid-1800s a rather abrupt change occurred in the style of artwork used to decorate clothing with beads, quills, and embroidery. Rather than the traditional patterns of curving lines and scrolls, designs became representational images of plants and flowers, influenced by the floral style prominent among the seventeenth- and eighteenth-century French.

Dances and Songs In their traditional music, the Iroquois had one type of wind instrument, the wooden "courting flute," which has six finger stops and is blown from the end. Single-tone rhythm instruments provided the only musical accompaniment for ceremonial dancing and singing. Rattles were made by placing dried corn kernels inside various materials, including turtle shells, gourds, bison horns, or folded and dried bark. The traditional drum was about six inches in diameter, made like a wooden pail, and covered with stretched animal skin; just the right amount of water was sealed inside to produce the desired tone when the drum was tapped with a stick.

Eventually, the Onondaga discovered that non-Indians would be willing to pay to see their ceremonial dances, and they experimented with public performances. In 1893 the annual Green Corn Festival was delayed several weeks for the convenience of the audience, and the council house was filled three times with spectators who paid 15 cents admission.

Holidays The annual cycle of festivals consists of six regular festivals, which are still observed among the Iroquois. In addition, ceremonies are held as needed for wakes, memorial feasts, burials, adoptions, or sealing of friendships. In traditional Iroquois culture, the new year began with the Mid-Winter Festival, which was held in late January or early February when the men returned from the fall hunt. It lasted five days, followed by another two or three days of game playing. This was a time of spiritual cleansing and renewal and included a ritual cleaning of homes. Public confessions were made, and penitents touched a wampum belt as a pledge of reform. Playing a traditional dice game commemorated the struggle between the Creator and his evil twin brother for control over the earth. Thanks were offered to the Creator for protection during the past year. Dreams were always considered to be supernatural messages, and everyone was obliged to help the dreamer by fulfilling the needs or desires expressed in the dream; particular attention was devoted to dream-guessing during the Mid-Winter Festival. On a pre-festival day, names were conferred on babies, young adults, and adoptees so they could participate in the upcoming ceremonies.

In the spring, when the sap rose, it was time for the Thanks-to-the-Maple Festival. This one-day

celebration included social dances and the ceremonial burning of tobacco at the base of a maple tree. In May or June, corn seeds saved from the previous year were blessed at the Corn Planting Ceremony. This was a half-day observance in which the Creator was thanked and spirit forces were implored for sufficient rain and moderate sun. Ripening strawberries in June signaled time for the Strawberry Festival. Dancers mimicked the motions of berry pickers. This one-day celebration was a time for giving thanks.

In August or early September, the corn was ready to eat. This event was marked by the Green Corn Festival, which involved ceremonies on four successive mornings. The first day included general thanksgiving, a Feather Dance honoring those who worked to put on the festival, and the naming of children. The second day saw more dances and the bestowing of names on young adults and adoptees. The third day was dedicated to personal commitment and sacrifice and included a communal burning of tobacco. Speeches and dancing were followed by a feast. On the fourth day the ceremonial dice game was played (like at the Mid-Winter Festival). Finally, the women who worked the fields sang thanksgiving for the crops.

When all the crops had been harvested and stored away, and before the men left for the fall hunt, the Harvest Festival was held. This one-day celebration took place in October. Many of these holidays, including the Green Corn Festival, the Strawberry Festival, and the Harvest Festival, are still celebrated today as an important part of Iroquois heritage.

Health Care Issues and Practices Traditional Iroquois rituals addressed both physical and mental health issues. Medicine men or women used herbs and natural ointments to treat maladies such as fevers, coughs, and snake bites. Wounds were cleaned, broken bones were set, and medicinal emetics were administered. Another type of healer, known as a conjurer, sang incantations to combat maladies caused by witchcraft. They might remove an affliction from the patient's body by blowing or sucking. Twice a year groups of False Faces, or Iroquois who wore sacred ceremonial masks to bring about healing, visited each house in the village, waving pine boughs and dispelling illness. Those who had been previously healed in one of these visits became a False Face in future events. Shamans were empowered to combat disorders caused by evil spirits.

In the realm of mental health, modern psychologists see the value in the Iroquois practice of dream-guessing, an ancient ritual that took place during the Ceremony of the Great Riddle during the Midwinter Festival. The Iroquois would tell their dreams to their tribe, and an expert would offer meaning; the greater community could also offer suggestions for the dream's meaning. Everyone in the community had a responsibility to resolve conflicts and unmet needs made evident through any person's dreams.

Many of the Iroquois reservations in the twenty-first century have embraced modern medical practices, including on-site medical clinics and modern drug prescriptions. The traditional medicines and herbal remedies, however, still exist, particularly among the older generation, who continue to gather plants to use for traditional medicinal purposes and still honor their ancestral healing practices. Many Iroquois, for instance, use masks to protect themselves from evildoers and to keep illness away from their homes.

Death and Burial Rituals When a person died, everyone who had similar names gave them up until a period of mourning was completed. Later, if another person was adopted into the clan, he was often given the name of the deceased person whose place he or she took. A wake was held the night following a death. After a midnight meal, the best orators of the village spoke about the deceased and about life and death in general. The body was placed on a scaffold for several days on the chance that the person only appeared dead and might revive, which happened occasionally. After decomposition began, the remains might be buried, or the cleaned bones might be housed in or near the family lodge. When the village relocated, all of the unburied skeletons were interred in a common grave. By the end of the nineteenth century, burials were conducted according to European customs.

Upon death both the soul and the ghost left the body. Using food and tools offered by the survivors, the soul journeyed to the land of the dead. The ghost, on the other hand, became a spiritual inhabitant of the village. At a yearly Feast of the Dead, tobacco and songs were offered to the resident ghosts. Many of these practices are still alive today within the Iroquois Confederacy, as a way to honor ancestors and preserve heritage.

Recreational Activities Traditional Iroquois games ranged from lively field contests like lacrosse to more sedentary activities involving the bouncing of dried fruit-pit "dice" from a wooden bowl. The games were played both as entertainment and as elements of periodic ceremonies. A favorite winter game called "snow-snake" involved throwing a long wooden rod and seeing how far it would slide down an icy track smoothed out on a snowy field.

FAMILY AND COMMUNITY LIFE

The Iroquois tribes were organized into eight clans, which were grouped in two moieties: Wolf, Bear, Beaver, and Turtle; and Deer, Snipe, Heron, and Hawk. In ancient times, intermarriage was not allowed within each four-clan group, but eventually intermarriage was only forbidden within each clan. Tribal affiliation did not affect clan membership; for example, all Wolf clan members were considered to be blood relatives, regardless of whether they were members of the Mohawk, Seneca, or other Iroquois tribes. At birth, each person becomes a member of the clan of his or her mother. Within a tribe, each clan was led by the clan mother, who was usually the oldest woman in the group. In consultation with the other women, the clan mother chose one or more men to serve as clan chiefs. Each chief was appointed for life, but the clan mother and her advisors could remove him from office for poor behavior or dereliction of duty.

In ancient times adultery among the Iroquois was rare. When it was discovered, the woman was whipped, but the man was not punished. If a couple decided to separate, both of their families would be called to a council. The parties would state their reasons for wanting a divorce, and the elders would try to work out a reconciliation. If those efforts failed, the marriage ended. When a divorce occurred in ancient times, fathers kept their sons and mothers kept their daughters; by the early eighteenth century, however, mothers typically kept all of the children.

Gender Roles Traditionally, Iroquois men worked outside of the home, while the women tended to life within the home. The men were the hunters, getting meat and fish for the community, as well as the warriors, defending their tribe from outside threats. The women, on the other hand, ran the longhouses, which could house as many as six different families. They were responsible for the farming, the cooking, the sewing, and the tending of the children. The women also organized the tribe's ceremonies and festivals, making them the ones responsible for preserving the Iroquois culture. The Iroquois was a matriarchal society, and women held a great deal of power within each tribe. In the twenty-first century, the gender roles are more equally divided, with men and women sharing equally in the household responsibilities. Clan mothers still exist, though they no longer choose the chief. The community now elects its chief, which can be either man or woman, and the term is no longer for life, but rather usually only a few years.

Education Iroquois children attending reservation schools study not only the subjects typically taught at non-Indian schools but also their tribal culture and history. The stated goals of the Akwesasne Freedom School, for example, are "to facilitate learning so that the students will have a good self-concept as Indians, promote self-reliance, promote respect for the skills of living in harmony with others and the environment and master the academic and/or vocational skills necessary in a dualistic society" (*The Native North American Almanac*, edited by Duane Champagne, 1994). Although the Akwesasne Freedom School is a unique school as part

An Iroquois in traditional dress stands in front of a longhouse. These longhouses were built to house up to 20 related families. NATHAN BENN / ALAMY

An Iroquois in traditional dress stands in front of a longhouse. These longhouses were built to house up to 20 related families. NATHAN BENN / ALAMY

of the Mohawk nation, most Iroquoian nations have some sort of tribal education in place to teach their children about native culture. The Onondagas have a kindergarten-through-eighth-grade school on the reservation, while most students attend a public high school off native land. This is a common occurrence among many of the Iroquois nations; most reservations do not have an official school for native students to attend. The native education of Iroquois language, culture, and art is handled through community centers with education programs geared toward teaching Iroquois heritage to the younger generations. For example, both the St. Regis Mohawk tribe and Tuscarora tribe have youth programs that focus on native culture. The 2010 Census found that 87 percent of Iroquois over the age of twenty five had a high school diploma or higher, and 17 percent had a bachelor's degree or higher.

Courtship and Weddings Traditionally, an Iroquois man and woman wishing to marry would tell their parents, who would arrange a joint meeting of relatives to discuss the suitability of couple. If no objections arose, a day was chosen for the marriage feast. On the appointed day the woman's relatives would bring her to the groom's home for the festivities. Following the meal, elders from the groom's family spoke to the bride about wifely duties, and elders from the bride's family told the groom about a husband's responsibilities. Then the two began their new life together.

EMPLOYMENT AND ECONOMIC CONDITIONS

Although the Haudenosaunee's bond to the land remains, most no longer live as farmers. Census data from 2010 show that 65 percent of the Iroquois people lived in urban areas. Ties to the homeland and the tribal culture are strong, however, and those who live off the reservation return from time to time to visit relatives and to renew themselves spiritually.

In a modern rendition of their ancient sojourns away from the village to hunt, Iroquois men today may support their families by living and working in a city but returning home periodically. In particular, there is a cohesive group of Native Americans, including many Mohawk, living in Brooklyn, New York, during the week but returning to their families on weekends.

Iroquois men, especially Mohawk, are famous as ironworkers in construction, capable of walking steel girders high in the air unhampered by any fear of heights. Consequently, for over a century they have been in demand around the country for skyscraper and bridge building projects, including such landmarks as the World Trade Center and the Golden Gate Bridge. Fathers pass their ironworking tools on to their sons (or sometimes daughters) in an atmosphere reminiscent of ancient rituals.

Cara E. Richards of Cornell University conducted an acculturation study focusing on the Onondaga tribe during the 1950s and early 1960s. At that time 70 percent of the tribal women who held jobs worked as domestics in off-reservation homes. This put them in the position of interacting with upper- and middle-class families in home environments that exposed them to radio and television programs, non-Indian lifestyles, modern home appliances, and different types of foods. Onondaga men, on the other hand, worked primarily in factories or on construction sites. Although they interacted with non-Indian men, there was little exchange of cultural information. Differential patterns of acculturation resulted, in which the women were more comfortable and successful in relating to non-Indian agencies, including law enforcement. The 2010 Census indicated that about 7.3 percent of the employed Iroquois were engaged in construction. Educational services, including health care and social assistance, accounted for 21 percent of the jobs held by Iroquois people; 14 percent of the employed Iroquois worked in manufacturing; and another 14 percent were engaged in "arts, entertainment, and recreation, and accommodation and food services."

Economic activity varies markedly among the various Iroquois reservations. For example, the Onondaga Reservation does not offer services for tourists, but the Mohawk welcome tourists to their museum and marinas. The Seneca Nation has three casinos, all of which offer diverse employment opportunities for its tribal members. Resolving the question of gambling on the reservations is also an important issue. In 1990 the controversy erupted into a gun battle that left two Mohawk dead. The Onondaga Council of Chiefs issued a "Memorandum on Tribal Sovereignty" that said: "These businesses have corrupted our people and we are appalled at the Longhouse people who have become part of these activities. They have thrown aside the values of our ancient confederacy for personal gain". On the other hand, the Oneida tribe saw a dramatic decrease in unemployment after building a bingo hall in 1985; first-year profits of over $5 million were used by the tribe to acquire additional land adjacent to the reservation. Gambling still remains a debated issue within the Iroquois Confederacy in the twenty-first century. In 2002 the Seneca Nation signed a Gaming Compact with New York State, allowing them to build three Las Vegas–style casinos.

POLITICS AND GOVERNMENT
The legendary Great Peace forged by Deganawidah and Hiawatha produced an unwritten but clearly defined framework for the Iroquois Confederacy (a written constitution was developed in about 1850). This framework was preserved by a symbolic design in the "Hiawatha Belt," a type of wampum belt with shapes to symbolize each of the five original Iroquois nations and the peace treaty that they agreed upon. Three principles, each with dual meanings, formed the foundation of the Confederacy government. The Good Word signified righteousness in action as well as in thought and speech; it also required justice through the balancing of rights and obligations. The principle of Health

referred to maintaining a sound mind in a sound body; it also involved peace among individuals and between groups. Thirdly, Power meant physical, military, or civil authority; it also denoted spiritual power. The founders envisioned the resulting peace spreading beyond the original Confederacy members, so that eventually all people would live in cooperation. Law and order remained the internal concern of each tribe, but the Confederacy legally prohibited cannibalism.

Under the structure of the Confederacy, the fifty clan chiefs (called *sachems*) from all the tribes came together to confer about questions of common concern. A chairman called the Tadadaho (named after the legendary Onondaga chief) oversaw the discussion, which continued until a unanimous decision was reached. If no consensus could be achieved, each tribe was free to follow an independent course on that matter. The Confederacy functioned well for generations, fostering peace among the Six Nations. Even when the tribes failed to agree regarding an external dispute, such as one between the French and the Dutch, they would find a way to fight their respective enemies without confronting another Confederacy tribe. However, they were unable to do this during the American Revolution. The Confederacy nearly collapsed in the wake of that war, and traditionalists are still trying to rebuild it. During the latter half of the twentieth century, it strengthened significantly.

In 1802 the Mohawk living within the United States officially discarded their traditional clan-based structure and established an elective tribal government. In 1848 a faction of Seneca instituted a similar change, establishing the Seneca Nation. Voting rights were denied to Seneca women, who had historically chosen the tribal leaders; women's suffrage was not reinstated until 1964. Other Iroquois tribes eventually followed suit, either abandoning their ancestral governments or modifying them to incorporate elections. Traditionalists fought to maintain the ancient structure, however, and today two competing sets of governments exist on several reservations. Violence occasionally erupts between the opposing factions.

The United States government has tried in various ways to relocate, assimilate, or disband Indian tribes. A core group of the Iroquois people has steadfastly resisted these efforts. In 1831 some Seneca and Cayuga moved to Indian Territory (now Oklahoma) as part of the federal removal effort; other Iroquois factions held their ground until the policy was overturned in 1842 and ownership of some of the Seneca land was restored. In 1924 Congress passed legislation conferring U.S. citizenship on all American Indians; the Haudenosaunee rejected such status.

The Iroquois have actively worked to reclaim sacred artifacts and ancestral remains from museums. In 1972 a moratorium was enacted prohibiting archaeologists from excavating native burial sites in New York state; tribal members would be notified

Jeanne Shenandoah, who issues passports for the Haudenosaunee, a confederacy of several Iroquois nations, displays an Onondaga Nation passport at the Onondaga Nation Communications Center in Nedrow, N.Y., near the Onondaga Territory. DAVID LASSMAN /AP IMAGES

to arrange proper reburials for remains unearthed accidentally. Wampum belts held by the New York State Museum in Albany were removed from public display in deference to the Indians' belief that they should not be treated as curiosities and were finally returned to the Onondagas (as Keeper of the Central Fire for the Iroquois League) in 1989. Years of effort were rewarded in the early 1990s and the 2000s when the Smithsonian Institution and its National Museum of the American Indian (opened in 2004) committed to returning human remains, burial artifacts, sacred objects, and other articles of cultural patrimony to Indian tribes.

While most of the six nations have their own sovereign government, the Iroquois are still active in local, state, and national government, especially as it relates to their cultural preservation. Other political interests of the Iroquois have revolved around land claims and gambling rights, both of which would preserve the economic well-being of the Iroquois tribes. This includes the 2002 Seneca Gaming Compact with the State of New York and the Onondaga land claim in the early 2000s. The St. Regis Mohawk Tribe, in particular, has an active lobbyist group that works for tribal laws and native rights in the United States.

Although disputed by some, there is significant evidence that the Iroquois Confederacy served as a model or inspiration for the U.S. Constitution. Benjamin Franklin and Thomas Paine were well acquainted with the League. John Rutledge, chairman of the committee that wrote the first draft of the Constitution, began the process by quoting some passages from the Haudenosaunee Great Law. The Iroquois form of government was based on democracy and personal freedom and included elements equivalent to the modern political tools of initiative, referendum, and recall. In 1987 Senator Daniel Inouye from Hawaii sponsored a resolution that would

commemorate the Iroquois' contributions to the formation of the federal government.

NOTABLE INDIVIDUALS

Academia Arthur C. Parker (Seneca, 1881–1955) was a leading authority on Iroquois culture as well as museum administration. He joined the New York State Museum at Albany as an archaeologist in 1906 and became director of the Rochester Museum of Arts and Sciences in 1925. He wrote fourteen major books and hundreds of articles.

John Mohawk (Seneca, 1945–2006) taught Native American law and history at SUNY Buffalo. He wrote extensively on the Iroquois philosophy and approach to government. He founded *Akwesasne Notes*, a quarterly activist magazine, and the Indigenous Press Network, a computerized news service focusing on Indian affairs.

Activism Sherrill Elizabeth Tekatsitsiakwa "Katsi" Cook (Mohawk, 1952–), a midwife and lecturer on women's health, is active is the Akwesasne Environment Project. Her health-related writings have appeared in national magazines as well as in medical books.

Oren Lyons (1930–) is an Onondaga chief who has led political delegations to numerous countries in support of the rights of indigenous people. Twice named an All-American lacrosse goalkeeper, he led his 1957 team at Syracuse University to an undefeated season and was eventually enrolled in the sport's Hall of Fame. He was a successful amateur boxer in both the U.S. Army and in the Golden Gloves competition. He worked as a commercial artist for several years before returning to the reservation to assume his position as faithkeeper. An author and illustrator, he has served as chairman of American Studies at the State University of New York (SUNY) at Buffalo and as publisher of *Daybreak*, a national quarterly newspaper of Native American views. In 1992 he became the first indigenous leader to address the United Nations General Assembly.

Art Richard W. Hill (1950–) followed in his father's footsteps and became an ironworker in construction before enrolling in the School of the Art Institute of Chicago. His watercolor paintings included a series on Iroquois culture, and he also documented the culture through photography. Since the early 1970s he has curated numerous art shows, prepared museum exhibits for such clients as the Smithsonian Institution, and written many articles about history and art. A past director of the North American Indian Museums Association, he also taught at the State University of New York at Buffalo.

Using the knowledge she acquired when earning bachelor's and master's degrees in zoology, Carol Snow (Seneca) wrote and illustrated a dozen reports on endangered and rare species for the Bureau of Land Management. As an artist, in 1980 she created a technique incorporating ink and acrylic paint, which she employed in her renderings of Native American and wildlife themes.

Government Robert L. Bennett (Oneida, 1954–) and Louis R. Bruce Jr. (Mohawk, 1906–1989) served in the 1960s and early 1970s as commissioners of the U.S. Bureau of Indian Affairs. Ely Parker (Seneca, 1828–1895), the first Native American to hold that post, had been appointed by Ulysses S. Grant in 1869.

Literature Maurice Kenny (1929–), a Mohawk poet, received the American Book Award in 1984 for *The Mama Poems*. He had previously been nominated for a Pulitzer Prize. His work has been widely anthologized, and he has been writer in residence at North County Community College in Saranac Lake, New York. He has also received the National Public Radio Award for Broadcasting.

Amber Coverdale Sumrall (Mohawk) is a writer and poet whose works include the collection *Refuge* (2007). She has edited or coedited numerous anthologies and has also lectured and taught workshops on the topic of disabilities.

Daniel Thompson (Mohawk, 1953–) is a photographer, graphic artist, and editor of several publications, including the *Northeast Indian Quarterly*, published by Cornell University. He writes poetry in both English and Mohawk and is working to devise an improved written form for the Mohawk language. He has also served as news director for the Mohawk radio station.

Roberta Hill Whiteman (Oneida, 1947–) is a poet whose work has been published in anthologies and magazines including *American Poetry Review*. She is also the author *Star Quilt* (1984), a poetry collection reflecting upon her childhood in the Oneida community; and the collection *Philadelphia Flowers* (1996). She has been involved with Poets-in-the-Schools programs in at least seven states and has taught at the University of Wisconsin–Eau Claire.

Stage and Screen Jay Silverheels (Mohawk, 1918–1980) was born on the Six Nations Indian Reservation in Ontario. Silverheels was an actor perhaps best known for his portrayal of Tonto, the loyal Indian sidekick in the Lone Ranger television series, which ran from 1949 to 1957. His noted performances include his depiction of the Apache Indian chief Geronimo, in *Broken Arrow* (1950), a film acclaimed by many as the first picture to portray Native Americans in a sympathetic light, as well as three Lone Ranger films. Silverheels was the first Native American to be given a star on Hollywood's Walk of Fame.

Gary Dale Farmer (Cayuga, 1953–), born on the Six Nations Indian Reservation, is an actor, film producer, and activist. Farmer has appeared in numerous movies, perhaps most notably *Dead Man* (1995), in which he starred alongside Johnny Depp. He also appeared on the television series *Miami Vice* and *China Beach*. After 1989 Farmer began lecturing on

MISCONCEPTIONS AND STEREOTYPES

"Hiawatha" is one of the most widely recognized Indian names among non-Indian Americans, thanks to Henry Wadsworth Longfellow's epic 1855 poem *The Song of Hiawatha*. Unfortunately, his character is a classic case of mistaken identity. The real subject of the poem is an Ojibwe hero named Nanabozho, who was confused with the Iroquoian Hiawatha in a mid-nineteenth century work by Henry Rowe Schoolcraft that inspired Longfellow.

The Longfellow poem, at least, presented a sympathetic image of an Iroquois-named character. In his eloquent history of the Tuscarora Indians, Chief Elias Johnson wrote in 1881: "Almost any portrait that we see of an Indian, he is represented with tomahawk and scalping knife in hand, as if they possess no other but a barbarous nature. Christian nations might with equal justice be always represented with cannon and balls, swords and pistols, as the emblems of their employment and their prevailing tastes."

Elias Johnson, **Legends, Traditions and Laws of the Iroquois, or Six Nations, and History of the Tuscarora Indians.**

Native American culture and issues on many campuses in the United States and Canada, focusing on media, environmental, and social topics relevant to Native communities. In 1998 Farmer had a role in the well-received film *Smoke Signals*, which earned him an Independent Spirit Award nomination. In 2008 and 2009 Farmer's blues band, Gary Farmer and the Troublemakers, released two albums.

Graham Greene (Oneida, 1952–) is a film actor who has found success in both Canada and the United States. Greene is one of the most visible Native American actors working on the stage and in film today. He is best known for his roles in *Dances with Wolves* (1990), for which he was nominated for an Academy Award for Best Supporting Actor, and *Thunderheart* (1992). Among the many films in which Greene has appeared are *Maverick* (1994), *Die Hard: With a Vengeance* (1995), and the *Twilight* films (2009 and 2012).

MEDIA

PRINT

Akwesasne Notes and Indian Times

This quarterly magazine is published by the Mohawk tribe.

P.O. Box 868, Akwesasne
New York 13655
Phone: (518) 358-9531
Email: info@indiantime.net
URL: www.indiantime.net

Ka Ri Wen Ha Wi

This monthly newsletter contains reservation news and items about the Akwesasne Library/Cultural Center.

Akwesasne Library
321 State Route 37
Hogansburg, New York 13655
Phone: (518) 358-2240
Fax: (518) 358-2649
URL: www.akwesasneculturalcenter.org

The Seneca Nation of Indians Official Newsletter

This quarterly publication prints news and special interest pieces about the Seneca Nation.

90 Ohiyo Way
Salamanca, New York 14779
Phone: (716) 945-1790
URL: http://sni.org/departments/newsletter/

RADIO

CKON-FM (97.3)

CKON is a radio station owned and operated by the Mohawk tribe on the St. Regis Reservation in New York. It broadcasts music twenty-four hours a day, including country, adult contemporary, rock, and blues segments. In addition, it airs hourly local news summaries, community announcements (sometimes in Mohawk or French), and live coverage of local lacrosse games.

Larry Edwards, General Manager
P.O. Box 1260
Akwesasne, New York 13655
Phone: (518) 358-3426
Fax: (518) 358-9456
Email: ckonfm@yahoo.com
URL: www.ckonfm.com

ORGANIZATIONS AND ASSOCIATIONS

The Onondaga Nation

A sovereign government, the Onondaga Nation works to promote its culture and heritage while moving the nation into the twenty-first century through the maintenance of its laws and language.

Jake Edwards
3951 Route 11
Onondaga Reservation
Nedrow, New York 13120
Phone: (315) 492-1922
Fax: (315) 469-4717
Email: admin@onondaganation.org
URL: www.onondaganation.org

St. Regis Mohawk Tribe

The St. Regis Mohawk Tribe's goal is a self-sufficient government and the promotion of the tribe's history and values.

Chief Paul O. Thompson
St. Regis Reservation
412 State Route 37
Akwasasne, New York 13655
Phone: (518) 358-2272

Fax: (518) 358-3203
Email: public.information@srmt-nsn.gov
URL: www.srmt-nsn.gov

Seneca Nation of Indians

The largest of the six nations of the Iroquois, the Seneca Nation has over 8,000 enrolled members and aims to support its people through various efforts, including cultural activities, education, employment opportunities, and advocacy.

Barry E. Snyder, President
90 Ohiyo Way
Salamanca, New York 14779
12837 Route 438
Irving, New York 14081
Phone: (716) 945-1790 (Allegany) or (716) 532-4900 (Cattaraugus)
Email: sni@localnet.com
URL: www.sni.org

Tonawanda Band of Senecas

The Tonawanda Seneca Nation offers support to the environmental protection of tribal lands as well as other issues affecting the Tonawanda.

Chief Roger Hill
7027 Meadville Road
Basom, New York 14013
Phone: (716) 542-4244
Fax: (716) 542-4244
Email: tonsenec@buffnet.net
URL: http://www.epa.gov/region2/nations/tonow.htm

MUSEUMS AND RESEARCH CENTERS

Akwesasne Cultural Center/Akwesasne Museum

This museum displays traditional Mohawk artifacts and basketry, contemporary Iroquois artifacts, and ethnological exhibitions.

Akwesasne Library
321 State Route 37
Hogansburg, New York 13655
Phone: (518) 358-2240
Fax: (518) 358-2649
URL: www.akwesasneculturalcenter.org

The Iroquois Indian Museum

The Iroquois Indian Museum features the history of the Iroquois and displays contemporary arts and crafts. A library is available for research.

P.O. Box 7
Caverns Road
Howes Cave, New York 12092
Phone: (518) 296-8949
Fax: (518) 296-8955
Email: info@iroquoismuseum.org
URL: www.iroquoismuseum.org

The National Shrine of the Blessed Kateri Tekakwitha and Native American Exhibit

The shrine displays artifacts and maintains the only completely excavated and staked-out Iroquois village in the United States.

Fr. Mark Steed
P.O. Box 627
Fonda, New York 12068
Phone: (518) 853-3646
Email: office@katerishrine.com
URL: www.katerishrine.com

The Oneida Nation Museum

This museum preserves the culture of the Wisconsin
tribe and serves as a point of contact for the Oneida
Reservation.

Rita Lara, Director
W892 County EE
DePere, Wisconsin 54155
Phone: (414) 869-2768
Email: rlara@oneidanation.org
URL: www.oneidanation.org

The Rochester Museum and Science Center

This museum offers changing exhibits as well as a
permanent display, "At the Western Door," that
focuses on relations between the Seneca Indians and
European colonists. Also on display are a furnished
1790s Seneca cabin, six life-size figure tableaus, and
over 2,000 artifacts.

George McIntosh, Director, Collections
657 East Avenue
Rochester, New York 14603-1480
Phone: (716) 271-4320
URL: www.rmsc.org

The Seneca-Iroquois National Museum

Located on the Allegany Reservation, this museum houses
300,000 articles portraying the life and culture of
the Seneca and other Iroquois Indians, including
wampum belts, costumes, games, and modern art.

Jaré Cardinal, Director
814 Broad Street
Salamanca, New York 14779
Phone: (716) 945-1760
URL: www.senecamuseum.org

SOURCES FOR ADDITIONAL STUDY

Axtell, James. *The European and the Indian: Essays in the Ethnohistory of Colonial North America.* New York: Oxford University Press, 1981.

Barreiro, José, ed. *Indian Roots of American Democracy.* Ithaca, NY: Akwe:kon Press, Cornell University, 1992.

Brandão, José António, and René Cuillerier. *Nation Iroquoise: A Seventeenth-Century Ethnography of the Iroquois.* Lincoln: University of Nebraska Press, 2003.

Bruchac, Joseph. *New Voices from the Longhouse: An Anthology of Contemporary Iroquois Writing.* Greenfield Center, NY: Greenfield Review Press, 1989.

Campisi, Jack, and Laurence M. Hauptman. *The Oneida Indian Experience: Two Perspectives.* New York: Syracuse University Press, 1988.

The Native North American Almanac, Duane Champagne, Ed. Detroit, MI: Thomson Gale, 1994.

Fenton, Willam N. *The Great Law and the Longhouse: A Political History of the Iroquois Confederacy.* Norman: University of Oklahoma Press, 1998.

Harvey, Arden. "The Fire that Never Dies," *National Geographic*, September 1987.

Johnson, Elias. *Legends, Traditions and Laws of the Iroquois, or Six Nations, and History of the Tuscarora Indians.* New York: AMS Press, 1978 (reprint of 1881 edition).

Johnson, Michael. *Tribes of the Iroquois Confederacy.* Oxford: Osprey, 2003.

Josephy, Alvin M. Jr. *Now That the Buffalo's Gone: A Study of Today' American Indians.* OK: University of Oklahoma Press, 1984.

Morgan, Lewis H. *League of the Iroquois.* Secaucus, NJ: Citadel Press, 1984.

Snow, Dean R. *The Iroquois.* Cambridge, MA: Blackwell, 1996.

Spittal, W. G., ed. *Iroquois Women: An Anthology.* Ohsweken, Ontario: Iroqrafts Ltd, 1990.

Tooker, Elisabeth. *Lewis H. Morgan on Iroquois Material Culture.* Tucson: University of Arizona Press, 1994.

ISRAELI AMERICANS

Laura C. Rudolph

OVERVIEW

Israeli Americans are immigrants or descendants of immigrants from Israel, a country in the Middle East. Israel is bordered by Lebanon to the north, Syria and Jordan to the east, Egypt to the southwest, and the Mediterranean Sea to the west. Despite its small territory, Israel has varied climates, with mountainous regions, deserts, and coastal areas. Israel measures 7,992 square miles (20,700 square kilometers), making it slightly larger than the state of Massachusetts.

According to a July 2012 estimate from the *CIA World Factbook*, Israel has a population of 7.5 million people from various ethnic backgrounds. Approximately 75 percent are Jews who have immigrated there from nearly every corner of the world. The rest are largely Arabs, the majority of whom are Muslim (nearly 17 percent), with smaller numbers of Christians, Druze, Circassians, and Samaritans. Compared with the rest of the Middle East, Israel has a very high standard of living, mostly due to its market economy, which depends on the export of agricultural products, electronic technology, and cut diamonds.

Israelis first began to immigrate to the United States in the 1950s and 1960s, after the founding of Israel in 1948, settling on both the East and West Coasts. In the following decades, particularly through the 1980s and 1990s, Israelis, many of whom were highly skilled and highly educated, came to the United States in search of employment and a desire to be involved in the global economy. This, and continuing tensions between Israel and Palestine, has sent Israelis to the United States today.

The 2010 U.S. Census estimated that nearly 130,000 people claiming Israeli ancestry were living in the United States. New York and California have the greatest number of Israeli Americans, with Florida, New Jersey, and Massachusetts also home to large populations.

HISTORY OF THE PEOPLE

Early History The origins of the modern state of Israel can be traced to as far back as 2000 BCE, to the events described in the first five books of the Old Testament that comprise the Hebrew Bible, or Torah. According to the Torah, God promised the Israelites a land where they would be able to prosper, so long as they were faithful to Him. The Israelites found this "Promised Land" in Canaan, an area of ancient Palestine where they settled and established a Hebrew nation. Over the next two millennia, according to biblical tradition, the Hebrew people left, returned to, reconquered, occupied, and again lost their homeland. By the sixth century BCE, the Hebrew people were tolerated in Israel but the area was controlled by the Persian Empire.

The Hebrew presence in Israel proved untenable under the Roman occupation, which began in about 63 BCE. The Hebrews were exiled and those who remained were annihilated. The Romans renamed Jerusalem Aelia Capitulina, decreed the city permanently off-limits to Hebrews, and renamed the entire province "Palaestina." In what is known as the *Diaspora*, exiled Jews dispersed widely throughout other lands such as Rome and Egypt; eventually many settled in Eastern Europe.

During this period, the spread of other religions fueled new claims to Palestine. In 638 CE, Jerusalem became an Islamic holy city, in accordance with the belief that the prophet Muhammad had ascended to heaven from within the city. Islamic claims to Jerusalem generated centuries of conflict with Christians. Around 1100 CE, the Christians began a series of crusades to wrest the Holy Land from the Muslims. By the sixteenth century, Palestine was part of the Ottoman Empire. The Jews, many of whom were suffering at the hands of Christians, quietly began returning to Palestine.

Jewish settlements in Palestine grew slowly during the next three centuries. However, during the 1870s and 1880s, Jews fleeing *pogroms* (a term for the massacre of helpless people) in Eastern Europe began flooding into Palestine in what is known as the First Aliyah, the mass waves of Jews "ascending to the land." As the persecution of the Jews in Europe continued, Theodore Herzl in *The Jewish State* (1896) proposed the idea of an all-Jewish state in Palestine. Herzl's book led to the formation of a movement termed Zionism. Proponents of Zionism lobbied for an independent Jewish nation, a nation where Jews could live free from religious persecution. In 1897 the first Zionist Congress introduced the formation of the World Zionist Organization (WZO). The WZO soon began purchasing land in Palestine.

In 1904, Jews fleeing pogroms in Russia arrived in Palestine, thus creating the Second Aliyah. As more Jewish immigrants arrived, tensions increased between Jews and Palestinian Arabs. At this time, Palestine was a protectorate of Great Britain. In 1917 the British issued the Balfour Declaration, which advocated the establishment of a Jewish state in Palestine. The Nazi persecution of the Jews during World War II resulted in a flood of immigrants from Europe to Palestine.

Following the end of World War II, Palestine was handed over to the United Nations. In November 1947, the United Nations voted to partition Palestine into separate Jewish and Arab states, and Jerusalem was proclaimed an international territory. On May 14, 1948, David Ben-Gurion, the first prime minister, declared the state of Israel an independent nation.

Modern Era The declaration of Israel's independence precipitated immediate internal and external crises for the new nation. Although some countries (including the United States and the Soviet Union) were quick to recognize Israel, the League of Arab States refused to do so, on the ground that the separation of territory privileged Jewish holy land while ignoring the religious significance of that land to the Arab community. In 1948 Israel was invaded by Iraq, Jordan, Egypt, Syria, and Lebanon. Israel was able to repel the invaders and, in the process, actually expanded its boundaries. Although the United Nations arranged a cease-fire agreement between the five neighboring Arab countries and Israel, more obstacles loomed ahead. In particular, tensions dramatically increased between the Israelis and the Palestinian Arabs, many of whom had been displaced from their land.

In 1950 Israel enacted the Law of Return, which guaranteed Israeli citizenship to all Jews. The number of immigrants continued to grow, and Israel's economy and military slowly gained strength. In 1967 the armies of Egypt, Jordan, and Syria again invaded Israel. Israel routed the invaders and captured large amounts of territory from its Arab neighbors. By the end of the war, Israel had gained control of the Golan Heights, the West Bank, the Gaza Strip, and the Sinai Peninsula. It also annexed Jerusalem. Dismayed by the growth of Israeli power in the region, the Palestinian Arabs formed the Palestinian Liberation Organization (PLO). In 1979 Egypt and Israel signed the Camp David peace accords. Egypt officially recognized Israel as an independent nation while Israel returned control of the Sinai Peninsula, which had been captured in the 1967 war, to Egypt.

Although a peace agreement had been reached between Egypt and Israel, the Palestinians continued to resent Israeli occupation of the Gaza Strip and West Bank. During the late 1980s, the Palestinians and Israelis mutually agreed to seek peace, but several attempts to broker a peace agreement between the two peoples were unsuccessful. In 1993, after a series of intense negotiations, the Palestinians and Israelis signed the Oslo peace accords. The Palestinians were given control of the Gaza Strip and parts of the West Bank and were offered the opportunity to hold democratic elections in those areas under their control. In return, the Palestinians agreed to halt violent attacks against Israel. Many Palestinians and Israelis were critical of the agreement, however, and tension between the two peoples remained high.

In 2000, U.S. President Bill Clinton, Israeli Prime Minister Ehud Barak, and Palestinian leader Yasser Arafat met for the ultimately unsuccessful Middle East Peace Summit at Camp David, ending with Arafat rejecting a plan for a new Palestinian state. This led Israel's next prime minister, Ariel Sharon, to counter Arafat, defeating his Second Intifada and building the Israeli West Bank barrier. The years 2006 and 2008 saw the Second Lebanon War and the Gaza War, respectively. Though a cease-fire has been ordered, Israel is still experiencing political tensions with Palestine and Syria.

SETTLEMENT IN THE UNITED STATES

Israelis began immigrating to the United States soon after Israel's independence in 1948. Although estimates vary greatly, anywhere from 100,000 to 500,000 immigrants arrived in America in the 1970s and 1980s, although the official numbers were much lower (90,000 according to the 1990 U.S. Census). The actual number of Israeli immigrants to the United States has been a subject of intense debate since the 1980s. Many Israeli citizens immigrated there from other countries, and when these Israelis immigrate to the United States, they often list their native country on census forms, rather than "Israel." This may explain in part the low number of Israeli Americans (130,000) recorded on the 2010 U.S. Census, a figure incongruent with the significant number of Israeli communities in larger cities.

Several key factors contributed to increased Israeli immigration into the United States during the last two decades of the twentieth century. Many Israeli immigrants cited the political unrest in the Middle East and the relative insecurity of the region as their primary reason for emigrating. Shortly after the Yom Kippur War in 1973, an event that left many Israelis shaken and disillusioned, the number of immigrants rose dramatically. It is important to note that many Israelis are exposed to American culture by virtue of the close relationship between Israel and the United States. American fashions, fads, and forms of entertainment are commonplace in Israel. In many cases, the "Americanization" of Israel added to the immigrants' desire to take advantage of the economic and educational opportunities in the United States. During the 1980s and 1990s, Israel produced more qualified and educated workers than there were skilled positions, a situation that resulted in fierce competition within the Israeli job market. Heavy taxation and a lack of available housing also dismayed many Israelis. Israelis looked to the United States as a place to fulfill

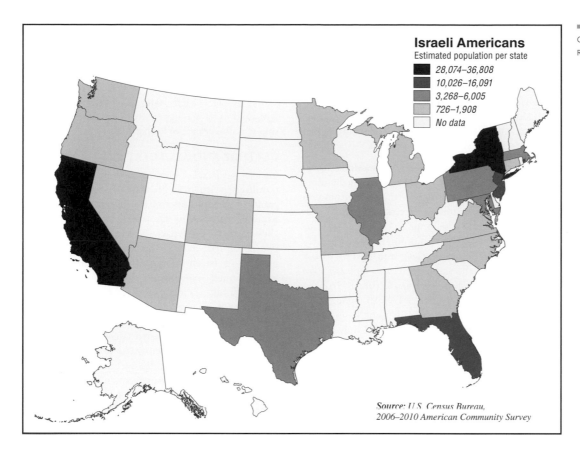

Israeli Americans
Estimated population per state

- 28,074–36,808
- 10,026–16,091
- 3,268–6,005
- 726–1,908
- No data

Source: U.S. Census Bureau, 2006–2010 American Community Survey

financial and educational goals in a manner not possible in Israel. As one Israeli immigrant stated in the book *Migrants from the Promised Land*, "It is not for nothing that they [the United States] are referred to as the land of endless opportunities. There are opportunities in every area of life, everywhere. I don't say that here things are blocked, they're not blocked … just smaller, more compact."

However, financial and educational fulfillment were not the only incentives for Israeli immigrants. During the 1990s, many Israelis immigrated as a result of their ideological dissatisfaction with Israel. For some, the ideal of an egalitarian community free from religious persecution had paradoxically resulted in an excessive amount of intervention from a highly stratified government that favored Ashkenazic Jews (Jews of European origin). Mizrahi Jews (those of North African and Middle Eastern ancestry) have long been the victims of ethnic discrimination by Ashkenazic Jews, who represent the overwhelming majority of Israelis. The socioeconomic discrepancies that arose from discrimination in Israel led many Mizrahi Jews to seek economic opportunities elsewhere. Twenty-first-century immigrants come to the United States seeking both better job prospects and political asylum.

The main areas of Israeli settlement in the United States include New York, California, Michigan, Florida, and Illinois. However, pockets of Israeli settlement can be found throughout the country. Israeli immigrants are fairly mobile and tend to migrate to several locations in the United States. Chain migrations are often a determining factor in the immigrants' choice of residence. The heaviest concentrations of Israeli Americans are located in New York and Los Angeles, which contain nearly half of those living in the United States. Not surprisingly, Israeli Jews gravitate toward other Jews, and a sizable number live in older, established Jewish neighborhoods such as Queens and Brooklyn in New York City, and West Hollywood and the San Fernando Valley in Los Angeles. Similarly, Israeli Arabs tended to settle near other Arabs, particularly in the industrial cities of the Midwest, such as Chicago and Detroit.

LANGUAGE

The official languages of Israel are Hebrew and Arabic. The vast majority of Israelis speak Hebrew, which dates back to 2000 BCE, though this Hebrew differs from the modern Hebrew spoken by native Israelis today. Israeli Americans generally learn the English language faster than other immigrant groups, and according to American Community Survey estimates for 2009–2011, only 13.6 percent of Israeli Americans are not proficient in English. However, immigrants continue to place an importance on Hebrew as a link to both their Jewish faith and their Israeli background. Hebrew is spoken at home by 80 percent of first-generation Israeli Americans, although the percentages decrease as the immigrants become more entrenched in American culture. In addition, the older Ashkenazic Jews speak Yiddish, which is a peculiarly Eastern European mixture of German and Hebrew, while the Mizrahi Jews speak Ladino. The use of both languages is decreasing in the United States, especially by the younger generations, although Yiddish-speaking Israeli Americans are more likely to be found among those who have settled in New York.

Greetings and Popular Expressions Israeli Americans can still be heard using some of the more common phrases of their native languages. Common Hebrew greetings and other expressions include: *shalom* (shah-LOHM)—hello or good-bye; *boker tov* (BOH-ker TOHV)—good morning; *erev tov* (EH-rev TOHV)—good evening; *todah* (toh-DAH)—thank you; *bevakasha* (be-vah-kuh-SHAH)—please; *ken* (KEN)—yes; *loh* (LOH)—no; *sleekha* (slee-KHAH)—excuse me; *mazel tov* (MAH-zl TAWV)—good luck; *chag sameach* (KHAHG Sah-MEHY-ahkh)—a happy holiday; and *l'shanah tovah* (li-SHAH-nuh TOH-vuh)—a good year.

RELIGION

Judaism represents the foundation of the state of Israel. Israeli Judaism is both national and secular, and does not necessarily include observance of the faith. Expression of a person's Jewish heritage is not restricted simply to the synagogue or to certain days of the year, but encompasses all daily activities, whether in the workplace, government, or during recreation. Observance of the Jewish holidays, the Hebrew language, and Jewish traditions are all performed on a national level. This has led to a greater secularization of Judaism within Israel, though most Israeli immigrants tend to be more involved in religious practices than American Jews.

Even if they are not entirely comfortable with American Judaism, Israeli Americans are fearful that their children will lose their Jewish identity altogether and embrace only American values. The majority of Israeli Americans reluctantly choose to place their children in American Jewish schools and day care centers. These children then become accustomed to American Jewish practices, sometimes generating conflict and tension between Israeli American parents and their children. To rectify this, some Israeli immigrants send their children to Israel-style schools in communities with large immigrant populations.

Toward the end of the twentieth century, American Jews sought to improve relations with Israeli Americans. During the 1980s, the American Jewish community began to encourage Israeli Americans to become more involved in Jewish community centers, organizations, and federations. Israeli Americans responded to these overtures favorably and began to forge bonds with American Jews. Many Israeli Americans discovered that their practice of the Jewish religion increased considerably after they immigrated to the United States. As they did in Israel, Israeli Americans continued to worship with those of similar ethnic background. The traditional discrimination between the Mizrahi and Ashkenazic Jews remains strong in the United States. Generally, the Mizrahi Jews tend to have a higher rate of synagogue membership and observance of kosher food laws.

CULTURE AND ASSIMILATION

On average, Israeli Americans have enjoyed a smoother transition to American life than other groups of immigrants. A good number of Israeli immigrants are well educated and possess specialized job skills that have allowed them to bypass the often-frustrating experiences of less trained immigrants. In addition, a number of Israeli immigrants have relatives living in the United States, which further eases the adjustment. Within a short period of time, many Israeli Americans attain a relative degree of financial security. Many Israeli Americans are accustomed to the close-knit community and shared ideological experience of Israel. In order to compensate for this loss, Israeli Americans have formed extensive and vibrant communities within the larger American culture, particularly in the Los Angeles and New York areas. This network of organizations ensures that many Israeli Americans remain connected to Israeli culture and the Hebrew language. The extensive Israeli network includes Hebrew newspapers, radio and television broadcasts, and Internet communities, as well as organizations such as the Israeli Flying Clubs, the Israeli Musicians Organization, and the Israeli Organization in Los Angeles (ILA).

The Israeli American network has provided a valuable service to immigrants, many of whom initially intended to remain in the United States only long enough to achieve their educational or financial goals before returning to Israel. An overwhelming majority of Israeli immigrants believe they will eventually return to Israel and are thus reluctant to fully assimilate into American culture; a sizable number of Israeli immigrants, however, eventually become permanent citizens, particularly through marriage. It is estimated that over a third of Israeli immigrants marry U.S. citizens. Likewise, a number of Israeli immigrants have established businesses in the United States, which further strengthens their ties to America. However, even those immigrants who eventually become naturalized continue to remain active in Israeli organizations long after the initial settling process. A strong identification with Israel, coupled with the stigma attached to immigration, helps explain why the majority of immigrants continue to refer to themselves as "Israelis" as opposed to "Americans" or even "Israeli Americans."

Traditions and Customs Israelis have a variety of traditions, the majority of which are connected to the Jewish religion; those immigrants of the Jewish religion keep the traditions alive in the United States.

Israeli American painter Uri Blayer shown here in Deadhorse Canyon at the Deadhorse Point State Park in Utah. VITO PALMISANO / GETTY IMAGES

The Torah outlines the strict observance of certain rules called the 613 Holy Obligations, as well as certain holidays and the weekly Sabbath. Other traditions associated with these celebrations have evolved over the centuries. Special foods, objects, and songs are all equally important to Jewish celebrations and the observance of the Sabbath, although they are not explicitly referred to in the Torah. During Rosh Hashanah, it is customary to send cards to friends and family bearing the words "L'shana tovah," which means "to a good and healthy year." Other traditions reflect geographical differences. For example, the Eastern European Jews began the tradition of eating gefilte fish to break the Yom Kippur fast. The custom of eating *cholent*, a stew prepared the night before the Sabbath, also emerged because cooking on the Sabbath is strictly forbidden.

Other customs are only loosely based on the Jewish religion and originate from earlier superstitions, such as the belief in the "evil eye." For example, it is customary to hold a baby shower after the baby is born. A baby's name is revealed only at the naming ceremony, and a red ribbon is tied to the baby's crib. These folk customs originated as precautions designed to fend off the evil forces accompanying the good fortune of a baby's birth. Although the traditions related to the practice of Judaism are still diligently observed, many of the superstitions have gradually been forgotten.

Israeli Americans observe *tevilah*, a purification rite similar to baptism, in the tradition of their Jewish faith. The circumcision ceremony (*brit milah*) occurs on the eighth day after the birth of a baby boy. The Covenant of Circumcision celebrates the covenant between God and Abraham and is traditionally performed by a *mohel*, a person who is specially trained in circumcision. The celebration is an important family ritual and the duties of those who take part in the ceremony are strictly designated: those who carry the baby are the baby's chosen godfather (*kvatter*) and godmother (*kvatterin*). Although there is generally not a special naming ceremony for Jewish girls, a special prayer is said at synagogue, at which time the daughter receives her Hebrew name.

Cuisine Israeli cuisine is savory and flavorful, and it reflects the influence of its diverse cultural inheritance as well as the strict dietary laws practiced by Jews. A faction of Israeli Jews observe the *kashrut*, which is a set of food restrictions outlined in the Old Testament book of Leviticus. Though not many Israeli Jews keep strictly kosher, the acceptable foods to eat when keeping kosher include meat from animals with cloven hoofs that ruminate (chew their cuds), breads, fish with scales and fins, fruits and vegetables, poultry, and kosher dairy products. Foods that are not acceptable (termed *trefa*) include pork, fish that do not have scales and fins (like lobster

CHICKEN SCHNITZEL

Ingredients

1 kosher chicken breast, boneless and butterflied

salt

pepper

flour

eggs

bread crumbs

2 tablespoons olive oil

Preparation

Separate chicken breast into 2 pieces and pound each to ¼ inch thin. Sprinkle with salt and fresh pepper. Dip into flour, being sure to get entire piece coated. Dip chicken into egg, coating well. Then dip the chicken into the bread crumbs. Set aside.

Heat olive oil in a skillet over low-medium heat. When oil is hot, sauteé each chicken cutlet until bottom is golden. Flip and cook other side until golden.

Recipe courtesy of Robert Lebow

or shrimp), and meals that combine meat and dairy products. In addition, meat is butchered in a special manner in order to observe the rule that forbids the drinking of blood. Both the Mizrahi and the Ashkenazi Jews have contributed to Israel's unique cuisine: the former introduced *shashlik* (cubed meat such as lamb or chicken) and *kebabs* (minced meats), and the latter contributed *schnitzels*, *goulashes*, and *blintzes*. Israeli Americans have brought this food to the United States, with restaurants and groceries that feature foods from their home country.

There is a strong Middle Eastern influence in Israeli cooking. Some favorite dishes include *hummus* (a dip that combines mashed chickpeas and tahini, a sesame paste); *falafel* (fried balls made from ground chickpeas); *fuul* (fava beans); and *mashi* (stuffed pita breads). Israelis enjoy sweet desserts including *baklava* (a dessert of wheat, honey, and nuts) and *katayeef* (cheese, wheat, sugar, and honey). Although kosher food is readily available in the United States, many Israeli Americans have opened restaurants that serve the Middle Eastern dishes prominent in Israeli cuisine.

Dances and Songs Israeli folk dancing is admired around the world, including in the United States, and there are thousands of different dances that are performed. Traditional dances include circle, line, or partner dances that are intricately choreographed. Some of the more popular dances include "Al Kanfe Hakesef," "Lechu Neranena," "Ahavat Itamar," "Al Tiruni," "Bakramim," and "Bat Teiman." Since Israeli folk dancing has long been admired by American Jews, several Jewish organizations have established community folk dancing classes. Klezmer music, a traditional music of Eastern European Jews, is also popular in Israel and became increasingly popular in the United States during the late 1990s. Traditional klezmer songs include "Az Der Rebbe Elimeylekh," "A Heymisher Bulgar," and "A Nakht in Gan Eden."

Not all Israeli music, however, is religious or inspired by folk tradition. Israeli and Israeli American musicians are also involved in mainstream musical genres, including rock, pop, and jazz.

Holidays Communities with large Israeli American populations often hold celebrations on Israeli Independence Day, which occurs on 5 Iyar according to the Hebrew lunar calendar (falling in April or May in the United States). Los Angeles, for example, holds an Israeli Festival to coincide with Israeli Independence Day. Synagogues sometimes hold a special prayer service. In many cases, it is a time for Israeli Americans to congregate and celebrate their culture and their homeland.

Some Israeli Americans also celebrate Jewish holidays, which are public holidays in Israel. The holidays are based on the Hebrew lunar calendar, which contains twelve 28-day cycles, for a total of 336 days a year, with an extra month added periodically. The holidays do not, therefore, fall on the same day every year, although they remain seasonal. The Jewish New Year begins in the fall with the celebration of Rosh Hashanah, which means "the Head of the Year" and is celebrated in September or October. As the sun sets on the first day of the first month, Jewish families gather together to say a blessing over wine and bread and to reflect on the significance of the holiday and renewal of the world. It is customary to bake *challah* bread in the form of a circle as a symbol of the cyclical year. Yom Kippur, the holiest day of the Jewish calendar, occurs on the tenth day of the New Year. The ten days between Rosh Hashanah and Yom Kippur are known as the "days of awe" and are meant to provide a quiet, reflective time in which Jews can cleanse their souls and focus on their relationship with God. There is a strict fast on the night before Yom Kippur, and the day and nighttime are usually spent in the synagogue. Special prayers are recited, including the *Kol Nidre*, *Musaf*, *Minchah*, *Neilah*, and ending with the symbolic intonation of "*L'shana ha-ba-ah b'Yerushalayim*," which means "next year in Jerusalem." The phrase is spoken as a wish of hope for the new year, both that the Messiah will return to rebuild the Holy City and that peace will find its way to Jerusalem.

The sukkot, or "festival of the booths," is celebrated immediately after the end of Yom Kippur and commemorates the exodus of the Jews from Egypt. At this time, it is customary to construct huts in order to observe the rule that Jews "live in nature" during the duration of the festival. Hanukkah, the "festival of the light," lasts for eight days in November or December. Hanukkah celebrates the victory of the Maccabees over the Syrians in 165 BCE. After the defeat, the oil for the Temple miraculously lasted for eight days until it could be renewed. During Hanukkah, candles in a menorah are lit for each one of the eight days. Traditional foods associated with this holiday include those cooked in oil and dairy foods. Purim, "the feast of lots," is a joyous celebration that takes place in late winter and celebrates the victory of the Jewish community in Persia by Queen Esther. It is customary to fast the day before Purim, called the "Fast of Esther." Passover, "the festival of freedom," takes place in March or April, and celebrates the time when the Jews put a sign on their doors that enabled God to "pass over" his chosen people when he delivered ten plagues upon their Egyptian captors. The Passover Seder celebrates not only the end of winter but also the release of oppressed Jews throughout the world. Shavuot, the "festival of weeks," occurs seven weeks after Passover and commemorates the anniversary of the receiving of the Ten Commandments by Moses on Mount Sinai. Shavuot is also considered an agricultural celebration, as it celebrates the festival of the first fruits when wheat is harvested. A custom practiced during Shavuot is staying up all night to read the Torah.

Other festivals or holidays include the Yom Ha'Shoa, which takes place in the spring and commemorates those who died in the Holocaust. Yom Hazikaron is the Israeli Memorial Day and is a day of remembrance for those who died in battle for Israel. Yom Ha-Atzma'ut takes place in April or May on the day after Yom Hazikaron and celebrates the day Israel declared its independence.

Israeli Americans often express disappointment about the way that Jewish holidays are celebrated in the United States. Although American Jews celebrate Jewish holidays, Israeli Americans are accustomed to a national celebration and find it difficult to adjust to the fact that Jewish holidays are ordinary days to the majority of Americans. Israeli Americans usually prefer to celebrate Israeli holidays with each other, particularly those that American Jews are not comfortable observing.

Health Care Issues and Practices Israeli Americans have not been prone to any specific medical conditions and generally tend to enjoy good health. Most Israelis Americans, like other Americans, have health insurance that is covered by their employers; those who are self-employed provide coverage for themselves and their employees. There are several nationwide organizations of Israeli health professionals in the United States.

Death and Burial Rituals Following a death in a Jewish family, the funeral is usually held within twenty-four hours after death. During this time, a *shomer* (person who stays in the same room) guards the body, which is never to be left alone before the burial. In accordance with custom, the casket remains closed and no embalming or cosmetology are performed. The casket is made of wood so that nature may follow its course quickly. All mirrors in the house are covered, so that vanity may not be allowed to interfere with the mourning and grief owed to the dead. At the graveside service, there is a ceremonial tearing of the mourner's skirt, ribbon, or shirt, which is called *keriah*. The mourners recite a prayer (*kaddish*) over the dead. During the next seven days, the family of the deceased sits *shivah*, and friends and family come to mourn and pay their respects. After a period of eleven months, the grieving process is considered over.

FAMILY AND COMMUNITY LIFE

The constant pressure of living in an insecure and dangerous environment has fostered the importance of the family and community among Israelis. Moreover, Judaism encourages strong family relationships, and many observances of the religion, such as the weekly Sabbath, serve to draw the family together. Most immigrants are married and place a strong emphasis on raising children. Because Israeli American parents are accustomed to relying on a national community of resources that aid in the socialization of their children, they often express disappointment with the lack of support systems available in the United States.

Israeli Americans often express disappointment about the way that Jewish holidays are celebrated in the United States. Although American Jews celebrate Jewish holidays, Israeli Americans are accustomed to a national celebration and find it difficult to adjust to the fact that Jewish holidays are ordinary days to the majority of Americans.

One of the greatest concerns of Israeli Americans is the preservation of their identity and their values within the alien culture of the United States. Israeli Americans are often unable to foster an Israeli identity in their more "Americanized" children. One Israeli American mother described the dilemma in a 1994 article by Steven J. Gold titled "Israeli Immigrants in the United States": "There is a big gap between Israelis and their kids that were born here. This is a special problem for the Israelis because we are raising a generation that are Americans, beautiful American children. Highly educated, high achievers, but still, American children. You cannot raise Israeli children in [the] United States, for heaven's sake."

In order to expose their children to Israeli culture, Israeli Americans and the Israeli government have created various programs and workshops to help strengthen U.S. bonds with Israel. Toward the end of the twentieth century, the American Jewish community began to establish similar programs through such groups as the New York Board of Jewish Education, which sponsors folk-dance groups, parent workshops, summer camps, and religious training. Tzabar, the American branch of Tzofim (Israeli Scouts), enrolls groups of children between the ages of ten and nineteen. Each summer, over 200 Israeli Americans spend a summer in Israel as part of Chetz V'Keshet, a program similar to Outward Bound.

Gender Roles The Jewish faith is often considered inherently patriarchal and, over the centuries, women have played a nominal role in Jewish religious communities worldwide. Traditionally, men were the heads of household, while wives and daughters were restricted to running the household and caring for children. Education was not considered necessary for women and in many instances was forbidden. During the last few generations, however, Jewish women across the world have made tremendous strides in gaining access to educational and career opportunities; Israel has even had a female prime minister, Golda Meir. Female Israeli American immigrants tend to be as educated as their male counterparts and are often able to secure high-status jobs within the United States. However, nearly one-half of all married Israeli American women choose to stay at home in order to raise their children.

Education Israeli Americans value education highly and often immigrate in order to take advantage of the excellent university programs available throughout the United States. According to the 2010 U.S. Census, 52.3 percent of Israeli American men and 53.2 percent of women had a college degree, and only 5.7 percent of Israeli Americans did not finish high school.

Although Israeli immigrants appreciate the large number of educational institutions available in the United States, they are cautious about placing their children in public schools. Some Israeli Americans fear that negative values such as low achievement, lack of respect toward parents, and American individualism are being taught to their children. Similarly, Israeli American parents are disturbed by the availability of illegal drugs and sexual permissiveness in some American schools. Israeli immigrants generally prefer to place their children in private schools that emphasize values that are more similar to those taught in the Israeli educational system. Israeli Americans have also relied on a number of instructional courses and after-school programs for their children, such as the AMI, which is an Israeli Hebrew course.

Courtship and Weddings Jewish weddings are lavish and festive occasions that are filled with many traditions. The ceremony takes place under a *chupah* (marriage canopy, which symbolizes the bridal chamber and the home that the couple is creating together). The wedding begins with a procession in which the groom (*chatan*) and the bride (*kalah*) are led to the chupah by their parents, where seven blessings (*sheva*

berachot) are chanted before the bride and groom drink a glass of wine as a symbol of the sharing of their lives. After the couple exchange rings, they sign the marriage contract, or *ketubah*. The couple is then pronounced husband and wife, and the groom steps on a glass as everyone shouts *mazel tov*. Following the ceremony, a large reception takes place, at which there is much singing and dancing.

EMPLOYMENT AND ECONOMIC CONDITIONS

Israeli Americans often find well-paying, highly skilled jobs within the American workforce. Even during the initial adjustment period to life in the United States, Israeli Americans are much less likely to use welfare than other immigrant groups, and they tend to have a high employment rate overall. Almost half of all male Israeli Americans in New York and Los Angeles are managers, administrators, professionals, or technical specialists, and another quarter are employed in sales. Israeli American professionals include doctors, architects, entertainers, small business owners, and teachers. A fairly large number of Israeli American women teach Hebrew.

As is typical of other Jewish immigrants, Israeli Americans are extremely entrepreneurial and have a high rate of self-employment in the United States. The 2010 Census found that one-tenth of Israeli Americans were self-employed. Over half of Israeli Americans found work in management, business, science, and the arts. Other immigrants opened businesses such as restaurants, nightclubs, and retail shops within the Israeli communities to serve the growing needs of Israeli immigrants. Many newly arrived immigrants view their work in Israeli American businesses as a type of apprenticeship before opening their own business. Although Israeli employers feel a sense of obligation toward other Israelis, they are aware that the employees will eventually become competitors, a situation that sometimes creates conflicts.

The average income for Israeli immigrants is high compared to the rest of the country. In 2010 the Census Bureau reported that Israeli American men earned a median annual income of $62,000 (compared to $42,000 for American men overall). Israeli American women made median earnings of $51,000 (compared to $31,000 for American women overall).

POLITICS AND GOVERNMENT

Many Israeli Americans expect to return to Israel and are more inclined to follow Israeli, rather than American, politics. Sometimes referred to as "transnationals," over 85 percent of Israeli Americans read Israeli newspapers and 58 percent listen to Hebrew broadcasts. Many Israeli Americans retain ownership of their homes in Israel and make frequent trips between Israel and the United States. Those Israeli Americans who do become naturalized U.S. citizens continue to follow events in Israel and tend to vote for American political candidates who support Israeli

Former Chief of Staff during President Obama's first term and Mayor of Chicago Rahm Emanuel (1959–) speaks at an Obama campaign fundraiser at Chicago's Navy Pier, 2011. SCOTT OLSON / GETTY IMAGES

interests. For instance, according to exit polls, 85 percent of Israeli Americans voted for Republican candidate Mitt Romney in the 2012 presidential election because of his strong commitment to Israel.

Israeli Americans generously support the state of Israel, and they have enough political clout to ensure that Israel remains a focal point of American interests. There has been so much financial, military, and cultural exchange between the two countries that some Israelis refer to Israel as the "fifty-first" state of the United States. Historically, the Israeli government has discouraged immigration to the United States. However, during the late 1990s, the Israeli government began to encourage the formation of services and organizations specifically designed to assist Israeli American immigrants. Today, Israeli Americans are becoming more and more vocal in U.S. politics, especially as it relates to the United States' relationship with Israel. For example, during the 2012 elections, many Israeli Americans used English-language news sources like *Israel Today* to voice their support for either Mitt Romney or Barack Obama, particularly focusing on how each candidate's policies might affect Israeli politics.

NOTABLE INDIVIDUALS

Academia Nadav Safran (1925–2003) received national recognition for his expertise on the Middle East. During his tenure at Harvard University, he published the following books, all of which were well received: *Egypt in Search of Political Community: An Analysis of the Intellectual and Political Evolution of Egypt, 1804–1952* (1961); *From War to War: The Arab-Israeli Confrontation, 1948–1967* (1969); *Israel: The Embattled Ally* (1978); and *Saudi Arabia: The Ceaseless Quest for Security* (1985). Amos Tversky (1937–1996) was considered one of the leading authorities on mathematical models in psychology and was a professor of psychology at Stanford University. He coauthored the following publications: *Mathematical Psychology: An Elementary Introduction* (1970) and *Decision Making: Descriptive, Normative, and Prescriptive Interaction* (1988).

Business The Nakash brothers (Joe, Ralph, and Avi), established Jordache Enterprises, Inc., in 1969. Their trademark Jordache jeans enjoyed immediate success and were soon distributed worldwide. By the late 1990s they had amassed a fortune of over $600 million. In 2004 the company introduced the Jordache Vintage line to celebrate thirty-five years in the fashion industry.

Music Itzhak Perlman (1945–), a world-renowned violinist, has appeared with the New York Philharmonic, the Cleveland Orchestra, the Philadelphia Orchestra, and other orchestras throughout the United States. He received the Leventritt Prize in 1964, fifteen Grammy awards between the years 1977 and 1987, and the Medal of Liberty in 1986. In November 2007, Perlman took the position of artistic director and principal conductor for the Westchester Philharmonic. Pinchas Zukerman (1948–), is also a world-renowned violinist and the recipient of the Leventritt Prize. He was selected as the music director of the St. Paul Chamber Orchestra in Minnesota, where he served from 1980 to 1987. From 1990 to 1992, he was the guest conductor of the Dallas Symphony Orchestra. Zukerman began teaching at the Manhattan School of Music in New York in 1993.

Politics Rahm Emanuel (1959–) was elected mayor of Chicago in 2011. Son of an Israeli immigrant, Emanuel grew up in Chicago, briefly serving as a civilian volunteer with the Israel Defense Forces. In his political career, Emanuel worked as a senior advisor to President Bill Clinton in the 1990s and as White House chief of staff to President Barack Obama from 2009 to 2010. He is Chicago's first Jewish mayor.

Stage and Screen Theodore Bikel (1924–) is an award-winning actor and singer. He has appeared in staged productions of *The Sound of Music* (1959–1961) and *Fiddler on the Roof* (1968–1996). He has also appeared in *The African Queen* (1951), *The Defiant Ones* (1958), for which he received an Academy Award nomination, *My Fair Lady* (1964), *Sands of the Kalahari* (1965), and *Crime and Punishment* (2002). He also hosted a weekly radio program titled "At Home with Theodore Bikel" (1958–1963), and recorded various folk songs. He has been the recipient of the Emmy Award (1988) and the Lifetime Achievement Award from the National Foundation for Jewish Culture (1997).

Natalie Portman (1981–) is an Israeli-born American actress. She first appeared in the 1994 film *The Professional*. She achieved mainstream success with her roles in the *Star Wars* prequel trilogy (1999, 2002, and 2005), *V for Vendetta* (2006), and *The Other Boleyn Girl* (2008). She received much critical acclaim for her lead role in *Black Swan* (2011), which won her an Academy Award, a Golden Globe Award, a BAFTA Award, a Screen Actors Guild Award, and an Independent Spirit Award.

MEDIA

PRINT

Ha'aret

An Israeli, Hebrew- and English-language daily, which is distributed across the country.

Natasha Mozgovya, Chief U.S. Correspondent
Email: mozgovaya@gmail.com
URL: www.haaretz.com

Viewpoint

Established in 1920, the quarterly publication of the National Council of Young Israel contains news of interest to the Israeli-Jewish communities.

Esther Altman, Editor
111 John Street
Suite 600
New York, New York 10038
Phone: (212) 929-1525
Fax: (212) 727-9526
Email: ealtmann@youngisrael.org
URL: http://www.youngisrael.org

RADIO

WELW-AM

WELW presents *Shalom America* on Sunday mornings.

Raymond Somich, General Manager
P.O. Box 1330
Willoughby, Ohio 44096
Phone: (440) 946-1330
Email: email@wlew.com
URL: www.welw.com

WRSU-FM

Israel Hour broadcasts on Rutgers University's college radio station.

126 College Avenue
New Brunswick, New Jersey 08901
Phone: (732) 932-7800
URL: www.israelhour.com

WUNR-AM

The Yiddish Voice broadcasts on WUNR.

Chasia Segal
The Yiddish Voice
c/o WUNR
60 Temple Place
Boston, Massachusetts 02114
Phone: (617) 738-8484
Email: radio@yv.org
URL: www.yiddishvoice.com

ORGANIZATIONS AND ASSOCIATIONS

America-Israel Cultural Foundation

Encourages, promotes, and sustains cultural excellence in Israel. Provides scholarships in music, the visual and design arts, filmmaking, dance, and theater to gifted students; advanced-study fellowships to teachers and young professionals; and grants to institutions and special projects in Israel. Allocates approximately $2.3 million for underwriting over 600 scholarships, projects, and institutions. Sponsors Israel Philharmonic Orchestra, Tel Aviv Museum of Art, Jerusalem Film and Television School, Batsheva Dance Company, and the Beit Zvi School of Drama.

David Homan, Executive Director
1140 Broadway
Suite 304
New York, New York 10001
Phone: (212) 557-1600
Fax: (212) 557-1611
URL: www.aicf.org

America Israel Friendship League

Seeks to maintain and strengthen the mutually supportive
relationship between people of the United States and
Israel. Seeks to promote the friendship between the
two democracies.

Dr. Alex Grobman, Executive Director
134 East 39th Street
New York, New York 10016
Phone: (212) 213-8630, ext. 230
Fax: (212) 683-3475
Email: agrobman@aifl.org
URL: www.aifl.org

Chabad West Coast Headquarters

Nationwide organization that addresses Jewish issues;
lends aid and sponsors events for Jewish immigrants,
including newly arrived Israelis.

Rabbi Boruchs Cunin, Director
741 Gayley Avenue
Los Angeles, California 90024
Phone: (310) 208-7511
URL: www.chabad.org

MUSEUMS AND RESEARCH CENTERS

Center for Israel Studies (CIS)

American University's Center for American Studies is
a national leader in the study of the history and
culture of Israel. The center takes a multi-disciplinary

approach to further understanding of Israel's
complex culture.

Laura Katz Cutler, Acting Director
4400 Massachusetts Avenue NW
Washington, D.C. 20016
Phone: (202) 885-3780
Email: cutler@american.edu
URL: www.american.edu/cas/israelstudies

SOURCES FOR ADDITIONAL STUDY

Blumberg, Arnold. *The History of Israel.* Westport, CT: Greenwood Press, 1998.

Cohen, Yinon. "Socioeconomic Dualism: The Case of Israeli-Born Immigrants in the United States." *International Migration Review* 23 (1989): 267–88.

Gold, Steven J. "Israeli Immigrants in the United States: The Question of Community." *Qualitative Sociology* 17 (1994): 325–45.

———— and Bruce A. Phillips. "Israelis in the U.S." *American Jewish Yearbook 1996.* New York: The American Jewish Committee, 1996: pp. 51–104.

Kushner, Tony, and Alisa Solomon, eds. *Wrestling with Zion: Progressive Jewish-American Responses to the Israeli-Palestinian Conflict.* New York: Grove Press, 2003.

Mittelberg, David, and Mary C. Waters. "The Process of Ethnogenesis Among Haitian and Israeli Immigrants in the United States." *Ethnic and Racial Studies* 15, no. 3 (July 1992): 412–35.

Ritterband, Paul. "Israelis in New York." *Contemporary Jewry* 7 (1986): 113–26.

Rosenthal, Mirra, and Charles Auerbach. "Cultural and Social Assimilation of Israeli Immigrants in the United States." *International Migration Review* 26, no. 3 (Fall 1992): 982–91.

Sobel, Zvi. *Migrants from the Promised Land.* New Brunswick, NJ: Transaction Books, 1986.

ITALIAN AMERICANS

George Pozzetta

OVERVIEW

Italian Americans are immigrants or descendants of people from Italy, a country in southern Europe. Moored by Alpine mountains in the north, the boot-shaped Italian Peninsula juts into the central Mediterranean Sea. Along its European frontier, Italy shares borders with, from west to east, France, Switzerland, Austria, and Slovenia. In addition, Italy surrounds the Vatican City and San Marino, both of which are classified as independent countries. The nation's land mass, which includes the two major islands of Sicily and Sardinia and numerous smaller islands, measures 116,324 square miles (301,200 square kilometers)—double the size of the state of Florida. With the exception of the broad North Italian Plain at the foot of the Alps, the peninsula is crosscut through much of its length by the Apennine mountain chain. The obstacles created by the highlands, valleys, and gorges found in the mountain regions fostered strong cultural and linguistic differences among the Italian people.

According to a census conducted by the Italian national statistics office (Istat) in 2011, Italy had a population of roughly 60 million people. The vast majority of Italian citizens are Roman Catholic. Beginning in the 1980s, after hundreds of years of losing citizens to emigration, Italy experienced increased immigration. The majority of immigrants have been from former Communist Bloc countries in Eastern Europe, such as Romania and Hungary. The next largest group has been from North Africa, particularly in the aftermath of the Arab Spring of 2010. By 2011, foreign residents made up about 8 percent of the total population. Italy was a founding member of the European Union (EU) in 1999. The service sector makes up 72.8 percent of the country's GDP (gross domestic product), followed by industry (25.3 percent) and agriculture (1.9 percent). Like much of the EU, Italy was hit hard by the economic crisis that began in 2007 and was caused by, among other things, high public debt and a rising unemployment rate. However, Italy has fared better than many of its European neighbors. As of 2010 its economy was still ranked the tenth largest in the world, and it was listed as the third-largest economy in the Eurozone in 2012.

Italians began arriving in the United States in small numbers as early as the founding of the republic.

This first group consisted of skilled craftsmen and artisans from northern Italy. Italians did not migrate to the United States in large numbers until the late 1800s. Four and a half million Italians, most of them from southern Italy, moved to the United States between 1880 and 1920. Primarily adult men, they came to find work with the intention of making money and returning home. Immigration slowed down in the 1920s due to the passage of restrictive immigration laws. The first such law was the Emergency Quota Act of 1921, which imposed numerical limits on European immigration. The quota system allowed entrance to 3 percent of the population from a given country living in the United States at the time of the 1910 U.S. Census. Congress deliberately used the 1910 Census rather than the 1920 Census in order to favor immigrants from northern Europe. The majority of southern and eastern European immigrants, including Italians, had arrived after the cutoff date. The Immigration Act of 1924 reduced the flow of southern and eastern European immigration even further, reducing the quota from 3 percent of the 1910 numbers to 2 percent of the 1890 U.S. Census. Such restrictive policies remained in place for decades, until the laws underwent a complete overhaul in 1952. After World War II the United States experienced another wave of immigration from Italy. But by the mid-1970s, the numbers had decreased due to an improved economy and political stability in their native land. Between 2000 and 2010, the total number of Italians who immigrated to the United States was less than 14,000.

The National Italian American Foundation estimated that as of 2010 there were more than 17 million people in the United States who identified themselves as Italian American, comprising close to 6 percent of the total population. Areas with the largest concentration of Italian Americans were New York, New Jersey, and California.

HISTORY OF THE PEOPLE

Early History Italy's modern state traces its roots to the founding of the city of Rome in 753 BCE. Romans engaged in territorial expansion and conquest of neighboring lands, devising effective colonization policies that ultimately sustained a widespread realm. By 172 BCE Rome controlled all of the Italian Peninsula and began moving outward into the Mediterranean basin. At its peak, the Roman Empire extended from the British Isles to the Euphrates River. The *pax romana*, or period of peace and stability, began to crumble, however, by the end of the first century CE. The sack of Rome by the Visigoths in 410 CE presaged the more complete disintegration of the empire in the later fifth and sixth centuries. With its political integration shattered, the country remained fragmented until the late nineteenth century. Italy was, in the view of many Europeans, a "mere geographic expression."

Italy is a relatively young nation-state, achieving full unification only during the *Risorgimento* ("Resurgence") of 1860–1870. Prior to this, the peninsula consisted of often mutually antagonistic kingdoms, duchies, city-states, and principalities. Some of these regions had a history of autonomous rule, while others came under the periodic control of foreign powers as a result of recurrent wars and shifting political alliances. Over the centuries, therefore, powerful regional loyalties emerged, which persisted until well after unification. Although local cultural variations remained notable, the most significant internal distinctions have been those stemming from the contrast between a relatively prosperous, cosmopolitan, urban north and a more rustic economically depressed, agricultural south.

Southern Italy (*Mezzogiorno*), the source of more than 75 percent of immigration to the United States, was an impoverished region possessing a highly stratified, virtually feudal society. The bulk of the population consisted of artisans (*artigiani*), petty landowners or sharecroppers (*contadini*), and farm laborers (*giornalieri*), all of whom eked out meager existences. For various reasons, including security, residents typically clustered in hill towns situated away from farmland. Each day required long walks to family plots, adding to the toil that framed daily lives. Families typically worked as collective units to ensure survival.

The impact of unification on southern Italy was disastrous. The new constitution heavily favored the north, especially in its tax policies, industrial subsidies, and land programs. The hard-pressed peasantry shouldered an increased share of national expenses while attempting to compete in markets dominated more and more by outside capitalist intrusions. These burdens only exacerbated existing problems of poor soil, absentee landlords, inadequate investment, disease, and high rates of illiteracy. With cruel irony, as livelihoods became increasingly precarious, population totals soared. Italy jumped from 25 million residents in 1861 to 33 million in 1901 to more than 35 million in 1911, despite the massive migration already underway.

Modern Era Italy joined the turn-of-the-century European land grab in Africa, invading and annexing Eritrea, Somalia, and Libya, thus creating the beginnings of a modern Italian empire. The Italian army also attempted to conquer Ethiopia (1895) but suffered a humiliating defeat. With the 1920s came the secularization of politics and the rise of Fascism. There has been a struggle between Fascism and anti-Fascist groups, such as socialists, labor unionists, and communists, in Italy ever since. Fascist dictator Benito Mussolini came to power in 1922 with a goal of expanding the Italian empire. Italian forces returned to Ethiopia in 1935, this time succeeding in turning the country into a colony. In 1939 Italy invaded Albania and made it a protectorate.

Mussolini's decision to enter World War II in 1940 initially received popular support, but once Italy was defeated and forced to give up its colonies, the move was subsequently seen as disastrous. Mussolini was overthrown in a coup in 1943 and executed in 1945, the same year the war ended. In 1946 a referendum ended the monarchy and instituted a republican form of government. Italians held their first democratic elections in April 1948, creating a parliamentary democracy led by a coalition of Italian Christian democrats and communists. This so-called First Republic lasted until the fall of communism in Europe in the early 1990s, at which point the electorate called for sweeping reforms. The old parties disappeared or changed names, regionalism in the north threatened Italian unity, and for a brief time the National Alliance (formerly a neo-Fascist party) joined a coalition government. In spite of the changes, the country remained a parliamentary republic. Center-left coalitions dominated the landscape from the mid-1990s to 2001. Since then, the government has shifted between the center-left and more conservative parties.

The Italian economy boomed in the 1950s and again in the 1980s, but in the 1990s and 2000s, Italy experienced a sharp reduction in real wages, benefits, and social services as well as an increasingly privatized industrial sector. A "brain-drain" occurred in the corporate and research fields as young professionals left Italy for economic opportunities in other countries. Another consequence of economic decline was renewed pressure on young women to marry and have children in order to ensure social reproduction and to preserve the full-time job market for men.

Greece's request for a bailout from the European Union in early 2010 highlighted the growing economic crisis in Europe and caused interest rates to soar on Italy's massive national debt. In 2011 the Italian Parliament passed austerity measures—including spending cuts, tax increases, and economic change—in its bid for lower interest rates and stronger support from the EU's wealthier member nations, Germany in particular. Italy's prime minister, Silvio Berlusconi, objected to the austerity measures, and the already scandal-plagued leader resigned in protest. Berlusconi had dominated Italian politics since the early 1990s, but by 2011 his credibility had been seriously undermined by sex scandals, right-wing pro-Fascist rhetoric, and criminal convictions for tax evasion. The three-time prime minister, also a media mogul and owner of A.C. Milan football club, was replaced by a technocrat, Mario Monte. Monte stepped down in mid-2012 amid growing public dissatisfaction with the way he was handing the crisis. A national presidential election was scheduled for April 2013, with the vote for prime minister set for May of the same year. In late 2012 Europe's Central Bank bought bonds from Italy, helping lower the country's interest rates and stave off a financial collapse.

SETTLEMENT IN THE UNITED STATES

After the American Revolution in the late 1800s, a small flow of largely northern Italian skilled artisans, painters, sculptors, musicians, and dancers came to the new nation, filling economic niches. With the failure of the early-nineteenth-century liberal revolutions in Italy, these immigrants were joined by a trickle of political refugees, the most famous of whom was military leader Giuseppe Garibaldi. By the second half of the century, American cities also typically included Italian street entertainers, tradesmen, statuette makers, and stoneworkers, who often established the first beachheads of settlement for the migrations to come. Many of these pioneers were merely extending generations-old migratory patterns that had earlier brought them through Europe. As an old Italian proverb instructed, "*Chi esce riesce*" (He who leaves succeeds).

This initial Italian movement dispersed widely throughout the United States, but its numbers were too small to constitute a significant presence. By 1850, the heaviest concentration was in Louisiana (only 915 people), the result of Sicilian migration to New Orleans and its environs. Within a decade, California contained the highest total of any state—still a mere 2,805—and New York, soon to become home to millions of Italian immigrants, counted 1,862.

Everything changed with the mass migration from Italy that began in the 1880s. From 1876 to 1924, more than 4.5 million Italians arrived in the United States, with more than 2 million coming in the years 1901–1910 alone. Despite these massive numbers, it should be noted that roughly two-thirds of Italian emigrants went elsewhere, especially to Europe and South America. Immigration to the United States before and after this period accounted for approximately 1 million additional arrivals—a considerable movement in its own right—but the era of mass migration remains central to the Italian immigrant experience.

The first phase consisted primarily of temporary migrants—"sojourners"—who desired immediate employment, maximum savings, and quick repatriation. The movement was predominately composed of young, single men of prime working age (fifteen to thirty-five) who clustered in America's urban centers. Multiple trips were commonplace, and ties to American society, such as learning English, securing citizenship, and acquiring property, were minimal. With eyes focused on the old-world *paese* (village),

at least half of the sojourners returned to Italy with the goal of working in the United States and sending wages home to the wives and children left behind before returning home themselves, although in some years return rates were much higher. Such mobility earned Italians the sobriquet "birds of passage," a label that persisted until women and families began to migrate and settlement became increasingly permanent in the years following 1910.

Migrants brought with them their family-centered peasant cultures and their fiercely local identifications, or *campanilismo*. They typically viewed themselves as residents of particular villages or regions, not as "Italians." The organizational and residential life of early communities reflected these facts, as people limited their associations largely to kin and *paesani* (fellow villagers). The proliferation of narrowly based mutual aid societies and *feste* (feast days) honoring local patron saints were manifestations of these tendencies. Gradually, as immigrants acclimated to the American milieu, in which others regarded them simply as Italians, and as they increasingly interacted with fellow immigrants, *campanilismo* gave way to a more national identity. Group-wide organization and identity, nonetheless, have always been difficult to achieve.

In terms of settlement, immigrants were (and are) highly concentrated. Using kin- and village-based chain migration networks to form "Little Italies," they clustered heavily in cities in the Northeast Region (the Mid-Atlantic and New England states) and the Midwest, with outposts in California and Louisiana. More than 90 percent settled in only eleven states—New York, New Jersey, Pennsylvania, Massachusetts, California, Connecticut, Illinois, Ohio, Michigan, Missouri, and Louisiana—and approximately 90 percent congregated in urban areas. These patterns largely hold true today, although immigrants have branched out to locations such as Arizona and Florida. In every settlement area, there has been, over time, a slow but steady shift from central cities to suburbs.

Immigrants often sought out Little Italies as a result of the hostility they encountered in American society. As a despised minority rooted in the working class and seemingly resistant to assimilation, Italians suffered widespread discrimination in housing and employment. American responses to the immigrants occasionally took uglier forms as Italians became the victims of intimidation and violence, the most notorious incident being the 1890 lynching of eleven Italians in New Orleans. Italian mass migration coincided with the growth of an American feeling of "nativism" that identified southern and eastern Europeans as undesirable elements. Inspired by the pseudoscientific findings of eugenics and social Darwinism, late-nineteenth-century nativists often branded southern Italians as especially inferior. Powerful stereotypes centering on poverty, clannishness, illiteracy, high disease rates, and an alleged proclivity toward criminal activities underscored the view that southern Italians were a degenerate "race" that should be denied entry to the United States. Criticism of Italians became integral to the successful legislative drives to enact the nativist Literacy Test in 1917 and National Origins Acts in 1921 and 1924. Although the dominant culture frequently scorned Italians in the early part of the twentieth century, for the most part they tended to perceive Italians as white. However, the 1924 legislation classified southern Italians as nonwhite in an attempt to preserve the homogeneity of the U.S. population. According to an article in a scholarly journal at the time, "Both laws express the determination that the U.S. is to be a white man's country." Northern Italians were quick to classify their southern compatriots as "dark" in order that they, the northerners, be seen as part of the dominant culture.

Within Little Italies, immigrants created New World societies. A network of Italian-language institutions—newspapers, theaters, churches, mutual aid societies, recreational clubs, and debating societies—helped fuel an emerging Italian American ethnic culture. Aspects of folk, popular, and high culture intermixed in this milieu, yielding an array of entertainment options. Saloons or club buildings in larger urban centers often featured traditional Italian puppet and marionette shows while immigrant men sipped wines and played card games of *mora*, *briscola*, and *tresette*. By the early 1900s, a lively Italian-language theater brought entertainment to thousands and sustained the careers of professional acting troupes and noted performers such as the comedic genius Eduardo Migliacco, known as "Farfariello." On a more informal level, Italian coffeehouses often presented light comedies, heroic tragedies, and dialect plays sponsored by drama clubs. Italian opera was a staple in most American urban centers, and working-class Italian music halls attracted customers by offering renditions of Neapolitan or Sicilian songs and dances. Band performances and choral recitals were regularly staged on the streets of Italian settlements. Although illiteracy rates among immigrants often ran well above 50 percent, newcomers in larger cities had access to Italian-language bookstores stocked with poetry, short stories, novels, and nonfiction. In 1906 one New York bookseller published a 176-page catalog to advertise his merchandise.

The cultural patterns of Little Italies were constantly evolving, providing for a dynamic interplay between older forms brought from Italy and new inventions forged in the United States. Many immigrants attempted to re-create old-world celebrations and rituals upon arrival in the United States, but those that directly competed with American forms soon fell away. The celebration of Epiphany (January 6), for example, was the principal Christmastime festivity in Italy, featuring the visit of *La Befana*, a kindly old witch who brought presents for children. In the United States the more popular Christmas Eve and Santa Claus displaced this tradition.

Even those cultural forms more sheltered from American society were contested. Immigrant settlements were not homogenous entities. Various members of the community fought for the right to define the group, and the ongoing struggle for dominance invariably employed cultural symbols and events. The commercial and political elites (*prominenti*)—usually aided by the Italian Catholic clergy—sought to promote Italian nationalism as a means of self-advancement. These forces invested great energy in celebrations of Italian national holidays (such as *venti di settembre*, which commemorates Italian unification), and in the erection of statues of such Italian heroes as Columbus, the poet Dante, and military leader Giuseppe Garibaldi.

These activities were challenged by a variety of leftist radicals (*sovversivi*), who sought very different cultural and political goals. Anarchists, socialists, and syndicalists such as Carlo Tresca and Arturo Giovannitti considered Italian Americans as part of the world proletariat, and they celebrated holidays (*Primo Maggio*—May Day) and heroes (Gaetano Bresci, the assassin of Italian King Umberto) reflecting this image. These symbols also played roles in mass strikes and worker demonstrations led by the radicals. Meanwhile, the majority of Italian Americans continued to draw much of their identity from the peasant cultures of the old-world *paese*. Columbus Day, the preeminent Italian American ethnic celebration, typically blended elements of all these components, with multiple parades and competing banquets, balls, and public presentations.

World War I proved an ambiguous interlude for Italian immigrants. Italy's alliance with the United States and the service of many immigrants in the U.S. military precipitated some level of American acceptance. The war also produced, however, countervailing pressures that generated more intense nationalism among Italians and powerful drives toward assimilation—"100 percent Americanism"—in the wider society. Immigration restrictions after 1924 halted Italian immigration, although the foreign-born presence remained strong (the 1930 U.S. Census recorded 1,623,000 Italian-born residents—the group's historic high). As new arrivals slowed and the second generation matured during the 1920s and 1930s, the group changed.

Several critical developments shaped the character of Italian America during the interwar years. National Prohibition provided lucrative illegal markets, which some Italian Americans successfully exploited through bootlegging operations. During the 1920s and early 1930s, the "gangster" image of Italians (exemplified by Al Capone) was perpetuated

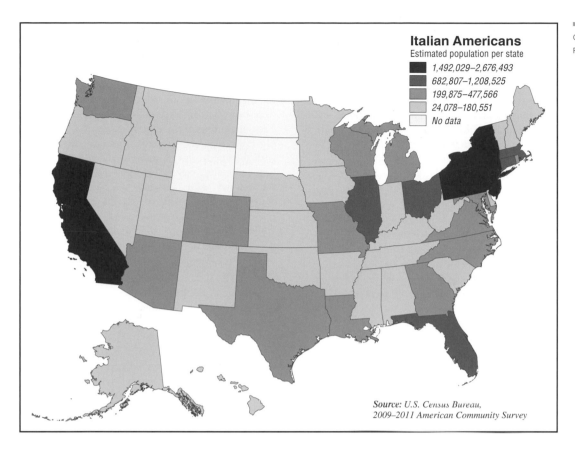

Italian Americans
Estimated population per state

- 1,492,029–2,676,493
- 682,807–1,208,525
- 199,875–477,566
- 24,078–180,551
- No data

*Source: U.S. Census Bureau,
2009–2011 American Community Survey*

through films and popular literature. The celebrated murder case of anarchists Nicola Sacco and Bartolomeo Vanzetti further molded the group's national image, underwriting the conception of Italians as dangerous radicals.

The Great Depression overtook earlier economic gains, often forcing Italian Americans back into their family-centered ethnic communities. Here, the emerging second generation found itself in frequent conflict with the first. Heavily influenced by the traditional *contadino* culture passed on from their parents, the second generation uneasily straddled two worlds. Traditional notions of proper behavior, stressing collective responsibilities toward the family, strict chastity and domestic roles for females, rigid chaperonage and courting codes, and male dominance, clashed with the more individualist, consumer-driven American values children learned in schools, stores, and on the streets. Problems of marginality, lack of self-esteem, rebellion, and delinquency were the outcomes.

Partly because of these dynamics, the community structures of Little Italies began to change. The more Americanized second generation began to turn away from older, Italian-language institutions founded by immigrants, many of which collapsed during the Depression. Italian theaters and music halls, for example, largely gave way to

vaudeville, nickelodeons, organized sports, and radio programming. During the 1920s and 1930s, these transformations were also influenced by Mussolini's Fascist regime, which sponsored propaganda campaigns designed to attract the support of Italian Americans. The *prominenti* generally supported these initiatives, often inserting Fascist symbols (the black shirt), songs ("Giovinezza"—the Fascist anthem), and holidays (the anniversary of the March on Rome) into the ichnography and pageantry of America's Little Italies. A small but vocal anti-Fascist element existed in opposition, and it substituted counter values and emblems. Memorials to Giacomo Matteotti, a socialist deputy murdered by Fascists, and renditions of the communist song "Bandiera Rossa" and the Italian national anthem "Inno di Garibaldi" became fixtures of anti-Fascist festivities. Thus, the political world of Italian America remained divided.

Any doubts regarding American Italians' loyalties to the United States were firmly quashed when Italian Americans rushed to aid the American struggle against the Axis powers after Italy declared war on the United States in 1941. More than 500,000 Italian Americans joined the U.S. military, serving in all theaters, including the Italian campaign. The war effort and ensuing anticommunist crusade stressed conformity, loyalty, and patriotism, and in the 1940s and 1950s it appeared that Italian Americans had comfortably settled into the melting pot. The second generation especially benefited from its war service and the postwar economic expansion, which yielded new levels of acceptance and integration. In the 1950s, they experienced substantial social mobility and embraced mass consumerism and middle-class values. Under the GI Bill, Italian American veterans had access to funds for higher education and housing.

Since the end of World War II, more than 600,000 Italian immigrants have arrived in the United States. A large percentage came shortly after passage of the Immigration Act of 1965, at which time yearly totals of Italian immigrants averaged about 23,000. Beginning in 1974, the numbers steadily declined as a result of improved economic conditions in Italy and changing policies in other immigrant-receiving nations. In 1990 the numbers of Italians wanting to move to the United States had fallen below the quota, and only 3,300 Italians immigrated that year. But 831,922 Italian-born residents remained in the country, guaranteeing that Italian language and culture were still part of the American cultural mosaic. According to the 2010 U.S. Census, 14,000 Italians had immigrated to the United States since 2000. That census reported approximately seventeen million Italian Americans, comprising 5.9 percent of the total U.S. population.

LANGUAGE

Italian is a Romance language derived directly from Latin; it utilizes the Latin alphabet, but the letters *j*, *k*, *w*, *x*, and *y* are found only in words of foreign origin. "Standard" Italian—based on the Tuscan dialect—is a relatively recent invention and was not used universally until well into the twentieth century. Numerous dialects were the dominant linguistic feature during the years of mass immigration. The 2010 U.S. Census reported that 93 percent of Italian Americans speak English only, and only 1.7 percent are less than fluent in English.

Italian dialects did not simply possess different tonalities or inflections. Some were languages in their own right, with separate vocabularies and, for a few, fully developed literatures (e.g., Venetian, Piedmontese, and Sicilian). Italy's mountainous terrain produced conditions in which proximate areas often possessed mutually unintelligible languages. For example, the word for "today" in standard Italian is *oggi*, but *ancheuj* in Piedmontese, *uncuó* in Venetian, *ste iorne* in Sicilian, and *oji* in Calabrian. Similarly, "children" in Italian is *bambini*, but it becomes *cit* in Piedmontese, *fruz* in Friulian, *guagliuni* in Neapolitan, *zitedi* in Calabrian, and *picciriddi* in Sicilian. Thus, language barriers encouraged *campanilismo*, further fragmenting the emerging Italian American world.

According to the 2010 U.S. Census, Italian was the fifth most common language taught in American colleges and universities. It was the seventh most

commonly spoken language, with more than one million Italian speakers living in the United States. Cities with Italian-speaking and Sicilian-speaking communities include Buffalo, New York; Chicago; Miami; New York City; and Philadelphia. However, the majority of Italian speakers in the United States were over the age of sixty-five. The College Board, a national nonprofit organization devoted to providing every high school student in the United States with the opportunity to receive college-level instruction and college credit, provides high schools around the country with curricula, assessment tools, and district guidance on thirty-four advanced placement (AP) subjects. Due to a perceived lack of interest, the College Board did not offer Italian language as an AP class until 2006, and after only three years, the organization dropped the class because of insufficient enrollment.

Aware of these facts, numerous Italian American organizations and individuals are actively promoting the teaching and learning of Italian among the younger generations. In cities such as Houston, Texas; New York City; San Francisco; and Seattle, Washington, there are institutions devoted exclusively to Italian-language instruction, offering daytime and evening classes. Groups such as the National Council for the Promotion of Italian Language and the National Italian American Foundation (NIAF) offer scholarships to students, grants to Italian-language teachers, and heritage travel funds to Italian Americans interested in developing their language skills. Every summer the NIAF runs an Italian immersion summer camp for children ages eight to eighteen. Web-based groups have launched campaigns to increase Italian language-learning opportunities, such as ItalianAware's book campaign aimed at expanding the New York Public Library System's collection.

Greetings and Popular Expressions Very soon after the Italians' arrival, all dialects became infused with Americanisms, quickly creating a new form of communication often intelligible only to immigrants. The new patois was neither Italian nor English, and it included such words as *giobba* for job, *grossiera* for grocery, *bosso* for boss, *marachetta* for market, *baccausa* for outhouse, *ticchetto* for ticket, *bisiniss* for business, *trocco* for truck, *sciabola* for shovel, *loffare* for the verb "to loaf," and *carpetto* for carpet. Angelo Massari, who immigrated to Tampa, Florida, in 1902, described preparations in his Sicilian village prior to leaving it:

> I used to interview people who had returned from America. I asked them thousands of questions, how America was, what they did in Tampa, what kind of work was to be had. … One of them told me the language was English, and I asked him how to say one word or another in that language. I got these wonderful samples of Sicilian American English

from him: *tu sei un boia, gud morni, olraiti, giachese, misti, sciusi, bred, iessi, bud* [you are a boy, good morning, alright, jacket, mister, excuse me, bread, yes, but]. He told me also that in order to ask for work, one had to say, 'Se misti gari giobbi fo mi?' [Say, mister got a job for me?].

Angelo Massari, The Wonderful Life of Angelo Massari, *trans. Arthur Massolo. New York: Exposition Press, 1965: 46–47.*

RELIGION

Although Italian immigrants were overwhelmingly Roman Catholic, their faith was a personal, folk religion of feast days and peasant traditions that often had little to do with formal dogma or rituals. As such, its practices differed greatly from those encountered in America's Irish-dominated Catholic Church. Unlike Irish Americans, most Italians possessed no great reverence for priests (who had sometimes been among the oppressors in Italy) or the institutions of the official Church, and they disliked what they regarded as the impersonal, puritanical, and overly doctrinal Irish approach to religion. As in Italy, men continued to manifest anticlerical traditions and to attend church only on select occasions, such as weddings and funerals.

For their part, the Irish clergy generally regarded Italians as indifferent Catholics—even pagans—and often relegated them to basement services. The Irish American hierarchy agonized over the "Italian Problem," and suspicion and mistrust initially characterized relations between the groups, leading to defections among the immigrant generation and demands for separate parishes. The disproportionately low presence of Italian Americans in the church leadership today is at least partially a legacy of this strained relationship. Protestant missionaries were not unaware of these developments. Many attempted to win converts but met with very little success. Catholic churches in the United States responded to pressure from different immigrant populations to preserve their faith as it had been handed down in the home country. The Church established so-called national parishes—parishes that were organized around the worshippers' ethnic background rather than their geographical proximity. Within the new framework, Italian American Catholics developed parish schools, national social networks, and mutual aid societies. Italian parishes proliferated after 1900. In many settlements, parish churches became focal points providing a sense of ethnic identity, a range of social services, and a source of community adhesion.

Italian-immigrant Catholicism centered on the local patron saints and the beliefs, superstitions, and practices associated with the *feste*. Feast days not only assisted in perpetuating local identities but also served as a means for public expression of immigrant faith. In the early years, feast days replicated those of the homeland. Festivals were occasions for great celebration, complete with music, parades, dancing, eating, and fireworks displays. At the high point, statues of local saints such as San Rocco, San Giuseppe, or San Gennaro were carried through the streets of Little Italies in a procession.

Worshippers lined the streets as processions moved toward the parish church, and they vied to pin money on the statue, place gifts on platforms, or make various penances (walking barefoot, crawling, licking the church floor [*lingua strascinuni*], reciting certain prayers). Irish prelates frequently attempted to ban such events, viewing them as pagan rituals and public spectacles. A cluster of beliefs focusing on the folk world of magic, witches, ghosts, and demons further estranged Italians from the church hierarchy. Many Italian immigrants were convinced, for example, of the existence of the evil eye (*malocchio* or *jettatura*), and believed that wearing certain symbols, the most potent of which were associated with horns (*corni*), or garlic amulets provided protection from its power.

As the second and subsequent generations grew to maturity, most strictly old-world forms of religious observance and belief were discarded, leading to what some have called the "hibernization" of Italian American Catholicism. Many feast day celebrations remain, although, in some cases, they have been transformed into mass cultural events that draw thousands of non-Italians. The San Gennaro *feste* in Manhattan's Little Italy is a case in point: once celebrated only by Neapolitans, it now attracts heterogeneous crowds from hundreds of miles away.

CULTURE AND ASSIMILATION

The integration of Italians into American life in the early twentieth century was a result of changes in both the group and the larger society. Italians were beginning to make a commitment to permanent settlement. This process was substantially underway by 1910, cresting in the 1920s when new immigration fell off. After this, perpetuation of the old-world public culture became increasingly difficult, although the family-based value structure was more resilient. During the 1920s and 1930s, the second generation continued to display many of its hallmarks: children of immigrants still held largely blue-collar jobs and were underrepresented in schools, tied to Little Italy residences, and attracted to in-group marriages—choices that demonstrated the continuing power of parental mores.

Changing contexts, however, diminished the "social distance" that separated Italians from other Americans. In the 1930s, second-generation Italian Americans joined forces with others in labor unions and lobbied for benefits. They also began to make political gains as part of the Democratic Party's New Deal coalition. Also for the first time, the national popular culture began to include Italian Americans among its heroes. In music, sports, politics, and cinema the careers of Frank Sinatra, Joe DiMaggio, Fiorello LaGuardia, Don Ameche, and others suggested that national attitudes toward Italians were in transition.

Italian Americans at Sorrento Caffe in Little Italy in Manhattan. DBTRAVEL / DBIMAGES / ALAMY

World War II was a critical benchmark in the acceptance of Italian Americans. Their wholehearted support of America's cause and their disproportionately high ratio of service in the military legitimized them in the eyes of America. The war also transformed many Little Italies, as men and women left for military service or to work in war industries. Upon their return, many newly affluent Italian Americans left for suburban locations and fresh opportunities, further eroding the institutions and *contadino* culture that once thrived in ethnic settlements.

The Cold War pushed the group further into the mainstream as Italian Americans joined in the anticommunist fervor gripping the nation. Simultaneously, structural changes in the economy vastly expanded the availability of white-collar, managerial positions, and Italian Americans jumped to take advantage. Beginning in the 1950s, they pursued higher education in greater numbers than ever before, many receiving aid as a result of the GI Bill. Such developments put them into more immediate and positive contact with other Americans, who exhibited greater acceptance in the postwar years.

Ironically, a resurgent Italian American ethnicity emerged at the same time, as the group experienced increasing integration into the larger society. Italian Americans were active participants in the ethnic revival of the 1960s and 1970s. As American core values came under assault in the midst of Vietnam, Watergate, and the rising counterculture, and the nation's urban centers

became torn by riots and civil protest, Italian Americans felt especially vulnerable and besieged. Unlike other ethnic groups, they had remained in urban enclaves, manifesting high rates of home ownership, where they now found themselves in contact and conflict with African Americans. Many interpreted the ensuing clashes in cultural terms, seeing themselves as an embattled minority defending traditional values in the face of new compensatory government programs. In response, ethnic traditions surrounding family, neighborhood, and homes gained heightened visibility and strength. New Italian American organizations and publications fostering ethnic identity came into being, and many old rituals experienced a resurgence, most notably the celebration of the *feste*.

Intermarriage rates increased after the 1950s, especially among the third and fourth generations who were now coming of age. By 1991, the group's overall in-marriage rate was just under 33 percent, above the average of 26 percent for other ethnic groups. But among those born after 1940—by now a majority in the Italian American population—the rate was only 20 percent, and these marriages crossed both ethnic and religious lines.

Once a marginalized, despised minority, Italian Americans are now among the most highly accepted groups according to national surveys measuring "social distance" indicators (Italians ranked fourteenth in 1926, but fifth in 1977). All of the statistical data point to a high level of structural assimilation in American society, although Italian American ethnicity has not disappeared. That Italian American identity has lost much of its former negative weight is suggested further by recent census figures for ancestry group claiming. The 1980 census recorded 12.1 million individuals who claimed Italian ancestry (5.4 percent of the national population). By 1990 this figure had risen to 14.7 million (5.9 percent), and by 2010 it had risen to seventeen million, indicating that ethnicity remains an important and acceptable component of self-identification for substantial numbers of Italian Americans.

Despite strong evidence of integration, Italian Americans retain distinguishing characteristics. They are still geographically concentrated in the old settlement areas, and they display a pronounced attachment to the values of domesticity and family loyalty. Italian Americans still rely heavily on personal and kin networks in residential choices, visiting patterns, and general social interaction. Perhaps most distinctive, the group continues to suffer from stereotypes associating it with criminal behavior, especially in the form of organized crime and the mafia. These images have persisted despite research documenting that Italian Americans possess crime rates no higher than other segments of American society and that organized crime is a multiethnic enterprise. Television and film images of Italian Americans continue to emphasize criminals, "lovable or laughable dimwits" who engage in dead-end jobs, and heavily accented, overweight "mamas" with their pasta pots.

These representations have hampered the movement of Italian Americans into the highest levels of corporate and political life. The innuendos of criminal ties advanced during Geraldine Ferraro's vice-presidential candidacy in 1984 and during Mario Cuomo's aborted presidential bids illustrate the political repercussions of these stereotypes, and many Italian Americans believe that bias has kept them underrepresented in the top echelons of the business world. Such negative stereotyping persists, with TV shows like *The Sopranos*, which aired from 1999 to 2006, playing off the Italian American stereotype of mobsters, and the reality show *Jersey Shore* (2009–2012), which many saw as a negative portrayal of Italian Americans. Since the 1970s, such organizations as the Americans of Italian Descent, the Sons of Italy in America, and the National Italian American Foundation (NIAF) have mounted broad-based antidefamation campaigns protesting such negative imagery. These groups have succeeded in getting advertisements pulled off the air, language changed in the movies, and even getting the U.S. attorney general's office to stop using the term "mafia" in its criminal prosecutions.

Cuisine Historically, the difficult conditions of daily life in Italy dictated frugal eating habits. Most peasants consumed simple meals based on whatever vegetables or grains (lentils, peas, fava beans, corn, tomatoes, onions, and wild greens) were prevalent in each region. A staple for most common folk was coarse black bread. Pasta was a luxury, and peasants typically ate meat only two or three times a year on special holidays. Italian cuisine was—and still is—regionally distinctive, and even festive meals varied widely. The traditional Christmas dish in Piedmont was *agnolotti* (ravioli), while *anguille* (eels) were served in Campania, *sopa friulana* (celery soup) in Friuli, and *bovoloni* (fat snails) in Vicenza.

In the United States, many immigrants planted small backyard garden plots to supplement the table and continued to raise cows, chickens, and goats whenever possible. Outdoor brick ovens were commonplace, serving as clear ethnic markers of Italian residences. With improved economic conditions, pastas, meats, sugar, and coffee were consumed more frequently.

"Italian cooking" in the United States has come to mean southern Italian, especially Neapolitan, cuisine, which is rich in tomato sauces, heavily spiced, and pasta-based. Spaghetti and meatballs (not generally known in Italy) and pizza are perhaps the quintessential Italian dishes in the United States. More recently, northern Italian cooking—characterized by rice (*risotto*) and corn (*polenta*) dishes and butter-based recipes—has become increasingly common in homes and restaurants. Garlic (*aglio*), olive oil (*olio d'oliva*), mushrooms (*funghi*), and nuts (*nochi*) of various types are common ingredients found in Italian cooking. Wine (*vino*), consumed in moderate amounts,

RISOTTO

Ingredients

5 cups chicken stock

1 pinch saffron threads (optional)

5 tablespoons butter

1 medium onion, finely chopped

1 clove garlic, finely chopped

1½ cups arborio rice

1 cup parmesan cheese, grated

salt and black pepper

Preparation

Bring stock to a boil, then reduce to a low simmer. Ladle a little stock into a small bowl; add the saffron threads and let infuse.

Melt 4 tablespoons of butter in a large sauce pan until foaming. Add onions, stirring frequently, and cook for 2 minutes, then add garlic and cook for 1 more minute. Cook only until softened, not brown. Add the rice and stir until the grains start to swell and burst; then add a few ladles of stock, saffron liquid, and salt and pepper to taste. Stirring constantly over low heat until liquid has been absorbed. Keep adding stock, letting the rice absorb the liquid before adding more.

After about 20–25 minutes, the rice should be just tender and the risoto golden and creamy. Take off heat and add parmesan cheese and remaining 1 tablespoon butter, mixing until butter has melted.

Season to taste with salt and pepper.

Transfer to serving plates and serve hot with additional parmesan cheese.

Serves 5

is a staple. Overall, Italian dishes have become so popular that they have been accepted into the nation's dietary repertoire, but not in strictly old-world forms. Americanized dishes are generally milder in their spicing and more standardized than old-world fare.

Dances and Songs Italian immigrants utilized traditional costumes, folk songs, folklore, and dances for special events, but like many aspects of Italian life, they were so regionally specific that they defy easy characterization. Perhaps the most commonly recognized folk dance, the *tarantella*, for example, is Neapolitan, with little diffusion elsewhere in the peninsula.

Holidays The major national holidays of Italy—*Festa della Republica* (June 5), *Festa dell'Unità Nazionale* (November 6), and *Festa del Lavoro* (May 1)—are no longer occasions of public celebration among Italian Americans. Some religious holidays, such as *Epifania di Gesù* (January 6), receive only passing notice. Most

ITALIAN PROVERBS

Italian proverbs tend to reflect the conditions of peasant and immigrant lives:

- Work hard, work always, and you will never know hunger.

- He who leaves the old way for the new knows what he loses but knows not what he will find.

- Buy oxen and marry women from your village only.

- The wolf changes his skin but not his vice.

- The village is all the world.

- Do not miss the Saint's day, he helps you and provides at all times.

- Tell me who your friends are and I will tell you what you are.

- He who respects others will be respected.

Italian Americans celebrate Christmas Day, New Year's Day, and Easter Day, but usually without any particular ethnic character. The principal occasions of public celebration typically revolve around Columbus Day, the quintessential Italian American national holiday, and the *feste* honoring patron saints. These events have, in general, become multiday celebrations virtually devoid of any religious or Italian national connotation and involving numerous non-Italians.

In New Orleans, Louisiana, St. Joseph's Day (March 19) is celebrated by some members of the Italian American community. The tradition began in Sicily, the origin of much of New Orleans' Italian American population. The day is commemorated by the building of temporary three-tiered alters, loaded with food offerings for the saint. The altars are found in private homes, churches, some restaurants, and public places associated with Italians, with the general public invited. Visitors to the altars are often given *lagniappe* (a sack of cookies and fava beans, a good luck charm) to take home.

Preparations for St. Joseph's Day begin several weeks in advance with the baking of cookies, breads, and cakes. Cookies, such as twice-baked biscotti and sesame-seed varieties, are shaped into forms with religious significance. Bread, cannoli, seafood, and vegetable dishes are also found on the altar. Such dishes include *forschias* and pasta Milanese covered with *mudriga*. Mudriga, made of breadcrumbs and sugar, is also called "St. Joseph's sawdust." No meat is found because the holiday almost always falls during Lent. In addition to food, the altar often has an image of St. Joseph, homegrown flowers, candles, and palm branches.

FAMILY AND COMMUNITY LIFE

The family (*la famiglia*) rests at the heart of Italian society. Family solidarity was the major bulwark from which the rural population confronted a harsh society, and the family unit (including blood relatives and relatives by marriage) became the center of allegiances. Economically and socially, the family functioned as a collective enterprise, an "all-inclusive social world" in which the individual was subordinated to the larger entity. Parents expected children to assist them at an early age by providing gainful labor, and family values stressed respect for the elderly, obedience to parents, hard work, and deference to authority.

Gender Roles The traditional Italian family was "father-headed, but mother-centered." In public, the father was the uncontested authority figure, and wives were expected to defer to their husbands. At home, however, females exercised considerable authority as wives and mothers and played central roles in sustaining familial networks. Still, male children occupied a favored position of superiority over females, and strong family mores governed female behavior. Women's activities were largely confined to the home, and strict rules limited their public behavior, including access to education and outside employment. Formal rituals of courting, chaperonage, and arranged marriages strictly governed relations between the sexes. Above all, protection of female chastity was critical to maintaining family honor.

Family and kin networks also guided migration patterns, directing precise village flows to specific destinations. During sojourner migrations, the work of women in home villages sustained the family well-being in Italy and allowed male workers to actively compete in the world labor market. In the United States, the extended family became an important network for relatives to seek and receive assistance. Thus, migration and settlement operated within a context of family considerations.

Attempts to transfer traditional family customs to the United States engendered considerable tension between generations. More educated and Americanized children ventured to bridge two worlds, with the individualist notions of American society often clashing with their parents' family-centered ethos. Still, strong patterns of in-marriage characterized the second generation, and many of their parents' cultural values were successfully inculcated. These carryovers resulted in a strong attachment to neighborhoods and families, consistent deference to authority, and blue-collar work choices. The second generation, however, began to adopt American practices in terms of family life (seen, for example, in smaller family size and greater English-language usage), and the collective nature of the unit began to break down as the generations advanced.

According to the American Community Survey conducted between 2005 and 2007, there was a significant gap between Italian American men and women in terms of full-time employment. A total of 59.5

percent of Italian American men held full-time jobs, while only 40.5 percent of Italian American women held full-time jobs. Italian American women were almost three times more likely to be single parents than their male counterparts.

Education The peasant culture placed little value on formal instruction, seeking instead to have children contribute as soon as possible to family earnings. From the peasant perspective, education consisted primarily of passing along moral and social values through parental instruction (the term *buon educat* means "well-raised or behaved"). In southern Italy, formal education was seldom a means of upward mobility because public schools were not institutions of the people. They were poorly organized and supported, administered by a distrusted northern bureaucracy, and perceived as alien to the goals of family solidarity. Proverbs such as "Do not let your children become better than you" spoke to these perceptions, and high rates of illiteracy testified to their power.

These attitudes remained strong among immigrants in America, many of whom planned a quick repatriation and saw little reason to lose children's wages. Parents also worried about the individualist values taught in American public schools. The saying "America took from us our children" was a common lament. Thus, truancy rates among Italians were high, especially among girls, for whom education had always been regarded as unnecessary since tradition dictated a path of marriage, motherhood, and homemaking.

Antagonism toward schools was derived not only from culture, but also from economic need and realistic judgments about mobility possibilities. Given the constricted employment options open to immigrants (largely confined to manual, unskilled labor) and the need for family members to contribute economically, extended schooling offered few rewards. From the parental viewpoint, anything threatening the family's collective strength was dangerous. Generations frequently clashed over demands to terminate formal education and find work, turn over earnings, and otherwise assist the family financially. Prior to World War I, less than 1 percent of Italian American children were enrolled in high school.

As the second generation came of age in the 1920s and 1930s and the United States moved toward a service economy, however, education received greater acceptance. Although the children of immigrants generally remained entrenched in the working class (though frequently as skilled workers), they extended their education, often attending vocational schools, and could be found among the nation's clerks, bookkeepers, managers, and sales personnel. The economic downturn occasioned by the Depression resulted in increased educational opportunities for some immigrants due to limited job prospects.

Italian Americans were well situated in post–World War II America to take advantage of the national expansion of secondary and higher education. They hastened to enroll in GI Bill programs and in the 1950s and 1960s began to send sons and daughters to college. By the 1970s, Italian Americans averaged about twelve years of formal education; in 1991 the group slightly surpassed the national mean of 12.7 years. As of 2010, 32.2 percent of Italian Americans over age twenty-five had a college degree or higher, compared to the national average of 29.9 percent.

Philanthropy The philanthropic activity of Italian Americans has focused primarily on its own community by promoting Italian studies, Italian American studies, and language study. Philanthropists such as Joseph and Elda Coccia have made generations donations to establish libraries and have endowed chairs and centers of study, while the Columbus Citizens Foundation, the Order of Columbus, and the NIAF have provided grants for younger Italian Americans as well as adult learners to study language and culture. One of the notable exceptions is the Golisano Foundation, established in 1985, which provides grants to individuals with developmental disabilities and their families and has invested in hospitals and rehabilitation centers. Since the late 1990s, the foundation has donated more than $200 million toward charitable causes.

EMPLOYMENT AND ECONOMIC CONDITIONS

Throughout the years of mass migration, Italians clustered heavily in the ranks of unskilled, manual laborers. In part, this seems to have been due to cultural preference—men favored outdoor jobs dovetailing old-world skills—and immigrant strategies that sought readily available employment in order for the men to return quickly to Italy with money in their pockets. But they were also relegated to such work by American employers who regarded Italians as unsuited for indoor work or heavy industry. Immigrants thus frequently engaged in seasonal work on construction sites and railroads, in mines, and on public works projects. Male employment often operated under the "boss system," in which countrymen (*padroni*) served as middlemen between groups of immigrant workers and American employers. Married women generally worked at home, either concentrating on family tasks or other home-based jobs such as keeping boarders, attending to industrial homework, or assisting in family-run stores. In larger urban centers, unmarried women worked outside the home in factories that manufactures garments, artificial flowers, or costume jewelry, and in sweatshops and canneries, often laboring together in all-Italian groups.

Some Little Italies were large enough to support a full economic structure of their own. In these locations, small import stores, shops, restaurants, fish merchants, and flower traders proliferated, offering opportunities for upward mobility within the ethnic enclave. In many cities, Italians dominated certain urban trades such as fruit and

Italian immigrant laborers pose during construction of the New Troy, Rensselaer & Pittsfield Electric Railway in Lebanon Valley, New York. MICHAEL MASLAN HISTORIC PHOTOGRAPHS / CORBIS

vegetable peddling, confectioniering, rag picking, shoe-shining, ice-cream vending, and stevedoring. A portion of the immigrants were skilled artisans who typically replicated their old-world crafts of shoemaking and repairing, tailoring, carpentry, and barbering.

The dense concentration of Italian Americans in blue-collar occupations persisted into the second generation, deriving from deliberate career choices, negative attitudes toward formal education, and the economic dynamics of the nation. Italians had begun to make advances out of the unskilled ranks during the prosperous 1920s, but many gains were overshadowed during the Great Depression. Partially in response to these conditions, Italians—both men and women— moved heavily into organized labor during the 1930s, finding the CIO industrial unions especially attractive. Union memberships among Italian Americans rose significantly; by 1937, the AFL International Ladies Garment Workers Union (with vice president Luigi Antonini) counted nearly 100,000 Italian members in the New York City area alone. At the same time, women were becoming a presence in service and clerical positions.

The occupational choices of Italian Americans shifted radically after World War II, when structural changes in the American economy facilitated openings in more white-collar occupations. Italian Americans were strategically situated to take advantage of these economic shifts, being clustered in the urban areas where economic expansion took place and ready to move into higher education. Since the 1960s, Italian Americans have become solidly grounded in the middle-class, managerial, and professional ranks. As a group, by 1991 they had equaled or surpassed national averages in income and occupational prestige. In 2010, 39.2 percent of Italian Americans were in professional or managerial positions, as compared to the national average of 36.6 percent. The average income for Italian Americans was also slightly higher than the national average.

POLITICS AND GOVERNMENT

Italians were slow to take part in the American political process. Due to the temporary nature of early migration, few took the time to achieve naturalization in order to vote. Anti-government attitudes, exemplified in the *ladro governo* ("the government as thief") outlook, also limited participation. Hence, Italian voters did not initially translate into political clout. Early political activity took place at the urban machine level, where immigrants commonly encountered Irish Democratic bosses offering favors in return for support, but often blocking out aspiring Italian politicians. In such cities, those Italians seeking office frequently drifted to the Republican Party.

Naturalization rates increased during the 1920s, but the next decade was marked by a political watershed. During the 1930s, Italian Americans joined the Democratic New Deal coalition, many, in doing so, becoming politically active for the first time. The careers of independent/sometime-Republican Fiorello LaGuardia and leftist Vito Marcantonio benefited from this expansion. As a concentrated urban group with strong union ties, Italians constituted an important component of President Franklin Roosevelt's national support. The Democratic hold on Italians was somewhat shaken by Roosevelt's "dagger in the back" speech condemning Italy's attack on France in 1940, but, overall, the group maintained its strong commitment to the Party. In the early 1970s, only 17 percent of Italian Americans were registered Republicans (45 percent were registered Democrats), although many began to vote Republican in later presidential elections. Both President Ronald Reagan and President George H. W. Bush were supported by strong Italian American majorities. Overall, the group has moved from the left toward the political center. By 1991, Italian American voter registration was 35 percent Republican and 32 percent Democratic.

The political ascent of Italian Americans came after World War II with the maturation of the second and third generations, the acquisition of increased education and greater wealth, and a higher level of acceptance by the wider society. Italian Americans were well-represented in city and state offices and had begun to penetrate the middle ranks of the federal government, especially the judicial system. By the 1970s and 1980s, there were Italian American cabinet members, governors, federal judges, and state legislators. Only four Italian Americans sat in Congress during the 1930s, but more than thirty served in the 1980s; in 1987 there were three Italian American U.S. senators. The candidacy of Geraldine Ferraro for the Democratic vice presidency in 1984, the high profile of New York governor Mario Cuomo in American political discourse during the 1980s and 1990s, and the appointment of Antonin Scalia (1986) and Samuel Alito (2006) to the Supreme Court are indicative of the group's political importance. In 2000, eighty-two of the country's one thousand largest cities had Italian American mayors.

As of 2012, four of the two hundred members of the Italian American Congressional Delegation were U.S. senators and twenty-five were U.S. representatives of Italian ancestry. Italian American Nancy Pelosi served as speaker of the house in the U.S. House of Representatives from 2007 through 2011.

Since World War II, most Italian Americans have remained largely uninvolved in—even ignorant of— the political affairs of Italy, no doubt a legacy of World War II and the earlier brush with Fascism. They have been very responsive, however, to appeals for relief assistance during periodic natural disasters such as floods and earthquakes.

NOTABLE INDIVIDUALS

Italians constitute such a large and diverse group that notable individuals have appeared in virtually every aspect of American life.

Academia Lorenzo Da Ponte (1749–1838) taught courses on Italian literature at Columbia University and sponsored the first Italian opera house in Manhattan in the 1830s. Prior to becoming president of Yale University in 1977, A. Bartlett Giamatti (1938–1989) was a distinguished scholar of English and comparative literature. He resigned his presidency

to become president of Major League Baseball's National League in 1986 and was named MLB commissioner three years later. Peter Sammartino (1904–1992) taught at the City College of New York and Columbia University before founding Fairleigh Dickinson University. He published fourteen books on various aspects of education.

Art Constantino Brumidi (1805–1880), a political exile from the liberal revolutions of the 1840s, became known as "the Michelangelo of the United States Capitol." He painted the interior of the dome of the Capitol in Washington, D.C., from 1865 to 1866, as well as numerous other areas of the building. Ralph Fasanella (1914–1997), a self-taught primitive painter whose work has been compared to that of Grandma Moses, was grounded in his immigrant background. Frank Stella (1936–) pioneered the development of "minimal art," involving three-dimensional "shaped" paintings and sculpture. His work has been exhibited in museums around the world.

Business Amadeo P. Giannini (1870–1949) opened a storefront bank in the Italian North Beach section of San Francisco in 1904. Immediately after the 1906 earthquake he began granting loans to residents to rebuild. Later, Giannini pioneered in branch

One of the classic Italian neighborhoods in the U.S. is San Francisco's North Beach. In this picture, the wares at a Salumeria are on display. JUSTIN SULLIVAN / GETTY IMAGES

banking and in financing the early film industry. His Bank of America eventually became the largest bank in the United States.

Lido Anthony "Lee" Iacocca (1924–) became president of Ford Motor Company in 1970. He left Ford after eight years to take over the ailing Chrysler Corporation, which was near bankruptcy. He rescued the company, in part through personal television ads that made his face instantly recognizable. Iacocca also spent four years as chairman of the Statue of Liberty/Ellis Island Foundation, which supported the refurbishment of these national monuments.

Fred DeLuca (1948–) borrowed $1,000 to open his first sandwich shop at the age of seventeen. As of 2012, the creator of the Subway franchise owned 13,136 Subways in sixty-four countries and had a net worth of $3 billion.

Film, Television, and Theater Francis Ford Coppola (1939–) earned international fame as the director of *The Godfather* (1972), an adaptation of Mario Puzo's best-selling novel. The film won three Academy Awards, including Best Picture. Among numerous other films, Coppola has made two sequels to *The Godfather*; the second film of this trilogy, released in 1974, also won multiple awards, including the Academy Award for Best Picture. His daughter, Sofia Coppola, is an acclaimed screenwriter and film director in her own right. In 2003 she became the first American woman to be nominated for an Academy Award for Best Director (for *Lost in Translation*).

Martin Scorsese (1942–), film director and screenwriter, directed *Mean Streets* (1973), *Taxi Driver* (1976), *Raging Bull* (1980), and *Goodfellas* (1990), among others, all of which draw from the urban, ethnic milieu of his youth. He won the Academy Award for Best Director for 2006's *The Departed* (2006).

Sylvester Stallone (1946–), has gained fame as an actor, screenwriter, and director. He is perhaps best known as the title character in both *Rocky* (1976), which won an Academy Award for Best Picture (and spawned five sequels), and the *Rambo* series.

Don Ameche (1908–1993), whose career spanned several decades, performed in vaudeville, appeared on radio serials ("The Chase and Sanborn Hour"), and starred in feature films. Ameche first achieved national acclaim in *The Story of Alexander Graham Bell* (1939) and appeared in many films, earning an Academy Award for Best Supporting Actor for his performance in *Cocoon* (1985).

Ernest Borgnine (born Ermes Effron Borgnino, 1917–2012) spent his early acting career portraying villains, such as the brutal prison guard in *From Here to Eternity*, but captured the hearts of Americans with his sensitive portrayal of a Bronx butcher in *Marty* (1955), for which he won an Academy Award. Borgnine also appeared on network television as Lieutenant Commander Quintin McHale on *McHale's Navy*, a comedy series that ran on ABC from 1962 to 1965.

Liza Minnelli (1946–), stage, television, and motion picture actress and vocalist, won an Academy Award for *Cabaret* (1972), an Emmy for *Liza with a Z* (1972), and a Tony Award for *The Act* (1977).

Jay Leno (1950–) was born in New York to a Scottish mother and a first-generation Italian American father. He started a comedy troupe while a student at Emerson College. He began his career as a professional standup comedian at the age of twenty-three. In 1992, Leno replaced Johnny Carson as the host of NBC's *The Tonight Show*. Leno has been the host of talk shows ever since.

Rachel Ray (1968–) is Italian American on her mother's side. She grew up in New York and Cape Cod, where her family owned and managed several restaurants. Ray hosts her own daytime talk show, and she is a celebrity chef with three cooking shows on the Food Network as well as a successful author.

Law Antonin Scalia (1936–) was appointed to the U.S. Supreme Court by President Ronald Reagan in 1986. Before his appointment he practiced at a law firm, taught at University of Chicago Law School, worked for the Nixon and Ford administrations, and served on the bench for the U.S. District Court for the District of Columbia.

Samuel Alito (1950–) was appointed to the U.S. Supreme Court by President George W. Bush in 2006. Prior to his appointment, he served as U.S. attorney for the district of New Jersey and as a judge for the U.S. Circuit Court for the Third Circuit.

Literature Gay Talese (1932–) began his career as a reporter for the *New York Times* but later earned fame for his national best sellers, including *The Kingdom and the Power* (1969), *Honor Thy Father* (1971), and *Thy Neighbor's Wife* (1980). Talese's *Unto the Sons* (1992) dealt with his own family's immigrant experience.

John Ciardi (1916–1986), poet, translator, and literary critic, published more than forty books of poetry and criticism. He profoundly impacted the literary world as the longtime poetry editor of the *Saturday Review*. Ciardi's translation of Dante's *Divine Comedy* is regarded as definitive.

Pietro DiDonato (1911–1992) published the classic Italian immigrant novel, *Christ in Concrete*, in 1939 to critical acclaim. He also captured the immigrant experience in later works, including *Three Circles of Light* (1960) and *Life of Mother Cabrini* (1960). The poetry of Lawrence Ferlinghetti (1919–) captured the essence of the Beat Generation during the 1950s and 1960s. His San Francisco bookstore, City Lights Books, became a gathering place for literary activists.

Mario Puzo (1920–1999) published two critical successes, *Dark Arena* (1955) and *The Fortunate Pilgrim* (1965), prior to *The Godfather* in 1969, which sold more than ten million copies and reached vast audiences in its film adaptations. Helen Barolini (1925–), poet, essayist, and novelist, explored the experiences of Italian American women in her *Umbertina* (1979) and *The Dream Book* (1985). Don DeLillo (1936–) is a first-generation Italian American and highly acclaimed author. His novels include such works as *Great Jones Street* (1973), *White Noise* (1985), and *Libra* (1988).

Music and Entertainment Francis Albert "Frank" Sinatra (1915–1998) began singing with the Harry James Band in the late 1930s, moved to the Tommy Dorsey Band, and in the early 1940s became America's first teen idol, rising to stardom as a "crooner." Moving into film, Sinatra launched a career in acting in 1946. The leader of the Rat Pack, who won an Academy Award for his performance in *From Here to Eternity* in 1953, made thirty-one films, released at least eight hundred records, and participated in numerous charity affairs.

Mario Lanza (1921–1959) was a famous tenor who appeared on radio, in concert, on recordings, and in motion pictures. Vocalist and television star Perry Como (born Pierino Roland Como, 1912–2001) hosted one of America's most popular television shows in the 1950s. Frank Zappa (1940–1993), musician, vocalist, and composer, founded the influential rock group Mothers of Invention in the 1960s and was noted for his social satire and musical inventiveness.

Politics Mario Cuomo (1932–) is a first-generation Italian American. When he was a child, his family owned a store in Queens. Cuomo attended public school in New York City and received his undergraduate and law degrees from St. Johns. Following law school he clerked for a judge on the New York Court of Appeals. He gained a reputation as an outstanding attorney for his representation of clients in public housing cases. He entered the political arena when he was elected New York's secretary of state in 1975. He was the fifty-second governor of New York from 1983 to 1994, and his son, Andrew Cuomo, became the fifty-sixth governor of New York in 2011.

Fiorello LaGuardia (1882–1947) gained national fame as the three-term energetic mayor of New York City (1934–1945). Earlier, LaGuardia sat for six terms as a Republican representative in the U.S. Congress. Known as "The Little Flower," LaGuardia earned a reputation as an incorruptible, hardworking, and humane administrator.

John O. Pastore (1907–2000) was the first Italian American to be elected a state governor (Rhode Island, 1945). Beginning in 1950, he represented that state in the U.S. Senate. Geraldine Ferraro (1935–2011) became the first American woman nominated for vice president by a major political party when she ran with Democratic presidential candidate Walter Mondale in 1984. Her earlier career included service as an assistant district attorney in New York and two terms in the U.S. Congress.

John J. Sirica (1904–1992), chief federal judge, U.S. District Court for the District of Columbia, presided over the Watergate trials. He was named *Time* magazine's Man of the Year in 1973. Rudolph W. Giuliani (1944–) served for many years as U.S. attorney for the Southern District of New York and waged war against organized crime and public corruption. He served as mayor of New York City from 1994 through 2001.

Nancy Pelosi (1940–) was elected to the United States House of Representatives in 1987. She served as speaker of the house from 2007 to 2011 (the first woman and the first Italian American to hold that position), and she became minority leader in 2011. As of 2013, she was the highest-ranking female politician in American history.

Religion Father Eusebio Kino (1645–1711) was a Jesuit priest who worked among the native people of Mexico and Arizona for three decades, establishing more than twenty mission churches, exploring wide areas, and introducing new methods of agriculture and animal-raising. Francesca Xavier Cabrini (1850–1917), the first American to be sainted by the Roman Catholic Church, worked with poor Italian immigrants throughout North and South America, opening schools, orphanages, hospitals, clinics, and novitiates for the Missionary Sisters of the Sacred Heart.

Science and Technology Enrico Fermi (1901–1954), a refugee from Benito Mussolini's Fascist regime, is regarded as the "father of atomic energy." Fermi was awarded the 1938 Nobel Prize in physics for his identification of new radioactive elements produced by neutron bombardment. He worked on the Manhattan Project during World War II to produce the first atomic bomb, achieving the world's first self-sustaining chain reaction on December 2, 1942.

Salvador Luria (1912–1991) was a pioneer of molecular biology and genetic engineering. In 1969, while he was a faculty member at the Massachusetts Institute of Technology, Luria was awarded the Nobel Prize for his work on viruses. Rita Levi-Montalcini (1909–2012) was awarded a Nobel Prize in 1986 for her work in cell biology and cancer research. Emilio Segre (1905–1989), a student of Fermi, received the 1959 Nobel Prize in physics for his discovery of the antiproton. Robert Gallo (1937–), a biomedical researcher best known for his discovery of the human immunodeficiency virus (HIV) and the role it plays in causing AIDS, subsequently developed a blood test for HIV.

Sports Joseph "Joe" DiMaggio (1914–1999), the "Yankee Clipper," is perhaps best-known for his fifty-six-game hitting streak in 1941. (The record still stands.) In a career spanning 1936 to 1951, DiMaggio led the New York Yankees to ten world championships and retired with a .325 lifetime batting average. He was voted the greatest living player in baseball in 1969.

At the time of his death, Vincent Lombardi (1913–1970) was the winningest coach in professional

Italian immigrants arrive at Ellis Island, c. 1920. AKG-IMAGES / NEWSCOM

football and the personification of tenacity and commitment in American sports. As head coach of the Green Bay Packers, Lombardi led the team to numerous conference, league, and world titles during the 1960s, including two Super Bowls (1967 and 1968). Rocky Marciano (born Rocco Thomas Francis Marchegiano, 1924–1969) is boxing's only undefeated heavyweight champion. Known as the "Brockton Bomber," Marciano won the heavyweight championship over Jersey Joe Walcott in 1952 and held it until he retired in 1956. Rocky Graziano (born Rocco Barbella, 1922–1990), middleweight boxing champion, is best known for his classic bouts with Tony Zale. Lawrence "Yogi" Berra (1925–), a Baseball Hall of Famer who played for the New York Yankees for seventeen years, also coached and managed several professional baseball teams, including the New York Mets and the Houston Astros.

MEDIA

RADIO

ICN Radio

Broadcast news, music, cultural programs and sports in Italian twenty-four hours a day, seven days a week. For twenty-three years, ICN has provided Italian radio in a four-state area: New York, New Jersey, Connecticut, and Pennsylvania. The station is also streaming on the web at ICNRadio.com.

Maria Pirraglia Suriano
475 Walnut Street
Norwood, New Jersey 07648
Phone: (201) 358-0700
Email: icnradio@yahoo.com

PRINT

Since the mid-1800s, more than two thousand Italian American newspapers have been established, representing a full range of ideological, religious, professional, and commercial interests. By 1980, about fifty newspapers were still in print. As of 2012, only one Italian-language Italian American daily paper was in print, but several print magazines and online publications were written by and for Italian Americans either in English or in both languages.

Ambassador Magazine

Established in 1985, *Ambassador* is published three times a year by the National Italian American Foundation (NIAF), an organization representing thousands of Italian Americans in business, government, entertainment, and education.

Don Oldenburg
Phone: (202) 939-3108
Email: don@niaf.org
URL: www.niaf.org/publications/ambassador/ambassador_magazine.asp

America Oggi (*America Today*)

Currently the only Italian-language daily newspaper in the United States, it was founded in 1989 by numerous journalists from *Il Progresso Italo-Americano*, an Italian-language daily newspaper in circulation from 1888 to 1988. As of 2013, it is available online.

Andrea Mantineo, Editor
Anna Letizia Soria, Web Manager
475 Walnut Street
Norwood, New Jersey 07648
Phone: (212) 268-0250
Fax: (212) 268-0379
Email: americoggi@aol.com
URL: www.americaoggi.info

Italian America Magazine

Full-color quarterly magazine published in English by the Order of the Sons of Italy.

Dona De Sanctis, Editor
219 E Street NE
Washington, D.C. 20002
Phone: (202) 546-8168
Email: ddesanctis@osia.org
URL: www.osia.org/ia-magazine/about-ia.php

Italian Americana: Cultural and Historical Review

An international journal published by the University of Rhode Island's College of Continuing Education.

Carol Bonomo Albright, Editor
80 Washington Street
Providence, Rhode Island 02908
Phone: (401) 277-5306
Fax: (401) 277-5100
Email: it.americana@yahoo.com

The Italian Tribune

Heavily illustrated journal published weekly and featuring articles by Italian American contributors.

Joan Alagna, Editor
7 North Willow Street
Suite 8C
Montclair, New Jersey 07042

Phone: (973) 860-0101
Fax: (201) 485-8967
Email: mail@ItalianTribune.com
URL: www.italiantribune.com

The Italian Voice (*La Voce Italiana*)

Provides regional, national, and local news coverage; published weekly in English.

Cesarina A. Earl, Editor
P.O. Box 9
Totowa, New Jersey 07511
Phone: (973) 942-5028

PRIMO

PRIMO magazine is a publication for and about Italian Americans featuring in-depth articles on Italian American history, heritage, neighborhoods, accomplishments, and current events. Published every ten weeks, every issue of *PRIMO* features articles on travel, food, and wine and reports on one or more of Italy's diverse regions.

2125 Observatory Place NW
Washington, D.C. 20007
Phone: (202) 363-3742
Email: editor@flprimo.com
URL: www.onlineprimo.com

Sons of Italy Times

Publishes news biweekly concerning the activities of Sons of Italy lodges and the civic, professional, and charitable interests of the membership.

John B. Acchione, III, Editor
170 South Independence Mall West
Suite 718E
Philadelphia, Pennsylvania 19106-3323
Phone: (215) 592-1713
Fax: (215) 592-9152
Email: info@sonsofitalypa.org

ORGANIZATIONS AND ASSOCIATIONS

American Italian Historical Association

Founded in 1966 by a group of academics as a professional organization interested in promoting basic research into the Italian American experience. The association encourages the collection and preservation of primary source materials and supports the teaching of Italian American history.

George Guida, President
209 Flagg Place
Staten Island, New York 11304
Email: gguida@citytech.cuny.edu

Italian American Studies (formerly Italian Cultural Exchange in the United States [ICE])

Promotes knowledge and appreciation of Italian culture among Americans.

Jim Grossman, Executive Director
27 Barrow Street
New York, New York 10014
Phone: (212) 255-0528

Italian Historical Society of America

Perpetuates Italian heritage in America and gathers historical data on Americans of Italian descent.

Dr. John J. LaCorte, Director
410 Park Avenue
Suite 1530
New York, New York 10022
Email: mail@italianhistorical.org
URL: www.italianhistorical.org

The National Italian American Foundation (NIAF)

A nonprofit organization designed to promote the history, heritage, and accomplishments of Italian Americans and to foster programs advancing the interests of the Italian American community.

John Viola, Chief Operating Officer
1860 19th Street NW
Washington, D.C. 20009
Phone: (202) 387-0600
Email: info@niaf.org
URL: www.niaf.org

Order Sons of Italy in America (OSIA)

Established in 1905, the organization is composed of lodges located throughout the United States. It seeks to preserve and disseminate information on Italian culture and encourages the involvement of its members in all civic, charitable, patriotic, and youth activities. OSIA is committed to supporting Italian American cultural events and fighting discrimination.

Philip R. Piccigallo, Executive Director
219 E Street, NE
Washington, D.C. 20002
Phone: (202) 547-2900
Fax: (202) 546-8168
URL: www.osia.org

MUSEUMS AND RESEARCH CENTERS

American Italian Renaissance Foundation

Focuses on the contributions of Italian Americans in Louisiana. Its research library also includes the wide-ranging Giovanni Schiavo collection.

Joseph Maselli, Director
537 South Peters Street
New Orleans, Louisiana 70130
Phone: (504) 522-7294
URL: www.airf.org

The Balch Institute for Ethnic Studies

Contains many documents addressing the Italian American experience in Pennsylvania and elsewhere, most notably the Leonard Covello collection. A published guide to the holdings is available.

Kim Sajet, President and CEO
1300 Locust Street
Philadelphia, Pennsylvania 19107
Phone: (215) 732-6200
Email: balchlib@hslc.org
URL: http://libertynet.org/~balch

The Center for Migration Studies

Houses a vast collection of materials depicting Italian American activities. It features extensive records of Italian American Catholic parishes staffed by the Scalabrini order. The center also provides published guides to its collections.

Donald M. Kerwin, Jr., Director
27 Carmine Street
New York, New York 10014
Phone: (212) 337-3080
Email: cms@cmsny.org
URL: www.cmsny.org

Immigration History Research Center (IHRC), University of Minnesota

IHRC is the nation's most important repository for research materials dealing with the Italian American experience. The center holds major documentary collections representing a wide cross section of Italian American life, numerous newspapers, and many published works. A published guide is available.

Ericka Lee, Director
Elmer L. Anderson Library
222-21st Avenue South
Suite 311
Minneapolis, Minnesota 55455
Email: ihrc@umn.edu.
URL: www.umn.edu/ihrc

The New York Public Library, Manuscripts Division

Holds many collections relevant to the Italian American experience, most notably the papers of Fiorello LaGuardia, Vito Marcantonio, Gino C. Speranza, and Carlo Tresca.

42nd Street and Fifth Avenue
New York, New York 10018-2788
Phone: (212) 930-0801
URL: www.nypl.org/locations/schwarzman/manuscripts-division

SOURCES FOR ADDITIONAL STUDY

Alba, Richard. *Italian Americans: Into the Twilight of Ethnicity*. Englewood Cliffs: Prentice-Hall, 1985.

Battistella, Graziano. *Italian Americans in the '80s: A Sociodemographic Profile*. New York: Center for Migration Studies, 1989.

Gabaccia, Donna. "Italian American Women: A Review Essay," *Italian Americana* 12, no. 1 (1993): 38–61.

Gambino, Richard. *Blood of My Blood*. New York: Anchor, 1975.

Gesualdi, Louis J. *The Italian/American Experience: A Collection of Writings*. Lanham, MD: University Press of America, 2012.

Mangione, Jerre, and Ben Moreiale. *La Storia: Five Centuries of the Italian American Experience*. New York: HarperCollins, 1992.

Morreale, Ben, Robert Carola, and Leslie Caron Carola, eds. *Italian Americans: The Immigrant Experience*. Baltimore/Washington: Metro Books, 2008.

Orsi, Robert A. *The Madonna of 115th Street: Faith and Community in Italian Harlem, 1880–1950*. New Haven: Yale University Press, 1988.

Pozzetta, George E. "From Immigrants to Ethnics: The State of Italian-American Historiography." *Journal of American Ethnic History* 9, no. 1 (1989): 67–95.

Stille, Alexander. *The Sack of Rome: How a Beautiful European Country with a Fabled History and a Storied Culture Was Taken Over by a Man Named Silvio Berlusconi*. New York: Penguin, 2006.

JAMAICAN AMERICANS

N. Samuel Murell

OVERVIEW

Jamaican Americans are immigrants or descendants of people from Jamaica, an island country in the Caribbean Sea. One of the four large islands of the Greater Antilles, Jamaica measures 4,441 square miles and is slightly smaller than the state of Connecticut. It is located roughly 600 miles southeast of Florida, just south of Cuba and west of Haiti and Puerto Rico. Kingston, Jamaica's capital and the largest English-speaking city south of Miami, is Jamaica's chief commercial and administrative center. Jamaica's ample coastline, particularly its northern shores, are lined with many miles of white-sand beaches that attract thousands of tourists annually. The eastern third of the island is made up of mountainous terrain, including the Blue Mountains, famous for the high-quality coffee cultivated on their slopes.

Jamaica's motto, "Out of Many, One People," is a national ideal for its diverse population, recorded in 2011 at approximately 2.7 million. The 2001 Jamaican census reported that 91.2 percent of Jamaicans were black, 6.2 percent were of mixed ethnicity, and 2.6 percent were of unknown ethnicity. Centuries of intermarriage among races accounts for the diverse physical features found in the Jamaican population. In addition to English, many Jamaicans speak Jamaican Patois (pronounced "patwa")—also referred to as Jamaican Creole—a mixture of English and African dialects. According to the *CIA World Factbook*, approximately 80 percent of Jamaican citizens have some form of association with Christianity. Protestants have traditionally outnumbered Catholics by a wide margin, and Rastafari, a twentieth-century religious movement, claims a following of approximately 8 percent of the population. Agriculture, manufacturing, and tourism are the main industries in the country. Many Jamaicans live below the poverty level, and the country has a 14 percent unemployment rate.

Jamaicans first began arriving in North America in significant numbers in the early seventeenth century, when many were forced into slavery and transported by ship to the settlement of Jamestown, Virginia. This forced emigration continued over the next two centuries in direct relation to the Caribbean slave trade. Although Britain abolished slavery in 1834, the slave trade in the United States remained active until 1865.

The first major wave of voluntary Jamaican immigration to the United States began in the early 1900s, and by 1930 roughly 100,000 black immigrants in the United States reported being of British Caribbean descent. In the late 1960s, European immigration laws became more rigid just as similar restrictions in the United States were being relaxed, making it easier for waves of Jamaican immigrants to enter the United States over the following decades.

The U.S. Census Bureau's American Community Survey (ACS) estimated in 2011 that there were 986,897 people of Jamaican descent living in the United States, with the largest populations residing in New York and Florida. Approximately 49 percent of Jamaican Americans live in the Northeast, 43 percent in the South, 5 percent in the West, and 4 percent in the Midwest. The states with the highest numbers of Jamaican Americans include Georgia, New Jersey, Connecticut, Maryland, Pennsylvania, California, and Massachusetts. Many Jamaicans immigrated to the United States in the mid-to-late twentieth century seeking employment opportunities and improved economic conditions. While some Jamaican Americans have found success in the realms of literature, music, education, public service, politics, and sports, a large number of Jamaican immigrants reside in lower-middle-class neighborhoods and work blue-collar jobs in urban centers along the East Coast.

HISTORY OF THE PEOPLE

Early History As early as 600 CE, Jamaica was settled by a native tribe called the Arawaks, who called the island Xaymaca. In 1494 Christopher Columbus claimed the island for Spain and forced the native population into servitude. In 1509 Juan de Esquivel began transporting Jamaican Arawaks to the nearby island of Hispaniola to serve as slaves. Within a few decades, Jamaica's native population had been wiped out by disease, kidnapping, enslavement, and genocidal methods of war. Africans, who had been brought to the island by the slave trade, soon constituted Jamaica's majority population. From 1509 until the early 1660s, Jamaica was sparsely populated and used mainly as a Spanish-held way station for galleons en route to Cuba and the Spanish mainland. During this time, Jamaica also became a headquarters for pirate ships, who sought to control the island in order to control the valuable waters surrounding it. After a failed expedition to the larger Spanish Caribbean, the British successfully captured Jamaica in 1655. The island continued to be run by pirates until 1670, when Spain officially ceded Jamaica to Britain with the Treaty of Madrid. As Britain sought to take control, a number of black slaves living on the island fled into its interior mountain ranges. Known as the Maroons, this group waged what is considered Jamaica's only successful black resistance movement. For centuries, the Maroons menaced British troops, looted plantations, and recruited other slaves, carrying them off to the mountains in retaliation against British abuses. The Maroons' successful guerrilla warfare abated after their chiefs signed successive peace treaties with the British government in 1739 and 1795.

Britain eventually turned the island of Jamaica into a vast sugar plantation based on slave labor. The one-crop sugar economy in Barbados, another British colony, was in sharp decline by 1650, causing many planters from that island to relocate to Jamaica with their slaves. They were followed by hundreds of British colonials and hundreds of thousands of enslaved Africans. By 1730 Jamaica's 75,000 slaves were producing 15,500 tons of sugar per year, and the island replaced Barbados as Britain's most prized colony. In 1808 the slave population exceeded 324,000 and produced 78,000 tons of sugar. At one point, English rulers attempted to balance the white-to-black population ratio by shipping criminals, prisoners of war, prostitutes, and other undesirable persons from Britain to Jamaica as a form of punishment. Nevertheless, when the British Parliament passed the Slave Trade Act in 1807—which abolished the slave trade but not slavery itself—blacks outnumbered whites in Jamaica by as many as ten to one.

Although under British law, no new African slaves could be transported to Jamaica after January 1, 1808, the new rules regarding slavery were relatively lax, and slaves could still be legally moved between the Caribbean islands. The antislavery campaign in Britain continued to intensify, and in 1831 a black Baptist preacher named Sam Sharpe alleged that their "free paper" had come to the island but that the government was concealing it from slaves. Sharpe led a large revolt in western Jamaica, known as the Baptist War, which resulted in massive destruction of property and a bloody and brutal clampdown by the government. This violent slave resistance, along with the unprofitability of slavery and mounting pressure from abolitionists, forced Britain to abolish the institution altogether in 1834. For the next several years, blacks in Jamaica continued to fight bitter and often futile battles to free themselves from the savage institution of slavery, many becoming apprentices for their former masters until unrestricted freedom was granted on August 1, 1838.

Modern Era Blacks in the post-emancipation Jamaica of the mid-to-late nineteenth century lived in freedom but had no rights or access to property. They were exploited by the white ruling class and treated with contempt by British governors, whose fiscal policies were designed to benefit only whites. In the wake of the American Civil War, which ended in 1865, the unheeded plea of the peasant masses for farmland erupted into a second major revolt in Jamaica. The Morant Bay Rebellion of 1865, led by Baptist deacon Paul Bogle and supported by politician George William Gordon, would prove to be a major crossroads in the nation's history. The ruling class suppressed the rebellion with ruthless force, with almost 400 suspects, including dozens of innocent Baptist peasants, executed on order of the island's governor, Edward Eyre. In the aftermath of the rebellion, the British government ordered an inquiry, which found Eyre's actions to be "excessive, barbarous, reckless, and criminal." As a result, the Jamaican assembly renounced its powers, and the island nation was converted to a crown colony with a local representative body. While this new political system limited the powers of the governor and the assembly, it also allowed the white colonial representatives in charge to dominate and exploit the black masses.

As late as the 1930s, the British-ruled political system continued to be closed to most native Jamaicans. In the post-World War I period, blacks voiced their discontent by supporting trade unions and other organizations led by political activists, such as the Pan-Africanism of Marcus Garvey and the Workers and Tradesmen's Union of A. G. S. Coombs and Alexander Bustamante. Frustration and anger over the country's persistent political inequity and economic hardship came to a head in 1938, when members of the working class staged a national strike against the West Indies Sugar Company (WISCO), which had failed to live up to its promises of new jobs, higher wages, and better working conditions in its massive, centralized new factory in the parish of Westmoreland. Bustamante, William Grant, and Norman Manley played key roles in this organized political agitation, which resulted in better workers' compensation. The strike also put new political leaders in the spotlight and renewed interest in political change. The People's National Party (PNP) and the Jamaica Labour Party (JLP) were born in the throes of these upheavals. In 1944 Jamaica was granted limited self-government and universal adult suffrage, and in 1962 the country finally achieved its independence from Britain, with Bustamante, a member of the JLP, serving as its first prime minister.

Jamaica today is a constitutional monarchy and a member of the British Commonwealth under the rule of the Queen of England as represented by a prime minister elected by the people and a Jamaican governor general. The first ten years of Jamaican independence included a great deal of political unrest and social upheaval. Although the government was

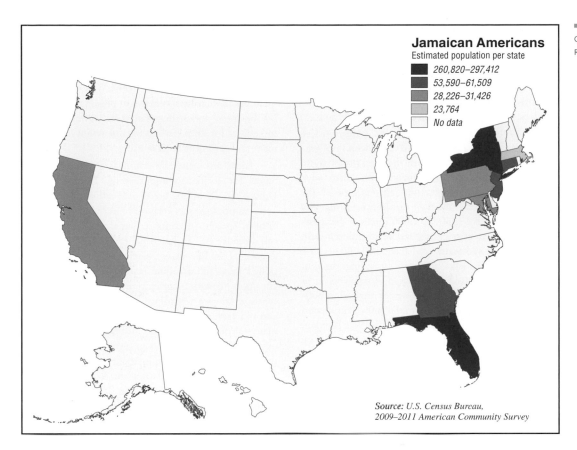

Jamaican Americans
Estimated population per state

- 260,820–297,412
- 53,590–61,509
- 28,226–31,426
- 23,764
- No data

Source: U.S. Census Bureau, 2009–2011 American Community Survey

a parliamentary democracy, political competition in the late 1960s and early 1970s slowly erupted into a more tense political battle in which violence became increasingly more common during national elections. Both the PNP and the JLP began employing the use of armed gangs. Michael Manley of the PNP was elected prime minister in 1972. Manley, who adopted a left of center position at a time when larger Cold War geopolitics pervaded the world, instituted a variety of educational, political, and social reforms in an attempt to bring together the country's upper and working classes. However, many upper-class Jamaicans, English landowners, and foreign investors opposed Manley's socialist views, and Edward Seaga of the JLP, whose allegiances during the Cold War were more aligned with the United States, was elected to office in 1980. Seaga attempted to balance power between the executive branch and parliament and promoted relations with the United States. In 1989 Manley was reelected to office, with the PNP retaining control of the executive branch until 2007, when the JLP returned for a short term under Bruce Golding. The two-party Jamaican political system is now much more stabilized, and the violent political unrest of the first quarter-century of the country's independence has largely dissipated. As of 2012, the prime minister of Jamaica was Portia Simpson-Miller, with Patrick Allen serving as governor general.

SETTLEMENT IN THE UNITED STATES

The documented history of black immigration from Jamaica and other Caribbean islands to the United States dates back to 1619, when twenty voluntary indentured workers from Jamaica arrived in Jamestown, Virginia, on a Dutch frigate. They lived and worked as "free persons," even after a Portuguese vessel arrived in 1629 with the first shipload of black slaves. Because Jamaica was a major way station and clearing house for slaves en route to North America, the history of Jamaican immigration to the United States is closely tied to slavery and post-emancipation migration. Much of Jamaica's current population consists of the descendants of freed African slaves who continued to make the island their home even after Britain's abolition of slavery in 1834.

The abolition of slavery in Jamaica predates the emancipation of slaves in the United States by more than thirty years. After 1838, when Jamaica's slaves were officially freed, European and American colonies with expanding sugar industries in the Caribbean imported large numbers of immigrants to meet their labor shortages. After slavery was abolished in the United States in 1865, American planters imported temporary workers, called "swallow migrants," to harvest crops on a seasonal basis. These workers, many of them Jamaicans, returned to their native countries after each season's harvest. Work began on the Panama

Canal in 1881, and between the start of the project and the beginning of World War I, the United States recruited more than 250,000 Caribbean workers, approximately 90,000 of them Jamaican, to work on the canal. During World Wars I and II, the United States recruited Jamaican men for service on U.S. military bases that were established on the island.

Since the start of the twentieth century, there have been three distinct waves of Caribbean immigration to the United States, with the majority of those immigrants coming from Jamaica. The first wave began around 1900 and extended through the 1920s, bringing a modest number of Caribbean immigrants to the country. By 1930, 178,000 documented first-generation black immigrants and their children were living in the United States, and about 100,000 of those were from the British Caribbean, including Jamaica. The second and weakest immigration wave began in the late 1930s and lasted until new immigration policies were implemented in the mid-1960s. This second influx was attributable in part to World War II, when many Jamaicans were drawn to the United States by the shortage of able-bodied migrant laborers resulting from the draft. In 1952 U.S. Congress passed the McCarran-Walter Act, which discriminated against black immigrants by establishing a quota system in which certain ethnic groups were deemed more "desirable" than others. The statute allowed only 100 Jamaicans into the country annually, and following its enactment, many Jamaicans began migrating to Britain rather than to the United States.

The final and largest wave of Jamaican immigration to the United States began in 1965 and has continued into the twenty-first century. As Britain began restricting the number of immigrants it accepted from its former Caribbean colonies, the 1965 Hart-Celler Act abolished the national origins quota system, thus changing US immigration policy and opening the way for a surge in Jamaican immigration. In 1976 Jamaicans began relocating to the United States in even larger numbers after new immigration legislation began allowing a maximum of 20,000 persons per country in the Western Hemisphere to enter the country annually. According to the U.S. Census Bureau, the number of Jamaican Americans living in the United States has increased significantly over the last half century, growing from 24,759 in 1960 to 951,000 in 2009. The American Community Survey in 2011 placed the total number of documented Jamaican Americans at just under one million, but this number does not account for Jamaican immigrants who are living in the country illegally.

The number of Jamaicans immigrating to the United States became so large that it caused a national crisis in Jamaica in the late twentieth century. While many of Jamaica's early emigrants were migrant workers, indentured servants, and even slaves, recent immigration waves have seen an exodus of skilled professionals, technicians, doctors, and lawyers. Consequently, Jamaica has a shortage of workers needed to provide the country's essential services, such as postal supervisors, health-care professionals, teachers, and other public servants. During the 1970s and early 1980s, about 15 percent of Jamaica's population left the country. In the early 1990s, Jamaica's government began offering incentives to persons with technical, business, and managerial skills willing to return to Jamaica for short periods of time to aid in management and technical skills training.

Jamaicans generally immigrate to the United States for socioeconomic reasons. In general, the United States offers better education, more work opportunities, greater religious choice, and more freedom of speech. In contrast, Jamaica in the past several decades has experienced economic hardship, a dwindling middle class, scarcity of professional and skilled jobs, and a failing economy still largely reliant upon plantation agriculture. Since the nineteenth century, Jamaica's distribution of arable crown lands and old plantations has been largely uneven, leaving many farmers without plots sufficient for subsistence or cash-crop farming. This in turn has contributed to the country's high unemployment statistics and poverty rates. Economic inflation and low salaries in the 1970s lowered the country's standard of living even further. When companies and corporations lost confidence in the democratic socialist government and anti-American rhetoric of Michael Manley's first term as president, the flight of capital from Jamaica and the shift in US capital investments worsened the situation. Jamaica's huge foreign debt and the International Monetary Fund's (IMF) restructuring of the economy further exacerbated the island's economic woes in the 1980s and 1990s. An increase in crime, fueled by unemployment and aggravated by the deportation of criminals from the United States back to Jamaica, forced thousands of Jamaicans to flee the island in search of safety. In recent years, unemployment and underemployment in Jamaica have risen above 50 percent, wages have continued to fall, the dollar has weakened, and the cost of goods and services has continued to increase.

The Jamaican mentality that one must "go ah foreign" and then "return to him country" to "show off" evidence of success has become a rite of passage for many Jamaicans. This attitude began to develop in the nineteenth and early twentieth centuries, when settlers in the United States began importing Jamaicans willing to work on various projects. Before long, Jamaicans began to see emigration as an attractive solution to the harsh social and economic conditions on the island. Besides seeking better work opportunities, some Jamaicans have left their home country to escape religious persecution. Many members of the Rastafari movement, for example, have sought a fresh start in the United States, although a central theme of the Rastafari ideology is the concept of repatriation to Africa for the descendants of those forced out of the continent by the Atlantic slave trade. Education is also a common reason for Jamaican immigration to the United States, with many Jamaican students and trainees studying at U.S. institutions and some choosing not to return to Jamaica upon completion of their studies.

The northeastern and southern regions of the United States are home to the largest concentrations of Jamaican immigrants, many of them undocumented. Jamaican Americans have largely settled along the eastern coast of the United States due to the region's accessibility, abundance of job opportunities, access to colleges and universities, and existing family and community connections. Despite the heavy concentration of Jamaican Americans in certain regions, the 2010 U.S. Census shows that Jamaicans now live in every state in the country, a strong validation of the popular Jamaican saying, "Anywhere you go in the world, you meet a Jamaican." Florida, New York, Georgia, New Jersey, and Connecticut are the states with the highest population of Jamaican Americans. Other states with smaller, but significant, numbers of people of Jamaican descent are Maryland, Pennsylvania, California, and Massachusetts.

LANGUAGE

English is Jamaica's official language and is spoken in variations that range from British English to Jamaican Patois, a mixture of English and African dialects that is widely considered its own distinct language. Most middle-class and upper-class Jamaicans adapt their speech to the social context of the moment. In general, they speak British English in formal discourse or political discussions and shift to Jamaican Patois in informal conversation and gossip. A large number of rural and blue-collar Jamaicans, however, speak Jamaican Patois all the time, as they experience great difficulty in switching to standard English. Thousands of Jamaicans in the United States also speak mainly Jamaican Patois, in many ways to keep their conversations private. In recent years, some Rastafaris (followers of the Rastafari movement) have developed their own non-Western vocabulary and Afro-Jamaican way of speaking, which has crossed over into the pop-culture lexicon in the United States due to the popularity of Jamaican reggae music.

Greetings and Popular Expressions The following are common colloquial Jamaican greetings: "Cool man"; "Wah the man ah seh?"; "How di dahta doin'?"; "Me soon come man" (See you soon); "Likle more" (See you later); "How you doin' man?"; "Wah 'appen man?"; "Mawning Sah!"; and "How yu deh do?" Some similar Rastafari greetings are: "Hail the man"; "I an I"; "Selassi I"; "Jah, Ras Tafari"; and "Hey me bredren" (Hello, brother).

RELIGION

The majority of Jamaica's population is Christian, with small Hindu, Muslim, Jewish, and Bahá'í communities. The older and more established Christian denominations are the Baptists, Methodists, Anglicans, Roman Catholics, Moravians, Presbyterians, and Congregationalists. Jamaica's most vibrant religious experiences come from the less formal Protestant religious denominations, including the Pentecostals, Church of God, Associated Gospel Assembly, Open Bible Standard Churches, Seventh Day Adventists, Jehovah's Witnesses, the Missionary Church, and a number of independent churches referred to as "evangelical."

A number of Afro-Caribbean revivalist religious groups also exist in Jamaica. Among these are Myalism, Bedwardism, Pocomania, Kumina, Nativism (or the Native Baptist Church), and Rastafari. Myalism, one of the oldest religions from Africa, involves the practice of magic and spirit possession. It is community-centered and refuses to accept negatives in life, such as sickness, failure, and oppression. Kumina, which began around 1730 and is related to Myalism, involves membership in Kumina "bands" that are inherited at birth, rather than by conversion or voluntary membership. The Native Baptist Church began as an indigenous church among black slaves who were taken from North America to Jamaica when their employers migrated to the island as Baptist loyalists. One of the distinguishing characteristics of the Native Baptist Church is immersion baptism, in which the convert is fully submerged in water during the baptismal rites.

Most first-generation Jamaican Americans cherish traditional family values, placing a strong emphasis on religion, the care of elders, the sanctity of marital vows, and the punishment of disobedient children.

Rastafari, Jamaica's most recognized Afro-Caribbean religion, was founded in 1930 by wandering Jamaican preachers who were inspired by the teachings of political activist Marcus Garvey. Followers of the Rastafari movement are monotheistic, worshipping a god they call Jah. Rastafaris established their beliefs based on messianic interpretations of Christian scripture and the idea that Haile Selassie, emperor of Ethiopia from 1930 until 1974, is divine. Distinguishing features of Rastafaris are unshorn hair woven into dreadlocks, adherence to a strict vegetarian diet called Ital, the smoking of marijuana for sacramental purposes, and the wearing of brightly colored, loose-fitting clothing. The Rastafari movement has made its presence felt worldwide, branching out across all lines of ethnicity. There are millions of Rastafari followers in the United States, with the country's largest Rasta community located in Brooklyn, New York.

Baptisms Jamaicans practice two types of baptism: infant baptism and adult baptism (also called confirmation). Among Catholics, Anglicans, Lutherans, Presbyterians, Disciples of Christ, and Methodists, a priest or minister baptizes an infant by sprinkling water on its head. When the child reaches the age of accountability (generally in the midteens), a confirmation ceremony is performed. In other Protestant and Afro-Caribbean Christian traditions, a person is blessed at dedication (or birth) but is baptized only after voluntarily confessing his or her faith in Christ. In this baptism by immersion, a minister of religion or elder of the faith submerges the "initiate" in water, typically in a river, sea, or baptismal font located near the sanctuary. Because these practices are similar to the standard baptismal rites of many Christian religions in the United States, most churchgoing Jamaican Americans continue to follow them.

CULTURE AND ASSIMILATION

Jamaican immigrants generally fall into the following two categories: those who come to the United States to stay, and those who plan to earn money in the United States and then return to their native land. Jamaicans who plan to make the country their home tend to live in predominately Jamaican neighborhoods in metropolitan areas on the Eastern Seaboard, immersing themselves in the community and forging their identities around it. Some Jamaican Americans, however, choose to settle in the country's predominately white, upper-middle-class suburbs, securing professional careers and assimilating into mainstream American culture. As for those Jamaicans planning a brief stay in the United States as "birds of passage," many reside in predominately Jamaican neighborhoods in major metropolitan areas and work in blue-collar jobs for several years before returning home. These Jamaicans are typically motivated by the need to provide for their families. Remittances from the United States are a major part of the Jamaican economy, and family members who are able to travel to and live in the United States, even if temporarily, are encouraged to do so in order to support family members back home. Other temporary immigrants come to the United States to obtain an education or job training before returning to pursue their careers in Jamaica. Most early Jamaican immigrants intended to return to their native country. Since the 1970s, however, more Jamaicans have sought permanent residence in the United States, likely due to declining social and economic conditions back home.

In addition to acclimating to severe weather variations, especially in northern states, Jamaican immigrants must make many other adjustments to adapt to American society. Life in the United States is far more fast-paced than island living, and making lifestyle adjustments can prove trying for newcomers. Jamaicans who become naturalized American citizens often struggle with how to best split their national allegiances between Jamaica and the United States. As with other immigrant groups, Jamaican Americans who are resident aliens enjoy the same privileges as

American citizens and thus enjoy more security and stability than undocumented immigrants, who exist in a state of vulnerability.

The first and second waves of Jamaican immigrants, most of them black, were subject to the same social prejudices and institutional racism that African Americans faced in the early and mid-twentieth century. Although more recent Jamaican immigrants are unlikely to encounter such blatant forms of racism, they may nevertheless be subject to the effects of subtle discrimination and stereotypes based on skin color and ethnicity. Jamaican immigrants often become much more conscious of their "blackness" when they arrive in the United States. Although Jamaica is not immune to color distinctions, blacks are a majority in the country, and many are highly respected leaders.

Many Jamaican Americans, particularly those who settle in large urban areas, must also learn to adjust to life in some of the toughest neighborhoods in the United States. To make those adjustments, many immigrants become streetwise early on, learning the safe areas in which to walk, work, and live. Unfortunately, a number of Jamaican youths have become active in the gang and drug culture of New York City, Miami, Los Angeles, Boston, and Washington, D.C., and some have even been named in organized-crime raids by the Federal Bureau of Investigation (FBI) and other law-enforcement bodies. Many Jamaicans in the United States find themselves unfairly associated with marijuana due to its role in the Rastafari movement and its prominence in reggae music, both of which have gained mainstream popularity over the past quarter century.

Working-class Jamaican Americans have certain characteristics that set them apart from other immigrant groups. They tend to dress differently (especially the Rastafaris), speak with a different accent, and favor certain types of foods. In some parts of New York City and Miami, working-class Jamaican Americans often live as a self-contained group with distinct social and economic habits. They use special verbal expressions and linguistic codes to communicate, mostly in Jamaican Patois. They are likely to be hardworking, confident, and proud of their Jamaican heritage and the positive international reputation their home country receives from its associations with reggae and sports. Reggae, along with Rastafari, has had an influence on many Americans, with many adopting aspects of Jamaican culture, including dress, mannerisms, and speech patterns. Although often described as assertive and not easily dominated, Jamaican immigrants generally establish good relations with other groups in their communities. Jamaicans own or operate many of the successful Caribbean businesses in the communities where they live. They are able to maintain strong and friendly social, religious, economic, and political ties with both black and white American institutions and communities simultaneously. Many Caribbean nurses and nurse's aides are Jamaican, while a number of Jamaican American scholars and professionals have established strong careers and solid reputations at U.S. universities and other institutions of learning.

Nevertheless, Jamaican Americans and African Americans have a history of conflict, often a result of stereotypes and misconceptions. For example, some Jamaicans believe that their hard work ethic, ambitions to achieve, community-building efforts, and strong family values are superior to those of African Americans. Caribbean immigrants also have a tendency to believe that, because they refrain from using antiwhite rhetoric in social, political, and economic discussions, they have healthier relations with whites than African Americans do. Meanwhile, some African Americans see Jamaican Americans as interlopers who are making it more difficult for them to find jobs and live peacefully in their neighborhoods. The fact that Jamaican Americans have dual national allegiances and, as a result, often pursue different social and political agendas than African Americans, adds to the misunderstanding.

Evidence shows that, with time, many of the differences between African Americans and Jamaican Americans will become less distinct. Marriage patterns, for example, demonstrate that while first-generation Jamaican Americans tend to marry and have children with other members of their immigrant group, marriages between second- or third-generation Jamaican Americans and African Americans are not uncommon. Members of these later generations generally have regular contact with African Americans in schools and in their communities, resulting in similar life experiences. The combined efforts of Jamaican Americans and African Americans in dealing with racial prejudices and injustice in their neighborhoods have also helped improve relations between the two groups.

Traditions and Customs Although Jamaica's population is predominantly black, small enclaves of East Indians, Chinese, Lebanese, Europeans, Jews, and other ethnic groups enhance the rich cultural heritage of the country. The motto "Out of Many, One People" brings Jamaicans together to celebrate a wide variety of local, national, and international cultural events throughout the year.

Many aspects of Jamaican culture are celebrated by Jamaicans living in the United States, including traditional cuisine, folklore, and storytelling. Jamaican music is more popular than ever in the United States, particularly reggae. Through the music of Bob Marley, Jimmy Cliff, and Peter Tosh and films like *Countryman* (1982), *Cool Runnings* (1993), and *Wah Do Dem* (2009), the culture surrounding the Rastafari movement has become a major influence on American pop culture over the past quarter century.

Festivals The Caribbean Festival and Jamaican Independence Celebration, which commemorates Jamaica's independence from England, is held each year in U.S. cities that are home to large Jamaican populations, including Chicago, New York City, and Miami. Although Carnival takes place in Jamaica in April and May, many Jamaican Americans in New York celebrate the holiday on Labor Day, when crowds of Caribbean Americans and others gather in the borough of Brooklyn for a huge Carnival celebration featuring festive floats, elaborate costumes, and traditional dances and music. Other Caribbean Carnivals are held throughout the year in U.S. cities with strong Caribbean communities. Another notable festival held in Jamaica is the Accompong Maroon Festival, held in January, which also includes dancing, parades, floats, and general revelry.

Holidays Most Jamaicans and Jamaican Americans celebrate traditional Christian holidays, including Christmas, Good Friday, Ash Wednesday, and Easter. Additional holidays include Boxing Day and, unofficially, Bob Marley's birthday (February 6). During National Heroes Day, held each year on the third Monday in October, local communities come alive with music, folk dances, and colorful dress to commemorate seven national heroes in the country's history.

Independence Day, Jamaica's grandest holiday, is held on August 6 to celebrate Jamaica's independence from British rule. During the celebration, Jamaicans pay homage to those who fought for the country's independence and partake in entertainment, music, dance, and parades, often attired in traditional costumes. Jamaican Americans typically observe these holidays by staging activities in their local communities.

Music Many Jamaican festivals celebrate the country's rich musical tradition. Although the origins of reggae are disputed, one theory attributes its beginnings to 1960s recording artist Count Ossie, who merged native Jamaican, Afro-Caribbean, and Afro-American musical rhythms with rock music and other influences to create a distinctively black genre of music. At the core of reggae music, popularized most notably by Bob Marley, is a journey into black consciousness and African pride and a corresponding plea for liberation. Reggae began as a working-class medium of expression and social commentary and is the first distinctly Caribbean music to become global in scope. Each summer since 1993, Jamaica has staged a large music festival in Montego Bay called Reggae Sumfest, which has attracted top reggae stars like Stephen Marley, Mighty Diamonds, and Frankie Paul. Several reggae festivals are also held in the United States, such as Reggae on the River in Humboldt County, California.

Jamaica also has many other musical forms. Calypso and soca music, usually performed by Trinidadian artists, feature a festive mix of Afro-Caribbean rhythms with witty lyrics and finely tuned steel drums. Jamaican American musician and actor Harry Belafonte is credited with popularizing the calypso style of music in the United States. Other popular music genres in Jamaica include dub poetry

A Jamaican woman plays steel drums in her neighborhood Labor Day Parade in Brooklyn, 1978. PHOTOGRAPH BYTED SPIEGEL. CORBIS REPRODUCED BY PERMISSION.

The National Dance Theatre Company of Jamaica (NDTC) is a world-renowned dance troupe that celebrates the unique traditional dance and rich musical heritage of Jamaica and other Caribbean islands. Formed in 1962 by Rex Nettleford and Eddie Thomas, the NDTC has made numerous tours to the United States, the United Kingdom, Canada, and other countries.

Cuisine Food is a communal aspect of Jamaican culture, and an old adage on the island suggests that a person always cook as if they are expecting company, for you never know who might show up. The national dish in Jamaica is ackee and saltfish (a type of fruit served with salted cod). However, other dishes, such as curried goat and rice or fried fish and bammy (a flat, baked cassava bread), are just as popular. Patties (a flaky pastry containing various fillings and spices), turtle soup, and pepper pot may contain pork or beef, as well as greens like okra or callaloo (a leafy green similar to spinach). Pimenta (also known as allspice), ginger, and peppers are commonly used, and many Jamaican dishes are known to be quite spicy. Other Jamaican American foods include plantains, rice and peas, cow foot, goat head, jerk chicken, pork, oxtail soup, stew peas and rice, liver and green bananas, rundown (a stew of coconut milk), callaloo and dumplings, mannish water (a soup made from goat intestines), and hard dough bread and pastries.

Dessert is usually fruit or a dish containing fruit. One example is matrimony, a mixture of orange sections, star apples, or guavas in coconut cream with guava cheese melted over the top. Other desserts are cornmeal pudding, sweet potato pudding, plantain tarts, and totos (small coconut cakes). Jamaica Blue Mountain Coffee, various British teas, and carrot juice are popular nonalcoholic beverages, while rum, Red Stripe lager, Dragon Stout, and Guinness stout are popular alcoholic beverages.

Many Jamaican Americans have adapted their diets to fit mainstream American culinary options, although ingredients for traditional dishes can be found in certain pockets of the United States. Specific sections of Miami and New York City, such as Flatbush and Utica, are home to grocery stores filled with a variety of Caribbean foods, including sugar cane, jelly coconut, and yams. With these options available, many Jamaican Americans tend to cook traditional cuisine at home while eating the food of different cultures when dining out.

Traditional Dress Because Jamaica is a tropical island abundant in vibrant foliage, its traditional dress tends to incorporate bright infusions of color. The colors of the Jamaican flag are black, green, and gold, although many people mistake the Rastafari colors of red, green, and gold (derived from the Ethiopian flag) as Jamaica's national colors.

The traditional folk costume for Jamaican women is a bandanna skirt worn with a matching

(chanted verses), dancehall (music with rap rhythms, reggae beats, and rude or suggestive lyrics), and ska (music with an emotionally charged, celebrative beat). Like most Americans, Jamaican immigrants in the United States tend to listen to a great variety of music, including jazz, reggae, calypso, soca, ska, rap, classical music, gospel, and "high-church" choirs.

Dances and Songs More than thirty distinctive dances are performed in Jamaica, all of which have been identified as having African, European, or Creole roots. One of the most popular Jamaican Creole dances is John Canoe (also called Jonkunnu), which features numerous characters whose movements are designed to match their roles. Although it is considered a secular dance, John Canoe is performed mainly at Christmas time. Among Jamaican Americans, traditional dances and songs are generally associated with the aforementioned festivals held in neighborhoods with large Jamaican immigrant communities.

head scarf and a white blouse. The blouse is typically embroidered and features a ruffled neck and sleeves. Jamaican women sometimes wear a dress of the same material and styling, referred to as a quadrille dress. Traditional Jamaican clothing for men consists of trousers worn with a short-sleeved shirt of the same bandanna material. Jamaicans wear these costumes on Independence Day, on National Heroes Day, and during other national celebrations. In New York City, Miami, and other large U.S. cities, many Jamaican Americans wear traditional costumes while participating in Caribbean Carnival celebrations.

Recreational Activities Jamaica's primary sports are cricket and soccer. Cricket is more than a sport in Jamaica—it is a way to express patriotism and an occasion to celebrate individual heroism. Other popular sports among Jamaicans include horse racing, tennis, basketball, netball, track and field, and triathlon. The island is also home to a number of activities designed specifically for tourists, including golf, boating, scuba diving, fishing, and polo. Many Jamaican Americans excel at athletics, particularly in baseball, basketball, soccer, and track and field.

Health-care Issues and Practices There are no documented medical problems that are unique to Jamaicans. In the 1950s and 1960s, polio appeared in some communities in Jamaica but was controlled by medical treatment. Since the 1980s, drug abuse, alcoholism, heart disease, and AIDS have plagued Jamaicans. Additionally, crime and economic hardship have taken a heavy toll on the health and life expectancy of those living in the country.

In 1994 the government of Jamaica stated that most violent crimes committed in the country were drug related. Many of the Caribbean drug kingpins in New York City at that time had been trained in the slums of Kingston. Perry Henzell's 1972 movie *The Harder They Come*, starring reggae superstar Jimmy Cliff, vividly depicts this underworld lifestyle. The distribution and use of marijuana and crack cocaine often accompany Jamaican gang members who immigrate to the United States, thus perpetuating drug abuse problems among Jamaicans living abroad.

FAMILY AND COMMUNITY LIFE

Most first-generation Jamaican Americans cherish traditional family values, placing a strong emphasis on religion, the care of elders, the sanctity of marital vows, and the punishment of disobedient children. The emotional bond between parents and children is very strong, often stronger than the bond between spouses. Parents with legal status are often active in civic and political affairs and take an interest in their children's education by joining the parent-teacher association (PTA), attending school board meetings, and participating in programs designed to address racism, crime, and poor test scores.

THE ITAL DIET

Followers of the Rastafari movement, including Jamaican American Rastafaris, often adhere to a strict vegetarian regimen called the Ital diet. While Rastas can find vegetarian options at a variety of restaurants across the United States, they tend to prepare much of their food at home according to the rituals of their religion. The word *Ital* is derived from the English word *vital*, and the goal of the diet is to eat fresh, healthful, often uncooked fruits, vegetables, grains, and fish in order to increase one's "life energy." Many of the Rastafari dietary restrictions are based on biblical readings and the teachings of their religion. Traditional Rastafaris refrain from consuming alcohol or caffeine, although many Jamaican American adherents to the religion do drink coffee and spirits.

Unfortunately, the modern Jamaican American family is plagued by many problems. Immigration restrictions and financial limitations often make it difficult for an entire family to immigrate to the United States at the same time. This situation is particularly common for lower income families or for immigrants who plan on working in the United States for only a brief period of time before returning to Jamaica. One parent often leaves Jamaica months or even years before the other family members, thus making it difficult to keep family values intact. In modern times, Jamaican women are more likely than men to migrate to the United States first. In some cases, during long periods of separation, one spouse may sever ties with his or her Jamaican family and begin a new family in the United States.

Because parents typically migrate first, children are often made to live with relatives or friends until they are able to join their parents in the United States. These children are sometimes left unsupervised in Jamaica, making them vulnerable to being introduced to drugs and crime at a young age. Some teens and young adults drop out of school during this time, believing their impending emigration means they have no need to complete their studies. Once in the United States, many Jamaican children are left on their own for hours every day while their parent or parents work multiple jobs to make ends meet. The end result, as with many immigrant families, is a fair amount of dysfunction within the family unit. The situation described, although not applicable to all Jamaican Americans, is most acute among blue-collar Jamaican immigrants.

Courtship and Weddings In traditional Jamaican weddings, the bride's parents are responsible for supplying the bridal gown and the reception, while the groom and his parents provide the ring and the new home. In rural Jamaica, weddings are community events, as a public invitation to observe the ceremony

JAMAICAN PROVERBS

Before the 1960s, working-class Jamaicans used numerous Jamaican Patois sayings and verbal expressions. In recent years, Jamaicans have begun to use the language and its proverbial expressions more often. Animal characters are used quite frequently in Jamaican proverbs. Examples include the following:

- When Jon Crow wan go a lowered, im sey a cool breeze tek im.

- When tiger wan' nyam, him seh him favor puss.

- Cow seh siddung nuh mean ress.

- Every dawg have im day.

- Yu see yu neighbor beard on fire, yu tek water an wet yu own.

- When man can't dance, him say music no good.

- One time nuh fool, but two times fool, him a damn fool.

- Mi t'row mi corn but mi nuh call nuh fowl.

- One one cocoa full basket.

There are many anglicized African proverbs that are popular in Jamaica. For example:

- When the mouse laughs at the cat, there is a hole nearby.

- No matter how long the night, the day is sure to come.

- No one tests the depth of a river with both feet.

- He who is bitten by a snake fears a lizard.

- If you are greedy in conversation, you lose the wisdom of your friend.

- When a fowl is eating your neighbor's corn, drive it away or someday it will eat yours.

Often the purpose of these sayings is to give caution, to play with social and political conventions, to make uncomplimentary remarks, to crack smutty jokes, or to give a new twist to a conversation. These sayings are also used to teach morality, values, and modes of conduct.

is also considered an invitation to attend the reception. Wedding receptions in Jamaica include a great amount of food and a large supply of rum and other beverages. The wedding menu includes traditional Jamaican cuisine, usually starting off with mannish water. For the main course, guests are often given a choice between stewed chicken or beef, curry goat and white rice, or fried chicken with rice and peas or kidney beans. A light salad is typically served with the meal, along with sorrel (rum punch), and cake is served afterward. Among poorer people, port wine is used for toasting the couple. In the United States, substantial variations of these practices exist, with most Jamaican Americans choosing to follow Western traditions in their wedding ceremonies and celebrations.

EMPLOYMENT AND ECONOMIC CONDITIONS

Jamaican American employment is quite diverse. A large number of older Jamaican women work for low wages in U.S. cities, often as domestic workers or caregivers. However, many recent Jamaican immigrants have brought technical and professional skills with them to the United States, allowing them to secure higher-paying jobs. Before 1970, white-owned institutions and corporations were generally more likely to hire skilled and educated Jamaicans than to hire African Americans, giving some African Americans the impression that Jamaicans were favored in the job market.

Despite decades of progress, Caribbean American and African American blacks continue to suffer job discrimination in the United States. Undocumented immigrants from Jamaica and those who are in a transitional stage of residency are particularly vulnerable to injustice and exploitation. Unskilled immigrants often work for long hours at multiple part-time, low-paying jobs in order to make ends meet. In New York City during the 1970s, many Jamaican Americans benefitted from affirmative action policies that allowed them greater access to better housing and jobs in the areas of Flatbush, Crown Heights, Bedford Stuyvesant, and elsewhere. Some Jamaican Americans have used open enrollment at the City University of New York to improve their skills and obtain higher-paying jobs.

A significant number of Jamaican Americans have found success in entrepreneurial enterprises. Since the late 1970s, Jamaican businesses in New York City have proliferated. These businesses include grocery stores, beauty salons, restaurants, travel agencies, real estate brokerages, bakeries, bars, music and record shops, and disco and dance clubs. This trend has spread to other U.S. cities with large Jamaican populations, including Miami, Oakland, Chicago, and Washington, D.C.

While most Jamaican Americans lead highly productive lives and contribute to their new communities in a variety of ways, some choose to make a living in the United States through more nefarious means.

Due to the high level of poverty and unemployment in Jamaica, juxtaposed against the booming tourism industry and constant influx of affluent foreigners, crime has become a way of life for some Jamaicans. Gang activity, the drug trade, robbery, and murder have flourished in the country's postindependence period, and some Jamaicans have carried over these "professions" to their new lives in the United States. In the late twentieth century, the US government began deporting Jamaicans convicted of crimes, sending them back to their home country.

POLITICS AND GOVERNMENT

Jamaicans have been involved in issues of political significance in the United States since the early 1800s. In 1827 Jamaica-born John B. Russwurm cofounded and coedited the first black press in the United States, *Freedom's Journal*. Russwurm's vocal political views and his criticism of slavery forced him to leave the paper under pressure from contributors and his own colleagues. After slavery was abolished in the British West Indies in 1834, a number of Jamaicans supported the Back to Africa movement, which encouraged people of African descent to return to the African continent. Many other Jamaicans worked in collaboration with their black American counterparts to lobby for the abolition of slavery in the United States.

In the early twentieth century, Marcus Garvey, a Jamaican living in the United States, began advocating and popularizing the Pan-African movement, which seeks to unify all people of African descent. In building the first significant black nationalist movement in the United States, Garvey established the Universal Negro Improvement Association (UNIA), which helped cement the bonds of racial consciousness between blacks of African and Caribbean descent. Most members of the UNIA in the United States were from the West Indies, particularly Jamaica. In 1922 Garvey was arrested and imprisoned for mail fraud, a move widely believed to be motivated by the U.S. government's unease with Garvey's activism. Garvey was released from prison and deported in 1927. Two years later, he established the People's Political Party (PPP) in Jamaica, which called for many reforms, including minimum wages, guaranteed employment, social security benefits, workers' compensation, land reform, and the creation of a Jamaican university.

For Jamaicans and Jamaican Americans alike, art and literature are oftentimes directly linked to the struggle for equality, and Garvey's teachings helped inspire an entire generation of black poets and writers during the Harlem Renaissance. For example, W. A. Domingo, a Jamaica-born Harlem Renaissance figure and writer, supported black rights and advocated Jamaica's independence. Domingo sought to deemphasize the differences between African Americans and West Indian Americans, arguing that both groups, as black Americans, experience the same effects of racial oppression and discrimination. In contrast, Claude McKay, a Jamaica-born Harlem Renaissance poet, became disillusioned with the nationalism of Marcus Garvey and, along with several other Caribbean writers, founded a more radical organization called the African Blood Brotherhood.

Jamaican Americans were notably vocal and assertive during the black struggles of the early twentieth century, often paving the way for blacks to enter professions not previously open to them. Jamaican Americans who experienced racial discrimination in the workplace and in their communities combined political efforts to address the concerns of the entire black population. In the 1930s, Jamaican American political activity reached new levels as Jamaican, Trinidadian, Guyanese, and other Caribbean immigrants began playing an important role in the Democratic Party in New York City. In 1991 Una Clarke, a Jamaican immigrant, became the first Caribbean-born woman elected to New York City's legislature. In more recent years, Jamaican Americans have continued to rise to prominence at the local and national levels.

Relations with Jamaica Jamaica and the United States have never engaged in a major military confrontation, and U.S. involvement in Jamaica has included little intervention. There has never been a need for a Bay of Pigs invasion, as in Cuba, a vertical insertion, as in Grenada, or a military occupation, as in Haiti and the Dominican Republic. The United States did not contemplate annexing Jamaica as it did Puerto Rico and Cuba during the Spanish-American War of

A Jamaican American master mechanic from the Bronx, New York. JOE DE MARIA KRT / NEWSCOM

1898. The first U.S. military bases in Jamaica did not exist until World War II, when the British requested aid from the United States. Thus, Jamaicans generally viewed American soldiers as necessary allies, rather than as an obtrusive colonial force. Today, American tourists visit the island in large numbers, adding substantially to the Jamaican economy. A busy flow of air traffic exists between Jamaica and the United States, serving both American tourists and those Jamaicans who make frequent business trips to the United States. Jamaican Americans make regular remittances to family members in Jamaica, and many visit their home country regularly, maintaining dual residency and even voting in local elections.

The relationship between the governments of the United States and Jamaica has generally been very cordial. In recent decades, however, the US government has used economic and diplomatic clout to influence the political and fiscal direction of Jamaica. In the late 1970s and 1980s, the United States used clandestine activities to destabilize Michael Manley's democratic socialist government. Consequently, Jamaican political analysts and politicians heavily criticized the United States for supporting political violence in Jamaica during elections. While the United States accepted a greater number of Jamaican immigrants during this period of political unrest, the country deported thousands of Jamaican American prisoners back to the island from the late 1990s through the turn of the century. This practice strained relations between the two countries, as many of the deportees went on to commit crimes in their homeland. Jamaica also refused to support the 2003 US invasion of Iraq, although many Jamaican Americans served in the U.S. armed forces during the war. Other events that affect Jamaican views of the US government lie in governmental overthrows and skirmishes in the Caribbean that the United States supports or fails to support. One such instance occurred in 2004, when the United States supported the overthrow of Jean-Bertrand Aristide, then president of Haiti, while many Jamaicans and Jamaican Americans endorsed Aristide's rule.

NOTABLE INDIVIDUALS

Jamaican immigrants have contributed substantially to political, cultural, religious, and educational life in the United States. Jamaican American writers, athletes, teachers, musicians, poets, journalists, artists, professors, sports writers, actors, and other professionals have greatly enriched the American culture in many ways.

Academia Jamaica-born John B. Russwurm (1799–1851) graduated from Bowdoin College in 1826, making him one of the first blacks to graduate from an American university. Russwurm went on to distinguish himself as cofounder of *Freedom's Journal*, the first black-owned and operated newspaper published in the United States. Leonard Barrett, born in Jamaica, was an emeritus professor of religion at

Temple University who authored several books focusing on Jamaica's traditional religions and folklore. Orlando Patterson (1940–) is a professor of sociology at Harvard University. His book *Freedom in the Making of Western Culture* (1991) won the National Book Award in the nonfiction category. George Beckford (1934–1990) was a renowned agricultural economist, professor, and author. Born and raised in rural Jamaica, Beckford concentrated much of his work on the Caribbean plantation systems and societies that emerged as a result of European colonialism.

Journalism Michelle Bernard (1963–) is a political and legal analyst for MSNBC and a columnist for the *Washington Examiner*. Born in the United States to Jamaican American parents, Bernard has served as president of several women's political forums and is author of *Women's Progress: How Women Are Wealthier, Healthier, and More Independent than Ever Before* (2007). Jamaica-born Carl Williams is the editor and founder of *Black Culture* magazine.

Literature Claude McKay (1889–1948) migrated from Jamaica to the United States in 1912 and became an important voice in the Harlem Renaissance. McKay was the author of four novels, among them *Home to Harlem* (1928) and *Banana Bottom* (1933), and published several other books and a collection of poetry during his lifetime. June Jordan (1936–2002) was a prolific, award-winning Jamaican American poet, author, and activist. Opal Palmer Adisa (1954–) is a Jamaica-born poet, novelist, and storyteller who moved to the United States in 1979. Adisa's work has been widely anthologized. Stacey-Ann Chin (1972–) is a spoken-word poet whose work has appeared in a number of prestigious publications, including the *New York Times*. Chin, who was born and raised in Jamaica but now lives in New York City, is also a prominent activist in the gay and lesbian community. Colin Channer (1963–) is a novelist and short story writer whose work presents themes told from a Jamaican perspective. Because the dialogue in his novels and short stories is often written in Jamaican Patois, Channer is sometimes referred to as a "reggae writer." Kwame Dawes (1962–), who was raised in Jamaica but later became a resident of the United States, is an award-winning poet, author, editor, actor, and musician.

Military During World Wars I and II, the Allies recruited Jamaicans living on the island and in the United States to serve in the armed forces. Since then, a number of Jamaican Americans have served in the U.S. military. Most notable is Colin Powell (1937–), a retired four-star general in the U.S. Army who fought in the Vietnam War and went on to serve as the chairman of the joint chiefs of staff, the highest military position in the U.S. Department of Defense, from 1989 to 1993. Powell was born in New York City to Jamaican immigrants. Following his military career, Powell went on to serve as secretary of state under President George W. Bush from 2001 to 2005. Another notable Jamaican American member of the U.S. military was Vincent

Terrelonge (1923–), who during World War II served with the 332nd Fighter Group (popularly known as the Tuskegee Airmen), the first African American military aviators in the history of the U.S. armed forces.

Music A notable Jamaican American musician is Harry Belafonte (1927–), best known for his album *Calypso* (1956), which is credited with popularizing the Caribbean calypso style of music in the United States. Well-known Jamaican American hip-hop artists include Busta Rhymes (1972–), Sean Kingston (1990–), and the Notorious B.I.G. (1972–1997).

Politics and Public Service James S. Watson (1882–1952) was born in Jamaica and went on to become one of the first black judges in the United States, serving in the state of New York from 1930 until 1950. Colin Powell, as mentioned in the section covering notable Jamaican Americans in the U.S. military, is perhaps the most recognizable Jamaican American in politics and public service. Following his military career, Powell went on to serve as secretary of state under U.S. President George W. Bush from 2001 to 2005. Other more recent Jamaican American public servants include Kamala Harris (1964–), who in 2011 was elected as attorney general of California, and Anthony Brown (1961), elected as lieutenant governor of Maryland in 2007.

Sports Charles "Chili" Davis (1960–) was the first Major League Baseball (MLB) player born in Jamaica. Davis started his MLB career with the San Francisco Giants in 1981 and went on to play for several other teams. As of 2013 Davis was the hitting coach for the Oakland Athletics. Patrick Ewing (1962–) is a retired National Basketball Association (NBA) Hall of Fame player who spent most of his career with the New York Knicks. Ewing was born in Kingston, Jamaica, and immigrated with his family to Massachusetts in 1975. His son Patrick Ewing Jr. (1984–) is also a professional basketball player. American track and field stars Inger Miller (1972–), a 1996 Olympic gold medalist, and Natasha Hastings (1986–), a 2008 Olympic gold medalist, are both of Jamaican descent. Jeff Cunningham (1976–) is a Major League Soccer (MLS) player with the San Antonio Scorpions who held the MLS record for regular-season goals as of 2013. Cunningham was born in Jamaica and immigrated to Florida as a teenager.

Stage and Screen Grace Jones (1948–) is a Jamaica-born singer, actress, and model. Robert Wisdom (1953–), born in Washington, D.C., to Jamaican parents, is an actor best known for his role as Howard "Bunny" Colvin on the popular HBO television series *The Wire* (2002–2008). Madge Sinclair (1938–1995) was a Jamaican American actress who starred in the films *Convoy* (1978) and *Coming to America* (1988). Sinclair also appeared in the television miniseries *Roots* (1977), for which she received an Emmy Award nomination.

MEDIA

PRINT

Caribbean Life

Caribbean Life is an online news source addressing Caribbean and Caribbean American issues, with sections that include news, entertainment, and classifieds.

Kenton Kirby, Editor
One Metrotech Center
Suite 1001
Brooklyn, New York 11201
Phone: (718) 260-2500
Email: carribeanlife@cnglocal.com
URL: www.caribbeanlifenews.com

Everybody's, the Caribbean-American Magazine

Founded in 1977, *Everybody's* is a print and online magazine that caters to the Caribbean American community.

1630 Nostrand Avenue
Brooklyn, New York 11226
Phone: (718) 941-1879
Fax: (718) 941-1886
Email: info@everybodysmag.com
URL: www.everybodysmag.com

The Gleaner

Based in Jamaica and with offices in the United States, Canada, and England, the *Gleaner* is a Jamaican daily newspaper covering news, sports, entertainment, classifieds, and more.

(U.S. office): 172-06 Jamaica Avenue
Jamaica, New York 11433
Phone: (U.S. office): (718) 657-0788
Email: feedback@jamaica-gleaner.com
URL: www.jamaica-gleaner.com

New York Carib News

Founded in 1981 by Karl Rodney, the former president of the Jamaican Progressive Party, the *New York Carib News* is an online news source covering Caribbean news, entertainment, politics, religion, and more.

35 West 35th Street
Suite 705
New York, New York 10001
Phone: (212) 944-1991
Fax: (212) 944-2089
Email: info@nycaribnews.com
URL: http://nycaribnews.com

The Star

The Star is a daily newspaper based in Kingston, Jamaica, that is read by many Jamaican Americans.

7 North Street
P.O. Box 40
Kingston, Jamaica West Indies
Phone: (876) 922-3400
Email: star@gleanerjm.com
URL: www.jamaica-star.com

RADIO

WINN FM 98.9 (West Indies News Network)

Provides online news radio for the West Indies.

> Lorraine Wilkin, Chief Operations Officer
> Unit C24
> The Sands Complex
> Newtown Bay Road,
> Basseterre, St. Kitts West Indies
> Phone: (718) 285-6984
> Email: lorraine@winnfm.com
> URL: www.winnfm.com

ORGANIZATIONS AND ASSOCIATIONS

Atlanta Jamaican Association (AJA)

A nonprofit organization that seeks to promote friendship and understanding between Jamaican Americans and the greater Atlanta community.

> Errol Ritchie, President
> P.O. Box 2207
> Lithonia, Georgia 30058
> URL: www.ajaatlanta.org

Friends of Jamaica Seattle (FOJS)

Promotes understanding and appreciation of Jamaican culture and heritage and provides assistance to Jamaicans and persons of Jamaican heritage living in the Pacific Northwest.

> 15704 NE 1st Street
> Bellevue, Washington 98008
> Phone: (425) 641-1438
> Email: info@fojs.org
> URL: http://fojs.org

Jamaican American Association of Northern California (JAANC)

Established in 1975, the JAANC is a nonprofit organization that aims to advance the relationship between Jamaican Americans and other Americans in northern California through cultural awareness, education, and resources.

> Newton C. Gordon, Chairman
> 810 Clay Street
> Oakland, California 94607
> Phone: (510) 854-6413
> URL: www.jaanc.org

Jamaican American Cultural Association (JACA)

An organization dedicated to providing educational support for children of Caribbean descent living in Jamaica and in Charlotte, North Carolina.

> Gaynor Russell, President
> P.O. Box 34005
> Charlotte, North Carolina 28234
> Email: jacacharlotte@gmail.com
> URL: www.jaca1.com

SOURCES FOR ADDITIONAL STUDY

Alleyne, Mervyn C. *Roots of Jamaican Culture*. London: Pluto Press, 1988.

Barrett, Leonard E. *The Rastafarians*. Boston: Beacon Press, 1997.

Campbell, Mavis Christine. *The Maroons of Jamaica 1655–1796: A History of Resistance, Collaboration & Betrayal*. Granby, MA: Bergin & Garvey, 1988.

Carty, Hilary S. *Folk Dances of Jamaica: An Insight*. London: Dance Books, 1988.

Davis, Stephen. *Bob Marley: Conquering Lion of Reggae*. London: Plexus, 1993.

Horst, Heather A., and Andrew Garner. *Jamaican Americans*. New York: Chelsea House, 2007.

Kessner, Thomas, and Betty Boyd Caroli. *Today's Immigrants, Their Stories: A New Look at the Newest Americans*. New York: Oxford University Press, 1981.

Luntta, Karl. *Jamaica Handbook*. Chico, CA: Moon Publications, 1991.

Senior, Olive. *Encyclopedia of Jamaican Heritage*. St. Andrew, Jamaica: Twin Guinep Publishers, 2003.

Sherlock, Philip Manderson, and Hazel Bennett. *The Story of the Jamaican People*. Princeton, NJ: M. Wiener Publishers, 1998.

JAPANESE AMERICANS

Stanley E. Easton and Lucien Ellington

OVERVIEW

Japanese Americans are immigrants or descendants of immigrants from Japan, a country in East Asia. An archipelago lying off the eastern coast of the Asian continent, Japan consists of four main islands—Honshu, Hokkaido, Kyushu, and Shikoku—as well as 3,900 smaller islands. To Japan's north is the Russia-controlled island of Sakhalin, while the People's Republic of China and South Korea lie to the country's west. Much of Japan is extremely mountainous, and almost the entire population lives on only one-sixth of the total land area. Of the world's major nations, it has the highest population density per square mile of habitable land. Japan has a total land area of 145,825 square miles (377,688 square kilometers), making it approximately the size of California.

According to the Japanese Ministry of Internal Affairs and Communications' Statistics Bureau, in 2011 Japan had a population of approximately 128 million people. Japan has one of the most homogeneous populations in the world. Fewer than 2 million non-ethnically Japanese (or under 1.5 percent of the total Japanese population) live in Japan. Koreans constitute more than half of the ethnic minorities in the country. Japan is also home to two indigenous minority groups, the Ainu and the Burakumin. The Ainu, a Caucasian group, number around 24,381 and live mainly on special reservations in central Hokkaido. The Burakumin, with a population estimated at two million, are often referred to as an outcast group. Although they now have the same legal status as their fellow citizens, the Burakumin have for centuries faced severe discrimination and relegation to the country's low-status occupations. According to 2012 statistics from the Japanese Ministry of Internal Affairs and Communications, Japan's predominant religion is Shinto, with 83.9 percent of the population practicing this indigenous religion. Buddhism, a Korean and Chinese import, is practiced by 71.4 percent of the population. Followers of Christianity constitute 1 percent of the Japanese population, while 7.8 percent list "other" for religious beliefs. Japanese people identifying as both Buddhist and Shinto are not uncommon, as many in the nation practice more than one religion. Despite the country's lack of natural resources, Japan's economy is the third largest in the world and is based primarily on exports of manufactured goods.

The first Japanese immigrants began arriving in the United States in the 1860s, following the termination of Japan's self-imposed national isolation. A number of these immigrants were adult contract laborers, recruited by representatives from American sugar and silk companies in need of workers. Between 1895 and 1908, approximately 130,000 Japanese workers arrived in the United States, settling predominantly in the Northwest and California, as well as in Hawaii, which was at that time an independent country. Members of this first wave of Japanese immigrants, most of whom were male, are referred to as the Issei. Although the United States subsequently restricted the flow of Chinese and Japanese immigrants, thousands of Japanese women traveled to join their husbands and fiancés already in the United States. The U.S. government ultimately put a stop to all Japanese immigration with the Immigration Act of 1924. Between 1965 and 1985, large waves of Japanese immigrants, men and women, came to the United States to attend university, find professional work, or join spouses who were American citizens. Starting in the mid 1980s, a time of economic prosperity in Japan, the number of Japanese people immigrating to the United States dropped steadily for more than twenty years. Those numbers began to increase again in 2000. According to a 2000 report from the United States Immigration and Naturalization Service (INS), approximately 4,000 Japanese people immigrated to the United States in 1999. By 2001 that number had reached 10,464. In the first decade of the twenty-first century, approximately 8,455 Japanese immigrants a year on average received permanent resident status in the United States, according to the United States Department of Homeland Security (DHS).

The 2010 United States Census estimated the Japanese American population, which includes people of exclusively Japanese descent and those who report having Japanese ancestry in combination with other races, at 1.3 million, or about 5.6 percent of the total Asian American population. Of that 1.3 million, approximately 775,000 are of exclusively Japanese ancestry. Although many Japanese immigrants still live in Hawaii, California and New York state are now home to the largest populations of Japanese Americans. Washington State is also home to a significant number of Japanese Americans.

HISTORY OF THE PEOPLE

Early History The oldest identified human remains found in Japan date from around 30,000 BCE. The region took its first steps toward political unification in the late fourth and early fifth centuries CE under Yamato chiefs, who developed an imperial line now believed to be the oldest in the world. Ancient and medieval Japan were culturally undeveloped compared to neighboring China, and from early in its history, Japan imported and incorporated into its own culture many Chinese practices, philosophies, and customs, including architecture, agricultural methods, Confucianism, and Buddhism.

Japan's medieval and early modern eras were marked by long periods of continuous warfare as rival families struggled for power. The country's first recorded contact with Europe came in 1543, when Portuguese traders landed off southern Kyushu. In 1603, through military conquest, Tokugawa Ieyasu was named Japan's first shogun, establishing himself as ruler of the entire country. During the Tokugawa era, foreigners were expelled from Japan, and the country largely isolated itself from the rest of the world for a period lasting more than two centuries. In 1854 Commodore Matthew Perry of the United States Navy sailed to Japan and demanded that its ruling shogun sign a treaty establishing formal diplomatic relations with the United States, ultimately forcing Japan to begin trading with the West and ending its extended, self-imposed period of isolation.

Modern Era Japan's modern history began in 1868 with the overthrow of the Tokugawa shogunate and the founding of the Meiji dynasty. In the decades that followed, Japan feverishly modernized in an attempt to end Western efforts at dominance. By the early twentieth century, Japan possessed a rapidly industrializing economy and a strong military. In 1894 Japan put its improved armed forces to the test when it invaded China, marking the beginning of the First Sino-Japanese War, fought primarily for control of Korea. The two countries signed a treaty the following year, granting Korea independence but allowing Japan control of Taiwan, the Liaodong Peninsula, and the Penghu Islands. The treaty also required China to pay Japan significant reparations. Japan's achievements in the war, despite China's larger army and more abundant resources, demonstrated its success in adopting a Western-style military. Tensions between the two countries began escalating once again in the 1930s, and in 1937 a scuffle between Japanese and Chinese troops ignited the Second Sino-Japanese War, a conflict that would last until 1945. In October 1937 the Japanese army captured the Chinese city of Shanghai, and two months later the Chinese capital city of Nanking also fell to the Japanese. In the six weeks that followed, a period now referred to as the Nanking Massacre, Japanese troops pillaged the city, raping thousands of women and killing an estimated 250,000 people. The Battle of Nanking also served to heighten tensions between Japan and the United States, as the Japanese military had fired on American troops during the conflict. By 1940 the Japanese government had signed a pact with Germany and Italy to fight against common enemies in the global conflict that would ultimately develop into World War II. Japan's bombing of Pearl Harbor on December 7, 1941, compelled the previously neutral United States to join the Allied Powers. In 1945 the U.S. military dropped an atomic bomb on Hiroshima, Japan, destroying five square miles of the city and killing more than 140,000 people. Three days later, the U.S. military dropped a second atomic bomb, this one on the Japanese city of Nagasaki, killing another 74,000 people and injuring many more.

In August 1945 a devastated Japan accepted the surrender terms of the Allied Powers. U.S. general Douglas MacArthur led the occupation and reconstruction efforts, enacting punitive economic measures and political and social reforms on Japan. Japan was forced to adopt a constitution and create a democracy with the emperor as figurehead. The country was also forbidden to rebuild an army, was required to adopt universal suffrage, and to officially separate the Shinto religion and the state. In the years following the war, Japan was in shambles, with most of its cities severely damaged, its industries destroyed, its infrastructure in disrepair, and food shortages all too common. Rigid censorship of the press forbade criticism of the United States. Ultimately, MacArthur shifted away from punitive measures and toward helping the Japanese achieve self-sufficiency. His policies encouraged the shift from a state-managed economy to a market economy with a focus on exports. This period of American occupation resulted in significant political and economic changes for Japan. The country became a democracy, renounced militarism, and resumed steady economic growth. American occupation of Japan ended in 1952, except in Okinawa, which the United States occupied until 1972, and Iwo Jima, occupied until 1968. In exchange for leaving U.S. troops on Japanese soil and for insisting on Japan's demilitarization, the United States in 1960 agreed to protect Japan from its neighbors. Japan became a critical ally to the United States during the Vietnam War and the Cold War, providing the United States with military bases from which to operate in that region of the world. The United States in turn provided security for Japan, which was positioned between two giant Communist countries. Relations between Japan and the United States cooled toward the end of the Cold War in the early 1990s, when Japan was in the midst of political turmoil and an economic downturn.

Following World War II, with no option to grow its military, the Japanese government focused on stimulating economic growth. The Japanese were aided in this by the United States, who facilitated Japan's entry into the U.S. market and supported Japanese restrictions on imports and foreign investment. Japan's economic recovery was so swift that Japanese industries

Male Japanese immigrants wearing samurai garb. AKG-IMAGES / ULLSTEIN BILD

were successfully competing with American industries by the 1970s. Experts have attributed the success of Japan's economic recovery to cooperation between manufacturers, suppliers, and distributors, as well as to the rise of strong unions, guaranteed lifetime employment, and close ties between the government and the business sector. Japanese economic growth slowed in the mid-1980s, when the United States increased its restrictions on trade, accused Japanese companies of unfair trade practices, and turned its attention to expanding U.S. exports to Japan. By the end of the 1980s, Japan's trade surplus was quite large, as was the trade deficit of the United States. When growth slowed in Japan, a burst of speculation artificially inflated land values and created an asset bubble, while low interest rates encouraged investors to pour money into inflated properties. The bubble burst in 1991, and the Japanese government was forced to bail out banks and companies previously considered too large to fail. Close to two decades of slow-to-no growth followed, and as of early 2013 the Japanese economy was continuing to shrink. In spite of its financial woes, Japan remains a stable democracy and continues to rank among the world's top economic superpowers.

SETTLEMENT IN THE UNITED STATES

In 1835 American settlers established the sugar plantation system in Hawaii, which was then an independent monarchy. The sugar plantations required large numbers of workers to cultivate and harvest the cane fields and to operate the sugar refineries. Beginning around 1852, the plantation owners began importing Chinese laborers.

By 1865 many Chinese laborers in Hawaii were leaving the plantations for other jobs. Hawaii's foreign minister, a sugar planter, wrote to an American businessman in Japan, telling him the region was in need of Japanese agricultural workers. On May 17, 1868, a ship sailed from the Japanese city of Yokohama for Honolulu with 148 Japanese people aboard. These people—140 men, six women, and two children—included samurai, cooks, *sake* brewers, potters, printers, tailors, woodworkers, and one hairdresser. Plantation labor was harsh. Ten-hour workdays were standard, and the monthly wage was four dollars, of which the plantation owners withheld 50 percent. Forty of these first Japanese farm laborers returned to Japan before completion of their three-year contracts. Once back home, thirty-nine of them signed a public statement charging the planters with cruelty and breach of contract.

On May 27, 1869, the Pacific Mail Steamship Company's S. S. Great Republic picked up a party of samurai, farmers, tradesmen, and women in Japan and transported them to San Francisco. These people had been displaced from their homes by the overthrow of the Tokugawa shogunate and the restoration of the Meiji emperor. Japanese entrepreneurs from this group established the 600-acre Wakamatsu Tea and Silk Farm Colony on the Sacramento River in Placerville, California. The colony failed in less than two years because the mulberry trees and tea seedlings perished in the dry California soil. A few of the settlers returned to Japan, while the rest drifted away from the colony seeking new beginnings.

In 1882 U.S. Congress passed the Chinese Exclusion Act, which prohibited further Chinese immigration. In 1886 Hawaii and Japan signed a labor convention that led to large numbers of Japanese contract workers immigrating to Hawaii. Meanwhile, the increase of Japanese immigrants in California gave rise to anti-Japanese sentiment, and in 1906 the school board in San Francisco ordered the segregation of Japanese American students. Ninety-three students of Japanese ancestry, along with a number of Korean students, were ordered to attend a school that had already been established for Chinese immigrant children. The Japanese government was insulted. President Theodore Roosevelt, wishing to maintain harmonious relations with Japan, condemned anti-Japanese agitation and the school segregation order. Roosevelt advocated naturalization of the Issei but never sponsored the introduction of a bill to accomplish it. Political reaction against Roosevelt in California was fierce, and several anti-Japanese bills were introduced in the state legislature in 1907. Roosevelt reacted by calling San Francisco school officials and California legislative leaders to Washington, and after a week of negotiations, the representatives from California agreed to allow Japanese children (excluding overage students and those

with limited English) to attend regular public schools. Roosevelt, in turn, promised to limit Japanese labor immigration. In late 1907 and early 1908, Japan and the United States corresponded on the matter. Japan agreed to stop issuing passports to laborers wishing to immigrate to the United States, while the United States agreed to allow Japanese who had already been to the United States to return and to accept immediate family members of Japanese immigrants already in the country. This arrangement was known as the "Gentlemen's Agreement."

Under the Gentlemen's Agreement, some Japanese immigration to the United States continued. Between 1908 and 1924, many new Japanese immigrants were women brought over by husbands already living in the United States. Between 1909 and 1920, the number of married Japanese women living in Hawaii doubled, while the number living on the U.S. mainland quadrupled. Most of the Japanese women who migrated to Hawaii and the United States during that period were referred to as "picture brides." Marriages were arranged by parents, while go-betweens brokered agreements between families. Couples were usually married while the bride was in Japan and the groom was in the United States, with husband and wife meeting for the first time upon their arrival at the pier in Honolulu, San Francisco, or Seattle, using photographs to identify one another. This wave of immigration changed the nature of the Japanese American community from a primarily male migrant laborer group to a family-oriented community seeking permanent settlement.

Job prospects were generally dismal for highly educated Japanese Americans living on the U.S. mainland. Racial discrimination resulted in unemployment or underemployment for many. Their situation, however, was not as difficult as that of Japanese immigrants living in Hawaii, which had been annexed by the United States in 1898. Japanese plantation workers on the islands, calling for improved wages and living conditions, organized multiple strikes throughout the first two decades of the twentieth century. The labor movement was met with great resistance, and thousands of Japanese workers were evicted and displaced as a result, while leaders were arrested and jailed. By the 1920s the U.S. government was viewing the politically active Japanese community in Hawaii, which comprised approximately 40 percent of the islands' population, as a threat to national security.

The terms of the Gentlemen's Agreement became null and void with the passage of the Immigration Act of 1924, a restrictive law reflecting growing antiforeigner sentiment in the United States. The act limited immigration by implementing strict quotas and restricting the entry of any people who, due to their racial or ethnic background, were not eligible for U.S. citizenship. The Naturalization Act of 1790 had made all nonwhite persons ineligible for naturalization, and so the 1924 law essentially halted all Japanese immigration to the United States.

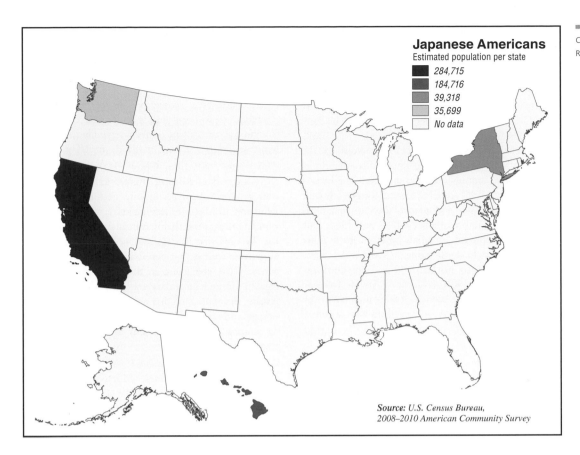

Japanese Americans
Estimated population per state

- 284,715
- 184,716
- 39,318
- 35,699
- No data

Source: U.S. Census Bureau,
2008–2010 American Community Survey

Immediately following the bombing of Pearl Harbor in 1941, U.S. officials in Hawaii began rounding up Japanese Americans. An internment camp was established on a flat, barren coral island in Honolulu called Sand Island, where detainees were treated harshly. Officials did not intern Japanese American agricultural workers in Hawaii considered essential to the territory's survival, but these workers were required to carry alien registration cards at all times and were subject to a curfew. Meanwhile, Japanese Americans on the U.S. mainland were also being rounded up. Between 1942 and 1945, approximately 110,000 people of Japanese heritage were sent to live on internment camps. Few in the United States protested these incursions on the rights of Japanese Americans.

At the end of 1941, there were 1,500 second-generation Japanese Americans enlisted in U.S. Army units in Hawaii. These soldiers were disarmed and rearmed at least twice during the course of the war. Japanese American troops from Hawaii were eventually joined by other Japanese American soldiers, mostly volunteers and draftees from mainland internment camps, to form a segregated battalion. This battalion, known as the 442nd Regimental Combat Team, would become the most decorated infantry regiment in the history of the U.S. Army. In all, about 33,000 Japanese Americans served the United States in World War II.

Other Japanese Americans were unwilling to serve a country that would enlist them while simultaneously subjecting their families to internment. In 1943 about 200 Nisei at the Heart Mountain Relocation Center in Wyoming formed the Fair Play Committee (FPC) to resist conscription into the armed services. The FPC published a manifesto protesting denial of their rights as citizens without due process, charges filed against them, or any evidence of wrongdoing. In 1944, following the largest draft resistance trial in U.S. history, 63 Nisei resisters confined at Heart Mountain internment camp were sentenced to three years in federal prison. In 1947, after the men had already served two years of their sentences, President Harry S. Truman pardoned them.

Since the start of their internment, Japanese Americans sought to argue the unconstitutional nature of it. In 1942 Mitsuye Endo, a Japanese American woman who had been removed from her home in Sacramento and sent to live on an internment camp, brought a petition in U.S. federal court challenging her internment as a violation of her civil rights. The U.S. Supreme Court in its 1944 verdict did not argue Endo's initial confinement but did find that her continued detention was unconstitutional, as the United States conceded it had no reason to question her loyalty. The court ordered Endo's immediate release. One day before the ruling, and in anticipation of it, the U.S. government announced the end of its exclusion order. The last of the internment camps was closed in 1945.

In 1952 the McCarran-Walter Act ended the ban on Japanese immigration, but the new law was still racially discriminatory. Approximately 100 to 200 immigrants per Asian country were allowed into the United States each year, while quotas on immigrants from European countries were far more lax. The McCarran-Walter Act also removed all racial barriers to naturalization. As a result, more than 46,000 Japanese immigrants, including many elderly Issei, became naturalized citizens by 1965.

The Immigration Act of 1965 abolished the national origin quotas and annually permitted the admission of 20,000 immigrants per country into the United States. Between 1965 and 1985, there were nearly four times as many Asian immigrants entering the United States as there had been between 1849 and 1965. Due to a booming economy in Japan, however, the number of Japanese people immigrating to the United States dropped significantly in the 1970s and remained low until 1999. Whereas in 1960 Japanese Americans made up 52 percent of the Asian American population, by 1985 only 15 percent of Asian Americans were Japanese.

After four decades of lobbying on the part of the Japanese American community, U.S. Congress passed the Civil Liberties Act of 1988. Through the law, the U.S. government acknowledged the fundamental injustice of the internment of Japanese Americans during World War II. The government also formally apologized for that injustice and granted reparations in the amount of $20,000 for each survivor.

At the turn of the twenty-first century, the United States began to see a rise in Japanese immigration. The number of Japanese immigrants entering the United States rose from 4,217 in 1999 to 10,464 in 2001. Women made up the majority, or 65 percent, of these immigrants. Recent increases have been attributed to a persistently weak economy in Japan since the 1990s, Japanese women seeking better job opportunities, and a new wave of Japanese women coupling with U.S. citizens, often through Internet dating. The 2010 United States Census counted 1.3 million people of Japanese descent living in the United States; however, only 775,000 were exclusively of Japanese ancestry. Today Japanese Americans live in all fifty states, with close to half residing in California. Other states with large populations of Japanese Americans include Hawaii, New York, and Washington.

LANGUAGE

The Japanese language is unique in that it has no close relationship to any other language, such as English does to German or French does to Spanish. The origins of Japanese are obscure, and only Korean can be considered to belong to the same linguistic family. A popular misconception is that the Japanese language is similar to Chinese, but although many *kanji* (characters used in modern Japanese writing) were borrowed from classical Chinese, the two spoken languages do not have a single basic feature in common. Spoken Japanese was in existence long before kanji reached Japan. While there is some variation in dialect throughout Japan, variance in pronunciation and vocabulary is, in general, quite small.

Many linguists assert that Japanese is the world's most difficult written language. Written Japanese consists of three types of characters: *kanji*, *hiragana*, and *katakana*. Kanji, which means "Chinese characters," are ideograms, or pictorial representations of ideas. Kanji were imported into Japan sometime during the fifth century CE from China via Korea. Although there are said to be some 48,000 kanji in existence, only about 4,000 are commonly used. In 1946 Japan's Ministry of Education identified 1,850 kanji (called *tōyō kanji*) as essential for official and general public use. In 1981 that list was superseded by a similar but larger one (called *jōyō kanji*) containing 1,945 characters. These characters are taught to all students in elementary and secondary school. Kanji are used in writing the main parts of a sentence, such as verbs and nouns, and are the most difficult Japanese characters to compose, requiring as many as twenty-three separate strokes.

Because spoken Japanese existed before kanji reached Japan, the Japanese adopted Chinese ideograms to represent spoken Japanese words. The Japanese words, of course, sounded different than the corresponding Chinese words, so it became important to develop a writing system to represent the Japanese sounds. Therefore, the Japanese developed two sets of characters, hiragana and katakana, from original Chinese characters. Each *kana*, as these two systems are called, is a separate phonetic syllabary, and each hiragana character has a corresponding katakana character. Hiragana and katakana characters are similar to English letters in that each character represents a separate phonetic sound. Hiragana are written in a cursive style and are used to represent verb endings, adverbs, conjunctions, and various sentence particles. Katakana, which are used mainly in writing foreign words, are written in a more angular, stiff style. Both hiragana and katakana are easy to write when compared with kanji.

In modern written Japanese, kanji, hiragana, and katakana are combined. Traditionally, Japanese is written vertically and read from top to bottom and right to left. Now most business writing is done horizontally, as it is easier to include numerals and English words. Although the written Japanese language is complex and in some ways illogical, it holds an aesthetic appeal for the Japanese and contributes to a feeling that they are unique among the world's peoples.

According to the 2010 United States Census, 445,471 people in the United States over the age of five speak Japanese at home. Among the rest of the Japanese American population, English is the primary language. For a variety of reasons, including the complicated nature of the written language, many third and fourth generation Japanese Americans cannot write the language of their ancestors.

Some useful daily expressions include: *Ohayōgozaimasu*—Good morning; *Konnichiwa*—Hello; *Kombanwa*—Good evening; *Sayōnara*—Goodbye; *Oyasumi nasai*—Good night; *Okaeri nasai*—Welcome home; *O-genki desu ka*—How are you; *Dōmo arigatō gozaimasu*—Thank you very much; and *Chotto matte kudasai*—Wait just a moment, please.

RELIGION

Shinto is an indigenous Japanese religion based on purification and fertility rituals, ancestor cults, and seasonal festivals that developed informally over hundreds of years. The concepts of harmony, gratitude, purity, and filial piety are central. Shinto is not monotheistic like many religions in the West. Rather, its gods, or *kami*, are many, and these supernatural beings are present in both animate and inanimate objects. Shinto was the only religion in Japan until Buddhism was introduced from China in 538 CE. Buddhism became so popular that branches of the two religions merged, becoming what is known as Ryobu Shinto ("Dual Shinto"). Many Japanese people continue to practice Shinto and Buddhism side by side in the early twenty-first century. Shinto rituals are reserved for birth and marriage, while Buddhist rituals and beliefs govern end of life and funerals.

Shinto underwent significant changes in the second half of the nineteenth century as Japan shifted from the Tokugawa shogunate, a feudal system of government, to the Meiji dynasty, a centralized system ruled by an emperor. The new Meiji emperor designated Shinto as the national religion, and shrines were separated from Buddhist temples, regulated, and placed under government control. The Shinto practice of worshipping an imperial ancestor was co-opted to legitimize the emperor and lend the Meiji dynasty the appearance of being the restoration of an ancient tradition. Shinto became a much more elaborate and formal system, with a highly organized structure of priests, shrines, and patriotic teachings. The religion was used as a tool to justify policies of expansion and empire. All Japanese people were expected to practice Shinto, regardless of their beliefs.

The first waves of Japanese immigrants brought their beliefs and practices with them to the United States. A survey conducted of Issei who came to the country before 1924 found that 78 percent identified as Buddhist, while only 3.5 percent identified as Shinto. Another 9.3 percent said they were Christian, and 9 percent reported being atheist. One possible explanation for the small number of people reporting Shinto as their religion is that the study did not provide the option of claiming multiple beliefs. Another explanation is that Shinto was such an ingrained part of Japanese ethnic identity that belief in it was simply assumed.

As soon as Japanese immigrants began arriving in the United States, Christian missionaries started to work at converting them. The Methodists were particularly successful in this effort, converting some Japanese immigrants as early as 1877, a full eleven years before Japan legally allowed its citizens to emigrate. By the latter part of the nineteenth century and the early years of the twentieth century, Japanese Christian churches and missions had been established in various California cities, as well as in Tacoma, Washington, and Denver, Colorado. In addition to religious services, these early Japanese Christian organizations usually offered English classes and social activities. While the Methodist church remained popular, other denominations, such as the Presbyterians, Baptists, Congregationalists, Episcopalians, and Catholics, also claimed converts.

Organized Buddhism was somewhat slow in attempting to minister to the spiritual needs of Japanese Americans. The first record of Japanese Buddhist priests in the United States was in 1893, when four traveled from Japan to attend the World Parliament of Religions in Chicago. The priests had limited contact, however, with Japanese Americans. In 1899 two ministers from the Jodo Shinshu sect in Kyoto (Jodo Shinshu translates to "Pure Land Buddhism") immigrated to San Francisco to minister to Japanese Americans. By 1914 the Buddhist Churches of America (BCA) had been established.

By the early years of the twentieth century, a number of Buddhist churches had been founded on the West Coast. The Immigration Act of 1924 and growing anti-Japanese sentiment led to an increase in the number of Buddhist temples during this era. Japanese American internment and its immediate aftermath around the time of World War II led to even greater interest in traditional Japanese religions, including Buddhism and a revival of what some refer to as "informal Shintoism." Japanese Americans living in internment camps found practicing these religions helped them to resist the "Americanization" efforts of the U.S. government. Many Japanese American Buddhist temples and Japanese American Christian churches continue to foster ethnic consciousness and liberal protest for Japanese Americans.

Japanese Americans enjoy a higher economic position and greater socioeconomic mobility now than at any other time in American history.

After World War II, during the Allied occupation of Japan, the U.S.-led Japanese government ordered the disestablishment of government-run Shinto, which it referred to as "State Shinto." Two branches of Shinto were set up in its place, called "Shrine Shinto" and "Denominational Shinto." The strong connection between Shinto and Japanese imperialism in the minds of most mainstream Americans made it difficult to practice any form of the religion in the United States

Three Japanese American children eat their bento lunches in 1985. A bento is typically packed in a box-shaped container and includes rice, meat or fish, and pickled or cooked vegetables. CORBIS / MICHAEL YAMASHITA. REPRODUCED BY PERMISSION.

for many decades after World War II. The first Shinto shrine in the United States, called the Tsubaki Grand Shrine of America, was built in 1987 in Stockton, California. In 2001 the shrine was moved to Granite Falls, Washington. Since that time, seven additional Shinto shrines have been built in the United States, all of them located in Hawaii.

As of 2013 the BCA was the dominant Buddhist denomination in the United States. Japanese American Buddhists continue to perform rituals honoring their ancestors at home, in temples, and at the cemetery. Some Japanese American Christian churches observe these rituals as well. Another common practice among modern Japanese American Buddhists is honoring the memory of ancestors by making financial donations to organizations dedicated to preserving cultural traditions.

According to a 2012 survey conducted by the Pew Research Center, 33 percent of Japanese Americans identify as Protestant, 25 percent are Buddhist, 4 percent are Catholic, and 32 percent are unaffiliated with any particular religion. Shinto was not mentioned in the survey.

CULTURE AND ASSIMILATION

Since they first began arriving in the United States, Japanese Americans have built Buddhist temples and Christian churches. They have built halls to serve as language schools and as places for theater performances, films, judo lessons, poetry readings, potlucks, and parties. They have constructed sumo rings, baseball fields, and bath houses. They have also established hotels, restaurants, bars, and billiard parlors, as well as shops that provide Japanese food and herbal medicines.

The Issei experienced many restrictions upon their arrival in the United States, facing discrimination and prejudice from the earliest days of immigration until after World War II. They were excluded from some occupations, restricted from owning land, and denied the opportunity to become U.S. citizens until 1952. The Issei's pleasure was largely in seeing the success of their children. Despite their poverty, the Issei developed large, close-knit families. They encouraged their children, the Nisei, to leave their farming communities, become educated, and obtain white-collar jobs. This drove the Nisei into close associations and friendships with Caucasians. The Nisei were generally educated in American schools and learned what many refer to as "white, middle-class American values." Hierarchical thinking, characteristic of Japanese culture, led to pressure to achieve academically and to compete successfully in the larger Caucasian-dominated society.

Between 1915 and 1967, the proportion of Japanese Americans living in predominantly Japanese American neighborhoods fell from 30 percent to 4 percent. With the end of World War II, prejudice and discrimination against Japanese Americans declined. According to a 2009 study conducted by the Japanese American Citizens League (JACL), the majority of Japanese Americans now live in largely integrated neighborhoods, although as a group they retain regional proximity. Most later generations are unfamiliar with the first-generation Japanese American world characterized by communal association and close social control. Whereas only 10 percent of the second generation Nisei married outside their ethnic group, about 50 percent of the third generation Sansei did.

Many Japanese Americans have indicated a desire to know more about their cultural roots. In the JACL's 2009 study, 67 percent of Japanese Americans said they felt they knew little of Japanese culture, while close to 40 percent expressed the desire to know more. In an effort to preserve Japanese culture, some Japanese Americans participate in Japanese-centered community festivals, volunteer with the elderly in their communities, get involved with Japanese political and legal organizations, and patronize the Japanese arts.

The degree to which later generations of Japanese Americans have assimilated into the predominant culture is unusual for a nonwhite group. In his book *Generations and Identity: The Japanese American* (1993), sociologist Harry H. L. Kitano observed that early Japanese Americans developed a congruent Japanese culture within the framework of American society. This was due to necessity rather than choice, as there was little opportunity for those first generations to enter into the social structure of the larger community. Most Japanese Americans today feel more able to enter into that social structure, so while later generations continue to identify as Japanese Americans, they also partake more easily in a larger society that is not as hostile toward them as it was toward their predecessors. Nonetheless, even later generations of Japanese Americans have indicated that identity remains important and that some degree of perceived racism still exists.

Americans of Japanese descent have the highest rate of intermarriage with members of other ethnic groups. The 2010 United States Census reported that 763,325 people identified themselves as Japanese American, while another 540,961 identified themselves as Japanese in combination with one or more other races. The high rate of assimilation has caused some in the Japanese American community to express concern over the loss of their cultural heritage. It is uncertain whether newer generations of Japanese Americans will retain their Japanese traditions and customs and pass them on to the next generations.

Traditions and Customs In Japanese tradition, a crane represents 1,000 years. On special birthdays, 1,000 red, hand-folded *origami* cranes are displayed to convey wishes for a long life. Certain birthdays are thought to be auspicious or calamitous in a person's life. For men, the forty-second birthday is considered the most calamitous, while for women it is the thirty-third year. Especially festive celebrations are held on these birthdays to ward off misfortune. The sixty-first birthday is considered the beginning of the auspicious years and the beginning of a person's second childhood (the term "second childhood" in Japanese translates as both a sixtieth birthday and as one's dotage, or the onset of senility). Traditionally, a person in his or her second childhood wears a crimson cap. The seventy-seventh birthday is marked by the wearing of a loose red coat (called the *chanchan ko*) over one's clothes. The most auspicious birthday is the eighty-eighth, when the honoree wears both the crimson cap and the chanchan ko.

Cuisine A distinctive trait of Japanese cuisine is the practice of keeping dishes separate, rather than mixing them or even letting them touch on the plate. Japanese food is served on platters big enough to serve the entire table. One style of platter used to keep food separate is called a bento box. These low-sided boxes are usually rectangular in shape, with different compartments for holding meat, fish, and other dishes. People serve themselves from the large platters, taking some of each dish and putting it in a small bowl and adding rice. The bowls can be used for tea or soup as well. The main utensils are chopsticks and flat-bottomed spoons. Rice is a staple that accompanies most meals, including breakfast.

Traditional ingredients in Japanese cuisine include rice, beans, eggs, flour, fruits, mushrooms, meat, seafood, and oil. Traditional meals usually include rice and a few main dishes, along with pickles and a bowl of soup on the side. Historically, oil, red meat, and fat are used sparingly, although that has changed somewhat with the advent of processed foods and foreign culinary influences. Common dishes include miso soup, tempura (lightly breaded and fried vegetables, meat, or seafood), teriyaki (a sweet sauce of soy and ginger served over vegetables, meat, or seafood), sashimi (raw seafood without rice), and sushi (raw seafood and rice rolled in seaweed). Green tea

and sake (plum wine) are traditional Japanese beverages. Lunches away from home are often packed in bento boxes. Traditionally made of lacquered wood, contemporary bento boxes are made from a wide variety of materials. In recent years these containers have found popularity in the United States, where they are often sold as children's lunch boxes.

Japan has several regional cuisines, the most notable of which are Kanto and Kansai. Kanto is known for strong broths with udon noodles (round noodles similar to spaghetti), while Kansai is known for lighter flavors and clear broths. For many decades, Japanese Americans could find ingredients for these foods only at stores owned and operated by fellow Japanese immigrants. In the 1980s, however, sushi began to gain popularity in American culture, and ramen noodle restaurants have also become popular. Japanese restaurants can now be found in most U.S. cities, while a limited number of Japanese ingredients are available

Two Japanese American girls are wearing traditional kimonos at the National Cherry Blossom Festival in Washington, D.C. CORBIS / NIK WHEELER. REPRODUCED BY PERMISSION.

at many national grocery chains and at gourmet shops and stores that cater specifically to Japanese Americans or Asian Americans. One dish that has been adapted from Japanese cooking in the United States is *spam musubi*, a sushi look-alike made with rice, spam, seaweed, and *furikake* (a Japanese condiment made of dried fish, sesame seeds, salt, and sugar). Spam musubi is very popular in Hawaii. Another popular Japanese-American hybrid dish is a kind of fried pork cutlet called *tonkatsu*. A number of American restaurants—including Brushstroke in New York City, Nobu in Los Angeles, and Bamboo in Portland, Oregon—offer an array of excellent Japanese food ranging from the traditional to the experimental.

Traditional Costumes In Japan, clothes are divided into two categories: Japanese clothing (*wafuku*) and Western clothing (*yofuku*). Traditional Japanese clothes are designed to reflect the season in which they are to be worn. Kimonos, robes that wrap around the body and tie with sashes and a wide *obi* (a sort of cummerbund), are the most notable example of traditional dress. Kimonos are designed to be worn only during a specific season or occasion. Lined kimonos, for example, are to be worn during the colder months and are replaced with unlined kimonos in June. Colors suitable for the summer months include light pinks, purples, greens, and grays, while seasonal flowers or scenes and classical court patterns that create a sense of coolness are also ideal for that time of year. Before World War II, both men and women wore kimonos, but Western dress became the standard everyday wear for most Japanese after the war. For the most part, kimonos are now worn by women only on special occasions, such as weddings, funerals, coming-of-age ceremonies, and festivals. Brides may choose to wear a kimono for their wedding ceremonies. Men rarely wear kimonos for any occasion, wearing a black tie as formal wear. Other traditional garments include *yukatas* (casual robes) and *happi* (short robes).

Traditional Arts and Crafts Japan has a rich tradition of art dating back thousands of years. The earliest forms of art in Japan included clay sculpture and bronze mirrors, while calligraphy and painting became popular with the rise of Zen Buddhism. Garden design, screen art, and ceramics were also popular. Perhaps the best known representations of Japanese art, however, are the famous woodblock prints filled with vibrant and realistic images and dazzling colors. The tradition of creating these woodblock prints dates back to the Edo period (1603–1868). Original prints and reproductions from this era can be found in museums, homes, and restaurants across the United States.

Dances and Songs Sword dancing became popular early in Japanese culture and continues to be appreciated in Japan, where solo and mock battle dances are still performed today. Another popular form of traditional dance is fan dance, including the parasol dances performed in Kabuki theater, a traditional form of Japanese theater that involves singing, dancing, and highly stylized performances.

There are many traditional styles of music in Japan, some of which were imported from China thousands of years ago and have been adapted to suit Japanese tastes and culture. *Gagaku* is a kind of court music that originated in China and Korea. Theatrical music characterized by bamboo flutes and drums is often played for performances in Kabuki and *Nohgaku* (a form of classical Japanese musical drama). *Minyo* is a style of Japanese folk music involving singing accompanied by an instrument. The *shamisen* is a traditional Japanese instrument that resembles a guitar with three strings. The *koto* is a type of zither with thirteen strings. Many Japanese people in the late twentieth and early twenty-first centuries have eschewed traditional music in favor of popular Western music, but the old forms are still played in the country. Modern musicians like the Yoshida Brothers have introduced younger generations to traditional instruments like the shamisen with their updated musical style.

Early generations of Japanese Americans attempted to retain their cultural heritage through Japanese language schools and social clubs, where they performed traditional dances and music. These practices fell off as Japanese organizations were dismantled during World War II, a time when it was considered dangerous to stress one's Japanese heritage. More recently, Japanese Americans have revived some of the old traditions. Taiko drum performances are an example of Japanese music that is still being performed by Japanese Americans. Taiko drums are drums in a variety of shapes and sizes that are played with a stick. In Japan, the taiko was historically used to motivate soldiers before battle or for military marches. Although taiko drum performances have increased in popularity in the twenty-first century, the first taiko group in the United States, the San Francisco Taiko Dojo, formed in 1968.

Holidays The New Year (*shogatsu*) is the most important holiday in Japan. For centuries Japan used the same calendar as China and Korea, but in 1873 the country switched to the Gregorian calendar. The Japanese now celebrate the New Year during the first three days in January. In Japanese American communities, many still celebrate the New Year in very much the same manner as the Issei, following the customs of Meiji-era Japan. The New Year is a time for debts to be paid and quarrels to be settled. It is an occasion when houses are cleaned, baths are taken, and new clothes are worn. On New Year's Eve, many Japanese Americans go to temples and shrines. Shinto shrines are especially popular. Just inside the red tori gate, worshippers wash their hands and rinse their mouths with water from a special basin. A priest then cleanses the worshippers by sprinkling them with water from a leafy branch and blesses them by waving a wand of white prayer papers. The worshippers sip sake, receive amulets (charms), and give money.

In Japanese American homes where the traditions are observed, offerings for the New Year are set in various places of honor around the house. The offerings consist of two *mochi* (rice cakes), a strip of *konbu* (seaweed), and citrus arranged on "happiness paper" depicting one or all of the seven gods of good luck. The offerings symbolize harmony and happiness from generation to generation.

At breakfast on New Year's Day, many Japanese Americans eat *ozoni* (toasted mochi) in a broth with other ingredients, such as vegetables and fish. Mochi is eaten for strength and family cohesiveness. Sometimes children compete with each other to see if they can eat mochi equal to the number of their years.

Friends, neighbors, and family members visit one another on New Year's Day. Special foods served on this day include *kuromame* (black beans), *kazunoko* (herring eggs), *konbumaki* (seaweed roll), *kinton* (mashed sweet potato and chestnut), and *kamaboko* (fish cakes). Sushi, sashimi, cooked red snapper, and *nishime* (vegetables cooked in stock) are commonly provided for guests. At many celebrations, the Japanese cheer of "*Banzai! Banzai! Banzai!*" rings out. The salute, which originated around 200 BCE, means "10,000 years." In the early twenty-first century, the Japanese tradition of bringing a gift of fruit or vegetables for the host at a dinner party is still common among Japanese Americans, especially when the host is also Japanese American.

Health-care Issues and Practices Japanese Americans are generally healthier than other Americans. A 1990 study conducted at the University of Hawaii found that the Issei and Nisei had lower rates of heart disease and breast and lung cancer than their white counterparts. However, the increased adoption of a Western diet among Japanese Americans and the resulting increase in saturated fat consumption has resulted in a higher risk for those conditions in third and fourth generations. According to a 2007 needs assessment published by the University of Maryland School of Public Health, Japanese Americans are increasingly at risk for stomach and colon cancers, possibly connected to increased consumption of sugar and fat. As a group, Japanese men have higher rates of liver cancer than the overall American population, due to significant alcohol consumption. They are also at greater risk for type two diabetes. Japanese Americans have the lowest infant death rate of any ethnic group in the United States. In 1986, 86 percent of babies born to Japanese American mothers were born to women who received early prenatal care, compared to 79 percent for Caucasians and 76 percent for all races. Relatively few Japanese American infants had low birth weight, and only 8 percent of Japanese American births were preterm, compared to 10 percent for all races. Asian Americans have fewer birth defects

SHIKATA GA NAI: JAPANESE PROVERB

A common phrase that originated in internment camps but continues to be used is *Shikata ga nai* ("It cannot be helped now"). Initially this saying was meant to encourage people to look forward instead of focusing on loss and suffering. The phrase has come to have a broader meaning of, "Focus on the things that can be changed rather than those that cannot." The underlying message is one of revitalization rather than debilitation.

than Native Americans, Caucasians, and African Americans, but more than Hispanic Americans. In 1987 less than 1 percent of recorded drug abusers in the United States were Asian Americans.

According to the 2010 United States Census, the life expectancy for Japanese Americans is 84.5 years. In a 2007 report published by the Centers for Disease Control and Prevention (CDC), only 5 percent of the Japanese American population reported fair to poor health, with little difference between men and women. According to the same report, only one in ten Japanese American adults was without health insurance, as compared to 16.7 percent of the general U.S. population. Japanese Americans were also shown to be the least likely ethnic group in the United States to delay or not receive medical care due to cost. Approximately 96 percent had been to the dentist within the previous five years, and less than 4 percent of adults were obese, with one in ten considered underweight.

A 1990 University of Hawaii study found that many Japanese Americans consider mental illnesses to be shameful, tending to use mental health services only as a last resort with severe disorders, such as schizophrenia. Similarly, a 2007 University of Maryland needs assessment found that Japanese Americans in Maryland underused mental health services in comparison to other ethnic groups, preferring to seek help from family members or close friends, rather than from mental health professionals. A number of Japanese Americans have entered the psychiatric field, however, perhaps indicating a growing acceptance of professional mental health care.

FAMILY AND COMMUNITY LIFE

Communalism did not develop in Japanese communities as it did among populations in China. In the fifteenth and sixteenth centuries, Japan's land-based lineage communities gave way to downsized extended families. Only the eldest son and his family remained in the parental household. Other sons established separate

EARLY JAPANESE LANGUAGE SCHOOLS

Concerned that living abroad would cause their offspring to lose connection to their homeland, early immigrants from Japan established programs in the United States to teach Japanese language and culture. The first of these schools opened in Hawaii in 1890. By 1912 there were eighteen Japanese schools in California. Soon, however, class and religious divisions emerged within the immigrant community in response to the direction of the schools. The school's organizers tended to be traditional Buddhist groups who believed in maintaining their cultural differences and supporting the labor movement, while Japanese American converts to Christianity favored assimilation and wanted to avoid controversy. In the lead-up to World War II, the schools were criticized by some in the U.S. government as being anti-American, a few even going so far as to call them hatching places for treasonous plots that promoted loyalty to the Japanese emperor. The U.S. government eventually closed all Japanese language schools in California and Hawaii during the war. Although the schools were later revived, enrollment has never again reached prewar levels.

"branch" households when they married. A national consciousness arose in Japan, whereas in China the primary allegiance remained to the clan-based village or community. Thus, Japanese immigrants were prepared to form nuclear families and rear children in the United States without the support of a larger extended family or community, much in the way modern American families have evolved.

The "picture bride" system, which brought several thousand Japanese women to the United States in the early twentieth century, was fraught with misrepresentation. Often old photographs were used to hide the age of a prospective bride, and the men were sometimes photographed in borrowed suits. The system led to a degree of disillusionment and incompatibility in marriages. Once in the United States, the women were trapped, unable to return to Japan. Many Issei women were employed outside the household, working for wages or shared labor on family farms in California and other states on the mainland. Two-income families found it easier to rent or purchase land, at least until 1920, when new laws made land ownership illegal for Japanese Americans in California.

By 1930, 52 percent of Japanese Americans were second generation. In the years preceding World War II, most Nisei were children and young people, many of them attempting to adapt to their adopted country in spite of the troubled lives of their parents.

Gender Roles In Japan traditional gender roles have been slow to change. Studies published in 1999 and 2001 showed that wives in Japan were still expected to be homemakers, while husbands were still the main providers. Most wives call their husbands *shujin* ("main person"), and husbands call their wives *kanai* ("inside the home"). Women who go against these expectations face social ostracism and discrimination in the workplace. The Japanese Educational Foundations Law, passed in 1947, guarantees equal access to education, but hiring, promotion, and pay remain unequal. In 2002 Japanese women were found to be making 34 percent less than their male counterparts.

Japanese American women seem to fare better when it comes to gender equality, although the percentage of Japanese American women not working outside the home might still be considered high when compared to other ethnic groups. According to the 2010 United States Census, approximately 52 percent of Japanese American women were not employed outside the home. Of the women who were employed, 48.5 percent were in the sectors of management, business, science, or art. Another 13.6 percent were in the service industry, and 27 percent were in sales or office work.

Education With the strong encouragement of their parents, most of the Nisei obtained high school and, in many cases, university educations, leaving their parents' family farms or small businesses in search of greater opportunities. Discrimination against Japanese Americans, coupled with the shortage of jobs during the Great Depression, thwarted many Nisei dreams. The next generation of Japanese Americans, however, fared far better, with more than three-fourths graduating from high school and close to half receiving college and graduate degrees. The 2010 United States Census showed the high school graduation rate at 96 percent for Japanese American men and 94.3 percent for Japanese American women, while 49.8 percent of Japanese American men and 43.7 percent of Japanese American women attained a college degree or higher. Of those Japanese Americans with college degrees or higher, 12.6 percent pursued a professional degree or a degree in science, management, or administration, while another 22.8 percent pursued degrees in education, health care, or social services.

Courtship and Weddings Japanese weddings are traditionally small, private ceremonies during which the bride and groom perform elaborate rituals in the presence of their families. One such ritual involves sharing sake. First the groom and then the bride sip from three sake cups. They then share the cups with parents and other family members to symbolize the union of the two families. Shinto ceremonies are fairly standard among the Japanese, although some prefer weddings that observe Buddhist customs. Among Japanese Americans, some couples combine Eastern and Western traditions by including Christian observances. Cash gifts are expected at most Japanese weddings, and they are to be given in envelopes called *shugi-bukuro*. The amount of the cash gift will sometimes be specified on the invitation and generally has to do with the invitee's relationship to the couple. At a wedding dinner, a whole red snapper is displayed at the head table. The fish represents happiness and must be served whole, as cutting it would mean eliminating happiness.

Relations with Other Americans Economic competition between the United States and Japan in the 1980s resulted in the rise of anti-Japanese sentiment in popular culture. In movies like *Back to the Future II* and in the novels of popular writers like Michael Crichton and James Michener, Japanese businessmen were depicted as demanding overlords and conniving, unethical schemers.

Many white Americans, particularly well-educated white Americans, perceive Japanese Americans as a "model minority group" because of their reputation for hard work and advanced education. While this stereotype is not necessarily a negative one, many Japanese Americans feel that they are pigeonholed as good workers but are not seen as aggressive enough to occupy top managerial and leadership positions.

EMPLOYMENT AND ECONOMIC CONDITIONS

The Issei, who came to the United States in the late 1800s and early twentieth century, worked mostly on the West Coast as seasonal agricultural workers, as railroad workers, and in canneries. Working conditions were generally abysmal, and the Issei were barred from the better factory and office jobs, due largely to racism and pressure from organized labor. As a result, many Issei became small-scale vegetable farmers or created small businesses, such as hotels and restaurants, to serve others in their ethnic group. The term "ethnic economy" is often used to describe these activities of pre-World War II Japanese Americans. The Issei were remarkably successful in both these endeavors for several reasons. Small businessmen, farmers, their families, and their work associates toiled an incredible number of hours and saved much of what was earned. The Issei community was also well organized, and small businesses and farms could rely upon their tightly knit ethnic group for capital, labor, and business opportunities. This ethnic solidarity paid off economically for the Issei. By the eve of World War II, 75 percent of Seattle's Japanese residents were involved in small business, and Japanese farmers were responsible for the production of the majority of vegetables in Los Angeles County.

The economic success of some Japanese Americans eventually led to a substantial backlash, which was spearheaded by elements of the majority population who felt their livelihoods threatened. Unions were consistently anti-Japanese, and California agricultural groups assumed leadership roles in the land limitation laws referred to as Alien Land Laws. The state of California in 1913 enacted legislation stating that people not eligible for citizenship, as well as corporations owned by such people, had to comply with the land ownership provisions of the U.S.-Japan

An 8-year-old Japanese American girl practices a piano lesson at home in Long Beach, California. KAYTE DEIOMA / PHOTOEDIT

Treaty of 1911. Because that treaty made no mention of the right of Japanese people on American soil to own land, the legislation held that no such right existed. Further restrictions were passed in 1920 that forbade the sale or lease of land to a noncitizen. In addition, noncitizen parents of citizens could not hold land in guardianship for their children, and any land considered to be illegally held or owned could be confiscated by the state of California. Between 1920 and 1925, the number of acres owned by the Issei declined from 74,769 to 41,898, while the acreage leased plummeted from 192,150 to 76,797.

No event in history has resulted in more economic change for Japanese Americans than World War II. Before the war, Japanese Americans constituted mostly a self-contained ethnic economy. The internment of Japanese Americans and societal changes in attitudes toward the Japanese destroyed much of their prewar economic status. Many Japanese American farmers, because of the internment, either sold their land or were unable to lease their prewar holdings again. Likewise, many Japanese American family businesses were sold or closed. A comparison of prewar and postwar economic statistics in Los Angeles and Seattle illustrates these changes. Prior to World War II, Japanese Americans in Seattle operated 206 hotels, 140 grocery stores, 94 cleaning establishments, 64 market stands, and 57 wholesale produce houses. After World War II, only a handful of these businesses remained. In Los Angeles, 72 percent of Japanese Americans were employed in family enterprises before World War II. By the late 1940s, only 17.5 percent of Japanese Americans earned their livelihood through family businesses.

While their internment forced these economic changes upon Japanese Americans, other societal factors also contributed to the end of the Japanese American ethnic economy. The prewar racial prejudice against Japanese Americans declined substantially in the late 1940s and 1950s. Japan no longer constituted a geopolitical threat, and many Americans were becoming more sympathetic about the issue of minority rights. As a result, the large majority of Japanese Americans in the postwar years began assimilating into the larger economy.

Japanese Americans today are well represented in professional occupations, including medicine, law, science, business, and technology. Japanese Americans also have higher levels of education and comparable to slightly higher incomes on average than the majority population in the United States. Studies documenting the absence of Asian Americans from top corporate management and public sector administrative positions provide some evidence that there remains a "glass ceiling" for Japanese Americans in the larger economy. Still, Japanese Americans enjoy a higher economic position and greater socioeconomic mobility now than at any other time in American history.

According to the 2010 United States Census, 52 percent of Japanese Americans held managerial positions in the business, finance, or professional sectors. The annual average income for Japanese Americans was reported as $91,000 per household. At the time of the census, only 3.6 percent of Japanese American men were unemployed, far below the national average of just under 9 percent.

POLITICS AND GOVERNMENT

In February 1903, 500 Japanese and 200 Mexican farmworkers in Oxnard, California, formed the Japanese Mexican Labor Association, the first farmworkers union in California. The union called a strike for better wages and working conditions, and membership soon grew to include 1,200 workers, or about 90 percent of the Mexican and Japanese agricultural workers in the area. On March 23 a striker was shot and killed and two were wounded in a confrontation with the Western Agricultural Contracting Company, the region's major labor contractor. Negotiations led to a settlement by the end of March. Despite such effective organization and leadership, the American Federation of Labor denied the Japanese Mexican Labor Association a charter.

In Hawaii there were twenty strikes by Japanese plantation workers in 1900 alone. In 1908 Japanese agricultural laborers from the major plantations in Oahu formed the Higher Wage Association, and in 1909 the group asked for a wage increase. In May of that year, 7,000 Japanese workers struck all major plantations on the island of Oahu. The strike lasted four months. The planters branded the strike as the work of agitators and evicted the strikers from plantation-owned homes. By June, more than 5,000 displaced Japanese were living in makeshift shelters in downtown Honolulu. The leaders of the Higher Wage Association were arrested, jailed, and tried on conspiracy charges.

In 1920 Japanese workers struck Hawaiian plantations for higher wages, better working conditions, and an end to discriminatory wages based on race and ethnic background. The strike lasted six months and cost the plantation owners an estimated $11.5 million. The union viewed their cause as part of the American way, but Hawaii's ruling class—the plantation owners and their allies—called the strike anti-American and painted it as a movement to take control of the sugar industry. The planters evicted more than 12,000 workers from their homes. Many deaths resulted from unsanitary conditions in the tent cities that arose.

After World War II, many Japanese Americans left internment camps or the armed services and immediately went to work to secure their rights and redress the wrongs committed against them. In Hawaii, Daniel K. Inouye, a decorated veteran, entered politics, serving in the U.S. House of Representatives from 1959 until 1962, when he was elected to the U.S. Senate. Along with three other Japanese American legislators (Senator Spark M. Matsunaga of Hawaii and Representatives Norman Y. Mineta and Robert T. Matsui of California), Inouye sponsored a bill that would require the U.S. government to apologize for the wartime internment of Japanese Americans and offer tax-free cash payments of $20,000 to each of the 60,000 victims still living. Congress enacted the bill in 1988, but because the necessary funds were not appropriated, a second bill had to be passed in 1989. The Reparations Act of 1989 designated $1.6 billion in payment to the victims of the internment and their descendants.

According to a 2009 National Asian American Survey, 82 percent of Japanese Americans reported they were "more likely to vote" than not. The majority (60 percent) identified as Democrats. In 2003 the Japanese American Political Action Committee (JAAMPAC) registered with the Federal Election Commission. JAAMPAC stated their goals as supporting Japanese American candidates running for office, promoting legislation that is helpful to Japanese Americans, and opposing candidates and legislation that is not favorable to the Japanese American community.

Japanese Americans have participated in U.S. politics on all levels. On the national level, Senator Daniel Inouye (D-HI) served in the U.S. Senate from 1963 until his death in 2012, and Senator Mazie Hirono (D-HI) took office in 2013. Several Japanese Americans have served or are currently serving in the U.S. House of Representatives, including Mike Honda (D-CA), Patricia Saiki (R-HI), Bob Matsui (D-CA), and, perhaps most notably, Patsy Mink (D-HI), who served twelve terms and authored the Title IX Amendment of the Higher Education Act. At least two Japanese Americans have served as presidential cabinet members. Norman Mineta was the secretary of transportation for George W. Bush, and Eric Shinseki, a retired four-star general, began serving as President Barack Obama's secretary of veterans affairs in 2009.

Japanese Americans have a history of promoting the civil and human rights of other minority groups.

In 1954 the JACL actively supported ending school segregation during the landmark Supreme Court case Brown v. Board of Education. In 1965 the JACL supported immigration reform. Japanese American organizations today are active in promoting anti-hate crime legislation and in opposing legislation that discriminates against immigrants.

NOTABLE INDIVIDUALS

Academia Eiichiro Azuma is a Japanese American historian and academic with an endowed chair at the University of Pennsylvania, where he has taught since 2001. Azuma has published many articles and books, including the award-winning work *Between Two Empires: Race, History and Transnationalism in Japanese America*, published in 2005.

Harry H. L. Kitano (1926–2002) was a professor of sociology at the University of California, Los Angeles (UCLA), where he held an endowed chair in Japanese American studies. Born in San Francisco to Japanese immigrants, Kitano spent several years during World War II living in a Utah internment camp with his family.

Mari Matsuda, born in Hawaii in 1956, is a lawyer, an activist, and an academic. In 1998 the UCLA School of Law granted Matsuda tenure, making her the first tenured female Asian American law professor in the United States. She went on to teach at Stanford Law School and Georgetown University Law Center before returning to Hawaii, where she currently teaches at the William S. Richardson School of Law.

Ronald Takaki (1939–2009), a second-generation Japanese American born in Hawaii, was a historian, an ethnographer, and an academic. He taught the first black history class offered at UCLA and went on to teach for many years at the University of California, Berkeley, as a professor of Asian American studies. Takaki authored several well-known books on the subjects of race and racial stereotypes in American history, including *Strangers from a Different Shore*, published in 1989.

Architecture Minoru Yamasaki (1912–1986) was one of the most prominent architects of the twentieth century, best known for his design of the Twin Towers of the World Trade Center in New York City.

Art Isamu Noguchi (1904–1988) was perhaps the most celebrated Japanese American sculptor of the twentieth century. His work extended beyond sculptures to include significant architectural projects and stage designs, including designs for the Martha Graham Dance Company.

Ruth Asawa (1926–) is a Nisei artist known for her wire sculptures and bronzed "baker's clay" sculptures. Asawa cofounded the Ruth Asawa San Francisco School of the Arts (SOTA), a public, tuition-free visual and performing arts high school.

Isami Doi (1903–1965) was a painter and printmaker who exhibited his works widely. Born and raised in Hawaii, Doi studied art at the University of Hawaii, at Columbia University, and in Paris.

Toyo Miyatake (1895–1979) was an accomplished photographer. Born in Japan, Miyatake immigrated to the United States as a child and eventually settled in the Little Tokyo section of Los Angeles, where he opened a photography studio and was considered a leader in the community. Miyatake's most famous photographs depict the lives of Japanese Americans living in the Manzanar, California, internment camp during World War II, where Miyatake and his family were also interned.

Yoko Ono (1933–), born in Japan and raised mostly in that country, is internationally known as the widow of John Lennon, founding member of the Beatles. Ono is an artist, musician, filmmaker, and activist.

Government John Fujio Aiso (1909–1987) was director of the Military Intelligence Service Language School (MISLS), which trained about 6,000 persons in the Japanese language for use in intelligence work during World War II. In 1953 Aiso became the first Japanese American judge.

George Ryoichi Ariyoshi (1926–) served as governor of Hawaii from 1974 to 1986. He was the first Japanese American lieutenant governor and governor in U.S. history.

Samuel Ichiye Hayakawa (1906–1992) was an accomplished academic and political figure. He served from 1968 to 1973 as president of San Francisco State College, where he gained national attention for his strong stand against student protesters. Hayakawa, a Republican, went on to serve as a U.S. senator representing California from 1977 to 1983.

Daniel K. Inouye (1924–2012) of Hawaii was the first Nisei elected to U.S. Congress. A Democrat, he served in the House of Representatives from 1959 to 1963. He was elected to the U.S. Senate in 1962, where he remained until his death in 2012. Inouye was also a decorated veteran who served in World War II.

Doris Matsui (1944–) is the U.S. Representative for California's sixth congressional district, an office she assumed in 2005 as a member of the Democratic Party. Matsui was born on an internment camp in Arizona and was raised in California.

Kenneth P. Moritsugu (1945–) is a physician and public health administrator. A rear admiral in the United States Public Health Service Commissioned Corps (PHSCC), Moritsugu served as Surgeon General of the United States from 2006 until 2007.

Clarence Takeya Arai (1901–1964) was a key figure in the founding of JACL. Arai, a lawyer, was active in Republican politics in the state of Washington in the 1930s. He and his family were forced to relocate to an internment camp in Minidoka, Idaho, during World War II.

Journalism James Hattori, a native of California, is a television correspondent who has worked for CBS News and CNN.

Harvey Saburo Hayashi (1866–1943), born and raised in Japan, was a pioneering Issei in the rural Japanese American community of Kona, Hawaii, where he served as both physician and newspaper editor. In 1897 he founded the newspaper the *Kona Hankyo*, which would be published for the next forty years. Hayashi also established a Japanese cemetery and a Japanese language school in Kona.

William Kumpai Hosokawa (1915–2007), a Nisei born in Seattle, was a prominent journalist, editor, and author who worked at the *Denver Post* and the *Rocky Mountain News*. Hosokawa published a number of books about the experiences of Japanese Americans, many of which were inspired by the time Hosokawa spent interned at the Heart Mountain Relocation Center in Wyoming during World War II. For more than forty years following the war, Hosokawa published a column in the *Pacific Citizen* newspaper that most often focused on his personal observations of the internment of Japanese Americans.

Michiko Kakutani (1955–) is a Pulitzer Prize–winning journalist who writes book reviews for the *New York Times*. She is considered one of the leading literary critics in the United States.

Ken Kashiwahara (1940–) was one of the first Asian American journalists to work in network television. Before his retirement in 1998, Kashiwahara spent twenty-five years covering major national and international news as a correspondent with ABC News.

Sachi Koto (1951–) is a television journalist who worked as a CNN news anchor for fourteen years.

James Yoshinori Sakamoto (1903–1955) began the first Nisei newspaper, the *Japanese American Courier*, in 1928. He was a strong supporter of the JACL from its inception and served as the organization's national president from 1936 to 1938.

Law Lance Allan Ito (1950–) is a highly respected superior court judge in Los Angeles who gained national prominence when he presided over the O. J. Simpson murder trial in 1995.

Literature Velina Hasu Houston (1957–) is an award-winning playwright, essayist, poet, and screenwriter. She is best known for her plays and poetry exploring the experiences of Japanese American women. Houston's plays include *Asa Ga Kimashita*, *American Dreams*, and *Tea*.

Atsushi Iwamatsu (1908–1994)—better known by his pseudonym, Taro Yashima—was a successful author and illustrator of children's books. Several of the books he published in the 1950s and 1960s were runners-up for the Caldecott Medal, one of the most prestigious children's book awards in the United States.

Tooru J. Kanagawa (1906–2002) was a journalist and decorated veteran of the 442nd Regimental Combat Team, a fighting unit of the U.S. military during World War II comprised entirely of Japanese Americans who

volunteered for service. Kanagawa published his first novel, *Sushi and Sourdough*, at the age of 83.

Toshio Mori (1910–1980) was one of the earliest Japanese Americans to publish a book of fiction. Most of his short stories and novels, many of which remain unpublished, feature Japanese American characters.

Julie Otsuka (1962–) is a celebrated author best known for her historical fiction novels that explore the lives of Japanese Americans. Her 2011 novel *The Buddha in the Attic* won the 2012 PEN/Faulkner Award for Fiction and was a 2011 National Book Award finalist.

Music Hiroshima is a pop music group composed almost entirely of third-generation Japanese American musicians. The band, which reached the height of its popularity in the mid-1980s and 1990s, is best known for blending traditional Japanese instruments into popular Western music.

James Iha (1968–) is a rock musician who cofounded and served as the guitarist for the 1990s alternative rock band the Smashing Pumpkins. Iha has since played with other alternative rock groups, including A Perfect Circle.

Midori Goto (1971–) is a celebrated violinist who has performed with many of the world's greatest orchestras. She made her debut at the age of eleven, playing with the New York Philharmonic symphony orchestra. In 2001 Goto won the Avery Fisher Prize, a prestigious award given to American musicians for outstanding achievement in classical music. In 2007 Goto was named a United Nations Messenger of Peace.

Seiji Ozawa (1935–) is a conductor who served as music director for the Toronto Symphony Orchestra and the San Francisco Symphony Orchestra in the 1960s and early 1970s. In 1973 Ozawa became music director of the Boston Symphony Orchestra, a position he held for twenty-nine years.

Science Leo Esaki (1925–) is a Nobel Prize–winning physicist who invented the tunnel diode, a type of semiconductor diode. Esaki immigrated to the United States in 1960 to work for the International Business Machines Corporation (IBM).

Makio Murayama (born in 1912) was a biochemist best known for his groundbreaking research on sickle cell anemia.

Hideyo Noguchi (1876–1928) was a microbiologist who devoted his career to fighting diseases, including bubonic plague, syphilis, Rocky Mountain spotted fever, and yellow fever. Noguchi is credited with discovering the agent of syphilis as the cause of progressive paralytic disease in 1911.

Jokichi Takamine (1854–1922) was a chemist who developed a starch-digesting enzyme (called *Takadiastase*) that was useful in medicines. In 1901 Takamine isolated adrenaline from the suprarenal gland and was the first scientist to discover gland hormones in pure form.

Gordon Hisashi Sato (1927–) is a Japanese American cell biologist who has received accolades for his work in biotechnology. In 1984 he was elected to the United States National Academy of Sciences (NAS). Sato is also the founder of the Manzanar Project, named after the internment camp where he and his family were confined during World War II. The organization attempts to use biotechnology to attack such issues as poverty and global warming.

Ryuzo Yanagimachi (1928–) is a Japanese-born scientist who is considered a pioneer in the fields of in vitro fertilization and cloning. Yanagimachi was elected to the NAS in 2001.

Yoichiro Nambu (1921–) is a renowned physicist who is considered one of the founders of string theory. Born in Tokyo, Nambu moved to the United States in 1952. In 2008 he was awarded a half share of the Nobel Prize in Physics.

Osamu Shimomura (1928–) is a prominent organic chemist and marine biologist. In 2008 he won the Nobel Prize in Chemistry for his discovery of green fluorescent protein, a major breakthrough that enabled scientists to study the insides of living cells. Born in Kyoto and educated in Japan, Shimomura moved to the United States in 1960 to conduct research at Princeton University.

Sports Bryan Ezra Tsumoru Clay (1980–) is a decathlete whose mother was a first-generation Japanese American. Clay won the gold medal in the 2008 Summer Olympics for the decathlon and won the silver medal in the 2004 Summer Olympics.

Hideo Nomo (1968–) is a former Major League Baseball (MLB) player who pitched for the Los Angeles Dodgers and the Kansas City Royals, among other teams. In 1995 Nomo became the first Japanese-born Japanese major league baseball player to permanently relocate to play in the United States.

Kristi Yamaguchi (1971–) is a former professional figure skater who won numerous awards during her career, including the women's gold medal in figure skating at the 1992 Winter Olympics. Yamaguchi is a fourth-generation Japanese American whose grandparents were interned during World War II. In 2005 Yamaguchi was inducted into the U.S. Olympic Hall of Fame.

Stage and Screen Philip Kan Gotanda (1951–), a prominent playwright and filmmaker, is best known for his musicals and plays depicting the Asian American experience. His plays include *The Avocado Kid*, *The Wash*, *Song for a Nisei Fisherman*, *Bullet Headed Birds*, *The Dream of Kitamura*, *Yohen*, *Yankee Dawg You Die*, and *American Tattoo*.

Sessue Hayakawa (1890–1973) was a leading figure in silent film and is widely considered to be the first Asian American movie star. Born and raised in Japan, Hayakawa lived in the United States intermittently throughout his movie career. After an absence of many years, he returned to Hollywood in the

Japanese American Iciro Suzuki of the Seattle Mariners with Derek Jeter of the New York Yankees. Both American League All-Stars look on during introductions before the 2009 MLB All-Star Game at Busch Stadium in 2009 in St. Louis, Missouri. DILIP VISHWANAT / GETTY IMAGES

1950s and was nominated for an Academy Award for his acting in the film *The Bridge on the River Kwai*.

Makoto (Mako) Iwamatsu (1933–2006) was the founding artistic director of the East West Players, an Asian American theater company in Los Angeles. He was nominated for an Academy Award for his supporting role as a Chinese coolie in the 1966 film *The Sand Pebbles*.

Nobu McCarthy (1934–2002) was a Japanese Canadian film actress, stage director, and model. She began acting in the 1950s and 1960s, depicting mostly stereotypical Asian characters, such as geisha girls and "lotus blossoms." Her later film roles would prove to be more rounded. McCarthy was also a member of the East West Players in Los Angeles, where she served as artistic director during the late 1980s and early 1990s.

Jeff Matsuda (1970–) is an award-winning concept artist, comics artist, and animator.

Noriyuki "Pat" Morita (1932–2005) was a popular television and film actor in the 1980s. He is best known for starring as the kind-hearted karate instructor in the 1984 film *The Karate Kid*, for which he was nominated for an Academy Award for best supporting actor.

Sono Osato (1919–) is a noted dancer who danced with the American Ballet Theatre and the Ballets Russes. Osato also served as the principal dancer in several Broadway musicals and worked briefly as an actress in film and television.

Chiyoko (Pat) Suzuki (1930–), a Japanese American singer and actress, became the first Nisei to star in a Broadway musical when she performed in *Flower Drum Song* in 1958.

Miyoshi Umeki (1929–2007) was the first Asian performer to win an Academy Award, which she received for her supporting role in the 1957 movie *Sayonara*.

MEDIA

PRINT

The Hawaii Hochi

A bilingual newspaper published and sold in Hawaii. The publication is intended to keep Japanese Americans who are not fluent in English informed about the United States. In 2012 the paper celebrated 100 years in operation.

Mamoru Tanji
917 Kokea Street
Honolulu, Hawaii 96817
Phone: (808) 845-2255
Fax: (808) 847-7215
URL: www.hawaiihoichi.com

The Rafu Shimpo

A bilingual newspaper based out of Los Angeles. It is the main source of Japanese American news in southern California.

Yoko Otsuki, Executive Assistant
701 East Third Street
Suite 130
Los Angeles, California 90013
Phone: (213) 629-2231
Fax: (213) 687-0737
URL: www.rafu.com

RADIO

Bible Broadcasting Network (BBN) Japanese Radio

A conservative Christian station that airs Bible teachings in Japanese.

11530 Carmel Commons Boulevard
Charlotte, North Carolina 28226
Phone: (704) 523-5555
URL: www.bbnradio.org

Japan-A-Radio

Plays Japanese pop and anime programs.

URL: www.japanaradio.com

KALI-FM (106.3 FM)

A Vietnamese radio station that airs a Japanese-language news broadcast every weekday from 7 a.m. to 9 a.m. The station serves the community of Santa Ana, California.

20300 South Vermont Avenue
Suite 200
Torrance, California 90502
Phone: (877) 595-3424
URL: www.kalifm.com

ORGANIZATIONS AND ASSOCIATIONS

Japan-America Society of the State of Washington (JASSW)

A nonprofit organization that seeks to promote mutual understanding and friendship between the people of Japan and Washington by providing a forum for the exchange of ideas and information.

Dale Watanabe, Executive Director
1511 Third Avenue
Suite 805
Seattle, Washington 98101
Phone: (206) 374-0108
Fax: (206) 374-0175
Email: jassw@jassw.org
URL: www.jassw.org

Japanese American Citizens League (JACL)

An educational, civil, and human rights organization founded in 1929 with 115 chapters and 25,000 members.

Priscilla Ouchida, National Executive Director
1765 Sutter Street
San Francisco, California 94115
Phone: (415) 921-5225
Fax: (415) 931-4671
Email: jacl@jacl.org
URL: www.jacl.org

Japan Hour Broadcasting

Founded in 1974, it produces radio and television programs in Japanese for Japanese residents in the United States and English-language programs on Japan to promote American understanding of Japan and U.S.-Japanese relations.

Raymond Otami, Executive Director
151-23 34th Avenue
Flushing, New York 11354
URL: http://channelnewsasia.com

Japan Society (JS)

A leading American organization committed to deepening mutual understanding between the United States and Japan in a global context.

Motoatsu Sakurai, President
333 East 47th Street
New York, New York 10017
Phone: (212) 832-1155
Fax: (212) 755-6752
URL: www.japansociety.org

The Nippon Club

The only Japanese social club in the United States. Based in New York City, the club seeks to contribute to the continued business and cultural exchange between Japan and the United States by hosting events, workshops, and cultural classes.

Tsutomu Karino, Executive Director
145 West 57th Street
New York, New York 10019
Phone: (212) 581-2223
Fax: (212) 581-3332
Email: info@nipponclub.org
URL: www.nipponclub.org

MUSEUMS AND RESEARCH CENTERS

Asian American Curriculum Project (formerly the Japanese American Curriculum Project)

A nonprofit organization that seeks to bring a wide variety of Asian American curriculum materials, including Japanese American resources, to schools, libraries, and the general public.

529 East 3rd Avenue
San Mateo, California 94401
Phone: (650) 375-8286
Fax: (650) 375-8797
Email: aacp@asianamericanbooks.com
URL: www.asianamericanbooks.com

Japanese American Cultural & Community Center (JACCC)

A performing and visual arts center founded in 1980.

244 South San Pedro Street
Suite 505
Los Angeles, California 90012
Phone: (213) 628-2725
Fax: (213) 617-8576
Email: jaccc@ltsc.org
URL: www.jaccc.org

Japanese American National Museum

The first national museum dedicated to preserving and sharing the history of Japanese Americans.

100 North Central Avenue
Los Angeles, California 90012
Phone: (213) 625-0414
Fax: (213) 625-1770
Email: hnrc@janm.org
URL: www.janm.org

Japanese American Society for Legal Studies

Established in 1964, this organization published an annual periodical on law in Japan. After the twenty-seventh volume was issued in 2002, the American branch was dissolved. The Japanese branch continues to operate.

Professor Kichimoto Asaka
University of Tokyo Faculty of Law 7-3-1 Hongo
Bunkyo-ku
Tokyo 113-0033 Japan
Email: kichi@j.u-tokyo.ac.jp>
URL: /www.kichi.j.u-tokyo.ac.jp/jasls.html

U.S.-Japan Culture Center (USJCC)

Seeks to promote mutual understanding between the United States and Japan by helping scholars, government officials, businesspersons, and the public increase their knowledge of relations between the two countries.

Mikio Kanda, Executive Director
5416 Nevada Avenue NW
Washington, D.C. 20015
Phone: (202) 342-5800
Fax: (202) 342-5802
Email: info@usjpcc.com
URL: www.usjpcc.com

SOURCES FOR ADDITIONAL STUDY

Akiba, Daisuke. *Japanese Americans*. New York: Sage Publications, 2005.

Eiichiro, Azuma. *Between Two Empires: Race, History and Transnationalism in Japanese America*. New York: Oxford Press, 2004.

Hane, Mikiso. *Modern Japan: a Historical Survey*. Boulder, CO: Westview Press, 2013.

Hosokawa, Bill. *Nisei: The Quiet Americans*. New York: William Morrow, 1969.

Ichioka, Yuji. *Before Internment: Essays in Prewar Japanese American History*. Eds. Gordon H. Chang and Eiichiro Azuma. Palo Alto, CA: Stanford University Press, 2006.

Kingston, Jeff. *Contemporary Japan: History, Politics, and Social Change Since the 1980s*. Malden, MA: John Wiley & Sons, 2013.

Kitano, Henry H. L. *Generations and Identity: The Japanese American*. Needham Heights, MA: Ginn Press, 1993.

———. *Japanese Americans: The Evolution of a Subculture*. Cliffs, NJ: Prentice Hall, 1969.

Lyman, Stanford M. *Chinatown and Little Tokyo: Power, Conflict, and Community Among Chinese and Japanese Immigrants in America*. Millwood, NY: Associated Faculty Press, 1986.

Montero, Darrel. *Japanese Americans: Changing Patterns of Ethnic Affiliation Over Three Generations*. Boulder, CO: Westview Press, 1980.

Nakano, Mei T. *Japanese American Women: Three Generations 1890–1990*. Berkeley, CA: Mina Press, 1990.

Okihiro, Gary Y. *Common Ground: Reimagining America*. Princeton, NJ: Princeton University Press, 2001. Print.

Takahashi, Jere. *Nisei/Sansei: Shifting Japanese American Identities and Politics*. Philadelphia: Temple University Press, 1997.

Takaki, Ronald. *Double Victory: A Multi-Cultural History of America in World War II*. Boston: Little, Brown and Company, 2000.

———. *Strangers from a Different Shore: A History of Asian Americans*. Boston: Little, Brown and Company, 1998.

Jewish Americans

Jim Kamp

OVERVIEW

Jewish Americans share a common heritage and identity as passed down from generation to generation. For many Jews the binding force is Judaism, a term usually referring to the Jewish religion but sometimes used to refer to Jewish culture as well. One does not have to be religious to be Jewish; indeed, there are atheists who nonetheless consider themselves Jewish. In general, people in the United States who view themselves as Jewish by birth, conversion, or affiliation are Jewish. Over the years Jews have had a disproportionately large representation in American government, business, academia, and entertainment, despite facing significant discrimination. On the whole, however, Jews have found greater acceptance in the United States than in any other country.

Unlike many American ethnic groups, Jewish Americans do not descend from a single country or region. Although ancient Jews came from the Middle East, over the centuries many peoples have mixed together in Jewish communities throughout the world. Most Jews now consider the State of Israel to be the Jewish homeland. Located in the Middle East with an area of about 8,000 square miles (20,770 square kilometers), Israel is slightly larger than New Jersey. It is bordered to the north by Lebanon, to the east by Syria and Jordan, to the southwest by Egypt, and to the west by the Mediterranean Sea. With a population of approximately 8 million–6 million of whom are Jewish–Israel is home to about 40 percent of the world's Jews, according to estimates by the North American Jewish Data Bank. In addition, there are approximately 3.37 million people living in the West Bank and Gaza Strip.

Jewish immigrants arrived in North America as early as the seventeenth century. Between 1881 and 1924 the United States saw its largest wave of Jewish immigration. Because of the anti-Jewish sentiment in Russia following Tsar Alexander II's assassination, some 2.4 million Eastern European Jews fled to the United States. By 1920 most of them had settled in large cities in New York, New Jersey, Massachusetts, Pennsylvania, Maryland, Ohio, Michigan, Illinois, and Missouri. Further waves of Jewish immigration occurred because of unrest or persecution elsewhere in the world, such as Germany during the 1930s,

Europe after World War II, and the former Soviet Union beginning in the 1990s. More recent Jewish immigrants have tended to be less educated and more economically vulnerable than the Jewish American population as a whole.

According to the Jewish Data Bank, there were about 5.7 million Jews in 2010, or about 2 percent of the U.S. population. The "enlarged Jewish" population in the United States, which includes those who are related to Jews or whose paternal relatives are Jewish, is estimated to be more than 6.5 million. U.S. cities with more than 200,000 Jewish Americans include New York, Philadelphia, Boston, Chicago, San Francisco, Los Angeles, Washington, D.C., and Broward, Florida.

HISTORY OF THE PEOPLE

Early History Jewish history dates back four thousand years–to the time of Abraham, the biblical figure credited with introducing the belief in a single God. Abraham's monotheism marked the beginning not only of Judaism but also of Christianity and Islam, which branched from Judaism later. The Jewish holy book, the Torah—much of which makes up the first five books of the Old Testament—describes how Abraham, following God's instructions, led his family out of Mesopotamia to Canaan, later renamed Palestine, then Israel. Abraham and his descendants were called Hebrews.

For hundreds of years these tribes lived in Canaan and comprised all of Hebrew civilization. Food shortages instigated a 420-year exile in Egypt, followed by the Exodus, led by Moses, back to the "Promised Land." Social tensions and foreign invasions split the Hebrew people into several tribes over the next several centuries, including one tribe that occupied a region known as Judah, with Jerusalem as its capital. Members of this tribe became known as Jews. The Jews of Judah were captured by Babylonians in 586 BCE and exiled, but they remained faithful to their traditions and monotheistic religion. Fifty years later the Jews returned to Israel after the Persians defeated the Babylonians.

For centuries Jewish culture thrived in Palestine, until the Roman occupation beginning in 63 BCE. By 70 CE, when the Romans destroyed the Jewish

Temple in Jerusalem, Jews had begun migrating to the outer regions of the Roman Empire, including the Near East, North Africa, and southwestern, central, and eastern Europe. In 135 CE the Romans officially banned Judaism, which marked the beginning of the diaspora, or the dispersal of Jews. Forced out of Palestine, Jews in exile concentrated less on establishing a unified homeland and more on maintaining Judaism through biblical scholarship and community life.

European Jews were historically divided into two main groups: the Sephardim, Jews of Spain and Portugal, and the Ashkenazim, Jews from German-speaking countries in central and eastern Europe. Approximately 80 percent of today's Jews are considered Ashkenazi. In medieval Europe, Sephardic Jews enjoyed more freedom and cultural acceptance than the Ashkenazi Jews, who faced persecution and even expulsion from some regions. However, by the beginning of the Spanish Inquisition in 1492, Sephardic Jews in Spain faced similar oppression, violence, and expulsion. As a result, Sephardic Jews spread out to Mediterranean countries, and the majority of Ashkenazi Jews moved east to Poland, which became the center of European Jewry.

The disintegration of the Polish state in the eighteenth century disrupted community life and caused many people to migrate elsewhere. By the nineteenth century, Jews in eastern Europe were primarily split between Prussia, Austria, and Russia. The governments in these countries, however, oppressed Jews through military conscription, taxation, and expulsion. Though relatively impoverished, the four million Jews in the Pale of Settlement (a region encompassing eastern Poland and western Russia) maintained their Jewish traditions through close community life.

Everybody had something to give me for help. It wasn't a question of money, it was a question of being a human being to a human being. And in those days people were apparently that way. There were so many nice people that were trying to help us when we came to this country.

Clara Larsen in 1908, cited in *Ellis Island: An Illustrated History of the Immigrant Experience*, edited by Ivan Chermayeff et al. (New York: Macmillan, 1991).

By contrast, Jews in western Europe fared much better economically and socially after the Protestant Reformation. Northern European cities with large Protestant populations, such as London, Hamburg, and Amsterdam, increasingly opened their doors to Jews. Many western European Jews attained significant wealth and status, generally through banking and trade. By the mid-nineteenth century, however, political turmoil had brought upheaval to western European Jewish communities, prompting many to emigrate. Many Jews immigrated to the United States or attempted to return to their ancestral homeland in the Middle East.

Modern Era For centuries Jews sustained a commitment to establishing a homeland for Jews at some point. The longing to return to Zion, the hill on which Jerusalem was built, remained a vague dream until 1896, when Theodor Herzl published *The Jewish State*, which called for modern Palestine to be the home for Hebrew culture. The following year the first Zionist Congress convened in Basel, Switzerland, marking the beginning of Zionism as an official movement. By 1914 some 12,000 American Jews had become Zionists. The movement was bolstered by the 1934 publication of Rabbi Mordecai M. Kaplan's influential *Judaism as a Civilization*, which argued that Judaism as a religion reflected the totality of the Jewish people's consciousness. Kaplan asserted that, as such, Jewish culture deserved its own central location: Palestine. In the 1930s about 250,000 Jews returned to Palestine from Europe—until Britain, which had become the colonial ruler after the end of World War I, began restricting immigration in 1936.

The influx of so many Jews contributed to growing instability in Palestine. In October 1933, Arab-led riots were directed at the British government and Jewish communities. In 1936, Arab nationalists revolted against the British government and to some extent against Jewish settlers. Though this revolt was quickly quashed, it instigated major changes in the region, including Britain's endorsement of a separate Jewish state. Though Britain sought to placate local Arabs during World War II, Jewish immigration—much of it illegal—continued as much of the world was closed off to Jews escaping Europe and the Holocaust during the war. Following the war, Jewish guerilla units began fighting the severely weakened British government, culminating in a deadly bombing of the British military headquarters in Tel Aviv in July 1946.

The insurgency made it clear to Britain that a permanent, independent solution would be necessary for Palestine, and the question was referred to the newly created United Nations. In November 1947 the United Nations approved a resolution to partition Palestine into Arab and Jewish regions. When Israel declared itself a nation on May 14, 1948, President Harry Truman decided to officially recognize Israel despite a long-standing warning from the U.S. State Department that such recognition could anger oil-producing Arab countries, and despite the rapid escalation of civil war between Arab and Jewish groups.

From its very declaration of independence, Israel has endured considerable conflict with many of its Arab neighbors, erupting into international armed conflict in 1948 (Arab-Israeli War), 1967 (Six-Day War), 1973 (Yom Kippur War), 1982 (first Lebanon war), and 2006 (second Lebanon war), in addition to numerous strikes of military installations, terrorist bases, and other targets in hostile nations. Israel emerged clearly victorious in most of these conflicts, eventually expanding its territory in Palestine to include everything but the "occupied territories" of the Gaza Strip in the southwest; the West Bank, a large area in the east of the country; and the Golan Heights, on the border with Syria. Throughout its history, Israel has grappled with continued violence with Palestinians in and near these territories, which flared up with particular intensity in 1987 (the First Intifada), 2001 (the Second Intifada), and 2012 (the Gaza War). All told, thousands of Israelis have been killed in violence throughout the nation's history, along with tens of thousands of Palestinians. Though Israel has achieved peaceful relations with most of its bordering nations (except Syria and Lebanon), the quest for internal peace between it and the Palestinians remains unresolved.

Despite this, Israel has emerged as a stable, prosperous, and militarily powerful nation, with a thriving culture and bustling cities. Though its land base is quite small, it has successfully developed intensive agriculture and industry, and its desert location has made it an international leader in green energy and water conservation. It is also one of the world's leaders in start-up technology companies and research and development firms. Tourism—particularly religious tourism, for global Jews as well as Christians and followers of other faiths—is an important industry, with millions of people visiting the nation annually.

SETTLEMENT IN THE UNITED STATES

The first Jewish immigrants to settle in colonial America were twenty-three Sephardic Jews, who settled in New Amsterdam in 1654 even though they faced resistance from the Dutch authorities. In the seventeenth and eighteenth centuries, Sephardic Jews came from Spain and other Mediterranean countries as well as from England, Holland, and the Balkans, establishing themselves in cities along the eastern seaboard, including New York City; Philadelphia; Newport, Rhode Island; Charleston, South Carolina; and Savannah, Georgia. Synagogues were built in each of these cities, attracting further immigration. Jewish businessmen from these cities were supported by influential businessmen from Sephardic communities in London and Amsterdam. The number of Jews in colonial America grew slowly but steadily, so that by 1776 there were approximately 2,500 Jews in the colonies.

A wave of German and central European Jewish immigration during the mid-nineteenth century represented the first major Jewish population explosion in the United States. Challenges to the monarchies of central Europe in the 1840s caused considerable social unrest, particularly in rural villages. Wealthy Jews could afford to escape the turbulence by moving to cities such as Vienna or Berlin, but poorer Jews could not. Consequently, many chose to immigrate to the United States. While there were just 6,000 Jews in the United States in 1826, the number of Jewish Americans climbed above 50,000 by 1850 and rose to 150,000 only a decade later.

During this period Jewish Americans also began to spread westward, alongside much of the American population. By the mid-nineteenth century, there were approximately 160 Jewish communities from New York to California, with Jewish population centers in the major hubs along the trade routes from east to West. Cities such as Cleveland, Cincinnati, Chicago, and St. Louis all became centers of Jewish business, cultural, and religious life. Jewish peddlers and retailers also followed the economic growth of the cotton industry in the South and the discovery of gold in the west. Most of the Jewish immigrants from this period were young, single Germans hoping to escape unfavorable economic conditions and repressive legislation that restricted marriage. Individuals would typically immigrate with others from their community and continue their congregation in the new world.

The largest wave of Jewish immigrants to the United States were eastern European Jews who came to the United States between 1881 and 1924. During these years one-third of the Jewish population in eastern Europe emigrated because of changing political and economic conditions. The assassination of Russian Tsar Alexander II in 1881 ushered in a new era of violence and anti-Jewish sentiment. Pogroms, or massacres, by the Slavs against the Jews had occurred since the mid-seventeenth century, but the pogroms of 1881 and 1882 were particularly numerous and intense, wiping out entire villages and killing hundreds of Jews. Also, industrialization made it difficult for Jewish peddlers, merchants, and artisans to sustain themselves economically. As a result, a mass exodus of Jews from eastern Europe occurred, with approximately 90 percent bound for the United States. During the late nineteenth and early twentieth century, tens of thousands and sometimes hundreds of thousands of Jews arrived in the United States annually. The immigration of some 2.4 million eastern European Jews boosted the American Jewish population from roughly a quarter million in 1881 to 4.5 million by 1924.

Many of these eastern European Jews gravitated toward big cities in the East and Midwest. The result was that by 1920 Jews had their greatest population centers in New York City; Newark, New Jersey; Boston; Philadelphia; Baltimore; Pittsburgh; Cleveland; Detroit; Chicago; and St. Louis. Within these cities, eastern European Jews established their own communities and maintained their cultural heritage and identity much more so than the nineteenth-century German Jewish immigrants, who had been eager to assimilate into American culture.

During this period of major immigration to the United States—not only by Jews but also by other eastern and southern Europeans—conflicts began growing between the general American population and immigrant populations filling its urban neighborhoods with unfamiliar tongues and practices. Nativist concerns about immigrants stealing jobs, introducing disease, and threatening the character of the United States inflamed tensions in a country seemingly unprepared for the influx. Jewish immigrants, like Italians, Poles, and Greeks, were segregated and shut out from many professions and communities.

U.S. officials sought to relieve the tension by restricting immigration. The Immigration Restriction Act of 1924, intended to curb immigration of unskilled laborers and "undesirable" groups (specifically, those from southern and eastern Europe), decreased the annual number of Jewish immigrants from more than 100,000 to about 10,000. U.S. immigration policy remained strict, even during World War II when the need to emigrate was a matter of life and death for Jews in Nazi-controlled countries. Although some American activists tried to rescue Jews from the horrors of the Holocaust, many Jewish refugees were actively turned away by the U.S. government. At the 1938 Evian Conference, the United States, Britain, and thirty other nations discussed the emerging Jewish refugee problem in Europe, but the United States and Britain would not agree to accept substantial numbers of refugees, and the conference was considered a failure. The U.S. attitude was epitomized by the 1939 refusal to allow the *St. Louis*, a ship carrying nine hundred passengers—mostly Jewish refugees from Germany—to land in Florida after it had been refused admission to Cuba. The ship was forced to return to Europe, where a third of its passengers are believed to have perished in the Holocaust.

The 150,000 Jews who managed to immigrate to the United States between 1935 and 1941 were primarily middle-class, middle-aged professionals and businessmen, and many settled in New York, Chicago, and San Francisco. These refugees from Nazi Germany represented a different type of immigrant from the young, working-class Jews who emigrated from eastern Europe at the beginning of the twentieth century. About six million Jews, or two-thirds of Europe's Jewish population, perished in the Nazi-led Holocaust. It has been estimated that as many as 200,000 Jews might have been saved from the Holocaust had the United States been more open to their immigration during the war.

The United States finally acknowledged the need for a coherent policy of accepting Jewish refugees in 1944. Following the war, hundreds of thousands of Jews remained displaced in Europe. In 1945 President Harry Truman chose to open U.S. borders to many of these displaced people via executive order. About 23,000 Jews entered under the so-called Truman Directive before Congress further loosened restrictions for refugees in 1948. Between 1945 and 1952 nearly 140,000 Jewish refugees settled in the United States. Following this, Jewish immigration leveled off for several decades, even after immigration laws were further loosened in the 1960s. The most recent major immigration wave occurred during the late 1980s, when political and economic changes in the Soviet Union prompted hundreds of thousands of Soviet Jews to immigrate to Israel and the United States. Immigration from Israel has been slower overall. About 5,000 Israelis—mostly Jewish—have immigrated to the United States annually since the 1990s—a total not much higher than who have left the United States for Israel in the same period.

Jewish American settlement trends in the twentieth and early twenty-first centuries have shown population decreases in the Midwest and increases in Los Angeles and Miami—similar to the patterns following World War II, when the population of American Jews decreased in Midwestern cities such as Chicago, Detroit, and Cleveland and increased in Los Angeles, Miami, and Washington, D.C. Beginning in the 1950s, many Jewish Americans, particularly older people, left Northeastern cities for warmer climes, especially Florida and California, where new synagogues and community centers increased steadily to accommodate the growing Jewish population. For each major city with a significant Jewish population, there has been a steady trend of outward movement toward the suburbs. The young and middle-aged professionals led this movement, while working-class, Orthodox, and older Jews continue to inhabit the old neighborhoods in the cities' cores.

Jewish population in relation to the general U.S. population peaked in 1937 at 3.7 percent. Limits on immigration and a Jewish birthrate of less than two children per family—lower than the overall national average—have since lowered the Jewish proportion of the American population to less than 3 percent. This proportion has remained relatively stable, even as the American Jewish population approached six million in 2011. More than 40 percent of Jewish Americans still live in the Northeast. According to 2011 estimates by the Jewish Data Bank, the largest Jewish population centers are the metropolitan areas of New York City (1.54 million), Los Angeles (519,000), Miami (484,000), the San Francisco Bay Area (390,000), Chicago (291,800), Washington, D.C. (215,600), Philadelphia (214,600), and Boston (210,500).

LANGUAGE

One of the strongest unifying links between Jews throughout the world is the Hebrew language. From the time of Abraham in 2000 BCE until the Babylonians captured Judah in 586 BCE, Hebrew was the everyday language of Jews. Since then, Jews have generally adopted the vernacular of the societies in

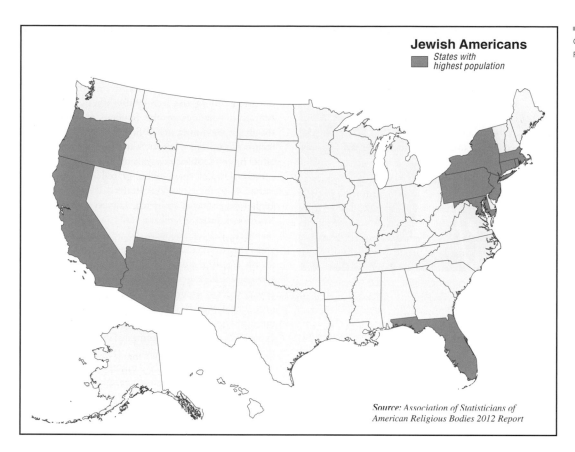

Jewish Americans

▮ States with
highest population

*Source: Association of Statisticians of
American Religious Bodies 2012 Report*

which they have resided, including Arabic, German, Russian, and English. Hebrew had largely disappeared as an everyday language by 200 CE, but it continued to be spoken and read in sacred contexts. Most of the Torah is written in Hebrew, and religious services are held mostly in Hebrew, though progressive synagogues typically make greater use of the language of the community. The use of Hebrew in religious worship enables Jews from all parts of the world to have a common bond. In the twentieth century, Hebrew regained its status as an everyday language in Israel, where it is the official language.

During the diaspora, as Jews left Palestine to settle in various parts of Europe, two distinctly Jewish languages emerged. The Sephardic Jews of Spain and Portugal developed Ladino, a mixture of Spanish and Hebrew, and Ashkenazi Jews in central and eastern Europe spoke Yiddish, a combination of medieval German and Hebrew. These two languages were spoken by immigrants when they came to the United States but were not typically passed on to the next generation. The exception to this occurred during the beginning of the twentieth century, when Russian Jews helped Yiddish gain a strong foothold in the United States through Yiddish newspapers and theater. Many "Yiddishisms" found their way into American speech, particularly in New York and other areas with heavy concentrations of Jews. At its high point in 1920, Yiddish was spoken by half of the Jewish population in

the United States. By 1940, however, the proportion of American Jews who spoke Yiddish had dropped to one-third. Today, some Jewish Americans are attempting to revitalize Yiddish as a language uniquely capable of transmitting Jewish cultural heritage. In 2011 the U.S. Census Bureau estimated that roughly 155,000 Americans spoke Yiddish at home, about one-third of them reporting that they spoke English "less than very well." This was down from about 180,000 Yiddish speakers in 2000.

Greetings and Popular Expressions Commonly heard Hebrew expressions include the following: *Shalom* (peace)—a general greeting; *Shalom lekha* ("hello" and "goodbye")—an everyday greeting; *Barukh ha-ha* (Blessed be the one who comes)—a general welcome to guests, often used at weddings or circumcision ceremonies; *Mazel tov* (good luck)—a wish for luck commonly used at births, bar and bat mitzvahs, and weddings; *Le-hayyim* ("To life," or "Cheers")—a traditional toast wishing someone good health; *Ad me'ah ve-esrim shana* (May you live until 120)—an expression meaning good wishes for a long life; *Tizkeh le-shanim* (Long life to you)—an expression wishing someone happy birthday or happy anniversary; *Hag same'ah* (A happy holiday)—a general holiday greeting used for all Jewish festivals; *L'shana tova* (Good year)—a shortened version of "May you be inscribed in the Book of Life for a good year," which is wished during Rosh Hashanah, the Jewish New Year.

An Orthodox Jewish woman makes her way down 34th Street in Manhatten with a baby carriage. DAVID GROSSMAN / ALAMY

RELIGION

The basic message of Judaism is that there is one all-powerful God. Originally established as a response to polytheism and idol worship, Judaism was quite successful in perpetuating a belief in monotheism—it is the parent religion of both Christianity and Islam. The basic difference between these three religions centers on the Messiah, or savior of the world. While Christians believe the Messiah was Jesus Christ and Muslims believe in several divinely inspired prophets, Jews believe the Messiah has not yet appeared.

The basic beliefs common to all Jews, except atheists and agnostics, were articulated by Torah scholar Moses Maimonides (1135–1204). Known as the Thirteen Principles of the Faith, they are: (1) God alone is the creator; (2) God is One; (3) God is without physical form; (4) God is eternal; (5) humans pray only to God; (6) the words of the prophets are true; (7) the greatest prophet was Moses; (8) today's Torah is the one God gave to Moses; (9) the Torah will not be replaced; (10) God knows people's thoughts; (11) the good are rewarded and the evil are punished; (12) the Messiah will come; and (13) the dead will be revived.

The centerpiece of Judaism is the Torah. Strictly speaking, the Torah refers to the first five books of the Bible (Five Books of Moses), but it can also mean the entire Old Testament or all of Jewish law, including the Talmud and the Midrash. The Talmud is oral law handed down through the generations that interprets the written law, or Torah. The Talmud consists of the Mishnah, which is the text version of the oral law as compiled by Rabbi Judah the Patriarch in 200 CE, and the Gemara, which is the collected commentary on the Mishnah. The Midrash refers to the collection of stories or sermons, or *midrashim*, which interpret biblical passages. Taken as a whole, Jewish law is known as *halakhah*, which guides all aspects of Jewish life.

Two other vital components of Judaism are the rabbi and the synagogue. Since the Middle Ages, rabbis have served as spiritual leaders of communities. Though equal with the rest of humanity in the eyes of God, the rabbi was chosen by the community as an authority on Jewish law. Rabbis were paid to teach, preach, and judge religious and civic matters. The role of the rabbi was well established in Europe, but American synagogues were reluctant to preserve the social and economic position of rabbis. Congregation members no longer felt the need for such an authoritative figure. Consequently, some congregations hired ministers rather than rabbis in order to restrict the influence of their religious leaders. Today many congregations continue to be led by rabbis, who perform traditional duties as well as a variety of other functions, including visiting the sick and attending to wedding and funeral services. The synagogue is the place for Jewish worship, study, and social meetings. Although synagogues have generally played a secondary role to Jewish secular organizations in the United States, the post-World War II years saw a revival in the importance of the synagogue in Jewish life. The synagogue expanded to become the center of community life and the organization through which Jewish children developed a Jewish identity. Membership in synagogues rose dramatically, though attendance at services did not increase proportionately. Today the synagogue still has a key importance to forming that community.

Most Jewish Americans do not fully practice traditional Judaism or regularly attend religious services. Just under half are synagogue members, and only about one-fifth said they attended religious services more than once a month in 2011, according to surveys by the American Jewish Data Bank. A greater proportion—29 percent—said they did not attend any religious services in the year. Thus, for many Jewish Americans, their identity has more to do with Jewish culture or heritage than with religion.

That said, most Jewish Americans still identify with one of American Judaism's four primary branches: Orthodox, Conservative, Reform, and Reconstructionist. Roughly 10 percent of American Jews are Orthodox, 35 percent are Reform, 26 percent are Conservative, and 2 percent are Reconstructionist, while another 25 percent identify as "Just Jewish," according to the Jewish Data Bank.

Though not known as such, Jews were all basically Orthodox until the eighteenth century. Orthodoxy as a separate branch of Judaism developed in eastern and central Europe during the eighteenth and nineteenth centuries, when the Jewish Enlightenment and Emancipation ushered in a new era of freedom of thought and living. Rejecting such changes, Orthodox Jews sought to maintain Jewish traditions through strict observance of Jewish law as expressed in the Torah. Through the early twentieth century, most Jewish immigrants were Orthodox when they arrived in the United States, but economic pressure and differences in social climate between Europe and the United States caused many to abandon Orthodoxy. As a result, Orthodox Judaism has been practiced by only a small minority of American Jews.

For many years the dominant branch of American Judaism has been Reform. Unlike Orthodox Jews, members of Reform Judaism view Jewish laws as adaptable to the changing needs of cultures over time. As a result, Reform Jews look to the Bible for basic moral principles. They do not believe in a literal reading of the Bible and have felt free to disregard outdated passages, such as those that make reference to animal sacrifice. Although some Jews maintain that Judaism has always been Reform, Reform Judaism as a distinct segment of Judaism can be traced to the eighteenth-century German Jewish Enlightenment. Some Reform synagogues began to appear in Germany in the early nineteenth century, but the branch gained its largest following among German Jews who immigrated to the United States during the mid-nineteenth century. In general, Reform Judaism represents the most liberal strain of Judaism: Reform was the first to let women become rabbis (1972); it is accepting of intermarriage (Jews marrying non-Jews) and converts; it consecrates same-sex marriage; and it does not stress such traditional teachings as the coming of the Messiah or the need for separate nationhood (Israel). These liberal views reflect Reform's emphasis on reason over tradition, a shift that represents a transformation of the traditional Jewish identity into a Jewish American identity.

As assimilation has proceeded and intermarriage greatly increased, many Reform Jews seeking to reinforce their Jewish identity have rediscovered traditional practices such as keeping kosher households, wearing yarmulkes (a special head covering worn as a symbol of respect), and studying Hebrew, the use of which has increased in religious services. In May 1999 the Central Conference of American Rabbis, meeting in Pittsburgh, adopted a new platform, known as the Pittsburgh Principles. The document, while not requiring such observances, strongly recommended the study and practice of *mitzvot* (the 613 holy obligations found in the Torah and Talmud), many of which are obligatory in more conservative Jewish sects.

With a theological perspective that falls somewhere between Orthodoxy and Reform, Conservative Judaism is the third main branch of American Judaism. Conservative Judaism first developed in nineteenth-century Germany and gained an American following by the early 1900s. The American roots of this branch of Judaism can be traced to the 1887 founding in New York City of the Jewish Theological Seminary, which has since become the center of Conservative Judaism and home to the world's largest repository of books on Judaism and Jewish life. With its blend of tradition and openness to change within the confines of Jewish law, Conservative Judaism steadily attracted new members until World War II, when membership sharply increased. Theologically, Conservatives look to the Talmud and its interpretations of the Torah as an example of their own views on the evolving nature of Jewish law. As long as change does not violate the basic tenets outlined in the Torah, it is welcomed by Conservatives. Thus, religious ceremonies do not have to be in Hebrew, and women can serve as rabbis. Because Conservatives have not formally articulated their ideology, individual congregations are able to style themselves around the needs of the community. Conservatives constituted the largest branch of Judaism in the United States until the end of the twentieth century, when a shift in membership made Reform Judaism the largest branch.

Another segment of American Judaism is Reconstructionist Judaism, which is sometimes lumped together with Reform and Conservative Judaism as Progressive Judaism. Developed in the 1920s and 1930s by Rabbi Kaplan and influenced by the thinking of American pragmatist philosopher John Dewey, Reconstructionism emphasizes democratic culture and humanistic values. Reconstructionists value Jewish traditions not merely for their religious significance, but because such traditions reflect Jewish culture. Thus, Judaism is more a way of life than a religion. Reconstructionists who learn Hebrew, observe Jewish holidays, and eat kosher foods do so not out of a sense of obligation but as a way of preserving Jewish culture.

CULTURE AND ASSIMILATION

From the earliest days of Jewish immigration to the late nineteenth century, Jewish Americans for the most part desired to assimilate into American society. Jews had left Europe because of poor social and economic conditions and were eager to establish themselves in an open, expanding society. This was not always easy, as many in mainstream American culture regarded the Jews with suspicion or outright hatred. But as their numbers remained small, and most were from western Europe in this period, their challenges were less significant than those of the Eastern European Jews who arrived later. The religious freedom guaranteed by the U.S. Constitution, coupled with the increasing prosperity of nineteenth-century Jewish Americans from Germany, enabled Jews to enjoy considerable acceptance in American society.

The basic division between Jewish Americans during the nineteenth century was between Polish and German congregations. However, in large population centers such as New York, subgroups emerged to accommodate the local traditions of various Dutch, Bavarian, English, and Bohemian Jewish Americans. The desire to assimilate to American culture was felt in the larger synagogues, where decorations were added and sermons were changed from German to English or abandoned altogether.

Beginning in 1881, the immigration of eastern European Jews marked the first significant resistance to acculturation. These immigrants tended to be poor, and they settled in tight-knit communities where they retained the traditions and customs from the old world. They consciously avoided assimilation into American culture and continued to speak Yiddish, which further separated them from other Americans. Some American institutions applied pressure to assimilate into mainstream culture by banning the use of Yiddish in public programs. But by the beginning of the twentieth century, the ban had been removed as efforts to limit Americanization became more popular among American Jews. Increasingly, rapid assimilation into American culture was viewed as unnecessary and harmful to Jewish identity. Still, a conflict remained between younger and older generation Jews over how much Americanization was desirable.

Over the years, however, most Jewish Americans assimilated into mainstream American society, practicing their beliefs and maintaining aspects of their culture while participating in their communities in just the same way as adherents of any other faith. A few ultra-Orthodox communities, primarily in the New York metropolitan area but also scattered around the country, are an exception. At the same time, mainstream American culture has become more tolerant and even welcoming of Jewish practices and beliefs. In some communities, mostly those with heavy Jewish concentrations, the major Jewish holidays have become part of the official government calendar and even some public school calendars. Since the 1980s, Hanukkah has even been celebrated in the White House.

Yet anti-Semitism, or discrimination against Jews, remains an undeniable part of Jewish American history, continuing in some instances to this day. The arrival of eastern European immigrants prompted the first significant tide of anti-Semitism in the United States. During the 1880s, clubs and resorts that once welcomed Jews began to exclude them. European anti-Semitism followed immigrants to the United States, perpetuating various negative stereotypes of Jews as clannish, greedy, parasitic, vulgar, and physically inferior. To mitigate these sentiments, some Jewish Americans developed aid societies to provide jobs and relief funds to help eastern European Jews fit into American society. In addition, American-born German Jews fought against restrictive legislation and formed philanthropic societies that funded schools, hospitals, and libraries for eastern European Jews. The hope was that if the hundreds of thousands of newly arriving Russian Jews had access to homes, jobs, and health care, the decreased burden on American public institutions would ease ethnic tensions.

Despite efforts to reduce ethnic hatred and stereotyping, discrimination against Jews continued into the twentieth century. Housing restrictions and covenants against Jews became more common just prior to World War I. During the 1920s and 1930s, Jews faced significant difficulty obtaining employment in large corporations or in fields such as journalism. Jews were also increasingly subjected to restrictive quotas in higher education. In particular, Jewish enrollment dropped by as much as 50 percent at Ivy League schools such as Harvard and Yale during the 1920s. By the 1930s most private institutions had Jewish quota policies in place. In politics, one of the motivating forces behind the Immigration Restriction Act of 1924 was the negative image that some held of immigrant Russian Jews, who were thought to live a lowly, animal-like existence. This "dirty Jew" stereotype was based on a perception of ghetto Jews—and a larger stereotype of all eastern Europeans—who were forced to endure squalid living conditions out of economic necessity. Another stereotype was of the Jew as Communist sympathizer and revolutionary, a characterization stemming from the belief that Jews were responsible for the Russian Revolution. All of these negative stereotypes were reinforced in American literature of the 1920s and 1930s. Authors such as Thomas Wolfe, F. Scott Fitzgerald, and Ernest Hemingway all depicted Jewish caricatures in their novels, and poets such as T. S. Eliot and Ezra Pound freely expressed their anti-Semitism.

Fueled by the Great Depression and the rise of German Nazism, Jewish discrimination and anti-Semitism reached a peak during the 1930s. One of the more influential American voices of anti-Semitism was Roman Catholic priest Charles E. Coughlin (1891–1979), who argued that the Nazi attack on Jews was justified because of the Communist tendencies of Jews. Coughlin blamed New York Jews for the hard economic times, a message intended to appeal to Coughlin's Detroit audience of industrial workers hurt by the Depression.

At the end of World War II, when the atrocities of the Nazi Holocaust became widely known, anti-Semitism in the United States diminished considerably. Although some Jews in academia and Hollywood lost positions as a result of the growing American fear of communism, Jews generally enjoyed improved social conditions after 1945. Returning war veterans who took advantage of the G.I. Bill to enroll in college created a demand for university professors that Jewish Americans helped fulfill, and entrance quotas restricting admission of Jewish students at universities were gradually abandoned. As discrimination waned, Jews enjoyed substantial representation in academia, business, entertainment, and such professions as finance, law, and medicine. In short, Jews during the postwar years resumed their positions as contributing and often leading members of American society, and their position remained strong into the first decades of the twenty-first century.

Traditions and Customs American Jewish traditions and customs primarily derive from the practice of Judaism. The most important Jewish traditions stem from the *mitzvot*, which are the 613 holy obligations found in the Torah and Talmud. Consisting of 248 positive commandments (Thou shall's) and 365 negative commandments (Thou shall not's), the mitzvot fall into three categories: *Edot*, or "testimonies," are rules that help Jews bear witness to their faith (for example, rules on what garments to wear); *Mishpatim* (judgments) are rules of behavior found in most religions (for example, the rule against stealing); and *Hukim* (statutes) are divine rules that humans cannot fully understand (for example, dietary rules). No one person can possibly fulfill all 613 *mitzvot*, because they include laws for different people in different situations. Even the most Orthodox Jew in modern times is expected to observe less than half of the obligations.

Immigrant Jews passed on Jewish traditions in the home, but subsequent generations have relied on religious schools to teach the traditions. These schools have helped Jewish American parents accommodate their goal of having their children become familiar with Jewish tradition without interfering with their children's integration into American culture. Today, many Jewish American children attend congregation school a few hours a week for three to five years. During this time, they learn Hebrew and discover the essential traditions and customs of Jewish culture.

The practice of observing and celebrating Jewish children's *bar mitzvah* (boys) or *bat mitzvah* (girls) when they turn thirteen is widespread throughout Jewish American communities. The coming-of-age ceremony initiates the young man or woman into the religious community. After reading from the Torah in synagogue, they become an adult. A celebration (*seudat mitzavah*) follows the service. These celebrations are sometimes very elaborate and large affairs, involving many guests, music, food, and gift-giving. Bat mitzvahs for girls were not introduced until the twentieth century, and while they are common in the Reform and Conservative groups, they remain rare among Orthodox Jews.

Another common Jewish custom is that of giving babies two names—an everyday name and a Hebrew name used in synagogue and on religious documents. The naming of the baby occurs after birth at a baby-naming service or, for many male babies, when they are circumcised. Since the emergence of Judaism some four thousand years ago, Jews have observed the tradition of *brit milah* (covenant of circumcision). The practice of cutting the foreskin of male babies probably served a hygienic purpose originally, but circumcision has come to represent the beginning of life in the Jewish community. To be sure, many non-Jews are circumcised as well. Nonetheless, circumcision is traditionally associated with the keeping of the covenant between Abraham and God as well as with physical and ethical purity. The *brit milah* must occur eight days after birth, unless the baby is sick. The ceremony (*bris*) traditionally takes place in the home or a synagogue and is usually performed by a *mohel*, an observant Jew who may be a rabbi, doctor, or simply one skilled in the technique. After the circumcision, which occurs very quickly and without much pain, a celebration of food, prayers, and blessings follows.

POTATO KUGEL

Ingredients
8 potatoes

2 onions

6 eggs

½ cup oil

4 tablespoons flour

1 tablespoon salt

1 teaspoon pepper

Preparation
Preheat oven to 400°F.

In a large bowl, mix eggs, oil, flour, salt and pepper. Set aside.

Coarsely grate the potatoes and onion by hand or food processor. Let stand 3–5minutes. Squeeze out excess liquid. Add grated potatoes to the egg-flour mixture. Mix with spoon until smooth.

Pour into a greased 9 by 13 inch baking dish.

Bake, uncovered, for 1 hour or until golden brown on top and a knife inserted in the middle comes out clean.

Serves 12

Recipe courtesy of Marty Fischhoff

Cuisine Much of what is commonly regarded as Jewish American cuisine comes from eastern European traditions and was brought to the United States by Ashkenazi Jews. It is often quite similar to dishes eaten by non-Jews in those countries, though sometimes modified to follow Jewish dietary laws. The cuisine is often hearty but simple, and almost never spicy. Popular dishes—some of which are eaten on specific holidays—include *matzo* balls, dumplings traditionally made with chicken fat, matzo meal flour, and eggs, and served in chicken soup; *latkes*, fried potato pancakes traditionally eaten at Hanukkah; gefilte fish, a ground fish stuffing shaped into a ball or stuffed inside a whole fish; and borscht, a beet soup. Jewish Americans also enjoy bagels with cream cheese and lox (smoked salmon), and challah, a sweet, egg-rich bread eaten on the Sabbath. Most American cities with a major Jewish population have restaurants that serve these dishes, sometimes alongside other general American "comfort foods." Jewish delis featuring bagels and meats like pastrami, corned beef, and chopped liver are also quite common in American cities and are popular with Jews and non-Jews alike.

Sephardic Jewish Americans eat a cuisine more similar to the Mediterranean diet, including fresh vegetables, rice, and couscous. Their dishes tend to feature more spices, including cumin, cardamom, turmeric, and cilantro. Israeli cuisine has also grown more popular in the United States in recent years, though in the United States it is very similar to Lebanese or other Middle Eastern dishes, including *falafel* (chickpea fritters), hummus, and pita.

Like most Americans, Jewish Americans are concerned with health and convenience in cooking and increasingly substitute vegetable oil for chicken fat or use instant or prepackaged *matzo* balls. Jewish American women, who traditionally do the cooking for their families, also increasingly use cookbooks where once they would have learned cooking methods from their relatives. Being well integrated in American society, most Jewish Americans also enjoy a wide range of foods not specific to their culture.

Many Jews, particularly Orthodox Jews, observe *kashrut*. Delineated in the Book of Leviticus and dating back to 1200 BCE, *kashrut* is a system of food laws for eating *kosher* foods and avoiding *trefa* foods. Kosher foods are simply ones that are, according to Jewish law, fit for Jews; they include fruits, vegetables, grains, meat from cud-chewing mammals with split hooves (such as sheep, cows, and goats), fish with scales and fins (such as salmon, herring, and perch), domesticated birds (such as chickens, turkeys, and ducks), and milk and eggs from kosher mammals and birds. *Trefa* foods are forbidden by Jewish law due to biblical decree, not because such foods are unfit for human consumption. They include meat from unkosher mammals (such as pigs, rabbits, and horses), birds of prey (such as owls and eagles), and water animals that do not have both scales and fins (such as shrimp, lobster, crab, and squid). *Kashrut* also prescribes that the slaughter of animals shall be painless. Thus, a Jewish butcher studies the anatomy of animals to learn the precise spot where killing may occur instantaneously. After the animal is killed, the blood must be completely drained and the body inspected for signs of disease. Finally, *kashrut* involves keeping meat and dairy separate. Jewish law has interpreted the biblical commandment not to "stew a kid in its mother's milk" to mean that meat and dairy products cannot be prepared or consumed together. These strict rules are not observed as closely as they once were—mainly because Orthodox Jews are no longer the majority. According to the Jewish Data Bank, about 21 percent of Jewish Americans say they observe kosher rules at home.

Holidays Because there is a separate Jewish calendar based on the lunar cycle, Jewish holidays occur on different secular days every year. The first holiday of the Jewish year is the celebration of the new year, Rosh Hashanah, which occurs sometime in September or October. It is a ten-day period in which Jews reflect on their lives during the previous year. Three basic themes are associated with this holiday: the anniversary of the creation of the world; the day of judgment; and the renewal of the covenant between God and Israel. On the night before the beginning of Rosh Hashanah, one popular custom is to eat honey-dipped apples so that the new year will be a sweet one. Yom Kippur, the "Day of Atonement," occurs at the end of Rosh Hashanah. For twenty-five hours observant Jews fast while seeking forgiveness from God and from those against whom they have sinned. There are five services at the synagogue throughout the day, most centering on the themes of forgiveness and renewal.

In the winter, usually in December, Jews celebrate the festival of Hanukkah. This is a joyous eight-day period that celebrates the rededication of the Temple in Jerusalem in 164 BCE; that year the Jews, led by Judah the Maccabee, successfully reclaimed the Temple from the Syrians. When the Maccabees prepared to light the perpetual flame in the Temple, they found only one jar of oil, enough for just one day. Miraculously, the oil lasted eight days, until a new supply of oil arrived. Thus, the celebration of Hanukkah, also known as the Festival of Lights, involves lighting candles for each night of the festival, one on the first night, two on the second, and so forth. Over time, Hanukkah has become a time of family celebration with games and presents for children. It has been suggested that Hanukkah has become a more commercialized holiday in the United States because it occurs at roughly the same time as Christmas, Americans' most significant gift-giving holiday.

Other holidays and festivals round out the Jewish year. In late winter Jews celebrate Purim, a period of great drinking and eating to commemorate the biblical time when God helped Esther save the Jews from the evil, tyrannical Haman, who wanted to destroy them. In late March or early April, Jews participate in the weeklong festival of Passover, which marks the Jewish Exodus from Egypt. The Passover supper, or *seder*, is the central feature of this celebration and is a gathering of family and friends (with an empty chair for the symbolic "unexpected guest," Elijah), who eat a traditional meal that includes unleavened bread (*matzah*), parsley, apples, nuts, cinnamon, raisins, and wine. Among Jewish Americans, it is increasingly common to invite non-Jews to participate in the seder.

Several other holidays are celebrated by some Jewish Americans, but not as prominently or as consistently as the four mentioned above. Seven weeks after Passover, *Shavout* is celebrated, marking the giving of the Torah by God and the season of wheat harvest. In autumn Jews celebrate *Sukkot*, a seven-day festival honoring the time when the Israelites spent forty years in the desert after the Exodus before returning to Palestine. Because the Israelites spent this time living in the wilderness, this holiday season is observed by building a temporary shelter called a *sukkah*. Though a sukkah is small and typically does not protect well against the increasingly harsh fall weather, Jews are expected to spend as much time as possible in it as a sign of their joy and gratitude for all that God has provided.

Health Care Issues and Practices Jewish Americans generally consider good health to be very important, following teachings and traditions that emphasize the importance of individual good health for the benefit of the community. They are also supportive of expanding access to health care. This is particularly true for Reform Jews—the Union for Reform Judaism adopted a position statement in favor of free, universal health care in 1971. According to surveys by the American Jewish Committee in 2010, Jewish Americans were more likely than the general population to support the health care reforms instituted under the Obama administration.

Jewish Americans are also disproportionately likely to have a number of genetic diseases. The Jewish Genetics Disease Center at New York's Mount Sinai School of Medicine is one of several centers researching these diseases, which include the following:

Bloom syndrome: a disease causing shortness in height (usually less than 5 feet), redness of skin, and susceptibility to respiratory tract and ear infections. Afflicted men usually experience infertility, and both sexes have an increased risk of cancer. Approximately 1 in 120 Ashkenazi Jews are carriers, and children from two carriers have a 25 percent chance of contracting the disease. About 1 in 50,000 Ashkenazi Jews have Bloom syndrome, comprising roughly one-third of those afflicted with the disease.

Riley-Day syndrome (Familial dysautonomia): a congenital disease of the nervous system resulting in stunted growth, inadequate pain and heat perception, and lack of tears. In the United States, 1 in 30 Ashkenazi Jews carry the gene, and the risk of recurrence in affected families is 25 percent. Only about 600 diagnoses have been made, nearly all of them in Ashkenazi Jews, since the disease was first identified in 1949. Recent research may help provide treatment options through stem-cell therapy. A person must inherit the gene from both parents in order to have the syndrome.

Gaucher's disease: a rare disease that can occur at any age. In its mildest form—the form most common to Jews—it is characterized by easy bruising, orthopedic problems, anemia, and a variety of other symptoms. The more advanced forms of the disease are usually fatal in infancy or childhood. About 9 percent of Ashkenazi Jews carry the recessive gene, and 1 in 450 Ashkenazi Jewish babies are afflicted.

Mucolipidosis IV: a genetic disease involving the deterioration of the central nervous system in babies who later develop mild or more severe retardation. The disease is often misdiagnosed as cerebral palsy. Most of the afflicted have been Ashkenazi Jews; 1 in 100 are carriers of the gene. The disease only occurs when both parents are carriers, with 25 percent of babies from such parents being afflicted.

Niemann-Pick disease: a usually fatal disease characterized by a buildup of fatty materials causing

enlargement of the spleen, emaciation, and degradation of the central nervous system. Afflicted babies typically die before the age of three, but survival into young adulthood is possible in milder cases, and treatment options are expanding. Around 1 in 40,000 Ashkenazi Jews are afflicted with Type A of the disease. The disease only occurs when both parents are carriers, with 25 percent of babies from such parents developing the disease.

Tay-Sachs disease: a biochemical disorder causing retardation in babies as early as the fourth month and leading to a deterioration of the central nervous system that ends in death, usually around age four or five. Approximately 1 in 27 Ashkenazi Jews are carriers, with the risk that 25 percent of babies from two carriers will have Tay-Sachs. There is no known treatment for the disease, which is also disproportionately common among French Canadians and Cajuns of Louisiana.

Torsion dystonia: a disease involving an increasing loss of motor control affecting children between the ages of four and sixteen. The disease often begins with immobility in one limb, progressing over several years to near-total immobility. In the United States, 1 in 70 Ashkenazi Jews are carriers, with 1 out of every 20,000 Jewish babies developing the disease.

FAMILY AND COMMUNITY LIFE

As Jews spread throughout Europe and the United States after being forced out of Palestine, their cultural heritage depended on strong family and community relations. One of the chief ways in which Jewish Americans, particularly Orthodox Jews, have maintained family and community values has been through the observance of *Shabat*, the Sabbath. Observing Shabat, or "the day of delight," is one of the Ten Commandments and is essentially a matter of taking a break from work to devote one day of the week to rest, contemplation, and family and community togetherness. Just prior to the Sabbath, which lasts from sunset

JEWISH PROVERBS

- A half-truth is a whole lie.

- Bygone troubles are a pleasure to talk about.

- If a man is destined to drown, he will drown even in a spoonful of water.

- If you can't bite, don't show your teeth.

- If you are bitter at heart, sugar in the mouth won't help you.

- What you don't see with your eyes, don't invent with your mouth.

- Rejoice not at thine enemy's fall—but don't rush to pick him up, either.

- A bird that you set free may be caught again, but a word that escapes your lips will not return.

- A slave shows his true character not while he is enslaved, but when he becomes a master.

- As you do, so will be done to you.

- Charity is the spice of riches.

- Do not be wise in words—be wise in deeds.

- Do not meet troubles halfway.

- Don't approach a goat from the front, a horse from the back, or a fool from any side.

- Don't be sweet, lest you be eaten up; don't be bitter, lest you be spewed out.

on Friday to Saturday night, the family must complete all the preparations for the day because no work should be done once the Sabbath begins. Traditionally, the mother starts the Sabbath by lighting candles and saying a special prayer. Afterward, the family attends a short service in the synagogue, then returns home for a meal and lighthearted conversation, perhaps even singing. The following morning the community gathers in the synagogue for the most important religious service of the week. On Saturday afternoon observant Jews will continue to refrain from work and either make social visits or spend time in quiet reflection. A ceremony called *havdalah* (distinction) takes place Saturday night, marking the end of Sabbath and the beginning of the new week. The relative importance of Shabbat and the synagogue for American Jews has declined over the years. In 2010, according to the Jewish Data Bank, about 28 percent of American Jews lit Shabat candles.

In fact, the history of Jews in the United States reflects an ongoing secularization of Jewish values.

Beginning in the nineteenth century, Jewish community centers developed as an important nonsectarian counterpart to synagogues. Modeled after the Young Men's Hebrew Association, Jewish community centers became dominated by the 1920s by professionals who wanted to establish a central place for younger Jews to acquire such American values as humanism and self-development. While such community centers continue to play a role in areas heavily populated by Jews, many of today's American Jews no longer associate with a synagogue or community center.

Courtship and Weddings According to Judaism, marriage is the fulfillment of one of God's purposes for human beings. Consequently, all Jews, including rabbis, are intended to experience both the joy and hardship of matrimony. To facilitate the finding of a mate, matchmakers play a role in bringing together suitable but perhaps reluctant individuals. The matchmaker only helps the process along; according to Jewish law the final choice must be made freely by both partners.

Traditionally, intermarriage between Jews and Gentiles has been forbidden. From ancient days through the twentieth century, a Jew in Palestine or Europe who married a Christian faced ostracism from family and community. Jews who immigrated to the United States during the colonial period and after, however, intermarried with non-Jews relatively frequently. This tolerance of religious freedom lasted until the 1880s, when the arrival of Russian Jews ushered in a conservative era with a more traditional view of intermarriage. For the first half of the twentieth century, intermarriage among Jews remained low, with only about 5 percent choosing to marry non-Jews. By the 1960s and 1970s, however, intermarriage became more common, with as many as 20 to 30 percent of Jews choosing non-Jewish mates, and by the 1990s this had risen to 52 percent. It continued to hover around 50 percent into the twenty-first century. Increased assimilation and intermarriage sparked concern over the continued existence of American Jewry and debates about who should be considered "Jewish."

Jewish weddings are marked by several distinct traditions. The ceremony occurs under a *huppah*, a canopy open on all four sides, symbolizing the openness of the bride and groom's new home. Jewish weddings happen in many places, including synagogues, hotels, or outdoors, but the huppah is almost always present. Under the huppah, the bride circles the groom seven times, the couple is blessed, and they both drink from the same cup of wine, a sharing that demonstrates that from this point forward they will share a life together. The heart of the ceremony, the only part required to make the marriage legally binding, occurs next. The groom places a ring on the right-hand index finger of the bride, proclaiming, "Behold you are consecrated to me by this ring according to the law of Moses and Israel." If at least two people witness her accepting the ring, the marriage is complete. The ceremony is rounded out by the signing of the marriage contract (the *ketubah*), the singing of seven blessings (the *Sheva brahot*), and the traditional smashing of the glass by the husband. Breaking a glass symbolizes the destruction of the Temple in Jerusalem and the fact that the couple will have to face hard times together. When the glass is broken, guests shout "*Mazel tov*" (good luck), and a wedding feast ensues.

When a Jewish American marries a non-Jew, the wedding ceremony may incorporate some or all of these elements, or the couple may hold two ceremonies: one Jewish ceremony and one Christian or secular.

Funerals Jewish funerals and mourning are characterized by a sense of frankness toward the reality of death. Funerals occur soon after a person dies, usually within a day or two unless family travel plans or the observance of Sabbath delays the service for an extra day. Arrangements for the deceased are traditionally handled by the *hevra kadisha* (holy society), which is a volunteer organization within the synagogue responsible for preparing the body. Such preparation does not involve makeup or embalming but instead consists of dressing the person in white, perhaps wrapping the deceased with his or her prayer cloth, or *tallit*. In modern times, the *hevra kadisha* are sometimes assisted by professionals, but not for profit. The ceremony is usually short and is followed by burial at the cemetery, where family members recite the *Kaddish*, a traditional prayer celebrating God and life.

For Orthodox survivors, four stages of mourning have evolved over the years, which encourage expression of grief so that the healing process may occur without delay. From the time a person dies until the funeral, mourners cease working, gather together, and do not generally receive visitors, primarily because any comfort at this point is premature and only causes unnecessary strain. The second stage occurs during the first week after the funeral, when the family observes *shiva*. At this time, mourners open their homes to visitors who offer their sympathy. The next stage is *shaloshim*, which lasts for three weeks after *shiva* and is marked by a resumption of work and other obligations, but entertainment is avoided. Finally, there is a last phase of light mourning for spouses or immediate family members that ends eleven months after the funeral. By the anniversary of a person's death, mourning is complete according to Jewish custom.

Gender Roles Jewish culture over the centuries has been male-dominated. Women's roles were limited to household activity, including raising children and performing minor religious functions, such as lighting the Sabbath candles. Although women are subject to the same negative biblical commandments as men, they are not expected to observe the same positive commandments. For example, men are expected to pray three times a day at fixed times, while women only pray once at a time of their choosing.

This difference has been variously attributed to the demanding nature of women's household duties and to men's higher proclivity to sin. For centuries, women could not study the Torah and could not receive a formal education. Orthodox Jews have eased their stance against education for women but have nevertheless maintained that women should serve a secondary role to their husbands. Other Jews have taken a more liberal view, holding that women are equals who can fully participate in religious ceremonies. In Reform and Conservative Judaism, women are permitted to become rabbis. Many Jewish women rabbis played a role in the American feminist movement of the 1960s and 1970s. The movement liberated women from having to serve traditional roles, and Jewish women such as Congresswoman Bella Abzug (1920–1998) and authors Gloria Steinem (1934–) and Betty Friedan (1921–2006) paved the way for women to enter a variety of fields once dominated by men.

Education Jewish Americans have long placed strong emphasis on the importance of education. In the nineteenth century, the ability to read gave German Jewish immigrants a competitive edge over other German immigrants. Later, American-born Jews pursued education as a means of entering such professions as law and medicine.

Religious education was once taught in a *cheder*, an eastern European elementary school for boys. While girls generally did not have access to formal education, boys would attend the *cheder* all day long, studying the Hebrew prayer book and the Torah. In the United States, the *cheder* played a secondary role to public schools. As priorities changed with acculturation, the *cheder* diminished in significance. However, the Talmud Torah school, a charitable school first established in Europe, began to usurp the role of the *cheder* as a place for Judaic instruction. Today, many children from observant Jewish American families attend some type of religious school a few hours each week for three to five years in order to learn Jewish history, traditions, and customs as well as the Hebrew language.

Jewish Americans faced considerable discrimination in higher education well into the twentieth century. Yet over time these discriminatory practices were curbed, and Jewish Americans began to achieve considerable academic success. A 2008 study by the Pew Forum on Religious and Public Life found that more than 59 percent of Jewish Americans had a college or graduate degree, more than twice the proportion of the general population. Jewish Americans are also well represented among the faculty of American academic institutions. Estimates say as many as 10 percent of American professors are Jewish, and many institutions, including Harvard and Yale, have had a Jewish president.

Philanthropic Traditions The Jewish philanthropic tradition reaches back to biblical times. The practice of *tzedakah*, or charity, is considered one of

Jews' primary duties in life, taught to children and emphasized in religious practice. In agrarian times, one common form of tzedakah was to allocate a portion of the harvest for the poor, who were free to take crops from certain parts of a farm. During the Middle Ages, Jewish self-governing communities called *kehillahs* would ensure that the community's poor would have the basic necessities of life. The spirit of the kehillah survived into the twentieth century in the United States in the form of *landsmanshaft*, separate societies existing within congregations in cities such as New York. The landsmanshaft were made up of townspeople from congregations who pooled resources to provide such benefits as insurance, cemetery rights, free loans, and sick pay to those who needed it.

The tradition of lending assistance began in the synagogue, but over the years philanthropic organizations became increasingly independent. Organizations such as the Order of B'nai B'rith and the Young Men's Hebrew Association became major sponsors of charitable projects. These and other benevolent societies were responsible for the establishment of Jewish orphanages, hospitals, and retirement homes in major cities across the United States throughout the nineteenth century.

Jewish American philanthropy increased tremendously during the twentieth century. Scientific philanthropy—a method of providing aid through modern methods and without assistance from religious institutions—gained favor at the turn of the century in response to the problem of helping settle the large waves of Russian immigrant Jews. One outgrowth of this movement was the establishment of the National Conference of Jewish Charities, which formed national agencies to deal with immigrant issues. During World War I, Jewish philanthropic efforts were consolidated through the establishment of the American Jewish Joint Distribution Committee, an organization formed to provide relief to eastern European Jews suffering from famine and pogroms. By raising more than $66 million by 1922, the committee was able to expand its relief efforts to include health care and economic reconstruction programs that reached some 700,000 Jews in need of assistance. Several organizations supplied economic relief to European Jews during and after World War II. One such organization, the United Jewish Appeal, was initially established to help Holocaust survivors and to promote Israel as a homeland for Jews. During the postwar decades, however, it blossomed into the one of the largest private charities in the United States, providing financial aid to Israel and Jews worldwide.

In the latter twentieth century and beyond, the Jewish philanthropic tradition has extended beyond the Jewish community. Mazon, for example, was founded in the 1980s as a national hunger relief organization that is funded by Jews who voluntarily donate 3 percent of the costs of such celebrations as weddings and bar mitzvahs. Additionally, many Jewish American children complete a mitzvah project in which they raise money for a specific charity in preparation for their bar or bat mitzvah.

EMPLOYMENT AND ECONOMIC CONDITIONS

Jewish Americans have generally attained a high level of economic prosperity through keen business sense and dedication to education and hard work. Such prosperity has been achieved over the course of several centuries, dating back to medieval Europe when Jews first became associated with the world of finance and trade. Excluded from craft guilds, Jews took on the jobs that Christians were prohibited from performing, such as money lending and tax collecting. In time Jews became involved in trade and the clothing business as well. By the time the Sephardic Jews began settling in the United States in the seventeenth and eighteenth centuries, most earned their livings as independent retailers; they were bakers, tailors, merchants, and small business owners.

Jewish Americans in the mid-nineteenth century were predominantly tailors or peddlers. Many of those who worked in cities were tailors or were otherwise affiliated with the garment business. Those who sought their fortune outside of the city were usually peddlers, who played a key role in bringing merchandise from the city to the country. The successful peddler could eventually earn enough to set up his own retail store on the outskirts of town or in rural areas. Credit was at the heart of the emerging network of these retail businesses. German Jews were the chief creditors at the time, and they would minimize their credit risks by dealing with relatives whenever possible. Attitudes among some Christians opposing usury—the charging of interest for loans—limited many Jews' clientele in the nineteenth century.

The close connection between creditor and businessman led to the emergence of a Jewish business elite between 1860 and 1880 that had established profitable ventures in such fields as investment banking, the garment industry, shoe manufacturing, and meat processing. By the end of the century, Jewish Americans were no longer primarily tailors or peddlers (those trades represented just 3 percent and 1 percent, respectively, of Jewish Americans in the 1890 U.S. Census). Instead, Jews had attained a substantial measure of wealth by becoming retailers, bankers, brokers, wholesalers, accountants, bookkeepers, and clerks; together, these occupations represented 67 percent of all Jewish Americans at that time.

The immigration of Russian Jews in the early twentieth century brought vast numbers of workers into the clothing industry in large cities. Newly arriving immigrants would work in the factories for long hours, often seventy or more hours a week, honing their skills and developing their own specialties. As with the German Jews before them, the Russian Jewish Americans worked their way into more affluent positions over the years, becoming business owners and professionals. Although German Jewish Americans comprised the majority of the one thousand clothing manufacturers in the late nineteenth century, by the eve of World War I Russian Jewish Americans owned more than 16,000 garment factories and employed more than 200,000 people. The slowing of immigration during and immediately after World War I, coupled with increasing wages in the garment industry, enabled Russian Jewish Americans to raise their standard of living and attain the same socioeconomic status as German Jewish Americans by the 1920s.

The educated professional has long been a highly valued member of Jewish culture. The entrepreneurial success of first-generation Jewish Americans enabled subsequent generations to move into the professional ranks of society. In large eastern and Midwestern cities such as New York and Cleveland, a disproportionate share of Jewish doctors, lawyers, and dentists represented two to three times the proportion of the Jewish population in those cities. For example, Jews in the 1930s comprised 25 percent of the population of New York City yet accounted for 65 percent of all lawyers and judges in the city.

As with the general population, Jews enjoyed considerable economic prosperity during the postwar years. After World War II, perhaps owing to the recognition of their peoples' suffering in the Holocaust, or to greater awareness of Jews' contributions to American society and economy, the institutional discrimination against Jews that had developed during the late nineteenth and early twentieth centuries largely disappeared. With unprecedented access to education and advancement in American society, younger Jews entered colleges and embarked upon successful professional careers at about twice the rate of the preceding generation. Since that time, Jewish Americans have excelled in a range of professional fields, including management, communications, real estate, law, medicine, entertainment, and academia. Their success has been remarkable. The Pew Religious Forums estimates that 46 percent of Jewish Americans earn more than $100,000 a year, while only 5 percent live under the poverty line—about a third of the national average.

The major exceptions to this general prosperity are more recent Jewish immigrants, particularly those who came from the nations of the former Soviet Union after 1980. A 2001 report by the United Jewish Communities found that 38 percent of these immigrants lived in poverty, and half were considered to be "low-income." This reflects the fact that many of these immigrants came to the United States to escape from impoverished conditions elsewhere. It may also be that their plight is often ignored amid the general perception of Jewish Americans as wealthy and comfortable; this has been a cause for concern among groups that advocate for recent Jewish immigrants.

POLITICS AND GOVERNMENT

Since the first Jews arrived in colonial America, Jewish Americans have enjoyed a high degree of political freedom and have taken an active role in politics and government. Although early Jewish settlers faced some political and social discrimination, laws restricting Jewish religious and business activities were generally not enforced. By 1740, Parliament granted Jewish aliens the right to citizenship without having to take a Christian oath. Once the United States gained its independence, the Mikveh Israel Congregation urged the Constitutional Convention to make a provision guaranteeing the freedom of religious expression, which became a reality with the passage of the First Amendment in 1789. Although they have faced considerable discrimination over the centuries, Jews have been involved in all levels of American civic and political life, with the presidency and vice presidency being the only major elected offices a Jew has not held.

Over the years Jews have developed a rich political tradition of fighting for social justice as liberals and radicals primarily affiliated with the Democratic Party. Jews have been staunch supporters of Democratic political leaders. When in 1944 President Roosevelt's New Deal policies caused the president to lose popularity, 90 percent of Jews continued to support him. The tendency to side with a liberal candidate, no matter how unpopular, continued through 1972, when Democratic presidential candidate George McGovern won only 38 percent of the popular vote but garnered more than 60 percent of the Jewish vote. Although the 1970s saw the emergence of a notable conservative movement among Jewish Americans, led by Nathan Glazer, Irving Kristol, Sidney Hook, and Milton Friedman, the majority of Jews have continued their allegiance to the Democratic Party. In 2008, according to the Pew Religious Forum, 66 percent of American Jews identified as Democrat or leaning Democrat, and they were more likely than other major American religious groups to have liberal views on abortion, homosexuality, and the environment. They were also more likely to believe that the United States should play a major role in world affairs, perhaps owing to concerns about Israel, their history of marginalization, and dedication to human rights for all groups.

Jewish Americans were active participants in the American labor movement. During the first part of the twentieth century, Jewish union leaders had strong ties to the Socialist Party and the Jewish Socialist Federation. This support reflected a socialist leaning on the part of Russian Jews who had participated in the failed Russian Revolution of 1905. The Socialist Party enjoyed its greatest success in New York City between 1914 and 1917, when Socialist Meyer London was elected to represent the Lower East Side in the U.S. Congress and more than a dozen Socialists won seats in city government.

Influenced by eastern European socialist thought and American free enterprise, Jewish Americans found

One of the most distinguished intellectuals in the United States, Jewish American Noam Chomsky was voted the world's top public intellectual in 2005. In addition to his academic accomplishments, which include advances in linguistics and analytical philosophy, Chomsky has been a strong political activist and advocate for human rights. CHINAFOTOPRESS / GETTY IMAGES

With approximately 80,000 Jewish families among its ranks by the mid-1920s, this union provided health care and cemetery services and involved itself in Jewish culture by sponsoring Yiddish newspapers, schools, and theaters.

Military Service Throughout U.S. history, Jews have served with distinction in the U.S. military. Jewish Americans served at most of the major battles of the American Revolution, and wealthy Jews supported the struggle for independence by making crucial donations for supplies and weaponry. Just as the Civil War divided North against South, so too did it divide the American Jews. While most Jewish American soldiers served in the Union army, many Jews in the South remained loyal to the Confederate cause. Several prominent Jews supported the South, notably Judah P. Benjamin (1811–1884), the Confederate secretary of war and secretary of state. Jewish Americans also figured prominently in the two world wars, with 250,000 Jewish Americans serving in World War I and 550,000 in World War II.

The participation of Jewish Americans in the country's major wars demonstrates that, although they are generally known as a peaceful people, Jews are prepared to fight for causes they perceive as just. For some Jewish Americans, this principle extends beyond national concerns. The Jewish Defense League (JDL), for example, is a militant organization established in New York in 1968 by radical Rabbi Meir Kahane (1932–1990). The JDL's guiding principle is "Never Again," a reference to the Nazi Holocaust. The group's method of combating worldwide anti-Semitism with violence has made the JDL controversial among Jews and non-Jews alike. It was declared a hate group by the Southern Poverty Law Center in 2002, after the discovery of a JDL plot to assassinate a congressman. The JDL represents a very tiny group of Jewish Americans, however. The vast majority prefer peaceful protest to combat injustice.

NOTABLE INDIVIDUALS

Countless Jewish Americans have made significant contributions to American culture, politics, and research over the years. Only a partial listing of notable names is possible.

Academia Jewish Americans have been particularly influential in academia. Notable Jewish scholars include historians Daniel J. Boorstin (1914–2004), Henry L. Feingold (1931–), Barbara Tuchman (1912–1989), and Howard Zinn (1922–2010); linguist Noam Chomsky (1928–); and philosophers Ernest Nagel (1901–1985), a logical positivist influential in the philosophy of science, and Norman Lamm (1927–), Yeshiva University chancellor and founder of the Orthodox periodical *Tradition*. Several Jewish Americans have headed Ivy League academic institutions: Rick Levin (1947–) is an economist who became president of Yale in 1993; Larry Summers (1954–),

themselves on both sides of the labor disputes of the early twentieth century. The clothing industry provided the battleground. For a time Russian Jewish American manufacturers refused to recognize unions, many of which contained a significant proportion of Jewish members. Tensions came to a head during two major strikes: "the uprising of twenty thousand," which involved Jewish and Italian American young women striking against shirtwaist manufacturers in 1909, and "the great revolt," a massive strike in 1911 involving thousands of cloak makers. Both strikes pitted thugs and police against union workers. The workers received community support from various Jewish benefactors, ranging from wealthy women who posted bail for the arrested workers to lawyers and community leaders who helped mediate settlements. As a result of the strikes, the work week was lowered to fifty hours and permanent mediation procedures were established. Two key unions at the time were the International Ladies' Garment Workers' Union and the Amalgamated Clothing Workers of America, both of which included a significant number of Jewish members. Another union with significant Jewish membership was Arbeter Ring, or Workmen's Circle.

an economist who was secretary of the treasury under President Bill Clinton, was president of Harvard University from 2001 to 2006; and Judith Rodin (1944–), president of the University of Pennsylvania from 1994 to 2004, was the first female Ivy League president.

Film Jewish Americans have had an enormous influence in Hollywood. By the 1930s Jews dominated the film industry, as almost all of the major production companies were owned and operated by eastern European Jews. These companies include Columbia (Jack and Harry Cohn), Goldwyn (Samuel Goldwyn, born Samuel Goldfish), Metro-Goldwyn-Mayer (Louis B. Mayer and Marcus Loew), Paramount (Jesse Lasky, Adolph Zukor, and Barney Balaban), Twentieth Century-Fox (Sol Brill and William Fox), United Artists (Al Lichtman), Universal (Carl Laemmle), and Warner Brothers (Sam, Jack, Albert, and Harry Warner).

Notable Jewish film directors include George Cukor (1899–1983), Mel Brooks (Melvyn Kaminsky, 1926–), Stanley Kubrick (1928–1999), Woody Allen (Allen Konigsberg; 1935–), Nora Ephron (1941–2012), Steven Spielberg (1947–), J. J. Abrams (1966–), and Judd Apatow (1967–).

Government Mordecai M. Noah (1785–1851) was the most widely known Jewish political figure of the first half of the nineteenth century. A controversial figure, Noah was U.S. consul in Tunis from 1813 to 1815, when he was recalled for apparently mismanaging funds. He went on to serve as an editor, sheriff, and judge. In 1825 he created a refuge for Jews when he purchased Grand Island in Niagara River. The refuge city, of which Noah proclaimed himself governor, was to be a step toward the establishment of a permanent state for Jews.

In 1916 noted legal scholar Louis Brandeis (1856–1941) became the first Jewish American U.S. Supreme Court justice. His liberalism and Jewish heritage sparked a heated five-month congressional battle over his nomination. After his confirmation, Brandeis used his power to help Zionism gain acceptance among Jews and non-Jews alike. Other prominent Jewish Supreme Court justices include Benjamin Cardozo (1870–1938), a legal realist whose opinions foreshadowed the liberalism of the Warren court; and Felix Frankfurter (1882–1965), who prior to his Supreme Court appointment had been influential in promoting New Deal policies as a key adviser to President Franklin D. Roosevelt. Ruth Bader Ginsberg (1933–) became the first Jewish American woman on the Supreme Court in 1999, followed by Elena Kagan (1960–) in 2010. Justice Stephen Breyer (1938–), appointed in 1994, is also Jewish.

In 1964 Arizona Republican Senator Barry Goldwater (1909–1998) became the first person of Jewish descent (on his father's side) to be a major party's presidential candidate. Henry Kissinger (Heinz Kissinger, 1923–), the first Jewish secretary

of state (under Presidents Nixon and Ford), was an architect of the détente strategy toward the Soviet Union and the opening of relations with the People's Republic of China. Kissinger received the Nobel Peace Prize in 1973. Connecticut Democratic senator Joe Lieberman (1942–), as Al Gore's running mate in 2000, was the first practicing Jew on a major party's presidential ticket. Debbie Wasserman Schultz (1966–) of Florida became chair of the Democratic National Committee in 2011.

After the 2012 elections, ten Jewish Americans were members of the U.S. Senate: Richard Blumenthal (Connecticut, 1946–), Barbara Boxer (California, 1940–), Ben Cardin (Maryland, 1943–), Dianne Feinstein (California, 1933–), Al Franken (Minnesota, 1951–), Frank Lautenberg (New Jersey, 1924–), Carl Levin (Michigan, 1934–), Bernie Sanders (Vermont, 1941–), Charles Schumer (New York, 1950–), and Ron Wyden (Oregon, 1949–). With the exception of Sanders, who is an Independent, all are Democrats. Twenty-two members of the House of Representatives were Jewish as of the 2012 elections, all but one Democratic. Eric Cantor of Virginia (1963–), the sole Republican Jewish congressman, was serving as the first Jewish majority leader. Three Jewish Americans were mayors of major cities in 2012: Michael Bloomberg (1942–) of New York, Rahm Emanuel (1959–) of Chicago, and Carolyn Goodman of Las Vegas.

Journalism During the late nineteenth century Jewish immigrant Joseph Pulitzer (1847–1911) operated a chain of newspapers, many of which often featured stories of public corruption. Upon his death, he left funds for the Columbia University School of Journalism and for the coveted annual prizes in his name. Since then, many Jewish journalists have won the Pulitzer Prize, including commentator and investigative journalist Carl Bernstein (1944–), best known for uncovering the Watergate scandal; *Washington Post* columnist David Broder (1929–2011); syndicated columnist and satirist Art Buchwald (1925–2007); syndicated columnist Ellen Goodman (1941–); *New York Times* reporter and author David Halberstam (1934–2007); renowned investigative journalist Seymour Hersh (1937–); and stylist, humorist, and former presidential speechwriter William Safire (1929–2009). Other notable Jewish journalists include sportscaster Howard Cosell (William Howard Cohen; 1920–1995), NBC television journalist Marvin Kalb (1930–), investigative journalist I. F. Stone (Isador Feinstein; 1907–1989), *60 Minutes* television journalist Mike Wallace (Myron Leon Wallace; 1918–2012), television anchor and interviewer Barbara Walters (1931–), and *New York Times* columnists David Brooks (1961–) and Paul Krugman (1953–).

Literature Jewish Americans have had a major impact on American literature from the early days of Jewish immigration to America. In fact, the poem

"The New Colossus," which is inscribed on the Statue of Liberty, was written by Jewish American Emma Lazarus (1849–1887). But the impact of Jewish American writers was especially notable in the twentieth century. Famous Jewish American novelists include Saul Bellow (Solomon Bellows; 1915–2005), Nobel laureate and Pulitzer Prize–winning author of *The Adventures of Augie March* and *Mr. Sammler's Planet*; J. D. Salinger (1919–2010), author of *The Catcher in the Rye*; E. L. Doctorow (1931–), author of *Ragtime* and *Billy Bathgate*; Joseph Heller (1923–1999), author of *Catch-22* and numerous satirical works; novelist and poet Erica Jong (Erica Mann; 1942–), author of *Fear of Flying*; Norman Mailer (1923–2007), Pulitzer Prize–winning author of *The Naked and the Dead* and *Tough Guys Don't Dance*; Philip Roth (1933–), National Book Award–winning author of *Portnoy's Complaint* and *Everyman*; Michael Chabon (1963–), Pulitzer Prize–winning author of *Wonder Boys* and *The Amazing Adventures of Kavalier and Clay*; Nicole Krauss (1974–), author of *The History of Love*; and Jonathan Safran Foer (1977–), author of *Everything Is Illuminated* and *Extremely Loud and Incredibly Close*.

Jewish Americans have also made an impact as playwrights. Famous Jewish American playwrights include Lillian Hellman (1907–1984), author of *The Children's Hour* and *The Little Foxes*; Pulitzer Prize winner Arthur Miller (1915–2005), writer of *Death of a Salesman* and *The Crucible*; David Mamet (1947–), Pultizer Prize winner and author of *American Buffalo* and *Glengarry Glen Ross*; Pulitzer Prize winner Wendy Wasserstein (1950–2006), best known for *The Heidi Chronicles*; and Tony Kushner (1956) best known for the Pulitzer Prize–winning *Angels in America*.

Notable Jewish American poets include Allen Ginsberg (1926–1997), famous Beat generation poet and author of "Howl"; Stanley Kunitz (1905–2006), author of "Green Ways"; National Book Award winner

Author and Nobel Prize laureate Elie Wiesel helped millions to understand and remember the Holocaust through his autobiographical novel, *Night*. NANCY R. SCHIFF / HULTON ARCHIVE / GETTY IMAGES

Adrienne Rich (1929–2012); and Pulitzer Prize winner Louise Glück (1943–).

Notable Jewish Americans in the field of political essays and memoirs include Emma Goldman (1869–1940), Russian native and famous anarchist; Irving Howe (1920–1993), notable socialist and author of *World of Our Fathers* and *How We Lived*; Alfred Kazin (1915–1998), writer of the immigrant experience, including *New York Jew*; MacArthur Fellow Susan Sontag (1933–2004), author of *Against Interpretation*; and Holocaust survivor and Nobel Peace Prize laureate Elie Wiesel (1928–), author of *Night*.

Music From Broadway to *Billboard* magazine, Jewish Americans have had a major impact on American music, as composers, performers, producers, and more.

In the world of musical theater and film composition, famous Jewish Americans include Irving Berlin (1888–1989), writer of "Blue Skies," "God Bless America," and "White Christmas"; George Gershwin (1898–1937), composer of *Of Thee I Sing* and *Porgy and Bess* (musicals) and "Rhapsody in Blue"; Richard Rodgers (1902–1979), co-composer, with Oscar Hammerstein, of *Oklahoma!*, *Carousel*, *South Pacific*, *The King and I*, and *The Sound of Music*; and pianist, composer, and conductor Leonard Bernstein (1918–1990), composer of *West Side Story* and *Candide* (musicals) and *On the Waterfront* (film score).

Notable Jewish American classical performers/composers include pianist Arthur Rubinstein (1887–1982); violinist Jascha Heifetz (1901–1987); pianist Vladimir Horowitz (1904–1989); violinist Nathan Milstein (1904–1992); violinist Itzhak Perlman (1945–); operatic soprano Beverly Sills (Belle Silverman; 1929–); and composer Aaron Copland (1900–1990). Jewish Americans in the world of jazz composing and performance have included swing clarinetist Benny Goodman (1909–1986) and saxophonist Stan Getz (1927–1991).

Jewish Americans have also made impressive contributions to American popular music. Among the most notable are Burt Bacharach (1928–); Bob Dylan (Robert Zimmerman; 1941–); Neil Diamond (1941–); Carole King (Carole Klein; 1941–); Paul Simon (1941–); Art Garfunkel (1941–); Joey Ramone (1951–2001) of the punk band the Ramones; Lou Reed (1942–) of the Velvet Underground; David Lee Roth (1954–) of Van Halen; Barbra Streisand (1942–); Paula Abdul (1962–); reggae rocker Matisyahu (Matthew Miller; 1979–); and Russian-born singer-songwriter Regina Spektor (1980–). All three members of the hip-hop group the Beastie Boys (Michael "Mike D" Diamond, 1965–; Adam "MCA" Yauch, 1964–2012; and Adam "Ad-Rock" Horovitz, 1966–) were Jewish.

Science and Medicine Perhaps the best-known thinker of the twentieth century is Albert Einstein (1879–1955), the German Jewish physicist who had completed his most important scientific work before coming to the United States in 1934. Though most famous for his theory of relativity, for which he won the Nobel Prize in 1922, Einstein played a critical role in American history as part of a team of scientists who researched atomic power during World War II. At that time, Jewish émigrés joined native-born Jews in the famous Manhattan Project, which led to the detonation of the first atomic bomb in 1945. Einstein was part of the "brain drain" of Jews from Nazi Germany, which also included psychoanalysts Erich Fromm (1900–1980), Bruno Bettelheim (1903–1990), and Erik Erikson (1902–1994), as well as social scientists Hannah Arendt (1906–1975) and Leo Strauss (1899–1973).

Robert Oppenheimer (1904–1967) worked with Einstein on the Manhattan Project. Jonas Salk (1914–1995) and Albert Sabin (1906–1993) discovered polio vaccines during the 1950s, and Robert Hofstadter (1916–1970) won the Nobel Prize for creating a device for measuring the size and shape of neutrons and protons. Medical science pioneer Joseph Goldberger (1874–1929) laid the foundation for modern nutritional science with his study of the dietary habits of poor whites and blacks in the South. Chemist Isaac Asimov (1920–1992) popularized science with his five hundred fiction and nonfiction books on science. Following Asimov's example, Stephen Jay Gould (1941–2002) reached millions of readers with his highly readable accounts of natural history, and biogeographer Jared Diamond (1937–) won the Pulitzer Prize for *Guns, Germs, and Steel* (1997).

Scores of Jewish Americans have won the Nobel Prize in science, reflecting their high academic achievements. Albert Michelson (1852–1931), who measured the speed of light, was the first American to win the Nobel Prize in science. Other Jewish American Nobel laureates include Gertrude Elion (1918–1999), developer of numerous pharmaceuticals; neuropsychiatrist Eric Kandel (1929–); Arthur Kornberg (1918–2007), who unlocked the secrets of DNA; and his son Roger Kornberg (1947–), who has achieved similar discoveries with RNA.

Sports Many children of Jewish immigrants at the beginning of the twentieth century gravitated toward sports to break up the routine of daily life. Boxing was especially popular, with Jewish boxing champions Abe Attell (Albert Knoehr; 1884–1969), Barney Ross (Barnet Rasofsky; 1909–1967), and Benny Leonard (Benjamin Leiner; 1896–1947) all hailing from New York's Lower East Side.

Beyond boxing, Jewish Americans have made their mark in many other sports. Members of the National Jewish Sports Hall of Fame in New York include such luminaries as Red Auerbach (basketball coach, 1917–2006), Isaac Berger (weightlifting, 1936–), Hank Greenberg (baseball, 1911–1986), Sandy Koufax (baseball pitcher, 1935–), Sid Luckman (NFL quarterback, 1916–1998), Dick Savitt (tennis, 1927–), and Mark Spitz (nine-time Olympic gold medalist swimmer, 1950–).

Stage and Screen A great number of Jewish Americans have been successful on screen, including the Marx Brothers—Chico (Leonard; 1887–1961), Harpo (Adolph; 1888–1964), Groucho (Julius; 1890–1977), Gummo (Milton; 1894–1977), and Zeppo (Herbert; 1901–1979); Kirk Douglas (Issur Danielovitch; 1916–); Walter Matthau (1920–2000); Lauren Bacall (Betty Joan Perske; 1924–); Sammy Davis Jr. (1925–1990); Gene Wilder (Jerome Silberman; 1935–); Dustin Hoffman (1937–); Paul Rudd (1969–); Winona Ryder (1971–); Sarah Michelle Gellar (1977–); siblings Maggie (1977–) and Jake (1980–) Gyllenhaal; Joseph Gordon-Levitt (1981–); and Natalie Portman (Natalie Hershlag, 1981–).

Jewish Americans have left a lasting impact in comedy as well. Notable Jewish American comedians include Jack Benny (Benjamin Kubelsky; 1894–1974), George Burns (Nathan Birnbaum; 1896–1996), Henny Youngman (Henry; 1906–1998), Milton Berle (Milton Berlinger; 1908–2002), Jerry Lewis (1926–), Joan Rivers (1933–), Gilda Radner (1946–1989), Albert Brooks (1947–), Billy Crystal (1947–), Jerry Seinfeld (1954–), Bob Saget (1956–), Jon Stewart (Jonathan Stuart Leibowitz, 1962–), Ben Stiller (1965–), Adam Sandler (1966–), Sarah Silverman (1970–), and Seth Rogen (1982–).

MEDIA

PRINT

Commentary

Published monthly by the American Jewish Committee, this influential Jewish magazine addresses religious, political, social, and cultural topics.

John Podhoretz, Editor
561 7th Avenue
16th Floor
New York, New York 10018
Phone: (212) 891-1400
Email: letters@commentarymagazine.com
URL: www.commentarymagazine.com

The Jewish Daily Forward

Published in English and Yiddish by the Forward Association. With a circulation of more than 25,000 in English and around 5,500 in Yiddish, the daily paper covers local, national, and international news, with special emphasis on Jewish life, from a progressive perspective.

Jane Eisner, Editor in Chief
125 Maiden Lane
New York, New York 10038
Phone: (212) 889-8200
Fax: (212) 447-6406
Email: newsdesk@forward.com
URL: www.forward.com

Jewish Press

The largest independent weekly Jewish newspaper in the United States, the paper covers issues and events related to Jewish life from a more Orthodox perspective. Established in 1949, it has a circulation of about 50,000.

Jason Maoz, Editor
4915 16th Avenue
Brooklyn, New York 11204
Phone: (800) 992-1600
or
Phone: (718) 330-1100
Email: editor@jewishpress.com
URL: www.jewishpress.com

Lilith

Founded in 1976, this monthly magazine calls itself "independent, Jewish, and frankly feminist." It covers issues of interest to Jewish women, as well as original fiction and poetry, social change, and more. It is named for the legendary first woman on Earth, created before Eve.

Susan Weidman Schneider, Editor in Chief
250 West 57th Street
Suite 2432
New York, New York 10107-0172
Phone: (212) 757-0818
Email: info@lilith.org
URL: www.lilith.org

Reform Judaism

Published by the Union of American Hebrew Congregations, this quarterly concentrates on religious, political, and cultural issues of concern to Reform Jews. It is received three times a year by more than 300,000 households.

Aron Hirt-Manheimer, Editor
633 Third Avenue
New York, New York 10017
Phone: (212) 650-4240
Email: rjmagazine@urj.org
URL: www.reformjudaismmag.org

TELEVISION

Jewish Life Television (JLTV)

Calling itself "America's Chosen Network," JLTV was launched in 2006 and is the country's first and only full-time Jewish television network. Available on a variety of cable and satellite outlets, it broadcasts from bureaus in Los Angeles, Washington, D.C., Israel, and Russia and reaches more than nine million households.

Phil Blazer, CEO and President
16501 Ventura Boulevard
Suite 504

Encino, California 91436
Phone: (818) 786-4000
Email: pblazer@jltv.tv
URL: www.jltv.org

Jewish Television Network (JTN)

Founded in 1981 at American Jewish University, JTN
produces television programming for a variety
of outlets, including news, music, comedy, and
documentaries about Israel, Judaism, and Jewish life
in the United States and abroad.

Harvey Lehrer, Senior Director
15600 Mulholland Drive
Bel Air, California 90077
Phone: (310) 440-1229
Email: info@jewishtvnetwork
URL: www.jewishtvnetwork.org

ORGANIZATIONS AND ASSOCIATIONS

American Jewish Committee (AJC)

Founded in 1906, the AJC is an influential organization
dedicated to the protection of religious and
civil rights for Jewish people and all minorities
internationally. Representing numerous Jewish
American communities, the AJC sponsors
educational programs, maintains its own library,
and publishes the noted journal *Commentary*. It has
twenty-six regional offices around the nation.

David Harris, Executive Director
165 East 56th Street
New York, New York 10022
Phone: (212) 751-4000
Email: info@ajc.org
URL: www.ajc.org

American Jewish Joint Distribution Committee (JDC)

Founded in 1914, the JDC is a charitable organization
created by the American Jewish Relief Committee,
the Central Committee for Relief of Jews of the
Union of Orthodox Congregations, and the People's
Relief Committee. In addition to providing economic
assistance to needy Jews in more than seventy
countries, the organization fosters community
development through an assortment of educational,
religious, cultural, and medical programs.

Darrell Friedman, Interim CEO
711 Third Avenue
New York, New York 10017-4014
Phone: (212) 687-6200
Fax: (212) 682-7262
Email: info@jdc.org
URL: www.jdc.org

Anti-Defamation League (ADL)

Founded in 1913, the ADL was created by B'nai B'rith, an
international organization founded in 1843 to foster
Jewish unity and protect human rights. The ADL was
established to counter the rising tide of anti-Semitism
during the early twentieth century, but it has since
expanded its focus to protect against defamation
and discrimination of any group of people. Though
the ADL has broadened its mission and sought to

improve interfaith relations, one of the group's
primary goals is to further American understanding
of Israel. The ADL sponsors a number of bulletins,
including its Anti-Defamation League Bulletin, as well
as articles, monographs, and educational materials.

Abraham H. Foxman, National Director
605 Third Avenue
New York, New York 10158
Phone: (212) 885-7700
URL: www.adl.org

92nd Street Y

Founded in 1874 from the merger between the Young
Men's Hebrew Association, the Young Women's
Hebrew Association, and the Clara de Hirsch
Residence, the 92nd Street Y provides Jewish cultural,
social, educational, and recreational programs for
300,000 Jews and other residents of New York
City. The association serves a variety of functions
by maintaining several facilities in Manhattan and
Rockland County, New York, including residence
facilities for Jewish men and women between the
ages of eighteen and twenty-seven, men's and
women's health clubs, swimming pools, gymnasiums,
concert halls and art galleries, and a library
containing more than 30,000 volumes on Jewish life
and thought. Scholarships are also offered to Jewish
undergraduate and graduate students.

Sol Adler, Executive Director
1395 Lexington Avenue
New York, New York 10128
Phone: (212) 415-5500
URL: www.92y.org

World Jewish Congress, American Section (WJC)

Founded 1936, the WJC is an international organization
representing three million Jews in one hundred
countries. The American Section of the WJC
represents twenty-three Jewish organizations. Guided
by its mission to protect human rights worldwide,
the WJC serves a consultative capacity with various
international governing bodies, including the United
Nations, UNESCO, UNICEF, International Labour
Organization, and Council of Europe. The WJC is
responsible for such periodicals as World Jewry,
Journal of Jewish Sociology, and Patterns of Prejudice.

Betty Ehrenberg, Executive Director, WJC North
America
501 Madison Avenue
17th Floor
New York, New York 10022
Phone: (212) 755-5770
Fax: (212) 755-5883
Email: info@worldjewishcongress.org
URL: www.worldjewishcongress.org

MUSEUMS AND RESEARCH CENTERS

American Jewish Historical Society (AJHS)

Founded in 1892 in an effort to gather, organize, and
disseminate information and memorabilia related
to the history of American Jews. The society has
a branch in Massachusetts and is a partner in the
Center for Jewish History in New York, providing

access to more than twenty-five million books, documents, manuscripts, pictures, and miniatures.

Jonathan Karp, Executive Director
15 West 16th Street
New York, New York 10011
Phone: (212) 294-6160
Fax: (212) 294-6161
Email: jkarp@ajhs.org
URL: www.ajhs.org

The Jewish Museum of New York

This museum boasts the largest collection in the Western Hemisphere of materials related to Jewish art and culture. Founded in 1904, the collection now comprises 25,000 items, including paintings, drawings, prints, sculpture, ceremonial objects, coins, broadcast material, and historical documents.

Anne Scher, Director of Communications
1109 Fifth Avenue
New York, New York 10128
Phone: (212) 423-3200
Email: info@thejm.org
URL: www.thejm.org

United States Holocaust Memorial Museum

Opened in 1994 on the National Mall in Washington, D.C., the Holocaust Museum presents a moving tribute to the millions of Jews and others who suffered and were killed in Nazi concentration camps during World War II. The museum features photographs, documents, and video related to the Holocaust and other genocides worldwide, with the goal of inspiring citizens to "confront hatred, prevent genocide, and promote human dignity."

Sara Bloomfield, Director
100 Raoul Wallenberg Place SW
Washington, D.C. 20024-2150
Phone: (212) 488-0400
Email: www.ushmm.org/museum/contact
URL: www.ushmm.org

YIVO Institute for Jewish Research

A secular research institute dedicated to scholarship on all aspects of the American Jewish experience, with particular emphasis on Yiddish language and

literature. Established in 1925, the institute has gathered a massive collection of some twenty-four million documents, photographs, manuscripts, audiovisuals, and other items related to Jewish life. It is another partner in the Center for Jewish History in New York, along with the American Jewish Historical Society, and also organizes public lectures, continuing education classes, and Yiddish language instruction.

Jonathan Brent, Executive Director
15 West 16th Street
New York, New York 10011
Phone: (212) 246-6080
Fax: (212) 292-1892
Email: yivomail@yivo.cjh.org
URL: www.yivoinstitute.org

SOURCES FOR ADDITIONAL STUDY

Chametsky, Jules, John Felstiner, Hilene Flanzbaum, and Kathryn Hellerstein, eds. *Jewish American Literature: A Norton Anthology*. New York: W. W. Norton, 2000.

Diner, Hasia. *The Jews of the United States, 1654–2000*. Berkeley: University of California Press, 2006.

Goldstein, Eric. *The Price of Whiteness: Jews, Race and American Identity*. Princeton: Princeton University Press, 2007.

Hertzberg, Arthur. *The Jews in America: Four Centuries of an Uneasy Encounter*. New York: Columbia University Press, 1998.

Howe, Irving. *World of Our Fathers*. New York: Harcourt Brace Jovanovich, 1976.

Sachar, Howard M. *A History of the Jews in America*. New York: Knopf, 1993.

Sarna, Jonathan D. *American Judaism: A History*. New Haven, CT: Yale University Press, 2005.

Sorin, Gerald. *Tradition Transformed: The Jewish Experience in America*. Baltimore: Johns Hopkins University Press, 1997.

Waskow, Arthur I. *Seasons of Our Joy: A Handbook of Jewish Festivals*. New York: Summit, 1991.

JORDANIAN AMERICANS

Olivia Miller and Norman Prady

OVERVIEW

Jordanian Americans are immigrants or descendants of immigrants from Jordan, a kingdom near the Mediterranean Sea in the area of southwest Asia known as the Middle East. Its neighbors are Israel and the semi-autonomous Palestinian territories to the west, Syria to the north, Iraq to the northeast, and Saudi Arabia to the east and south. Amman, the largest city, is the capital. Most of Jordan is a plateau averaging about 900 meters above sea level. The eastern part of the country is largely desert. The western part has a less arid climate because of its proximity to the Mediterranean Sea and the Dead Sea, which lies between Jordan and Israel. Jordan is the site of the city of Petra, an archeological treasure that was the religious center for the Nabataeans, an ancient nomadic Arab people. Jordan's land area is approximately 35,000 square miles (almost 92,000 square kilometers), about the size of Indiana.

According to the Central Intelligence Agency (CIA) World Factbook, Jordan's population in 2012 was about 6,500,000. Ninety-eight percent of the people were Arab, and the remaining 2 percent included Assyrians, Armenians, Circassians, Mandeans, and tiny minorities of non-Arabs originating elsewhere, among them Shishans—also known as Chechens—and Kurds. Of the Arabs living in Jordan, more than half are Palestinian people who began migrating to Jordan in significant numbers in 1947 after the United Nations General Assembly called for the formation of the State of Israel. Palestinians tend to live in the western part of the country, near Israel. Another third of population are Jordanian Bedouins, a nomadic people who migrated to the area in large numbers between the fourteenth and eighteenth century. While significant portions of the Bedouin population have assimilated into Jordanian society and adopted a sedentary lifestyle, those who have maintained the group's traditional culture live in the desert in the southern and eastern portions of the country. The 2007 CIA World Factbook also recorded a substantial number (450,000 to 1 million) of refugees from Iraq living in Jordan. About 92 percent of Jordanians are Sunni Muslims. Nearly 8 percent are Christian, and less than 1 percent are Shia Muslim. Since 1999, when King Abdullah II introduced free-trade policies, creating an economic boom, Jordan has become one of the Middle East's more competitive economies, though it

is not as wealthy as Gulf States such as Saudi Arabia, Oman, and the United Arab Emirates. Despite recent advances, Jordan's economy continues to be impeded by chronic water scarcity, lack of raw materials, reliance on oil imports, a high national debt, and political instability throughout the region.

Jordanians began immigrating to the United States after World War II, when the 1948 establishment of the State of Israel increased tensions in the area. The first Jordanians to arrive tended to settle in large cities, especially Chicago and New York City. The number of immigrants climbed substantially in the subsequent decades, primarily as a result of wars in the Middle East. Although Jordanian immigrants tended to be well educated, those who arrived in the large waves of the 1960s and 1970s often had to accept retail or factory work below their level of schooling, and many returned home after the wars. After the 1980s most Jordanian immigrants came to the United States to pursue an education. Higher percentages of these immigrants have remained in the United States, where they have found professional jobs.

According to the U.S. Census Bureau's American Community Survey (ACS) one-year estimates, 72,730 Jordanians lived in the United States in 2011. This total appears low when compared to the Homeland Security data indicating that more than 80,000 Jordanians obtained permanent resident status between 1990 and 2010 alone. One likely reason for the discrepancy is that Jordanians responding to the ACS may self-identify as Palestinian rather than Jordanian. The 2010 ACS estimates for 2006 to 2010 indicate that the majority of Jordanian immigrants settled in California. Other states with large Jordanian American populations included Texas, Illinois, and New York. Smaller communities can also be found in Michigan, New Jersey, Florida, and Ohio.

HISTORY OF THE PEOPLE

Early History As an independent nation, Jordan is relatively young. The land it occupies, however, was inhabited by the earliest humans. The archaeological record indicates that people who survived by hunting and gathering lived in the area during the Paleolithic and Mesolithic eras. During the Neolithic period, which began about 10,000 BCE, agriculture, written language, organized religion, political structures,

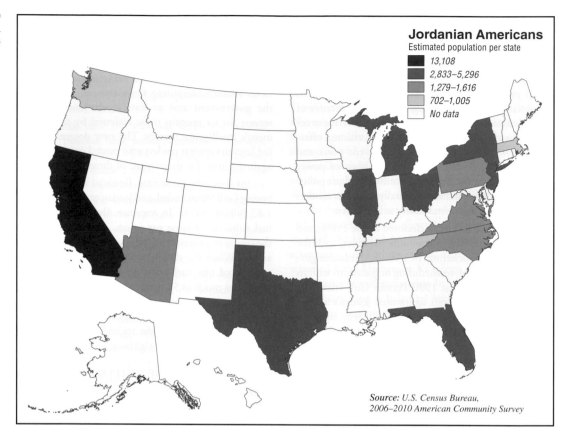

Jordanian Americans
Estimated population per state

- 13,108
- 2,833–5,296
- 1,279–1,616
- 702–1,005
- No data

Source: U.S. Census Bureau,
2006–2010 American Community Survey

According to the U.S. Immigration and Naturalization Service, 5,762 new Jordanian immigrants arrived in the 1950s. In the 1960s this number almost doubled when 11,727 Jordanians immigrated, and the numbers soared again in the 1970s, with 27,535 arrivals. This spike in numbers was a result of two Arab-Israeli Wars—the Six Day War in 1967 and the Yom Kippur War in 1973—and the Jordanian Civil War (1970–1971). Jordanians fleeing wartime conditions found temporary asylum in the United States and returned home when they felt it was safe to do so.

According to the Department of Homeland Security's *Yearbook of Immigration Statistics: 2011*, approximately 2,500 Jordanians obtained legal permanent resident status each year of the 1980s. Again many came to pursue an education. This wave of immigrants, whose departure from Jordan was provoked by economic necessity, as diminished foreign aid and the large budget deficit took their tolls, included more Muslims than the prior waves had. Most Jordanians who came in the 1980s hoped to find professional jobs at higher salaries than they received in Jordan. These immigrants brought their families and were more likely to stay than the people who had come in previous decades.

Between 1990 and 2010 the average number of Jordanian immigrants climbed to 4,000 per year, according to the *Yearbook of Immigration Statistics:*

2011. The First Gulf War, in 1991, and tensions that lingered in the area drove the increase. Many of the immigrants during this period were Christians seeking to escape religious friction within Jordan. Others were members of the international business community who chose to leave jobs in the Middle East because of ongoing violence there. Like those who came before them, members of the most recent wave of Jordanian immigrants were well educated and sought professional positions. The largest numbers of Jordanian Americans reside in California.

LANGUAGE

Arabic, which shares its Semitic roots with Hebrew, Aramaic, and certain Ethiopic languages, is Jordan's official language. Most Jordanians read and write in Standard (as opposed to Classical, or Quranic) Arabic and converse in their local dialects. The majority speak a dialect that is also common in Lebanon, Syria, and Iraq. Residents whose native language is not Arabic (for example, Circassians or Armenians) are usually also proficient in Arabic. Before the arrival of Palestinian refugees in the wake of the wars with Israel, the Levantine Bedawi Arabic dialect was the language of Jordan. It remains the language of the army and is used in many television programs for Bedouin people or to promote Bedouin culture.

Many Jordanians among the middle and upper classes speak English, so Jordan's radio and television stations offer some English programming. A daily English newspaper is published in Amman, and a weekly newspaper offers a French section. Additionally, some Jordanians who have business or cultural connections in Europe speak French and German, and Jordanian television offers some daily programming in French.

Jordanian Americans have access to national newspapers published in Arabic. Local Arabic newspapers are published in some U.S. communities with large Arab populations, such as metropolitan Detroit. Jordanian Americans tend to become proficient in English but also to continue speaking Arabic at home and in their communities. According to the 2011 ACS one-year estimates, just 20 percent of Jordanian Americans speak only English in their homes. Almost 80 percent of those surveyed indicated that they spoke "a language other than English"—in this case, presumably Arabic—at home, and 28 percent reported that they spoke English "less than well."

Greetings and Popular Expressions In Arabic the Hashemite Kingdom of Jordan is called *Urdoun*. *Ahlan wa sahlan* means "welcome," and *marhab* means "hello." *Mat el malak, ash el malak,* or "The king is dead; long live the king," is an expression that was heard frequently after the death of Hussein and the swearing in of King Abdullah to signify both grief and optimism. *Inshallah*, or "God willing," is often used to state intention, whereas the term *bismallah*, "in the name of God," accompanies many daily deeds, such as eating, drinking, and driving.

RELIGION

Jordan's constitution guarantees freedom of religion, but the country's official religion is Sunni Islam, and the government supports Sunni institutions. The monarch and the monarch's successors must be Muslims and sons of Muslims.

The religious affiliations of Jordanian Americans contrast sharply with those of homeland Jordanians. Jordan's government states that the country is 92 percent Muslim and 8 percent Christian, whereas the Jordanian American community has a 92 percent majority who are Christian, with the remaining 8 percent Muslim. The largest group of Jordanian American Christians belongs to the Eastern Orthodox Church, the second-largest to the Roman Catholic Church, and the remainder to a variety of Protestant and evangelical churches. Jordanian American Christians and Muslims often share their church buildings and mosques with compatible congregations from other Arab groups and with institutions bolstering Jordanian or Arab identity and cultural continuity.

CULTURE AND ASSIMILATION

As comparative newcomers to the United States, Jordanian Americans tend to be much less Americanized than groups with longer histories here.

Guided by family and friends, these new Americans understandably find comfort in neighborhoods established by others from their home country. In such surroundings they continue their familiar social activities, shopping habits, and religious practices. Jordanian Americans fluent in English have greater communication and interaction with the larger community, as do those whose educational levels are higher and whose jobs have demanded that they adapt. People from urban areas of Jordan have adjusted more quickly to American city life than those from rural Jordan, and younger Jordanian Americans have often assimilated more quickly than their parents.

Traditions and Customs Although Jordan is modern and Western-oriented, Islamic ideals and beliefs provide the conservative foundation of the country's customs, laws, and practices. For instance, because the Muslim holy day is Friday, the work week for Jordanian government offices and most businesses is Saturday through Thursday. Along with religion, hospitality is an important value that dictates many typical Jordanian behaviors.

Elements of Jordanian American life provide cultural continuity with the homeland. Among these are events offering music and dancing, which are typically provided by larger, mixed-Arab groups. The events range from stage presentations to shows on the radio or cable television in many major metropolitan areas of the United States. Additionally, some cable networks show Arab movies. Ongoing exposure to traditional entertainment is especially comforting to new immigrants and supportive for longer-term residents.

Cuisine Much of Jordanian cuisine is based on traditional Bedouin cooking. A good example is *mensef*, a national dish that has altered little over the years. Usually, a whole sheep is roasted. Large chunks of the roasted meat are served with rice on a tortilla-like bread called *shraaq*. Toppings consist of a yogurt-based sauce, chopped parsley, and fried nuts. *Mensef* is usually eaten with the fingers. The guests of honor at a feast are presented with the softly cooked eyes of the sheep, which are considered a delicacy.

A Jordanian meal usually begins with several varieties of *mezze*, or hors d'oeuvres, such as *humus* (chickpea, tahini, and garlic spread), *fuul* (a paste of fava beans, garlic, and lemon), *kube* (deep-fried herbed minced meat and cracked wheat), *tabouleh* (cracked wheat salad with tomatoes onions, and parsley), and *felafel* (deep-fried chickpea balls). Lentils, *adas* in Arabic, are a common ingredient in Jordanian dishes, and there are many recipes for *shorabat 'adas*, lentil soup. *Magloube* is a dish consisting of meat, fish, or vegetable stew served with rice. One typical *magloube* recipe calls for alternating layers of chicken, fried eggplant, and rice. *Magloube* is often served with a lettuce and tomato salad and plain yogurt. *Musakhan* is a chicken dish with onions, olive oil, and pine nuts, baked in the oven on a thick loaf of Arabic bread.

Mahshi Waraq 'inab are grape leaves stuffed with rice, minced meat, and spices. Also popular in Jordan and among Jordanian Americans is the famous Middle Eastern shish kebab, consisting of chunks of lamb or marinated chicken speared on a wooden stick and cooked over a charcoal fire with tomatoes and onions. *Shwarma*, spit-cooked sliced lamb, is served on flatbread with vegetables as a sandwich.

Jordanian foods are seasoned with garlic, lemon, and spices typical of the Mediterranean, including cumin, coriander, and especially saffron. Arabic unleavened bread, or *khobz*, is eaten with almost everything. A meal finishes with dessert or fresh fruits and Arabic coffee, without which no meeting, formal or informal, is complete. Arabic coffee is normally served continuously during social occasions. A guest may signal that no more is wanted by slightly tilting the cup when handing it back; otherwise it will be refilled. The local Jordanian alcohol, *arak*, is an anise-flavored beverage that is served mixed with water over ice. Traditionally, lunch is the main meal in Jordan, while breakfast and supper are light.

Jordanian cuisine is popular among Americans in large urban centers. Restaurants such as the Petra House in Portland, Oregon, and the Bedouin Tent and the Bedouin Express in Brooklyn have drawn large crowds and have established a reputation for serving delicious and affordable meals.

Traditional Dress As late as the 1980s, the style of any Middle Eastern costume conveyed the wearer's ethnic and regional identity as well as the identity of its maker. Jordanian men traditionally wore an ankle-length, cool, loose-fitting garment with a high neck and long sleeves called a *kandoura* or *dishdash*. The headdress, a *taqia* or *qahfa*, was a skullcap covered by a long cloth, usually white, called a *gutra*, secured by a wool rope, known as *al iqal* or *al ghizam*. The headdress was wound around the crown to protect the head and neck from the blistering sun. The *bisht*, a sleeveless flowing black or beige cloak trimmed with gold (the material depended on the social status of the wearer), was the preferred outfit for ceremonial occasions. Many people throughout the Arabian Peninsula still wear traditional dress, with minor variations, because it is suitable for the desert climate. In the United States, however, Jordanian men typically wear Western clothing rather than the *kandoura* and *qahfa*.

Bedouin men typically carried weaponry of some kind. The *khanjar*, a curving double-edged blade, six to eight inches long, with a hilt of local horn overlaid with silver, was once necessary for defense and has since become a status symbol. The *khanjar*'s curving wooden scabbard is more extensively decorated: the upper part is usually covered with engraved silver, and the lower section consists of strips of leather overlaid with silver and adorned with silver rings and wire, often in a geometric pattern. The tip is capped with silver. Some *khanjar* scabbards are also trimmed with gold. Other popular weapons were a single-edged dagger with a tapered blade and a straight carved wooden scabbard overlaid with silver at both ends; and the *yirz*, an axe combining a three-foot shaft with a four-inch steel head. The *saif*, a double-edged sword; and the scimitar-like *qattara* are usually only seen in museums or in ceremonial dances. Silver and copper were used to decorate containers for gunpowder and long-barreled pistols. Bedouin men also carried less deadly items such as beautifully decorated silver purses, pipes, toothpicks, ear-cleaning spoons, and tweezers, all hanging from silver chains. Modern rifles and cartridge belts slung around the waist were eventually added to the customary dress of the Bedouin. Jordanian men in the United States do not engage in these practices.

Jordanian women dress in accordance with social positions and Islamic injunctions. As with men, traditional dress among women is still very popular. Bedouin women, for practical and financial reasons, wear wool and cotton garments, whereas urban women favor silks, brocades, satins, and chiffons. Women's clothing is often intricately ornamented. In rural and other less populated areas, the *burqa* (a full-length garment that includes a veil of coarse black silk with a central stiffened rib resting on the nose, leaving only the eyes clearly visible) is still worn in the street, particularly by older women and women of the lower and lower-middle classes. Other Muslim women wear the more fitted but still all-enveloping black *abaya*, a robe-like dress made from lightweight cloth embroidered with tapestried threads. The *kandoura*, a loose, full-sleeved dress reaching to the midcalf, exquisitely embellished on the cuffs and collar, is usually made of colorful material, with its quality and design varying with the economic status of the wearer. Older Bedu, or Bedouin women of the village, and sometimes the younger ones, still make and wear the traditional dress, a long black *thobe*, its hems, yokes, and sleeves decorated with tiny embroidered stitches that form complex and colorful patterns. Women may heavily decorate their eyes and hands, as these are often the only visible parts of their bodies. They accentuate their eyes with kohl and apply henna to their palms, and sometimes the soles of their feet, in intricate designs. Many Jordanian women in larger urban areas such as Amman, as well as those who have immigrated to the United States, compromise between Eastern and Western dress, opting for Western slacks or jeans and long-sleeved tops rather than *kandouras* but in many cases wearing headscarves that reveal the face.

Many tribal women still carry their savings around their necks, wrists, or ankles in the form of jewelry. These pieces have at various times included intricately designed necklaces of beads and coins; elaborate forehead decorations of coins and chains; ornate looped or dangling earrings, including inverted pyramids with embossed geometric designs; heavy bossed bracelets covering much of the lower arm; elaborate, hinged anklets; and rings for fingers, toes, and noses, sometimes inset with bone or horn and studded with stone, glass, or coral. Many fine examples of silver Bedouin jewelry can still be found in markets and museums. Jordanian American women are fond of jewelry, although they rarely display it extravagantly in public, and they use Western-style purses to carry personal items.

Dances and Songs Bedouin musical traditions are important in Jordan. The most popular of the Jordanian Bedouin singers is Omar Al-Abdallat, who has achieved fame with a number of patriotic songs and has a wide audience throughout the region. Jordan also has a vibrant popular music scene, boasting a number of successful rap artists and heavy metal and indie bands. The leading rapper in the country is Tareq Abu Kwaik, who has named his solo musical venture El Far3i. Heavy metal has encountered great resistance from mainstream Jordanians. The genre is linked to Satanism in the popular imagination, and shows are often closed down by police. Some heavy metal artists have chosen to leave the country in order to freely pursue their careers. First-generation Jordanian Americans are more likely to listen to traditional music than are later generations, who typically prefer Western-style popular music and are not likely to keep tabs on the contemporary music scene in Jordan.

Holidays Although Islam is the state religion in Jordan, Christians are encouraged to celebrate religious holidays openly, and Christmas is a holiday on the national calendar. Malls and shops have Christmas trees and other holiday decorations, Christians attend Christmas mass and exchange gifts, and restaurants offer lunch and dinner specials featuring dishes that celebrate the season. Easter is not recognized in Jordan, though many Christians are lobbying the government to declare it an official public holiday. Jordanian Christians celebrate Easter by attending a liturgy and having a large midday meal with friends and family. Jordanian American Christians celebrate Christmas and Easter in much the same way as Americans do. Both Jordanian and Jordanian American Muslims observe the major holidays on the Muslim calendar, adhering to the traditions that are common to Sunni Muslims. Holidays include Eid al-Adha (Feast of the Sacrifice of Ibrahim/Abraham), Eid al-Fitr (Feast of Breaking the Fast of Ramadan), Isra wal Mi'raj (the Ascension of Mohammad), and Mawlid al-Nabi (Mohammad's birthday). Jordanian Americans also celebrate Western secular holidays such as Valentine's Day, the Fourth of July, Halloween, and Thanksgiving. This is especially true if they have children, who participate in festivities at school.

Jordanians observe Independence Day on May 25, Labor Day on May 1, Army Day on June 10, and King Abdullah's accession to the throne on June 9. Each year the Eastern Orthodox Church in Jordan recognizes

Independence Day by offering special prayers for the king. Universities and other organizations hold symposiums and round tables to honor Jordan's history. At night the larger cities have fireworks shows. Jordanians celebrate King Abdullah II's accession to the throne with a large gathering in Amman, where thousands of citizens converge to pledge their support to the monarch and promise to maintain national security and stability by honoring their fellow citizens' human rights. While Jordanian Americans are more likely to observe religious holidays than national holidays, organizations such as the Jordanian American Association of New York celebrate national holidays by holding formal ceremonies at which dignitaries from the Jordanian Embassy address crowds. Jordanian music and food are presented at such events.

> *The religious affiliations of Jordanian Americans contrast sharply with those of homeland Jordanians. Jordan's government states that the country is 92 percent Muslim and 8 percent Christian, whereas the Jordanian American community has a 92 percent majority who are Christian, with the remaining 8 percent Muslim.*

Health Care Issues and Practices The Jordanian diet is seasonal; it contains high amounts of fiber and not much meat. Jordanian Americans consume more meat and other high-fat foods, as well as more processed food. Consequently they experience higher rates of certain cancers, diabetes, and cardiovascular diseases than their compatriots at home.

Despite having limited access to fresh water, Jordanians are among the healthiest people in the Middle East, and the country's health care facilities are known to be clean, efficiently run, and affordable. A 2008 report in the *Jordan Times* indicated that the country took in more than $1 billion annually in medical tourism revenues—fees from nationals of other countries who preferred treatment in Jordan. *Medical Tourism* magazine listed that number at $650 million. Jordan's medical schools are widely regarded to be among the best in the region. Life expectancy in the country, for both men and women, is close to eighty years of age, and infant mortality rates are considerably lower than the region's average. One notable exception to this is that cancer rates in Jordan are higher than average, with more than 4,000 new cases reported per year since 2007. A 2010 report on *AMEinfo.com*, an online Middle East business publication, recorded some medical experts as projecting that the annual number of new cancer cases could climb as high as 19,000 by 2050. The report suggested that the primary causes of these high cancer rates were smoking and poor diet.

In February 1999 the Cyprus Institute of Neurology and Genetics, in collaboration with two

JORDANIAN PROVERBS

Common Jordanian proverbs include the following:

- When elephants begin to dance, smaller creatures should stay away.

- The dogs may bark but the caravan moves on.

- Eat whatever you like, but dress as others do.

- The hand of God is with the group.

- He that plants thorns must never expect to gather roses.

- If I am a prince and you are a prince, who will lead the donkeys?

- If begging should unfortunately be thy lot, knock at the large gates only.

- Judge a man by the reputation of his enemies.

- A kind word can attract even the snake from his nest.

- Knowledge acquired as a child is more lasting than an engraving on stone.

- The man who can't dance says the band can't play.

- Older than you by a day, wiser than you by a year.

- Silence is the door of consent.

- Trust in God, but tie your camel.

- The wound of words is worse than the wound of swords.

- All sunshine makes the desert.

- The ass went seeking for horns and lost his ears.

- Beware of one who flatters unduly, for he will also censure unjustly.

- Dawn does not come twice to awaken a man.

- Death is a black camel that lies down at every door. Sooner or later you must ride the camel.

Jordanian hospitals, identified a new form of nerve and muscle-wasting hereditary disease that strikes a particular tribal population of Jordanians. The disease causes selective weakness and wasting of the nerves controlling the muscles of the hands and feet while not necessarily affecting the arms and legs. The researchers were able to isolate the gene on chromosome nine that causes the crippling motor neuropathy, which is unique to people of the ancient Roman-Greek Jordanian city of Jerash and is transmitted among those who intermarry. The disorder is recessive, meaning both parents may carry the gene and still not pass it to their children, although the risk is greater in this case than if only one parent is a carrier. The disease's victims have been strictly Arab Jordanians, all from the Jerash area, and have included no Palestinians.

There is a minimal amount of health-related data on Jordanian Americans. According to the 2011 ACS one-year estimates, more than 80 percent of Jordanian Americans have some form of health insurance in the United States, with more than 46 percent on private policies.

Death and Burial Rituals Jordanian Americans have modified their homeland custom of quick burials to conform to common U.S. practices. They generally use the facilities and services of a funeral director instead of having a home-based rite. Jordanian American Christians might display the body for several days while family and friends visit and offer their sympathies. Jordanian American Muslims, however, do not display the body. Well-wishers usually send food to the home of the deceased person's immediate family every day until the burial. Following the burial, family and friends gather for a meal and to share memories. Visiting might continue for forty days afterward.

FAMILY AND COMMUNITY LIFE

Jordanians' upbringing emphasizes generosity, warmth, openness, and friendliness. The ideals of tribal unity and respect for the family form the core of Jordanian society. Jordanian Americans typically live in tight-knit nuclear families and have frequent contact with members of their extended families. Children are taught to respect the authority of everyone older than them, and they respond to directives from uncles and aunts as they would to those of their parents. Adult children are expected to help take care of elderly parents, who tend to move in with one of their children when they are no longer able to live independently. Public care for the elderly is not an acceptable option for most Jordanian American families.

Jordanian Americans are expected to choose a Jordanian spouse of similar religious and economic background. Marriages are not arranged, but children are expected to follow their parents' advice when selecting a partner. It is not uncommon for a Jordanian American male to go to Jordan in search of a bride. According to Jordanian tradition brought to the United States, the bride, groom, and both families plan the wedding, and the groom and his family pay for it. Divorce is uncommon among Jordanian Americans. If a couple has marital problems, parents and relatives from both families intervene with the goal of preserving the marriage. If children are involved, the culture dictates that the wife and husband resolve their problems for the children's benefit.

Gender Roles As with many other Arab nations, Jordan's traditional patriarchal culture has experienced a continuing campaign for women's rights. Since the 1960s increasing numbers of women have entered the workforce. As women's educational levels have risen, they have begun to delay marriage and tend to have fewer children, partly because of the economic strain of supporting a large family. Still, marriage and childbearing continue as the basis of women's status.

In 1988 Nadia Hijab, a Palestinian policy analyst, published a study of employed Jordanian women (most of whom were single). She found that opportunity and need trumped cultural attitudes in the decision to seek employment. In the mid-1980s, when unemployment surged, Jordan's leaders pressured women to return to their homes. Publicly and privately, Jordanians hotly debated the issue. Letters to newspapers took sides both for and against women's employment. Hijab found that by 1985 pressure on women to stay out of the workforce had acquired an almost "official" status. Then-prime minister Zaid ar Rifai stated that employed women should stop working if they paid more than half of their salaries to foreign maids who sent the currency abroad.

In the 1990s Jordanian women began to organize to change their nation's attitudes. In 1992 they established a policy forum, the Jordan National Committee for Women (JNCW), to involve women in national development and economic activities, promote enhanced legal status among women, and increase their participation in decision making. In the late 1990s the United Nations Development Fund for Women collaborated with the JNCW in a meeting in Amman to discuss how to eliminate violence against women in Muslim society. Jordanian women began to lead women's movements in other Arab countries. In 1999 Queen Noor (the widow of King Hussein and queen dowager of Jordan) spoke out against "crimes of honor," specifically the murders of women by husbands whom they had allegedly dishonored through immodest or otherwise unacceptable behavior. In 2003 a constitutional amendment implemented a gender quota system in the Parliament. This step demonstrated Jordan's sincerity in creating gender equality.

In general, Jordanian American women adhere to traditional Jordanian values in their living arrangements, considering the male as head of the household. According to the 2011 ACS one-year estimates, almost 70 percent of the 22,799 Jordanian American women older than fifteen years of age were either currently married or widowed. Only 3 percent of the 21,364 Jordanian women eighteen and older were raising children without a spouse. In addition, just 3 percent of the female adults lived alone, and 0.3 percent lived with another person out of wedlock. The 2011 ACS indicated that 8,136 Jordanian American women between

sixteen and sixty-five—almost half of the female population in that age range—were employed. More than 80 percent of those employed women held jobs in management, science, business, sales, or some form of office work. Jordanian American women who work are still expected to do the majority of the domestic work.

Education According to the *Jordan Times*, Jordan's literacy rate in 2011 was greater than 93 percent. This figure is consistent with a 2006 report from the World Health Organization that estimated the country's literacy rate at slightly more than 90 percent. Enrollment in the primary grades increased from 71 percent in 1994 to 98 percent in 2006. During the same period enrollment in the secondary grades increased from 63 percent to 97 percent. Enrollment in higher education has fluctuated, involving between 79 and 85 percent of the population, with women constituting nearly half of enrollment. The first nine years of education are compulsory and free; the next three are free but not compulsory. In 2011 the Ministry of Education implemented a program to rehabilitate student dropouts. That year almost 1,800 students who had left school returned to class at one of forty-seven centers in Jordan established to provide vocational and academic training to people who had not completed secondary education.

Jordanian American families place a premium on education. Parents are very active in their children's schools, regardless of their own levels of education. They value education not only because it improves children's future prospects but also because it brings honor to the family. According to the 2011 ACS one-year estimates, nearly 90 percent of Jordanian Americans had obtained a high school degree, and almost 40 percent of the Jordanian American population twenty-five years and older had earned a bachelor's degree. Before 2000 Jordanian Americans were earning bachelor's degrees at slightly higher rates than the average for Arab immigrants in the United States. This trend changed in the first decade of the twenty-first century, however, as the 2011 ACS reported that 45 percent of the Arab American population twenty-five years and older had earned a bachelor's degree.

EMPLOYMENT AND ECONOMIC CONDITIONS

Jordanian Americans are well represented in the American labor force. According to the 2011 ACS one-year estimates, 50,555 Jordanian Americans aged sixteen and older (almost 70 percent of the entire Jordanian American community) held jobs in the United States. More than 40 percent of these work in management, science, business, or the arts, and another 30 percent work in sales or office positions. Nearly 10 percent are self-employed. Families earned an average annual income of nearly $80,000. These high numbers can be explained to some degree by the fact that many Jordanians come to the United States to pursue advanced degrees in medicine and engineering.

AMERICAN-JORDANIAN TEAMWORK

The U.S. government first established diplomatic relations with Jordan in 1949 and began providing limited military aid to the country in 1950. The United States became Jordan's principal source of assistance in 1957 after the British cut financial ties with its former protectorate. During the 1970 to 1971 Jordanian Civil War, the United States supported King Hussein against the Palestinian insurgents without intervening directly. Tension between Jordan and the United States arose when King Hussein made frequent requests for weapons to quell widespread demonstrations during the 1980s. Protest came from university students clamoring for more civil rights and from citizens enraged over skyrocketing gas prices. During this time the U.S and Jordan managed to remain on largely cordial terms, however, with the U.S. government providing specialized training for Jordan's military and high-ranking officers. The United States considered Hussein one of the most moderate Middle Eastern leaders and often relied on him to assist in peace negotiations in the region. Shortly before his death he was instrumental in developing a peace agreement between Israel and the Palestinians. Jordan and Egypt remain the only Arab nations to sign peace treaties with Israel, making Jordan one of the few voices of moderation in the Middle East.

Whereas members of the early waves of Jordanian immigrants tended to return to Jordan after earning degrees and obtaining some professional training abroad, since the economic troubles of the late 1980s and 1990s more Jordanian immigrants have pursued careers in the United States.

POLITICS AND GOVERNMENT

When Jordanians began arriving in the United States in the latter half of the twentieth century, their new country was undergoing far-reaching social change. Old and newer civil rights laws have helped immigrants feel they do not have to submerge their ethnic identity to fully participate in American society. As a result, Jordanian Americans and members of other groups have felt increasingly secure in taking part in local and national political activity, both inside and outside their own groups' interests.

Jordanian expatriates follow contemporary events in Jordan closely and have tended to support their families back in Jordan and local political groups with cash remittances. In the early 2010s Jordan was beset by a number of political issues. Although the country has a history of religious tolerance, fundamentalist groups such as the Islamic Action Front and various radical Salafi movements have gained traction there, partly as a consequence of the country's floundering economy and partly because of considerable sectarian tension in neighboring Syria. A November 2012 report in *Al Bawaba*, an

Arab online business journal, indicated that remittances increased by 5.5 percent during the first 10 months of 2012, topping out at more than $3 billion. In March 2013 a group of Jordanian American professionals and intellectuals petitioned President Barack Obama to increase political and economic aid to Jordan in order to help the country continue transitioning toward a democratic state. The petitioners also urged the government "to use its influence and prestige around the world to end the bloody conflict in Syria and support the Syrian people's aspirations of peace, freedom, and democracy."

NOTABLE INDIVIDUALS

Activism Lily Bandak is a renowned photographer who founded an organization to help disabled workers in Arab nations. Born in Amman, Jordan, Bandak has lived in the United States since 1960. She has served as the personal photographer of Mrs. (Jehan) Anwar Sadat, King Hussein, and Queen Noor and has also photographed Yasser Arafat. In 1978 the government of Egypt invited her to document the people and monuments of that country and compiled the photographs in the book *Images of Egypt*. She was the first photographer to have work accepted into the permanent collection of the White House. In 1984 Bandak was diagnosed with multiple sclerosis. In 1994 she set up the Bandak Foundation, which encourages people with disabilities to enter the workforce and participate fully in society.

Journalism Daoud Kuttab (1955–) is a Palestinian who immigrated to the United States from Jordan and obtained American citizenship. In 2008 he created the Community Media Network, which is registered in Jordan. In 1997 he moved to Amman and established the Arab world's first Internet radio station, AmmanNet. (www.ammannet.net).

Literature Diana Abu-Jaber (1960–), a second-generation Jordanian American, won the Oregon Book Award for her first novel, *Arabian Jazz* (1993), which was also a finalist for the PEN/Hemingway Award. Her novel *Crescent* (2003) won the Pen Center Award for Literary Fiction, and her most recent book *Birds of Paradise* (2011) won the National Arab American Book Award.

The poet and scholar Lisa Suhair Majaj (1960–), a Palestinian American raised in Jordan, received the 1995 prize for the best published poem of the year from the New England Poetry Club. Her volume *Geographies of Light* (2009) won the Del Sol Press Annual Poetry Prize.

The poet and activist Suheir Hammad (1973–) was born in Amman and immigrated to the United States when she was five. She was a featured narrator in the documentaries *Lest We Forget* (2003) and *The Fourth World War* (2004) and starred in the feature film *Salt of This Sea*(2008). Her volumes of poetry include *Born Palestinian, Born Black* (1996), *ZaatarDiva* (2005), and *Breaking Poems* (2008).

Science Omar Yaghi (1965–), born in Amman, is the James and Neeltje Tretter Chair Professor of

Chemistry at the University of California, Berkeley. His research laboratories produce compounds with clean energy and carbon dioxide storage applications.

Sports Justin Abdelkadar (1987–), whose paternal grandfather emigrated from Jordan, played forward for the Detroit Red Wings hockey team beginning in 2009. Drew Haddad, (1978–), an American football player of Jordanian descent, was drafted in 2000 to play wide receiver for the Buffalo Bills. He also played for the Indianapolis Colts, and he finished his career with the San Diego Chargers.

MEDIA

Jordan Times

An independent, English-language political newspaper published daily except on Friday in Jordan by the Jordan Press Foundation. Many Jordanian Americans read the paper.

Samir Barhoum, Editor in Chief
Phone: (962) 6-5600-800, extension 2392
Email: editor@jordantimes.com
URL: http://jordantimes.com

ORGANIZATIONS AND ASSOCIATIONS

Bandak Arab African Foundation

A nonprofit organization in the United States that urges Middle Eastern governments, particularly Jordan's, to help people with disabilities in the workforce.

345 New London Road
Newark, Delaware 19711
Phone: (302) 737-4055

Embassy of the Hashemite Kingdom of Jordan

The U.S. Embassy of Jordan seeks to foster relations between the kingdom and the United States by processing passports and visas for people from the United States who wish to visit Jordan, providing news coverage to Jordanian Americans and others with an interest in Jordan, and acting as a liaison between the two countries.

3504 International Drive NW
Washington, D.C. 20008
Phone: (202) 966-2664
Fax: (202) 966-3110
Email: hkjembassydc@jordanembassyus.org
URL: http://jordanembassyus.org

Sisterhood Is Global Institute

Established in 1998, the institute seeks to deepen the understanding of women's human rights at the local, national, regional, and global levels and to strengthen the capacity of women to exercise their rights. With members in seventy countries, the institute currently maintains a network of more than 1,300 individuals and organizations. It has a regional office in Jordan that was inaugurated by Princess Basma Bint Talal.

4343 Montgomery Avenue
Suite 201
Bethesda, Maryland 20814

Phone: (301) 654-2774
Fax: (301) 654-2775
Email: wlp@learningpartnership.org
URL: http://play.learningpartnership.org/en/partners/jordan

Justin Abdelkader, #8 of the Detroit Red Wings, is Jordanian on his paternal side. DAVE REGINEK / NHLI VIA GETTY IMAGES

SOURCES FOR ADDITIONAL STUDY

Hijab, Nadia. *Womanpower: The Arab Debate on Women at Work*. Cambridge Middle East Library Series. Cambridge, UK: Cambridge University Press, 1988.

Hitti, Philip K. *History of the Arabs from the Earliest Time to the Present*. New York: St. Martin's Press, 1956.

Jureidini, Paul A., and R. D. McLaurin. *Jordan: The Impact of Social Changes on the Role of the Tribes*. Washington Papers, No. 108, Center for Strategic and International Studies, Georgetown University. New York: Praeger, 1984.

Massad, Joseph M. *Colonial Effects: The Making of National Identity in Jordan*. New York: Columbia University Press, 2001.

Metz, Helen Chapin. *Jordan: A Country Study*. Washington, D.C.: Federal Research Division, Library of Congress, 1991.

Tobin, Sara. "Ramadan Blues: Debates in Pop Music and Popular Islam in Amman, Jordan." *Digest of Middle East Studies* 21, no. 2 (2013).

ANNOTATED BIBLIOGRAPHY

Acuña, Rodolfo, and Guadalupe Compean. *Voices of the U.S. Latino Experience.* Westport, CT: Greenwood Press, 2008. The history of Latinos in the United States derived from letters, memoirs, speeches, articles, essays, interviews, treaties, government reports, testimony, and more.

Aguirre, Adalberto. *Racial and Ethnic Diversity in America: A Reference Handbook.* Santa Barbara, CA: ABC-CLIO, 2003. Examines, through current and historical census data, the populations and social forces that contribute to the racial and ethnic diversity of the United States.

Alba, Richard D., and Victor Nee. *Remaking the American Mainstream: Assimilation and Contemporary Immigration.* Cambridge, MA: Harvard University Press, 2003. Demonstrates the importance of assimilation in American society by looking at language, socioeconomic attachments, residential patterns, and intermarriage.

Alba, Richard D., and Mary C. Waters. *Next Generation: Immigrant Youth in a Comparative Perspective.* New York: New York University, 2011. An examination of second-generation immigrant youth in the United States and Western Europe.

American Ethnic Writers. Rev. ed. Pasadena, CA: Salem Press, 2009. Compiles and describes the works of African American, Asian American, Jewish American, Hispanic/Latino, and Native American writers.

Anderson, Wanni W., and Robert G. Lee, eds. *Displacements and Diasporas: Asians in the Americas.* New Brunswick, NJ: Rutgers University Press, 2005. An interdisciplinary look at the experiences of Asians in North and South America and how they have been shaped by the social and political dynamics of the countries in which they have settled as well as by their countries of origin.

Angell, Carole S. *Celebrations around the World: A Multicultural Handbook.* Golden, CO: Fulcrum, 1996. A month-by-month look at festivals from around the world.

Anglim, Christopher. *Encyclopedia of Religion and the Law in America.* 2nd ed. Amenia, NY: Grey House, 2009. Covers topics from prayer in schools to holiday displays on public property; includes a description of major cases.

Atwood, Craig D., et al. *Handbook of Denominations in the United States.* 13th ed. Nashville: Abingdon Press, 2010. This frequently updated handbook serves as a guide to the many denominations that make up the American religious experience.

Axtell, Roger E. *Gestures: The Do's and Taboos of Body Language around the World.* Rev. ed. New York: Wiley, 1998. Lists, illustrates, and explains the meaning of gestures from eighty-two countries around the world.

Banks, James A., ed. *Encyclopedia of Diversity in Education.* Thousand Oaks, CA: SAGE, 2012. A guide to research and statistics, case studies, best practices, and policies.

———, ed. *Handbook of Research on Multicultural Education.* 2nd ed. San Francisco: Jossey-Bass, 2004. A guide to advances in the research of multicultural education.

———. *Teaching Strategies for Ethnic Studies.* 8th ed. Boston: Pearson/Allyn & Bacon, 2009. Examines the current and emerging theory, research, and scholarship in the fields of ethnic studies and multicultural education.

Barkan, Elliott Robert, ed. *Immigrants in American History: Arrival, Adaptation, and Integration.* Santa Barbara, CA: ABC-CLIO, 2013. Covers the arrival, adaptation, and integration of immigrants into American culture from the 1500s to 2010.

Barkley, Elizabeth F. *Crossroads: The Multicultural Roots of America's Popular Music.* 2nd ed. Upper Saddle River, NJ: Pearson Prentice Hall, 2007. A comparative exploration of the music of Native Americans, European Americans, African Americans, Latino Americans, and Asian Americans.

Bayor, Ronald H., ed. *The Columbia Documentary History of Race and Ethnicity in America*. New York: Columbia University Press, 2004. Seeks to shed light on the many ways in which immigration, racial histories, and ethnic histories have shaped contemporary American society.

————, ed. *Multicultural America: An Encyclopedia of the Newest Americans*. Santa Barbara. CA: Greenwood, 2011. Profiles fifty of the largest immigrant groups in the United States.

Benson, Sonia, ed. *The Hispanic American Almanac: A Reference Work on Hispanics in the United States*. 3rd ed. Detroit: Gale, 2003. Examines the history and culture of Hispanic Americans with coverage of events, biographies, and demographic information.

Berlin, Ira. *The Making of African America: The Four Great Migrations*. New York: Viking, 2010. Interprets the history of African Americans by examining the forced migration of slavery, the relocation of slaves to interior southern states, the migrations to the north, and the more recent arrival of immigrants from African and Caribbean nations.

Berzok, Linda Murray, ed. *Storied Dishes: What Our Family Recipes Tell Us about Who We Are and Where We've Been*. Santa Barbara, CA: Praeger, 2011. An exploration of family history through recipes.

Bird, Stephanie Rose. *Light, Bright, and Damned Near White: Biracial and Triracial Culture in America*. Westport, CT: Praeger, 2009. Explores the challenges for, and psychological issues of, people with ethnically mixed ancestry.

Blank, Carla. *Rediscovering America: The Making of Multicultural America, 1900–2000*. New York: Three Rivers Press, 2003. A retelling of American history through the contributions of women, African Americans, Asian Americans, Hispanic Americans, and Native Americans, immigrants, artists, "renegades, rebels, and rogues."

Bona, Mary Jo, and Irma Maini, eds. *Multiethnic Literature and Canon Debates*. Albany: State University of New York Press, 2006. Critiques the debate over the inclusion of multiethnic literature in the American literary canon.

Boosahda, Elizabeth. *Arab-American Faces and Voices: The Origins of an Immigrant Community*. Austin: University of Texas Press, 2003. Looking at the long history of Arab Americans in the United States, this book includes personal interviews, photographs, and historical documents.

Bowler, Shaun, and Gary M. Segura. *The Future Is Ours: Minority Politics, Political Behavior, and the Multiracial Era of American Politics*. Thousand Oaks, CA: SAGE, 2012. A data-based examination of whether and how minority citizens differ from members of the white majority in political participation.

Brettell, Caroline. *Constructing Borders/Crossing Boundaries: Race, Ethnicity, and Immigration*. Lanham, MD: Lexington Books, 2008. Essays on a diverse range of immigrant populations from past to present that look at the boundaries and borders created by the social construction of race and ethnicity.

Bronner, Simon J., ed. *Encyclopedia of American Folklife*. Armonk, NY: M. E. Sharpe, 2006. Looks at the oral and written literary traditions, songs, and stories that make up a community's identity.

Brooks, Christopher Antonio, ed. *The African American Almanac*. 11th ed. Farmington Hills, MI: Gale Cengage Learning, 2011. A continually updated work from Gale's series of multicultural reference sources. Provides chronology, biography, events, and demography.

Buenker, John D., and Lorman A. Ratner, eds. *Multiculturalism in the United States: A Comparative Guide to Acculturation and Ethnicity*. Rev. ed. Westport, CT: Greenwood Press, 2005. Discusses how American culture has affected immigrants as well as how it has been shaped by them.

Cannato, Vincent J. *American Passage: The History of Ellis Island*. New York: Harper, 2009. Tells the story of Ellis Island from 1892 to 1924 using a variety of primary sources.

Carlisle, Rodney P., general ed. *Multicultural America*. 7 vols. New York: Facts On File, 2011. Presents the social history, customs, and traditions of ethnic groups throughout American history.

Carter, Susan B., ed. *Historical Statistics of the United States: Earliest Times to the Present*. 5 vols. New York: Cambridge University Press, 2006. Provides a historical perspective on statistics about the U.S. population, economy, government, and international relations.

Cesari, Jocelyne, ed. *Encyclopedia of Islam in the United States*. Westport, CT: Greenwood Press, 2007. Based on primary documents, this encyclopedia provides historical context for the current state of the practice of Islam in the United States.

Chi, Sang, and Emily Moberg Robinson, eds. *Voices of the Asian American and Pacific Islander Experience*. Santa Barbara, CA: Greenwood, 2012. Explores the experiences, views, and politics of recent Asian immigrants, emphasizing the diversity of experiences and viewpoints of individuals within the different nationalities and generations. Based on primary documents.

Ciment, James, and John Radzilowski, eds. *American Immigration: An Encyclopedia of Political, Social, and Cultural Change*. 2nd ed. 4 vols. Armonk, NY: M. E. Sharpe, 2013. American immigration from historic and contemporary perspectives. Primary documents include laws and treaties, referenda, Supreme Court cases, historical articles, and letters from 1787 to 2013.

Cohen, Selma Jeanne, ed. *International Encyclopedia of Dance*. 6 vols. New York: Oxford University Press, 2004. The definitive reference book for dance, documenting all types and styles of dance from around the world and throughout history.

Condra, Jill, ed. *The Greenwood Encyclopedia of Clothing through World History*. 3 vols. Westport, CT: Greenwood Press, 2008. Examines the history of clothing from all corners of the globe from pre-history to modern times.

Coontz, Stephanie, ed. *American Families: A Multicultural Reader*. 2nd ed. New York: Routledge, 2008. Brings together articles that look at the ethnic and racial diversity within families.

Cullum, Linda, ed. *Contemporary American Ethnic Poets: Lives, Works, Sources*. Westport, CT: Greenwood Press, 2004. Presents the lives and works of seventy-five poets.

Cordry, Harold V. *The Multicultural Dictionary of Proverbs: Over 20,000 Adages from More than 120 Languages, Nationalities and Ethnic Groups*. Jefferson, NC: McFarland, 1997. Presents 1,300 headings arranged by nationality, with a focus on European cultures.

Daniels, Roger. *Coming to America: A History of Immigration and Ethnicity in American Life*. 2nd ed. New York: Perennial, 2002. An overview of immigration to the United States from the colonial era to the beginning of the twenty-first century.

Danilov, Victor J. *Ethnic Museums and Heritage Sites in the United States*. Jefferson, NC: McFarland, 2009. A directory of all ethnic heritage sites in the United States.

Danky, James P., and Wayne A. Wiegand, eds. *Print Culture in a Diverse America*. Urbana: University of Illinois Press, 1998. Examines the multicultural world of reading and readers in the United States.

Davis, Rocío G., ed. *The Transnationalism of American Culture: Literature, Film, and Music*. New York: Routledge, 2012. A study of the border-crossing aspects of literature, film, and music.

Dinnerstein, Leonard, and David M. Reimers. *Ethnic Americans: A History of Immigration*. 5th ed. New York: Columbia University Press, 2009. Chapters examine the history of immigration to the United States chronologically, from the fifteenth century to 2008.

Dinnerstein, Leonard, Roger L. Nichols, and David M. Reimers. *Natives and Strangers: A History of Ethnic Americans*. 5th ed. New York: Oxford University Press, 2010. Examines the history of American ethnic groups and their impact on the character and social fabric of the United States.

Dodge, Abigail Johnson. *Around the World Cookbook*. New York: DK Publishing, 2008. A children's cookbook with fifty step-by-step recipes for preparing ethnic cuisine.

Ellicott, Karen, ed. *Countries of the World and Their Leaders Yearbook 2014*. 2 vols. Detroit: Gale, 2014. U.S. Department of State reports looking at all social, political, legal, economic, and environmental aspects for selected countries of the world.

Fleegler, Robert L. *Ellis Island Nation: Immigration Policy and American Identity in the Twentieth Century*. Philadelphia: University of Pennsylvania Press, 2013. Uses World War II films, records of Senate subcommittee hearings, and anti-Communist propaganda to view the evolution in the debate over immigration in the United States.

Franco, Dean J. *Ethnic American Literature: Comparing Chicano, Jewish, and African American Writing*. Charlottesville: University of Virginia Press, 2006. Provides a comparative approach to American ethnic literature.

Frazier, John W., Eugene L. Tettey-Fio, and Norah F. Henry, eds. *Race, Ethnicity, and Place in a Changing America*. 2nd ed. Albany: State University of New York Press, 2011. Looks at how race and ethnicity affects all aspects of everyday life.

Fredrickson, George M. *Diverse Nations: Explorations in the History of Racial and Ethnic Pluralism*. Boulder, CO: Paradigm Publishers, 2008. A comparative exploration of slavery and race relations in the United States, Europe, South Africa, and Brazil.

Gillota, David. *Ethnic Humor in Multiethnic America*. New Brunswick, NJ: Rutgers University Press, 2013. Investigates the role of humor in the national conversation on race and ethnicity and the response of contemporary comedians to multiculturalism.

Gilton, Donna L. *Multicultural and Ethnic Children's Literature in the United States*. Lanham, MD: Scarecrow Press, 2007. The history of and contemporary trends in U.S. multicultural children's literature.

Glenn, Evelyn Nakano. *Unequal Freedom: How Race and Gender Shaped American Citizenship and Labor*. Cambridge, MA: Harvard University Press, 2002. A comparative look at the history of inequality and specifically how labor and citizenship have been defined, enforced, and challenged in the United States.

González, Alberto, et al., eds. *Our Voices: Essays in Culture, Ethnicity, and Communication*. 5th ed. New York: Oxford University Press, 2012. Short first-person accounts that examine the varieties of intercultural communication covering discourses of gender, race, and ethnicity.

Sherrow, Victoria. *Encyclopedia of Hair: A Cultural History*. Westport, CT: Greenwood Press, 2006. Everything about hair across cultures and throughout time.

Shinagawa, Larry Hijime, and Michael Jang. *Atlas of American Diversity*. Walnut Creek, CA: AltaMira Press, 1998. A visual exploration through maps and charts of the social, economic, and geographic state of an ethnically diverse United States.

Shorris, Earl. *Latinos: A Biography of the People*. New York: W. W. Norton, 1992. Looks at Latino history from the time of the Spanish conquest of North and South America.

Snodgrass, Mary Ellen. *World Clothing and Fashion: An Encyclopedia of History, Culture, and Social Influence*. Armonk, NY: M. E. Sharpe, 2013. Approaches fashion from a global, multicultural, social, and economic perspective, covering prehistory to the present time.

Spickard, Paul R., ed. *Race and Immigration in the United States: New Histories*. New York: Routledge, 2012. Each essay looks at a particular aspect of immigrant experience, drawing attention to the ways the experiences differ depending on country of origin.

Statistical Abstract of the United States. Washington, DC: U.S. Gov. Print. Off., 1878–2012. The *Statistical Abstract* was compiled and published annually by the U.S. Census Bureau through 2012; beginning in 2013 it was instead published digitally by ProQuest. Provides an annual update of statistics about the characteristics and conditions of most aspects of life in the United States. For the historical perspective see *Historical Statistics of the United States: Earliest Times to the Present*, edited by Susan B. Carter.

Stave, Bruce M. Salerno, John F. Sutherland, and Aldo Salerno. *From the Old Country: An Oral History of European Migration to America*. New York: Maxwell Macmillan International, 1994. A compilation of oral histories describing the experience of migration and all aspects of the transition to life in a new country.

Strobel, Christoph. *Daily Life of the New Americans: Immigration since 1965*. Santa Barbara, CA: Greenwood, 2010. A history of twentieth- and twenty-first-century American immigrants through first-person and biographical narratives.

Stuhr, Rebecca. *Autobiographies by Americans of Color 1980–1994: An Annotated Bibliography*. Troy, NY: Whitston, 1997.

Stuhr, Rebecca, and Deborah Stuhr Iwabuchi. *Autobiographies by Americans of Color, 1995–2000: An Annotated Bibliography*. Albany, NY: Whitston, 2003. These two works together provide a comprehensive bibliography with extensive annotations for autobiographical works and oral histories.

Takaki, Ronald T. *A Different Mirror: A History of Multicultural America*. Boston: Little, Brown, 1993.

———. *Double Victory: A Multicultural History of America in World War II*. Boston: Little, Brown, 2000.

———. *Strangers from a Different Shore: A History of Asian Americans*. Boston: Little, Brown, 1989. Ronald Takaki was a pioneer in the field of ethnic studies. His books were among the very first to carefully and comprehensively explore the history and contemporary experiences of immigrants who crossed the Pacific to North America.

Thernstrom, Abigail M., and Stephan Thernstrom, eds. *Beyond the Color Line: New Perspectives on Race and Ethnicity in America*. Stanford, CA: Hoover Institution Press, Stanford University, 2002. Examines social, political, and economic changes that have taken place within ethnic America and the persistence of attitudes that create conditions of inequality.

Thernstrom, Stephan, ed. *Harvard Encyclopedia of American Ethnic Groups*. Cambridge, MA: Belknap Press of Harvard University, 1980. Although this work has never been updated, it continues to serve as a foundational text on the history and makeup of the population of the United States.

Thompson, William N. *Native American Issues: A Reference Handbook*. 2nd ed. Santa Barbara, CA: ABC-CLIO, 2005. An assessment of the problems faced by Native Americans, both historically and in the twenty-first century.

Ueda, Reed, ed. *A Companion to American Immigration*. Malden, MA: Blackwell, 2006. Scholarly essays on a range of topics, including law, health, politics, prejudice and racism, housing, education, labor, internationalism, and transnationalism.

Upton, Dell, ed. *America's Architectural Roots: Ethnic Groups That Built America*. New York: Preservation Press, 1986. An illustrated overview of the ethnic derivations of American architecture.

U.S. Census Bureau. *2000 Census of Population and Housing: Population and Housing Unit Counts* and *Summary Social, Economic, and Housing Characteristics*. Washington, DC: U.S. Dept. of Commerce, Economics, and Statistics Administration, U.S. Census Bureau, 2003. Two separate publications from the United States decennial census providing demographic and economic statistics on all populations within the United States.

Verbrugge, Allen, ed. *Muslims in America*. Detroit: Greenhaven Press, 2005. Looks at different aspects of life for Muslims in the United States, including gender, family, college life, politics, and the repercussions of 9/11, with narratives of personal experiences.

Vigdor, Jacob L. *From Immigrants to Americans: The Rise and Fall of Fitting In*. Lanham, MD: Rowman & Littlefield, 2009. A view of the challenges of belonging in the United States, with chapters on economics, linguistics, citizenship, neighborhoods, and family.

Walch, Timothy, ed. *Immigrant America: European Ethnicity in the United States*. New York: Garland, 1994. Examines the experiences of European immigrants to specific regions of the United States.

Waldman, Carl. *Encyclopedia of Native American Tribes*. 3rd ed. New York: Facts On File, 2006. Covers more than 200 American Indian tribes of North America.

Walkowitz, Rebecca L., ed. *Immigrant Fictions: Contemporary Literature in an Age of Globalization*. Madison: University of Wisconsin Press, 2006. A look at contemporary literature by immigrant authors from China, Eastern Europe, and other countries. Includes interviews.

Webb, Lois Sinaiko, and Lindsay Grace Roten. *The Multicultural Cookbook for Students*. Rev. ed. Santa Barbara, CA: Greenwood Press, 2009. Recipes are arranged by region and country and are preceded by an account of the geography, history, and culinary traditions of their country of origin.

Weil, François. *Family Trees: A History of Genealogy in America*. Cambridge, MA: Harvard University Press, 2013. A history of the practice of genealogy from its early methodology to the use of the database Ancestry.com and DNA testing; from a preoccupation with social status to an acceptance and celebration of diverse ethnic heritage.

Welsch, Janice R., and J. Q. Adams. *Multicultural Films: A Reference Guide*. Westport, CT: Greenwood Press, 2005. Provides brief synopses and critiques of motion pictures that explore race and ethnicity.

Wertsman, Vladimir. *What's Cooking in Multicultural America: An Annotated Bibliographic Guide to Over Four Hundred Ethnic Cuisines*. Lanham, MD: Scarecrow Press, 1996. An annotated bibliography to cookbooks, covering the cuisines of more than four hundred ethnic groups from all continents.

Wills, Chuck. *Destination America*. New York: DK Pub., 2005. Through personal accounts, letters, diaries, photographs, statistics, maps, and charts, examines the reasons immigrants leave home to travel to the United States and the conditions of their lives once they arrive.

York, Sherry. *Ethnic Book Awards: A Directory of Multicultural Literature for Young Readers*. Worthington, OH: Linworth, 2005. Provides an alphabetical listing of titles winning various book awards, including the Coretta Scott King, Carter G. Woodson, and Tomás Rivera Mexican American Children's book awards.

PERIODICALS

African American Review (1992–). Terre Haute: Dept. of English, Indiana State University. Print and online. Continues *Black American Literature Forum* (1976–1991). History and criticism of African American literature.

Amerasia Journal (1971–). Los Angeles: University of California, Los Angeles; and Yale Asian American Students Association. Print and Online. An interdisciplinary journal studying all aspects of Asian American society, jointly published by the UCLA Asian American Studies Center and the Yale Asian American Students Association.

Callaloo (1976–). Baltimore, MD: Johns Hopkins University Press. Print and Online. An African diaspora literary journal founded at Southern University in Baton Rouge, Louisiana, and now sponsored by Texas A&M University and published by Johns Hopkins University Press.

Ethnic NewsWatch (1998–). ProQuest Information and Learning. Online. Newspaper articles from the ethnic American presses. Dates of coverage depend on arrangements with each particular newspaper. Searchable via keywords and broad ethnic group.

Ethnic Studies Review: The Journal of the National Association for Ethnic Studies (1996–). Tempe, AZ: National Association for Ethnic Studies. Print and Online. A multidisciplinary international journal devoted to the study of ethnicity, ethnic groups and their cultures, and intergroup relations. Preceded by *Explorations in Ethnic Studies*.

Hispanic American Historical Review (HAHR) (1918–). Durham, NC: Duke University Press. Print and Online. Covers Latin American history and culture.

International Migration Review: IMR (1966–). New York: Center for Migration Studies. Print and Online. A quarterly interdisciplinary, peer-reviewed journal created to encourage and facilitate the study of all aspects of international migration.

Journal of American Ethnic History (1981–). Champaign: University of Illinois Press. Print and Online. Addresses various aspects of American immigration and ethnic history, including history of emigration, ethnic and racial groups, Native Americans, immigration policies, and the processes of acculturation.

Journal of Intercultural Studies (1980–). Melbourne: River Seine Publications. Print and Online. Covers cultural studies, sociology, gender studies, political science, cultural geography, urban studies, race, and ethnic studies.

MELUS: Society for the Study of the Multi-Ethnic Literature of the United States (1974–). Storrs: University of Connecticut, Dept. of English. Provides interviews and reviews that explore and bring light to the multiethnic character of American literature.

Multicultural Education (1993–). San Francisco: Caddo Gap Press. An independent quarterly magazine featuring research on promising pedagogical practices in art, music, and literature.

Rebecca Stuhr